Photoshop® CS2 Bible

Deke McClelland and Laurie Ulrich Fuller

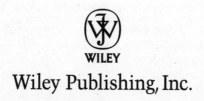

Wiley Publishing, Inc.

Photoshop® CS2 Bible

Published by
Wiley Publishing, Inc.
111 River St.
Hoboken, NJ 07030-5774
www.wiley.com

Copyright © 2005 by Wiley Publishing, Inc., Indianapolis, Indiana

Published simultaneously in Canada

ISBN-13: 978-0-7645-8972-0

ISBN-10: 0-7645-8972-5

Manufactured in the United States of America

10 9 8 7 6 5 4 3

1O/QV/QX/QV/IN

For general information on our other products and services or to obtain technical support, please contact our Customer Care Department within the U.S. at (800) 762-2974, outside the U.S. at (317) 572-3993 or fax (317) 572-4002.

Wiley also publishes its books in a variety of electronic formats. Some content that appears in print may not be available in electronic books.

Library of Congress Control Number: 2005924607

About the Authors

Deke McClelland. Born near Verona in 1511, he was once the most popular portrait painter in all of Florence. His career came to a grinding halt a few centuries later with the advent of photography. Broken, penniless, and deeply resentful, Deke dedicated his energies to the development of a pathogen so insidious that it would one day contaminate each and every photograph on the planet. Code named the Pernicious Instrument of eXtreme EviL (or "pixel" for short), Deke smuggled his terrible creation into The New World and set it free. When his invention turned out to help rather than hurt photography, he went quite mad. He now inflicts his revenge by writing educational books and hosting training videos.

His most sinister books are the award-winning *Photoshop CS2 Bible* and *Photoshop CS2 Bible, Professional Edition*, now in their 12th year with more copies in print than any other guides on computer graphics. Other subversive titles include *Photoshop CS For Dummies* and *Photoshop Elements For Dummies* (both Wiley Publishing, Inc.).

In 1989, Deke won the Benjamin Franklin Award for Best Computer Book. Since then, he has received similarly diabolical honors from the Society for Technical Communication (once in 1994 and twice in 1999), Photo>Electronic Imaging (1999), the American Society of Business Press Editors (1995 and 2000), the Western Publications Association (1999), and the Computer Press Association (1990, 1992, 1994, 1995, 1997, and twice in 2000). In 1999, Book Bytes named Deke its Author of the Year. In 2002, the National Association of Photoshop Professionals voted Deke into the Photoshop Hall of Fame.

During his fall from grace, Deke has also managed to become an Adobe Certified Expert, a member of the PhotoshopWorld Instructor Dream Team, a featured speaker on the 2003 Photoshop Fling cruise of the Eastern Caribbean, and a contributing editor for *Macworld* and *Photoshop User* magazines. Few now believe there is any hope for him.

Laurie Ulrich Fuller. An artist through heredity and education, a teacher by nature, and a writer since she was old enough to pick up a crayon, Laurie Ulrich Fuller is a graphic artist, computer trainer, and the author and co-author of more than 25 books on computers, software, and the Web. Laurie has written hundreds of training manuals for universities and corporate training centers, and in the past 15 years, she's personally trained thousands of people to make more creative and effective use of their computers. Her classroom has recently expanded to include total strangers she'll never lay eyes on — through CD-based training products available from both Total Training and VTC.

In the early 1990's, after spending way too many years working for other people, Laurie started her own firm, Limehat & Company, Inc. This venture allowed her to put her experience, ideas, and contacts to good use, providing consulting, training,

Web design, and Web hosting services with a focus on the special needs of growing companies and non-profit organizations. If you're wondering where the name "Limehat" came from, it's a long story, but suffice to say it goes back to a childhood taunt heard on the school bus, regarding a plaid hat that nearly turned the then-six-year-old Laurie into a social pariah.

When not writing about or teaching people to use computers, Laurie can be found supporting a variety of animal advocacy groups — through protests, writing educational articles, and maintaining her other organization's Web site. She also enjoys her family, gardening, antiques, old houses, and adding to her collections of books, movies, and Wallace Nutting artwork.

You can find out more about Laurie's work, experiences, and both personal and professional interests at www.planetlaurie.com. You can find out more about Photoshop, the Photoshop Bibles, and check out online Photoshop tutorials, tips, tricks, and expert advice at www.photoshopbible.com. Laurie welcomes reader mail at laurie@photoshopbible.com.

To my husband, Robert, who is quite wonderful.
— Laurie

Credits

Acquisitions Editor
Tom Heine

Project Editor
Cricket Krengel

Copy Editor
Kim Heusel

Editorial Manager
Robyn Siesky

Vice President & Executive Group Publisher
Richard Swadley

Vice President & Publisher
Barry Pruett

Project Coordinator
Shannon Schiller

Graphics and Production Specialists
Andrea Dahl
April Farling
Denny Hager
Joyce Haughey
Barbara Moore
Barry Offringa
Lynsey Osborn
Heather Ryan

Quality Control Technicians
John Greenough
Leeann Harney
Jessica Kramer
Carl William Pierce

Proofreading
TECHBOOKS Production Services

Indexing
TECHBOOKS Production Services

Preface

Hello and welcome to the *Photoshop CS2 Bible*, the bestselling book on Photoshop in publishing history. We've done our best to cover everything thoroughly, accurately, and whenever we could, entertainingly Of course, we hope you learn a lot, but we also hope you have a wonderful time while you're at it, because if you're not having fun, what's the point? Of course not every minute of life can (or some might argue should) be fun, but heck—this is a book on Photoshop—we're not studying some dry, sobering topic.

As you prepare yourself for the thrills and excitement you're about to experience, let us tell you a little something about this book. Now in its 11th year, the *Photoshop Bible* is the longest continuously published title on Adobe Photoshop. Not coincidentally, it also happens to be the bestselling reference guide on the topic, with more than 14 U.S. editions, dozens of localized translations in foreign lands, and more than a million copies in print worldwide. This makes it not only the most successful book of its kind but also one of the most successful books on any electronic publishing topic ever printed.

Of course, "bestseller" doesn't necessarily translate to "best"—remember those homely Cabbage Patch dolls? But the *Photoshop Bible* seems to have withstood the test of time, and while it may be inertia we have to thank for the continued success of this book, it is our hope that the book's enduring appeal is at least in part the result of the time and effort put into it.

The driving philosophy behind the *Photoshop Bible* is a simple one: Even the most intimidating topic can be made easy if it's explained properly. This goes double when the subject of the discussion is something as modest as a piece of software. Photoshop isn't some remarkable work of nature that defies our comprehension. It's nothing more that a commercial product designed by a bunch of regular people for the simple purpose of being understood and put to use by a bunch of regular people like you. If we can't explain something that inherently straightforward, shame on us.

We've made it our mission to address every topic directly, and we haven't spared you our personal opinions and experience, even if they're not entirely flattering to the software. As great as Photoshop is, not every tool is as efficient or intuitive or fun to use as it could be, and sometimes there are workarounds or more unorthodox ways of doing things, and we share those insights without hesitation. You'll find everything here, from the practical benefits of creating accurate masks to the theoretical wonders of designing your own custom layer styles. We weren't born with this knowledge, and there were plenty of times during the years leading up to this book's creation and during the writing of the books when we were learning right along with you — any good teacher learns the most from his or her students and in preparing to teach said students. When we don't know how (or sometimes why something works, we do the research and figure it out, sometimes discussing features directly with the programmers and sometimes taking advantage of other sources. Our job is to find out the answers, make sure those answers make sense, and pass them along to you as clearly as we can.

About This Edition of the Book

It is the primary goal to make every update to the *Photoshop Bible* special and even more valuable than its predecessor, particularly for those of you who purchase the book on a regular basis (with each new revision of the software), and this edition is no exception. Naturally, we cover all the new features, including Photoshop's new file organization, printing, and publishing workspace known as The Bridge, support for 32 bit/channel images, and new tools — including the Spot Healing Brush, and the Red Eye Removal tool, new blur, sharpen, and distortion filters, and the somewhat tinkered-with Layers palette. Smart Objects, including Smart Guides, and the new Adobe versions of the Open and Save dialog boxes are also covered. This book has been scrutinized from head to toe, thoroughly dissected, filled to the breaking point with all sorts of tips and tricks to improve your workflow and enhance your images, and finally carefully reassembled into the weighty tome you hold in your hands. This book is also unique in that it has grown a co-author, who has revised content throughout the book, and added the content on new features. In addition, she has created the artwork for the book throughout. Feel free to blame her for its added weight, especially if you drop it on your foot.

Like all versions of the *Photoshop Bible*, this is a reference guide, not a tutorial. We do not make the images in this book available for download for two reasons. First, many are commercial stock images; understandably, their photographers would frown on our giving away their artwork for free. Second, the techniques discussed in this book are designed to work on *your* images — there's nothing being done to the images shown in this book that you can't do to your own photos, drawings, and scanned artwork of any type. Because this isn't a tutorial (although there are procedural bits that help you perform more complex tasks in a step-by-step fashion), you can jump right in, making practical use of these techniques immediately — you'll learn faster and better that way, too. So don't go whining that we aren't personally sending you the images and stopping by to check on your progress — we care about you and all, but hey — we have our own lives, you know?

Why two Photoshop CS2 Bibles?

When you pulled this book off the bookstore shelf or found it online, you may have noticed a similarly titled book nearby: the *Photoshop CS2 Bible, Professional Edition*.

If you didn't, you should see it soon because it's due out shortly after this book hits the shelves. Either way, you may logically be wondering: Why two *Photoshop Bibles*?

The *Professional Edition*, which first arrived on the scene a couple months after the *Photoshop 7 Bible* was published, exists for a few main reasons. As the amount of information that was needed to cover in the *Photoshop Bible* increased, so did the size of the book, until it was topping out at more than 1,100 pages. It became pretty clear that there was a demand for a tighter, more streamlined book; one that assumed a solid understanding of the program and focused on more advanced features and techniques. Coincidentally, there was also a sizable call for more color in the *Photoshop Bible*. Thus, the *Photoshop Bible, Professional Edition* was born: A hardcover, full-color (and thus more expensive), slimmed-down, more advanced book.

Which Photoshop CS2 Bible is right for you?

Don't for an instant think that the book you currently hold in your hands is some sort of dime-store, slapdash, inferior model. In fact, as we mentioned earlier, there's a great deal of information in this book that you simply won't find in the *Professional Edition*. That's because we've made sure that this edition, sometimes referred to as the *"standard edition,"* is a comprehensive, cradle-to-grave resource guide that contains tips and insights valuable to all levels of Photoshop users. Topics included in the standard edition that aren't covered in the *Professional Edition* include navigation, preferences, tool presets, workspaces, resampling and resolution, file formats, color channels and models, the eyedropper tool, gradients, the basic selection tools, paths, text, Color Settings, and CMYK printing. Additionally, you get the comprehensive guide to Photoshop's default keyboard shortcuts found at the back of this book, and that alone makes the term "standard edition" a serious understatement.

That said, if you own one of the previous editions of the *Photoshop Bible* or you're fairly experienced with Photoshop, the *Photoshop CS2 Bible, Professional Edition* might well be more up your alley. Topics that receive either exclusive or dramatically expanded coverage in the *Professional Edition* include Levels, Curves, hue and saturation adjustments, the Channel Mixer, pattern creation, layer styles, history, the Render filters, actions, batch renaming and processing, arbitrary and displacement maps, the Custom filter, the sRGB color space, and Adobe ImageReady CS2. Additionally, the *Professional Edition* is where you'll find in-depth coverage of Photoshop CS2's powerful Camera Raw capabilities (though we explore the basics in this edition, too).

Our goal was to create two independent books with as little overlap as possible. For what it's worth, the areas of overlap revolve mostly around Photoshop CS2's upgraded capabilities, such as the Bridge, the use of the new filters, Photoshop's Web-specific features and capabilities. We're not advising that you get both books, but some readers will, and we want them to be absolutely satisfied with that decision.

Conventions

Every computer book conforms to its own special brand of logic, and this one is no exception. While we generally abhor conformity and convention, the book does have some features that we figured you'd want to find and be able to count on — so here they are:

Vocabulary

Call it *computerese*, call it *technobabble*, call it the indecipherable gibberish of incorrigible propeller-head geeks. Whatever you call it, we can't explain Photoshop in graphic (pardon the pun) detail without occasionally reverting to the specialized language of the trade. However, to help you keep up, we can and have italicized vocabulary words (such as *bit depth*) with which you may not be familiar or which are used in an unusual context. An italicized term is followed by a definition.

If you come across a strange word that is *not* italicized (*that* bit of italics was for emphasis), look it up in the index to find the first reference to the word in the book.

Commands and options

To distinguish the literal names of commands, dialog boxes, buttons, and so on, we capitalize the first letter in each word (for example, *click the Cancel button*). The only exceptions are option names, which can be six or seven words long and filled with prepositions such as *to* and *of*. Traditionally, prepositions and articles (*a, an, the*) don't appear in initial caps, and this book follows that time-honored rule, too.

When discussing menus and commands, we use an arrow symbol to indicate hierarchy. For example, *Choose File ⇨ Open* means to choose the Open command from the File menu. If you have to display a submenu to reach a command, we list the command used to display the submenu between the menu name and the final command. *Choose Image ⇨ Adjustments ⇨ Invert* means to choose the Adjustments command from the Image menu and then choose the Invert command from the Adjustments submenu.

The whole platform thing

This is a cross-platform book, which means it's written for both Windows and Macintosh users. Photoshop is virtually identical on the two platforms, so it makes little difference. However, the PC and Mac keyboards are different. The Ctrl key on the PC translates to the Command key (⌘) on the Mac. Alt translates to Option, and because Apple's mice do not include right mouse buttons, right-clicking on the PC becomes Control-clicking on the Mac. Throughout this book, we try to make things as unambiguous as possible by mentioning the Windows keystroke first with the

Macintosh equivalent second, usually in parentheses. You'll also find that select figures of dialog boxes and other parts of the Photoshop workspace were shot in both operating systems — there are Mac figures and Windows figures where the two differ greatly. We don't want anyone to feel left out, unrepresented, unloved, or unappreciated.

Version names and numbers

A new piece of software comes out every 15 minutes. That's not a real statistic, mind you, but it's probably not far off. When it comes to Photoshop, it started (surprisingly enough) with version 1.0, and the numbering of versions ended with Photoshop 7. With the release of Photoshop CS in 2003, Adobe abandoned numbering, but has gone back to it now (sort of) by calling this year's model Photoshop CS2. This book will refer to older versions, but without being overly specific. While there were multiple releases of the major versions, when we write *Photoshop 7*, we mean Versions 7.0 and 7.0.1, *Photoshop 6*, means Versions 6.0 and 6.0.1; *Photoshop 5* means Versions 5.0, 5.0.2, and 5.5; *Photoshop 4* means Versions 4.0 and 4.0.1; *Photoshop 3*, means Versions 3.0, 3.0.1, 3.0.3, 3.0.4, and 3.0.5 — well, you get the idea.

Icons

Like just about every computer book currently, this one includes compelling and visually arresting icons that focus your peepers on important information. The icons make it easy for people who like to just skim books to figure out what the heck's going on, to "cut to the chase" in some cases, or to just provide "the highlights". Icons exist not only for those with short attention spans, but for people who are just so darn busy that reading an entire page is just unimaginable. On the whole, the icons are self-explanatory, but here's an explanation of them anyway.

The Caution icon warns you that a step you're about to take may produce disastrous results. Well, perhaps "disastrous" is an exaggeration. Inconvenient, then. Uncomfortable. For heaven's sake, be careful.

The Note icon highlights some little tidbit of information we've decided to share with you that seemed at the time to be at least remotely related to the topic at hand. You might learn how an option came into existence, why a feature is implemented the way it is, or how you might use the feature in an unconventional way, or skip its use altogether.

The New Feature icon explains an option, a command, or a feature that is either bright, shiny and new to this latest revision, or it's something that's been changed more than slightly. If you're already familiar with previous versions of Photoshop, you might just want to plow through the book looking for Photoshop CS2 icons and see what new stuff is out there. A description of what's new can also be found at the beginning of Chapter 2, if you're interested in a quick tour — again, those in search of instant gratification need not be put off by the girth of this book — we've accommodated both the cover-to-cover reader and those of you who'll hardly crack the binding, but will want to know that when they need us, we're there.

This book is bursting with tips and techniques. If we were to highlight every one of them, entire pages would be gray with light bulbs popping out all over the place. The Tip icon calls attention to shortcuts that are specifically applicable to the Photoshop application. For the bigger, more useful power tips, you'll have to — gasp — actually read the text.

The Cross-Reference icon tells you where to go for information related to the current topic. It's about as straightforward as an icon can get, so you won't have any trouble with this one.

Contact

Even in its millionth edition, scanned by the eyes of hundreds of thousands of readers and scrutinized intensely for months at a time by the authors and our editors, we bet someone, somewhere will still manage to locate errors and oversights. If you notice those kinds of things and have a few spare moments, please let us know what you think. We always appreciate readers' comments really, we do.

If you want to share your insights, comments, or corrections, send a note to authors@photoshopbible.com. Don't fret if you don't get a response immediately. While every letter does get read and every constructive idea anyone bothers to send is considered, it would be impossible, due to volume, to respond to everyone.

Please, do not write to ask why your copy of Photoshop is misbehaving on your specific computer. Neither of the authors of this book were involved in developing Photoshop, we are not employed by Adobe, and we are not trained in product support. Adobe can answer your technical support questions way better than anyone can, so leave it to the experts.

Now, without further ado, you should turn the page and advance forward into the great untamed frontier of image editing. Soon, you will know things you never knew before, you will see things you never saw before, and you will gain insights and burn unwanted fat, just from the expenditure of pure thinking energy and lifting the book onto your lap. (Such results are not typical.) But whatever you do, don't take this book to bed, fall asleep, and let it topple onto your face — the injuries could be quite disfiguring.

Contents at a Glance

Preface vii

Part I: Welcome to Photoshop 1
Chapter 1: Introducing Photoshop CS2. 3
Chapter 2: Inside Photoshop. 11
Chapter 3: Image Management. 71

Part II: Painting and Retouching. 165
Chapter 4: Defining Colors 167
Chapter 5: Painting and Brushes. 215
Chapter 6: Filling and Stroking 265
Chapter 7: Retouching and Restoring 307

Part III: Selections, Masks, and Filters 353
Chapter 8: Selections and Paths 355
Chapter 9: Masks and Extractions 423
Chapter 10: Corrective Filtering 469
Chapter 11: Distortions and Effects 541

Part IV: Layers, Objects, and Text 611
Chapter 12: Working with Layers. 613
Chapter 13: The Wonders of Blend Modes 679
Chapter 14: Shapes and Styles 735
Chapter 15: Fully Editable Text 769

Part V: Color and Output 809
Chapter 16: Essential Color Management 811
Chapter 17: Mapping and Adjusting Colors. 837
Chapter 18: Printing and Publishing with Photoshop 917

Appendix: The Keyboard, Menus, and Making Photoshop Your Own 987

Index 1029

Contents

Preface vii

Part I: Welcome to Photoshop — 1

Chapter 1: Introducing Photoshop CS2 3

What Is Photoshop? 3
Image-Editing Theory 4
    Bitmaps versus vectors 4
    The ups and downs of painting 5
    The downs and ups of drawing 6
    When to use Photoshop 7
    When to use a drawing program 7
What's New in Photoshop CS2 8
Summary 10

Chapter 2: Inside Photoshop 11

Dive in with the Splash Screen 12
The Welcome Screen 12
The Photoshop Workspace 13
    The Info Palette 16
    The tools 20
    The Toolbox controls 28
    The Options bar 30
    Tool presets 31
    The Preset Manager 33
    The floating palettes 34
    Rearranging and docking palettes 36
Navigating in Photoshop 39
    The view size 40
    The Zoom tool 41
    The Zoom commands 42
    The magnification box 43
    Creating a reference window 45
    Scrolling in the window 45
    The Navigator palette 47

Customizing the Interface 48
Summary 70

Chapter 3: Image Management 71

Size Versus Resolution 71
Changing the Printing Resolution 72
Changing the Page-Layout Resolution 74
What's the Best Resolution? 74
The Resolution of Screen Images 76
How to Open, Duplicate, and Save Images 76
Creating a new image 78
Opening an image 83
Using the Bridge 89
A typical Bridge session 91
Opening images from the Bridge 93
Your Bridge view options 94
Selecting images 98
Rotating images 99
Adding an image to Favorites 100
Managing the cache 110
Renaming files 111
Using the File Info command 112
Duplicating an image 115
Saving an Image to Disk 116
Adding an extension to Mac files 116
Saving previews 117
Choosing other save options 117
The Save for Web dialog box 120
File Format Roundup 122
The native format 122
Special-purpose formats 123
Interapplication formats 131
The mainstream formats 139
The formats nobody talks to 144
Still can't get that file open? 148
Adding Annotations 148
Making a note of it 149
Speaking your mind 149
Managing annotations 150
Resampling and Cropping 152
Resizing versus resampling 152
Cropping 154
Summary 163

Part II: Painting and Retouching   165

Chapter 4: Defining Colors 167

Specifying Colors 167
Using the Color Picker 169
Typing Numeric Color Values 171
Working in Different Color Modes 172
    RGB 172
    HSB 174
    CMYK 174
    CIE's Lab 177
    Understanding Lab anatomy 178
    Indexed Color 179
    Grayscale 181
    16 and 32 bits per channel 182
    Black and white (bitmap) 183
Using Color Libraries 188
    Predefined colors 188
    The Color palette 190
    The Swatches palette 192
    Swatches presets 194
    The Eyedropper tool 195
    The Color Sampler tool 196
Introducing Color Channels 198
    For those of you who just said "So?" 199
    How channels work 199
    Switching and viewing channels 200
Trying Channels on for Size 202
    RGB channels 202
    CMYK channels 204
    Lab channels 206
Other Channel Functions 206
Color Channel Effects 210
    Improving the appearance of color scans 210
    Using multichannel techniques 212
Summary 213

Chapter 5: Painting and Brushes 215

Get to Know the Paint and Edit Tools 215
    The paint tools 217
    The edit tools 218
Basic Techniques 220
    Painting a straight line 221
    Painting a perpendicular line 221
    Painting with the Smudge tool 224

Sponging color in and out 226
Using the Color Replacement tool 228
Undoing your damage 230
Brush Size and Shape 230
Selecting a brush shape 231
Making your own brush shape 233
Defining a custom brush 237
Saving and loading brush sets. 238
Brush Dynamics 240
Brush dynamic basics 241
Shape dynamics. 241
Additional brush dynamics 246
Noise, Wet Edges, and the rest 248
Undoing pressure-sensitive lines 249
Opacity and Strength, Flow and Exposure 250
Brush Modes 252
The 25 paint tool modes 253
The three Dodge and Burn modes 261
Summary 263

Chapter 6: Filling and Stroking **265**
Filling Selections with Color or Patterns 266
The Paint Bucket tool 266
The Fill command 272
Backspace- and Delete-key Techniques. 274
Using the Paint Bucket Inside a Selection 275
Applying Gradient Fills 277
Using the Gradient tool. 278
Gradient options 279
Gradient styles 282
Creating custom gradations 284
Editing solid gradients 285
Creating noise gradients 290
Saving and managing gradients 292
Gradations and brush modes 293
Applying Strokes and Arrowheads 297
Stroking a selection outline 298
Applying arrowheads to straight lines 300
Appending arrowheads to curved lines 302
Summary 305

Chapter 7: Retouching and Restoring. **307**
Cloning and Healing. 309
The Clone Stamp tool. 310
The Healing Brush tool. 314
The Spot Healing Brush 319

The Patch tool. 320
The Red Eye tool 322
Retouching Photographs 323
Restoring an old photograph 327
Eliminating distracting background elements. 331
Stepping Back through Time 336
Using the traditional undo functions 337
The History palette 338
Painting away the past 342
Summary 352

Part III: Selections, Masks, and Filters   353

Chapter 8: Selections and Paths. 355

How Selections Work 355
Geometric Selection Outlines 359
Free-form Outlines. 362
Magnetic Selections 364
Using the Magnetic Lasso tool 365
Modifying the Magnetic Lasso options. 366
The World of the Wand 367
Adjusting the tolerance 368
Making the Wand see beyond a single layer. 371
Ways to Change Selection Outlines 372
Quick changes. 372
Manually adding and subtracting. 373
Power-User tricks 374
Adding and subtracting by command 375
Softening selection outlines 380
Moving and Duplicating Selections 385
The role of the Move tool 385
Making precise movements 385
Cloning a selection 386
Moving a selection outline independently of its contents 389
Scaling or rotating a selection outline 389
How to Draw and Edit Paths 392
Paths overview 393
Drawing paths with the Pen tool 396
Editing paths 402
Filling paths 408
Painting along a path 408
Converting and saving paths 412
Importing and Exporting Paths 414
Swapping paths with Illustrator. 415
Exporting to Illustrator. 416
Retaining transparent areas in an image. 416
Summary 421

Chapter 9: Masks and Extractions. 423

Painting and Editing Inside Selections 425
Working in Quick Mask Mode 429
    How the Quick Mask mode works 430
    Changing the red coating 435
    Gradations as masks 436
Generating Masks Automatically 442
    The Magic Eraser 442
    The more magical Background Eraser 444
    The still more magical Extract command 447
    Using the Color Range command 453
    A few helpful Color Range hints. 456
Creating an Independent Mask Channel 457
    Saving a selection outline to a mask channel 457
    Converting a mask to a selection 459
    Viewing mask and image. 460
Building a Mask from an Image 461
Summary 468

Chapter 10: Corrective Filtering 469

A First Look at Filters 470
    Corrective filters 470
    Destructive filters. 471
    Effects filters. 472
How Filters Work 473
    External plug-ins 474
    Previewing filters 474
    Reapplying the last filter 476
    Nudging numerical values 476
Fading a Filter 476
    Creating layered effects 478
    Filtering inside a border 478
    Undoing a sequence of filters 478
Heightening Focus and Contrast. 480
    Using the Unsharp Mask filter. 480
    Using the preset sharpening filters. 487
    Sharpening grainy photographs 487
    Smart Sharpen. 489
    Using the High Pass filter 492
    Converting an image into a line drawing. 493
Blurring an Image 494
    Applying the Gaussian Blur filter 495
    The preset blurring filters 496

Anti-aliasing an image 497
Directional blurring. 499
Using the Lens Blur filter. 508
Applying a Box Blur. 512
Using the Shape Blur 515
Working with Surface Blur 518
Softening a selection outline. 520
Noise Factors. 526
Adding noise. 526
Removing noise with Despeckle 530
Averaging pixels with Median 530
Sharpening a compressed image 531
Cleaning up scanned halftones 535
Using the Average filter 537
Summary 539

Chapter 11: Distortions and Effects. 541
Bizarre Effects 542
What about the others? 552
One final note about RAM 552
The Filter Gallery 553
The Pixelate Filters 555
Creating a Mezzotint 556
Edge-Enhancement Filters 557
Embossing an image 557
Tracing around edges 560
Creating a metallic coating 561
Distortion Filters. 562
The fun-house mirror. 564
Twirling spirals 566
Zigging and zagging. 569
Creating parallel Ripples and Waves 571
Distorting an image along a curve 579
Changing to Polar Coordinates 580
Working with Lens Correction. 582
Distorting with the Liquify command 585
Creating a vanishing point. 595
Adding Clouds and Spotlights 601
Creating clouds 602
Using the Fibers filter. 603
Lighting an image 604
Summary 609

Part IV: Layers, Objects, and Text — 611

Chapter 12: Working with Layers 613

Sending a Selection to a Layer 616
Other Ways to Make a Layer 617
Layer Basics 620
Switching between layers 620
Switching layers from the keyboard 622
Selecting similar layers. 622
Understanding transparency 623
Modifying the background layer 625
Reordering layers. 627
Displaying layer edges 629
Automated matting techniques 630
Blending layers 632
Fusing several layers 634
Deleting layers. 635
Saving a flattened version of an image 635
Selecting the Contents of Layers 635
Drop Shadows 637
Moving, Linking, and Aligning Layers 642
Linking and unlinking. 642
Organizing layers in Groups 644
Creating and Using Smart Objects. 647
Creating a new Smart Object 648
Editing Smart Objects 649
Locking layers. 651
Using guides and Smart Guides 652
Setting up the grid 656
Using the Measure tool. 658
Applying Transformations 660
Transforming the entire image 660
Transforming layers and selected pixels. 661
Warping layers 664
Numerical transformations 666
Masking and Layers 667
Preserving transparency. 667
Creating layer-specific masks 670
Pasting inside a selection outline. 673
Masking groups of layers 673
Working with Layer Comps. 675
Summary 678

Chapter 13: The Wonders of Blend Modes. 679

Opacity and Fill 681
Blend Modes 684
Advanced Blending Options 701
    Blending interior layer effects. 702
    Masking and unmasking effects 705
    Dumping whole color channels 708
    Making knockouts. 708
Dropping Out and Forcing Through. 712
    Color range sliders 713
    Fuzziness. 716
Whole Image Calculations 719
    The Apply Image command 720
    Add and Subtract 724
    The Calculations command 728
    Combining masks 730
Summary 734

Chapter 14: Shapes and Styles. 735

Drawing Shapes 736
    The pros and cons of shapes 736
    The shape tools 738
    Drawing the shape 739
    Combining and editing shapes 742
    Editing for inner beauty 745
Skin-Deep Beauty: Layer Styles 747
    The advantages of layer effects 755
    Inside the Layer Style dialog box 756
Modifying and Saving Effects. 764
    Disabling effects. 764
    Duplicating effects 765
    Scattering effects to the four winds 765
    Saving effects as styles. 766
Summary 767

Chapter 15: Fully Editable Text. 769

The Five Flavors of Text 770
Text as Art 771
Using the Type Tool 775
Creating Vertical Type 777
Creating and Manipulating Text in a Frame 778

Applying Character Formatting 781
Font 782
Size 784
Leading 785
Kerning 787
Fractional Widths and System Layout 789
Tracking 789
Horizontal and vertical scaling 789
Baseline 790
Color 791
Applying Paragraph Formatting 793
Alignment 793
Roman Hanging Punctuation 794
Justification 794
Indents and paragraph spacing 796
Hyphenation 797
Line breaks and composition methods 798
Checking your spelling 798
Finding and Replacing Text 799
Fitting Type on a Path 801
Warping Text 804
Editing Text as Shapes 806
Summary 808

Part V: Color and Output — 809

Chapter 16: Essential Color Management — 811

A Typical Color-Matching Scenario 812
Setting up the source monitor 813
Selecting the ideal working space 816
Embedding the profile 818
Setting up the destination space 819
Defining color management policies 819
Converting the color space 820
Color Conversion Central 822
Description 822
Working spaces 822
Color management policies 825
More options 827
Custom CMYK Setup 830
Saving and Loading Color Settings 832
Synchronizing Bridge Color Settings 834
Summary 836

Chapter 17: Mapping and Adjusting Colors 837

Color Effects and Adjustments. 837
When Colors Need Therapy 839
Quick and Automatic Color Effects 840
   Invert 840
   Equalize 842
   Threshold 843
   Posterize 848
Quick and Automatic Corrections. 849
   Gray areas 849
   The Auto Levels command 850
   The Auto Contrast command 851
   The Auto Color command 851
Adjusting Hues and Colorizing Images 853
   Using the Hue/Saturation command 853
   Colorizing images. 861
   Shifting selected hues 861
   Shifting predefined colors 862
   Filtering colors 864
   Using the Variations command 865
   Using the Match Color command. 867
   Enhancing colors in a compressed image 870
Making Custom Brightness Adjustments 871
   The Histogram palette 872
   The Levels command. 875
   The Curves command 882
   Gradient maps. 887
   Practical applications: Continuous curves 888
   Practical applications: Arbitrary curves. 891
   The Shadow/Highlight command 891
   Correcting exposure 895
Adjustment Layers 898
   The advantages of layer-based corrections 901
   Correcting a flat image using layers 903
Correcting Camera Raw Images 904
   Making color adjustments 906
   Sharpening and smoothing 908
   Correcting for the camera lens 909
   Tweaking the profile 912
   Opening and saving images with Camera Raw 912
   Saving your Camera Raw settings. 913
   Applying your saved Camera Raw settings 914
Summary 915

Chapter 18: Printing and Publishing with Photoshop 917

Understanding Printing Terminology 918
Printing Composites. 921
    Choosing a printer through Windows 923
    Choosing a printer on a Mac. 923
    Setting up the page 924
    Specifying a transfer function 935
    Printing pages 936
Creating Color Separations. 939
    Outputting separations. 940
    Color trapping. 941
Printing Duotones 942
    Creating a duotone 942
    Reproducing a duotone 944
    Editing individual duotone plates. 945
Spot-Color Separations 946
Optimizing Images for Web Publication. 947
Choosing the Right Web Graphic Format 947
    Graphic Interchange Format. 948
    JPEG File Interchange Format 949
    Portable Network Graphics Format 950
    The Save For Web Dialog Box 951
Optimizing Images into GIF and PNG-8 Formats 954
    Optimization presets 956
    Custom GIF and PNG-8 optimization settings 956
Optimizing Images into JPEG and PNG-24 Formats 961
    Optimization presets 961
    Custom JPEG and PNG-24 optimization settings 962
Resizing Images 962
Creating Animated GIF Images 963
Slicing and Dicing an Image 965
    Creating slices. 967
    Editing slices 968
    Setting slice options 968
    Saving slices 971
Publishing from the Bridge. 971
    Printing contact sheets. 974
    Creating a picture package 975
    Creating a Web Photo Gallery 978
    Creating a PDF presentation. 981
    Using Photomerge to create a panorama 983
Summary 986

Appendix: The Keyboard, Menus, and Making Photoshop Your Own **987**

   Hidden Shortcuts and Modifiers. 988
      Windows Alt-key combos 988
      The shortcut menu 989
      Toolbox shortcuts 990
      Palette shortcuts 991
   Customizing Keyboard Shortcuts 993
      Customizing menus. 995
      Creating a new menu set 996
   The Great-Grandmother of All Shortcut Tables 997

Index. 1029

Welcome to Photoshop

P A R T

I

In This Part

Chapter 1
Introducing
Photoshop CS2

Chapter 2
Inside Photoshop

Chapter 3
Image Management

Introducing Photoshop CS2

✦ ✦ ✦ ✦

In This Chapter

An introduction
to Photoshop

How image
editing works

The difference
between pixels
and vectors

The new features in
Photoshop CS2

✦ ✦ ✦ ✦

What Is Photoshop?

Maybe you already know what Photoshop is and what it does.
You may be one of the people who have been using it since its
first version and you use it every day. On the other hand, you
might be one of the larger group of people who have a general
sense of what Photoshop is and does but have little or no
experience using it. It is our intention to make this book useful
for both camps — and with this, the first chapter, there may
be some review for the former group and some startling reve-
lations for the latter. As you move forward and get to "What's
New in Photoshop CS2" the playing field should level out, and
as you move through the rest of the book, no matter what level
of user you are now, there is a great deal of new and useful
information throughout.

So what exactly is Photoshop and what does it do? Adobe
Photoshop — Photoshop is the name of the software, Adobe
Systems is the name of the company that develops and sells
it — is a professional-level image-editing application. It allows
you to create images from whole cloth or, more likely, modify scanned artwork and digital photographs. Photoshop
is available for use on computers equipped with either
Microsoft Windows or Apple's Macintosh operating system,
currently OS X.

Mind you, Photoshop isn't just any image-editing application.
It's the most powerful, most ubiquitous image-editing application in the world. Despite hefty competition, where professional
image editing is concerned, Photoshop's not just the market
leader — it's the only game in town.

Such a lack of competition is rarely a good thing, because
stagnation can often result. But in Photoshop's case, the his-
torically lopsided sales advantage has provided Adobe with a
clear incentive to reinvest in Photoshop and regularly enhance,
and even overhaul, its capabilities. It's as if each new version
of Photoshop is competing with its own previous versions for

the hearts and minds of the digital art community. Meanwhile, other vendors have had to devote smaller resources to playing catch-up. Some, such as Jasc Software, with its Windows-only Paint Shop Pro, have hung in there and remained commercially viable. But such success stories are few and far between. Although competitors have provided some interesting and sometimes amazing capabilities, the sums of their parts have more often than not fallen well short of Photoshop's.

As a result, Photoshop rides a self-perpetuating wave of market leadership. It wasn't always the best image editor, nor was it the first. But its deceptively straightforward interface combined with a few terrific core functions made it a hit from the moment of its first release. More than a dozen years later — thanks to substantial capital injections from Adobe and highly creative programming on the parts of Photoshop's engineering staff and its originator, Thomas Knoll — Photoshop has evolved into the most popular program of its kind.

Image-Editing Theory

Like any *image editor*, Photoshop enables you to alter photographs and other scanned artwork. You can retouch an image, apply special effects, swap details between photos, introduce text and logos, adjust color balance, and even sharpen the focus of a photograph. Photoshop also provides everything you need to create artwork from scratch, including a suite of vector drawing tools and a highly specialized painting palette. These tools are fully compatible with pressure-sensitive tablets, so you are not limited to creating only those images you can successfully draw with a mouse.

Bitmaps versus vectors

Image editors fall into the larger software category of *painting programs*. In a painting program, you draw a line, and the application converts it to a string of tiny square dots called *pixels*. The painting itself is called a *bitmapped image*, but *bitmap* and *image* are equally acceptable terms.

Note   Photoshop uses the term *bitmap* exclusively to mean a black-and-white image, the logic being that each pixel conforms to one *bit* of data, 0 or 1 (off or on). To avoid confusion — and because forcing a distinction between working with exactly two colors or anywhere from 4 to 16 million colors is entirely arbitrary — the term bitmap is used more broadly to mean any image composed of a fixed number of pixels, regardless of the number of colors involved.

What about other graphics applications, such as Adobe's own Illustrator? Applications such as Illustrator, Macromedia FreeHand, and CorelDraw fall into a different category of software called *drawing programs*. Drawings comprise *vector objects*, which are independent, mathematically defined lines and shapes. For this reason, drawing programs are sometimes said to be *vector-based* or *object-oriented*.

As luck would have it, Photoshop bridges the gap between conventional painting and drawing programs quite nicely by providing many of the best features of both. In addition to its wealth of image-editing and organic-painting capabilities, Photoshop permits you to add vector-based text and shapes to your photographic images. These features may not altogether take the place of a drawing program, but they help to make Photoshop an increasingly flexible and dynamic image-creation environment.

The ups and downs of painting

As you might expect, painting programs and drawing programs have their own strengths and weaknesses. The strength of a painting program is that it offers a straightforward approach to creating images. For example, although many of Photoshop's features are complex — some of them extremely so — its core painting tools are as easy to use and familiar as a pencil. You alternately draw and erase until you reach a desired effect, just as you've been doing since childhood.

In addition to being simple to use, each of Photoshop's core painting tools is fully customizable. It's as if you have access to an infinite variety of crayons, colored pencils, pastels, airbrushes, watercolors, and so on, all of which are erasable. The simplicity and customization potential make these tools fun to use, and you'll find yourself creating artwork that you would never have had the time or patience to attempt manually.

Because painting programs rely on pixels, they are ideally suited to electronic photography. Whether captured with a scanner or digital camera, an electronic photograph is composed of thousands or even tens of millions of colored pixels. A drawing program such as Illustrator may let you import such a photograph and apply very simple edits, but Photoshop gives you complete control over every pixel, entire collections of pixels, or independent elements of pixels. As witnessed by a quick examination of the pictures in this book, a photograph can become anything.

The downside of paintings and electronic photos is that they are ultimately finite in scale. Because a bitmap contains a fixed number of pixels, the *resolution* of an image — the number of pixels in an inch, a centimeter, or some other defined space — changes with respect to the size at which the image is printed. Print the image small, and the pixels become tiny, which increases the resolution of the image. Like the millions of cells in your body, tiny pixels become too small to see and thus blend together to form a cohesive whole, as in the first image in Figure 1-1. Print the image large and the pixels grow, which decreases the resolution. Large pixels are like cells viewed through a microscope; once you can distinguish them independently, the image falls apart, as in the second example in the figure. The results are jagged edges and blocky transitions. The only way to remedy this problem is to increase the number of pixels in the image, which increases the size of the file.

Cross-Reference Bear in mind that this is a very basic explanation of how images work. For a more complete description that includes techniques for maximizing image resolution and quality, check out Chapter 3.

Figure 1-1: When printed small, an image appears smooth and sharp (left). But when enlarged, the now-visible individual pixels create a grainy image (right).

The downs and ups of drawing

The process of creating a vector-based drawing might more aptly be termed "constructing," because you actually build each of the lines and shapes, point by point, and stack them on top of each other to create a finished image. Each of these objects is independently editable — one of the main advantages of an object-oriented approach — but you're still faced with the task of building your artwork one chunk at a time.

Because a drawing program defines lines, shapes, and text as mathematical equations, these objects automatically conform to the full resolution of the output device, whether it's a laser printer, an imagesetter, or a film recorder. The drawing program sends the math to the printer and the printer *renders* the math to paper or film. In other words, the printer converts the drawing program's equations to printer pixels. Your printer offers far more pixels than your screen — a 600-dots-per-inch (dpi) laser printer, for example, offers 600 pixels per inch (dots equal pixels), whereas most screens are limited to 150 pixels per inch or fewer. So the printed drawing appears smooth and sharply focused regardless of the size at which you print it, as shown in Figure 1-2.

get the point

Figure 1-2: Whether printed small or viewed through a high-level zoom, this image remains crisp and clear.

Another advantage of drawings is that they take up relatively little space on a hard drive. The file size of a drawing depends on the quantity and complexity of the objects the drawing contains. Thus, the file size has almost nothing to do with the size of the printed image, which is just the opposite of the way bitmapped images work. A thumbnail drawing of a garden that contains hundreds of leaves and petals consumes several times more space than a poster-sized drawing that comprises three rectangles.

When to use Photoshop

Because of their specialized tools and methods, painting programs and drawing programs fulfill distinct and divergent purposes. Photoshop and other painting programs are best suited to creating and editing the following kinds of artwork:

✦ Scanned photos, including photographic collages and embellishments that originate from scans

✦ Images captured with any type of digital camera

✦ Still frames captured from videotape or film

✦ Realistic artwork that relies on the play between naturalistic highlights, midranges, and shadows

✦ Impressionistic artwork and other images created for purely personal or aesthetic purposes

✦ Logos and other display type featuring soft edges, reflections, or tapering shadows

✦ Special effects that require the use of filters and color enhancements that you simply can't achieve in a drawing program

When to use a drawing program

You're probably better off using Illustrator or some other drawing program if you're interested in creating more stylized artwork, such as the following:

✦ Poster art and other high-contrast graphics that heighten the appearance of reality

✦ Architectural plans, product designs, or other precise line drawings

✦ Business graphics, such as graphs, charts, and diagrams that reflect data or show how things work

✦ Traditional logos and text effects that require crisp, ultrasmooth edges

✦ Brochures, flyers, and other single-page documents that mingle artwork, logos, and body-copy text (such as the text you're reading now)

If you're serious about computer graphics, you should own at least one painting program and one drawing program. If I had to rely exclusively on two graphics applications for producing still, two-dimensional images, I would choose Photoshop and Illustrator. Adobe has done a fine job of establishing symmetry between the two programs so that they share common interface elements and keyboard shortcuts. Learn one and the other makes a lot more sense.

What's New in Photoshop CS2

While at first glance it doesn't appear that CS2 is a major upgrade from CS (or from version 7, if you happened to skip the upgrade to CS), that doesn't mean that it isn't a worthwhile investment; on the contrary, you'll find that new tools and new options for individual tools and the program as a whole make it a very important upgrade for users of all levels. Many of these improvements don't smack you in the face when you first open the application — you might not notice them until you go to do some image restoration, tinker with color or light correction, or attempt to organize your images. To give you a quick tour of what's new and improved, a list of the most significant upgrades/changes and notes as to where to find coverage of the features in the book follows — bear in mind there are a lot of smaller upgrades and changes beyond this very basic list, and you'll discover them throughout the rest of the book and in your own travels with Photoshop:

✦ **New Workspace Presets (Chapter 2).** In previous versions, you could save workspaces — configurations of palette and tool placements that were conducive to specific images or types of work. In CS2, you can choose from nine new workspace presets, designed for different tasks such as creating Web graphics, working with type, or correcting color.

✦ **The Bridge (Chapter 3).** When you upgraded from version 7 to Photoshop CS, you probably noticed the File Browser. You may not have used it much, however, because while it was a major improvement simply because such a tool was added, it wasn't the most efficient or intuitive tool. Replacing the File Browser in CS2 is the Bridge, a workspace that you can invoke through several avenues. The Bridge provides tools for searching for, sorting, organizing, and using your images for a variety of print and online distribution products — from photo album pages to a gallery of Web images.

✦ **Animation (Chapter 18).** Previously available only in ImageReady, Photoshop CS2 enables you to create animations from your images, building frames and establishing the playback rules for them. It's rumored that ImageReady will be going away in future releases of Photoshop, so this is just the beginning of the integration of ImageReady's tools for creating Web graphics.

✦ **Keyboard and Menu Customization (Chapter 2).** Now you can create your own keyboard shortcuts and customize the appearance of menus and menu commands. If you aren't a big shortcut user now, this enhancement may turn you into a keyboard shortcut junkie — the ability to make the software work the way your mind approaches your tasks is a major enhancement.

ImageReady?

Photoshop's companion program, ImageReady CS2, remains a great tool for preparing images for the Web — to animate them, to create rollovers, and to create and edit sliced images. ImageReady may disappear, however, in subsequent releases of Photoshop, and is not significantly changed in CS2. You'll find, too, that one of ImageReady's chief uses has been usurped by Photoshop — you can now animate your images right in Photoshop, with no need to go out to ImageReady to create, edit, test, and save the animation.

✦ **The New Spot Healing Brush (Chapter 7).** You had the Healing Brush in CS, and now it's joined by the Spot Healing Brush. With this tool, you can make quick, small restorations within your photos. Rather than manually selecting the area to be healed and the content to use in healing it, the spot healing brush makes quick restorations with one click of the mouse. No need to sample a source for the healing content — just click on the spot, stain, nick, or small tear, and voila — the healing happens.

✦ **Red-Eye Removal (Chapter 7).** If you've used Photoshop Elements (Adobe's bargain-priced photo-editing program), you may have been impressed with its red-eye removal tool. Complex in Elements 2 and vastly improved in Elements 3, this tool has now joined the Photoshop CS2 toolbox, and is much like the Spot Healing Brush in its simplicity and ease of use. Just set the pupil size and degree of darkening you require, and click to exorcise the demon glow.

✦ **Warp (Chapter 12).** When transforming a layer — a list of distortions previously limited to resizing, rotating, skewing, or adding perspective — you can now warp the content, clicking and dragging from any of a series of handles along a grid that appears over the selected layer's content. You can now bend, twist, and stretch your images into any number of shapes and in any number of directions.

✦ **Vanishing Point (Chapter 11).** Need to create the look of a vanishing point, to create an accurate perspective? Choose Vanishing point from the Filter menu, and create the perspective, edit it, and apply it to your image through a series of tools in a handy dialog box, much like the Liquify dialog box.

✦ **Smart Objects (Chapter 12).** Turn layers — individual layers or groups thereof — into objects that can be edited outside the image, in their own window, and exported easily to other images.

✦ **Smart Guides (Chapter 12).** Taking the ubiquitous Guides feature to a new level, Smart Guides allow you to visually align and distribute layers more easily. When Smart Guides are turned on, the guides you place on-screen are accompanied by additional guides to show you when layers are lined up — when top, bottom, or sides are aligned. The color of your Smart Guides is customizable through the Preferences dialog box.

✦ **New Blur and Sharpen Filters (Chapter 10).** To the list of Blur filters, add the Box, Shape, and Surface blur, substantially expanding your ability to soften and blend content. The Sharpen filters now include Smart Sharpen, a customizable sharpening tool.

✦ **Correct Exposure (Chapter 17).** Found in the Image, Adjustments submenu, this command allows you to quickly and easily correct a photo that was over- or underexposed. A simple set of Exposure, Offset, and Gamma sliders gives you total control over the process.

✦ **Lens Correction (Chapter 11).** This new filter enables you to create a fully customizable lens through which to distort your layer content. The distortion can be restorative or truly destructive, bending content around a curve that you design.

✦ **Image Variables (Chapter 3).** Store various visibility and type options for a single image, naming each set of variables for future use.

✦ **New HDR (High Dynamic Range) Mode (Chapter 4).** You can now preview and process images in 32 bits/channel mode.

Summary

Whether you consider CS2 a major upgrade or a small set of changes, this chapter's goal has been to familiarize you with what to expect in terms of new coverage throughout the rest of this book. Some features have been improved, some added, some have simply been moved. In any case, you're now ready to move forward and focus on the individual features and tasks covered in the book's subsequent chapters, and to begin exploring Photoshop CS2's new and improved features on your own.

✦   ✦   ✦

Inside Photoshop

✦ ✦ ✦ ✦

In This Chapter

Getting comfortable
with the Photoshop
desktop

Finding your favorite
tools and making
new friends

Checking out your
tool options

Saving and managing
tool presets

Zooming in on
your images

Scrolling from the
keyboard

Navigating the
workspace

Using Photoshop's
Preferences to make
yourself at home

✦ ✦ ✦ ✦

There are things we can count on in just about any computer application these days — toolbars, menus, keyboard shortcuts (some of them common to many applications), and dialog boxes that appear when the toolbar buttons and menu commands are used. All of the common features help us devote our time to the features that vary by application — the things that make each application unique.

You'll find all the aforementioned familiar features in Photoshop, which should make your first impression a favorable one. At first glance, the workspace — the default arrangement of Toolbox, menu bar, and a handful of palettes — looks simple enough. Upon further inspection, of course, you'll find that Photoshop has a lot more going on than, say, your word processor or e-mail application, and that can be a bit daunting. Photoshop has palettes and options bars, and its dialog boxes can be a bit intimidating to a new user. Photoshop CS2 even has a separate workspace for file management, called The Bridge.

If you're new to Photoshop, all of this can be a lot to absorb, but absorb it you will, and through this chapter, you'll get a lot more comfortable with the Photoshop workspace, its tools, menus, and with the process of navigating it all. If you're not new to Photoshop, this chapter will show you some new features (a new tool or two, some relocated tools, some new workspace capabilities), and you may even discover some things that aren't new to Photoshop but that are new to you.

The Bridge — that name is a trifle dramatic, but fear not — is covered in Chapter 3, where its role as an image file management tool is thoroughly discussed. In Chapter 18, you'll see The Bridge used to print and publish various multiple-image creations. For now, though, let's fire up Photoshop and start poking around!

Dive in with the Splash Screen

Shortly after you launch Photoshop, the *splash screen* appears. A splash screen is not a phenomenon unique to Photoshop—many applications have one. The splash screen's role is to announce the application's launch, maybe offer some marketing information, and to explain the launching process by showing the names of plug-in modules as they load and listing the various initialization procedures. In Photoshop, the splash also lists the names of Photoshop's developers, going all the way back (the first names) to the beginning, when Photoshop 1.0 was just a baby.

Tip   If you're a Windows user, you can access the splash screen at any time by choosing Help ➪ About Photoshop. On the Mac, choose About Photoshop from the Photoshop menu. After a few seconds, the list of programmers and copyright statements at the bottom of the screen starts to scroll. Press Alt (or Option on the Mac) to make the list scroll more quickly. To make the splash screen go away, just click it.

Note   If you've ever tried to launch Photoshop on a networked computer while another computer on the network is already running a copy of Photoshop using the same serial number, you're familiar with the message "Could not initialize Photoshop because So-and-So is already running a copy of Adobe Photoshop with this serial number." There are two important things to note here: One is that you can work around this by simply detaching the second computer from the network before you launch Photoshop. After the application is open, renetwork the computer, and you'll be up and running. And the other important thing to note is that with Mac OS X, this network problem doesn't occur.

The Welcome Screen

In Photoshop CS, Adobe changed the way you access online help and other resources, and this change, along with several others, continues in CS2. After the initial splash screen disappears, Photoshop presents you with the Welcome Screen, shown in Figure 2-1, which provides you with several choices. You can view Tutorials, Tips and Tricks, Color Management Setup, or a listing of What's New. Be aware that most of these options require that you have access to the Internet. If you want to dismiss the screen and go about your business, click Close. If you want to disable the screen so it does not appear every time you launch the program, deselect the Show this dialog at startup option. Either way, you can return to the Welcome Screen at any time by choosing Help ➪ Welcome Screen.

Note   As in previous versions, you can still get to the Adobe Web site by clicking the icon at the top of the toolbox or by choosing Help ➪ Photoshop Online.

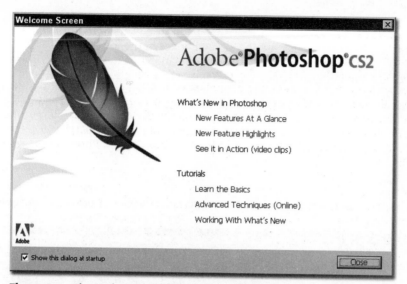

Figure 2-1: The Welcome Screen offers a series of support options and other resources for Photoshop CS2. If you don't ever want to see it again, just deselect the Show this dialog at startup option.

The Photoshop Workspace

After the launch process is complete, the Photoshop workspace appears in the foreground. Figure 2-2 shows the Photoshop CS2 workspace as it appears for a Windows user when an image is open and all palettes are visible. Figure 2-3 shows the same scenario as it appears on a Mac running Mac OS X.

Many of the elements that make up the Photoshop workspace are familiar to people who are acquainted with the Windows or Macintosh operating system environments. For example, the menu bar lives at the top of the workspace (as it lives at the top of the window for virtually all applications) and provides access to menus and commands. Even the way the menus work should be comfortable to users of both operating systems. At the top of the window, you have a title bar, and you can drag the title bar to move the application window (assuming it's not already maximized). In either OS, you will have scroll bars in your windows if there's more to be seen than will fit in the window at its current size.

Other Photoshop workspace features that may be less familiar include:

✦ **Image window.** Photoshop lets you open multiple images at one time — you can open them simultaneously from the Open dialog box, or one at a time, over the course of a work session, either way. The nice thing is that each open image resides in its own window. On the Mac, click the green zoom button in the upper-left corner of the title bar to resize the window to fit the image. Also worth noting on the Mac are the special boxes in the lower-left corner of the image window (see Figure 2-3). The magnification box tells you the current view size, and the Info palette can tell you important things about image size and computer resources. (To see the Info palette, you may need to increase the horizontal size of your image window by dragging it from the lower-right corner.)

Color Picker

Options bar

Toolbox   Menu bar   Title bar   Image window   Palettes   Docking well

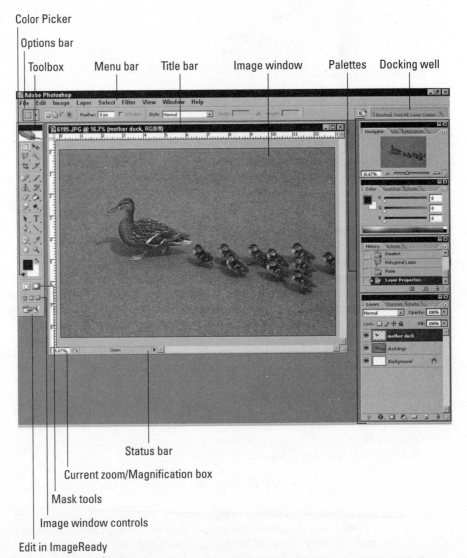

Status bar

Current zoom/Magnification box

Mask tools

Image window controls

Edit in ImageReady

Figure 2-2: The Photoshop CS2 workspace as it looks for a user running Windows

Figure 2-3: The Photoshop CS2 workspace as it looks on a Mac running OS X

✦ **Status bar (Windows only).** Just above the Windows taskbar sits Photoshop's status bar, which provides running commentary on the active tool and image. (If the status bar doesn't appear on your screen, choose Window ➪ Status Bar.) The left end of the status bar features the magnification box and the Info palette, both of which are described in the preceding paragraph.

For complete information on the magnification box, read the section "Navigating in Photoshop" later in this chapter. The very next section explains the Info palette.

✦ **Toolbox.** The Toolbox icons provide one-click access to the various Photoshop tools. To select a tool, click its icon. Then use the tool by clicking or dragging with it inside the image window.

The bottom four rows of the Toolbox contain controls for changing your paint colors, entering and exiting the quick mask mode, changing the screen area available for image display, and switching to Adobe ImageReady (which ships with Photoshop).

✦ **Floating palettes.** Photoshop CS2 offers a total of 16 palettes, not including the Toolbox and the Options bar, which are technically palettes as well. Each palette is said to be "floating," which means that it's independent of the image window and of other palettes. Palettes can be grouped together or dragged apart to float separately according to your tastes. For more information on palettes, see the upcoming section "The floating palettes." To see the whole list of palettes, click your Window menu.

✦ **Docking well.** The gray bar at the end of the Options bar is the docking well. You can drag palettes to the well to save screen space but still keep the palettes easily accessible. For more information, see the section "Rearranging and docking palettes" later in this chapter.

Note Unfortunately, the docking well is visible only if you use a screen resolution with a horizontal pixel display of more than 800 pixels.

The Info Palette

The Info palette is Photoshop's way of keeping you informed of important things — the size of the image, the tool that's in use, where your image is on the page (if it were to be printed), how much memory you're using — a lot of stuff you may or may not want to know at any given time. You don't have to display the Info palette if you don't want to (it's displayed in Figure 2-4), or you may be thrilled that it's there and feel queasy when you can't see it — but it's there if you need it. The following sections explain all the wonderful things it can tell you.

Figure 2-4: The Info palette provides one-stop shopping for all your image information needs. Here, the Info Palette Options dialog box (displayed by clicking the palette menu button) shows the info you can choose to see.

Document size

By default, the Info palette contains two numbers divided by a slash. The first number is the size of the base image in memory. The second number takes into account any additional layers in your image. If you're interested in how the values are calculated, here goes:

Photoshop calculates the first value by multiplying the height and width of the image (both in pixels) by the *bit depth* of the image, which is the size of each pixel in memory. Consider a typical, full-color, 640 × 480-pixel image. A full-color image takes up 24 bits of memory per pixel (which is why it's called a 24-bit image). There are 8 bits in a byte, so 24 bits translates to 3 bytes. Multiply that by the number of pixels and you get 640 × 480 × 3 = 921,600 bytes. Because there are 1,024 bytes in a kilobyte, 921,600 bytes is exactly 900K. Try it yourself — open a 640 x 480-pixel RGB image and you'll see that the first number in the Info palette reads 900K. Now you know why.

It's the second value, however, the one that factors in the layers, that represents the real amount of memory that Photoshop needs. If the image contains one layer only, the numbers before and after the slash are the same. Otherwise, Photoshop measures the opaque pixels in each layer and adds approximately 1 byte of overhead per pixel to calculate the transparency. The second number also grows to accommodate paths, masks, spot-color channels, undoable operations, and miscellaneous data required by the image cache.

Of course, it's not necessary that you be able to predict these values, which is a good thing, because predicting the second value is virtually impossible. Photoshop asks no help when calculating the values in the information, but it's a good idea to know what's going on as you start adding layers to an image. The larger the preview numbers grow, the more work Photoshop has to do and the slower it's likely to perform, depending on your system configuration — memory, processor, available hard-drive space, and so on.

Image position

If you want to position a picture precisely on a page before printing, use the Print with Preview command in the File menu (see Chapter 18 for details). To get a rough idea of the current image position, however, click and hold on the Info palette. Photoshop displays a pop-up window showing the size and placement of the image in relation to the paper. The preview also shows the approximate placement of crop marks and other elements requested in the Show More Options section of the Print with Preview dialog box.

Tip

Press Alt (or Option on the Mac) and click the Info palette to view the size, channels, and resolution of the image.

You can also Ctrl-click (⌘-click on the Mac) the Info palette to see the tile sizes. Photoshop uses *tiles* to calculate pixel manipulations. If you confine your work to a single tile, it will probably go faster than if you allow a little to run over into a second tile. Click the right-pointing arrowhead next to the Info palette to display a pop-up menu of seven options. The first option — Document Sizes — is selected by default. This option displays the image-size values described in the preceding section. You can find out what information the other choices provide in the next few sections.

Tip

The prefix displayed before the values in the Info palette indicates which of the options is active: Doc shows that Document Sizes is selected; Scr, Scratch Sizes; and Eff, Efficiency. When the Timing option is active, an *s* appears after the numerical value. If a tool name appears in the Info palette, you know that the final option, Current Tool, is active. Similarly, if you see a color profile statement, such as "Untagged RGB," or a couple of measurements, such as "640 pixels x 480 pixels," you're looking at the Document Profile or Document Dimensions setting, respectively.

Image color profile

If you work regularly with many different color profiles, you may find the Document Profile option quite useful. When you select this option, the name of the current color profile appears in the Info palette.

Cross-Reference

For more information on color profiles, see Chapter 16, where you'll find everything you need to know about color profiles — how to apply them and what they do.

Document measurements

Similar to Alt- or Option-clicking the Info palette, selecting Document Dimensions gives you a quick readout of the width-by-height measurements of your document. The unit of measurement is set in the Units & Rulers panel of Photoshop's Preferences dialog box, and conveniently enough, you'll learn more about setting such preferences later on in this chapter.

Memory consumption and availability

When you select Scratch Sizes, Photoshop changes the values in the Info palette to represent memory consumption and availability. The first value is the amount of room required to hold the currently open images in RAM. The second value indicates the total amount of RAM that Photoshop has to work with. For the program to run at top efficiency, the first number must be smaller than the second.

In earlier versions of Photoshop, the number before the slash was generally equal to between three and five times the size of all open images, including layers. Ever since we have had the ability to undo multiple levels (going back multiple states through the History palette), however, this value can grow to more than 100 times as big as any one image. This is because Photoshop has to store each operation in memory on the off chance that you may want to undo to a previous point in time. For each and every action, Photoshop nudges the first value upward until you reach the ceiling of undoable operations.

The second value is simply equal to the amount of memory available to your images after the Photoshop application itself has loaded. For example, suppose Photoshop has 100MB of RAM at its disposal. The code that makes up the Photoshop application consumes about 15MB, so that leaves 85MB to hold and edit images.

If the second value is bigger than the first, all is happiness and Photoshop is running as fast as your particular brand of computer permits. But if the first value is larger, Photoshop has to dig into its supply of *virtual memory*, a disk-bound adjunct to RAM. Virtual memory makes Photoshop run more slowly because the program must swap portions of the image on and off your hard drive. The simple fact is, hard drives have moving parts and RAM does not. That means disk-bound virtual memory is slower than real memory.

To increase the size of the value after the slash, you have to get more RAM to your images in one of the following ways:

✦ Purchase more RAM. Installing an adequate supply of memory is the single best way to make Photoshop run more quickly. Not sure how? Consult your manufacturer, or get help from the company from whom you buy the RAM.

✦ Quit other applications so that only Photoshop is running.

✦ Quit Photoshop and remove any filters that you don't need from the Plug-Ins folder (which resides in the same folder as the Photoshop application). Important — you shouldn't throw the filters away, just move them to a location outside the Plug-Ins folder so they don't load into RAM when you launch Photoshop.

✦ Choose Memory & Image Cache in the Preferences submenu and increase the Memory Usage value as explained later in this chapter.

Operating efficiency

When you select the Efficiency option, Photoshop lists the amount of time it spends running operations in RAM compared with swapping data back and forth between the hard drive. A value of 100 percent is the best-case scenario. It means Photoshop never has to rely on scratch files. Low values indicate higher reliance on the hard drive and, as a result, slower operations. Adobe recommends that if the value falls below 75 percent, you should either assign more memory to Photoshop or purchase more RAM for your computer.

The Efficiency option is a reality check. If it seems Photoshop is dragging its feet, and you hear it writing to your hard drive a little too often, you can refer to the Efficiency rating to see whether performance is as bad as you suspect. Keep in mind, hearing Photoshop occasionally write to disk is not in and of itself cause for concern. All versions of Photoshop since 3.0 automatically copy open images to a disk buffer in case using virtual memory is later warranted. In fact, this is the reason Adobe added the Efficiency option to Version 3.0.1 — to quash fears that a few sparks from your hard drive indicated anything less than peak performance.

Photoshop operations timing

If you select Timing, the Info palette tells how long Photoshop took to perform the last operation (including background tasks, such as transferring an image to the system Clipboard). Adobe may have added this option to help testing facilities run their Photoshop tests. But built-in timing helps you as well.

For example, suppose you're trying to decide whether to purchase a new computer. You read a magazine article detailing the newest super-fast system. You can run the same filters with the same settings on your computer and see how much slower your results are, all without picking up a stopwatch.

The active tool

Select the Current Tool option, and Photoshop displays the name of the active tool. Why do you need such a condescending option? Surely you're not so far gone that you need Photoshop telling you what you already know. Adobe's intention is not to drum you over the head with redundant information but to offer a helping hand if you find the tool configuration confusing. Also, on the PC, the tool name serves as a companion to the tool description to the right of it in the status bar. Now you see not just what the tool does, but what the tool is.

Still, this option may prove to be as rarely useful to everyday image editing as Timing. Use it if you're having problems when first using Photoshop and then set it back to Document Sizes, Scratch Sizes, or Efficiency. The original three options continue to be the best.

The tools

When multiple tools share a single Toolbox slot, you select the tool you want from a menu-style list, as shown in Figure 2-5. A tiny triangle in the lower-right corner of a Toolbox button indicates that multiple tools share that button. You can click the triangle and then click the name of the tool you want to use. Or, to do the job with one less click, just drag from the icon onto the name of the tool and then release the mouse button.

Tip   You can cycle between the tools in the pop-up menu by Alt-clicking (Win) or Option-clicking (Mac) a tool icon. Pressing the key that appears to the right of the tool names also does the trick — however, depending on a tool setting that you establish in the Preferences dialog box, you may need to press Shift (see the section "General preferences").

Also, when you position your cursor over a tool, Photoshop tells you the name of the tool and how to select it from the keyboard. If you find the tool tips irritating, see the section "General preferences" to find out how to turn them off.

Drag from the button - (the pop-up menu appears)

and then drag out to the tool you want to use.

Figure 2-5: Drag from any tool icon with a triangle to display a pop-up menu of alternate tools.

Each tool has been cataloged in the following list, with tool icons, quick summaries, and the chapter (if any) to which you can refer for more information. No need to read the list word for word; just use it as a reference to get acquainted with the new program. Unless otherwise noted, each of the following descriptions tells how to use the tool in the image window. For example, if an item says drag, you click the tool's icon to select the tool, and then click and drag in the image window; you don't drag on the tool icon itself. Of course, you probably knew that!

Rectangular marquee (Chapter 8). Drag with this tool to enclose a portion of the image in a rectangular *marquee*, which is a pattern of moving dash marks indicating the boundary of a selection.

Shift-drag to add to a selection; Alt-drag (Win) or Option-drag (Mac) to delete from a selection. The same goes for the other marquee tools, as well as the lassos and Magic Wand. As an alternative to using these time-honored shortcuts, you can click mode icons in the Options bar to change the behavior of the selection tools.

Elliptical Marquee (Chapter 8). Drag with the Elliptical Marquee tool to enclose a portion of the window in an oval marquee.

Single-Row Marquee (Chapter 8). Click with the Single-Row Marquee tool to select an entire horizontal row of pixels that stretches all the way across the image. You can also drag with the tool to position the selection. You rarely need the Single-Row Marquee, but when you do, here it is.

Single-Column Marquee (Chapter 8). Same as the Single-Row Marquee, except the Single-Column Marquee tool selects an entire vertical column of pixels. Again, not a particularly useful tool.

Move (Chapter 8). Drag to move a selection or layer. In fact, the Move tool is the exclusive means for moving and cloning portions of an image. You can also Ctrl-drag (Win) or ⌘-drag (Mac) selections with any tools except the Shape, Path, and Slicing tools, but only because Ctrl (⌘ on the Mac) temporarily accesses the Move tool.

Lasso (Chapter 8). Drag with the Lasso tool to select a free-form portion of the image. You can also Alt-click (Win) or Option-click (Mac) with the Lasso to create a straight-sided selection outline.

Polygonal Lasso (Chapter 8). Click hither and yon with this tool to draw a straight-sided selection outline (just like Alt-clicking or Option-clicking with the standard lasso). Each click sets a corner point in the selection.

Magnetic Lasso (Chapter 8). As you drag with the Magnetic Lasso tool, the selection outline automatically sticks to the edge of the foreground image. Bear in mind, however, that Photoshop's idea of an edge may not jibe with yours. Like any automated tool, the Magnetic Lasso sometimes works wonders, and other times it's more trouble than it's worth.

Tip   The Magnetic Lasso automatically lays down points as you drag. If you don't like a point and want to get rid of it, press Backspace (Win) or Delete (Mac).

Magic Wand (Chapter 8). Click with the Magic Wand tool to select a contiguous area of similarly colored pixels. To select noncontiguous areas, click in one area and then Shift-click in another. Deselect the Contiguous tool option and click once to select similar colors throughout the image.

Crop (Chapter 3). Drag with the Crop tool to enclose the portion of the image you want to retain in a rectangular boundary. Photoshop tints areas outside the boundary to help you better see which image areas will go and which will stay when you apply the crop. The crop boundary sports several square handles you can drag to resize the cropped area. Drag outside the boundary to rotate it; drag inside to move it. Press Enter or Return to apply the crop or Esc to cancel.

Slice (Chapter 18). The Slice tool and its companion, the Slice Select tool, come into play when you're creating Web graphics. You can cut images into rectangular sections — known as slices — so that you can apply Web effects, such as links, rollovers, and animations, to different areas of the same image. Drag with the Slice Tool to define the area that you want to turn into a slice.

Slice Select (Chapter 18). If you don't get the boundary of your slice right the first time, click the slice with this tool and then drag one of the side or corner handles that appear. Or drag inside the boundary to relocate it.

Press Ctrl (Win) or ⌘ (Mac) when the Slice tool is active to temporarily access the Slice Select tool, and vice versa.

Healing Brush (Chapter 7). The Clone Stamp tool (also known to long-time Photoshop users as the Rubber Stamp tool) has always seemed like a miracle worker when removing unwanted elements from images. Although excellent results were possible, you still had to be careful that the texture and shading of the cloned area matched the area you were replacing. Although the Healing Brush tool seems at first use just like the Clone Stamp tool, its special "healing" process lets you clone details from one area without obscuring the texture and shading of the other.

Spot Healing Brush (Chapter 7). This tool is new to Photoshop CS2 and works similarly to the Healing Brush — it clones other content over offending material and makes it match the new surroundings. It's different from the Healing Brush in that it is simpler to use, fixes one spot at a time, and is best used for small problems — small stains, cuts, scratches, or small items in the image itself that you want to eradicate.

Patch (Chapter 7). Similar to the Healing Brush, the Patch tool lets you use the same "healing" technology by making selections and dragging them to new locations. It's generally useful for healing larger areas of the image.

Color Replacement (Chapter 5). Hailing from Photoshop's younger sibling, Photoshop Elements, the Color Replacement tool lets you paint over an existing color in the image to replace it with the foreground color. Its main reason for existence is to make it easy to fix red-eye — but now that there is also a tool specifically for that purpose, you may have to find another reason to use it.

Brush (Chapter 5). Drag with the Brush tool to paint soft lines. If you're thinking that sounds kind of dull, wait until you learn about the multitude of settings available to you in the Brushes palette.

Pencil (Chapter 5). Drag with the Pencil tool to paint jagged, hard-edged lines. Its main purpose is to clean up individual pixels when you're feeling fussy.

Clone Stamp (Chapter 7). This tool copies one portion of the image onto another. Alt-click (Win) or Option-click (Mac) the part of your image you want to clone, and then drag to clone that area to another portion of the image.

Pattern Stamp. The Pattern Stamp tool lets you paint with a pattern. Either choose a preset or define your own pattern using Edit ➪ Define Pattern and then paint away.

Red Eye Removal (Chapter 7). First found in Photoshop Elements, this tool is much appreciated by users of Photoshop CS2. Used to get rid of the bizarre glow in the eyes of those too close to the camera's flash, this simple tool restores the pupil based on simple Options bar settings that you can customize for individual cases of the dreaded demonic red eye.

History Brush (Chapter 7). The History Brush reverts portions of the image to any of a handful of previous states throughout the recent history of the image. To specify the state that you want to revert to, click in the first column of the History palette. It's like an undo brush but way, way better.

Art History Brush (Chapter 7). Like the History Brush, the Art History Brush paints with pixels from a previous image state. But with this brush, you get a variety of brush options that create different artistic effects.

Eraser (Chapter 7). Drag with the Eraser tool to paint in the background color or erase areas in a layer to reveal the layers below. Alt-drag (Win) or Option-drag (Mac) to switch to the Erase to History mode, which reverts the image to a previous state just as if you were using the History Brush.

Background Eraser (Chapter 9). The Background Eraser rubs away the background from an image as you drag along the border between the background and foreground. If you don't wield this tool carefully, though, you wind up erasing both background and foreground.

Magic Eraser (Chapter 9). The Magic Eraser came from the same gene pool that produced the Magic Wand. When you click with the Magic Wand, Photoshop selects a range of similarly colored pixels; click with the Magic Eraser, and you erase instead of select.

Gradient (Chapter 6). Drag with this tool to fill a selection with a gradual transition of colors, commonly called a *gradient*. You can click the gradient icon in the Toolbox and select a gradient style from the Options bar.

Paint Bucket (Chapter 6). Click with the Paint Bucket tool to fill a contiguous area of similarly colored pixels with the foreground color or a predefined pattern.

Blur (Chapter 5). Drag with the Blur tool to diffuse the contrast between neighboring pixels, which blurs the focus of the image. You can also Alt-drag (Win) or Option-drag (Mac) to sharpen the image.

Sharpen (Chapter 5). Drag with this tool to increase the contrast between pixels, which sharpens the focus. Alt-drag (Win) or Option-drag (Mac) when this tool is active to blur the image.

Smudge (Chapter 5). The Smudge tool works just as its name implies; drag with the tool to smear colors inside the image.

Dodge (Chapter 5). Drag with the Dodge tool to lighten pixels in the image. Alt-drag (Win) or Option-drag (Mac) to darken the image.

Burn (Chapter 5). Drag with the Burn tool to darken pixels. Press Alt (Win) or Option (Mac) to temporarily access the Dodge tool and lighten pixels.

Sponge (Chapter 5). Drag with the Sponge tool to decrease the amount of saturation in an image so the colors appear more drab and eventually gray. You can also increase color saturation by changing the Mode setting in the Options bar from Desaturate to Saturate.

Path Selection (Chapter 8). Click anywhere inside a path to select the entire path. If you click inside a path that contains multiple subpaths, Photoshop selects the subpath under the tool cursor. Shift-click to select additional paths or subpaths. You also use this tool and the Direct Selection tool, described next, to select and manipulate lines and shapes drawn with the shape tools.

Direct Selection (Chapter 8). To select and edit a segment in a selected path or shape, click it or drag over it with this tool. Press Shift while using the tool to select additional segments. Or Alt-click (Option-click on the Mac) inside a path or shape to select and edit the entire object.

Horizontal Type (Chapter 15). Also known simply as the Type tool, click with this tool to add vector text to your image.

Vertical Type (Chapter 15). The Vertical Type tool behaves just like the Horizontal Type tool, except that your text is oriented vertically in the image.

Horizontal Type Mask (Chapter 15). As you might expect, this tool creates horizontal type. The twist is that the type appears not directly in the image but rather as a mask, with an active selection around the shapes of the letters.

Vertical Type Mask (Chapter 15). Combine the verticality of the Vertical Type tool with the maskiness of the Horizontal Type Mask tool, and you have—what else?—the Vertical Type Mask tool. Use it to create an active selection of vertically oriented text.

Pen (Chapter 8). Click and drag with the Pen tool to set points in the image window. Photoshop draws an editable path outline—much like a path in Illustrator—that you can convert to a selection outline or stroke with color.

Freeform Pen (Chapter 8). Drag with this tool to draw freehand paths or vector masks. Photoshop automatically adds points along the path as it sees fit. If you select the Magnetic option in the Options bar, the Freeform Pen morphs into the Magnetic Pen. Deselect the option to return to the Freeform Pen.

Add Anchor Point (Chapter 8). To insert a point in a path, click a path segment with this tool.

Delete Anchor Point (Chapter 8). Click a point to remove it without interrupting the outline of the path. Photoshop automatically draws a new segment between the neighboring points.

Convert Point (Chapter 8). Points in a path come in different varieties, some indicating corners and others indicating smooth arcs. The Convert Point tool enables you to change one kind of point to another. Drag a point to convert it from a corner to an arc. Click a point to convert it from an arc to a sharp corner.

Rectangle (Chapter 14): One of the five vector drawing tools, this tool draws rectangles filled with the foreground color. Just click and drag to create a rectangle; Shift-drag to draw a square.

Rounded Rectangle (Chapter 14). Prefer your boxes with nice, curved corners instead of sharp, 90-degree angles? Drag or Shift-drag with the Rounded Rectangle tool.

Cross-Reference

You can opt to create rasterized shapes and lines with the Rectangle, Rounded Rectangle, Ellipse, Polygon, Line, and Custom Shape tools. See Chapter 14 for details.

Ellipse (Chapter 14). You look pretty smart to me, so you probably already figured out that you drag with this tool to draw an ellipse and Shift-drag to draw a circle.

Polygon (Chapter 14). By default, dragging with this tool creates a five-sided polygon. Controls available in the Options bar enable you to change the number of sides or set the tool to create star shapes.

Line (Chapter 14). Drag with the Line tool to create a straight line. But before you do, travel to the Options bar to set the line thickness and specify whether you want arrowheads at the ends of the line.

Custom Shape (Chapter 14). After you draw a shape with one of the other drawing tools, you can save it as a custom shape. Thereafter, you can re-create that shape by selecting it from the Options bar and then dragging with the Custom Shape tool. You also can choose from a variety of predefined shapes when working with the Custom Shape tool.

Notes (Chapter 3). Use this tool to create a little sticky note on which you can jot down thoughts, ideas, and other pertinent info that you want to share with other people who work with the image — or that you simply want to remember the next time you open the image. After you create the note, Photoshop displays a note icon in the image window; double-click the icon to see what you had to say.

Audio Annotation (Chapter 3). If you prefer the spoken word to the written one, you can annotate your images with an audio clip, assuming that you have a microphone and sound card for your computer. As with the Notes tool, an audio icon appears in the image window after you record your message. Clicking the icon plays the audio clip.

Eyedropper (Chapter 4). Click with the Eyedropper tool on a color in the image window to make that color the foreground color. Alt-click (Win) or Option-click (Mac) a color to make that color the background color.

Color Sampler (Chapter 4). Click as many as four locations in an image to evaluate the colors of those pixels in the Info palette. After you set a point, you can move it by dragging it to a different pixel.

Measure (Chapter 12). The Measure tool lets you measure distances and directions inside the image window. Just drag from one point to another and note the measurement data in the Info palette or the Options bar. You can also drag the endpoints of your line to take new measurements. And by Alt-dragging (Win) or Option-dragging (Mac) an endpoint, you can create a sort of virtual protractor that measures angles.

Hand (Chapter 2). Drag inside the image window with the Hand tool to scroll the window so you can see a different portion of the image. Double-click the Hand tool icon to magnify or reduce the image so it fits on the screen in its entirety. When the Hand tool is active, you can click buttons in the Options bar to display the image at the actual-pixels, fit-on-screen, or print-size view sizes.

Zoom (Chapter 2). Click with the Zoom tool to magnify the image so you can see individual pixels more clearly. Alt-click (Win) or Option-click (Mac) to step back from the image and take in a broader view. Drag to enclose the specific portion of the image you want to magnify. And finally, double-click the Zoom tool icon inside the Toolbox to restore the image to 100 percent view size.

You can modify the performance of any tool but the Measure tool by adjusting the settings in the Options bar. To change the unit of measurement used by the Measure tool, double-click the ruler or choose Edit ➪ Preferences ➪ Units & Rulers (Photoshop ➪ Preferences ➪ Units & Rulers in Mac OS X) to display the Units & Rulers panel of the Preferences dialog box. Then select the unit from the Rulers pop-up menu. Or even quicker, right-click (Win) or Control-click (Mac) the ruler or click the plus sign in the lower-left corner of the Info palette and select a measurement unit from the resulting pop-up menu.

The Toolbox controls

Well, that's about it for the Photoshop CS2 tools, except for a few more tools that are known as controls, which are for selecting colors, views of the workspace, masking modes, and hopping to ImageReady to edit the active image.

 Foreground color. Click the foreground color icon to bring up the Color Picker dialog box. Select a color and press Enter or Return to change the foreground color, which is used by the Pencil, Paintbrush, Airbrush, Gradient, and shape tools.

Note

I'm not sure why, but many users make the mistake of double-clicking the foreground or background color icons when they first start using Photoshop. A single click is all that's needed. Experienced users don't even bother with the Color Picker — they stick to the more convenient Color palette.

Background color. Click the background color icon to display the Color Picker and change the background color, which is used by the Eraser and Gradient tools. Photoshop also uses the background color to fill a selected area on the background layer when you press the Backspace or Delete key.

Switch colors. Click the switch colors icon to exchange the foreground and background colors.

Default colors. Click this icon to return to the default foreground and background colors _ black and white, respectively.

Tip

At any time, you can quickly make the foreground color white by clicking the default colors icon and then clicking the switch colors icon. Or just press D (for default colors) and then X (for switch colors).

 Marching ants. Click this icon to exit Photoshop's Quick Mask mode and view selection outlines as animated dotted lines that look like marching ants, hence the name. (Adobe calls this the "standard" mode, but "marching ants" mode better describes how it works.)

 Quick Mask. Click here to enter the Quick Mask mode, which enables you to edit selection boundaries using painting tools. The marching ants vanish and the image appears half covered by a translucent layer of red, like a rubylith in traditional pasteup. The red layer covers the deselected — or masked — portions of the image. Paint with black to extend the masked areas, thereby subtracting from the selection. Paint with white to erase the mask, thereby adding to the selection.

Cross-Reference

The Quick Mask mode is too complex a topic to sum up in a few sentences. If you can't wait to find out what it's all about, check out Chapter 9.

Standard window. Click this icon to display the foreground image in a standard window, as shown earlier in Figures 2-2 and 2-3. Every image appears in the Standard Window mode when you first open it.

Full Screen with Menu Bar. If you can't see enough of your image inside a standard window, click this icon. The title bar and scroll bars disappear, as do all background windows and the Windows taskbar, but the menu bar and palettes remain visible, as shown in Figure 2-6. (You can still access other open images by choosing their names from the Window menu.) A light gray background fills any empty area around the image.

Note

This is similar to the effect that you get when you click the Maximize button in the upper-right corner of the image window on a PC. However, you probably want to avoid maximizing images; use the Toolbox controls instead. Photoshop has a habit of resizing a maximized window whenever you zoom with the commands on the View menu. If you use the Toolbox controls, you don't have that problem.

Figure 2-6: The Full Screen with Menu Bar view gives you a bit more elbow room for your image.

Tip When the image doesn't consume the entire image window, the empty portion of the window appears gray when you're working in the Standard Window mode or the Full Screen with Menu Bar mode. To change the gray area to a different color — such as black — select a color and Shift-click in the gray area with the Paint Bucket tool.

◾ **Absolute Full Screen.** If you still can't see enough of your image, click the rightmost of the image window controls to see the photo set against a neutral black background. (You can't change the color of this backdrop — it's always black.) The menu bar disappears, limiting your access to commands, but you can still access many commands using keyboard shortcuts. Only the Toolbox and palettes remain visible.

As noted in the tool tips, pressing F lets you cycle through the Standard Window, Full Screen with Menu Bar, and Absolute Full Screen modes. If you need access to a menu command when working in the Absolute Full Screen mode, press Shift+F to display the menu bar. Press Shift+F again to hide it.

Tip If Photoshop's screen elements interfere with your view of an image, you can hide all palettes — including the Toolbox and Options bar — by pressing Tab. To bring the hidden palettes back into view, press Tab again.

You can hide the palettes but leave the Toolbox and Options bar on-screen by pressing Shift+Tab. Press Shift+Tab again to bring the palettes back. (Pressing Tab while the standard palettes are gone hides the Toolbox and Options bar.) If the rulers are turned on, they remain visible at all times. Press Ctrl+R (⌘-R on the Mac) to toggle the ruler display off and on.

Tip If you don't want to hide the palettes, you can reposition an image in either Full Screen mode by dragging it with the Hand tool. Or press the space bar and drag when any other tool is selected.

Tip Here's one more tip for good measure: Shift-click the icon for Absolute Full Screen to switch the display mode for all open images. Then press Ctrl+Tab (Control-Tab on the Mac) to cycle through the open images. This same trick works for the Standard and Full Screen with Menu Bar modes.

Go to ImageReady. Click this icon to switch to ImageReady, Photoshop's companion Web graphics program.

The Options bar

Spanning the width of the Photoshop window, and found just below the menu bar, the Options bar (labeled back in Figures 2-2 and 2-3) contains the major controls for the tools in the Toolbox. There's an Options bar for every tool, and through them, you establish settings for the active tool by selecting options, clicking icons, dragging sliders, and choosing options from pop-up menus in the bar. You can think of the Options bar as just another floating palette, albeit a long, skinny one. There is a difference, though — you'll use different tactics to hide, display, and relocate the Options bar than you do a regular palette:

✦ Choose Window ➪ Options or double-click any tool icon in the Toolbox to toggle on the display of the Options bar. (You should see a check mark to the left of the command when the Options bar is visible.) Choose Window ➪ Options again to toggle off the display of the Options bar. You also can press Tab to toggle on and off the display of the Options bar and all other palettes.

✦ By default, the Options bar is docked at the top of the program window. Drag the vertical handle at the left end of the bar to relocate it. If you drag the Options bar to the top or bottom of the window, the bar becomes docked again.

✦ Unfortunately, you can't change the size or shape of the Options bar.

You can attach regular palettes to the Options bar by dragging them into the docking well at the right end of the bar. The section "Rearranging and docking palettes" gives you the full story.

Tool presets

For tools that you use the same way much of the time — like the Brush, Gradient, or Type tool — you can establish presets that save you the time of resetting the tool to your favorite options each time you use it. Imagine that you often use a Brush set to a particular shape, size, and opacity. Rather than having to use the Options bar and Brushes palette every time you want to use those particular settings, imagine further that you can call up a preset group of settings for the tool and know that the exact same settings are now in force. This not only saves you time, but it assures you consistency between and within images where the same settings are required for identical effects.

To create a tool preset, select a tool and adjust the settings until they're perfect. Set up the ideal gradient and direction settings for the Gradient tool, a frequently used tolerance for the Magic Wand, or a combination of font, size, and alignment options for the Type tool. After setting up your "dream" tool, use any of the following three techniques to make it a preset you can call upon at any time:

✦ Choose Window ➪ Tool Presets to display the Tool Presets palette, which is stashed in the docking well by default. Then click the new tool preset icon at the bottom of the palette (labeled in Figure 2-7).

✦ Click the current tool icon in the Options bar; then click the new tool preset icon below the flyout menu arrow in the upper-right corner of the drop-down palette.

✦ Choose New Tool Preset from either the Tool Presets floating palette menu or the palette menu accessible from the drop-down palette in the Options bar (shown in Figure 2-7).

New Tool Preset button

Figure 2-7: Click the current tool icon in the Options bar or choose
Window ➪ Tool Presets to display options for creating new tool presets.

Any of these methods will take you to a small dialog box where you can type a
descriptive name for your tool settings — it can be helpful to choose a name that
reminds you of what image or situation you set up the tool for ("complexion brush")
or to pick a name that describes what the tool does ("softens skin"). Some tools
also have a check box where you can choose to include or exclude a particular
setting from the preset, such as the color for the Brush tool or the pattern for the
Pattern Stamp tool. Click OK, and your newly named group of tool settings will
appear in the list. From here on out, clicking the preset will load that group of settings into the Options bar. If you're having a hard time finding a preset, make sure
the Current Tool Only option is checked; this will make presets for only the current
tool appear in the list.

Whether you access the Tool Presets menu from the Options bar or from the Tool
Presets palette, you can choose from the following additional options:

✦ Rename Tool Preset and Delete Tool Preset let you perform those functions on
   the currently selected tool preset.

✦ Sort By Tool is active only if the Current Tool Only option is deselected; it
   groups the presets in the list by tool.

✦ Show All Tool Presets and Show Current Tool Presets toggle off and on the Current Tool Only check box.

✦ There are three options for viewing the list: Text Only, which lets you see the most options on-screen at one time; Small List, which adds a small icon; and Large List, which gives you the icon along with larger text.

✦ Reset Tool and Reset All Tools are carryovers from Photoshop 6, letting you restore either the current tool or all tools to their default settings. This has no effect on your collection of tool presets.

✦ Reset Tool Presets, Load Tool Presets, Save Tool Presets, and Replace Tool Presets all let you deal with groups of presets. Reset takes you back to the default set of tool presets, giving you the option to append the default set to the current set or to replace it entirely with the default set; Load gives you access to previously saved groups of presets; Save lets you save the group of presets to disk for future use, and Replace wipes out the current group of presets in favor of the pre-saved group of your choice.

✦ Preset Manager takes you to Adobe's gift to the obsessively organized: the Preset Manager dialog box. Here you can store and manage all of your preset collections, as explained in the next section.

The Preset Manager

Tool presets are the latest addition to the Preset Manager, a wonderful innovation introduced in Photoshop 6. This feature lets you organize and store presets in eight categories: Brushes, Swatches, Gradients, Styles, Patterns, Contours, Custom Shapes, and Tools. In addition to choosing Preset Manager from the palette menus of the Tool Presets, Brushes, Swatches, and Styles palettes, you can always access the Preset Manager dialog box (shown in Figure 2-8) by choosing Edit ⇨ Preset Manager. Then choose a category from the Preset Type pop-up menu.

Figure 2-8: The Preset Manager dialog box lets you store and organize presets for eight categories.

If you click the right-pointing arrowhead to the left of the Done button, a pop-up menu appears with some of the same options found in the Tool Presets palette menu. For example, you can choose to replace the current preset collection with another or return to the default collection. To append a collection, click Load. Alternatively, click a collection name in the pop-up menu, in which case you have the choice of appending or replacing the current collection with the new one. In addition, you can click a preset and then click Delete to remove the preset or Rename to change the preset's name. If you want to dump or rename a bunch of presets, Shift-click them and then click Delete or Rename. To select all presets, press Ctrl+A (⌘-A on the Mac). If you press Alt (Option on the Mac), you get a scissors cursor with which you can click a preset to delete it.

Tip   Probably the best reason for using the Preset Manager is to create a new preset collection out of presets from an existing set or sets. Load the collection that you want to use as a basis for the new set, and then Shift-click to select presets for the new set — or press Ctrl+A (⌘-A on the Mac) to select all presets — and click Save Set. Give the collection a name and store it in the suggested folder.

Note   To protect you from yourself, Photoshop has set it up so that you can't overwrite any existing preset files. Also, after you add a new preset, you must save it as part of a collection, either through the palette menu or the Preset Manager. Otherwise, Photoshop deletes the preset if you replace the current preset collection with another.

The floating palettes

When you first launch Photoshop, all the palettes appear in one of two places — on-screen and in the docking well — that is, except for two of them: the Character and Paragraph palettes. With the default workspace in use, the Navigator, Histogram, Color, Swatches, Styles, History, Actions, Layers, Channels, and Paths palettes are out loose, and the Brushes, Tool Presets, and Layer Comps palettes are up in the Docking well.

The Character and Paragraph palettes, which don't appear by default in either place, can only be displayed if you choose Character or Paragraph from the Window menu or click the Palettes button in the Options bar while a type tool is active. Other than that, these palettes look and behave just like the other palettes, which look and behave much like they have since version 3. Each palette contains most or all elements labeled in Figure 2-9 (note that on the Mac, the Close button is positioned on the far left side of the title bar), but some palettes have a few kinks. For example, some palettes don't let you resize them, and some palettes have scroll bars while others don't. These aren't huge, glaring differences, but they're enough to keep things interesting. Sort of.

Tip   Photoshop automatically snaps palettes into alignment with other palettes as you drag them on the workspace. To snap a palette to the edge of the screen, Shift-click its title bar. You can also Shift-drag the title bar to move the palette around the perimeter of the screen or to snap the palette from one edge of the screen to the other. (This tip works also with the Toolbox.)

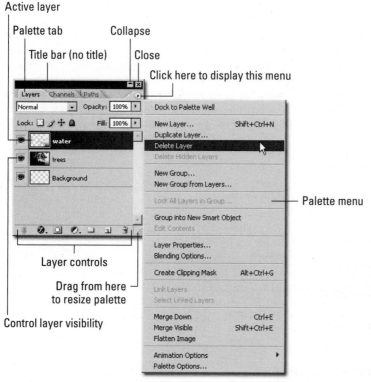

Figure 2-9: Most palettes include the same basic elements as the Layers palette, shown here.

Four elements are unique to floating palettes:

✦ **Palette options.** Each floating palette offers its own collection of options. These options may include icons, pop-up menus, slider bars, you name it.

✦ **Palette menu.** Click the right-pointing arrowhead to display a menu of commands specific to the palette. These commands enable you to manipulate the palette options and adjust preference settings.

✦ **Palette tabs.** Click a palette tab to move it to the front of the palette group. (You can also select the palette commands from the Window menu, but it's more convenient to click a tab.)

✦ **Collapse box.** Click the collapse box to decrease the amount of space consumed by the palette. If you previously enlarged the palette by dragging the size box, your first click reduces the palette back to its default size. After that, clicking the collapse box hides all but the most essential palette options.

Tip

In most cases, collapsing a palette hides all options and leaves only the tabs visible. But in the case of the Color and Layers palettes, clicking the collapse box leaves a sliver of palette options intact, as demonstrated in the middle example of Figure 2-10. To eliminate all options — as in the last example — Alt-click (or Option-click on the Mac) the collapse box. You can also double-click one of the tabs or in the empty area to the right of the tabs. And if your palette is located at the bottom edge of the screen, collapsing the palette will make it collapse downward, leaving the visible part of the collapsed palette hugging the bottom of the screen. These tricks work even if you've enlarged the palette by dragging the size box.

Click here

Alt (or Option)
+ Click here

OR Double-click here

Figure 2-10: The Color palette shown at full size (top), partially collapsed (middle), and fully collapsed (bottom)

Rearranging and docking palettes

Photoshop makes it easy to regroup palettes to suit the way you work. You can dock (attach) palettes to each other or to the Options bar. To attach a floating palette to the Options bar, as shown in Figure 2-11, drag the palette tab to the docking well. After you dock the palette, you see just the palette tab in the Options bar. Click the tab to display the palette, as shown in the figure. When you click outside the palette, the palette closes automatically. You can also dock palettes to the well by clicking the palette menu button and choosing Dock to Palette Well — this will dock the palette to the well when you close the palette — not at the time that you issue the menu command.

Note

If you don't see the docking well, you need to raise your monitor resolution. The docking well isn't accessible at monitor resolutions of 800 pixels wide or less.

When a box forms around the Docking well,
release the mouse and your palette is docked.

Drag by the tab

An outline
follows you

Figure 2-11: Attach palettes to the Options bar by dragging
them to the docking well.

In addition to docking palettes in the Options bar, you can dock palettes to each
other. Drag a palette tab to the bottom of another palette and release the mouse
button when just the bottom of the other palette appears highlighted. The dragged
palette grabs hold of the other palette's tail and doesn't let go — sort of like the
snap to we're all used to, but even stronger than that subtle pull. Now you can keep
both palettes visible but move, close, collapse, and resize the two as a single entity.

Tip   When you dock a resizable palette to another resizable palette, you can resize the
palettes like so:

✦ Position your cursor over the border between two stacked palettes until you
see the double-headed arrow cursor. Then drag down to enlarge the upper
palette and shrink the lower one. Drag up to enlarge the lower palette and
shrink the upper one. The overall size of the docked palettes doesn't change.

✦ Alt-drag (or Option-drag on the Mac) the border to resize the upper palette only.

Still not happy with your palette layout? You can shuffle palettes at will, moving a
single palette from one group to another or giving it complete independence from
any group. This also enables you to make your own groups, pairing or grouping
palettes that you use often — potentially making it so that you have only one palette
box on the workspace, stacked with the palettes you need all the time. To separate

a palette from its current group, drag its tab away from the palette and drop it on the workspace. To add a palette to another palette group, drag its tab onto the target palette group and release the mouse. It's pretty simple, and represents a big chance to customize the actual working efficiency of the workspace.

The Reset Palette Locations command (Window ➪ Workspace ➪ Reset Palette Locations) makes it easy to restore your palette setup to the neat and tidy defaults — palettes in their default groupings and locations and the Toolbox on the left side of the workspace. And that's great if you've been tinkering and creating your own palette groupings and moving things around and now you want everything to go back to its pristine, pre-tinkering state, but you can also take this concept one step further and save your own custom palette arrangements. These workspace presets, created by you, make it easy for multiple users to share the same Photoshop application; if your bizarre coworker can't function in the application unless the Toolbox is moved to the right side of the screen, you can choose Window ➪ Workspace ➪ Save Workspace, name the workspace Bizarre Workspace (or something less inflammatory, should said coworker not have a good sense of humor), and click Save. From then on, he or she can access the saved workspace in the Window ➪ Workspace menu, and you can access yours — or use the default arrangement if that's more to your liking. Of course, when Mr. or Ms. Bizarre Coworker gets the boot, you can choose Window ➪ Workspace ➪ Delete Workspace and choose from a pop-up list of all saved workspaces.

New Feature   If you thought saving workspace presets was cool, prepare yourself for something dangerously exciting. Not only does CS2 support the creation of workspace presets and allow you to go back to a default workspace arrangement, it also offers a series of task-specific presets already built in to the software. Choose from presets like Color and Tonal Correction, Painting and Retouching, Web Design, and Working with Type — plus several others, from a group of nine different presets. Simply choose Window ➪ Workspace and then make a selection from the bottom section of the menu, as shown in Figure 2-12.

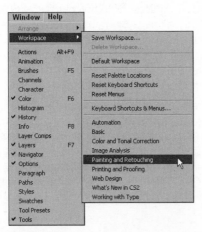

Figure 2-12: Not sure how to group your palettes and arrange your on-screen tools for a particular job? Let Photoshop take a whack at it and choose one of the built-in workspace presets that are new with CS2.

Tabbing through the options

As mentioned earlier, you can hide the palettes by pressing Shift+Tab and you can hide the palettes, Toolbox, and Options bar by pressing Tab. This keyboard trick doesn't work, however, if an option box is active.

For example, suppose you click in the R (Red) option box in the Color palette. This activates the option. Now press Tab. Rather than hiding the palettes, Photoshop advances you to the next option box in the palette, G. This function of the Tab key is common to virtually all Windows and Mac-based software, whenever you're working in a dialog box — the dialog box functions like a form (like those you might fill in at a Web site, for example), and the Tab key moves you from field to field. To move backward through the options, press Shift+Tab. This "trick" applies to the Options bar as well as to the standard palettes.

To apply an option box value and return focus to the image window, press Enter or Return. This deactivates the palette options. If an option box remains active, certain keyboard tricks — such as pressing a key to select a tool — won't work properly. Photoshop either ignores the shortcut or beeps at you for pressing a key that the option box doesn't like.

While you're working in the image window, you can return focus to the Options bar from the keyboard. When you press Enter or Return, Photoshop displays the Options bar, if it's not already visible. If the Options bar offers an option box for the active tool, Photoshop highlights the contents of the option box. You can then tab around to reach the option you want to change, type a new value, and press Enter or Return to get out.

Tip
You can see your open images side by side — for comparison, to drag layers from one to the other, or just to see all the images you have open without having to drag them around and resize them manually. This is done by choosing Window ⇨ Arrange ⇨ Tile Horizontally or Tile Vertically. Your other options in this submenu include Cascade, which stacks the open image windows with their title bars visible. You can also open a new window for the active image by choosing New Window for X, where "X" is the name of the active image.

Navigating in Photoshop

All graphics and desktop publishing programs provide a variety of navigational tools and functions that enable you to move around the screen; hop, skip, and jump from place to place; and examine the fine details while you take in the big picture. Sounds like a lot of activity, doesn't it? When it comes to this to and fro, Photoshop is no exception.

The view size

You can change the *view size*—the size at which an image appears on-screen—so you can either step back to see more of or all of an image all at once or get in really close to concentrate on individual pixels. Each change in view size is expressed as a *zoom ratio*, which is the ratio between screen pixels and image pixels. Photoshop displays the zoom ratio as a percentage value in the title bar as well as in the magnification box—and in the lower-left corner of the image window. The 100 percent zoom ratio shows one image pixel for each screen pixel (and is therefore equivalent to the old 1:1 zoom ratio, as it was expressed in Photoshop 3 and earlier, for all you Photoshop history buffs out there). A 200 percent zoom ratio doubles the size of the image pixels on-screen, a 300 percent zoom triples the size, and so on.

Actual pixels

Photoshop calls the 100 percent zoom ratio the *actual-pixels* view. This is the most accurate view size because you can see the image as it really is. Reduced view sizes drop pixels; magnified view sizes stretch pixels. Only the actual-pixels view displays each pixel without a trace of screen distortion—good to know if you think your image looks a bit choppy or noisy, and you're not sure if that's how it really looks or if it's just the screen size you're using at the time. A quick change to Actual Pixels view ends all doubt.

You can switch to this most accurate of view sizes at any time using one of the following techniques:

✦ Choose View ➪ Actual Pixels.

✦ Press Ctrl+Alt+0 (⌘-Option-0 on the Mac). That's the number 0, not the letter *O*.

✦ Double-click the zoom tool icon in the toolbox.

✦ Click the Actual Pixels button, which appears in the Options bar when the zoom tool is selected.

Fit on screen

When you first open an image, Photoshop displays it at the largest zoom ratio (up to 100 percent) that permits the entire image to fit on-screen. Assuming you don't change the size of the image, you can return to this "fit-on-screen" view size in one of the following ways:

✦ Choose View ➪ Fit on Screen.

✦ Press Ctrl+0 (or ⌘-0 on the Mac).

✦ Double-click the Hand tool icon in the Toolbox.

✦ Select the Zoom tool and then click the Fit on Screen button in the Options bar.

Strangely, any of these techniques may magnify the image beyond the 100 percent view size. When working on a very small image, for example, Photoshop enlarges the image to fill the screen, even if this means maxing out the zoom to 1,600 percent. Personally, I prefer to use the fit-on-screen view only when working on very large images, because it usually causes a good deal of distortion — not to the image in reality, but to its display in the image window.

You may not love Fit on Screen view because while Photoshop does the best job of previewing an image when you can see all pixels — that is, at 100 percent view size, in Fit on Screen view, the percentage you get is rather arbitrary. You never know what percentage you'll get when you choose this command — all you know is that the entire image will be visible within the image window.

Print size

You can switch to yet another predefined view size by choosing View ⇨ Print Size. This command theoretically displays the image on-screen at the size it will print. (You set the print size using Image ⇨ Image Size, as explained in Chapter 3.) When the Zoom tool is active, you also can click the Print Size button in the Options bar to turn on the print-size view.

In practice, "print-size" view isn't particularly reliable. Photoshop assumes that your monitor displays exactly 72 pixels per inch, even on the PC, where the accepted screen resolution is 96 pixels per inch. But it's all complete nonsense, whatever the assumption. Monitor resolutions vary all over the map. And high-end monitors let you change screen resolutions without Photoshop even noticing.

The long and the short of it is this: Don't expect to hold up your printed image and have it exactly match the print-size view on screen. It's a rough approximation, designed to show you how the image will look when imported into InDesign, QuarkXPress, PageMaker, or some other publishing program — nothing more.

The Zoom tool

Obviously, the aforementioned zoom ratios aren't the only ones available to you. You can zoom in as close as 1,600 percent and zoom out to 0.2 percent.

The most straightforward way to zoom in and out of your image is to use the Zoom tool, and here are some techniques to try:

✦ Click in the image window with the Zoom tool to magnify the image in pre-set increments — from 33.33 percent to 50 to 66.67 to 100 to 200 and so on. Photoshop centers the zoomed view at the point where you click (or comes as close as possible).

✦ Go the other way and Alt-click (Win) or Option-click (Mac) with the Zoom tool to reduce the image incrementally — 200 to 100 to 66.67 to 50 to 33.33 and so on. Again, Photoshop tries to center the new view on the click point.

Tip

Drag with the Zoom tool to draw a rectangular marquee around the portion of the image you want to magnify. Photoshop magnifies the image so the marqueed area fits just inside the image window. (If the horizontal and vertical proportions of the marquee do not match those of your screen — for example, if you draw a tall, thin marquee or a really short, wide one — Photoshop favors the smaller of the two possible zoom ratios to avoid hiding any detail inside the marquee.)

✦ If you want Photoshop to resize the window when you click with the Zoom tool, select the Resize Windows to Fit option in the Options bar. The check box appears only when the Zoom tool is the active tool.

✦ Turn off the Ignore Palettes check box in the Options bar if you want Photoshop to stop resizing the window when the window bumps up against a palette anchored against the side of the program window. Select the option to resize the window regardless of the palettes. The palettes then float over the resized window.

✦ If you have multiple image windows open, you can control the zoom ratio on all of them at the same time. Simply Shift-click with the Zoom tool in any image window. Alternatively, you can eliminate the need for the Shift key by selecting the Zoom All Windows option in the Options bar.

✦ Use the Window, Arrange, Match Zoom, Match Location, or Match Zoom and Location commands to control the zoom on two or more open images. Zoom in (or out) on one of your open images, and maybe even pan the image to one side or another. Then choose Window, Arrange, Match Zoom and Location, and voila! Both images are zoomed to the same percentage, and the image content is placed in the same position within the image window.

Tip

To access the Zoom tool temporarily when some other tool is selected, press and hold Ctrl (or ⌘ on the Mac) and the space bar. Release both to return control of the cursor to the selected tool. To access the Zoom Out cursor, press Alt (or Option on the Mac) with the space bar. These keyboard equivalents work from inside many dialog boxes, enabling you to modify the view of an image while applying a filter or color correction.

The Zoom commands

You can also zoom in and out using the following commands and keyboard shortcuts:

✦ Choose View ➪ Zoom In or press Ctrl+plus (+) (⌘-plus on the Mac) to zoom in. This command works exactly like clicking with the Zoom tool except you can't specify the center of the new view size. Photoshop merely centers the zoom in keeping with the previous view size.

✦ Choose View ➪ Zoom Out or press Ctrl+minus (–) (⌘-minus on the Mac) to zoom out.

Tip The General panel of the Preferences dialog box (Ctrl+K on the PC and ⌘-K on the Mac) includes an option called Zoom Resizes Windows. If you select this option, Photoshop resizes the image window when you use the Zoom commands. To override the setting temporarily, press Alt (or Option on the Mac) as you press the keyboard shortcut or select the menu command. Similarly, if you deselect the option in the Preferences dialog box, you can add Alt or Option to turn window-zooming on temporarily.

If Photoshop is unresponsive to these or any other keyboard shortcuts, it's probably because the image window has somehow become inactive. (It can happen in Windows if you so much as click the taskbar.) Just click the image window's title bar and try again — you may also want to momentarily minimize the window, and then restore it — the process can aide in refreshing the window to give you the view you want if it wasn't responding properly before.

The magnification box

Another way to zoom in and out without changing the window size is to type a value into the magnification box, located in the lower-left corner of the Photoshop window (or image window on the Mac). Select the magnification value, type a new one, and press Enter or Return. Photoshop zooms the view without zooming the window. (Neither the Resize Windows to Fit option in the Options bar nor the Zoom Resizes Windows option in the Preferences dialog box affect the magnification box.)

Figure 2-13 starts with a specially sized window at 25 percent. Two different zoom ratios are typed in the magnification box — 57.8 percent and 18.9 percent — alternately enlarging and reducing the image in the confines of a static window.

You might like to know more about the magnification box:

✦ You can type values in the magnification box as percentages, ratios, or "times" values. To switch to a zoom value of 250 percent, for example, you can type 250%, 5:2, or 2.5x.

✦ You can specify a zoom value in increments as small as 0.01 percent. So if a zoom value of 250.01 doesn't quite suit your fancy, you can try 250.02. It's unlikely that you'll need this kind of precision, but isn't it great to know that it's there?

Tip When you press Enter or Return after typing a magnification value, Photoshop changes the view size and returns focus to the image window. If you aren't exactly certain what zoom ratio you want to use, press Shift+Enter (Shift-Return on the Mac) instead. This changes the view size while keeping the magnification value active; this way, you can type a new value and try again.

Figure 2-13: To zoom an image without changing the window size, type a zoom ratio in the magnification box and press Enter or Return. You can also deselect the Resize Windows to Fit option in the Options bar when working with the Zoom tool.

Creating a reference window

In the past, paint programs provided a cropped view of your image at the actual-pixels view size to serve as a reference when you worked in a magnified view. Photoshop does not, but you can easily create a second view of your image by choosing Window ➪ Arrange ➪ New Window, as in Figure 2-14. Use one window to maintain a 100 percent view of your image while you zoom and edit inside the other window. Both windows track the changes to the image.

Figure 2-14: You can create multiple windows to track the changes made to a single image by choosing the New Window command from the Arrange submenu of the Window menu.

Scrolling in the window

In the standard window mode, you have access to scroll bars, as you do in just about every other major application. But as you become more proficient with Photoshop, you'll use the scroll bars less and less. One way to bypass the scroll bars is to use the keyboard equivalents listed in Table 2-1. If you're using a Mac that lacks the Page Up and Page Down keys — such as an older-model PowerBook — try the Control key equivalents in the third column. These may also come in handy when the Page Up and Page Down keys don't always behave properly, as on new PowerBook and iBook keyboards that require you to press a separate Fn key.

Tip   Legend has it that some artists use the Page Up and Page Down shortcuts to comb through very large images at 100 percent view size. This way, they can make sure all their pixels are in order before going to print.

Table 2-1		
Scrolling from the Keyboard		
Scrolling Action	*Keystroke*	*Alternate Keystroke (Mac Standard Keyboard Only)*
Up one screen	Page Up	Control-K
Up slightly	Shift+Page Up	Control-Shift-K
Down one screen	Page Down	Control-L
Down slightly	Shift+Page Down	Control-Shift-L
Left one screen	Ctrl+Page Up (⌘-Page Up)	⌘-Control-K
Left slightly	Ctrl+Shift+Page Up (⌘-Shift-Page Up)	⌘-Control-Shift-K
Right one screen	Ctrl+Page Down (⌘-Page Down)	⌘-Control-L
Right slightly	Ctrl+Shift+Page Down (⌘-Shift-Page Down)	⌘-Control-Shift-L
To upper-left corner	Home	Control-A
To lower-right corner	End	Control-D

Tip   To access the Hand tool temporarily when some other tool is selected, press and hold the space bar. Releasing the space bar returns the cursor to its original appearance. This keyboard equivalent even works in many dialog boxes.

Tip   You can scroll multiple image windows at the same time by Shift-dragging in any one image with the Hand tool. If you don't want to use the Shift key, select the Scroll All Windows option in the Options bar. You can also use the Spacebar+Shift+Drag method if you want to scroll multiple image windows without first selecting the Hand tool.

The Navigator palette

As shown in Figure 2-15, the Navigator palette is the best thing to happen to zooming and scrolling since Photoshop was introduced. If you routinely work on large images that extend beyond the confines of your relatively tiny screen, you'll want to get up and running with this palette as soon as possible — it makes life so much easier, you won't know how you got along without it.

Figure 2-15: Navigate, preview, and zoom, all in one palette

If the Navigator palette isn't visible, choose Window ➪ Navigator. You can then use the palette options as follows:

✦ **View box.** Drag the view box inside the image thumbnail to reveal some hidden portion of the photograph. Photoshop dynamically tracks your adjustments in the image window. "This is really very cool," you're saying now.

Tip

"Are you kidding? There's more?" Yes. Press Ctrl (or ⌘ on the Mac) to get a Zoom cursor in the Navigator palette. Then Ctrl-drag (or ⌘-drag on the Mac) to resize the view box and zoom the photo in the image window.

You can also Shift-drag to constrain dragging the view box to only horizontal or vertical movement.

✦ **Box color.** You can change the color of the view box by choosing the Palette Options command from the palette menu. The default is red, but if your image has a lot of red in it or if you just don't like red, try yellow or bright lime green — something that stands out against even a bright color image.

✦ **Magnification box.** This value works like the one in the lower-left corner of the image window — just type a new zoom ratio and press Enter or Return.

✦ **Zoom out.** Click the zoom out button to reduce the view size in the same predefined increments as the Zoom tool. This button doesn't alter the size of the image window, regardless of any window resizing options you set for the other zoom controls.

✦ **Zoom slider.** Move the slider triangle and watch what happens. Drag to the left to zoom out; drag right to zoom in. Again, Photoshop dynamically tracks your changes in the image window. Dang, it's nice to zoom on the fly.

✦ **Zoom in:** Click the big mountains to incrementally magnify the view of the image without altering the window size. Of course, the small mountains zoom out, and they, too, do not alter the window size.

✦ **Size box:** If you have a large monitor, you don't have to settle for that teeny thumbnail of the image. Drag the size box to enlarge both palette and thumbnail to a more reasonable size.

Customizing the Interface

Every program gives you access to a few core settings so you can modify the program to suit your personal needs. These settings are known far and wide as *preferences*. Photoshop ships with certain recommended preference settings already in force — known coast to coast as *factory defaults* — but just because these settings are recommended doesn't mean they're right. In fact, I disagree with quite a few of them. But why quibble when you can change the preferences according to your merest whim?

You can modify preference settings in two ways. You can make environmental adjustments in Windows by using Edit ➪ Preferences ➪ General; on the Mac, that's Photoshop ➪ Preferences ➪ General. Or you can change the operation of specific tools by adjusting settings in the Options bar. Photoshop remembers environmental preferences, tool settings, and even the file format under which you saved the last image by storing this information to a file each time you exit the program.

Tip

You can dump the preferences file using this trick: Close the program, and then relaunch it. Immediately after you launch the program, press and hold Ctrl+Shift+Alt (⌘-Shift-Option on the Mac). Photoshop displays a dialog box asking for your permission to delete the preferences file. Click Yes.

Deleting the preferences file is also a good idea if Photoshop starts acting funny. Photoshop's preferences file has always been highly susceptible to corruption, possibly because the application writes to it so often. Whatever the reason, if Photoshop starts behaving erratically, trash that preferences file. You'll have to reset your preferences, but a smooth-running program is worth the few minutes of extra effort. It's a good thing that Photoshop saves actions, color settings, custom shapes, contours, and the like separately from the *Prefs* file. This means that you can delete your *Prefs* file without worrying about harming your scripts, color conversions, and other custom settings.

Tip

After you get your preferences set as you like them, you can prevent Photoshop from altering them further by locking the file. On the PC, right-click the Adobe Photoshop CS *Prefs.psp* file in Windows Explorer and choose Properties from the pop-up menu. Then select the Read Only option in the Properties dialog box and press Enter. On the Mac, go to the Finder, track down the Adobe Photoshop CS *Prefs* file, and choose File ⇨ Show Info (⌘-I on the Mac). Then select the Locked option in the Info dialog box. From now on, Photoshop will start up with a consistent set of default settings.

That's a good tip, and it's included in the name of comprehensive coverage. But you may not want to lock your *Prefs* file because you may periodically want to modify your settings and want Photoshop to remember the latest and greatest. Instead, make a backup copy of your favorite settings. After a few weeks of working in the program and customizing it to a more or less acceptable level, copy the preferences file to a separate folder on your hard drive (someplace you'll remember!). Then if the preferences file becomes corrupt, you can replace it quickly with your backup.

Under Windows, the Preferences command appears on the Edit menu. In Mac OS X, it's found on the Photoshop menu. Choosing the command displays a long submenu of commands, but you needn't ever use them if you remember a simple keyboard shortcut: Ctrl+K (⌘-K on the Mac).

Meanwhile, Back at the Factory...

To restore Photoshop's factory default settings, delete the Adobe Photoshop *Prefs.psp* (simply *Prefs* on the Mac) file when the application is *not* running. The next time you launch Photoshop, it creates a new preferences file automatically. On the PC, you can find the preferences file in the Application Data/Adobe/Photoshop/8.0/Adobe Photoshop CS Settings folder. Under Windows 2000 and XP, the Application Data folder is located in the Documents and Settings/*User Name* folder. In earlier versions of Windows, the Application Data folder is in the Windows folder. In Mac OS X, follow this path: Home folder ⇨ Library ⇨ Preferences ⇨ Adobe Photoshop CS Settings. (Depending on your system setup, the program may choose a different storage folder.) You can also search for the preferences file by name using Sherlock on the Mac or the built-in search tool in Windows. Under Windows 2000 and XP, you must first turn on the visibility of hidden files. To do so, choose Tools ⇨ Folder Options, click the View tab, and then select the Show Hidden Files and Folders option.

This shortcut brings up the Preferences dialog box, which provides access to nine panels of options representing every one of the Edit ⇨ Preferences commands. Select the desired panel from the pop-up menu in the upper-left corner of the dialog box, as demonstrated in Figure 2-16. Or press the Ctrl key (or ⌘-key on the Mac) equivalent for the panel as listed in the pop-up menu. You can also click the Prev and Next buttons or press Alt+P and Alt+N, respectively (⌘-Option-P and ⌘-Option-N on the Mac) to cycle from one panel to the next.

Tip

Photoshop always displays the first panel, General, when you press Ctrl+K (or ⌘-K on the Mac). If you prefer to go to the panel you were last using, press Ctrl+Alt+K (⌘-Option-K on the Mac).

To accept your settings and exit the Preferences dialog box, press Enter or Return. Or press Escape to cancel your settings. Okay, so you already knew that, but here's one you might not know: Press and hold Alt (or Option on the Mac) to change the Cancel button to Reset. Then click the button to restore the settings that were in force before you entered the dialog box.

Figure 2-16: Select a panel of options from the pop-up menu, or click the Prev and Next buttons to advance from one panel to the next.

The following sections examine the Preferences panels, in the order in which they appear in the Figure 2-16 pop-up menu. How each option works is explained, and what are considered the optimal setting are included in parentheses. (The figures, however, show the default settings.) Out of context like this, Photoshop's preference settings can be a bit confusing. In later chapters, some additional light is shed on the settings you may find most useful.

General preferences

The General panel, shown in Figure 2-17, contains a miscellaneous supply of what are arguably the most important Preferences options.

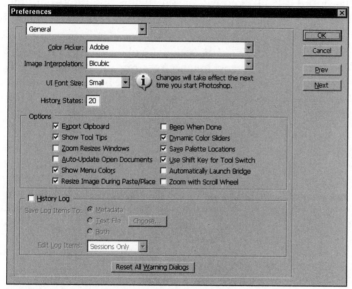

Figure 2-17: The General panel provides access to the most important environmental preference settings.

✦ **Color Picker (Adobe).** When you click the foreground or background color control icon in the Toolbox, Photoshop displays any Color Picker plug-ins that you may have installed plus one of two standard Color Pickers: the Adobe Color Picker or the one provided by the operating system. If you're familiar with other Windows graphics programs, the system's color picker may at first seem more familiar. But Photoshop's color picker is better suited to photographic work.

✦ **Image Interpolation (Bicubic).** When you resize an image using Image ➪ Image Size or transform it using Layer ➪ Free Transform or one of the commands in the Layer ➪ Transform submenu, Photoshop has to make up — or *interpolate* — pixels to fill in the gaps. You can change how Photoshop calculates the interpolation by choosing one of five options from the Image Interpolation pop-up menu.

If you select Nearest Neighbor (Faster), Photoshop simply copies the next-door pixel when creating a new one. This is the fastest setting (hence the label "Faster"), but it invariably results in jagged effects.

The second option, Bilinear, smoothes the transitions between pixels by creating intermediate shades. Photoshop averages the color of each pixel with four neighbors — the pixel above, the one below, and the two to the left and right. Bilinear takes more time but, typically, the softened effect is worth it.

Still more time intensive is the default setting, Bicubic, which averages the color of a pixel with its eight closest neighbors — one up, one down, two on the sides, and four in the corners. The Bicubic setting boosts the amount of contrast between pixels to offset the blurring effect that generally accompanies interpolation.

You also have two Image Interpolation settings: Bicubic Smoother and Bicubic Sharper. Based on the standard Bicubic option, these settings are further optimized for different sizing operations. Bicubic Smoother is designed to produce the smoothest possible transitions between pixels, ideal when resizing a grainy or noisy image. It is also the option of choice on those rare occasions when you decide to enlarge an image. Bicubic Sharper is designed to preserve the sharpness and detail of an image when you reduce it, eliminating the need to apply Unsharp Mask after downsampling. Although these new interpolation options can be useful, they're best used on a case-by-case basis from inside the Image Size dialog box (see Chapter 3).

Tip   The moral is this: Select Bicubic to turn Photoshop's interpolation capabilities on and select Nearest Neighbor to turn them off. The Bilinear setting is a poor compromise between the other options — too slow for roughing out effects and too remedial to be worth your time.

✦ **UI Font Size.** This sets the font size to use for Small User Interface fonts, which are fonts used in small devices, such as handheld organizers, cell phones, and so forth. It's set to Small by default, and your alternates are Medium and Large. As the "i" (appears as "!" on the Mac) balloon indicates, changes will take effect the next time you start Photoshop.

✦ **History States (your call).** This value controls how many steps you can undo using the History palette. The right value depends on the amount of RAM you're willing to devote to Photoshop. If you're working with limited memory, I suggest that you lower the value to 5 or 10. Otherwise, raise the value as you see fit, remembering that the more states the program retains, the more you strain your system.

✦ **Export Clipboard (on).** When selected, this option tells Photoshop to transfer a copied image from the program's internal Clipboard to the operating system's Clipboard whenever you switch applications. This enables you to paste the image into another running program. Turn this option off if you plan to use copied images only within Photoshop and want to reduce the lag time that occurs when you switch from Photoshop to another program. Even with this option off, you can paste images copied from other programs into Photoshop.

✦ **Show Tool Tips (on).** When on, this option displays little labels and keyboard shortcuts when you hover your cursor over a tool or palette option. The tool tips don't impede Photoshop's performance, so there is no reason to turn off this option.

✦ **Zoom Resizes Windows (off).** Select this option to force Photoshop to resize the image window when you zoom in or out on your image by choosing a Zoom command from the View menu or by using the keyboard shortcuts, Ctrl+plus (⌘-plus on the Mac) and Ctrl+minus (⌘-minus on the Mac). This one's really a matter of personal choice—you'll do no harm to yourself or the planet if leave it off, as it is by default in Windows, or leave it on, as it is by default on the Mac. Either way, you can temporarily choose the opposite setting by pressing Alt (or Option on the Mac) as you choose the Zoom command.

✦ **Auto-Update Open Documents (off).** This option creates and maintains a link between an open image and the image file on disk. Any time the image on disk updates, Photoshop updates the image on-screen in kind. This feature is an amazing help when you're editing images with another artist over a network. Imagine that you and a coworker each have the same server file open in separate copies of Photoshop. Your coworker makes a change and saves it. Seconds later, your copy of Photoshop automatically updates the image on your screen. Then you make a change and save it, and Photoshop relays your modifications to your coworker's screen.

So what happens if you're both editing the image simultaneously? Whoever saves first gets the glory. If your coworker saves the image before you do, any changes that you haven't saved are overwritten by the other person's work.

Tip

However, you can snatch victory from the jaws of defeat simply by pressing Ctrl+Alt+Z (⌘-Option-Z on the Mac), which undoes your coworker's edits and retrieves yours. Quickly save your image to lob your changes over the net. Ooh, psych! With any luck, your coworker won't understand Photoshop well enough to know that your changes can be undone just as easily. But just to be safe, better hide this book from prying eyes.

✦ **Show Menu Colors (on).** This option, new in Photoshop CS2, allows you to take advantage of the ability to apply colors to menu commands (Edit ⇨ Menus). If this is off, your settings through that feature don't show.

✦ **Resize Image During Paste/Place (on).** This option determines whether or not your image will be resized when you paste content or place a layer from another image into the image window. I usually turn this option off, because I find that I don't remember it's on and am then surprised (rarely pleasantly so) when the image resizes.

✦ **Beep When Done (off).** You can instruct Photoshop to beep at you whenever it finishes an operation that displays a Progress window. This option may be useful if you doze off during particularly time-consuming operations.

✦ **Dynamic Color Sliders (on).** When selected, this option instructs Photoshop to preview color effects in the slider bars of the Color palette. When the option is turned off, the slider bars show the same colors regardless of your changes. Unless you're working on a slow computer, leave this option on. On a fast machine, Photoshop takes a billionth of a second longer to calculate the color effects and it's well worth it.

✦ **Save Palette Locations (on).** When this option is selected, Photoshop remembers the location of the Toolbox and floating palettes from one session to the next. If you deselect this option, Photoshop restores the default palette positions the next time you restart the program.

✦ **Use Shift Key for Tool Switch (on).** When two or more tools share the same slot in the Toolbox, you can press the keyboard shortcut associated with the tools to cycle through the tools. This Preferences option determines whether you must press Shift along with the shortcut. I recommend that you turn this option off — one extra keystroke per function adds up over the course of a day, you know.

Note   In this book, it is assumed that you have deselected this option when tool shortcuts are presented.

✦ **Automatically Launch Bridge (off).** The Bridge can be started automatically when Photoshop is launched — if you select this option, the Bridge opens and runs in the background. Because the very powerful Bridge saps much of the system resources you may prefer to deselect this option and activate it only when you need it.

Cross-Reference   The Bridge is discussed fully in Chapters 3 and 18.

✦ **Zoom with Scroll Wheel (off).** Because this is off by default, you can use the scroll wheel (predominantly for Windows users) to move up and down in an image window that's not set to Fit on Screen or where whatever zoom you're using allows the entire image to be seen in the image window. If you turn this on, scrolling forward with the scroll wheel will zoom in, and scrolling backward will zoom out. If you use the scroll wheel a lot in Photoshop and other applications, turning this on can be annoying, because you'll keep forgetting it's on and then wonder why the stupid image keeps growing whenever you scroll up.

✦ **History Log (your call).** This option lets you save information about the list of edits and operations applied to your images. For starters, select the History Log option and select a radio button to specify whether you want to save the log along with the image's metadata, in a separate text file, or both. If you select the Metadata option, you'll be able to view the log information in the History panel of the File Info dialog box (Ctrl+Alt+I or ⌘-Option-I). If you select the Text

File radio button, Photoshop prompts you to specify a name and location for the log file. Naturally, the Both radio button saves the log information to metadata and a text tile.

Use the Edit Log Items pop-up menu to specify the type of information you'd like to save to the log. The Sessions Only option simply keeps track of every time you launch and quit Photoshop and open and close files. Choose the Concise option to log the session information plus the data that's recorded in the History palette. Choose Detailed to log detailed information about every edit performed on an image, giving you a permanent record of the steps you took to achieve the final results.

✦ **Reset All Warning Dialogs.** Every now and then, Photoshop displays a warning dialog box to let you know that the course you're on may have consequences you hadn't considered. Some dialog boxes include an option that you can select to tell Photoshop that you don't want to see the current warning any more. If you click the Reset All Warning Dialogs button in the Preferences dialog box, Photoshop clears all the Don't Show This Warning Again options so that you once again get all available warnings. Photoshop responds to your click of the reset button by displaying a warning dialog box telling you that all warning dialog boxes will be enabled if you go forward.

File Handling

When in the Preferences dialog box, press Ctrl+2 (or ⌘-2 on the Mac) to advance to the File Handling panel. Figures 2-18 and 2-19 show the panel as it appears on the PC and the Mac, respectively.

Figure 2-18: The File Handling panel as it appears on the PC

Figure 2-19: The File Handling panel as it appears on the Mac

Every option in the File Handling panel affects how Photoshop saves images to disk. The following list explains how the options work and the recommended settings:

✦ **Image Previews (Ask When Saving).** When Always Save is active (as by default), Photoshop saves a postage-stamp preview so that you can see what an image looks like before opening or importing it. On the Mac, you can select as many as four kinds of image previews, as follows.

The Icon option creates a preview icon that you can view from the Finder desktop. You may not find this to be worth the extra hard drive space it takes up, and too many custom icons can cause problems with older versions of the system software.

When you select one of the Thumbnail options, Photoshop creates a postage-stamp preview that appears in the Open dialog box when you select a file. The Macintosh Thumbnail option saves the preview in a part of the file known as the resource fork, but Windows doesn't recognize resource forks. So if you ever plan on previewing the image on a PC, you should select the Windows Thumbnail option as well.

The fourth option, Full Size, creates a 72-dpi preview that can be used for placement in a page-layout program.

The problem with previews is that they slightly increase the size of the file. This is fine when doing print work — a thumbnail isn't going to add that much — but when creating Web graphics, every byte counts. That's why I prefer to select Ask When Saving from the Image Previews pop-up menu. This option makes the preview options available in the Save dialog box so that you can specify whether you want previews on a case-by-case basis when you save your images.

✦ **Append File Extension (Ask When Saving).** Available only on the Mac, this option adds a three-character extension to the end of a file name to make your Mac images compatible with Windows and DOS programs. For example, a layered composition saved in the Photoshop format gets a *.psd* extension. You might like to set this option to Ask When Saving; that way, you can decide whether or not to include a PC-style extension from inside the Save dialog box on a file-by-file basis.

Tip

Actually, you can set the Append File Extension option to Never and still access extensions when saving images. Just press Option when selecting a file format and Photoshop automatically slaps on an extension. Read more about this process in Chapter 3.

✦ **File Extension (Use Lower Case)/Use Lower Case (on).** Called File Extension on the PC and Use Lower Case on the Mac, this option decides whether the three-character extension at the end of a file name is uppercase or lowercase. Lowercase is the better choice because it ensures compatibility with other platforms, particularly UNIX, the primary operating system for Web servers. (UNIX is case-sensitive, so a file called *Image.psd* is different from *Image.PSD*. Lowercase extensions eliminate confusion.)

✦ **Ignore EXIF sRGB tag (off)/Ignore EXIF profile tag (off).** This is a controversial feature, but I'm coming down on the side of the default. Virtually every modern digital camera embeds information about when and how a photo was captured (date, f-stop, flash setting, and so on) in the image file. Part of this so-called EXIF data (short for Exchangeable Image File) is a color profile, which is meant to convey the source of the photo so Photoshop knows how to handle its colors. It's a great idea, but there's a big problem. Most vendors make no attempt to profile their specific cameras, instead defaulting to sRGB (the color profile of last resort for just about every printer and scanner sold today). It's also been said that there is so little quality control that the profile is nearly meaningless. However, "nearly meaningless" is better than nothing. Better to have a vague sense of where your images come from than no sense at all. So it is recommended that you leave this option deselected.

✦ **Ask Before Saving Layered TIFF Files (on).** If you add a layer to a TIFF file that formerly consisted of only a background layer and then try to save the file, having this option selected opens the TIFF Options dialog box. This dialog box lets you choose between JPEG, ZIP, and the traditional LZW compression for TIFFs, as well as other options discussed in Chapter 3. These are useful options, so I say leave this turned on. You will also be prompted that saving a TIFF with layers may create a larger file, at which point you can accept that and move on, or stop the process and go back to merge your layers.

✦ **Enable Large Document Format (.psb) (on).** Starting with Photoshop CS, images of any file size or pixel dimension are now supported with a file format called Large Document Format (PSB). You can open PSB files regardless of the status of this option, but if you want to save to the PSB format, this option must be selected. If you regularly work with images that weigh in at 2GB or more, select this option. Otherwise, feel free to turn it off.

Cross-Reference   For more information on the PSB format, consult Chapter 3.

✦ **Maximize PSD File Compatibility (Ask).** This option is pure evil, yet it is set to "Ask" by default, which means that you will be prompted about maximizing file compatibility when saving a new PSD file. If you never change another preference setting, you should set this one to Never. Of course, this begs the question, "Why did Adobe set to Ask by default, if it's so evil?" The answer? Who knows, but this option should be named Double My File Sizes Just Because.

Even Adobe's designers would be hard-pressed to defend use of this option, but here's the tragic backstory: The option ensures backward compatibility between Photoshop CS2 and programs that support the Photoshop file format but don't recognize layers. It's a nice idea, but it comes at a very steep price. To ensure compatibility, Photoshop has to insert an additional flattened version of a layered image into every native Photoshop file. As you can imagine, this takes up a considerable amount of hard drive space, doubling the file size in the most extreme situations.

So set this option to Never. And when you want cross-application compatibility, save an extra TIFF version of your file (as explained in Chapter 3) — it's worth the extra time, and it only has to be done when you want that cross-application compatibility, not every single time you save a PSD file.

Note   Actually, there is one situation where you might find the Maximize PSD File Compatibility option useful. It permits older versions of After Effects or Illustrator to open files that contain layer effects that were added to Photoshop after those products shipped. If this rare scenario applies to you, then Ask might be the appropriate setting for this otherwise evil option.

✦ **Enable Version Cue Workgroup File Management (on).** This option invokes a spinoff of WebDAV technology, which is a means for multiple users to share and modify documents over a network. Although not currently widely implemented, Adobe and others hope to see WebDAV (or just DAV, as it's sometimes called) grow into a standard means of collaboration. We're not just talking about interoffice networks here; in the DAV world of the future, artists can collaborate with each other remotely from points around the globe.

Probably, most of you won't need this option, and those of you who do will be forced into it by some maniacal IT manager. For those in such a position, here's how it works. Selecting this option inserts a Version Cue icon in the Open dialog box. Clicking the Version Cue icon enables you to check out files and work on collaborative efforts. If, after clicking the Version Cue icon, you need to work on a local file, simply click the Local Files icon in the Open dialog box.

✦ **Recent file list contains (10) files (your call).** This option determines how many file names appear when you choose the Open Recent command, which displays a list of the images that you worked on most recently. You can simply click an image name to open the image. The default number of file names is 10, but you can raise it to 30. Raising the value doesn't use resources that would otherwise be useful to Photoshop, so type whatever value makes you happy — the more images you tend to work with in a given day, the higher a value you may want to set for this option.

Display & Cursors

Press Ctrl+3 (⌘-3 on the Mac) to sidle up to the Display & Cursors options, which appear in Figure 2-20. These options affect the way colors and cursors appear on-screen. Here's how the options work, along with recommended settings:

✦ **Color Channels in Color (off).** An individual color channel contains just 8 bits of data per pixel, which makes it equivalent to a grayscale image. Photoshop provides you with the option of colorizing the channel according to the primary color it represents. For example, when this option is selected, the Red color channel looks like a grayscale image viewed through red acetate. Most experts agree the effect isn't helpful, though, and it does more to obscure your image than make it easier for you to see what's happening. Leave this option deselected and read Chapter 4 for more information.

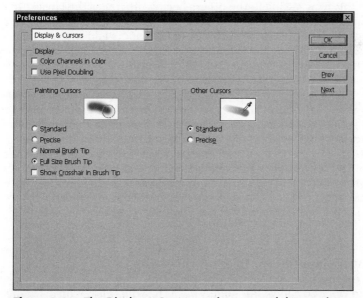

Figure 2-20: The Display & Cursors options control the way images and cursors appear on-screen. Here we see the default settings.

✦ **Use Pixel Doubling (off).** When you're editing huge images on a less-than-robust computer, this option can help speed up operations but not by much. When you select the option, Photoshop displays selected areas using a low-resolution proxy. This option goes into effect with selections and while moving layers.

✦ **Painting Cursors (Brush Size).** When you use a paint or edit tool, Photoshop can display one of four cursors — Standard, Precise, Normal Brush Tip, or Full Size Brush Tip. The Standard cursor looks like a paintbrush, a pencil, a finger (if you're smudging), or whatever tool you're using. These cursors are great if you have problems keeping track of what tool you selected, but otherwise they border on childish and make precision nearly impossible — imagine trying to erase a row of single pixels with a cursor that looks like a big picture of an eraser. Not easy.

The Precise and two Brush Size options are more functional. The Precise option displays a cross-shaped cursor — called a cross hair — regardless of which tool is active. The cross hair is great because it prevents the cursor from blocking your view as you edit, but it has a significant drawback — sometimes it's hard to see your cursor unless you're zoomed in very close to your image On the other hand, the Normal Brush Size option displays a circle that's 50 percent of the size and shape of the active brush in the Brushes palette, and allows you to be precise as well as providing a sense of the effect the Brush tool in question will have, at least in terms of how wide a swath you'll be painting, smudging, blurring, sharpening, or erasing. The Full Size Brush Tip option is the default setting, and shows your brush tip in the actual size you have set. Most artists prefer this final setting to the others because it comes the closest to showing the cursor the way it really is, and because it's a circle (and you can see through it), it affords more accuracy in tight spots and where a high level of precision is required. You can also add to the precision by selecting the Show Crosshair in Brush Tip option, which does just that — it places a cross hair in the middle of the Normal or Full Size brush tip cursor.

When Standard or Brush Size is selected, you can access the cross-hair cursor by pressing the Caps Lock key. When Precise is selected from the Painting Cursors options, pressing Caps Lock displays the brush size.

✦ **Other Cursors (Standard).** Again, you can select Standard to get the regular cursors or Precise to get cross hairs. You may want to leave this option set to Standard because you can always access the cross-hair cursor by pressing Caps Lock. The Precise option locks you into the cross hair whether you like it or not.

Transparency & Gamut

Press Ctrl+4 (⌘-4 on the Mac) to switch to the Transparency & Gamut panel shown in Figure 2-21. The options in this panel change how Photoshop displays two conceptual items — transparent space behind layers and RGB colors that can't be expressed in CMYK printing.

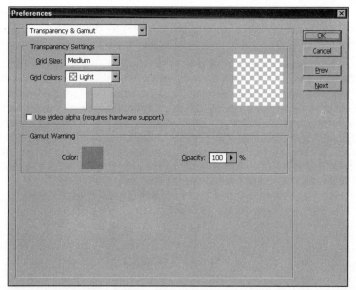

Figure 2-21: The options in this panel affect how Photoshop represents transparency and out-of-gamut colors. For the most part, you just want to select colors that you don't often see in your images, so you can tell Transparency from an actual pattern in your image.

The options are arranged into two groups — Transparency Settings and Gamut Warning — as explained in the following sections.

Transparency settings

Photoshop images rest on a layer of absolute transparency, and by default, Photoshop represents this transparency as a gray checkerboard pattern. When you view a layer independently of others, Photoshop fills the see-through portions of the layer with the checkerboard, so having the checkerboard stand out from the layer itself is essential. You can customize the size of the checkers and the color of the squares using the Grid Size and Grid Colors pop-up menus, and you can also set the Opacity of the checkerboard (it's set to 100 percent by default). You can also click the color swatches to define your own colors — when you click either one, the Color Picker opens.

Tip

To lift colors from the image window (for use in your checkerboard, or anything else you're coloring, for that matter), move your cursor outside the Color Picker (if that dialog box is open), or the Preferences dialog box to get the Eyedropper. Click a color to change the color of the white checkers; Alt-click (or Option-click on the Mac) to change the gray ones.

If you own a TrueVision NuVista+ board or some other 32-bit device that enables chroma keying, you can select the Use Video Alpha option to view a television signal in the transparent area behind a layer. Unless you work in video production, you needn't worry about this option.

Gamut warning

If Photoshop can display a color on-screen but can't accurately print the color, the color is said to be *out of gamut.* You can choose View ➪ Gamut Warning to coat all out-of-gamut colors with gray (or any other color you choose by clicking the Color block in the dialog box). You may find that you prefer using the View ➪ Proof Colors (Ctrl+Y or ⌘-Y) command instead — but if you use View ➪ Gamut Warning, you don't have to accept gray as the out-of-gamut coating.

Units & Rulers

The Units & Rulers panel is the fifth panel in the Preferences dialog box; hence, you reach the panel by pressing Ctrl+5 (⌘-5 on the Mac). Shown in Figure 2-22, this panel offers options that enable you to change the predominant system of measurement used throughout the program.

Tip   Whenever the rulers are visible, the Units & Rulers panel is only a double-click away. Choose View ➪ Rulers (Ctrl+R or ⌘-R) to display the rulers (if they're not already showing), and then double-click either the horizontal or vertical ruler to open the dialog box.

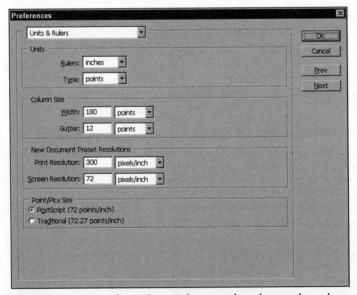

Figure 2-22: Go to the Units & Rulers panel to change the column and pica settings and set the unit of measurement.

Rulers

You can set the unit of measurement with the Units option in the Preferences dialog box. But there's an easier way: Just right-click (Control-click on the Mac) anywhere on the ruler to display a pop-up menu of unit options and then click the unit you want to use. You can display the same pop-up menu by clicking the plus sign in the lower-left corner of the Info palette.

When you're first learning Photoshop, and if you're coming from the print design world, you may be tempted to go with inches or picas as your Unit of choice. Another option? Use pixels. Why? Because you can change the resolution of an image at any time and the only constant is pixels. An image measures a fixed number of pixels high by a fixed number of pixels wide — that's it. You can print those pixels as large or as small as you want, but the pixels are the one constant. Another reason? If your images might ever end up on the Web, you'll want to be thinking in pixels because that's how Web pages are measured, too.

To learn more about resolution, read Chapter 3.

Type

Photoshop enables you to set the unit of measure used for the Type tool independently of the ruler units. You can work in points, pixels, and millimeters; select your unit of choice from the Type pop-up menu.

Check out Chapter 15 for more information and insights about type in Photoshop.

Column Size

The Column Size options enable you to size images according to columns in a newsletter or magazine. Type the width of your columns and the size of the gutter in the Width and Gutter option boxes. Then use File ➪ New or Image ➪ Image Size to specify the number of columns assigned to the width of the image. You can read more about these commands in more detail in Chapter 3.

New Document Preset Resolutions

One nifty feature, first introduced in Photoshop 7, is the listing of preset sizes you get when you create a new document by choosing File ➪ New. The New Document Preset Resolutions preferences let you set a default resolution for these presets for both print and screen. This can be especially helpful for setting different print resolutions if you commonly work at something other than the default of 300 pixels per inch. Adjusting the Print Resolution preference changes the number of pixels in the document when you choose the Letter preset, for example. For general purposes though, the defaults are just fine here.

Point/Pica Size

The last option in the Units & Rulers panel, Point/Pica Size, may be the most obscure of all Photoshop options. First you need to know that exactly 12 points are in a pica, and about 6.06 picas are in an inch. What—you mean you didn't know that?

Because picas are almost evenly divisible into inches, the people who came up with the PostScript printing language decided to throw out the difference and define a pica as exactly ⅙ inch. This makes a point exactly ½ inch.

But a few purists didn't take to it—you know those purists, they're always making trouble. They found their new electronic documents weren't quite matching their old paste-up documents, and apparently this was more than they could bear. So Adobe caved and had to go back and add the Traditional (72.27 points/inch) option to keep everyone happy.

You may find that you prefer the nontraditional PostScript definition of points. This way, a pixel on-screen translates to a point on paper when you print an image at 72 ppi (the standard screen resolution). The purists may not like it, but computer imaging makes more sense when you can measure points and pixels without resorting to a calculator—life is complicated enough, thank you!

Guides, Grid & Slices

The Guides, Grid & Slices version of the Preferences dialog box can be accessed by pressing Ctrl+6 (⌘-6 on the Mac). If your computer isn't on and glowing at your side right now, you can see the dialog box in Figure 2-23. This dialog box lets you modify the colors of any guides you place in the image window and specify the size of the grid that you use to help line things up. It also provides tools for customizing Smart Guides, which you can read more about in Chapter 12.

Tip   You can display the Preferences dialog box and go directly to the Guides, Grid & Slices panel by double-clicking a guide with the Move tool or Ctrl+double-clicking (⌘-double-clicking on the Mac) with another tool. (To create a guide, drag from the horizontal or vertical ruler into the image.)

These options are explained in more detail in Chapter 12 but, for the moment, here are some brief descriptions.

Guides

Select a color for horizontal and vertical ruler guides from the Color pop-up menu. To lift a color from the image, move your cursor outside the Preferences dialog box and click in the image window with the Eyedropper. You can also view guides as solid lines or dashes by selecting an option from the Style pop-up menu.

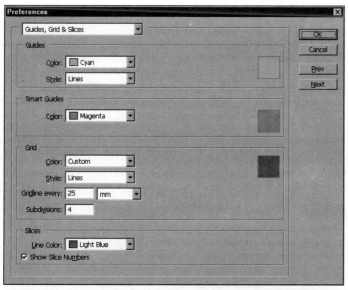

Figure 2-23: Use these options to adjust the size of the grid and change the way that ruler guides, Smart Guides, the grid, and your slices appear on-screen.

Smart Guides

These snappy little guides appear when you have Smart Guides turned on through the View ➪ Show submenu. Pink by default, they show up to help you line up one layer's content with another, letting you know when the top, bottom, sides, and/or center of the content in transit is aligned to nearby content in the image. Through this portion of the dialog box, you can change the Color of the Smart Guides, using the list to choose from eight alternatives to the default Magenta, or click the color swatch to the right of the Color option and use the Color Picker to make your selection. What should you do? Pick a color that doesn't occur in your image (or that doesn't appear in great quantity) because the Smart Guides appear fleetingly — just as you're moving the layers around, and only while you're close to perfect alignment — so you need to be able to spot them quickly and easily.

Grid

Choose a color for the grid from the Color menu, or Alt+click (Option-click on the Mac) in the image window to lift a color from the image. Then decide how the grid lines look by selecting a Style option. The Dots setting is the least intrusive.

The Gridline Every value determines the increments for the visible grid marks on-screen. But the Subdivisions value sets the real grid. For example, if you request a grid mark every 1 inch with four subdivisions, Photoshop snaps selections and layers in ¼-inch increments (1 inch divided by 4).

Slices

Like setting the color for guides and the grid, the Slices preference lets you choose a color for the lines that illustrate exactly where you've sliced up your image for posting on the Web. You can turn on and off the visibility of the slice numbers here as well.

Plug-Ins & Scratch Disks

Press Ctrl+7 (or ⌘-7 on the Mac) to advance to the panel shown in Figure 2-24. Each time you launch Photoshop, the program searches for plug-in modules and identifies one or more scratch disks. You have to tell Photoshop where to find the plug-ins and where the temporary scratch files should go.

Figure 2-24: Tell Photoshop where to find plug-ins and where to put scratch files using these options.

Additional Plug-Ins Folder

By default, the plug-ins are located in a folder cleverly disguised with the name Plug-Ins, which resides in the same folder as the Photoshop application. But you can tell Photoshop to also look for plug-ins in some other folder — a useful option if you install all your third-party plug-ins to some central location outside the Photoshop folders. To specify the second plug-ins location, select the option and then click Choose to select the folder.

Legacy Photoshop Serial Number

As you might have noticed when you installed it, Photoshop CS2 continues the new era in Adobe serial numbers first introduced with Photoshop 7. No longer are they a mixture of numbers and letters; it's all just numbers and dashes now. Some third-party plug-ins, however, serialize themselves to the old-style Photoshop serial number format. So if you're upgrading to Photoshop CS2 and you have an old serial number from Photoshop 6 or earlier, you can type it here.

Scratch Disks

By default, Photoshop assumes you have only one hard drive, so it stores its temporary virtual memory documents — called *scratch files* — on the same drive that contains your system software. If you have more than one drive available, though, you might want to tell Photoshop to look elsewhere. In fact, Photoshop can use up to four drives.

Adobe advises against using removable media such as SyQuest, MO, and Zip drives as a scratch disk. Removable media is typically less reliable and slower than a permanent drive. (A Jaz cartridge is more stable than Zip or the others, but still not as reliable as a fixed hard drive.) Using a removable drive on an occasional basis isn't the end of the world, but if you use it regularly, you may end up crashing more often, in which case you'll probably want to add a new hard drive.

Changes affect the next session

As the note at the bottom of the Plug-Ins & Scratch Disks panel warns, "Scratch disks will remain in use until you quit Photoshop." This means that you have to exit and restart Photoshop in order to see your new settings here go into effect. Potentially annoying, yes, but necessary given that Photoshop will have to reacquaint itself with your hardware if you're suddenly informing it of an additional drive or partition and want it to make use of it as a scratch disk or location for your plug-ins.

If you find restarting simply unacceptable, there is a workaround. To access the plug-ins and scratch disk settings during the launch cycle, after double-clicking the Photoshop application icon or choosing Photoshop from the Windows Start menu, press and hold Ctrl and Alt (⌘ and Option keys on the Mac). If you're using a Mac, Photoshop greets you with a message requesting that you locate the Plug-Ins folder. After you do so, press and hold ⌘ and Option again. After a few seconds, a screen of the scratch disk options appears. Specify the disks as desired and press Enter or Return. Your new settings now work for the current session — no restarting necessary. In order to use this workaround, you need to know that you want to make these changes before you start Photoshop.

Memory & Image Cache

Photoshop offers a caching scheme that speeds operations at reduced view sizes, and you can adjust this feature by pressing Ctrl+8 (or ⌘-8 on the Mac) in the Preferences dialog box. This displays the Memory & Image Cache panel shown in Figure 2-25.

Cache Levels

Photoshop has been criticized for its lack of a "pyramid-style" file format capable of storing an image several times over at progressively smaller and smaller image sizes, called *downsamplings*. Photoshop's alternative is image caching. Rather than saving the downsamplings to disk, Photoshop generates the reduced images in RAM. The Cache Levels value determines the number of downsamplings, which permits the program to apply operations more quickly at reduced view sizes. For example, if you choose a color correction command at the 50 percent view size, it previews much faster than normal because Photoshop has to modify a quarter as many pixels on-screen.

However, Photoshop must cache downsamplings in RAM, which takes away memory that could be used to hold the image. If you have lots of RAM (say, 512MB or more) and you frequently work on large images (20MB or larger), you'll probably want to raise the value to the maximum, 8. The lost memory is worth the speed boost. If you have little RAM (say 256MB or less) and you usually work on small images or Web graphics (4MB or smaller), you may want to reduce the Cache Levels value to 1 or 2. When files are small, RAM is better allocated to storing images rather than caching them.

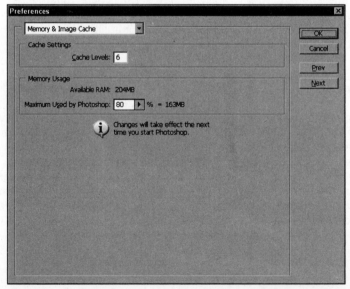

Figure 2-25: Photoshop's caching capabilities speed the processing of very large images. This is also where you specify how much memory goes to Photoshop.

Memory Usage

Mac OS X and Windows 95, NT 4, and 2000 offer dynamic memory allocation, which means that each application gets the memory it needs as it needs it. But Photoshop has a habit of using every spare bit of RAM it can get its hands on, which can cause problems in such an environment. Left to its own devices, it might gobble up all the RAM and bleed over into the operating system's virtual memory space, which is less efficient than Photoshop's own scratch disk scheme.

The Memory Usage option helps you place some limits on Photoshop's ravenous appetite. The option lists the amount of RAM available to all applications after the operating system loads into memory. You can then decide how much of that memory should go to Photoshop. If you like to run lots of applications at the same time — your word processor, Web browser, spreadsheet program, drawing program, and Photoshop, for example — set the Maximum Used by Photoshop value to 50 percent or lower. But if Photoshop is the only program running — and if you have less than 256MB of RAM — raise the value to 70 to 80 percent.

Caution

It is recommended that you not take the Maximum Used by Photoshop value any higher than 80 percent, particularly on a low-capacity machine (256MB or less). Doing so permits Photoshop to fill up RAM that the operating system might need, which makes for a less stable working environment. As noted earlier, if Photoshop is going too slow for you and hitting the scratch disk too often, buy more RAM — don't play dangerous games with the little RAM you do have.

Type

Housing just four simple options, the Type preferences dialog box, shown in Figure 2-26, lets you choose from the following:

✦ **Use Smart Quotes.** On by default, Smart Quotes that "know" if they're at the beginning or end of a word or phrase and curl accordingly. If you turn this off, you'll get straight quotes. Straight quotes can be useful if you're typing measurements, where a single straight quote means feet and two straight quotes mean inches.

✦ **Show Asian Text Options.** Off by default, if you want to see Chinese, Japanese, and Korean type options in the Character and Paragraph palettes, turn this option on. If you don't, don't.

✦ **Show Font Names in English.** This option, which is on by default, really pertains to non-Roman fonts, and whether or not you want to see their Roman names. You do, for familiarity's sake, so leave this on.

✦ **Font Preview Size.** This option lets you choose between Small, Medium (the default), and Large. The preview is found in the Type tool's Options bar, and certainly Small is going to be less visually effective than Medium, and Large is great for people with their monitors set to a high resolution — say 1024 × 768 or greater.

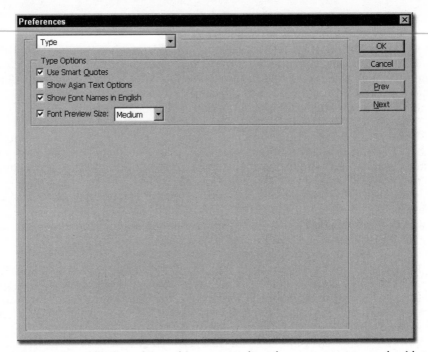

Figure 2-26: Tell Photoshop a thing or two about how you want to work with type.

Summary

In this chapter, every effort was made to help you become comfortable with the Photoshop desktop, tools, palettes, and the interface in general. You learned about new tools (and found out where in-depth coverage can be found elsewhere in the book) and discovered how to view your tool options and save presets for tools, presets, and the workspace.

Key to getting to know Photoshop is getting around in Photoshop, and toward that end you also learned about zooming in on your images, scrolling from the keyboard, and navigating the workspace. Finally, you learned how to use Photoshop's Preferences to make yourself at home — so hopefully by now, you have your feet up and are ready to move forward and find out about file management, covered in the next chapter.

✦   ✦   ✦

Image Management

In This Chapter

Scaling an image for the printer and for the screen

Opening and saving images in Photoshop CS2

Searching for and viewing images, and managing image data with the Bridge

Exploring JPEG, GIF, PDF, and dozens of other file formats

Rendering object-oriented EPS images

Annotating images with text and audio comments

Changing the number of pixels in an image

Using the Crop tool and Crop command

Using the Crop and Straighten Photos command

The colored pixels that make up an *image* work much like the tiles in a mosaic. If you enlarge the pixels, they look like an unrelated collection of colored squares. Reduce the size of the pixels, and they blend together to form an image that looks like a standard photograph. Photoshop deceives the eye, counting on the distance that printing or normal on-screen viewing puts between the person's eye and the image pixels, and in most cases, the deception is successful.

Of course, there are differences between pixels and mosaic tiles. Pixels come in 16 million distinct colors. Also, you can resample, color separate, and crop electronic images.

In this chapter, you learn about the way images are constructed, how to change their resolution, how to crop out what you don't want, how to save your files (including an exhaustive discussion of file formats and choosing the right ones for the way your files will be used), and ways to better organize and view your saved images.

Size Versus Resolution

If you haven't already guessed, the term *image size* describes the physical dimensions of an image. *Resolution* is the number of pixels per linear inch in the final printed image. The term linear is used because you measure pixels in a straight line. If the resolution of an image is 72 *ppi* — that is, pixels per inch — you get 5,184 pixels per square inch (72 pixels wide × 72 pixels tall = 5,184).

Assuming the number of pixels in an image is fixed, increasing the size of an image decreases its resolution, and vice versa. An image that looks good when printed on a postage stamp, therefore, probably looks jagged when printed as an 11 x 17-inch poster.

Figure 3-1 shows a single image printed at three different sizes and resolutions. The smallest image is printed at twice the resolution of the medium-sized image; the medium-sized image is printed at twice the resolution of the largest image.

Figure 3-1: These three images contain the same number of pixels but are printed at different resolutions. Doubling the resolution of an image reduces it to 25 percent of its original size.

One inch in the smallest image includes twice as many pixels vertically and twice as many pixels horizontally as an inch in the medium-sized image, for a total of four times as many pixels per square inch. Therefore, the smallest image covers one-fourth the area of the medium-sized image.

The same relationships exist between the medium-sized image and the largest image. An inch in the medium-sized image comprises four times as many pixels as an inch in the largest image. Consequently, the medium-sized image consumes one-fourth the area of the largest image.

Changing the Printing Resolution

When printing an image, a higher resolution translates to a sharper image with greater clarity. Photoshop lets you change the resolution of a printed image in one of two ways:

✦ Choose Image ➪ Image Size to access the controls that enable you to change the pixel dimensions and resolution of an image. Then type a value into the Resolution option box, either in pixels per inch or pixels per centimeter.

Caution

A good idea (although not essential) is to deselect the Resample Image option, as demonstrated in Figure 3-2. If you leave it selected, Photoshop may add or subtract pixels, as discussed later in this chapter. Of course, if you're shrinking an image for posting on the Web, resampling the image is necessary. For non-Web images, deselecting resampling instructs Photoshop to leave the pixels intact but merely change how many of them print per inch. This is especially important when going from a lower resolution to a higher one.

Image Size

Pixel Dimensions: 538.3K

Width: 525   pixels

Height: 350   pixels

OK   Cancel   Auto...

Document Size:

Width: 3.5   inches

Height: 2.333   inches

Resolution: 150   pixels/inch

☑ Scale Styles
☑ Constrain Proportions
☐ Resample Image: Bicubic

Turn this option off

Figure 3-2: Deselect the Resample Image option to maintain a constant number of pixels in an image and to change only the printed resolution.

✦ Alternatively, you can ask Photoshop to scale an image during the print cycle. You hand down this edict with the Print with Preview command. Choose File ➪ Print with Preview or press Ctrl+Alt+P (⌘-Option-P on the Mac) to open the dialog box. You can type specific Width and Height values or type a percentage value into the Scale option box. Lower values reduce the size of the printed image and thereby increase the resolution; higher values lower the resolution. (Chapter 18 contains more information about scaling images as well as the other settings in the Print with Preview dialog box.)

Photoshop saves the Resolution setting with the image; the scale settings in the Print with Preview box affect only the current print job. Together, the two determine the printed resolution. Photoshop divides the Resolution value in the Image Size dialog box by the Scale percentage from the Print with Preview dialog box. For example, if the image resolution is set to 72 ppi and you reduce the image to 48 percent, the final printed image has a resolution of 150 ppi (72 divided by 0.48).

Note   With apologies to the non-mathematically inclined readers out there, it's important to remind you that whenever you use a percentage in an equation, you first convert it to a decimal. For example, 100 percent is 1.0, 64 percent is 0.64, and 5 percent is 0.05. This little piece of nontrivia will help you make sense of the discussions of image size, resolution, and so on throughout this chapter and the rest of the book.

Tip   To avoid confusion, most people rely exclusively on the Resolution value and leave the Print with Preview dialog box Scale value set to 100 percent. The only exception is when printing tests and proofs. Because inkjet and other consumer printers offer lower-resolution output than high-end commercial devices, you may find it helpful to proof larger images so that you can see more pixels. Raising the Scale value lets you accomplish this without upsetting the Resolution value. Just be sure to restore the value to 100 percent after you make your test print.

Changing the Page-Layout Resolution

The Scale value in the Print with Preview dialog box value has no effect on the size and resolution of an image imported into an object-oriented application, such as QuarkXPress or Illustrator. But these same applications do observe the Resolution setting from the Image Size dialog box.

Specifying the resolution in Photoshop is a handy way to avoid resizing operations and printing complications in your page-layout program. For example, when images were created for this book, their resolution was preset so the production team had only to import the images in preparation for the printing process.

Tip   Photoshop is as good as or better at adjusting pixels than any other program. So prepare an image as completely as possible in Photoshop before importing the image into another program.

What's the Best Resolution?

After all this explanation of pixels and resolution, you may still be wondering what the best resolution would be for any image — images that will be printed, displayed on-screen, or both. The answer is frustrating to some and freeing to others: The resolution is entirely up to you, and there's no hard and fast rule. You're best off using the highest resolution possible, of course, because the higher the resolution, the cleaner, crisper, and more detailed the image will be, but there are no absolute right answers. The images in this book vary from 150 ppi for figures that show black-and-white images, dialog boxes, and other parts of the workspace to 300 ppi for the images that appear in color. Now, despite the lack of an established rule for determining resolution, here are a few guidelines to help you make intelligent choices:

✦ Most experts recommend that you set the Resolution value to somewhere between 150 percent and 200 percent of the screen frequency of the final output device. The *screen frequency* is the number of halftone dots per linear inch, measured in *lpi* (short for *lines per inch*). So ask your commercial printer what screen frequency he uses — generally 120 lpi to 150 lpi — and multiply that times 1.5 or 2.

✦ More specifically, for high-end photographic print work, it's hard to go wrong with the standard Resolution value of 267 ppi. That's around 200 percent of 133 lpi, arguably the most popular screen frequency. When in doubt, most professionals aim for 267 ppi.

✦ If you're printing on a home or small-office printer, the rules change slightly. Different manufacturers recommend different optimum resolutions for their various models, but the average is 250 to 300 ppi. Experiment to see how low you can go, though — sometimes you can get by with fewer pixels than the manufacturer suggests. And don't forget that the quality of the paper you use may be more to blame than a lack of pixels for a lousy print — copier-quality paper absorbs the ink and colors, and detail can be lost to that. You want bright white paper that won't suck up all the ink. Most papers you can buy at the office-supply store or printer will be marked clearly as to what kind of printing they're best used for — photos, brochures, flyers, informal publications, and so on.

✦ What if you don't have enough pixels for 267 ppi? Say that you shoot a digital snapshot that measures 768 x 1024 pixels and you want to print it at 6 x 8 inches. That works out to a measly 128 ppi. Won't that look grainy? Probably. Should you add pixels with Image Size or some other command? No, that typically won't help. You have a finite number of pixels to work with, so you can print the image large and a little grainy, or sharp and small. The choice is yours.

✦ What if you have a photograph or slide and you can scan it at any resolution you want? Flatbed scanners typically offer two maximum resolutions, a true optical maximum and an interpolated digital enhancement. The lower of the two values is invariably the true optical resolution. Scan at this lower maximum setting. Then use Image ⇨ Image Size to resample the image down to the desired size and resolution, as explained in the section "Resampling and Cropping" near the end of this chapter.

Finally, just take the pixels you have and try to make them look the best you can. Then print the image at the size you want it to appear, or for images that will be viewed solely online or on-screen, make sure they look good on the monitor and leave it at that — the Save for Web dialog box (discussed later in this chapter and again in Chapter 18) can help you make sure your image is both visually appealing *and* browser-friendly in terms of fast-loading for your onsite patrons. Overall, if you focus on the function of your image first and worry about resolution and other technical issues second, you'll produce better art.

The Resolution of Screen Images

Regardless of the Resolution and Scale values, Photoshop displays each pixel on-screen according to the zoom ratio (covered in Chapter 2). If the zoom ratio is 100 percent, for example, each image pixel takes up a single screen pixel. Zoom ratio and printer output are unrelated.

This same rule applies outside Photoshop as well. Other programs that display screen images — including multimedia development applications, presentation programs, and Web browsers — default to showing one image pixel for every screen pixel. This means that when you're creating an image for the screen, the Resolution value has limited impact. Some people might recommend that screen images should be set to 72 ppi on the Mac or 96 ppi for Windows, and while there's nothing wrong with doing this, anything over 72 ppi should be fine, considering that the load time is king when it comes to Web images — unlike print, where the image quality is primary. On the Web, you want the image to look good, but to load fast — even if that means sacrificing image quality somewhat.

When publishing for the screen, just scan or capture at a high resolution — 300 ppi or more — make your corrections, retouches, edits, and so on — and then use the Save for Web dialog box to optimize the image for the Web. The dialog box contains a preview that lets you choose the right format, quality, and color range, and the software does the work of setting the resolution for you. You'll also get a load-time estimate so you can decide whether you want to sacrifice some of the clarity in order for your image to load in under a minute. The Save for Web dialog box is discussed later in this chapter, and also in Chapter 18.

So, in the end, all that counts is the 100 percent view. That means you want the image to fit inside the prospective monitor when you choose View ➪ Actual Pixels (Ctrl+Alt+0 on the PC or ⌘-Option-0 on the Mac) inside Photoshop. The term *prospective* monitor is used because although you may use a 17-inch monitor when you create the image, you may need the final image to fit on a 13-inch display. So even though your monitor probably displays at least 1,024 x 768 pixels, many Web and screen artists prepare for the worst-case scenario, 800 x 600 pixels.

How to Open, Duplicate, and Save Images

Before you can work on an image in Photoshop — whether you're creating a brand-new document or opening an image from disk — you must first load the image into an image window. Here are the basic ways to create an image window:

✦ **File ➪ New.** Create a new window by choosing File ➪ New or by pressing Ctrl+N (⌘-N on the Mac). After you fill out the desired size and resolution specifications (or accept the defaults, based on any content from another image you may have copied to the Clipboard) in the New dialog box, Photoshop confronts you with a stark, white, empty canvas. You then face the ultimate test of your artistic abilities—painting from scratch—unless, of course, you have content in other images that you can bring in and play with in the new image window. For information on how to click and drag layers and selections from one image into another image, see Chapter 12.

✦ **File ➪ Open.** Choose File ➪ Open or press Ctrl+O (⌘-O on the Mac) to open images scanned in other applications, images purchased from stock photo agencies, slides and transparencies digitized to a Kodak Photo CD, or an image you previously edited in Photoshop. Photoshop CS2's Bridge feature also gives you access to Adobe Stock Photos. While you're in the Open dialog box, click the Use Adobe Dialog button, and see the dialog box shown in Figure 3-3. The dialog box functions nearly identically to the default dialog box (see the Use OS Dialog button that appears when you're in the Adobe version), but it provides a few more tools—for opening images into the Bridge (Photoshop CS2's new file organization workspace) and for setting up Projects.

✦ **File ➪ Browse.** This command opens the Bridge, a separate workspace that allows you to organize and print your images. In Windows, if you have an open image on-screen, this command appears as Close and Go to Bridge.

Note

You can also open the Bridge by clicking the Go To Bridge button (found just to the left of the palette dock). The Bridge is discussed later in this chapter and also in Chapter 18.

Figure 3-3: The Adobe Open dialog box is a new feature in Photoshop CS2—use it if you want a totally Adobe experience. Otherwise, the default OS dialog box will serve you well.

✦ **File ⇨ Open Recent.** A variation on the Open command, Open Recent displays a list of the images that you recently opened. Click an image name to crack open the image file without taking that tedious trip to the Open dialog box. You can set the number of files that you want to appear in this list in the File Handling panel of the Preferences dialog box.

✦ **Edit ⇨ Paste.** Photoshop automatically adapts a new image window to the contents of the Clipboard (provided those contents are bitmapped). So if you copy an image in a different application or in Photoshop and then choose File ⇨ New, Photoshop enters the dimensions and resolution of the image into the New dialog box. You can just accept the settings and choose Edit ⇨ Paste to introduce the image into a new window. Photoshop pastes the Clipboard contents as a new layer. This technique is useful for editing screen shots captured to the Clipboard or for testing effects on a sample of an image without harming the original.

✦ **File ⇨ Import.** If you own a scanner or a digital camera, it may include a plug-in module that lets you transfer an image directly into Photoshop. Just copy the module into Photoshop's Plug-Ins folder and then run or relaunch the Photoshop application. To initiate a scan or to load an image into Photoshop, choose the plug-in module from the File ⇨ Import submenu.

After you choose the command, Photoshop launches the device's download software. If you're scanning, select the scanner settings and initiate the scan as usual; the scanned picture appears in a new image window in Photoshop. If you're transferring images from a digital camera, the camera software typically creates thumbnail previews of images in the camera's memory so that you can select the ones you want to transfer to Photoshop.

Tip

Save your images to disk immediately after you scan or download them; unlike some other programs, Photoshop doesn't automatically take this step for you. Also, if your digital camera stores images on removable memory cards (CompactFlash, SmartMedia, Memory Stick, and the like), it's a good idea to invest in a card reader or adapter that enables your computer to see the memory card as just another hard drive. You can then just drag and drop images from the memory card to your computer's hard drive, a process that, depending on your camera, may be much faster and more convenient than transferring images using a cable connection.

Creating a new image

Whether you're creating an image from scratch or transferring the contents of the Clipboard to a new image window, choose File ⇨ New or press Ctrl+N (⌘-N on the Mac) to open the New dialog box shown in Figure 3-4. If the Clipboard contains a selection or a layer within another image, the Width, Height, and Resolution option boxes show the size and resolution of this content. Otherwise, you can type your own values in one of six units of measurement: pixels, inches, centimeters, millimeters, picas, or points. If you're uncertain exactly what size image you want to create, enter a rough approximation. You can always change your settings later.

Tip When in doubt about the size of your new image, go for bigger rather than smaller. If you have a general sense that the image will need to print at 3 inches by 4 inches, go for 4 inches by 5 inches, or even use one of the preset sizes, such as 4 x 6. You can always crop away unwanted periphery, and it's better to have too much room than not enough.

Figure 3-4: Use the New dialog box to specify the size, resolution, and color mode of your new image.

The Preset pop-up menu gives you easy access to several popular document sizes, common settings for working in print or on the Web, and several presets for video and film formats such as NTSC, PAL, and HDTV. Photoshop also lets you select the pixel aspect ratio of your document. You'll find more information about pixel aspect ratios later in this chapter.

Tip You also have the New Document Preset Resolutions settings in the Units & Rulers panel of the Preferences dialog box, which let you set a default resolution for print or screen; the resolutions you set in the Preferences dialog box appear when you select certain options from the Preset menu.

Note When you select one of the video presets from the Preset pop-up menu, Photoshop automatically adds guides to your image that are specific to that setting. These guides delineate areas known in the video industry as the action-safe and title-safe zones. Because most television screens crop a certain amount off the borders of a video image, it's extremely helpful to be aware of what will and won't be visible on any given television set. These days, you'll be safe on most televisions if you keep your graphics within the outermost, or action-safe, zone. You can quickly toggle the visibility of these guides on and off by pressing Ctrl+; (semicolon) (⌘-; on the Mac). You'll find a more in-depth look at guides in Chapter 12.

If you don't like Photoshop's preset document sizes, you can easily create your own. The moment you make any sort of change to one of Photoshop CS2's predefined presets, you get access to the Save Preset button. Click it to open the New Document Preset dialog box, shown in Figure 3-5. Here you can type a name for the new preset and specify which of your current settings you'd like to include. This is a great feature that can be a huge timesaver when you're creating a large batch of identically sized files. If you later decide you want to delete a custom document preset, simply select it from the Preset pop-up menu in the New dialog box, and click Delete Preset.

Figure 3-5: The New Document Preset dialog box lets you name and save custom document presets.

Tip

Although Photoshop matches the contents of the Clipboard by default, you can also match the size and resolution of other images:

✦ Press Alt (or Option on the Mac) when choosing File ➪ New or press Ctrl+Alt+N (⌘-Option-N on the Mac) to override the contents of the Clipboard. Photoshop displays the size and resolution of the last image you created, whether or not it came from the Clipboard. Use this technique when creating many same-sized images in a row.

✦ You can also match the size and resolution of the new image to any other open image. Any images you currently have open appear at the bottom of the Preset pop-up menu.

Units of measure

The Width and Height pop-up menus contain the six common units of measure mentioned earlier: pixels, inches, centimeters, millimeters, points, and picas. But the Width pop-up menu offers one more: Columns. If you want to create an image that fits exactly within a certain number of columns when it's imported into a desktop-publishing program, select this option. You can specify the width of a column and the gutter between columns by pressing Ctrl+K and Ctrl+5 (⌘-K and ⌘-5 on the Mac) to display the Units & Rulers preferences. Then type values into the Column Size option boxes.

The Gutter value affects multiple-column images. For example, if you accept the default setting of a 15-pica column width and a 1-pica gutter, and you specify a one-column image in the New dialog box, Photoshop makes it 15 picas wide. If you ask for a two-column image, Photoshop adds the width of the gutter to the width of the two columns and creates an image 31 picas wide.

The Height pop-up menu in the New dialog box lacks a Column option because vertical columns have nothing to do with the image height.

Tip

You can set the default unit of measurement for the Width and Height pop-up menus in the Units & Rulers panel of the Preferences dialog box. (Select the value from the Rulers pop-up menu; the Type menu sets the measurement unit for text-related controls.) But if the dialog box isn't already open, here are two quicker options:

✦ Press Ctrl+R (or ⌘-R on the Mac) to display the rulers, and then right-click (or Control-click on the Mac) anywhere in the rulers to display a pop-up menu of units. Click the unit you want to use.

✦ Display the same pop-up menu by pressing F8 to display the Info palette and then clicking or dragging the cross icon (next to the X and Y coordinate values) in the palette's lower-left corner. Click the unit you prefer.

New image size

In most cases, the on-screen dimensions of an image depend on your entries in the Width, Height, and Resolution option boxes. If you set both the Width and Height values to 10 inches and the Resolution to 72 ppi, the new image will measure 720 x 720 pixels. An exception occurs if you choose pixels as your unit of measurement. In this case, the on-screen dimensions depend solely on the Width and Height options, and the Resolution value only determines the size at which the image prints.

Color Mode

Use the Color Mode pop-up menu to specify the number of colors that can appear in your image. Choose Bitmap to create an image consisting of only black and white pixels, and choose Grayscale to access only gray values. RGB Color, CMYK Color, and Lab Color all provide access to a full range of colors, although their methods of doing so differ. You can read all about these color modes and how they work in Chapters 4, 16, and 17.

In addition to specifying the color mode, Photoshop lets you set the bit depth of your image in the New dialog box. The bit depth determines the amount of color information available to each individual pixel in the image. Choosing 1 bit limits your image to black and white pixels and thus can be used only in Bitmap mode. The option you'll probably use most often is 8 bit, which is standard fare for most full-color images. Choosing 16 bit gives your image a much greater number of available colors, providing you with a more accurate color representation and finer color controls. But the 16-bit option also greatly increases the file size and limits your editing options. For more information on using 16-bit mode, see Chapter 4 — where you can also read about taking an existing image and bumping it up to 32-bit mode, using the Image ⇨ Mode ⇨ 32 Bits/Channel command.

Cross-Reference

RGB stands for red-green-blue, CMYK for cyan-magenta-yellow-black, and Lab for luminosity and two abstract color variables: *a* and *b*. To learn how each of these color modes works, read Chapter 4.

Background Contents

The New dialog box also provides a Background Contents pop-up menu that enables you to change the color of the background for the new image. You can fill the new image with white, with the current background color (which might be white anyway, of course), or with no color at all. This last setting, Transparent, results in a floating layer with no background image whatsoever (represented by a gray and white checkerboard pattern), which can be useful when editing one layer independently of the rest of an image or when preparing a layer to be composited with an image. For an in-depth examination of layering, see Chapter 12.

If you do select a transparent background, you must later flatten the layers if you want to save the image to a format that doesn't support layers. (See the upcoming discussion on saving an image to disk for information about options that retain layers when saving.) The advantage of the Transparent setting, however, is that Photoshop doesn't create a new layer when you press Ctrl+V (⌘-V on the Mac) to paste the contents of the Clipboard. In the long run, you don't gain much — you still must flatten the image before you save it to some formats — but at least you needn't fuss with two layers, one of which might be an unwanted background layer.

Color Profile

At the very bottom of the New dialog box, you'll find an Advanced option (click the button with the two little carat symbols on it). The Advanced settings offer options for selecting a Color Profile and the Pixel Aspect Ratio for your image.

In the first option, Color Profile, you can determine the color space in which your new image will exist. Essentially, the color profile of an image provides the information necessary to make sense of how an image should be displayed or printed based on the circumstances under which the image was created. For an in-depth look at the sometimes daunting world of color management, check out Chapter 16.

Pixel Aspect Ratio

The second and final setting in the Advanced section of the New dialog box lets you set the Pixel Aspect Ratio for your image. Computer monitors display images with an assortment of perfectly square pixels. The pixels that make up an image on a television, however, are of a more rectangular nature. The result is that an image created with square pixels in Photoshop will look somewhat squashed when imported into video-editing software and output onto a television screen.

Luckily, Photoshop can help. By selecting a nonsquare pixel aspect ratio or choosing any of the nonsquare video presets, you can work with a preview of the image that more accurately represents its appearance in your final film or video project. It's important to note, however, that these settings don't actually alter the pixels in your image. They simply present them to you in a way that more closely matches your specific destination. You always have the option of displaying the pixels in a square ratio by choosing View ➪ Pixel Aspect Ratio Correction to turn the option off. Toggling this option off can at times be helpful because it eliminates the need for Photoshop to do any scaling and provides you with a higher-quality preview.

Tip

If you decide to change the pixel aspect ratio of an image after you've begun to edit it, simply choose Image ⇨ Pixel Aspect Ratio and select a new setting from the submenu.

Note

It's important to note that choosing a nonsquare aspect ratio affects the behavior of many tools. For example, if you Shift-drag with the Elliptical Marquee tool to draw a circular selection outline, a different number of pixels are selected depending on whether you're working with square or nonsquare pixels. This pertains to all shape tools and even brushes. A 90-pixel circular brush used on an NTSC image, for example, will paint a circle 90 pixels tall and 100 pixels wide.

Naming the new image

The New dialog box provides a Name option. If you know what you want to call your new image, you can type the name now. You don't have to, of course, as you won't be officially naming the file until you save it with the File ⇨ Save command. Through the resulting Save As dialog box, Photoshop asks you to specify the location of the file and confirm the file's name. Therefore, don't feel compelled to name your image anything in the New dialog box — the only reason to use this option is to help you keep your images organized on-screen, as the name you provide in the New dialog box appears on the image window title bar, replacing the generic "Untitled."

Caution

Photoshop supports long file names, and you're welcome to use them, but you should be aware of the implications. If you send a file to someone using Windows 3.1, DOS, or some other ancient operating system, the long file name gets truncated to eight characters with a tilde symbol (~) and number. This can happen also when exchanging files between PCs and Macs, depending on how you do it. If you swap files to a Mac using a PC-formatted floppy disk, Zip disk, or the like, the file names get the ax when the disk is popped into the Mac. But if you network your PC to a Mac using PC MACLAN (from Miramar Systems, www.miramarsys.com) or the like, the long file names come through swimmingly.

Opening an image

Photoshop provides a File menu command, Open Recent, which displays a list of the images you worked on in recent Photoshop sessions. Click the name of the image you want to open. You set the number of files that appear on the list by typing a value in the Recent File List Contains option box, found on the File Handling panel of the Preferences dialog box, which you access by pressing Ctrl+K and then Ctrl+2 (⌘-K and ⌘-2 on the Mac). The maximum value is 30.

Tip

Some tricks for Mac people: ⌘-click the title bar of an open image to display a pop-up menu showing the folder hierarchy for the image file. Click any folder to open it and display all image files therein. Then simply double-click the image file you want to open. (In Mac OS X, this trick works in any application, not just Photoshop.)

Also, the icon in the title bar gives you an instant hint as to whether or not your image has been edited since it was last saved. If the image has unsaved changes, the title bar icon appears faded. (Mac OS X users can also look at the red Close button in the title bar; if it contains a black dot, the image has been edited since it was last saved.)

Of course, you can always open images the old-fashioned way by choosing File ⇨ Open or pressing its keyboard shortcut, Ctrl+O (⌘-O on the Mac), to display the Open dialog box. On the PC, you also can double-click an empty spot in the Photoshop program window to open the dialog box.

The default Open dialog box behaves just like the ones in other Windows and Macintosh applications, with a folder bar at the top, a scrolling list of files, and the usual file management and navigation options. You can also open multiple files at one time. To select a range of files on the PC and in Mac OS X, click the first file name and then Shift-click the last file in the range. Ctrl-click (⌘-click in Mac OS X) to add a single file to the group you want to open. Ctrl-click or ⌘-click again to deselect a file from the group.

The Photoshop version of the Open dialog box (not to be confused with the Adobe Open dialog box, discussed just a few paragraphs from here) also includes a few controls that most other programs lack. You can read about these options in the next sections. But first, a few other brief notes about opening files:

✦ When you choose File ⇨ Open, Photoshop displays the folder that contained the last file you opened. Similarly, when you save a file, the folder you saved last is selected automatically.

✦ When you open an image, Photoshop may display a dialog box telling you that the color profile of the image doesn't match the default color profile you've established. You have the option of converting the image to the default profile or leaving well enough alone. See Chapter 16 for help with this issue.

Tip   When opening an image, you may occasionally encounter a dialog box warning you that some data in the file cannot be read and will be ignored. Well, it's a bunch of bunk. If this happens to you, just click OK to dismiss the warning and open the image as usual.

The Adobe Open dialog box (displayed by clicking the Use Adobe Dialog button in the lower-left corner of the default Open dialog box) offers the same options as the default Open dialog box. You can click the Look in drop-down list to choose from disks, drives, and other places to look for your file. You can also click the icons on the left side of the dialog box to look on the Desktop and in particular folders. In the main area of the dialog box (seen in Figure 3-6), you can view the images in the open folder or drive in the same ways that you can in the default Open dialog box—in Details view, where file name, size, status, type, and date modified are displayed, Icons, Thumbnails, or Tiles view. Wait—Tiles? Yes, as shown in Figure 3-6, Tiles view shows an icon for the image—indicating format—and some basic stats for the image, including name, size, and date/time modified.

Figure 3-6: The Tiles view in the Adobe version of the Open dialog box offers enlarged image icons and file information that rivals the familiar Details view's list of file statistics.

Tip

Click the Project Tools button (looks like a little briefcase) in the upper right of the dialog box to access a menu that includes commands for accessing the Bridge, creating a new project, editing file properties, creating new folders, and looking or restoring deleted files. This menu also offers a command for going back to the "OS Dialog" (OS standing for Operating System), which you can also do by clicking the Use OS Dialog button that has replaced the Use Adobe Dialog button in the lower-left corner of the dialog box. There is also an Adobe dialog version of the Save and Save As dialog boxes — look for coverage of these later in this chapter.

Viewing the thumbnail

To help you assess an image before you open it, Photoshop displays a thumbnail preview of the selected file in the Open dialog box, as shown in Figure 3-7. On the Mac, the column view found in Open dialog boxes automatically displays a preview of graphic files. On the PC, Photoshop automatically displays thumbnails for any files saved in the native format (PSD). If you're running Windows 2000, the operating system may generate thumbnails for files saved in other formats.

On the Mac, the thumbnail space may appear empty, which means the file does not contain a Photoshop-compatible preview. The file may have been created by a piece of hardware or software that doesn't support thumbnails, or the thumbnail feature may have simply been turned off when the image file was saved. To generate thumbnails when saving images in Photoshop, press Ctrl+K and then Ctrl+2 (⌘-K and

⌘-2 on the Mac) to display the File Handling panel of the Preferences dialog box. Then select the Macintosh Thumbnail option if you're using a Mac or set the Image Previews pop-up menu to Always Save if you're using a PC. Alternatively, you can set the Image Previews pop-up menu to Ask When Saving, in which case Photoshop gives you the option of adding a thumbnail to the image inside the Save dialog box.

Figure 3-7: You can see a preview of an image if you previously saved it in Photoshop with the thumbnails option selected.

Previewing outside Photoshop

Tip

The Open dialog box isn't the only place where you can preview an image before you open it. To preview an image file directly in Windows Explorer under Windows XP or 2000, simply navigate to the folder in which the image is located and click the file to highlight it. A section on the left side of the folder window, labeled Details under Windows XP, displays a high-quality image preview, provided a preview was saved along with the image. Alternatively, you can view thumbnail previews for an entire folder of images by choosing View ❙ Thumbnails from the menu bar at the top of the folder window.

Mac OS X is pretty clever about generating previews of graphic files all on its own. Depending on the file format, you can generally get a preview of a graphic file, no matter what the thumbnail saving settings were. Select an image in the Finder and press ⌘-I to access the Get Info command. Twirl down the arrow next to the word Preview to view a miniature version of the image, as pictured in Figure 3-8. You can also open and view PSD files through Apple's own Preview application.

Figure 3-8: The Get Info command in Mac OS X can show previews of many different graphic file types.

Opening elusive files on a PC

The scrolling list in the Open dialog box contains the names of the documents that Photoshop recognizes it can open. If you can't find a desired document on your PC, it may be because the Files of Type pop-up menu is set to the wrong file format. To view all supported formats, either select All Formats from the Files of Type pop-up or type *.* in the File Name option box and press Enter.

If a file lacks an extension, the Open dialog box won't be able to identify it. This unusual situation may arise in one of two ways. On rare occasions, a file transmitted electronically (through the Internet, for example) loses its extension en route. But more likely, the file comes from a Macintosh computer. The Mac doesn't need file extensions — the file type identification resides in the resource fork — so many Mac users never give a thought to three-character extensions.

You can solve this problem by renaming the file and adding the proper extension or by choosing File ➪ Open As (Ctrl+Alt+O). If you choose Open As, Photoshop shows you all documents in a directory, whether it supports them or not. Just click the extension-less file and select the correct file format from the Open As pop-up menu. Provided that the image conforms to the selected format option, Photoshop opens the image when you press Enter. If Photoshop gives you an error message instead, you need to select a different format or try to open the document in a different application.

Opening elusive files on a Mac

If you can't find a document in the Open dialog box on your Mac, it may be because Photoshop doesn't recognize the document's four-character type code. The type code for a document created or last edited on a Macintosh computer corresponds to the file format under which the image was saved (as explained in the upcoming section on file formats).

For example, TIFF is the type code for a TIFF image, JPEG is the code for a JPEG image, GIF is the code for a GIF image, and so on. However, if you transferred a document from another platform, such as a Windows machine or a Unix workstation, it probably lacks a type code. In the absence of a type code, Photoshop looks for a three-character extension at the end of the file name, such as *.tif* or *.jpg* or *.gif*. But if the extension is as much as a character off — *.tff* or *.jpe* or *.jif*, for example — Photoshop won't know what to do.

To see *all* documents regardless of their type code or extension, select All Documents from the Show pop-up menu in the Open dialog box, as shown in Figure 3-9. When you click on a document in the scrolling list, the Format option displays the format that Photoshop thinks the file was saved in — if it has any thoughts to offer. If you disagree, click the Format option and select the correct file format from the pop-up menu. As long as the image conforms to the selected format option, Photoshop opens the image when you press Return. If you get an error message instead, either select a different format or try to open the document in a different application.

Tip

Normally, Mac users don't see a file's four-character type code because it's hidden inside the resource fork. Unless, that is, you're willing to purchase a special utility, such as Prairie Group's DiskTop (www.prgrsoft.com), SkyTag's File Buddy (www.filebuddy.com), or Apple's ResEdit (www.apple.com). All three are great, but DiskTop is more convenient for the simple day-to-day tasks of viewing and modifying type codes and other invisible resources.

Finding lost files on a Mac

If you know the name of a file — or at least part of the name — but you can't remember where you put it, click the Find button, type some text in the resulting option box, and press Return. Photoshop searches the disk in a fairly random fashion and takes you to the first file name that contains the exact characters you typed.

Figure 3-9: Select the All Documents option to access any document regardless of its four-character type code.

If the first file name isn't the one you're looking for, click the Find button again to find the next file name that contains your text. If you want to search for a different string of characters, click Find and type some different text.

Using the Bridge

The Bridge replaces the File Browser for accessing, organizing, and storing data about your images. To call the Bridge a feature seems like a gross understatement. The Bridge is really an application unto itself — it has its own workspace, menus, tools, and opens as a separate application in terms of how the operating system (Windows or Mac) sees it.

New Feature The Bridge is new to Photoshop CS2.

You can access the Bridge without opening Photoshop at all, or you can use either one of these methods for opening it from within Photoshop:

✦ **The Go to Bridge button.** Click this button (shown in Figure 3-10), found to the left of the palette dock. The Bridge opens in its own window shortly thereafter.

Figure 3-10: Click this button to access the Bridge. Photoshop remains open, and the Bridge opens in its own window.

✦ **Choose File ➪ Browse.** This opens the Bridge in its own window.

✦ **Choose File ➪ Close and Go to Bridge.** This closes the active image and opens the Bridge in its own window. You would do this when you're finished with an image and ready to go find another one, using the Bridge tools for accessing images. The Bridge interface appears in Figure 3-11.

Figure 3-11: The Bridge workspace provides a menu bar, tabbed panels on the left, a large viewing area for looking at your files and folders, and navigational tools for moving around in the workspace. It's kind of like the old File Browser on steroids.

A typical Bridge session

The sequence of events that takes you to and through the Bridge might go something like this — you remember you need to find a particular photo but you're not sure of the file name. Or, you want to check and see if you have all the photos you should have stored in a particular folder or on a particular CD. The Open dialog box doesn't show you all of your photos at once, and hopping out to the Finder (Mac) or Explorer (Windows) to look at thumbnails is too time-consuming. What to do? Fire up the Bridge.

Using any of the aforementioned methods — clicking the Go to Bridge button or using the File ⇨ Browse command — you open the Bridge and begin looking for or at your photos. If you know where the photo is stored and just want to see all the images in a particular folder or on a specific disk, you can use the Folders panel on the left side of the workspace. Figure 3-12 shows the Folders panel, with a folder selected, its contents displayed as thumbnails in the main viewing area of the Bridge workspace.

Folder panel   Name of currently open folder appears here

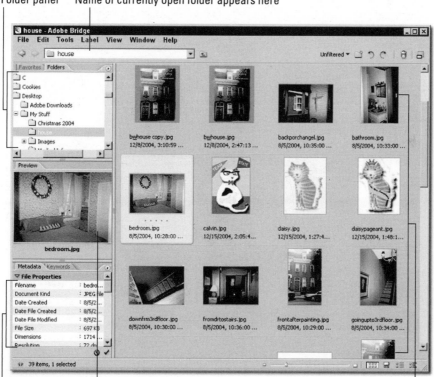

Metadata panel   Preview of an image   Thumbnails of images in selected folder

Figure 3-12: Navigate the folder tree — clicking folders and their subfolders — until you have the one you need selected. Once you select a folder, its contents appear on the right — in whatever view you choose from the View menu or using the view buttons in the lower-right corner of the workspace.

Tip   You can resize the different parts of the Bridge workspace by clicking and dragging the walls of the various panels. Drag to the right to widen the panel of tabs on the left; drag up and down on the dividers between the Favorites/Folders, Preview, and Metadata/Keyword panel areas. By resizing different areas of the workspace, you can rob space from information that you don't care about to make more room for the stuff you need to see more clearly or in its uncluttered entirety.

Assuming you're now looking at an array of thumbnails of the subfolders and images within the folder, drive, or disk you've chosen from the tree, now you can click an individual photo and view its data (see the Metadata panel in the lower left, shown in Figure 3-13) or change your view to Details (View ⇨ As Details) so that you can see the name, size, and date/time the file was last modified.

Selected image file

Metadata for selected file   Details view

Figure 3-13: In Details view, you trade a thumbnail for the file's statistics — and if the Metadata panel is showing, you see the same information and then some.

Meta-what?

What the heck is Metadata? The Metadata panel lets you view and edit more information about your images than you ever thought possible. By default, it's divided into three sections: File Properties, IPTC, and Camera Data (EXIF). The Exchangeable Image File format (EXIF) is a standard for appending nonpixel information — known as *metadata* — to an image file. EXIF is most widely used by digital cameras to describe a photograph's history, including the date and time it was shot, the make and model of the camera, the flash setting, and the focal length. In the Camera Data (EXIF) section of the Metadata panel, you may be able to find out all kinds of wonderful information about digital photographs that you shot and edited years ago.

Opening images from the Bridge

If you want to open a particular file, just double-click it. If it was not already open, Photoshop opens in its own window (the Bridge remains open, too), with the selected file open in its own image window. If Photoshop was already open, it becomes the active application and displays the selected file in its own image window — so the final outcome is the same, whether the Bridge tells Photoshop to open and show you your image, or if you had Photoshop open, ready, and waiting.

You can also select multiple images, too — just click them and press Shift to select a series of files, or Ctrl (Windows) or Command (Mac) to select random files from the same folder. Once they're all selected, you can drag them to a different folder, or to a disk as represented in the Folders panel on the left. You can also rate the images, or turn them into Favorites, which you can then access as a separate group through the Favorites panel (sharing a panel with Folders) on the left side of the Bridge workspace.

Tip

If you want to open or move everything but the file or files you have selected, choose Edit ➪ Invert Selection. The Edit menu also houses commands for selecting everything in the open folder (Select All), deselecting (Deselect All), and viewing only certain files — such as only those files that are labeled. Find out about applying labels later in this section on the Bridge.

Your Bridge view options

The whole point of the Bridge is to give you a powerful, yet simple way to view your images and access information about them. Of course, being able to open the files after viewing them is important too, but you can do that through Photoshop itself. No, the big plus to the Bridge are the image viewing options, each accessible through the View menu (big surprise, eh?). You can also use the view buttons in the lower-right corner of the workspace.

✦ **Slide show.** Choose View ➪ Slide Show, or press Ctrl+L (⌘-L on the Mac) to see a one-image-at-a-time view of the images in a particular folder or on a particular disc. Once the show is over (press Esc to stop the show at any time), you return to whichever view you were in when you invoked the show. A slide show in progress appears in Figure 3-14.

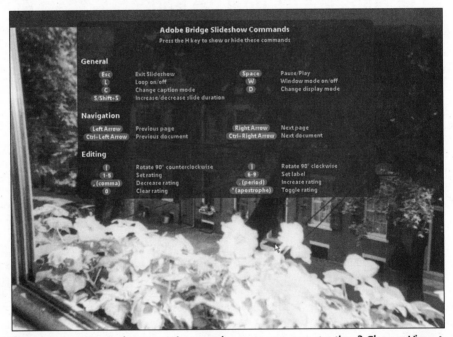

Figure 3-14: Want to have your images shown to you one at a time? Choose View ➪ Slide Show. When the show starts, instructions for navigating the show are displayed (you can see the first image behind them) — press H to hide the instructions once you've taken note of them.

✦ **Thumbnails.** You may find this view to be your favorite for looking at folders or discs with lots of files on them — you see the image, helping you find and choose images, but because the view of the image is tiny, you can see lots of them at one time. You also see the date of the file's last modification, and if you position the mouse over the thumbnail, a tip appears for a few seconds, telling you the format, size, and the dimensions of the file. Figure 3-15 shows Thumbnails view with a tip displayed.

File tip pertains to   Mouse over an image to see a tip

Selected file   Drag slider to change thumbnail size

This icon indicates the file is open in Photoshop

Figure 3-15: In Thumbnails view, you can see small versions of each image, plus some key info about the files. With the floating tip that appears when you mouse over an image, you can view metadata on the selected image as well as the details for another image at the same time.

Tip

Adjust the number of thumbnails seen simultaneously by clicking and dragging the Thumbnail Size slider (lower right of the workspace, under the thumbnails viewing area). Drag to the left to increase the thumbnail size, which means you see fewer of them at a time. Drag to the right to shrink the thumbnails and see many files at once.

✦ **Filmstrip.** This view is really very cool, in that you can see a nice, big preview of the images, one at a time, plus you can see thumbnails of a series of images all at once, along the bottom of the viewing area (see Figure 3-16). To see the bigger view of the image, click once on the thumbnail.

✦ **Details.** If you choose View ➪ As Details, you see both thumbnails (resizable with the Thumbnail Size slider, mentioned earlier) as well as seeing much of the metadata that is also stored in the Metadata panel on the right side of the window. You can see the file name, date and time of creation, date last modified (including the time, down to the second), the size of the file, the format, and the dimensions. Figure 3-17 shows Details view.

Figure 3-16: Filmstrip view gives you an enlarged preview along with a series of thumbnails. Click and drag the Thumbnail Size slider to see more thumbnails at once — the smaller the thumbnails, the larger the preview of the selected image.

Drag slider to change thumbnail size in Details (or any) view

Figure 3-17: Details view shows you pertinent data as well as a handy thumbnail of each image.

✦ **Versions and Alternates.** This view allows you to keep track of versions of your images — the subsequently saved versions that you've created (using the File ⇨ Save Version command) for sharing, backup, or to prepare the image for Web use. When you switch to this view (View ⇨ As Versions and Alternates), the view changes to display a very Details-like view — with the addition of a second column (see Figure 3-18) that shows information about alternate versions of the files. For files with no alternates, the words "No versions to display" appear in the column.

Note

You can move and resize the panels on the left side of the Bridge workspace much like you can move and resize the palettes in Photoshop. Click the panel's tab itself and drag it up or down to regroup the tabs within the right-hand panel. You can group the palettes in any configuration you want — for example, you can drag them all so that they share a single box so less vertical space is taken up in the left-hand panel. To determine which tabs are displayed, use the View menu to select and deselect them by name. A check mark indicates that the panel is currently displayed.

Figure 3-18: Got lots of versions of a single starting image? Keep track of the ancestors and offspring of any file with Versions and Alternates view.

Selecting images

You can select images — choosing from those displayed in the main viewing area — by clicking them with your mouse or by making selection command choices from the Edit menu (shown in Figure 3-19). You can also select images by searching for them (see coverage of the Find dialog box later in this section of this chapter). Once found, the images meeting your Find dialog box criteria can be selected en masse or by clicking the one that you really wanted to find.

To select images with your mouse, click once on the single image you want, or to gather more images, press Shift to select a series — as shown in Figure 3-18 — or press Ctrl (⌘ on the Mac) to select random images. Once selected, the images can be moved to a new folder (drag them to the target folder on the Folder panel on the left side of the workspace) or opened in Photoshop — just press Enter while they're selected.

Caution

If yours is not the latest and greatest computer with lots of memory, you may want to avoid opening several images at once. Start small — open one or two images, and if things don't slow down too much, you can open additional images until you notice the application becoming a bit clumsy. You may be prompted that your virtual memory setting is too low, and if you're a Windows user, Windows will beef up the memory allocation to meet your needs at the time.

Selection options in the Edit menu   Contiguous images are selected with the Shift key

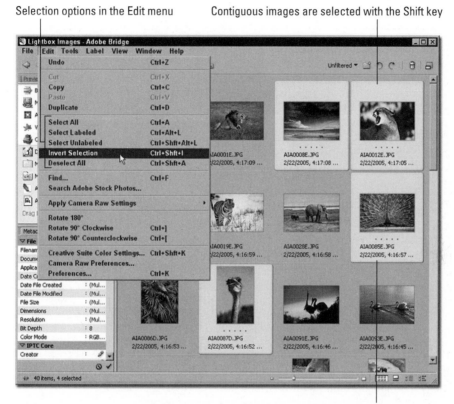

Non-contiguous images are selected with Ctrl (or ⌘ on the Mac)

Figure 3-19: Select images by mouse or by menu.

Rotating images

In Photoshop, you can rotate the image canvas, turning an image that was scanned lengthwise or upside down that you want to see turned around. The change made through the Image ➪ Rotate Canvas command is actually applied to the image itself. In the Bridge, you can rotate images, but only for the purpose of viewing them within the Bridge — the change in the rotation of an image within the Bridge is not made a part of the file itself — the image rotation will not be changed if you open the image in Photoshop.

As shown in Figure 3-20, you can right-click (or ⌘-click on the Mac) any image and choose Rotate 180, 90 Clockwise, or 90 Counterclockwise from the pop-up menu. The displayed thumbnail or filmstrip display is then changed to the rotation you chose. You can also access these rotation commands in the Edit menu.

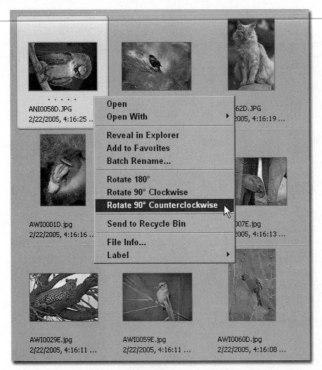

Figure 3-20: Tired of cocking your head to the right to view an image thumbnail? Rotate the display and give your neck a break.

Tip   In the upper-right corner of the workspace is a series of buttons — Unfiltered, Create a New Folder, and then the two rotation buttons: Rotate 90 Clockwise and Rotate 90 Counterclockwise. You can use these on whichever image is selected at the time — or, use them to rotate multiple selected images all at once.

Adding an image to Favorites

Like the sites you've added to your Favorites (or Bookmarks) in your Web browser, images that you want to be able to come back to quickly and easily (and frequently) can also be turned into Favorites, accessible through the Favorites panel on the left side of the Bridge workspace. Figure 3-21 shows the Favorites list, which includes locations on the computer, folders, and images.

Tip   If you're not a big Bridge user and want your oft-used images to be easily accessible, increase the number of files that can be included in the File ➪ Open Recent submenu (in Photoshop). Choose Edit ➪ Preferences ➪ File Handling and increase the Recent file list contains setting to 30. If 30 is way more than you need for this list, choose some lower number that makes it possible for the file(s) you want to see in the list to remain there even with the other files you'll open and use throughout the day or week, which could potentially push your desired files off the list.

Right-click and use the pop-up menu to add new favorites

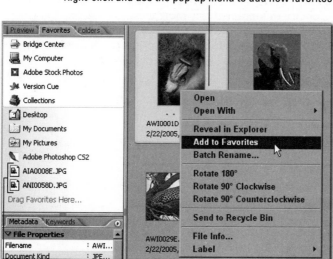

Images already added to Favorites

Figure 3-21: Are there images you use often and navigating to them via the Open dialog box is a pain? Add them to the Bridge Favorites list, and they're always right where you need them.

To add an image to Favorites, just right-click (or ⌘-click if you're on the Mac) and choose Add to Favorites from the pop-up menu. You can also choose File ➪ Add to Favorites. Once added to Favorites, you can remove an image from favor by right-clicking the image in the Favorites list (or ⌘-clicking on the Mac) and choosing Remove from Favorites from the pop-up menu. Note that if you only want to add a single image to the Favorites, be sure that only that image is selected when you right-click it — if you have multiple files selected, even if you right-click (or Control+click on the Mac) that one file, all of the selected files become Favorites.

Tip

When you click an image in the Favorites list, the Bridge assumes you want to open it in Photoshop — so don't click the image in the list unless you want that to happen.

Labeling and rating images

Humans' affinity for ranking and rating things is obvious — there are entire books of top-ten lists, and a popular late-night talk host compiles a funny top-ten list for each show. Applying value, even if it's totally subjective, is something most of us can't resist. The Bridge, being aware of this, gives you the ability to rate and label your images — ranking them with stars (from one star to five stars) and applying color-coded labels. As shown in Figure 3-22, the Label menu offers five ratings and five color labels, plus the ability to incrementally increase and decrease the existing rating for any image. You can also right-click an image (or ⌘-click on the Mac) and use the Image command in the pop-up menu to access the Label color options.

Figure 3-22: Here, the selected elephant image to the right of the Label menu already has a two-star rating and a yellow label — from the Label menu, the rating is about to be increased.

Viewing and using metadata

Metadata, as described earlier in this chapter, is a cornucopia of file information, divided into three sections. You can scroll through them in the Metadata panel, shown in Figure 3-23. You can look at File Properties (the most commonly used, and therefore visible without scrolling), IPTC Core data, and Camera Data (EXIF). For many of your files, the vast majority of these bits of data will be blank — clicking the little pencil icon next to any currently blank or editable fields opens a text box into which you can type the appropriate information.

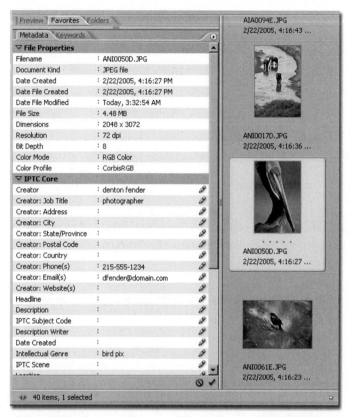

Figure 3-23: The Metadata panel lists all sorts of useful information about your images — plus some information you may place in the "Who Cares?" category.

If you click the Metadata panel's options menu button (triangle button on the top right of the panel's tab), you're presented with the following commands/options:

✦ **Find.** This command opens the Find dialog box (surprisingly enough), through which you can type various Criteria to find a file on any drive or in any folder to which your computer has access. Type your specifics — Look In (type a location, or click Browse), indicate whether or not to Include Subfolders in the search, and whether or not to Find All Files. In the Criteria section (see Figure 3-24), you can choose from among several items such as Filename...contains...*.jpg (for example), and then click the plus sign (+) to add another level of Criteria, such as Date Created...is... 04/23/2004. The "*.jpg" and "04/23/2004" are just examples of what you can ask the Bridge to look for — you can set up as many as 13 levels of Criteria. Filename, File Size, Date Created, Date Modified, Label, Rating, Keywords, Description, Comments, or All Metadata are among your choices for which aspect of the file's data to use in finding it.

Figure 3-24: Use the Find dialog box to locate a file based on any of the stored information about the file.

✦ **Increase Font Size and Decrease Font Size.** These commands change the display font size for the data in the Metadata panel.

✦ **Preferences.** This opens the Preferences dialog box (shown in Figure 3-25) through which you can customize the Bridge. You can customize General settings (default Thumbnail display options, the contents of the Favorites panel), the Metadata that's stored, Label colors, File Type Associations (which applications are used, by default, to open various graphic file types), Advanced (file size limits, Language, and Cache settings), and Adobe Stock Photos options.

✦ **Append Metadata.** Using preset templates, you can establish new data that will be stored about individual files.

✦ **Replace Metadata.** Instead of adding to the Metadata, this command allows you to choose from data templates that replace the metadata that appears by default.

Viewing and adding Keywords

Next to the Metadata panel tab is the Keywords panel tab, shown in Figure 3-26. Keywords are searchable text that is associated with individual images, stored with the file's data to help you locate files easily. Keywords are one of the Criteria you can set in the Find dialog box used to search for files — for example, if you're looking for all your vacation photos, you can tell Photoshop to find all files with "Vacation" in the Keyword list.

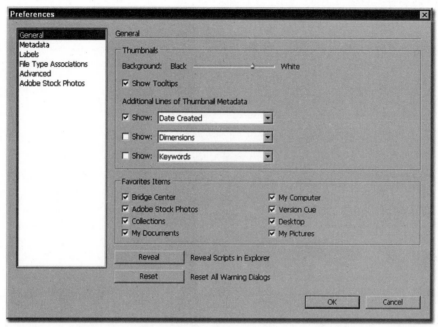

Figure 3-25: Click General, Metadata, Labels, or any of the other Bridge areas listed on the left to display those preferences options in the main dialog box.

To view the Keywords for any file, click the file in the main display area, and then click the Keywords tab on the left. A series of words — names, places, and categories such as "Birthday" and "Wedding" appear with check boxes next to them. Boxes with check marks indicate an association with that keyword.

To add your own keywords to the list, click the Keywords panel options menu button (that triangle again), and choose New Keyword. An "Untitled Key" entry appears in the list (see the menu and the resulting Untitled Key in Figure 3-27) and becomes highlighted; you can type a new keyword to replace the sample text. The new word is made part of the Other Keywords category.

To set up a new category, click the Options button and choose New Keyword Set. An Untitled Set appears, and you can again replace the sample text with a set name of your choice. After making a new set, you need to use the New Keywords command to create keywords for the set. For example, if you create a set called "Family," you can create keywords for individual people ("Mom" or "Uncle Emil") and/or you can create keywords for family events, like "Christmas" or "Bar Mitzvahs."

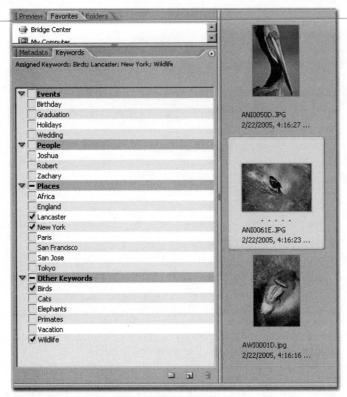

Figure 3-26: The Keywords panel allows you to associate your images with words that will help you find the images later.

Once you've created your own keywords and sets, additional commands become available in the Keywords panel options menu. Rename and Delete commands appear, and you can use them to do just what you'd expect—rename a selected keyword or set, or delete a keyword or set you no longer need.

Note   The Find command appears in the Keywords options menu, just as it does in the Metadata menu. The resulting dialog box is the same.

To apply a keyword to an individual image, select the image, and then place check marks in the boxes next to one or more of the words in the Keywords panel. You can check as many boxes as you want, and if you think of any other words that you might want to use in searching for the selected image in the future, use the New Keyword command to create them.

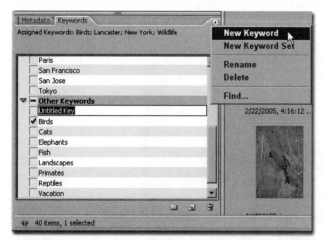

Figure 3-27: Type the new keyword where the Untitled Key entry appears. It can be a good preparatory step to go into the Keywords panel and build all the keywords you can think of using for any images — that way, the words are there and waiting whenever you're ready to begin associating them with your images.

Choosing Suite Color Settings

The Creative Suite (referenced by the "CS" in Photoshop CS2) is a group of Adobe applications that are typically used — if not at the same time — together in terms of sharing files. The movie clips edited in Adobe Premiere may end up edited as still shots in Photoshop, for example, or the still photos you edit in Photoshop might end up in a GoLive Web site or used for page layout with InDesign. You get the idea.

What assists the suite in operating as a cohesive unit is the synchronization of color settings. Through the Bridge, you can make sure Photoshop holds up its end of the bargain, working with the dialog box shown in Figure 3-28. To display and work with this dialog box, choose Edit ➪ Creative Suite Color Settings. There are a series of 17 different settings — from Monitor Color, which works with most video settings, to settings for North America, Europe, and Japan. There are prepress, general-purpose, and Web settings for each region, and default settings for prepress and Web graphics, too.

Figure 3-28: Check the available color settings for the Creative Suite.

To synchronize the settings, you can select one from within the dialog box. This sets up the suite applications — as many as you have installed on your computer from the same version of the suite — to work together with the same color settings.

Tip   To access the settings files, click the Show Saved Color Settings Files button, which opens an Explorer window with a folder tree on the left and the settings files on the right. If the right side of the window is empty, you have no saved color settings files.

Setting Camera Raw preferences

Camera Raw, a file format supported by Photoshop, is discussed later in this chapter and elsewhere in this book (see Chapter 17). You can set your Camera Raw preferences through the Bridge, using the Edit menu (or the Bridge menu if you're on a Mac). Once the Camera Raw Preferences dialog box (shown in Figure 3-29) is open, you can choose how image settings will be saved (pick a format; Sidecar ".xmp" files is the default), choose how sharpening will be applied, and set up the Camera Raw cache, which includes deciding where the cache file will be saved (find out more about cache later in this chapter) and how much space to allocate to cache files.

Figure 3-29: Customize where and how Camera Raw preferences are applied.

Selecting and saving a Bridge workspace

The old saying, "A place for everything, and everything in its place" is a philosophy that many tidy people live by. It's also a good motto for Photoshop users, because productivity hinges on easy access to the tools you need. Keyboard shortcuts can help put things at your fingertips (literally), but they don't always help enough when it comes to using palettes, tools, and so forth. Photoshop is sensitive to this and gives you the Window ⇨ Workspace ⇨ Save Workspace command. The Bridge is similarly helpful, offering a Window ⇨ Workspace ⇨ Save Workspace command of its own.

When you choose this command, the Save Workspace dialog box appears, giving you the chance to apply a relevant name to the workspace, and to choose a keyboard shortcut (Ctrl + any of the function keys from F6 through F12, except F10, for Windows users) that will invoke the saved workspace configuration. You also have an option to Save Window Location as Part of Workspace — meaning if you have the Bridge window sized and positioned the way you want it, you can save that position, too.

Note

"What about preset workspaces?" you may ask. Good question. If you choose Window ⇨ Workspace, you can choose from four different workspaces — Lightbox, File Navigator, Metadata Focus, or Filmstrip Focus. Each workspace caters to a different perspective on your images — looking at particular images in specific folders, expanding the Metadata panel area so that the content can be read without scrolling left to right, or letting the Filmstrip view take over the whole workspace.

Managing the cache

You may spend several minutes generating previews, rotating thumbnails, and ranking images inside the Bridge. Because not a single one of these functions or their impact on the image display in the Bridge is saved with the image file, you might wonder how Photoshop prevents you from losing your work. It does this by saving a cache file that records all changes made to an entire folder full of images.

This all happens in the background without any assistance from you, but problems can crop up. Imagine these two possible problem scenarios:

✦ **Sharing images over a network.** There is one cache file per folder and each resides in a system folder on your computer. This is called a *local cache* because it resides locally on your machine — important because a networked version of Photoshop running on a different computer cannot share a local cache file. If you and a coworker are browsing through images on a server and you rotate a few thumbnails or assign a few rankings, you might assume that the coworker can see what you just did. She can't, though, because her local cache is different than yours.

✦ **Browsing images on a CD.** Suppose that you start with a folder of 200 images. After giving Photoshop a few minutes to generate the thumbnails, you rotate and rank the images as you see fit. Then you burn the images to a CD, having faith that the thumbnails, rotations, and ranks will be maintained. When you put the CD in your drive and view it in the File Browser, however, Photoshop starts generating the thumbnails all over again — the rotation and ranks have been lost. The cache remains intact, but it's linked to the folder, not the CD. Photoshop, therefore, has to create a new cache for the CD, so that after you re-perform your work, the CD will browse as expected from that point on — *but only on this one machine.* Other computers will require their own local caches.

See how messy and complicated this can get? These two scenarios are just the tip of the iceberg, as the saying goes — there's a lot more going on under the surface than you might ever imagine.

There has to be a solution, right? It can't be that you have to lose all your work at the slightest change in display or other settings, nor can it be that you have to spend all your time worrying about this caching process. There is, in fact, a solution — just choose Tools ➪ Cache ➪ Export Cache, and without any additional help from you, Photoshop exports three cache files. The files are AdobeP8T.tb0, which contains the thumbnails, AdobeP8P.tb0, which contains the previews, and AdobeP8M.md0, which contains the metadata, including rotation and ranking information. From that point on, the three cache files are available to other users on a network, you can burn them to a CD, or you can keep them with a folder on the off chance you move the folder or rename it.

Caution Exporting is a manual process, so don't expect Photoshop to update your changes. If you change a rotation or ranking and want to make it available to other users or computers, choose Export Cache again. When burning image CDs, get in the habit of choosing Export Cache immediately before writing the CD; this will ensure that the cache is as up to date as possible.

If you tend to spend days and nights combing through a seemingly endless parade of images, your cache files can grow fairly quickly. Luckily, you can delete, or *purge*, the cache just as easily as you can export it. From the Bridge Tools menu, choose Cache ➪ Purge Cache for This Folder or Purge Central Cache — whichever is appropriate for your situation. You can either clear the cache of the particular folder you're currently viewing or clear the Photoshop cache files from your hard drive completely.

Tip You can create cache files for your current file's subfolders by choosing Tools ➪ Cache ➪ Build Cache for Subfolders (using the Bridge Tools menu).

Renaming files

To rename a handful of specific files, click and Shift-click their thumbnails to select them. To rename all files in a folder, choose Select All or Deselect All from the Edit menu. Then right-click (Control-click on the Mac) and choose Batch Rename (or choose Tools ➪ Batch Rename from the Bridge menu bar) to display the dialog box pictured in Figure 3-30.

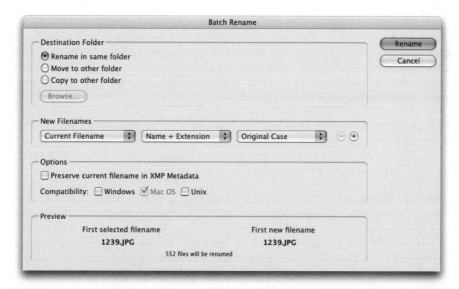

Figure 3-30: Use the Batch Rename command to rename multiple files in a single operation. You can select naming options from a pop-up menu or type your own name.

You have the option of renaming files in the folder where they currently reside (the most common choice) or moving them to a different folder. If you click Move to New Folder, the File Browser asks you to select a destination. Note that *moving* means just that — Photoshop relocates the files as opposed to copying them to the new location.

You can specify up to six File Naming variables, though two or three are usually sufficient. The three Document Name options retain or change the case of the name currently assigned to the file. Alternatively, you can type your own name in an option box.

Caution   To ensure that your images are named so that they'll work on any computer, select all three Compatibility options. (Either Windows or Mac OS will already be selected, depending on your platform.) Then click OK to apply your changes. Note that, as with other File Browser operations, renaming is not undoable. So be sure all settings are correct before you click OK. If you have any doubt how the command will work, experiment on a few trial images before renaming important files.

Using the File Info command

As we've seen, an image file can contain a lot more information than the image data. On top of pixels, alpha channels, color profiles, and all the other image data you can cram into your image files, you can add a variety of reference information — where you shot the picture, who owns the image copyright, your thoughts on the photo, potential uses for the prints, and so on.

Despite the abundance of data already available to you through the ridge Metadata panel, sometimes you need to be able to edit and access more information than a little panel can hold. That's when you should choose File ➪ File Info from the File Browser's menu bar or press Ctrl+Alt+I (⌘-Option-I on the Mac) to display the File Info dialog box, shown in Figure 3-31.

To switch from one File Info area to another, press Ctrl+1 through Ctrl+8 (⌘-1 through ⌘-5 on the Mac) or select the panel name from the list on the left side of the window. On the PC, Alt+N and Alt+P navigate you to the next and previous panel, respectively. Here's a brief overview of the options on each panel:

✦ **Description.** The options in this panel are fairly straightforward. For example, if you want to create a caption, type it in the Description option box, which can hold up to 2,000 characters. If you select Description in the Output section of the Print with Preview dialog box, the caption appears below the image when you print it from Photoshop. You can also add a copyright notice to your image. If you choose Copyrighted Work from the Copyright Status pop-up menu, a copyright symbol (©) appears in the image window title bar and in the information box at the bottom of the screen on the PC or at the bottom of the image window on the Mac. This symbol tells people viewing the image that they can go to the Description panel to get more information about the owner of the image copyright. Choose Public Domain if you want to make it clear that the work isn't copyrighted (an Unmarked image might actually be a neglected copyrighted one).

You can also include the URL for your Web site, if you have one. Then, when people have your image open in Photoshop, they can come to this panel and click Go to URL to launch their Web browser and jump to the URL.

Tip

Click the down arrow to the right of an option to reveal a pop-up menu containing information that you've previously entered for the option in other images. For example, if you've listed yourself as the author of another image you recently worked on, you can click the arrow next to the Author option and select your name.

Figure 3-31: You can document your image in encyclopedic detail using the wealth of options in the File Info dialog box.

Note

Because only people who open your image in Photoshop have access to the information in the File Info dialog box, you may want to embed a digital watermark in your image as well. Many watermarking programs exist, ranging from simple tools that merely imprint copyright data to those that build in protection features designed to prevent illegal downloading and reproduction of images. Photoshop provides a watermarking utility from Digimarc as a plug-in on the Filters menu; before using the plug-in, visit the Digimarc Web site (www.digimarc.com) to find out which, if any, of the Digimarc watermarking schemes best suits the type of work you do.

✦ **Camera Data.** Following the Description options you'll find two panels of Camera Data values. This is where the EXIF information discussed earlier in the chapter is displayed. EXIF data is written by the digital camera, not the user, so these fields cannot be altered.

✦ **Categories.** The Categories panel may seem foreign to anyone who hasn't worked with a news service. Many large news services use a system of three-character categories to file and organize stories and photographs. If you're familiar with this system, you can type the three-character code in the Category option box and even throw in a few supplemental categories up to 32 characters long.

✦ **History.** If you've selected the History Log option in the General panel of the Preferences dialog box, this panel displays the history data for the image. Otherwise, it's blank. (For complete details on setting up the History Log, see Chapter 2.)

✦ **Origin.** This panel provides more option boxes for entering specific information about how the image came to be, including the date, the location, and a headline. Click the Today button to automatically enter the current date and time in the Date Created field. You can use the Urgency pop-up menu to indicate the editorial timeliness of the photo.

✦ **Advanced.** The Advanced panel displays all the information you've set for the image in metadata's XMP format. On a PC, file information is only saved in image file formats that support saving extra data with the file. This includes the native Photoshop (*.psd*) format, EPS, PDF, JPEG, and TIFF. On a Mac, file information is saved with an image regardless of the format you use. Photoshop merely tacks the text onto the image's resource fork. If you need the metadata of an image to travel with the image file, regardless of platform, application, or operating system, saving an XMP file is the way to go. XMP, which stands for *eXtensible Metadata Platform,* is essentially a text file containing metadata that can be assigned to an image and read by many applications. The Advanced panel lets you save this type of file with the metadata you're currently viewing. From this panel, you can also open an XMP file and use it in place of your current metadata, as well as add the information from an XMP file on top of your image's metadata. Selecting any of the categories of metadata in the Advanced panel and clicking Delete will clear that specific data from your image file.

Perhaps the most useful metadata-related feature in Photoshop is the capability to create metadata templates. If you have a collection of images with the same author or origin information, you don't want to have to go through the task of opening the File Info dialog box and manually entering metadata (or importing an XMP file) for each and every one. Photoshop can take care of this for you. Creating a metadata template is simple: Just open the File Info dialog box for any one of the images and enter the common characteristics of the group. Next, click the right-pointing arrowhead in the upper-right corner of the dialog box and choose Save Metadata Template. You'll be asked to type a name but not a location (Photoshop does that for you). Click Save and you're finished. Photoshop automatically adds the metadata template to the pop-up menu in the File Info dialog box, so you can easily access it.

You can assign your saved metadata templates to multiple files at once in the File Browser. Simply select the files to which you want to assign the metadata and choose Edit ➪ Replace Metadata to display a submenu that contains all the templates you've saved. If you want to add metadata from a saved template but keep the original characteristics of your image (such as name, description, or source), choose Edit ➪ Append Metadata instead and select a template. One of the advantages of appending versus replacing metadata in an image is that appending adds any keywords saved in the template to the existing keywords in the image.

Duplicating an image

Have you ever wanted to try an effect without permanently damaging an image? Photoshop offers multiple undos, and you'll get a kick out of using the History palette to see before and after views of your image (as explained in Chapter 7). But what if you want to apply a series of effects to an image independently and compare them side by side? And save the variations as separate files? Or perhaps even merge them? This is a job for image duplication.

To create a new window with an independent version of the foreground image, choose Image ➪ Duplicate. A dialog box appears, requesting a name for the new image. Just like the Name option in the New dialog box, this option is purely an organizational tool that you can use or ignore. If your image contains multiple layers, Photoshop will, by default, retain all layers in the duplicate document. Or you can merge all visible layers into a single layer by selecting the oddly named Duplicate Merged Layers Only option. (Hidden layers are ignored.) Press Enter or Return to create your new, independent image. Bear in mind that this image is unsaved; you need to choose File ➪ Save to save any changes to disk.

Tip If you're happy to let Photoshop automatically name your image and you don't care what it does with the layers, press and hold Alt (or Option on the Mac) and choose Image ➪ Duplicate. This bypasses the Duplicate Image dialog box and immediately creates a new window.

Saving an Image to Disk

The first rule of image editing — and of working on computers in general — is to save the file frequently. If your computer or Photoshop crashes while you're working on an image, all edits made during the current editing session are lost.

To save an image for the first time, choose File ➪ Save or press Ctrl+S (⌘-S on the Mac) to display the Save dialog box. Name the image, select the drive and folder where you want to store the image file, select a file format, and press Enter or Return.

After you save the image once, choosing the Save command updates the file without bringing up the Save dialog box. To save the image with a different name, location, or format, choose File ➪ Save As.

You can execute the Save As command also by pressing Ctrl+Shift+S (⌘-Shift-S on the Mac). As for the Save a Copy command found in some earlier versions of Photoshop, that function is provided through the As a Copy option in the Save As dialog box. By the way, if your only reason for using Save As is to change the file format, it's perfectly acceptable to overwrite (save over) the original document, assuming you no longer need the previous copy of the image. Granted, your computer could crash during the Save As operation, but because Photoshop actually creates a new file during any save operation, your original document should survive the accident. Besides, the chance of crashing during a Save As is extremely remote — no more likely than crashing during any other save operation.

Tip   To speed the save process, you might want to save an image in Photoshop's native format until you've finished working on it. Then, when the file is all ready to go, you can choose File ➪ Save As and save the image in whatever compressed format is needed. This way, you compress each image only once during the time you work on it.

If you have multiple files open, you can close them in one step by choosing File ➪ Close All. Or better yet, press Ctrl+Shift+W (⌘-Shift-W on the Mac). Photoshop prompts you to save any images that haven't yet been saved and closes the others automatically.

Adding an extension to Mac files

On the Mac, the Preferences dialog box includes an option that lets you append a three-character file extension to your files. Again, this option is located in the File Handling panel, so press ⌘-K, ⌘-2 to get to it. There are two general recommendations for this option—first, leave the Use Lower Case option selected, because it ensures fewer conflicts if and when you post your images on the Web. Second, go ahead and append extensions to your file names.

Why add PC file extensions on a Mac? Obviously, it makes life easier when sharing images with PCs. More importantly, it's another form of insurance. If you're a Mac person and you ever find yourself using a PC, you're going to have tons and tons of old Macintosh image files that you'd like to open and reuse. With file extensions, you'll have no problem. Without them, good luck. The file extension is the only way a Windows application has to identify the file format. If there's no file extension, you have to tell the application which format to use. Although I don't question the basic record-keeping capabilities of your brain, you probably have better things to remember than what file format you used five years ago.

Tip   As mentioned in Chapter 2, you can automatically append an extension from the Save dialog box regardless of your preference settings. Press Option, choose an option from the Format pop-up menu, and there it is.

Saving previews

In Chapter 2, it was recommended that you set the Image Previews option in the File Handling preferences panel (Ctrl+K, Ctrl+2 on the PC or ⌘-K, ⌘-2 on the Mac) to Ask When Saving. If you followed this sage advice, the Save dialog box on the PC offers a Thumbnail option. On the Mac, it offers several Image Previews option. For print work, you should generally select the Thumbnail option on a PC and both the Macintosh and Windows Thumbnail options on a Mac. Previews consume extra hard-drive space, but it's well worth it in exchange for being able to see files before opening them. Why save a Windows thumbnail on a Mac? If you ever swap files between platforms, it will come in handy.

The only reason *not* to save a thumbnail with an image is if you plan to post the picture on the Web. In that case, the file has to be as streamlined as possible, and that means shaving away the preview.

Choosing other save options

Certain save options that once upon a time were available only through the Save a Copy command now appear in the Save dialog box all the time. You also get access to these options when you choose Save As or press its keyboard shortcut, Ctrl+Shift+S (⌘-Shift-S on the Mac). Figure 3-32 shows the dialog box.

Figure 3-32: A look at the Save As dialog box, which incorporates the old Save a Copy command as a save option

Note   There's a Use Adobe Dialog button in the Save As dialog box, which opens the Adobe Save dialog box — just like there's an Open dialog box in Adobe format, as described earlier in this chapter. Once you click the Use Adobe Dialog button, the dialog box changes, and you see the version shown in Figure 3-33. Note that that dialog box has a Use OS Dialog button you can click to go back to the default Save As dialog box.

Note that the options you can select vary depending on the image file and the selected file format. If an option is dimmed, it either doesn't apply to your image or isn't supported by the file format you chose. And if your image includes features that won't be saved if you go forward with the current dialog box settings, Photoshop gives you the heads up by displaying a warning message at the bottom of the dialog box.

Figure 3-33: Should you use the Adobe Save dialog box? Yes, if you prefer it. The layout is slightly different, and it gives you access to the Bridge and Version Cue (see list on left) information.

✦ **As a Copy.** Select this option to save a copy of the image while leaving the original open and unchanged — in other words, to do what the Save a Copy command did in Photoshop 5.5 and earlier. The result is the same as duplicating an image, saving it, and closing the duplicate all in one step.

The whole point of this option is to enable you to save a flattened version of a layered image or to dump other extraneous data, such as masks. Just select the file format you want to use and let Photoshop do the rest for you.

✦ **Annotations.** Select this option to include any annotations that you created using the notes and audio annotation tools. You can find out how to annotate your images in the section "Adding Annotations" later in this chapter.

✦ **Alpha Channels.** If your image contains an alpha channel — Photoshop's techy name for an extra channel, such as a mask (discussed in Chapter 9) — select the Alpha option to retain the channel. Only a few formats — notably Photoshop, PDF, PICT, PICT Resource, TIFF, and DCS 2.0 — support extra channels.

✦ **Spot Colors.** Did you create an image that incorporates spot colors? If so, select this option to retain the spot-color channels in the saved image file. You must save the file in the native Photoshop, PDF, TIFF, or DCS 2.0 format to use this option.

✦ **Layers.** TIFF and PDF can retain independent image layers, as can the native Photoshop format. Select the option to retain layers; deselect it to flatten the image.

If you're working with a layered image and select a file format that doesn't support layers, a cautionary message appears at the bottom of the dialog box. However, Photoshop doesn't prevent you from going through with the save, so be careful. All layers are automatically merged when you save the file in a nonlayer format. However, when you close the file, Photoshop reminds you that you haven't saved a version of the image that retains all data and gives you the opportunity to do so.

✦ **Use Proof Setup.** This option relates to Photoshop's color profile options. If the current view's proof setup is a "convert to" proof, Photoshop converts the image to the selected proofing space when saving.

✦ **ICC Profile (Win)/Embed Color Profile (Mac).** If you're saving your image in a file format that supports embedded ICC profiles, selecting this option embeds the profile. The current profile appears next to the option name. See Chapter 16 for advice about working with color profiles.

The Save for Web dialog box

If your image is bound for the Web, you want to use the File ⇨ Save for Web command rather than simply choosing File ⇨ Save or Save As. While you can access the two Web-preferred formats, JPEG and GIF, through the Save As dialog box, the Save for Web dialog box (shown in Figure 3-34) does much more than just save your image — it provides the following abilities and information:

✦ **View side-by-side versions of the image.** On the left (see Figure 3-34) is the original; on the right (in a 2-up view), the optimized version. This enables you to see if the optimization process has degraded the file at all.

✦ **Preview File Sizes and Load Times.** Under the optimized view, the current file format (per your choice on the right side of the dialog box, using the Preset drop list), the file size, and how long that file would take to load for a site visitor using a 28.8 kbps modem is displayed. The quality setting chosen on the upper-right side of the dialog box also appears in this area.

✦ **Choose the right format for the file.** GIF, JPG, or PNG? While these options are discussed later in this chapter, you can make your pick through the Preset drop-down list at the top on the right side of the Save for Web dialog box. From GIF 128 Dithered to PNG-8 128 Dithered (with 10 options in between), you can choose from any Web-safe format, in any configuration.

Figure 3-34: The Save for Web dialog box provides one-stop shopping for images that you'll be using online. Choose from the right formats for Web use, tweak their settings to make them load as fast as possible, and customize their appearance for maximum effectiveness on the Web.

✦ **Set the file quality or color density.** If you've opted to save the file as a JPEG (which you should if it's a photo), there's a Quality slider. If you chose GIF (for line art or drawings with solid colors), you have a Colors option that allows you to set the image to display from 2 to 256 colors.

✦ **Customize the image.** Using options that vary depending on which Preset you chose, you can totally customize the quality and display behavior of the file. Choose the Transparency, Dither, Lossy, and Matte settings (for GIF images), or choose to make your JPEG appear in Progressive fashion, with or without Blur.

✦ **Animate your GIF images.** If the image is already saved as a GIF file, you can use the buttons along the bottom of the right side of the dialog box (under the Color Table) to animate the image, layer by layer. You can create animated GIF images from simple on-off affairs to more elaborate movie-like graphics. Read more about this in Chapter 18.

After making your choices in the Save for Web dialog box, all you have to do is click Save, which opens a Save dialog box through which you can name and choose a location for your file. By default, if the file is already saved in PSD or another format (prior to your opening the Save for Web dialog box), Photoshop will attempt to give the file that same name—with the extension for the format you chose for the Web-bound file. If the file name you gave it previously is not Web-friendly—bearing capital letters and punctuation other than dashes—edit the name accordingly.

And speaking of file formats, in the next section you'll learn more about different formats supported by Photoshop, their uses, benefits, and possible drawbacks.

File Format Roundup

Photoshop CS2 supports more than 25 file formats from inside both the OS and Adobe versions of the Open and Save dialog boxes. It can support even more through the addition of plug-in modules that attach commands to the File ⇨ Save As, File ⇨ Import, and File ⇨ Export submenus.

File formats represent different ways to save a file to disk. Some formats provide unique image-compression schemes that save an image in a manner that consumes less space on a hard drive. Other formats enable Photoshop to trade images with different applications running under Windows, the Mac, or some other platform.

The native format

Like most programs, Photoshop offers its own native format—that is, a format optimized for Photoshop's particular capabilities and functions. This PSD format saves every attribute that you can apply in Photoshop—including layers, extra channels, file info, and so on—and is compatible with versions 3 and later of the program. Of course, when you open files in earlier versions of Photoshop, you lose file attributes related to later versions, such as annotations, color proof options, and so on.

Note   Photoshop isn't the only application that uses PSD as its native format; PSD is also the native format used by Photoshop's close relatives ImageReady and Photoshop Elements.

Tip   Perhaps not surprisingly, Photoshop can open and save more quickly in its native format than in any other format. The native format also offers image compression. Like TIFF's LZW compression, the Photoshop compression scheme does not result in any loss of data. But Photoshop can compress and decompress its native format much more quickly than it can TIFF, and the compression scheme is better able to minimize the size of mask channels (as explained in Chapter 9).

The downside of the Photoshop format is that relatively few applications other than Photoshop support it, and those that do don't always do a great job. Some applications, such as Corel Photo-Paint and Adobe After Effects, can open a layered Photoshop image and interpret each layer independently. But most of the others limit their support to flat Photoshop files. To accommodate these programs, you can either deselect the Layers option in the Save dialog box to save a flattened version of the image or set the Maximize PSD File Compatibility option in the Preferences dialog box to Ask or Always.

There's another way to look at this, however. If you think about the fact that Photoshop's native format was never intended to be an interapplication standard. It's not like a DOC file created by Microsoft Word, which is meant to be compatible with any other word processor. You can save your Photoshop creations in a variety of formats, making it possible to work with other programs, but the PSD format isn't so transferable. It's actually easier to set the Maximize PSD File Compatibility to Never, which you can read about in Chapter 2. If you need to share an image you've created or edited in Photoshop with someone who doesn't have Photoshop, just save it in a format that person can use — like TIFF or JPEG. And always keep a PSD version for yourself, so that flattening the file for someone else doesn't rob you of future editing capabilities in Photoshop.

Special-purpose formats

With so many file formats from which to choose, you can imagine that most are not the kinds you'll be using on a regular basis. In fact, apart from the native Photoshop format, you'll probably want to stick with TIFF, JPEG, and GIF for Web images and EPS when preparing images for placement in InDesign, QuarkXPress, and other layout programs.

Many of the other formats are provided simply so that you can open an image created on another platform, saved from some antiquated paint program, or downloaded from the Web. These formats are covered in other places in the book — Chapter 18 for Web-safe formats, for example. Moving forward here, you learn about the more robust formats — from BMP to TGA, and lots of other alphabet soup in between.

Microsoft Paint's BMP

BMP (*Windows Bitmap*) is the native format for Microsoft Paint (included with Windows) and is supported by a variety of Windows and DOS applications. Photoshop supports BMP images with up to 16 million colors. You also can use RLE (*Run-Length Encoding*), a lossless compression scheme specifically applicable to the BMP format.

Note   The term *lossless* refers to compression schemes that conserve disk space without sacrificing any data in the image, such as BMP's RLE and TIFF's LZW (*Lempel-Ziv-Welch*). The only reasons not to use lossless compression are that it slows down the open and save operations, although this isn't as much of an issue on newer machines, and it may prevent less-sophisticated applications from opening an image. (Lossy compression routines, such as JPEG, sacrifice a user-defined amount of data to conserve even more space, as explained later.)

The most common use for BMP is to create images for use in help files and Windows wallpaper. In fact, designing your own Windows wallpaper can be a fun way to share your Photoshop skills with coworkers, family, and with yourself, too. For the best results, make sure you set your image to exactly the same pixel dimensions as your screen (which you can check from the Settings panel in the Display control panel). To conserve memory, you may want to reduce the number of colors in your wallpaper image to 256 using Image ➪ Mode ➪ Indexed Color.

When you save the wallpaper image, Photoshop displays the options shown in Figure 3-35. Generally, you'll want to select the Windows and Compress (RLE) options, but it really doesn't matter when creating wallpaper. Don't mess with the Depth options. Either you reduced the bit depth using the Indexed Color command as directed previously or you didn't. There's no sense in changing the colors during the save process.

Figure 3-35: Select the options shown here when saving a BMP image for use as a desktop background. Leave the Depth setting alone.

To load the wallpaper onto your PC desktop, right-click anywhere on the desktop and choose the Properties command. This brings up the Display Properties dialog box. Go to the Background tab, and click Browse to locate your BMP image on disk. After you find it, double-click it to select it, and then click Apply to see how the image looks. You can tweak its appearance on the desktop by choosing from the three Picture Display options—Stretch, Center, or Tile.

Camera Raw

When opening images from a digital camera, Photoshop gives you the ability to work with Camera Raw files. These are the untouched, pristine files generated by mid-level to high-end digital cameras before the image is run through various in-camera compression and color-correction passes. Think of Camera Raw as the digital equivalent of a film negative. Camera Raw files are proprietary, meaning that cameras manufactured by Canon, Fuji, Minolta, and others produce different types of files. Luckily, Photoshop supports a variety of Camera Raw file formats. When you open a supported Camera Raw file, it appears in a special Camera Raw dialog box, where you can make minute adjustments to colors, brightness levels, and other values in your image with virtually no loss in quality. You'll find more information on the Camera Raw dialog box in Chapter 17.

Cineon

Cineon is a film- and video-related format supported by Photoshop. Developed by Kodak and used for years as the standard for transferring computer-based images to film, Cineon is a robust, high-quality format and one of the few capable of saving images in 16-bit mode. When Cineon files are used with the Cineon Digital Film System, they can be output to film with absolutely no loss in image quality.

CompuServe's GIF

In the old days, the CompuServe online service championed GIF (short for *Graphics Interchange Format*) as a means of compressing files so you could quickly transfer photographs over your modem. Like TIFF, GIF uses LZW compression, but unlike TIFF, GIF is limited to just 256 colors.

Over the years the GIF format has grown slightly more sophisticated. You can save an image with or without transparency by choosing File ➪ Save and then choosing CompuServe GIF from the Format pop-up menu. When you index (reduce) the image to 256 colors — which you can do either before or during the file save process — select the Transparency option in the Indexed Color dialog box if you want any transparent areas of the image to remain transparent when you view the image file in a Web browser.

Tip   GIF files can be animated through the Save for Web dialog box. Save the file in GIF format through Photoshop's Save As dialog box, and then open the Save for Web dialog box to access animation tools that turn image layers into components that can be made to move or blink on and off for one loop or an endless series of repeating actions.

PC Paintbrush's PCX

PCX doesn't stand for anything. Rather, it's the extension PC Paintbrush assigns to images saved in its native file format. Although the format is losing favor, many PCX images are still in use today, largely because PC Paintbrush is the oldest painting program for DOS. Photoshop supports PCX images with up to 16 million colors. You can find an enormous amount of art, usually clip art, in this format. However, don't save files to PCX unless a client specifically demands it. Other formats are better.

Adobe's paperless PDF

PDF (*Portable Document Format*) is a variation on the PostScript printing language that enables you to view electronically produced documents on-screen. This means you can create a publication in QuarkXPress or InDesign, export it to PDF, and distribute it without worrying about color separations, binding, and other printing costs. Using a program called Adobe Reader, you can open PDF documents, zoom in and out of them, and follow hypertext links by clicking highlighted words. Adobe distributes Mac, Windows, and Unix versions of the Adobe Reader for free, so almost anyone with a computer can view your stuff in full, natural color.

PDF files come in two flavors: those that contain just a single image and those that contain multiple pages and images. You can only save single-page PDF files using the File ➪ Save command. To save multipage PDF files, you must use the new PDF Presentation command, discussed in Chapter 18. When opening either a single-image or multipage PDF file, Photoshop will always rasterize the contents of the file.

You open PDF files in different ways depending on what elements of the file you want to access:

✦ Use File ➪ Open to open a particular page in a multipage PDF file. After selecting the page you want to view, you can set the image size and resolution of the rasterized file. You also can choose File ➪ Place to add a page as a new layer to an open image; in this case, you can't control the size and resolution before adding the page. However, you can scale the page after the fact as you can any layer.

✦ Choose File ➪ Import ➪ PDF Image to bring up a dialog box that enables you to open a particular image in the PDF file.

✦ Choose File ➪ Automate ➪ Multi-Page PDF to PSD to turn each page in the PDF file into a separate Photoshop image file.

The real question, however, is why would you *want* to open or place a PDF file in Photoshop instead of viewing it in Adobe Reader, which provides you with a full range of document-viewing tools not found in Photoshop? Furthermore, because you can save only single-page PDF files, why on earth would you save to PDF in Photoshop?

There are really only two scenarios where Photoshop's PDF functions may be of use:

✦ You want to see how images in a PDF document will look when printed on a high-resolution printer. Open the PDF file using File ➪ Open, set the resolution to match that of the output device, and eyeball those images on-screen. This "soft-proofing" technique enables you to spot defects that may not be noticeable in draft proofs that you output on a low-res printer.

✦ You need a convenient way to distribute images for approval or input. You can save an image as a PDF file and send it to clients and colleagues, who can view the image in Acrobat or Adobe Reader if they don't have Photoshop. You can even add text or voice annotations to your PDF file. In addition to annotations, Photoshop PDF supports layers, transparency, embedded color profiles, spot colors, duotones, and more. This enables you to route an image for approval without having to flatten the image or otherwise strip it of its Photoshop features. Of course, features not supported by Adobe Reader aren't accessible to the viewer.

When you save to PDF in Photoshop, you have a choice of two encoding options, as shown in Figure 3-36. Choose ZIP only for images that feature large expanses of a single color; otherwise, opt for JPEG. Keep the Quality option set to Maximum to maintain the best print quality, just as you do for regular JPEG files.

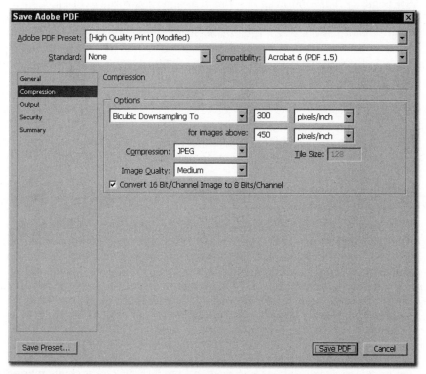

Figure 3-36: Click any one of the five items listed on the left to display a new set of options. Here, the Compression options are displayed.

If you select JPEG encoding, you need a PostScript Level 2 or later printer to output your PDF file. Also be aware that separating files into individual plates can be problematic.

When saving to PDF, you also encounter several other options:

✦ **Save Transparency.** If your image has transparency and you're saving it as a PDF without layers, the Save Transparency option determines whether or not the transparency will be maintained.

✦ **Image Interpolation.** Selecting this option enables other programs to interpolate the image when resampling to another size.

✦ **Downgrade Color Profile.** Here's an option you'll probably never use. PDF doesn't support version 4 ICC profiles. Selecting this option converts them to version 2 profiles so that they'll work in PDF. The thing is, you probably don't have a version 4 ICC profile anyway, in which case this option is dimmed. For more on ICC profiles, see Chapter 16.

✦ **PDF Security.** This option allows you to assign passwords to PDF documents — if users don't know the password, they can't open the document. To set the security information, select the PDF Security option and click Security Settings. You can set the user password here, along with a master password, which can prevent others from changing the user password. The Encryption Level options take effect only when the document is being opened with Adobe Acrobat; you can choose the version of Acrobat and determine whether options such as saving changes and printing are allowed.

✦ **Include Vector Data** and **Embed Fonts.** Select these two options to retain any vector graphics and font data, respectively. Alternatively, you can select Use Outlines for Text to save text as character outlines that are editable in the PDF file.

Apple's PICT

PICT (*Macintosh Picture*) was the native graphics format for Mac OS 9. (Mac OS X has adopted PDF as its standard graphics file format.) Based on the QuickDraw display language that the system software uses to convey images on-screen, PICT handles object-oriented artwork and bitmapped images with equal aplomb. It supports images in any bit depth, size, or resolution. PICT even supports 32-bit images, so you can save a fourth masking channel when working in the RGB mode.

If you've installed QuickTime on the Mac, you can subject PICT images to JPEG compression. But although PICT's compression options may look similar to JPEG's, they are actually significantly inferior. The differences become especially noticeable if you open an image, make a change, and again save it to disk, effectively reapplying the compression.

In most cases, you'll want to use the JPEG format instead of PICT when compressing images. JPEG images are compatible with the Web; PICT images are not. Also, more Windows applications recognize JPEG than PICT, and it's extremely difficult to find a Windows program that can handle PICT files with QuickTime compression.

In fact, the only reason to use PICT is low-end compatibility. If you're trying to save an image in a format that your mom can open on her Mac, for example, PICT may be a better choice than JPEG. Heck, you can open PICT files inside a word processor, including everything from SimpleText to Microsoft Word. Just be sure mom has QuickTime loaded on her machine.

When you save a PICT image, Photoshop also lets you set the bit depth. You should always stick with the default option, which is the highest setting available for the particular image. Don't mess around with these options; they apply automatic pattern dithering, which is a bad thing.

If you're using a PC, you may need to open a PICT file a Mac friend sends you. Photoshop can do this, but one thing may trip you up: On the Mac, you have the option of saving PICT files with a variety of JPEG compressions supplied by Apple's QuickTime. Unless you have QuickTime installed on your PC—which you might if you do a lot of surfing on the Web—you won't be able to open compressed PICT images.

PICT resource

PICT resources were the images contained in the resource fork of a Mac file in OS 9. (Windows programs can't recognize resource forks, so this section is only relevant to Mac users.) The only reason you would want to save a PICT resource is if you are creating an OS 9 startup screen, and the most likely reason to open one is to extract images from the OS 9 Scrapbook. However, because Photoshop CS2 (and its predecessor, CS) no longer runs under OS 9, you can be fairly confident that you won't be using this format. For the time being, however, Photoshop continues to support the format.

Pixar workstations

Pixar has created some of the most memorable computer-animated short films and features in recent memory. From the desk lamps playing with a beach ball in *Luxo, Jr.* to the artistic triumphs that were *Toy Story, Monsters, Inc.*, and *Finding Nemo,* Pixar continues to blaze a trail in this spectacular new art form.

Pixar works its 3-D magic using mondo-expensive proprietary workstations. Photoshop enables you to open a still image created on a Pixar machine or to save an image to the Pixar format so you can integrate it into a 3-D rendering. The Pixar format supports grayscale and RGB images.

PNG for the Web

The PNG (pronounced *ping*) format enables you to save 16-million color images without compression for use on the Web. Although PNG has been generally supported by Netscape Navigator and Microsoft Internet Explorer since 1997, these main two browsers still can't be counted on to fully support all the features of PNG. Couple that info with the obvious fact that you can't count on the general public to have anywhere near the most recent version of any software application, and using PNG begins to seem like a dicey proposition. It's a great format, though, offering full-color images without the pesky visual compression artifacts you get with JPEG.

Large Document Format (PSB)

Recently, many applications have adopted the capability to work with and save files more than 2GB in size. If you're editing nonlinear video, the need to use gigantic files makes perfect sense. Image-editing applications like Photoshop have been slower to adopt support for such huge files, but Photoshop has leapt into the fray with its new Large Document Format (PSB). Finally, you won't need to figure out a work-around when designing that billboard for the surface of the moon.

Photoshop is capable of opening and saving existing PSB files by default, but if you want to create a Large Document Format file from scratch, you need to select the Enable Large Document Format (.psb) option in the File Handling panel of the Preferences dialog box (that's Ctrl+K, Ctrl+2 on the PC and ⌘-K, ⌘-2 on the Mac). Keep in mind that images saved in PSB format cannot be opened in other applications or previous versions of Photoshop.

Note   Another format that you can use for storing enormous files is Photoshop Raw, but it's not nearly as capable as PSB. Most important, the image needs to be flattened, meaning you can kiss your layers goodbye. Photoshop Raw can be useful for other purposes, though, as is explained shortly.

Scitex image processors

Some high-end commercial printers use Scitex printing devices to generate color separations of images and other documents. Photoshop can open images digitized with Scitex scanners and save the edited images to the *Scitex CT* (*Continuous Tone*) format. Because you need special hardware to transfer images from the PC to a Scitex drive, you'll probably want to consult with your local Scitex service bureau technician before saving to the CT format. The technician may prefer that you submit images in the native Photoshop, TIFF, or JPEG format. The Scitex CT format supports grayscale, RGB, and CMYK images.

TrueVision's TGA

TrueVision's Targa and NuVista video boards enable you to overlay computer graphics and animation onto live video. The effect is called *chroma keying* because, typically, a key color is set aside to let the live video show through. TrueVision designed the TGA (*Targa*) format to support 32-bit images that include 8-bit alpha channels capable of displaying the live video. Support for TGA is widely implemented among professional-level color and video applications on the PC.

Acrobat TouchUp Image

If your preferences are set correctly in Adobe Acrobat, you can select any image file in a PDF document, right-click it (Control-click on the Mac), and choose to edit the image externally in Photoshop. Acrobat creates a temporary file with a long, indecipherable name, called a TouchUp Image, and opens Photoshop. After you save the file and return to Acrobat, the changes you made are incorporated automatically. A quick tip: Make sure you don't alter the dimensions of an image you're touching up — doing so will alter the layout of the PDF file — and remember to flatten any layers you may have created before you return to Acrobat.

Wireless Bitmap

Hey, those crude little graphics found on handheld wireless devices have to come from somewhere, right? Why not Photoshop? Photoshop can open and save in WBMP (*Wireless Bitmap*) format, an up-and-coming standard for cell phones and personal digital assistants. To save an image to the Wireless Bitmap format, the image must be in Bitmap mode, with only black and white pixels.

Interapplication formats

In the name of interapplication harmony, Photoshop supports a few software-specific formats that permit you to trade files with popular object-oriented programs, such as Illustrator and QuarkXPress. Every one of these formats is a variation on EPS (*Encapsulated PostScript*), which is based in turn on Adobe's industry-standard PostScript printing language.

Rasterizing an Illustrator or FreeHand file

Photoshop supports object-oriented files saved in the EPS format. EPS is specifically designed to save object-oriented graphics that you intend to print to a PostScript output device. Just about every drawing and page-layout program on the planet (and a few on Mars) can save EPS documents.

Prior to version 4, Photoshop could interpret only a small subset of EPS operations supported by Illustrator (including the native *.ai* format). But then Photoshop 4 came along and offered a full-blown EPS translation engine, capable of interpreting EPS illustrations created in FreeHand, CorelDraw, Deneba's Canvas, and more. You can even open EPS drawings that contain imported images, something else version 3 could not do.

When you open an EPS or native Illustrator document, Photoshop *rasterizes* (or *renders*) the artwork — that is, it converts the artwork from a collection of objects to a bitmapped image. During the open operation, Photoshop presents the Rasterize Generic EPS Format dialog box (see Figure 3-37), which enables you to specify the size and resolution of the image, just as you can in the New dialog box. Assuming the illustration contains no imported images, you can render it as large or as small as you want without any loss of image quality.

Figure 3-37: You can specify the size and resolution at which Photoshop renders an EPS illustration.

Tip

If the EPS illustration does contain an imported image or two, you need to know the resolution of the images and factor this information into the Rasterize Generic EPS Format dialog box. Select anything but Pixels from both the Width and Height pop-up menus and leave the suggested values unchanged. Then type the setting for the highest-resolution imported image in the Resolution option box. (If all the images are low resolution, you may want to double or triple the Resolution value to ensure that the objects render smoothly.)

You should always select the Anti-aliased option unless you're rendering a very large image — say, 300 ppi or higher. *Anti-aliasing* blurs pixels to soften the edges of the objects so they don't appear jagged. When you're rendering a very large image, the difference between image and printer resolution is less noticeable, so anti-aliasing is unwarranted.

Photoshop renders the illustration to a single layer against a transparent background. Before you can save the rasterized image to a format other than native Photoshop, you must eliminate the transparency by choosing Layer ⇨ Flatten Image. Or save a flattened version of the image to a separate file by choosing the As a Copy option in the Save dialog box.

Tip Rendering an EPS illustration is an extremely useful technique for resolving printing problems. If you regularly work in Illustrator or FreeHand, you no doubt have encountered *limitcheck errors*, which occur when an illustration is too complex for an imagesetter or other high-end output device to print. If you're frustrated with the printer and tired of wasting your evening trying to figure out what's wrong (sound familiar?), use Photoshop to render the illustration at 300 ppi and print it. Nine times out of 19, this technique works flawlessly.

If Photoshop can't *parse* the EPS file — a techy way of saying Photoshop can't break down the individual objects — it attempts to open the PICT (Mac) or TIFF (Windows) preview. This exercise is usually futile, but occasionally you may want to take a quick look at an illustration to, say, match the placement of elements in an image to those in the drawing.

Placing an EPS illustration

If you want to introduce an EPS graphic into the foreground image rather than render it into a new image window of its own, choose File ⇨ Place. Unlike other File menu commands, Place supports only EPS illustrations and PDF files.

After you import the EPS graphic, it appears inside a box — which Photoshop calls a *bounding box* — with a great big X across it. You can move, scale, and rotate the illustration into position before rasterizing it to pixels. Click and drag a corner handle to resize the image; drag outside the image to rotate it. You can also nudge the graphic into position by pressing the arrow keys. When everything is the way you want it, press Enter (or Return on the Mac) or double-click inside the box to rasterize the illustration. If the placement isn't perfect, don't worry. The graphic appears on a separate layer, so you can move it with complete freedom. To cancel the Place operation, press Esc instead of Enter or Return.

Saving an EPS image

When preparing an image for placement in a drawing or page-layout document that will be printed to a PostScript output device, many artists prefer to save the image in the EPS format. Converting the image to PostScript up front prevents the drawing or page-layout program from doing the work. The result is an image that prints more quickly and with less chance of problems. (Note that an image does not *look* any different when saved in EPS. The idea that the EPS format somehow blesses an image with better resolution is pure nonsense.)

A second point in the EPS format's favor is clipping paths. As explained graphically at the end of Chapter 8, a clipping path defines a free-form boundary around an image. When you place the image into an object-oriented program, everything outside the clipping path becomes transparent. While some programs — notably InDesign and PageMaker — recognize clipping paths saved with a TIFF image, many programs acknowledge a clipping path only when saved in the EPS format.

Third, although Illustrator has remedied the problems it had importing TIFF images, it still likes EPS best, especially where screen display is concerned. Thanks to the EPS file's fixed preview, Illustrator can display an EPS image on-screen very quickly compared with other file formats. And Illustrator can display an EPS image both in the preview mode and in the super-fast artwork mode.

So if you want to import an image into Illustrator, QuarkXPress, or another object-oriented program, your best bet is EPS. On the downside, EPS is an inefficient format for saving images thanks to the laborious way that it describes pixels. An EPS image may be three to four times larger than the same image saved to the TIFF format with LZW compression. But this is the price we pay for reliable printing.

Caution

Absolutely avoid the EPS format if you plan on printing your final pages to a non-PostScript printer. This defeats the entire purpose of EPS, which is meant to avoid printing problems, not cause them. When printing without PostScript, use TIFF or JPEG.

To save an image in the EPS format, choose Photoshop EPS from the Format pop-up menu in the Save dialog box. After you press Enter or Return, Photoshop displays the dialog box shown in Figure 3-38. The options in this dialog box work as follows:

✦ **Preview.** Technically, an EPS document comprises two parts: a pure PostScript-language description of the graphic for the printer and a bitmapped preview so you can see the graphic on-screen. On a PC, select the TIFF (8 bits/pixel) option from the Preview pop-up menu to save a 256-color TIFF preview of the image. On a Mac, select the Macintosh (8 bits/pixel) option from the Preview pop-up menu to save a 256-color PICT preview of the image. Or select the Macintosh (JPEG) option for a 24-bit preview (which in most cases takes up less room on disk, thanks to the JPEG compression). If you plan on passing off the image to a Windows colleague, select TIFF (8 bits/pixel). The 1-bit option provides a black-and-white preview only, which is useful if you want to save a little room on disk. Select None to include no preview and save even more disk space.

✦ **Encoding.** If you're saving an image for import into Illustrator, QuarkXPress, or some other established program, select the Binary encoding option (also known as *Huffman encoding*), which compresses an EPS document by substituting shorter codes for frequently used characters. The letter *a*, for example, receives the 3-bit code 010, rather than its standard 8-bit ASCII code, 01100001 (the binary equivalent of what we humans call 97).

Figure 3-38: When you save an image in the EPS format, you can specify the type of preview and tack on some printing attributes.

Sadly, some programs and printers don't recognize Huffman encoding, in which case you must select one of the less efficient ASCII options. ASCII stands for *American Standard Code for Information Interchange*, which is fancy jargon for text-only. In other words, you can open and edit an ASCII EPS document in a word processor, provided you know how to read and write PostScript.

Tip

Actually, this can be a useful technique if you have a Mac file that won't open on a PC, especially if the file was sent to you electronically. Chances are that a Mac-specific header got into the works. Open the file in a word processor and look at the beginning. You should see the four characters *%!PS*. Anything that comes before this line is the Macintosh header. Delete the gobbledygook before *%!PS*, save the file in text format, and try again to open the file in Photoshop.

Caution

The remaining Encoding options are JPEG settings. JPEG compression not only results in smaller files on disk but also degrades the quality of the image. Select JPEG (Maximum Quality) to invoke the least degradation. Better yet, avoid the JPEG settings altogether. These options work only if you plan to print your final artwork to a PostScript Level 2 or Level 3 device. Earlier PostScript printers do not support EPS artwork with JPEG compression and will choke on the code.

So to recap, ASCII results in really big files that work with virtually any printer or application. Binary creates smaller files that work with most mainstream applications but may choke some older-model printers. And the JPEG settings are compatible exclusively with Level 2 and later PostScript printers.

✦ **Include Halftone Screen.** Another advantage of EPS over other formats is that it can retain printing attributes. If you specified a custom halftone screen using the Screens button in the Page Setup dialog box, you can save this setting with the EPS document by selecting the Include Halftone Screen option. But be careful—you can just as easily ruin your image as help it. Read Chapter 18 before you select this option.

✦ **Include Transfer Function.** As described in Chapter 18, you can change the brightness and contrast of a printed image using the Transfer button in the Page Setup dialog box. To save these settings with the EPS document, select the Include Transfer Function option. Again, this option can be dangerous when used casually.

✦ **PostScript Color Management.** Like JPEG compression, this option is compatible with Level 2 and 3 printers only. It embeds a color profile, which helps the printer to massage the image during the printing cycle to generate more accurate colors. Unless you plan on printing to a Level 2 or later device, leave the option deselected. (For more information about color profiles, read Chapter 16.)

✦ **Include Vector Data.** Select this option if your file contains vector objects, including shapes, nonbitmap text, and layer clipping paths. Otherwise, Photoshop rasterizes the objects during the save process. When you select the option, Photoshop displays a warning in the dialog box to remind you that if you reopen the file in Photoshop, you rasterize any vector objects that you saved with the file.

✦ **Transparent Whites.** When saving bitmap mode images as EPS files in Photoshop, the four options previously discussed drop away, replaced by Transparent Whites. Select this option to make all white pixels in the image transparent.

Although Photoshop EPS is the only format that offers the Transparent Whites option, many programs — including Illustrator and InDesign — treat white pixels in black-and-white TIFF images as transparent as well.

✦ **Image Interpolation.** Select this option if you want another program to be able to interpolate the image when resampling it to another size. For example, suppose you import an EPS image into InDesign and scale it to 400 percent. If Image Interpolation is deselected, InDesign just makes pixels in the image four times larger, as if you had used the nearest neighbor interpolation in Photoshop. If select Image Interpolation, however, InDesign applies bicubic interpolation to generate new pixels. (For details on nearest neighbor and bicubic interpolation, see Chapter 2.) Unless you have a reason for doing otherwise, select this option.

QuarkXPress DCS

Quark developed a variation on the EPS format called DCS (*Desktop Color Separation*). When you work in QuarkXPress, PageMaker, and other programs that support the format, DCS facilitates the printing of color separations. Before you can use DCS, you have to convert your image to the CMYK color space using Image ➪ Mode ➪ CMYK Color. (DCS 2.0 also supports grayscale images with spot-color channels.) Then open the Save dialog box and select Photoshop DCS 1.0 or 2.0 from the Format pop-up menu.

Photoshop 5 introduced support for DCS 2.0 to accommodate images that contain extra spot-color channels, as explained in Chapter 18. If you add a Pantone channel to an image, DCS 2.0 is the only PostScript format you can use. If your image doesn't contain any extra channels beyond the basic four required for CMYK, DCS 1.0 is the safer and simpler option.

After you press Enter or Return, Photoshop displays an additional pop-up menu of DCS options, which vary depending on whether you've selected DCS 1.0 or 2.0, as shown in Figure 3-39. The DCS 1.0 format invariably saves a total of five files: one master document (which is the file that you import into QuarkXPress) plus one file each for the cyan, magenta, yellow, and black color channels (which are the files that get printed). The DCS 2.0 format can be expressed as a single file (tidier) or five separate files (better compatibility).

Either way, the DCS pop-up menu gives you the option of saving a 72-ppi PostScript composite of the image inside the master document. Independent from the bitmapped preview — which you specify as usual by selecting a Preview option — the PostScript composite makes it possible to print a low-resolution version of a DCS image to a consumer-quality printer. If you're using a black-and-white printer, select the 72-pixel/inch grayscale option; if you're using a color printer, select the final option. Be forewarned, however, that the composite image significantly increases the size of the master document on disk. The two options at the bottom of the options dialog boxes for DCS 1.0 and 2.0, Include Vector Data and Image Interpolation, work just as described earlier for the Photoshop EPS format.

Figure 3-39: The extra options for the DCS 1.0 format (top) and those for the DCS 2.0 format (bottom)

Premiere Filmstrip

Adobe Premiere Pro is a popular video-editing application for the PC. The program is a wonder when it comes to fades, frame merges, and special effects, but it offers no frame-by-frame rotoscope-style animating capabilities. For example, you can neither draw a mustache on a person in the movie nor can you make brightly colored brushstrokes swirl about in the background—at least, not in Premiere.

You can export the movie to the Filmstrip format, though, which is a file-swapping option exclusive to Photoshop and Premiere. A Filmstrip document organizes frames in a long vertical strip. A gray bar separates each frame. The number of each frame appears on the right; the SMPTE (Society of Motion Picture and Television Engineers) time code appears on the left. The structure of the three-number time code is minutes:seconds:frames, with 30 frames per second.

Caution   If you change the size of a Filmstrip document inside Photoshop in any way, you cannot save the image back to the Filmstrip format. Feel free to paint and apply effects, but stay the heck away from the Image Size and Canvas Size commands.

Tip   While there really isn't much coverage of the Filmstrip format anywhere else in this book, it's useful to pass along a few quick Filmstrip tips:

✦ First, you can scroll up and down exactly one frame at a time by pressing Shift+Page Up or Shift+Page Down, respectively.

✦ Second, you can move a selection exactly one frame up or down by pressing Ctrl+Shift+up arrow (⌘-Shift-up arrow on the Mac) or Ctrl+Shift+down arrow (⌘-Shift-down arrow on the Mac).

✦ If you want to clone the selection as you move it, press Ctrl+Shift+Alt+up arrow (⌘-Shift-Option-up arrow on the Mac) or Ctrl+Shift+Alt+down arrow (⌘-Shift-Option-down arrow on the Mac).

And finally, you can select several sequential frames and edit them simultaneously by following the next set of steps:

STEPS: Selecting Sequential Frames in a Movie

1. **Select the first frame you want to edit.** Select the Rectangular Marquee tool by pressing M. Then click and drag around the area you want to edit in the movie. (This is the only step that takes any degree of care or coordination whatsoever.)

2. **Switch to the Quick Mask mode by pressing Q.** The areas around the selected frame are overlaid with pink.

3. **Set the Magic Wand Tolerance value to 0.** Select the Magic Wand tool. Then, in the Options bar, type 0 for the Tolerance value and deselect the Anti-aliased option.

4. **Click inside the selected frame (the one that's not pink) with the Magic Wand tool.** This selects the unmasked area inside the frame.

5. **Press Ctrl+Shift+Alt+down arrow (⌘-Shift-Option-down arrow on the Mac) to clone the unmasked area to the next frame in the movie.** When you exit the Quick Mask mode, both this frame and the one above it will be selected.

6. **Repeat several times.** Continue to press Ctrl+Shift+Alt+down arrow until you're rid of the pink stuff on all the frames you want to select.

7. **Exit the Quick Mask mode by pressing Q again.** All frames appear selected.

8. **Edit the frames to your heart's content.**

If you're new to Photoshop, half of these steps, if not all of them, probably went right over your head. If that's the case, don't feel bad. If you want to learn more about selections and cloning, see Chapter 8. In Chapter 9, you can explore the Quick Mask mode and other masking techniques. After you finish reading those chapters, return to this section to see if it doesn't make a little more — that is if working with movie frames in Photoshop is of any interest.

The process of editing individual frames as just described is sometimes called *roto-scoping*, named after the traditional technique of using live-action film as a source when creating animated sequences. You also can try out some scratch-and-doodle techniques, which is where an artist scratches and draws directly on frames of film. If this isn't enough, you can emulate *xerography,* in which an animator makes Xerox copies of photographs, enhances the copies using markers or whatever else is convenient, and shoots the finished artwork, frame by frame, on film. In a nutshell, Photoshop extends Premiere's functionality by adding animation to its standard supply of video-editing capabilities.

You can save an image in the Filmstrip format through the Save dialog box. But remember, you can save in this format only if you opened the image as a Filmstrip document and did not change the size of the image.

The mainstream formats

The formats discussed so far are all very interesting and they fulfill their own niche purposes. But two formats — JPEG and TIFF — are the all-stars of digital imagery. You'll probably use these formats the most because of their outstanding compression capabilities and almost universal support among graphics applications.

JPEG

The JPEG format is named after the people who designed it, the Joint Photographic Experts Group. JPEG is the most efficient and essential compression format currently available and is likely to be the compression standard for years to come. JPEG is a lossy compression scheme, which means it sacrifices image quality to conserve space on disk. You can control how much data is lost during the save operation, however.

When you save an image in the JPEG format, you're greeted with the JPEG Options dialog box (see Figure 3-40). The most vital option in this dialog box is the Quality setting, which determines how much compression Photoshop applies to your image.

Figure 3-40: The JPEG Options dialog box provides a total of 13 compression settings, ranging from 0 (heaviest compression) to 12 (best quality).

Select an option from the Quality pop-up menu or click and drag the slider from 0 to 12 to specify the quality setting. Of the named options, Low takes the least space on disk but distorts the image rather severely; Maximum retains the highest amount of image quality but consumes more disk space. Of the numbered options, 0 is the most severe compressor and 12 does the least damage.

Note   JPEG evaluates an image in 8-x-8-pixel blocks, using a technique called *Adaptive Discrete Cosine Transform,* or ADCT. It averages the 24-bit value of every pixel in the block (or the 8-bit value of every pixel in the case of a grayscale image). ADCT then stores the average color in the upper-left pixel in the block and assigns the remaining 63 pixels smaller values relative to the average.

Next, JPEG divides the block by an 8 x 8 block of its own called the *quantization matrix*, which homogenizes the pixels' values by changing as many as possible to zero. This process saves the majority of disk space, but loses data. When Photoshop opens a JPEG image, it can't recover the original distinction between the zero pixels, so the pixels become the same, or similar, colors. Finally, JPEG applies lossless Huffman encoding to translate repeating values to a single symbol.

In most instances, it's a good idea to use JPEG only at the Maximum Quality setting (10 or higher), at least until you gain some experience with it. The smallest amount of JPEG compression saves more space than any non-JPEG compression format and still retains the most essential detail from the original image.

Check the coverage of the Save for Web dialog box earlier in this chapter, and Chapter 18 for more information on the JPEG format and its use for images that will be displayed online.

JPEG is a *cumulative compression scheme*, meaning that Photoshop recompresses an image every time you save it in the JPEG format. There's no disadvantage to saving an image to disk repeatedly during a single session, because JPEG always works from the on-screen version. But if you close an image, reopen it, and save it in the JPEG format, you inflict a small amount of damage. Use JPEG sparingly. In the best of all possible worlds, you should save to the JPEG format only after you finish all work on an image. Even in a pinch, you should apply all filtering effects before saving to JPEG, because these have a habit of exacerbating imperfections in image quality.

JPEG is best used when compressing continuous-tone images (images in which the distinction between immediately neighboring pixels is slight). Any image that includes gradual color transitions, as in a photograph, qualifies for JPEG compression. JPEG is not the best choice for saving screen shots, line drawings (especially those converted from EPS graphics), and other high-contrast images. These are better served by GIF if you want to post them on the Web or by a lossless compression scheme, such as TIFF with LZW. The JPEG format is available when you are saving grayscale, RGB, and CMYK images.

Occupying the bottom half of the JPEG Options dialog box are three radio buttons, designed primarily to optimize JPEG images for the Web. If your image is destined for print, just select the first option, Baseline ("Standard"), and be done with it. For Web graphics, select the Baseline Optimized option to make images display on-screen line by line or select the Progressive option to make images display in multiple passes.

TIFF

Developed by Aldus in the early days of the Mac to standardize an ever-growing population of scanned images, TIFF (*Tagged Image File Format*) is the most widely supported image-printing format across both the Macintosh and PC platforms. Unlike EPS, it can't handle object-oriented artwork, but otherwise it's unrestricted. In fact, TIFF offers a few tricks of its own that make it very special.

In Photoshop, TIFF supports up to 24 channels, the maximum number permitted in any image. In fact, TIFF is the only system other than DCS 2.0, "raw," and the native Photoshop format that can save more than four channels. To save a TIFF file without extra mask channels, deselect the Alpha option in the Save dialog box. (For an introduction to channels, read Chapter 4.) Even more impressive, TIFF supports multiple layers. If you want layers to remain independent when you save the file, you can select the Layers option in the Save dialog box.

When you save an image as a TIFF file, Photoshop displays the TIFF Options dialog box (see Figure 3-41), which offers the following controls:

✦ **Compression.** You can choose among three different types of compression: LZW (Lempel-Ziv-Welch), ZIP, or JPEG. Here are the major differences:

- **LZW:** Like Huffman encoding (previously described in the section "Saving an EPS image"), LZW digs into the computer code that describes an image and substitutes frequently used codes with shorter equivalents. But instead of substituting characters, as Huffman does, LZW substitutes strings of data. Because LZW doesn't so much as touch a pixel in your image, it's entirely lossless. Most image editors and desktop-publishing applications — including Illustrator, FreeHand, InDesign, PageMaker, and QuarkXPress — import LZW-compressed TIFF images, but a few still have yet to catch on.

- **ZIP:** The problem with LZW (from a programming perspective) is that it's regulated by a patent. And whenever a bit of technology costs money to use, you can bet somebody out there is trying to come up with a free equivalent. Hence ZIP, a competing lossless compression scheme used in PDF documents. Why use it? Theoretically, it's a bit smarter than LZW and can on occasion deliver smaller image files. On the other hand, Photoshop is currently one of the few programs to support ZIP compression in a TIFF file. So unless you discover big savings when using ZIP, you should stick with LZW until ZIP support becomes more widespread.

- **JPEG:** If two lossless compression schemes aren't enough options, the TIFF format also permits you to apply lossy JPEG compression. Long-time Photoshop users may balk at JPEG compression inside TIFF options. After all, one of the major benefits of TIFF is that it ensures optimum image quality; by applying JPEG compression, which results in loss of image data, you defeat the purpose. But now that TIFF supports layers, JPEG inside TIFF permits you a unique opportunity to cut the size of your layered image files in half. Experience shows that JPEG in TIFF results in only a modest loss of data. And because JPEG does not affect the transparency mask — which defines the outlines of the layers — the layers continue to exhibit nice, sharp edges.

Figure 3-41: Photoshop offers a myriad of compression schemes for TIFF files.

Note

If names such as Huffman, LZW, and ZIP ring a faint bell, it may be because these are the same compression schemes used by StuffIt, PKzip, WinZIP, and other file compression utilities. For this reason, using an additional utility to compress a TIFF image that you've already compressed using LZW, ZIP, or JPEG makes no sense. Neither do you want to compress a standard JPEG image, because JPEG takes advantage of Huffman encoding. You may shave off a few K, but this isn't enough space to make it worth your time and effort.

Caution

Also be aware that some programs may gag on compressed TIFF files, regardless of which compression scheme you apply. If an application balks at opening your Photoshop TIFF file, try resaving the file with no compression.

✦ **Byte Order.** Every once in a while, Photoshop chooses to name a straightforward option in the most confusing way possible. Byte Order is a prime example, and it relates to the two variations of TIFF, one for the PC and the other for the Mac. This probably has something to do with the arrangement of 8-bit chunks of data, but do you care? Probably not. More likely, you're sure about your choice of either wanting to use a PC or a Mac, regardless of TIFF variations.

✦ **Save Image Pyramid.** Select this option to save *tiled* TIFF files. This variation of the standard TIFF file-saving algorithm divides your image into tiles and then stacks the tiles in a pyramid. Each level of the pyramid represents your image at a different resolution, with the highest-resolution version serving as the base of the pyramid. The idea is that an application can use the low-resolution tiles to perform certain image-processing tasks and dig down to the high-resolution version only when absolutely necessary. When you're working with very large image files, this approach not only speeds up certain editing tasks but also puts less strain on your computer's resources. (If you're familiar with the FlashPix format, the concept is the same.)

Unless you're saving your image for use in a program that you know supports tiled TIFF images, however, deselect this option. Photoshop itself can't take advantage of the tiled technology, and many applications can't open tiled images at all.

✦ **Save Transparency.** If the image contains transparent areas, select this option to retain the transparency. Otherwise, transparent areas become white.

✦ **Layer Compression.** Not only can you decide whether you want to use lossless or lossy image compression, but Photoshop lets you specify how you want to save the layers themselves. The choices speak for themselves; RLE saves more quickly but makes bigger files, and the reverse is true for ZIP. Alternatively, you can choose to discard the layers altogether and save a flattened copy of your file.

The formats nobody talks to

Nope, the discussion of formats is not quite complete. There are two more, the odd men out. Why are they formatting pariahs? One format has a purpose so specific that Photoshop can open files saved in the format but it can't save to the format. The other is not so much a format but a manual file can opener that may come in handy for prying open a file from an unknown source.

Photo CD YCC images

Photoshop can open Eastman Kodak's Photo CD and Pro Photo CD formats directly. A Photo CD contains compressed versions of every image in each of the five scan sizes provided on Photo CDs — from 128 x 192 pixels (72K) to 2,048 x 3,072 pixels (18MB).

The Pro Photo CD format can accommodate each of the five sizes included in the regular Photo CD format, plus one additional size — 4,096 x 6,144 pixels (72MB) — that's four times as large as the largest image on a regular Photo CD. As a result, Pro Photo CDs hold only 25 scans; standard Photo CDs hold 100. Like their standard Photo CD counterparts, Pro Photo CD scanners can accommodate 35mm film and slides. But they can also handle 70mm film and 4 x 5-inch negatives and transparencies. The cost can be an issue, as scanning an image to a standard Photo CD costs between $1 and $2, but scanning it to a Pro Photo CD costs about $10. Your budget will determine which path makes the most sense for you.

Both Photo CD and Pro Photo CD use the YCC color model, a variation on the CIE (Commission Internationale d'Eclairage) color space, which is discussed in Chapter 4. YCC provides a broader range of color — theoretically, every color your eye can see. By opening Photo CD files directly, you can translate the YCC images directly to Photoshop's Lab color mode, another variation on the CIE color space that ensures no color loss.

When you open a Photo CD image, a Photo CD dialog box appears divided into three main sections: Image Info, Source Image, and Destination Image. The Image Info section simply tells you the type of film on which the image was shot and the type of scanner used to scan the image to CD. Selections that you make in the Source and Destination areas tell Photoshop how you want it to open the image. Here's what you need to know:

- ✦ **Pixel Size.** Select which of the available image sizes you want to use from this pop-up menu.

- ✦ **Profile.** Use this pop-up menu to select the kind of film from which the original photographs were scanned. You can select from one of the variations on Kodak's film brands — E-6 for Ektachrome or K-14 for Kodachrome — or settle for the generic Color Negative V3.0 Film option. Your selection determines the method Photoshop uses to transform the colors in the image.

- ✦ **Resolution.** This setting determines the output resolution and size at which Photoshop opens the image. You get the same number of image pixels no matter what — that's controlled by the Pixel Size option. In other words, changing this value is no different than changing the Resolution value in the Image Size dialog box with the Resample Image option deselected.

- ✦ **Color Space.** Select an option from this pop-up menu to specify the color model you want to use. Select RGB to open the image in the RGB mode; select LAB to open the image in the Lab mode. You can also select from 8 Bits/Channel to edit the image in 24-bit color or 16 Bits/Channel to open the image in 48-bit color.

- ✦ **Orientation.** The preview in the left side of the dialog box shows you the original orientation of the image. If you want to change that orientation, click the other Orientation radio button. The preview updates to show you the new orientation.

Photoshop cannot save to the Photo CD format. And frankly, there's little reason you'd want to do so. Photo CD is strictly a means for transferring slides and film negatives onto the world's most ubiquitous and indestructible storage medium, the CD-ROM.

Note

Kodak also offers a product called Picture CD, which is quite different from Photo CD — don't get the two confused. With Picture CD, consumers can drop off rolls of undeveloped film and receive both traditional prints and a CD containing scanned versions of their pictures. Picture CD images are provided in the JPEG format, so none of the Photo CD file-opening features discussed here apply. You open Picture CD images like any other JPEG file.

Opening raw documents

A *raw document* is a plain binary file stripped of all extraneous information. It contains no compression scheme, specifies no bit depth or image size, and offers no color mode. Each byte of data indicates a brightness value on a single color channel, and that's it. Photoshop offers this function specifically so you can open images created in undocumented formats, such as those created on mainframe computers.

To open an image of unknown origin on a PC, choose File ➪ Open As. On a Mac, choose File ➪ Open and select All Documents from the Show pop-up menu. Then select the desired image from the scrolling list and choose Photoshop Raw (*.RAW) from the Open As pop-up menu (or Format pop-up menu on the Mac). After you press Enter or Return, the Raw Options dialog box appears, featuring these options:

✦ **Width, Height.** If you know the dimensions of the image in pixels, type the values in these option boxes.

✦ **Swap.** Click this button to swap the Width value with the Height value.

✦ **Count.** Type the number of color channels in this option box. If the document is an RGB image, type 3; if it is a CMYK image, type 4.

✦ **Interleaved.** Select this value if the color values are stored sequentially by pixels. In an RGB image, the first byte represents the red value for the first pixel, the second byte represents the green value for that pixel, the third the blue value, and so on. If you deselect this option, the first byte represents the red value for the first pixel, the second value represents the red value for the second pixel, and so on. When Photoshop finishes describing the Red channel, it describes the Green channel and then the Blue channel.

✦ **Depth.** Select the number of bits per color channel. Most images contain 8 bits per channel, but scientific scans from mainframe computers may contain 16.

✦ **Byte Order.** If you specify 16 bits per channel, you must tell Photoshop whether the image comes from a Mac or a PC.

✦ **Header.** This value tells Photoshop how many bytes of data at the beginning of the file consist of header information it can ignore.

✦ **Retain When Saving.** If the Header value is greater than zero, you can instruct Photoshop to retain this data when you save the image in a different format.

✦ **Guess.** If you know the Width and Height values, but you don't know the number of bytes in the header — or vice versa — you can ask Photoshop for help. Fill in either the Dimensions or Header information and then click Guess to ask Photoshop to take a stab at the unknown value. Photoshop estimates all this information when the Raw Options dialog box first appears. Generally speaking, if it doesn't estimate correctly the first time around, you're on your own. But hey, the Guess button is worth a shot.

Tip
If a raw document is a CMYK image, it opens as an RGB image with an extra masking channel. To display the image correctly, choose Image ➪ Mode ➪ Multichannel to free the four channels from their incorrect relationship. Then recombine them by choosing Image ➪ Mode ➪ CMYK Color.

 Note
Don't confuse Photoshop Raw with Camera Raw, which is the untreated image created by a digital camera before processing. Camera Raw is as impressive as Photoshop Raw is bland. You take a closer look at Camera Raw in Chapter 17.

Saving a raw document

Photoshop also lets you save to the raw document format. This capability is useful when you create files you want to transfer to mainframe systems or output to devices that don't support other formats, such as the Kodak XL7700.

 Caution
Do not save 256-color indexed images to the raw format or you will lose the color lookup table and, therefore, all color information. Be sure to convert such images first to RGB or one of the other full-color modes before saving.

When you save an image in the raw document format, Photoshop presents the dialog box shown in Figure 3-42. The dialog box options work as follows:

✦ **File Type.** This option defines information for the resource fork, so it's only pertinent to Mac users. (Under Windows, the option is always dimmed. Feel free to ignore it.) Type the four-character file type code (TIFF, PICT, and so on) in this option box. (You should check the documentation for the application you plan to use to open the raw document.) If you plan to use this file on a computer other than a Mac, you can type any four characters you like; only Macs use this code.

Figure 3-42: When saving a raw document on a Mac, type the file type and creator codes and specify the order of data in the file.

✦ **File Creator.** Again, this option is relevant only on a Mac. Type the four-character creator code, which tells the system software which application created the file. By default, the creator code is 8BIM, Photoshop's code. Ignore this option unless you have a specific reason for changing it — for example, to open the image in a particular Macintosh application. (You won't hurt anything by changing the code, but you will prevent Photoshop from opening the image when you double-click the document icon at the Finder desktop.) On Windows machines, the 8BIM default code is selected for you and the option is dimmed.

✦ **Header:** Type the size of the header in bytes. If you type any value but 0, you must fill in the header using a data editor, such as Norton Disk Editor.

✦ **Save Channels In.** Select the Interleaved Order option to arrange data sequentially by pixels, as described earlier. To group data by color channel, select the Non-interleaved Order option.

Still can't get that file open?

File format specs are continually evolving. As a result, programs that provide support for a particular format may not support the specific version of the format used to save the file you're trying to open. For example, JPEG is notorious for causing problems because there were several private implementations in the early days. As a result, some JPEG files can be read only by the originating application.

If you can't open a file in Photoshop, you may have another program that can read and write the problem format. Try the problem file in every program you have, and hope you get lucky.

You may also want to try a program such as HiJaak, TransverterPro, DeBabelizer Toolbox, or DeBabelizer Pro from Equilibrium (www.equilibrium.com). A great format converter, DeBabelizer Pro handles every format Photoshop handles, as well as Dr. Halo's CUT, Fractal Design Painter's RIFF, the animation formats PICS, FLI, and ANM, as well as Unix workstation formats for Silicon Graphics, Sun Microsystems, and others.

Adding Annotations

Adobe PDF has become the "it" file format for sharing and reviewing documents, but you don't need to export to PDF to add comments to your images. Borrowing from Adobe Acrobat, Photoshop offers tools that let you attach written notes and audio clips that you can view and play right from the image window. The following section has the details.

Making a note of it

Photoshop enables you to slap the digital equivalent of a sticky note onto your image. The notes can be viewed in Adobe Acrobat (assuming that you save the image as a PDF) as well as in Photoshop. You can jot down ideas that you want to remember later, for example. Or, if you're routing an image for approval, you can ask questions about a certain image element — or, more likely, explain why a part of the picture looks the way it does and why changing it would be a mistake of life-altering proportions.

The Photoshop Notes tool works like its counterpart in Adobe Acrobat: Click in the image window to display a blank note or drag to create a custom-sized note. If you don't want to use the name that appears in the note's title bar (it defaults to the name you typed when you installed Photoshop), type the desired name in the Author box in the Options bar. Next, type your comments — all the standard text-editing techniques apply — and then click the Close box in the upper-left corner of the note window. Your note shrinks to a little note icon, as shown in the figure. Double-click the icon to redisplay the note text, as shown in Figure 3-43.

When you save your image, be sure to save in the native Photoshop format or PDF and select the Annotations option in the Save dialog box. Otherwise, you lose all your notes. For information on how to delete individual notes in an open image and how to customize and import notes, see the section "Managing annotations."

Speaking your mind

If you like to speak your mind rather than put your thoughts in writing, check out the Audio Annotation tool. This tool works like the Notes tool except that it inserts an audio recording of your voice rather than a text message into the file. Of course, you need a microphone, speakers, and a sound card installed in your computer to use this feature, and so does the intended recipient of the file — if you'll be sharing the file with a coworker or other associate. Photoshop retains audio annotations only when you save the image file using the Photoshop native format or PDF, as with text notes. Be aware, too, that audio files increase file size significantly — which will probably make e-mailing the file out of the question.

The Audio Annotation tool shares a button with the Notes tool in the Toolbox. Press N to toggle between the two tools (or Shift+N, depending on your preference setting for switching tools). Click in your image at the spot where you want the icon representing your message to appear. When the Audio Annotation dialog box appears, click Start to begin your recording and then talk into the microphone. Click Stop when you've said all you have to say.

Figure 3-43: After adding text-based notes or audio comments to an image, save the file in PDF so that others can access the annotations when viewing the image in Adobe Reader.

Photoshop represents your audio message with a little speaker icon in the image window. Double-click the icon to play the message.

Managing annotations

If you're a solo artist and the only approval of your work you need is your own, you may not have much reason to use the Notes or Audio Annotation tools. Then again, even if you do work alone, you may be forgetful or so busy that real notes or even thoughts just get lost in the shuffle. Whatever the reason you want to commit ideas and so forth to memory, annotations are a terrific way to remind yourself exactly what you're trying to accomplish in an image. And why not store a recording of your baby's first words with a picture of the kid? If someone wants to look at the picture in the first place, chances are this feature will be entertaining. Whether you're using annotations for fun or profit, employ the following strategies to manage audio and text annotations:

✦ Use the Font and Size controls in the Options bar to change the font and type size in an open note.

✦ Click the Color icon to change the color of the icon and title bar for any new note you create. This option comes in handy if several people will be reviewing the image and contributing their thoughts and ideas. You can assign a different color to each author. To change the color of an existing note, open the note and click the Color icon. This time, you affect only the open note — other notes by the same author don't change.

✦ You can move and copy annotations between image windows. Just click the icon and use the Cut, Copy, and Paste commands as you do to move and copy any selection.

✦ If an icon blocks your view of the image, you can click and drag it out of the way. However, when you open the note, its window appears in the icon's original location. Click and drag the size box in the lower-right corner of an open note to shrink the window if necessary. You can also drag the title bar of a note to reposition it on-screen.

✦ Choose View ➪ Show ➪ Annotations to toggle the display of annotation icons on and off. Alternatively, choose View ➪ Show ➪ All and View ➪ Show ➪ None to hide and display icons and other interface elements, such as selection marquees, guides, and so on.

✦ To delete a single annotation, click its icon and press Delete. Or right-click (Control-click on the Mac) the icon and choose Delete Note or Delete Audio Annotation. If you want to delete all annotations, choose Delete All Annotations or click the Clear All button in the Options bar.

Tip

If you send out several copies of the same image for approval, you don't have to open each copy individually to read the annotations. Instead, open just one copy and then import the annotations from the other files. Choose File ➪ Import ➪ Annotations, select the files containing the annotations, and click Open. Photoshop gathers up all the annotations and dumps them into your open image.

Caution

Remember to save your image as a PDF, a TIFF, or in the native Photoshop file format to retain annotations in a file. And if you're sending an annotated file to other people for viewing, tell them that they need to use Adobe Acrobat 4.0 or higher to access the annotations.

Resampling and Cropping

After you bring up an image — whether you created it from scratch or opened an existing image stored in one of the formats from the seemingly endless list discussed in the preceding pages — its size and resolution are established. Neither size nor resolution is carved in stone, however. Photoshop provides two methods for changing the number of pixels in an image: resampling and cropping.

Resizing versus resampling

Typically, when people talk about *resizing* an image, they mean enlarging or reducing it without changing the number of pixels in the image, as demonstrated back in Figure 3-1. By contrast, *resampling* an image means scaling it so the image contains a larger or smaller number of pixels. With resizing, an inverse relationship exists between size and resolution — size increases when resolution decreases, and vice versa. But resampling affects either size or resolution independently. The resampled and original images have identical resolutions, but the resized image has twice the resolution of its companions.

Resizing an image

To resize an image, use one of the techniques discussed near the beginning of this chapter. To recap briefly, the best method is to choose Image ➪ Image Size, deselect the Resample Image option, and type a value into the Resolution option box. See Figure 3-2 to refresh your memory.

Resampling an image

You also use Image ➪ Image Size to resample an image. The difference is that you leave the Resample Image option selected, as shown in Figure 3-44. As its name implies, the Resample Image option is the key to resampling.

When Resample Image is selected, the Resolution value is independent of both sets of Width and Height values. (The only difference between the two sets of options is that the top options work in pixels and the bottom options work in relative units of measure, such as percent and inches.) You can increase the number of pixels in an image by increasing any of the five values in the dialog box; you can decrease the number of pixels by decreasing any value. Photoshop stretches or shrinks the image according to the new size specifications.

At all times, you can see the new number of pixels Photoshop will assign to the image, as well as the increased or decreased file size. In Figure 3-44, for example, the first Width value has been changed to 669 pixels. The Pixel Dimensions value at the top of the dialog box reflects the change by reading *883.9K (was 1.00M)*, which shows that the file size has decreased.

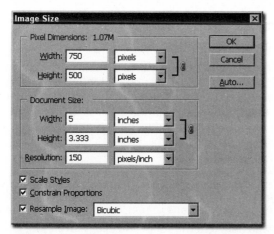

Figure 3-44: With the Resample Image option selected, you can modify the number of pixels in your image.

To calculate the pixels in the resampled image, Photoshop must use its powers of interpolation, as explained in Chapter 2. The interpolation setting defaults to the one chosen in the Preferences dialog box, but you can also change the setting right inside the Image Size dialog box. Simply select the desired method from the Resample Image pop-up menu. Bicubic generally results in the smoothest effects, as does Bicubic Smoother — it does its best to reinterpret your image with the smoothest pixel transitions possible. Bicubic Sharper is recommended for preserving the sharpness of an image that you're reducing, or downsampling. Bilinear is faster than any of the other options, but doesn't provide the smoothest results. Nearest Neighbor turns off interpolation so Photoshop merely throws away the pixels it doesn't need or duplicates pixels to resample up.

Here are a few more random items you should know about resampling with the Image Size dialog box:

✦ This may sound wrong, but you generally want to avoid adding pixels. When you resample up, you're asking Photoshop to make up details from thin air, and the program isn't that smart. Simply put, an enlarged image almost never looks better than the original; it merely takes up more disk space and prints slower.

Tip   Resampling down, on the other hand, is a useful technique. It enables you to smooth away photo grain, halftone patterns, and other scanning artifacts. One of the most tried-and-true rules is to scan at the maximum resolution permitted by your scanner and then resample the scan down to, say, 72 or 46 percent (with the interpolation set to Bicubic Sharper, naturally). By selecting a round value other than 50 percent, you force Photoshop to jumble the pixels into a regular, homogenous soup. You're left with fewer pixels, but these remaining pixels are better. And you have the added benefit that the image takes up less space on disk.

✦ To make an image tall and thin or short and fat, you must first turn off the Constrain Proportions option. This enables you to edit the two Width values entirely independently of the two Height values.

✦ Layer styles in Photoshop are dynamic, meaning you never lose the ability to edit their values. Accordingly, the look of a style you've applied to a layer can change when you resample an image. Select the Scale Styles option to avoid unwanted changes in your image's layer styles when you resample. It's important to note, however, that this option is available only if Constrain Proportions is also selected.

You can resample an image to match precisely the size and resolution of any other open image. While the Image Size dialog box is open, choose the name of the image you want to match from the Window menu.

✦ If you need help resampling an image to the proper size for a print job, choose Help ⇨ Resize Image to open the Resize Image Wizard. The dialog box walks you through the process of resampling step by step.

If you ever get confused inside the Image Size dialog box and want to return to the original size and resolution settings, press Alt (or Option key on the Mac) to change the Cancel button to Reset. Then click Reset to start from the beginning.

Photoshop remembers the setting of the Resample Image option and uses this same setting the next time you open the Image Size dialog box. This can trip you up if you record an action in the Actions palette that uses the Image Size command. Suppose that you create an action to resize images, deselecting the Resample Image option. If you later resample an image — selecting Resample Image — the option stays selected when you close the dialog box. The next time you run the action, you end up resampling instead of resizing. Always check the status of the option before you apply the Image Size command or run any actions containing the command.

Cropping

Another way to change the number of pixels in an image is to *crop* it, which means to clip away pixels around the edges of an image without harming the remaining pixels. (The one exception occurs when you rotate a cropped image or use the perspective crop feature, in which case Photoshop has to interpolate pixels to account for the rotation.)

Cropping enables you to focus on an element in your image. For example, the left side of Figure 3-45 shows an image with some unwanted content in the periphery — visual distractions that aren't necessary (see image on left). By cropping down to the content seen on the right, a real portrait is created.

Figure 3-45: Focus your viewer's eyes on the really important part of the picture by cropping away all distractions.

Photoshop offers several cropping options, including the capability to crop nonrectangular selections, automatically trim away transparent areas from the borders of an image, correct perspective effects while cropping, and crop and straighten crooked scans. You can read about all these features in the upcoming sections.

Changing the canvas size

One way to crop an image is to choose Image ⇨ Canvas Size, which displays the Canvas Size dialog box shown in Figure 3-46. The options in this dialog box enable you to scale the imaginary canvas on which the image rests separately from the image itself.

Canvas Extension Color pop-up menu lets you specify a color when you increase the canvas area in your image. You can choose the current Background or Foreground color, Black, White, or Gray, or Other to select a color using Photoshop's Color Picker dialog box. Keep in mind that you can select a color only when you're working with an image that contains a background layer. Otherwise, Photoshop will fill the newly expanded canvas area with transparent pixels. Either way, if you reduce the canvas, you crop the image. Just type the new desired pixel dimensions in the Width and Height boxes.

Selecting the Relative option allows you to change the height or width (or both the height and the width) of the canvas by a specific pixel amount. For example, type 2 in each option box to change a 100 x 100-pixel image into a 102 x 102-pixel image; type −2 to crop it down to a 98 x 98-pixel image. Not only can this save you from having to do a little math, but it can really be quite useful when you want to add the same number of pixels to a batch of different-sized files.

Figure 3-46: Choose Image ⇨ Canvas Size to crop an image or to add empty space around the perimeter of an image.

Click inside the Anchor grid to specify the placement of the image on the new canvas. For example, if you want to add space to the bottom of an image, enlarge the canvas size and then click the upper-middle square. If you want to crop away the upper-left corner of an image, create a smaller canvas size and then click the lower-right square. The Anchor grid offers little arrows to show how the canvas will shrink or grow.

To shrink the canvas so that it exactly fits the image, try the Image ⇨ Trim command. With the Trim command, you can automatically clip away empty canvas areas on the outskirts of your image, using the dialog box shown in Figure 3-47. To snip away empty canvas, select the Transparent Pixels option. Then specify which edges of the canvas you want to slice off by using the four Trim Away option. Alternatively, you can tell Photoshop to trim the image based on the pixel color in the top-left corner of the image or the bottom-right corner — just click the appropriate Based On radio button. For example, if you have a blue stripe running down the left edge of your image and you select the Top Left Pixel Color option, Photoshop clips away the stripe. No trimming occurs unless the entire edge of the image is bounded by the selected color.

Figure 3-47: To quickly snip away transparent areas from the edges of an image, use the Image ⇨ Trim command.

Tip   When you want to enlarge the canvas but aren't concerned with making it a specific size, try this timesaving trick: Click and drag with the Crop tool to create a crop marquee and then enlarge the crop marquee beyond the boundaries of the image (see the next section if you need help). When you press Enter or Return to apply the crop, the canvas grows to match the size of the crop marquee.

Using the Crop tool

In general, the Canvas Size command is most useful for enlarging the canvas or shaving a few pixels off the edge of an image. If you want to crop away a large portion of an image, the Crop tool is a better choice — if only because you can actually see what you're doing and see the crop happen as it happens.

Press C or click the crop icon in the toolbox to activate the tool, and then click and drag to create a rectangular marquee that surrounds the portion of the image you want to retain. You can see what will be cropped away if you proceed, because the content outside the box you've created is now darker than what's inside the box—it's an overlay, which you can choose not to see if you don't want to, as you'll discover in the following list of cropping tips:

✦ To help you distinguish the borders of the crop marquee, Photoshop displays a colored, translucent overlay on the area outside the crop box—similar to the way it indicates masked versus unmasked areas when you work in the Quick Mask mode. If you hate the overlay, deselect the Shield option in the Options bar. You also can click the neighboring color box to change the overlay color and set the overlay opacity through the Opacity pop-up menu. Note that these controls don't appear in the Options bar until after you create your initial crop marquee.

✦ You have the option of permanently discarding the pixels you crop or simply hiding them from view. Before you drag with the Crop tool, click the Delete or Hide option in the Options bar to signify your preference. If you choose Hide, you can bring the hidden regions back into view by enlarging the canvas or by using the Image ➪ Reveal All command.

Tip   As you drag, you can press the space bar to move the crop boundary temporarily on the fly. To stop moving the boundary and return to resizing it, release the space bar.

If you don't get the crop marquee right the first time, you can move, scale, or rotate it at will. Here's what you do:

✦ Click and drag inside the crop marquee to move it.

✦ Drag one of the square handles to resize the marquee. You can Shift-drag a handle to scale the marquee proportionally (the same percentage vertically and horizontally). You can also drag the sides of the marquee to resize it.

✦ Drag outside the crop marquee to rotate it, as explained in the next section. This may strike you as weird at first, but it works wonderfully.

✦ Drag the origin point (labeled in Figure 3-48) to change the center of a rotation.

✦ Select the Perspective option in the Options bar, and you can click and drag corner handles to distort the image. This will correct any convergence problems that occur when shooting images at an angle. For example, let's say you have a billboard in perspective, so that it declines toward the horizon. Using the Perspective option, you can crop the billboard and remove its perspective so it appears flat.

Crop tool   Origin point

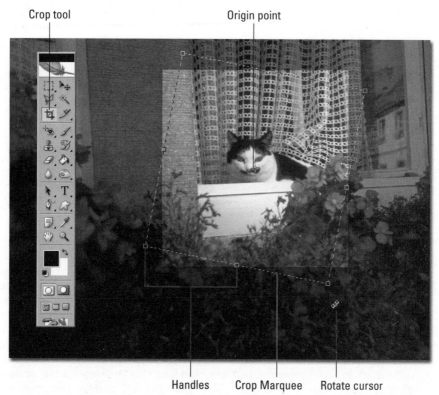

Handles   Crop Marquee   Rotate cursor

Figure 3-48: When rotating a crop boundary, align the marquee with an obvious axis in your image to determine the proper angle.

Although Perspective is a solid feature, it can prove confusing. For one thing, you can't preview the results of your changes before applying the crop. Also, in an attempt to conserve important detail, Photoshop tends to stretch the image after applying the perspective. This is actually a good thing — better to stretch an image than trash data — but it requires you to reverse the stretch in a second operation. If this bothers you, you may be better off tackling perspective problems using the Free Transform command, covered in Chapter 12, and do your cropping afterward.

When the marquee surrounds the exact portion of the image you want to keep, apply the crop by pressing Enter (or Return on the Mac) or double-clicking inside the marquee. You also can click the OK (check mark) button at the right end of the Options bar.

If you change your mind about cropping, you can cancel the crop marquee by pressing Esc or clicking the Cancel button, the universal "no" symbol next to the check mark in the Options bar.

Rotating the crop marquee

As stated earlier, you can rotate an image by clicking and dragging outside the crop marquee. Straightening a crooked image, however, can be a little tricky. Rarely, if ever, does one's first (or sometimes second) attempt to straighten an image by rotating it manually (in Free Transform mode) work the way you want it. Either you rotate it too far or not far enough. If your rotation fails to give you the straightening effect you want, choose Edit ➪ Undo (Ctrl+Z or ⌘-Z) and try again. Do not try using the tool a second time to rotate the already rotated image. If you do, Photoshop sets about interpolating between already interpolated pixels, resulting in more lost data. Every rotation gets farther away from the original image.

Tip

A better solution is to do it right the first time. Locate a line or general axis in your image that should be straight up and down. Rotate the crop marquee so it aligns exactly with this axis. In Figure 3-48, the crop marquee was rotated so one edge bisects the vertical content on the right. After you arrive at the correct angle for the marquee, drag the handles to size and position the boundary properly. As long as you don't drag outside the marquee, its angle remains fixed throughout.

Yet another solution is to use the Measure tool. Just click and drag with the tool along the axis you want to make vertical. Choose Image ➪ Rotate Canvas ➪ Arbitrary, and the angle of rotation you just sampled with the Measure tool is automatically added to the Rotate Canvas dialog box. Just click OK, and the transformation is complete.

Cropping an image to match another

You can crop an image so it matches the size and resolution of another image in two ways:

✦ Bring the image you want to crop forward and choose Image ➪ Canvas Size. Then, while inside the Canvas Size dialog box, select the name of the image you want to match from the Window menu. Of course, the image you want to match has to be open, so that it can be selected from the Window menu (look at the very bottom of the menu).

Tip

This method doesn't give you much control when cropping an image, but it's a great way to enlarge the canvas and add empty space around an image.

✦ Better yet, use the Crop tool in its fixed-size mode. First, bring the image you want to match to the front. Then select the Crop tool and click the Front Image button in the Options bar. The Width, Height, and Resolution options automatically update to show the size and resolution of the front image.

Now bring the image you want to crop to the front and drag with the Crop tool as normal. Photoshop constrains the crop marquee to the proportions of the targeted image. After you press Enter or Return, Photoshop crops, resamples, and rotates the image as necessary.

Note The next time you select the Crop tool, it starts out in fixed-size mode. To return the tool to normal, click the Clear button in the Options bar.

Cropping a selection

Another way to crop an image is to create a selection and then choose Image ➪ Crop. One advantage of the Crop command is that you needn't select the Crop tool if the Marquee tool is already active. One tool is all you need to select and crop. As with the Crop tool, you can press the space bar while you draw a marquee to move it on the fly. It's quite simple to get the placement and size exactly right — the only thing you can't do is rotate.

Another advantage of the Crop command is flexibility. After drawing a selection, you can switch windows, apply commands, and generally use any function you like prior to choosing Image ➪ Crop. The Crop tool, by contrast, is much more limiting. After drawing a cropping marquee, you can't do anything but adjust the marquee until you press Enter or Return to accept the crop or Esc to dismiss it.

And finally, you can use the Crop command on selections of any shape, even feathered selections and multiple noncontiguous selections. Of course, your image canvas remains rectangular no matter what the selection shape. Photoshop simply crops the canvas to the smallest size that can hold all selected areas.

Cropping and straightening crooked scans

When it comes to scanning images, you have two basic options: Scan each and every image in a separate pass, which can be hopelessly time consuming, or scan a group of images together. In the past, if you scanned your images as a group, you had to go at them with the Marquee tool, slice them up, separate them into layers, duplicate the layers into new images, rinse and repeat. It was arduous and soul numbing to say the least, not to mention the fact that you then needed to rotate every new image to compensate for slightly skewed scanning. With the release of Photoshop CS, however, Adobe streamlined all these steps into one simple command, and this ability remains in CS2.

Naturally, you need to begin with a one-layer scanned image consisting of the photos you want to crop out, such as the one on the left side of Figure 3-49. Then choose File ➪ Automate ➪ Crop and Straighten Photos. As if by magic, Photoshop detects each of the photos in your master scanned image, straightens them according to their borders, copies them to the Clipboard, and pastes them into new image windows, as shown on the right side of Figure 3-49.

Note   It's important to note, however, that the Crop and Straighten Photos command only fixes images that were scanned crookedly, not photos that were taken with a shaky hand. For a quick trick that makes correcting crooked photos a snap, see Chapter 12.

Figure 3-49: The Crop and Straighten Photos command in Photoshop takes the pain out of separating and straightening multiple photos in a single scanned image.

If you want to crop out and straighten only certain images from your scan, draw a selection border around the area you want to isolate and carry on as you normally would. If the command repeatedly splits one scanned image into two, select that particular scanned image, press and hold Alt (Option key on the Mac), and repeat the process. This tells Photoshop that the selected area represents only one scanned image. Keep in mind that the Crop and Straighten Photos command doesn't even need real photos to work its wonders. For example, suppose you have a sheet full of drawings that you want to divide into separate images. You can simply draw a clear border around each drawing and scan in the page. Because Photoshop is now intelligent enough to detect the borders inside of a multi-image scan, you're one leap closer to a collection of mini-masterpieces.

Summary

In this chapter, you learned to resize an image for the printer and for the screen, keeping the needs of your image and your goals for its use in mind. In addition, core skills for opening and saving images were covered, along with techniques for searching for and viewing images, and managing image data with the Bridge. You also learned about pixel depth, dimensions, and resolution, resampling an image, and cropping images to rid them of unnecessary edge content.

File formats were covered, too — you explored JPEG, GIF, PDF, and many other file formats, and learned about rendering object-oriented EPS images. Using Photoshop's less-often-used but very important tools for annotating and adding voice commentary to images, you learned to extend the editing process beyond the image itself.

✦   ✦   ✦

Painting and Retouching

◆   ◆   ◆   ◆

In This Part

Chapter 4
Defining Colors

Chapter 5
Painting and Brushes

Chapter 6
Filling and Stroking

Chapter 7
Retouching and
Restoring

◆   ◆   ◆   ◆

Defining Colors

From cell phones that take pictures to Web sites that let you print and share your latest batch of vacation photos, color images have never been more prevalent and universally accessible. Even someone on a meager budget can afford a low-end digital camera, an inkjet printer, and some photo paper — thus making the taking and printing of color photos something just about anyone can do. This also puts the use of color images for commercial use — brochures, ads — within the reach of more organizations, resulting in their producing more color themselves or expecting the graphic artists they employ to do the same. For those who still find the color brochure to be too expensive, a full-color Web site is entirely doable.

Photoshop, of course, is not typically the domain of the family photographer or the small business. At least in the past it hasn't been, due to its price tag, and it's still a more serious tool for more serious photographers and graphic artists. Photoshop's "lite" cousin, Elements, brings much of Photoshop's power to the home and small-business user, and that, too, will make color photos, their capture and manipulation, even more commonplace.

In the meantime, check out Photoshop's color tools. With color, color everywhere, it's important to know how to use Photoshop's tools to select colors, edit them, apply them, and tinker with them. It's important to know how Photoshop looks at and interprets color, and how you can enhance its ability to give you the color results you're looking for. So let's get started.

Specifying Colors

To begin this foray into the world of color, Photoshop provides four color controls in the toolbox, as shown in Figure 4-1. These icons work as follows:

♦ **Foreground color.** The foreground color icon indicates the color you apply when you use the Paint Bucket, Pencil, Brush, or one of the type tools, and also if you Alt-drag (Option-drag on the Mac) with the Smudge tool. The foreground color also begins any gradation created

◆ ◆ ◆ ◆

In This Chapter

Using the color controls in the toolbox

Selecting and defining colors in the Color Picker dialog box

Examinations of the RGB, HSB, CMYK, Lab color, and HDR modes

Converting images to 16 bits per channel

Creating grayscale and black-and-white images

Introductions to the Trumatch and Pantone color standards

Using the Color palette, Eyedropper, and color sampler

Understanding how color channels work

Using channel editing commands in the Channels palette

Improving the appearance of poorly scanned images

◆ ◆ ◆ ◆

with the Gradient tool in its default state. Photoshop uses the current foreground color to fill any shape you create with the shape tools, and if you make a selection and then click inside it with the Paint Bucket or use the Edit ➪ Fill command, the foreground color fills it up. Remember that you can also apply the foreground color to a standard selection by pressing Alt+Backspace (Option-Delete on the Mac).

To change the foreground color, click the foreground color icon to display the Color Picker dialog box. Then select a new color in the Color palette, or click anywhere in an open image window with the Eyedropper tool. You also can set the foreground color by clicking a swatch in the Swatches palette. (All are explained later in this chapter.)

Figure 4-1: Photoshop's color selection tools include Foreground color, Background color, and tools for going back to the default colors and swapping foreground for background colors. You can also see the Eyedropper in this figure.

✦ **Background color.** The active background color indicates the color you apply with the Eraser tool when you're working on the background layer. By default, the background color also ends any custom gradation created with the Gradient tool. To change the background color, click the background color icon to display the Color Picker dialog box. Or define the color by using the Color palette, clicking a swatch in the Swatches palette, or Alt-clicking (Option-clicking on the Mac) any open image window with the Eyedropper tool.

You can apply the background color to a selection by pressing Backspace or Delete, or by choosing Background Color from the Use list in the Fill dialog box opened by choosing Edit ➪ Fill. Note that if the selection is floating or exists on any layer except the background layer, pressing Backspace or Delete actually deletes the selection instead of filling it. For complete safety, use Ctrl+Backspace (⌘-Delete on the Mac) to fill a selection with the background color.

✦ **Switch colors.** Click this icon (or press X) to swap the current foreground and background colors.

✦ **Default colors.** Click this icon (or press D) to make the foreground color black and the background color white, according to their factory default settings. If you're editing a layer mask or an adjustment layer, the default colors are reversed, as explained in Chapter 12.

Using the Color Picker

When you click the foreground or background color icon in the toolbox or the Color palette, Photoshop displays the Color Picker dialog box, which is shown in Figure 4-2. My assumption that you're also looking at the Adobe Color Picker on your computer screen is based on my assumption that you read Chapter 2, wherein the downsides of using an OS-based picker are discussed. If you aren't sure which picker you've selected, or if you'd like to pick a different picker (apologies to Peter Piper and his pickled peppers), check the General panel of the Preferences dialog box.

All alliteration aside, I present you now with the many elements and options offered by the Color Picker dialog box:

✦ **Color slider.** Use the color slider to home in on the color you want to select. Click and drag up or down on either of the slider triangles to select a color from a particular 8-bit range. The colors represented inside the slider correspond to the selected radio button. For example, if you select the H (Hue) radio button, which is the default setting, the slider colors represent the full 8-bit range of hues. If you select S (Saturation), the slider shows the current hue at full saturation at the top of the slider, down to no saturation — or gray — at the bottom of the slider. If you select B (Brightness), the slider shows the 8-bit range of brightness values, from solid color at the top of the slider to absolute black at the bottom. You also can select R (Red), G (Green), or B (Blue), in which case the top of the slider shows you what the current color looks like when subjected to full-intensity red, green, or blue (respectively), and the bottom of the slider shows every bit of red, green, or blue subtracted.

✦ **Color field.** The color field shows a 16-bit range of variations on the current slider color. Click inside it to move the color selection marker and select a new color. The field plots colors against the two remaining attributes not represented by the color slider. For example, if you select the H (Hue) radio button, the field displays colors according to brightness vertically and saturation horizontally

Note

Slider and field always work together to represent an entire 16-million-color range. The slider displays 256 colors, and the field displays 65,000 variations on the slider color; 256 times 65,000 is roughly 16 million. No matter which radio button you select, you have access to the same colors; only your means of accessing them changes.

Figure 4-2: Use the Color Picker dialog box to specify a new foreground or background color from the 16-million-color range.

✦ **Current color.** The color currently selected from the color field appears in the top rectangle immediately to the right of the color slider. Click OK or press Enter or Return to make this the current foreground or background color (depending on which color control icon in the Toolbox you originally clicked to display the Color Picker dialog box).

✦ **Previous color.** The bottom rectangle to the right of the color slider shows how the foreground or background color — whichever one you are in the process of editing — looked before you displayed the Color Picker dialog box. Click Cancel or press Esc to leave this color intact.

✦ **Alert triangle.** The alert triangle appears when you select a color that Photoshop can't print using standard process colors. The box below the triangle shows the closest CMYK equivalent, invariably a duller version of the color. Click either the triangle or the box to bring the color into the printable range. Pressing Ctrl+Shift+Y (⌘-Shift-Y on the Mac) or choosing View ⇨ Gamut Warning automatically grays out any colors not allowed in the CMYK spectrum.

✦ **Web-safe alert cube.** This little cube appears if you select a color that's not included in the so-called Web-safe palette, a 216-color spectrum that's supposedly ideal for creating Web graphics. If you click either the cube or the swatch below it, Photoshop selects the closest Web-safe equivalent to the color you originally selected.

✦ **Only Web Colors.** This option changes the display in the Color Field so that it displays delineated sections of Web-safe colors. The rest of the options in the dialog box work the same way when you're in Only Web Colors mode, except that you're limited to choosing from the 216 colors that can be reliably reproduced in a Web browser.

Typing Numeric Color Values

In addition to selecting colors using the slider and color field, you can type specific color values in the option boxes in the lower-right region of the Color Picker dialog box. Novices and intermediates may find these options less satisfying to use than the slider and field. These options, however, enable artists and print professionals to specify exact color values, whether to make controlled adjustments to a color already in use or to match a color used in another document. The options fall into one of four camps:

✦ **HSB.** These options stand for hue, saturation, and brightness. Hue is measured on a 360-degree circle. Saturation and brightness are measured from 0 to 100 percent. These options permit access to more than 3 million color variations.

✦ **RGB.** You can change the amount of the primary colors red, green, and blue by specifying the brightness value of each color from 0 to 255. These options enable access to more than 16 million color variations.

✦ **Lab.** This acronym stands for luminosity, measured from 0 to 100 percent, and two arbitrarily named color axes, a and b, whose brightness values range from –120 to 120. These options enable access to more than 6 million color variations.

✦ **CMYK.** These options display the amount of cyan, magenta, yellow, and black ink required to print the current color. When you click the alert triangle, these are the only values that don't change, because they make up the closest CMYK equivalent.

At the bottom of the dialog box, the value next to the pound sign (#) shows you the hexadecimal value for the chosen color (see Figure 4-2). This value comes into play only if you're creating Web graphics — and maybe not even then.

When creating graphics for use on a Web page, you'll want to make sure that the Only Web Colors option is selected, so that you can easily select only Web-safe colors for use in your artwork. Every color in the 216-color Web-safe palette has a numeric value based on the hexadecimal numbering system. Each value includes a total of three pairs of numbers or letters, one pair each for the R, G, and B values. When you create a color tag in HTML code, you type the hexadecimal value for the color you want to use. Fortunately, you can create a Web page without having to write your own HTML code; page-creation programs like GoLive and Macromedia Dreamweaver do the work for you. But if you prefer to do your own coding or if you have been given a hexadecimal number and told to use that color in your design (say, by a client who already has Web content that you have to work with or enhance), make note of the hexadecimal value in the Color Picker dialog box.

Tip

The hexadecimal number can be useful if you want to precisely match a color on an existing Web page and don't have a client telling you what color that is. Just look at the HTML coding for the page (in Internet Explorer, for example, choose View ➪ Source), note the hexadecimal value in the appropriate color tag, and type that value in the Color Picker dialog box.

You may find the numerical range of your various color options somewhat confusing. For example, the CMYK options enable you to create 100 million unique colors, whereas the RGB options enable the standard 16 million variations, and the Lab options enable a measly 6 million. Despite this deficit, Lab is the largest color space, theoretically encompassing all colors from both CMYK and RGB. The printing standard CMYK provides by far the fewest colors, the opposite of what you might expect. Huh? These statistics seem misleading and unrelated to what we think of as the reality of displayed and printed color. To find out more about color models and how they really work, read on.

Working in Different Color Modes

The four sets of option boxes in the Color Picker dialog box represent color models — or, if you prefer, color modes, which more closely matches the Image ➪ Mode command terminology, wherein you choose a mode for your image. *Color models* are different ways to define colors on both the screen and the printed page.

Outside the Color Picker dialog box, you can work in any one of these color models by choosing a command from the Image ➪ Mode submenu. In doing so, you generally change the colors in your image by dumping a few hundred, or even thousand, colors with no equivalents in the new color model. The only exception is Lab, which in theory encompasses every unique color your eyes can detect.

Rather than discuss the color models in the order in which they occur in the Mode submenu, let's talk about them in logical order, starting with the most common and widely accepted color model, RGB. The Multichannel mode, meanwhile, is not even a color model. Rather, Image ➪ Mode ➪ Multichannel enables you to separate an image into independent channels, which you then can swap around and splice back together to create special effects. For more information, see the section "Using multichannel techniques" later in this chapter.

Cross-Reference   Duotone mode is not covered here. The Image ➪ Mode ➪ Duotone command represents an alternative method for printing grayscale images, so it is discussed in Chapter 18.

RGB

RGB is the color model of light. RGB comprises three primary colors — red, green, and blue — each of which can vary between 256 levels of intensity (called brightness values, as discussed in previous chapters). The RGB model is also called the *additive primary model* because a color becomes lighter as you add higher levels of red, green, and blue light. All monitors, projection devices, and other items that transmit or filter light — including televisions, movie projectors, colored stage lights, and even stained glass — rely on the additive primary model. This, in case you were wondering, is why RGB is the color mode for Web graphics.

Red, green, and blue light mix as follows:

✦ **Red and green.** Full-intensity red and green mix to form yellow. Subtract some red to make chartreuse; subtract some green to make orange. All these colors assume a complete lack of blue.

✦ **Green and blue.** Full-intensity green and blue with no red mix to form cyan. If you try hard enough, you can come up with 65,000 colors in the turquoise/jade/sky-blue/sea-green range.

✦ **Blue and red.** Full-intensity blue and red mix to form magenta. Subtract some blue to make rose; subtract some red to make purple. All these colors assume a complete lack of green.

✦ **Red, green, and blue.** Full-intensity red, green, and blue mix to form white, the absolute brightest color in the visible spectrum.

✦ **No light.** Low intensities of red, green, and blue plunge a color into blackness.

As far as image editing is concerned, the RGB color model is ideal for editing images on-screen because it provides access to the entire range of 24-bit screen colors. Furthermore, you can save an RGB image in every file format supported by Photoshop except GIF and the two DCS formats. As shown in Table 4-1, grayscale is the only other color mode compatible with a wider range of file formats.

Table 4-1
File-Format Support for Photoshop CS Color Models

	Bitmap	*Grayscale*	*Duotone*	*Indexed*	*RGB*	*CMYK*	*Lab*
Photoshop	Yes	Yes	Yes	Yes	Yes	Yes	Yes
BMP	Yes	Yes	No	Yes	Yes	No	No
DCS 1.0	No	No	No	No	No	Yes	No
DCS 2.0	Yes	Yes	Yes*	No	No	Yes	No
EPS	Yes	Yes	Yes	Yes	Yes	Yes	Yes
GIF	Yes	Yes	No	Yes	No	No	No
JPEG	No	Yes	No	No	Yes	Yes	No
PCX	Yes	Yes	No	Yes	Yes	No	No
PDF	Yes	Yes	No	Yes	Yes	Yes	Yes
PICT	Yes	Yes	No	Yes	Yes	No	No
PNG	Yes**	Yes	No	Yes	Yes	No	No
Scitex CT	No	Yes	No	No	Yes	Yes	No
TIFF	Yes	Yes	No	Yes	Yes	Yes	Yes

* You can save a duotone in DCS 2.0 only after first converting the image to the Multichannel mode. For more information, consult Chapter 18.

** PNG supports Bitmap mode only on the Mac.

Note Table 4-1 lists color models in the order in which they appear in the Image ⇨ Mode submenu. Again, the Multichannel mode is skipped because it is not a true color model.

On the negative side, the RGB color model provides access to a wider range of colors than you can print. If you are designing an image for full-color printing, therefore, you can expect to lose many of the brightest and most vivid colors in your image. The only way to avoid any color loss whatsoever is to have a professional scan your image to CMYK and then edit it in the CMYK mode. Colors can get clipped when you apply special effects, and the editing process can be exceptionally slow. The better solution is to scan your images to RGB and edit them in the Lab mode, as explained in the section "CIE's Lab."

HSB

Way back in Photoshop 2, the Modes submenu provided access to the HSB — hue, saturation, brightness — color model, now relegated to the Color Picker dialog box and the Color palette (discussed later in this chapter). *Hue* is pure color, the stuff rainbows are made of, measured on a 360-degree circle. Red is located at 0 degrees, yellow at 60 degrees, green at 120 degrees, cyan at 180 degrees (midway around the circle), blue at 240 degrees, and magenta at 300 degrees. This is basically a pie-shaped version of the RGB model at full intensity and is the basis of the color wheel you often see offered as a tool for selecting complementary and opposite colors — colors' relationships (what goes with what) can be demonstrated on that wheel.

Saturation represents the purity of the color. A zero saturation value equals gray. White, black, and any other colors you can express in a grayscale image have no saturation. Full saturation produces the purest version of a hue.

Brightness is the lightness or darkness of a color. A zero brightness value equals black. Full brightness combined with full saturation results in the most vivid version of any hue.

CMYK

In nature, our eyes perceive pigments according to the *subtractive color model.* Sunlight contains every visible color found on Earth. When sunlight is projected on an object, the object absorbs (subtracts) some of the light and reflects the rest. The reflected light is the color you see. For example, a fire engine is bright red because it absorbs all the light that is not red — meaning all blue and green — from the white-light spectrum.

Pigments on a sheet of paper work the same way. You can even mix pigments to create other colors. Suppose you paint a red brushstroke, which absorbs green and blue light, over a blue brushstroke, which absorbs green and red light. You get a blackish mess with only a modicum of blue and red light left, along with a smidgen of green because the colors weren't absolutely pure.

But wait — every child knows red and blue mix to form purple. So what gives? What gives is that what you learned in elementary school is only a clumsy approximation of the truth. Did you ever try mixing a vivid red with a canary yellow only to produce an ugly orange-brown glop? The reason you didn't achieve the bright orange you wanted is because red starts out darker than bright orange, which means you must add a great deal of yellow before you arrive at orange. And even then, the yellow had better be an incredibly bright lemon yellow, not some deep canary yellow with a lot of red in it.

Commercial subtractive primaries

The subtractive primary colors used by commercial printers — cyan, magenta, and yellow — are for the most part very light. Cyan absorbs only red light, magenta absorbs only green light, and yellow absorbs only blue light. On their own, these colors unfortunately don't do a good job of producing dark colors. In fact, at full intensities, cyan, magenta, and yellow all mixed together don't get much beyond a muddy brown. That's where black comes in. Black helps to accentuate shadows, deepen dark colors, and, of course, print real blacks.

In case you're wondering how colors mix in the CMYK model, it's basically the opposite of the RGB model. Because pigments are not as pure as primary colors in the additive model, though, some differences exist:

✦ **Cyan and magenta.** Full-intensity cyan and magenta mix to form a deep blue with a little violet. Subtract some cyan to make purple; subtract some magenta to make a dull medium blue. All these colors assume a complete lack of yellow.

✦ **Magenta and yellow.** Full-intensity magenta and yellow mix to form a brilliant red. Subtract some magenta to make vivid orange; subtract some yellow to make rose. All these colors assume a complete lack of cyan.

✦ **Yellow and cyan.** Full-intensity yellow and cyan mix to form a bright green with a hint of blue. Subtract some yellow to make a deep teal; subtract some cyan to make chartreuse. All these colors assume a complete lack of magenta.

✦ **Cyan, magenta, and yellow.** Full-intensity cyan, magenta, and yellow mix to form a muddy brown.

✦ **Black.** Black pigmentation added to any other pigment darkens the color.

✦ **No pigment.** No pigmentation results in white (assuming white is the color of the paper).

Editing in CMYK

If you're used to editing RGB images, editing in the CMYK mode can require some new approaches, especially when editing individual color channels. When you view a single color channel in the RGB mode (as discussed later in this chapter), white indicates high-intensity color, and black indicates low-intensity color. It's the opposite in CMYK. When you view an individual color channel, black means high-intensity color and white means low-intensity color.

This doesn't mean RGB and CMYK color channels look like inverted versions of each other. In fact, because the color theory is inverted, they look much the same. But if you're trying to achieve the full-intensity colors mentioned in the preceding section, you should apply black to the individual color channels, not white as you would in the RGB mode.

Should I edit in CMYK?

RGB doesn't accurately represent the colors you get when you print an image because the RGB color space contains many colors — particularly very bright colors — that CMYK can't touch. This is why when you switch from RGB to CMYK, the colors appear somewhat dull.

For this reason, many people advocate working exclusively in the CMYK mode, but you might want to reconsider just blindly following this advice. Although working in CMYK eliminates color disappointments, it is also much slower because Photoshop has to convert CMYK values to your RGB screen on the fly.

Furthermore, your scanner and monitor are RGB devices. No matter how you work, a translation from RGB to CMYK color space must occur at some time. If you pay extra to purchase a commercial drum scan, for example, you simply make the translation at the beginning of the process — Scitex has no option but to use RGB sensors internally — rather than at the end. In fact, nearly every color device on Earth is RGB except the printer.

You should wait to convert to the CMYK mode until right before you print. After your artwork is finalized, choose Image ➪ Mode ➪ CMYK Color and make whatever edits you deem necessary. For example, you might want to introduce a few color corrections, apply some sharpening, and even retouch a few details by hand. Photoshop applies your changes more slowly in the CMYK mode, but at least you're slowed down only at the end of the job, not throughout the entire process.

Before converting an image to the CMYK color space, make certain Photoshop is aware of the monitor you're using and the printer you intend to use. These two items can have a pronounced effect on how Photoshop generates a CMYK image. You learn how to set up your personal RGB and CMYK color spaces in Chapter 16.

The advice about converting to CMYK before printing applies only to professional printing situations. If you're just in your home office printing to your inkjet printer, you should leave your image in RGB mode when you print. Your printer will handle the CMYK conversion internally, with no effort required from you.

Previewing the CMYK color space

While you're editing in RGB mode, you can *soft proof* your image — display a rough approximation of what the image will look like when converted to CMYK and printed. To display colors in the CMYK color space, choose View ➪ Proof Colors. You also can press Ctrl+Y (⌘-Y on the Mac). This command is a toggle, so you can also use the menu or keyboard shortcut to turn this preview off.

Before you proof your colors, however, you should select the output you want to preview from the View ➪ Proof Setup submenu. Photoshop creates the proof display based on your selection. You can preview the image using the current CMYK working space, choose Custom to specify a particular output device, or preview the individual cyan, magenta, yellow, and black plates. The plates appear as grayscale images unless you colorize them by selecting the Color Channels in Color option in the Display & Cursors panel of the Preferences dialog box (that's Ctrl+K, Ctrl+3 on the PC and ⌘-K, ⌘-3 on the Mac). If you work with an older-model color inkjet printer tnat prints using just cyan, magenta, and yellow, you can choose the Working CMY Plates option to see what your image will look like when printed without black ink.

View ➪ Gamut Warning (Ctrl+Shift+Y on the PC or ⌘-Shift-Y on the Mac) is a companion to Photoshop's CMYK preview commands that covers so-called out-of-gamut colors — RGB colors with no CMYK equivalents — with gray. You may find this command less useful because it demonstrates a problem without suggesting a solution. You can desaturate the grayed colors with the Sponge tool (which is explained in Chapter 5), but this doesn't accomplish anything that Photoshop won't do automatically. A CMYK preview is much more serviceable and representative of the final CMYK image.

CIE's Lab

RGB isn't the only mode that responds quickly and provides a bountiful range of colors. Photoshop's Lab color space comprises all the colors from RGB and CMYK and is every bit as fast as RGB. Many high-end users prefer to work in this mode, and even if you don't consider yourself "high end," give it a shot to see if you like it.

Whereas the RGB mode is the color model of your luminescent computer screen and the CMYK mode is the color model of the reflective page, Lab is independent of light or pigment. Perhaps you've already heard the bit about how, in 1931, an international color organization called the Commission Internationale d'Eclairage (CIE) developed a color model that, in theory, contains every single color the human eye can see. Then, in 1976, the CIE came up with two additional color systems. One of those systems was Lab, and the other was either a big secret or somebody lost the minutes to the meeting where the systems were devised, because we don't know what the other one was.

The beauty of the Lab color model is it fills in gaps in both the RGB and CMYK models. RGB, for example, provides an overabundance of colors in the blue-to-green range but is stingy on yellows, oranges, and other colors in the green-to-red range. Meanwhile, the colors missing from CMYK are as numerous as the holes in the Albert Hall. Lab gets everything right.

Understanding Lab anatomy

The Lab mode features three color channels, one for luminosity and two others for color ranges, known simply by the initials *a* and *b*. Upon hearing luminosity, you might think, "Of course, just like HSL," but that's not entirely so. To make things confusing (weren't they already?), Lab's *luminosity* is like HSB's brightness. White indicates full-intensity color.

Meanwhile, the *a* channel contains colors ranging from deep green (low-brightness values) to gray (medium-brightness values) to vivid pink (high-brightness values). The *b* channel ranges from bright blue (low-brightness values) to gray to burnt yellow (high-brightness values). As in the RGB model, these colors mix together to produce lighter colors. Only the brightness values in the luminosity channel darken the colors. So you can think of Lab as a two-channel RGB with brightness thrown on top. Now it's clear why in elementary school, you learn that red and blue make purple — can you imagine the reaction of an average five-year-old if you read him or her the beginning of this paragraph? "Pass me the crayons and shut up!"

Now, because it's very likely you're all over the age of five, take a closer look at how all of this works by trying the following simple experiment — there are no figures to accompany this exercise, because, as you may have noticed, this book is printed in black and white.

STEPS: Testing Out the Lab Mode

1. **Create a new image in the Lab mode — say, 300 x 300 pixels, setting the Background Contents option to White.**

2. **Press D to return the default colors to the Toolbox.** The foreground color is now black and the background color is white.

3. **Press Ctrl+2 (⌘-2 on the Mac).** This takes you to the *a* channel.

4. **Click the Gradient tool in the Toolbox.**

5. **In the Options bar, select the Foreground to Background option from the Gradient pop-up menu, select the Linear gradient style, and select Normal from the Mode pop-up menu.** (See Chapter 6 if you need help using these controls in the Options bar.)

6. **Shift-drag with the Gradient tool from the top to the bottom of the window.** This creates a vertical black-to-white gradation.

7. **Press Ctrl+3 (⌘-3 on the Mac).** This takes you to the *b* channel.

8. **Shift-drag from left to right with the Gradient tool.** Photoshop paints a horizontal gradation.

9. **Press Ctrl+~ (tilde) (⌘-~ on the Mac) to return to the composite display.** Now you can see all channels at once. If you're using a 24-bit monitor, you should be looking at a window filled with an incredible array of super bright colors. In theory, these are the brightest shades of all the colors you can see. In practice, however, the colors are limited by the display capabilities of your RGB monitor.

Using Lab

Because the Lab mode is device independent, you can use it to edit any image.
Editing in the Lab mode is as fast as editing in the RGB mode and several times
faster than editing in the CMYK mode. If you plan on printing your image to color
separations, you may want to experiment with using the Lab mode instead of RGB,
because Lab ensures no colors are altered when you convert the image to CMYK,
except to change colors that fall outside the CMYK range. In fact, any time you convert an image from RGB to CMYK, Photoshop automatically converts the image to
the Lab mode as an intermediate step.

Tip   If you work with photo CDs often, open the scans directly from the Photo CD format
        as Lab images. Kodak's proprietary YCC color model is nearly identical to Lab, so
        you can expect an absolute minimum of data loss; some people claim that no loss
        whatsoever occurs.

Indexed Color

Choose Image ➪ Mode ➪ Indexed Color to display the dialog box shown in Figure 4-3.
This command permits you to strip an image of all but its most essential colors.
Photoshop then generates a color look-up table (LUT) that describes the few remaining colors in the image. The LUT serves as an index, which is why the process is
called *indexing*.

Tip   Before the advent of the Save for Web dialog box, which was added to Photoshop
        in version 5, you needed to use the Indexed Color dialog box to prepare images
        for the Web — especially GIF images. However, with the Save for Web dialog box
        (accessed by choosing File ➪ Save for Web, or pressing the very finger-intensive Alt+
        Shift+Ctrl+S, or Opt-Shift-⌘-S on the Mac), you have the ability to both strip out
        colors and preview your results.

Photoshop doesn't let you apply the Indexed Color command to Lab or CMYK
images. And although you can apply Indexed Color to a grayscale image, you don't
get any control over the indexing process; Photoshop doesn't let you reduce the
image to fewer than 256 colors, for example. So if you want to index a Lab or CMYK
image or custom-prepare a grayscale image, choose Image ➪ Mode ➪ RGB to convert the image to the RGB mode and then choose Image ➪ Mode ➪ Indexed Color.
You also cannot index an image that you've converted to the 16 Bits/Channel mode,
which is discussed shortly. If you want to index such an image, you must first choose
Image ➪ Mode ➪ 8 Bits/Channel.

Caution   Don't expect to be able to edit your image after indexing it. Most of Photoshop's
           functions — including the Gradient tool, all the edit tools, and the filters — will
           refuse to work. Others, such as Feathering and the Brush tool, produce undesir-
           able effects. If you plan on editing an 8-bit image much in Photoshop, convert it to
           the RGB mode, edit it as desired, and then switch back to the Indexed Color mode
           when you finish.

Figure 4-3: Use the Palette option to select the kinds of colors that remain in the image. Use the Colors option to specify how many colors remain.

Now that you have all the warnings and special advice, the following list provides a brief rundown of the options inside the Indexed Color dialog box, along with some recommended settings for Web graphics:

✦ **Palette.** This pop-up menu tells Photoshop how to compute the colors in the look-up table. You have lots of options here, but only a handful are really useful. If your image already contains fewer than 256 colors, the Exact option appears by default, in which case you should just press Enter or Return and let the command do its stuff. The Web option converts your image to the 216 so-called "Web-safe" colors. The Adaptive option selects the most frequently used colors in your image, which typically delivers the best possible results. The Perceptual and Selective options are variations on Adaptive. But where Adaptive maintains the most popular colors, Perceptual is more intelligent, sampling the colors that produce the best transitions. The Selective option tries to maintain key colors, including those in the Web-safe palette. The Adaptive, Perceptual, and Selective options each come in two flavors: Local and Master. Choose Local if you want Photoshop to consider the colors in only the current image. If you have several images open and want to create a palette based on all the images, choose Master.

Tip

Select Perceptual for images in which smooth transitions are more important than color values. Use Selective when an image contains bright colors or sharp, graphic transitions. And if an image contains relatively few colors and you want to maintain those colors as exactly as possible, go for Adaptive.

✦ **Colors.** You can specify the number of colors in the palette by typing a number in this option box. As you can guess, fewer colors result in smaller files. For GIF images, I generally start with 64 colors. If the image looks okay, I try going even lower.

✦ **Forced.** This option enables you to lock in important colors so that they don't change. Black and White locks in black and white. Primaries protects 8 colors — white, red, green, blue, cyan, magenta, yellow, and black. And Web protects the 216 colors in the Web-safe palette. If you choose Custom, you can select the colors that you want to lock in.

✦ **Transparency.** If an image is set on a layer against a transparent background, selecting this option maintains that transparency. Bear in mind, however, that transparency in a GIF file is either on or off; there are no soft transitions as in a Photoshop layer.

✦ **Matte.** The Matte option works in collaboration with the Transparency option. (If an image has no transparency — that is, all layers cover one another to create a seamless opacity — the Matte option is dimmed.) When you select Transparency, the specified Matte color fills the translucent pixels in the image. When Transparency is deselected, the Matte color fills all translucent and transparent areas.

✦ **Dither.** This option controls how Photoshop mimics the colors that you asked it to remove from an image. The None setting maps each color in the image to its closest equivalent in the look-up table, pixel for pixel. This results in the harshest color transitions, but it is frequently the preferable option. Diffusion dithers colors randomly to create a naturalistic effect. Pattern dithers colors in a geometric pattern, which is altogether ugly. Noise mixes pixels throughout the image, not merely in areas of transition.

✦ **Amount.** When you choose Diffusion as the dithering mode, you can modify the amount of dithering by raising or lowering this value. Lower values produce harsher color transitions but decrease the file size. It's a trade-off. Keep an eye on the image window to see how low you can go.

✦ **Preserve Exact Colors.** This option is available only when the Diffusion option is selected from the Dither pop-up menu. When selected, this option turns off dithering inside areas of flat color that exactly match a color in the active palette. As mentioned before, you may often get better-looking images if you apply no dithering. But if you decide to dither, select the Preserve Exact Colors option. Even if you can't see a difference on your screen, it may show up on another screen.

Grayscale

Grayscale is pretty neat because it frees you from all the problems and potential expense of working with color and provides access to every bit of Photoshop's power and functionality. Anyone who says you can't do as much with grayscale as you can with color probably *likes* what Ted Turner did to great old movies like *It's a Wonderful Life*. Let's not even talk about it, it's too depressing. Anyway, you can print grayscale images to any laser printer, reproduce them in any publication, and edit them on nearly any machine. In addition to being universally printable and displayable, they look great, they remind you of classic movies (before Ted got his hands on 'em), and they make a humongous book, such as this one, affordable. What could be better?

Beyond discussing how neat Grayscale is, however, there isn't a whole lot to say about it. You can convert an image to the Grayscale mode regardless of its current mode, and you can convert from Grayscale to any other mode just as easily. In fact, choosing Image ➪ Mode ➪ Grayscale is a necessary step in converting a color image to a duotone or black-and-white bitmap. (You also can use the Channel Mixer command to create a custom grayscale version of a color image, as you learn near the end of this chapter.)

Search your channels before converting

When you convert an image from one of the color modes to the Grayscale mode, Photoshop normally weights the values of each color channel in a way that retains the apparent brightness of the overall image. For example, when you convert an image from RGB, Photoshop weights red more heavily than blue when computing dark values. This is because red is a darker-looking color than blue (much as that might seem contrary to popular belief).

Tip

If you choose Image ➪ Mode ➪ Grayscale while viewing a single color channel, Photoshop retains all brightness values in that channel only and abandons the data in the other channels. This can be an especially useful technique for rescuing a grayscale image from a bad RGB scan.

So before switching to the grayscale mode, be sure to look at the individual color channels — particularly the red and green channels (the blue channel frequently contains substandard detail) — to see how each channel might look on its own. To browse the channels, use the following shortcuts (on the Mac, substitute the ⌘ key for Ctrl): Press Ctrl+1 for red, Ctrl+2 for green, and Ctrl+3 for blue. Or Ctrl+1 for cyan, Ctrl+2 for magenta, Ctrl+3 for yellow, and Ctrl+4 for black. Or even Ctrl+1 for luminosity, Ctrl+2 for *a*, and Ctrl+3 for *b*. You read about color channels in more detail later in this chapter.

16 and 32 bits per channel

The potential number of colors an image can contain depends on the image's bit depth. A pixel 2 bits long can be one of four colors, and each additional bit doubles the number of colors available to the pixel. A typical RGB image contains 8 bits per channel, or a total of 24 bits (3 channels × 8 bits = 24 bits), which translates to 2^{24} = 16.8 million colors. You can increase the bit depth of an image by choosing Image ➪ Mode ➪ 16 Bits/Channel to convert the image to 16-bit mode, which gives you 2^{48} = 281.5 trillion colors. If you choose 32 Bits/Channel, you're looking at 2^{96}, which is equal to — well, a heck of a lot of colors.

Note When your images are in 32 Bits/Channel mode, they're considered HDR — High Dynamic Range — images, which are typically used in 3D rendering and advanced special effects software for animation. Photoshop's support for these images is increasing in recent versions, yet remains limited in Photoshop CS2. You can choose View, 32-bit Preview Options to choose the Method (Exposure and Gamma or Highlight Compression), and if you select the former, use the sliders to set the Exposure and Gamma levels for the preview.

 Tip Want to make your image a 32 Bits/Channel image? The command will be dimmed until you raise your RGB image to 16 bits/channel. After you increase the bits per channel in the image to 16, you can increase it again to 32 and take advantage of HDR viewing options.

When you consider that even the largest images don't contain more than a couple million pixels, and each pixel can display only one color, 281.5 trillion colors might seem like overkill. In most cases it probably is, but 16-bit mode, and certainly 32-bit mode, does offer one big advantage: You can apply multiple color adjustments without noticeably damaging your image. And now that most of Photoshop's features are applicable to images in 16-bit mode (fewer are applicable in 32-bit mode) — prior to version CS, many commonly used features, such as layers, text, and paint tools, were unavailable — it's more practical for everyday image editing.

But Photoshop's 16-bit and 32-bit modes have their drawbacks. Most significantly, when you double the bit depth of an image, you double the size of the file in memory, which can make for some very large and unwieldy files. You have a limited choice of file formats, including TIFF and PSD, but not JPEG, and most of the commands on the Filter menu are unavailable to images in 16-bit or 32-bit mode. Also note that the 16 Bits/Channel command is applicable to RGB, CMYK, Lab, and grayscale images but not indexed or black-and-white files, and only RGB images can be set to 32-bits/channel.

Black and white (bitmap)

Choose Image ➪ Mode ➪ Bitmap to convert a flattened grayscale image to exclusively black-and-white pixels. This may sound like a boring option, but it can prove useful for gaining complete control over the printing of grayscale images. After all, output devices such as laser printers and imagesetters render grayscale images as a series of tiny dots. Using the Bitmap command, you can specify the size, shape, and angle of those dots.

When you choose Image ⇨ Mode ⇨ Bitmap, Photoshop displays the Bitmap dialog box, shown in Figure 4-4. Here you specify the resolution of the black-and-white image and select a conversion process. The options work as follows:

✦ **Output.** Specify the resolution of the black-and-white file. If you want control over every single pixel available to your printer, raise this value to match your printer's resolution. As a general rule, try setting the Output value somewhere between 200 to 250 percent of the Input value.

Figure 4-4: The Bitmap dialog box converts images from grayscale to black and white.

✦ **50% Threshold.** Select this option from the Use pop-up menu to change every pixel that is darker than 50 percent gray to black and every pixel that is 50 percent gray or lighter to white. Unless you are working toward some special effect — for example, overlaying a black-and-white version of an image over the original grayscale image — this option most likely isn't for you. (And if you're working toward a special effect, Image ⇨ Adjustments ⇨ Threshold is the better alternative.)

✦ **Pattern Dither.** To *dither* pixels is to mix them up to emulate different colors. In this case, Photoshop mixes up black and white pixels to produce shades of gray. The Pattern Dither option (in the Use pop-up menu) dithers an image using a geometric pattern. Unfortunately, the results are pretty ugly, as demonstrated in the left example in Figure 4-5. And the space between dots has a tendency to fill in, especially when you output to a laser printer.

Figure 4-5: Compare the results of selecting the Pattern Dither option (the choppy-looking one on the left) to the Diffusion Dither option (the smoother one on the right).

✦ **Diffusion Dither.** Select this option from the Use pop-up menu to create a mezzotint-like effect, as demonstrated in the right example in Figure 4-5. Again, because this option converts an image into thousands of stray pixels, you can expect your image to darken dramatically when it is output to a low-resolution laser printer and reproduced. So be sure to lighten the image with something like the Levels command (as described in Chapter 17) before selecting this option.

✦ **Halftone Screen.** When you select this option from the Use pop-up menu and press Enter or Return, Photoshop displays the dialog box shown in Figure 4-6. These options enable you to apply a dot pattern to the image, as demonstrated in Figure 4-7. Type the number of dots per inch in the Frequency option box and the angle of the dots in the Angle option box. Then select a dot shape from the Shape pop-up menu. Figure 4-7 shows examples of three dot patterns applied to a photo of a zebra, each with a frequency of 24 lines per inch.

Cross-Reference

You can learn all about screen patterns and frequency settings in Chapter 18.

Figure 4-6: This dialog box appears when you select the Halftone Screen option in the Bitmap dialog box.

Figure 4-7: Three examples of halftone cell shapes (from left to right): Diamond, Line, and Cross. In all cases, the Frequency value was set to 24.

✦ **Custom Pattern.** To use a custom dither pattern, select this option from the Use pop-up menu and open the Custom Pattern palette, as shown in Figure 4-8. The palette includes a number of predefined patterns that ship with Photoshop as well as any custom preset patterns that you may have defined using Edit ⇨ Define Pattern. Simply click the icon for the pattern you want to use — the smaller or more intricate the pattern, the more detail you'll retain in the image. If you use a large-scale pattern, you may not recognize anything in the photo — which can be a good thing, if that's the effect you're looking for. Figure 4-8 also shows two examples of predefined patterns (Gravel and Woven) used as custom halftoning patterns.

Tip

To access additional preset patterns, choose Load Patterns from the palette menu (click the right-pointing triangle in the upper-right corner of the palette to display the menu). You can find the patterns in the Patterns folder, which lives inside the Presets folder. To delete a pattern from the palette, click its icon and choose Delete Pattern from the palette menu.

Figure 4-8: Two examples of employing repeating patterns as custom halftoning patterns — you can still make out the zebra's head, but he's become a design unto himself, thanks to the patterns' effects.

Cross-Reference   For a complete guide to creating and defining patterns in Photoshop, see Chapter 7.

Caution   Photoshop lets you edit individual pixels in the so-called Bitmap mode, but that's about the extent of it. After you go to black-and-white, you can neither perform any serious editing nor expect to return to the Grayscale mode and restore your original pixels. So be sure to finish your image editing before choosing Image ⇨ Mode ⇨ Bitmap. Even more important, make certain to save your image before converting it to black and white, and maybe save a backup copy of the image to go back to in case you discover problems after converting it to Bitmap mode. I would say that saving is always good idea prior to performing any color conversion, and when making any kind change that will limit the use of Photoshop's tools for editing an image, making a backup copy of the image is a smart thing to do.

Using Color Libraries

In addition to the Color Picker dialog box, Photoshop provides a handful of additional techniques for selecting colors. The next several sections explain how to use the Color Libraries dialog box, the Color palette, and the Eyedropper tool. When you've finished reading it, words like *Pantone* and *sampling* will become allegedly valuable additions to your vocabulary, and you can use them to dazzle your friends — at least the ones who don't know anything about Photoshop or commercial printing.

Predefined colors

If you click the Color Libraries button in the Color Picker dialog box, Photoshop displays the Color Libraries dialog box shown in Figure 4-9. In this dialog box, you can select from a variety of predefined colors by choosing the color family from the Book pop-up menu, moving the slider triangles up and down the color slider to specify a general range of colors, and ultimately, selecting a color from the color list on the left. If you own the swatchbook for a color family, you can locate a specific color by typing its number on the keyboard.

The color families represented in the Book pop-up menu fall into seven brands: ANPA (now actually NAA, as will be explained shortly), DIC, Focoltone, HKS, Pantone, Toyo, and Trumatch. At the risk of offending a few of these companies, you're likely to find certain brands more useful than others. The following sections briefly introduce the brands in order of their impact, from smallest to greatest, on the American market — with apologies to readers in other parts of the world, of course.

Tip   The most popular use for predefined colors in Photoshop is in the creation of duotones, tritones, and quadtones (described in Chapter 18). You can also use predefined colors to match the colors in a logo or some other important element in an image to a commercial standard. And you can add an independent channel for a predefined color and print it to a separate plate, as discussed later in this chapter.

Figure 4-9: The Color Libraries dialog box enables you to select predefined colors from brand-name libraries such as Pantone, Focoltone, and Trumatch.

Focoltone, DIC, Toyo, and HKS

Focoltone, Dianippon Ink and Chemical (DIC), Toyo, and HKS have a very small impact on the market and are foreign color standards with followings abroad. Focoltone is a British company, and DIC and Toyo are popular in the Japanese market, but have very few subscribers outside Japan. HKS formerly was provided only in the German and French versions of Photoshop, but enough people asked for it to be included in other languages that it now is available in all versions of the program.

Newspaper Association of America

American Newspaper Publishers Association (ANPA) is now part of NAA, which stands for Newspaper Association of America, and has updated its color catalog. NAA provides a small sampling of 45 process colors (mixes of cyan, magenta, yellow, and black ink) plus five spot colors (colors produced by printing a single ink). The idea behind the NAA colors is to isolate the color combinations that reproduce most successfully on inexpensive newsprint and to provide advertisers with a solid range of colors from which to choose, without allowing the color choices to get out of hand.

Trumatch

Designed entirely using a desktop system and created especially with desktop publishers in mind, the Trumatch Colorfinder swatchbook features more than 2,000 process colors, organized according to hue, saturation, and brightness. Each hue is broken down into 40 tints and shades. Reducing the saturation in 15 percent increments creates tints; adding black ink in 6 percent increments creates shades. The result is a guide that shows you exactly which colors you can attain using a desktop system. If you're wondering what a CMYK blend will look like when printed, you need look no further than the Trumatch Colorfinder.

As if the Colorfinder weren't enough, Trumatch provides the ColorPrinter Software utility, which automatically prints the entire 2,000-color library to any PostScript-compatible output device. The utility integrates EfiColor and PostScript Level 2, thereby enabling design firms and commercial printers to test the entire range of capabilities available to their hardware. Companies can provide select clients with swatches of colors created on their own printers, guaranteeing that what you see is darn well what you'll get.

Pantone

On the heels of Trumatch, Pantone released a 3,006-color Process Color System Guide (labeled Pantone Process in the Book pop-up menu) priced at around $85. Pantone also produces the foremost spot-color swatchbook, the Color Formula Guide. Then there's the Solid to Process Guide, which enables you to figure out quickly if you can closely match a Pantone spot color using a process-color blend or if you ought to give it up and stick with the spot color.

Pantone spot colors are ideal for creating duotones and adding custom colors to an image for logos and the like, both discussed in Chapter 18. Furthermore, Pantone is supported by every computer application that aspires to the color prepress market. As long as the company retains the old competitive spirit, you can, most likely, expect Pantone to remain the primary color-printing standard for years to come.

The Color palette

Another means of selecting colors in Photoshop is to use the Color palette, shown in Figure 4-10. The Color palette is convenient, it's always there, and it doesn't hog your screen like the Color Picker dialog box. Frankly, this is the tool I use most often to select colors in Photoshop.

To display the palette, choose Window ➪ Color or press F6. If you want, you can dock the palette in the docking well, making it easily grabable whenever you need it. For details on how to dock a palette, go back to Chapter 2. Either way, you use the elements and options in the palette as follows:

Figure 4-10: The Color palette as it appears normally (top) and with the Web Color Sliders option selected (bottom).

✦ **Foreground color** or **background color.** Click the foreground or background color icon in the Color palette to specify the color you want to edit. If you click the foreground or background color icon when it's already highlighted — as indicated by a double-line frame — Photoshop displays the Color Picker dialog box.

✦ **Sliders.** Click and drag the triangles in the slider controls to edit the highlighted color. By default, the sliders represent the red, green, and blue primary colors when a color image is open. You can change the slider bars by choosing a different color model from the palette menu.

✦ **Option boxes.** Alternatively, you can type numerical values in the option boxes to the right of the sliders. Press Tab to advance from one option box to the next; press Shift+Tab to go to the previous option.

✦ **Alert triangle** and **cube.** Photoshop displays the alert triangle when a color falls outside the CMYK color gamut. The color swatch to the right of the triangle shows the closest CMYK equivalent. Click the triangle or the color swatch to replace the current color with the CMYK equivalent.

If you select the Web Color Sliders option from the palette menu, the alert cube appears to indicate colors that aren't included in the Web-safe palette. The palette also displays the hexadecimal values for the color, as shown in Figure 4-10. And as you drag the sliders, they automatically snap to Web-safe hues. To limit the palette so that it displays only Web-safe colors, choose Make Ramp Web Safe from the palette menu.

Tip
If you're writing your own HTML code to set up a Web page, you can use the Color palette to help you grab the hexadecimal number for any color you're using on the page. After you define a Web color, choose Copy Color as HTML from the palette menu to save the hexadecimal code for the color to the Clipboard. You can then paste the code into an HTML file by choosing Edit ➪ Paste in the Web application.

✦ **Color bar.** The bar along the bottom of the Color palette displays all colors in the CMYK spectrum. Click or drag inside the color bar (your mouse pointer turns to an eyedropper when you're pointing in or on the bar) and make the color you choose the current foreground or background color. Which color it becomes depends on whether the foreground or background icon is selected. The sliders update as you drag. Alt-click (Option-click on the Mac) or drag to lift the background color if the foreground icon is selected or the foreground color if the background color is selected.

You needn't accept the CMYK spectrum in the color bar, however. To change to a different spectrum, just choose the spectrum from the palette menu. Or Shift-click the color bar to cycle through the available spectrums. You can opt for the RGB spectrum, a black-to-white gradation (Grayscale Ramp), or a gradation from the current foreground color to the current background color (Current Colors). The color bar continuously updates to represent the newest foreground and background colors.

Notice the black and white squares at the right end of the color bar? You can click 'em to set a color to absolute black or white. But if all you want to do is set the foreground color to black, don't bother with the Color palette — just press D. For white, press D and then X. The first shortcut restores the foreground and background colors to black and white, respectively; pressing X swaps the colors to make white the foreground color and black the background color.

The Swatches palette

Choose Window ➪ Swatches to display the Swatches palette, shown in Figure 4-11, which lets you collect colors for future use, sort of like a list of favorites. You can also use the palette to set the foreground and background colors.

Here's how to take advantage of the Swatches palette:

✦ Click a color swatch to make that color the foreground color. Ctrl-click (⌘-click on the Mac) to set the background color.

✦ To add the current foreground color to the reservoir, Shift-click an existing color swatch to replace the old color or click an empty swatch to append the new color. In either case, your cursor temporarily changes to a Paint Bucket. After you click, you're asked to give the swatch a name. Type the name and click OK. If you later want to change the name, just double-click the swatch to redisplay the name dialog box.

Tip   You can bypass the dialog box and add an unnamed color to the palette by Alt-clicking (Option-clicking on the Mac) an empty space in the palette.

✦ To delete a color from the palette, Alt-click (Option-click on the Mac) a color swatch. Your cursor changes to a pair of scissors and cuts the color away.

✦ The Swatches palette includes a New icon (it's the one that looks like a page) and a Trash icon, similar to those you find in the Layers palette. The icons provide alternative methods of adding and deleting colors: Click the New icon to add a new swatch in the current foreground color; Alt-click (or Option-click on the Mac) to display the Name dialog box and then add the color. Drag a swatch to the Trash icon to delete it from the palette.

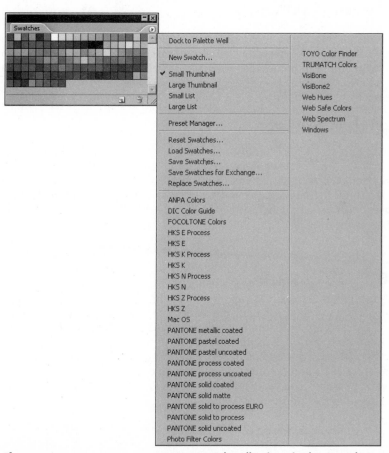

Figure 4-11: You can create custom swatch collections in the Swatches palette.

You can also save and load color palettes on disk using options in the palette menu. Load Swatches appends swatches stored in a swatches file to the current set of swatches; Replace Swatches replaces the current swatches with the ones in the file. Save Swatches lets you create a new swatch collection and save it to disk.

The Presets folder, located inside the main Photoshop folder, contains folders for all available preset items — tool presets (see Chapter 2) and color swatches are only two of them. The Photoshop Only folder, found inside the Color Swatches folder of the Presets folder, contains palettes for the major color libraries from Pantone, Trumatch, and others. You can load these palettes by simply selecting them from the palette pop-up menu. You're then given the choice of appending the swatches to the existing swatches or replacing the current swatches altogether. Custom swatch sets that you create also appear on the palette menu, but only after you close and restart Photoshop.

Tip

When a color library palette is loaded, positioning your cursor over a color swatch displays a tool tip showing the name of that color. If you prefer to select colors by using the color names, select Small List from the palette menu. Now you see a scrolling list of colors instead of just the swatches.

Swatches presets

You can also create and manage swatch collections using the Preset Manager dialog box. Choose Preset Manager from the Swatches palette menu, choose Edit ➪ Preset Manager, and then choose Swatches from the Preset Type pop-up menu, or choose Edit ➪ Preset Manager, and then press Ctrl+2 (⌘-2 on the Mac) to display the Swatches presets panel, shown in Figure 4-12. The presets panel shows the current swatch set.

Many functions in the Swatches panel of the Preset Manager duplicate those offered by the Swatches palette. If you click the arrowhead to the upper left of the Done button (see the figure), a pop-up menu appears that's nearly identical to the Swatches palette menu. You can choose the Replace Swatches command on the pop-up menu to replace the current swatch collection with another or choose Reset Swatches to return to the default swatch collection. To append a collection, click Load. Alternatively, click a collection name in the pop-up menu, in which case you have the choice of appending or replacing the current collection with the new one. To create a new swatch collection comprised of colors from an existing set, Shift-click the swatches you want to include, click Save Set, and then name the collection and store it in the Color Swatches folder.

Cross-Reference

For complete details on using the Preset Manager, see Chapter 2.

Figure 4-12: To easily create a new swatch collection using just some colors from an existing collection, head for the Preset Manager.

The Eyedropper tool

The Eyedropper tool — which you can select by pressing I — provides the most convenient and straightforward means of selecting colors in Photoshop. The process is so straightforward, in fact, that you may be surprised that there is so much to say about it — but there is, so you might as well read on:

✦ **Selecting a foreground color.** To select a new foreground color, click the desired color inside any open image window with the Eyedropper tool. (This assumes the foreground icon in the Color palette is selected, which it will be by default, unless you've tinkered with the palette. If the background icon is selected, Alt-click or Option-click with the Eyedropper tool to lift the foreground color.) You can even click inside the image window of an open, yet inactive image to lift a color without bringing that window to the foreground.

Tip

To select a color on your computer screen that isn't contained in one of Photoshop's image windows, click inside an image window with the Eyedropper, and then drag the tool outside the window. This means that you can select a color found on the Photoshop workspace, or on your Windows or Mac desktop, should the Photoshop window not be obscuring the desktop beneath it. As you drag the Eyedropper, you'll see it pick up all the colors you pass — to select one of the colors as you drag over it, just release the mouse and see that color appear in the Foreground Color block (or the Background Color block, if that's what you have selected in the Color palette).

✦ **Selecting a background color.** To select a new background color, Alt-click (Option-click on the Mac) the desired color with the Eyedropper tool. (Again, this assumes that the foreground icon is selected in the Color palette. If the background icon is selected, click with the Eyedropper to lift the background color.)

✦ **Skating over the color spectrum.** You can animate the foreground color icon by clicking and dragging with the Eyedropper tool. As soon as you achieve the desired color, release the mouse button. To animate the background color icon, Alt-drag (or Option-drag on the Mac) with the Eyedropper tool. The icon color changes as you move the Eyedropper tool. Again, swap these procedures if the background color icon is selected in the Color palette.

✦ **Sampling multiple pixels.** Normally, the Eyedropper tool selects the color from the single pixel you click. If you prefer to average the colors of several neighboring pixels, however, select either the 3 by 3 Average or 5 by 5 Average option from the Sample Size pop-up menu in the Options bar. Or right-click (Control-click on the Mac) with the Eyedropper to display a pop-up menu of sampling options near the cursor. In this case, you get one additional option, Copy Color as HTML, which works just as it does when you select it from the Color palette pop-up menu. Photoshop determines the hexadecimal code for the color and sends the code to the Clipboard so that you can use Edit ⇨ Paste to dump the code into an HTML file.

Tip   To access the Eyedropper tool temporarily (and set a new Foreground color) when using a Type, Paint Bucket, Gradient, Line, Pencil, or Brush tool, press and hold Alt (or Option on the Mac). The Eyedropper cursor remains in force for as long as Alt or Option is pressed, and then when you release the key, you return to the tool that you were using before activating the Eyedropper. To set the Background color, switch to the Eyedropper tool by pressing I and then Alt-click (Option-click on the Mac) in an image window.

The Color Sampler tool

Found in the same Toolbox flyout as the Eyedropper, the Color Sampler tool looks like the Eyedropper with a little cross-hair target. Unlike the Eyedropper, however, which lifts foreground and background colors, the Color Sampler merely measures the colors of pixels so that you can monitor how the pixels react to various color changes.

Select the Color Sampler and click somewhere inside the image window. By default, the tool is set to Point Sample (see the Options bar's Sample Size) and Photoshop adds a cross-hair target to indicate the point you clicked. You can also switch to 3 by 3 Average or 5 by 5 Average to sample groups of pixels instead. When you begin using the Color Sampler, Photoshop opens the Info palette (or brings it to the top of its palette group—it is grouped by default with the Navigator and Histogram palettes—if it was already open) and adds a new color measurement item labeled #1. This item corresponds to the target in the image, which is also labeled #1. Click again and you add a second target and a corresponding item #2 in the Info palette. You can add up to four targets to an image, as demonstrated in Figure 4-13, which also shows the Info palette and four targets' worth of information.

Cross-Reference

The Color Sampler is intended primarily for printers and technicians who want to monitor the effects of color corrections on specific points in an image. If you apply Image ⇨ Adjustments ⇨ Levels, for example, Photoshop constantly updates the items in the Info palette to reflect your changes (for more detail, see Chapter 17). But you can also sample points in an image to monitor the effects of filters (see Chapters 10 and 11), blend modes (Chapter 13), and edit tools, such as Dodge and Burn (Chapter 5). The Color Sampler is just another way to monitor changes to an image.

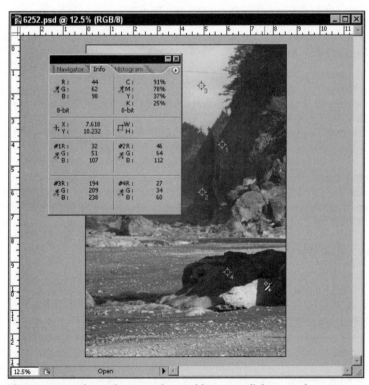

Figure 4-13: The Color Sampler tool lets you click on and measure the colors of four points in your image. You can also measure a fifth point by merely moving the cursor around, without clicking.

Here are a few more techniques of interest when color sampling:

✦ Photoshop limits you to four color targets. If you try to create a fifth one, the program generates an error message. If you want to measure a different point in the image, you can either position your cursor over the point and note the top set of color values in the Info palette (as in Figure 4-13) or move one of the existing targets to the spot you now want to sample.

✦ To move a target inside the image window, click and drag it with the Color Sampler tool. You can move a target also by pressing Ctrl (Win) or ⌘ (Mac) and dragging the target with the Eyedropper tool. Press and hold Shift to constrain the drag to a 45-degree angle.

✦ To delete a target, Alt-click (Win) or Option-click (Mac) it. To delete all targets, click the Clear button in the Options bar.

✦ The Info palette grows to more than twice its normal size when you start clicking with the Color Sampler. To hide the sampler information without deleting targets, click the Info palette's collapse box or choose Color Samplers from the palette menu. If you go the second route, you have to choose Color Samplers again to bring the samples back.

✦ By default, the sampler items in the Info palette measure colors in the active color space. If you want to track a target in a different color space, click the item's Eyedropper icon in the Info palette or right-click (Control-click on the Mac) the target in the image window. Either way, you get a pop-up menu of color-space alternatives, including Grayscale, RGB, and several others that you may recall from previous explanations in this chapter.

Tip

To select the Color Sampler, press I when the Eyedropper is active or Alt-click (Option-click on the Mac) the Eyedropper icon. Or press I repeatedly to cycle between the Eyedropper, Color Sampler, and Measure tool (add Shift if you selected the Use Shift Key for Tool Switch option in the Preferences dialog box). You can temporarily access the Color Sampler any time the Eyedropper is active by pressing Shift. You can also use this convenient trigger when a color correction dialog box such as Levels or Curves is open, as explained in Chapter 17.

Introducing Color Channels

It might surprise you, especially in a chapter devoted to color, to read that Photoshop approaches a full-color image not as a single collection of 24-bit pixels but as three or four bands of 8-bit (grayscale) pixels. This is because Photoshop is really a grayscale editor, even though it offers tools for applying, tweaking, printing, and displaying color. How does this work in a color image? An RGB file contains a band of red, a band of green, and a band of blue, each of which functions as a separate grayscale image. A Lab image likewise contains three bands, one corresponding to luminosity and the others to the variables a and b. A CMYK file contains four bands, one for each of the process-color inks. These bands are known as *channels*.

Channels frequently correspond to the structure of an input or output device. Each channel in a CMYK image, for example, corresponds to a different printer's plate when the document goes to press. The cyan plate is inked with cyan, the magenta plate is inked with magenta, and so on. Each channel in an RGB image corresponds to a pass of the red, green, or blue scanner sensor over the original photograph or artwork. Only the Lab mode is device independent, so its channels don't correspond to any piece of hardware.

For those of you who just said "So?"

You're not alone in thinking that channels are something you don't really need to think about. Like many people, you use Photoshop to edit the way a photo looks and prints, and isolating one of the aforementioned channels is something you've never had to do in the past (assuming you've used Photoshop before, even momentarily), and your photos look just fine, thank you.

But what would you do if your client is self-publishing a book about bird-watching and wants you to use what turn out to be some really below-average photos? Given that many bird sightings are fleeting, irreproducible events, you can't say, "Man, these are awful. Can you go out again and get a new shot of this yellow-bellied sapsucker?" No, you have to go with what he's given you, and that's it. So you're faced with tinkering endlessly with Photoshop's commands found in the Image ⇨ Adjustments submenu, and maybe some filters, and that fails to fix up these really abysmal images. Then, suddenly, it hits you that you've never really looked at that Channels palette. Maybe it can help you, maybe there's something there. You choose Window ⇨ Channels, and before you stand four bands in the palette, one labeled RGB, one labeled Red, another Green, and finally Blue (this is an RGB image in this dream sequence). You click the different bands (much like activating layers in the Layers palette) and you look at the channels in your image.

How channels work

So now that you're hopefully sold you on the value of channels, how do you use them? First, some math (don't yawn, pay attention).

For a typical full-color image, Photoshop devotes 8 bits of data to each pixel in each channel, thus permitting 256 brightness values, from 0 (black) to 255 (white). Therefore, each channel is actually an independent grayscale image. At first, this may throw you off. If an RGB image is made up of Red, Green, and Blue channels, why do all the channels look gray?

Photoshop provides an option in the Display & Cursors panel of the Preferences dialog box (that's Ctrl+K, Ctrl+3 on the PC and ⌘-K, ⌘-3 on the Mac) called Color Channels in Color. When selected, this function displays each channel in its corresponding primary color. But although this feature can be reassuring — particularly to novices — it's equally counterproductive.

When you view an 8-bit image composed exclusively of shades of red, for example, it's easy to miss subtle variations in detail that may appear obvious when you print the image. You may have problems accurately gauging the effect of filters and tonal adjustments. I mean, face it, red isn't a friendly shade to stare at for a half hour of intense editing. So leave the Color Channels in Color option deselected and temporarily suspend your biological urge for on-screen color. With a little experience, you'll be able to better monitor your adjustments and predict the outcome of your edits in plain old grayscale.

Cross-Reference   You can add channels above and beyond those required to represent a color or grayscale image for the purpose of storing masks, as described in Chapter 9. But even then, each channel is typically limited to 8 bits of data per pixel — meaning that it's just another grayscale image. Mask channels do not affect the appearance of an image on-screen or when it is printed. Rather, they serve to save selection outlines, as Chapter 9 explains.

Switching and viewing channels

To access channels in Photoshop, display the Channels palette by choosing Window ⇨ Channels. Every channel in the image appears in the palette — including any mask channels — as shown in Figure 4-14. Photoshop even shows a thumbnail view of each channel so that you can see what it looks like.

To switch to a different channel, click a channel name in the Channels palette. The channel name becomes selected — like the Blue channel in Figure 4-14 — showing that you can now edit it independently of other channels in the image.

Tip   To edit more than one channel at a time, click one channel name, and then Shift-click another. You can also Shift-click an active channel to deactivate it independently of any others.

When you select a single channel, Photoshop displays that one channel's content in the active image window. However, you can view additional channels beyond those that you want to edit. To specify which channels appear and which remain invisible, click in the boxes in the far-left column of the Channels palette. Click the Visibility icon (an eye, as appears in the Layers palette, also used there to also hide and display) to make the eye disappear and therefore hide that channel. Click where there is no eye and an eye appears, thus displaying the channel.

When only one channel is visible, that channel appears as a grayscale picture in the image window (possibly colorized in accordance with the Color Channels in Color option in the Preferences dialog box). However, when more than one channel is visible, you always see color. If both the Blue and Green channels are visible, for example, the image appears blue-green. If the Red and Green channels are visible, the image has a yellow cast, and so on.

Figure 4-14: Photoshop displays tiny thumbnails of each color channel in the Channels palette.

In addition to the individual channels, Photoshop provides access to a *composite view* that displays all colors in an RGB, a CMYK, or a Lab image at once. (The composite view does not show mask channels; you have to specify their display separately.) The composite view is listed first in the Channels palette and is displayed by default. Notice that when you select the composite view, the names of all individual color channels in the Channels palette become highlighted along with the composite channel. This shows that all the channels are active. The composite view is the default in which you will perform the majority of your image editing.

Press Ctrl (or ⌘ on the Mac) plus a number key to switch between color channels. Depending on the color mode you're working in, Ctrl+1 (⌘-1 on the Mac) takes you to the Red (RGB), Cyan (CMYK), or Luminosity (Lab) channel — the first band in the palette; Ctrl+2 takes you to the Green, Magenta, or *a* channel; and Ctrl+3 takes you to the Blue, Yellow, or *b* channel. In CMYK mode, Ctrl+4 displays the Black channel. Other Ctrl-key equivalents — up to Ctrl+9 — take you to mask or spot-color channels (if there are any). To go to the composite view, press Ctrl+~ (tilde) (⌘-~ on the Mac), of course. Tilde, in case you aren't familiar with it, is typically the Shift value of the key to the left of 1, or on some keyboards, to the right of the spacebar.

Note   You do not need to press Shift to execute a keyboard shortcut that includes the tilde character or any other Shift value character.

The shortcuts are slightly different when you're working on a grayscale image. You access the image itself by pressing Ctrl+1 (⌘-1 on the Mac). Ctrl+2 (⌘-2 on the Mac) and higher take you to extra spot-color and mask channels.

Tip
When editing a single channel, you may find it helpful to monitor the results in both grayscale and full-color views. Choose Window ➪ Arrange ➪ New Window to create a new window for the image, and then press Ctrl+~ (tilde) to set it to the color composite view. Then return to the first window and edit away on the individual channel. One of the amazing benefits of creating multiple views in Photoshop is that the views may show entirely different channels, layers, and other image elements — so create as many new windows of the image in progress as you need.

Trying Channels on for Size

Of course, if you're like most people, you need to see or use something to understand it. Luckily, channels are something you can both see and use, and the following sections show you exactly how to use channels for each of the major image color modes, and how to control what's seen in the Channels palette.

RGB channels

Suppose that the Alaskan seal is an RGB image. Figure 4-15 compares a grayscale composite of this same image (created by choosing Image ➪ Mode ➪ Grayscale) with the contents of the Red, Green, and Blue color channels from the original color image. The Green channel is closest to the grayscale composite because green is such a dominant color in the image. The Red channel differs the most from the grayscale composite, simply because the image doesn't have much red. The overall darkness of the Red channel bears this out. The pixels in the Blue channel are lightest in the water because — you guessed it — the water is rich with blue (and in this case, oil, but that's another story).

As you look at Figure 4-15, you probably notice that each of the channel versions of the image has its own unique and interesting qualities. For example, the Red channel is darker overall, and the oily water looks more dense and, well, oily. You can feel the weight of the water and the ripples around the seal look less like clean, clear water. The Blue channel looks more washed out overall, and you focus more on the seal, and the name of the ship in the background. Both versions of the image make a similar statement, but in different ways. The Green channel, being closest to the grayscale composite of the image, doesn't say anything that the image as a whole doesn't say on its own.

Grayscale composite

Red channel

Green channel

Blue channel

Figure 4-15: A grayscale composite of an image from the Exxon Valdez oil spill, with views of the same photo's Red, Green, and Blue color channels

The point? If you see that one of your channels, when viewed on its own, creates an interesting version that you might like to keep, remember that when converting a color image to grayscale, you have the option of retaining the image exactly as it appears in one of the channels. You can also calculate a grayscale composite by choosing Image ➪ Mode ➪ Grayscale when viewing all colors in the image in the composite view. To retain a single channel only, switch to that channel, and then choose Image ➪ Mode ➪ Grayscale. Instead of the usual *Discard color information?* message, Photoshop displays the message *Discard other channels?* If you click OK, Photoshop throws out the other channels in favor of the interesting single channel you've elected to keep. Of course, you might want to save a backup copy of the image before doing any of this, so that you can go back to the color, multichannel image at any time.

When the Warning dialog box appears, select the Do Not Show Again option if you don't want Photoshop to ask for permission to dump color information or channels when you convert to grayscale. But do so at your peril if you're one of those mere humans who forgets things from time to time — without the warning, you might not realize that you have a single channel selected and end up tossing the other channels when all you meant to do was convert to grayscale. Of course, if you fail to heed my warning here, and you grow to miss the warning, click Reset All Warning Dialogs on the General panel of the Preferences dialog box.

CMYK channels

If only to show you the interesting single-channel versions of this photo in CMYK and Lab modes, Figures 4-16 and 4-17 (respectively) show the channels from the image after it was converted to these two color modes. In Figure 4-16, the image has been converted to the CMYK mode with each of the individual channels captured. Because this color mode relies on pigments rather than light, as explained in the section "CMYK," dark areas in the channels represent high color intensity.

The CMY channels have more contrast than their RGB pals, but the basic brightness distribution is the same. Here's another graphic demonstration of color theory. You would think that the CMY channels would be very similar to the RGB channels — one color model would simply be the other turned on its head, with cyan pairing up with blue, magenta with red, and yellow with green. But they don't — and as a result, Photoshop has to boost the contrast of the CMY channels and throw in black to punch up those shadows.

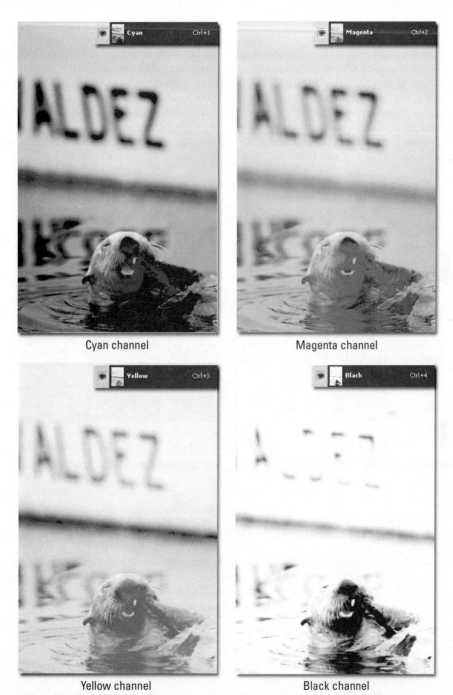

Cyan channel

Magenta channel

Yellow channel

Black channel

Figure 4-16: The contents of the cyan, magenta, yellow, and black channels from the image first seen in Figure 4-15

Lab channels

To create Figure 4-17, the original images was converted to the Lab mode. The image in the luminosity channel looks similar to the grayscale composite in Figure 4-15 because it contains the lightness and darkness values for the image. The *a* channel maps the greens and magentas, while the *b* channel maps the yellows and blues, so both channels are working hard to provide color information for this photograph. Certainly there are differences — the seal is much darker in the *a* channel, and there is a dark halo around the seal's head and the letters on the side of the ship in the *b* channel — but the two channels carry roughly equivalent amounts of color information.

Lightness channel (luminosity)	"a" channel (greens are darkest)	"b" channel (blues are darkest)

Figure 4-17: The contents of the luminosity channel and the *a* and *b* color channels after converting the original image to Lab mode

Other Channel Functions

In addition to viewing and editing channels using any of the techniques discussed in future chapters of this book, you can choose commands from the Channels palette menu and select icons along the bottom of the palette (labeled back in Figure 4-14). The following items explain how the commands and icons work.

Cross-Reference You may notice "see Chapter 9" (or words to that effect) every so often as these options are explained because many of them are specifically designed to accommodate masks, the main topic of Chapter 9. This list is designed to introduce you to *all* the options in the Channels palette, even if you'll need more background to use a few of them. After the options are introduced, you'll revisit the ones that have a direct effect on managing the colors in your image.

✦ **Palette Options.** Even though this is the last command in the menu, it's the easiest, so you can start with it. When you choose Palette Options, Photoshop displays four Thumbnail Size radio buttons, enabling you to change the size of the thumbnail previews that appear along the left side of the Channels palette. Why might you want to change the thumbnail size? Most likely so that you can see the image and see the differences between the individual channels' views from within the palette — large gives you the best view, and None, of course, gives you, well, None. The default is small, and for the terminally wishy-washy, there's medium.

Have you ever wondered what those thumbnail icons in the Palette Options dialog box are supposed to show? No? Well, shame on you for not being more inquisitive. Whether you want to know or not, you're gonna find out. They're silhouettes of tiny Merlins (wizards) on a painter's palette. Want proof? Switch to the Layers palette and choose Palette Options and you'll see them in color. But how do I know they're specifically Merlins? Press Alt (Option on the Mac) when choosing Palette Options to see the magician up close. This is a real "Easter egg" here — going back to Photoshop 2.5.

✦ **New Channel.** Choose this command to add a mask channel to the current image. The Channel Options dialog box appears, requesting that you name the channel. You also can specify the color and translucency that Photoshop applies to the channel when you view it with other channels. We explain how these options work in Chapter 9.

You can also create a new channel by clicking the Create New Channel icon at the bottom of the Channels palette (it's the one that looks like a little page with a dog-eared corner). Photoshop creates the channel without displaying the dialog box. To force the dialog box to appear, Alt-click (Option-click on the Mac) the page icon.

How many channels can one image contain? The answer used to be 24, but as of the release of Photoshop CS, you can have up to 56 total channels, regardless of color mode — and of course in Photoshop CS2, you can still have all 56 of 'em.

✦ **Duplicate Channel.** Choose this command to create a duplicate of the selected channel, either inside the same document or as part of a new document. (If the composite view is active, the Duplicate Channel command is dimmed because you can duplicate only one channel at a time.) The most common reason to use this command is to convert a channel into a mask. Again, you can find real-life applications in Chapter 9.

You can duplicate a channel also by dragging the channel name onto the new channel icon. No dialog box appears; Photoshop merely names the channel automatically. To copy a channel to a different document, drag the channel name and drop it into an open image window. Photoshop automatically creates a new channel for the duplicate.

✦ **Delete Channel.** To delete a channel from an image, click the channel name in the palette and choose this command. You can delete only one channel at a time. The Delete Channel command is dimmed when any essential color channel is active or when more than one channel is selected.

Tip

If you're all tuckered out and choosing a command is too much effort, just drag the channel onto the delete channel icon (the little trash icon in the lower-right corner of the Channels palette). You can also click the trash icon, in which case Photoshop asks you if you really want to delete the channel — a nice little reminder and your last chance to rethink. Of course, if you are absolutely sure and don't want Photoshop questioning your intentions, you can bypass this warning by Alt-clicking (Option-clicking on the Mac) the trash icon.

✦ **New Spot Channel.** Photoshop lets you add spot-color channels to an image. Each spot-color channel prints to a separate plate, just like spot colors in Illustrator or QuarkXPress. When you choose the New Spot Channel command, Photoshop asks you to specify a color and a Solidity (see Figure 4-18). Click the color square to display the Color Picker and then as needed, click the Color Libraries button to bring up the Color Libraries dialog box, from which you can select a Pantone or other spot color. The Solidity option in the New Spot Channel dialog box lets you set the opacity of the ink, perfect for special effects inks like Day-Glo fluorescents and metallics.

Tip

To create a spot-color channel without choosing a command, Ctrl-click (⌘-click on the Mac) the page icon at the bottom of the Channels palette. For more information on spot-color channels, see Chapter 18.

Figure 4-18: Create a spot channel and then specify its color and density. The more solid the color, the more the ink in the new channel will obscure the other inks in the image.

✦ **Merge Spot Channel.** Select a spot-color channel and choose this command to merge the spot color with the RGB, Lab, or CMYK colors in the image. Most spot colors don't have precise RGB or CMYK equivalents, so you will lose some color fidelity in the merge. Adobe includes this command to enable you to proof an image to a typical midrange color printer.

✦ **Channel Options.** Choose this command or double-click the channel name in the palette's scrolling list to change the settings assigned to a spot-color or mask channel. The Channel Options command is dimmed when a regular, everyday color channel is active.

✦ **Split Channels.** When you choose this command, Photoshop splits off each channel in an image to its own independent grayscale image window with the channel color appended to the end of the window name. The Split Channels command is useful as a first step in redistributing channels in an image before choosing Merge Channels, which is demonstrated later in this chapter.

✦ **Merge Channels.** Choose this command to merge several images into a single multichannel image. The images you want to merge must be open, grayscale, and absolutely equal in size — the same number of pixels horizontally and vertically — so be sure to verify these common attributes before proceeding. When you choose Merge Channels, Photoshop displays the Merge Channels dialog box, shown in Figure 4-19. It then assigns a color mode for the new image based on the number of open grayscale images that contain the same number of pixels as the foreground image.

Figure 4-19: The two dialog boxes that appear after you choose Merge Channels enable you to select a color mode for the merged image (top) and associate images with color channels (bottom).

You can override Photoshop's choice by selecting a different option from the Mode pop-up menu. (Generally, you won't want to change the value in the Channels option box because doing so causes Photoshop to automatically select Multichannel from the Mode pop-up menu. You'll find out more about multichannel images in the section "Using multichannel techniques.")

After you press Enter or Return, Photoshop displays a second dialog box, which also appears in Figure 4-19. In this dialog box, you can specify which grayscale image goes with which channel by choosing options from pop-up menus. When working from an image split with the Split Channels command, Photoshop automatically organizes each window into a pop-up menu according to the color appended to the window's name.

Color Channel Effects

Now that you know how to navigate among channels and apply commands, it's time to talk about *why* you'd do such things. The most pragmatic applications for channel effects involve the restoration of bad color scans, and if you use a color scanner, you know what is meant by "bad color scans." Everyone has ended up with scans that look like everyone in the photo was terminally embarrassed, nauseated, or under water. The excess red, green/yellow, or blue can be eliminated with some of the Image ⇨ Adjustment submenu tools, of course, but with channels, you can target the specific problems with color and also with clarity and the lack of clean edges within the image and fix them efficiently.

Improving the appearance of color scans

The following are a few channel-editing techniques you can use to improve the appearance of poorly scanned full-color images. Keep in mind that these techniques don't work miracles, but they can make a big difference.

Note Don't forget that you can choose Window ⇨ Arrange ⇨ New Window to maintain a constant composite view. Or you can click the Visibility icon (the eye) in front of the composite view in the Channels palette to view the full-color image, even when editing a single channel.

✦ **Aligning channels.** Every so often, a scan may appear out of focus even after you use Photoshop's sharpening commands to try to correct the problem, as discussed in Chapter 10. If, on closer inspection, you can see slight shadows or halos around colored areas, one of the color channels probably is out of alignment. To remedy the problem, switch to the color channel that corresponds to the color of the halos. Then select the move tool (by pressing V) and use the arrow keys to nudge the contents of the channel into alignment. Use the separate composite view (created by choosing Window ⇨ Arrange ⇨ New Window) or click the eyeball in front of the composite channel to monitor your changes.

✦ **Channel focusing.** If all channels seem to be in alignment (or, at least, as aligned as they're going to get), one of your channels may be poorly focused. Use the Ctrl-key (or ⌘-key on the Mac) equivalents to search for the responsible channel. If you find it, use the Unsharp Mask filter to sharpen it as desired. You may also find it helpful to blur a channel, as when trying to eliminate moiré patterns in a scanned halftone. (For a specific application of these techniques, see Chapter 10.)

✦ **Bad channels.** In your color channel tour, if you discover that a channel is not so much poorly focused as simply rotten to the core — complete with harsh transitions, jagged edges, and random brightness variations — you may be able to improve the appearance of the channel by mixing other channels with it.

Suppose that the blue channel is awful, but the red and green channels are in fairly decent shape. The Channel Mixer command lets you mix channels together, whether to repair a bad channel or achieve an interesting effect. Choose Image ⇨ Adjustments ⇨ Channel Mixer and press Ctrl+3 (⌘-3 on the Mac) to switch to the blue channel. Then raise the Red and Green values and lower the Blue value to mix the three channels together to create a better blue. To maintain consistent brightness levels, it's generally a good idea to use a combination of Red, Green, and Blue values that add up to 100 percent, as in Figure 4-20. If you can live with the inevitable color changes — and you may not be able to, in which case a channel mask will be required — the appearance of the image should improve dramatically.

Figure 4-20: Here the Channel Mixer command is used to repair the blue channel by mixing percentages of the red and green channels. The red and green channels themselves remain unaffected.

Note that Channel Mixer is also a great command for creating custom grayscale images. Rather than choosing Image ⇨ Mode ⇨ Grayscale and taking what Photoshop gives you, you can choose the Channel Mixer command and select the Monochrome option. Then adjust the Red, Green, and Blue values to mix your own grayscale variation.

Incidentally, the Constant slider simply brightens or darkens the image across the board. Usually, you'll want to leave it set to 0, but if you're having problems getting the color balance right, give it a nudge with your mouse or the arrow keys.

Using multichannel techniques

The one channel function not looked at so far is Image ⇨ Mode ⇨ Multichannel. When you choose this command, Photoshop changes your image so that channels no longer have a specific relationship to one another. They don't mix to create a full-color image; instead, they exist independently within the confines of a single image. The multichannel mode is generally an intermediary step for converting between different color modes without recalculating the contents of the channels. Multichannel is also the only Mode option if you use the Merge Channels command and have only two images open — the other modes are dimmed.

In terms of multichannel's use in converting between different color modes, when you normally convert between the RGB and CMYK modes, Photoshop maps RGB colors to the CMYK color model, changing the contents of each channel as demonstrated back in Figures 4-15 and 4-16. But suppose, just as an experiment, that you want to bypass the color mapping and instead transfer the exact contents of the red channel to the cyan channel, the contents of the green channel to the magenta channel, and so on. You convert from RGB to the multichannel mode and then from multichannel to CMYK as described in the following steps.

STEPS: Using the Multichannel Mode as an Intermediary Step

1. **Open an RGB image.** If the image is already open, make sure that it is saved to disk.

2. **Choose Image ⇨ Mode ⇨ Multichannel.** This eliminates any relationship between the formerly Red, Green, and Blue color channels.

3. **Click the new channel icon at the bottom of the Channels palette.** Or choose the New Channel command from the palette menu and press Enter or Return to accept the default settings. Either way, you add a mask channel to the image. This empty channel will serve as the black channel in the CMYK image. (Photoshop won't let you convert from the multichannel mode to CMYK with less than four channels.)

4. **Press Ctrl+I (⌘-I on the Mac).** Unfortunately, the new channel comes up black, which would make the entire image black. To change the channel to white, press Ctrl+I (⌘-I on the Mac) or choose Image ⇨ Adjustments ⇨ Invert.

5. **Choose Image ⇨ Mode ⇨ CMYK Color.** The image looks washed out and a tad dark compared to its original RGB counterpart, but the overall color scheme of the image remains more or less intact. This is because the Red, Green, and Blue color channels each have a respective opposite in the cyan, magenta, and yellow channels.

Web-Ready? JPEG and GIF

When preparing images for the Web, the two most common file formats are JPEG and GIF, as you learned in Chapter 18. This image shows two images in their most appropriate formats — JPEG for the photo on the top, and GIF for the original artwork on the bottom.

The parrot appears in four states, each created by selecting a Quality for the JPEG image in the Save for Web dialog box, which is covered in both Chapters 3 and 18. The first image (upper left) is at Maximum. The second version of the parrot is set to High (upper right), and the third and fourth examples are set to Medium and Low (bottom left and right, respectively). The High and Medium quality images are barely distinguishable from the Maximum image, but the Low quality image shows a lot of the compression artifacts that JPEG is known for.

The bottom set of images is better suited to GIF, also covered in Chapter 18. The artist Mimi Shapiro, who gave her kind permission for me to use her work in this book, created this original artwork (you can view her other artwork at www.manhattanarts.com/profiles/MimiShapiro/). This artwork was scanned from the original painting and the Save for Web dialog box used to create the four GIF versions seen here. Clockwise from the upper left, the images are at 256 colors, 128 colors, 64 colors, and the last at 32 colors.

Lab Channel Effects

One of the advantages of Photoshop's Lab mode is that it permits you to edit colors in an image, independently of the brightness values. To demonstrate this, the top left image shows an unedited photo of an orange sunset. After converting the photo to Lab (Image ⇨ Mode ⇨ Lab), the A channel was inverted, using the Ctrl + I (⌘- I on the Mac) command, and the result appears in the second image (upper right).

In the third image, on the lower left, the B channel was given the Auto Levels treatment (Image ⇨ Adjustments ⇨ Auto Levels), which enhanced the contrast. In the fourth image (lower right), the two effects were combined, and as you can see, radical color changes occurred, yet no detail was lost or lighting adjusted.

You can read more about Lab mode in Chapter 4.

The Channel Mixer

Another way to really play with colors without upsetting the detail in an image is to replace one color channel with another or to swap the content of two or more channels using the Image ➪ Adjustments ➪ Channel Mixer command. Starting with an RGB version of the orange sunset, the Red channel was replaced with the contents of the Green channel. The result is a dark yellow sunset in the upper left. Restoring the Red channel to its original state and then cloning the Green channel into the Blue channel turned everything pink, as shown in the upper right. In the lower left image, the Red and Blue channels were swapped, and in the fourth image (bottom right), the Red and Green channels were swapped, and the Blue value dropped to 50%.

Color modes and channels are discussed in Chapter 4.

The Sponge Tool

Although the edit tools are less powerful than many of Photoshop's filters and color adjustment commands, they can be useful for applying spontaneous creative effects. In this sequence of images, for example, a young man's face (the original appears at the top) is given a mask using the Burn tool and the Sponge (see middle image). Additional use of the Burn tool is seen above the eyes and alongside the nose, as well as along the outer edges of the mask. In the bottom image, saturation and darkening are strategically increased, and the Sponge was also applied to the hair and the eyes, to increase the saturation of these areas.

You can read more about the Sponge and Burn tools in Chapters 2 and 4, and about using the Pen tool to make selections (as was done here to create the shape of the mask) in Chapter 8.

Color Replacement

This row of mailboxes is given a new coat of several different colors of paint, thanks to the Color Replacement command. Taking the top image to the bottom image required that I change the Limits option to Find Edges. This forces the tool to resist painting beyond a ridge of high-contrast pixels until you lead with your cursor. This one change can resolve the problems typically seen when using this tool — color replacement that spills out of the desired area.

To learn all about the Color Replacement tool, see Chapter 5.

Brush Modes

These images show a series of brushstrokes applied using several brush modes. In each case, the brushstrokes were drawn with the Brush tool — and only the mode and Opacity settings change from chair to chair — the brushstrokes are identical.

Over the course of the 12 chairs, the following brush modes are used, by row:

Top row, from left: Darken, Multiply, Linear Burn

Second row, from left: Lighten, Screen, Linear Dodge

Third row, from left: Overlay, Linear Light, Pin Light

Fourth row, from left: Hard Mix, Difference, and Exclusion

You can read more about brush modes in Chapter 5.

The Paint Bucket

Used properly, the Paint Bucket can be a powerful tool for coloring scanned line art. Start by creating an independent layer for each color in the image, and then use the Paint Bucket with its All Layers option turned on — this allows you to fill one layer based on the content of the others. The two examples on this page apply color to a black and white drawing by artist Mimi Shapiro. The top image is the black and white drawing and the bottom is the result of using the Paint Bucket to fill areas with color. Because the drawing had varying shades of gray used to fill the shapes — the base, tablecloth, flowers, and the background — the Paint Bucket's Tolerance setting could be tweaked to control the application of color to like shades of gray, and using the Contiguous option, the fill could be confined to desired areas within a single layer.

Read more about the Paint Bucket in Chapters 2 and 6, and learn about creating layers from selections in Chapters 8 and 12.

Healing and Patching

In this fairly unsettling image, a young man's eyes are removed, replaced by skin grafts. This example shows the use of the man's own skin to cover his eyes. Here, the Patch Tool was used to take skin from the cheeks and patch the eyes — eyelids, eyeballs ... everything.

To use the Patch tool, first select the area you want to cover up — in this case, selections that completely surrounded the eyes, as shown in the top image. Feather the selection slightly so that the patching won't be too obvious, and then with the Patch tool activated, drag the selection outline over the area to be used for the patch (middle image). As soon as you release the mouse, the content from the source area fills the original target, and the eyes are gone (bottom image).

Find out more about using the Patch tool and its various options in Chapter 7.

... and Cosmetic Surgery

Use the Healing Brush for the quickest, most pain-free cosmetic surgery ever. Activate the Healing Brush to apply a custom pattern, and the wrinkles on this man's face are magically removed. In the top set of images, the original photo is accompanied by the Fill dialog box and the Add Noise filter. The low level of noise was used to create a pattern (see background behind the two dialog boxes, created with the Fill command), and that pattern was applied with the Healing Brush. In the lower set of images, you can see the gray strokes that show where the healing is to be applied. In the second of these images, the man's face is virtually devoid of wrinkles, and the smooth, yet realistic pattern is what makes it possible.

Read more about creating custom patterns in Chapter 6, and learn to use the Healing Brush in Chapter 7.

Masking Defined

The top image shows an elliptical selection outline, rotated a few degrees counter-clockwise and feathered by a Radius value of 64 pixels. Of course, the feathering isn't obvious while the marching ants are visible — it isn't until the mask is created (or you use Quick Mask) that you can see the soft edges made by the selection. In the middle image, you see the Mask, all by itself, a feathered white ellipse. White represents the selected area the black around it represents the deselected area.

In the bottom image, the mask and original image are viewed together, the mask appearing as a red wash on the image. The areas within the mask are not washed in red, but the areas outside of it are. If this prospect is a problem because your image has a lot of red in it to start with, you can set your mask to a different color; choose something that will stand out in your image.

Learn more about creating masks in Chapter 9.

Gradient Quick Mask

Among other things, Quick Mask mode affords you the option of feathering one portion of a selection independently of another. For example, if you were to take the skeleton in the upper left and make it look as though it were floating in the sky as shown in the second image from the left, you would begin by selecting the mask with the Pen tool, and then switching to Quick Mask mode (second image from the right). Then you draw a black-to-transparent gradient from the top of the skeleton to its toes (see the mask in the Channels palette in the far right of the top row).

In the final image, the skeleton appears to be floating in the sky, and he's been distorted with Free Transform — adding to the illusion that he's floating up and away from the ground.

Read more about creating masks and using Quick Mask mode in Chapter 9, and find out more about using Free Transform in Chapters 10 and 12.

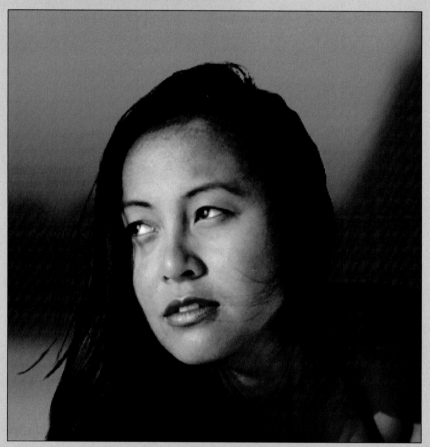

Photorealistic Mask

What do you do when you want to composite a complex image (see top left image) with a new background? You create a complex mask for the image, as discussed in Chapter 9. The process involves duplicating the channel with the most contrast, and then using the High Pass filter and the Levels command (Image ⇨ Adjustments ⇨ Levels) to create the mask seen in the top right image.

Finally, the mask is used to copy the desired content (the girl's face and hair) and paste it against a new background as illustrated in the bottom image. Depending on the accuracy of your mask and its inclusion of fine detail around the content's edges, the composite should look quite natural, as though the girl was always posed in front of a dark sunset.

Unsharp Mask

The Unsharp Mask filter, discussed in Chapter 10, is probably Photoshop's most useful corrective filter. It works by sharpening the focus of an image by increasing the contrast of edge details. You can apply the filter to an entire image, to independent channels, or to a selection within an image.

The top left figure shows the original image, a beautiful male lion in profile. In the upper right, the same image is shown with the Unsharp Mask filter applied to the entire image. The middle row shows various channels: the left is the Red channel only, the middle shows Red and Green channels, and the middle right image is the Green channel only. Finally, in the bottom row, the left image shows the Unsharp Mask applied to the Green and Blue channels, the middle shows the Blue channel only, and the right shows the Blue and Red channels.

Gaussian Blur

Gaussian Blur is one Photoshop's most useful filters. Use it in the creation of masks, depth effects, and more. In the examples here, the Gaussian blur filter is used to simulate a diffuse glow around the subject. The top image shows the result of applying the filter with a Radius value of 8 pixels. This makes the image look out of focus, which seems like a problem because the subject needs to be sharp and clear. This is where the Fade command comes in.

The middle image shows the results of choosing Edit ➪ Fade, and setting the Mode to Darken. By doing this, Photoshop keeps only those pixels from the blur effect that appear darker than their counterparts in the original image. This results in an overall darkening of the image, with blurry transitions isolated to the lighter areas around the edge of the subject.

The bottom image shows the results of reapplying the Gaussian Blur filter, then choosing Edit ➪ Fade, and setting the Mode to Linear Dodge with an Opacity of 80%. This brings some lightness back to the subject, creating the effect of an image shot in soft focus under powerful direct light, while keeping the details of the image fully intact.

Read more about the Gaussian Blur filter in Chapter 10.

Focus a Digital Image

While digital camera technology has improved greatly in the last year or so, lower-end digital cameras will still produce images with jagged edges, artifacts, and other blemishes. Even in the higher-end cameras, these blemishes stem from lower resolutions, heavy-handed compression schemes (all based on JPEG), or both.

The image shown on this page was taken with a digital camera, and as you can see in the top left example, it's a bit noisy and not well focused. In the top right example, the noisiness is gone, but the Median and Gaussian Blur-induced smoothness has robbed the image of its details. The bottom image shows a focused image, with little or no graininess, yet no blurry smoothing, either.

Using a series of filters — Median, Gaussian Blur, and finally Unsharp Mask, the photo was improved greatly. You can read the step-by-step instructions for transforming this photo in Chapter 10.

Sketch Filters

Most of Photoshop's Sketch filters (Filter ⇨ Sketch) recolor an image entirely in the current foreground and background colors you have selected. Starting with the original image at the top, the foreground and background colors were set to medium green and light turquoise. The next image down shows the Halftone Pattern filter applied (Filter ⇨ Sketch ⇨ Halftone Pattern). The result looks almost as if the image were being displayed on an old monochrome computer monitor.

To combine the texture from this image with colors from the original, use the Fade command. In the third image, the Fade command was used and the Mode set to Overlay (Edit ⇨ Fade Halftone Pattern, Mode: Overly). To lose the foreground and background color entirely, use the Luminosity mode, as in the final image.

6. **Press Ctrl+Shift+L (⌘-Shift-L on the Mac).** Or choose Image ⇨ Adjustments ⇨ Auto Levels. This punches up the color a bit by automatically correcting the brightness and contrast.

7. **Convert the image to RGB and then back to CMYK.** The problem with the image is that it lacks any information in the black channel. So although it may look okay on screen, it will lose much of its definition when printed. To fill in the black channel, choose Image ⇨ Mode ⇨ RGB Color, and then choose Image ⇨ Mode ⇨ CMYK Color. Photoshop automatically generates an image in the black channel in keeping with the standards of color separations (as explained in Chapter 18).

Keep in mind that these steps are by no means a recommended procedure for converting an RGB image to a CMYK image. Rather, they merely suggest one way to experiment with channel conversions to create a halfway decent image. You can likewise experiment with converting between the Lab, multichannel, and RGB modes, or Lab, multichannel, and CMYK.

Tip If you want to really manipulate the colors in an RGB or a CMYK image, there's nothing like replacing one color channel with another to produce spectacular (or at least quite interesting) effects — and the Channel Mixer is your manipulation tool of choice. You can try swapping the Red and Blue channels in an RGB image, setting red to 0 and blue to 100, then flip that around, setting red to 100 and blue to 0. You can mix and match your CMYK image channels, too, tinkering with the sliders until you get bored.

Summary

In this chapter, you learned about using the color controls in the toolbox, selecting and defining colors in the Color Picker dialog box, and all about the RGB, HSB, CMYK, Lab color, and HDR modes. You learned how to convert images to 16 and 32 bits per channel, and how to create grayscale and black-and-white images.

You learned to apply colors using the Color palette, Eyedropper, and color sampler, and found out how color channels work. You also learned to use channel editing commands in the Channels palette, and how to improve the appearance of poorly scanned images.

✦　　✦　　✦

Painting and Brushes

In This Chapter

Exploring Photoshop's paint and edit tools

Applying the airbrush control

Painting straight and perpendicular lines

Smudging and sponging colors

Using the new Color Replacement tool

Changing the brush size, shape, and hardness

Saving and loading custom brush sets

Painting with a pressure-sensitive drawing tablet

Creating lines that fade away or taper to a point

Using scatter, texture, and other dynamics

Adjusting opacity and flow

Working with brush modes

There was a time when you couldn't browse the aisles at a software store and not see painting programs everywhere. It seemed that virtually every software manufacturer had one on the market, each of them doing many of the same things. The excitement over being able to create artwork with one's computer kept some of them in business for a while, but in the end, well, that ended. There are still a few of them out there, and only one real survivor — Corel's Painter (*www.corel.com*). Corel's market share is quite tiny, though, and the other "competitor," Jasc's Paint Shop Pro, really isn't a painting program — the word Paint simply appears in its title.

So what led to the demise of these many painting programs? Photoshop. While the program was originally designed to be (and remains) an image-editing program, it has always had painting tools, and it turned out that most people wanted to edit images rather than paint them from scratch. Imagine that — all the people who tell you they can't even draw stick figures suddenly become da Vinci when seated in front of a computer screen! The proximity, therefore, of painting tools with image-editing tools gave people what they really wanted. Over the years and versions, Photoshop's painting tools have become even better, and this sealed the fate of any would-be competitors. Photoshop simply offers users what they want, and makes it possible to create virtually any kind of image, for just about any printed or electronic purpose.

Get to Know the Paint and Edit Tools

Photoshop provides two basic varieties of brush tools. There are paint tools, which allow you to apply colors to an image, and there are edit tools, which modify existing colors in an image. Both types of tools work the same way — you activate the tool and drag your cursor within the image window, much like you drag a brush across a canvas or a sheet of paper.

Now, don't think that these tools require any sort of artistic ability, because they don't. If you can drag a mouse or a tablet's pen, you can paint and edit with Photoshop. The tools are designed to cater to users of all levels, and provide simple ways to apply straight, curved, and free-form strokes to an image as well as more complex tool options that make it possible for true visionaries with great eye-hand coordination to create serious works of art.

So what are these tools? Photoshop CS2 provides the big two that you'll find in any fledgling or accomplished artist's studio: the Brush and the Pencil. You also get seven editing tools: Blur, Sharpen, Smudge, Dodge, Burn, Sponge, and the new Color Replacement tool. Figure 5-1 shows all the tools along with the keyboard shortcuts for selecting them.

Figure 5-1: Sharing three spots in the Toolbox, you'll find all nine of Photoshop's painting and editing tools.

You'll know when a button in the toolbox represents multiple tools — a small triangle appears in the lower-right corner of the button. When you see that triangle, you can click and hold the button to display a flyout menu of tools, as shown in Figure 5-1. Of course, unlike that illustration, you can't activate three different tools and show their flyout menus simultaneously — you can only activate one button (and its flyout menu) at a time. To activate any tool, you can select it from the toolbox and click on it in the flyout menu, or you can skip using your mouse entirely and just press the keyboard shortcut. When more than one tool shares a single shortcut, you can simply press Shift along with the shortcut key (B, for example, to select the Brush or Pencil) and the tool you want appears in the toolbox and on the Options bar at the top of the workspace. If you want to avoid having to press two keys, you can deselect the Use Shift Key for Tool Switch option in the General Preferences dialog box, and then all you have to do is keep pressing the single keyboard shortcut key until the tool you want is selected.

The paint tools

The paint tools apply strokes of color. In most cases, you'll be painting with the foreground color, though you can also create multicolored brushstrokes using the Color Dynamics options in the Brushes palette, as you'll see later. Here's how the paint tools work:

✦ **Brush.** This tool paints a line of any thickness that you specify (using the Options bar). You can make the line sharp or blurry, but it's always slightly soft — that is to say, the edges of the brushstroke blend to some extent with the background. Known as *anti-aliasing*, this softness produces halftone dots when printing, ensuring smooth transitions between a brushstroke and its surroundings.

Normally, the Brush tool applies a continuous stream of color and stops applying paint whenever you stop dragging. However, if you activate the Airbrush function by clicking the Airbrush icon next to the Flow setting in the Options bar, the color continues to build as long as you press the mouse button, even when holding the cursor in a stationary position. In Figure 5-2, the first line was painted with soft brush and the Airbrush option off. To make the second line, I turned on the Airbrush setting and reduced the Flow value to 50 percent. The result is a buildup of color at the corners and at the end of the stroke.

Tip   To invoke the Airbrush function from the keyboard, press Shift+Alt+P (or Shift-Option-P on the Mac). Pressing Shift+Alt+P again turns the function off. If you think remembering the P will be difficult, it won't be — P stands for Paint.

✦ **Pencil.** Like the Brush tool, the Pencil paints a line of any thickness in the foreground color. However, whereas Brush tool lines are always soft, Pencil lines are always hard edged, with no interaction between the Pencil line and background colors. At high resolutions, Pencil lines appear sharp. At low resolutions, Pencil lines have jagged edges.

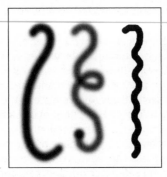

Figure 5-2: Three lines painted in black — the first two with the Brush, the third with the Pencil. Use of the Airbrush and reduced Flow create the differences between the two brushstrokes.

When you select the Pencil tool, a unique check box, Auto Erase, appears in the Options bar. When selected, this option instructs Photoshop to paint with the background color — thereby erasing — whenever you begin painting on an area already colored with the foreground color.

Tip

As when painting in real life, one of the imperatives of painting in Photoshop is switching out the color of your brush. The Colors palette is handy, and is certainly more convenient than opening the Color Picker to change colors, but it's not immediate enough. You need something that can keep up with the speed of your creative ideas. The solution is the Eyedropper. As introduced in Chapter 4, you can use the Eyedropper to sample colors from an image by Alt-clicking (Option-clicking on the Mac) when using either the Brush or Pencil tool. While pressing Alt or Option, click your mouse on a color you want to use, and that becomes your new Foreground color. Voila!

The edit tools

Rather than applying color, the edit tools influence existing colors in an image. Figure 5-3 shows the effect of dragging with each of the edit tools, except the Sponge and Color Replacement tools, both of which work best with color images. Future sections cover these tools in more detail, but here's a brief introduction:

✦ **Blur.** The first of the two focus tools, the Blur tool blurs an image by reducing the amount of color contrast between neighboring pixels.

✦ **Sharpen.** The second focus tool selectively sharpens by increasing the contrast between neighboring pixels.

✦ **Smudge.** The Smudge tool smears colors in an image. The effect is rather like dragging your finger across wet paint. Although simple, this tool can be effective for smoothing out colors and textures. See the section "Painting with the Smudge tool" for more information.

✦ **Dodge.** The first of three toning tools, the Dodge tool lets you lighten a portion of an image by dragging across it. Named after a traditional darkroom technique, the Dodge tool is supposed to look like a little paddle. Before computers,

Tools versus Filters

As you work with Photoshop's Filters, you'll notice that there are also Blur and Sharpen filters, and you might wonder how these differ (or if they differ) from the Blur and Sharpen tools. I find that the Blur tool, while it requires scrubbing with the mouse, is more effective and controllable than the Blur filter. There are other Blur filters, such as Gaussian, Motion, Smart, Radial, Box, Shape, and Surface, which provide very effective and dramatic results — but the plain old Blur filter is not my first choice for blurring edges or background content. The Sharpen filter, on the other hand, is a bit better than the Sharpen tool, in that it provides an effective, yet subtle effect. I find that the Sharpen tool usually ends up creating a mess of randomly colored pixels and even at a low Strength setting, and more often than not, I end up cursing its results and using Undo.

a technician would wave such a paddle (or anything, really) over photographic paper to prevent light from hitting the paper, thereby leaving areas less exposed.

✦ **Burn.** The Burn tool is the Dodge tool's opposite, darkening an area as you drag over it. Again referencing old darkroom techniques, technicians would create a mask over the developing print, using their hands or a piece of paper with a hole cut in it. The mask would protect areas of photographic paper that had already been exposed and darken the area inside the hole. Photoshop's metaphor for this is found in the Burn tool's button, which depicts a hand in the shape of an O.

✦ **Sponge.** The Sponge tool has two modes — Saturate and Desaturate. In Desaturate mode, the Sponge tool robs an image of color when working inside a color image, or contrast when working in grayscale. If you switch to Saturate mode, the Sponge tool adds more color (in color images), or contrast in grayscale images.

✦ **Color Replacement.** The Color Replacement tool was added to Photoshop CS In Photoshop CS, the tool was grouped in the toolbox with the healing brush and patch tools. In CS2, it has been promoted to share a button with the Brush and Pencil tools. At its most basic level, the Color Replacement tool provides a great way to get rid of any color in favor of a preferred shade. Through the tool's Options bar, you can pick which color goes and which color replaces it. The intricacies of the tool's use are covered in detail later.

Tip Some tools are often used together — not at the same time, of course, but you'll find yourself hopping from one to the other and wishing you could do so more quickly. The Sharpen and Blur tools are an example of this, as you often need to soften one area and add more focus to another, all in the same image. To access the Sharpen tool temporarily when the Blur tool is selected, press and hold Alt or Option while using the tool. The Sharpen tool remains available only as long as you press Alt (or Option on the Mac). Likewise, you can press Alt (or Option on the Mac) to access the Blur tool when the Sharpen tool is selected. You can use the same Alt/Option technique with other likely pairs such as the Dodge and Burn tools.

Figure 5-3: The effects of dragging with five of Photoshop's edit tools. The boundaries of each line are highlighted so you can clearly see the distinctions between line and background.

Basic Techniques

Maybe you're among the people who think they can't draw at all. While I believe that every person is more creative and artistic than he or she believes (and that it's the belief part that determines one's ability), Photoshop makes it possible for anyone to paint and draw. In this section, it's my goal to help you unleash your creativity and free your artistic soul — with Photoshop's painting and editing tools as the means to that end.

Painting a straight line

With the Brush and Pencil tools, it's easy to draw straight lines. All you need is the tool and the Shift key. Pressing Shift while you drag the tool keeps the line straight and eliminates the little bumps and detours that occur when you try to create a freehand straight line. You can use the same technique with the Blur, Sharpen, Smudge, Dodge, and Burn tools.

If you find the Shift key technique to be too limiting, Photoshop also provides a Line tool (one of the Shape tool variants) that lets you draw straight lines. It's a surprisingly flexible tool that permits you to draw vector-based layers or pixel-based lines, and you can even add arrowheads.

Cross-
Reference

The Line tool and others like it are explained in greater detail in Chapter 14.

So, try this Shift technique with the Brush and Pencil tools. First, using the Brush tool, click at one point in your image and then press Shift and click at another point. Photoshop connects the start and endpoints with a straight stroke of paint. Try it again with the Pencil tool, and enhance your experiments by trying different Brush and Pencil presets to see the results. You can also create free-form polygons by continuing to Shift-click with the Brush or Pencil tool, creating a series of straight lines as shown in Figure 5-4. Figure 5-4 shows effects created by Shift-clicking with the Brush tool. Note that different brush sizes were used throughout the image, and that at no point did I drag the mouse — every line shown was created by Shift-clicking with the Brush tool and then made more visually interesting with blending modes.

Cross-
Reference

For more information on blending modes, see Chapter 13.

Painting a perpendicular line

To create a perpendicular line — that is, a line that is either vertical or horizontal — with any of the paint or edit tools, press Shift while dragging with the tool. Releasing Shift returns the line to free form, as illustrated in Figure 5-5, which shows a mix of straight, perpendicular, and free-form lines. For example, I started by pressing Shift to draw a vertical line. I released Shift, pressed it again, and drew a freehand line for the top of the cat's head. For the ear, I pressed Shift again and clicked at the point of the ear and at the bottom of the ear. The body and the tail were drawn freehand. After pressing Shift again to draw a short horizontal and a short vertical line, I repeated the steps and created the mirror image.

Tip

Note that you can press Shift in mid-drag to snap the line back into perpendicular alignment.

Figure 5-4: This image was created entirely with the Brush tool, set to different weights and presets, and always using the Shift key (and no dragging) to make the lines straight. After drawing the lines (two sets, on two separate layers), a drop shadow, outer glows, and bevel blending modes were applied to create a 3-D look.

Remember one thing, however, as you create serial straight lines: When you press Shift to create a subsequent straight line, instead of a line going in the direction you want, you get a diagonal line connecting your last straight line with the starting point of your next one. You can avoid this by clicking once without the Shift key before clicking with the Shift key to make the next straight line. As long as you don't move the mouse on the non-Shift-accompanied click, the technique will not reveal itself in your resulting image. Photoshop's further tendency to snap to creating perpendicular lines is another potential problem, but you can use this to your advantage. For example, to create the lines shown in Figure 5-6, I dragged from right to left with the brush tool. I painted by intermittently pressing and releasing Shift as I dragged. In each case, pressing Shift snapped the line to the horizontal axis, the location of which was established by the beginning of the drag. After drawing the lines, I applied fill colors, and then used the Watercolor filter to create a more visually interesting effect for this stylized still life.

Cross-Reference You can read more about applying fills in Chapter 6, and about Filters in Chapters 10 and 11.

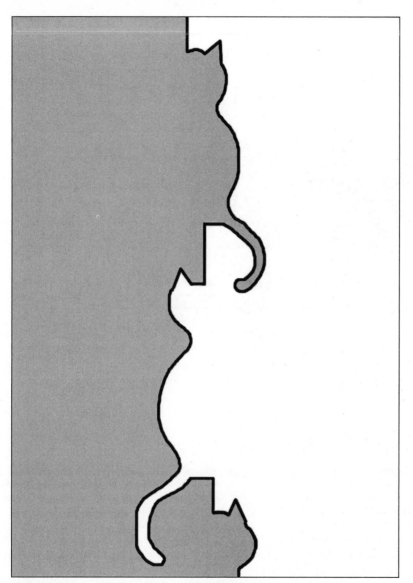

Figure 5-5: Combining freehand dragging and the use of the Shift key enables you to draw a variety of lines.

Figure 5-6: To create the lines shown here, I pressed and released Shift while dragging with the Brush tool. Fills and filters complete the finished effect.

Painting with the Smudge tool

Many first-time Photoshop artists misuse the Smudge tool to soften color transitions, which is the purpose of the Blur tool. The Smudge tool is designed to smear colors by shoving them into each other. The process bears more resemblance to finger painting than to any traditional photographic-editing technique.

In Photoshop, the performance of the Smudge tool depends in part on the settings of the Strength and Finger Painting controls in the Options bar. Here's what you need to know about these options:

✦ **Strength.** The Smudge tool works by stamping the image hundreds of times throughout the length of a brushstroke. The effect is that the color appears to get pushed across the length of the stroke. The Strength value determines the intensity of each stamping, so higher values push colors the farthest. A Strength setting of 100 percent equates to infinity, meaning the Smudge tool pushes a color from the beginning of your drag until you release your mouse button. Figure 5-7 shows three examples.

Smudge at 50%   Smudge at 75%

Figure 5-7: Two identical drags with the Smudge tool subjected to different Strength settings: 50 percent (left), and 75 percent (right). In each case, the smudge began at the same spot in the image and dragged for the same duration.

✦ **Finger Painting.** In the distant Photoshop past, the people at Adobe called this effect *dipping*, which may accurately express the results of this option. When you select this option, the Smudge tool begins by applying a very small amount of the current foreground color, which it eventually blends in with the colors in the image. It's as if you dipped your finger in a color and then dragged it through an oil painting. Use the Strength setting to specify the amount of foreground color applied. If you turn on Finger Painting and set the Strength to 100 percent, the smudge tool behaves like the Brush tool. Figure 5-8 shows examples of Finger Painting with the Smudge tool when the foreground color is set to white.

Tip

You can reverse the Finger Painting setting by pressing Alt (Option on the Mac) and dragging. If the option is off, Alt-dragging dips the tool into the foreground color. If Finger Painting is turned on, Alt-dragging smudges normally.

Finger Painting smudge at 50%   Finger Painting smudge at 75%

Figure 5-8: The same two drags pictured in Figure 5-7, but this time with the Finger Painting option turned on and the foreground color set to white

The Use All Layers option instructs the Smudge tool to grab colors in all visible layers and smudge them into the current layer. Whether the option is on or off, only the current layer is affected; the background and other layers remain intact. Figure 5-9 shows the same smudged path with Use All Layers off and then with the option on — you can see how colors from the other layer (a pastel mask on top of the front-most petal in the flower) is included in the smudge in the latter example.

Sponging color in and out

The Sponge tool is actually a really simple tool that works in one of two modes — Desaturate or Saturate. You choose the mode from the tool's Options bar, and then choose how much color the sponge removes or adds, respectively, by adjusting the Flow setting. When you pick one of the modes, this is what happens:

> ✦ **Desaturate.** When set to Desaturate, the Sponge tool reduces the saturation of the colors over which you drag. When you're editing a grayscale image, the tool reduces contrast.
>
> ✦ **Saturate.** If you select Saturate, the Sponge tool increases the saturation of the colors over which you drag or increases contrast in a grayscale image.

Smudge Mask only at 65%   Smudge Mask and underlying
                                 layer together at 65%

Figure 5-9: With Use All Layers off in the example on the left, the 65% smudge only affects the content and colors of the active layer. When Use All Layers is turned on (in the example on the right), content from pattern-filled layer beneath the photo is included in the 65% smudge, resulting in more dramatic effects.

You can switch between the Desaturate and Saturate modes from the keyboard. Press Shift+Alt+D (Shift-Option-D on the Mac) to select the Desaturate option. Press Shift+Alt+S (Shift-Option-S on the Mac) for Saturate. No matter which mode you choose, higher Flow settings produce more dramatic results. Figure 5-10 shows an image that was both saturated and desaturated, with a Flow setting of 50.

Tip   You might find it helpful to turn on the Airbrush setting in the Options bar when using the Sponge tool (as well as the other toning tools, Dodge and Burn). This way, you can gradually build up effects. When you find a section of an image that needs more sponging than most, hold your cursor in place, watch Photoshop airbrush in the effect, and then move the cursor when you see that the desired effect has been achieved.

Figure 5-10: Sponge on, Sponge off. The Sponge applied to a rectangular selection on the left added color, and the Sponge applied to a rectangular selection on the right removed color.

Using the Color Replacement tool

The Color Replacement tool works by taking a color sample from the area in which you first click and then applying the foreground color to any area that matches the sample. For example, if you were trying to change the color of someone's clothing in a photo, you could use the Color Replacement tool to sample the unwanted color and then replace it with another color. This requires only that you set the Foreground color to the desired shade, and then activate the Color Replacement tool (found sharing a button with the Brush and Pencil tools) and drag it over the parts of your image where the offending color can be found. In Figure 5-11, a little boy's coat goes from navy blue to bright red (with an obvious stroke through the boy's coat to make the change visible in black and white).

You control the behavior and sensitivity of the Color Replacement tool using the settings in the Options bar. Here's how they break down:

✦ **Brush.** You don't get a whole lot of brush choices when using the Color Replacement tool. The minimalist controls found in the Brush option bear a closer resemblance to Photoshop 6-era brushes than the snazzy, robust Brushes palette available to a number of the other tools.

✦ **Mode.** This setting tells the tool how to combine the newly painted pixels with the existing ones in your image. By default, the Mode option is set to Color, and you're generally going to want to leave it there. Because the Color mode affects hue and saturation, or the color values of an image, but doesn't affect luminance, or lightness values, it's generally the way to go.

✦ **Sampling.** The Sampling option lets you set how Photoshop will decide what color you're replacing. The first option, Continuous, causes the tool to keep sampling colors, nonstop, for as long as you're using the tool.

Much more useful than Continuous is the second Sampling option, Once (its results appear in Figure 5-11). This sets the color on which you click when you begin your drag as the target of your replacement. This means that for as long as you continue dragging, only the original color will be affected. The third and final Sampling setting is Background Swatch. Choosing this option tells the color replacement tool to alter only pixels in your image that share a color with the current background color. It can be a neat way of providing even more control over what the tool will affect, but I still recommend you stick with the Once setting.

✦ **Limits.** The Limits option lets you set even more guidelines for determining which pixels the tool will affect. Select Discontiguous to replace colors anywhere you drag with the tool. Select Contiguous to replace colors only in areas that are contiguous with, or connected by color to, the color currently under your cursor. The Find Edges option is designed to work the same way as Contiguous while better preserving edge details in the image.

✦ **Tolerance.** The Tolerance value determines how exact of a color match is required to deem a pixel suitable for replacement. Lower values replace colors similar to the sampled color, and higher values replace a broader range of colors. Most of your work with the Color Replacement tool will live or die based on this setting, and it can be a bit tricky to get it right. Keep in mind that a value that works for one section of color in an image may not be the correct setting to affect a lighter or darker section of the same color in the image.

✦ **Anti-alias.** This option lets you toggle anti-aliasing, or softening, on or off. It's almost certainly a good idea to keep it turned on.

Figure 5-11: The navy blue coat is recolored, and now the boy's wearing red — although it all appears as shades of gray here. You can see the stroke through the boy's coat, however, indicating the path of the Color Replacement tool.

Undoing your damage

If you make a mistake in the course of painting an image, stop and choose Edit ⮑ Undo or press Ctrl+Z (⌘-Z on the Mac). If this doesn't work, press Ctrl+Alt+Z (⌘-Option-Z on the Mac) to step back through a sequence of paint strokes.

Cross-Reference
You can also undo a brushstroke by selecting a previous state in the History palette. As explained in Chapter 7, the History palette lists brushstrokes and other changes according to the tool you used to create them.

If you like the basic look of a brushstroke but you'd like to fade it back a bit, choose Edit ⮑ Fade or press Ctrl+Shift+F (⌘-Shift-F on the Mac). The Fade command lets you reduce the Opacity or change the blend mode of the brushstroke you just finished painting. (If you have since clicked with another tool, the command may appear dimmed, indicating that you've lost your chance.) The Fade command is applicable to all paint and edit tools, as well as other operations in Photoshop, so you'll be seeing a lot of it throughout this book.

Brush Size and Shape

Now that you have a feel for the purpose and basics of using the paint and edit tools, let's take a look at how you modify the performance of these tools. For example, every tool behaves differently according to the size and shape of your cursor, known as the *brush tip*. Different styles of brush tips are known as *brush shapes*, or just plain *brushes* (not to be confused with the Brush tool, which people sometimes call "the brush" as well). The concept behind the brush shape is very simple. A big, round brush paints in broad strokes. A small, elliptical brush is useful for performing hairline adjustments. And if that's not enough — which it rarely is — there is a world of options in between these two extremes, plus an assortment of specialized brushes that will come in handy in unique situations.

Selecting a brush shape

Provided that a paint or edit tool (other than the Color Replacement tool, which does not offer a full set of brushes to choose from) is active, there are a handful of ways to modify the brush shape in Photoshop:

✦ **Right-clicking.** Right-click anywhere in the image window (Control-click on the Mac) to display a small palette of preset brush shapes complete with a menu of additional options, as seen in Figure 5-12. Scroll through the list of brush shapes, click the one you want to use, and then press Enter or Return to hide the palette. You can also press Escape to hide the palette and leave the brush shape unchanged.

Note The Presets palette previews how the brush looks both when you click and when you drag. If your computer setup includes a pressure-sensitive drawing tablet, or if you've adjusted the Fade parameter in the brush's Shape Dynamics settings (as I explain in the upcoming "Shape dynamics" section), the strokes appear to taper, as in the figure. Otherwise, they appear uniform. To dispense with the stroke previews, choose Large Thumbnail from the palette menu. To restore the stroke previews, choose Stroke Thumbnail.

✦ **Brushes palette.** Choose Window ➪ Brushes or press F5 to display the Brushes palette, which appears on the left side of Figure 5-13. Click Brush Presets in the top-left corner of the palette to see a list of predefined brush shapes. You also get a large preview of the active brush shape at the bottom of the palette. Bear in mind, it will appear tapered only if you select the Shape Dynamics option on the left side of the palette.

The primary advantage of the Brushes palette is that you can define your own brush shapes and adjust various exciting dynamics, as I discuss in the next section. If all you want to do is select a predefined brush, right-clicking (or Control-clicking) is generally simpler.

Note By default, the Brushes palette is wider than Photoshop's other palettes, which means it doesn't stack well on the right side of your screen. You have two ways of working around this. One is to get in the habit of pressing F5 to show or hide the palette at a moment's notice. The other is to turn off the Expanded View command in the Brushes palette menu, which lets you shrink the preset brush list to Photoshop's standard palettes width, as in the right example in Figure 5-13.

Figure 5-12: The Presets palette lets you select from a list of predefined brush shapes and load other ones from disk.

✦ **Master Diameter.** With the Presets palette or Brushes palette on-screen, you can change the size of the brush by adjusting the Master Diameter value. Measured in pixels, this value represents the thickest stroke the brush will paint. (It can get thinner based on the Shape Dynamic settings, as I explain later in this chapter.) This means you're never locked into a preset brush diameter, even when painting with custom (nonround) brushes.

Tip

Changing the brush diameter is so useful you can do it from the keyboard. Press the left bracket key ([) to make the brush smaller. Press the right bracket key (]) to make the brush bigger. Keep an eye on the brush icon in the Options bar to see how much smaller or larger the brush diameter gets.

✦ **Preset shortcuts:** You can cycle between presets even when no palette is visible. Press , (comma) to toggle to the previous brush shape in the list. Press . (period) to select the next brush shape. You also can press Shift+, (comma) to select the first brush shape in the list (1 pixel wide) and Shift+. (period) to select the last brush.

Figure 5-13: The Brushes palette can fully expand (left) or reduce (right). The advantage of the reduced view is that it stacks well with Photoshop's other palettes and won't obscure as much of your workspace.

By default, your cursor outline reflects the active brush shape. If your cursor looks like a cross hair or tool icon instead, press Ctrl+K (⌘-K on the Mac) to open the Preferences dialog box, then press Ctrl+3 (⌘-3 on the Mac) for the Display & Cursors panel, and select Brush Size from the Painting Cursors radio buttons. Now you can create a brush as big as 2,500 pixels in diameter and have your cursor grow accordingly.

Tip When you use a very small brush, four dots appear around the cursor perimeter, making the cursor easier to locate. If you need a little more help, press Caps Lock to access the more obvious cross-hair cursor.

Making your own brush shape

To create a custom brush shape, click Brush Tip Shape in the Brushes palette, which displays the options shown in Figure 5-14. Photoshop displays thumbnails for the predefined brushes in the top-right quadrant of the palette. Select a brush to serve as a starting point for your custom creation, and then you can tweak the settings until you've created the brush you have in mind.

✦ **Diameter.** This option determines the width of the brush. If the brush shape is elliptical instead of circular, the Diameter value determines the longest dimension. You can type any value from 1 to 2,500 pixels.

Caution   Brush shapes with diameters of 15 pixels or higher are too large to display accurately in the Options bar; the stroke preview at the bottom of the Brushes palette is accurate to no higher than 50 pixels. Therefore, you should essentially ignore the previews of such brushes, rather than assume that you've done something wrong with the setup.

Figure 5-14: To change the size, shape, and hardness of a brush, click Brush Tip Shape in the Brushes palette.

✦ **Flip X** and **Flip Y.** Select the Flip X option to flip the brush shape into a mirror image of itself. Select the Flip Y option to flip the brush shape upside-down. These options are most obvious when you're using one of the more detailed brushes or a brush preset you've created from an image.

✦ **Angle.** This option pivots a brush shape on its axis. Unless the brush is elliptical, though, you won't see a difference. So it's best to first adjust the Roundness value and then adjust the Angle.

✦ **Roundness.** Type a Roundness value of less than 100 percent to create an elliptical brush shape. The value modifies the height of the brush as a percentage of the Diameter value, so a Roundness of 50 percent results in a short, fat brush.

Tip   You can adjust the angle of the brush dynamically by dragging the gray arrow inside the box to the right of the Angle and Roundness options. Drag the handles on either side of the black circle to make the brush shape elliptical, as demonstrated in Figure 5-15. Drag the arrow tip to angle the brush. Or try this trick: Click anywhere in the white box to move the arrow to that point.

Figure 5-15: Drag the black handles and gray arrow to change the roundness and angle of the brush, respectively. The Roundness and Angle values update automatically, as does the preview of the brushstroke at the bottom of the palette.

✦ **Hardness.** Except when using the Pencil tool, brushes are always anti-aliased. You can further soften the edges of a brush by dragging the Hardness slider bar away from 100 percent. The softest setting, 0 percent, gradually tapers the brush from a single solid-color pixel at its center to a ring of transparent pixels around the brush's perimeter. Figure 5-16 shows how low Hardness percentages expand the size of a 200-pixel brush beyond the Diameter value (as demonstrated by the examples in the bottom row). Even a 100 percent hard brush shape expands slightly because it is anti-aliased. The Hardness setting is ignored when you use the Pencil tool.

Tip

Like Diameter, Hardness is one of those settings that you need regular access to. So the ever-helpful Photoshop lets you change the Hardness from the keyboard. Press Shift-[(Shift-left bracket) to make the brush softer; press Shift-] (Shift-right bracket) to make the brush harder. Both shortcuts work in 25 percent increments. For example, you have to press Shift-] four times to go from 0 percent Hardness to 100 percent.

✦ **Spacing.** In real life, a brush lays down a continuous coat of paint. But that's not how it works on the computer. Photoshop blasts out a stream of colored spots. The Spacing option controls how frequently the spots are emitted, measured as a percentage of the brush shape. For example, suppose the Diameter of a brush is 40 pixels and the Spacing is set to 25 percent (the default setting for all predefined brushes). For every 10 pixels (25 percent of 40) you drag with the Brush tool, Photoshop lays down a 40-pixel-wide spot of color. A Spacing of 1 percent provides the most coverage but also slows down the performance of the tool. If you deselect the Spacing option, the effect of the tool is wholly dependent on the speed at which you drag; this can be useful for creating splotchy or oscillating lines. Figure 5-17 shows examples.

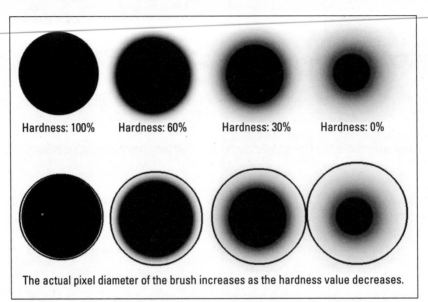

Hardness: 100%   Hardness: 60%   Hardness: 30%   Hardness: 0%

The actual pixel diameter of the brush increases as the hardness value decreases.

Figure 5-16: A 200-pixel brush as it appears when set to each of four Hardness percentages. In the bottom row, the brushes are on a separate layer and a black fringe is added so you can see the effective diameter of each Hardness value.

You may see ridges begin to appear at the default Spacing value of 25 percent, especially when painting with a mouse. If you notice lumps in your brushstrokes, lower the Spacing to 15 percent, which ensures a good mix of speed and smoothness. When using a soft-edged brush, lower Spacing values result in a denser, fatter stroke, and higher values result in a lighter, thinner stroke. High Spacing values are great for creating dotted lines.

After you edit a brush, you can save the brush for later use by clicking the tiny page icon at the bottom of the palette. Photoshop suggests a name, which you can then change. To save a brush without being asked to name it, Alt-click the Page icon (or Option-click on the Mac). Photoshop stores the brush with your program preferences so that it's preserved between editing sessions.

If you delete the preferences file (as discussed in Chapter 2), you lose your custom brushes. To ensure that your custom brushes are saved in case you delete the preferences file or for use on another machine, choose Save Brushes from the Palette menu. See the section "Saving and loading brush sets" for more information.

To delete a brush from the list, switch back to the Brush Presets view and drag the brush to the trash icon at the bottom of the palette.

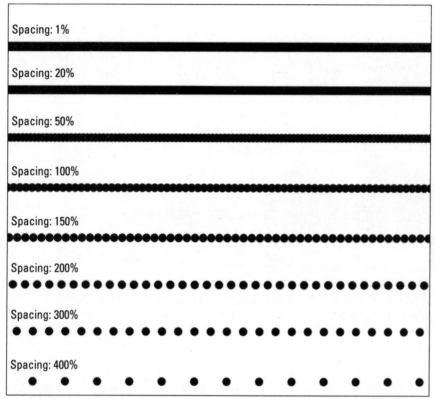

Spacing: 1%

Spacing: 20%

Spacing: 50%

Spacing: 100%

Spacing: 150%

Spacing: 200%

Spacing: 300%

Spacing: 400%

Figure 5-17: Examples of lines drawn with the Brush tool subject to different Spacing values. Values greater than 100 percent are useful for creating dotted-line effects.

Defining a custom brush

Photoshop allows you to not only modify the size and roundness of a brush, but define a custom brush as well. Start by making a new image and doodling the shape of your brush tip —to test and experiment with the procedure. Doodle a bit with the brush, and don't worry about creating the perfect custom brush just yet. Next, use the rectangular marquee tool to select the doodle. You don't have to be particularly careful; just select the general area around the doodle, as shown in Figure 5-18. Photoshop is smart enough to distinguish the confines of the brush from its background.

For more information on the Rectangular Marquee tool, see Chapter 8.

Next, choose the Define Brush command from the Edit menu. Photoshop invites you to give your brush a name; if you're not feeling inspired, just press Enter or Return and accept the default name, Sampled Brush #1.

Figure 5-18: After selecting a doodle against a white background, choose
Edit ⇨ Define Brush and type a name to turn the doodle into a custom
brush.

After you define a custom brush, you can tweak it just like any other brush inside
the Brush Tip Shape panel of the Brushes palette. You can adjust the Diameter,
Angle, and Roundness (height versus width) of your new brush. The only option
that appears dimmed is Hardness; you have to accept the sharpness of the brush as
it was originally defined. A custom brush will even grow and shrink according to
stylus pressure if you're using a graphic tablet, or you can use the left and right
bracket [ ] keys.

To restore a custom brush to its original size, click Use Sample Size in the Brush Tip
Shape panel of the Brushes palette.

Saving and loading brush sets

After you define a handful of brushes you may want to save them for use on a differ-
ent computer or to avoid losing them in the event of any problem that might require
you to reinstall Photoshop. Photoshop saves multiple brushes at a time to libraries.
The program also ships with several predefined libraries, which you can find in the
Presets/Brushes folder inside the folder that contains the Photoshop application.
Brush libraries have the *.abr* file extension.

You can save brush sets — as well as load and edit them — by choosing commands
from the Brushes palette menu when the Brush Presets panel is displayed. You can
also choose commands from the Presets palette that you get when right-clicking

with a paint or edit tool (other than the Color Replacement tool). You can manage libraries by choosing Edit ➪ Preset Manager, which is shown in Figure 5-19 with the Brushes panel at the forefront. If you're already working in the Preset Manager, press Ctrl+1 (⌘-1 on the Mac) to get to the Brushes panel.

Figure 5-19: Choose Edit ➪ Preset Manager to display the central headquarters for loading, saving, and editing brush sets.

By default, the Brushes palette displays a list of nearly 70 predefined brushes, including both elliptical and custom varieties. You can't delete this brush set, but you can prevent brushes you don't use from taking up space in the palette. You also can load or create a different set, combine two or more sets, and add or delete brushes from your custom brush sets. Here's the drill:

✦ **Save a brush set.** To save all brushes currently displayed in the Brushes palette, choose Save Brushes from the palette menu. If you want to save only some of the brushes as a set, however, choose Edit ➪ Preset Manager. Shift+click the brushes you want to save, and then click the Save Set button. If you want to select non-contiguous brushes, use the Ctrl key (Windows) or the Cmd key (Mac) as you click on the brushes you want to save.

Regardless of where you initiate the save, Photoshop takes you to the Save dialog box, where you can name your brush set. By default, brushes are saved in the Presets/Brushes folder. The next time you start Photoshop, your new brush set appears on the Brushes palette menu along with other available sets.

✦ **Use a different brush set.** If you want to put the current brush set away and use a different set, choose Replace Brushes from the Brushes palette menu and select the brush set you want to use. Alternatively, click the arrowhead at the top of the scrolling list of icons in the Preset Manager dialog box to display a similar menu, and then choose Replace Brushes from that menu.

✦ **Load multiple brush sets.** You can keep multiple brush sets active if you want. After loading the first set, choose Load Brushes from the Brushes palette menu or click Load in the Preset Manager dialog box. Photoshop appends the second brush set onto the first. If you want to keep using the two sets together, you may want to save them as a new, custom brush set.

✦ **Delete a brush.** To delete a brush from the current brush set, select it from the Brush Presets panel of the Brushes palette and click the trash icon. Or choose Delete Brush from the palette menu.

Want to give a bunch of brushes the axe? Cut them loose through the Preset Manager dialog box. Select the brushes you no longer want, and then click Delete.

✦ **Restore default brushes.** To return to the default Photoshop brush set, choose Reset Brushes from the menu in the palette or the dialog box. You then have the option of either replacing the existing brushes with the default brushes or simply adding them to the end of the palette.

✦ **Rename a brush.** If you want to rename a brush, select it in the Preset Manager dialog box and click Rename. Or, even easier, double-click the brush-stroke in the Brush Presets panel of the Brushes palette.

If you want your new brush names to live in perpetuity, resave the brush set. Otherwise, the names will revert to their original labels when and if you replace the brush set.

Brush Dynamics

Photoshop has long permitted you to vary the size, opacity, and color of paint according to input from a pressure-sensitive drawing tablet. Available from companies such as Wacom (www.wacom.com), pressure-sensitive drawing tablets respond to how hard you press on the stylus (the pen that is drawn across the surface of the tablet), as well as the angle of the stylus and other attributes.

Even if you don't have a tablet, Photoshop permits mouse users to enjoy much of the same flexibility as their stylus-wielding colleagues. Whether you use a stylus, a mouse, or even a finger on a notebook trackpad, you can introduce an element of spontaneity into what seems at times like an absolute world of computer imaging.

Photoshop calls these imaginative options *brush dynamics*, and they open up a lot of opportunities for faking pressure sensitivity. For example, you can make a brush shape twirl as you paint. You can add noise to the edges of a stroke. You can spray shapes, add texture, combine brushes, or even paint in rainbows. And most of the settings work every bit as well with, say, the Sponge tool as they do with the Brush tool. You may find this tinkering and experimenting with brush dynamics to be rather addictive, so pack a lunch or bring a thermos of strong coffee with you when you first sit down to play.

Brush dynamic basics

To access Photoshop's brush dynamics when a paint or edit tool (other than the Color Replacement tool) is active, open the Brushes palette (press F5 if it's hidden) and select the Shape Dynamics option on the left side of the palette. This simultaneously activates and displays the first of six panels — Scattering, Texture, and so on — devoted to brush dynamics. Photoshop also provides a series of options in the central portion of the palette (starting with Noise and ending with Protect Texture) that apply minor effects without displaying additional panels of options.

Note that all check boxes and options are available when using the Brush tool, but they come and go for the other paint and edit tools. For example, the Wet Edges option is unavailable when using the Pencil tool, Color Dynamics is dimmed when using the Dodge and Burn tools, and so on. Even so, the sheer amount of options available for even the most limited of the edit tools verges on fantastic, especially when compared with older versions of Photoshop. Also, each tool observes an independent set of defaults. So activating, say, Shape Dynamics, Texture, and Smoothing for the Brush tool does not turn them on for other tools. However, they will again be turned on the next time you return to the Brush tool.

If you want to save a group of brush dynamics for use with a variety of tools, click the Page icon along the bottom of the Brushes palette. Brush dynamics are considered part of a saved brush shape and transfer from one tool to another. To save a group of brush dynamics for use with a single tool, visit the Tool Presets palette (Window ➪ Tool Presets) and choose New Tool Preset from the palette menu. It's equivalent to designing a custom tool that you can select from the Options bar, as discussed back in Chapter 2.

Tip   As you experiment with these options, don't forget to keep one eye on the big stroke preview at the bottom of the palette. It really is useful, especially when trying out settings that you haven't used before or combining options to achieve specific effects.

Shape dynamics

Inside the Brushes palette, click the Shape Dynamics option — the name, not the check box — to display the panel of options illustrated in Figure 5-20. Notice that the panel is divided into three sections, which start with the words Size Jitter, Angle Jitter, and Roundness Jitter. These options permit you to vary the diameter, angle, and roundness, respectively, of the brush over the course of a single stroke. But the repetition of the word "Jitter" may be misleading. It implies (to many users) that each group of options is related to jittering — Photoshop's word for random brush shape fluctuations — when in fact, jittering is a minor element of shape dynamics.

Figure 5-20: The Shape Dynamics panel, with a drawing made with the displayed brush settings

The diameter settings

The first group of options controls the thickness of the brushstroke. The most important of these is the Control pop-up menu, which links the diameter of the brush to one of several variables. If you own a pressure-sensitive tablet, the most obvious setting is Pen Pressure, which is the default. This turns the brush into a traditional, pressure-sensitive painting tool, growing when you bear down on the stylus and shrinking with you let up.

Note   Three settings — Pen Pressure, Pen Tilt, and Stylus Wheel — require compatible hardware. If your only pointing device is a standard mouse, as is typical, selecting one of these options displays a triangular warning icon. This is Photoshop's way of telling you that, although you are welcome to select the option, it isn't really going to work. If you get the message in error — say, you get a warning for Pen Pressure even though you have a tablet installed — try clicking with the stylus on the Brushes palette. If that doesn't work, open the control panel or utility that manages the tablet to make sure the tablet is properly installed.

Cross-Reference   As it turns out, you can take advantage of the Pen Pressure option even if you don't own a pressure-sensitive tablet. In Photoshop, you can simulate pressure by stroking a paint or edit tool along a path. For complete information, see Chapter 8.

In addition to Pen Pressure, the Control pop-up menu lets you select among the following options:

✦ **Off.** Select this option to turn off the capability to vary the thickness of the brushstroke. You can still add random variations to the thickness using the Size Jitter value.

✦ **Fade.** This option works every bit as well whether you use a mouse or tablet. Select Fade to reduce the size of the brush over the course of the drag, and then type a value in the option box on the right to specify the distance over which the fading should occur. This distance is measured in steps — that is, the number of spots of color the brush plops down before reducing the size of the brush to its minimum (defined by the Minimum Diameter setting). The default value is 25#, which means 25 spots of color. Exactly how long such a stroke is in, say, inches, depends on the Diameter and the Spacing values in the Brush Tip Shape panel. In other words, be prepared to experiment.

The Fade option can be most useful in the creation of a specular reflection, or in layman's terms, a sparkle. Figure 5-21 shows before and after versions of an image to which I applied a sparkle, or glow, using a series of strokes with a soft brush. The brush settings included a diameter of 20 pixels and a Fade value of 100 steps. To make each stroke, I clicked in the center and Shift-clicked farther out (creating a straight line). To complete the effect, I clicked once in the center of the sparkle with a very large, very soft brush.

✦ **Pen Tilt.** The tilt of a pen is its angle with respect to the tablet. Straight up and down, the pen communicates no tilt; at a severe angle, the pen communicates maximum tilt. When you set the Control option to Pen Tilt, you do two things. First, you vary the size of the brush according to pressure, just as you do when using Pen Pressure. Second, you add an element of vertical scaling so that the brush shape is oblong during a tilt. This scaling is defined by the Tilt Scale slider. All in all, it's an interesting idea, but for my money, Pen Tilt works more predictably when applied to roundness.

✦ **Stylus Wheel.** If tablet owners account for 10 percent of Photoshop users, airbrush owners account for about 1 percent of tablet users. That's still enough people to populate a small town, so Photoshop might as well support them. Unlike the scroll wheels included with many PC mice — which are exceptionally useful for scrolling Web pages and Word documents — the wheel on an airbrush locks into position. This means you can nudge it higher or lower and leave it there. Although typically associated with properties such as Flow (which you can set from the Other Dynamics panel), the airbrush wheel is surprisingly useful for diameter as well. Move the wheel up, the brush gets thick and stays thick; move the wheel down, and you lock in a fine line, all in the middle of painting a brushstroke. This all sounds great, so is there a downside? Why, yes! A Wacom airbrush can cost upwards of $100, not including the tablet. So it's not a spur-of-the-moment gift for most of us.

Figure 5-21: Need more shine? Add some with a customized brush.

Accompanying the Control pop-up menu are three slider bars:

✦ **Minimum Diameter.** Use this option to determine the thinnest a brushstroke can go. You can go as low as 1 percent.

✦ **Tilt Scale.** Available only when you set the Control option to Pen Tilt, this setting stretches the height of the brush to make it elliptical when you tilt the stylus, and attempts to mimic the way painting with a real brush feels. You can do this just as well with the roundness options, though, so you may not use this setting – then again, you might like it. It's up to you and your personal preferences.

✦ **Size Jitter.** Use this slider to add an element of randomness to the thickness of a brushstroke. It doesn't matter whether you use a mouse or a stylus; the brush will jitter every bit as well either way. Higher values produce a wider range of jitter. Keep an eye on the preview at the bottom of the palette to get a sense of what different settings will do.

Angle and roundness

Now that you understand the diameter settings, the angle and roundness settings are pretty simple stuff. But to confirm your knowledge and make sure that we're all on the same page, here's how they work:

✦ **Angle Control.** As with diameter, you can link the angle of the brush to such variables as Pen Pressure, Pen Tilt, and Stylus Wheel. More pressure or tilt equals more rotation of the brush. Naturally, the changes show up best with elliptical or asymmetrical brushes. You can also link the angle to Fade, which rotates the brush over the course of a specific number of steps, and then returns the brush to its normal angle (as specified in the Brush Tip Shape panel).

But this Control pop-up menu adds two more settings: Direction and Initial Direction. The first rotates the brush according to the direction of your drag. A horizontal drag is considered the normal angle; when dragging vertically, the brush rotates 90 degrees. For maximum effect, after setting this option to Direction, go to the Brush Tip Shape panel and set the Angle value to 90 degrees (or something close) with an elliptical brush. Then raise the Spacing value to something higher than 100 percent.

Meanwhile, the Initial Direction option rotates the brush according to the very start of your drag and then locks it into position. It's a nice idea, but the angle is locked down about 2 pixels into your drag, which means Photoshop is aware of your initial direction before you are.

✦ **Angle Jitter.** This option rotates the brush randomly as you paint. As always, be sure to adjust the roundness of the brush so you can see the randomness at work.

✦ **Roundness Control.** Set this option to Fade to reduce the roundness to its minimum over the course of a specified number of steps. You can also associate the roundness with Pen Pressure, Pen Tilt, or Stylus Wheel. Of these, Pen Tilt makes by far the most sense to me because that's what Pen Tilt does in real life.

✦ **Minimum Roundness.** This value determines the minimum roundness, or maximum flatness, of the brush available to the Control and Jitter settings. If the Control option is set to Off and the Roundness Jitter is 0 percent, the Minimum Roundness slider is dimmed.

✦ **Roundness Jitter.** Use this option to introduce random variations in roundness to your brushstroke.

✦ **Flip X Jitter and Flip Y Jitter.** Two check boxes at the bottom of the Shape Dynamics panel give you the ability to flip the jitter on its x-axis, y-axis, or both at once, much like you can flip the brush shape. Flipping the jitter on its axis may be more control than most of us will ever need, but it was nice of Photoshop's designers to make this option available.

Additional brush dynamics

For many, the Shape Dynamics settings will be enough. They certainly permit you to achieve an enormous range of effects. But if you're feeling ambitious, you can venture much deeper. Fortunately, the other panels of options — Scattering, Texture, and so on — follow the same logic we've seen thus far and you'll find they're quite simple to deal with, based on your having looked at the Shape Dynamics settings already.

Figure 5-22 demonstrates several dynamic permutations as applied to the Scattered Leaves predefined custom brush. Here's how these options work:

✦ **Scattering.** Highlight the Scattering option to spread the position of the spots of color around the brushstroke. When using a custom brush, such as Scattered Leaves in Figure 5-22, the effect is like spraying a pattern of images. Raise the Scatter value to increase the spread. Select Both Axes to scatter the brush spots along the stroke as well as perpendicularly to it. Use the Control pop-up menu to link it to stylus pressure or some other variable. Finally, use the Count options to increase the population of brush spots.

✦ **Texture.** Select this option to apply a texture to a brushstroke, useful for conveying a surface such as paper or canvas. After selecting a predefined texture, set the Scale and Depth values to determine the size and degree of texture applied. Use the Mode option to define how brush and texture mix. (You can find out more about modes in the "Brush Modes" section near the end of this chapter, but for now, just experiment with an eye on the preview.)

If you want to vary the depth of texture throughout a stroke, turn on the Texture Each Tip option. Then use the Control option to vary the depth according to, say, stylus pressure, or add some random Depth Jitter.

✦ **Dual Brush.** The Dual Brush panel lets you mix two brushes together. Select the second brush from the list of thumbnails and use the Mode option to specify how the brushes intermix. You can also throw in settings such as Spacing, Scatter, and Count, all of which affect the second brush. Figure 5-23 shows another example, complete with settings in the Brushes palette. Notice how by mixing a standard round brush with one of Photoshop's predefined Dry Brush options, a complex brush that imparts its own texture is generated.

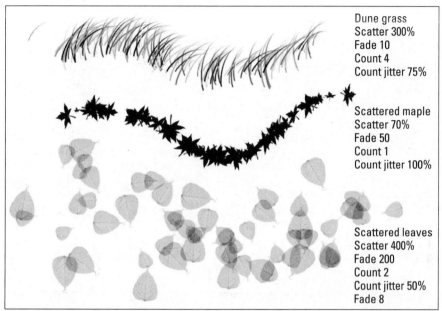

Dune grass
Scatter 300%
Fade 10
Count 4
Count jitter 75%

Scattered maple
Scatter 70%
Fade 50
Count 1
Count jitter 100%

Scattered leaves
Scatter 400%
Fade 200
Count 2
Count jitter 50%
Fade 8

Figure 5-22: Several brush dynamics applied to various Brush presets -- Dune Grass, Scattered Maple Leaves, and Scattered Leaves. By varying the Scatter value, the preset's scattering effect can be heightened (see bottom sample) or tightened (see middle example).

✦ **Color Dynamics.** Use these options to vary the color of the stroke between the foreground and background colors depending on a fade or stylus pressure. You can also apply random changes to the hue, saturation, and brightness. The final slider bar, Purity, increases or decreases the saturation of colors throughout the brushstroke.

✦ **Other Dynamics.** The final set of brush dynamics permits you to associate the opacity, strength, flow, or exposure of the brush, depending on what tool you're using. I discuss each of these attributes in more detail in the section "Opacity and Strength, Flow and Exposure." If you happen to own an airbrush, settings such as the Flow and Exposure are what the wheel was originally designed for.

Tip

You'll notice that you have the ability to lock the settings you choose in the various brush dynamics panels. Click the Lock icon next to a panel name in the Brushes palette to toggle the lock option on or off. When a panel is locked, Photoshop retains the panel's settings even if you select a new brush preset that would normally contain different settings.

Figure 5-23: The look of chalk, achieved with a Brush. A larger-sized brush, with the Flow reduced, created the look of the blackboard having been wiped before the drawing was done. Neat, huh?

Noise, Wet Edges, and the rest

The list along the left side of the Brushes palette ends with five options that you can use to add highlights and constraints to your brushstrokes. Not all options work with all tools — none is compatible with the Smudge tool, for example — but when available, they're as effective as they are easy to use. And they work equally well with a mouse or a tablet.

✦ **Noise.** This option randomizes the pixels along the edge of a brushstroke. Because the option affects only the edge, softer brushes result in more noise. The middle line in Figure 5-24 shows an example.

✦ **Wet Edges.** When you select the Wet Edges option, the brush creates a translucent line with darkened edges, much as if you were painting with watercolors. Soft brush shapes produce more naturalistic effects. The final example in Figure 5-24 shows a soft brushstroke painted in black.

✦ **Airbrush.** This option duplicates the Airbrush icon in the Options bar. When turned on, paint builds up even when you hold the cursor in place, as if you were spraying color from a real airbrush. The Airbrush option is not available when using the pencil tool or any of the three focus tools (Blur, Sharpen, and Smudge).

Figure 5-24: Three lines painted in black with the brush tool. The left was painted without dynamics (soft), the middle was painted with Noise, and the right, with Wet Edges.

- ✦ **Smoothing.** If you have difficulty drawing smooth lines and curves, turn this option on to even out the rough spots. It slows down Photoshop's tracking time a little, but it may be worth it in many cases. Adobe recommends this option when using a stylus, but I've found it most helpful when using optical mice, which are notoriously bad at tracking evenly on patterned surfaces, such as wood tabletops.

- ✦ **Protect Texture.** If you plan on painting a lot of textured lines and you want your textures to match, select this option. It maintains a consistent pattern from one brushstroke to the next. The effect can be subtle, but I usually advise working with this option turned on.

Undoing pressure-sensitive lines

In the old days, pressure-sensitive lines were a pain to undo. Because a stylus is so sensitive to gradual pressure, you can unwittingly let up and repress the stylus during what you perceive as a single drag. If, after doing so, you decide you don't like the line and press Ctrl+Z (⌘-Z on the Mac), Photoshop deletes only the last portion of the line because it detected a release midway.

This is why it's a good idea to get in the habit of using Ctrl+Alt+Z (⌘-Option-Z on the Mac). Each time you press this shortcut, you take another step back in the history of your image, permitting you to eliminate every bit of a line regardless of how many times you let up on the stylus.

See Chapter 7 for complete information on Photoshop's multiple undos.

Create a new layer (by pressing Ctrl+Shift+N on the PC or ⌘-Shift-N on the Mac) before you paint with or without a stylus. Then you can refine your lines and erase them without harming the original appearance of your image. (You can do this without layers using the history brush, again explained in Chapter 7, but a relatively old-fashioned layer tends to be less hassle.)

Opacity and Strength, Flow and Exposure

Another way to change the performance of a paint or edit tool is to adjust the Opacity and Flow values, which also go by the terms Strength and Exposure, respectively, depending on the tool you're using. When available, these controls appear in the Options bar. Regardless of which setting you want to change, you click the triangle to display a slider bar, drag the slider to raise or lower the value, and then press Enter or Return. Alternatively, you can double-click the option box, type a value, and press Enter.

Here's a look at how these options work:

✦ **Opacity.** The Opacity value determines the translucency of colors applied with the Brush or Pencil tool. The option is available also when using the Gradient tool, Paint Bucket tool, History Brush tool, both stamp tools, and the Eraser tool, all of which I discuss in future chapters. At 100 percent, the applied colors appear opaque, completely covering the image behind them. (Exceptions occur when using the Brush tool with Wet Edges active, which produces a translucent stroke, and when applying Mode options, discussed in the "Brush Modes" section.) At lower settings, the applied colors mix with the existing colors in the image.

You can change the opacity of brushstrokes or edits that you just applied by choosing Edit ➪ Fade or pressing Ctrl+Shift+F (⌘-Shift-F on the Mac). Then drag the Opacity slider in the Fade dialog box. While you're in the dialog box, you can apply one of Photoshop's brush modes to further change how the modified pixels blend with the original ones.

✦ **Strength.** When using the Blur or Sharpen tool, the Opacity option changes to Strength. The value determines the degree to which the tool changes the focus of the image; 1 percent is the minimum and 100 percent is the maximum. Strength also appears when using the Smudge tool, in which case it governs the distance the tool drags colors in the image. Another difference between Strength and Opacity is that the default Opacity value for each tool when you begin using Photoshop is 100 percent but the default Strength value is 50 percent. Whether Strength is stronger than Opacity or these tools merely happen to know their own Strength is uncertain; but 50 percent is the baseline.

✦ **Flow.** The Flow option appears when using the Brush, Sponge, and Eraser tools, both stamp tools, and the History Brush. Although it is always accompanied by the Airbrush icon, you can use Flow and Airbrush independently. The Flow value controls the opacity of each spot of color a tool delivers. So as a tool lays each spot of color onto the previous spot, the spots mix together and become more opaque. This means three things. First, a particular Flow setting produces a more opaque line than an equivalent Opacity setting. In Figure 5-25, for example, a Flow value of 50 percent comes in slightly darker than an Opacity value of 50 percent. Second, Flow results in a progressive effect that compounds as a brushstroke overlaps itself, also demonstrated in the figure. Third, because Flow works on a spot-by-spot basis, you can increase or decrease the opacity of a line further by lowering or raising, respectively, the Spacing value in the Brush Tip Shape panel.

When using the Brush, History Brush, Stamp, and Eraser tools, you can combine Opacity and Flow values to achieve unique effects. You can also add the Airbrush, which compounds Flow further by adding spots of color when you slow down a brushstroke or hold the cursor still.

✦ **Exposure.** Available when using the Dodge or Burn tool, Exposure controls how much the tools lighten or darken the image, respectively. As with Flow, Exposure compounds when you corner or overlap a brushstroke, and includes an airbrush variation. A setting of 100 percent applies the maximum amount of lightening or darkening, which is still far short of either absolute white or black. As with Strength, the default is 50 percent.

Tip

You can change the Opacity, Strength, or Exposure setting for the active tool in 10 percent increments by pressing a number key on the keyboard or keypad. Press 1 to change the setting to 10 percent, press 2 for 20 percent, and so on, all the way up to 0 for 100 percent. If you want to change the Opacity, Strength, or Exposure setting in 1 percent increments just press two keys in a row. Press 4 twice for 44 percent, 0 and 7 for 7 percent, and so on. This works whether or not the Options bar is visible. Get in the habit of using the number keys and you'll thank yourself later.

Changing the Flow value on the fly is trickier but still possible. When the Sponge tool is active, Flow works just like Opacity: Type a number to change the value in 10 percent increments; type two numbers to enter a specific value. But what about the Brush tool and others that offer both Opacity and Flow? Typing a number changes the Opacity value *unless* the Airbrush icon is active, in which case typing a number changes Flow. If the Airbrush is turned off, press Shift plus a number key to change the Flow value. When the Airbrush is turned on, pressing Shift plus a number key changes the Opacity value.

Opacity 50%   Opacity 50%   Opacity 50%
Flow 100%   Flow 50%   Flow 50%
                                          Spacing 10%

Figure 5-25: Here you can see the difference between Opacity, which controls an entire brushstroke (left), and Flow, which affects individual spots of paint (middle). Tighter Spacing values also heighten the effect of Flow (right).

Brush Modes

When certain painting or editing tools are active, the Options bar provides access to Photoshop's brush modes. The brush modes control how the colors applied by the tool mix with existing colors inside an image or layer. Figure 5-26 shows which brush modes are available when you select various tools.

With the exception of the specialized modes available for the Dodge, Burn, and Sponge tools, these brush modes are merely variations on the blend modes available in the Layers palette, which are discussed in Chapter 13. The difference is that the blend modes in the Layers palette mix colors between layers but the brush modes in the Options bar mix colors inside a single layer. Because of this subtle distinction, the modes are covered twice, once in the following section and again in Chapter 13. The latter discussion is more detailed, so if you don't get all the info you need here, read Chapter 13 to find out more.

Figure 5-26: The specific Mode settings in the Options bar vary depending on which tool is active. The Mode pop-up menu changes to Range when using the Dodge or Burn tool.

Tip   You can change brush modes from the keyboard by pressing Shift+plus (+) or Shift+minus (–). Shift+plus takes you to the next brush mode listed in the pop-up menu; Shift+minus selects the previous brush mode. It's a great way to cycle through the brush modes without losing your place in the image.

The 25 paint tool modes

Photoshop offers a total of 25 brush modes when you use the Brush, the Pencil, or any of the other tools shown along the left side of Figure 5-26. (An additional mode, Threshold, is an alternative to Normal in certain color modes.) The brush modes are organized into six groups, and the individual modes — what they do and how you might use them — are described here.

Tip   Just as you can cycle from one brush mode to the next from the keyboard, you can jump directly to a specific brush mode as well. Just press Shift+Alt (Win) or Shift-Option (Mac) and a letter key. For example, Shift+Alt+N (Shift-Option-N on the Mac) selects the Normal mode; Shift+Alt+C (Shift-Option-C on the Mac) selects the Color mode. The letter key for each brush mode is in parentheses along with its description.

✦ **Normal (N).** Choose this mode to paint or edit an image normally. A paint tool coats the image with the foreground color, and an edit tool manipulates the existing colors in an image according to the Opacity, Strength, Flow, and Exposure values.

Two color modes prevent Photoshop from rendering soft or translucent edges. The Black-and-White and Indexed modes (Image ➪ Mode ➪ Bitmap and Image ➪ Mode ➪ Indexed Color) simply don't have enough colors to go around. When painting in such a low-color image, Photoshop replaces the Normal brush mode with Threshold (L), which results in harsh, jagged edges, just like a stroke painted with the Pencil tool. You can alternatively dither the soft edges by selecting the Dissolve mode.

✦ **Dissolve (I).** Dissolve scatters a random pattern of colors to simulate translucency. The pattern shows up along the edges of opaque brushstrokes or inside translucent strokes, like those in Figure 5-27. Note that this mode and the two that follow are not applicable to the edit tools. To get something resembling Dissolve with, say, the Smudge tool, try applying the Noise setting in the Brushes palette.

✦ **Behind (Q).** This mode is applicable exclusively to layers with transparency. When Behind is selected, the paint tools apply color behind the image on the active layer, showing through only in the transparent and translucent areas. Figure 5-28 shows a painting made from a photo — essentially using the photo as a sort of paint-by-numbers guide after which the photo was removed from the image — in which I started by painting the black and very dark areas, then built the midtones on top of that, and finally the lightest shades. The finished product, with a black background (on a separate layer) appears in the fourth block. It's important to note that when working on an image without layers or on the background layer of a multilayered image, the Behind mode is dimmed.

✦ **Clear (R).** When working on a layer other than *Background*, the Clear mode turns the Brush, Pencil, or Paint Bucket into an erasing tool, clearing away pixels. Given that the Eraser tool already emulates the behavior of both the Brush and Pencil tools (as explained in Chapter 7), there's not a lot of reason to use Clear mode with either of these tools. However, it creates a unique effect when combined with the Paint Bucket, as explained in Chapter 6.

✦ **Darken (K).** The first of the four darkening modes, Darken applies a new color to a pixel only if that color is darker than the pixel's present color. Otherwise, the pixel is left unchanged. The mode works on a channel-by-channel basis, so it might change a pixel in the green channel, for example, without changing the pixel in the red or blue channel. For more information on channels, see Chapter 4.

✦ **Multiply (M).** The Multiply mode combines the foreground color with an existing color in an image to create a third color, darker than the other two. Using the multiply analogy, cyan times magenta is blue, magenta times yellow is red, yellow times cyan is green, and so on. Discussed in Chapter 4, this is the subtractive (CMYK) color theory at work. The effect is almost exactly like drawing with felt-tip markers, except the colors don't bleed.

In Figure 5-29, three roses are used to illustrate the darkening modes. The left flower uses the Darken mode, but because the new petal is the same color as the rest of the rose, it has not effect. The middle flower uses Multiply mode, creating a new color where the new petal overlaps the rose. In the right flower, the Linear Burn mode creates a darker, more colorful shade where the new petal overlaps.

Figure 5-27: Vertical lines were painted with the Normal (left) and Dissolve (right) mode set to 50 percent opacity. The diagonal lines were painted with the Normal (left) and Dissolve (right) mode set to 100 percent opacity. The soft shapes beneath the layer containing the straight lines shows the translucency achieved through the use of Dissolve mode.

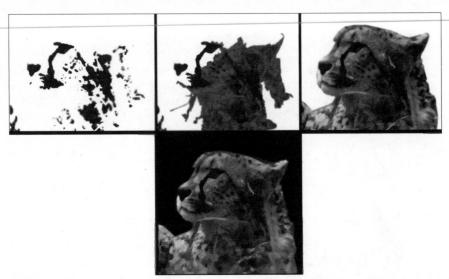

Figure 5-28: To build up the layers of color, draw the darkest colors first and then apply progressively lighter colors using the brush tool set to the Behind mode.

✦ **Color Burn (B)** and **Linear Burn (A).** The two Burn modes are designed to simulate colored versions of the Burn tool. Typically (though not always), Color Burn results in a darker, more colorful stroke than Multiply. Linear Burn is darker still and more muted, as shown in the last example in Figure 5-29. When combined with low Opacity values, the two modes can be interesting, but I wouldn't go so far as to call them particularly helpful.

✦ **Lighten (G).** Leading the lightening modes is the appropriately named Lighten, which ensures that Photoshop applies a new color to a pixel only if the color is lighter than the pixel's present color. In Figure 5-30, the Lighten mode was applied to the left rose, applying color only where a lighter color already existed (only on the white outside the rose).

✦ **Screen (S).** The inverse of the Multiply mode, Screen combines the foreground color with each colored pixel you paint to create a third color, lighter than the other two. Red on green is yellow, green on blue is cyan, blue on red is magenta. In other words, Screen obeys the rules of the additive (RGB) color theory. In the middle rose in Figure 5-30, the Screen mode created a new color that is lighter than the original rose, but only where the paint was applied on top of the original color.

✦ **Color Dodge (D)** and **Linear Dodge (W).** Intended to emulate the Dodge tool, these modes radically lighten an image. Color Dodge produces the more color-ful effect; Linear Dodge works out to be the lightest. In Figure 5-30, in the left rose, the Linear Dodge mode lightens the original rose to white. It applied the paint color only outside the rose. As with the Burn modes, you're likely to have the most luck with the two Dodge modes at low Opacity values.

Figure 5-29: Examples of three of the four darkening modes applied to drawings of a rose, using two colors — a light pink for the flower, and a bright green for the stem and leaves. A new petal is added to the three identical roses, each time painted in a different mode. In all cases, the Opacity setting is 100 percent.

✦ **Overlay (O).** The seven modes starting with Overlay are cousins, each multiplying the dark pixels in an image and screening the light pixels. Of the seven, Overlay is the kindest and arguably the most useful. It enhances contrast and boosts the saturation of colors, rather like a colored version of the Sponge tool set to Saturate. The first image in Figure 5-31 shows the Overlay mode in action. It increased the contrast and added color. Note the areas where the two new petals overlap.

✦ **Soft Light (F)** and **Hard Light (H).** The Soft Light mode applies a subtle glazing of color to an image. Even black or white applied at 100 percent Opacity does no more than darken or lighten the image, but it does slightly diminish contrast. In Figure 5-31, the Soft Light mode lightened and reduced contrast. Meanwhile, Hard Light produces a much stronger effect, even stronger than Overlay. Of the modes you've seen so far, only Normal is more opaque.

Figure 5-30: This time, three of the four lightening modes are applied to the rose. Note that Linear Dodge (right) has a tendency to send the colors to white where it overlaps existing color. The same is true of Color Dodge.

✦ **Vivid Light (V)** and **Linear Light (J).** Vivid Light works like a more colorful variation on the Hard Light mode, much like a Color Burn and Color Dodge effect combined. Linear Light turned the overlapping petal area white in Figure 5-31. And it lightened the original rose color by an increase in contrast. Try one of these modes when you want to simultaneously burn the darkest colors in an image and dodge the lightest ones.

✦ **Pin Light (Z).** This peculiar mode drops out all but the so-called "high-frequency" colors, which are the lightest, darkest, and most saturated color values, as illustrated in the first example in Figure 5-32. The actual paint color only appears where it was applied to white. It is almost never useful for brushing, though it can come in handy when applied to layers, as discussed in Chapter 13.

Figure 5-31: The medium Overlay, subtle Soft Light, and extreme Linear Light modes are applied to the drawn rose, this time with two new petals to show the overlap results.

✦ **Hard Mix (L).** This new mode paints using the Vivid Light brush mode and then applies a threshold operation to each color channel. The result is a stark, high-contrast mix consisting of only eight primary colors: red, green, blue, cyan, magenta, yellow, white, and black.

Cross-Reference

For more information on thresholds, see Chapter 17.

✦ **Difference (E).** When a paint tool is set to the Difference mode, Photoshop subtracts the brightness value of the foreground color from the brightness value of the pixels in the image. If the result is a negative number, Photoshop simply makes it positive. The result of this complex-sounding operation is an inversion effect, as shown on the middle rose in Figure 5-32. Painting with black has no effect on an image; painting with white inverts it.

Tip Because the Difference mode inverts an image, it results in an outline around the brushstroke. You can make this outline thicker by using a softer brush shape, which you get by pressing Shift+[(left bracket).

Figure 5-32: Three petals are added to the rose here, and in each of the three roses, the modes — Pin Light, Difference, and Exclusion — have obvious results on the existing color, where colors overlap, and where paint is applied to the white around the rose.

✦ **Exclusion (X).** Exclusion inverts an image in much the same way as Difference, except colors in the middle of the spectrum mix to form lighter colors, as shown on the left rose in Figure 5-32.

✦ **Hue (U).** Understanding this and the next few modes requires a color theory recap. Remember how the HSL color model calls for three color channels? One is for hue, the value that explains the colors in an image; the second is for saturation, which represents the intensity of the colors; and the third is for luminosity, which explains the lightness and darkness of colors. If you choose the Hue brush mode, therefore, Photoshop applies the hue from the fore-ground color without changing any saturation or luminosity values in the existing image.

Note All HSL brush modes — Hue, Saturation, Color, and Luminosity — are exclusively applicable to color and are therefore unavailable when painting in grayscale images.

✦ **Saturation (T).** If you choose this mode, Photoshop changes the intensity of the colors in an image without changing the colors themselves or the lightness and darkness of individual pixels.

✦ **Color (C).** This mode combines Hue and Saturation to change the colors in an image and the intensity of those colors without changing the lightness and darkness of individual pixels.

Tip In concert with the Brush tool, the Color mode is most often used to colorize grayscale photographs. Here's how it works: Open a grayscale image and then choose Image ⇨ Mode ⇨ RGB Color to convert the image to the RGB mode. Then select the Brush tool — with or without the airbrush turned on — and set the Mode pop-up menu to Color. From that point on, you have only to select the colors you want to use and start painting.

✦ **Luminosity (Y).** The opposite of the Color mode, Luminosity changes the lightness and darkness of pixels, but leaves the Hue and Saturation values unaffected.

The three Dodge and Burn modes

The three modes available with the Dodge and Burn tools are accessed through the Range pop-up menu in the Options bar. As with other brush modes, you can select the Dodge and Burn modes from the keyboard. Just press Shift+Alt (Win) or Shift-Option (Mac) and the letter in parentheses as follows:

✦ **Midtones (M).** Selected by default, the Midtones mode applies the Dodge or Burn tool equally to all but the very lightest or darkest pixels in an image. Midtones enables you to adjust the brightness of colors without blowing out highlights or filling in shadows.

✦ **Shadows (S).** When you select this mode, the Dodge or Burn tool affects dark pixels in an image more dramatically than light pixels. As illustrated in Figure 5-33, medium values are likewise affected, so the Shadows option modifies a wider range of colors than Midtones.

✦ **Highlights (H).** This option lets you lighten or darken the midtones and lightest colors in an image.

Selecting Shadows when using the Dodge tool or Highlights when using the Burn tool has an equalizing effect on an image. For example, the first brushstroke in Figure 5-33 shows the Shadows option combined with the dodge tool. As a result,

Photoshop paints an almost consistent brightness value across the course of a white-to-black gradient. The same is true for the last brushstroke, which combines Highlights with the Burn tool.

Figure 5-33: Here you can see have black-and-white strokes on a gradient background. Across the top, the Dodge tool, set to Shadows, Midtones, and Highlight Range, has been applied. On the bottom image, the Burn tool's three ranges are applied.

Summary

In this chapter, you explored Photoshop's paint and edit tools, learned how to apply the airbrush control, and to paint straight and perpendicular lines. You also learned to use the Smudge and Sponge tools to play with your image colors, and to use the Color Replacement tool.

In mastering all brush-based tools, you learned to change the brush size, shape, and hardness, to save and load custom brush sets, and how to work with a pressure-sensitive drawing tablet.

Customizing brushes was discussed at length, and you learned to create lines that fade away or taper to a point, to use scatter, texture, and other dynamics that adjust opacity and flow, and finally, you learned to work with brush modes.

✦   ✦   ✦

Filling and Stroking

✦ ✦ ✦ ✦

In This Chapter

Applying color with
the Paint Bucket tool
and Fill command

Filling a selection
with custom patterns

Having fun with
the Backspace or
Delete key

Creating an
antique framing effect
with the Paint Bucket

Using the
Gradient features

Designing your own
multicolor gradation

Using the Gradient
tool with the Dissolve
brush mode

Creating
outlines and borders

Attaching
an arrowhead
to any stroke

✦ ✦ ✦ ✦

I t's probably a good idea to make sure everyone's clear on the terminology here, before we dive into the use of Photoshop's fill and stroke tools. To *fill* a selection or a layer is to put color inside it; to *stroke* a selection or a layer is to put color around it. You can *fill* a layer or a selection or shape; you place a *stroke* around that filled area. You might prefer the term *outline* to *stroke*, but an outline is typically a border, a line placed around something to encase it, like a fence or a wall, to delineate it from the stuff surrounding it. Outlines are solid, uniform, and one thinks of them as being straight lines with sharp corners. A stroke, on the other hand, is more like an embrace of color, and perhaps texture (depending on the nature of the stroke). To be more technical about it, *stroke* is also the PostScript term, and given that all this desktop publishing and graphics stuff started in the PostScript world, it's a good idea to stick with it. *Stoke* is also the term Photoshop uses, so that's that. So there.

Whatever you call them, though, Photoshop's fill and stroke functions are so straightforward that you may have long since dismissed them as minor players in the entire cast of Photoshop's characters. But the truth is, you can do a whole lot of things with them and they're worthy of more investigation and your time in mastering them. In this chapter, for example, I show you how to fill selections using keyboard shortcuts, how to create interesting framing effects, how to make the most of Photoshop's gradient options, and how to add an arrowhead to a curving line — all in addition to the really basic things every Photoshop user needs to know.

Filling Selections with Color or Patterns

How do you fill the layer, shape, or selection? Let us count the ways:

✦ **Paint Bucket tool.** Also known as the Fill tool, the Paint Bucket shares a flyout with the Gradient tool in the toolbox. You can apply the foreground color or a repeating pattern to areas of related color in an image by clicking in the image window with the tool. For example, if you want to turn all midnight blue pixels in an image into red pixels, set the foreground color to red and then click one of the blue pixels. Note that you can't use this tool on images that you converted to Bitmap mode.

✦ **Fill command.** Choose Edit ➪ Fill to fill a selection with the foreground color or a repeating pattern. You don't need to select a portion of the image to access the Fill command. If you choose the command while no selection is active, Photoshop fills the entire layer.

Tip   To choose the Fill command without even moving the mouse, press Shift+Backspace (Shift-Delete on the Mac).

✦ **Backspace (Win) and Delete (Mac) key techniques.** After selecting part of a single-layer image — or part of the background layer in a multilayered image — you can fill the selection with the background color by pressing Backspace (Win) or Delete (Mac). You can also fill any layer with the background color without a selection by pressing Ctrl+Backspace (Win) or ⌘-Delete (Mac). To fill with the foreground color, press Alt+Backspace (Win) or Option-Delete (Mac).

✦ **Gradient tool.** Drag across a layer or selection with a Gradient tool to fill it with a multicolor gradation in one of five gradient styles. You choose a gradient style by clicking an icon in the Options bar. Press G (or Shift+G, depending on your preferences setting for tool toggles) to toggle the Gradient and Paint Bucket tools, which occupy the same flyout menu in the toolbox.

✦ **Layer fills.** Photoshop provides two additional ways to fill an entire layer. You can use the dynamic fill and Layer Style features to fill a layer with a solid color, gradient, pattern, or special-effect fills.

The next sections explain the first four fill options.

Cross-Reference   To find out more about dynamic fills and layer styles, turn to Chapter 14.

The Paint Bucket tool

Unlike the very basic and limited paint bucket tools in other painting programs that apply paint exclusively within outlined areas or areas of solid color, the Photoshop Paint Bucket tool offers several useful and powerful adjustment options. When you activate the Paint Bucket tool its Options bar appears, giving you access to those adjustment options. If you don't see the Options bar, press Enter or Return, double-click the paint bucket icon in the toolbox, or choose Window ⇨ Options.

Once you're looking at the Paint Bucket's Options bar, here are the controls you can play with:

✦ **Fill.** In this pop-up menu, choose whether you want to apply the foreground color or a repeating pattern. If you choose the latter, you can use one of Photoshop's preset patterns or one you create using Edit ⇨ Define Pattern. The Define Pattern command is covered in Chapter 7. Note that Photoshop lets you create multiple patterns; you're not limited to one custom pattern, and once created, they can be applied in any image.

✦ **Pattern.** If you select Pattern from the Fill pop-up, click the Pattern icon (or the adjacent triangle) to display the Pattern drop-down palette, as shown in Figure 6-1. The palette contains icons representing the patterns in the current preset. Click the pattern you want to use.

You load, replace, edit, and create pattern presets just as you do tool and brush presets (see Chapters 2 and 5, respectively), working either in the Preset Manager dialog box or the Pattern palette menu.

Figure 6-1: The Paint Bucket's Options bar includes the opportunity to fill with a pattern, rather than the current foreground color. Click the Pattern field to apply a pattern and where you see the mouse pointer in the figure to access other pattern groups.

✦ **Tolerance.** Raise or lower the Tolerance value to increase or decrease the number of pixels affected by the Paint Bucket tool. The Tolerance value represents a range in brightness values, as measured from the pixel that you click with the Paint Bucket.

Immediately after you click a pixel, Photoshop reads the brightness value of that pixel from each color channel. Next, the program calculates a color range based on the Tolerance value — which can vary from 0 to 255. The program adds the Tolerance to the brightness value of the pixel you clicked to determine the top of the range and subtracts the Tolerance from the pixel's brightness value to determine the bottom of the range. For example, if the pixel's brightness value is 100 and the Tolerance value is 32, the top of the range is 132 and the bottom is 68.

Figure 6-2 shows the result of clicking the same pixel three separate times, each time using a different Tolerance value — once set to a lower-than-default 20, once at 32 (the default), and once at 100. Because of the variety of colors in the background, it took a high Tolerance setting to fill the background. Of course, the tool's specificity is a good thing when you want to only fill areas based on very specific pixels — as you can see, when the Tolerance did its job and filled the background, nearly all of the flower and much of the butterfly was filled, too.

✦ **Anti-aliased.** Select this option to soften the effect of the Paint Bucket tool. As demonstrated in the left example of Figure 6-3, Photoshop creates a border of translucent color between the filled pixels and their unaffected neighbors. If you don't want to soften the transition, deselect the Anti-aliased option. Photoshop then fills only those pixels that fall inside the Tolerance range, as demonstrated in the right example of the figure.

✦ **Contiguous.** When you select this option, Photoshop fills only contiguous pixels, that is, pixels that both fall inside the Tolerance range and touch another affected pixel. If you instead want to fill all pixels within the Tolerance range — regardless of where those pixels lie — deselect the check box. For what it's worth, the option was left selected when creating Figures 6-2 and 6-3.

✦ **All Layers.** Select this option to make the Paint Bucket see beyond the current layer. When the option is selected, the tool takes all visible layers into account when calculating the area to fill. Mind you, it fills only the active layer, but the way it fills an area is dictated by all layers.

✦ **Mode.** This menu offers a selection of blend modes, which determine how and when color is applied. As demonstrated in Figure 6-4, the Clear mode creates a hole in the image, leaving transparency in its wake. The Soft Light mode (see the middle panel) effects are obvious, and Overlay does an interesting job of increasing contrast and boosting saturation. (Note that Clear is dimmed when working on a flat image or a Background layer.)

Cross-Reference

For a complete description of all the blend modes, their uses and effects, see Chapter 13.

Figure 6-2: The background (the blurred colors behind the flower and butterfly) is only slightly filled with the white foreground color when using a low Tolerance, half-filled at the default Tolerance, and totally filled when set at a high Tolerance.

Figure 6-3: Where the fill runs into the butterfly's wing, the anti-aliased example (left) is cleaner, with fewer dark pixels remaining along the edge. Where anti-aliasing is off (right), the edge is choppy.

✦ **Opacity.** Type a new value or press a number key to change the translucency of a color applied with the Paint Bucket. (Press 0 for full opacity, 9 for 90 percent opacity, and so on.)

In Figure 6-5. you can see the All Layers option in use. The first image shows a flat version of the image, with no fill colors. Layers were created for the background, the butterfly, and the flower, so that changes to each part of the image could easily be edited without risking a change to the background colors affecting similar colors in the other areas of the image. To fill each layer, the All Layers option is selected and the Paint Bucket used as normal. This way, Photoshop respected any outlines within the background when coloring the various layers, and we can deal with the fill on each layer separately, even though the fill was applied in one fell swoop.

Tip

To limit the area affected by the Paint Bucket, select a portion of the image before using the tool. As when using a paint or edit tool, the region outside the selection outline is protected from the Paint Bucket. To see an interesting application of this, skip ahead to the section "Using the Paint Bucket inside a selection."

When working on a layer, you can protect pixels by locking the layer's transparency in the Layers palette.

Cross-Reference

You can find out more about the locking options and every other exciting aspect of Layers in Chapter 12.

Tip

You can use the Paint Bucket to color the empty window area around your image. First, make your image window larger than your image, so you can see some gray canvas area around the image. Now Shift-click with the Paint Bucket to fill the canvas area with the foreground color. This technique can come in handy if you're creating a presentation or you simply don't care for the default shade of gray.

Figure 6-4: The results of selecting three of the many Mode options available when using the Paint Bucket — Soft Light gently lightens as it fills (top), Clear deletes as it fills (middle), and Overlay enhances contrast (bottom).

Figure 6-5: Despite the butterfly and flowers selections being on their own layers (see the after image [bottom]), the Use All Layers option is on and therefore the fill applies to content within all the layers of the image. The top figure (before) has only one layer.

The Fill command

The one problem with the Paint Bucket tool is its lack of precision. Although the tool is undeniably convenient, the effects of the Tolerance value are so difficult to predict that you typically have to click with the tool, choose Edit ➪ Undo when you don't like the result, adjust the Tolerance value, and reclick several times before you fill the image as desired.

A better option is to choose Edit ➪ Fill or press Shift+Backspace (Shift-Delete on the Mac). (If you prefer function keys, try Shift+F5.) In this way, you can define the exact area of the image you want to color using the entire range of Photoshop's selection tools. For example, instead of putting your faith in the Paint Bucket tool's Anti-aliased option, you can draw a selection outline that features hard edges in one area, anti-aliased edges elsewhere, and downright blurry edges in between.

If you want to fill an entire layer, you don't need to create a selection outline before choosing Fill. The program assumes that you want to fill the whole layer if it doesn't see a selection outline.

 Cross-Reference Dynamic fills and layer styles provide additional ways to fill a layer; see Chapter 14 for details on how these fills differ from those you create with the Fill command.

Selection outline or no, choosing the Fill command displays the dialog box shown in Figure 6-6. In this dialog box, you can apply a translucent color or pattern by typing a value in the Opacity option box. You can also choose a brush mode from the Mode pop-up menu.

Figure 6-6: The Fill dialog box combines the opacity and brush mode options available for the Paint Bucket with an expanded collection of fill content options.

If you display the Use pop-up menu, you see a collection of fills that you can apply. Foreground Color and Pattern behave the same as they do for the Paint Bucket tool. When you select Pattern, the Custom Pattern option becomes available, as shown in Figure 6-6. Click the icon to display the Pattern drop-down palette, which also works just as described in the preceding section. Click an icon to select a pattern; click the right-pointing arrow to display the palette menu and load a different pattern preset.

Cross-Reference To find out how to load, save, edit, and create custom pattern presets, see Chapter 5. You use the same techniques for brush presets and pattern presets.

You can also fill a selection with the background color and such monochrome options as Black, White, and 50% Gray. Black and White are useful if the foreground and background colors have been changed from their defaults; 50% Gray fills the selection with the absolute medium color without having to mess around with the Color palette. History enables you to revert the selected area to a previous appearance, as you'll see in Chapter 7.

The Preserve Transparency option gives you the same result as locking the active layer's transparency in the Layers palette, which you can read about in Chapter 12. If you select Preserve Transparency, you can't fill transparent pixels in the active layer. Deselect Preserve Transparency, and you can fill the selection outline uniformly. (The option is dimmed when you're working on the background layer or if you already locked the layer's transparency in the Layers palette.)

Backspace- and Delete-key Techniques

Of all the fill techniques, the Backspace key (Delete key on the Mac) is by far the most convenient and, in most respects, every bit as capable as the others. The key's only failing is that it can neither fill a selection with a repeating pattern nor revert a selection to a previous state. But with the exception of those two items, you can rely on the Backspace or Delete key for the overwhelming majority of your fill needs.

Try these techniques for using Backspace (Win) or Delete (Mac):

✦ **Background color, method 1.** To fill a selection on the background layer with solid background color, press Backspace (Win) or Delete (Mac). The selection outline remains intact.

✦ **Background color, method 2.** Press Ctrl+Backspace (⌘-Delete on the Mac) instead. Ctrl+Backspace or ⌘-Delete fills the selection with the background color, no matter where the selection is.

Caution The problem with pressing Backspace (Delete on the Mac) is that it's unreliable. If the selection is floating, as explained in Chapter 8, the Backspace (or Delete on the Mac) key deletes it. The key also erases pixels on a layer. So there's no time like the present to get into a new habit.

✦ **Foreground color.** To fill a selection or a layer with solid foreground color, press Alt+Backspace (Win) or Option-Delete (Mac). This works when filling floating and nonfloating selections alike.

✦ **Black or white.** To fill an area with black, press D to get the default foreground and background colors and then press Alt+Backspace (Option-Delete on the Mac). To fill an area with white, press D for the defaults and then Ctrl+Backspace (⌘-Delete on the Mac).

✦ **Preserve transparency.** You can fill only the opaque pixels in a layer — regardless of whether you locked the layer's transparency in the Layers palette — by pressing Shift. Press Shift+Alt+Backspace (Shift-Option-Delete on the Mac) to fill a selection with the foreground color while preserving transparency. Press Ctrl+Shift+ Backspace (⌘-Shift-Delete on the Mac) to fill the opaque pixels with the background color.

Learn more about this technique in Chapter 12.

Using the Paint Bucket Inside a Selection

With all the plusses and minuses of using the Paint Bucket and Fill commands, they do make it easier to achieve certain results. In this section, you learn how to create a frame around your image. The steps utilize the Backspace (Windows) and Delete (Mac) keys to apply the fills, as well as other techniques and tools that review some previously and yet-to-be discussed features (assuming you're reading this book's chapters in order). Figure 6-7 shows the final result of this procedure.

STEPS: Creating an Antique Framing Effect

1. **Select the portion of the image you want to frame.** Use the Rectangular Marquee tool. Make certain the image extends at least 20 pixels outside the boundaries of the selection outline, and be sure to use a photo with content that goes to the very edges — this effect won't look right against a plain white background. Think of the 20-pixel overlap like the edges of a printed photo that sit inside the frame, holding the image in place.

2. **Specify a radius.** Choose Select ⇨ Feather, or press Ctrl+Alt+D (⌘-Option-D on the Mac). Then specify a Radius value somewhere in the neighborhood of 6 to 12 pixels. The values work for nearly any resolution of image. (If you enter too high a value, the color you are going to add with the Paint Bucket will run out into the image.)

3. **Choose Select ⇨ Inverse, or press Ctrl+Shift+I (⌘-Shift-I on the Mac).** This selects everything but the original marquee-d selection of your photo.

Figure 6-7: Create this antique frame effect by filling a feathered selection with the Paint Bucket tool.

4. **Press D to make certain the background color is white.** Then press Ctrl+Backspace (⌘-Delete on the Mac) to fill the selected area with the background color.

5. **Select the Paint Bucket tool.** If the Options bar isn't visible, press Enter or Return to display it. Make sure the Fill option is set to Foreground. Then type 20 or 30 in the Tolerance option box and select the Anti-aliased option. (You can also experiment with this last option deselected.)

6. **Click inside the feathered selection to fill it with black.** The result is an image that fades into gray and then into black, like the edges of a worn slide or photograph, as shown in Figure 6-7.

Figure 6-8 shows a variation on this effect that you can produce using the Dissolve brush mode. Rather than setting the Tolerance value to 20, increase it to 60. Then select the Dissolve option from the Mode pop-up menu in the Options bar. When you click inside the feathered selection with the Paint Bucket tool, you create a frame of random pixels, as illustrated in the figure.

Figure 6-8: Select Dissolve from the Mode pop-up menu in the Options bar to achieve a speckled frame effect.

Applying Gradient Fills

Without demanding that you whip out a thesaurus to find a list of other words that you could substitute for "gradient," suffice to say it is a progression of colors that fade gradually into one another, as demonstrated in Figure 6-9. You specify a few (as little as two) key colors in the gradation, and Photoshop automatically generates the hundred or so colors in between to create a smooth transition.

Note   If you're accustomed to using gradients in a drawing program — such as Illustrator or FreeHand — you'll find that in many ways Photoshop is better. Because Photoshop is a pixel editor, it lets you blur and mix colors in a gradation if they start *banding* — that is, if you can see a hard edge between one color and the next when you print the image. And Photoshop's gradients never choke the printer or slow it down, no matter how many colors you add. In Illustrator, each band of color in an object-oriented gradation is expressed as a separate shape — so that one gradation can contain hundreds, or even thousands, of objects. Gradations in Photoshop are simply colored pixels, no more or less complicated than the pixels in any of the images we've looked at thus far in this book.

Figure 6-9: The distance dragged from starting point (upper left) to ending point (lower right) determines the span of the gradient from Foreground to Background color. You can also apply preset gradients, using the Gradients Options bar.

Using the Gradient tool

The Gradient and Paint Bucket tools share a toolbox slot and a keyboard shortcut — press G to toggle between the two tools (or Shift+G, depending on whether you selected the Use Shift Key for Tool Switch option in the Preferences dialog box, as discussed in Chapter 2). But unlike the Paint Bucket, which fills areas of similar color according to the Tolerance setting, the Gradient tool affects all colors within a selection — or if you don't make a selection, it applies to an entire layer.

To use the tool and apply the default gradient, click on the Gradient button in the toolbox, and then drag inside the selection, as shown in Figure 6-9. The point at which you begin dragging (the upper-left corner in the figure, in this case) defines the location of the first color in the gradation. The point at which you release (the lower-right corner, as shown in the figure) defines the location of the last color. If multiple portions of the image are selected, the gradation fills all selections continuously. Photoshop doesn't stop and apply the gradient to the individual selections — it follows your mouse path across selections, skipping the intervening areas that are not within the selection.

Gradient options

As with other tools in Photoshop, the Gradient tool has its own Options bar, which you can see in Figure 6-10 (or on your own computer, if you're playing along). If you don't see the Options bar, press Enter or Return when the Gradient tool is active or double-click the tool icon in the toolbox.

Figure 6-10: The Options bar gives you quick access to all Gradient tool options — including a list of gradient presets.

The following list explains how the controls in the Options bar work. In all cases, you must adjust the options before using the Gradient tool. They do not affect existing gradations:

✦ **Gradient preview.** The selected gradient appears in the gradient preview, labeled in Figure 6-10. Click the preview to open the Gradient Editor dialog box, discussed in the section "Creating custom gradations."

✦ **Gradient drop-down palette.** Click the triangle adjacent to the preview to display the Gradient palette, which contains icons representing gradients in the current gradient presets. Click the icon for the gradient you want.

Note

In the default gradient preset, the first two gradations are dependent on the current foreground and background colors. The others contain specific colors bearing no relationship to the colors in the toolbox.

You load gradient presets using the same techniques described in detail in the brush preset discussion in Chapter 5, but here's the short story:

• Click the triangle near the top of the drop-down palette to display the palette menu. The Photoshop collection of presets and any presets that you defined on your own appear at the bottom of the palette menu. Click a preset group by name to access those presets instead of or in addition to the default set of presets. The preset groups' names — like Metals and Pastels — are fairly revealing.

- To append a preset from disk — such as when a coworker gives you a preset file — choose Load Gradients from the palette menu or click Load in the Preset Manager dialog box. If you want to replace the current preset instead, choose Replace Gradients from the palette menu or click Replace in the dialog box. To return to the default gradients, choose Reset Gradients from the palette menu, either from the Options bar palette or the one in the Preset Manager dialog box.

Tip   You can edit a gradient and perform the aforementioned preset manipulations from the Gradient Editor dialog box, too. The section "Creating custom gradations" covers this dialog box in detail.

✦ **Gradient style.** Click an icon to select the gradient style. The section "Gradient styles" explains the five styles.

✦ **Mode and Opacity.** These options work as they do for the paint and edit tools, the Fill command, and every other tool or command that offers them as options. Select a different brush mode to change how colors are applied; lower the Opacity value to make a gradation translucent. Remember that you can change the Opacity value by pressing number keys as well as by using the Opacity control in the Options bar. Press 0 for 100 percent opacity, 9 for 90 percent opacity, and so on.

✦ **Reverse.** When active, this option begins the gradation with the background color and ends it with the foreground color. Use this option when you want to start a radial or other style of gradation with white, but you want to keep the foreground and background colors set to their defaults.

✦ **Dither.** Remember how we said Photoshop doesn't give you *banding* when you print a gradient? Well, that's not totally true. In the old days, Photoshop drew its gradients one band at a time, and each band was filled with an incrementally different shade of color. The potential result, known as banding, made it so that you could clearly distinguish the transition between two or more bands of color. The Dither option helps to eliminate this problem by mixing up the pixels between bands (much as Photoshop dithers pixels when converting a grayscale image to black and white), smoothing the transitions between them. It's generally safe to deselect the Dither option if you're working on an image in 16-bit mode, as it's essentially unnecessary and banding won't occur anyway. If you're not working in 16-bit mode, you should leave this option turned on unless you want to use banding to create a special effect.

Tip   If you're not sure you're working in 16-bit mode check the Image, Mode submenu and see where the check mark is. If you're in 16-bit mode, it appears next to the 16 bits/channel mode.

✦ **Transparency.** You can specify different levels of opacity throughout a gradation. For example, the Soft Stripes effect (available from the Gradient palette when the Special Effects preset is loaded) lays down a series of alternately black and transparent stripes. But you needn't use this transparency information. If you prefer to apply a series of black and white stripes instead, you can make all portions of the gradation equally opaque by deselecting the Transparency option.

For example, in Figure 6-11, Soft Stripes is applied as a radial gradation in two separate swipes (first to a selection in the middle image, and again on the bottom image). Both times, the Opacity setting is changed to 50 percent, so the eye would never be completely obscured. (The Opacity setting works independently of the gradation's built-in transparency, providing you with additional flexibility.) In the top gradation (middle example), the Transparency option is selected, so the white stripes are completely transparent. In the bottom gradation, Transparency is turned off, so the white stripes become 50 percent opaque (as prescribed by the Opacity setting).

Figure 6-11: With the Opacity value set to 50 percent, the Soft Stripes gradient is applied to the middle and bottom eyes. Transparency is selected in the middle eye, so that you can see through what would otherwise be the white stripes. Transparency is deselected in the bottom eye, and the gradient is applied to a smaller elliptical marquee.

Gradient styles

You select the gradient style by clicking the gradient style icons in the Options bar (refer to Figure 6-10 to identify these icons). Illustrated in Figure 6-12, the five styles are:

✦ **Linear.** A linear gradient progresses in bands of color in a straight line between the beginning and end of your drag. The top two examples in Figure 6-12 show linear gradations created from black to white, and from white to black. The point labeled "B" marks the beginning of the drag; "E" marks the end.

✦ **Radial.** A radial gradation progresses outward from a central point in concentric circles, as in the second row of examples in Figure 6-12. The point at which you begin dragging defines the center of the gradation, and the point at which you release defines the outermost circle. This means the first color in the gradation appears in the center of the fill. So to create the gradation on the right side of Figure 6-12, you must set the foreground color to white and the background color to black (or select the Reverse option in the Options bar).

✦ **Angle.** The angle gradient style creates a fountain of colors flowing in a counterclockwise direction with respect to your drag, as demonstrated by the middle two examples of Figure 6-12. This type of gradient is known more commonly as a *conical gradation* because it looks like the bird's-eye view of the top of a cone.

Of course, a real cone doesn't have the sharp edge between black and white that you see in Photoshop's angle gradient. To eliminate this edge, create a custom gradation from black to white to black again, as explained in the "Adjusting colors in a solid gradation" section later in this chapter.

✦ **Reflected.** The fourth gradient style creates a linear gradation that reflects back on itself. Photoshop positions the foreground color at the beginning of your drag and the background color at the end, as when using the linear gradient style. But it also repeats the gradient in the opposite direction of your drag, as demonstrated in Figure 6-12. It's great for creating natural shadows or highlights that fade in two directions.

✦ **Diamond.** The last gradient style creates a series of concentric diamonds (if you drag at a 90-degree angle) or squares (if you drag at a 45-degree angle, as in Figure 6-12). Otherwise, it works exactly like the radial gradient style.

Figure 6-12: Examples of each of the five gradient styles created using the default foreground and background colors (left column) and with the foreground and background colors reversed (right column). B marks the beginning of the drag; E marks the end.

Creating custom gradations

The secret passageway to the Gradient Editor dialog box shown in Figure 6-13 is the color preview that appears at the left end of the Options bar. If you click the preview, you display the Gradient Editor dialog box. If you click the neighboring triangle, you display the Gradient palette, as shown earlier in Figure 6-10.

Figure 6-13: Click the gradient preview in the Options bar to display the Gradient Editor dialog box, which enables you to design custom gradations.

Here are some important points about the Gradient Editor:

✦ The scrolling list at the top of the dialog box mirrors the Gradient drop-down palette in the Options bar and the Gradients panel of the Preset Manager dialog box. If you click the triangle at the top of the scrolling list, you display a virtual duplicate of the palette menu.

Tip

If you want to see gradient names instead of icons in the list, choose Text Only from the dialog box menu. Or choose Small List or Large List to see both icon and gradient name.

✦ To create a new gradient, find an existing gradient that's close to what you have in mind. Then type a name for the gradient in the Name option box and click New. The new gradient appears in the scrolling list, and you can edit the gradient as you see fit.

Caution

Even though the gradient appears in the dialog box (as well as in the Gradient palette and the Preset Manager dialog box), it's vulnerable until you save it as part of a preset. If you make further edits to the gradient or replace the current gradient preset, the original gradient is a goner. Deleting your main Photoshop preferences file also wipes out an unsaved gradient. See the section "Saving and managing gradients" for more details.

✦ You can create *noise gradients* as well as solid-color gradations. If you select Noise from the Gradient Type pop-up menu, Photoshop introduces random color information into the gradient, the result of which is a sort of special-effect gradient that would be difficult to create manually.

✦ The options at the bottom of the dialog box change depending on whether you select Solid or Noise from the Gradient Type pop-up. For solid gradients, Photoshop provides a Smoothness slider, which you can use to adjust how abrupt you want to make the color transitions in the gradient.

Tip

For greater control when creating or editing a gradient, make the dialog box wider by dragging the size box in the lower-right corner.

Editing solid gradients

If you select Solid from the Gradient Type pop-up menu, you use the options shown in Figure 6-14 to adjust the gradient. Note that this is a doctored screen shot and all the options are visible in the figure; normally, only some of the options associated with the active stops are available.

The *fade bar* (labeled in Figure 6-14) shows the active gradient. The starting color is represented by a *color stop* (see the triangle on top of a square) on the left; the ending color stop appears on the far right. The upside-down stop markers on the top of the fade bar are *opacity stops*. These stops determine where colors are opaque and where they fade into translucency or even transparency.

Figure 6-14: Use these controls to adjust the colors and transparency in a solid gradient.

To select either type of stop, click it. The triangle portion of the stop appears black to indicate that it is active. After you select a stop, diamond-shaped *midpoint markers* appear between the stop and its immediate neighbors. On the color-stop side of the fade bar, the midpoint marker represents the spot where the two colors mix in exactly equal amounts. On the transparency side, a marker indicates the point where the opacity value is midway between the values that you set for the stops on either side of the marker.

You can change the location of any stop or marker by dragging it. Or you can click a stop or marker to select it and then type a value in the Location option box below the fade bar:

✦ When numerically positioning a stop, a value of 0 percent indicates the left end of the fade bar; 100 percent indicates the right end. Even if you add more stops to the gradation, the values represent absolute positions along the fade bar.

✦ When repositioning a midpoint marker, the initial setting of 50 percent is at equal points between two stops, 0 percent is all the way over to the left stop, and 100 percent is all the way over to the right. Midpoint values are, therefore, measured relative to stop positions. In fact, when you move a stop,

Photoshop moves the midpoint marker along with it to maintain the same relative positioning. If you type a value below 5 percent or more than 95 percent, Photoshop politely ignores you.

Tip Pressing Enter or Return after you type a value into the Location option box is tempting, but don't do it. Photoshop dumps you out of the Gradient Editor dialog box, which you might not be ready to leave just yet.

Adjusting colors in a solid gradation

When editing a solid gradation, you can add colors, delete colors, change the position of the colors in the gradient, and control how two colors blend together. After clicking a color stop to select it, you can change its color in several ways:

✦ To change the color to the current foreground color, open the Color pop-up menu, as shown in Figure 6-15, and select Foreground. You can also select Background to use the background color instead.

When you select Foreground or Background, the color stop becomes filled with a grayscale pattern instead of a solid color. If you squint real hard and put your nose to the screen, you can see that the pattern is actually a representation of the Foreground and Background color controls in the toolbox. The little black square appears in the upper-left corner when the foreground color is active, as shown in the first stop on the fade bar in Figure 6-15.

If you change the foreground or background color after closing the Gradient Editor dialog box, the gradient changes to reflect the new color. When you next open the Gradient Editor, you can revert the stop to the original foreground or background color by selecting User Color from the pop-up menu.

Foreground color stop   Background color stop

Color midpoint marker

Figure 6-15: A look at the color stop options in the Gradient Editor dialog box

✦ To set the color stop to some other color, click the Color swatch or double-click the color stop to display the Color Picker and define the new color. Select your color and press Enter or Return.

Tip

You may have noticed that when you open the Gradient Editor dialog box, Photoshop automatically selects the Eyedropper tool for you and displayed that tool's controls in the Options bar. Why did it do that? Because you can click with the Eyedropper in an open image window to lift a color from the image and assign that color to the selected color stop. You can also sample a color from anywhere on-screen by first clicking with the Eyedropper in an image window and then dragging outside it.

To change the point at which two colors meet, drag the midpoint marker between the two stops. Or click the midpoint marker and type a new value into the Location box. A value of 0 puts the midpoint marker flush against the left color stop; a value of 100 moves the stop all the way over to the right stop.

You add or delete stops as follows:

✦ To add a color stop, click anywhere along the bottom of the fade bar. A new stop appears where you click. Photoshop also adds a midpoint marker between the new color stop and those to its left and right. You can add as many color stops as your heart desires. To define the color of the stop, double-click the new color stop (double-click an existing stop if you want to change its color) and watch as the Color Picker dialog box opens. Make a selection, click OK, and voila! Your new color stop is created and its color is set.

Tip

If your goal is a gradient that features tons of random colors, you may be able to create the effect you want more easily by using the Noise gradient option. See the section "Creating noise gradients" for more information.

✦ To duplicate a color stop, Alt-drag (Option-drag on the Mac) it to a new location along the fade bar. One great use for this is to create a reflecting gradation.

For example, select Foreground to Background from the scrolling list of gradients and click New to duplicate the gradient. After naming your new gradient — something like Foreground to Background to Foreground, for example — click the background color stop and change the Location value to 50. Then Alt-drag (Option-drag on the Mac) the foreground color stop all the way to the right. This new gradient is perfect for making true conical gradations with the angle gradient style, as demonstrated in Figure 6-16.

✦ To remove a color stop, drag the stop away from the fade bar. Or click the stop and click Delete. The stop icon vanishes and the fade bar automatically adjusts as defined by the remaining color stops.

Figure 6-16: A true "cone" is created (right). Two gradations with the angle gradient style, one using the standard Foreground to Background gradient (left) and the other with a reflected Foreground to Background to Foreground style (right).

Adjusting the transparency mask

If you like, you can include a *transparency mask* with each gradation. The mask determines the opacity of different colors along the gradation. You create and edit this mask independently of the colors in the gradation.

To create a transparency mask, you play with the opacity stops across the top of the fade bar. When you click an opacity stop, the transparency options become available below the fade bar and the color options dim.

To add an opacity stop, click above the fade bar. By default, each new stop is 100 percent opaque. You can modify the transparency by selecting a stop and changing the Opacity value. The fade bar updates to reflect your changes. To reposition a stop, drag it or type a value in the Location option box.

Midpoint markers represent the spot where the opacity value is half the difference between the opacity values of a pair of opacity stops. In other words, if you set one opacity stop to 30 percent and another to 90 percent, the midpoint marker shows you where the gradient reaches 60 percent opacity. You can relocate the midpoint marker, and thus change the spot where the gradient reaches that midrange opacity value, by dragging the marker or typing a new value in the Location option box.

Creating noise gradients

Adobe describes a noise gradient as a gradient that "contains random components along with the deterministic ones that create the gradient." For those of us who speak one of the known languages on the planet, this means that Photoshop adds random colors to the parameters that you set in the Gradient Editor dialog box. Did that clear things up? OK, try looking at Figure 6-17, which shows examples of three noise gradients. You could create these same gradients using the regular Solid gradient controls, but it would take you forever to add all the color and midpoint stops required to produce the same effect.

Figure 6-17: Three Noise gradients — with 50% Roughness (top), 100% Roughness (middle), and finally, 100% Roughness plus Transparency (bottom)

To create a noise gradient, select Noise from the Gradient Type menu in the Gradient Editor dialog box, as shown in Figure 6-18. You can adjust the gradient as follows:

✦ Raise the Roughness value to create more distinct bands of color, as in the middle example in Figure 6-17. Lowering the Roughness value results in softer color transitions, as you can see from the top example, which are set at one-half the Roughness value of the middle example.

✦ Use the color sliders at the bottom of the dialog box to define the range of allowable colors in the gradient. You can work in one of three color modes: RGB, HSB, or Lab. Select the mode you want from the pop-up menu above the sliders.

Figure 6-18: Use the Noise gradient option to create gradients like the ones you see in Figure 6-17.

✦ The Restrict Colors option, when selected, adjusts the gradient so that you don't wind up with any oversaturated colors. Deselect the option for more vibrant hues.

✦ If you select Add Transparency, Photoshop adds random transparency information to the gradient, as if you had added many opacity stops to a regular gradient. In the bottom example of Figure 6-18, we started with the gradient from the middle example, selected the Add Transparency option, and left the Roughness value at 100.

✦ Click Randomize and Photoshop shuffles all the gradient colors and transparency values to create another gradient. If you don't like what you see, just keep clicking Randomize until you're satisfied. Note that each click of Randomize produces a radically different gradient, so if you find a gradient that's close to what you're looking for, you might want to save it as a preset and continue tweaking it by hand.

Tip   For some really cool effects, try applying special effects filters to a noise gradient. Figure 6-19 shows the results of applying the Gaussian Blur, Twirl, and Ripple filters on the original noise gradient shown in the left-most example.

Figure 6-19: Four areas are selected along a rectangle, filled with a Noise Gradient. From left to right: Roughness set to 100%, Gaussian Blur filter set to 5 pixels, Twirl set at an angle of 300 degrees, and Ripple at 999% and set to Large. Experiment with other filters at various settings and see what cool results you get.

Saving and managing gradients

When you define a new gradient, its icon appears in the palette, the Preset Manager dialog box, and the Gradient Editor dialog box. But if you replace the current gradient set or edit the gradient, the original gradient is deleted. You also lose the gradient if you delete your Photoshop CS2 preferences file because that's where the temporary gradient information is stored.

Tip   If you want to delete your preferences file, press Ctrl+Alt+Shift (or ⌘-Opt-Shift if you're on a Mac) as the application starts. A prompt asks if you really want to delete your preferences, and if you respond affirmatively, they're gone!

If you want to preserve a gradient, you must save it as part of a *preset* — which is nothing more than a collection of gradients. Photoshop ships with several gradient presets stored in the Gradients folder, which resides inside the Presets folder in the main Photoshop program folder. You also can create as many custom presets as you like. Gradient presets have the *.grd* file extension.

You can save all the gradients in the active preset — including any custom gradients that you define — by clicking Save in the Gradient Editor dialog box or by choosing Save Gradients from the Gradient palette pop-up menu. But if you want to save only some of the current gradients as a preset, choose Preset Manager from the Gradient palette pop-up menu and then display the Gradients panel, shown in Figure 6-20, by pressing Ctrl+3 (⌘-3 on the Mac) or by choosing Gradients from the Preset Type pop-up menu. Shift-click the gradients you want to save and then click Save Set. If you want to dump the selected gradients into an existing preset, select the preset file and press Enter or Return. Alternatively, you can type a new preset name to create a brand-new preset that contains only the selected gradients.

Figure 6-20: To select specific gradients and save them as a new preset, use the Preset Manager.

To delete a gradient, Alt-click (Option-click on the Mac) its icon in the palette, the Preset Manager, or the Gradient Editor dialog box. To delete multiple gradients, Shift-click the gradients in the Preset Manager and then click Delete. Save the preset immediately if you want the deleted gradients gone for good; otherwise, they remain an official part of the preset and reappear the next time you load the preset.

Gradations and brush modes

All standard brush modes are available when you apply gradations, and they make a tremendous impression on the performance of the gradient tool. This section examines one way to apply a brush mode in conjunction with the tool. Naturally, this section barely scrapes the surface of what's possible, but it may inspire you to experiment and discover additional effects on your own.

The following steps tell you how to use the Dissolve mode with a radial gradation to create a planet with a ring around it, kind of like your very own Saturn. Figures 6-21 through 6-24 show this mini-universe in progress. Feel free to tinker with the steps — preferably after trying them my way once, just to get the hang of it — and create your own solar system, complete with stars and moons. You get extra credit if you can figure out how to use a brushstroke to create the look of a comet.

Cross-Reference   These steps involve the use of the Elliptical Marquee tool. Generally it's an easy tool to use. But if you find that you have problems making it work according to my instructions, you can find additional information in Chapter 8.

STEPS: Creating a Gradient Planet and Saturn-like Ring

1. **Create a new image window.** Make it 1000 x 750 pixels. Set the image to RGB mode, but remember you're seeing it here in grayscale.

2. **Create a new layer.** Name the layer **Planet**.

3. **Fill the Background layer with Black.**

4. **Switch back to the Planet layer, making it the active layer.**

5. **Select a perfect circle.** Using the Elliptical Marquee tool, shift-draft anywhere in the cosmos. Release Shift after you release the mouse button. Try to form a planet that's roughly 350 pixels in diameter.

6. **Click the Gradient tool.**

7. **Click the triangle to the right of the Gradient on the Options bar.** Choose Copper from the presets.

8. **Click OK.**

9. **Choose a Radial gradient style.**

10. **Drag from just outside the upper-left "corner" of your ellipse to just inside the opposite side, on the lower right.** This creates the gradient seen in Figure 6-21.

Figure 6-21: With a black background and a circle selected and filled with a Radial gradient, we have the look of nice, round planet.

11. **Create a new layer (call it** Ring**), and draw an elliptical marquee on it as shown in Figure 6-22.** This requires using the Subtract from Selection option on the Marquee Options bar to cut the smaller ellipse out of the center. The hole you create should be as big as the planet is wide, at some point close to its equator. Don't feel bad if you have to take a few whacks at this.

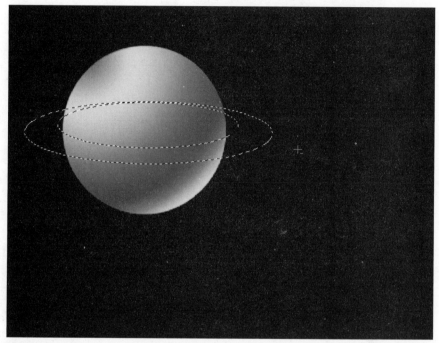

Figure 6-22: Draw the rings with two concentric elliptical marquee selections.

12. **Using the Gradient tool, choose the Spectrum gradient, set to Radial style.**

13. **Using the Options bar, choose Dissolve for the blending Mode.**

14. **Drag across the selection.** Your results appear in Figure 6-23.

15. **Activate the Eraser tool and erase the portion of the ring that should be hidden behind the planet.** The ring layer should be on top of the Planet layer (if it's not, drag it up within the Layers palette so that it is the top-most layer).

16. **To make it look as though the ring is spinning around the planet, apply the Radial Blur filter to the Ring layer.** Set the Amount to 10, and use the Spin method. The results are shown in Figure 6-24.

17. Add some stars to your universe with the Brush tool, set to White. Apply them randomly, and try different sizes to achieve the look of stars at varying distances from the viewer's position.

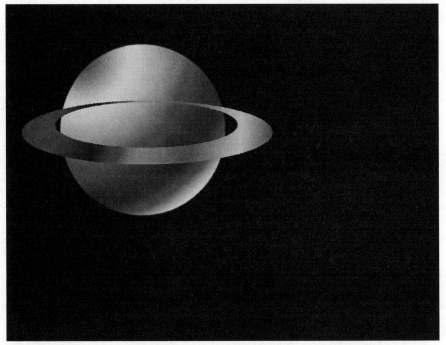

Figure 6-23: The ring, temporarily in front of (rather than around) the planet, is filled with a full spectrum of colors, creating a striped ring around the planet.

Figure 6-24: Now the ring looks like it encircles and spins around the planet. You can use the Transform command to rotate the ring a bit, if you want it to appear at an angle — this may require tinkering with the Eraser to adjust the edges of the ring where it appears to run behind the planet.

Applying Strokes and Arrowheads

Photoshop is nearly as adept at drawing lines and outlines as it is at filling selections — and like the fill tools and commands, Photoshop's tools for drawing lines and outlines are as varied. By "drawing lines" in this section, we don't mean the same lines we talk about in Chapter 5; the word "lines" here refers to outlines and borders. The following sections discuss how to apply a border around a selection outline — which is practical, if not terribly exciting — and how to create arrowheads — which can yield more interesting results than you might think.

To further clarify what we mean by lines, bear in mind that we're talking about *raster* lines — that is, lines made of pixels that you create with the Line tool set to the Fill Pixels mode. To find out how to use the tool to produce vector lines and work paths, see Chapters 14 and 8, respectively. Some Line tool techniques discussed here apply to the Line tool also when it's set to vector mode or work path mode.

Stroking a selection outline

Stroking is useful for creating frames and outlines. Generally, you can stroke an image in Photoshop in four ways:

✦ **Stroke command.** Select the portion of the image that you want to stroke and choose Edit ➪ Stroke to display the Stroke dialog box shown in Figure 6-25. Or, if you're working on a multilayered image, you can choose the Stroke command without making a selection; Photoshop then applies the stroke to the entire layer, unless the layer in question is the Background layer, which can only be stroked if it is unlocked and is no longer serving as the Background layer.

In the Stroke dialog box, type the thickness of the stroke in the Width option box. The default unit of measurement here is pixels, but you can use inches and centimeters as well. Just type the value and then the unit abbreviation (*px* for pixels, *in* for inches, or *cm* for centimeters).

Figure 6-25: Use the options in the Stroke dialog box to specify the thickness of a stroke and its location with respect to the selection outline.

You can also set the stroke color from within the dialog box. Click the color swatch to select a color from the Color Picker — don't forget that you have full access to the Eyedropper tool while the Color Picker is open, so any color on your screen is fair game and can be selected. Press Enter or Return to close the Color Picker and return to the Stroke dialog box after you've made your selection.

Tip

Select a Location radio button to specify the position of the stroke with respect to the selection outline. When in doubt, select Inside from the Location radio buttons. This setting ensures that the stroke is entirely inside the selection outline in case you decide to move the selection. If you select Center or Outside, Photoshop applies part or all of the stroke to the deselected area around the selection outline — unless, of course, your selection extends to the edge of the canvas, in which case you wind up with no stroke at all for Outside and half a stroke inside the selection outline for Center.

The Stroke dialog box also includes Mode, Opacity, and Preserve Transparency options that work like those in the Fill dialog box.

✦ **Border command.** Select a portion of the image and choose Select ➪ Modify ➪ Border to retain only the outline of the selection. Specify the size of the border by typing a value in pixels in the Width option box and press Enter or Return. To fill the border with the background color, press Ctrl+Backspace (⌘-Delete on the Mac). To fill the border with the foreground color, press Alt+Backspace (Option-Delete on the Mac). To apply a repeating pattern to the border, choose Edit ➪ Fill and select the Pattern option from the Use pop-up menu.

✦ **Layer Style effects.** If you want to stroke an entire layer, try the options provided by the Layer Style feature. Choose Layer ➪ Layer Style ➪ Stroke to display the Layer Style dialog box shown in Figure 6-26. At first glance, the options here appear to mirror those you find in the regular Stroke dialog box. They do, as long as you select Color from the Fill Type pop-up menu. This menu offers two other options. You can fill the stroke with a gradient or a pattern, or you can adjust the pattern and gradient on the fly and preview the results in the dialog box. For example, you can scale the gradient and change its angle — two things you can't do in the regular Gradient Editor dialog box, so their availability through the pop-up menu is even more convenient. By using the settings shown in the figure, a plain, old black-to-white gradient has been adapted to produce the shadowed frame effect you see in the preview (the small block on the right side of the dialog box — just in case you were expecting an image preview).

Cross-Reference

The Layer Style dialog box in covered detail in Chapter 14, so if you have any questions about or problems with the stroke options, look there for help.

✦ **Canvas Size trick.** Okay, so this one is a bit unorthodox, and probably was not intended for this purpose, but it works, so here you go. To create an outline around the entire image, choose Image ➪ Canvas Size, select the Relative option, and type twice the desired border thickness in pixels in the Width and Height options.

For example, to create a 1-pixel border all the way around, type 2 pixels for the Width value (1 for the left side and 1 for the right) and 2 pixels for the Height value (1 for the top and 1 for the bottom). (You could also deselect the

Relative option and add 2 pixels to the existing Width and Height values if you're inordinately fond of doing math.) Leave the Anchor option set to the center tile so that the added canvas is applied on all sides of the image. Choose Other from the Canvas Extension Color pop-up menu to open the Color Picker dialog box. Select a color and click OK to return to the Canvas Size dialog box. When you press Enter or Return, Photoshop enlarges the canvas size according to your specifications and fills the new pixels around the perimeter of the image with the color you chose. Simple, logical, and it works. Who could ask for more?

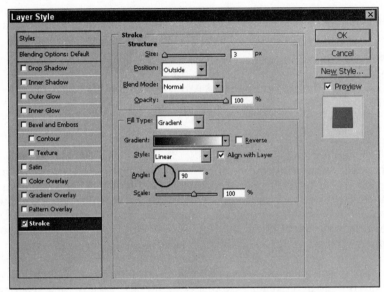

Figure 6-26: With the Stroke options in the Layer Style dialog box, you can stroke a layer with a solid color, gradient, or pattern. You also can adjust the angle and scale of gradients to create the effect shown in the preview.

Applying arrowheads to straight lines

The one function missing from all the operations in the preceding list is applying arrowheads. This is not because we forgot to discuss it — rather, it's because, in Photoshop, you can apply arrowheads only to straight lines drawn with the Line tool.

The Line tool is grouped with the drawing tools — the tools you use for drawing shapes like rectangles, ellipses, polygons, and custom shapes. You can cycle between the tools by pressing U (or Shift+U, depending on your preferences setting for switching tools). The Line tool can create three different kinds of shapes. You can paint raster lines, that is, lines made up of pixels or you can draw vector-based lines on a new shape layer, as explained in Chapter 14. Finally, you can create a work path using the Line tool, which is discussed in Chapter 8.

You specify which type of line you want to create by clicking one of the three icons near the left end of the Options bar, which you can see labeled in Figure 6-27. If you don't see the Options bar, press Enter or Return, or double-click the Line tool icon in the toolbox.

Paths   Click to display line options

Fill Pixels

Shape Layers

Figure 6-27: The arrowhead options appear in this drop-down palette.

Tip

When choosing the type of line you're going to create, remember that the Shape Layers option creates a...surprise! shape layer (containing a vector shape, which you can later rasterize by right-clicking the layer and choosing Rasterize Shape from the pop-up menu), Paths creates a path from the line you draw, and Fill Pixels creates a raster line. If you choose Fill Pixels, the line you draw becomes part of the active layer (unless you're on a Shape or Type layer), so be careful to create a new layer for the raster line if your goals for further editing require the line to be on its own editable layer.

Regardless of which type of line you're creating, you set the width of the line by typing a value into the Weight box in the Options bar. Then you add arrowheads using the drop-down options palette shown in the figure. To display the options, click the triangle at the end of the strip of shape icons. Use the Arrowheads options as follows:

✦ **Start.** Select this option to add an arrowhead to the beginning of a line drawn with the Line tool.

✦ **End.** Select this option to add an arrowhead to the end of a line. This sounds like something you probably didn't explained to you, but it's surprising how many people don't realize that the way the line is drawn, from where you begin to drag to where you stop dragging, determines the start and finish of the line and therefore which end is the pointy end of the arrow.

✦ **Width.** Type the width of the arrowhead in this option box. The width is measured as a percentage of the line weight, so if the Weight is set to 6 pixels and the Width value is 500 percent, the width of the arrowhead will be 30 pixels. This opportunity to do some multiplication can be very exciting for you math fans out there.

✦ **Length.** Type the length of the arrowhead, measured from the base of the arrowhead to its tip, as a percentage of the line weight.

✦ **Concavity.** You can specify the shape of the arrowhead by typing a value between negative and positive 50 percent in the Concavity option box. Figure 6-28 shows examples of a few Concavity settings applied to an arrowhead 50 pixels wide and 100 pixels long, the top arrow at –50 percent and the bottom at 50 percent.

Figure 6-28: Various arrowhead concavity settings are in use on the left, and Outer Glow and Bevel blending modes were also applied to the arrows and the target.

Appending arrowheads to curved lines

Applying arrowheads to straight lines is a simple matter. Applying an arrowhead to a stroked selection outline is a little trickier, but still possible. The following steps explain the process:

Note   For the effect shown in this example, you need raster arrowheads, so click the Fill Pixels icon in the Options bar (see Figure 6-27). Now your Line tool creates raster lines rather than vector lines (Shape Layer) or work paths (Paths).

STEPS: Adding an Arrowhead to a Free-Form Stroke

1. **Create a new layer.** Display the Layers palette by pressing the F7 key. Then click the little page icon at the bottom of the palette to create a new layer.

2. **Draw and stroke a selection.** Draw any selection outline you like. Stroke it by choosing Edit ⇨ Stroke and applying whatever settings strike your fancy. Remember the value you type in the Width option. In Figure 6-29, the Lasso tool was used to draw a free-form line and a 5-pixel black stroke set to 50 percent Opacity was applied.

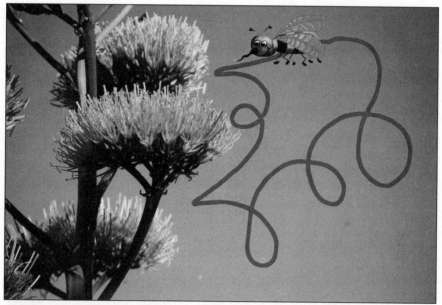

Figure 6-29: Here we created a new layer, drew a free-form shape with the Lasso tool, and stroked it with a 5-pixel black outline at 50 percent Opacity.

3. **Press Ctrl+D (⌘-D on the Mac).** This deselects all portions of the image.

4. **Erase the portions of the stroke you don't need.** Select the Eraser tool by pressing E. Then drag to erase through the stroke layer without harming the layer below. Erase the areas of the stroke where you want to add arrowheads. By erasing a chunk of the line, you're creating a beginning and an end to the line — here, the path of a bee from flower to flower.

5. **Select the Line tool and click the Fill Pixels icon in the Options bar.**

6. **Specify the line weight and arrowhead settings.** Type the line weight you used when stroking the selection outline into the Weight option box (in this

case, 5 pixels). Next, display the line options drop-down palette. Just click the triangle at the end of the strip of shape icons, as shown in Figure 6-27. Select the End option and deselect the Start option. Then specify the width, length, and concavity of the arrowhead as desired.

7. **Set the foreground color as needed.** Because a black stroke at 50 percent Opacity has been applied, the foreground color has been set to 50 percent gray. (Click the stroke with the Eyedropper to change the foreground color to the stroke color.)

8. **Zoom in to the point in the image where you want to add the arrowhead.** You have to get in close enough to see what you're doing, as in Figure 6-30.

9. **At the tip of the stroke, draw a very short line exactly the length of the arrowhead, illustrated in Figure 6-30.** This may take some practice to accomplish. Start the line a few pixels in from the end of the stroke to make sure that the base of the arrowhead fits snugly. If you're unhappy with your first attempt at this, choose Edit ➪ Undo or press Ctrl+Z (⌘-Z on the Mac) and try again — you will get the hang of it.

Figure 6-30: Use the Line tool to draw a line no longer than the arrowhead. This appends the arrow to the end of the stroke. You may want to zoom in tight on the end of the stroke (as done here) in order to have the control you need.

And that's it! From then on, you can continue to edit the stroke as you see fit. In Figure 6-31, for example, you erased a series of strips across the stroke to create a dashed-line effect, which, through its lack of uniformity, expresses a halting path taken by the bee that appears at the end of the line. Feel free, when creating this on your own, to choose the insect, bird, or other flying creature/machine of your choice and to set your line's specs accordingly — fatter, stronger lines for an airplane, loopy, choppy lines for a helicopter, light, graceful lines for a tiny bird, for example. Remember that mastering Photoshop isn't just about identifying all the tools and understanding what each one does — although that sure does help — it's about figuring out how to make Photoshop express what you have in mind.

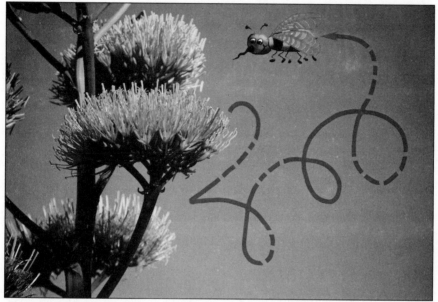

Figure 6-31: You finished by erasing pieces of the line at varying intervals to create dashes that show changes in the bee's speed as he continues on his path.

Summary

In this chapter, you learned to apply color with the Paint Bucket tool and Fill command, including the use of Fill tools and commands for filling a selection with custom patterns.

For interesting fills, you also learned about using the Gradient features, and designing your own multicolor gradations. You also learned about using the Gradient tool with the Dissolve brush mode, and how to create outlines and borders, and how to work with Stroke commands, including the ability to attach an arrowhead to any stroke.

✦　　✦　　✦

Retouching and Restoring

✦ ✦ ✦ ✦

In This Chapter

An overview of
Photoshop's image
restoration tools

Touching up dust,
hair, and other
scanning artifacts

Using the Healing
Brush, Spot Healing
Brush, and Patch
tools

Restoring a
damaged
photograph

Eliminating
background
elements from
an image

Traveling through
time with the History
palette

Painting away
mistakes with the
Eraser and History
Brush tools

Getting rid of red eye

✦ ✦ ✦ ✦

You now have an extensive set of editing disciplines —
smearing and sponging, filling and stroking, and the art of
painting — under your belt (assuming you're reading this tome
from cover to cover, which of course you are). Hopefully, your
belt has a few more holes so we can let it out a bit to make room
for the world of Photoshop's retouching and restoring tools.

These tools — the stamps, healing and patching tools, Erasers,
History Brushes, and red-eye removal tools — enable you to
repair damaged images, erase mistakes, and restore operations
from your recent past. In short, they make it possible for you to
perform the sorts of miracles that simply weren't possible in
the days before computer imaging. From new, but poorly composed or developed photos to vintage photos showing decades
of wear and tear, you can bring new life to all your photos and
scanned documents, all without the slightest fear of damaging
the originals, be they electronic or printed.

Very briefly, here's how the restoring and retouching tools work:

- ✦ **Clone Stamp and Pattern Stamp.** Use the Clone Stamp
  tool to replicate pixels from one area in an image to
  another. This one feature makes the Clone Stamp ideally
  suited to removing dust, repairing minor defects, and eliminating distracting background elements. Alt-click (Option-
  click on the Mac) the Clone Stamp icon in the toolbox or
  press S or Shift+S to switch to the Pattern Stamp tool. This
  tool paints with a repeating image tile selected from
  Photoshop's library of predefined patterns or defined
  using Edit ➪ Define Pattern or Filter ➪ Pattern Maker.

- ✦ **Healing Brush, Spot Healing Brush, and Patch tools:**
  The Brush tool is an expanded version of the Clone
  Stamp tool that merges texture detail from one portion
  of an image with color and brightness values from

another. This permits you more flexibility when retouching imperfections, particularly when repairing tricky defects, such as scratches and wrinkles. Click the Healing Brush icon to display the flyout menu, or press J or Shift+J to switch to the Patch tool, which allows you to repair entire selections at a time. Like the Stamp tool, the Healing Brush and Patch tools alternatively let you retouch with a pattern.

✦ **Eraser.** When used in a single-layer image or on the background layer, the Eraser tool paints in the background color. When applied to a layer, it erases pixels to reveal the layers below.

Cross-Reference

The Eraser tool includes two variations, the Background Eraser tool and Magic Eraser tool (see Figure 7-1), which automatically extract background details from a layer. Because their specific purpose is to extract and they work only with layered images, they're discussed independently of the standard Eraser tool in Chapter 9.

Figure 7-1: The main tools you'll use for restoring, repairing, and retouching photos are found in four buttons in the Toolbox — and you can view your steps and go back in time as needed with the History palette, here shown with several retouching steps taken.

✦ **History Brush and Art History Brush.** The History Brush tool allows you to selectively revert to any of several states listed in the History palette. To select the *source state* that you want to paint with, click in the first column of the History palette. A brush icon identifies the source state, as illustrated by the Lasso item in Figure 7-1. If Photoshop displays a little "not-allowed" cursor when you try to use the History Brush tool, it means you can't paint from the selected state. Click another state in the History palette and try again.

Alt-click the History Brush icon or press Y or Shift+Y to switch to the art History Brush tool, which lets you apply impressionistic effects based on the active source state in the History palette. It's not a terribly useful tool, but it can be a lot of fun.

✦ **Red Eye tool.** This tool removes red eye (or any unwanted glow in the eyes of the photo's subjects) through the use of two settings — Pupil Size and Darken Amount. Almost scarily simply, you can click on a glowing pupil and darken it without creating that glass-eyed doll look that can often result from manually darkening a pupil or painting out the glow with the Brush tool or by using the Burn tool, the latter of which often results in a strangely colored pupil.

New Feature

The Red Eye tool, which very conveniently removes those annoying demon eyes, is a new feature in Photoshop CS2.

Okay. These are the very abridged introductions to Photoshop's restoring and retouching tools, but at least you've got a general idea of how they work and why you'd use them. Now you're ready to rush headlong into the riveting, pulse-pounding details of how each and every one can be used to repair virtually any kind of photographic mishap or mishandling.

Cloning and Healing

Let's start with the Clone Stamp tool, which works by duplicating specified portions of an image and placing those cloned portions on top of existing content. Unlike a copy and paste that creates a new layer with the obscuring content, the Clone Stamp covers up things you don't want and places the obscuring content on the active layer. The process of using this tool is very simple, and has just a few options to keep in mind. The basic steps include selecting the tool — which you can do by pressing S and then Alt (or Option on the Mac) — and click in the image window to specify the portion of the image you want to clone. This is termed the *source point*. After sampling the source point, you can paint the cloned content onto any other part of the image — or even another image that's open at the same time. As you'll find as you read on, you can control the Clone Stamp tool's effects by choosing a brush preset and Mode, and choosing how the cloned content is sampled as you drag your mouse to paint the clone over the image.

Closely related to the Clone Stamp tool is the Healing Brush tool, which clones multiple attributes of an image at a time. Press J to select the tool. Then, as with the Clone Stamp, Alt-click (or Option-click on the Mac) in the image to set the source of the clone. Note that the Clone Stamp and Healing Brush share a common source point, so setting the source for one tool sets it for both. Drag with the Healing Brush tool to mix the texture from the source point with the highlights, shadows, and colors of pixels that neighbor the brushstroke — unlike the Clone Stamp, which deposits the cloned material with its source lighting and color intact. The Healing Brush actually updates the cloned material so that it blends in with its new surroundings.

Of course, you can probably think of a few ways to use this. That pesky kid who makes faces in all family photos can now be replaced (or his smirk replaced with a normal expression, borrowed from a more mature sibling), that mud puddle in front of your house can be filled in with nice green grass, and those scratches, tears, and stains in your old and/or improperly stored photos can now be repaired, using clean content from elsewhere in the same image or from an image with compatible content. You can also use these tools artistically — not just as a repair mechanism — to improve by cloning and healing all sorts of interesting content from one place or image to another.

The Clone Stamp tool

The Clone Stamp tool is the simpler of the two tools. Although easy to use, there are a few options that you can use to control the tool and achieve different results — and these require a little practice. If you just click the Clone Stamp and start dragging, Photoshop will balk and throw a prompt in your face warning you that you must first define a source point. This is done by pressing Alt (Windows) or Option (Mac) and requires only that you choose the source point in your mind before you click it.

How cloning works

To clone part of an image, Alt-click (Option-click on the Mac) in the image window to specify a point of reference in the portion of the image you want to clone. Then click or drag with the tool in some other region of the image to paint a cloned spot or line. You'll click if you want to place a single clone of the source point on some other place in the image, or drag if you want to create a series of clones in one continuous stretch. In Figure 7-2, the cloned content (the source point) is identified on the left, and its use is obvious on the right — both a single click to deposit the cloned content once, and an example of dragging with the Clone Stamp.

It's worth noting that the Clone Stamp tool clones the image as it existed before you began using the tool for as long as you hold down the mouse button. Even when you drag over an area that contains a clone, the tool references the original appearance of the image. This means there may be a visual disconnect between what the Clone Stamp tool seems to be sourcing and what it paints. This is actually a good thing, however, because it avoids repetition of detail, a dead giveaway of poor retouching.

Tip

Photoshop lets you clone not only within the image in which you're working but from a separate image window as well. This technique makes it possible to merge two different images, as demonstrated in Figure 7-3. To achieve this effect, Alt-click (Option-click) to set a source point in one image, bring a second image to the foreground, and then drag with the Clone Stamp tool to copy from the first image. You can also clone between layers, assuming the layers are unlocked. Just Alt-click (Option-click) one layer and then switch to a different layer and drag.

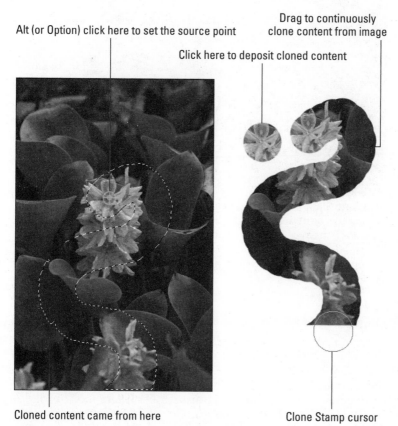

Alt (or Option) click here to set the source point

Drag to continuously clone content from image

Click here to deposit cloned content

Cloned content came from here

Clone Stamp cursor

Figure 7-2: After Alt-clicking (Option-clicking on the Mac) at the point indicated by the target cursor, a single click duplicates a portion of the flower, while a continuous drag with the Clone Stamp creates the painted stroke of cloned content.

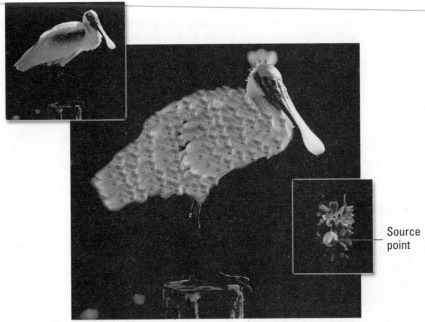

Source
point

Figure 7-3: The Clone Stamp tool placed this content from one image into another — replacing this bird's feathers with flower petals. By dragging in short, repeated strokes, the pattern of feathers is mimicked, and using a soft brush preset, the diffused edges on the bird in the original photo are maintained. The "before" image appears reduced on the left, and the source point within the flower is highlighted on the lower right.

Cloning options

When the Clone Stamp tool is active, the Options bar gives you access to the standard Brush, Mode, and Opacity settings that you get when using the Brush tool. These options enable you to mix the cloned image with the original to get different effects, as explained in Chapter 5. You also get the Flow value and Airbrush icon, which make it possible for you to build up brushstrokes where they overlap and at points where you click without moving the cursor.

You'll also find the Use All Layers option, which lets you clone from multiple layers at a time, very useful for cloning from the composite image onto a new layer. For more information on this option, see Chapter 5.

An option that you haven't seen before presents both a wrinkle and a real opportunity to get some interesting effects with the Clone Stamp tool. It's the Aligned option, which locks the relative source of a clone from one Alt- or Option-click to the next. Huh? OK, try this. Think of the locations where you Alt-click (Option-click on the Mac) and begin dragging with the Clone Stamp tool to opposite ends of an imaginary straight line, as illustrated in Figure 7-4. When Aligned is selected, the length and angle of this imaginary line remains fixed until the next time you Alt-click. As you drag, Photoshop moves the line, cloning pixels from one end of the line and laying them down at the other. The benefit is that regardless of how many times you start and stop dragging with the stamp tool, all brushstrokes match up as seamlessly as pieces in a puzzle.

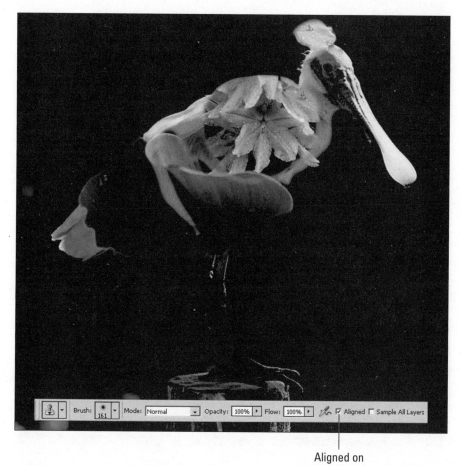

Aligned on

Figure 7-4: With the Aligned option selected, the cloned content stays in synch with the source points, a new one set each time you click and drag to place cloned content in target areas. By dragging over the bird's body, flowers and leaves are strategically placed to mimic feathers and a leafy wing.

Note The glow around the cloned areas is added through blending modes (see Chapter 13) and was applied only to make it more clear to you where the cloning was applied.

If you want to clone from a single portion of an image repeatedly, deselect the Aligned option — note that this option was off in Figure 7-3, where the repeated pattern of feathers was desirable, yet total uniformity in terms of what was cloned was not desirable, as no two feathers are the same, even if they're growing in a uniform pattern. Figure 7-5 shows how, with the Aligned option selected, Photoshop clones from the same point every time you paint a new line with the Clone Stamp tool. As a result, each of the brushstrokes brings in some of the photo of the flower, but the strokes don't line up with each other as they did in Figure 7-4.

Aligned off

Figure 7-5: If you deselect the Aligned option, Photoshop clones only from the point at which you Alt- or Option-clicked to set your source point. Here, the flowers are repeated each time the mouse was clicked, and the same part of the original image appears in each of the cloned areas.

The Healing Brush tool

Way back in Photoshop 7 the nearly magical Healing Brush tool was presented to grateful photographers, restorers, and just plain folks with photos in need of help. Even now, its powers seem amazing, and almost too good to be true.

If you thought the Clone Stamp tool was the bee's knees (and you were right), get ready for the cat's pajamas. Open a photo that needs some work. For the example shown in Figure 7-6, a vintage photo with some serious scars on it is a great subject on which to demonstrate the tool. Because there are places that are unmarked, we can use them to cover the scars — but unlike the Clone Stamp, which could be used to take the clean content and duplicate it on top of the scars, the Healing Brush will not only clone that clean content but relight and color it to meet the needs of its new surroundings. The Spot Healing Brush tool, which we'll discuss shortly, does the same thing, but with small troubled areas — thus the tool's name including the word "Spot."

Anyway, in Figure 7-6, see the before (left) and after (right) versions, wherein large scars — scuffs and scrapes with decades of dirt ground into them — are repaired with the Healing Brush tool.

Figure 7-6: Set the "way-back machine" to a time before this photo had been scuffed, scraped, and generally abused by storing it loose in a drawer full of other photos, pencils, rubber bands, and other bits and pieces that have no business bumping into a precious glimpse of relatives past.

To make the changes seen in Figure 7-6, select the Healing Brush tool by pressing J, which you can remember because it's the only letter missing from the words *heal, patch, mend, fix, knit, remedy, salvage, cobble,* and *requite.* Or, just click the tool with your mouse — it may be easier that way. Next, press Alt (or Option) and click in the image to identify the texture that you want to match. Then paint over a spot, scratch, scar, or wrinkle and watch as the Healing Brush lives up to its name.

How the healing works

In getting to know the Healing Brush tool, you quickly discover two things. When it works, it works incredibly well, better than any other retouching technique available in Photoshop. But when it doesn't work, it fails completely, in that it can bring in colors and shades that don't match their surroundings at all. What is the best way to avoid such a scenario and only have the Healing Brush make you happy? Take a little time to learn how the Healing Brush really works, and you'll learn not only how best to use it, but when to use the Clone Stamp tool instead.

Assuming you're on board for the whole "take a little time" idea, let's take a moment and reveal some of the magic. The Healing Brush tool blends the pixels from the source point with the original pixels of your stroke made with the Healing Brush. In that respect, it works a little bit like the Clone Stamp tool combined with a brush mode — changing colors and lighting at the same time it's applying . . . well, in this case applying content, in the case of the Brush tool, applying paint. Instead of the rather simplistic technique of blending two pixels at a time as a brush mode does the Healing Brush blends cloned pixels with those just outside the brushstroke, drawing information from those pixels to determine how to adjust the cloned content. The idea is that the pixels you're painting over are messed up, but the pixels just beyond the brushstroke are in good shape and should be emulated.

Figure 7-7 illustrates this concept. The Healing Brush tool has been used to clone portions of a photo onto a fabric background. The smooth image from the left is cloned onto the fabric, and the fabric's texture is smoothed away by the photo content applied by the Healing Brush. The lighting is also adjusted, achieved by Photoshop burning and dodging the healed content based on the source point. Bear in mind that it does all this according to the colors, highlights, and shadows that it encounters in tracing the very outer perimeter of the brushstroke, which is highlighted by the line drawn on the right side of Figure 7-7.

What can we deduce from this?

✦ First, the Healing Brush tool replaces the texture as you paint just as surely as if you were using the Clone Stamp tool. If you want to mix textures, you'll need to employ a brush mode, as explained in the next section.

✦ Second, the manner in which the color and shading are mixed is directly linked to the size and hardness of your brush. Bear in mind that Photoshop is looking at the outside edge of the brushstroke. As illustrated, back in Chapter 5 (on painting), the outer edge of the brush grows as the Hardness value shrinks. Therefore, you can count on soft brushes to cause the Healing Brush to factor in more surrounding colors and shading than hard brushes will.

So what if it all goes wrong and undesirable results appear where healing was expected? Just click Undo, or use the History palette to go back to before the healing began. Then tinker with your brush settings, changing the size and softness, until you get the results you are looking for. If all else fails, try the Clone Stamp tool — you may like the results. It could just be that the extra magic applied by the Healing Brush tool wasn't what was needed after all.

Source point   Target area

A single click of the Healing Brush repeats the source content

One continuous stroke of the Healing Brush created this content

Figure 7-7: The Healing Brush tool applies photo content to fabric, and incorporates the lighting and textures from the source point into the very different target area.

Healing options

Despite its powers and the intuitive way it applies content, there aren't many ways you can customize the behavior of the Healing Brush tool. It permits you neither to use custom brushes nor to apply any of the settings in the Brushes palette. To modify a brush, click the Brush icon in the Options bar. This gives you access to Photoshop 6-style brush-tip settings along with a single dynamic that lets you link brush size to pen pressure or airbrush wheel.

You also have no control over Opacity or Flow. While this is a surprising omission, you can work around this problem by choosing Edit ⇨ Fade, as you discover later. The brush modes are limited to just eight, and in each case, the mode merges cloned and original pixels, and then performs the additional healing blending. By way of example, Figure 7-8 shows four of the eight modes in use while the Healing Brush applied a single stroke (one stroke per Mode) to a gradient background. Thanks to the dodging and burning applied by the Healing Brush, dark modes like Multiply and light modes such as Screen can be substantially compromised. In fact, most of the brush modes have little effect, as you can see in the figure — the strokes are not very different, and the differences you can see are subtle. This can either result in your finding the use of the modes to be a waste of time, or you may revel in their subtlety. Your choice.

Figure 7-8: Examples of the Healing Brush combined with four different Healing Brush modes across the same textured fabric as seen in Figure 7-7.

The exception is Replace. Unique to the Healing Brush tool, the Replace mode clones pixels without any blending, just as if you were painting with the Clone Stamp tool set to Normal. The question is, why in the world would you want to do this, particularly when the Healing Brush set to Replace offers far fewer options than the highly customizable Clone Stamp tool? The answer is to test effects. Thanks to its blending routine, the Healing Brush sometimes takes several seconds to apply. But when set to Replace, it takes no time at all. You can test a brushstroke, make sure it's cloning the right area, undo it, switch back to Normal, and paint the real thing. Replace is so useful that it's worth remembering its shortcut, Shift+Alt+Z (Shift-Option-Z on the Mac). Press Shift+Alt+N (Shift-Option-N) to return to Normal.

Other options include the Source buttons, which determine whether the Healing Brush tool clones pixels (Sampled) or paints with a predefined texture (Pattern). You also have the Aligned option, which aligns multiple brushstrokes to a fixed source point, as described in the section "Cloning options." The Aligned options for the Healing Brush and Clone Stamp tools are linked, so selecting one selects the other as well.

Tip Don't forget the Healing Brush tool's Use All Layers setting in the Options bar. Much like the similarly named option available to the Clone Stamp and Smudge tools (discussed in Chapter 5), selecting Use All Layers factors in information from every visible layer during the healing process. This can be a great asset because it allows you to create a new layer and perform all your pixel manipulation on it while retaining the original pixels on the layers below.

The Spot Healing Brush

New in Photoshop CS2, the Spot Healing Brush tool works very much like the Healing Brush tool in terms of its results, but the mechanism is a bit different when it comes to your role in the process. Instead of having to sample content and set a source point, all you have to do is click the tool on top of the offending spot — a small scratch, stain, blemish, or any other small area of unwanted content. If you attempt to sample by pressing Alt (Windows) or Option (Mac), you're prompted that if you want to manually set a source point, you should use the Healing Brush tool.

There are some drawbacks. As shown in Figure 7-9, Photoshop guesses which content to use in repairing the problem, and it can guess wrong. In the figure, you can see that the Proximity Match created a repair that is too light, and Create Texture created and unwanted texture (inset).

Of course, with a quick Undo, the bad results are reversed, and a click with the Spot Healing Brush tool on the other end of the scratch solves the problem, because there were more appropriate pixels nearby. Two more clicks along the scratch and it is gone (see the "After" version on the right where the scratch is gone, although a problem created by the healing process remains). It's a great tool for a quick fix, but it does have its shortcomings. You can also try using a larger brush to do the repair in a single click, but you risk the area considered "proximity" including content that you don't want used in the healing process.

Note There are options for this simple tool — you can go with the default Proximity Match, which heals the spot you click on using neighboring pixels; or you can click the Create Texture option, which heals and creates a texture based on nearby pixels. This can work well, or it can be a problem if the texture Photoshop creates is visually effective. As shown in Figure 7-9, a texture on the face isn't a good thing — and its source is difficult to anticipate. The other option, Sample All Layers, enables Photoshop to draw its healing information from pixels on . . . well, you guessed it — all layers.

Figure 7-9: The Spot Healing Brush in Proximity Match mode works great when there is nothing but clear sailing next to the spot you're trying to heal. Here you can see its two healing types — Proximity Match and Create Texture — at work, and you can also see how the tool can sometimes go wrong.

The Patch tool

If you prefer to heal a selected area all at once, choose the Patch tool from the Healing Brush flyout menu in the toolbox. You can also press J — or if you did not deselect the Use Shift Key for Tool Switch option in the Preferences dialog box, press Shift+J instead.

You can use the Patch tool in one of two ways:

✦ **Define destination, drag onto source.** Assuming the Source option is selected in the Options bar, as it is by default, use the Patch tool to draw an outline around the portion of the image you want to heal. This creates a selection outline. In Figure 7-10, for example the large scratched area of the vintage photo is selected. Next, click and drag the selection outline to move it to a new location. The spot where you release the mouse button determines the source for the clone. In the "After" version, the selection has been dragged to an area of the background that is clear of scratches and scuffs, and that smooth territory has been cloned on top of the scratch, patching it.

✦ **Define source, drag onto destination.** The former method seems a bit counterintuitive, or backward, to some people. If it seems backward to drag the offending content onto good content, then just swap things around. Choose Destination as the Patch method on the Options bar, and select an area to use as the patch. Then drag that onto the stuff you want to obscure. Of course, this requires that you either guess the shape of the patch by looking at the target area as you drag to select within the source area (where the good content is), or you can make the selection first, in the bad area, then move it to the good area, and *then* activate the Patch tool.

Figure 7-10: Like cutting a swatch of fabric that's just a bit larger than the hole in your jeans, you can patch your photo rips and tears with content from a clean spot on the photo. You can drag the patch to the problem, or drag the problem to the patch (as shown here).

If you're wondering how the Patch tool's selection process works, it's just like the standard Lasso tool. You can add to a selection by Shift-dragging or delete by Alt-dragging (Option-dragging on the Mac), and you can soften a patch by using Select ➪ Feather or modify it in the Quick Mask mode, thus giving the Patch tool more room along the edge of the selection to sample colors and shades. For complete information on creating and editing selections, read Chapter 8.

The Patch tool lacks Opacity and brush mode controls, and you can't use it between layers or between different images. All work has to be performed on a single layer, which ultimately limits its potential. On the plus side, you can patch a selection with a predefined pattern by clicking the Use Pattern button in the Options bar.

Note The Patch tool also gives you a preview of unaltered source pixels in your selected area while you're still dragging it around. This gives you a better idea of how the size and shape of the area from which you're pulling texture will fit when it combines with your original destination. You also have a Transparent option in the Options bar, which when selected enables the Patch tool to pull the texture but none of the color information from wherever you drag.

The Red Eye tool

Allegedly because of their large pupils, animals, especially those with some nocturnal vision capabilities, tend to become the most frequent victims of red eye in photos. Children are often victims, too, but that's often because one of them is either the adored subject and the photographer (mom or dad) gets too darn close when taking the picture, or the little darling moves in closer to the camera just as the picture's taken. The proximity of the lens and the flash is also a potential culprit, but with many cameras, you can't adjust this distance—the flash is atop the camera, and the lens is in a fixed position, too. Whatever the cause and whomever the victim, red eye is one of the most common problems faced by amateur photographers, especially the "home user" of cameras with a flash. As shown in Figure 7-11, you can get rid of it quickly with Photoshop CS2's new Red Eye tool, a simple, fast tool for darkening and washing the glow right out of the demonically glowing pupil.

Note Red isn't always the color of the glow — sometimes, as shown in Figure 7-11, the glow is yellow (well, it appears light gray here, but take my word for it). In fact, rarely is the glow a single color — as you also see in this figure, where the glow is brightest in the center of the very large pupil. In the color version of this photo, it goes from canary yellow in the center to a burnt orange around the edges.

The Red Eye tool is bizarrely simple to use, and it's quite effective — to a point. It has two options — Pupil Size and Darken Amount, both set to 50% by default. You can drag the options' sliders to accommodate larger or smaller pupils and more or less of a glow in the subject's eyes. Remember to use different settings for each of the eyes if the subject was not facing the camera head-on — if he or she was at an angle, the eye farthest from the camera will have a smaller pupil and may have less of a glow going on.

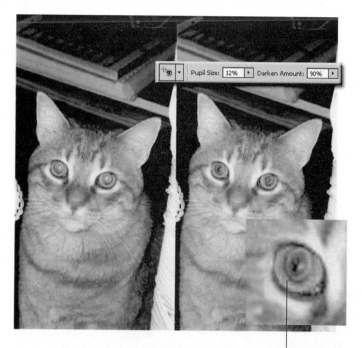

Be sure to center the tool or you risk washing out the iris as well

Figure 7-11: Don't worry about selecting the pupil and painting or burning the glow away as you might have in previous versions of Photoshop. Instead, use the Red Eye tool to exorcise that glow and restore the look of sanity to your photos' subjects.

Now about that "to a point" comment. The tool works by washing out the color (as though you've used the Sponge tool in Desaturate mode) and it also darkens it (as if the Burn tool was used). In color photos, or in close-ups where the eye is quite visible in detail, this may not be a good thing, as having black or dark gray pupils in a color photo looks, well, weird. You may prefer to use the Burn tool yourself and use other color-adjustment tools to get rid of the red or yellow, essentially going back to one of the many manual methods of getting rid of red eye used in the past when this tool was not available. Figure 7-11 shows the almost grayscale-looking pupils, and as noted in the figure, shows the downside of not quite centering the tool when clicking the pupil — some of the iris has been relieved of its color as well, as seen in the left eye and shown in the zoomed inset.

Retouching Photographs

Having seen how the Clone Stamp, Healing Brush, Spot Healing Brush, Patch, and Red Eye tools work, the following sections examine a few sample uses for the tools. For example, say you have a snapshot lying around, one that's really a good picture of someone you love, but it's in terrible shape, like the scanned photo shown in Figure 7-12. The problems are many — nicks and scratches in the photo's surface (damage from improper storage and rough handling of the print), the photo is faded (age), and blurry (poor photographic and/or development). You probably don't need to *imagine* such a photo — you probably have many of them lying around the house, or if you're a professional photographer, your non-photographer relatives are creating these horrors on every holiday and vacation.

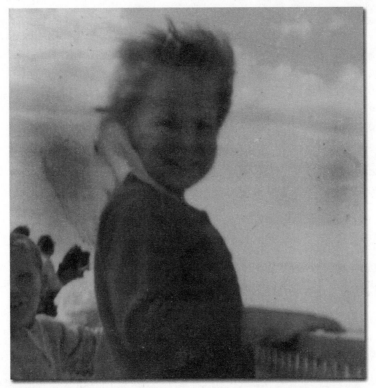

Figure 7-12: This is a very lovable shot, of a child on a boat in 1965 at Cape Cod. The many problems shown in this zoomed-in view of the photo have Photoshop solutions.

Now, of course, there are some non-Photoshop solutions you can try, first. Try cleaning your scanner's glass, if you're scanning a printed photo. Try tinkering with the scanner's settings for contrast and sharpness a bit (don't go wild, these can cause more problems than they solve, depending on the scanner's software), and try increasing the resolution of your scan if lack of detail and color is a problem. Beyond that, you have what you have and Photoshop is really your only solution.

So let's look at those solutions, some or all of which may be used depending on the photo, or perhaps only one of them will work — it really depends on the photo in question:

✦ **Dust & Scratches filter.** Try this if your image is sharp and clear but has a lot of dust and scuffs on it — tiny, minor ones. This filter won't get rid of major scratches, but it will remove some of the "white noise" that can accumulate on a poorly stored or roughly handled photo.

✦ **Clone Stamp, Healing Brush, Spot Healing Brush, and Patch tools**. Yes, one or more of these, used to fix small and large problems, can be your salvation. They can also lead to back- and headaches, as the more problems you have, the longer you'll spend fixing the photo, bent over the monitor at a high, eye-scorching zoom, fixing the flaws. Figure 7-13 shows an "after" version of the photo in 7-12, where the Spot Healing Brush and Clone Stamp tools were used to clean up the bigger flaws, and the aforementioned Dust & Scratches filter was used on portions of the image — the sky, any place that didn't have too much detail to worry about losing — to do a general cleanup.

Figure 7-13: After a general sweep with the Dust & Scratches filter and some focused cleanup with the Clone Stamp and Spot Healing Brush tools, the photo looks much better — the stain in the sky behind the subject is gone and the tiny flaws have been softened and healed away.

As you discover in Chapter 10, the Dust & Scratches filter has one big downside — along with the dust, scratches, and tiny flaws it miraculously removes, it also removes a lot of your detail. Of course, you can tinker with the filter's settings to mitigate this a bit, but if you let the filter work hard enough to really rid the photo of the tiny flaws, you lose the tiny details, too. Oh, well — Photoshop giveth, and Photoshop taketh away.

Not liking the loss of detail, in Figure 7-14, you can see the results of a final touch-up with the Smart Sharpen filter, which is new in Photoshop CS2. This filter, also discussed in Chapter 10, goes over the image and adds back some of the detail lost to the Dust & Scratches filter. Of course, it can't re-create lost details, but it does add to the differences between adjacent pixels, eliminating that fuzzy, blurry look.

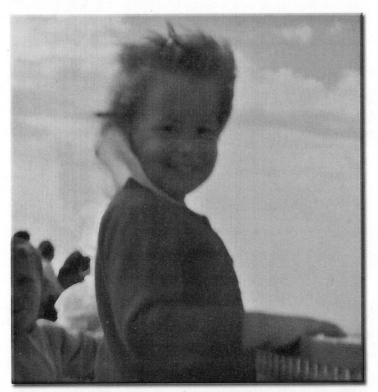

Figure 7-14: The final touch is to sharpen the image using the Smart Sharpen filter. The result is by no means perfect — Photoshop can't produce detail out of thin air — but the photo, one that I really love, is really suitable for framing now.

The lesson to draw from all this is that the Dust & Scratches filter may suffice for purging fibers and defects from a low-quality photo like this one, but it's hardly a professional-level tool. In almost all cases, the better alternative is to roll up your sleeves, get real with your image, and fix its flaws manually — not to mention lovingly — with the Healing Brush and Clone Stamp tools. You'll be glad you did.

Restoring an old photograph

Old photos present some unique problems. First, depending on their age, they may have been around for decades — maybe even a century — and even the most carefully stored photo of that vintage is going to show signs of its age. Add to that the fact that in the late nineteenth and early twentieth centuries, photos were printed on paper that doesn't hold up well — it was often textured, which can affect your scan adversely, and the paper dried out and crumbled, making what might have been an easily fixable fold or scrape into a huge scar that requires major restoration.

Figure 7-15 shows an old photo, one that was treated relatively well, but not stored in an environmentally controlled place. It was in a photo album since the 1960s, and before that, it was kept in a box. The photo was taken in 1887, and was scanned at 300 dpi as a color photo — despite it not really being "in color." Scanning it as a color photo brings in more information and allows the photo to be brought back to its sepia-tone glory with less loss of detail.

Despite the photo's rough condition, Photoshop's many restoration tools were able to restore it, as evidenced by Figure 7-16. After about an hour and a few hundred brushstrokes, the image was nearly back to its original state. If an hour sounds like a long time to fix a few rips and scrapes, bear in mind that photographic restoration is a labor-intensive activity that relies heavily on your talents and your mastery of Photoshop. The job of Photoshop's restoration tools is to make your edits believable, but they do little to automate the process. Retouching calls for a human touch, and that's where you come in.

The main trick in all this is to Alt-click (Option-click on the Mac) with the Clone Stamp or Healing Brush tools in an area that looks like it'd do a good job of covering up a blemish and then click or drag over the blemishes. For tiny spots where you aren't sure where to grab the coverup material, use the Spot Healing Brush tool — just restrict its use to where there are clean pixels all around the spot — because that's where Photoshop will derive its content to cover the blemish you click on. Rather than take you back through a boring description of every click and drag to bring the photo in Figure 7-15 up to the way it looks in Figure 7-16, here are some tips for ways to restore even the most damaged, faded, beat-up photo:

✦ **Toss the bad channels.** Most images in this kind of condition are black-and-white. Scan them in color and then look at the individual color channels (see Figure 7-17) to see which grayscale version of the image looks best.

✦ **View actual pixels.** When possible, work at 100 percent view size or larger. It's difficult to judge scratches and other defects accurately at smaller zoom ratios, but if you must, stick with the "smooth views" — 50 percent and 25 percent.

✦ **Keep an eye on the source.** Keep the original photo next to you as you work. What looks like a scratch on-screen may actually be a photographic element, and what looks like an element may be a scratch. Only by referring to the original image can you be sure.

Tip

Don't crop until you're finished retouching the image. You'd be surprised how useful that extra garbage around the perimeter is when it comes to covering up really big tears.

Figure 7-15: Portraits were serious business in the days when not everyone had access to a camera or a photographer. Smiling, even for a child, was virtually unheard of. Though treated reverentially over the years, it looks like this little guy knew how his photo would end up.

✦ **Vary the brush hardness.** Use hard brush shapes against sharp edges. But when working in general areas such as the shadow, the ground, and the wall, mix it up between soft and hard brushes using the shortcuts Shift+[and Shift+]. Staying random is the best way to avoid harsh transitions, repeating patterns, and other digital giveaways.

✦ **Keep it short.** Paint in short strokes. This helps keep things random, but it also means you don't have to redraw a big, long brushstroke if you make a mistake.

Tip

Use your History when you make a mistake. Don't automatically press Ctrl+Z (⌘-Z for you Mac people). In many cases, you'll be better off using the History Brush tool to paint back the image as it appeared before the last Healing Brush or Clone Stamp tool operation. You'll learn more about the History Brush later in this chapter.

Figure 7-16: The same image after about an hour of work with the Clone Stamp, Spot Healing Brush, and the Healing Brush tools

✦ **Deselect the Aligned option.** Another way to stay random is to change the source of your clone frequently. That means Alt-clicking (Option-clicking on the Mac) after every second or third brushstroke. And keep the Aligned option deselected. An aligned clone is not a random one.

✦ **Try out brush modes.** Feel free to experiment with the brush modes and, when using the Clone Stamp tool, the Opacity setting. You can also tinker with Mode settings for the Healing Brush tool, experimenting with lightening and darkening modes to see which one gives you the best results — of course, each picture and its individual flaws will dictate which one of the tools and which settings for it work best.

Red   Green   Blue

Figure 7-17: When each channel is viewed separately, it's clear that the green channel looks best, with best contrast, fewest splotches, and crispest edges. Blue is way too dark and blotchy, and the red channel is nearly faded out to nothing.

Tip

You also can try applying Edit ➪ Fade to change the opacity and brush mode of the pixels you just cloned. This little trick can be extremely useful when using the Healing Brush tool because it means you can introduce an Opacity value into the proceedings where none existed previously. Curious? After applying a Healing Brushstroke, choose Edit ➪ Fade or press Ctrl+Shift+F (⌘-Shift-F on the Mac). You get an Opacity value and no Mode option, exactly the opposite of what you see in the Options bar when using the tool.

✦ **Keep the grain.** Don't attempt to smooth out the general appearance of grain in the image. Grain is integral to an old photo and hiding it usually makes the image look faked. If your image gets too smooth, or if your cloning results in irregular patterns, select the problem area and apply Filter ➪ Noise ➪ Add Noise. Enter very small Amount values (2 to 6 percent). Monochromatic noise tends to work best. If necessary, press Ctrl+F (⌘-F on the Mac) to reapply the filter one or more times.

With Photoshop's History Brush tool at your side, there's really no way to permanently harm an image. You can even let four or five little mistakes go and then correct them all at once with the History Brush. Just click to the left of the state in the History palette that directly precedes the first state where things went wrong, and then drag with the History Brush. It's so effective and liberating, you'll wish life had a History palette — click and drag and that whopping error in judgment is . . . um . . . history.

Anyway, to paint back to the original scanned image, click in front of the very top item in the History palette — this brings things back to how they were before you did anything beyond opening or importing (scanning) the image. Again, there's more info to come on using the History palette, so stay tuned to this chapter.

Eliminating distracting background elements

The Clone Stamp and Healing Brush tools also come in handy for eliminating background action that competes with the central elements in an image. For example, Figure 7-18 shows a photo of a little girl and her dad, both facing away from mom, the photographer. It's a sweet photo, but it has a few distracting elements — the stain from tape at the bottom (this can be cropped out if you don't mind losing the white frame, so common in photos going back to the 1960s) and the person sunbathing in front of the subjects. If the photo were just of these two people standing on the boardwalk, looking out at the beach, it'd be great. What to do? Whack that sunbather, and send her back to her overpriced rented beach house, towel and all. You could even get rid of the edge of the towel in the lower left, while you're at it.

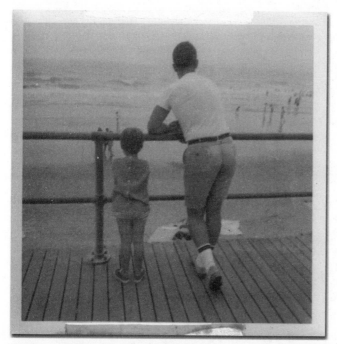

Figure 7-18: Don't leave distracting elements, even seemingly insignificant ones, in your photos. The photographer probably didn't even notice the sunbather in this photo, but once the image was printed, the visual "noise" she creates is obvious.

Note   Remember as you read these steps that cloning away an image element is something of an inexact science. It requires considerable patience and a little bit of trial and error. So regard the following steps as an example of how to approach the process of editing an image rather than as a specific procedure that works for all images. You will undoubtedly need to adapt the process to suit the specific needs of your image.

STEPS: Eliminating Distracting Elements from an Image

1. **Clone a spot in the sand near the edge of the sunbather's towel.** Set the brush to a size that encompasses a reasonable amount of sand, but keep the brush size small enough that you can fit it between the bars on the railing the two subjects are leaning on. Figure 7-19 shows the Clone Stamp tool poised above its first section of towel, one click under its belt.

Tip   Make sure the Clone Stamp tool is set to a soft-edged brush, so that there are no obvious edges to the cloned content.

2. **Clone away the towel and sunbather, getting as close to the edges of the railing and the subject's legs as you can without risking cloning them out of the photo, too.** Figure 7-20 shows this in progress.

Figure 7-19: Clone the content that will obscure the unwanted portion of the image — in this case sand will be used to bury the sunbather.

3. **Shrink your Clone Stamp brush and zoom in.** You need to get in tight on the subjects' legs now, so you can clone away the sunbather and her towel right up to the legs. This is again why you want a soft-edged brush, so you don't get a hard edge that makes the subjects look like cutouts that were pasted onto a photo of the beach. Figure 17-21 shows a zoomed-in view and a smaller Clone Stamp brush at work. As you get in tight on corners and in crevices, you can go as low as a 1- or 2-pixel brush, because zoomed in as tight as you are, it won't seem that small and it won't be hard to see the brush cursor, as you can see in Figure 7-21, where a very small brush is in use.

4. **Keep cloning.** Just keep cloning along, clicking and dragging up to the edge of the subjects' legs. Get as close as you can, and keep zooming in if you need to, so you don't clone anything you want to keep.

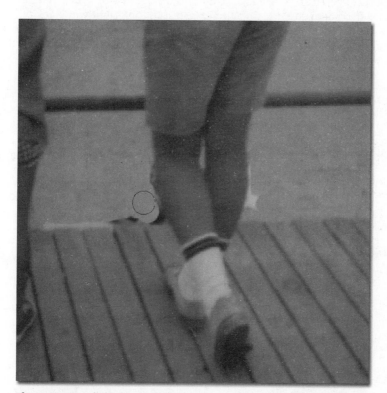

Figure 7-20: Click, drag, and just keep applying sand from the source point.

Tip

If you really feel like you can't come right up to the edge without cloning the legs, too, then select them with the Magnetic Lasso (or whichever Lasso you feel most comfortable with) and copy them to a new layer. You can then hide that new layer and clone right up to and onto the original legs and then redisplay the legs after the fact. Of course, a little feather on the selection will keep the edges soft enough to seem like they belong once they're back in the picture.

5. **Use the Blur tool, set to a low Strength, and gently smooth out any edges where the cloning along the legs and railings was too obvious.** You can also use the Eraser tool, set to a soft-edged brush, to clean up the edges of the legs (and railings) if you put them on their own layer, per the tip that precedes this step.

6. **Look for any obvious patterns or repetitions in the sand.** The one risk with the Clone Stamp tool, even with the Aligned option deselected, is that the cloned content will look cloned. This is especially likely when you're cloning natural substances like fabric, grass, or in this case, sand with footprints and other irregular high and low spots in it. You want to keep the random, natural look, so if you see any places where the cloning looks obvious, clone on top of it, grabbing from a source point that's nowhere near the unwanted pattern. Of course, keep the color and texture of the sand in mind, and don't go grab wet sand from near the tide line and expect it to look right way back on the dry sand near the subjects. Figure 7-22 shows the final result — after blurring, recloning to get rid of patterns, and a teeny-tiny bit of Burn-tool used to darken the front edges of the boards so they didn't look cut off.

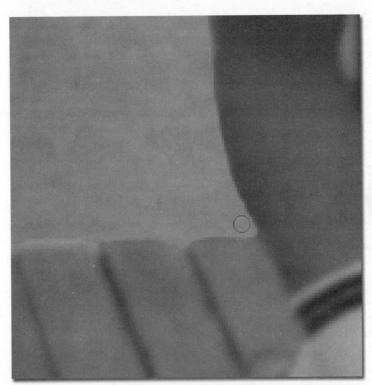

Figure 7-21: Get closer, closer, closer and clone, clone, clone.

Hopefully, as you experimented with this procedure, you found that cloning with the Clone Stamp tool requires you to alternate between patching and whittling away. There are no rights and wrongs, no hard-and-fast rules. Anything you can find to clone is fair game. As long as you avoid totally messing up the foreground image, you can't go wrong (well, then there is *one* hard-and-fast rule). If you're careful and diligent, no one but you will notice your alterations.

Caution Any time you edit the contents of a photograph that was created by someone other than yourself, you tread on sensitive ground. Although some have convincingly argued that electronically retouching an image is, theoretically, no different than cropping a photograph — a technique available and in use since the first daguerreotype — photographers have certain rights under copyright law that cannot be ignored. A photographer may have a reason for including an element you want to eliminate. So, before you edit any photograph, be sure to get permission either from the original photographer or from the copyright holder. For the photos used in this chapter, the permission came from one of the authors, who either appears in or is related to the subjects.

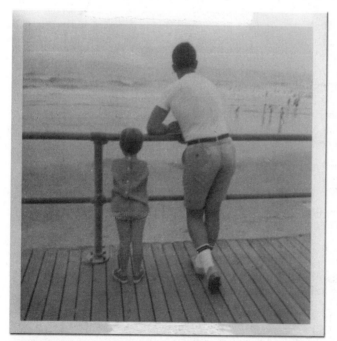

Figure 7-22: With a little softening, some tight, tiny cloning, and in this case, a little "cheating" with the Burn tool to darken an edge or two, this photo is now free of distracting elements — even that stain from the tape and some other beach combers.

Stepping Back through Time

One of the most annoying things about Photoshop — and there aren't that many truly annoying things, so given that this merits mentioning, you know it's really annoying — is that you can't undo more than your last step using the Edit, Undo (Ctrl/⌘ + Z) command. You can press Ctrl + Alt + Z (or ⌘ + Option + Z on the Mac) to undo more than one thing, but the ubiquitous Ctrl/⌘ + Z –the shortcut that allows multiple undos in every other piece of software under the sun — can't be used for more than one step backward. If you've ever seen or used Photoshop Elements, you know that you can undo several times in a row with Ctrl/⌘ + Z in *that* application, so it's not like having multiple Undos is something that's against the rules at Adobe.

With the release of Photoshop 5, the software gods at Adobe gave us the History palette, which is a great and powerful tool for going back in time and undoing many steps either serially or as a group. You'll learn a great deal more about it in the ensuing paragraphs, but it still is not as convenient as pressing Ctrl/⌘ + Z repeatedly and watching your last several steps be undone. Sorry, I just had to say that.

No matter. The History palette is great, and this is the spot in the book where you're gonna learn all about it. Here are just a few of the marvelous things you can do with the History palette:

✦ **Undo-independent stepping.** Step backward by pressing Ctrl+Alt+Z (⌘-Option-Z on the Mac); step forward by pressing Ctrl+Shift+Z (⌘-Shift-Z). Every program with multiple undos does this, but Photoshop's default keyboard equivalents are different. Why? Because you can backstep independently of the Undo command, so that even backstepping is undoable.

✦ **Before and after.** Revert to a point in history to see a "before" view of your image and then fly forward to see the "after" view. From then on, Ctrl+Z (⌘-Z on the Mac) becomes a super-undo, toggling between the before and after views. The opportunities for comparing states and changing your mind are mind-boggling.

✦ **Real time travel.** If before and after aren't enough, how about animated history? You can drag a control to slide dynamically forward and backward through operations. It's as if you recorded the operations to videotape, and now you're rewinding and fast-forwarding through them.

✦ **Sweeping away mistakes.** Select a point in the history of your image and paint back to it using the History Brush. You can let the mistakes pile up and then brush them away. This brush isn't a paintbrush; it's a hand broom. Want even more variety? Use the Art History Brush to paint back to the image using various artistic styles.

✦ **Take a picture, it'll last longer.** You can save any point in the History palette as a snapshot. That way, even several hundred operations after that point in history are long gone, you can revisit the snapshot.

✦ **It was a very good year.** Each and every image has its own history. After performing a few hundred operations on Image A, you can still go back to Image B and backstep through operations you performed hours ago. The caveat is that the history remains available only as long as an image is open. Close the image, and its history goes away.

✦ **Undo the Revert command.** Back in the days before Photoshop 5.5, you couldn't undo the Revert command. Now, the History palette tracks Revert. So if you don't like the image that was last saved to disk, you can undo the reversion and get back to where you were. Also notice that when you choose File ➪ Revert, Photoshop does not ask you to confirm the reversion. There's no reason for a warning because Revert is fully undoable.

The only thing you can't do through the History palette is travel forward into the future — say, to about three days from now when you've finished your grueling project, submitted it to your client, and received your big fat paycheck. Believe it or not, that's actually good news. The day Adobe can figure out how to do your work for you, your clients will hire Photoshop and stop hiring you.

Using the traditional undo functions

Before going any further with the History palette, let's make sure you're totally familiar with Photoshop's more traditional reversion functions. If you already know about this stuff, leaf on ahead to the next section.

✦ **Undo.** To restore an image to the way it looked before the last operation, choose Edit ➪ Undo or press Ctrl+Z (⌘-Z on the Mac). You can undo the effect of a paint or edit tool, a change made to a selection outline, or a special-effect or color-correction command. You can't undo disk operations, such as opening or saving. Photoshop does enable you to undo an edit after printing an image, though. You can test an effect, print the image, and then undo the effect if you think it looks awful. But to perform such an undo, you have to press Ctrl+Alt+Z (⌘-Option-Z on the Mac) to backstep through history.

✦ **Revert.** Choose File ➪ Revert to reload an image from disk. In most programs, this is the last-resort function, the command you choose after everything else has failed. But in Photoshop, it's a very useful tool. Forget what the image looked like last time you saved it? Choose the Revert command. Don't like it? Press Ctrl+Z (⌘-Z on the Mac) to undo it. That's right, you can undo a reversion — what'll they think of next?

To restore the image to the way it looked when you originally opened it — which may precede the last-saved state — scroll to the top of the History palette and click the topmost item. (This assumes that you haven't deselected the Automatically Create First Snapshot option in the History Options dialog box.)

✦ **Selective reversion.** To revert a selected area to the way it appeared when it was first opened — or some other source state identified in the History palette — choose Edit ➪ Fill or press Shift+Backspace (Shift-Delete on the Mac). Then select History from the Use pop-up menu and press Enter or Return.

Tip

Better yet, just press Ctrl+Alt+Backspace (⌘-Option-Delete on the Mac). This one keystroke combination fills the selection with the source state. With this or with Shift+Backspace, you set the source state for the reversion by clicking in the left column of the History palette, as explained in the next section.

✦ **The Erasers.** Click and drag in the background layer with the Eraser tool to paint in the background color. You're essentially erasing the image back to bare canvas. Or apply the Eraser to a layer to delete pixels and expose underlying layers.

Tip

You can also Alt-drag (Option-drag on the Mac) with the Eraser tool to revert to the targeted state in the History palette. Or select Erase to History in the Options bar and just drag. But you're better off using the History Brush for this purpose. The History Brush offers more capabilities, including most notably brush modes.

Where warranted, these functions are explained in greater detail in the following sections. But first, the next few paragraphs look at the main office for reversion in Photoshop, the History palette.

The History palette

First, you want to actually see the History palette; if it's not on-screen now, choose Window ➪ History. This displays the History palette, which is shown in Figure 7-23. The History palette records each significant operation — everything other than settings and preferences (for example, selecting a new foreground color) — and adds it to a list. The oldest operations appear at the top of the list with the most recent operations at the bottom.

Each item in the list is called a *state*. Each item in the palette represents a step taken by you in the building and/or editing of the image, creating a condition at a moment in time — in other words, a state. Although it is similar in usage, don't confuse this type of state with the states in the Layer Comps palette. You learn all about the Layer Comps palette in Chapter 12.

Photoshop automatically names each item according to the tool, command, or operation used to arrive at the state — the nomenclature is pretty obvious, so it won't leave you wondering what was going on at a given point in time as displayed in the palette. The icon next to the name helps to identify the state further. But the best way to find out what a state is like is to click it. Photoshop instantaneously undoes all operations performed after that state and returns you to the state so that you can inspect it in detail. To redo all the operations you just undid in one fell swoop, press Ctrl+Z (⌘-Z on the Mac) or choose Edit ⇨ Undo State Change.

That one action — clicking a state — is really the core of what you need to know to travel forward and backward through time in Photoshop. If that's all you ever learn, you'll find yourself working with greater speed, freedom, and security than is possible in virtually any other graphics application. But this represents only the first in a long list of the History palette's capabilities. Here's the rest of what you might want to know:

✦ **Changing the number of undos.** By default, Photoshop records the last 20 operations in the History palette. When you perform the 21st operation, the first state is shoved off the list. To change this behavior, choose Edit ⇨ Preferences ⇨ General or press Ctrl+K (⌘-K on the Mac), which opens the Preferences dialog box, and then type your preferred number of undoable operations in the History States option box. If your computer is equipped with 128MB of RAM or less, you might want to lower the value to 5 or 10 to maintain greater efficiency. On the other hand, if you have plenty of RAM — say, 1GB or more — feel free to increase the number of states. The History palette can hold up to 1,000 states, and while that's probably more than you want to use — after all, some states take up a lot of memory when working on a single image, 100 states may be a good idea when, on rare occasions, you need that much flexibility.

✦ **Undone states.** When you revert to a state by clicking it, every subsequent state is dimmed to show that it's been undone. You can redo a dimmed state simply by clicking it. But if you perform a new operation, all dimmed states disappear. You have one (count it, *one*) opportunity to bring them back by pressing Ctrl+Z (⌘-Z); if you perform another new operation, the once-dimmed states are gone for good. For an exception to this behavior, see the very next paragraph.

✦ **Working with nonsequential states.** If you don't like the idea of losing your undone states — every state is sacred, after all — choose the History Options command in the palette menu and select the Allow Non-Linear History option (see Figure 7-24). Undone states no longer drop off the list when you perform a new operation. They remain available on the off chance that you might want to revisit them. It's like having multiple possible time trails.

Snapshot

States | Opened state   Palette menu

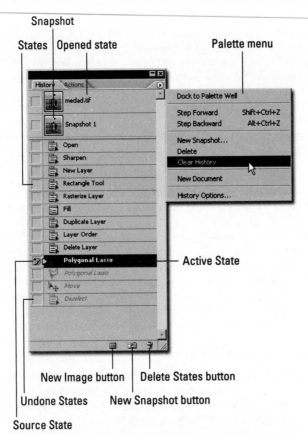

New Image button | Delete States button

Undone States   New Snapshot button

Source State

Figure 7-23: The History palette records each significant event as an independent state. To return to a state, just click it.

Figure 7-24: Choose History Options from the History palette menu and select the Allow Non-Linear History option to permit Photoshop to keep states that you have undone.

Note

Selecting the Allow Non-Linear History option does not permit you to undo a single state without affecting subsequent states. For example, let's say you paint with the Airbrush, smear with the Smudge tool, and then clone with the Clone Stamp tool.

You can revert to the airbrush state and then apply other operations without losing the option of restoring the smudge and clone. But you can't undo the smudge and leave the clone intact. Operations can only occur in the sequence they were applied.

✦ **Stepping through states.** You can press Ctrl+Alt+Z (⌘-Option-Z) to undo the active step or Ctrl+Shift+Z (⌘-Shift-Z) to redo the next step in the list. Backstepping goes up the list of states in the History palette; forward-stepping goes down. So bear in mind that if the Allow Non-Linear History option is selected, backstepping may take you to a state that was previously inactive.

✦ **Flying through states.** Click and drag the right-pointing active state marker (labeled in Figure 7-23) up and down the list to rewind and fast-forward, respectively, through time. If the screen image doesn't appear to change as you fly by certain states, it most likely means those states involve small brushstrokes or changes to selection outlines. Otherwise, the changes are quite apparent.

✦ **Taking a snapshot.** Every once in a while, a state comes along that's so great, you don't want it to fall by the wayside 20 operations from now. To set a state aside, choose New Snapshot or click the little camera icon at the bottom of the History palette (labeled in Figure 7-23). To rename a snapshot after you create it, just double-click its name at the top of the History palette and type a new one. Or you can name a snapshot as you create it by pressing Alt (or Option on the Mac), clicking the little camera icon, and typing a name in the dialog box.

Photoshop lets you store as many snapshots as your computer's RAM permits. Also worth noting, the program automatically creates a snapshot of the image as it appears when it's first opened. If you don't like this opening snapshot, you can change this behavior by deselecting the Automatically Create First Snapshot option in the History Options dialog box — but this may not be wise because having an opening state to go back to can really be a great thing if everything goes horribly awry and you just want to go back to square one. It doesn't really hurt anything to keep this one initial state hanging around, like it now or not.

✦ **Creating a snapshot upon saving the image.** Select the Automatically Create New Snapshot When Saving option in the History Options dialog box to create a new snapshot every time you save your image. This is useful if you find yourself venturing down uncertain roads from one save to the next, and want the ability to backstep not only to the last saved state (which you can do by choosing File ⇨ Revert), but to the one before that and the one before that.

✦ **Saving the state permanently.** The problem with snapshots is that they last only as long as the current session. If you quit Photoshop or the program crashes, you lose the entire history list, snapshots included. To save a state so you can refer to it several days from now, choose the New Document command or click the leftmost icon at the bottom of the History palette. You can also drag and drop a state onto the icon. Either way, Photoshop duplicates the state to a new image window. Then you can save the state to the format of your choice.

✦ **Setting the source.** Click to the left of a state to identify it as the *source state*. The History Brush icon appears where you click. The source state affects the performance of the History Brush, Art History Brush, Fill command, and Eraser if you select Erase to History. The keystroke Ctrl+Alt+Backspace (⌘-Option-Delete on the Mac) fills a selection with the source state.

✦ **Trashing states.** If your machine is equipped with little RAM or you're working on a particularly large image, Photoshop may slow down as the states accumulate. If it gets too slow, you may want to purge the History palette. To delete any state as well as those before it, drag the state to the trash icon at the bottom of the palette. Your image updates accordingly. If the Allow Non-Linear History option is selected, clicking the trash can deletes just the active state.

Tip

To clear all states from the History palette, choose the Clear History command from the palette menu. This doesn't immediately empty RAM, just in case you change your mind and decide you want to undo. Photoshop purges memory for real only after you perform another operation. If you want the memory emptied right away — and you're *positive* that you have no desire whatsoever to undo — press Alt (Option on the Mac) and choose the Clear History command. And if you're really hankering to purge, choose Edit ➪ Purge ➪ Histories, which gets rid of *all* states for *all* open documents.

Painting away the past

The History palette gives you a very simple, yet powerful way to step backward and forward in time. It's very linear (despite that Allow Non-Linear option), and it's very simple and reliable. But what if you want to step a little to the left or right? What if simply going back to before you selected and deleted something isn't enough for you?

As luck would have it, Photoshop offers three more liberating alternatives to the linear world of the History palette: the Eraser tool, the History Brush tool, and the Art History Brush tool. The Eraser tool washes away pixels to reveal underlying pixels or exposed canvas. The History Brush tool takes you back to a kinder, simpler state; the Art History Brush tool does the same but enables you to paint using special artistic effects. Although the functions of these tools overlap slightly, they each have a specific purpose, as becomes clear in the following sections.

Cross-Reference

As you work with any of these tools, remember that you can use the Edit ➪ Fade command to blend the altered pixels with the originals, just as you can when applying a filter. You can adjust both the opacity and the blend mode of the erased or painted pixels. Chapter 17 explores the Fade command in detail.

The Eraser tool

When you work with the Eraser tool, you can select from three Eraser styles, all available from the Mode pop-up menu in the Options bar pictured in Figure 7-25. These are Brush, Pencil, and Block. Block is the ancient 16 × 16-pixel square Eraser that's great for hard-edged touch-ups. The other options work exactly like the tools for which they're named.

In addition to the Mode settings, the Options bar provides access to the Brush option, the Opacity and Flow values, and the Airbrush icon, all of which work as described in Chapter 5. All options are available when using the Brush-style Eraser, none is applicable to the Block style, and Flow and airbrush dim when painting with a Pencil-style Eraser.

Figure 7-25: When the Eraser tool is selected, the Mode pop-up menu offers a choice of Eraser styles rather than the brush modes available to the painting and editing tools.

Although the Eraser tool is pretty straightforward, there's no sense in leaving any stone unturned. So here's everything you ever wanted to know about the art of erasing:

✦ **Erasing on a layer.** When you're working on the Background layer, the Eraser merely paints in the background color. Not very exciting. What distinguishes the Eraser tool from the other brushes, though, is layers. If you click and drag on a layer and deselect the Lock buttons for transparency and image pixels in the Layers palette, the Eraser tool removes paint and exposes portions of the underlying image. The Eraser tool suddenly performs like that pink thing at the end of your pencil.

If you select the transparency Lock button in the Layers palette, Photoshop won't let the Eraser bore holes in the layer or alter areas that are already transparent. Instead, the Eraser paints opaque pixels in the background color. If you select the option for locking image pixels, you can't erase or paint any part of the layer. For more information on locking layers, see Chapter 12.

✦ **Erasing lightly.** Change the Opacity setting in the Options bar to make portions of a layer translucent in inverse proportion to the Opacity value. For example, if you set the Opacity to 90 percent, you remove 90 percent of the opacity from the layer and, therefore, leave 10 percent of the opacity behind. The result is a nearly transparent stroke through the layer.

✦ **Erasing versus using layer masks.** As described in Chapter 12, you can also erase holes in a layer using a layer mask. But unlike the Eraser — which eliminates pixels for good — a layer mask doesn't do any permanent damage. On the other hand, using the Eraser tool doesn't increase the size of your image as much as a layer mask does. Of course, you can argue that *any* operation — even a deletion — increases the size of the image in RAM because the History palette has to track it. But even so, the Eraser remains more memory-efficient than a layer mask. With the speed and power of most modern computers, this is hardly the issue that it once was.

✦ **Erasing with the Pencil tool.** When you work with the Pencil tool — not the Eraser's Pencil mode but the actual Pencil tool — Photoshop presents you with an Auto Erase option in the Options bar. Turn it on to draw in the background color any time you click or drag on a pixel that is already colored in the foreground color. This technique can be useful when you're drawing a line against a plain background. Set the foreground color to the color of the line; set the background color to the color of the background. Then use the Pencil tool to draw and erase the line until you get it just right.

Note   Unlike the Eraser tool, the Pencil tool always draws either in the foreground or background color, even when used on a layer.

✦ **Erasing to history.** Press Alt (Option on the Mac) as you drag with the Eraser to paint with the source state identified by the History Brush icon in the History palette. It's like scraping away the paint laid down by the operations following the source state. Also, instead of pressing Alt, you can select the Erase to History option in the Options bar. In this case, dragging with the Eraser tool reverts and Alt-dragging (Option-dragging on the Mac) paints in the background color or erases the active layer.

Note   In the old days, people used the term "Magic Eraser" to mean the Eraser tool set to the Revert mode. But when Photoshop 5.5 introduced the official Magic Eraser tool, which deletes a range of similarly colored pixels each time you click in the image window (see Chapter 9), this use of the term disappeared. So the old Magic Eraser is the modern History Eraser. Confused yet?

The History Brush tool

Painting with the History Brush tool — which you can select from the keyboard by pressing Y — is like painting with the Eraser tool when Erase to History is selected. Just click and drag with the History Brush to selectively revert to the source state targeted in the History palette. You also can vary the translucency of your strokes using the Opacity setting in the Options bar. But that's where the similarities end. Unlike the part-time history Eraser, the dedicated History Brush tool lets you take advantage of brush modes. By choosing a different brush mode from the Mode pop-up menu in the Options bar, you can mix pixels from the changed and saved images to achieve interesting, and sometimes surprising, effects.

Tip   It's a good idea to get in the habit of using the History Brush tool instead of using the Eraser's Erase to History function. Of course, with Pencil and Block, the Eraser offers more styles. But when weighed against brush modes, these styles aren't much of an advantage. The History Brush is also more intuitive because its icon matches the source state icon in the History palette.

As you play with the History Brush tool, keep in mind that you don't have to limit yourself to painting into the past. Just as the History palette lets you skip back and forth through time, the History Brush lets you paint to any point in time. The following steps provide an example of how you can use the History palette to establish an alternative reality and then follow up with the History Brush tool to merge that reality with the present.

STEPS: Painting Backward

1. **Open an image that you want to take with you on your voyage back in time.** Figure 7-26 is the image used in this example.

2. **Apply some filters.** Here, Watercolor and Plastic Wrap have been applied to a portion of the image, as shown in Figure 7-27. You can try any filters you like, perhaps suggested by your image content.

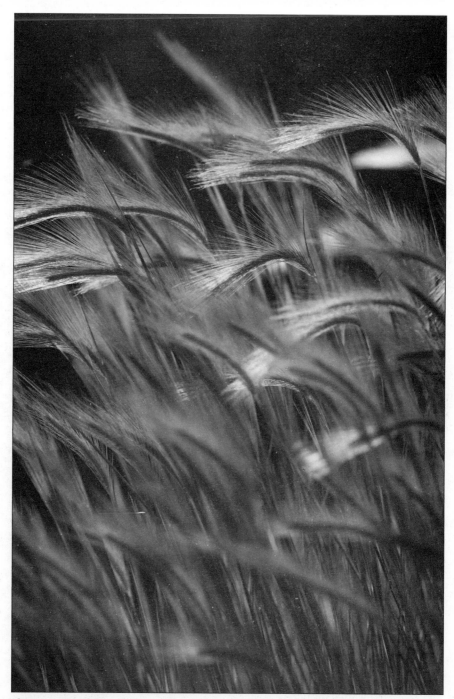

Figure 7-26: These waving stalks will soon be watercolored and wrapped in plastic. How environmentally unfriendly!

3. **Using the History palette's menu, choose Palette Options and select the Allow Non-Linear History option.** Press Enter or Return.

4. **Click back on the first state in the History palette, the Opening state.** This appears as the file name (6196.jpg in this case).

5. **Because you selected the Allow Non-Linear History option, you can now click in front of the state where the filter you'd like to paint with was used.** In the case of this example, you'll go back to Watercolor, which makes this filter the source state.

Figure 7-27: So that there'd be some stalks left to paint with the History Brush, filters are applied to only part of the image. You can see the selection surrounding the filtered portion.

6. **Turn on the History brush, and start painting.** As you see in Figure 7-28, the Watercolor filter, as applied in Step 2, is applied by painting.

Figure 7-28: Apply the filter you chose as your source state with the History Brush.

7. **If you want, you can set another of your previously used filter states as the source state and paint again, or you can stop now and admire your results.**

The Art History Brush tool

The Art History Brush tool lets you create impressionistic effects with the aid of the History palette. To get a sense of how it works, open any image, such as the one shown in Figure 7-29. Press D to get the default foreground and background colors, select the standard Brush tool, and paint wildly all over your image.

Figure 7-29: Any photo will do.

Select the Art History Brush tool, which shares a flyout menu and keyboard short-cut (Y) with the History Brush tool. Bring up the History palette and make sure the first snapshot is identified as the source state (assuming that you haven't made any unauthorized changes to the image since you opened it). Now paint inside your black image. Each stroke reveals a bit of your original photograph in painterly detail, as illustrated in Figure 7-30.

If you want to go even wilder, try applying various filters, maybe even an Artistic fil-ter, so that you'll be painting with a painted or drawn filter — sort of trippy in terms of the irony. Anyway, you might end up with something like the now artistically fil-tered photo shown in Figure 7-31.

Like the History Brush tool, the Art History Brush tool paints from the source state specified in the History palette. But it does so by painting tens or even hundreds of tiny brushstrokes at a time, swirling and gyrating according to settings you select in the Options bar. Many of these settings you've seen several times before. As shown in Figure 7-32, you have the standard Brush controls, a reduced Mode option, and the tried-and-true Opacity value. But starting with the Style option, the Art History Brush tool goes its own way:

Figure 7-30: After painting a random series of black brushstrokes all over the image (top), the Art History Brush is selected and used to paint in a rough translation of the original (bottom). Cool, no?

Figure 7-31: Using Artistic filters (Rough Pastels and Underpainting), the image is now . . . like . . . art. Art like you'd see at a Starving Artists sale or on the wall in a hotel, but it's art, just the same.

✦ **Style.** The Art History Brush tool paints with randomly generated worms and corkscrews of color. You can decide the basic shapes of the creepy crawlies by selecting an option from the Style pop-up menu, displayed in Figure 7-32. Combine these options with different brush sizes to vary the detail conveyed by the impressionistic image. Tight styles and small brushes give you better detail; loose styles and big brushes produce less detail.

✦ **Area.** This value defines the area covered by a single spot of corkscrews. Larger values generally mean more corkscrews are laid down at a time, reducing the value for a sparser look. You can get some very interesting effects by raising the Area value to its maximum, 500 pixels, and clicking inside the image without moving the cursor. Watch those worms writhe.

✦ **Tolerance.** This value limits where the Art History Brush can paint. A value of 0 lets the brush paint anywhere; higher values let the brush paint only in areas where the current state and source state differ dramatically in color.

Figure 7-32: You have several History Brush styles illustrated here Tight Short, Loose Medium, Dab, Tight Curl, and Loose Curl, all revealing the blacked-out image.

Source state limitations

Photoshop displays the Cancel cursor if you try to paint with the History Brush or Art History Brush using a source state that's a different width or height than the current image. One pixel of difference, and the source state is a dead issue. This same restriction applies to Edit ⇨ Fill, Ctrl+Alt+Backspace (⌘-Option-Delete on the Mac), and any other history technique.

You may also see the Cancel cursor if the layer is locked or the source state lacks an equivalent layer. To find out exactly what the problem is, click the image with the Cancel cursor to display an explanatory alert message. If the problem relates to the source state, move the source state icon in the History palette to a point after you modified the width or the height of the image. The crop tool and the Image ⇨ Image Size, Canvas Size, Rotate Canvas, and Crop commands can mix up the History Brush tool. If you applied one of these operations in the very last state, you have to back-step before that operation or find some alternative to the History Brush.

Summary

This chapter provided an overview of Photoshop's image restoration tools, and showed you how to touch-up dust, hair, and other scanning artifacts, removing them from your images. You also learned to use the Healing Brush, Spot Healing Brush, and Patch tools, and to use these and other tools to restore damaged photographs.

In addition, this chapter showed you how to eliminate background elements from an image, and to move backward through time with the History palette. You also learned to paint away mistakes with the Eraser and History Brush tools, and how to get rid of red eye.

✦   ✦   ✦

Selections, Masks, and Filters

P A R T

◆ ◆ ◆ ◆

In This Part

Chapter 8
Selections and Paths

Chapter 9
Masks and
Extractions

Chapter 10
Corrective Filtering

Chapter 11
Distortions and
Effects

◆ ◆ ◆ ◆

Selections and Paths

A selection tells Photoshop what portion of your image or layer that you want to address — that is, where it is you intend to make a deletion, change, or addition. It's like selecting text in a word processing document — dragging through some of the text tells that word processor which text you want bolded, indented, whatever. If you don't tell Photoshop which part of the image you're about to deal with, it assumes your next move should affect the entire active layer.

With that said, it should also be noted that no other program gives you as much control over the size and shape of selections as Photoshop. You can finesse selection outlines with unparalleled flexibility, alternatively adding to and subtracting from selected areas and moving and rotating selections independently of the pixels inside them. You can even mix masks and selection outlines together, as covered in Chapter 9.

That's why this chapter and the one that follows are the most important chapters in this book — and you probably want to pay close attention to the fundamental concepts and approaches documented throughout this chapter. Although each and every technique couldn't be labeled "essential" — lots of artists get by without paying much attention to paths, for example, while other artists swear by them — a working knowledge of selection outlines is key to using Photoshop successfully.

How Selections Work

If you want to edit a portion of an image without fear that you might accidentally mess up another portion of the image, you must first *select* it, indicating the boundaries of the area you want to edit (see Figure 8-1). To select part of an image in an image editing program, you surround it with a selection outline

✦   ✦   ✦   ✦

In This Chapter

Special tricks that work with only the marquee tools

Using the Polygonal and Magnetic Lasso tools

Working with the Magic Wand

Manual and automatic methods for editing selection outlines

An in-depth examination of the Feather command

Moving and cloning selections and selection outlines

Using Photoshop's pen tools

Transforming selection outlines and paths independently of the image

Painting along an open path

Creating, saving, and exporting clipping paths

✦   ✦   ✦   ✦

or a marquee, which tells Photoshop where to apply your editing instructions. The selection outline appears as a moving pattern of dash marks, colloquially termed *marching ants* — by users who had probably been sitting in front of the computer screen for too long, looking at the marquee.

Marching ants indicate selection

Figure 8-1: The dashed line, while static in this image, seems to move within the image window, so there's no doubt as to which part of the picture is selected.

Visible selection outlines can be helpful sometimes, but they can just as readily impede your view of an image. If they do manage to annoy you, press Ctrl+H (⌘-H on the Mac) to get rid of them. Pressing Ctrl+H (Win) or ⌘-H (Mac) toggles the View ➪ Extras command, which hides and displays all on-screen aids so you also lose guides, the grid, note icons, slices, and target paths. If you want to hide just the selection "ants," choose View ➪ Show ➪ Selection Edges to toggle the command off. Choose the command again to toggle the ants back on. You also can control which items disappear when you press Ctrl+H (⌘-H on the Mac) by choosing View ➪ Show ➪ Show Extras Options. In the resulting dialog box, select the items that you want Photoshop to display at all times.

As for creating selections, you have at your disposal a whole bunch of tools and options, all shown in Figure 8-2 and described briefly in the following list. You can access most of the tools by using keyboard shortcuts, which appear in parentheses.

Figure 8-2: Selection tools abound in Photoshop. Add to this the Options bars that appear as each of these tools is selected (shown in later figures) and well, it's almost decadent.

Note   When multiple tools share the same shortcut, you press the key once to activate the tool that's visible in the toolbox and press the key repeatedly to cycle through the other tools. This assumes that you have deselected the Use Shift Key for Tool Switch option in the Preferences dialog box. Otherwise, press Shift and the shortcut key to cycle through the following tools:

✦ **Rectangular Marquee (M).** Long a staple of painting programs, this tool enables you to select rectangular or square portions of an image.

✦ **Elliptical Marquee (M).** The Elliptical Marquee tool works like the Rectangular Marquee except it selects elliptical or circular portions of an image.

✦ **Single-Row and Single-Column.** The Single-Row and Single-Column tools enable you to select a single row or column of pixels that stretches the entire width or height of the image. These tools are used so rarely that Adobe didn't give them keyboard shortcuts.

✦ **Lasso (L).** Click and drag with the Lasso tool to select a free-form portion of an image. Unlike the lasso tools in most painting programs, which shrink selection outlines to disqualify pixels in the background color, Photoshop's Lasso tool selects the exact portion of the image you enclose in your drag.

✦ **Polygonal Lasso (L).** Click different points in your image to set corners in a straight-sided selection outline. This is a great way to select free-form areas if you're not good at controlling the mouse with the Lasso tool — your "sides" in the polygonal selection can be so small that in the end, the edges of the selection are as smooth and curvy as any Lasso-made selection. You can also achieve the same effect by Alt-clicking or Option-clicking with the Lasso tool; you can learn more about this later in this chapter.

✦ **Magnetic Lasso (L).** Click with the Magnetic Lasso along the edge of an image element that you want to select independently from its background. Then move (you don't have to drag) the Magnetic Lasso around the edge of the element. It's a tricky tool to use, but its options bar, which makes it easier, is discussed later in the chapter.

✦ **Magic Wand (W).** First introduced by Photoshop (not by any of its competitors), this tool lets you select a contiguous region of similarly colored pixels by clicking inside the region. For example, you might click inside the boundaries of a face to isolate it from the hair and background elements. Novices tend to gravitate toward the Magic Wand because it seems like such a miracle tool, but you may find that it can be the least predictable tool of the bunch.

✦ **Pen (P).** The Pen tool is difficult to master, but it's the most accurate and versatile of the selection tools. You use the Pen tool to create a *path*, which is an object-oriented breed of selection outline. You click and drag to create individual points in the path. You can edit the path after the fact by moving, adding, and deleting points. You can even transfer a path by dragging and dropping between Photoshop, Illustrator, and FreeHand. For a discussion of the Pen tool, read the section "How to Draw and Edit Paths."

✦ **Freeform Pen and Magnetic Pen (P).** If you hate setting points but you need to create a clipping path, the Freeform Pen is the tool for you. You just click and drag with the tool as if you were selecting with the Lasso tool and let Photoshop define the points automatically. Obviously, you can't expect the same level of accuracy that you get from the standard Pen tool, but it's very simple to use.

Selecting the Magnetic option in the Options bar transforms the Freeform Pen into the Magnetic Pen, which once upon a time was a tool in its own right. The Magnetic Pen is basically an object-oriented version of the Magnetic Lasso tool. Click to set the first point and then move your mouse and watch Photoshop create the other points automatically. It's not a great tool, but it can prove handy when selecting image elements that stand out very clearly from their backgrounds.

✦ **Shape tools (U).** To draw paths in simple geometric shapes — rectangles, polygons, and so on — give the shape tools a shot. First, put the tools in the path mode by clicking the Paths icon at the left end of the Options bar. Then simply click and drag to create the path. To find out more about working with these tools, visit Chapter 14.

✦ **Path and shape selection tools.** Use the Path Selection tool (the black arrow) and the Direct Selection tool (the white arrow) to select and edit paths and vector shapes. You can read more about these tools later in the section "How to Draw and Edit Paths."

Cross-Reference

Photoshop's Horizontal Type Mask tool and Vertical Type Mask tool are also technically selection tools because Photoshop converts each character of type to a selection outline. But type involves other issues that would merely confuse the contents of this chapter, so type and its uses as a selection tool are found in Chapter 15. Also, if your purpose for selecting an area is to separate it from its background, you should investigate the Extract command and the Magic Eraser and Background Eraser (covered in Chapter 9).

If this were all you needed to know to use the selection tools in Photoshop, the application would be on par with the average paint program. Part of what makes Photoshop exceptional, however, is that it provides literally hundreds of options, commands, and tricks to increase the functionality of every selection tool. Furthermore, all of Photoshop's selection tools work together in perfect harmony. You can exploit the specialized capabilities of multiple selection tools to create a single selection boundary, or maybe just tweak the way one selection tool works to achieve the desired effect. After you understand which tool best serves which purpose, you can isolate any element in an image, no matter how complex or how delicate its outline.

Geometric Selection Outlines

Tools for creating simple geometric selection outlines occupy the first slot in the Photoshop toolbox. By default, the Rectangular Marquee tool appears on the Toolbox button, and with good reason — it's probably the most often-used selection tool. You select its alternates — the Elliptical, Single-Row, and Single-Column Marquee tools — from the flyout menu that appears when you click and drag from the Marquee tool icon.

Tip

Press M to select the tool that's currently visible in the toolbox. Press M again to toggle between the Rectangular and Elliptical Marquee tools. Alternatively, Alt-click (Win) or Option-click (Mac) the tool icon to toggle among all four marquee tools.

The marquee tools are more versatile than they may appear at first glance. You can adjust the performance of each tool as follows:

✦ **Constraining to a square or circle.** Press and hold Shift after beginning your drag to draw a perfect square with the Rectangular Marquee tool or a perfect circle with the Elliptical Marquee tool. (Pressing Shift before dragging also works if no other selection is active; otherwise, this adds to a selection, as explained later in this chapter.)

✦ **Drawing a circular marquee.** Remember to press Shift after you begin to drag, and assuming you've selected the Elliptical Marquee tool to make the selection, the ellipse (which most people tend to think of as an oval) becomes a circle. Pretty simple, huh?

✦ **Drawing out from the center.** Press and hold Alt (Option on the Mac) after you begin dragging to draw the marquee from the center outward instead of from corner to corner. (Again, pressing Alt or Option before dragging works if no selection outline is active; otherwise, this subtracts from the selection.) This technique is especially useful when you draw an elliptical marquee. Locating the center of the area you want to select is frequently easier than locating one of its corners — particularly because ellipses don't have corners.

✦ **Moving the marquee on the fly.** While drawing a marquee, press and hold the space bar to move the marquee rather than resize it. When you get the marquee in place, release the space bar and keep dragging to modify the size. The space bar is most helpful when drawing elliptical selections or when drawing a marquee out from the center — this eliminates the guesswork, so you can position your marquees exactly on target.

✦ **Selecting a single-pixel line.** Use the Single-Row or Single-Column tools to select a single row or column (respectively) of pixels stretching across the width or length of your image. I use these tools to fix small mishaps, such as a missing line of pixels in a screen shot or to delete random pixels around the perimeter of an image. You can also use it to create perpendicular lines in a fixed space — giving you more control over the length of the line than you have if you use the Line tool (one of the Shape tool's variants).

✦ **Constraining the aspect ratio.** If you want to create an image that conforms to a certain aspect ratio, you can constrain either a rectangular or an elliptical marquee so that the ratio between height and width remains fixed, no matter how large or small a marquee you create. To accomplish this, select Fixed Aspect Ratio from the Style pop-up menu in the Options bar, as shown in Figure 8-3. Type the desired ratio values in the Width and Height option boxes.

Figure 8-3: Select Fixed Aspect Ratio from the Style pop-up menu in the Options bar to constrain the width and height of a rectangular selection outline.

Tip

If you work with a digital camera, you may find this feature especially helpful. Digital cameras typically produce images that fit the 4 x 3 aspect ratio used by computer screens and televisions. If you want to crop an image to a standard photo size — say, 6 x 4 inches — type 6 and 4, respectively, in the Width and Height option boxes. Then drag the marquee around to select the portion of the picture you want to retain, as shown in the figure, and choose Image ⇨ Crop.

Remember that you're just establishing the image aspect ratio here, not setting the output width and height. So you could just as easily type 2 and 3 in the Width and Height option boxes. The size of the final, cropped image depends on how large you draw the marquee and the Resolution value you set in the Image Size dialog box.

✦ **Sizing the marquee numerically.** If you're editing a screen shot or some other form of regular or schematic image, you may find it helpful to specify the size of the marquee numerically. To do so, select Fixed Size from the Style pop-up menu and type size values in the Width and Height option boxes. To match the selection to a 640 x 480-pixel screen, for example, change the Width and Height values to 640 and 480, respectively. Then click in the image to create the marquee.

Note

You can set the marquee size in any unit of measurement you like. Just type the number followed by one of these units: px (pixels), in, mm, cm, pt (points), pica, or %.

✦ **Drawing feathered selections.** A Feather option box is available in the Options bar when you use any of the marquee tools. To *feather* a selection is to blur its edges beyond the automatic anti-aliasing afforded by most tools. For more information on feathering, refer to the coverage of softening selections found later in this chapter.

✦ **Creating jagged ellipses.** By default, elliptical selection outlines are anti-aliased. If you don't want anti-aliasing — you might prefer harsh edges when editing screen shots or designing screen interfaces — deselect the Anti-aliased option. (This option is dimmed when you use the Rectangular Marquee because anti-aliasing is always off for this tool.)

Cross-Reference

Photoshop novices often misunderstand the Rectangular and Elliptical Marquee tools and expect them to create filled and stroked shapes. For these tasks, Photoshop provides the shape tools, which can create filled vector and raster shapes. You can apply strokes and other effects to these shapes if you like. Chapter 14 takes you on a guided tour of the shape tools.

Free-form Outlines

In comparison to the Rectangular and Elliptical Marquee tools, the Lasso tool provides a rather limited range of options. Generally speaking, you click and drag in a free-form path around the image you want to select. The few special considerations are as follows:

✦ **Feathering and anti-aliasing.** Just as you can feather rectangular and elliptical marquees, you can feather selections drawn with the Lasso tool by first selecting the Feather option in the Options bar. To soften the edges of a lasso outline, select the Anti-aliased option.

Note   Although you can adjust the feathering of any selection after you draw it by choosing Select ➪ Feather, you must specify anti-aliasing before you draw a selection. Unless you have a specific reason for doing otherwise, leave the Anti-aliased option deselected (as it is by default).

✦ **Drawing polygons.** When you press and hold Alt (Option on the Mac), the Lasso tool functions like (and the icon even looks like) the Polygonal Lasso tool. (*Polygon*, incidentally, means a shape with multiple straight sides.) With the Alt or Option key pressed, click to specify corners in a free-form polygon, as shown in Figure 8-4. If you want to add curves to the selection outline, drag with the tool while still pressing Alt or Option, as the center inset in Figure 8-4 shows. Photoshop closes the selection outline the moment you release both the mouse button and the Alt or Option key.

Tip   You can extend a polygon selection outline to the absolute top, right, or bottom edges of an image. You can also Alt-click (Win) or Option-click (Mac) with the Lasso tool beyond the confines of the image window — clicking and creating a selection that exceeds the image window's dimensions. To prove that the selection shape you drew was retained, if you move the selection so that the portions that were outside of the window are now within it, you can see the corners and sides you drew. Figure 8-4's annotations show where the selection went beyond the edges of the image window.

✦ **The Polygonal Lasso tool.** If you don't want to bother with pressing Alt (Win) or Option (Mac), select the Polygonal Lasso. When the Lasso is active, you can switch to the Polygonal Lasso by pressing L or Shift+L, depending on your Use Shift Key for Tool Switch setting in the Preferences dialog box. Or drag from the Lasso tool icon to display the Lasso flyout menu and select the Polygonal Lasso that way. Then click inside the image to set corners in the selection. Click the first point in the selection or double-click with the tool to complete the selection outline. To create free-form curves with the Polygonal Lasso tool, press Alt (or Option on the Mac) and drag.

Tip   If you make a mistake while creating a selection outline with the Polygonal Lasso, press Backspace (Delete on the Mac) to eliminate the last segment you drew. Keep pressing Backspace or Delete to eliminate more segments in the selection outline. This technique works until you close the selection outline and it turns into marching ants.

Adobe added the Polygonal Lasso for those times when Alt-clicking (Option-clicking on the Mac) isn't convenient. If no portion of the image is selected, it's no trick to Alt-click (Win) or Option-click (Mac) with the standard Lasso to draw a straight-sided selection. But if some area in the image is selected, pressing Alt or Option tells Photoshop that you want to subtract from the selection outline. For this reason, it's often easier to use the Polygonal Lasso — although you still can make it work by pressing Alt or Option after you click with the Lasso tool, as explained later in this chapter.

Figure 8-4: Very few free-form selections are all curves — and this butterfly is a good example. The Alt (Option) key has been added when straight edges were needed (as in the top left inset), and the selection even strayed off the image window at one point (the lower left inset), but Photoshop kept track of the mouse and was right there when I strayed back.

Magnetic Selections

In the old days of black-and-white painting programs — most notably MacPaint on the Mac — black pixels were considered foreground elements and white pixels were the background. To select a black element, you had only to vaguely drag around it with the lasso tool and the program would automatically omit the white pixels and "shrink" the selection around the black ones.

The Magnetic Lasso tool is Adobe's attempt to transfer shrinking into the world of color. Under ideal conditions a selection drawn with the Magnetic Lasso automatically shrinks around the foreground element and omits the background. Naturally, it rarely works this miraculously, but it does produce halfway decent selection outlines with very little effort — provided that you know what you're doing.

Using the Magnetic Lasso tool

Typically, when people have a problem using the magnetic lasso tool, it's because they're trying to make the process too complex. Work less, and the tool works better. Here are the basic steps for using this unusual tool:

STEPS: Making Sense of the Magnetic Lasso Tool

1. **Select an image with very definite contrast between the foreground image and its background.** The content in Figure 8-5 is a good example of when you'd be compelled to use the Magnetic Lasso, because the central object stands out against the background and the tool will have no trouble discerning its edges. Here's something that Photoshop can really sink its teeth into.

2. **Select the Magnetic Lasso.** If any tool but a Lasso tool is active, press L to grab the Lasso that's showing in the toolbox. Then press L as necessary to cycle to the Magnetic Lasso.

3. **Click anywhere along the edge of the foreground element.** Note the starting point, labeled in Figure 8-5 — of course, your image and its content may suggest another strategy.

4. **Move the cursor around the edge of the foreground element.** Just move the mouse, don't drag — that is, there's no need to press the mouse button. As your cursor passes over the image, Photoshop lays down a line along the edge of the element, as Figure 8-5 shows. If you don't like the placement of the line, back up the cursor and try moving along the edge again. The Magnetic Lasso also lays down anchor points at significant locations around the image. If you don't like where the program puts a point, press Backspace (or Delete on the Mac). Each time you press Backspace or Delete, Photoshop deletes the most recent point along the line. To set your own anchor points, just click.

5. **When you make it all the way around to the beginning of the shape, click the first point in the outline to close the selection.** Or just double-click to close with a straight edge.

Tip

To create a straight segment while working with the Magnetic Lasso tool, press Alt (Option on the Mac), click to set the start of the segment, and click again at the endpoint. The next time you click without holding down Alt or Option, the tool reverts to its normal magnetic self.

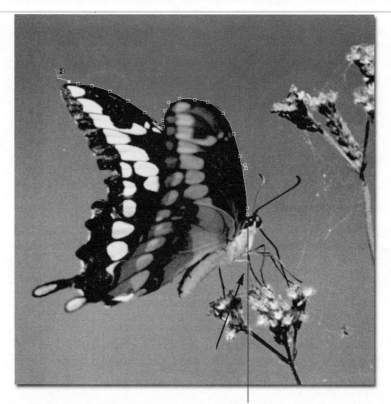

Starting point

Figure 8-5: Drag as long as you see the Magnetic Lasso doing its job — that is, following the edge of your desired content and creating a nice, tight selection up against that edge. When it wavers, click to keep the tool on track. You can also press Backspace to back up when the tool goes astray.

Modifying the Magnetic Lasso options

You modify the performance of the Magnetic Lasso tool by adjusting the values in the Options bar. The Feather and Anti-aliased options define the softness of the final selection outline, just as they do for the standard Lasso tool. The others control how the Magnetic Lasso positions lines and lays down points:

✦ **Width.** This option determines how close to an edge you have to move the cursor for Photoshop to accurately see the image element. Large values are great for smooth elements that stand out clearly from their backgrounds. If you raise the Width to 20, for example, you can move the cursor 20 pixels away from the edges of the content you're trying to select and Photoshop still shrinks the selection tight around the content's edge. That gives even the shakiest mouse-users a pretty workable margin for error and makes your life easier. When you're selecting small areas or where there is little difference between what you want to select and the surrounding pixels, you need a low value to keep Photoshop from veering off to the wrong edge.

Tip   The great advantage to the Width value is that you can change it on the fly by pressing a bracket key. Press [(left bracket) to lower the Width value; press] (right bracket) to raise the value. Shift+[lowers the value to its minimum, 1, and Shift+] raises it to the maximum, 256.

If you have a pressure-sensitive tablet and select the Pen Pressure option, you can control the edge-tracking accuracy by adjusting how hard you press on the pen. Bear down to be careful; let up to be more casual about the selection's accuracy. Because this is the way you probably work naturally, you'll be able to adjust the width as needed without even thinking much about it.

✦ **Edge Contrast.** This is the simplest of the options. It tells Photoshop how much contrast there has to be between the element you're trying to select and its background to even be recognized. If the foreground element stands out clearly, you may want to raise the Edge Contrast value to avoid selecting random flack around the edges. If the contrast between foreground and background is subtle, lower the value.

✦ **Frequency.** This option tells the Magnetic Lasso when to lay down points. As you drag with the tool, the line around the image changes to keep up with your movements. When some point in the line stays still for a few moments, Photoshop decides it must be on target and anchors it down with a point. If you want Photoshop to anchor points more frequently, raise the value. For less frequent anchoring, lower the option. High values tend to be better for rough edges; lower values are better for smooth edges.

Most of the time, you can rely on the bracket keys to adjust the Width and leave the Frequency and Edge Contrast values set to their defaults. When dealing with a low-contrast image, lower the Edge Contrast value to 5 percent or so. And when selecting unusually rough edges, raise the Frequency to 70 or more. But careful movements with the Magnetic Lasso tool go further than adjusting any of these settings.

The World of the Wand

Using the Magic Wand tool seems like — what's the word — magic, right? You just click with the tool and it selects all colors that fall within a selected range. The problem, though, and where the magic can kind of wear off is in getting the wand to recognize the same range of colors that you see on-screen. For example, if you're editing a photo of a red flower amongst pink flowers, how do you tell the Magic Wand to select the red one and leave the pink ones alone?

For some users, adjusting the Wand seems too complicated and it can be kind of frustrating to use. Other times, it seems like a gift from on high, in that it selects exactly what you want, without any falderal. Its success as a selection tool depends on several factors, so don't write it off as too difficult, yet don't assume it's cake, either. Just read on and then play with the tool and try it in different selection scenarios.

When the Magic Wand is active, you'll see the following four controls in the Options bar:

✦ **Tolerance.** This option determines the range of colors the tool selects when you click with it in the image window.

✦ **Anti-aliased.** This option softens the selection, just as it does for the Lasso tools.

✦ **Contiguous.** When selected, this option tells Photoshop to select a contiguous region of pixels emanating from the pixel on which you click — this means that if you click a pixel in that hypothetical red flower, only the red pixels in that flower, touching the pixel you clicked (or touching one of the pixels that were touching the pixel you clicked) can be selected. Red pixels in a flower on the other side of the image cannot. To select all similarly colored pixels throughout the picture, deselect the option.

✦ **Use All Layers.** Select this option to take all visible layers into account when defining a selection.

You now know all you need to know about the Anti-aliased and Contiguous options; the next two sections explain Tolerance and Use All Layers.

Adjusting the tolerance

You may have heard the standard explanation for adjusting the Tolerance value: You can type any number from 0 to 255 in the Tolerance option box. Type a low number to select a small range of colors; increase the value to select a wider range of colors.

When you click a pixel with the Magic Wand tool, Photoshop first reads the brightness value that each color channel assigned to that pixel. If you're working with a grayscale image, Photoshop reads a single brightness value from the one channel only; if you're working with an RGB image, it reads three brightness values, one each from the red, green, and blue channels; and so on. Because each color channel permits 8 bits of data, brightness values range from 0 to 255.

Next, Photoshop applies the Tolerance value, or simply *tolerance*, to the pixel. The Tolerance describes a range that extends in both directions — lighter and darker — from each brightness value.

Suppose you're editing a standard RGB image. The Tolerance is set to 32 (as it is by default). You click with the Magic Wand on a turquoise pixel, whose brightness values are 40 red, 210 green, and 170 blue. Photoshop subtracts and adds 32 from each brightness value to calculate the Magic Wand range that, in this case, is 8 to 72 red, 178 to 242 green, and 138 to 202 blue. Photoshop selects any pixel that both falls in this range and, if the Contiguous option is turned on, can be traced back to the original pixel through an uninterrupted line of other pixels that also fall within the range.

From this information, you can draw the following basic conclusions about the Magic Wand tool:

✦ **Clicking on midtones maintains a higher range.** Because the Tolerance range extends in two directions, you cut off the range when you click a light or dark pixel, as demonstrated in Figure 8-6. In all cases, the Contiguous option is selected, and in the top two boxes, a pixel with a brightness level of 150 was clicked. In the upper-right example, the Tolerance value is set to 75, and the range shrinks. But when a pixel with a brightness value of 10 is clicked, as in the bottom gradations (Tolerance set to 32 on the left, 75 on the right), the range shrinks to 0 to 70. Clicking on a medium-brightness pixel, therefore, permits the most generous range.

✦ **Selecting brightness ranges.** Many people have the impression that the Magic Wand selects color ranges. The Magic Wand, in fact, selects brightness ranges within color channels. So if you want to select a flesh-colored region — regardless of shade — set against an orange or a red background that is roughly equivalent in terms of brightness values, you probably should use a different tool.

✦ **Selecting from a single channel.** If the Magic Wand repeatedly fails to select a region of color that appears unique from its background, try isolating that region inside a single-color channel. You'll probably have the most luck isolating a color on the channel that least resembles it. For example, to select the sky shown in Figure 8-7, each color channel was examined closely to see which provided the greatest contrast between the elements in the photo. Experiment with this technique and it will prove even more useful over time.

Note

Here's one more important twist in the Tolerance story: The Magic Wand is affected by the Sample Size option that you select for the Eyedropper tool. If you select Point Sample, the Wand bases its selection solely on the single pixel that you click. But if you select 3 by 3 Average or 5 by 5 Average, the Wand takes into account 9 or 25 pixels, respectively. As you can imagine, this obscure option can have a noticeable effect on the extent of the selection that you get from the Wand. Try clicking the same spot in your image using each of these Sample Size settings, using the same Tolerance value throughout, to see what I mean.

Figure 8-6: Note the results of clicking a pixel with a brightness value of 140 (top row) and a brightness value of 10 (bottom row) with the Tolerance set to the default of 32 and then at 75.

Figure 8-7: Make your selection within the channel that provides the most difference in brightness — between your desired content and the rest of the image.

Making the Wand see beyond a single layer

The Use All Layers option enables you to create a selection based on pixels from different layers (see Chapter 12 for more about layers). With the image in use thus far (the butterfly) in mind, imagine that the butterfly is on its own layer, the flowers on another layer, and the sky behind them on yet a third layer. Without using the

Sample All Layers option for the Magic Wand, one could only select the blue in the butterfly's wings, and not the blue in the sky or the blue in the flowers — at least not at the same time.

Mind you, while the Sample All Layers option enables the Wand to consider pixels on different layers when creating a selection, it does not permit the Wand to actually select content on two separate layers. Strange as this may sound, no selection tool is capable of that. Every one of the techniques explained in this chapter is applicable to only a single layer at a time. The Sample All Layers option merely allows the Wand to draw selection outlines that appear to encompass colors on many layers.

Well, if it's not actually sampling and selecting all the content on all the layers, what good is this? Well, imagine that you want to change all the blue in the image to purple — using any number of tools to tweak the blue and change its color. With the help of Sample All Layers, you can draw a selection outline that encompasses all the pixels that match the sampled pixel, and then you can hop between layers (with that same selection in place) and make the color changes to each individual layer. Of course, it would be easier if you could literally select content on multiple layers, but the ability to map out a selection that will work on all the individual layers will just have to do.

Ways to Change Selection Outlines

If you don't draw a selection outline correctly the first time, you have two options. You can draw it again from scratch, which can be really tedious and time consuming, or you can change your botched selection outline, correcting the selection. Now, which one sounds more appealing? Assuming you chose the latter solution, it's time to talk about Photoshop's tools for changing the nature of selections — removing some or all of them, adding new stuff to them, resizing them, and changing their edges.

Quick changes

First, here are some fast and easy changes you can make. The following list explains how a few commands work. You'll find them all in the Select menu along with handy keyboard shortcuts you can use.

✦ **Deselect (Ctrl+D or ⌘-D).** You can deselect the selected portion of an image in three ways. You can select a different portion of the image; click anywhere in the image window with the Rectangular Marquee tool, the Elliptical Marquee tool, or the Lasso tool; or choose Select ➪ Deselect. Remember, though, when no part of a layer is selected, the entire layer is susceptible to your changes. If you apply a filter, choose a color-correction command, or use a paint tool, you affect every pixel of the layer.

✦ **Reselect (Ctrl+Shift+D or ⌘-Shift-D).** If you accidentally deselect an image, you can retrieve the most recent selection outline by choosing Select ➪ Reselect. It's a great function that operates entirely independent of the Undo command and History palette, and it works even after performing a long string of selection-unrelated operations. (You can restore older selections from the History palette, but that usually means undoing operations along the way.)

✦ **Inverse (Ctrl+Shift+I or ⌘-Shift-I).** Choose Select ➪ Inverse to reverse the selection. Photoshop deselects the portion of the image that was previously selected and selects the portion of the image that was not selected. This way, you can begin a selection by outlining the portion of the image you want to protect, rather than the portion you want to affect, and then swap the two portions.

Tip   You can also access the Inverse and Deselect commands from a shortcut menu in the image window. Right-click (Control-click on the Mac) to make the menu appear underneath your cursor.

Manually adding and subtracting

Imagine a portrait. How would you go about selecting both eyes and not selecting or otherwise affecting any other portion of the face? Well, if you're new to the selection tools, you might think that you'd have to select one eye and then do whatever you want to it, and then go select the other eye and repeat whatever was done to the first eye. This, however, is not tapping one of Photoshop's best set of options — found in the first group of four buttons on the Options bar for the Marquee, Lasso, Magic Wand, and even the Shape, Pen, and Path tools (though the buttons are not the first group on the Options bar for the last three tools listed).

With these buttons, Photoshop lets you add a bit more to a selection, whittle away at a selection, and create new selections out of overlapping areas within two or more selections. This makes it possible, too, to combine selection tools — starting out, for example, with the Marquee, and then tacking on a selection made with the Lasso or the Magic Wand. You can use the buttons (shown in Figure 8-8), or you can use these handy-dandy keyboard shortcuts:

✦ **Adding to a selection outline.** To increase the area enclosed in an existing selection outline, Shift-drag with one of the marquee or lasso tools. You also can Shift-click with the Magic Wand tool or Shift-click with one of the marquee tools when the Fixed Size option is active (as described in the section "Geometric selection outlines" earlier in this chapter).

✦ **Subtracting from a selection outline.** To take a bite from an existing selection outline, press Alt (Win) or Option (Mac) while using one of the selection tools.

✦ **Intersecting one selection outline with another.** Another way to subtract from an existing selection outline is to Shift+Alt-drag (Shift-Option-drag on the Mac) around the selection with the Rectangular Marquee, Elliptical Marquee, or Lasso tool. You also can Shift+Alt-click (Shift-Option-click on the Mac) with the Magic Wand tool. Shift+Alt-dragging instructs Photoshop to retain only the portion of an existing selection that also falls inside the new selection outline.

If the keypress techniques seem cumbersome, use the selection state buttons (labeled in Figure 8-8) at the left end of the Options bar to set your selection tool to the Add, Subtract, or Intersect mode. After clicking a button, simply drag to alter the selection outline. To toggle the tool back to the normal operating mode, click the first button in the bunch. Note that the keyboard techniques described in the preceding list work no matter what button you select in the Options bar. For example, if you click the Intersect button, Alt-dragging (Option-dragging on the Mac) still subtracts from the selection outline. Remember, too, that you can switch selection tools and then use the Add to, Subtract from, or Intersect with buttons, creating a selection that's created with a combination of tools.

Subtract from selection

New selection

Add to selection

Intersect with selection

Figure 8-8: You can use the selection state buttons as well as the Shift and Alt keys (Shift and Option keys on the Mac) when modifying a selection outline.

Tip

When you're working with the Magic Wand, you can right-click (Control-click on the Mac) to display a shortcut menu that contains the Add, Subtract, and Intersect mode options. Click the mode you want to use.

Tip

Photoshop displays special cursors to help you keep track of a tool's selection state. Suppose that you select part of an image and the Lasso tool is active. When you press Shift or click the Add button in the Options bar, Photoshop appends a little plus sign to the Lasso cursor to show you're about to add. A minus sign indicates that you're set to subtract from the selection outline; a multiply sign appears when you work in Intersect mode. If you're pressing keys to switch tool modes, Photoshop temporarily selects the corresponding selection state button in the Options bar as well.

Power-User tricks

The roles of the Shift and Alt keys (or Shift and Option keys on the Mac) in adding, subtracting, and intersecting selection outlines can interfere with your ability to take advantage of other functions of the selection tools. For example, when no portion of an image is selected, you can Shift-drag with the Rectangular Marquee tool to draw a square. But after a selection is active, Shift-dragging adds a rectangle — not a square — to the selection outline.

This is one reason for the selection state buttons in the Options bar. After you click a button, the tool adds, subtracts, or intersects, with no additional keypresses on your part, depending on which button you click. But if you want to hide the Options bar or you just prefer pressing keys to clicking buttons, you can control the selection tools from the keyboard without giving up any selection flexibility.

The trick is to learn when to press Shift and Alt (or Option on the Mac). Sometimes you have to press the key before you begin your drag; other times you must press the key after you begin the drag but before you release. For example, to add a square to a selection outline with the Rectangular Marquee tool, Shift-drag, release Shift while keeping the mouse button pressed, and press Shift again to snap the rectangle to a square. The same goes for adding a circle with the Elliptical Marquee tool.

The following list introduces you to a few other techniques. They may seem a little elaborate or complicated but with a little practice, they will become second nature — really, they will. Before you try any of them, be sure to select Normal from the Style pop-up menu in the Options bar.

To keep things visually simple in the text, the following list refers only to Windows users' keystrokes and commands. On a Mac, press Option instead of Alt.

- ✦ **Subtract a square or a circle from a selection.** Alt-drag, release Alt, press Shift, drag until you get it right, release the mouse button, and then release Shift.

- ✦ **Add a rectangle or an ellipse by drawing from the center outward.** Shift-drag, release Shift, press Alt, and hold Alt until after you release the mouse button. You can even press the space bar during the drag to move the marquee around, if you like.

- ✦ **Subtract a marquee drawn from the center outward.** Alt-drag, release Alt, press Alt again, and hold the key down until after you release the mouse button.

- ✦ **Add a straight-sided area to an existing selection.** Shift-drag with the tool for a short distance. With the mouse button still down, release Shift and press Alt. Then click around as you normally would, while keeping the Alt key down.

- ✦ **Subtract a straight-sided area.** Alt-drag with the Lasso, release Alt, press Alt again, and click around with the tool.

The last two might be easier if you switch to the Polygonal Lasso instead of using the regular Lasso. In fact, one of the reasons Adobe provided the Polygonal Lasso tool was to accommodate people who don't want to have to press Alt or Option many times during the creation of a selection—so by all means, use the tool and make your life easier.

Adding and subtracting by command

Photoshop provides several commands under the Select menu that automatically increase or decrease the number of selected pixels in an image according to numeric specifications. The commands in the Select ➪ Modify submenu work as follows:

✦ **Border.** This command selects an area of a specified thickness around the perimeter of the current selection outline and deselects the rest of the selection. For example, to select a 20-pixel-thick border around the current selection, choose Select ➪ Modify ➪ Border, type 20 in the Width option box, and press Enter or Return. But what's the point? After all, if you want to create an outline around a selection, you can accomplish this in fewer steps by choosing Edit ➪ Stroke, right? The Border command, however, broadens your range of options. You can apply a special effect to the border, move the border to a new location, or even create a double-outline effect by first applying Select ➪ Modify ➪ Border and then applying Edit ➪ Stroke.

✦ **Smooth.** This command rounds off the sharp corners and weird anomalies in the outline of a selection. When you choose Select ➪ Modify ➪ Smooth, the program asks you to type a Sample Radius value. Photoshop smoothes out corners by drawing little circles around them; the Sample Radius value determines the radius of these circles. Larger values result in smoother corners.

Tip   The Smooth command is especially useful in combination with the Magic Wand. After you draw one of those weird, scraggly selection outlines with the Wand tool, use Select ➪ Modify ➪ Smooth to smooth out the rough edges. It's also helpful when you have used the Polygonal Lasso to make a more controlled selection along curvy edges — use the Smooth command to eliminate any of the angles you may inadvertently create as you click and move the mouse to make the selection.

✦ **Expand and Contract.** Both of these commands do exactly what they say, either expanding or contracting the selected area by a specified amount. For example, if you want an elliptical selection to grow by 8 pixels, choose Select ➪ Modify ➪ Expand, type 8, and that's it.

Tip   Both Expand and Contract have a flattening effect on a selection. To round things off, apply the Smooth command with a Sample Radius value equal to the number you just typed in the Expand Selection or Contract Selection dialog box. This isn't the technique for making very precise selections, but that's the downside (and one that's usually worth it, for all the effort it saves you) of using automated commands.

In addition to the Expand command, Photoshop provides two other commands — Grow and Similar — that increase the area covered by a selection outline. Both commands resemble the Magic Wand tool because they measure the range of eligible pixels by way of a Tolerance value. In fact, the commands rely on the same Tolerance value that you set for the Magic Wand (in the Options bar). So if you want to adjust the impact of either command, you must first select the Magic Wand and then apply the commands:

✦ **Grow.** Choose Select ➪ Grow to select all pixels that both neighbor an existing selection and resemble the colors included in the selection, in accordance with the Tolerance value. In other words, Select ➪ Grow is the command equivalent of the Magic Wand tool. If you feel constrained because you can click only one pixel at a time with the Magic Wand tool, you may prefer to select a small group of representative pixels with a marquee tool and then choose Select ➪ Grow to initiate the Wand's magic.

✦ **Similar.** Another member of the Select menu, Similar works like Grow, except the pixels needn't be adjacent. When you choose Select ⟹ Similar, Photoshop selects any pixel that falls within the Tolerance range, regardless of the location of the pixel in the foreground image.

Note

Although both Grow and Similar respect the Magic Wand's Tolerance value, they pay no attention to the other Wand options — Contiguous, Use All Layers, and Anti-aliased. Grow always selects only contiguous regions; Similar selects noncontiguous areas. Neither can see beyond the active layer nor produce anti-aliased selection outlines.

One of the best applications for the Similar command is to isolate a complicated image set against a consistent background whose colors are significantly lighter or darker than the image. Figure 8-9, which features just such a scenario, contains some sample selections made to "train" Photoshop as to what the Similar command should look for when choosing pixels for selection. The following steps explain how to separate this image into its major parts, using the Similar command in combination with a few other techniques you may find helpful in your own work.

Figure 8-9: Before choosing Select ⟹ Similar, select a few sample portions of the background for Photoshop to use as a basis for its selection range.

STEPS: Isolating a Complex Image Set Against a Plain Background

1. **Use the Rectangular Marquee tool to select some representative portions of the background.** Figure 8-9 shows some Rectangular Marquee selections that encompass portions of the background that are fairly representative of that portion of the image. Remember, you make multiple selections by Shift-dragging with the tool or switching to the Add to Selection mode on the Marquee tool's Options bar.

2. **Click the Magic Wand tool icon and type a Tolerance value in the Options bar.** For the image shown in Figure 8-9, a Tolerance value of 20, a relatively low value, was used so that only very minor inconsistencies in the background would prevent the Wand from working. If your background is less homogenous, you may want to type a higher value so that more of the background can be selected automatically. Make certain you select the Anti-aliased option.

3. **Choose Select ⇨ Similar.** Photoshop should select the entire background — if it doesn't, tweak the Tolerance setting and try again.

4. **Choose Select ⇨ Inverse, or press Ctrl+Shift+I (⌘-Shift-I on the Mac).** Photoshop selects the foreground image and deselects the background, as shown in Figure 8-10.

5. **Modify the selection as desired.** If too few pixels are selected, try choosing the Similar command again. You might also have luck with Select ⇨ Grow. Or you can modify the selection using Shift and Alt (Option on the Mac).

6. **You've isolated your complex image.** Way to go! Now you can filter your image, colorize it, or perform whatever operation inspired you to select this image in the first place. If you want to superimpose the image onto a different background, you can copy the image to the Clipboard (Ctrl+C or ⌘-C), open the desired background image, and then paste the first image in place (Ctrl+V or ⌘-V). A result you might like (picture it with your image in use) is shown in Figure 8-11. The image could stand some tinkering with the paint and edit tools, but it's not half bad for an automated selection process.

Note

Whenever you introduce a selection into another image — by copying and pasting or by dragging the selection and dropping it into another image window — Photoshop automatically assigns the selection to a new layer. This is a great safety mechanism because it prevents you from permanently affixing the selection to its new background. But it also limits your file format options when saving an image; you can't save in a format other than the native Photoshop format, PDF, or TIFF without first flattening the image. For the whole story on layers, read Chapter 12.

Figure 8-10: After selecting the entire background, press Ctrl+Shift+I (⌘-Shift-I on the Mac) to reverse what's selected and what's not. Now the bird and the flower are the only thing that's selected.

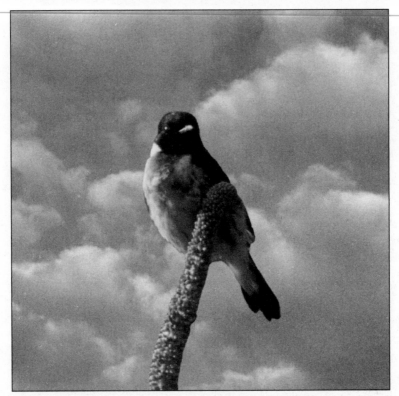

Figure 8-11: Now the bird is perched against the sky. Later, we can blur his edges a bit so he looks less stark against the new background, and we can adjust the lighting on his feathers to match his new setting.

Softening selection outlines

Sometimes, you want to make sure that whatever you're selecting, or the hole left by deleting it, has a soft edge — for artistic reasons or simply to make the changes or deletion less jarring to the image, avoiding any hard, obvious edges. When you feel the need for such an effect, you can soften a selection in two ways. The first method is *anti-aliasing*, introduced in Chapter 5. Anti-aliasing is an intelligent and automatic softening algorithm that mimics the appearance of edges you'd expect to see in a sharply focused photograph.

Note Where did the term *anti-alias* originate? Anytime you try to fit the digital equivalent of a square peg into a round hole — say, by printing a high-resolution image to a low-resolution printer — the data gets revised during the process. This revised data, called an *alias*, is frequently inaccurate and undesirable. Anti-aliasing is the act of revising the data ahead of time, essentially rounding off the square peg so it looks nice as it goes into the hole. According to a reader who spent time at MIT's Architecture Machine Group, "We did the first work with displaying smooth lines. We called the harsh transitions *jaggies* and the display process *dejaggying*. Somehow, this easy-to-understand term slid sideways into 'alias' (which it isn't, really, but it's too late to change)." Now you know.

When you draw an anti-aliased selection outline in Photoshop, the program calculates the hard-edged selection at twice its actual size. The program then shrinks the selection in half using bicubic interpolation (described in Chapter 2). The result is a crisp image with no visible jagged edges.

The second softening method, *feathering*, is more dramatic. Feathering gradually dissipates the selection outline, giving it a blurry edge. Photoshop accommodates partially selected pixels; feathering fades the selection both inward and outward from the original edge.

You can specify the number of pixels affected either before or after drawing a selection. To feather a selection before you draw it with a Marquee or Lasso tool, type a value in the Feather option box, found in the Options bar. To feather a selection after drawing it, choose Select ➪ Feather or press Ctrl+Alt+D (⌘-Option-D on the Mac). You also can right-click (Control-click on the Mac) in the image window and then choose Feather from the pop-up menu that appears next to your cursor.

The Feather Radius value determines the approximate distance over which Photoshop fades a selection, measured in pixels in both directions from the original selection outline. Figure 8-12 shows the effects of feathering a selection. In the first example, no feathering was used. In the second example, a 24-pixel feather was applied, and the resulting selection has a very soft edge. A pattern was also made from a selection on the stalk on which the bird is sitting, and this was used to fill the background — and then a Gaussian Blur was applied to it. If you missed it, creating patterns from selections within your image was covered in Chapter 6, and the Blur filters are covered in Chapter 10.

Figure 8-12: One with, one without. In the second image, the Feather was set to 10 pixels, creating this fuzzy frame around the deletion.

The math behind the feather

You, like previous readers who've written to ask, might wonder why feathering blurs a selection outline more than the number of pixels stated in the Feather Radius value. A radius of 4 pixels actually affects a total of 20 pixels: 10 inward and 10 outward. The reason revolves around Photoshop's use of a mathematical routine called the *Gaussian bell curve*, which exaggerates the distance over which the selection outline is blurred.

Tip   If exact space is an issue, you can count on the Feather command affecting about 2.7 times as many pixels as you type in the Feather Radius option box, both in and out from the selection. That's a total of 5.4 times as many pixels as the radius in all.

Putting feathering to use

You can use feathering to remove an element from an image while leaving the background intact, a process described in the following steps. The image in Figure 8-13 has some problem items in it — namely, a particular child who insists on making a crazy face every time a camera is pointed in his direction — but the one that can be removed without causing any family discord is the bright dot of light in the left side of the photo. In Figure 8-13, a selection has been drawn around the offending spot.

Figure 8-13: Got something to hide? The smoother the edges of the patch you use to obscure it, the more convincing your cover up.

STEPS: Removing an Element from an Image

1. Draw a selection around the element using the Lasso tool. As shown in Figure 8-13, the offending spot is encircled in an elliptical marquee selection.

2. Drag the selection outline over a patch in the image. Now that you've specified the element you want to remove, you must find a patch — that is, some portion of the image to cover the element in a manner that matches the surroundings. In Figure 8-14, the best match was clearly from some of the wall to the right of the spot. To select this area, move the selection outline independently of the image merely by dragging it with the selection tool (the Marquee in this case). Dragging a selection with a selection tool moves the outline without affecting the pixels, unlike dragging a selection with the Move tool, which moves whatever's in the selection. Make certain you allow some space between the selection outline and the element you're trying to cover.

3. Choose Select ➪ Feather, or press Ctrl+Alt+D (⌘-Option-D on the Mac). Type a small value (8 or less) in the Feather Radius option box — just enough to make the edges fuzzy. Then press Enter or Return to initiate the operation.

4. Clone the patch onto the area you want to cover. Select the Move tool by pressing V. Then Alt-drag (Option-drag on the Mac) the feathered selection to clone the patch and position it over the element you want to cover, as shown in Figure 8-15. To align the patch correctly, choose Select ➪ Hide Extras or press Ctrl+H (⌘-H on the Mac) to hide the marching ants and then nudge the patch into position with the arrow keys.

Figure 8-14: After drawing a circle around the spot with the Marquee tool, the selection outline was moved to the right to select another portion of the wall. Feathering the selection is the next step.

Figure 8-15: Next, I used the Move tool to Alt-drag (Option-drag on the Mac) the feathered selection over the bright spot. As long as you have something to use in covering the offending content, this technique can mask just about anything, and often with fewer steps and better results than the Clone Stamp.

Moving and Duplicating Selections

In the preceding steps, you discovered that you can either move the selected pixels or the empty selection outline to a new location, and with feathering the selection, make the moved content blend in with its new surroundings. Now it's time to examine these techniques in greater depth.

The role of the Move tool

To move selected pixels, you need the Move tool. This might seem rather obvious, but there are so many other ways to select and reposition content that you may not realize exactly what the Move tool does and how many other tools it can replace (or at least shove slightly to the side) if you use it properly. When you want to use it, you can select the Move tool at any time by pressing V (for *mooV*). One of the chief advantages of using the Move tool is that there's no chance of deselecting an image or harming the selection outline. Drag inside the selected area to move the selection; drag outside the selection to move the entire layer, selection included. Layers are covered in more detail in Chapter 12.

Tip

To access the Move tool on a temporary basis, press and hold Ctrl (⌘ on the Mac). The Move tool remains active as long as you hold Ctrl or ⌘. This shortcut works when any tool except the Hand tool, the Direct Selection or Path Selection tool, or any Pen, Shape, or Slice tool is active. If you have any interest in keyboard shortcuts, it's worth committing this to memory. It will save you heaps of time, as you will probably spend a lot of time Ctrl-dragging (⌘-dragging on the Mac) in Photoshop.

Making precise movements

Photoshop provides three methods for moving selections in prescribed increments. In each case, the Move tool is active, unless otherwise indicated:

✦ First, you can nudge a selection in 1-pixel increments by pressing an arrow key on the keyboard or nudge in 10-pixel increments by pressing Shift while pressing an arrow key. This technique is useful for making precise adjustments to the position of an image. Note that a series of consecutive nudges is recorded in the History palette (see Chapter 7) as only one history state, regardless of how much you move the selection. Choosing Undo will take the selection back to its original position in the image.

Tip

To nudge a selected area when the move tool is not active, press Ctrl (Win) or ⌘ (Mac) and an arrow key. Press Ctrl+Shift (Win) or ⌘-Shift (Mac) and an arrow key to move in 10-pixel increments. After the selection is floating — that is, after your first nudge — you can release the Ctrl or ⌘ key and use only the arrows (assuming a selection tool is active).

✦ Second, you can press Shift during a drag to constrain a move to a 45-degree direction — that is, horizontally, vertically, or diagonally.

✦ And third, you can use the Info palette to track your movements and to help locate a precise position in the image.

To display the Info palette, shown in Figure 8-16, choose Window ➪ Info or press F8. The first section of the Info palette displays the color values of the image area beneath your cursor. When you move a selection, the other eight items in the palette monitor movement as follows:

✦ **X, Y.** These values show the coordinate position of your cursor. The distance is measured from the upper-left corner of the image in the current unit of measure. The unit of measure in Figure 8-16 is pixels.

✦ **ΔX, ΔY.** These values indicate the distance of your move as measured horizontally and vertically.

✦ **A, D.** The A and D values reflect the angle and direct distance of your drag.

✦ **W, H.** These values reflect the width and height of your selection.

Figure 8-16: The Info palette provides a world of numerical feedback when you move a selection.

Cloning a selection

When you move a selection, you leave a hole in your image in the background color, as shown in the top half of Figure 8-17. If you prefer to leave the original in place during a move, you have to *clone* the selection — that is, create a copy of the selection without upsetting the contents of the Clipboard. Photoshop offers several ways to clone a selection:

✦ **Alt-dragging (Option-dragging on the Mac).** When the Move tool is active, press Alt (Option on the Mac) and drag a selection to clone it. Figure 8-17 shows a selection that was moved once and Alt-dragged three times. You know the guy in the picture just *loves* that he not only appears once in a paper crown, but three additional times.

✦ **Ctrl+Alt-dragging (⌘-Option-dragging on the Mac).** If some tool other than the Move tool is active, press Ctrl+Alt (⌘-Option on the Mac) and drag the selection to clone it. This is probably the technique you'll use most often.

✦ **Alt+arrowing (Option-arrowing on the Mac).** When the Move tool is active, press Alt (Win) or Option (Mac) and one of the arrow keys to clone the selection and nudge it one pixel away from the original. If you want to move the image multiple pixels, press Alt+arrow (Option-arrow on the Mac) the first time only. Then nudge the clone using the arrow key alone. Otherwise, you'll create a bunch of clones, which probably isn't what you want to do.

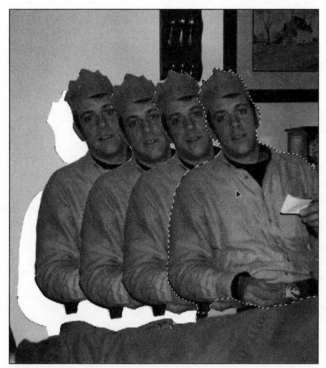

Figure 8-17: When you move a selection, you leave a gaping hole in the selection's wake — and you can also see the edges where you may have missed some of the desired content (see edges of hole). When you clone an image, you leave a copy of the selection behind. To illustrate this point, the selection was moved once, and then duplicated three times.

✦ **Ctrl+Alt+arrowing (⌘-Option-arrowing on the Mac).** If some other tool is active, press Ctrl and Alt (⌘ and Option on the Mac) and an arrow key. Again, press only Alt (or Option on the Mac) the first time, unless you want to create a string of clones.

✦ **Drag-and-drop.** Like about every other program on the planet, Photoshop lets you clone a selection between documents by dragging it with the move tool from one open window and dropping it in another, as demonstrated in Figure 8-18. As long as you manage to drop into the second window, the original image remains intact and selected in the first window. Notice that the layer from the image on the right appears smaller in the left image where it was dropped because the image on the left was captured at a higher resolution.

Tip

Don't worry about exact positioning during a drag-and-drop; first get the selection into the second window and then worry about placement.

Cross-Reference

You can drag-and-drop multiple layers if you link the layers first. For more information on this subject, see Chapter 12.

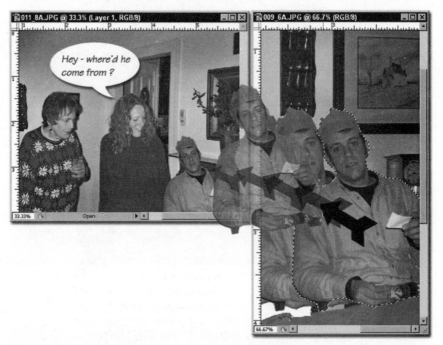

Figure 8-18: Use the Move tool to drag a selection from one open window and drop it into another. This creates a clone of the selection in the target window.

✦ **Shift-drop.** If the two images are exactly the same size — pixel for pixel — press Shift when dropping the selection to position it in the same spot it occupied in the original image. This is called *registering* the selection.

Tip

If an area is selected in the destination image, Shift-dropping positions the selection you're moving in the center of the selection in the destination image. This tip works regardless of whether the two images are the same size.

✦ **Ctrl-drag-and-drop (⌘-drag-and-drop on the Mac).** Again, if some other tool than the Move tool is selected, you must press Ctrl (Win) or ⌘ (Mac) when you drag to move the selected pixels from one window to the other.

Moving a selection outline independently of its contents

After all this talk about the Move tool and the Ctrl key (⌘ key on the Mac), you may be wondering what happens if you drag a selection while the Marquee, Lasso, or Wand tool is active — right after you've used one or more of them to make the selection, presumably. The answer is, you move the selection outline independently of the image. This technique, which was used earlier in this chapter in the steps "Removing an Element from an Image," serves as yet another means to manipulate selection outlines. It also enables you to take a selection from one portion of an image to another portion of the image or to an entirely different image window— without bringing any image content with you.

Tip You can nudge a selection outline independently of its contents by pressing an arrow key when a selection tool is active. Press Shift and an arrow key to move the outline in 10-pixel increments.

You can also can drag and drop empty selection outlines between images. Again, the selection tool — the Marquee, Lasso, or Magic Wand — must be active. Just drag the outline from one image window and drop it into another. The difference is that only the selection outline gets cloned; the pixels remain behind. This is a great way to copy pixels back and forth between images. You can set up an exact selection outline in Image A, drag it into Image B with the Marquee tool, move it over the pixels you want to clone, and Ctrl-drag-and-drop (⌘-drag-and-drop on the Mac) the selection back into Image A. Add the use of the Feather option (to soften the selection edges, remember?) and you've got a seamless edit in Image A, and Image B won't even know what hit it.

So remember: The selection tools affect only the selection outline. The selection tools never affect the pixels themselves; that's the Move tool's job, as you'll see as you read on.

Scaling or rotating a selection outline

In case you were distracted while reading the last two sentences, here's the important thing to remember: Selection outlines stay independent — and entirely changeable — as long as a selection tool is active. In addition to moving a selection outline, you can transform it by choosing Select ➪ Transform Selection.

When you select this command, Photoshop displays a transformation boundary framed by eight handles, as shown in Figure 8-19. This is also known as a *bounding box*. You can drag the handles to adjust the outline as described in the upcoming list. In addition, the Options bar gives you access to a slew of mysterious option boxes, as shown at the top of the figure. You can type specific values to relocate, size, rotate, and skew the selection outline precisely.

Figure 8-19: Much like using the Transform and Free Transform commands on actual image content, after choosing Select ➪ Transform Selection, you can scale the selection outline (top) and rotate it (bottom), all without affecting the image in the slightest.

The handles and Options bar controls work just as they do for the Edit ➪ Free Transform command, which is covered in riveting detail in Chapter 12. To save you the backbreaking chore of flipping ahead four chapters, though, let's cut to the chase here:

✦ **Scale.** Drag any of the handles to scale the selection, as shown in Figure 8-19. Shift-drag to scale proportionally, Alt-drag (Option-drag on the Mac) to scale with respect to the origin (little cross hair/circle thing labeled in the figure). You can move the origin just by dragging it.

Alternatively, type a scale percentage in the W (width) and H (height) boxes in the Options bar. By default, Photoshop maintains the original proportions of the outline. If that doesn't suit you, click the Constrain Proportions button (it looks like a little chain) between the two boxes.

Note

See that little replica of the transformation boundary near the left end of the Options bar? The black square represents the current origin. You can click the boxes to relocate the origin to one of the handles. Use the X and Y values to change the position of the origin numerically. Click the triangular delta symbol, labeled in Figure 8-19, to measure positioning relative to the transformation origin.

✦ **Rotate.** Type a value in the Rotate option box or drag outside the transformation boundary to rotate the selection, as in the second example in Figure 8-19. The rotation always occurs with respect to the origin.

Tip

To rotate the outline by 90 or 180 degrees, right-click (Control-click on the Mac) the image window and choose the rotation amount you want from the resulting pop-up menu.

✦ **Flip.** You can flip a selection outline by dragging one handle past its opposite handle, but this is a lot of work. The easier way is to right-click (Control-click on the Mac) inside the image window and choose Flip Horizontal or Flip Vertical from the pop-up menu.

✦ **Skew and distort.** To skew the selection outline, Ctrl-drag (⌘-drag on the Mac) a side, top, or bottom handle. Or type values in the H (horizontal) and V (vertical) skew boxes in the Options bar. To distort the selection, Ctrl-drag (Win) or ⌘-drag (Mac) a corner handle.

✦ **Warp.** Photoshop's Warp capabilities now extend to selections as well as image content. In Warp mode, you can distort the selection using the grid and additional handles shown in Figure 8-20. You can drag any of the grid intersections, the gray solid handles on the perimeter, the corner box handles, or points along any of the gridlines.

You can click the Warp list (shown in Figure 8-20) and select a preset grid. The grid will appear in the shape you choose, and the Bend, Height, and Width fields become available. The top image in Figure 8-20 shows the default Custom warp grid in place. The image on the bottom shows a warp in progress. When you drag from a handle once, additional handles appear to allow you to change the angle of the corner or slide in question. To commit to your warp changes, click the check mark button (shown in Figure 8-19), or press Return or Enter. Esc abandons the Warp and restores your selection to its prewarp state.

Cross-Reference

Read more about warping image content in Chapter 12.

When you get the selection outline the way you want it, press Enter or Return or double-click inside the boundary. To cancel the transformation, press Escape. You can also click the check mark button near the right end of the Options bar to apply the transformation or click the "no" symbol button to cancel the operation.

Figure 8-20: Use the Warp mode grid to distort your selection — each gridline, grid intersection, and handle can be used by clicking and dragging with your mouse. Once a handle has been dragged, new handles appear to let you change the angle of the distortion.

How to Draw and Edit Paths

Now that you know all about the main, basic selection tools and how to manipulate their selections, it's time to move on to one of the more powerful, yet complex tools that can be used to create selections. Photoshop's path tools provide the most flexible and precise ways to define a selection short of masking, but they can be something of a mystery and a technical challenge to novices and intermediate-level users. Given that most people underestimate their knowledge of Photoshop (other than total novices, who know they have little or no experience), you may not know which level you're on — but don't worry. Most people take some time to grow comfortable with the Pen tool, for example, because it requires you to draw a selection outline one point at a time.

Note   If you're familiar with Illustrator's Pen tool and other path-editing functions, you'll find Photoshop's tools nearly identical. Users of other illustration programs, such as CorelDRAW, will also recognize many similarities with the Bezier tool, used to draw curved lines and shapes. Of course, Photoshop doesn't provide the breadth of options available in Illustrator and these other program's Pen/Bezier tools, but the basic techniques are the same. Photoshop also includes a set of path-drawing tools to help smooth out the learning curve — and the possibly undesirable paths you've drawn — for inexperienced users. You can use any of the shape tools — Rectangle, Rounded Rectangle, Line, Ellipse, Polygon, and Custom Shape — to draw a simple geometric path.

The following pages get you up and running with all the path features. You'll learn how to draw a path, edit it, convert it to a selection outline, and stroke it with a paint or edit tool. You'll be a path-drawing, editing, converting, painting maniac just a few pages from now.

Paths overview

You create and edit paths from scratch by using the various pen tools or shape tools. (Figure 8-2, earlier in this chapter, shows all the path-related tools along with their selection tool counterparts.) Path management options — which enable you to convert paths to selections, fill and stroke paths, and save and delete them — reside in the Paths palette, shown in Figure 8-21.

Figure 8-21: To save and organize your paths, display the Paths palette by choosing Window ⇨ Paths.

How paths work

Paths differ from normal selections because they exist on the equivalent of a distinct, object-oriented layer that sits in front of the bitmapped image. This setup enables you to edit a path with point-by-point precision with no fear that you'll accidentally make any change to the image, as you can when you edit ordinary selection outlines. After you get a path just so, you convert it to a standard selection outline, which you can then use to edit the contents of the image and treat like a regular selection outline.

The following steps explain the basic process of drawing a selection outline with the path tools. The individual steps are explained in greater detail later in the chapter, but this procedure should enable you to sort of sneak up to the pool and dip your toe in — diving comes later.

STEPS: Creating a Selection with the Path Tools

1. **Draw the path.** Make sure the Paths button is selected in the Options bar, and then use a Pen tool or a Shape tool to draw the outline of your prospective selection.

Note   If your goal is to select multiple areas of the image, draw outlines around all of them. A path can include as many separate segments as you like. Technically, the individual segments in a path are called *subpaths*.

2. **Edit the path**. If the path requires some adjustment, reshape it using the other path tools.

3. **Save the path.** When you get the path exactly as you want it, save the path by choosing the Save Path command from the Paths palette menu. Or double-click the *Work Path* item in the scrolling list.

4. **Convert the path to a selection.** You can make the path a selection outline by choosing the Make Selection command or by pressing Enter on the numeric keypad when a path or selection tool is active.

That's it. After you convert the path to a selection, it works like any of the selection outlines described earlier. You can feather a selection, move it, copy it, clone it, or apply one of the special effects described in future chapters. The path remains intact in case you want to do further editing or use it again.

Sorting through the path tools

Before you get into how you draw and edit paths, here's a quick introduction to the path tools. To start, take a look at the tools on the Pen tool flyout:

Pen. Use the Pen tool to draw paths in Photoshop one point at a time. Click to create a corner in a path; click and drag to make a smooth point that results in a continuous arc. Fear not, this tool is explained *ad nauseam* in the section "Drawing paths with the Pen tool" later in this chapter. You can select the Pen tool by pressing P; press P again to toggle to the freeform pen, described next. (As always, the shortcuts assume that you have deselected the Use Shift Key for Tool Switch option in the Preferences dialog box.)

Freeform Pen. Click and drag with this tool to create a path that automatically follows the twists and turns of your drag. Simplicity at its best; control at its lowest. Luckily, you can turn around and edit the path after you initially draw it, so the lack of control when drawing the path can be made up afterward as you edit it.

The **Magnetic Pen** doesn't actually appear in the toolbox. But if you select the Freeform Pen and then select the Magnetic option in the Options bar, the Freeform Pen dashes into a phone booth and becomes the Magnetic Pen. Click the edge of the foreground element you want to select and then move the cursor along the edge of the shape. Photoshop automatically assigns points as it deems appropriate.

Add Anchor Point. Click an existing path to add a point to it.

Delete Anchor Point. Click an existing point in a path to delete the point without creating a break in the path's outline.

Convert Point. Click or drag a point to convert it to a corner or smooth point. You also can drag a handle to convert the point. To access the Convert Point tool, press Alt (Win) or Option (Mac) when the Pen is active. Press Ctrl+Alt (⌘-Option on the Mac) when an Arrow tool (explained in the next section) is active. (The terms *anchor point, smooth point,* and others associated with drawing paths are explained in the upcoming section.)

You can use the Pen tool to add, delete, and convert points, too, providing that you select the Auto Add/Delete option in the Options bar. Pass the cursor over a segment in a selected path to toggle to the Add Anchor Point tool; move the cursor over a point to get the Delete Anchor Point tool. Press Alt (Option on the Mac) over a point to get the Convert Point tool.

If all you need is a simple, geometric path, you can save time by creating the path with the shape tools. The shape tools are covered in detail in Chapter 14, so there's no need to repeat everything here. Just know that after you select a shape tool, you shift it into Path-Drawing mode by clicking the Paths button in the Options bar, labeled in Figure 8-22. (The pen that appears on the button face serves as a reminder that you're in path country.) Photoshop sets the shape tools to that mode automatically if you select them while working on an existing path.

Figure 8-22: Click the Paths button in the Options bar to draw paths with the shape tools.

As you draw, Photoshop automatically adds whatever points are needed. You only need to worry about selecting a path overlap button, which determines how paths intersect and interact. See the next section to find out which button to choose when.

After you create a path, you can select it or edit it by using the two tools on the flyout directly above the pen tools flyout:

Path Selection tool (black arrow). This tool selects an entire path. Just click inside the path to select it. If you created subpaths, the tool selects only the one under your cursor. You also use this tool to select vector objects, as explained in Chapter 14.

Direct Selection tool (white arrow). This tool permits you to click and drag points and handles to reshape a path. You can access the tool when any other path tool is active by pressing and holding Ctrl (⌘ on the Mac). And you can Alt-click (Option-click on the Mac) inside a path to select the entire path without switching to the Path Selection (black arrow) tool.

From this point on, these two tools are referred to as the *black arrow* and *white arrow*. Why? Because Photoshop users are a visually oriented group, and it's a safe bet that you can find the right tool more quickly if you're told to "click with the black arrow" or "drag with the white arrow" than if you were to see the technical tool names in all references to the tools.

You can access the arrow tools from the keyboard by pressing A. You know the drill: Press A to switch to the tool that's currently active; press A again to toggle to the other tool. (Add Shift if you selected the Use Shift Key for Tool Switch option in the Preferences dialog box.)

Drawing paths with the Pen tool

When drawing with the regular Pen tool, you build a path by creating individual points. Photoshop automatically connects the points with segments, which are simply straight or curved lines. It will be hard not to drag (unless you're using the Freeform Pen), so be prepared to curse and start over a few times.

Adobe prefers the term *anchor points* rather than *points* because the points anchor the path into place. But most people just call them points. Given that *all* points associated with paths are anchor points, it's not like there's some potential for confusion, right? Right.

All paths in Photoshop are *Bézier* (pronounced bay-zee-ay) paths, meaning they rely on the same mathematical curve definitions that make up the core of the PostScript printer language. The Bézier curve model allows for zero, one, or two levers to be associated with each point in a path. These levers, labeled in Figure 8-23, are called *Bézier control handles* or simply *handles.* You can move each handle in relation to a point, enabling you to bend and tug at a curved segment like it's a piece of soft wire.

Figure 8-23: Click and drag with the Pen tool to create a smooth point and then adjust the curve using Bézier control handles.

The following list summarizes how you can use the Pen tool to build paths in Photoshop:

✦ **Adding segments.** To build a path, create one point after another until the path is the desired length and shape. Photoshop automatically draws a segment between each new point and its predecessor. (The next section gets specific about how you use the tool to create points.)

✦ **Closing the path.** If you plan to convert the path to a selection outline, you need to complete the outline by clicking again on the first point in the path. Every point will then have one segment entering it and another segment exiting it. Such a path is called a *closed path* because it completely encloses the desired area.

✦ **Leaving the path open.** If you plan to apply the Stroke Path command (explained later), you may not want to close a path. To leave the path open, so it has a specific beginning and ending, deactivate the path by saving it (choose the Save Path command from the Paths palette menu).

✦ **Extending an open path.** To reactivate an open path, click or drag one of its endpoints. Photoshop draws a segment between the endpoint and the next point you create.

✦ **Joining two open subpaths.** To join one open subpath with another, click or drag an endpoint in the first subpath and then click or drag an endpoint in the second.

✦ **Specifying path overlap.** You can set the path tools to one of four settings that control how Photoshop treats overlapping areas in a path when you convert the path to a selection.

To make your intentions known, click one of the buttons near the right end of the Options bar, labeled in Figure 8-24. The button you click remains in effect until you choose another button.

Add   Intersect

Subtract   Exclude

Figure 8-24: Click one of these buttons in the Options bar to control how Photoshop treats overlapping areas when you convert a path to a selection.

Note

These buttons also appear when you draw paths with the shape tools. With either set of tools, your choices are as follows:

- **Add to path area.** Select this button if you want all areas, overlapping or not, to be selected.

- **Subtract from path area.** Select this button to draw a subpath that eats a hole in an existing path. Any areas that you enclose with the subpath are not selected. Note that if you select a path and the Make Selection command is dimmed in the Paths palette, it's probably because you drew the path with the Subtract option in force.

- **Intersect path areas.** The opposite of Exclude, this option selects only overlapping areas.

- **Exclude overlapping path areas.** Any overlapping regions are not included in the selection.

You can change the overlap setting for a subpath after you draw it if necessary. Select the paths with the black arrow tool and then click the overlap button for the setting you want to use.

✦ **Deactivating paths.** At any time, you can press Enter or Return to *dismiss* — deactivate — the path. When you do, Photoshop hides the path from view. To retrieve the path, click its name in the Paths palette. Be careful with this one, though: If you dismiss an unsaved path and then start drawing a new path, you can lose the dismissed one. For more details, see the section "Converting and saving paths" later in this chapter.

✦ **Hiding paths.** If you merely want to hide paths from view, press Ctrl+H (⌘-H on the Mac), which hides selections, guides, and other screen elements as well. You can also press Ctrl+Shift+H (⌘-Shift-H on the Mac) or choose View ➪ Show ➪ Target Path to toggle the path display on and off. To select which items you want to hide with Ctrl+H (Win) or ⌘-H (Mac), choose View ➪ Show ➪ Show Extras Options.

To get a better sense of how the Pen tool works, click the arrow button at the right end of the row of path-drawing icons to access the Pen Options (or "Option," in this case). Here you can select the Rubber Band option. This tells Photoshop to draw an animated segment between the last point drawn and the cursor.

The anatomy of points and segments

Points in a Bézier path act like little road signs, each point steering the path by specifying how a segment enters it and how another segment exits it. You specify the identity of each little road sign by clicking, dragging, or Alt-dragging (Option-dragging on the Mac) with the Pen tool. The following items explain the specific kinds of points and segments you can create in Photoshop. See Figure 8-25 for examples.

✦ **Corner point.** Click with the Pen tool to create a corner point, which represents the corner between two straight segments in a path.

✦ **Straight segment.** Click at two different locations to create a straight segment between two corner points. Shift-click to draw a 45-degree-angle segment between the new corner point and its predecessor.

✦ **Smooth point.** Drag to create a smooth point with two symmetrical Bézier control handles. A smooth point ensures that one segment meets with another in a continuous arc.

✦ **Curved segment.** Drag at two different locations to create a curved segment between two smooth points.

✦ **Straight segment followed by curved.** After drawing a straight segment, drag from the corner point you just created to add a Bézier control handle. Then drag again at a different location to append a curved segment to the end of the straight segment.

✦ **Curved segment followed by straight.** After drawing a curved segment, Alt-click (Option-click on the Mac) the smooth point you just created to delete the forward Bézier control handle. This converts the smooth point to a corner point with one handle. Then click at a different location to append a straight segment to the end of the curved segment.

✦ **Cusp point.** After drawing a curved segment, Alt-drag (Option-drag on the Mac) from the smooth point you just created to redirect the forward Bézier control handle, converting the smooth point to a corner point with two independent handles, sometimes known as a *cusp point*. Then click and drag again at a new location to append a curved segment that proceeds in a different direction than the previous curved segment.

Straight segment   Click to begin curve

Drag and stop
to create curve

Click and drag again
to create second curve

Click again to create
second straight segment

Click on a point to activate Bézier handles

Figure 8-25: A path in progress, starting as a straight segment, containing two consecutive curved segments, ending with a straight segment. Points where the curved segments meet straight segments have visible Bézier handles.

Going free-form

If the Pen tool is still a little hard for you to use or for any reason seems like overkill, try the Freeform Pen tool. Just click the P key while you already have the standard Pen in use, and you're there. As you drag, Photoshop tracks the motion of the cursor with a continuous line. After you release the mouse button, the program automatically assigns and positions the points and segments needed to create the Bézier path, which you can then edit as though you drew it with the regular Pen.

Tip   Despite its popularity for drawing free-form, wavy paths, you can draw straight segments with the Freeform Pen: As you're dragging, press and hold Alt (Win) or Option (Mac). Then click around to create points. When you're finished drawing straight segments, drag again and release Alt (Option on the Mac).

Sometimes, even such a powerful tool (in the hands of such a capable artisan) can mess up. When the program finishes its calculations, a path may appear riddled with far too many points or equipped with too few. What to do? Fortunately, you can adjust the performance of the Freeform Pen to accommodate your personal drawing style using the Curve Fit control, which you can access by clicking the arrow at the end of the row of path-drawing tool icons in the Options bar. Set before you begin drawing (changing the setting won't affect existing paths), you can type any value between 0.5 and 10, which Photoshop interprets in screen pixels. The default value of 2, for example, instructs the program to ignore any jags in your mouse movements that do not exceed 2 pixels in length or width. Setting the value to 0.5 makes the Freeform Pen extremely sensitive; setting the value to 10 smoothes the roughest of gestures.

A Curve Fit from 2 to 4 is generally adequate for most folks, but you should experiment to determine the best setting. Like the Magic Wand's Tolerance setting, you can't alter the Curve Fit value for a path after you've drawn it. Photoshop calculates the points for a path only once, after you release the mouse button.

Going magnetic

To use the Magnetic Pen tool, first select the Freeform Pen tool and then select the Magnetic option in the Options bar. The Magnetic Pen works like a combination of the Magnetic Lasso and the Freeform Pen. As with the Magnetic Lasso, you begin by clicking anywhere along the edge of the image element you want to select. (For a refresher on magnetism, see Figure 8-5.) Then move the cursor — no need to drag — around the perimeter of the element and watch Photoshop do its work. To set an anchor point, click. When you come full circle, click the point where you started to close the path.

You can create straight segments by Alt-clicking (Option-clicking on the Mac), just as you can when using the Freeform Pen without Magnetic selected. And the Curve Fit option (in the Freeform Pen Options drop-down palette shown in Figure 8-26) controls the smoothness of the path. Lower values trace the edges more carefully; higher values result in fewer points and smoother edges. The other options here give you access to the Width, Contrast, Frequency, and Pen Pressure, all of which should be familiar from your playing with the Lasso tool earlier in this chapter.

Figure 8-26: While the Freeform Pen is active, select the Magnetic option in the Options bar to access the Magnetic Pen. Click the arrow at the left of the check box to display additional options.

Editing paths

If you take time to master the default Pen tool, you'll find yourself drawing accurate paths more and more frequently. Even after mastering the tool's use and features, however, don't feel bad if you don't get it right 100 percent of the time — or even 50 percent of the time. When you rely on the Freeform or Magnetic Pen tools, the results are rarely, if ever, totally accurate — simply because your arm and hand are not robotic. From your first fledgling steps through to the point where you've developed into a maestro, you'll rely heavily on Photoshop's capability to reshape paths by moving points and handles, adding and deleting points, and converting points to change the curvature of segments. So don't worry too much if your path looks terrible. The path-editing tools provide all the correction capabilities you could ever want or need.

Reshaping paths

The white arrow tool — known officially as the Direct Selection tool — represents the foremost path-reshaping function in Photoshop. To select this tool from the keyboard, first press A to select the black arrow tool and then press A again to toggle to the white arrow. Or just Alt-click (Win) or Option-click (Mac) the black arrow tool in the toolbox. You use the black arrow to select, relocate, and duplicate entire paths or subpaths, as explained in an upcoming section.

Tip   Press and hold Ctrl (Win) or ⌘ (Mac) to access the white arrow tool temporarily when one of the pen or path-editing tools is selected. When you release Ctrl or ⌘, the cursor returns to the selected tool. This is a great way to edit a path while you're drawing it.

However you choose to activate the white arrow, you can perform any of the following functions with it:

✦ **Select points.** Click a point to select it independently of other points in a path. Shift-click to select an additional point, even if the point belongs to a different subpath than other selected points. Alt-click (Win) or Option-click (Mac) a path to select all its points in one fell swoop. You can even marquee points by dragging a rectangle around them. You cannot, however, apply commands from the Select menu, such as All or Deselect, to the selection of paths.

✦ **Drag selected points.** To move one or more points, select them and then drag one of the selected points. All selected points move the same distance and direction. When you move a point while a neighboring point remains stationary, the segment between the two points shrinks, stretches, and bends to accommodate the change in distance. Segments located between two selected or deselected points remain unchanged during a move.

Tip   You can move selected points in 1-pixel increments by pressing arrow keys. If both a portion of the image and points in a path are selected, the arrow keys move the points only. Because paths reside on a higher layer, they take precedence in all functions that might concern them.

✦ **Drag a straight segment.** You also can reshape a path by dragging its segments. When you drag a straight segment, the two corner points on either side of the segment move as well.

Caution This technique works best with straight segments drawn with the default Pen tool. Segments created by Alt-clicking (Option-clicking on the Mac) with the Freeform or Magnetic Pen may include trace control handles that make Photoshop think that the segment is actually curved.

✦ **Drag a curved segment.** When you drag a curved segment, you stretch, shrink, or bend that segment.

Tip When you drag a curved segment, drag from the middle of the segment, approximately equidistant from both its points. This method provides the best leverage and ensures that the segment doesn't go flying off in some weird direction you hadn't anticipated.

✦ **Drag a Bézier control handle.** Select a point and drag either of its Bézier control handles to change the curvature of the corresponding segment without moving any of the points in the path. If the point is a smooth point, moving one handle moves both handles in the path. If you want to move a smooth handle independently of its partner, you must use the convert point tool, as discussed in the section "Converting points" later in this chapter.

Adding and deleting points and segments

The quantity of points and segments in a path is always subject to change. Whether a path is closed or open, you can reshape it by adding and deleting points, which, in turn, forces the addition or deletion of a segment:

✦ **Appending a point to the end of an open path.** If a path is open, you can activate one of its endpoints by clicking or dragging it with the Pen tool, depending on the identity of the endpoint and whether you want the next segment to be straight or curved. Photoshop is then prepared to draw a segment between the endpoint and the next point you create.

✦ **Closing an open path.** You also can use the technique just described to close an open path. Select one endpoint, click or drag it with the Pen tool to activate it, and then click or drag the opposite endpoint. Photoshop draws a segment between the two endpoints, closing the path and eliminating both endpoints by converting them to *interior points*, which simply means the points are bound on both sides by segments.

✦ **Joining two open subpaths.** You can join two open subpaths to create one longer open path. To do so, activate an endpoint of the first subpath and then, using the Pen tool, click or drag an endpoint of the second subpath.

✦ **Inserting a point in a segment.** Using the Add Point tool, click anywhere along an open or closed path to insert a point and divide the segment into two segments. Photoshop automatically inserts a corner or smooth point, depending on its reading of the path. If the point does not exactly meet your needs, use the Convert Point tool to change it. In addition to using the Add Point tool, you can select the Auto Add/Delete option in the Options bar. Then, whenever you pass the Pen tool cursor over a segment, you see the little plus sign next to your cursor, indicating that the Add Point tool is temporarily in the house. This trick works only if the path is selected, however.

✦ **Deleting a point and breaking the path.** The simplest way to delete a point and break the path is to select it with the white arrow and press Delete or Clear. (You also can choose Edit ➪ Clear, though why you would want to expend so much effort is beyond me.) When you delete an interior point, you delete both segments associated with that point, resulting in a break in the path. If you delete an endpoint from an open path, you delete the single segment associated with the point.

✦ **Removing a point without breaking the path.** Select the Delete Point tool and click a point in an open or closed path to delete the point and draw a new segment between the two points that neighbor it. The Delete Point tool ensures that no break occurs in a path.

Tip   To access the Delete Point tool when using the Pen tool, select the Auto Add/Delete option in the Options bar and then hover your cursor over a selected interior point in an existing path. You see the minus sign next to the cursor, indicating that the Delete Point tool is active. Click the point and it goes away. Alternately, you can remove a point when the Add Point tool is active by Alt-clicking (Option-clicking on the Mac), and vice versa.

✦ **Deleting a segment.** You can delete a single interior segment from a path without affecting any point. To do so, first click outside the path with the white arrow tool to deselect the path. Then click the segment you want to delete and press Delete. When you delete an interior segment, you create a break in your path.

Converting points

Photoshop lets you change the identity of an interior point. You can convert a corner point to a smooth point, and vice versa. You perform all point conversions using the convert point tool as follows:

✦ **Smooth to corner.** Click an existing smooth point to convert it to a corner point with no Bézier control handle.

✦ **Smooth to cusp.** Drag one of the handles of a smooth point to move it independently of the other, thus converting the smooth point to a cusp.

✦ **Corner to smooth.** Drag from a corner point to convert it to a smooth point with two symmetrical Bézier control handles.

✦ **Cusp to smooth.** Drag one of the handles of a cusp point to lock both handles back into alignment, thus converting the cusp to a smooth point.

Tip   Press Alt (Win) or Option (Mac) to access the Convert Point tool temporarily when one of the three pen tools is active and positioned over a selected point. To do the same when an arrow tool is active, press Ctrl+Alt (⌘-Option on the Mac).

Transforming paths

In addition to all the aforementioned path-altering techniques, you can scale, rotate, skew, and otherwise transform paths using the following techniques:

✦ To transform all subpaths in a group — such as shown in the left example of Figure 8-27 — select either arrow tool and click off a path to make sure all paths are deselected. Then choose Edit ➪ Free Transform Path.

✦ To transform a single subpath independently of others in a group, click it with the black arrow and then select the Show Bounding Box option in the Options bar. Or click the path with the white arrow and choose Edit ➪ Free Transform Path.

✦ Photoshop even lets you transform some points independently of others inside a single path, as demonstrated in the second example of Figure 8-27. Just use the white arrow to select the points you want to modify and then choose Edit ➪ Free Transform Points.

Figure 8-27: To transform multiple paths at once, deselect all paths and press Ctrl+T (⌘-T on the Mac). If you don't want to transform your entire path, you can transform a portion thereof or a series of points by selecting them and pressing Ctrl+T.

Tip   The keyboard shortcut for all of these operations is Ctrl+T (⌘-T on the Mac). If you select an independent path — or specific points inside a path — press Ctrl+Alt+T (⌘-Option-T on the Mac) to transform a duplicate of the path and leave the original unaffected.

While the topic of transformation is found in one central location— in a major section of Chapter 12 — it's probably a good idea to repeat some of the concepts here. Read on for a brief rundown of your transformation options after you press Ctrl+T (⌘-T on the Mac):

✦ **Scale.** To scale a path, drag one of the eight square handles that adorn the transformation boundary. Alt-drag (Win) or Option-drag (Mac) a handle to scale with respect to the origin point. You can move the origin by dragging it or by clicking one of the boxes in the little bounding box icon at the left end of the Options bar. To scale the path and maintain proportions, press the Shift key as you drag any of the corner handles.

✦ **Rotate.** Drag outside the boundary to rotate the paths or points, as demonstrated in Figure 8-27.

✦ **Flip.** Right-click (Control-click on the Mac) to access a pop-up menu of transformation options. Choose Flip Horizontal or Flip Vertical to create a mirror image of the path.

✦ **Skew.** Ctrl-drag (Win) or ⌘-drag (Mac) one of the side handles to slant the paths. Press Shift along with Ctrl or ⌘ to constrain the slant along a consistent axis.

✦ **Distort.** Ctrl-drag (Win) or ⌘-drag (Mac) one of the corner handles to distort the paths.

✦ **Perspective.** Press Ctrl+Shift+Alt (⌘-Shift-Option on the Mac) and drag a corner handle to achieve a perspective effect.

Note   You can't take advantage of the distortion or perspective feature when individual points are selected. These techniques apply to whole paths only.

✦ **Numerical transformations.** If you need to transform a path by a very specific amount, use the controls in the Options bar, which are the same ones you get when transforming a regular selection. Modify the values as desired and press Enter or Return.

✦ **Warp.** Click the Warp button on the Options bar while you're in Transformation mode for your path. The same grid and preset warp options that were discussed earlier in this chapter (remember the section on transforming selections?) appear for your warping pleasure.

When you finish stretching and distorting your paths, press Enter or Return or double-click inside the boundary to apply the transformation. You also can click the check mark button at the right end of the Options bar. To undo the last transformation in the transform mode, press Ctrl+Z (⌘-Z on the Mac). Or bag the whole thing by pressing Esc.

Tip   To repeat the last transformation on another path, press Ctrl+Shift+T (⌘-Shift-T on the Mac).

Moving and cloning paths

You can relocate and duplicate paths as follows:

✦ **Clone a path.** Click inside the path with the black arrow tool to select it. To select multiple subpaths, Shift-click them, or marquee-drag around them. Then Alt-drag (Option-drag on the Mac) to clone all selected paths.

✦ **Move a path.** After selecting the path with the black arrow, drag the path to its new home.

✦ **Align and distribute paths.** You can align two or more paths by selecting them with the black arrow and then clicking an alignment button in the Options bar. To space the paths evenly across the image, click one of the distribution buttons, which are shown in Figure 8-28. Press Enter or Return or click the check mark button in the Options bar to apply the transformation.

Figure 8-28: You can align and distribute multiple selected paths, just as you can layers and vector objects.

Merging and deleting paths

When the black arrow is selected, the Options bar contains a Combine button (see Figure 8-28). Clicking this button merges all selected subpaths into one. When Photoshop combines the subpaths, it does so according to which path overlap options were active when you drew the subpaths. Remember, you can select a subpath with the black arrow to change its overlap setting if necessary. Just select the subpath, and then click the appropriate overlap button in the Options bar (see Figure 8-28). Refer to the section "Drawing paths with the Pen tool" for more information about overlap options.

To get rid of a path, click inside it with the black arrow or drag around it with the white arrow. Then press Delete. It's that simple!

Filling paths

After you finish drawing a path, you can convert it to a selection outline as described in the section "Converting paths to selections," or you can paint it. You can paint the interior of the path by choosing the Fill Path command from the Paths palette menu, or you can paint the outline of the path by choosing Stroke Path. In either case, Photoshop applies the fill on the active image layer.

The Fill Path command works much like Edit ➪ Fill. After drawing a path, choose the Fill Path command or Alt-click (Option-click on the Mac) the fill path icon in the lower-left corner of the Paths palette. (The icon looks like a filled circle.) Photoshop displays a slight variation of the Fill dialog box discussed in Chapter 6; the only difference is the inclusion of two Rendering options. Type a value in the Feather Radius option box to blur the edges of the fill, as if the path were a selection with a feathered outline. Select the Anti-aliased option to slightly soften the outline of the filled area. If you simply click the fill path icon without pressing and holding a modifier key, the area within the path is automatically filled with the foreground color. The path, of course, is unaffected and can be moved to a new location and used again.

Note If you select one or more subpaths, the Fill Path command changes to Fill Subpaths, enabling you to fill only the selected subpaths. The fill path icon also affects only the selected subpaths.

When applying the fill, Photoshop adheres to the overlap option you used when creating the path. Suppose that you draw two round paths, one fully inside the other. If you drew both circles with the Add overlap option active, both circles get filled. If you drew the interior circle with the Invert option active, Photoshop fills only the area between the two paths, resulting in the letter *O*.

If the Fill Path command fills only part or none of the path, the path probably falls outside a selection outline. Choose Select ➪ Deselect or press Ctrl+D (⌘-D on the Mac) to deselect the image and then choose the Fill Path command again.

Painting along a path

Unlike the Fill Path command, which works a lot like the Edit ➪ Fill command, the Stroke Path command is altogether different from Edit ➪ Stroke. Edit ➪ Stroke creates outlines on an active selection, whereas the Stroke Path command enables you to paint a brushstroke along the contours of a path. This may not sound like such a big deal at first, but this feature enables you to combine all the flexible, artistic things about both the paint and edit tools with the structure and precision of a path.

To paint a path, choose the Stroke Path command from the Paths palette menu to display the Stroke Path dialog box shown in Figure 8-29. In this dialog box, you can choose the paint or edit tool with which you want to *stroke* the path (which only means to paint a brushstroke along a path). Photoshop drags the chosen tool along the exact route of the path, retaining any tool or brush shape settings that were in force when you chose the tool.

The Stroke Path dialog box includes a Simulate Pressure option, which is particularly useful for people who don't have a pressure-sensitive tablet. Provided you use appropriate settings in the Brushes palette, this option begins your stroke with a thin line, widens it as it reaches the middle, and then tapers it off as it reaches the end. The effect is similar to what you could achieve with a pressure-sensitive drawing tablet. Try experimenting with different settings in the Shape Dynamics dialog box (activated through the Brush Options bar), and tinker with pen pressure, pen shape, angle, and so forth. The more you play with this feature, the more you'll be able to anticipate the results of tweaking various settings and the more control you'll have over the tools in question — especially when they're applied to a path.

Figure 8-29: Select the paint or edit tool that you want Photoshop to use to stroke the path.

Tip

You can display the Stroke Path dialog box also by Alt-clicking (or Option-clicking on the Mac) on the Stroke Path icon, the second icon at the bottom of the Paths palette. If you prefer to bypass the dialog box, select a paint or edit tool and then either click the Stroke Path icon or simply press Enter or Return. Instead of displaying the dialog box, Photoshop assumes that you want to use the selected tool and strokes away. If any tool but a paint or edit tool is active, Photoshop strokes the path using the tool you previously selected in the Stroke Path dialog box.

Note

If you select one or more subpaths, the Stroke Path command becomes a Stroke Subpath command. Photoshop then strokes only the selected path, rather than all paths saved under the current name.

The following steps walk you through a project in which you can try stroking paths yourself with the Brush tool. Figures 8-30 through 8-32 show the progression and eventual outcome of a sample image.

STEPS: Stroking Paths with Paint Tools

1. **Draw a curved path similar to the one shown in Figure 8-30.** The path spirals downward, curving back and forth, gently, and then spirals back up over itself.

2. **Save the path.** Double-click the *Work Path* item in the Paths palette, type a name for the path, and press Enter (or Return on the Mac).

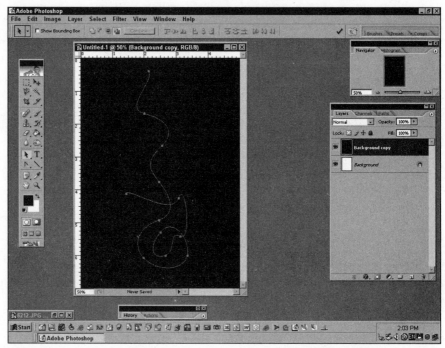

Figure 8-30: A series of curved segments, tweaked a bit afterward with the Convert Point tool

3. Use the Brushes palette to create a custom brush. For this example, the Brushes palette has been used to set up an 80-pixel brush (Spacing set to 60%, Angle at 35 degrees, Roundness set to 50), and then Shape Dynamics was used to set the Size Jitter to 50%. You can Alt-click (Option-click on the Mac) on the Stroke Path

icon at the bottom of the Paths palette to select the Simulate Pressure option, and let Photoshop stroke the path using a medium-gray color. The results are shown in Figure 8-31.

4. **Stroke the path again, using the Stroke Path command and new brush settings.** By decreasing the size of the second stroke (to just 40 pixels) and using a darker color, you get two overlapping strokes (or the appearance thereof). Figure 8-32 shows the result.

Tip

When you deselect the Spacing value in the Brush Tip Shape Options of the Brushes palette, Photoshop applies a single blob of paint for each point in a path.

Figure 8-31: The path with a specialized stroke applied. Turning on Simulate Pressure creates a tapered effect, similar to what you could achieve with a pressure-sensitive tablet.

Figure 8-32: A second stroke follows the first, because it follows a path.

Converting and saving paths

Photoshop provides two commands to switch between paths and selections, both of which are located in the Paths palette menu. The Make Selection command converts a path to a selection outline; the Make Work Path command converts a selection to a path. Regardless of how you create a path, you can save it with the current image, which enables you not only to reuse the path, but also to hide and display it as needed.

Converting paths to selections

When you choose the Make Selection command or Alt-click (Option-click on the Mac) the make selection icon, Photoshop displays the dialog box shown in Figure 8-33. You can specify whether to anti-alias or feather the selection and to what degree. You can also instruct Photoshop to combine the prospective selection outline with any existing selection in the image. The Operation options correspond to the keyboard functions discussed in the section "Manually adding and subtracting" earlier in this chapter.

Figure 8-33: When you choose the Make Selection command, you have the option of combining the path with an existing selection.

Photoshop offers several alternatives to convert a path to a selection outline, all of which are more convenient than the Make Selection command:

✦ **Press Ctrl+Enter (Win) or ⌘-Return (Mac).** As long as a path, shape, or selection tool is active, this keyboard shortcut converts the path to a selection.

✦ **Ctrl-click (Win) or ⌘-click (Mac) the path name.** If a tool other than a path, shape, or selection tool is active, you can Ctrl-click (Win) or ⌘-click (Mac) the name of a path in the Paths palette. The path needn't be active.

✦ **Ctrl+Shift+Enter or Ctrl+Shift-click (⌘-Shift-Return or ⌘-Shift-click on the Mac).** To add the path to an existing selection, press Shift with one of the previous techniques.

✦ **Alt+Enter or Ctrl+Alt-click (Option-Return or ⌘-Option-click on the Mac).** Naturally, if you can add, you can subtract.

✦ **Shift+Alt+Enter or Ctrl+Shift+Alt-click (Shift-Option-Return or ⌘-Shift-Option-click on the Mac).** Now we're starting to get into some obscure stuff, but what's possible is possible. You select the intersection of a path and a selection outline by pressing a whole mess of keys.

All these techniques offer the advantage of hiding the path when converting the path to a selection, giving you full, unobstructed access to your selection outline.

Caution By contrast, the Make Selection command leaves the path on-screen in front of the converted selection. If you try to copy, cut, delete, or nudge the selection, you perform the operation on the path instead.

Converting selections to paths

You turn a selection into a path by choosing the Make Work Path command from the Paths palette. When you choose the command, Photoshop produces a dialog box containing a single option, Tolerance. Unlike the Tolerance options you've encountered so far, this one is accurate to $\frac{1}{10}$ pixel and has nothing to do with colors or brightness values. Rather, it works like the Curve Fit option for the Freeform Pen and Magnetic Pen. That is, it permits you to specify Photoshop's sensitivity to twists and turns in a selection outline. The value you type determines how far the path can vary from the original selection. The lowest possible value, 0.5, not only ensures that Photoshop retains every nuance of the selection, but also can result in overly complicated paths with an abundance of points. If you type the highest value, 10, Photoshop rounds the path and uses few points. If you plan on editing the path, you probably won't want to venture any lower than 2.0, the default setting.

To bypass the Make Work Path dialog box and turn your selection into a path using the current Tolerance settings, click the Make Path icon at the bottom of the Paths palette.

Saving paths with an image

As mentioned at the beginning of the paths discussion, saving a path is an integral step in the path-creation process. You can store every path you draw and keep it right where you need it in case you decide later to reselect an area. Because Photoshop defines paths as compact mathematical equations, they take up virtually no room when you save an image to disk — so you can make as many paths as you need in a given image and not worry about the impact on your hard drive.

You save one or more paths by choosing the Save Path command from the Paths palette menu or by simply double-clicking the italicized *Work Path* item in the scrolling list. After you perform the save operation, during which you name the path, the path name appears in nonitalicized characters in the palette.

A path listed in the palette can include any number of separate paths. In fact, if you save a path and then set about drawing another one, Photoshop automatically adds the new path in with the saved path. To start a new path under a new name, you first must hide the existing path. Or click the new path icon — the little page at the bottom of the Paths palette — to establish an independent path. To hide paths, you can click the empty portion of the scrolling list below the last saved path name. You can even hide unsaved paths in this way. If you hide an unsaved path and then begin drawing a new one, however, the unsaved path is deleted, never to return again.

Importing and Exporting Paths

Paths are useful not only for working in Photoshop, but also for importing images into drawing programs, such as Illustrator and FreeHand, and into page-layout programs, such as InDesign and QuarkXPress. By saving a path as a clipping path, you can mask regions of an image so that it appears transparent when placed in other programs that support clipping paths.

In addition, you can swap paths directly with the most recent versions of Illustrator and FreeHand. That way, you can take advantage of the more advanced path-creation features found in those programs. You can even copy and paste paths into After Effects for use as masks or even motion paths.

The last few sections of this chapter explain some of these added uses for your Photoshop paths.

Swapping paths with Illustrator

You can exchange paths between Photoshop and Illustrator or FreeHand by using the Clipboard. This special cross-application compatibility feature expands and simplifies a variety of path-editing functions.

Caution   To avoid having problems transferring data between Photoshop and Illustrator, go into Illustrator, choose Edit ⇨ Preferences ⇨ Files & Clipboards, and select the AICB option. I also recommend that you select the Preserve Paths option when using Illustrator to alter Photoshop paths.

Suppose that you want to scale and rotate a path. Select the path in Photoshop with the black arrow tool and copy it to the Clipboard by pressing Ctrl+C (⌘-C on the Mac). Then switch to Illustrator, paste the path, and edit as desired. About 95 percent of Illustrator's capabilities are devoted to the task of editing paths, so you have many more options at your disposal in Illustrator than in Photoshop. When you finish modifying the path, copy it again, switch to Photoshop, and paste.

When you paste an Illustrator path into Photoshop, the dialog box shown in Figure 8-34 gives you the option of rendering the path to pixels (just as you can render an Illustrator EPS document using File ⇨ Open), keeping the path information intact, or creating a new shape layer. Select the Paths option to add the copied paths to the selected item in the Paths palette. (If no item is selected, Photoshop creates a new *Work Path* item.) You can then use the path to create a selection outline or whatever you want.

Figure 8-34: When pasting a path copied from Illustrator, Photoshop greets you with this dialog box.

Tip   Things can get pretty confusing in the Clipboard, especially when you're switching applications. If you copy something from Illustrator, but the Paste command is dimmed in Photoshop, you may be able to force the issue a little. If you're using a PC, you may simply need to wake up the Clipboard by opening the Windows Clipbook Viewer (Start ⇨ Programs ⇨ Accessories ⇨ System Tools ⇨ Clipbook Viewer). Don't worry if you see a message about an unsupported format or if the image looks like a complete mess. Just minimize the viewer window and try to paste again.

Note You can copy paths from Photoshop and paste them into Illustrator or some other drawing program regardless of the setting of the Export Clipboard option in the Preferences dialog box. That option affects only pixels. Paths are so tiny, Photoshop always exports them.

Exporting to Illustrator

If you don't have enough memory to run both Illustrator and Photoshop at the same time, you can export Photoshop paths to disk and then open them in Illustrator. To export all paths in the current image, choose File ⇨ Export ⇨ Paths to Illustrator. Photoshop saves the paths as a fully editable Illustrator document. This scheme enables you to trace images exactly with paths in Photoshop and then combine those paths as objects with the exported EPS version of the image in Illustrator. Whereas tracing an image in Illustrator can prove a little tricky because of resolution differences and other previewing limitations, you can trace images in Photoshop as accurately as you like.

Note Unfortunately, Illustrator provides no equivalent function to export paths for use in Photoshop, nor can Photoshop open Illustrator documents from disk and interpret them as paths. This means the Clipboard is the only way to take a path created or edited in Illustrator and use it in Photoshop.

Retaining transparent areas in an image

Adobe's object-oriented design programs, InDesign 2 and Illustrator 10 (and later), can read transparency straight from a native Photoshop (PSD) file. However, in virtually every other program — including popular applications like QuarkXPress and FreeHand — any image file, whether it contains transparent pixels or not, comes in as a fully opaque rectangle. Even if the image appeared partially transparent in Photoshop — on a layer, for example — the pixels will be filled with white or some other color. In cases like this, you need to establish a *clipping path* to mask portions of an image that you want to appear transparent. Elements that lie inside the clipping path are opaque; elements outside the clipping path are transparent. Photoshop enables you to export an image in the EPS format with an object-oriented clipping path intact. When you import the image, it appears premasked with a perfectly smooth perimeter, as illustrated by the clipped image in Figure 8-35.

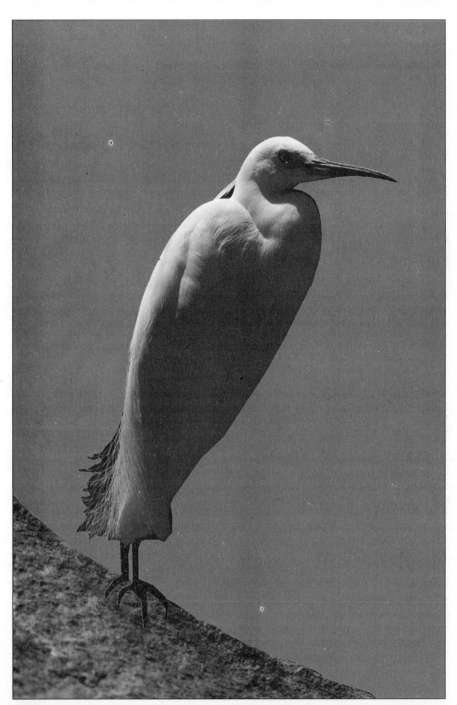

Figure 8-35: After defining the paths as clipping paths, the image was exported in EPS format, imported into Illustrator, and set against a gray background for contrast.

The following steps explain how to assign a set of saved paths as clipping paths.

STEPS: Saving an Image with Clipping Paths

1. Draw one or more paths around the portions of the image that you want to appear opaque. Remember, the areas outside the paths will be transparent.

2. Save the paths. Double-click the *Work Path* item in the Paths palette, type a path name, and press Enter or Return. You should try to use a name that's memorable, so you're not scratching your head six months or a year from now when you have to revisit this image and figure out what in the world you were thinking.

3. Choose the Clipping Path command from the Paths palette menu, as shown in Figure 8-36. Photoshop displays the dialog box shown at the top of the figure, asking you to select the saved path you want to assign as the clipping path. Don't go looking for your work path in this list — you can't make the *Work Path* a clipping path; you must save it as a named path first.

Note   If you like, type a value in the Flatness option box. This option enables you to simplify the clipping paths by printing otherwise fluid curves as polygons. The Flatness value represents the distance — between 0.2 and 100, in printer pixels — that the polygon may vary from the true mathematical curve. A higher value leads to a polygon with fewer sides. This means it looks chunkier, but it also prints more quickly. I recommend a value of 3. Many experts say you can go as high as 7 when printing to an imagesetter without seeing the straight edges. But it depends on how much of a perfectionist you are. If you're as much of a nerd about these things as I am, 3 will seem like a much safer bet.

4. Choose File ➪ Save As, select Photoshop EPS from the Format pop-up menu, and press Enter or Return. Select the desired Preview and Encoding settings and then press Enter or Return. Photoshop saves the EPS image with masked transparencies to disk.

Note   InDesign and PageMaker support clipping paths saved as TIFFs. So if you plan on placing the image in one of those programs, you can save the image in TIFF instead of EPS in Step 4.

Figure 8-37 shows an enhanced version of the clipped image shown in Figure 8-35. In addition to exporting the image with clipping paths in the EPS format, the paths were saved to disk by choosing File ➪ Export ➪ Paths to Illustrator. In Illustrator, the exported paths were used to create the outline around the clipped image. The background features repeated, reduced versions of the paths, and enlarged, black-filled versions of the path, as well, creating ominous-looking shadows of the bird. An Outer Glow was applied to the large birds, too. It may look like a complex job, but thanks to the paths, the only drawing required was the creation of the two initial Photoshop paths, and the rest was simple — adding type and a shape.

Figure 8-36: Choose the Clipping Path command from the Paths palette menu (bottom) and then select the path that you want to use from the Clipping Path dialog box (top).

Be prepared for your images to grow by leaps and bounds when imported into Illustrator. An EPS illustration such as the one shown in Figure 8-37 can consume six times as much space on disk as the original Photoshop image saved as a TIFF.

When used in excess, clipping paths can present problems for the most sophisticated printing devices. You should use a clipping path only when it's absolutely necessary and can't be avoided. If you want to place an image against a bitmapped background, for example, do it in Photoshop, not in Illustrator, QuarkXPress, or any other application. This will enable the image to print much faster, and will prevent most potential printing glitches — at least those caused by the image itself.

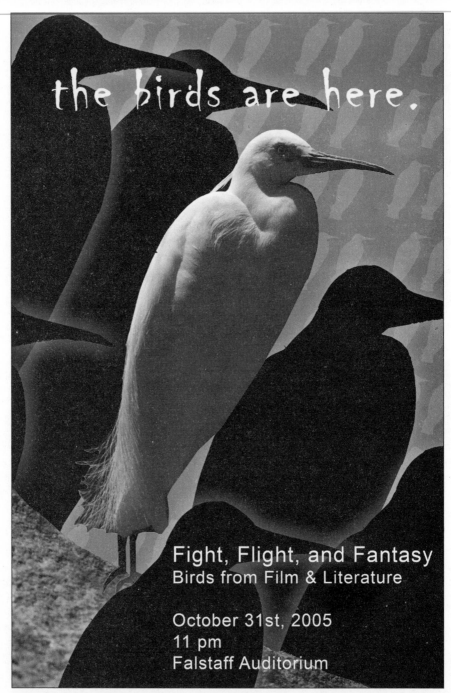

Figure 8-37: One simple photo, with paths created from its content, some type, and voila! — the result is this announcement that will send anyone with ornithophobia running from the room.

Summary

In this chapter, you learned special tricks that work with only the marquee tools, and found out how to gain greater control over your fine selections with the Polygonal and Magnetic Lasso tools. You also learned to select based on pixels with the Magic Wand, and to create paths and selections with the Pen tool.

Because selections are often in need of a tweak, you learned manual and automatic methods for editing selection outlines, and how to use the Feather command. You also learned to move and clone selections and selection outlines, and to fill and stroke your selections and paths.

✦   ✦   ✦

Masks and Extractions

✦   ✦   ✦   ✦

In This Chapter

An introduction
to masking

Painting inside a
selection outline

Using the Quick
Mask mode to modify
selection outlines

Drawing gradient
selections in the
Quick Mask mode

Using the Magic
Eraser, Background
Eraser, and Extract
command to clip
away the image
background

Selecting images
with the Color Range
command

Saving a selection
outline to a mask
channel

Converting channels
into selections

Creating a highly
accurate mask based
on the image itself

✦   ✦   ✦   ✦

Most Photoshop users don't use masks. It may be that masks seem complicated, or they may strike you as being more trouble than they're worth. It's quite likely you've played with the basic selection tools — namely the marquee tools, the lassos, and the Magic Wand — and felt that these were good enough. On occasion, you may even resort to the Pen tools, which let you draw precise curves and convert them to selections or clipping paths. You may, in fact, be so confident and content with these tools that you venture to wonder what more a skilled Photoshop craftsman could possibly need.

Quite a bit, as it turns out. Every one of the tools just mentioned is only moderately suited to the task of selecting images. The lasso tools let you create free-form selections, but none of the tools — not even the Magnetic Lasso — can account for differences in focus levels. The Magic Wand selects areas of color, but it usually leaves important colors behind, and the edges of its selection outlines often appear ragged and ugly. The Pen tool is extremely precise, but it results in mechanical outlines that may appear incongruous with the natural imagery they contain.

Masks offer all the benefits of the other tools. With masks, you can create free-form selections, select areas of color, and generate amazingly precise selections. Masks also address all the deficiencies associated with the selection tools. They can account for different levels of focus, they give you absolute control over the look of the edges, and they create selections every bit as natural as the image itself.

In fact, a mask *is* the image itself. Masks use pixels to select pixels. Masks are your way to make Photoshop see what you see using the data inherent in the photograph. Masks enable you to devote every one of Photoshop's powerful capabilities to the task of creating a selection outline. Masks are, without a doubt, the most accurate selection mechanism available in Photoshop.

If you're not entirely clear about what term *mask* means, then just continue reading. You'll be pleasantly surprised.

A mask is nothing more than your good ol' standard selection outline expressed as a grayscale image.

✦ Selected areas appear white.

✦ Deselected areas appear black.

✦ Partially selected parts of the image appear gray. Feathered edges are also expressed in shades of gray, from light gray near the selected area to dark gray near the deselected area.

Figure 9-1 shows a selection outline and its equivalent mask. The image to the left shows a selection outline delineated by Photoshop's traditional marching ants and softened with the feather command (Select ➪ Feather). These little insects only show you the gross area of the selection. If you look to the right, you see the same selection expressed as a mask. The selected area is white *(unmasked)* and the deselected area is black *(masked)*. You can't see the feathering effect in the selection outline — marching ants can't accurately express softened edges — but in the equivalent mask it's completely visible.

When you look at the Quick Mask view in Figure 9-1, you may wonder where the heck the image went. One of the wonderful things about masks is that you can view them independently of an image, as in Figure 9-1, or with an image, as in Figure 9-2. In the second figure, the mask is expressed as a color overlay. You can't tell here, but by default the color of the overlay is a translucent red, like a sheet of rubylith film used in printing. Areas covered with the rubylith are masked (deselected); areas that appear normal — without any red tint — are unmasked (selected). When you return to the standard marching ants mode, any changes you make to your image affect only the unmasked areas.

Figure 9-1: The outline of a feathered selection (left) and the physical mask itself (right)

Figure 9-2: In Quick Mask mode, you see how the mask actually affects the image.

Now that you know roughly what masks are (the definition becomes progressively clearer throughout this chapter), the question remains, what good are they? Because a mask is essentially an independent grayscale image, you can edit the mask using paint and edit tools, filters, color-correction options, and almost every other Photoshop function. You can even use the selection tools, as discussed in Chapter 8. With all these features at your disposal, you can't help but create a more accurate selection outline in a shorter amount of time.

Painting and Editing Inside Selections

Before diving into masking techniques, it's a good idea to start with a warm-up topic: *selection masking*. When you were in grade school, you may have had a teacher who nagged you to color within the lines. If so, your teacher would have loved this incredibly straightforward feature. In Photoshop, all selection outlines act as masks — hence the term *selection masking*. (And you thought this chapter was going to be hard.) Regardless of which tool you use to create the selection — Marquee, Lasso, Magic Wand, or Pen — Photoshop permits you to paint or edit only the selected area. The paint can't enter the deselected (or protected) portions of the image, so you can't help but paint inside the lines. If you dread painting inside an image because you're afraid you'll screw it up, selection masking is the answer.

Figures 9-3 through 9-6 show a biology class skeleton subject to some pretty free-and-easy use of the paint and edit tools. The following steps describe how these images were created using a selection mask.

STEPS: Painting and Editing Inside a Selection Mask

1. **Select the skeleton.** You can see the selection outline in the right example of Figure 9-3.

Figure 9-3: Starting with the image shown at left, a selection outline is drawn around the skeleton. The selection is then inversed, and the background, as you can see in the right-hand image, becomes the selection.

2. **Reverse the selection with the Inverse command.** You want to edit the area surrounding the head, so choose Select ⇨ Inverse (Ctrl+Shift+I under Windows or ⌘-Shift-I on the Mac) to reverse which areas are selected and which are not.

3. **Press Ctrl+Backspace (⌘-Delete on the Mac) to fill the selected area with the background color.** In this case, the background color is gray, as shown in the right half of Figure 9-3.

4. **Paint inside the selection mask.** But first choose View ⇨ Extras (Ctrl+H or ⌘-H). This toggles off those infernal marching ants, which enable you to paint without being distracted. (In fact, this is one of the most essential reasons for toggling the Extras command.)

5. **Select the Brush tool and express yourself.** With the foreground color set to black, click and drag around the perimeter of the skeleton to set it apart from its gray background, and then rough in an outline around the black using white, as shown in Figure 9-4.

Figure 9-4: Painting inside the selection mask with a 150-pixel brush

6. **Put the Smudge tool to work.** The tool's Strength value is set to 80 percent by pressing 8. Then, by clicking and dragging from inside the unselected area outward a few dozen times, a series of curlicues is created. As shown in Figure 9-5, the Smudge tool can smear colors from inside the protected area, but it does not apply these colors until you go inside the selection. This is an important point to remember because it demonstrates that although the protected area is safe from all changes, the selected area may be influenced by colors from protected pixels.

Figure 9-5: Clicking and dragging with the Smudge tool smears colors from pixels outside the selection mask without changing the appearance of those pixels.

7. **Add some embellishments.** As you can see in Figure 9-6, the selection mask comes in handy when using the Burn tool to darken around the eye sockets and teeth. Out of a desire to create fabulous hair, the new hair layer was duplicated a few times, a handful of filters (Filter ⇨ Distort ⇨ Ocean Ripple, as well as Filter ⇨ Pixelate ⇨ Pointillize) were applied, and the layers sandwiched using various blend modes (see Chapter 13).

Figure 9-6: Side Show Bob grabbing a live wire, or a failed design for a Grateful Dead album cover — you decide.

Working in Quick Mask Mode

Selection masks give you an idea of what masks are all about, but they only scrape the surface. The rest of this chapter revolves around using masks to define complex selection outlines.

The most straightforward environment for creating a mask is the *Quick Mask mode*. In the Quick Mask mode, a selection is expressed as a rubylith overlay. All deselected areas appear coated with red, and selected areas appear without red coating. You can then edit the mask as desired and exit the Quick Mask mode to return to the standard selection outline. The Quick Mask mode is — as its name implies — expeditious and convenient, with none of the trappings or permanence of more conventional masks. It's kind of like a fast-food restaurant — you use it when you aren't overly concerned about quality and you want to get in and out in a hurry.

How the Quick Mask mode works

Typically, you'll at least want to rough out a selection with the standard selection tools before entering the Quick Mask mode. Then you can concentrate on refining and modifying your selection inside the quick mask, rather than having to create the selection from scratch. (Naturally, this is only a rule of thumb. Feel free to violate it whenever you find it necessary.)

To enter the Quick Mask mode, click the Quick Mask mode icon in the Toolbox, as shown in Figure 9-7, or press Q. Starting with the same selection used on the head in the previous steps section (the selection was inverted yet again so that the background was selected), then Q was pressed and the image shown in Figure 9-7 resulted. The head receives the mask because it is not selected. (In Figure 9-7, the mask appears as a light gray coating; on your color screen, the mask appears in red.) The area outside the head looks the same as it always did because it's selected and, therefore, not masked.

Notice that the selection outline disappears when you enter the Quick Mask mode. This happens because the outline temporarily ceases to exist. Any operations you apply affect the mask itself and leave the underlying image untouched. When you click the marching ants mode icon (to the left of the Quick Mask mode icon) or press Q, Photoshop converts the mask back to a selection outline and again enables you to edit the image.

Note

If you click the Quick Mask mode icon and nothing changes on-screen, your computer isn't broken; you simply didn't select anything before you entered the Quick Mask mode. When nothing is selected, Photoshop makes the entire image open for editing. In other words, everything's selected. (Only a smattering of commands under the Edit, Layer, and Select menus require something to be selected before they work.) If everything is selected, the mask is white; therefore, the quick mask overlay is transparent and you don't see any difference on-screen. This is another reason why it's better to select something before you enter the Quick Mask mode —you get an immediate sense you're accomplishing something.

Also, Photoshop enables you to specify whether you want the red mask coating to cover selected areas or deselected areas. For information on how to change this setting, see the section "Changing the red coating."

In the Quick Mask mode, you can edit the mask in the following ways:

✦ **Subtracting from a selection.** Paint with black to add red coating and, thus, deselect areas of the image. This means you can selectively protect portions of your image by merely painting over them.

✦ **Adding to a selection:** Paint with white to remove red coating and, thus, add to the selection outline, as demonstrated in the top half of Figure 9-8. You can use the Eraser Tool to whittle away at the masked area (assuming the background color is set to white). Or you can swap the foreground and background colors so you can paint in white with one of the painting tools.

Quick Mask mode

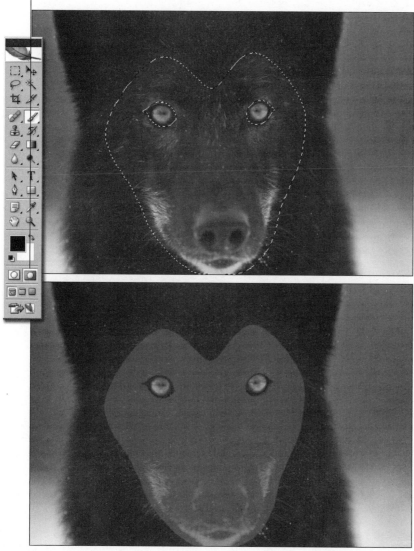

Figure 9-7: You can see the marching ants-style selection in the upper image, indicating that the eyes and most of the head are selected. Clicking the Quick Mask mode icon instructs Photoshop to express the selection temporarily as a rubylith overlay (bottom).

Figure 9-8: Painted in white with a soft-edged brush to enlarge the selected area (top). After switching out of the Quick Mask mode, the Brush and Smudge tools (bottom) have been used liberally.

✦ **Adding feathered selections.** If you paint with a shade of gray, you add feathered selections. You also can feather an outline by painting with black or white with a soft brush shape, as shown in Figure 9-8. Here, a soft-edged brush is applying white paint, adding a nice feathered edge to the top of the selection. Then after reentering the world of the marching ants, a little more painting and smudging creates the image on the bottom of the figure.

✦ **Cloning selection outlines.** If you have a selection outline that you want to repeat in several locations throughout the image, the Quick Mask is your friend. Select the transparent area with one of the standard selection tools, press and hold Ctrl+Alt (⌘-Option on the Mac), and drag the selection to a new location in the image, as shown in Figure 9-9. Although the Rectangular Marquee tool is used in the figure, the Magic Wand tool also works well for this purpose. To select an anti-aliased selection outline with the Wand tool, set the Tolerance value to about 10 and be sure the Anti-aliased option is selected. Then click inside the selection. It's that easy.

✦ **Transforming selection outlines.** You can scale or rotate a selection independently of the image, just as you can with the Transform Selection command (covered in Chapter 8). Enter the Quick Mask mode, select the mask using one of the standard selection tools, and choose Edit ➭ Free Transform or press Ctrl+T (⌘-T on the Mac). (See Chapter 12 for more information on Free Transform and related commands.)

These are only a few of the unique effects you can achieve by editing a selection in the Quick Mask mode. Others involve tools and capabilities not yet discussed, such as filters and color corrections.

When you finish editing your selection outlines, click the marching ants mode icon (to the left of the Quick Mask mode icon) or press Q again to return to the marching ants mode. Your selection outlines again appear flanked by marching ants, and all tools and commands return to their normal image-editing functions.

Tip

The Quick Mask mode offers a splendid environment for feathering one selection outline while leaving another hard-edged or anti-aliased. Granted, because most selection tools offer built-in feathering options, you can accomplish this task without resorting to the Quick Mask mode. But the Quick Mask mode enables you to change feathering selectively after drawing selection outlines, something you can't accomplish with Select ➭ Feather. The Quick Mask mode also enables you to see exactly how your actions affect the selection — which is something the marching ants aren't capable of.

Figure 9-9: To clone the eye selections, marquee around them. Then press Ctrl+Alt (⌘-Option on the Mac) and drag it into position below the original eye. This is done a second time and then repeated for the wolf's other eyeball (top).This makes it possible to switch out of Quick Mask mode and paint details into the new eye sockets (bottom).

Changing the red coating

By default, the protected region of an image appears in translucent red in the Quick Mask mode, but if your image contains a lot of red, the mask can be difficult to see. Luckily, you can change it to any color and any degree of opacity that you like. To do so, double-click the Quick Mask icon in the Toolbox (or double-click the Quick Mask item in the Channels palette) to display the dialog box shown in Figure 9-10.

✦ **Color Indicates.** Choose Selected Areas to reverse the color coating so that the translucent red coating covers selected areas and deselected areas appear normally. Choose Masked Areas (the default setting) to cover deselected areas in color.

Tip   You can reverse the color coating without ever entering the Quick Mask Options dialog box. Simply Alt-click (Win) or Option-click (Mac) the Quick Mask icon in the Toolbox to toggle between coating the masked or selected portions of the image. The icon itself changes to reflect your choice.

Figure 9-10: Double-click the Quick Mask mode icon to access the Quick Mask Options dialog box. You then can change the color and opacity of the protected or selected areas when viewed in the Quick Mask mode.

✦ **Color.** Click the Color icon to display the Color Picker dialog box and select a different color coating. (If you don't know how to use this dialog box, see Chapter 4.) You can lift a color with the Eyedropper after the Color Picker dialog box appears; just keep in mind that you probably want to use a color that isn't in the image so that you can see the mask better.

✦ **Opacity.** Type a value to change the opacity of the translucent color that coats the image. A value of 100 percent makes the coating absolutely opaque.

Change the color coating to achieve the most acceptable balance between being able to view and edit your selection and being able to view your image.

Gradations as masks

If you think that the Feather command is a hot tool for creating softened selection outlines, wait until you get a load of gradations in the Quick Mask mode. There's no better way to create fading effects than selecting an image with the Gradient tool.

Fading an image

In the following example, you'll create a gradient mask to fade part of an image into nothingness. Figure 9-11 brings the handy biology class skeleton in the left, which will fade in from the ground up onto the stormy plain over on the right.

Figure 9-11: You can create a linear gradient in the Quick Mask mode to make the skeleton (left) rise from the stormy plain (right).

Here's how: Switch to the Quick Mask mode by pressing Q. Then use the Gradient tool to draw a linear gradation from black to white. (Chapter 6 explains exactly how to do so.) The white portion of the gradation represents the area you want to select. To select the top portion of the mask shown in Figure 9-12, draw the gradation as shown in the first example of the figure.

Figure 9-12: After drawing a linear gradation in the Quick Mask mode over the bottom of the image (left), the image was hidden and the Add Noise filter applied with an Amount of 10 (right).

Banding can be a problem when you use a gradation as a mask. To eliminate the banding effect, apply the Add Noise filter at a low setting several times. To create the right example in Figure 9-12, apply Add Noise using an Amount value of 10 and the Uniform distribution option.

Tip   In the right example of Figure 9-12, the image is hidden so that only the gradient mask is visible. As the figure shows, the Channels palette lists the *Quick Mask* item in italics. This is because Photoshop regards the Quick Mask as a temporary channel. You can hide the image and view the gradient mask in black and white by clicking the eyeball in front of the color composite view, in this case RGB. Or just press tilde (~) to hide the image. Press tilde again to view the gradient mask and image together.

To apply the gradation as a selection, return to the marching ants mode by pressing Q. Then Ctrl-drag (⌘-drag on the Mac) the selected portion of the mask and drop it onto the stormy plain, as seen in Figure 9-13. Then press Ctrl+T (⌘-T) to enter the free transform mode. Scale and Distort the image by Ctrl-dragging (⌘-dragging) the corner handles (see Chapter 12). Further enhancement is achieved by adding an outer glow, and five little unfaded copies of the skeleton to stand in awe before the big guy.

Figure 9-13: The result of selecting the upper portion of the skeleton using a gradient mask and then Ctrl-dragging (⌘-dragging on the Mac) and dropping the selection onto the plain. Throw in a little more tweaking, and you've got a rather Bergman-esque tableau.

Applying special effects gradually

You also can use gradations in the Quick Mask mode to fade the outcomes of filters and other automated special effects. For example, applying a filter around the edges of the image that appears in Figure 9-14. Begin by deselecting everything in the image by pressing Ctrl+D (⌘-D on the Mac) and switching to the Quick Mask mode. Then select the Gradient tool, and choose the linear gradient style icon in the Options bar, and select the Foreground to Transparent gradient from the Gradient drop-down palette. You also want to select the Transparency option in the Options bar.

Figure 9-14: This time around, surround the foreground image with a gradual filtering effect.

Next, press D to make the foreground color black. Then drag with the Gradient tool from each of the four corners of the image inward to create a series of short gradations that trace around the focal point of the image, as shown in Figure 9-15. (The image is hidden here so that you see the mask in black and white.) Because the Foreground to Transparent option is selected, Photoshop adds each gradation to the previous gradation.

To jumble the pixels in the mask (preventing banding), apply Filter ⇨ Noise ⇨ Add Noise (in this case an Amount value of 10 was used). You see the effect in Figure 9-15.

Tip

Of course, as stated previously, white is selected and black is deselected. So now you need the edges to appear white and the inside to appear black — the opposite of what you see in Figure 9-15. No problem. All you do is press Ctrl+I (⌘-I on the Mac) to invert the image. Inverting inside the Quick Mask mode produces the same effect as applying Select ⇨ Inverse to a selection.

Figure 9-15: Inside the Quick Mask mode, each of the four corners has been dragged with the Gradient tool (as indicated by the arrows).

Finally, it's time to switch back to the marching ants mode by pressing Q. Apply Filter ⇨ Render ⇨ Difference Clouds to get the atmospheric effect you see in Figure 9-16. While somewhat less dynamic for the black and white version of the image shown here, when you try it, your color monitor will show the full effect.

Figure 9-16: For good measure, a little lightening was added to those clouds by nabbing such an image, adding it to a new layer, and using the selection to remove its center. Then the layer's opacity was lowered to 50 percent.

Tip   The corners of the mask in Figure 9-15 are soft and rounded, but you can achieve all kinds of corner effects with the Gradient tool. For harsher corners, select the Foreground to Background gradient and select Lighten from the Mode pop-up menu in the Options bar. For some *really* unusual corner treatments, try the Difference and Exclusion brush modes.

Generating Masks Automatically

In addition to the Quick Mask mode and selection masking, Photoshop offers a few tools that automate the masking process — well, *some* parts of the process. You still need to provide some input to tell the program exactly what you're trying to mask. These tools are the Magic Eraser, Background Eraser, and Extract command. You've already taken a look at the standard Eraser tool (Chapter 7), but in case you're skipping around, here's the rundown: The Eraser paints in the background color when used on the background layer. When applied to a layer, it erases pixels to reveal the layers below. The Magic Eraser works like the Fill tool but in reverse. When you click with the Magic Eraser, you delete a range of similarly colored pixels. The Background Eraser, as its name implies, erases the background from an image and leaves the foreground intact — or at least that's what happens if you use the tool correctly. Otherwise, it just erases everything.

Tip   You can cycle through the erasers by Alt-clicking (Option-clicking on the Mac) the eraser icon in the Toolbox or by pressing E (or Shift+E).

The Magic Eraser

As recently mentioned, the Magic Eraser, found on the same flyout as the regular Eraser, erases similarly colored pixels. If you're familiar with the Magic Wand, covered in Chapter 8, using the Magic Eraser is a cinch. The two tools operate virtually identically, except the Wand selects and the Magic Eraser erases.

When you click a pixel with the Magic Eraser, Photoshop identifies a range of similarly colored pixels, just as it does with the Magic Wand. But instead of selecting the pixels, the Magic Eraser makes them transparent, as demonstrated in Figure 9-17. Bear in mind that in Photoshop, transparency requires a separate layer. So if the image consists of only the background, Photoshop automatically converts the background into a layer with nothing underneath. As a result, you get the checkerboard pattern shown in the second example in the figure — transparency with nothing underneath.

Note The Lock buttons in the Layers palette affect the Magic Eraser. When you have no buttons selected, the Magic Eraser works as just described. But if you lock transparent pixels, the Magic Eraser paints opaque pixels in the background color and leaves transparent areas untouched. You can't use the Magic Eraser at all on a layer for which you've locked image pixels.

Figure 9-17: To delete a homogeneously colored background, such as the sky in this picture, click inside it with the Magic Eraser (bottom).

You can further alter the performance of the Magic Eraser through the controls in the Options bar, shown in Figure 9-18 and described in the following list. Except for the Opacity value, these options work the same way as the options for the Magic Wand:

✦ **Tolerance.** Just like the Magic Wand's Tolerance value, this one determines how similar a neighboring color has to be to the clicked color to be made transparent. A higher value affects more colors; a lower value affects fewer colors. (Remember, any change to the Tolerance value affects the *next* click you make; it does not affect the existing transparent area.)

✦ **Anti-aliased.** To create a soft fringe around the outline of your transparent area, leave this option selected. If you'd prefer a hard edge — as when using a very low Tolerance value, for example — deselect this option.

Figure 9-18: The Magic Eraser options are nearly identical to the options for the Magic Wand.

✦ **Contiguous.** Select this option and the Magic Eraser deletes *contiguous* colors only — that is, similar colors that touch each other. If you prefer to delete all pixels of a certain color — such as the background pixels in Figure 9-17 that are divided from the rest of the sky by the bat — deselect the Contiguous option.

✦ **Use All Layers.** When selected, this option tells Photoshop to factor in all visible layers when erasing pixels. The tool continues to erase pixels on only the active layer, but it erases them according to colors found across all layers.

✦ **Opacity.** Lower this value to make the erased pixels translucent instead of transparent. Low values result in more subtle effects than high ones.

The more magical Background Eraser

The Magic Eraser is as simple to use as a hammer, and every bit as indelicate. It pounds away pixels, but it leaves lots of color fringes and shredded edges in its wake. You might as well select an area with the Magic Wand and press Backspace (Win) or Delete (Mac). The effect is the same.

The more capable, more scrupulous tool is the Background Eraser. As demonstrated in Figure 9-19, the Background Eraser deletes background pixels as you drag over them. (Again, if the image consists only of a background, Photoshop converts the background into a new layer to accommodate the transparency.) The tool is intelligent enough to erase background pixels and retain foreground pixels provided that — and here's the clincher — you keep the cross in the center of the eraser cursor squarely centered on a background color pixel. Move the cross over a foreground pixel, and the background eraser deletes foreground pixels as well. As Figure 9-20 demonstrates, it's the position of the cross that counts.

> **Note** As is the case when you work with the Magic Eraser, the Lock buttons in the Layers palette affect the Background Eraser. In this case, locking image pixels prevents you from using the Background Eraser. Be aware that if you drag over a selection that's already partially transparent, locking transparent pixels does not protect the selection from the Background Eraser.

Figure 9-19: Click and drag around the edge of an image with the Background Eraser to erase the background but leave the foreground intact.

You can also modify the performance of the Background Eraser using the Options bar controls pictured in Figure 9-21. These options are a bit intimidating at first, but they're actually pretty easy to use:

✦ **Limits.** Choose Contiguous from this pop-up menu, and the background eraser deletes colors inside the cursor as long as they are contiguous with the color immediately under the cross. To erase all similarly colored pixels, whether contiguous or not, select Discontiguous. One additional option, Find Edges, searches for edges as you brush and emphasizes them. Although interesting, Find Edges has a habit of producing halos and is rarely useful.

✦ **Tolerance.** Raise the Tolerance value to erase more colors at a time; lower the value to erase fewer colors. Low Tolerance values are useful for erasing around tight and delicate details, such as hair.

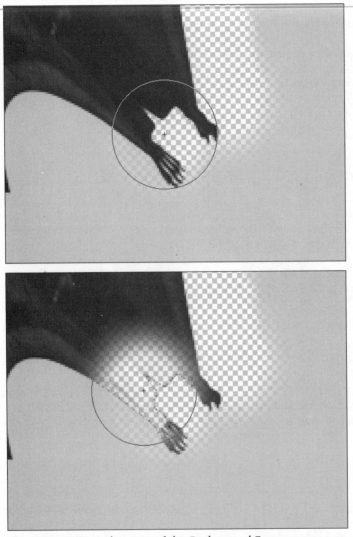

Figure 9-20: Keep the cross of the Background Eraser cursor over the background you want to erase (top). If you inadvertently move the cross over the foreground, the foreground gets erased (bottom).

Figure 9-21: The seemingly intimidating Background Eraser options are actually pretty intuitive.

✦ **Protect Foreground Color.** Select this option to prevent the current foreground color (by default, black) from ever being erased.

✦ **Sampling.** This pop-up menu determines how the Background Eraser determines what it should and should not erase. The default setting, Continuous, tells the eraser to continuously reappraise which colors should be erased as you drag. If the background is pretty homogenous, you might prefer to use the Once option, which samples the background color when you first click and erases only that color throughout the drag. Select Background Swatch to erase only the current background color (by default, white).

The still more magical Extract command

Like the Magic Eraser and Background Eraser, the Extract command aims to separate — extract, if you will — an image element from its surroundings. After you draw a rough highlight around the subject you want to retain, Photoshop analyzes the situation and automatically deletes everything but the subject. Extract is only slightly more powerful than the background eraser and several times more complex. Some images respond very well to the command, others do not. That said, Extract can produce reasonably good results if you get the steps right. So take Extract for a test drive, as follows:

STEPS: Extracting Content from its Surroundings

1. **Choose Filter ➪ Extract, or press Ctrl+Alt+X (⌘-Option-X on the Mac).** Either way, Photoshop displays the large Extract dialog box shown in Figure 9-22.

Often, it's easier to Shift-click around the perimeter of an image than drag manually. Shift-clicking creates a straight highlight from one click point to the next. As long as you do a reasonably careful job, the performance of the Extract command won't be impaired.

2. **Select the Edge Highlighter tool.** Most likely, this tool is already active, but if not, press B to select it.

Select the Smart Highlighting option in the Tool Options section of the Extract dialog box to get some assistance in drawing your outline. Smart Highlighting seeks out edges in the image and places the highlight along them. When you select Smart Highlighting, your cursor becomes a circle with four inward-pointing lines. Keep the center of the circle over the edge between the subject and the background as you drag. This feature works best when your subject has well-defined edges, of course. Note that you can't Shift-click with the tool to draw straight segments when Smart Highlighting is active.

3. **Outline the subject that you want to retain.** In this case, it would be the bat, as shown in Figure 9-23. Be sure to either completely encircle the subject or, if the subject is partially cropped, trace all the way up against the outer boundaries of the photograph.

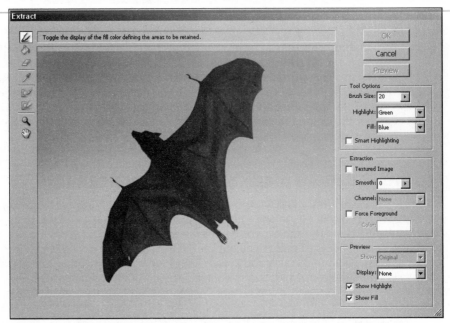

Figure 9-22: The Extract dialog box serves as a miniature masking laboratory, complete with a Toolbox and options.

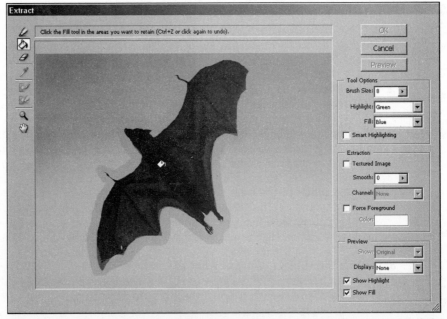

Figure 9-23: After tracing around the portion of the image you want to retain, click inside the outline with the Fill tool.

Ctrl-drag (Win) or ⌘-drag (Mac) to temporarily turn off Smart Highlighting without deselecting the option. Or go the opposite direction: Deselect the option and then Ctrl-drag (Win) or ⌘-drag (Mac) to temporarily take advantage of Smart Highlighting.

4. **As you trace, use the bracket keys, [and], to make the brush larger or smaller.** When you work with brushes from 1 to 9 pixels in diameter, each press of [or] changes the brush size by 1 pixel. The increment of change gets larger as you increase the brush size.

Small brush sizes result in sharper edges. Larger brush sizes are better for fragile, intricate detailing, such as hair, foliage, wispy fabric, bits of steel wool, thin pasta — you get the idea.

5. **If you make a mistake, press Ctrl+Z (⌘-Z on the Mac).** You get only one Undo level here — you can undo and redo only your last stroke with the Highlighter tool.

   If you want to erase more of the highlight, drag over the botched region with the Eraser tool (press E to access it from the keyboard) or press Alt (Option on the Mac) and drag with the Edge Highlighter tool. To delete the entire highlight and start over, press Alt+Backspace (Win) or Option-Delete (Mac).

6. **Navigate as needed.** If you can't see all of your image, you can access the Hand tool by pressing the space bar or clicking the Hand tool icon. You can also zoom by pressing Ctrl+plus or Ctrl+minus (⌘-plus or ⌘-minus on the Mac) or by using the Zoom tool.

7. **Select the Fill tool.** It's the one that looks like a paint bucket. To select the Fill tool from the keyboard, press G as you do to select the paint bucket in the regular Photoshop Toolbox.

8. **Click inside the subject of the image.** The highlighted outline should fill with color. If the fill color spills outside the outline, your outline probably has a break. Press Ctrl+Z (⌘-Z on the Mac) to undo the fill and then scroll the image with the Hand tool to find the break. Patch it with the Edge Highlighter and then click with the Fill tool again.

You also can click inside a filled area with the Fill tool or Eraser to remove the fill.

9. **Click Preview.** Before you can apply your prospective mask, you need to preview it so you can gauge the finished effect, as in Figure 9-24.

If you Shift-click with the Fill tool in Step 8, Photoshop fills the outline and processes the preview automatically, saving you the trouble of clicking Preview.

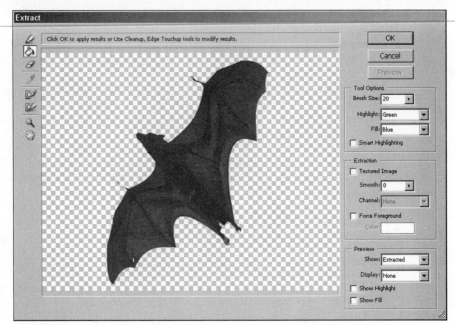

Figure 9-24: Click Preview to gauge the appearance of the final masked image.

10. **Edit the mask as needed.** You have several tools at your disposal. These tools are labeled in Figure 9-24, and you can read about them in the list following these steps.

11. **Click OK to delete the masked portion of the image.** If the image consisted of only a background, Photoshop converts it into a separate layer. You can then use the Move tool to drag the layer against a different background. In Figure 9-25, the bat has been set against a New Zealand sky. The composite isn't perfect, but it's not half bad for 5 to 10 minutes of work.

12. **After you exit the Extract window, fix any problems using the Background Eraser and History Brush.** Use the Background Eraser to erase stray pixels that you wish the Extract command had deleted. Use the History Brush to restore details that you wish the Extract command hadn't deleted.

Figure 9-25: Is the fruit bat from South America? Not that it matters — it's cruising over New Zealand now.

Back in Step 10, it was stated that you can refine the mask in the Extract dialog box. You can use the following techniques to touch up the mask before clicking OK to create it:

✦ **Drag with the cleanup tool (C) to change the opacity of the mask.** Press the number keys to adjust the pressure of the tool and thus alter the amount of opacity that the tool subtracts. To erase to full transparency, press 0, as you do when working with the Eraser on a layer. Press 9 for 90 percent transparency, 8 for 80 percent, and so on. Alt-drag (or Option-drag on the Mac) to add opacity.

✦ **Drag along the boundaries of the mask with the Edge Touchup tool (T) to sharpen the mask edges.** If the boundary between mask and subject isn't well defined, dragging with this tool adds opacity to the subject and removes it from the mask. In other words, it turns soft, feathery edges into crisp, clearly defined edges. Again, you can press the number keys to adjust the impact of the tool.

✦ **Raise the Smooth value to remove stray pixels from the mask.** A high value smoothes out the edges around the image and fills in holes. Basically, if your edges are a big mess, give this option a try.

✦ **Drag with the Edge Highlighter or Eraser Tool to edit the mask boundary.** When you select either tool, the original mask highlight reappears, and the tools work as they do when you initially draw the highlight. After you adjust the highlight, Shift-click inside it to redraw and preview the adjusted mask.

✦ **Choose an option from the Show pop-up menu to toggle between the original highlight and the extracted image preview.** You can press X to toggle between the two views without bothering with the pop-up menu.

That's 99 percent of what you need to know about the Extract command. For those of you who care to learn the other 1 percent, here's a quick rundown of the remaining options that appear along the right side of the Extract dialog box:

✦ **Highlight, Fill.** Use these pop-up menus to change the highlighter and fill colors. It doesn't matter what colors you use, as long as they show up well against the image.

✦ **Textured Image.** If your image is highly textured, try selecting this option. Much like the Smooth option, it helps smooth out jagged edges around the image.

✦ **Channel.** Advanced users may prefer to prepare the highlighter work by tracing around the image inside an independent mask channel, which you can create in the Channels palette before choosing the Extract command. Then load the mask by selecting it from the Channel pop-up menu. You can further modify the highlight using the Edge Highlighter and Eraser tools. One weirdness: When loading a mask, black in the mask channel represents the highlighted area and white represents the non-highlighted area. Strikes me as upside-down, but that's how it goes.

✦ **Force Foreground.** If the subject of your image is predominantly a single color, select Force Foreground and use the Eyedropper to sample the color in the image that you want to preserve. (Alternatively, you can define the color using the Color swatch, but it's much more work.) Then use the Edge Highlighter tool to paint over all occurrences of the foreground color. (Note that this option is an alternative to the Fill tool. When Force Foreground is selected, the Fill tool is dimmed.)

✦ **Display.** You don't have to preview the image against the transparent checkerboard background. You can also view it against white (White Matte) or some other color. Or you can view it as a mask, where white represents the opaque area and black the transparent area. (Ironically, you can't export the extraction as a mask—go figure.)

Tip

Press F to select the next display mode in the menu; press Shift+F to switch to the previous mode in the menu.

✦ **Show Highlight, Show Fill.** Use these options to hide and show the highlight and fill colors.

Tip

Before using the Extract command—or the Magic Eraser or Background eraser, for that matter—you may want to copy the image to a separate layer or take a snapshot of the image in the History palette. Either way, you have a backup in case things don't go exactly according to plan.

Using the Color Range command

Another convenient method for creating a mask is the Color Range command in the Select menu. This command enables you to generate selections based on color ranges. Use the familiar eyedropper cursor to specify colors that should be considered for selection and colors that you want to rule out. The Color Range command is a lot like the Magic Wand tool, except it enables you to select colors with more precision and to change the tolerance of the selection on the fly.

When you choose Select ➪ Color Range, Photoshop displays the Color Range dialog box shown in Figure 9-26. Like the Magic Wand with the Contiguous option deselected, Color Range selects areas of related color all across the image, whether or not the colors are immediate neighbors. Click in the image window to select and deselect colors, as you do with the Wand. But rather than adjusting a Tolerance value before you use the tool, you adjust a Fuzziness value any time you like. Photoshop dynamically updates the selection according to the new value. Think of Color Range as the Magic Wand on steroids.

Note

So why didn't the people at Adobe merely enhance the functionality of the Magic Wand instead of adding this strange command? The Color Range dialog box offers a preview of the mask—something a tool can't do—which is pretty essential for gauging the accuracy of your selection. And the Magic Wand is convenient, if nothing else. If Adobe were to combine the two functions, you would lose functionality.

When you move your cursor outside the Color Range dialog box, it changes to an eyedropper. Use it to click anywhere within your image to specify the color on which you want to base the selection, or click inside the preview, labeled in Figure 9-26. In either case, the preview updates to show the resulting mask.

You can also do the following:

✦ **Add colors to the selection.** To add base colors to the selection, select the Add Color tool in the Color Range dialog box and click inside the image window or preview. You can access the tool while the standard Eyedropper is selected by Shift-clicking (just as you Shift-click with the Magic Wand to add colors to a selection). You can even Shift-drag with the Eyedropper to add multiple colors in a single pass, something you can't do with the Magic Wand.

✦ **Remove colors from the selection.** To remove base colors from the selection, click with the Remove Color tool or Alt-click (Option-click on the Mac) with the Eyedropper. You can also drag or Alt-drag (Option-drag on the Mac) to remove many colors at a time.

Preview

Eyedropper | Remove color

Add color

Figure 9-26: The Color Range dialog box enables you to generate a mask by clicking and dragging with the Eyedropper tool and adjusting the Fuzziness value.

Tip

The Undo command works in the Color Range dialog box as well as out of it. If adding or removing a color sends your selection careening in the wrong direction, press Ctrl+Z (⌘-Z on the Mac).

✦ **Adjust the Fuzziness value.** This option resembles the Magic Wand's Tolerance value because it determines the range of colors to be selected beyond the ones you click. Increase the Fuzziness value to expand the selected area; decrease the value to contract the selection. A value of 0 selects only the clicked color. Unlike changes to Tolerance, however, changing the Fuzziness value adjusts the selection on the fly; no repeat clicking is required, as it is with the Wand tool.

Fuzziness and Tolerance also differ in the kind of selection outlines they generate. Tolerance entirely selects all colors within the specified range and adds anti-aliased edges. If the selection were a mask, most of it would be white with a few gray pixels around the perimeter. By contrast, Fuzziness entirely selects only the colors you click and Shift-click, and it partially selects the other colors in the range. That's why most of the mask is expressed in shades of gray. The light grays in the mask represent the most similar colors; the dark grays represent the least similar pixels that still fall within the Fuzziness range. The result is a tapering, gradual selection, much more likely to produce natural results.

✦ **Reverse the selection.** Sometimes it's easier to isolate the area you don't want to select than the area you do want to select. In which case, just select the Invert option to reverse the selection, changing black to white and white to black.

✦ **Toggle the preview area.** Use the two radio buttons below the preview area to control the preview's contents. If you select the first option, Selection, you see the mask that will be generated when you press Enter (Win) or Return (Mac). If you select Image, the preview shows the image.

Tip

Press and hold Ctrl (Win) or ⌘ (Mac) to toggle between the two previews. It's best to leave the option set to Selection and press Ctrl or ⌘ when you want to view the image.

✦ **Control the contents of the image window.** The Selection Preview pop-up menu at the bottom of the dialog box enables you to change what you see in the image window. Leave the option set to None — the default setting — to view the image normally in the image window. Select Grayscale to see the mask on its own. Select Quick Mask to see the mask and image together. Select Black Matte or White Matte to see what the selection would look like against a black or white background.

Although they may sound weird, the Matte options enable you to get an accurate picture of how the selected image will mesh with a different background. Figure 9-27 includes two Matte views to help you see how this particular selection looks against two backgrounds as different as night and day. Use the Fuzziness value in combination with Black Matte or White Matte to come up with a softness setting that will ensure a smooth transition.

✦ **Select by predefined colors.** Choose an option from the Select pop-up menu at the top of the dialog box to specify the means of selecting a base color. If you choose any option besides Sampled Colors, the Fuzziness value and Eyedropper tools become dimmed to show that they are no longer operable. Instead, Photoshop selects colors based on their relationship to a predefined color. For example, if you select Red, the program entirely selects red and partially selects other colors based on the amount of red they contain. Colors composed exclusively of blue and green are not selected.

The most useful option in this pop-up menu is Out of Gamut, which selects all the colors in an RGB or Lab image that fall outside the CMYK color space. You can use this option to select and modify the out-of-gamut colors before converting an image to CMYK.

✦ **Load and save settings.** Click Save to save the current settings to disk. Click Load to open a saved settings file. To use a settings file on a PC, it must end in the *.axt* extension.

None   Grayscale

Black Matte   White Matte

Figure 9-27: The options in the Selection Preview pop-up menu change the way the Color Range command previews the selection in the image window.

After you define the mask to your satisfaction, click OK or press Enter or Return to generate the selection outline. Although the Color Range command is more flexible than the Magic Wand, you can no more expect it to generate perfect selections than any other automated tool. After Photoshop draws the selection outline, therefore, you'll probably want to switch to the Quick Mask mode and paint and edit the mask to taste.

If you learn nothing else about the Color Range dialog box, at least learn to use the Fuzziness value and the Eyedropper tools. Basically, you can approach these options in two ways. If you want to create a diffused selection with gradual edges, set a Fuzziness value — 60 or more — and click and Shift-click two or three times with the Eyedropper. To create a more precise selection, type a Fuzziness value of 40 or lower and Shift-drag and Alt-drag (Option-drag on the Mac) with the Eyedropper until you get the exact colors you want.

A few helpful Color Range hints

You can add to or subtract from an existing selection using the Color Range command. Press Shift when choosing Select ➪ Color Range to add to a selection. Press Alt (or Option on the Mac) when choosing Color Range to subtract from a selection.

Tip
You can limit the portion of an image that Select ➪ Color Range affects by selecting part of the image before choosing the command. When a selection exists, the Color Range command masks only those pixels that fall inside it. Even the preview area reflects your selection.

If you get hopelessly lost when creating your selection and you can't figure out what to select and what to deselect, click with the Eyedropper tool to start over. This clears all the colors from the selection except the one you click. Or you can press Alt (Option on the Mac) to change the Cancel button to Reset, which returns the settings in the dialog box to those in force when you first chose Select ➪ Color Range.

Creating an Independent Mask Channel

Masks generated through the Quick Mask mode and Color Range command are tempo-rary. Once you let go of the selection, they're gone. Sometimes, this isn't a problem — you're only using the selection once, so what do you care? Other times, however, a selection is as much a work of art as the image you create with it is. You may need to work on it in stages; take a break, and come back to it when your brain isn't fried.

The simplest solution is to back up your selection, save your file, and then continue to work. In fact, anytime that you spend 15 minutes or more on a selection, you should save it.

Saving a selection outline to a mask channel

The following steps describe how to back up a selection to an independent mask chan-nel, which is any channel above and beyond those required to represent a grayscale or color image. Mask channels are saved along with the image itself, making them a safe and sturdy solution.

STEPS: Transferring a Selection to an Independent Channel

1. **Convert the selection to a mask channel.** One way to do this is to choose Select ➪ Save Selection or right-click (Control-click on the Mac) in the image window and choose Save Selection from the pop-up menu, which saves the selection as a mask. The dialog box shown in Figure 9-28 appears, asking you where you want to put the mask. In most cases, you'll want to save the mask to a separate channel inside the current image. To do so, make sure that the name of the current image appears in the Document pop-up menu. Then select New from the Channel pop-up menu, type any name for the channel that you like, and press Enter or Return.

   If you have an old channel you want to replace, select the channel's name from the Channel pop-up menu. The radio buttons at the bottom of the dialog box become available, permitting you to add the mask to the channel, sub-tract it, or intersect it. These radio buttons work like the equivalent options that appear when you make a path into a selection outline (as discussed in the preceding chapter), but they blend the masks together, instead. The result is the same as if you were adding, subtracting, or intersecting selection outlines, except it's expressed as a mask.

Load channel as selection

Save channel as selection

Create new channel

Delete current channel

Figure 9-28: The Save Selection dialog box enables you to convert your selection outline to a mask and save it to a new or existing channel.

Alternatively, you can save the mask to a new multichannel document all its own. To do this, choose New from the Document pop-up menu and press Enter or Return.

Tip   If you want to simply save the selection to a new channel and be done with it, just click the make channel icon at the bottom of the Channels palette (labeled in Figure 9-28). Photoshop automatically creates a new channel, converts the selection to a mask, and places the mask in the channel.

Regardless of which of these many methods you choose, your selection outline remains intact.

2. **View the mask in the Channels palette.** To do so, click the appropriate channel name in the Channels palette—automatically named *Alpha 1* unless you assigned a name of your own. In Figure 9-28, the contents of a channel called Existing Selection have been replaced, so this is where the mask now resides.

   This step isn't the least bit mandatory. It just lets you see your mask and generally familiarize yourself with how masks look. Remember, white represents selection, black is the deselected area, and gray is a partial selection.

Tip   If you didn't name your mask in Step 1 and want to name it now, double-click the Alpha 1 name in the Channels palette and type a new name.

3. **Return to the standard image-editing mode by clicking the first channel name in the Channels palette.** Better yet, press Ctrl+1 (⌘-1 on the Mac) if you're editing a grayscale image or Ctrl+tilde (⌘-tilde on the Mac) if the image is in color.

4. **Save the image to disk to store the selection permanently as part of the file.** A handful of formats—PICT, Pixar, PNG, TIFF, Targa, PDF, and native Photoshop—accommodate RGB images with an extra mask channel. But only TIFF, PDF, and the native Photoshop format can handle more than four channels, all saving up to a total of 56 channels.

Both the native Photoshop format and TIFF can compress masks so that they take up substantially less room on disk. The Photoshop format does this automatically. When saving a TIFF image, be sure to select the LZW Compression option. In both cases, this run-line compression is entirely safe. It does not change a single pixel in the image; it merely writes the code in a more efficient manner.

Tip   You can also save a quick mask to its own channel for later use. Here's how it works. When you enter the Quick Mask mode, the Channels palette displays an item called *Quick Mask*. The italic letters show that the channel is temporary and will not be saved with the image. (To clone it to a permanent channel, click and drag the Quick Mask item onto the page icon at the bottom of the Channels palette.) Now save the image to the TIFF or Photoshop format, and you're backed up.

Converting a mask to a selection

To retrieve your selection later, choose Select ➪ Load Selection. A dialog box nearly identical to the one shown in Figure 9-28 appears except for the addition of an Invert option. Select the document and channel that contain the mask you want to use. You can add the mask to a current selection, subtract it, or intersect it. Select the Invert option if you want to reverse the selected and deselected portions of the mask.

Want to avoid the Load Selection command? Ctrl-click (Win) or ⌘-click (Mac) the channel name in the Channels palette that contains the mask you want to use. For example, if you Ctrl-click the Existing Mask item in Figure 9-32, Photoshop loads the equivalent selection outline into the image window.

But wait, there's more:

✦ You can press Ctrl+Alt (⌘-Option on the Mac) plus the channel number to convert the channel to a selection. For example, Ctrl+Alt+4 converts the Existing Mask channel shown in Figure 9-28.

✦ You can also select the channel and click the far-left mask selection icon at the bottom of the Channels palette. But you may find that's just too much effort.

✦ To add a mask to the current selection outline, Ctrl+Shift-click (⌘-Shift-click on the Mac) the channel name in the Channels palette.

✦ Ctrl+Alt-click (⌘-Option-click on the Mac) a channel name to subtract the mask from the selection.

✦ And Ctrl+Shift+Alt-click (⌘-Shift-Option-click on the Mac) to find the intersection.

You can convert color channels to selections, too. For example, if you want to select the black pixels in a piece of scanned line art in grayscale mode, Ctrl-click (Win) or ⌘-click (Mac) the first item in the Channels palette. This selects the white pixels; press Ctrl+Shift+I (⌘-Shift-I on the Mac) or choose Select ➪ Inverse to reverse the selection to the black pixels.

Viewing mask and image

Photoshop lets you view any mask channel along with an image, just as you can view the mask and image together in the Quick Mask mode. To do this, click in the first column of the Channels palette to toggle the display of the eyeball icon. An eyeball in front of a channel name indicates that you can see that channel. If you are currently viewing the full-color image, for example, click in front of the mask channel name to view the mask as a translucent color coating, again as in the Quick Mask mode. Or if the contents of the mask channel appear by themselves on-screen, click in front of the composite name (RGB, CMYK, or LAB) to display the image as well.

Tip   When the mask is active, you can likewise toggle the display of the image by pressing tilde (~). Few people know about this shortcut, but it's a good one to assign to memory. It works whether the Channels palette is open or not, and it permits you to focus on the mask without moving your mouse all over the screen.

Using a mask channel is different than using the Quick Mask mode in that you can edit either the image or the mask channel when viewing the two together. You can even edit two or more masks at once. To specify which channel you want to edit, click the channel name in the palette. To edit two channels at once, click one and Shift-click another. All active channel names appear highlighted.

You can change the color and opacity of each mask independently of other mask channels and the Quick Mask mode. Double-click the mask channel thumbnail or choose the Channel Options command from the Channels palette menu. (This command is dimmed when editing a standard color channel, such as Red, Green, Blue, Cyan, Magenta, Yellow, or Black.) A dialog box similar to the one shown back in Figure 9-11 appears, but this one contains a Name option box so you can change the name of the mask channel. You can then edit the color overlay as described in the section "Changing the red coating" earlier in this chapter.

Tip　If you ever need to edit a selection outline inside the mask channel using the paint and edit tools, click the Quick Mask mode icon in the Toolbox. It may sound a little like a play within a play, but you can access the Quick Mask mode even when working in a mask channel. Make sure that the mask channel color is different than the quick mask color so you can tell what's happening.

Building a Mask from an Image

So far, everything discussed in this chapter has been pretty straightforward. Now it's time to see how the professionals do things. This final section explains every step required to create a mask for a complex image. This is it — the lowdown on how to select the image you never thought you could select, complete with wispy little details such as leaves, stray pieces of string, very small rocks, and hair. Of course, a pro with some deep pockets might go out and buy an expensive third-party masking add-on for Photoshop, but it's not like the program can't do some pretty amazing stuff right out of the box.

Figure 9-29 gives you an idea of the kind of image in question. The major challenges presented by the subject are the stray bits of hair roaming about her head and shoulders. Imagine trying to select those using the Magnetic Lasso or Magic Wand. It ain't happening. As demonstrated by the examples in Figure 4-16, these tools lack sufficient accuracy to do any good. You'd be fit to be tied by the time you finished selecting the hairs with the pen tools, and the edges aren't definite enough for Select ➪ Color Range to latch onto.

The solution is to mask your image manually, as shown in the following steps. Granted, masking techniques vary as widely as the artists who employ them, but there are a few tried-and-true formulas that can work for just about everyone. First, you want to examine the image's channels to find one that lends itself best to a mask. You're looking for high degrees of contrast, specifically around the edges. Once you've decided on a suitable channel, you copy it and boost the level of contrast using any of the weapons in Photoshop's arsenal that accomplish such things. For example, the High Pass filter (Filter ➪ Other ➪ High Pass) combined with adjustments to the channel's levels (Image ➪ Adjustments ➪ Levels) does a pretty good job. Some folks prefer Image ➪ Adjustments ➪ Curves, but the Levels command is more straightforward. From this point, it's a matter of painting/editing the mask until you're satisfied with it.

The results of removing this backround...   with the Magnetic Lasso

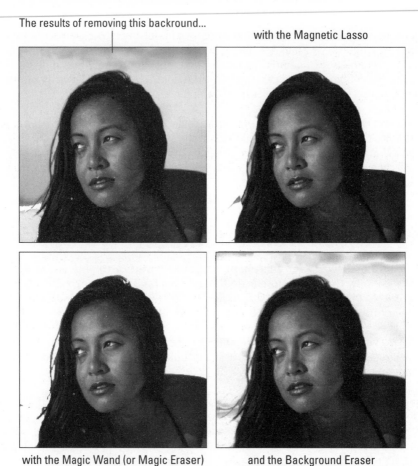

with the Magic Wand (or Magic Eraser)   and the Background Eraser

Figure 9-29: The details and indistinct transitions in this head of hair are too much for Photoshop's selection and extraction tools. This is a job for manual masking.

STEPS: Masking a Monstrously Complicated Image

1. **Browse the color channels.** Press Ctrl+1 (⌘-1 on the Mac) to see the Red channel, Ctrl+2 (⌘-2) for Green, and Ctrl+3 (⌘-3) for Blue. Note that this assumes you're working in an RGB image. You can also peruse CMYK and Lab images. If you're editing a grayscale image, you have only one channel, and that's Black.

   Figure 9-30 shows the three channels in the RGB image. Of the three, the Blue channel offers the most contrast between the hair and the background.

Red   Green   Blue

Figure 9-30: Of the three color channels, the Blue channel offers the best contrast.

2. **Clone the channel.** Click and drag the channel onto the little page icon at the bottom of the Channels palette to create a duplicate of the channel. Now you can work on the channel without harming the image itself.

3. **Choose Filter ⇨ Other ⇨ High Pass.** The next thing you want to do is to force Photoshop to bring out the edges in the image so you don't have to hunt for them manually. And when you think edges, think filters. All of Photoshop's edge-detection prowess is packed into the Filter menu. Several edge-detection filters are available — Unsharp Mask, Find Edges, and many others that are discussed in Chapters 10 and 11. But the best filter for finding edges in a mask is Filter ⇨ Other ⇨ High Pass.

   High Pass selectively turns an image gray. High Pass may sound strange, but it's quite useful. The filter turns non-edges completely gray while leaving edges mostly intact, thus dividing edges and nonedges into different brightness camps, based on the Radius value in the High Pass dialog box. Unlike in most filters, a low Radius value produces a more pronounced effect than a high one, thus locating more edges.

   Figure 9-31 shows the cloned Blue channel on the left with the result of the High Pass filter on the right, set to a Radius of 16, which is a nice, moderate value. The lower you go, the more edges you find and the more work you make for yourself. A Radius of 3 is accurate, but it'll take you an hour to fill in the mask. Granted, 10 is less accurate, but if you value your time, it's more sensible.

4. **Choose Image ⇨ Adjustments ⇨ Levels or press Ctrl+L (⌘-L on the Mac).** After adding all that gray to the image, follow it up by increasing the contrast. And the best command for enhancing contrast is Levels. This command is discussed in depth in Chapter 17. Here's the short version: Inside the Levels dialog box, increase the first Input Levels value to make the dark colors darker, and decrease the third Input Levels value to make the light colors lighter. (For now, ignore the middle value.)

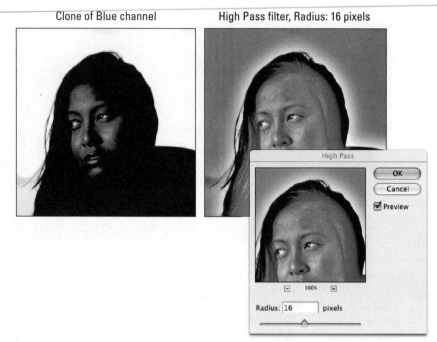

Clone of Blue channel   High Pass filter, Radius: 16 pixels

Figure 9-31: After cloning the Blue channel (left), the High Pass filter with a Radius value of 16 gets applied to highlight the edges in the image (right).

Figure 9-32 shows the result of increasing the first Input Levels value to 110 and decreasing the third value to 155. As you can see in the left-hand image, this provides some excellent contrast between the white hairs and black background.

To demonstrate the importance of the High Pass command in these steps, the right-hand image in Figure 9-32 shows what happens if you skip Step 3. The same Levels values are applied as in the left image, and yet the image is overly dark and quite lacking in edges.

5. Identify the edges. By way of High Pass and Levels, Photoshop typically presents you with a complex coloring book. Items that are dark in the original image have a white ethereal glow, while light items are just the reverse. Luckily for me, the woman is basically darker than her background. Sometimes, you may want to select areas and invert them (Image ⇨ Adjustments ⇨ Invert, or Ctrl+I for Windows/⌘-I for Mac) so all your outside edges are glowing uniformly. From here on, it's a matter of coloring inside the lines.

Figure 9-32: Here are the results of applying the Levels command to the mask after the High Pass step (left) and without High Pass (right). As you can see, High Pass has a positive effect on the edge detail.

6. Use the Lasso tool to remove the big stuff you don't need. To simplify things, get rid of the stuff you know you don't need. All you care about is the area where the woman meets her. Everything else goes to white or black.

In Figure 9-33, the area outside the woman is selected and filled with white by pressing Ctrl+Backspace (⌘-Delete on the Mac). A lot was accomplished with the Lasso tool, but not everything is as it should be. The areas inside the hair require some careful attention with the Brush tool.

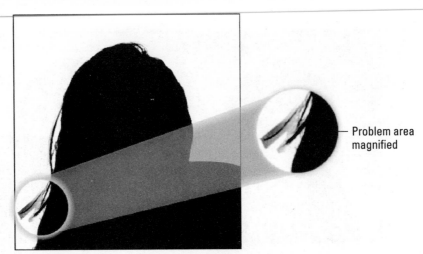

Figure 9-33: By selecting the area outside the woman and filling it with white, you can clearly distinguish the foreground and background. But that still leaves a few messy edges, identified by the circles.

Note   Be sure to press Ctrl+D (⌘-D on the Mac) to eliminate the selection before continuing to the next step.

7. **Paint inside the lines with the Brush tool.** This tends to be the most time-consuming part. Now you have to paint inside the lines to make the edge pixels black or white. For this image, the Brush tool was used with a hard brush size of about 5 to 10 pixels. Pressing X allowed switching between painting with black and white. The first image in Figure 9-34 shows the fruits of those labors. As you can see, a few judgment calls had to be made where the hair got so thick that background imagery wouldn't show through. You may even disagree with some of the brushstrokes. But it doesn't matter. Despite whatever flaws that may have introduced, this mask is more than accurate enough to select this person, as you'll see.

8. **Invert the mask.** You may or may not need to perform this step. Based on the condition of the edges after the High Pass command was used, the woman ended up black against a white background. But to select the woman, she needs to be white. Therefore, press Ctrl+I (⌘-I on the Mac) to swap the blacks and whites. If your foreground image ends up white after Step 7, you can obviously skip this step.

9. **Switch to the color composite view.** Press Ctrl+tilde (⌘-tilde on the Mac). Or if you're working in a grayscale image, press Ctrl+1 (⌘-1). By the way, now is a good time to save the image if you haven't already done so. Remember, TIFF is a terrific format for this purpose.

10. **Ctrl-click (or ⌘-click on the Mac) the mask channel to convert it to a selection.** This mask is ready to go prime time.

Figure 9-34: Problem areas are fixed by hand using the Brush tool (left). Then the entire mask is inverted so the area inside the woman's outline is white and the area outside is black (right). Depending on how you paint your mask, you may be able to skip Step 7.

11. **Ctrl-drag (or ⌘-drag on the Mac) the selection and drop it into a different image.** Figure 9-35 shows the result of dropping the woman into an evening background of orange sunset and sails. Thanks to the mask, she looks as natural in her new environment as she did in her previous one. In fact, an uninitiated viewer might have difficulty believing this isn't how she was originally photographed. But if you take a peek at Figure 9-31, you can confirm that Figure 9-35 is indeed an artificial composite. Be aware a few extra hairs were added to sell the composition, but in most cases, you won't need to bother.

The grayscale Figure 9-35 looks great, but your compositions may not fare quite so well in color, where fringing is a common problem. The solution may be to brush in color from the new background. By setting the Brush tool to the Color mode and then Alt-clicking (or Option-clicking on the Mac) in the Background layer to lift colors from the new background, you can introduce the background color into the masked layer in a realistic fashion.

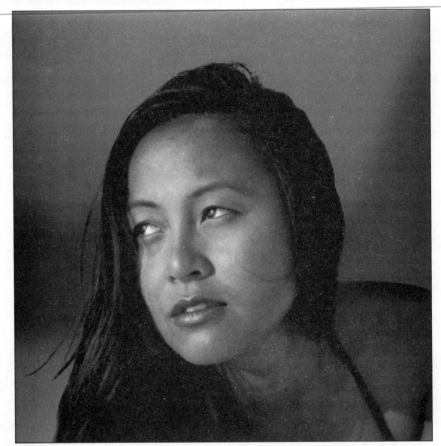

Figure 9-35: Thanks to masking, the woman has found a new life in a new environment.

Summary

In this chapter, you learned about creating and using masks to control which parts of the image can be edited, how to separate content from its surroundings, and how to use Quick Mask mode to mask content and create standard selections using tools other than the standard selection tools. These new skills will help you make more effective use of Photoshop's painting, fill, and retouching tools.

✦   ✦   ✦

Corrective Filtering

In Photoshop, filters enable you to apply automated effects to an image. Although named after photographers' filters, which typically correct lighting fluctuations and perspective, Photoshop can accomplish a great deal more. You can slightly increase the focus of an image, introduce random pixels, add depth to an imagebreak an image apart, or mimic a variety of artistic media, textures, natural and man-made substances, and distortions. Just about anything you can imagine doing to your photo can be achieved with one or more of the filters — and some of the most amazing results will be obtained through filter combinations, making for a nearly unlimited number of effects.

You might be approaching the whole concept of filters with some skepticism. If you're a veteran photographer or seasoned Photoshop user, you may be writing them off as little better than those layer styles discussed in Chapter 17, a bunch of "canned" effects that any old user can and will use. The thought of such conformity and standardization may be offending your creative sensibilities. If you're a new user, you may be either worried that the filters will be hard to use or that they're so easy you're going to head right for them, sure that they're the answer to your "but I don't have time to learn Photoshop!" blues.

In just about every one of those assumptions, you'd be...um...wrong. Filters are not cheats, they aren't "canned" effects, and they're not so uniform and conformist that your use of them will mark your photos as hopelessly pedestrian. With literally hundreds of combinations of individual filters' settings and combinations of filters that you can employ, uniformity is actually difficult to achieve — unless you're looking for that, say, between two of your photos that should look alike. If you're worried that filters are difficult to use, don't be — they're not. If you're thinking they're so easy you won't need to really learn Photoshop in order to use them, well, yes, you can just use them and hope for the best, but a good understanding of both Photoshop and the filters themselves is a good idea.

✦ ✦ ✦ ✦

In This Chapter

An overview of corrective, destructive, and effects filters

Mixing a filtered image with the original

Fixing the focus of an image with Unsharp Mask

Enhancing a grainy photograph using a custom edge mask

Highlighting edges with the High Pass filter

Creating glowing images with Gaussian Blur

Using the Blur filter

Feathering a selection using Maximum and Gaussian Blur

Sharpening images

Reducing moiré patterns in scanned images

✦ ✦ ✦ ✦

So, you're willing and eager to give filters a try. Good! This chapter and the one following it are all about filters — and the creative and practical uses thereof. The two chapters explain exactly how filters in general work, and with a focus on the most important (or often used) filters, the way specific controls work. You'll also learn about how to figure out which filter to use in specific situations, and get some good ideas for how to use them.

A First Look at Filters

You access Photoshop's special-effects filters by choosing commands from the Filter menu. These commands fall into two general camps, although the submenus don't break them down that way. In any case, you can pretty much place all the filters in one of two groups: *corrective* and *destructive*.

Corrective filters

Corrective filters are tools that you use to modify scanned or otherwise captured images and to prepare an image for printing or screen display. In many cases, the effects are subtle enough that the viewer won't even notice that you applied a corrective filter. As demonstrated in Figure 10-1, these filters include those that change the focus of an image, enhance color transitions, and average the colors of neighboring pixels. You can find these filters in the Filter ⇨ Blur, Noise, Sharpen, and Other submenus.

Many corrective filters have direct opposites. Blur is the opposite of Sharpen, Add Noise is the opposite of Median, and so on. This is not to say that one filter entirely removes the effect of the other; only reversion functions such as the History palette provide that capability. Instead, two opposite filters produce contrasting effects — and you may want to use both of them together, despite their contrasting results.

Corrective filters are the subject of this chapter — the more artistic and "special effect" filters, also known as the *destructive* filters are covered in Chapter 11. Although the corrective filters number fewer than their destructive counterparts, the coverage is extensive because they represent the functions you're most likely to use on a day-to-day basis.

Figure 10-1: Four corrective filters, including one each from the Sharpen, Blur, Other, and Noise submenus are applied to this photo. Clockwise from upper left, they are Unsharp Mask, Gaussian Blur, High Pass, and Median.

Destructive filters

The destructive filters produce effects so dramatic that they can, if used improperly, completely overwhelm your artwork, making the filter more important than the image itself. Many of the destructive filters reside in the Filter ⇨ Distort, Pixelate, Render, and Stylize submenus. A few examples of overwhelmed images appear in Figure 10-2.

Destructive filters produce very interesting effects, and many people gravitate toward them when first experimenting with Photoshop. These filters invariably destroy the original clarity and composition of the image, though, so that should be your goal before you apply them — unless you're just experimenting. Remember, as with anything you do to a photo and then regret, you can always use Undo or access the History palette to go back to a predestructive state.

Figure 10-2: The effects of applying four destructive filters, one each from the Distort, Pixelate, Stylize, and Render submenus. Clockwise from upper left, they are Ripple, Color Halfton, Diffuse (Anisotropic, ×3), and Difference Clouds.

Effects filters

Photoshop also provides a subset of destructive filters called the *effects* filters. These filters are easily applied through the Filter Gallery, which debuted in Photoshop with version CS. In previous versions, each effect filter had to be applied separately and there was no quick way of viewing how different effects would work with each other. All that has changed with the introduction of the Filter Gallery, which lets you access all effects filters in one convenient dialog box. Even more impressive, the Filter Gallery lets you stack as many of these filters as you want on top of one another to see how they interact. It's a great addition to the program, and one you explore in more detail in the next chapter.

In addition to the Filter Gallery dialog box, most of the effects filters also reside in the Filter ➪ Artistic, Brush Strokes, Sketch, and Texture submenus (see Figure 10-3 for some examples). A few have trickled out into other submenus, including Filter ➪ Distort ➪ Diffuse Glow, Glass, and Ocean Ripple; and Filter ➪ Stylize ➪ Glowing Edges. You'll see these in Chapter 11, too.

Figure 10-3: Here you see the impact of one filter each from the Filter ⇨ Artistic, Brush Strokes, Texture, and Sketch submenus. Clockwise from upper left, they are Plastic Wrap, Crosshatch, Stained Glass, and Reticulation.

How Filters Work

When you choose a command from the Filter menu, Photoshop applies the filter to the selected portion of the image on the current layer. If no portion of the image is selected, Photoshop applies the filter to the entire layer. Therefore, if you want to filter every nook and cranny of the current layer, press Ctrl+D (⌘-D on the Mac) to cancel any existing selection outline and then choose the desired command.

Tip

Some filters are applied immediately upon making a selection from a Filter sub-menu, and others open a dialog box. You can tell which ones will spawn a dialog box by looking at the submenus—if the command is followed by an ellipsis (...), a dialog box will open. If not, the filter will be applied with no questions asked, based on built-in defaults. You may be thinking, "Yeah, I know about dialog boxes!" but it's worth remembering to check for that ellipsis—even seasoned users can forget which filters are applied with no dialog box to allow for cus-tomization and which ones just . . . happen.

External plug-ins

Some filters are built into the Photoshop application. Others are external modules that reside in the Plug-Ins folder. This enables you to add functionality to Photoshop by purchasing additional filters from third-party collections such as Eye Candy, from Alien Skin. You can search the Web for Photoshop plug-ins to find more.

If you open the Plug-Ins folder inside the Photoshop folder, you see that it contains several subfolders. By default, Photoshop places the filters in the Filters and Effects subfolders, but you can place additional filters anywhere inside the Plug-Ins folder.

Previewing filters

For years, the biggest problem with Photoshop's filters was that none offered previews to help you predict the outcome of an effect. You just had to tweak the seemingly endless and often vaguely named settings and hope for the best. But today, life is much better. Photoshop 3 introduced previews, Version 4 made them commonly available to just about all of the filters, and subsequent versions have maintained this vastly improved status quo.

Photoshop offers two previewing capabilities:

✦ **Dialog box previews.** Labeled in Figure 10-4, the 100-×-100-pixel preview box is now a common feature of all filter dialog boxes. Click and drag inside the preview box to scroll the portion of the image you want to preview. Move the cursor outside the dialog box to get the square preview cursor (labeled in the figure). Click with the cursor to center the contents of the preview box at the clicked position in the image.

Click the zoom buttons (+ and –) to change the view of the image in the preview box. You can even take advantage of the standard Zoom tool by pressing Ctrl+spacebar or Alt+spacebar (⌘-spacebar or Option-spacebar on the Mac), depending on whether you want to zoom in or out.

✦ **Image window previews.** Most corrective filters — as well as a few destructive ones such as Mosaic and Emboss — also preview effects in the full image window. Just select the Preview option to activate this function. While the effect is previewing, a blinking progress line appears under the Zoom value in the dialog box. If you're working on a low computer, you'll probably want to deselect the Preview option to speed up the pace at which the filter functions.

 Note   Incidentally, the Preview option has no effect on the contents of the preview box. The latter continually monitors the effects of your settings, whether you like it or not.

Tip

Use the Preview option to compare the before and after effects of a corrective filter in the image window. Select it to see the effect; deselect it to see the original image. You can compare the image in the preview box also by clicking in the box. Click to see the old image; release to see the filtered image.

Preview Cursor   Image Window

Zoom percentage   Preview box

Zoom buttons

Figure 10-4: Most filter dialog boxes let you preview the effects of the filter in both the dialog box and the image window—you may want to move the dialog box aside so you can see some or all of the image window at the same time.

✦ Even though a dialog box is on-screen and active, you can zoom and scroll the contents of the image window. Ctrl+spacebar-click (⌘-spacebar-click on the Mac) to zoom in; Alt+spacebar-click (Option-spacebar-click on the Mac) to zoom out. Or you can zoom in and out by pressing Ctrl+plus and Ctrl+minus (⌘-plus and ⌘-minus on the Mac), respectively. Spacebar-drag to scroll. You can also choose commands from the View and Window menus.

Tip

One more tip: When you press Alt (Win) or Option (Mac), the Cancel button changes to Reset. Alt-click (Option-click on the Mac) this button to restore the settings that appeared when you first opened the dialog box. (These are not necessarily the factory default settings; they are the settings you last applied to an image.)

Six filters continue to offer no previews whatsoever: Radial Blur, Displace, Color Halftone, Extrude, Tiles, and De-Interlace. Of course, the filters that don't bring up dialog boxes at all don't need previews because there aren't any settings to adjust.

Reapplying the last filter

To reapply the last filter used in the current Photoshop session, choose the first command from the Filter menu or simply press Ctrl+F (⌘-F on the Mac). If you want to reapply the filter subject to different settings, press Alt (or Option on the Mac) and choose the first Filter command or press Ctrl+Alt+F (⌘-Option-F on the Mac) to redisplay that filter's dialog box.

Both techniques work even if you undo the last application of a filter. However, if you cancel a filter in progress, pressing Ctrl+F or Ctrl+Alt+F (⌘-F or ⌘-Option-F on the Mac) applies the last uncanceled filter.

Nudging numerical values

In addition to typing specific numerical values in filter dialog boxes, you can nudge the values using the up- and down-arrow keys. When working with percentage values, press an arrow key to raise or lower the value by 1. Press Shift-up arrow or Shift-down arrow to change the value in increments of 10. Note that with some destructive filters, you must use the arrow keys on the numeric keypad; the regular navigation arrow keys don't work.

If the value accommodates decimal values, it's probably more sensitive to the arrow key. Press an arrow for a 0.1 change; press Shift+arrow for 1.0.

Fading a Filter

In many cases, you apply filters to a selection or an image at full intensity — meaning that you marquee an area using a selection tool (or not, if you want an entire layer to be affected), choose a filter command, type whatever settings you want if a dialog box appears, and then watch as the filter is applied.

Mezzotint Filter

Here the Mezzotint filter (Filter ➪ Pixelate ➪ Mezzotint) has been applied, with the Type option set to Long Strokes. The left-hand column (from top to bottom) shows the results of applying the filter in RGB, Lab, and CMYK modes. Photoshop changes all pixels to either black or white, resulting in very high-contrast images. The right-hand column (from top to bottom) shows the result of fading the filter and setting the mode to Overlay at an Opacity of 40%, which helps to temper contrast and achieve a more subtle effect.

Emboss Filter

By itself the Emboss filter will make any image you apply it to look as if the details were gouged out of some slab of neutral gray rock. On the surface, this may seem pretty useless. But, if you try experimenting with blend mode options you'll see there's more to be gained from this filter than meets the eye.

The top image shows swirling spaceship Earth. Moving down, the second image shows the results of the Emboss filter. The remaining images show what you can do if you simply float a copy of the original image to another layer and start monkeying around with the blend mode options.

Twirl Drops

Distortion filters allow you to create some interesting effects without relying on an original image for inspiration. Starting with Photoshop's Gradient tool and the predefined Blue, Red, Yellow combination, applying the Twirl filter gives you the result shown in the first image at the upper left. The image in the upper right shows what happens if you copy the layer, flip it horizontally, and apply the Difference blend mode. By continuing to clone the layer and applying more transformations, the middle left and right images are created. The final image in the series is the result.

For more about distortion filters and the Twirl filter, read Chapter 11.

Polar to Rectangular

Filter ⇨ Distort ⇨ Polar Coordinates may be one of Photoshop's most bizarre filters — it can be used to literally turn an image inside out. In this series of images, the filter has been used to turn 10 pinches and 7 swirls into a series of waves (top row of images, left to right), and to take a perfectly nice man and turn him into distorted, freakish Fish Face Boy (second row, left to right). In the final image (bottom), the Twirl Drops from the previous page become a rainbow pool.

You can read all about the Polar Coordinates filter in Chapter 11.

Blend Modes

Blend modes allow you to mix colors and brightness values between independent layers. In the examples on this page, you see four blocks of content — a face, a gradient, a pattern, and a scenic background. In the final image at the bottom, you see the result of combining them and utilizing blend modes to make a truly beautiful composite. The layer palette appears in the bottom image, and lists what's been done to create the image:

The girl's face was subjected to the Screen mode, at 100% Opacity.

The Multiply mode was applied to the Gradient, at 80% Opacity.

The Pattern layer was left under the Normal blend mode, at 50% Opacity.

The Background layer is just that — the 100% Opacity, Normal layer at the very bottom of it all.

Difference Sandwich

By stacking cloned layers, as if they are the bread and meat in your sandwich, you can achieve interesting effects with layered filters and blend modes. As shown in the images on this page, in the top image, three cloned layers of the girl's face are subjected to Color Dodge, Multiply, and Normal (the bottom-most layer, as shown in the Layers palette next to the top image).

In the middle image, the top-most layer has been subjected to the Pin Light blend mode, and that's on top of a layer that has had the Screen blend mode applied to it. The Background layer is again a Normal layer, the original of the girl's face.

In the bottom image, Pin Light has been applied to both the top layer of bread and to the sandwich contents (the middle layer). These sit atop the Background layer (bottom slice of bread) and create the effects shown.

You can read about creating your own "Difference Sandwich" in Chapter 13.

Layer Effects

In this set of images, Layer effects have been applied. These preset styles seem like cheating to some old-school artists, but they're really not cheating or taking the easy way out. Despite the simplicity of applying them, these clever and well-planned combinations create some very cool effects you can't achieve otherwise.

On this page, you can see four versions of two shapes — a crown and flames — created with the Custom Shape tool. In the upper left, the flame has a metallic style and a stroke outline, and that's on top of the crown with embossing and a pattern overlay. In the upper right, the two effects are blended.

In the lower left, the crown is blended with the background, and in the lower right, the flames are blended with the crown once again.

The cumulative and combined effects are quite unique and would not be possible without layer styles — which are covered in detail in Chapter 14. You can read about Shape layers in Chapter 14, too.

Threshold Tricks

The Threshold command (Image ⇨ Adjustments ⇨ Threshold) converts all colors to either black or white, depending on their brightness values. You can refresh your memory on Threshold in Chapter 17.

This example features an original piece entitled "Knowledge," by artist Mimi Shapiro. Here, the composite image, consisting of sections of various photos and documents, appears in its original state in the top left image. In the second version of the image, the image was switched to Lab mode, with Threshold applied to the A and B channels. In the third and fourth images, in CMYK mode, Threshold was applied to various channels, creating the interesting color shifts shown.

Auto Adjustments

Photoshop's Auto adjustments include Auto Levels (which enhances contrast in an image on a channel-by-channel basis, often producing a color shift), Auto Contrast (which does not create a color shift), and Auto Color, which neutralizes the highlights, shadows, and midtones in the image — you usually get much more natural-looking results with this adjustment. The original, untouched image is at the top, followed by Auto Levels in the second image, Auto Contrast in the third, and Auto Color in the final image.

Want to know more about these Auto adjustments? Check out Chapter 17.

Original

Auto Levels

Auto Contrast

Auto Color

Original, red towel

Yellow Hue: +60

Green Hue: +120

Cyan Hue: -180
Saturation: +180

Royal Blue Hue: -120
Saturation: +240

Purple Hue: -60
Saturation: +300

Hue Saturation

This little boy has a different towel for each time he gets out of the pool — thanks to the Hue/Saturation command. By using the Hue/Saturation dialog box and its sliders to adjust colors and the levels of color in an image, layer, or selection, you can shift colors slightly or replace them entirely.

Each of the six images on this page has been subjected to various adjustments. In the top left is the original, untouched image with a red towel. Next to that, the towel is yellow, thanks to a Hue shift to +60. In the top right the green towel results from a Hue shift to +120. On the bottom row, the left image shows a cyan towel that was created by adjusting Hue to -180 and increasing Saturation to +180. In the middle, royal blue is achieved by setting Hue to -120 and Saturation to +240. Last but not least, a purple towel is created on the bottom right by adjusting Hue to -60 and Saturation to +300.

Go ahead and tinker with your own images and find out more about Hue/Saturation in Chapter 17.

Match Color

This set of images utilizes the Match Color command, covered in Chapter 17. Using two versions of the same photo — one with good coloring (top) and the other with weird coloring (second), a Match Color version is created (third). Then, using a selection within the good color version to help focus the Match Color command's attention on the key sunset color, the fourth image (bottom) was created. Here's how it all happened, in detail:

Starting with both the weird and the good color versions of the herons photo open, I took the weird version and applied Match Color by choosing Image ➪ Adjustments ➪ Match Color. Then, I set the Source option to the good version (available in the drop list because that image was open), and clicked OK. The third image (lower left) resulted.

Next, I made a small rectangular selection in the both the good and weird color versions, in the upper area of the sunset, and reopened the Match Color dialog box while pressing Alt (Option on the Mac) so that the Source image is reloaded. I turned on the Ignore Selection When Applying Adjustment checkbox, so that the change applies to the entire image (Image Statistics is also left on). The Color Intensity setting was raised, and the Fade value reduced, and the fourth image, on the bottom, was the result.

Boost JPEG Colors

This JPEG image of an Italian village was taken by Robert Yamaguchi. The original (top left) was filled with JPEG artifacts and required some tinkering to remove the artifacts yet bring out detail and color, too.

First, I used Hue and Saturation (Image ⇨ Adjustments ⇨ Hue/Saturation) to boost the Saturation to +80% (see the top right image). Then, the Median filter was applied (Filter ⇨ Noise ⇨ Median), with a Radius of 6 and Gaussian Blur was applied (Filter ⇨ Blur ⇨ Gaussian Blur) with a Radius of 4 (bottom left image).

Finally, the Color blend mode was applied, and Unsharp Mask was applied, too — with an Amount set to 120, and a Radius of 1.5. The results appear in the bottom right image.

Levels Correction

Image ⇨ Adjustments ⇨ Levels may be the one color correction tool you can't live without. As shown in the five images on this page — the top image is the uncorrected original — you can correct color for individual channels as well as for the composite image. Dialog boxes showing individual settings for each channel accompany the images. The second image shows the red channel corrected, the third image has the green channel corrected, and the fourth image has the blue channel corrected. The bottom image shows the composite corrected (RGB).

To make adjustments, simply choose the channel from the dropdown list at the top of the dialog box, and then enter Input levels or drag the three sliders at the bottom of the histogram. You can read all about the Levels dialog box and how to use it on your images in Chapter 17.

Uncorrected

Red channel corrected

Green channel corrected

Blue channel corrected

Composite corrected (RGB)

Gradient Map

The Gradient Map command (found in the Image ⇨ Adjustment submenu) maps brightness values in an image to colors inside a preset gradient. This can help you turn a regular photo into a duotone, tritone, or a brilliant many-colored image. The nine images shown on this page were subjected to the same three gradients, and then to the Gaussian Blur filter (middle row) and then the Color blend mode (bottom row).

Top row, left: The original image.

Top row, middle: The Blue, Yellow, Blue gradient is applied.

Top row, right: The Chrome gradient is applied.

Middle row, left: The Blue, Red, Yellow gradient is applied, with a Gaussian Blur set to a Radius of 4 pixels.

Middle row, middle: The Blue, Yellow, Blue gradient is now given a Gaussian Blur, again with a Radius of 4 pixels.

Middle row, right: The Chrome gradient is also subjected to a 4 pixel Radius Gaussian Blur.

Bottom row, left: The Blue, Yellow, Blue gradient is given the Color blend mode.

Bottom row, middle: The Blue, Red, Yellow gradient with Color blend mode.

Bottom row, right: The Chrome Gradient, as seen through the Color blend mode.

Read all about Gradient Maps in Chapter 17.

Curves Corrections

If the Levels command doesn't solve your color problems or give you the special color effects you're looking for, try Image ➪ Adjustments ➪ Curves. The Curves dialog box (shown in various states with each of the images on this page) allows you to adjust individual channels and control not just the amount of color but the contrast within that channel.

The images on this page include the top image, which is the result of Green channel adjustment (seen in the second image) and the Blue channel adjustment (in the third image). The Green channel adjustment included lightening that channel, and the Blue channel adjustment increased contrast.

The final adjustment, which is not reflected in the top image, shows an arbitrary channel adjustment applied to the Red channel. This adjustment results in vivid, unnatural reds, and a sort of psychedelic effect on the man's shirt and hair, and her sunglasses.

Read all about the Curves dialog box and how to use it in Chapter 17.

Duotones

A duotone is an image created by blending two or more inks. The term is also applied to indicate any image created by blending colored inks, whether it contains a single ink (monotone), three inks (tritone), or four inks (quadtone). Printing two or more inks increases the dynamic range of an otherwise grayscale image, producing darker blacks and richer midtones.

The examples shown here demonstrate the process of building up a grayscale image — in this case a vintage photo — starting with a navy monotone and ending in a rich quadtone. Each successive example has an added ink. Clockwise from the top left, you can see the starting navy, followed by orange, then teal, and finally deep red, which produces the fourth color, making the final quadtone.

You can read more about the Duotone mode in Chapter 4, printing duotones in Chapter 18, and about adding colors to an image in Chapter 17.

This probably sounds pretty normal, a procedure not unlike any other editing command, such as applying Levels or Variations. But what if you want to reduce the intensity of the filter — and the level of reduction isn't something you can tweak through the filter's dialog box? You can reduce the intensity of the last filter applied by choosing Edit ⇨ Fade or by pressing Ctrl+Shift+F (⌘-Shift-F on the Mac). This command permits you to mix the filtered image with the original, unfiltered one.

As shown in Figure 10-5, the Fade dialog box provides you with the basic tools of image mixing — an Opacity value and a blend mode pop-up menu. As also shown in Figure 10-5, the right-hand images show the effects of pressing Ctrl+Shift+F to Fade the previously-applied filters, and applying two successive blend modes, Screen (to the top-right image) and Vivid Light (to the lower-right image), with the Opacity values set to 100 and 65 percent, respectively.

Figure 10-5: The full-intensity versions of two filters are found on the left — Glowing Edges (upper left) and Bas Relief (lower left). When using Fade to apply them to the unfiltered original — reducing the intensity of the filters — you get the results seen on the right.

Creating layered effects

Caution

The drawback of the Fade command is that it's available only immediately after you apply a filter (or perform some other applicable edit). If you do anything after applying the filter — even something as benign as making a selection or saving the file — the Fade command dims, only to return when you apply the next filter.

Due to the fleeting, sensitive nature of the Fade command, you may find it more helpful to copy a selection to a separate layer by pressing Ctrl+J (⌘-J on the Mac) before applying a filter. This way, you can perform other operations, and even apply many filters in a row, before mixing the filtered image with the underlying original.

Filtering inside a border

And here's another reason to layer before you filter: If your image has a border around it — like the ones shown in Figure 10-6 — you don't want Photoshop to factor the border into the filtering operation. To avoid this, select the image inside the border and press Ctrl+J (Win) or ⌘-J (Mac) to layer it before applying the filter. The reason this works is that most filters take neighboring pixels into consideration even if they are not selected. By contrast, when a selection floats, it has no neighboring pixels, and therefore the filter affects the selected pixels only.

Figure 10-6 shows the results of applying the Motion Blur filter — when the image is anchored in place and when it's layered. In both cases, the 10-pixel border was not selected when the filter was applied. In the left example, the Motion Blur filter duplicates the left and right edges of the border. The problem vanishes when the filter is applied to a layered image, as seen on the right.

Even if the area outside the selection is not a really a border — perhaps it's just a comparatively dark or light area that serves as a visual frame — layering comes in handy. You should always layer the selection unless you specifically want edge pixels to be calculated by the filter.

Undoing a sequence of filters

If you needed yet another reason to layer before you filter, consider this. Copying an image to a layer protects the underlying image. If you just want to experiment a little, pressing Ctrl+J (⌘-J on the Mac) is often more convenient than restoring a state in the History palette. After applying four or five effects to a layer, you can undo all that automated abuse by Alt-clicking (Win) or Option-clicking (Mac) the trash can icon at the bottom of the Layers palette, which deletes the layer. The underlying original remains unharmed.

Figure 10-6: If the filtered content and the image border are on the same layer (left), the border can be affected by the filter, and that's rarely what you want to see happen. Protect your border by placing the filtered content on its own layer (right) — *before* applying the filter.

Heightening Focus and Contrast

If you've experimented at all with Photoshop, you've no doubt had your way with many of the commands in the Filter ⇨ Sharpen submenu. By increasing the contrast between neighboring pixels, the sharpening filters enable you to compensate for image elements that were photographed or scanned slightly out of focus.

The Sharpen, Sharpen More, and Sharpen Edges commands are easy to use and immediate in their effect. However, you can achieve better results and widen your range of sharpening options if you learn how to use the Unsharp Mask and High Pass commands, which are discussed at length in the following pages.

Using the Unsharp Mask filter

The first thing you need to know about the Unsharp Mask filter is that it has a weird name. The filter has nothing to do with unsharpening—whatever that is—nor is it tied into Photoshop's masking capabilities. Unsharp Mask is named after a traditional film-compositing technique (which is also oddly named) that highlights the edges in an image by combining a blurred film negative with the original film positive.

That's all well and good, but the fact is most Photoshop artists have never touched a stat camera (an expensive piece of machinery, roughly twice the size of a washing machine used by image editors of the late Jurassic, pre-Photoshop epoch). Even people who used to operate stat cameras professionally never had the time to delve into the world of unsharp masking. In addition—and much to the filter's credit—Unsharp Mask goes beyond traditional camera techniques.

To understand Unsharp Mask—or Photoshop's other sharpening filters, for that matter—you first need to understand some basic terminology. When you apply one of the sharpening filters, Photoshop increases the contrast between neighboring pixels. The effect is similar to what you see when you adjust a camera to bring a scene into sharper focus.

Two of Photoshop's sharpening filters, Sharpen and Sharpen More, affect whatever area of your image is selected. The Sharpen Edges filter, however, performs its sharpening operations only on the *edges between colors* in the image—those areas that feature the highest amount of contrast.

Unsharp Mask gives you both sharpening options. It can sharpen only the edges in an image or it can sharpen any portion of an image according to your exact specifications, whether it finds an edge or not. It fulfills the same purposes as the Sharpen, Sharpen Edges, and Sharpen More commands, but it's much more versatile. Simply put, the Unsharp Mask tool is the only sharpening filter you'll ever need.

When you choose Filter ➪ Sharpen ➪ Unsharp Mask, Photoshop displays the Unsharp Mask dialog box shown in Figure 10-7, which offers the following options:

✦ **Amount.** Type a value between 1 and 500 percent to specify the degree to which you want to sharpen the selected image. Higher values produce more pronounced effects.

Figure 10-7: Despite any conclusions you may draw from its somewhat confusing name, the Unsharp Mask filter sharpens images according to your specifications in this dialog box.

✦ **Radius.** This option determines the thickness of the sharpened edge. Low values produce crisp edges. High values produce thicker edges with more contrast throughout the image.

✦ **Threshold.** Type a value between 0 and 255 to control how Photoshop recognizes edges in an image. The value indicates the numerical difference between the brightness values of two neighboring pixels that must occur if Photoshop is to sharpen those pixels. A low value sharpens lots of pixels; a high value excludes most pixels from the running.

The preview options offered by the Unsharp Mask dialog box are absolutely essential visual aids that you're likely to find tremendously useful throughout your Photoshop career. Just the same, you'll be better prepared to experiment with the Amount, Radius, and Threshold options and less surprised by the results if you read the following sections, which explain these options in detail and demonstrate the effects of each.

Specifying the amount of sharpening

If Amount were the only Unsharp Mask option, no one would have any problems understanding this filter. If you want to sharpen an image ever so slightly, type a low percentage value. Values between 25 and 50 percent are ideal for producing subtle effects. If you want to sharpen an image beyond the point of good taste, type a value somewhere in the 300 to 500 percent range. And if you're looking for moderate sharpening, try out some value between 50 and 300 percent. Figure 10-8 shows the results of applying different Amount values while leaving the Radius and Threshold values at their default settings of 1.0 and 0, respectively.

Figure 10-8: The results of sharpening an image with the Unsharp Mask filter using eight different Amount values. The Radius and Threshold values used for all images were 1.0 and 0, respectively (the default settings).

If you're not sure how much you want to sharpen an image, try out a small value in the 25 to 50 percent range. Then reapply that setting repeatedly by pressing Ctrl+F

(⌘-F on the Mac). As you can see in Figure 10-9, repeatedly applying the filter at a low setting produces a nearly identical result to applying the filter once at a higher setting. For example, you can achieve the same effect by applying the Unsharp Mask filter three times at 50 percent or once at 250 percent.

Figure 10-9: Repeatedly applying the Unsharp Mask filter at 50 percent (top row) is nearly equivalent on a pixel-by-pixel basis to applying the filter once at higher settings (bottom row).

The benefit of using small values is that they enable you to experiment with sharpening incrementally. As the figure demonstrates, you can add sharpening bit by bit to increase the focus of an image. You can't, however, reduce sharpening incrementally if you apply too high a value; you must press Ctrl+Z (Win) or ⌘-Z (Mac) and start again, unless you catch your error immediately after applying the too-intense sharpening — if you do catch it right away, you can use the Edit ⇨ Fade command to apply the last filter at reduced intensity.

Cross-Reference

If you're a little foggy on how to access individual color channels, read Chapter 4.

Tip

As mentioned in Chapter 4, Photoshop is ultimately a grayscale editor, so when you apply the Unsharp Mask command to a full-color image, Photoshop actually applies the command in a separate pass to each of the color channels. Therefore, the command always results in color halos — it's just that the halos get mixed together, minimizing the effect. To avoid any haloing whatsoever, convert the image to the Lab mode (Image ⇨ Mode ⇨ Lab Color) and apply Unsharp Mask to only the Lightness channel in the Channels palette. (Do not filter the *a* and *b* channels.) This sharpens the brightness values in the image and leaves the colors 100 percent untouched.

Setting the thickness of the edges

The Unsharp Mask filter works by identifying edges and increasing the contrast around those edges. The Radius value tells Photoshop how thick you want your edges. Large values produce thicker edges than small values.

The ideal Radius value depends on the resolution of your image and the quality of its edges:

✦ When creating screen images — such as Web graphics — use a very low Radius value, such as 0.5. This results in terrific hairline edges that look so crisp, you'll think you washed your bifocals.

✦ If a low Radius value brings out strange imperfections — such as grain, scan lines, or JPEG compression artifacts — raise the value to 1.0 or higher. If that doesn't help, don't worry. You'll discover two very effective image-fixing techniques later in this chapter, one designed to sharpen grainy old photos and another that accommodates compressed images.

✦ When printing an image at a moderate resolution — anywhere from 120 to 180 ppi — use a Radius value of 1.0. The edges will look a little thick on-screen, but they'll print fine.

✦ For high-resolution images — around 300 ppi — try a Radius of 2.0. Because Photoshop prints more pixels per inch, the edges have to be thicker to remain nice and visible.

Tip   If you're looking for a simple formula, try 0.1 of Radius for every 15 ppi of final image resolution. That means 75 ppi warrants a Radius of 0.5, 120 ppi warrants 0.8, 180 ppi warrants 1.2, and so on. If you have a calculator, just divide the intended resolution by 150 to get the ideal Radius value.

You can, of course, type higher Radius values — as high as 250, in fact. Higher values produce heightened contrast effects, almost as if the image had been photocopied too many times, which is generally useful for producing special effects.

But don't take my word for it; you be the judge. Figure 10-10 demonstrates the results of specific Radius values. In each case, the Amount and Threshold values remain constant at 100 percent and 0, respectively.

Figure 10-11 shows the results of combining different Amount and Radius values. You can see that a large Amount value helps to offset the softening of a high Radius value. For example, when the Amount is set to 200 percent, as in the first row, the Radius value appears to mainly enhance contrast when raised from 0.5 to 2.0. However, when the Amount value is lowered to 50 percent, the higher Radius value does more to distribute the effect than to boost contrast.

Figure 10-10: The results of applying eight different Radius values, ranging from precise edges to very soft. The upper-left image is the original, untouched by any filter.

Figure 10-11: The effects of combining different Amount and Radius settings. High Amount settings are countered by higher Radius levels, and as the Amount drops to 50 percent with a Radius of 10, the results are subtle, yet effective—sharpening all over, without a change in contrast. The Threshold value for each image was set to 0 (the default setting).

Recognizing edges

By default, the Unsharp Mask filter sharpens every edge in a selection. However, you can instruct the filter to sharpen only the edges in an image by raising the Threshold value from 0 to some other number. The Threshold value represents the difference between two neighboring pixels — as measured in brightness levels — that must occur for Photoshop to recognize them as an edge.

Suppose that the brightness values of neighboring pixels are 10 and 20. If you set the Threshold value to 5, Photoshop reads both pixels, notes that the difference between their brightness values is more than 5, and treats them as an edge. If you set the Threshold value to 20, however, Photoshop passes them by. A low Threshold value, therefore, causes the Unsharp Mask filter to affect a high number of pixels, and vice versa.

In the top row of images in Figure 10-12, the high Threshold values result in tiny slivers of sharpness that outline only the most substantial edges in the owl's feathers, especially around the chest and edge of the face. As the Threshold value is lowered incrementally in the second and third rows, the sharpening effect takes over more and more of the owl's face, ultimately sharpening all details uniformly — even in the background behind the owl — in the lower-right example.

Figure 10-12: The results of applying nine different Threshold values. To best show off the differences between each image, the Amount and Radius values were set to 500 percent and 2.0, respectively.

Using the preset sharpening filters

So how do the Sharpen, Sharpen Edges, and Sharpen More commands compare with the Unsharp Mask filter? First of all, none of the preset commands permit you to vary the thickness of your edges, a function provided by Unsharp Mask's Radius option. Second, only the Sharpen Edges command can recognize high-contrast areas in an image. And third, all three commands are set in stone — you can't adjust their effects in any way (except, of course, to fade the filter after the fact). Figure 10-13 shows the effect of each preset command and the nearly equivalent effect created with the Unsharp Mask filter.

Figure 10-13: The effects of the three preset sharpening filters (top row) compared with the Unsharp Mask equivalents (bottom row). Unsharp Mask values are listed in the following order: Amount, Radius, Threshold.

Sharpening grainy photographs

Although Amount and Radius are great options that will serve you well, it's a good idea to use Threshold with caution. The Threshold concept is fine — it's useful to have some way to draw a dividing line between those pixels that you want to sharpen and those that you want to leave unchanged. The Threshold setting, however, functions like an on/off switch — and it can result in harsh transitions between sharpened and unsharpened pixels.

Consider the picture in Figure 10-14. Like so many vintage photographs, this particular image is a little softer than the portraits seen today. If you were to apply the Unsharp Mask — as in the second example in the figure — you would bring out as much film grain as image detail. The official Photoshop solution is to raise the Threshold value, but the option's intrinsic harshness results in a pockmarked effect, as shown on the right. Photoshop has simply replaced one kind of grain with another.

These abrupt transitions are not typical of Photoshop's normal approach. Paint brushes have anti-aliased edges, selections can be feathered, the Color Range command offers Fuzziness—in short, everything mimics the softness found in real life. Yet right here, in what may be Photoshop's most essential filter, there is no mechanism for softness whatsoever.

Now, to counteract this problem (while we await an improved Threshold from Adobe), you can use a very simple masking technique. Using a few filters, explored at greater length throughout this chapter and the next, you can devise a selection outline that traces the essential edges in the image—complete with fuzzy transitions—and leaves the non-edges unchanged. So with a vintage photograph scanned and open in the Photoshop workspace, follow these steps:

Original   Sharpened, Threshold 0   Sharpened, Threshold 20

Figure 10-14: The original photograph is a bit soft (left), a condition you can remedy with Unsharp Mask. Leaving the Threshold value set to 0 brings out the film grain (middle), but raising the value results in equally unattractive artifacts (right).

STEPS: Creating and Using an Edge Mask

1. **Duplicate one of the color channels.** Open the Channels palette and click and drag one of the color channels onto the little page icon. As the vintage photo is probably in grayscale, duplicate the one and only channel.

2. **Choose Filter ⇨ Stylize ⇨ Find Edges.** As explained in Chapter 11, the Find Edges filter automatically traces the edges of your image with thick, gooey outlines that are ideal for creating edge masks.

3. **Press Ctrl+I (⌘-I on the Mac).** Or choose Image ⇨ Adjustments ⇨ Invert. Find Edges produces black lines against a white background, but to select your edges, you need white lines against a black background. The Invert command reverses the lights and darks in the mask, as in the first example in Figure 10-15.

4. **Choose Filter ⇨ Other ⇨ Maximum.** The next step is to thicken the edges. The Maximum filter expands the white areas in the image, serving much the same function in a mask as Select ⇨ Modify ⇨ Expand serves when editing a selection outline. Type a Radius value and press Enter or Return. In this case, a Radius of 4 pixels works nicely, but for best results you should experiment with different values based on the resolution of your image.

5. **Choose Filter ➪ Noise ➪ Median.** To firm up the edges, choose the Median filter, type the same Radius value you did for the Maximum filter, 4 in this case, and press Enter or Return.

6. **Choose Filter ➪ Blur ➪ Gaussian Blur.** Unfortunately, the Maximum filter results in a bunch of little squares that don't do much for your cause. You can merge the squares into a seamless line by choosing the Gaussian Blur command and typing the same radius you typed for Maximum (4 in this case). Then press Enter or Return.

Figure 10-15: Copy a channel, find the edges, and invert (left). Next, apply a string of filters to expand and soften the edges (middle). After converting the mask to a selection outline, reapply Unsharp Mask with improved results (right). To see the original, look back at Figure 10-14, and view the far left image.

7. **Return to the standard composite view. In a color image, press Ctrl+~ (tilde) (or ⌘-~ on the Mac).** In a grayscale image, press Ctrl+1 (or ⌘-1 on the Mac).

8. **Convert the mask to a selection outline.** Ctrl-click (or ⌘-click on the Mac) the mask name in the Channels palette. Photoshop selects the most essential edges in the image without selecting the grain.

9. **Choose Filter ➪ Sharpen ➪ Unsharp Mask.** In the last example in Figure 10-15, the highest permitted Amount value, 500 percent, and a Radius of 2.0, were applied.

10. Whatever values you use, make sure the Threshold is set to 0.

Smart Sharpen

The Smart Sharpen filter is found in Photoshop CS2's Filter ➪ Sharpen submenu. Using a dialog box with more bells and whistles than the average Filter dialog box, yet not as graphical and friendly as the Filter Gallery, the Smart Sharpen filter lets you tweak the Amount and Radius settings you're familiar with from the Unsharp Mask filter, but adds a Remove field, with a list of three of the Blur filters — Gaussian, Lens, and Motion — and enables you to counteract them.

 The Smart Sharpen filter is new to Photoshop CS2.

Set to Advanced mode, the Smart Sharpen dialog box offers three tabs — Sharpen (see Figure 10-16), Shadow, and Highlight (see Figure 10-17), through which you can adjust the Sharpen and Fade Amount, Tonal Width, and Radius. Like most other filter dialog boxes, you can Preview your image in both the dialog box and the image window (thanks to the Preview option, which is selected by default), and unlike other filters, you can save your settings with the Save a Copy of the Current Settings icon, labeled in Figure 10-16. Once settings have been saved, you can access them through the Settings drop list, which lists only "Default" until you've created settings of your own.

Save a Copy of the Current Settings button

Figure 10-16: The Smart Sharpen filter uses familiar sharpening tools — Amount and Radius — plus a blur-fighting option in the Remove list, which defaults to Gaussian.

The additional fields in this unique dialog box offer the following features, and are shown in Figure 10-17:

✦ **Fade Amount.** In both the Shadow and Highlight tabs, this option works much like the Fade command discussed earlier in this chapter. Instead of applying the filter at full intensity, it applies it in concert with the unfiltered layer for a more subtle result. The default is 16 percent for Shadows, and 70 percent for Highlights.

✦ **Tonal Width.** This ranges from narrow (0) to broad (100), and determines the range of tones that will be incorporated into the sharpening effect. Increasing the Tonal Width on the Shadows tab will reduce contrast, and decreasing it on the Highlights tab increases contrast, deepening shadows and intensifying highlights.

Figure 10-17: The Shadows and Highlights tabs allow you to focus your sharpening attention on those aspects of the layer in question. Go for subtlety by increasing the Fade, and create more color diversity by expanding the Tonal Width.

So how do you use this newfangled filter? Well, the "Smart" aspect is the key to its use. Instead of applying sharpening to all the pixels on the layer, and like the rest of the Sharpen filters (except Sharpen Edges), applying the sharpening with equal intensity to all the pixels, this filter lets you focus on pure sharpening (see the Sharpen tab in Figure 10-17) with a nod to the possible presence of blurring, either from the photo itself, or from a Blur filter. The Shadows and Highlights tabs allow you to address the darkest and lightest pixels respectively, using a Fade setting to create less intense results in these two key areas of any photo.

In Figure 10-18, you see the different sharpening effects applied by switching among Gaussian Blur (left), Lens Blur (middle), and Motion Blur (right) in the Remove field of the Smart Sharpen dialog box. The three Remove options are displayed with identical Amount (300 percent) and Radius (5) settings. The More Accurate option is also selected. The Lens Blur gives the most grainy, artifact-filled sharpening effect, and Motion Blur is the least realistic — the cat's fur is strangely sharpened, as though he's been combed.

Drag the line or enter a new value to adjust the Angle

Figure 10-18: Depending on which type of blur you're trying to counteract, the Smart Sharpen filter targets different areas of the active layer. When Motion Blur is chosen from the Remove drop list, the Angle option activates, allowing you to counteract the direction of the motion's blur.

Using the High Pass filter

The High Pass filter falls more or less in the same camp as the sharpening filters but is not located under the Filter ➪ Sharpen submenu. This frequently overlooked filter enables you to isolate high-contrast image areas from their low-contrast counterparts.

When you choose Filter ➪ Other ➪ High Pass, Photoshop offers a single option: the familiar Radius value, which can vary from 0.1 to 250.0. As demonstrated in Figure 10-19, high

Radius values distinguish areas of high and low contrast only slightly. Low values change all high-contrast areas to dark gray and low-contrast areas to a slightly lighter gray. A value of 0.1 (not shown) changes all pixels in an image to a single gray value and is therefore useless.

Figure 10-19: Going, going, gone. The results of separating high- and low-contrast areas in an image with the High Pass filter set at nine different Radius values.

Converting an image into a line drawing

The High Pass filter is especially useful as a precursor to Image ➪ Adjustments ➪ Threshold (covered in Chapter 17), which converts all pixels in an image to black and white. As illustrated in Figure 10-20, the Threshold command produces entirely different effects on images before and after you alter them with the High Pass filter. In fact, applying the High Pass filter with a low Radius value and then issuing the Threshold command converts your image into a line drawing.

In the second row of examples in the figure, Threshold was followed with Filter ➪ Blur ➪ Gaussian Blur (the subject of the next section). The Gaussian Blur Radius value was set to 1.0. Like the Threshold option in the Unsharp Mask dialog box, the Threshold command results in harsh transitions; Gaussian Blur softens them to produce a more natural effect.

Why change your image to a bunch of slightly different gray values and then apply a command such as Threshold? One reason is to create a mask, as discussed at length in Chapter 9. (In Chapter 9, Levels was used instead of Threshold, but both are variations on the same theme.)

High Pass w/loss Radius settings

Threshold and Gaussian Blur

Opacity: 45%, Overlay Mode

Figure 10-20: Three different settings of the High Pass filter with low Radius values (top row), followed by the same images subject to Image ➪ Adjustments ➪ Threshold and Filter ➪ Blur ➪ Gaussian Blur (middle). Next, the second row was layered onto the first and modified with the Opacity and blend mode settings to create the third row.

You might also want to bolster the edges in an image. For example, to achieve the last row of examples in Figure 10-20, the images were layered before applying High Pass, Threshold, and Gaussian Blur. Next, the Opacity setting and the blend mode were adjusted to achieve an edge-tracing effect.

Note   It should be mentioned that Photoshop provides several automated edge-tracing filters — including Find Edges, Trace Contour, and the Gallery Effects acquisition, Glowing Edges. But High Pass affords more control than any of these commands and permits you to explore a wider range of alternatives. Also worth noting, several Gallery Effects filters — most obviously Filter ➪ Sketch ➪ Photocopy — lift much of their code directly from High Pass. Although it may seem at first glance a strange effect, High Pass is one of the seminal filters in Photoshop.

Blurring an Image

The commands under the Filter ➪ Blur submenu produce the opposite effects of their counterparts under the Filter ➪ Sharpen submenu. Rather than enhancing the amount of contrast between neighboring pixels, the Blur filters diminish contrast to create softening effects.

Applying the Gaussian Blur filter

The preeminent Blur filter, Gaussian Blur, blends a specified number of pixels incrementally, following the bell-shaped Gaussian distribution curve discussed earlier. When you choose Filter ➪ Blur ➪ Gaussian Blur, Photoshop produces a single Radius option box, into which you can enter any value from 0.1 to 250.0. As demonstrated in Figure 10-21, Radius values of 1.0 and smaller blur an image slightly; moderate values, between 1.0 and 5.0, turn an image into what might be seen if viewed through a dense fog; and higher values blur the image beyond recognition.

Figure 10-21: The results of blurring an image with the Gaussian Blur filter using nine different Radius values, ranging from slightly out of focus to what the heck is that?

STEPS: The Soft Focus Effect

1. Select a portion of the image if desired. If you want to apply the effect to only a portion of the image, feather the selection with a Radius in the neighborhood of 5 to 8 pixels. Duplicate the selection on its own layer, or if you want to work with an entire layer, duplicate the layer without making a selection first.

2. Choose Filter ➪ Blur ➪ Gaussian Blur to blur the duplicate layer. Type an unusually large value in the Radius option box — say, 8.0 — and press Enter or Return. The results are shown in the first example of Figure 10-21, where the Radius value was increased to 12.

3. Press Ctrl+Shift+F (⌘-Shift-F on the Mac) to open the Fade dialog box. To achieve the effect shown in the second example of Figure 10-22, you can reduce the Opacity value to 65 percent, making the blurred image slightly translucent. This way, you can see the hard edges of the original image through the filtered one.

4. You can achieve additional effects by selecting options from the Mode pop-up menu. The third example in Figure 10-22 was created by raising the Opacity back up to 100 percent and selecting the Darken mode option, which uses the colors in the filtered image to darken the original. Next, press Ctrl+F (⌘-F on the Mac) to reapply my Gaussian Blur settings, pressing Ctrl+Shift+F (⌘-Shift-F on the Mac) to bring back the Fade command, lowering the Opacity to 80 percent, and choosing the Linear Dodge mode, as seen in the last example of Figure 10-22.

Gaussian Blur, Radius: 5.5 pixels   Normal, 65% Opacity

Darken, 100% Opacity   ...with Linear Dodge, 80% Opacity

Figure 10-22: After applying Gaussian Blur (top left), the Fade command was used to lower the Opacity to 65 percent (top right) and to apply the Darken mode with 100 percent Opacity (bottom left). Overlaying another application of Gaussian Blur with Opacity at 80 percent and Linear Dodge mode in force created the final example in the figure.

The preset blurring filters

Neither of the two preset commands in the Filter ➪ Blur submenu, Blur and Blur More, can distribute its blurring effect over a bell-shaped Gaussian curve. For that reason, these two commands are less functional than the Gaussian Blur filter. However, just so you know where they stand in the grand Photoshop focusing scheme, Figure 10-23 shows the effect of each preset command and the nearly equivalent effect created with the Gaussian Blur filter.

Figure 10-23: The effects of the two preset blurring filters (top row) compared with their Gaussian Blur equivalents (bottom row), which are labeled according to Radius values.

Anti-aliasing an image

If you have a particularly jagged image, such as found in a 256-color GIF file, there's a better way to soften the rough edges than applying the Gaussian Blur filter. The best solution is to anti-alias the image. How? As described in Chapter 8, Photoshop anti-aliases a brushstroke or selection outline at twice its normal size and then reduces it by 50 percent and applies bicubic interpolation. You can do the same thing with an image.

Choose Image ⇨ Image Size and enlarge the image to 200 percent of its present size. Make sure that the Resample Image option is selected and set to Bicubic. (You can also experiment with Bilinear for a slightly different effect but don't use Nearest Neighbor.) Next, turn around and choose Image ⇨ Image Size again, but this time shrink the image by 50 percent.

Figure 10-24 shows a hand-drawn (on paper) doodle, along with the Gaussian Blur applied to the top detail sample (in the hopes of smoothing the drawn lines), and then an example of anti-aliasing applied to the bottom sample. The image subjected to Gaussian Blur with a very low Radius value (0.5) has turned out fuzzy, instead of smoothed. After applying anti-aliasing, however, the lines in the drawing are smooth, not fuzzy.

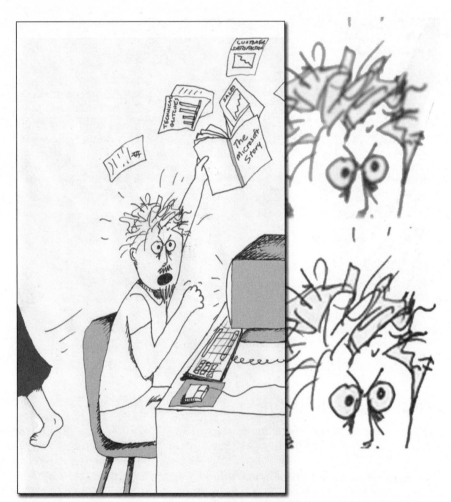

Figure 10-24: A doodle that's in need, indeed. Note the enlarged detail (top) showing the Gaussian Blur's results, compared with Antialiasing, which smoothes the lines without making them fuzzy (bottom). The secret? Bicubic interpolation, through the Images Size dialog box and the use of the Resample option.

Directional blurring

In addition to its everyday blurring functions, Photoshop provides two *directional blurring* filters, Motion Blur and Radial Blur. Instead of blurring pixels in feathered clusters like the Gaussian Blur filter, the Motion Blur filter blurs pixels in straight lines over a specified distance. The Radial Blur filter blurs pixels in varying degrees depending on their distance from the center of the blur. The following pages explain both filters in detail.

Motion blurring

The Motion Blur filter makes an image appear as if either the image or the camera was moving when you shot the photo. When you choose Filter ➪ Blur ➪ Motion Blur, Photoshop displays the dialog box shown in Figure 10-25. You type the angle of movement in the Angle option box. Alternatively, you can indicate the angle by clicking and dragging the straight line inside the circle to the right of the Angle option, as shown in the figure. (Notice that the arrow cursor actually appears outside the circle. After you begin dragging on the line, you can move the cursor anywhere you want and still affect the angle.)

Figure 10-25: Click and drag the line inside the circle to change the angle of the blur.

You then type the distance of the movement in the Distance option box. Photoshop permits any value between 1 and 999 pixels. The filter distributes the effect of the blur over the course of the Distance value, as illustrated by the examples in Figure 10-26.

Note Mathematically speaking, Motion Blur is one of Photoshop's simpler filters. Rather than distributing the effect over a Gaussian curve—which one might argue would produce a more believable effect—Photoshop creates a simple linear distribution, peaking in the center and fading at either end. It's as if the program took the value you specified in the Distance option, created that many clones of the image, offset half the clones in one direction and half the clones in the other—all spaced 1 pixel apart—and then varied the opacity of each.

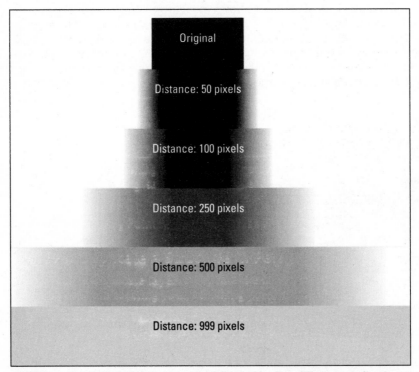

Figure 10-26: A single black rectangle followed by five different applications of the Motion Blur filter. Only the Distance value varied, as labeled. A 0-degree Angle value was used in all five examples.

Using the Wind filter

The problem with the Motion Blur filter is that it blurs pixels in two directions. If you want to distribute pixels in one absolute direction or the other, try the Wind filter, which you can use either on its own or with Motion Blur.

When you choose Filter ➪ Stylize ➪ Wind, Photoshop displays the Wind dialog box shown in Figure 10-27. You can select from three methods and two directions to distribute the selected pixels. Figure 10-28 compares the effect of the Motion Blur filter to each of the three methods offered by the Wind filter. Notice that the Wind filter does not blur pixels. Rather, it evaluates a selection in 1-pixel-tall horizontal strips and offsets the strips randomly inside the image.

Figure 10-27: Use the Wind filter to randomly distribute a selection in 1-pixel horizontal strips in one of two directions.

Figure 10-28: The difference between the effects of the Motion Blur filter (top left) and the Wind filter (clockwise from top right: Wind, Stagger, and Blast). In each case, From the Right was selected within the Direction section of the Wind filter dialog box.

For interesting results, try combining the Motion Blur and Wind filters to get both the illusion of action with the clarity preserved by Wind, which as stated, doesn't blur pixels. For example, as shown in Figure 10-29, the image on the right was cloned on three separate layers, stacked on top of each other. The top-most layer is an unfiltered clone of the original, with 60 percent Opacity and the Darken blend mode applied. The Motion Blur set to 25 percent Opacity in Normal mode was used on the middle layer. The bottom layer was subjected to the Wind filter, with the Wind method, and the layer is set at 100 percent Opacity in Normal mode. The result is the appearance of motion — those streaks coming off the elephant's tusks make it look as though he's coming at the camera — and with enough blur to counteract the unrealistic trails of color created by the Wind filter. The image on the left is the original, a photo of an elephant standing still, shown for comparison's sake.

Figure 10-29: Combining the Wind filter on one layer with the Motion Blur on another, and yet another unfiltered layer of the elephant in Darken mode creates the look of an elephant on the move.

Radial blurring

Choosing Filter ➪ Blur ➪ Radial Blur displays the Radial Blur dialog box shown in Figure 10-30. The dialog box offers two Blur Method options: Spin and Zoom.

Figure 10-30: Click and drag inside the Blur Center grid to change the point about which the Radial Blur filter spins or zooms the image.

If you select Spin, the image appears to be rotating about a central point. You specify that point by clicking and dragging in the grid inside the Blur Center box (as demonstrated in the figure). If you select Zoom, the image appears to rush away from you, as if you were zooming the camera while shooting the photograph. Again, you specify the central point of the Zoom by clicking and dragging in the Blur Center box. Figure 10-31 features examples of both settings.

After selecting a Blur Method option, you can type any value between 1 and 100 in the Amount option box to specify the maximum distance over which the filter blurs pixels. (You can type a value of 0, but doing so merely causes the filter to waste time without producing an effect.) Pixels farthest away from the center point move the most; pixels close to the center point barely move at all. Keep in mind that large values take more time to apply than small values.

Tip   Select a Quality option to specify your favorite compromise between time and quality. The Good and Best Quality options ensure smooth results by respectively applying bilinear and bicubic interpolation (as explained in Chapter 2). However, they also prolong the amount of time the filter spends calculating pixels in your image. The Draft option *diffuses* an image, which leaves a trail of loose and randomized pixels but takes less time to complete.

Original

Spin, 10 pixels, Good

Zoom, 30 pixels, Good

Figure 10-31: Two examples of the Radial Blur filter, with one
set to Spin and the other to Zoom, along with the original,
unfiltered image. Set to "Good" Quality, the head of the joyous
penguin was the center of the Spin (set to 10 pixels) and the
Zoom (set to 30 pixels).

Blurring with a threshold

The purpose of Filter ⇨ Blur ⇨ Smart Blur is to blur the low-contrast portions of an image while retaining the edges. This way, you can downplay photo grain, blemishes, and artifacts without harming the real edges in the image. If you're familiar with Filter ⇨ Pixelate ⇨ Facet, it may help to know that Smart Blur is essentially a customizable version of that filter.

The two key options in the Smart Blur dialog box (see Figure 10-32) are the Radius and Threshold sliders. As with all Radius options, this one expands the number of pixels calculated at a time as you increase the value. Meanwhile, the Threshold value works just like the one in the Unsharp Mask dialog box, specifying how different two neighboring pixels must be to be considered an edge.

Figure 10-32: The Smart Blur filter lets you blur the low-contrast areas of an image without harming the edges.

But the Threshold value has a peculiar and unexpected effect on the Radius. The Radius value actually produces more subtle effects if you raise the value beyond the Threshold. For example, take a look at Figure 10-33. Here you see a grid of images subject to different Radius and Threshold values. (The first value below each image is the Radius.) In the top row of the figure, the 5.0 Radius produces a more pronounced effect than its 20.0 and 60.0 cousins. This is because 5.0 is less than the 10.0 Threshold, while 20.0 and 60.0 are more.

Figure 10-33: Combinations of different Radius (starting, from left to right, at 5, then 20, then 60) and Threshold (10 in the top row, 30 in the second row, 80 in the bottom row) values. Notice that the most dramatic effects occur when the Radius is equal to about half the Threshold.

The Quality settings control the smoothness of the edges. The High setting takes more time than Medium and Low, but it looks smoother as well — shown in Figure 10-33, where the value was set to High to create all the effects demonstrated. The two additional Mode options enable you to trace the edges defined by the Threshold value with white lines. Overlay Edge shows image and lines, and Edge Only shows just the traced lines. About the only practical purpose for these options is to monitor the precise effect of the Threshold setting in the preview box. Otherwise, the Edge options are clearly relegated to special effects.

Tip　　The better way to blur low-contrast areas is to create an edge mask, as explained in the section "Sharpening grainy photographs." Just reverse the selection by choosing Select ⇨ Inverse and apply the Gaussian Blur filter.

Figure 10-34 shows how the masking technique compares with Smart Blur. In the first image, Unsharp Mask was applied with a Threshold of 20. Then Smart Blur was applied with a Radius of 2.0 and a Threshold of 20.0, matching the Unsharp Mask value.

In the second image, an edge mask was created — as explained in the procedure entitled "Creating and Using an Edge Mask" — and an Unsharp Mask was applied with a Threshold of 0. Next, Ctrl+Shift+I (⌘-Shift-I on the Mac) was pressed to reverse the selection and a Gaussian Blur was applied with a Radius of 2.0.

Unsharp Mask +   Unsharp Mask +
Smart Blur, Threshold: 20   Gaussian Blur, Edge Mask

Figure 10-34: The difference between relying on
Photoshop's automated Threshold capabilities (left)
and sharpening and blurring with the aid of an edge
mask (right). A little manual labor wins out over total
automation.

Using the Lens Blur filter

The Lens Blur filter is designed to simulate the type of optical blurring that occurs
in the real world. For years, photographers have experimented with depth of field
to determine the relative focus of foreground and background elements in their
photos. Although a crisp, uniformly in-focus image is appropriate in many circumstances, sometimes a shallow depth of field (where one section is sharply in focus
while others are blurred) can perfectly set the tone for an image. You can take pictures as crisp as you can manage and then perform the selective blurring later in
Photoshop. Not content to simply be a compound blur effect, however, the Lens
Blur filter also offers you a blissfully obsessive amount of control over Iris,
Highlight, and Noise settings.

Choose Filter ➪ Blur ➪ Lens Blur to bring up the large Lens Blur dialog box, shown in
Figure 10-35. On the left side of the dialog box is the image preview, which is scaled to
fit entirely inside the dialog box by default. If you want to adjust the zoom ratio, use
the plus and minus signs in the lower-left corner or click the right-pointing arrowhead
and choose an option from the resulting pop-up menu. As usual, you can press and
hold the space bar and drag over your image to position it within the preview area.
Next to the zoom options is the progress bar, which lets you know that Photoshop is
still working hard during some of the slower, more complex Lens Blur calculations.
The right side of the bulky Lens Blur dialog box contains the following options:

✦ **Preview.** When the Preview option is selected, the Lens Blur filter automatically updates the image preview every time you make an adjustment. For
  minute tweaking, this can be great, but sometimes this calculation-intense

filter can take a while to give you a result, in which case you may want to de-select this option. Even better is the ability to choose between the Faster and More Accurate preview options. Generally, it's a safe bet to leave this set to Faster. Remember, these option are only for previewing. As soon as you click OK, Photoshop renders the best possible result it can.

Figure 10-35: Bring your ideas into focus with the Lens Blur filter. Focus, blur — it works on many levels.

✦ **Depth Map.** Here's where the wonders of the Lens Blur filter really shine. The Depth Map you specify contains information that assigns an imaginary position in space to every individual pixel in your image. By default, the Source pop-up menu offers three options: None, which performs blurring on each pixel in your image uniformly; Transparency, which determines what gets blurred in an image based on the transparency values of the pixels; and Layer Mask, which bases blur levels on the grayscale values in an image's layer mask. Under the default settings, the black areas of the mask are treated as though they are in the foreground and the white areas are treated as though they are in the background, though you can reverse this by selecting the Invert option or by adjusting these settings manually, as you'll see in a moment. If you've added an alpha channel to your layer, it too is available to choose as a Depth Map from the Source pop-up menu.

Tip

The ability to create custom Depth Maps gives you the opportunity to individually tweak the blurriness of every single pixel in your image. You'll be astonished at the blurring power at your fingertips. Try this: Create a layer mask and draw a black-to-white transparency gradient in your image. Then apply the Lens Blur filter with the Source set to Layer Mask. The result will be an image that gradually increases in blurriness according to your gradient. Or add an alpha channel to your layer and use the Brush tool to paint in random splotches of blacks and grays to emulate the random, selective focus that's so popular right now among music video directors and people with broken camera lenses. Why, the possibilities are endless, though blurry in the distance.

In Figure 10-36, an alpha channel was added to the image, and a Depth Map was created using the Magnetic Lasso and Gradient tools. Next, Filter ➪ Blur ➪ Lens Blur was chosen, and the new alpha channel selected from the Source pop-up menu. As a result, the background came into sharp focus and the main subject of the photo was softened.

✦ **Iris.** The characteristics of genuine lens blur in a photograph can depend a lot on the shape of the iris in the camera lens that captured the photo. (An *iris* is a diaphragm comprised of plates that expand and contract to determine the amount of light entering the lens.) Photoshop's Lens Blur filter gives you a number of options for simulating many different types of irises. From the Shape pop-up menu you can select anything from a triangular iris to an octagonal one. Experiment with the various Shape options together with the Blade Curvature and Rotation settings to create different types of realistic details and imperfections in your lens blur effects. As the number of sides in the iris increases, along with the Blade Curvature, the blur highlights will become more and more smooth until they are virtually circular.

The Radius setting is where you adjust the amount of blur applied to your image. You can think of it as the Photoshop counterpart to a camera's f-stop (which regulates depth of field in real life), though the fact that Photoshop doesn't know the focal length of the lens that captured the image prevents you from getting a direct, mathematical correlation.

✦ **Specular Highlights.** When you blur an image through one of the other blurring filters in Photoshop, colors can get averaged and bright whites can become shades of gray. Photographers are well aware of the fact that no matter how much a photo is optically blurred, whites remain bright white. The Lens Blur filter accounts for this with the Specular Highlights section of the dialog box. Decrease the Threshold amount to add areas that will be affected by the highlights and increase the Brightness level to blast the image with pools of white. In addition to being optically accurate, Specular Highlights can also add a nice, otherworldly quality to an image.

Figure 10-36: Here, an alpha channel was created for use as a Depth Map (see palette inset). Then, the Lens Blur filter was applied, and the Blur Focal Distance set by clicking in the center of the main subject of the photo. The other pixels were blurred at a Radius value of 33 (right).

✦ **Noise.** When you apply a drastic blur to sections of an image, it tends to smooth out detail and color values. But as you've seen, the name of Lens Blur's game is realism, and no matter how blurry a photograph is, it would look unnatural to lose film's inherent grain detail. Thankfully, the Noise options can help artificially pull this detail back in. Adjust the Amount slider until the noise in the blurred section matches the original photo's noise in the in-focus section. Below the slider, select either Uniform or Gaussian to set the type of noise (for my money, Gaussian is the way to go). Finally, you can make sure the noise you generate won't affect the color in your image by selecting the Monochromatic option.

Applying a Box Blur

The Blur Box works a lot like the Gaussian Blur, as you have only a Radius slider to adjust the effect, but the results are faster, and the filter works differently in terms of which pixels its using to make the blur happen. The term "box" comes from the boxy direction that the pixel comparison takes. Each pixel is compared to the pixels directly above, below, and to the left and right — no diagonally positioned pixels are included. Figure 10-37 shows the Box Blur dialog box and the image window behind it. The Preview option is selected, and you can see the potential drawback of using this filter — a "boxy" look to the blur.

New Feature   The Box Blur is new to Photoshop CS2.

This boxy-ness is only really visible at high Radius settings — you can see the obvious vertical and horizontal streaks of blurring in the image window. Figure 10-38 shows two versions of the same image — one blurred at a Radius of 5 pixels, the second at 30 pixels.

Figure 10-37: Click and drag the Box Blur's Radius slider to adjust the intensity of the horizontal and vertical blurring effect.

5 pixels

30 pixels

Figure 10-38: Want a quick blur effect? Box Blur may be your answer — unless you're blurring in the Radius range of 20 to 80 pixels. Higher than that, and the blur is so extensive that the boxy look disappears. Lower than 20, and the boxy look is negligible.

Using the Shape Blur

You know those shapes you can choose from when you use the Custom Shape drawing tool? Well, they come back to serve you again when you choose Filter ⇨ Blur ⇨ Shape Blur. The resulting dialog box (seen in Figure 10-39) offers you a preview of the image, the ubiquitous zoom controls, and the oft-seen Radius slider. Below that, you have a palette of shapes, with an options menu button that displays the menu also seen in Figure 10-39.

 The Shape Blur is new to Photoshop CS2.

Figure 10-39: Pick a shape, or choose from different shape categories in the pop-up menu. Choose All to see the entire set of shapes with which you can blur your layer content.

To blur with a shape—the shape dictating the sweep of the tool's comparisons of each pixel's neighbors—simply click a shape in the palette, and watch the results appear in the dialog box and in the image window (if you have selected the Preview option).

The results? Well, as shown in Figure 10-40, you can see that like the Box Blur (which is really a shape blur perpetually set to a box shape) the Radius setting determines whether or not the shape used is visible within the blur results. At low settings (below 10 pixels—and 5 is as low as you can go), you can't really tell the results from a Gaussian blur, which compares each pixel to all of its immediate neighbors, resulting in no discernable shape. At higher Radius settings—higher than 20, but less than 100—you can really see the blur effect is tweaked by the shape you chose. This isn't to say that you could tell which shape was used if you were handed a photo that was blurred, with say, the little dog paw shape, but you can tell it's not a uniform Gaussian blur, either.

Figure 10-40: In the top-most image, the Radius is set low, and the blur is very Gaussian-like. On the bottom, the higher Radius setting shows the shape's effect.

Tip

The more simple the shape—arrows, triangles, boxes, anything angular without too many sides, nooks, or crannies—the more obvious and identifiable the shape's impact is. If you're looking for a blur that's not the regular old Gaussian effect, this might be the one for you—you can even choose a shape that's similar to your photo's key subject. In Figure 10-40, an elongated arrowhead was chosen (see Figure 10-39 for the shape chosen in the dialog box) because it's reminiscent of both the feathers on the bird and the foliage behind him.

Working with Surface Blur

The third new Blur filter—third because it's alphabetically after Box, and Shape—is intended for use in blurring images depicting shiny surfaces. It has interesting effects on non-shiny content, as shown in Figure 10-41, where the parrot seen in Figures 10-37 through 10-40 is shown, blurred at a Radius of 20 and a Threshold of 80. The result, because the image isn't particularly shiny to begin with, resembles a soft fog—as though the bird was captured on film during a soft, tropical rain.

In Figure 10-42, an image with both shiny and not-so-shiny content—an animal in oily water, courtesy of the Exxon Valdez—is subjected to the Surface Blur filter. Here we see that a low Radius and a higher Threshold result in more blurring of bright areas and less overall dimming. Increase the Radius, and the overall dimming occurs, killing some or all of the highlights that make the look of a bright, shiny subject.

Tip

If you don't want to lose detail in an image with shiny glass, chrome, or other glossy surfaces, select only those areas with a high shine that you need to tone down. Using low Radius and Threshold settings will assure subtle results, and the Preview makes it possible to make sure that your Surface Blur doesn't make your highlights look dirty compared to the rest of the shiny content.

Figure 10-41: The Surface Blur dialog box gives you two familiar sliders — Radius and Threshold — and here we see that when the photo isn't shiny or sparkly to begin with, you can achieve a cool, foggy result.

Figure 10-42: Use the Surface Blur to tone down the gloss or sparkle on a very shiny subject (original image at top). Adjust the Radius to 10 pixels or lower (5 here), and the Threshold to 20 or lower (15 here) if you want to keep the detail but lose any distracting or excessive shine.

Softening a selection outline

Gaussian Blur and other Blur filters are equally useful for editing masks as they are for editing image pixels. As mentioned earlier, applying Gaussian Blur to a mask has the same effect as applying Select ➪ Feather to a selection outline. But Gaussian

Blur affords more control. Where the Feather command affects all portions of a selection outline uniformly, you can apply Gaussian Blur selectively to a mask, permitting you to easily mix soft and hard edges within a single selection outline.

Another advantage to blurring a mask is that you can see the results of your adjustments on-screen, instead of relying on the seldom-helpful marching ants. For example, suppose you want to create a shadow that recedes away from a subject in your composition. You've managed to accurately select the foreground image — but how do you feather the selection exclusively inward, so that it appears smaller than the object that casts it? Although you can pull this off using selection commands such as Contract and Feather, it's much easier to apply filters such as Minimum and Gaussian Blur inside a mask.

Minimum and Maximum

Filter ➪ Other ➪ Minimum expands the dark portions of an image, spreading them outward into other pixels. Its opposite, Filter ➪ Other ➪ Maximum, expands the light portions of an image. In traditional stat photography, these techniques are known, respectively, as *choking* and *spreading*.

When you are working in the Quick Mask mode or an independent mask channel, applying the Minimum filter has the effect of incrementally contracting the selected area, subtracting pixels uniformly around the edges of the selection outline. The Minimum dialog box presents you with a single Radius value, which tells Photoshop how many edge pixels to delete. Just the opposite, the Maximum filter incrementally increases the size of white areas that add pixels uniformly around the edges of a selection.

Adding a cast shadow to a layer

The following steps describe how to use the Minimum and Gaussian Blur filters to contract and feather an existing selection outline to create a shadow that leans away from the foreground subject of a composition. Figures 10-43 through 10-45 illustrate the steps in the project. Figure 10-46 shows the final cast shadow.

STEPS: Filtering a Selection Outline in the Quick Mask Mode

1. **Select the foreground image.** These steps work best if you set your foreground object up on a separate layer. (To learn how, see Chapter 12.) To select the foreground object, convert the layer's transparency mask to a selection outline by Ctrl-clicking (⌘-clicking on the Mac) the layer thumbnail in the Layers palette.

2. **If you're working on a layer, switch to the background image.** The quickest route is Shift+Alt+[(or Shift-Option-[on the Mac).

3. **Press Q to enter the Quick Mask mode.** You can create a new mask channel if you prefer, but the Quick Mask mode is more convenient.

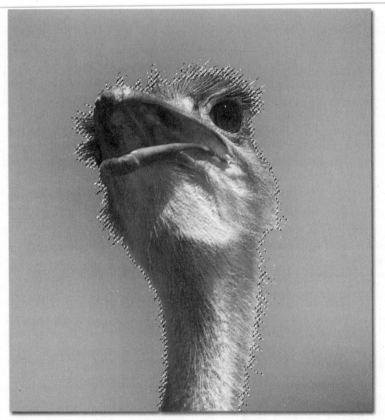

Figure 10-43: This content lives on an independent layer. To select it, Ctrl-click (or ⌘-click) the layer in the Layers palette.

4. **Choose Filter ⇨ Other ⇨ Minimum.** Type a Radius value to expand the transparent area into the rubylith. In Figure 10-44, a Radius value of 10 pixels was used. This expanded the size of the black, or masked, area and made the selection smaller.

5. **Choose Filter ⇨ Blur ⇨ Gaussian Blur.** To create a soft shadow, a Radius equal to the Radius used in the Minimum dialog box was typed, which was 10 pixels. Smaller values are also acceptable. The only potential problem with larger values is that they expand the shadow beyond the boundaries of the image, which in all probability is not the effect you want. When you click OK, Photoshop blurs the transparent area.

6. **Press Q to exit the Quick Mask mode.** Marching ants appear.

7. **Send the selection to an independent layer.** The easiest way to do this is to press Ctrl+J (⌘-J on the Mac). You now have a shadow filled with colors from the background layer.

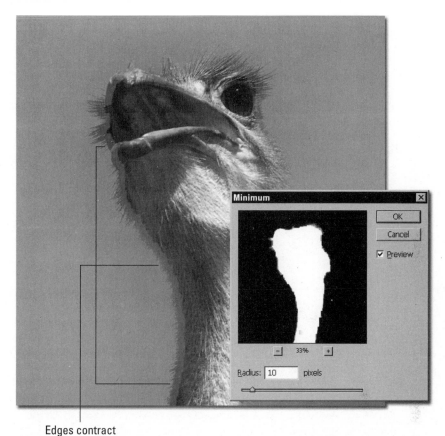

Edges contract

Figure 10-44: The Minimum filter decreases the size of the transparent area in the Quick Mask mode, thereby choking the selection outline.

8. **Choose the Multiply mode.** You can choose Multiply from the pop-up menu at the top of the Layers palette, or press Shift+Alt+M (Shift-Option-M on the Mac). As discussed in Chapter 13, this burns the shadow into its background, so it looks darker, as a shadow should. Because your foreground image is in the way, you may not be able to see the effect of this step, but don't worry — you will soon.

9. **Scale and distort the shadow.** Press Ctrl+T (or ⌘-T on the Mac) to invoke the Free Transform command. Then drag the top handles in the bounding box to scale the shadow; press Ctrl (⌘ on the Mac) and drag a handle to distort the shadow, as demonstrated in Figure 10-45. For the best effect, you'll need a big distortion. You may have to zoom out and expand the size of the image window to give yourself lots of room to work. When you get the effect you want, press Enter or Return to apply the distortion.

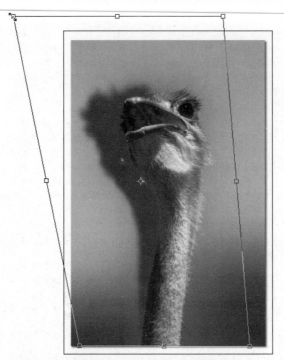

Figure 10-45: Press Ctrl+T (⌘-T on the Mac) to enter the Free Transform mode. Then Ctrl-drag (⌘-drag) a corner handle to distort the shadow.

Thanks to the fact that you applied the Multiply blend mode to the shadow, it appears darker than the rest of the background. You can adjust its opacity or fill it with a different color if you like. The background was filled with one of Photoshop's predefined patterns called Molecular, as shown in Figure 10-46. You could have achieved a similar effect using Select ➪ Modify ➪ Contract and Select ➪ Feather, but unless you have a special aversion to the Quick Mask mode, it's easier to be sure of your results when you can see exactly what you're doing using filters.

Figure 10-46: Words to the wise from this ostrich now appear against a pattern background.

Noise Factors

Photoshop offers four loosely associated filters in its Filter ➪ Noise submenu. One filter adds random pixels — known as *noise* — to an image. The other three, Despeckle, Dust and Scratches, and Median, average the colors of neighboring pixels in ways that theoretically remove noise from poorly scanned images. But in fact, they function nearly as well at removing essential detail as they do at removing extraneous noise. In the following sections, you learn how the Noise filters work.

Adding noise

Noise adds grit and texture to an image. Noise makes an image look like you shot it in New York on the Lower East Side and were lucky to get the photo at all because someone was throwing sand in your face as you sped away in your chauffeur-driven, jet-black Maserati Bora, hammering away at the shutter release. In reality, of course, a guy over at Sears shot the photo for you, after which you tooled around in your minivan trying to find a store that sold day-old bread. But that's the beauty of Noise. It makes you look cool, even when you aren't.

You add noise by choosing Filter ➪ Noise ➪ Add Noise. Shown in Figure 10-47, the Add Noise dialog box features the following options:

✦ **Amount.** This value determines how far pixels in the image can stray from their current colors. The value represents a color range rather than a brightness range and is expressed as a percentage. You can type a value as high as 400 percent. The percentage is based on 256 brightness values per channel if you're working with a 24-bit image and 32,768 brightness values for 16-bit images. So with a 24-bit image (8-bit channels), the default value of 12.5 percent is equivalent to 32 brightness levels, which is 12.5 percent of 256.

For example, if you type a value of 12.5 percent for a 24-bit image, Photoshop can apply any color that is 32 shades more or less red, more or less green, *and* more or less blue than the current color. If you type 400 percent, Photoshop theoretically can go 1,024 brightness values lighter or darker. But that results in colors that are out of range; therefore, they get clipped to black or white. The result is higher contrast inside the noise pixels.

✦ **Uniform.** Select this option to apply colors absolutely randomly within the specified range. Photoshop is no more likely to apply one color within the range than another, thus resulting in an even color distribution.

✦ **Gaussian.** When you select this option, you instruct Photoshop to prioritize colors along the Gaussian distribution curve. The effect is that most colors added by the filter either closely resemble the original colors or push the boundaries of the specified range. In other words, this option results in more light and dark pixels, thus producing a more pronounced effect.

✦ **Monochromatic.** When working on a full-color image, the Add Noise filter distributes pixels randomly throughout the different color channels. However, when you select the Monochrome option, Photoshop distributes the noise in the same manner in all channels. The result is grayscale noise. (This option does not affect grayscale images; the noise can't get any more grayscale than it already is.)

Figure 10-47: The Add Noise dialog box asks you to specify the amount and variety of noise you want to add to the selection.

Figure 10-48 compares three applications of Gaussian noise to identical amounts of Uniform noise.

Figure 10-48: The Gaussian option produces more pronounced effects than the Uniform option at identical Amount values.

Noise variations

Normally, the Add Noise filter adds both lighter and darker pixels to an image. If you prefer, however, you can limit the effect of the filter to strictly lighter or darker pixels. To do so, apply the Add Noise filter, and then apply the Fade command (Ctrl+Shift+F on the PC or ⌘-Shift-F on the Mac) and select the Lighten or Darken blend mode. Or you can copy the image to a new layer, apply the filter, and merge the filtered image with the underlying original.

Figure 10-49 shows sample applications of lighter and darker noise. After copying the image to a separate layer, the Add Noise filter was applied with an Amount value of 40 percent and Gaussian was selected. To create the top example in the figure, Lighten was selected from the blend mode pop-up menu. To create the bottom example, the Darken mode was selected. In each case, a layer of strictly lighter or darker noise was added while at the same time retaining the clarity of the original image.

Figure 10-49: You can limit the Add Noise filter to strictly lighter (top, 40 percent Add Noise, Lighten mode) or darker (bottom, 40 percent Add Noise, Darken mode) noise by applying the filter to a layered clone.

Chunky noise

You may find that your biggest frustration with the Add Noise filter is that you can't specify the size of individual specks of noise. No matter what you do, noise only comes in 1-pixel squares. It may occur to you that you can enlarge the noise dots in a layer by applying the Maximum or Minimum filter, but in practice, doing so simply fills in the image, because there isn't sufficient space between the noise pixels to accommodate the larger dot sizes.

Luckily, Photoshop provides several alternatives. One is the Pointillize filter, which adds variable-sized dots and then colors those dots in keeping with the original colors in the image. Though Pointillize lacks the random quality of the Add Noise filter, you can use it to add texture to an image.

To create the top image in Figure 10-50, Filter ➪ Pixelate ➪ Pointillize was used, with 5 in the Cell Size option box. After pressing Enter (Return on the Mac) to apply the filter, Ctrl+Shift+F (⌘-Shift-F on the Mac) was pressed to fade the filter, changing the Opacity value to 50 percent.

Figure 10-50: From top to bottom, noise was created with Pointillize, Halftone, and Grain. Experiment with different settings for each one on your own photos.

The Gallery Effects filters provide a few noise alternatives. Filter ➪ Sketch ➪ Halftone Pattern adds your choice of dot patterns, as shown in the middle example in Figure 10-50. But like all filters in the Sketch submenu, it replaces the colors in your image with the foreground and background colors. Filter ➪ Texture ➪ Grain is a regular noise smorgasbord, permitting you to select from ten different Grain Type options, each of which produces a different kind of noise. The bottom example in Figure 10-50 shows Grain in Clumped.

Removing noise with Despeckle

Strictly speaking, the Despeckle command probably belongs in the Filter ➪ Blur submenu, given that more than removing specks (or speckles), it blurs the image. Specifically, it blurs a selection while preserving its edges — the idea being that unwanted noise is most noticeable in the continuous regions of an image, rather than out along the perimeter. In practice, this filter is nearly the exact opposite of the Sharpen Edges filter — so it should be moved to Blur submenu, and called Blur Everything But The Edges.

How does it know where the edges are? The Despeckle command searches an image for edges using the equivalent of an Unsharp Mask Threshold value of 5. It then ignores the edges in the image and blurs everything else with the force of the Blur More filter, as shown in the upper-left image in Figure 10-51.

Figure 10-51: The effects of the Despeckle filter (upper left) and then the Median filter, the Radius values for which are noted in the images.

Averaging pixels with Median

Another command in the Filter ➪ Noise submenu, Median removes noise by averaging the colors in an image, one pixel at a time. When you choose Filter ➪ Noise ➪ Median, Photoshop produces a Radius option box. For every pixel in a selection, the filter averages the colors of the neighboring pixels that fall inside the specified radius — ignoring any pixels that are so different that they might skew the average — and applies the average color to the central pixel. You can type any value between 1 and 100. However, even at low settings like 16, significant blurring occurs, as you can see from the bottom-right example in Figure 10-51. At the maximum Radius value, you are left with a sort of soft, blurry gradient, with all image detail obliterated.

As with Gaussian Blur, you can achieve some interesting and useful effects by backing off the Median filter with the Fade command. But rather than creating a romantic, soft-yet-focused glow, Median clumps up details, giving an image a plastic, molded quality, as demonstrated by the examples in Figure 10-52. To create every one of these images, the Median filter was applied with a Radius of 5 pixels. For the second example, Ctrl+Shift+F (⌘-Shift-F on the Mac) was pressed to display the Fade dialog box, and the Opacity value was lowered to 65 percent. For the bottom-left image, Opacity was raised back up to 100 percent in the Fade dialog box and the Darken blend mode was applied. And for the final example, the Opacity was brought back down to 80 percent and the Linear Dodge mode was used.

Median Radius: 5 pixels   Normal Opacity: 65%

Darken Opacity: 100%   Linear Dodge Opacity: 80%

Figure 10-52: After applying the Median filter, the effect was reversed slightly using Edit ➪ Fade Median. The blend modes and Opacity values were varied — Darken with 100 % Opacity on the left, and Linear Dodge with 80% Opacity on the right.

Another difference between Gaussian Blur and Median is that Gaussian Blur destroys edges and Median invents new ones. This means you can follow up the Median filter with Unsharp Mask to achieve even more pronounced sculptural effects.

Sharpening a compressed image

A digital camera has gone from something that's nice to have to something you really must have if you're serious about electronic imaging. You can take as many images as you like, download them to your computer immediately, and place them into a printed document literally minutes after snapping the picture. The technology has improved greatly in the last year or so — with reasonably priced cameras ($200 to $400) having enough oomph (megapixels, bells and whistles) to create images that are vastly superior to the images people were taking with cameras at twice the price just two years ago. Of course, lower-end digital cameras will still produce images with jagged edges, artifacts, and other blemishes. These blemishes stem from lower resolutions, heavy-handed compression schemes (all based on JPEG), or both. Cameras that produce 5-megapixel images and that enable you to store uncompressed images as TIFFs are producing the better images, and the prices should continue to drop, placing such cameras within many people's budgetary reach.

If your digital images need some help, you can firm up the detail and smooth out the color transitions in your digital photos by applying a combination of filters — Median, Gaussian Blur, and Unsharp Mask — to a layered version of the image. The following steps should help you:

STEPS: Adjusting the Focus of Digital Photos

1. **Select the entire image and copy it to a new layer.** That's Ctrl+A, Ctrl+J (⌘-A, ⌘-J on the Mac). Figure 10-53 shows an image in need of sharpening.

2. **Choose Filter ⇨ Noise ⇨ Median.** A Radius value of 2 is almost always the optimal choice. But if the image is particularly bad, 3 may be warranted.

3. **Choose Filter ⇨ Blur ⇨ Gaussian Blur.** Now that you've gummed up the detail a bit and rubbed out most of the compression, use the Gaussian Blur filter with a Radius of 1.0 to blur the gummy detail slightly. This softens the edges that the Median filter creates. (You don't want any fake edges, after all.)

4. **Choose Filter ⇨ Sharpen ⇨ Unsharp Mask.** All this blurring demands some intense sharpening. So apply Unsharp Mask with a maximum Amount value of 500 percent and a Radius of 1.0 (to match the Gaussian Blur Radius). This restores most of the definition to the edges, as shown in Figure 10-54.

5. **Lower the layer's Opacity value.** By itself, the filtered layer is a bit too smooth. So mix the filtered floater and the underlying original with an Opacity value between 30 and 50 percent.

6. **Merge the image. Press Ctrl+E (Win) or ⌘-E (Mac) to send the layer down.**

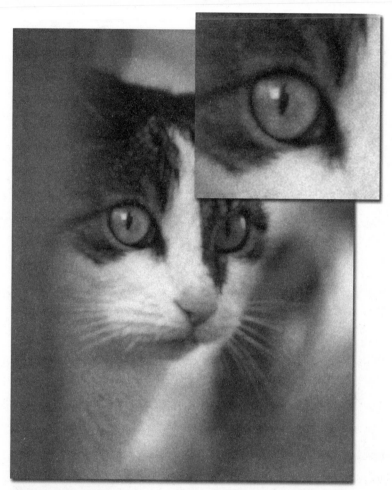

Figure 10-53: This image was captured with a low-end digital camera, with just 3 megapixels.

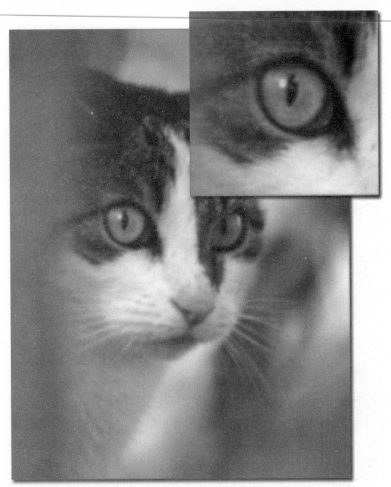

Figure 10-54: Thanks to Median, Gaussian Blur, and Unsharp Mask, the cat's face (see eye in detail) is smooth and clean, but a little too soft.

7. **Continue to correct the image as you normally would.** Fix blemishes that were part of the real subjects of the photo, clean up unwanted content, fix lighting, and so forth — whatever your photo requires. The finished result appears in Figure 10-55.

These steps also work well for sharpening other kinds of compressed imagery, including old photographs that you overcompressed without creating backups, and images that you've downloaded from the Internet. If applying the Unsharp Mask filter brings out the goobers, try these steps instead.

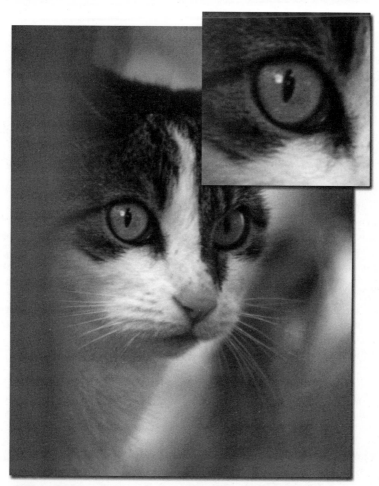

Figure 10-55: Sharp as a tack, the image looks great after a combination of filters, layers, and opacity adjustments.

Cleaning up scanned halftones

Photoshop offers one additional filter in the Filter ➪ Noise submenu called Dust & Scratches. The purpose of this filter is to remove dust particles, hairs, scratches, and other imperfections that may accompany a scan. The filter offers two options, Radius and Threshold. As long as the offending imperfection is smaller or thinner than the Radius value and different enough from its neighbors to satisfy the Threshold value, the filter deletes the spot or line and interpolates between the pixels around the perimeter.

But like so many of Photoshop's older automated tools, Dust & Scratches works only when conditions are extremely favorable. It's not that you should never use it; in fact, you may always want to give it a shot at a dusty image. If it doesn't work, don't be surprised—just get to work and eliminate the imperfections manually using the Clone Stamp tool or Healing Brush, as discussed in Chapter 7.

Now, as stated, Dust & Scratches was designed to get rid of the dirt from your scanner that ends up on your images. But another problem that the filter may be able to eliminate is moiré patterns. These patterns appear when scanning halftone images from books and magazines. The image shown in Figure 10-56 was scanned from a black-and-white newspaper image, and the original is really awful. It won't ever be a crisp, clean image, but it can be a lot better.

Caution When scanning published photographs or artwork, take a moment to find out if what you're doing is legal. It's up to you to make sure that the image you scan is no longer protected by copyright—most, but not all, works more than 75 years old are considered fair game—or that your noncommercial application of the image falls under the fair-use umbrella of commentary, criticism, or parody. It's better to be extremely safe than even slightly sorry, so be careful and thorough in your copyright research.

The Dust & Scratches filter can be pretty useful for eliminating moirés, particularly if you reduce the Threshold value below 40. These halftone imperfections come from the halftone dots required to print images in books and magazines, which create periodic inconsistencies known as moiré patterns

In Figure 10-56, you see an image subjected to the Dust & Scratches filter (the original appears first, on the left) with a Radius of 2 and a Threshold value of 20. The moirés are for the most part gone, but the edges have all but disappeared as well. In the third version of the image (on the right), the Gaussian Blur, Median, and Unsharp Mask filters have been applied, and the result is an image with no moiré, and with a bit more contrast and a bit more detail—an improvement over the middle image, which was simply subjected to the Dust & Scratches filter.

Tip Always scan halftone images at the highest resolution available to your scanner. Then resample the scan down to the desired resolution using Image ⇨ Image Size, as covered in Chapter 3. This step by itself goes a long way toward eliminating moirés.

Figure 10-56: The Dust & Scratches filter quickly eliminates the patterns (see left image), but can result in loss of details and edges (see middle image). Fix that with filters that blur and another that sharpens, as shown in the final image on the right.

Using the Average filter

Choosing Filter ➪ Blur ➪ Average will, on most color images, replace the image with a grayish wall of nothing. That gray void is what you usually end up with when you average all the varied color values in an image. Consequently, on its own, Average isn't really terribly useful. However, it does have some uses, when used with selections and blend modes.

When a portion of the image is selected, the Average filter makes calculations from and applies changes to only the selected area. Marquee over a patch of grass, and the averaged area becomes a flat, solid green. Use the Magic Wand to grab a handful of sky, and Average makes it smooth and perfect. Of course, these averages may not be all that photographic or impressive on their own; when you begin to blend averaged sections of an image with the original underlying pixels, the filter proves its value.

You can also experiment with blend modes to achieve stylized results, as shown in Figure 10-57. First, select different areas of the image using Select ➪ Color Range and apply the Average filter to each individually (top). Next, use a few blend modes and Opacity values on a copy of the image.

Figure 10-57: Three faces... with the original image on top, followed by a duplicate layer where the Average filter was applied to various selections. In the bottom image, a copy of the unfiltered chimp was placed on top of a copy of the Averaged image, and the top layer's Opacity was reduced to 90 percent with the Lighten mode applied. The underlying layer (with Average applied) was given a Gaussian Blur of 1 pixel.

Summary

In this chapter, you received an overview of corrective, destructive, and effects filters, and learned about mixing a filtered image with the original. Through the Sharpen filters, you learned to fix the focus of an image with Unsharp Mask, to use the new Smart Sharpen filter, and to enhance a grainy photograph using a custom edge mask. You also learned about highlighting edges with the High Pass filter, and creating glowing images with Gaussian Blur. New Blur filters were also covered, as was the removal of unwanted patterns through the use of combined blur and sharpen filters.

✦　　✦　　✦

Distortions and Effects

In This Chapter

Brief, but compelling descriptions of Photoshop's special effects filters

Applying filters via the Filter Gallery

Using the Pixelate and Mezzotint filters

Applying the Edge-Enhancement filters

Creating metallic effects with Bas Relief, Plastic Wrap, and Chrome

Twisting reality with Distort filters

Torturing your images with the new Lens Correction and Liquify tools

Using the new Vanishing Point filter

Changing a picture's atmosphere using Clouds

The complete inner workings of Lighting Effects

Corrective filters enable you to eliminate image flaws and apply special effects, and these were discussed in Chapter 10. *Destructive filters*, on the other hand, are devoted solely to special effects. There are nearly twice as many destructive filters as corrective filters, perhaps because they simplify the creation of special effects, from simple artistic medium-mimicry to total distortion — things you could not easily do from scratch with any of Photoshop's tools or corrective commands and filters.

Now, some Photoshop veterans will tell you that destructive filters aren't useful or they aren't as important or effective as the corrective ones. That's an entirely subjective position, and one that isn't really worth defending or attacking. Suffice to say that many veteran designers love the destructive filters and would miss them terribly if they went away. Whether you're a veteran or a newbie, you'll probably find yourself loving some of the destructive filters and not seeing the need for or sense in others. That's why, as they say, "they make chocolate and vanilla" — there's something for everyone.

In this chapter, there is no attempt to cover each and every one of the destructive filters. First of all, for most of them, once you've mastered a few of the different controls the filter dialog boxes offer, you don't need an explanation of the others. Second, you'd need a forklift to get this book from the shelf in your bookstore to the cashier (or you'd have to tip the mail carrier for lugging the book to your doorstep) if each one was covered.

Fear not — even with the filters that have been skipped in this chapter, you're going to find yourself a master of destruction after reading the next 70-plus pages, and no filter will elude you.

Bizarre Effects

The following is a list of some of the more interesting special effects filters. Many of them may not seem immediately useful, but the more creative your work, the more you'll find yourself making use of them:

✦ **Fragment.** Found in the Pixelate group of filters, this filter repeats an image four times in a square formation and lowers the opacity of each to give the illusion of the image being shaken—as though the photo was taken during an earthquake. Earthquake photography is not the technical purpose for this filter—it may not have a specific purpose at all—but it can be used alone or with other filters for interesting results, especially if you use it on a duplicate layer with reduced opacity. There are no options for controlling its effects, and it can make your eyes hurt if you stare at the photo for too long. It's as if your eyes suddenly went bad, and you're cursed with double vision.

✦ **Lens Flare.** Found in the Render submenu, this filter adds sparkles and halos to an image to suggest light bouncing off the camera lens. Even though many photographers work hard to avoid these sorts of reflections, lens flares can have artistic merit and this filter lets you add them after the fact. You can select from one of three Lens Type options, adjust the Brightness slider between 10 and 300 percent (though somewhere between 100 and 150 is bound to deliver the best results), and move the center of the reflection by clicking and dragging a point around inside the Flare Center box. In addition, you can Alt-click (Win) or Option-click (Mac) inside the preview to position the center point numerically. By way of example, Figure 11-1 shows the 35mm lens flare added to a photo that formerly had no light bouncing off the camera's lens.

Tip   The Alt or Option key can be very helpful to you in the Lens Flare and many other filter dialog boxes: If you press and hold Alt or Option as you drag the slider, you can see the preview update on the fly.

If you want to add a flare to a grayscale image, first convert it to the RGB mode. Then apply the filter and convert the image back to grayscale. The Lens Flare filter is applicable only to RGB images and is dimmed in the menu if your image is in Grayscale mode.

Before you write off Lens Flare as something too detail-obscuring or something you'd never need, consider this: Prior to choosing the filter, create a new layer, fill it with black, and apply the Screen blend mode by pressing Shift+Alt+S (Shift-Option-S on the Mac) with a nonpainting tool selected. Now apply Lens Flare. You get the same effect as you would otherwise, but the effect floats above the background image, protecting your original image from harm. You can even move the lens flare around and vary the Opacity value, giving you more control over the final effect.

Figure 11-1: Intensify the impact of the sun by adding a lens flare to any outdoor photo—here, the 35mm Prime flare is used (bottom). The original image appears at the top, and shows how even naturally dramatic lighting can be made more dynamic with this effect.

✦ **Diffuse.** Located in the Stylize submenu—as are the three filters that follow—Diffuse dithers the edges of color, much like the Dissolve brush mode dithers the edges of a soft brush. The results are hard to describe in terms of "makes it look like ____" or "mimics ____," but the results are pretty neat.

✦ **Solarize.** This filter has no dialog box, so you can't control it. It serves mostly to distort your colors, and may have a variety of creative purposes in the right situation—it's up to you. What it does is change all medium grays in the image to 50 percent gray, changes all blacks and whites to black, and remaps the other colors to shades in between. If you're familiar with the Curves command, the map for Solarize looks like a pyramid. What? You're not familiar with Curves? Go to Chapter 17.

✦ **Tiles.** This filter does its best to break an image up into a bunch of square, randomly spaced rectangular tiles. You specify how many tiles fit across the smaller of the image's width or height—a value of 10, for example, creates 100 tiles in a perfectly square image—and the maximum distance each tile can shift. You can fill the gaps between tiles with the foreground color, the background color, or an inverted or normal version of the original image. You can compare the Tiles filter to the Extrude filter (the next one discussed here) in Figure 11-2 (see top-right image—the original, unfiltered image is on the top left).

✦ **Extrude.** A functional cousin of the Tiles filter, Extrude breaks an image into tiles and forces them toward the viewer in three-dimensional space. The Pyramid option is a lot of fun, turning an image into a collection of spikes (see Figure 11-2, bottom left). When using the Blocks option, you can select a Solid Front Faces option that renders the image as a true 3-D mosaic (also shown in Figure 11-2, bottom right). The Mask Incomplete Blocks option simply leaves the image untouched around the perimeter of the selection where the filter can't draw complete tiles.

✦ **Diffuse Glow.** Filter ➪ Distort ➪ Diffuse Glow sprays a coat of dithered, background-colored pixels onto your image. It can be really helpful when you want the look of soft sunshine bathing your photo — just set your Background color to an orangey-yellow and it's dawn in springtime.

✦ **Custom.** The first of two custom effects filters in Photoshop, Filter ➪ Other submenu, Custom enables you to design your own *convolution kernel*, a function that allows neighboring pixels to be mixed together. The kernel can be a variation on sharpening, blurring, embossing, or a half-dozen other effects. You create your filter by typing numerical values in a matrix of options, represented by little boxes (see Figure 11-3 for the not-terribly-illustrative dialog box). This is one you just have to tinker with and if you like it, go for it. If not, move on.

✦ **Displace.** Located in the Distort submenu, Displace is Photoshop's second custom effects filter. It permits you to distort and add texture to an image by moving the colors of certain pixels in a selection. You specify the direction and distance that the Displace filter moves colors by creating a second image called a *displacement map*, or *dmap* (pronounced *dee-map*) for short. The brightness values in the displacement map tell Photoshop which pixels to affect and how far to move the colors of those pixels.

✦ **Artistic filters.** As a rule, the effects under the Filter ➪ Artistic submenu add a hand-painted or drawn quality to your image. Colored Pencil, Rough Pastels, and Watercolor are examples of filters that successfully emulate traditional mediums. Other filters — Fresco, Palette Knife, and Smudge Stick — may produce results that don't immediately remind you of the mediums after which they're named, but they have their uses, alone or in combination with other filters. Figure 11-4 shows a photo broken into four blocks, each of which is filtered to look like a wet or dry artistic medium.

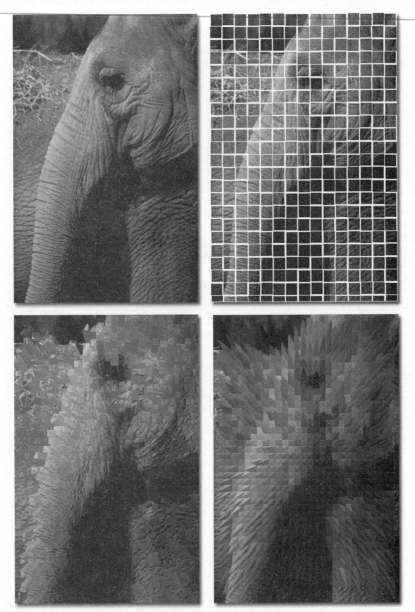

Figure 11-2: Very cool 3-D effects can be created with the Extrude filter. Can you think of any way to do this with other tools or modes? No, you can't — and that's the reason even the most unusual, hard-to-explain-the-purpose-of filter has a place in Photoshop. On the bottom row, Pyramid is applied to the bottom right, and Blocks to the bottom left. For comparison's sake, the Tiles filter is applied to the image, too (top right), and appears next to the unfiltered original (top left).

Figure 11-3: Type numbers into these little boxes and watch your photo's light, color, and clarity change — for the better or worse, depending on the numbers you type, where you type them, and what you were hoping for.

✦ **Brush Strokes filters.** The Brush Strokes filters could really have been packed into the Artistic group, because most of them mimic artistic tools such as pens, spray paint, and other methods for using ink. Some of them defy categorization (Accented Edges comes to mind here), but you'll find ways to use them regardless of where Adobe decided to store them.

✦ **Sketch filters.** Many of the Sketch filters replace the colors in your image with the current foreground and background colors, so be prepared to undo and then tinker with the Color settings before reapplying the filter for more pleasing results. If the foreground and background colors are black and white, the Sketch filter results in a grayscale image. Charcoal and Conté Crayon create artistic effects, Bas Relief and Note Paper add texture, and Photocopy and Stamp create extreme black-and-white results — not easy to imagine using every day, but... Figure 11-5 shows a group of Sketch filters (including Photocopy) in use.

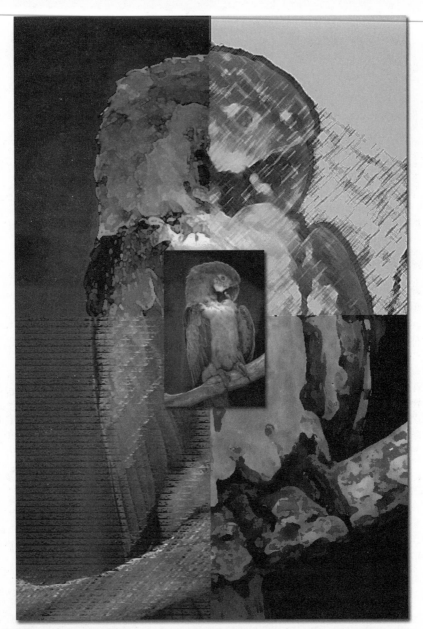

Figure 11-4: A photo goes from reality (inset) to Watercolor, Colored Pencil, Rough Pastels, and Fresco (clockwise from upper left). Try them yourself on an otherwise boring photo to mask blemishes, unwanted details, or just plain ugliness.

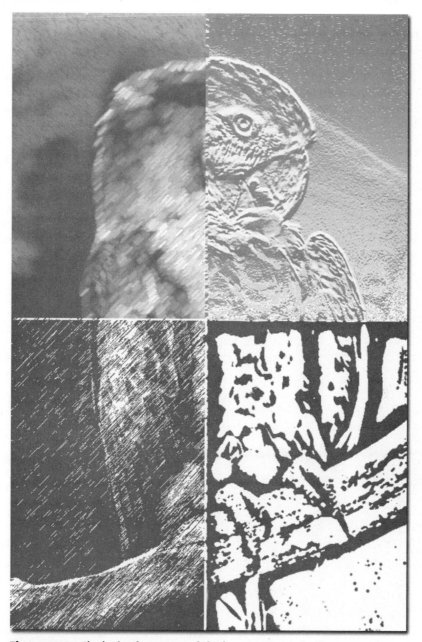

Figure 11-5: Clockwise from upper left, the parrot seen in Figure 11-4 has been Sketched with the Chalk & Charcoal, Bas Relief, Graphic Pen, and Photocopy filters.

Tip

To retrieve some of the original colors from your image after applying a Sketch filter, press Ctrl+Shift+F (⌘-Shift-F on the Mac) to display the Fade dialog box and try out a few Mode settings. Overlay and Luminosity are particularly good choices.

✦ **Texture filters.** As a group, the commands in the Filter ⇨ Texture submenu are very useful effects filters. Craquelure, Mosaic Tiles, and Patchwork (think tiny tiles) apply interesting depth textures to an image. Texturizer provides access to several scalable textures and permits you to load your own (as long as the pattern is saved in the Photoshop format), as demonstrated in Figure 11-6. Stained Glass creates polygon tiles like Photoshop's own Crystallize filter, only with black lines around the tiles — try applying this filter to a duplicate layer with reduced opacity for an interesting effect.

Note

Adobe decided that 3D Transform and Texture Fill are somewhat dated and not terribly useful, so as of the release of Photoshop CS, they don't install automatically with the program. But if you want them, they're on the Photoshop CD, and you'll need to install them manually to access them.

Figure 11-6: Filter ⇨ Texture ⇨ Texturizer lets you select from four built-in patterns — from sandstone to brick, to canvas, to burlap (top to bottom).

What about the others?

Some filters don't belong in either the corrective or destructive camp. Take Filter ⇨ Video ⇨ NTSC Colors, for example, and Filter ⇨ Other ⇨ Offset. Both are examples of commands that probably don't belong in the Filter menu (maybe the Image ⇨ Adjustments menu would have been a better choice), and you may or may not be excited about their results.

The NTSC Colors filter modifies the colors in your RGB or Lab image for transfer to videotape. Vivid reds and blues that might otherwise prove very unstable and bleed into their neighbors are curtailed. The problem with this function is that it's not an independent color space; it's a dialog box-less filter (meaning you can't control it) that changes your colors and is finished with them. If you edit the colors after choosing the command, you may very well reintroduce colors that are incompatible with NTSC devices and therefore warrant a second application of the filter. Conversion to NTSC — another light-based system — isn't as risky as conversion to CMYK pigments, but you may wish you could have better results than this filter gives you.

The Offset command moves an image a specified number of pixels. Why wasn't it covered in Chapter 8 with the other movement options? Because the command moves the image inside the selection outline while keeping the selection outline itself stationary. It's as if you had pasted the entire image into the selection outline and were now moving it around. The command is a favorite among fans of channel operations, a topic covered in Chapter 4. You can duplicate an image, offset the entire duplicate by a few pixels, and then mix the duplicate and original to create highlight or shadow effects.

Among the filters omitted in this chapter is Filter ⇨ Stylize ⇨ Wind, which is technically a destructive filter but is covered along with the Blur and Noise filters in Chapter 10.

As for the other filters in the Filter ⇨ Distort, Pixelate, Render, and Stylize submenus, keep reading this chapter to discover their details.

One final note about RAM

Why bring this up here, in a chapter on filters? Because RAM (and your other system resources) is a precious commodity when applying destructive filters. As mentioned in Chapter 2, scratch disk space typically enables you to edit larger images than your computer's RAM might permit. But all the filters in the Distort submenu and most of the commands in the Render submenu operate exclusively in memory. If they run out of physical RAM, they won't work.

The latest release of Photoshop is probably the most specific about the computer resources you must have to run it, compared to all of its predecessors, including Photoshop CS. From the speed of your processor to the amount of memory you have — that is, real RAM — you really want as robust a system as you can get. At a minimum you need a Pentium IV processor (if you're running Windows) and at least 512MB of RAM. You can consult your packaging for the exact system requirements for Photoshop CS2.

Tip If this possibility scares you, there is one potential workaround: When editing a color image, try applying the filter to each of the color channels independently. One color channel requires just a third to a fourth as much RAM as the full-color composite. Sadly, this technique does not help Lens Flare, Lighting Effects, or NTSC Colors. These filters are compatible only with full-color images, so when you're editing a single channel, they appear dimmed.

The Filter Gallery

Introduced in Photoshop CS, the Filter Gallery (shown in Figure 11-7) provides one-stop shopping for many of Photoshop's filters. If your last version of Photoshop was version 7 or earlier, you may gasp at the ease with which you can jump from filter to filter, adjust filter settings, and even stack filters on top of one another (like layers) — all in a single dialog box. If you've seen Photoshop Elements, you won't gasp (because the Gallery is part of Elements), but you'll probably say "It's about time!" and be glad to see it has become part of Photoshop.

To access the Filter Gallery, choose Filter ⇨ Filter Gallery. Some of the filters will open the Gallery as soon as you choose them from the various Filter submenus, and you'll get the hang of which ones do that and which ones don't. Avoid the surprise by opening the Gallery first, and making your filter choices from within it.

One of the really nice things about the Filter Gallery is the ability to see that large preview of the image within the Gallery itself. As with the Lens Blur filter dialog box discussed in Chapter 10, you can adjust the zoom level of the preview using the – and + icons or the pop-up menu under the right-pointing arrowhead next to the zoom percentage. Whenever there is more to the image than fits in the preview window, you can use your mouse (its cursor appears as the Hand tool) to pan up, down, left, or right, and view other parts of the preview in the window. Also similar to the Lens Blur filter is the progress bar that appears next to the zoom controls during particularly time-consuming renders.

The middle vertical section of the Filter Gallery dialog box is where you access the filters themselves. The filters are organized in an assortment of sections that correspond to their respective submenus in the Filter menu. Click the triangles to the left of the section names (or simply click a section name) to reveal the thumbnails, each altered to represent the effect of applying a particular filter. Click any of the thumbnails to apply the effect to your image, bring up a preview in the left side of the dialog box, and display the filter's settings on the right side of the dialog box.

Tip Want to see all the Gallery's filters without having to navigate the sections? Click the down arrow next to the displayed filter name (above the active filter's settings on the right side of the dialog box) and see a list of all the Gallery's filters — regardless of section — displayed in one long list.

Filter sections correspond to Filter menu's submenus.   Active filter settings

Image preview   Click here to enlarge preview

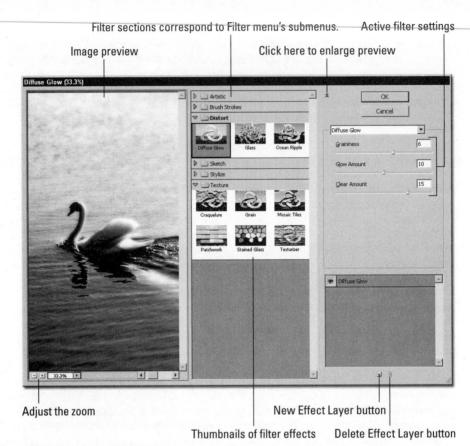

Adjust the zoom   New Effect Layer button

Thumbnails of filter effects   Delete Effect Layer button

Figure 11-7: The Filter Gallery gives you access to a large preview of your image (without having to drag a filter dialog box aside to see your image window) and access to each filter's controls. Very handy.

After you enable an effect, you can adjust its settings as you would any other filter. From here, you can more or less go wild—hop from section to section or filter to filter and play with the controls and watch the changes appear in the preview. Click the arrow icon to the left of the OK button to toggle the visibility of the filter area in the middle section of the dialog box and create more room for your image preview.

The real power of the Filter Gallery, however, is found in the bottom-right corner of the window (its features are labeled in Figure 11-7), where the applied filters are displayed in much the same manner as layers in the Layers palette. The filters also work in a similar fashion, if only because their stacking order plays a large role in determining how the final image looks. By default, you have only one layer of effects in the Filter Gallery, but adding additional layers is as easy as clicking the New Layer Effect button (it's the little page) at the bottom of the dialog box and then selecting a different filter from the thumbnails. Additionally, you can stack the same filter on top of itself again and again, varying the settings to create some interesting effects. Click the eyeball icons next to the filter layers to toggle the visibility of any of the effects. Reordering the layers of filters in the Filter Gallery is as simple as clicking one and dragging it up or down the stack—just like restacking layers in the Layers palette. To remove any of the filters, simply highlight its layer and click the trash icon.

Cross-Reference With all these references to layers, if you're not clear on their use or how to manage them, check out Chapter 12.

Moving on, key filters are analyzed and demonstrated—not all the filters in the whole Filters menu and submenus, as stated previously, but many of them and with enough detail to enable you to use any filter successfully—including some filters that are new to Photoshop CS2.

The Pixelate Filters

The Filter ➪ Pixelate submenu features a handful of commands that rearrange your image into clumps of color:

✦ **Color Halftone.** This highly practical filter allows you to suggest the effect of a halftone pattern. There is no Preview from the filter's dialog box, so if you don't like your results, just Undo and reopen the dialog box to tweak the settings and reapply. When applied to a CMYK image, Photoshop simulates a commercially reproduced color separation. Otherwise, the filter merely affects those channels that it can. For example, when working inside an RGB image, the Channel 4 value is ignored, because there is no fourth channel. When working on a grayscale image or mask, the Screen Angles value for Channel 1 is the only angle that matters.

✦ **Crystallize.** This filter organizes an image into irregularly shaped nuggets. You specify the size of the nuggets by typing a value from 3 to 300 pixels in the Cell Size option.

Tip If your image is set to a very high resolution or is quite large in terms of print size, you'll want to back the zoom off a bit (using the plus and minus buttons) to see the overall effect on the image before clicking OK. This applies to just about all the filters that offer a preview in their dialog box—you want to zoom in to adjust the specific settings and their per-pixel impact on the image, but zoom out to see how it's going to affect things overall.

✦ **Facet.** Facet fuses areas of similarly colored pixels to create a sort of hand-painted effect. There is no dialog box for this one, so if you don't see a big change, just repeat the filter a few times (Ctrl+F or ⌘-F, if you're on a Mac) until you can see an appreciable change.

✦ **Fragment.** Another filter with no dialog box, this one shakes things up—literally. It creates the look of a photo taken by a camera sitting on a paint-shaker.

✦ **Mezzotint.** This filter renders an image as a pattern of dots, lines, or strokes. See the section "Creating a mezzotint" for more information. There is no way to adjust the zoom percentage for the Preview in the dialog box (or to turn off the Preview), and your mouse has no panning ability in the dialog box. Just pick the Type of dots, lines, or strokes, and click OK to see what it does to your image.

✦ **Mosaic.** The Mosaic filter blends pixels together into larger squares. You specify the height and width of the squares by typing a value in the Cell Size option box. Obviously, the smaller the cells, the more recognizable your image details will remain.

✦ **Pointillize.** This filter is similar to Crystallize, except it separates an image into disconnected nuggets set against the background color. As usual, you specify the size of the dots by changing the Cell Size value.

Creating a Mezzotint

A *mezzotint* is a special halftone pattern that replaces dots with a random pattern of swirling lines and wormholes. Photoshop's Mezzotint filter is an attempt to emulate this effect. Although not entirely successful — true mezzotinting options can be properly implemented only as PostScript printing functions, not as filtering functions — they do lend themselves to some interesting interpretations.

The filter itself is straightforward. You choose Filter ➪ Pixelate ➪ Mezzotint, select an effect from the Type submenu, and press Enter or Return. A preview box enables you to see what each of the 10 Type options looks like. Figure 11-8 shows off four of the effects — dots, lines, and strokes — in fine, medium, and long varieties.

Figure 11-8: The results of applying the Mezzotint filter as Fine Dots (upper left), Course Dots (upper right), Medium Lines (lower left), and Long Strokes (lower right). The original (inset) detail is pretty much lost with all but the Fine Dots.

The Mezzotint line patterns are on par with the halftoning options offered when you select Mode ⇨ Bitmap, as discussed in Chapter 4.

When applied to grayscale artwork, the Mezzotint filter always results in a black-and-white image. When applied to a color image, the filter automatically applies the selected effect independently to each of the color channels. Although all pixels in each channel are changed to either black or white, you can see a total of eight colors — black, red, green, blue, yellow, cyan, magenta, and white — in the RGB composite view.

If the Mezzotint filter affects each channel independently, it follows that the color mode in which you work dramatically affects the performance of the filter. For example, if you apply Mezzotint in the Lab mode, you again whittle the colors down to eight, but a very different eight — black, cyan, magenta, green, red, two muddy blues, and a muddy rose. If you're looking for bright happy colors, don't apply Mezzotint in the Lab mode.

In CMYK, the filter produces roughly the same eight colors that you get in RGB — white, cyan, magenta, yellow, violet-blue, red, deep green, and black. However, the distribution of the colors is much different. The image appears lighter and more colorful than its RGB counterpart. This happens because the filter has a lot of black to work with in the RGB mode but very little — just that in the black channel — in the CMYK mode.

Edge-Enhancement Filters

The Filter ⇨ Stylize submenu offers access to a triad of filters that enhance the edges in an image. The most popular of these is undoubtedly Emboss, which adds dimension to an image by making it look as if it were carved in relief. The other two — Find Edges and Trace Contour — may have fewer practical applications, but you'll find creative use for them, too.

Embossing an image

The Emboss filter works by searching for high-contrast edges (just like the Sharpen Edges and High Pass filters), highlighting the edges with black or white pixels, and then coloring the low-contrast portions with medium gray. When you choose Filter ⇨ Stylize ⇨ Emboss, Photoshop displays the Emboss dialog box shown in Figure 11-9. The dialog box offers three options:

✦ **Angle.** The value in this option box determines the angle at which Photoshop lights the image in relief. For example, if you type a value of 90 degrees, you light the relief from the bottom straight upward. The white pixels therefore appear on the bottom sides of the edges, and the black pixels appear on the top sides. Figure 11-10 shows four reliefs lit from different angles and with different Height settings.

✦ **Height.** The Emboss filter accomplishes its highlighting effect by displacing one copy of an image relative to another. Using the Height option, you specify the distance between the copies, which can vary from 1 to 100 pixels. Lower values produce crisper effects, as demonstrated in Figure 11-10. Values above 4 work best if you also use a high Amount value. Together, the Height and Amount values determine the depth of the image in relief.

Figure 11-9: The Emboss dialog box lets you control the depth of the filtered image (Height and Amount) and the Angle from which the image is lit.

Tip　The Height value is analogous to the Radius value in the Unsharp Mask dialog box. You should therefore set the value according to the resolution of your image — 1 for 150 ppi, 2 for 300 ppi, and so on.

✦ **Amount.** Type a value between 1 and 500 percent to determine the amount of black and white assigned to pixels along the edges. Values of 50 percent and lower produce almost entirely gray images. Higher values produce sharper edges, as if the relief were carved more deeply.

Tip　To create a color-relief effect, apply the Emboss filter and then select the Luminosity option in the Fade dialog box. This retains the colors from the original image while applying the lightness and darkness of the pixels from the filtered selection. The effect looks something like an inked lithographic plate, with steel grays and vivid colors mixing together.

Tip　If you're not sure how you might use the Emboss filter (other than to create the illusion of a carving), think of Emboss as an extension of the High Pass filter. When considered this way, it takes on new meaning. You can use it to edit selection outlines in the Quick Mask mode, just as you might use the High Pass filter. You also can use it to draw out detail in an image.

Figure 11-10: Emboss-created reliefs lit from four different angles. Clockwise from top left: the Height and Amount increase, and the Angle changes from 90, to 0, to -90, to 180 degrees. Amount is set to 275 percent in each example. The Height starts at 1 pixel in the first example, and increases by 1 in each image.

Tracing around edges

Photoshop provides three filters that trace around pixels in your image and accentuate the edges. All three filters live in the Filter ⇨ Stylize submenu:

✦ **Find Edges.** This filter detects edges similarly to High Pass. Low-contrast areas become white, medium-contrast edges become gray, and high-contrast edges become black, as in the upper-left example in Figure 11-11. Hard edges become thin lines; soft edges become fat ones. The result is a thick, organic outline that you can overlay on an image to give it a waxy appearance. The original, unfiltered image appears in the inset in the upper-left corner of the figure.

✦ **Glowing Edges.** This Gallery Effects filter is a variation on Find Edges, with two important differences. Glowing Edges produces an inverted effect, changing low-contrast areas to black and edges to white, as shown in the upper-right and lower-left images in Figure 11-11. This filter also enables you to adjust the width, brightness, and smoothness of the traced edges by adjusting the Edge Width and Edge Brightness. The Smoothness setting reduces noise and heightens the intensity of the outline (see bottom-left example in Figure 11-11).

Tip   If you want black lines against a white background, change the image to Grayscale mode, and press Ctrl+I (or ⌘-I on the Mac) to invert the image.

✦ **Trace Contour.** Illustrated in Figure 11-11, this filter traces a series of single-pixel lines along the border between light and dark pixels. Choosing the filter displays a dialog box containing two settings: Level, and an Edge setting with two options: Upper and Lower. The Level value indicates the lightness value above which pixels are considered to be light and below which they are dark. For example, if you type 128 (medium gray), Trace Contour draws a line at every spot where an area of color lighter than medium gray meets an area of color darker than medium gray. The Upper and Lower options tell the filter where to position the line — inside the lighter color's territory (Upper) or inside the space occupied by the darker color (Lower).

Like Mezzotint, Trace Contour applies itself to each color channel independently and renders each channel as a 1-bit image. A collection of black lines surrounds the areas of color in each channel. The RGB, Lab, or CMYK composite view shows these lines in the colors associated with the channels. When you work in RGB, a cyan line indicates a black line in the Red channel (no red plus full-intensity green and blue becomes cyan). A yellow line indicates a black line in the Blue channel, and so on. You get a single black line when working in the Grayscale mode.

Tip   There's no end to the ways you can tweak one filter by combining it with another filter (or two) and various image adjustments. For example, while on the topic of metallic coatings and the gleaming highlights they promise, could there be another way to achieve that look without the problems that the Chrome filter can create? Absolutely — and the Find Edges filter can help. First, copy your image to a separate layer by pressing Ctrl+J (⌘-J on the Mac). Then apply the Gaussian Blur filter. A

Radius value between 1.0 and 4.0 produces the best results, depending on how liquid you want the edges to look. Next, apply the Find Edges filter. If the resulting image is too light, you might want to darken it using Image ⇨ Adjustments ⇨ Levels (raise the first Input Levels value to 100 or so, as explained in Chapter 17).

Figure 11-11: Find Edges (upper left) and Glowing Edges (upper right and lower left) have creative uses in their own right and can also be used to bring out the edges in a photo. The Trace Contour filter (lower right) maps lines between light and dark pixels.

Creating a metallic coating

The edge-tracing filters are especially fun to use in combination with Edit ⇨ Fade. If you want the look of a metal coating on your image, choose Filter ⇨ Sketch ⇨ Chrome, which turns your image (or a selection therein) to a melted pool of metallic slime. Chrome is best used with color images, and you may find that following it up with the Fade command gives you more subtle results that don't totally rob your image of any detail. Figure 11-12 shows Chrome applied normally (left) and with Fade (at 75 percent Opacity) used afterward (right).

Figure 11-12: Chrome can be very cool (left), but you may want to tone down its effects a bit with the Fade command (right). Here the fine detail of the bird is retained, while on the left, the full chrome effect is distracting from the subject. The inset in the lower right shows the original image.

Distortion Filters

For the most part, commands in the Distort submenu are related by the fact that they move colors in an image to achieve unusual stretching, swirling, and vibrating effects. They're rather like the transformation commands in the Edit menu in that they perform their magic by relocating and interpolating colors rather than by altering brightness and color values.

The distinction, of course, is that whereas the transformation commands let you scale and distort images by manipulating four control points, the Distort filters provide the equivalent of hundreds of control points, all of which you can use to affect different portions of an image. In some cases, you're projecting an image into a fun-house mirror; other times, it's a reflective pool. You can fan images, wiggle them, and change them in ways that have no correlation to real life, as illustrated in Figure 11-13.

Distortion filters are powerful tools. Although they are easy to apply, they are extremely difficult to use well. Here are some rules to keep in mind:

✦ **Practice makes perfect.** Distortion filters are like complex vocabulary words. You don't want to use them without practicing a little first. Experiment with a distortion filter several times before trying to use it in a real project. You may even want to write down the steps you take so that you can remember how you created an effect.

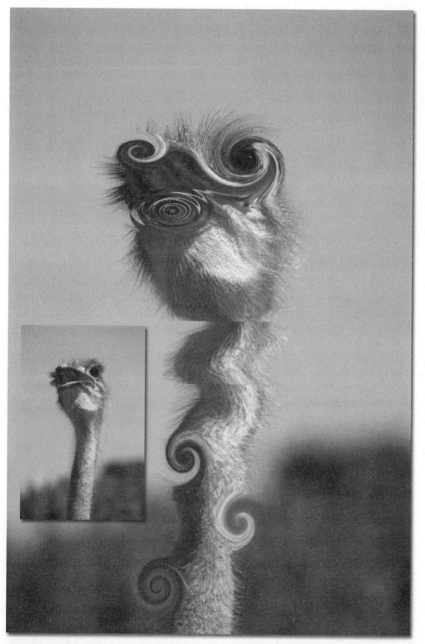

Figure 11-13: An innocent victim (inset) of the Distort family of filters applied in combination

✦ **Keep your eye on the clock.** Distortion filters are enormous time-wasters. Unless you know exactly how you want to proceed, you may want to avoid using them when time is short. The last thing you need when you're working under the gun is to get trapped trying to pull off a weird effect.

✦ **Apply selectively.** The effects of distortion filters are too severe to inflict all at once. You can achieve marvelous, subtle effects, however, by distorting feathered and layered selections. Although one would hardly call the image in Figure 11-13 subtle, no single effect was applied to the entire image.

✦ **Combine creatively.** Don't expect a single distortion to achieve the desired effect. If one application isn't enough, apply the filter again. Experiment with combining different distortions.

Distortion filters interpolate between pixels to create their fantastic effects. This means the quality of your filtered images depends on the setting of the Image Interpolation option in the General Preferences dialog box. If a filter produces jagged effects, the Nearest Neighbor option is probably selected. Try selecting the Bicubic or Bilinear option instead.

The fun-house mirror

Just about everyone has stood in front of a fun-house mirror and watched his or her face and/or body be squeezed, stretched, and otherwise twisted into a variety of shapes. Where it gets really weird is where your facial features are shrunken, as though your face was shrinking from the center, and where your face seems to expand from the center—making for a big nose and a receding brow-bone and chin. It's probably fun to play in front of such a mirror for the same reason kids dress up like scary characters for Halloween—when something's temporary and unreal, even something scary can be fun. In Figure 11-14, you'll see a photo turned into a fun-house mirror reflection, using the Pinch and Spherize filters to scrunch, stretch, and wrap what started out as a perfectly normal-looking face.

A positive Amount value in the Pinch dialog box produces an effect similar to a negative value in the Spherize dialog box. There is a slight difference between the spatial curvature of the 3-D calculations: Pinch pokes the image inward or outward using a rounded cone—we're talking bell-shaped, much like a Gaussian model. Spherize wraps the image on the outside or inside of a true sphere. As a result, the two filters yield subtly different results. Pinch produces a soft transition around the perimeter of a selection; Spherize produces an abrupt transition. If this doesn't quite make sense to you, just play with one, try out the same effect with the other, and see which you like better.

Another difference between the two filters is that Spherize provides the additional options of enabling you to wrap an image on the inside or outside of a horizontal or vertical cylinder, as shown in the last sample in Figure 11-14, where Vertical Only was used. To try out these effects, select the Horizontal Only or Vertical Only options from the Mode pop-up menu at the bottom of the Spherize dialog box.

Figure 11-14: Using Pinch and Spherize, you can create some truly scary results. From the upper left, the untouched photo appears, followed by some serious pinching (upper right), some spherizing (in the lower left) and a combination of the two in the lower right.

Tip

Both filters can affect only elliptical regions. If a selection outline is not elliptical, Photoshop applies the filter to the largest ellipse that fits inside the selection. As a result, the filter may leave behind a noticeable elliptical boundary between the affected and unaffected portions of the selection. To avoid this effect, select the region you want to edit with the Elliptical Marquee tool and then feather the selection before filtering it. This softens the effect of the filter and provides a more gradual transition (even more so than Pinch already affords).

One of the more remarkable properties of the Pinch filter is that it lets you turn any image into a conical gradation. First, you may want to blur the image to eliminate any harsh edges between color transitions. Then apply the Pinch filter at full strength (100 percent). Reapply the filter several more times. Each time you press Ctrl+F (⌘-F on the Mac) the center portion of the image recedes farther and farther into the distance.

Twirling spirals

The Twirl filter rotates the center of a selection while leaving the sides fixed in place. The result is a spiral of colors that looks for all the world as if you poured the image into a blender set to a very slow speed.

When you choose Filter ⇨ Distort ⇨ Twirl, you can type a positive value from 1 to 999 degrees to spiral the image in a clockwise direction. Type a negative value to spiral the image in a counterclockwise direction. Figure 11-15 shows a 30-degree spiral (top left) and a 100-degree spiral (top right) in both positive and negative directions. As you are probably already aware, 360 degrees make a full circle, so the maximum 999-degree value equates to a spiral that circles around almost three times, as shown in the bottom example in Figure 11-15.

Tip   The Twirl filter produces smoother effects when you use lower Angle values. Therefore, you're better off applying a 100-degree spiral 10 times rather than applying a 999-degree spiral once.

Figure 11-16 illustrates a droplet technique designed by Mark Collen. The steps to re-create it follow.

Figure 11-15: A lovely face, subjected to the Twirl filter. You can adjust the direction of the Twirl filter and also increase its intensity.

Figure 11-16: Although they appear as if they might be the result of the ZigZag filter, these images were created entirely by using the gradient tool, the Twirl filter, and a couple of transformations.

STEPS: Creating a Thick-Liquid Droplet

1. **Press D to restore the default foreground and background colors.**

2. **Shift-drag with the Rectangular Marquee tool to select a square portion of an image.**

3. **Create a linear gradation by dragging inside the selection outline with the Gradient tool.** Before you drag, select the linear gradient style in the Options bar and select the foreground to background gradient from the Gradients drop-down palette, also in the Options bar. Drag a short distance near the center of the selection from upper left to lower right, creating the black-to-white gradation shown in the top-left box in Figure 11-16.

4. **Choose the Twirl filter and apply it at –360 degrees so that the spiral moves counterclockwise.** To create the top-right image in the figure, the Twirl filter was applied three times. Each repetition of the filter adds another ring of ripples.

5. **Press Ctrl+J (or ⌘-J on the Mac) to copy the selection to a layer.**

6. **Choose Edit ⇨ Transform ⇨ Flip Horizontal.**

7. **Lower the Opacity value to 50 percent.** You can do this from the keyboard by selecting the Rectangular Marquee tool and pressing 5. The result appears in the lower-left example in Figure 11-16.

8. **Choose Edit ⇨ Transform ⇨ Rotate 90° CW.** This rotates the layer a quarter turn, thus creating the last image in the figure. You can achieve other interesting effects by choosing Lighten, Darken, and others from the brush modes pop-up menu.

Now that you've mastered this grayscale image technique, try it with color. Starting with a two- or three-color gradient preset, repeat Steps 1 through 4. Next, use copies of layers and apply the Difference blend mode to them. Wrap up with a the Spherize, ZigZag, and Lens Flare filters, and then try the Unsharp Mask to mutate the concentric rings into something a little more interesting.

Zigging and zagging

When you hear ZigZag filter, you may picture lightening bolts or other back-and-forth patterns. When it comes to a Photoshop filter, however, you know it won't be that simple. The ZigZag filter does arrange colors into zigzag patterns, but it does so in a radial fashion, meaning that the zigzags emanate from the center of the image like spokes in a wheel. The result is a series of concentric ripples, as shown in Figure 11-17 (see original image in the center inset). If you want parallel zigzags, check out the Ripple and Wave filters, described in the next section. (The ZigZag filter creates ripples and the Ripple filter creates zigzags — don't ask.)

When you choose Filter ⇨ Distort ⇨ ZigZag, Photoshop displays a dialog box offering the following options:

✦ **Amount.** Type an amount between negative 99 and positive 100 in whole-number increments to specify the depth of the ripples. If you type a negative value, the ripples descend below the surface. If you type a positive value, the ripples protrude upward.

✦ **Ridges.** This option box controls the number of ripples in the selected area and accepts any value from 0 to 20.

✦ **Style.** The options in this pop-up menu determine how Photoshop moves pixels with respect to the center of the image or selection.

• **Around Center:** Select this option to rotate pixels in alternating directions around the center without moving them outward. This is the only option that produces a true zigzag effect.

Figure 11-17: The ZigZag filter applied with Around Center, -50 Amount, Ridges 5 (upper left), Out from Center, 75 Amount, Ridges 10 (upper right), and Pond Ripples, Amount -50, Ridges 5 (lower left) Styles applied. The lower-right quadrant shows the Pond Ripples at the highest Amount (100) and Ridges (20) settings.

- **Out From Center:** When you select this option, Photoshop moves pixels outward in rhythmic bursts according to the value in the Ridges option box.

- **Pond Ripples:** This option is really a cross between the previous two. It moves pixels outward and rotates them around the center of the selection to create circular patterns.

Creating parallel Ripples and Waves

Photoshop provides four means to distort an image in parallel waves, as if the image were lying on the bottom of a shimmering or undulating pool. Of the four, the ripple filters — which include Ripple, Ocean Ripple, and Glass — are only moderately sophisticated, but they're also relatively easy to apply. The fourth filter, Wave, affords you greater control, but its options are among the most complex Photoshop has to offer.

The Ripple filter

To use the Ripple filter, choose Filter ➪ Distort ➪ Ripple. Photoshop displays the Ripple dialog box, giving you the following options:

✦ **Amount.** Type an amount between negative 998 and positive 999 in whole-number increments to specify the width of the ripples from side to side. Negative and positive values change the direction of the ripples, but visually speaking, they produce identical effects. The ripples are measured as a ratio of the Size value and the dimensions of the selection — all of which translates to, "Experiment and see what happens." You can count on getting ragged effects from any value over 300, as illustrated in Figure 11-18.

✦ **Size.** Select one of the three options in the Size pop-up menu to change the length of the ripples. The Small option results in the shortest ripples and therefore the most ripples. Combining the Small option with a relatively high Amount value results in a textured-glass effect. The Large option results in the longest and fewest ripples. Figure 11-19 shows an example of each Size option.

Tip

You can create a blistered effect by overlaying a negative ripple onto a positive ripple. Try this: First, copy the selection. Then apply the Ripple filter with a positive Amount value — say, 300. Next, paste the copied selection and apply the Ripple filter at the opposite Amount value, in this case, −300. Press 5 to change the Opacity value to 50 percent. The result is a series of diametrically opposed ripples that cross each other to create teardrop blisters.

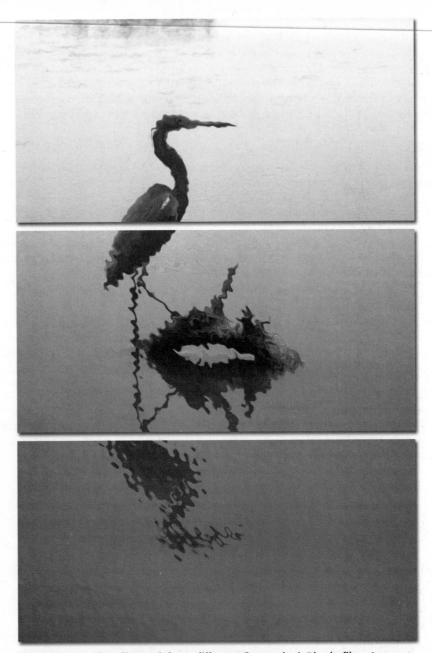

Figure 11-18: The effects of three different (increasing) Ripple filter Amount values. From the top, the Amount is set to 100 percent, then 300 percent in the middle, and finally 999 percent in the bottom.

Figure 11-19: The effects of the three different Ripple filter Size settings — Small (top), Medium (middle), and Large (bottom). In all three sections, an Amount of 300 percent was used.

Ocean Ripple and Glass

The Ocean Ripple and Glass filters are gifts from Gallery Effects. Both filters emulate the effect of looking at an image through textured glass. These two distorters so closely resemble each other that they would be better merged into one. But where the effects filters are concerned, interface design is as fickle and transitory as the face on the cover of *Tiger Beat Magazine*.

The Ocean Ripple filter's two parameters, Ripple Size and Ripple Magnitude, are illustrated in Figure 11-20. Compare the examples horizontally to observe an increase in Ripple Size values from 3 to the maximum of 15; compare vertically to observe an increase in Ripple Magnitude from 5 to the maximum of 20. As you can see, you can vary the Ripple Size value with impunity. But raise the Ripple Magnitude value, and you're looking through sculpted glass.

The principal difference between Glass and Ocean Ripple is that Ocean Ripple uses one preset distortion texture, and Glass gives you four to choose from, plus it lets you load your own (similar to Texturizer). You can invert the texture—high becomes low, low becomes high—and also scale it to change its size relative to the layer you're distorting. Figure 11-21 uses the Tiny Lens texture throughout, and demonstrates how different the effect can be depending on the Distortion and Smoothness settings. Compare the examples in the figure horizontally for proof that Distortion is perhaps the best-named parameter in all of Photoshop. Smoothness, on the other hand, is sort of like an "anti-Ripple Magnitude" setting. High Smoothness settings in Glass are analogous to low Ripple Magnitude settings in Ocean Ripple.

Figure 11-20: Raising the Ocean Ripple Size value spreads out the effect; raising the Ocean Ripple Magnitude adds more depth and contrast to the ripples. All three rows' Size increase from 3 to 8 to 15, with Magnitude remaining constant at 5 in the top row, 10 in the middle row, and 20 in the bottom row.

Figure 11-21: The higher the Distortion (increasing from left to right in both top and bottom rows) the more the image is obscured by the Glass. The Smoothness setting (5 in the top row, 12 in the bottom) improves image recognizability when paired with higher Distortion.

The Wave filter

To go from baby ripples to serious water damage, choose Filter ➪ Distort ➪ Wave. This displays the Wave dialog box shown in Figure 11-22, which offers the following options:

✦ **Number of Generators.** Think of Generators as rocks tossed into still water. The more rocks you throw (one at a time), the more pools of outward-flowing concentric waves you get. If the rocks are close to each other, the waves intersect and flow through and bounce off one another. As shown in Figure 11-23, the more rocks you throw in, the more extreme and complex the results. If you type a very high value in this field, however, be prepared to wait a few years for the preview to update. If you can't wait, press Esc, which turns off the preview until the next time you type a value in the dialog box.

✦ **Wavelength and Amplitude.** The Wave filter produces random results by varying the number and length of waves (Wavelength) as well as the height of the waves (Amplitude) between minimum and maximum values, which can range from 1 to 999. (The Wavelength and Amplitude options, therefore, correspond in theory to the Size and Amount options in the Ripple dialog box.) Figure 11-24 demonstrates an increase in Wavelength and Amplitude.

Figure 11-22: The Wave dialog box lets you decide how high the tide will rise as it undulates over your image.

Figure 11-23: The only difference between the examples in this figure is in the Number of Generators. Adding generators increases random action by creating more intersecting waveforms — here there is 1 Generator in the top word, 2 in the middle one, and 3 Generators in the bottom word.

Figure 11-24: With only 1 Generator, tinkering with Wavelength (increasing in each image from top to bottom) and Amplitude (increasing from top to bottom) adjusts the distance between and height of the waves.

✦ **Scale.** You can scale the effects of the Wave filter between 1 and 100 percent horizontally and vertically. Increasing Horizontal Scale makes the waves go back and forth as well as up and down.

✦ **Type.** You can select from three kinds of waves. The Sine option produces standard sine waves that rise and fall smoothly in bell-shaped curves, just like real waves. The Triangle option creates zigzags that rise and fall in straight lines, like the edge of a piece of fabric cut with pinking shears. The Square option has nothing to do with waves at all, but rather organizes an image into a series of rectangular groupings, reminiscent of Cubism. You might think of this option as an extension of the Mosaic filter. All examples in Figure 11-25 utilize a Number of Generators setting of 1 and demonstrate the Sine, Triangle, and Square settings.

✦ **Randomize.** The Wave filter is random by nature. If you don't like the effect you see in the preview box, click Randomize (as illustrated in the bottom example in Figure 11-25) to stir things up a bit. You can keep clicking the button until you get an effect you like.

✦ **Undefined Areas.** The Wave filter distorts a selection to the extent that gaps may appear around the edges. You can fill those gaps by repeating pixels along the edge of the selection, as in the figures, or by wrapping pixels from the left side of the selection onto the right side and pixels from the top edge of the selection onto the bottom.

Figure 11-25: Using Triangle and Square, your waves change shape. The bottom example demonstrates the Randomize option. Scale was also increased.

Distorting an image along a curve

The Distort command (Edit ➪ Transform ➪ Distort), which isn't discussed elsewhere in this book, creates four corner handles around an image. You click and drag each corner handle to distort the selected image in that direction. Unfortunately, you can't add other points around the edges to create additional distortions, which can be frustrating if you're trying to achieve a specific effect. If you can't achieve a certain kind of distortion using Edit ➪ Free Transform, the Shear filter may be your answer.

Shear distorts an image or a selection along a path. When you choose Filter ➪ Distort ➪ Shear, you get the dialog box shown in Figure 11-26. Initially, a single line that has two points at either end appears in the grid at the top of the box. When you click and drag the points, you slant the image in the preview. This, plus the fact that the filter is named Shear — Adobe's strange term for skewing (it appears in Illustrator as well) — leads many users to dismiss the filter as nothing more than a slanting tool. But in truth, it's more versatile than that.

You can add points to the grid line simply by clicking it. A point springs up every time you click an empty space in the line. Drag the point to change the curvature of the line and distort the image along the new curve. To delete a point, click and drag it off the left or right side of the grid. To delete all added points and return the line to its original vertical orientation, click Defaults.

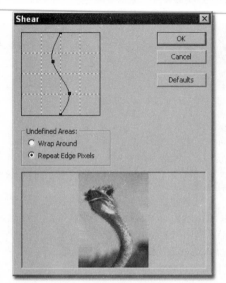

Figure 11-26: Click the grid line in the left corner of the Shear dialog box to add points to the line. Click and drag these points to distort the image along the curve.

The Undefined Areas options work just as they do in the Wave dialog box (described in the preceding section). You can either fill the gaps on one side of the image with pixels shoved off the opposite side by selecting the Wrap Around option or repeat pixels along the edge of the selection by selecting the Repeat Edge Pixels option.

Tip   Although Shear was conceived to create horizontal distortions, you may find you need to create a vertically based distortion instead. If you can't change the filter, why not change the image? Simply rotating the image on its side allows you to give the desired slant to the image.

Changing to Polar Coordinates

The Polar Coordinates filter is another one of those gems that a lot of people shy away from because it doesn't make much sense at first glance. When you choose Filter ➪ Distort ➪ Polar Coordinates, Photoshop presents a dialog box with two radio buttons, as shown in Figure 11-27. You can map an image from rectangular to polar coordinates or from polar to rectangular coordinates. Figure 11-28 shows the same symbol in Polar to Rectangular, the distorting filter applied to the image.

When you convert the image to Polar Coordinates (by selecting the Rectangular to Polar option in the Polar Coordinates dialog box), you look down on it from an extreme aerial view. This means that the entire length of the image becomes a single dot in the exact center of the polar projection. If you select the Polar to Rectangular option, the Polar Coordinates filter produces the opposite effect — instead of the entire image becoming a dot in the center of the project, the image flows from a polar center outward, in a rectangular shape.

Figure 11-27: A yin-yang symbol is seen in Rectangular to Polar, along with the Polar Coordinates dialog box.

Tip

The Polar Coordinates filter is a great way to edit gradations. After drawing a linear gradation with the Gradient tool (as discussed in Chapter 6), try applying Filter➪Distort➪ Polar Coordinates with the Polar to Rectangular option selected. (Rectangular to Polar just turns it into a radial gradation, sometimes with undesirable results.) You get a redrawn gradation with highlights at the bottom of the selection. Press Ctrl+F (⌘-F on the Mac) to reapply the filter to achieve another effect. You can keep repeating this technique until jagged edges start to appear. Then press Ctrl+Z (⌘-Z on the Mac) to go back to the last smooth effect.

Figure 11-28: Wrap the image in Polar to Rectangular instead.

Working with Lens Correction

The Lens Correction filter opens a very large dialog box, shown in Figure 11-29. Your image appears in the Preview area, with a grid as an overlay. You can turn the Preview and the Grid off (hide them), using the check boxes just down and to the right of the preview — but you'd be better off keeping them on, at least while you're tinkering with the settings on the right side of the dialog box.

Tip   If you can't see the grid (maybe it's the same color as the image — it's set to a medium gray by default), click the Color swatch and choose a color that will stand out against your image.

Speaking of settings, your choices are as follows:

✦ **Remove Distortion.** This adjusts the default lens distortion to create a concave lens (drag to the right) or a convex lens (drag to the left).

✦ **Chromatic Aberration.** Drag the Fix Red/Cyan Fringe and/or Fix Blue/Yellow Fringe sliders to further adjust the distortion.

✦ **Vignette Amount.** A vignette is typically a distinct darkening around the edges of an image. This was seen a lot in vintage portraits, creating a dark, cloudy frame around the main subject. This option allows you to darken or lighten the edges of the image by dragging the slider. If you leave the slider in the middle, there is no vignette effect added by the filter. Of course, if your image already has an unwanted vignette effect, you can counter it by dragging the slider toward the opposite of your problem — most likely toward Lighten to counteract a traditional vignette.

Figure 11-29: Create the look of viewing your image through either a concave or convex lens with the Lens Correction filter. Here, a slightly distorted photo of buildings in Italy will be corrected, the bulging appearance in the image center reversed.

✦ **Vignette Midpoint.** Drag this slider to change the center of the vignette effect's origin.

✦ **Transform Vertical Perspective.** Drag this slider to tilt the image away from you at the top (drag to the right) or away from you at the bottom (drag to the left).

✦ **Transform Horizontal Perspective.** Drag this slider to swing the image like a door — a door opening away from you to the left by dragging the slider to the right, or a door swinging away from you to the right by dragging the slider to the left.

✦ **Transform Angle.** Rotate the image with this option, either by dragging within the circle, or by entering an angle of rotation into the box.

✦ **Transform Edge.** Choose from Edge Extension, which (surprise) extends the ends of the image to the edges of the grid, Transparency (the default), which leaves the areas outside of the image yet within the grid transparent, and Background Color, which fills in around the image with the current background color. This option only becomes an issue when the lens has created space between the grid's edges and your image — through rotation, and perspective changes, or by dragging on the grid with your mouse to apply a lens effect to the image.

✦ **Transform Scale.** This option simply sizes the image within the grid. Drag to the right to increase its size, or drag to the left to decrease it. If you're correcting a bulging image (such as the one shown in Figure 11-29), increase the Scale to a level close to 100 plus the number shown in the Remove Distortion option — typically, this resolves any transparency or obvious expansion (if you have Edge Extension turned on for the Edge option). Figure 11-30 shows that with a +15.00 Remove Distortion level, a Scale of 114% improves the edges of the image.

The tools on the left side of the dialog box allow you to use your mouse to adjust the Lens Correction settings — from top to bottom, the Remove Distortion tool, Straighten tool, Move Grid tool, Hand tool, and Zoom tool either correspond with a slider on the right or help you control the Preview area. For example, if you prefer a more hands-on approach to using this filter, use the Remove Distortion tool to drag on the Preview of the image instead of dragging the Remove Distortion slider. You can adjust the Angle setting by dragging to draw a line on the Preview with the Straighten tool.

Figure 11-30 shows the image, still inside the Lens Correction dialog box, with a +15.00 Remove Distortion setting, the Vignette Amount and Midpoint both set to 0, and the Vertical and Horizontal Perspective options also left at 0. The Angle is unchanged, and the Edge is set to Edge Extension, with the Scale at 115 percent.

Figure 11-30: Eliminate the distortion through one or more of the Lens Correction dialog box options. You won't need all of them for every image, and here we see that only the Remove Distortion and Scale options required much tinkering.

Distorting with the Liquify command

The final essential distortion function isn't located under the Filter ➪ Distort submenu. In fact, in many respects, it's not a filter at all. The Liquify command is more of a separate distortion utility that just happens to run in Photoshop. It enables you to perform any number of distortions — you can warp, shift, twirl, expand, contract, and even copy pixels. It grants you multiple undos and redos before you apply the final effect. And unlike other distortion filters, which apply a uniform effect across a layer or selection, Liquify lets you modify pixels by pushing them around with a brush.

The result is a distortion filter that doubles as a powerful retouching tool. Consider the images in Figure 11-31. Thanks to the Liquify command, a calm and serene face was contorted into a mix of angered agitation.

Note
English teachers and ex-spelling-bee champions may notice the habitual misspelling of the word "liquefy" throughout this and the following pages. Rather than referring to the strictly accurate "Liquefy command," which would not match your screen, or the condescending "Liquify (sic) command," which gets old fast, we have just stuck with Adobe's inexplicable spelling.

Figure 11-31: From content to contorted, all with the Liquify command's exciting set of tools

Liquify basics

To enter the world of Liquify, choose the Liquify command from the Filter menu or press the keyboard shortcut Ctrl+Shift+X (⌘-Shift-X on the Mac). Photoshop displays the immense Liquify image window shown in Figure 11-32, which tops even the Extract window (see Chapter 9) in its wealth of tools and options.

The miniature toolbox on the left side of the window contains seven tools for distorting your image. You drag or click with the tools as explained in the next section. (You can even select tools from the keyboard, as indicated by keys in parentheses.) But before you begin, here are a few basic facts:

✦ All tools respond to the Brush Size setting on the right side of the window. Press the right and left bracket keys ([and]) to raise and lower the brush size by 2 pixels. This is a bit of a departure from Photoshop's standard painting tools, where pressing [or] routinely changes the brush size by 10 pixels or more. To change the brush size in the Liquify window more rapidly, press and hold [or]. Throughout, your cursor reflects the approximate brush size. Note, however, that most distortions affect the pixels at the center of the cursor more quickly than those on the perimeter.

✦ The Brush Density setting determines how much feathering the edges of your cursor will have while you are creating your distortions. A smaller Brush Density setting means that effects will be more localized to the center of the brush.

Figure 11-32: Choose Filter ➪ Liquify to shove pixels around in your image by dragging them with a brush.

✦ The Brush Pressure option controls the impact of the tools as you drag across your image; higher values produce more pronounced effects. If you work with a pressure-sensitive tablet, select the Stylus Pressure option to make Photoshop adjust the tool pressure based on the amount of pressure you put on the pen stylus.

✦ Available when you use the reconstruct, Twirl clockwise, Pucker, Bloat, and Turbulence tools, the Brush Rate option controls the strength of these tools when you click on a particular area but keep the cursor still. The higher the Brush Rate setting, the faster distortions will apply to the area.

✦ You can use the standard shortcuts Ctrl+plus to zoom in and Ctrl+minus to zoom out (⌘-plus and minus on the Mac). Use the scroll bars to reposition the image or press the space bar to get the Hand tool and drag the image inside the window. The Liquify window also provides Zoom (Z) and Hand (H) tools for your navigation pleasure.

✦ If you select a portion of your image before choosing Filter ➪ Liquify, by default any deselected areas are considered *frozen*, which just means that they're unaffected by the distortion tools. You can freeze and then *thaw* — make available for editing — portions of the image as explained in the section "Freezing and thawing pixels." You can even create partially frozen or thawed areas, which further limits the impact of the distortion tools. With the release of Photoshop CS, Adobe introduced a number of new ways to control which pixels are frozen and which are thawed. In addition to a selection, you can freeze and thaw pixels based on a combination of the transparency information in the image and even through a layer mask.

✦ By default, frozen regions are covered with a red translucent coating, just like masked areas in the Quick Mask mode. You can change the appearance of the overlay by selecting a new color from the Mask Color pop-up menu at the bottom of the Liquify window. If you don't want to see the coating at all, deselect the Show Mask option.

✦ If your image contains layers, you will see only the current layer against a transparent checkerboard background when you enter the Liquify window. To see other layers, select the Show Backdrop option in the bottom-right corner of the window. You can view all layers or select a specific layer from the nearby pop-up menu. The Opacity option controls how well you can see the other layers.

✦ Use the Mode pop-up menu in the Show Backdrop settings to specify exactly how the layer you're currently distorting interacts with the other layers in the image. Regardless of what you see, Photoshop lets you edit only the active layer.

✦ Select the Show Mesh option to display gridlines on top of the image. You can use the gridlines as a guide if you want to apply very precise distortions. You can even apply your distortions while viewing only the grid by deselecting the Show Image option. Set the grid size and color by selecting options from the Mesh Size and Mesh Color pop-up menus.

✦ You can save a distortion for later use by clicking Save Mesh. To use the mesh on a Mac or PC, the file name needs to end with the *.msh* extension. Click Load Mesh to load a distortion stored on disk. Note that Photoshop is smart enough to scale the mesh to fit the current image, so a mesh specifically designed for one image may turn out to be useful for another.

You Really Must Mesh

As with other Save buttons found throughout Photoshop's myriad dialog boxes, the Save Mesh button may strike you as the kind of option that could prove useful every once in a while. Be that as it may, you should use it *every time you use the Liquify command*. Yes, *every time*. The last thing you should do, right before you click OK, is click Save Mesh. Why? Because Photoshop does not automatically keep track of your previous Liquify settings. So if you spend 15 minutes or so working in the Liquify window, click OK, and then decide that the distortion doesn't work exactly as you had hoped, you're left with two unpleasant options: Choose Liquify and try to tweak the image further, which can result in incremental damage to the detail, or undo the previous operation and start over. But if you saved the mesh, you always have that last distortion to come back to. And the beauty is, a mesh is purely mathematical until it's applied. So you can use one mesh as a jumping-off point for another without doing incremental damage. Pixels get involved only after you click OK. So don't forget to save your mesh. Got that?

The Liquify tools

Okay, so much for the basics. You're itching to start, so here's how the distortion tools along the left side of the Liquify window work:

 Forward warp (W). Drag to shove the pixels under your cursor around the image. At first, it may feel a lot like the Smudge tool. But instead of smearing pixels, you're incrementally moving points in the mesh that distort the image. The first example in Figure 11-33 shows a few large-scale changes made with a large brush and the default Pressure value. When used properly, the Forward Warp tool is the Liquify command's most practical tool. To create the second image, the Forward Warp tool was set to a smaller brush size. But the biggest difference was in the length of the strokes. Instead of dragging, say, 10 to 20 pixels at a time, the brush was dragged just 1 or 2 pixels. As you can see, lots of little adjustments — in this case, somewhere in the neighborhood of 30 strokes — produces the best results.

Twirl clockwise (C). Click or drag to spin pixels under your cursor in a clockwise direction, or to the right.

This tool's companion, the Twirl counterclockwise tool, no longer owns a slot in the Liquify toolbox. But you can still access the Twirl counterclockwise tool by pressing Alt (Option on the Mac) when you drag with the Twirl clockwise tool. You can press and release Alt in mid-drag to switch the Twirl direction on the fly. Figure 11-34 shows the Twirl tool used with the Alt (or Option) key to change the Twirl direction.

Figure 11-33: Making big strokes with the Forward Warp tool produces wacky results (left); short, careful drags give you more control (right). But you have to be patient. It took 6 strokes to make the big changes on left and about 30 to make the subtle changes on right—broadening the nose, expanding the lips, raising the chin, and lifting the eyelids and brows.

Figure 11-34: Here the Twirl tool was used, twirling in two directions, thanks to the Alt (Option) key.

Pucker (S). Click and drag with this tool to move pixels toward the center of the brush cursor. The effect is similar to applying the Pinch filter with a positive Amount value. If you move your mouse down instead of dragging, Photoshop steadily increases the extent of the distortion until you release the mouse button.

Bloat (B). When you drag or move your mouse down with this tool, pixels underneath the cursor move outward. As is the case with the Pucker tool, the longer you hold down the mouse button, the more bloating you get.

Tip   Press Alt (or Option on the Mac) to toggle between the Pucker and Bloat functions on the fly.

The Pucker and Bloat tools are particularly valuable for removing weight or adding bulk. For example, in the first image in Figure 11-35, the Pucker tool was used to contort the face and head shape.

Push Left (O). As you click and drag with this tool, pixels underneath the cursor move in a direction perpendicular to your drag. For example, if you drag down, pixels flow to the right. Drag straight up, and pixels move to the left. To reverse the direction of the pixels, press Alt (Option on the Mac).

 Tip   At first, the Push Left tool may seem unwieldy, resulting in dramatic and sometimes unpredictable movements. But you can control it using two techniques. First, reduce the Brush Pressure value to 25 or lower. Figure 11-36 illustrates the difference between drags performed using Pressure settings of 50 and 20. Second, try using the Push Left tool in a straight line by clicking at one point and Shift-clicking at another, as you might with Photoshop's painting and editing tools. The result is a neat line, great for reducing flab along straight elements, such as arms and legs.

Figure 11-35: Armed with the Pucker tool, click and drag along the facial contours to reshape in ways a plastic surgeon can only imagine.

Mirror (M). Clicking and dragging with this tool creates a reflection, albeit one you might see in a fun-house mirror. As you drag, Photoshop copies pixels from the area perpendicular to the direction you move the cursor. So if you drag up, you clone pixels to the right of the cursor into the area underneath the cursor; drag down to clone pixels from left to right, as shown in Figure 11-37. Press Alt (Option on the Mac) to reflect from another direction on the fly.

Figure 11-36: Pushing things around lets you totally revamp a face, body, or any photographic content.

Figure 11-37: Using the Mirror tool, drag up on the left side and down on the right side. Pixels are reflected in a clockwise direction.

Turbulence (T). The Turbulence tool is a variation on the Forward Warp tool that distorts pixels in random directions as you drag. When you select this tool, Photoshop grants you access to a third Tool Options value labeled Turbulent Jitter. If the Brush Size value controls how many pixels are affected at a time and Brush Pressure controls the strength of the stroke,

Turbulent Jitter specifies just how much random variation is permitted. The minimum value of 1 causes the Turbulence tool to behave much like the Forward Warp tool; a maximum value of 100 mixes pixels in all directions.

Figure 11-38 illustrates a few examples. For purposes of demonstration, all four images were created using a very large Brush Size (ranging from 100 to 200, throughout all the samples), and the maximum Pressure value, 100. For each image in the top row, the brush was held in place for 15 seconds. The random variations built up from one moment to the next. Not surprisingly, a higher Turbulent Jitter value produced a more dramatic effect than a lower one.

Figure 11-38: Four variations created using the Turbulence tool, twice holding the mouse in place (top row) and twice dragging with the tool on the left and right sides of the face (bottom row).

After you drag with any of these tools, you can undo the effect by pressing Ctrl+Z (⌘-Z on the Mac). You also have the option of multiple undos. Press Ctrl+Alt+Z (⌘-Option-Z on the Mac) to backstep through your operations. Press Ctrl+Shift+Z (⌘-Shift-Z) to redo undone distortions. To learn how to go back in time nonsequentially and explore additional reversion options, read the section on reconstructing and reverting.

Freezing and thawing pixels

As mentioned earlier, if you make a selection in your image before choosing Filter ➪ Liquify, Photoshop automatically freezes unselected pixels when you enter the Liquify dialog box. Therefore, these unselected pixels are not affected by any distortions you apply. In previous versions of Photoshop (prior to CS), you couldn't thaw these pixels from within the Liquify window. But Photoshop lets you thaw pixels, freeze new ones, and determine frozen pixels based on transparency and layer masks in ways never before possible.

To freeze a portion of your image from the Liquify window, you have two options:

Freeze Mask (F). Press F to select the Freeze Mask tool and then click and drag over areas that you want to protect. You can adjust the brush size and pressure as you can when working with the distortion tools. But in this case, the Brush Pressure setting determines how deeply frozen the pixels become. At anything less than 100 percent, the pixels become partially distorted when you drag over them with a distortion tool. If you set the pressure to 50 percent, the distortion is applied with half the pressure used in unfrozen areas. Likewise, the Brush Density setting controls how deeply pixels become frozen toward the outside of the brush. To freeze the entire image, click Mask All in the Mask Options settings.

Thaw Mask (D). To thaw areas that you have frozen from the Liquify window, once again making them slaves to the distortion tools, paint over them with the Thaw Mask tool. The tool options affect this tool just as they do the Freeze Mask tool. To thaw the entire image, click None in the Mask Options settings.

Tip

Just as you can invert a selection outline or invert a mask in the Quick Mask mode, you can click Invert All to quickly freeze any unfrozen pixels and thaw any frozen ones.

Among the more complex features in the Liquify dialog box are the Mask Options settings, located below the Reconstruct Options. Above the None, Mask All, and Invert All buttons just mentioned, you're presented with five different buttons, each giving you a different option for interacting with the current mask. And each of those buttons has three options, when relevant; you can use information from the layer's current selection, transparency, or layer mask. From left to right, the options perform the following functions:

✦ **Replace selection** replaces the current mask, completely wiping out any freezing or thawing you've done and replacing it with a mask drawn from the layer's current selection, transparency, or layer mask.

✦ **Add to selection** keeps all thawed areas in the current mask and also thaws other areas according to the layer's current selection, transparency, or layer mask.

✦ **Subtract from selection** keeps all frozen areas in the current mask and also freezes other areas according to the layer's current selection, transparency, or layer mask.

✦ **Intersect with selection** only allows an area to stay thawed if it is thawed both in the current mask *and* according to the layer's current selection, transparency, or layer mask.

✦ **Invert selection** takes the current mask and inverts it, but only within the thawed areas according to the layer's current selection, transparency, or layer mask.

Reconstructing and restoring

In the Reconstruct Options section of the Liquify window, you see a Mode pop-up menu plus two buttons, Reconstruct and Restore All. You can use these options not only to revert an image to the way it looked before you applied a distortion, but also to redo a distortion so that it affects the image differently.

The following list outlines reversion possibilities:

✦ **Undo.** The Liquify window doesn't give you a History palette, but Ctrl+Alt+Z and Ctrl+Shift+Z still let you undo and redo sequences of operations (⌘-Option-Z and ⌘-Shift-Z on the Mac).

✦ **Reset.** To return everything back to the way it was the very first time you opened the Liquify window, Alt-click (Win) or Option-click (Mac) Cancel, which changes to Reset. Not only do you restore your original image, you restore the Liquify window's default settings.

Tip   Believe it or not, you can undo Reset and other reversion techniques. I know, it's too cool. Just press Ctrl+Z (⌘-Z on the Mac) to get your edits back.

✦ **Restore All.** To revert the image without resetting all values to their defaults, click Restore All. This affects frozen and thawed areas alike.

Liquify also offers a handful of reconstruction techniques that are more controlled and more complex than the reversion options. By selecting an option from the Mode menu and then clicking Reconstruct or clicking and dragging with the Reconstruct tool (R), you can reconstruct a distortion so that it extends from a frozen area into neighboring unfrozen pixels. The Reconstruct button affects all unfrozen areas, but dragging with the tool alters only pixels under your cursor, subject to the Brush Size and Pressure values.

Tip   All the reconstruction modes calculate the change to the image based on the warp mesh (grid). To get a better feel for how each mode works, deselect the Show Image option, select the Show Mesh option, and then apply a simple distortion across a portion of the grid. Freeze part of the distorted region and then keep an eye on the grid lines at the intersections between frozen and unfrozen regions as you try out each of these modes:

✦ **Revert.** The Revert mode restores unfrozen portions of the image to their original appearance, without regard to the borders between the frozen and unfrozen areas. Compare this to the Revert button, which restores frozen and unfrozen areas alike.

✦ **Rigid.** This mode extends the distortion only as needed to maintain right angles in the mesh where frozen and unfrozen areas meet. The result is unfrozen areas that look very much like they did originally but smoothly blend into the frozen areas.

✦ **Stiff.** Stiff interpolates the distortion so that the effect tapers away as you move farther from the boundary between the frozen and unfrozen areas.

✦ **Smooth and Loose.** These two modes extend the distortion applied to the frozen areas into the unfrozen areas. The Smooth setting tries to create smooth transitions between frozen and unfrozen areas. Loose shares more of the distortion from the frozen area with the unfrozen area. You'll achieve the most dramatic results when frozen and unfrozen areas have been distorted differently.

✦ **Displace, Amplitwist, and Affine.** The last three modes work exclusively with the reconstruct tool. Using these modes, you can apply one or more distortions that are in force at a specific reference point in the image. Click to set the reference point and then drag through unfrozen areas to distort them. Use the Displace mode to move pixels to match the displacement of the reference point; select Amplitwist to match the displacement, rotation, and scaling at the reference point; and choose Affine to match all distortions at the reference point.

Although Liquify certainly gives you plenty of ways to reconstruct distortions, predicting the outcome of your drags with the Reconstruct tool can be nearly impossible. So be prepared to experiment. And if you don't get the results you want, remember that you can undo a reconstruction just as easily as you can any distortion.

Creating a vanishing point

The Vanishing Point filter, which really goes beyond what you expect from a filter, is used to manipulate image content to create the illusion of perspective. Of course, the Edit ➪ Transform ➪ Perspective command allows you to take the four corners of a layer and move them to create a new perspective, but that's nothing compared to what Vanishing Point can do. Figure 11-39 shows the Vanishing Point dialog box, complete with some new and familiar tools on the left, a preview of the image in the middle, and controls across the top.

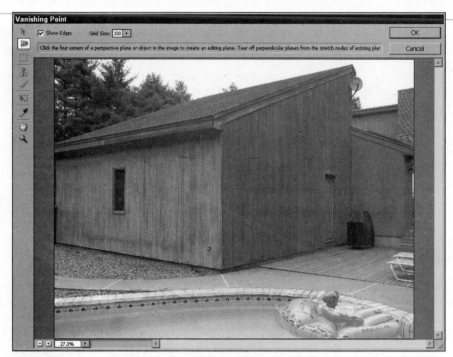

Figure 11-39: The Vanishing Point dialog box provides tools for creating and editing planes, cloning, stamping, sampling, panning, and zooming in on your image.

To use the Vanishing Point filter, follow these steps:

STEPS: Duplicate a Structure in Perspective

1. **Create a duplicate layer.** Duplicate the layer that has the content you want to work with in creating your vanishing point and content-in-perspective.

2. **Choose Filter ➪ Vanishing Point.** The Vanishing Point dialog box opens, as shown in Figure 11-39. The Create Plane tool is active as soon as the dialog box opens.

3. **Create a plane by clicking and dragging to create a four-sided plane, as shown in Figure 11-40.** If the resulting grid is yellow or red, you have not drawn a plane that follows a true perspective in your image.

4. **Repeat Step 3 to create a plane in the area of the image where you want to position content taken from the area within the first plane.** Figure 11-41 shows a second plane in place on the right side of the building.

Tip

If your grid is yellow or red, or if it's simply the wrong size, point to and drag the grid's side points to extend the edges of the grid to cover the area you wish to work in. If your resizing of the grid changes the perspective, the grid may change color, again indicating a problem with the perspective. Tinker with your grid until it's blue and the right size for your needs.

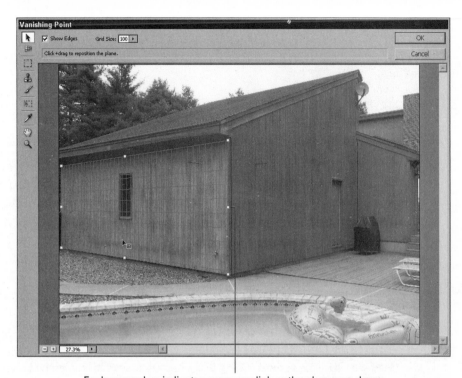

Each corner box indicates a mouse click as the plane was drawn

Figure 11-40: The editing plane encompasses the front of the building. The window on the front of the building will be duplicated, in perspective, on the right side.

5. **Clone the content from one plane to the next.** Click the Clone Stamp tool. You'll use this tool to clone content from the first plane into the second.

6. **Press the Alt key (or Option on the Mac) and click to set the source point for the clone-to-be.** Figure 11-42 shows the source point set in the window on the front of the building.

7. **Click Heal to turn the option on.** This ensures the colors and lighting in the cloned content match their new surroundings. You can also leave Aligned on so that you don't create any unwanted patterns if cloning a large area.

8. **Drag your mouse over the target area to draw content from the source point.** As shown in Figure 11-43, the window from the front of the garage is cloned to the right side of the building, and it appears in perfect perspective.

9. **Click OK to save the modifications to the duplicate layer.**

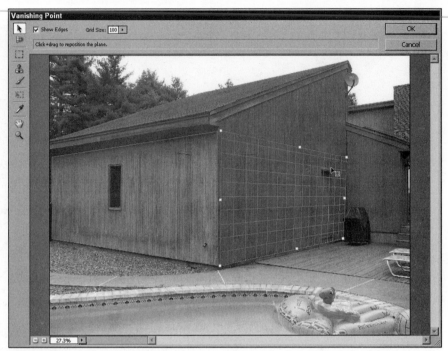

Figure 11-41: The second editing plane encompasses the side of the building, and follows the intended vanishing point. Because the grid is blue (although it appears light gray in this black and white image), one knows that the correct perspective is achieved.

Figure 11-44 shows the door from the right side of the building cloned to the front of the building—done by using the Marquee tool to select the door within the second plane, and then dragging the selection onto the front of the building. The perspective of the target plane is applied to the door, and it looks like it belongs there.

Tip   The Vanishing Point filter takes a lot of practice, and you'll find that using images with buildings, roads, and other solid structures with a lot of vertical and horizontal sides is your best bet for honing your vanishing point skills. Have fun!

Figure 11-42: The green (gray here) cross hair indicates the source point for the Clone Stamp.

Figure 11-43: No need for a home construction how-to manual here — a new window is placed on this building in just minutes.

Figure 11-44: Use the Marquee tool in the Vanishing Point dialog box to select content from one plane and place it in another. Drag with the Alt key pressed to make a duplicate in the target location.

Adding Clouds and Spotlights

The five filters in the Render submenu produce lighting effects. You can use Clouds and Difference Clouds to create a layer of haze over an image. Lens Flare creates light flashes and reflections (as shown earlier in the chapter). Lighting Effects lights an image as if it were hanging on a gallery wall. You also have the Fibers filter, which you may want to check out but then ignore — its results are a bit strange.

Creating clouds

The Clouds filter creates an abstract and random haze between the foreground and background colors. Difference Clouds works exactly like layering the image, applying the Clouds filter, and selecting the Difference blend mode in the Layers palette.

Why would Difference Clouds make special provisions for a single blend mode? Because you can create cumulative effects. Try this: Select a sky blue as the foreground color and then choose Filter ➪ Render ➪ Clouds. The results look like a nice, summer sky. Now choose Filter ➪ Render ➪ Difference Clouds. Not so nice and summer this time; instead, it's all blacks and oranges. Press Ctrl+F (or ⌘-F on the Mac) to repeat the filter; it's back to the blue sky. Keep pressing Ctrl+F (⌘-F on the Mac) over and over and notice the results. A pink tone starts to seep into the blue sky; a green tone seeps into the orange one. Multiple applications of the Difference Clouds filter generate organic oil-on-water effects. Figure 11-45 shows an example of Clouds and Difference Clouds — here in black and white, of course, but you can see the difference in the results — the one on the left could easily be added to fill in the sky on an outdoor photo, the one on the right might not be.

Figure 11-45: Clouds (left) and Difference Clouds (right)

Tip

To strengthen the colors created by the Clouds filter, press Shift when choosing the command. This same technique works when using the Difference Clouds filter as well. In fact, there may be no reason *not* to press Shift while choosing one of these commands, unless you have some specific need for washed-out effects.

Also, if you want to make a repeating texture using Clouds and Difference Clouds, make sure your image size is a square with pixel dimensions based on a power of two — something like 128 x 128 or 256 x 256 will work well. Your cloudy image will seamlessly tile, making it a perfect backdrop when you need something to fill in a large area.

Tip Tempted to use a Clouds filter-created image as your Web page background? Think again. First, background images are pretty passé for use on the Web, and second, even if a background image is appropriate in a table, frame, or layer (some smaller segment) of your Web pages, a background image that has any significant pattern or color diversity will make text hard to read and compete visually with any Web graphics placed on top of it.

Using the Fibers filter

Like the Clouds and Difference Clouds filters, the Fibers filter uses Perlin-based fractal noise to achieve a realistic randomness that, when stretched out in one direction, looks less like fluffy clouds and more like, well, fibers. This could be a problem for you if you don't want the fibers Photoshop gives you, because there is no way to vary the fibers greatly — you have two sliders (Variance and Strength) and one button (Randomize), and as you'll see, these don't do much more than change the appearance of the fibers — in the end, you still get fibers. If fibers are what you want, this will be a great thing, but if you were hoping for a fibrous texture made from the content of your image, this is not what you're getting here. Programs such as Adobe's After Effects give you lots of options for tweaking and adjusting the noise this filter generates, but Photoshop's Fibers filter is rather limited in terms of its flexibility, and therefore its uses.

If you're still interested in using this filter — and you should be, if only to see for yourself how you might be able to use it — choose Filter ➪ Render ➪ Fibers. This opens the Fibers dialog box, shown in Figure 11-46. In the preview box, you can view the fibers generated by the filter based on the values of your foreground and background colors. Increase the Variance slider value to create shorter strands of fiber with more contrast between the colors. Ramp up the Strength slider value to make your fibers stringier. Click Randomize to call up a new random seed for the noise; it's a good way to mix it up a bit if the need arises. Also seen in Figure 11-46 are the results of the Fiber filter (in the visible image window) with more Strength, shorter strands (higher Variance), and Randomize turned on.

Tip Sadly, there's no way to change the angle of the fibers generated by the Fibers filter to create a woven effect, but you can cheat your way around this. Apply the Fibers filter to a layer, duplicate it, and then rotate the top layer 90 degrees. Set the top layer to the Darken blend mode and you should wind up with a somewhat realistic interwoven pattern.

Figure 11-46: The Fibers filter dialog box and a preview of its effect on . . . well, anything. Behind the dialog box, you see the results of higher Variance and Strength settings, and the Randomize option applied.

Lighting an image

The complex Lighting Effects filter enables you to shine lights on an image, color, position, and focus the lights, specify the reflectivity of the surface, and even create a surface map.

Note The Lighting Effects filter is applicable exclusively to RGB images.

When you choose Filter ➪ Render ➪ Lighting Effects, Photoshop displays one of its most complex dialog boxes, as shown in Figure 11-47. The dialog box has two halves: one in which you position light with respect to a thumbnail of the selected image and one that contains an intimidating number of options, many with rather confusing or vague names. Read on as a valiant (and hopefully successful) attempt at making order and usefulness out of the confusion is made.

There's no way around it — this filter and its dialog box are complex. The easiest way to apply the filter is to choose one of the predefined lighting effects from the Style pop-up menu at the top of the right side of the dialog box, see how it looks in the preview area, and — if you like it — press Enter or Return to apply the effect.

If you want to create your own effects, you have to tinker with the settings a bit and risk some frustration. It can be worth it, though, for creating some striking lighting effects in your images. Here are the basic steps involved in creating a custom effect.

Footprint   Focus point

Handle   Trash icon   Hot spot   Color swatches

Preview area

Figure 11-47: The Lighting Effects dialog box lets you light an image as if it were hanging in a gallery, lying on a floor, or perhaps resting too near a hot flame.

STEPS: Lighting an Image

1. **Click and drag from the light icon at the bottom of the dialog box into the preview area to create a new light source.** Think of this area as the *stage* because it's as if the image is painted on the floor of a stage and the lights are hanging above it.

2. **Select the kind of light you want from the Light Type pop-up menu.** It's just below the Style pop-up menu. You can select from Directional, Omni, and Spotlight:

   - Directional works like the sun, producing a general, unfocused light that hits a target from an angle.

   - Omni casts light like a bare light bulb hanging in the middle of the room, shining in all directions from a center point.

   - Spotlight is a focused beam that is brightest at the source and tapers off gradually.

3. **Specify the color of the light by clicking the top Color Swatch.** You can also tinker with the Intensity slider to control the brightness of the light. If Spotlight is selected, the Focus slider becomes available. Click and drag the slider toward Narrow to create a bright laser of light; drag toward Wide to diffuse the light and spread it over a larger area.

4. **Move the light source by clicking and dragging at the *focus point* (if you've chosen a color for your light, the focus point appears as a colored circle in the preview area).** When Directional or Spotlight is selected, the focus point represents the spot at which the light is pointing. When Omni is active, the focus point is the actual bulb.

5. **If Directional or Spotlight is active, you can change the angle of the light by clicking and dragging the hot spot.** The *hot spot* represents the location in the image that's liable to receive the most light. When you use a Directional light, the hot spot appears as a black square at the end of a line joined to the focus point. The same holds true when you edit a Spotlight; the confusing thing is that there are four black squares altogether. The light source is joined to the focus point by a line; the three *handles* are not.

Tip To make the light brighter, click and drag the hot spot closer to the focus point. Dragging the hot spot away from the focus point dims the light by increasing the distance that it has to travel. It's like having a flashlight in the living room when you're in the garage—the light gets dimmer as you move away from it.

6. **With Omni or Spotlight in force, you can edit the elliptical footprint of the light.** When Omni is in force, a circle surrounds the focus point. When editing a Spotlight, you see an ellipse. Either way, this shape represents the *footprint* of the light, which is the approximate area of the image affected by the light. You can change the size of the light by clicking and dragging the handles around the footprint. Enlarging the shape is like raising the light source. When the footprint is small, the light is close to the image so it's concentrated and very bright. When the footprint is large, the light is high above the image, so it's more generalized.

Tip When editing the footprint of a Spotlight, Shift-drag a handle to adjust the width or height of the ellipse without affecting the angle. To change the angle without affecting the size, Ctrl-drag (or ⌘-drag on the Mac) a handle.

7. **Introduce more lights as you see fit.**

Tip Duplicate a light in the stage by Alt-dragging (Option-dragging on the Mac) its focus point. To delete the active light, drag the focus point onto the Trash icon below the preview area.

8. **Change the Properties and Texture Channel options as you see fit.** This is explained in detail after the steps.

9. **If you want to save your settings for future use, click Save.** Photoshop invites you to name the setup, which then appears as an option in the Style pop-up

menu. If you want to get rid of one of the presets, select it from the pop-up menu and click Delete.

10. Press Enter or Return to apply your settings to the image.

That's really about it — the only parts not yet discussed are the Properties and Texture Channel options. The Properties sliders control how light reflects off the surface of your image:

✦ **Gloss.** Is the surface dull or shiny? Click and drag the slider toward Matte to make the surface flat and nonreflective like dull enamel paint. Drag the slider toward Shiny to make it glossy, as if you had slapped on a coat of lacquer.

✦ **Material.** This option determines the color of the light that reflects off the image. According to the logic employed by this option, Plastic reflects the color of the light; Metallic reflects the color of the object itself.

✦ **Exposure.** Your options here are Under and Over — referring to exposure. This option controls the brightness of all lights like a dimmer switch. You can control a single selected light using the Intensity slider, but the Exposure slider offers the added control of changing all lights in the stage (preview) area and the ambient light (described next) together.

✦ **Ambience.** The last slider enables you to add *ambient light*, which is a general, diffused light that hits all surfaces evenly. First, select the color of the light by clicking the color swatch to the right. Then click and drag the slider to cast a subtle hue over the stage. Drag toward Positive to tint the image with the color in the swatch; drag toward Negative to tint the stage with the swatch's opposite. Keep the slider set to 0 — in the center — to cast no hue.

The Texture Channel options let you treat one channel in the image as a *texture map*, which is a grayscale surface in which white indicates peaks and black indicates valleys (as long as the White is High option is selected, that is. If you deselect that option, everything flips, and black becomes the peak). It's as if one channel has a surface to it. By selecting a channel from the pop-up menu, you create an emboss effect, much like that created with the Emboss filter except much better because you can light the surface from many angles at once and it's in color, too.

Choose a channel to serve as the embossed surface from the pop-up menu. Then change the Height slider to indicate more or less Flat terrain or huge Mountainous cliffs of surface texture.

Figure 11-48 shows an image lit with a total of five spotlights, two from above and three from below. In the first example, the Texture Channel option is set to None. In the second example, the Green channel is selected as the surface map. And in the third example, a separate mask channel is filled with a bunch of white and black dollops using Filter ➪ Pixelate ➪ Pointillize. Then the mask from the Texture Channel pop-up menu in the Lighting Effects dialog box is selected. The result is a really rough paper texture.

Figure 11-48: Not only can Lighting Effects enhance your images with simulated directional light, it can also be used to create textures.

Summary

In this chapter, you learned about Photoshop's special effects filters, including those available exclusively through the Filter Gallery. The plusses and minuses of all of Photoshop's special effects filters were discussed followed by more specific coverage of the Pixelate and Mezzotint filters, the Edge-Enhancement filters, and the Distort filters. This included the new Lens Correction filter and the always-exciting Liquify filter.

You also learned to create metallic effects with Bas Relief, Plastic Wrap, and Chrome, and how to use the Fade command to reduce the sometimes over-the-top results these and other filters can give you.

Coverage of new features continued with coverage of the Vanishing Point filter, which enables you to build and modify structures in your photos like never before, and was followed by a discussion of the Clouds and Lighting Effects filters.

✦　　✦　　✦

Layers, Objects, and Text

✦   ✦   ✦   ✦

In This Part

Chapter 12
Working with Layers

Chapter 13
The Wonders of
Blend Modes

Chapter 14
Shapes and Styles

Chapter 15
Fully Editable Text

✦   ✦   ✦   ✦

Working with Layers

✦ ✦ ✦ ✦

In This Chapter

Creating
and cloning layers

Floating the
background layer

Reordering layers

Using the
Matting commands

Merging layers

Converting
layers to selections

Making drop
shadows, halos,
and spotlights

Combining layers
using links and
groups

Moving,
scaling, rotating,
and aligning layers

Working
with Smart Objects

Using
the Measure tool

Selecting the Lock
Transparency option

Working
with layer masks

Working with the
Layer Comps palette

✦ ✦ ✦ ✦

Layers started out as little more than their name implies —
sheets of pixels that you could edit and transform independently of each other. But since the feature was introduced
in version 3, layers have become increasingly more sophisticated and complicated. Photoshop 4 introduced floating *adjustment layers* that let you correct colors without permanently
affecting a single pixel (see Chapter 17). Photoshop 5 gave us
layer effects, which included editable drop shadows, glows,
and edge bevels (see Chapter 14). Photoshop 6 permitted you
to bundle and color-code layers into logical clusters (this
chapter), blend color channels independently of each other
(Chapter 13), and even add vector-based lines and shapes
(Chapter 14) and object-oriented text (Chapter 15). Photoshop
7 gave you the ability to adjust the fill opacity and allowed for
easier renaming of layers, but otherwise maintained the status
quo. Photoshop CS dramatically improved the way you work
with layers by introducing layer comps (covered later in this
chapter).

**New
Feature** Photoshop CS2 has made more changes to the way layers
work, some considered improvements and others that are
simply a change in the way you do business — and all of these
are covered in this chapter. For example, the way you link layers has changed, as has the terminology with regard to layer
sets. The Layers menu has changed a bit, too, but all the functionality is still there. If you were a Photoshop CS user, you
won't be left scratching your head or worse, banging your
head on the desk.

Of course, even with all the improvements made to layers over
the years and releases, there's still room for improvement. For
example, one day it would be nice to see Photoshop integrate
parametric effects, in which filters such as Unsharp Mask and
Motion Blur are fully editable, interactive, and interchangeable,
on the order of Adobe's full-motion editor, After Effects. But in
the meantime, Photoshop's layers still provide us with a reward-
ing amount of freedom and flexibility — in fact, without them,
much of what we now assume can be done to photos would be
difficult, if not outright impossible.

For those of you who are new to Photoshop or for whom layers are something of a conceptual enigma, let's back up and talk about what they are, what they do, and why you love them (you really do, you know).

The first and foremost benefit of layers is that they add versatility. Because each layer in a composition is completely independent of other layers, you can change your mind at a moment's notice. Consider the top example in Figure 12-1. This photo started out as a picture of a cat sitting in the window (see the top image), looking out on some flowering shrubbery. Three additional cats were added, one added so that he's partially hidden by the curtain that was part of the original image. Another cat is peeking out from behind the added cat, and another from behind the shrubbery on the left side of the image. Finally, text is added to the image (middle).

Obviously crafted out of several other photos (the extra cats had to come from somewhere, right?), in the bottom image, the original cat from the windowsill has jumped down and now appears in the foreground, and the text has been moved up so as not to be obscured. What made all this possible? Layers. Without layers, once the image was built, you'd be hard-pressed to easily (just forget quickly) rearrange, resize, or remove anything from a photo. Because everything from the background to the smallest item in the image is on its own layer, everything was fluid and changeable.

Layers make it harder to make mistakes, they make it easier to make changes, and they expand your range of options. More than anything else, they permit you to restructure a composition and examine how it was put together after you assemble it. Layers can be very challenging or relatively simple to use — it depends on what you're doing with them and whether or not you've taken the time to get to know them, which is what you're about to do right now.

Figure 12-1: Thanks to the existence and inherent flexibility of layers, you can rearrange your image components, keeping them separate for easy editing, transformation, and removal.

Sending a Selection to a Layer

To its credit, Photoshop lets you establish a new layer in roughly a billion ways. If you want to add a selected portion of one image to another image, the easiest method is to Ctrl-drag (Win) or ⌘-drag (Mac) the selection and drop it into its new home, as demonstrated in Figure 12-2. Photoshop creates the new layer from the selection, in one fell swoop.

Figure 12-2: Ctrl-drag (or ⌘-drag on the Mac) a selected portion of an image and drop it into a different image window to introduce the selection as a new layer. As you can see in the Layers palette, the tabby cat is being moved into place as a new layer in front of the window and curtain, which is part of the image background layer.

Caution

Be sure to Ctrl-drag (⌘-drag on the Mac) or use the Move tool. If you merely drag the selection with the Marquee, Lasso, or Wand, you drop an empty selection outline into the new image window. Also, be aware that pressing Ctrl (Win) or ⌘ (Mac) delivers the Move tool. But if the Pen, Arrow, or Shape tool is active, you get the Arrow tool instead, which won't work for you. Press V to get the Move tool and then try dragging again.

When you drop the selection, the selection outline disappears. Not to worry, though. Now that the image resides on an independent layer, the selection outline is no longer needed. You can move the layer using the move tool, as you would move a selection. You can even paint inside what was once the selection by selecting the first of the Lock buttons in the Layers palette. Both the Move tool and the Lock buttons are covered in greater detail throughout this chapter.

If you want to clone a selection to a new layer inside the same image window — useful when performing complex filter routines and color corrections — choose Layer ➪ New ➪ Layer Via Copy — or simply press Ctrl+J (⌘-J on the Mac).

Other Ways to Make a Layer

Those are only two of many ways to create a new layer in Photoshop. Here are a few others:

✦ Copy a selection (Ctrl+C or ⌘-C) and paste it into another image (Ctrl+V or ⌘-V). Photoshop pastes the selection as a new layer.

✦ If you want to relegate a selection exclusively to a new layer, choose Layer ➪ New ➪ Layer Via Cut or press Ctrl+Shift+J (⌘-Shift-J on the Mac). Rather than cloning the selection, Layer Via Cut removes the selection from the background image and places it on its own layer.

✦ To convert a floating selection — one that you've moved or cloned — to a new layer, press Ctrl+Shift+J (⌘-Shift-J on the Mac). The Shift key is very important. If you press Ctrl+J (Win) or ⌘-J (Mac) without Shift, Photoshop clones the selection and leaves an imprint of the image on the layer below.

✦ To create an empty layer — to house, for example, a few brushstrokes without harming the original image — choose Layer ➪ New ➪ Layer or press Ctrl+Shift+N (⌘-Shift-N on the Mac). Or click the new layer icon at the bottom of the Layers palette (labeled in Figure 12-3).

✦ When you create a new layer, Photoshop positions it in front of the active layer. To create a new layer behind the active layer, Ctrl-click (Win) or ⌘-click (Mac) the new layer icon.

Incidentally, you can also create a new layer by choosing New Layer from the Layers palette menu. But as you can see in Figure 12-3, nearly all the palette commands are duplicated in the Layer menu. The only unique palette commands are Dock to Palette Well, which sends the Layers palette tab to the Options bar, and Palette Options, which lets you change the size of the thumbnails in front of the layer names. Turns out, you can perform the latter technique more easily by right-clicking (Win) or Control-clicking (Mac) in the empty space below the layer names and choosing an option.

Tip When you choose the Layer Via Copy or Layer Via Cut command or click the new layer icon, Photoshop automatically names the new layer for you. Unfortunately, the automatic names — Layer 1, Layer 2, and so on — are fairly meaningless and don't help to convey the contents of the layer.

If you want to specify a more meaningful name, add the Alt (Win) or Option (Mac) key. Press Ctrl+Alt+J (⌘-Option-J on the Mac) to clone the selection to a layer, press Ctrl+Shift+Alt+J (⌘-Shift-Option-J on the Mac) to cut the selection, or Alt-click (Option-click on the Mac) the new layer icon to create a blank layer. In any case, you see the dialog box shown in Figure 12-4. Type a name for the layer. If you like, you can also assign a color to the layer, which is helpful for identifying a layer name at a glance. Then press Enter or Return. For now, ignore the other options in this dialog box—you don't need to address them each time you use the dialog box, and anyway, you'll be getting to them later.

Figure 12-3: All but two of the commands in the Layers palette menu are duplicated in the Layer menu—and supported by buttons at the bottom of the Layers palette itself.

When creating a new layer from the keyboard, press Ctrl+Shift+Alt+N (⌘-Shift-Option-N on the Mac) to bypass the dialog box. Alt (Option on the Mac) works both ways, forcing the appearance of the dialog box some times and suppressing it others. The only time it produces no effect is when pasting or dropping an image.

Tip

To rename a layer, just double-click the name and type a new name directly in the Layers palette.

Figure 12-4: Press Alt (or Option on the Mac) to force the display of the New Layer dialog box, which lets you name the new layer.

Duplicating a layer

To clone the active layer, you can choose Layer ➪ Duplicate Layer. If that seems like the long way 'round the barn to you, try dragging the layer you want to duplicate down to the Create New Layer icon at the bottom of the Layers palette.

To specify a name for the cloned layer or to copy the layer into another image, Alt-drag (or Option-drag on the Mac) the layer onto the new layer icon. Always the thoughtful program, Photoshop displays the dialog box shown in Figure 12-5. You can name the cloned layer by typing something in the As option box. To jettison the layer to some other open image, choose the image name from the Document pop-up menu. Or choose New and type the name for an entirely different image in the Name option box, as the figure shows.

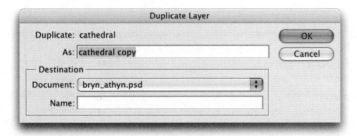

Figure 12-5: You can duplicate the layer into an entirely different image by Alt-dragging (or Option-dragging on the Mac) the layer onto the new layer icon in the Layers palette — this dialog box helps you complete the process.

Tip

You can clone a layer by simply Ctrl-Alt-dragging (or ⌘-Option-dragging on the Mac) it inside the image window. This way, you clone the layer and reposition it in one operation. Just be sure not to begin your drag inside a selection outline; if you do, you create a floating selection.

Layer Basics

Regardless of how you create a new layer, Photoshop lists the layer along with a little thumbnail of its contents in the Layers palette. The new layer appears highlighted to show that it's active, and the layer's name appears in bold. The little paintbrush icon in front of the layer name also indicates an active layer.

 Tip   If the thumbnails aren't big enough for you, click the palette's option menu button (the triangle pointing to the right, just above the Opacity setting), and choose Palette Options. In the resulting dialog box, you can choose from three sizes for the thumbnails (small is the default), and also choose to see either just the content of the layer (Layer Bounds) or Entire Document in the thumbnail.

Back in the Layers palette, to the left of the paintbrush icon is a column of eyeballs. These symbols invite you to hide and display layers temporarily. Click an eyeball to hide the layer — the eyeball disappears, and so does the layer's content within the image. Click where the eyeball previously was to bring it back and redisplay the layer. Whether hidden or displayed, all layers remain intact and ready for action — although some layer quality adjustments, such as the blending mode and Opacity, are dimmed if you click on a hidden layer. To make such adjustments to the layer, redisplay it, tweak the desired settings, and then rehide the layer if you still don't need to see it in the image.

 Tip   To view a single layer by itself, Alt-click (Win) or Option-click (Mac) the eyeball icon before the layer name to hide all other layers. Alt-click (Win) or Option-click (Mac) in front of the layer again to bring all the layers back into view.

Switching between layers

You can select a different layer by clicking its name in the Layers palette. The layer you click becomes active, enabling you to edit it.

 New Feature   You can now click and activate multiple layers — just click the first layer you want to select, and then press and hold Shift to select additional consecutive layers (next to each other in the Layers palette, not necessarily in the image) or Ctrl (⌘ on the Mac) to select nonconsecutive layers. Once the multiple layers are selected, you have limited abilities to do things to them — you can move them with the Move tool, and you can transform them as a unit. This is not the same as grouping them, which is discussed later in this chapter.

You can also link multiple layers and combine them into groups — as is also explained later. Once linked, you have the same ability to move and transform the layers (press Ctrl [⌘] + T to enter Free Transform mode) as you do when you simply Shift or Ctrl (⌘) + click the layers to select them. You cannot, however, paint, draw, fill, or apply filters to the selected or linked layers. If you do want to formally merge the layers, you can by turning them into a single layer, which can then be treated like any other layer. More about that later, too.

Here are some more layer-selection tips:

✦ Ctrl (⌘ on the Mac) gets you the Move tool. (If the Move tool is already selected, you don't have to press Ctrl or ⌘; Alt-right-clicking or Option-Control-clicking works just fine.)

✦ Right-clicking (or Control-clicking on the Mac) alone brings up a shortcut menu. When you right-click or Control-click with the Move tool — or Ctrl-right-click (⌘-Control-click on the Mac) with any other tool — Photoshop displays a pop-up menu that lists the layer that the image is on and any other layers in the image, as in Figure 12-6. (If a layer is completely transparent at the spot where you right-click or Control-click, that layer name doesn't appear in the pop-up menu.) Select the desired layer to go there.

Figure 12-6: Right-click (or Control + click on the Mac) an image to view a pop-up menu. The menu lists all the layers in the image that contain pixel data on the spot where you clicked.

Tip

If you'd prefer Photoshop to *always* go directly to the layer on which you click and avoid all these messy keyboard tricks, press V to select the Move tool. The first option in the Options bar is called Auto Select Layer. Select it. Now whenever you click a layer with the Move tool — or Ctrl-click (⌘-click on the Mac) with some other tool — Photoshop goes right to that layer.

Tip

There is also an Auto Select Groups option, which you may want to deselect — so that when you select a layer simply by clicking it, you don't necessarily select the entire group of which that layer may be a member. More about groups can be found later on in this chapter.

Switching layers from the keyboard

You can ascend and descend the layer stack also from the keyboard:

✦ **Alt+] (or Option-] on the Mac).** Press Alt+right bracket (Win) or Option-right bracket (Mac) to go to the next layer up in the stack. If you're already at the top layer, Photoshop takes you back around to the lowest one.

✦ **Alt+[(or Option-[on the Mac).** Press Alt+left bracket (Win) or Option-left bracket (Mac) to go down a layer. If the background layer is active, Alt+[or Option-[takes you to the top layer.

✦ **Shift+Alt+] (or Shift-Option-] on the Mac).** This takes you to the top layer in the image.

✦ **Shift+Alt+[(or Shift-Option-[on the Mac).** This activates the background layer (or the lowest layer if no background exists).

Note

These shortcuts work only with visible layers. Hidden layers will be skipped.

Note

While we haven't gotten into Layer Groups yet, it's important to note that Photoshop treats a closed group in the Layers palette (a *layer group*) as if it were a layer unto itself. So every one of these tricks skips to or over the group in a single bound. For the complete lowdown on layer groups including Photoshop CS2's support for nested layer groups, see the section on grouping layers found later in this chapter.

Selecting similar layers

New Feature

If you right-click (or Ctrl-click on the Mac) any layer in the Layers palette, a pop-up menu (shown in Figure 12-7) appears. Among the pop-up menu's commands is a new option, "Select Similar Layers." Similar? What does that mean? It means layers that have similar content in terms of size, shape, color, modes, and styles. It can be a great way to select several duplicate layers at once without having to hunt through (and possibly scroll through, if you have a lot of layers) a long list of layers in the palette to find the ones you want to select for moving, resizing, linking, or dragging to another image in the workspace. Figure 12-7 shows two layers selected, the result of choosing the highlighted menu command.

Figure 12-7: Choose Select Similar Layers to grab all the layers that have a lot in common.

Understanding transparency

Although the selection outline disappears when you convert a selection to a layer, no information is lost. Photoshop retains every nuance of the original selection outline—whether it's a jagged border, a little bit of anti-aliasing, or a feathered edge. Anything that wasn't selected is now transparent. The data that defines the opacity and transparency of a layer is called the *transparency mask*.

To see this transparency in action, click the eyeball icon in front of the background item in the Layers palette. This hides the background layer and enables you to view the new layer by itself. In Figure 12-8, the background (the black and white cat, the window, the shrubbery) is hidden (note the missing eyeball icon next to that layer) and only the orange tabby layer is visible—and all of that layer except for the cat is transparent and filled with a checkerboard pattern. Opaque areas look like the standard image, and translucent areas—where they exist—appear as a mix of image and checkerboard.

Figure 12-8: When you hide the background layer, you see a checkerboard pattern that represents the transparent portions of the layer.

Tip

If the checkerboard pattern is hard to distinguish from the image, you can change the appearance of the pattern. Press Ctrl+K and then Ctrl+4 (⌘-K and then ⌘-4 on the Mac) to go to the Transparency & Gamut panel of the Preferences dialog box. Then edit the colors as you see fit (as explained in Chapter 2).

If you apply an effect to the layer while no portion of the layer is selected, Photoshop changes the opaque and translucent portions of the image but leaves the transparent region intact. For example, if you press Ctrl+I (⌘-I on the Mac) or choose Image ➪ Adjustments ➪ Invert, Photoshop inverts the image but doesn't change a single pixel in the checkerboard area. If you click in the left column in front of the background item to bring back the eyeball icon, you may notice a slight halo around the inverted image, but the edge pixels blend with the background image as well as they ever did. The only difference is that this selection is independent of its background. You can do anything you want to it without running the risk of harming the underlying background.

Only a few operations affect the transparent areas of a layer, and most of these are limited to tools. You can paint on transparent pixels to make them opaque. You can clone with the Clone Stamp or smear pixels with the edit tools. To send pixels back to transparency, paint with the Eraser. All these operations change both the contents of the layer and the composition of the transparency mask.

Tip

You can fill all pixels also by pressing Alt+Backspace (Option-Delete on the Mac) for the foreground color and Ctrl+Backspace (⌘-Delete on the Mac) for the background color. To fill the pixels in a layer without altering the transparency mask, toss in the Shift key. Shift+Alt+Backspace (Shift-Option-Delete on the Mac) fills the opaque pixels with the foreground color; Ctrl+Shift+Backspace (⌘-Shift-Delete on the Mac) fills them with the background color. In both cases, the transparent pixels remain every bit as transparent as they ever were.

When a portion of the layer is selected, pressing plain old Backspace (Win) or Delete (Mac) eliminates the selected pixels and makes them transparent, revealing the layers below.

> **Note**
>
> Transparent pixels take up next to no space in memory, but opaque and translucent pixels do consume memory space. Thus, a layer containing 25 percent as many pixels as the background layer takes up roughly 25 percent as much space. Mind you, you shouldn't let this influence how you work in Photoshop, but it is something to keep in mind.

Modifying the background layer

At the bottom of the layer stack is the *Background layer*, the fully opaque layer that represents the base image. The background image is as low as you go. Nothing can be slipped under the background layer, and pixels in the background layer cannot be made transparent, unless you first convert the background to a floating layer. Blend modes and styles cannot be applied to the layer, nor can the background be changed in terms of its Opacity or Fill — you'll see these options become dimmed while the background layer is active.

To convert your Background layer to a floating layer, double-click the item labeled Background in the Layers palette. A dialog box appears. Type a name for the new layer — Photoshop suggests Layer 0 — and press Enter or Return. You can now change the order of the layer or erase down to transparency.

> **Tip**
>
> To skip the dialog box and accept Layer 0 as the new layer name, press Alt (Win) or Option (Mac) and double-click the Background item in the Layers palette.

In Figure 12-9, the background image (cat, house, shrubbery) has been converted to a layer. Had this particular image included a path that encircled the background layer's subject — or had the background content not completely filled the Background layer, you could Ctrl-click (⌘-click on the Mac) on the path to convert it to a selection outline and then press Ctrl+Shift+I (⌘-Shift-I on the Mac) to reverse the selection — this would select everything but the content on the layer, and that "everything but" could then be removed by pressing Delete. To demonstrate this in the image used thus far, the canvas size was increased to create white space around the image of the cat, window, shrubs, and so on. This area, then, can be cleared, leaving transparency around the layer's actual content.

> **Note**
>
> Although InDesign CS can easily handle layered Photoshop files complete with transparency, QuarkXPress 6.0 can't. As I mentioned in Chapter 8, if you want to export transparency to Quark, you must use a clipping path.

Figure 12-9: After converting the Background layer to a floating layer (called "Layer 0," the white space around the content (canvas area) was selected and deleted, leaving transparency in its wake.

Tip   To convert the active layer to a background layer when there is currently no background layer, choose Layer⇨New⇨Background From Layer. It doesn't matter whether the active layer is at the top of the stack, the bottom, or someplace in between — Photoshop takes the layer and makes a new background out of it.

To establish a blank background, create an empty layer by pressing Ctrl+Shift+N (⌘-Shift-N on the Mac) and then choose Layer ⇨ New ⇨ Background From Layer. In Figure 12-10, a pattern fill (Canvas, applied via the Edit ⇨ Fill command and Fill dialog box) was used to create a texture, framing the image on the previous background, now called "main image." The main image layer was then selected and Layer⇨Layer Style⇨Drop Shadow chosen, to add a drop shadow that makes the photo look like it's hovering over the textured paper backdrop. Drop shadows and other layer styles are discussed in Chapter 14.

Photoshop permits only one background layer per image. If an image already contains a background layer, the command Layer⇨New⇨Background From Layer changes to Layer From Background, which converts the background layer to a floating layer, as when you double-click the Background item in the Layers palette.

Figure 12-10: A new background layer is added below the main image layer (the former background) and a paper texture drop shadow were applied to give the composition a little false depth.

Reordering layers

Layers would be rather limited in terms of enabling you to rearrange your image content if you couldn't change their stacking order. Luckily, Photoshop makes it easy to move layers up and down in the stack, making things overlap when they didn't before, preventing overlaps where you don't want them, and placing content behind other content so you can either see it (by reducing the opacity of the uppermost layer) or so you can't see some or all of the underlying layer.

You can reorder layers in two ways. First, you can click and drag a layer name up or down in the scrolling list to move it forward or backward in layering order (your mouse pointer turns from a pointing hand to a little determined fist while you're dragging). The only trick is to make sure that the black bar appears at the point where you want to move the layer before you release the mouse button, as illustrated in Figure 12-11.

The second way to reorder layers is to choose a command from the Layer ⇨ Arrange submenu. For example, choose Layer ⇨ Arrange ⇨ Bring Forward to move the active layer up one level; choose Layer ⇨ Arrange ⇨ Send to Back to move the layer to just above the Background layer.

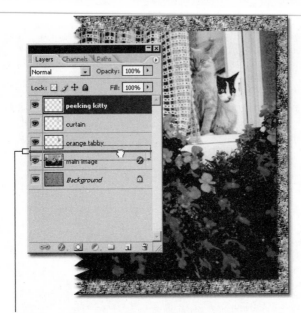

Black bar indicates Layer can be released

Figure 12-11: Here, the cat intended to appear to be peeking out from behind the tabby sitting on the windowsill is now on top — it needs to be moved down to fall beneath the "orange tabby" layer. The "curtain" layer was placed on top of the tabby layer already, so that it appears that the cat is partially hidden by the curtain.

You can move faster if you remember the following keyboard shortcuts:

✦ **Ctrl+Shift+] (or ⌘-Shift-] on the Mac).** Press Ctrl+Shift+right bracket (Win) or ⌘-Shift-right bracket (Mac) to move the active layer to the top of the stack.

✦ **Ctrl+Shift+[(or ⌘-Shift-[on the Mac).** This shortcut moves the active layer to the bottom of the stack, just above the background layer.

✦ **Ctrl+] (or ⌘-] on the Mac).** This nudges the layer up one level.

✦ **Ctrl+[(or ⌘-[on the Mac).** This nudges the layer down one level.

Note   You can neither reorder the background layer nor move any other layer below the background layer until you first convert the background to a floating layer, as explained in the preceding section.

Displaying layer edges

New Feature

When layer content is really tiny, or is right next to, slightly behind, or mostly obscured by other content, it can be hard to spot and even harder to click it with your mouse to move it. To make your layers easier to see and click on, no matter how small, see-through, or camouflaged they may be, Photoshop CS2 offers the View ➪ Show ➪ Layer Edges command.

To use the Layer Edges command feature, click on the layer you want to see highlighted by an edge (use the Layers palette to click on it). Then issue the View ➪ Show ➪ Layer Edges command to display the dark blue box you see in Figure 12-12, where the curtain layer is selected.

Figure 12-12: Turn on Layer Edges to display a helpful box that surrounds the active layer.

Once you turn this option on, whichever layer you activate — be it by selecting the layer by clicking on it in the Layers palette or by clicking the layer content directly with your mouse — will be encompassed by the dark blue box. If you press Shift or Ctrl (⌘ on the Mac) to select multiple layers, each of the selected layers will also be encompassed by its own box.

To stop seeing the boxes, you can either reselect the command to toggle it off, or turn off the view of all Extras (guides, slice borders, and so on) with the View ⇨ Extras command. This latter approach is rather radical, unless you want to eliminate all visual clutter in one sweeping command. To tweak which things to show and not show, use the View ⇨ Show submenu to click on and off those features you want to see.

Automated matting techniques

When you convert an anti-aliased selection to a layer, you sometimes take with you a few pixels from the selection's previous background. These *fringe pixels* can result in an unrealistic outline around your layer that really makes the selection-based layer stand out in its new location. Figure 12-13 shows this very problem in magnified detail from an early attempt to add the orange tabby to the windowsill image. Although the selection outline is accurate — it was done at a high zoom, with great care — a few dark pixels from around the cat (he used to be on a dark green background) came along with him.

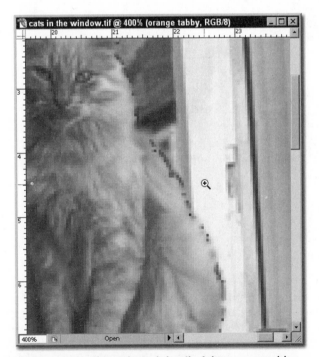

Figure 12-13: This enlarged detail of the orange tabby his new home on the windowsill demonstrates the extra, unwanted pixels that can accompany even the most carefully selected additions to your image.

You can instruct Photoshop to replace the fringe pixels with colors from neighboring pixels by choosing Layer ⇨ Matting ⇨ Defringe. Type the thickness of the perceived fringe in the Width option box to tell Photoshop which pixels you want to replace. To create the image shown in Figure 12-14, a value of 1 was typed. But even at this low value, the effect is pretty significant, leaving gummy edges in its wake.

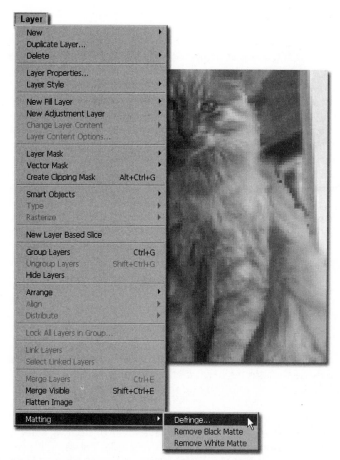

Figure 12-14: Here the Defringe command was set to a Width value of 1 to replace the pixels around the edges of the orange tabby layer with colors borrowed from neighboring pixels.

It's not that Defringe never works; sometimes the results will be satisfactory. But keep in mind that it's not available when a selection is active or when the layer has a layer mask or vector mask.

Photoshop provides two additional commands under the Layer ➪ Matting submenu: Remove Black Matte and Remove White Matte. Frankly, it's unlikely you'll have much call to use them, but here's their story:

✦ **Remove Black Matte.** This command removes the residue around the perimeter of a layer that was lifted from a black background.

✦ **Remove White Matte.** This command removes a white ring around a layer.

Adobe says that these commands were designed for compositing a scene rendered in a 3-D drawing program against a black or white background. But for other purposes, they almost never work.

Tip

If you encounter unrealistic edge pixels and the automatic matting commands don't solve your problem, you may be able to achieve better results by fixing the edges manually. First, switch to the layer that's making you crazy and Ctrl-click (Win) or ⌘-click (Mac) its name in the Layers palette. This creates a tight selection around the contents of the layer. Then choose Select ➪ Modify ➪ Contract and type the width of the fringe in the Contract By option box. Next, choose Select ➪ Feather or press Ctrl+Shift+D (⌘-Shift-D on the Mac) and type half of the Contract By value in the Feather Radius option box. Finally, press Ctrl+Shift+I (⌘-Shift-I on the Mac) to invert the selection and press Backspace (Delete on the Mac) to eliminate the edge pixels.

Blending layers

Photoshop lets you blend layers like no other program in the business. In fact, Photoshop does such a great job that it takes all of Chapter 13 to explain these options in detail. This section serves as an introduction so that you're at least aware of the basics. If you have bigger questions, Chapter 13 is waiting to tell all.

The Layers palette provides four basic ways to blend pixels between layers (see Figure 12-15). None of these techniques permanently changes as much as a pixel in any layer, so you can always return and reblend the layers at a later date.

✦ **Opacity value.** Type a value in the Opacity option box near the top of the Layers palette to change the opacity of the active layer or floating selection. If you reduce the Opacity value to 50 percent, for example, Photoshop makes the pixels on the active layer translucent, so the colors in the active layer mix evenly with the colors in the layers below.

Tip

If any tool other than a paint or edit tool is active — including the selection and navigation tools — you can press a number key to change the Opacity value. Press 1 for 10 percent, 2 for 20 percent, up to 0 for 100 percent. Or you can enter a specific Opacity value by quickly pressing two number keys in a row. For example, press 3 and then 7 for 37 percent.

✦ **Fill value.** The Fill option lets you adjust the opacity of pixel information in the layer — anything painted, drawn, or typed — without affecting the opacity of any layer effects that might be applied. For example, if you have a text layer with the Drop Shadow layer effect applied, lowering the Fill slider to 0 fades out the text itself, leaving just the ghostly drop shadow behind. As with all other blending-related options, the Fill option is explained in excruciating detail in Chapter 13.

✦ **Blend mode pop-up menu.** Choose an option from the blend mode pop-up menu — open in Figure 12-15 — to mix every pixel in the active layer with the pixels below it, according to one of several mathematical equations. For example, when you choose Multiply, Photoshop really does multiply the brightness values of the pixels and then divides the result by 255, the maximum brightness value. Blend modes use the same math as the brush modes covered in Chapter 5 (in fact, the two terms are sometimes used interchangeably). But you can accomplish a lot more with blend modes, which is why so much space is devoted to examining them in Chapter 13.

Tip

As with Opacity, you can select a blend mode from the keyboard when a selection or navigation tool is active. Press Shift+plus to advance incrementally down the list; press Shift+minus to inch back up. You can also press Shift+Alt (Win) or Shift-Option (Mac) and a letter key to select a specific mode. For example, Shift+Alt+M (Shift-Option-M on the Mac) selects the Multiply mode. Shift+Alt+N (Shift-Option-N on the Mac) restores the mode to Normal.

Figure 12-15: The blend mode pop-up menu and the Opacity and Fill option boxes enable you to mix layers without making any permanent changes to the pixels.

✦ **Blending Options.** Choose Layer ➪ Layer Style ➪ Blending Options, or double-click a layer thumbnail to display the Layer Style dialog box. The General Blending area of this dialog box provides access to a blend mode pop-up menu and an Opacity value, but it also offers a world of unique functions. As you learn in Chapter 13, you can hide one or more color channels, specify which colors are visible in the active layer, and force other colors to show through from the layers behind it. Select an item from the left-hand list to apply a layer style, as discussed in Chapter 14.

Fusing several layers

Although layers are wonderful and extremely helpful devices, they have their draw-backs — of course, none of these negative aspects outweighs its usefulness. Layers do expand the size of an image in RAM and ultimately lead to slower performance, and as noted in Chapter 3, only four formats — PDF, TIFF, the new PSB, and native PSD — permit you to save layered compositions. You can use layers in the construction of any image — it's just that when you go to save it in any format other than those four, your layers will be combined into a single layer, and further editing on an individual layer basis will be impossible. Of course, you can save a PSD or TIFF version of the artwork, too, and that way you'll retain an editable, layer-laden copy.

With the size and performance-eating problem in mind, you may want to put your image on a diet of sorts. To slim down your image, Photoshop provides the following methods for merging layers:

 New Feature   Choose Layer ➪ Merge Layers or Ctrl+E (⌘-E on the Mac) to merge two or more selected layers. This is a slight change from Photoshop CS, which had more merging options in terms of how the Merge commands appeared in the Layers menu. For example, if you had linked layers and went to the Layers menu, the command appeared as "Merge Linked" — now it appears as "Merge Layers," and Photoshop assumes you mean to merge the layers you have selected at the time.

✦ **Merge Visible (Ctrl+Shift+E or ⌘-Shift-E).** Choose the Merge Visible command to merge all visible layers into a single layer. If the layer is not visible — that is, if no eyeball icon appears in front of the layer name — Photoshop doesn't eliminate it; the layer remains independent.

Tip   To create a merged clone from two or more selected layers, press Alt when applying either the Layer ➪ Merge Layers or Layer ➪ Merge Visible commands. Pressing Alt (Win) or Option (Mac) and choosing Merge Layers — or pressing Ctrl+Alt+E (⌘-Option-E on the Mac) — clones the contents of the selected layer/s into the layer below it. Pressing Alt (Win) or Option (Mac) and choosing Merge Visible — or pressing Ctrl+Shift+Alt+E (⌘-Shift-Option-E on the Mac) — copies the contents of all visible layers to the active layer. The resulting layer in either case will have the word "merged" in parentheses following the name of the top-most layer that was included in the merge. The History palette will list the action as Stamp Layers — something handy to know in case you want to go back and Undo this.

 Tip   More useful is the ability to copy the merged contents of a selected area. To do so, choose Edit ➪ Copy Merged or press Ctrl+Shift+C (⌘-Shift-C on the Mac). You can then paste the selection into a layer or make it part of a different image.

✦ **Flatten Image.** This command merges all visible layers and throws away the invisible ones. The result is a single, opaque background layer. Photoshop does not give this command a keyboard shortcut because it's so dangerous. To take a safer, more conservative route, you may want to flatten an image incrementally using the two Merge commands — whittling away at the number of layers until you're ready to merge them all into one.

Caution   Note that Photoshop asks whether you want to flatten an image when converting from one color mode to another. You can choose not to flatten the image (by pressing D or clicking Don't Flatten) but this may come at the expense of some of the brighter colors in your image. As discussed in Chapter 13, many of the blend modes perform differently in RGB than they do in CMYK.

Deleting layers

You can also throw a layer away. Drag the layer name onto the trash can icon at the bottom of the Layers palette, click the trash can icon to delete the active layer, or right-click the layer (Control-click on the Mac) to be deleted and choose Delete Layer from the pop-up menu. So many choices.

Tip   When you click the trash can icon, Photoshop displays a message asking whether you really want to toss the layer. To give this message the slip in the future, Alt-click (Win) or Option-click (Mac) the trash can icon.

Tip   Here's a good one for you: If the active layer is linked to one or more other layers (see the upcoming section "Linking layers"), you can delete all linked layers in one fell swoop by Ctrl-clicking (Win) or ⌘-clicking (Mac) the trash can icon.

Saving a flattened version of an image

As already mentioned, only four file formats — PDF, TIFF, PSB, and the native Photoshop format — save images with layers. If you want to save a flattened version of your image — that is, with all layers fused into a single image — in some other file format, choose File ➪ Save As or press Ctrl+Shift+S (⌘-Shift-S on the Mac) and select the desired format from the Format pop-up menu. If you select a format that doesn't support layers — such as JPEG, GIF, or EPS — the Layers option is dimmed.

The Save As command does not affect the image in memory. All layers remain intact. So, if you select the As a Copy option with the Layers option deselected — which is a good idea, really — Photoshop doesn't even change the name of the image in the title bar. It merely creates a flattened version of the image on disk. Nevertheless, be sure to save a layered version of the composition as well, just in case you want to edit it in the future.

Selecting the Contents of Layers

It was mentions a few sections back that every layer (except the background) includes a *transparency mask*. This mask tells Photoshop which pixels are opaque, which are translucent, and which are transparent. Like any mask, Photoshop lets you convert the transparency mask for any layer — active or not — to a selection outline. In fact, you use the same keyboard techniques you use to convert paths to selections (as explained in Chapter 8) and channels to selections (Chapter 9):

✦ Ctrl-click (Win) or ⌘-click (Mac) an item in the Layers palette to convert the transparency mask for that layer to a selection outline.

✦ To add the transparency mask to an existing selection outline, Ctrl+Shift-click (Win) or ⌘-Shift-click (Mac) the layer name. The little selection cursor includes a plus sign to show you that you're about to add.

✦ To subtract the transparency mask, Ctrl+Alt-click (Win) or ⌘-Option-click (Mac) the layer name.

✦ To find the intersection of the transparency mask and the current selection outline, Ctrl+Shift+Alt-click (Win) or ⌘-Shift-Option-click (Mac) the layer name.

If you think you can't remember all these keyboard shortcuts, don't worry — you can use Select ➪ Load Selection instead. After choosing the command, select the Transparency item from the Channel pop-up menu. (You can even load a transparency mask from another open image if the image is exactly the same size as the one you're working on.) Then use the Operation radio buttons to merge the mask with an existing selection.

Selection outlines exist independently of layers, so you can use the transparency mask from one layer to select part of another layer. For example, to select the part of the background layer that exactly matches the contents of another layer, press Shift+Alt+[(Shift-Option-[on the Mac) to descend to the background layer and then Ctrl-click (Win) or ⌘-click (Mac) the name of the layer you want to match.

The most common reason to borrow a selection from one layer and apply it to another is to create manual shadow and lighting effects. After Ctrl-clicking (⌘-clicking on the Mac) on a layer, you can use this selection to create a drop shadow that precisely matches the contours of the layer itself. No messing with the Brush or the Lasso tool — Photoshop does the tough work for you.

Now, you might think with Photoshop's extensive range of layer styles, manual drop shadows and the like would be a thing of the past. After all, you have only to choose Layer ➪ Layer Style ➪ Drop Shadow and, bang, the program adds a drop shadow. But the old, manual methods still have their advantages. You don't have to visit a complicated dialog box to edit a manual drop shadow, and you can reposition a manual shadow from the keyboard (or with your mouse, if you press Ctrl (⌘) + T to enter transform mode, where you can scale, rotate, skew, and otherwise transform the shadow layer independently. The separate-layer approach gives you way more flexibility over the size, position, color, Opacity, and edges of the shadow than you can get through the Layer Styles dialog box (discussed later in this chapter). If you've forgotten how to move a shadow layer to indicate a light source, go back and revisit the ostrich in Chapter 10.

On the other hand, the old ways aren't necessarily always better. A shadow created with the Drop Shadow command takes up less room in memory, it moves and rotates with a layer, and you can edit the softness of the shadow long after creating it. You can also set the shadow to employ Global Light, which means any other shadows in the image (drop shadows applied as Layer Styles, that is) will have the same angle, indicating light coming from the same direction. This can save time and effort if you have more than one item shadowed in an image.

What you have is two equally powerful solutions, each with its own characteristic pros and cons. Luckily, you can easily master both, and then you'll be ready for any situation.

Cross-Reference The following sections explore manual drop shadows and highlights. For everything you ever wanted to know about the Layer Styles commands, read Chapter 14.

Drop Shadows

In these first steps, the joyous penguin (looking skyward, wings outstretched) is made to cast a drop shadow on the ground beneath and the wall behind him.

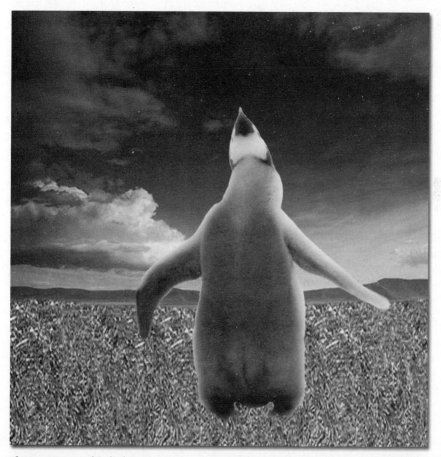

Figure 12-16: This little penguin is out of his element, but enjoying the sunshine. Soon, he'll cast the shadow to show the sun is coming from the right side of the photo.

STEPS: Creating a Drop Shadow

1. **Select the subject that you want casting the shadow (the penguin, here).** In this case, by pressing Ctrl (⌘ on the Mac) while clicking the penguin layer, a selection in the shape of the layer was created.

2. **Create a layer from the selected penguin.** Click and drag the layer with the content to be shadowed to the Create New Layer button in the Layers palette. A duplicate layer is created, with selected duplicate content in place. Click to select the new layer, and leave the selection in place.

3. **To create a softened drop shadow — indicative of a diffused light source — choose Select ⇨ Feather or press Ctrl+Alt+D (⌘-Option-D on the Mac).** The Radius value you type depends on the resolution of your image. As a general rule, dividing the resolution of your image by 20 can yield pretty good results. (Note that this isn't a hard and fast rule; by all means, forget about the math if necessary and do what looks right.) Then press Enter or Return to soften the selection.

4. **Fill the feathered area with black.** If necessary, press D to make the foreground color black. Then press Shift+Alt+Backspace (Shift-Option-Delete on the Mac) to fill only the area inside the transparency mask. A slight halo of dark pixels forms around the edges of the image.

5. **Press Ctrl (or ⌘ on the Mac) with the arrow keys to nudge the shadow to the desired location.** In this case, the shadow was nudged 25 pixels to the left. (Press Ctrl+Shift+arrow key or ⌘-Shift-arrow key to nudge the shadow in 10-pixel increments.)

6. **Lower the Opacity setting. If the shadow is too dark — black lacks a little subtlety — change the Opacity value in the Layers palette to change the opacity of the shadow.** Or press M to make sure a selection tool is active and then press a number key to change the opacity. Figure 12-17 shows the results so far.

Tip

If you don't like a black drop shadow, you can make a colored one with only slightly more effort. Instead of filling the shadow with black in Step 6, select a different foreground color and press Shift+Alt+Backspace (Shift-Option-Delete on the Mac). For the best result, select a color that is the complementary opposite of your background color. Next, choose Multiply from the blend mode pop-up menu in the Layers palette or press Shift+Alt+M (Shift-Option-M on the Mac). This burns the colors in the shadow into those in the lower layers to create a darkened mix. Finally, press a number key to specify the opacity.

Figure 12-17: A manually created drop shadow behind this formally attired fellow creates the look of depth — but the angle of the shadow isn't really very accurate for the light.

7. **Press Ctrl+T (⌘-T on the Mac) to apply Free Transform, and distort the shadow.** Ctrl-drag (⌘-drag on the Mac) on the corner handles to create a perspective distortion, as seen in Figure 12-18. This is an advantage of creating a drop shadow manually; it can easily be resized, filtered, and transformed to suit your whim.

Figure 12-18: The Free Transform command lets you distort the drop shadow to more accurately depict the direction from which light is shining on the penguin and give the illusion of depth to the image.

Tip

You can use the Burn tool to darken parts of the shadow—just scrub a little with the tool set to a low Exposure, ensuring you of very subtle results. Darken the shadow right beneath the feet or base of whatever's casting the shadow to reinforce the idea of the content sitting firmly on a surface, implying weight and a real connection to the surface beneath it.

8. **Press Ctrl+Shift+X (⌘-Shift-X on the Mac) to tweak with the Liquify filter.**
   The shadow didn't line up perfectly with the penguin, so the Liquify filter was used, and the shadow nudged around until things looked perfect, as shown in Figure 12-19.

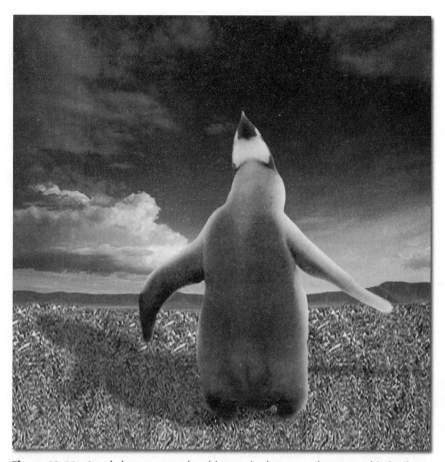

Figure 12-19: A truly happy penguin — his toes in the grass, the sun on his feathers, and a shadow cast behind him

Tip

Don't restrict your use of the tools and techniques described in the drop shadow procedure to creating just shadows. You can create glows — again, more flexibly than you can using the Outer or Inner Glow layer styles — or simply create a pool of color behind a subject. Filters can soften, add grain, or more light (read Chapters 10 and 11 for more information on Filters), and you can use the Liquefy tool to fine-tune the shape of the glow or pool.

Moving, Linking, and Aligning Layers

You can move an entire layer or the selected portion of a layer by clicking and dragging in the image window with the Move tool. If you have a selection in place, drag inside the marching-ants outline to move only the selection; drag outside the selection to move the entire layer.

Caution   If you have selected the Auto Select Layer option (it's a Move tool option) and forget that it's on, you may create a few stressful moments for yourself when attempting to move a layer that partially or completely overlaps another. You'll select the layer using the Layers palette or by right-clicking (Ctrl + clicking on the Mac) the layer you want, and then when you click and drag to move the layer you *think* is active, you'll really grab the top-most layer and move *that* one instead. If you find that this happens, just forgo the potential convenience of Auto Select Layer and turn the darn thing off.

Speaking of the Move tool, as mentioned in Chapter 8, you can temporarily access the Move tool when some other tool is active by pressing Ctrl (Win) or ⌘ (Mac). To nudge a layer, press Ctrl or ⌘ with an arrow key. Press Ctrl+Shift (⌘-Shift on the Mac) to nudge in 10-pixel increments.

If part of the layer disappears beyond the edge of the window, no problem. Photoshop saves even the hidden pixels in the layer, enabling you to drag the rest of the layer into view later.

Caution   If, while dragging a selection, you move your cursor outside the image window, Photoshop thinks you are trying to drag-and-drop pixels from one image to another and responds accordingly.

If you Ctrl-drag (or ⌘-drag on the Mac) the background image with no portion of it selected, you get an error message telling you that the layer is locked. If some portion of the layer is selected, however, you can drag that selected portion, and Photoshop will fill in the hole with the background color.

Tip   If you regularly work on huge images or your machine is old and kind of slow, Photoshop lets you speed the display of entire layers on the move. Press Ctrl+K and then Ctrl+3 (⌘-K and then ⌘-3 on the Mac) to display the Display & Cursors panel of the Preferences dialog box. Then select the Use Pixel Doubling option. From now on, Photoshop will show you a low-resolution proxy of a selection or a layer as you drag (or Ctrl-drag) it across the screen.

Linking and unlinking

There've been a few changes to the way you link and unlink layers in Photoshop CS2. Of course, there's no big change in your overall capabilities in terms of layer linking and unlinking, but the procedure for linking layers (and then unlinking them later) has changed a bit.

First, there is no longer any link check box or chain icon next to each layer. In Photoshop CS and its layer-supporting predecessors, in addition to the box where the eyeballs live, there was another column of boxes, which when clicked, would display a chain icon. This meant that the selected layers (you had to select them before clicking in the box) were linked. You could then unlink layers by clicking the chain icon and breaking the link.

In Photoshop CS2, the Link Layers button is on the bottom of the palette, and you use it to link and unlink selected layers. Figure 12-20 shows two linked layers, and the Link Layers button is labeled.

 Dragging inside a selection outline moves the selection independently of any linked layers. Dragging outside the selection moves all linked layers at once.

Linked layers indicated by chain link

Link Layers

Figure 12-20: Select the layers you want to link, and then click the Link Layers button, found at the lower-left end of the Layers palette buttons.

You can also link layers with the shortcut menu. As you may recall from the section "Switching between layers" earlier in this chapter, you can bring up a pop-up menu listing the layers in an image by Ctrl-right-clicking (or ⌘-Control-clicking on the Mac) an image element with any tool. If you're a Windows user, add Shift while selecting a layer from the pop-up menu to link or unlink the layer rather than switch to it.

When you drag-and-drop linked layers from one image window into another, all linked layers move together and the layers retain their original order. If you want to move just one layer without its linked buddies, drag the layer name from the Layers palette and drop it into another open image window.

Tip

If you press and hold Shift when dropping, Photoshop centers the layers in the document. If the document is exactly the same size as the one from which you dragged the layers, Shift-dropping lands the image elements in the same position they held in the original document. And finally, if something is selected in the document, the Shift-dropped layers are centered inside that selection.

New Feature

Another word about unlinking, a point that's related to what's new about linking and unlinking in CS2: When you have just two layers linked, unlinking is just as easy as previously stated — with the layers selected, click the Link Layers button, and the link is broken. The chain icon leaves the layers, and the link is no more. But what if you have more than two layers linked? Is it an all-or-nothing proposition? Nope. If you have three, four, or more layers linked, to unlink them all, right-click (or Ctrl+click on the Mac) any one of the linked layers and choose Select Linked Layers from the pop-up menu. To unlink just one or two (or any number, just not all) of the linked layers, select just those that you want to unlink and click the Link Layers button. The layers you didn't select remain linked, but the selected layers are no longer part of the chain gang.

Organizing layers in Groups

In previous versions, layers could be placed in *sets* — using the Folder button at the foot of the Layers palette, you could create a set and click and drag layers into it, and you could also create nested sets by creating sets within sets and dragging layers into the nested sets. It all worked like file management in Windows (or even on the Mac), where you have folders and subfolders, and files can be stored in them to keep your work organized. Sets served the same purpose in Photoshop, enabling you to organize your layers and deal with them in large, well, groups. That may be why the name was changed, huh?

New Feature

Speaking of gangs, which are really just groups with tattoos, grouping layers is new in Photoshop CS2.

Anyway, in Photoshop CS2, sets are called *groups,* and you call the process of creating them and placing layers in and taking layers out of them grouping and ungrouping layers. For those of you who are new to grouping layers, or if you're familiar with putting layers in the aforementioned sets, here's how the whole grouping/ungrouping thing works:

First, click the Create a New Group button (it's still a folder button) at the foot of the Layers palette. A generically named Group layer appears in the palette, called Group 1 (if it's your first in the current image). You can also Alt-click (or Option-click if you're on the Mac) the Create a New Group button and open the New Group dialog box shown in Figure 12-21. Through this dialog box, you can name your new group, choose a color for its display in the Layers palette, and choose a Mode and Opacity for it. You'll note that the default Mode is Pass Through, and that will be explained shortly.

Figure 12-21: Choose the Create a New Group command or Alt-click (Option-click on the Mac) the folder icon at the bottom of the Layers palette to create and name a new group.

Tip The Pass Through Mode option tells Photoshop to observe the blend modes assigned to the individual layers in the group. By contrast, if you apply a different blend mode such as Multiply to the group, Photoshop overrides the blend modes of the layers in the group and applies Multiply to them all.

The group appears as a folder icon in the Layers palette scrolling list. There's also a little triangle next to the folder icon, which you'll use to display and hide the list of grouped layers — not hide them in the image, but hide them in the palette.

To add a layer to the group, click and drag the layer name within the Layers palette and drop it on the folder icon. That little fist mouse pointer you saw in the coverage of restacking layers returns, and follows you as you drag the layer up or down to the group in which it belongs. Figure 12-22 shows a new group in place, with layers already in it and a layer being added.

Photoshop also lets you place groups inside of other groups, a process called *nesting*. Photoshop allows you to nest groups up to five levels deep. Nesting layer groups can be a great way to better organize your layers. To place one group inside another, simply drag-and-drop it onto the other group in the same manner you would a layer. As it does when you place a layer into a group, Photoshop applies the blend mode of the master group to every layer and nested group within it when the mode is not set to Pass Through.

Down-pointing triangle indicates
all member layers are displayed

New group

Layer being added

Right-pointing triangle indicates
groups layers are not displayed

Existing group members appear indented

Figure 12-22: A new group and its members — and a
member being brought to its first meeting

Here are some other ways to create and modify groups:

✦ Double-click a group name to rename it.

✦ Drag a group name up or down the palette to move it.

✦ When a group is expanded, you can drag a layer within the group, move a
layer out of the group, or drop a layer into the group at a specific position.

✦ To duplicate a group, drag it onto the folder icon at the bottom of the Layers
palette.

✦ Hate dragging all those layers into a group? Select the layers before creating
the group and choose Layer ➪ Group Layers. The new group is created, and the

selected layers are automatically its members. You can do this to create a nested group, too — just select layers already in a group and issue the Layer ➪ Group Layers command — a nested group, complete with members, is created.

✦ In case you're wondering, "Can I link layers in different groups?," yes, you can. If you're wondering, "Can I link groups together?," yes, it's possible not only to link groups, but also to link individual layers to entire groups. Pretty snazzy, huh?

✦ You know that you can click the triangle next to a folder icon to open or close the group and show or hide the layers and nested groups it contains. Alt-click (Option-click on the Mac) the triangle next to a folder icon to show or hide every element contained in the group, including nested groups and layer styles.

Anytime a group name is active in the Layers palette, you can move or transform all layers in the group as a unit, much as if they were linked. To move or transform a single layer in the group, just select that layer and go about your business as you normally would.

Tip

Hang on. What if you've got a group and you don't want it anymore? You want the layers, but don't want them grouped. What to do? Right-click (or Ctrl + click on the Mac) the Group layer, and choose Ungroup Layers from the pop-up menu. The group disappears, but the layers that were in it remain, in place, maintaining their original modes, opacity settings, and stacking order. If you want to delete an entire group, members (layers) and all, right-click (Ctrl-click on the Mac) and choose Delete Group.

Creating and Using Smart Objects

Why would you turn your layers into a Smart Object? If you want to edit the content outside of Photoshop and then bring it back seamlessly later, Smart Objects are the way to go. Of course, you could copy the layers to a new image, save the image in a vector-friendly format (such as EPS, for example) and then open the new image in Illustrator, edit it there, and then bring it back to Photoshop, open it, copy its contents and the paste them back into their original Photoshop image, but that would be really taking the long way home — that's a lot of steps and a lot of margin for error.

New Feature

While we're on the subject of organizing and grouping layers, new in Photoshop CS2 are Smart Objects — content from your images in the form or one or more layers that can be edited externally to the image in which they originally resided. A Smart Object can be edited in Photoshop (but in a separate image window) or edited in a vector-based program such as Adobe Illustrator. If you do edit a Smart Object outside of its original image, when the object is returned to the image, its changes are brought back with it, and in the case of an object edited in a vector-based program, the prodigal object will be rasterized upon its return to a Photoshop image.

Another reason is that Smart Objects can be scaled, rotated, skewed, or warped losslessly — meaning that no details are lost to the process of pixels being edited and created to fill in as the image content changes size, position, shape, and so on.

Essentially, turning content into a Smart Object protects it and makes it easier to move it back and forth between images and applications without the problems of loss of detail and wasted time and effort required in the past.

Creating a new Smart Object

To turn content into a Smart Object, simply select the layer or layers from within any Photoshop image — it can be a PSD or TIFF file, or saved in any other format that supports the use of layers. With the layer/s selected, choose Layer ⇨ Smart Objects ⇨ Group Into New Smart Object. After a brief pause (a Progress bar that states that it's "Merging Layers" will probably appear), your layer/s appear as shown in Figure 12-23. This Figure shows a Smart Object called "main window," which consists of three former layers — "bushes," "peeking kitty," and "main window." The three layers were combined into a single Smart Object, and the name of the top-most layer was applied to the object. You can rename an object the same way you'd rename a layer — just double-click the name in place and type a new one.

Three selected layers   Resulting Smart Object

Figure 12-23: Select three layers (see the "before" version of the Layers palette on the left) and turn them into a Smart Object (see right-hand version of the palette).

Tip   You can use the Layers palette to create your Smart Objects, too. Select the layer(s) to be made into an object, and right-click (Ctrl-click on the Mac) to display a pop-up menu. Choose Group into New Smart Object from the menu, and the object is created. The Layers ⇨ Smart Objects submenu commands — New Smart Object Via Copy, Edit Contents, Export Contents, and Replace Contents — are also found in the pop-up menu.

Editing Smart Objects

So you've made a Smart Object. Now what do you do with it? You can double-click the object layer in the Layers palette or choose Layers ⇨ Smart Objects ⇨ Edit Contents. A large prompt window opens, shown in Figure 12-24, which gives you valuable instructions—after you finish your edits (you'll be working in a new image window with the object layers' content in it), choose File ⇨ Save to keep your changes. If you don't do so, the changes won't be reflected in the original image. You can also save the changes to a new file—a new file name, format, and location—thus creating a new image from a Smart Object.

Figure 12-24: Take this good advice to make sure your edited Smart Object can return to the image from whence it came.

After clicking OK to acknowledge this great advice, you're presented with an image window, titled with the same name the Smart Object had when it was a layer in your original image. The format for the new image is PSB (large document format), and the image consists of the layer/s you grouped into the Smart Object. Figure 12-25 shows the resulting main window.psb file and its Layers palette.

Figure 12-25: One Smart Object becomes a new image with three (in this case) layers.

You can edit the new PSB file as you would any Photoshop file using virtually any of the tools, commands, filters, and so forth that you want. You can use the Transform tools to rotate, skew, scale, and even warp the content, too (but you'll find Distort and Perspective dimmed). Warping, another new Photoshop CS2 feature, is discussed later in this chapter.

 Tip   Handling PSB files hogs a lot of system resources. If you think you'll be creating and editing a lot of Smart Objects, and you see that your system slows down to a crawl (or even gives you "scratch disks are full" prompts while you're editing them), consider increasing your RAM.

Once you've finished your edits, you can use the File ➪ Save (Ctrl + S for Windows, ⌘ + S on the Mac) command to save the object, and then return to your original image — the original image reflects any changes you made to the size, position, stacking order, and actual content of the object's layers (including new layers) while you edited it as a PSB file. You can then convert the Smart Object back into a layer, using the Layers ➪ Smart Objects ➪ Convert to Layer command. Bear in mind that it will not be converted back into the multiple layers that may have made up the object from the beginning — instead, a single layer is created from the Smart Object as a whole. Your History palette tells the real story of what's happened at this point, too — the state that appears when a Smart Object is converted to a layer is "Rasterize Smart Object." This reminds you that the object is preserving its content for vector-based editing, and to become a native part of a Photoshop image once again, it must be rasterized, returned to being a lowly gaggle of pixels.

Exporting and replacing Smart Objects

To export a Smart Object, select Export Contents from the pop-up menu that appears when you right-click (or Ctrl-click) the object. A Save dialog box opens through which you can give your file a name (PSB is the default format, but you can pick another), and choose a location for the file. Once you've saved the file, it can be opened in Illustrator or any other vector-based editing program. You can also open it in Photoshop. Once the edits are performed, you can save the image and reopen the original image in Photoshop — "original image," refers to the one the original layers that became the object came from. The changes you made in the other program are reflected, and the content is rerasterized.

If you choose Replace Contents from the Layer ⇨ Smart Objects submenu, a Place dialog box opens through which you can select another image — any Photoshop-recognized file — and use it to replace the Smart Object in your active image. The image you select literally replaces the Smart Object content, and becomes a new layer in the image. You can then edit that layer, restack it to reveal original content beneath it, or apply any other Photoshop tool, command, or filter to the replacement content.

Locking layers

Just like a Smart Object can protect selected layers from loss of quality when transferred to and from an external editing program, the Layers palette can protect a layer from any kind of changes by allowing you to lock it. Photoshop also lets you lock only some attributes of a layer and leave other attributes unlocked, thus making this protection very flexible. Figure 12-26 labels the four Lock buttons available in the Layers palette. Here's how they work:

✦ **Lock transparency.** This button protects the transparency of a layer. When selected, you can paint inside a layer without harming the transparent pixels. This option is so useful, there is an entire section devoted to it (see "Preserving transparency" later in this chapter).

✦ **Lock pixels.** Select this button to prohibit further editing of the pixels in the active layer. Paint and edit tools will no longer function, nor will filters or other pixel-level commands. However, you'll still be able to move and transform the layer as you like. Note that selecting this button dims and selects the Lock Transparency button as well. After all, if you can't edit pixels, you can't edit pixels — whether they're opaque or transparent.

✦ **Lock position.** Select this button to prevent the layer from being moved or transformed. You can, however, edit the pixels.

✦ **Lock all.** To lock everything about a layer, select this button. You can't paint, edit, filter, move, transform, delete, or otherwise change a hair on the layer's head. About all you can do is duplicate the layer, move it up and down the stack, add it to a group, and merge it with one or more other layers. This button is applicable to layers and groups alike.

Lock Transparency

Lock Pixels

Lock Position

Lock All

Figure 12-26: The Lock buttons at the top of the Layers palette let you protect certain layer attributes.

Indicates a locked layer

Photoshop shows you which layers are locked by displaying two kinds of lock icons in the Layers palette. As labeled in Figure 12-26, the hollow lock means one attribute is locked; the filled lock means all attributes are locked.

Using guides and Smart Guides

Photoshop's grids and guides allow you to move selections and layers into alignment. When combined with the Move tool, they also enable you to create rows and columns of image elements and even align layers by their centers. This capability, along with the enhanced alignment indicators known as Smart Guides (you'll read about them shortly), enables you to achieve a much greater control over your image elements, aligning and distributing your layers "by eye" with unexpected accuracy.

Adding guides

To create a guide, press Ctrl+R (⌘-R on the Mac) or choose View ➪ Rulers to display the horizontal and vertical rulers. Then point to the ruler with your mouse — the top ruler to create a horizontal guide, the left-side ruler to create a vertical guide — and click and drag a guideline onto the image in Figure 12-27, you can see a vertical guide in place and two layers lined up against it.

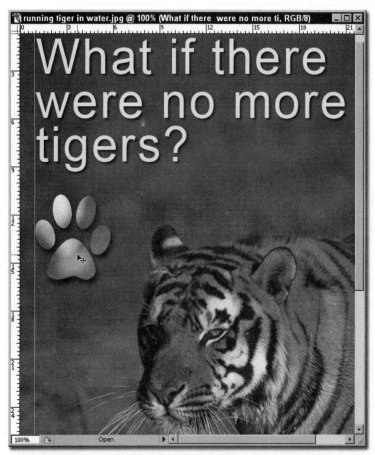

Figure 12-27: Click and drag from one of the rulers to create a guide, and then Ctrl-drag (⌘-drag on the Mac) each layer or selection into alignment.

Once you've created your guide or guides (drag as many as you need onto the image), you can use them to align and distribute your layers — against the guides, and against each other, using the guides to establish common vertical and horizontal planes.

To make sure your layers adhere to the guides, Ctrl-drag (Win) or ⌘-drag (Mac) as you move your layers and selections. In Figure 12-27, the text and the shape are aligned by their left sides along a vertical guide on the left side of the image. Each item is on its own layer, and the layers snap into alignment at their centers.

Note   Single-line text layers snap to horizontal guides a little differently than other kinds of layers. Rather than snapping by the top or bottom edge of the layer, Photoshop snaps a text guide by its baseline. It's just what you need when aligning type.

Showing, hiding, and controlling guides

Guides are straightforward creatures. A few minutes with the text below is all you need to master them:

✦ If you know the exact position where you want to put a guideline, choose View ➪ New Guide. After selecting from a horizontal or vertical guide, type the location of the guide as measured from the ruler origin, by default in the upper-left corner of the image. For example, type "1 in" for 1 inch, "2.5 cm" for 2.5 centimeters, or "200 px" for 200 pixels.

✦ You can show and hide all guides by choosing View ➪ Show ➪ Guides. When the guides are hidden, layers and selections do not snap into alignment.

✦ You can hide or show guides also by pressing Ctrl+H (or ⌘-H on the Mac). But be aware that this turns on or off the visibility of other elements, including the grid, selection outlines, paths, and notes. To hide and show just the guides, press Ctrl+semicolon (;) under Windows (or ⌘-semicolon [;] on the Mac).

Tip

You can preselect which items are hidden and shown with the Show Extras command by selecting and deselecting the items in the View ➪ Show menu.

✦ You can turn a guide's snappiness on and off by choosing View ➪ Snap To ➪ Guides. You can also press Ctrl+Shift+semicolon (⌘-Shift-semicolon on the Mac). Again, this shortcut affects the snappiness of *everything*, including the grid, the perimeter of the image, and Web slices (read about slices in Chapter 18).

Tip

To turn off the snappiness in the middle of a brushstroke or layer movement, press Ctrl (Win) or ⌘ (Mac) in mid-drag. Release Ctrl or ⌘ to return to snappy land.

✦ As with all image elements in Photoshop, you can move a guide with the Move tool. If some other tool is active, Ctrl-dragging (Win) or ⌘-dragging (Mac) also works.

✦ To lock all guides so you can't accidentally move them while you're trying to Ctrl-drag or ⌘-drag something else, press Ctrl+Alt+semicolon (⌘-Option-semicolon on the Mac) or choose View ➪ Lock Guides. Press Ctrl+Alt+semicolon again to unlock all guides.

Tip   When moving a guide, press Shift to snap the guide to the nearest ruler tick mark.

✦ To convert a horizontal guide to a vertical guide, or vice versa, press Alt (Win) or Option (Mac) while pointing to or moving the guide.

✦ If you rotate your document in exact multiples of 90 degrees or flip the image horizontally or vertically, your guides also rotate unless they are locked.

Tip   You can position a guide outside the image if you want. To do so, make the image window larger than the image. Now you can drag a guide into the empty canvas surrounding the image. You can then snap a layer or selection into alignment with the guide.

✦ To edit the color of the guides, Ctrl-double-click (Win) or ⌘-double-click (Mac) a guide to display the Guides, Grid & Slices panel of the Preferences dialog box. You can also change the guides from solid lines to dashed. (This is only for screen purposes, by the way. Guides don't print.)

✦ On the Mac, guides are saved with any file format. But on the PC, the only formats that let you save guides are Photoshop (PSD), JPEG, TIFF, PDF, and EPS.

✦ If you don't need your guides anymore, choose View ⇨ Clear Guides to delete them all at once.

Intelligent alignment with Smart Guides

Smart Guides (shown in action in Figure 12-28) flash on the image when your layer-in-motion is lined up against the items above, below, and beside it. Depending on the Smart Guides that appear — straight lines pointing toward the items against which the active layer is being aligned — you know if your layer is where you need it to be.

New Feature   Thanks to the advent of Smart Guides (new in Photoshop CS2), all this aligning and distributing has become a whole lot easier. Not that it was difficult before, but sometimes, unless you're zoomed in very tight on your image, you can't tell if you're really lined up with the guide, or if all the items you've lined up against the guide really are where you want them.

Smart Guide   Smart Guide

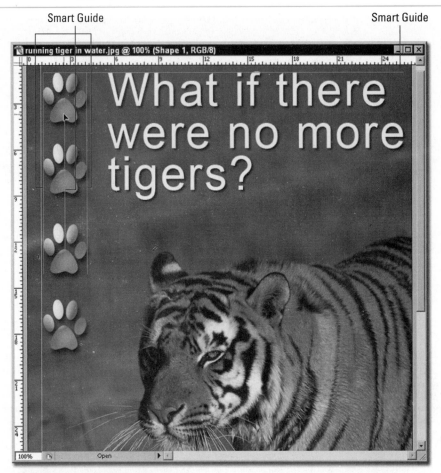

Figure 12-28: Pink lines flash and you know you're lined up properly. Smart Guides are a big help when aligning both horizontally and vertically, with or without ruler-derived guides in use.

Setting up the grid

For more control over the placement of layers in your image, Photoshop offers a grid, which is a regular series of snapping increments. Think of it like a ton of guides, positioned in uniform increments — and you don't have to drag each of them onto the image, because they all arrive at once when you choose View ⇨ Show ⇨ Grid. You can turn the snapping forces of the grid on and off by choosing View ⇨ Snap To ⇨ Grid.

You edit the grid in the Guides, Grid & Slices panel of the Preferences dialog box, which you can get to by pressing Ctrl+K and then Ctrl+6 (⌘-K and then ⌘-6 on the Mac) or by Ctrl-double-clicking (Win) or ⌘-double-clicking (Mac) on a guide. You can also go at it the traditional way, by choosing Edit ⇨ Preferences ⇨ Guides, Grid & Slices. The use of this dialog box is described in Chapter 2, but to save you leafing back right now, you type the major grid increments in the Gridline Every option box and type the minor increments in the Subdivisions option box, shown in Figure 12-29.

Figure 12-29: With the grid in place — set by tweaking the Grid Preferences — you have a customizable network of guides you can snap to or not snap to, positioning your layers along the vertical and horizontal lines.

Tip   Don't want to see the grid anymore? Choose View ⇨ Show ⇨ Grid. The checked Grid command will toggle off.

Using the Measure tool

The final method for controlling movements in Photoshop is the Measure tool. To activate it (it shares a button with the Eyedropper and Color Sampler tools), Alt-click (or Option-click on the Mac) the Eyedropper tool a couple of times to select it — or press Shift+I twice (if the Eyedropper is displayed) to activate the tool.

Once the tool's active, all you have to do is click and drag from one point to another point in the image window, and Photoshop itemizes the distance and angle between the two points in the Info palette. The Measure tool is even smart enough to automatically display the Info palette if it's hidden.

From that point on, any time you select the Measure tool in the current image, Photoshop displays the original measurement line. This way, you can measure a distance, edit the image, and press I to refer back to the measurement. If you've switched to the Eyedropper or Color Sampler tool at any point in the interim, Shift+I will bring back the Measure tool.

To measure the distance and angle between two other points, you can draw a new line with the Measure tool. Or drag the endpoints of the existing measurement line.

Photoshop accommodates only one measurement line per document. But you can break the line in two using what Adobe calls the "protractor" feature. Alt-drag (Win) or Option-drag (Mac) on one of the endpoints to draw forth a second segment. The Info palette then measures the angle between the two segments. As demonstrated in Figure 12-30, the D1 item in the Info palette lists the length of the first segment, D2 lists the length of the second segment, and A tells the angle between the segments.

Tip

The Measure tool is great for straightening crooked layers. After drawing a line with the Measure tool, choose Image ➪ Rotate Canvas ➪ Arbitrary. The Angle value automatically conforms to the A (angle) value listed in the Info palette. If you look closely, the two values may not exactly match. That's because Photoshop intelligently translates the value to between −45 and +45 degrees, which happens to be the simplest way to express any rotation. If you don't understand what I'm talking about, just trust in Photoshop. It does the math so you don't have to.

Alt + click (Opt + click on the Mac) here to draw next segment

Measure tool cursor   Angle is measured here

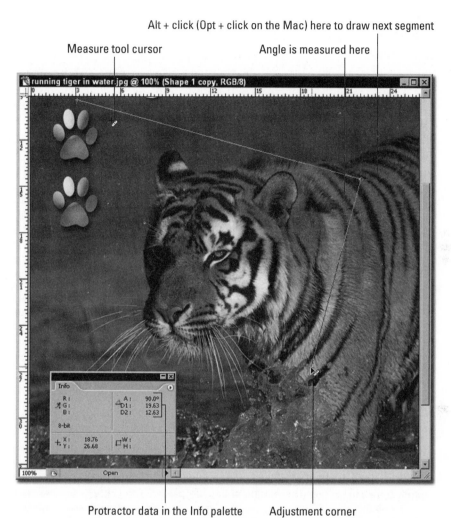

Protractor data in the Info palette   Adjustment corner

Figure 12-30: The distance from the footprint to the edge of a proposed crop around the tiger's head, and the 90-degree angle down from the outer edge is measured. The Info palette displays the data, and serves as a guide as you drag— it updates as the Measure tool's lines are drawn and adjusted.

Applying Transformations

Photoshop treats some kinds of edits differently than others. Edits that affect the geometry of a selection or a layer are known collectively as *transformations*. These transformations include scaling (resizing), rotating, flipping, slanting, and distorting. Technically, moving is a transformation as well, but you just need to activate the Move tool to do that. Transformations are a special breed of edits in Photoshop because they can affect a selection, a layer, multiple layers, or an entire image at a time.

Transforming the entire image

Photoshop has two varieties of transformations. Transformation commands that affect the entire image — including all layers, paths, channels, and so on — are listed in the Image menu. Those that affect layers and selected portions of layers are in the Edit menu, or in the case of selection outlines, in the Select menu.

The following list explains how to apply transformations to every pixel in an image, regardless of whether the image is selected or not:

✦ **Scale.** To resize the image, choose Image ➪ Image Size. Because this command is one of the most essential low-level functions in the program, this is covered in Chapter 3.

✦ **Rotate.** To rotate the entire image, choose a command from the Image ➪ Rotate Canvas submenu. To rotate an image scanned on its side, choose the 90° CW or 90° CCW command. (That's clockwise and counterclockwise, respectively.) Choose 180° to spin the image on its head. To enter some other specific value, choose Image ➪ Rotate Canvas ➪ Arbitrary.

Tip

To fix a crooked scanned image, for example, select the Measure tool from the Eyedropper flyout in the Toolbox (press I or Shift+I, depending on your preference settings, three times). Drag along what should be a vertical or horizontal edge in the image. If you like, note the A value in the Info palette. Then choose Image ➪ Rotate Canvas ➪ Arbitrary. The angle value is preset to the angle you just measured, and all you have to do is press Enter or Return and the job's complete. Voila!

Whenever you apply the Arbitrary command, Photoshop has to expand the canvas size to avoid clipping any of your image. This results in background-colored wedges at each of the four corners of the image. You need to either clone with the Clone Stamp tool to fill in the wedges or clip them away with the Crop tool.

✦ **Flip.** Choose Image ➪ Rotate Canvas ➪ Flip Horizontal to flip the image so left is right and right is left. To flip the image upside down, choose Image ➪ Rotate Canvas ➪ Flip Vertical.

No command is specifically designed to slant or distort the entire image. In the unlikely event you're keen to do this, you'll have to link all layers and apply one of the commands under the Edit ➪ Transform submenu, as explained in the next section. Or, after linking your layers, you can use the Warp command and tools, discussed shortly.

Transforming layers and selected pixels

To transform a layer or selection, you can apply one of the commands in the Edit ➪ Transform submenu. Nearly a dozen commands are here, all of which you can explore on your own. The following coverage isn't going to go into a discussion and provide a visual demonstration of each one of them—not because the authors are busy or lazy, but because the transformations are pretty straightforward—with one exception, the Warp command, which is both new to Photoshop CS2 and covered separately later in this chapter. In the meantime, you'll learn what you need to know about the main forms of transformation—Scale, Rotate, Skew, Distort, Perspective, and the Flip commands—by working with a command that's really much better for these sorts of manipulations, anyway, the Edit ➪ Free Transform command. Free Transform is so wonderful, a shortcut—Ctrl (Cmd) + T—was assigned to it. Imagine that—a *keyboard shortcut*. Sarcastic references to the abundance of keyboard shortcuts aside, with Free Transform, you can scale, flip, rotate, slant, distort, skew, and move a selection or layer in one continuous operation. This one command lets you get all your transformations exactly right before pressing Enter or Return to apply the final changes.

Once you've gone into Free Transform mode (by using the aforementioned keyboard or menu methods), Photoshop surrounds the layer or selection with an eight-handle marquee. While you're in this mode, you can't do anything except transform the image or cancel the operation—commands are dimmed, the "no" symbol appears if you mouse over things you can't use. It's Transform or nothing.

Note   You can reach a slightly less powerful version of Free Transform by selecting the Move tool and selecting the Show Bounding Box option in the Options bar. You don't have the ability to adjust the transformation origin, but it can be handy nevertheless.

Here's how to work in the Free Transform mode:

✦ **Scale.** Drag one of the eight square handles to scale the image inside the marquee. To scale proportionally, Shift-drag a corner handle. To scale about the central *transformation origin* (labeled in Figure 12-31), Alt-drag (Win) or Option-drag (Mac) a corner handle.

Tip   By default, the origin is located in the center of the layer or selection. But you can move it to any place inside the image—even outside the transformation box—by clicking and dragging it. The origin snaps to the grid and guides, as well as to the center or any corner of the layer.

✦ **Flip.** You can flip the image by dragging one handle past its opposite handle. For example, dragging the left side handle past the right side handle flips the image horizontally.

Tip   If you want to perform a simple flip, it's generally easier to choose Edit ➪ Transform ➪ Flip Horizontal or Flip Vertical. Better yet, right-click (Win) or Control-click (Mac) in the image window and choose one of the Flip commands from the shortcut menu. Quite surprisingly, you can choose any of the shortcut menu commands while working in the Free Transform mode.

Transformation origin   Skew cursor

Scale cursor

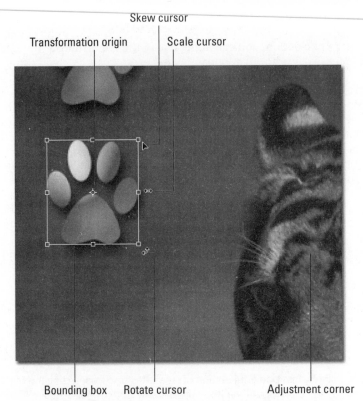

Bounding box   Rotate cursor   Adjustment corner

Figure 12-31: A bounding box appears around the layer content while you're in Free Transform mode. You only get one cursor while you're working (defined by where you point and what keys you press), but all of the cursors are magically included in this figure.

✦ **Rotate.** To rotate the image, click and drag outside the marquee, as demonstrated in the first example in Figure 12-31. Shift-drag to rotate in 15-degree increments.

✦ **Skew.** Ctrl-drag (Win) or ⌘-drag (Mac) a side handle (including the top or bottom handle) to slant the image. To constrain the slant, which is useful for producing perspective effects, Ctrl+Shift-drag (Win) or ⌘-Shift-drag (Mac) a side handle.

✦ **Distort.** You can distort the image by Ctrl-dragging (Win) or ⌘-dragging (Mac) a corner handle. You can tug the image to stretch it in any of four directions.

Tip

To tug two opposite corner handles in symmetrical directions, Ctrl+Alt-drag (or ⌘-Option-drag on the Mac) either of the handles.

✦ **Perspective.** For a one-point perspective effect, Ctrl+Shift-drag a corner handle. To move two points in unison, Ctrl+Shift+Alt-drag (or ⌘-Shift-Option-drag on the Mac) a corner handle.

✦ **Move.** Click and drag inside the marquee to move the image. This is useful when you're trying to align the selection or layer with a background image and you want to make sure the transformations match up properly.

✦ **Undo.** To undo the last modification without leaving the Free Transform mode altogether, press Ctrl+Z (⌘-Z on the Mac).

✦ **Zoom.** You can change the view size by choosing one of the commands in the View menu. You can also use the keyboard zoom shortcuts: Ctrl+space bar-click, Alt+space bar-click, Ctrl+plus, or Ctrl+minus on the PC or ⌘-space bar-click, Option-space bar-click, ⌘-plus, or ⌘-minus on the Mac.

✦ **Apply.** Press Enter or Return to apply the final transformation and interpolate the new pixels. You can also double-click inside the marquee or click the check mark button in the Options bar.

Note

If the finished effect looks jagged after you've applied the transformation, it's probably because you selected Nearest Neighbor from the Image Interpolation pop-up menu in the Preferences dialog box. To correct this problem, press Ctrl+Z (⌘-Z on the Mac) to undo the transformation and then press Ctrl+K (⌘-K on the Mac) and select the Bicubic option from the General panel of the Preferences dialog box. Then press Ctrl+Shift+T (⌘-Shift-T on the Mac) to reapply the transformation.

✦ **Cancel.** To cancel the Free Transform operation, press Esc, click the "no" symbol button in the Options bar, or press Ctrl+period (⌘-period on the Mac).

Tip

To transform a clone of a layer or selected area, press Alt (or Option on the Mac) when choosing the Free Transform command or press Ctrl+Alt+T (⌘-Option-T on the Mac).

If no part of the image is selected, you can transform multiple layers at a time by first linking them, as described in the "Linking layers" section earlier in this chapter. For example, in the picture with the series of footprint shapes up the left side, all of them, on separate layers, could have been linked and transformed as a unit.

Tip

To replay the last transformation on any layer or selection, choose Edit ➪ Transform ➪ Again or press Ctrl+Shift+T (⌘-Shift-T on the Mac). This is a great technique to use if you forgot to link all the layers that you wanted to transform. You can even transform a path or selection outline to match a transformed layer. It's a handy feature. In fact, throw the Alt or Option key in there, and the transformation can be repeated on a clone of the selected layer.

Note

Neither Free Transform nor any of the commands in the Edit ➪ Transform submenu are available when a layer is locked, either with the Lock Position or Lock All button. If a transformation command appears dimmed, therefore, the Lock buttons are very likely your culprits. Further, if you go to issue a command, click on a tool, or switch layers, and can't, chances are you forgot to commit to or abandon the transformation — press Enter if you want whatever you just did (scale, rotate, whatever) to be applied, or press Esc if you're not sure what's going on and how you might have left the transformation.

Warping layers

The Warp command allows you to totally disfigure (distort is too mild a term for what this feature does, and there's already a Transform ➪ Distort command, anyway). No, Warp lets you tug on, stretch, rip, and twist the content of a layer using a grid and bounding box to drag not just the sides and corners but the entire layer, in all different directions. A close-up of one of the footprint symbols in the process of being warped appears in Figure 12-32.

 New Feature   When it comes to transforming with that submenu of Edit ➪ Transform commands, there is one that's worth going into in detail — and it's new to Photoshop CS2.

Bounding box

Drag from a grid intersection

Drag from the handle on the bounding box

Use these controls to change the curve of the grid's sides

Figure 12-32: Grab any grid intersection, corner, or bounding box handle, and pull, stretch, twist, and generally abuse the selected layer.

When you grab the edges where the gridlines meet the bounding box, dragging creates the sort of handles you see when drawing Bezier curves with the Pen tool—

also shown in Figure 12-32, these handles let you change the direction and curve of the stretched sides of the grid (and the layer within it, being dragged right along with the grid), pulling it up, down, in, and out.

Once you've finished tormenting the layer, all you have to do is press Enter to commit to the transformation, or press Esc to abandon it and send the layer back to its pre-Warp state.

To really go to town on a layer and get some help in shaping the layer at the same time, you can click the Warp drop-down list, shown on the Options bar that appears when you activate the Warp command. Figure 12-33 shows the Options bar, drop-down list, and a footprint that's been subjected to the Arch Warp. Once a Warp preset has been applied, you can resize the Warp effect and click and drag from the single handle (looks like a little box along the perimeter of the bounding box, labeled in Figure 12-33) and flip the layer's content by dragging back through the layer itself.

Figure 12-33: Use the Warp tool's Options bar to apply a preset Warp to the layer, and then drag the lone grid handle to resize the layer and change the scale of the layer's distortion.

The Warp command's Options bar also offers numerical fields into which you can type the Bend (a percentage increase or decrease in it) or a Horizontal or Vertical percentage change, which will change the perspective of the preset Warp. For more about using such numerical transformation tools, keep reading—that's what the next section is all about.

Numerical transformations

To track your transformations numerically, display the Info palette (F8) before you apply the Free Transform command. Even after you initiate Free Transform, you can access the Info palette by choosing Window ➪ Info. You can also track and adjust the numerical equivalents of your mouse-driven transformations in the Options bar. Shown in Figure 12-34, the Options bar contains a series of numerical transformation controls anytime you enter the Free Transform mode. These values not only reflect the changes you've made so far, but also permit you to further transform the selection or layer by typing new values.

Figure 12-34: Normally, the options in the Options bar change only when you select a different tool, but choosing Free Transform adds a series of controls that permit you to transform a selection or layer numerically.

For the most part, the controls in the Options bar are straightforward. Click in the grid of nine squares to reposition the transformation origin. Use the X and Y values to change the location of the origin numerically. Click the triangular delta symbol to measure the movement relative to the transformation origin. Use the W and H values to scale the selection or layer. Click the link button to constrain the W and H values and resize the selection or layer proportionally. The angle value rotates; the H and V values skew.

Tip　Photoshop gives you the ability to control the values in the Options bar by "scrubbing," or dragging back and forth, over the icons or letters next to the editable values. When you see your mouse pointer turn to a two-headed arrow (at the tip of a pointing finger, labeled in Figure 12-34), you can drag over the position or scale values to increase or decrease them in increments of 1 pixel or 1 percentage point, respectively. Press and hold Alt (Option on the Mac) while scrubbing to change that to .1 pixel (or percentage point), and press and hold Shift to scrub the values in increments of 10. Scrubbing on the more sensitive angle and skew settings, however, raises or lowers them by .1 degree, and adding Shift changes the increment to 1 degree.

Probably, most people use the Options bar strictly for scaling and rotating—it's easy to picture the change that your entries into the Width, Height, and Set Rotation fields will do to the layer in question. You'd need the spatial awareness of a NASA navigation system to predict a numerical slant.

Masking and Layers

Layers offer special masking options unto themselves. You can paint inside the confines of a layer as if it were a selection mask; you can add a special mask for a single layer; or you can group multiple layers and have the bottom layer in the group serve as the mask. Although they're fairly complicated to use — you must be on your toes once you start juggling layer masks — these functions provide all sorts of image-editing and enhancement opportunities.

Preserving transparency

As you may recall, further discussion of the Lock Transparency button was promised when first mentioned in the section on locking layers. That further discussion begins here. Now, if you don't remember this, to refresh your memory, the Layers palette, with the Lock Transparency button labeled, appears in Figure 12-35.

Figure 12-35: The Lock Transparency button enables you to paint inside the layer's transparency mask without harming the transparent pixels.

When selected, this button prevents you from painting inside the transparent portions of the layer. And although that may sound like a small thing, it is in fact the most useful Lock option of them all. Suppose you want to paint inside the tiger shown in Figure 12-35. If this were a flat, non-layered image, you'd have to draw a selection outline carefully around the tiger to isolate him from the other pixels in the image. With layers, however, there's no need to do this, because the tiger lies on a different layer than his background, and a permanent selection outline exists because of this, telling Photoshop that there are both transparent and opaque pixels. Further, it tells Photoshop which pixels are which, and this creates the *transparency mask*.

The first example in Figure 12-36 shows the tiger on his own with the background hidden. The transparent areas outside the mask appear in the checkerboard pattern. When the Lock Transparency button is deselected, you can paint anywhere you want inside the layer. Selecting the Lock Transparency button activates the transparency mask and places the checkerboard area off-limits.

The bottom image in Figure 12-36 shows what happens after the Lock Transparency button is selected and the Clone Stamp tool is used to paint in the other content. No matter how large the Clone Stamp was (it was much larger than the tiger), the cloned content appears only within the tiger's portion of the layer — the transparent areas are protected by the mask.

Some more useful information about Lock Transparency:

✦ You can turn Lock Transparency on and off from the keyboard by pressing the standard slash character (/) right there on the same key with the question mark.

✦ The Lock Transparency button is dimmed when the background layer is active because this layer is entirely opaque.

Figure 12-36: The layered tiger as he appears on his own (top) and when content from another image has been clone stamped in with the Lock Transparency button turned on (bottom).

Creating layer-specific masks

In addition to the transparency mask that accompanies every layer (except the background), you can add a mask to a layer to make certain pixels in the layer transparent. Now, you might wonder if simply erasing portions of a layer wouldn't make those portions transparent — and you'd be right, it would. When you erase, however, you delete pixels permanently. By creating a layer mask, you make pixels temporarily transparent instead. You can return at any time in the future and bring those pixels back to life again simply by adjusting the mask. So layer masks add yet another level of flexibility.

To create a layer mask, select the layer you want to mask and choose Layer ➪ Add Layer Mask ➪ Reveal All. Or more simply, click the layer mask icon at the bottom of the Layers palette, as labeled in Figure 12-37. A second thumbnail preview appears to the left of the layer name, also labeled in the figure. A second outline around the preview shows the layer mask is active.

Tip   If the second outline is hard to see, check the icon directly to the right of the layer's eye icon. If the icon is a paintbrush, the layer — and not the mask — is active. If the icon is a square with a little dotted circle, the mask is active.

To edit the mask, simply paint in the image window. Paint with black to make pixels transparent. Because black represents deselected pixels in an image, it makes these pixels transparent in a layer. Paint with white to make pixels opaque.

Thankfully, Photoshop is smart enough to make the default foreground color in a layer mask white and the default background color black. This ensures that painting with the brush makes pixels opaque, whereas painting with the eraser makes them transparent, just as you would expect.

Photoshop offers a lot of bells and whistles to make the function of layer masks both convenient and powerful. Here's everything you need to know:

✦ **Reveal the selection.** If you select some portion of your layer, Photoshop automatically converts the selection to a layer mask when you click the layer mask icon at the bottom of the palette. The area outside the selection becomes transparent. (The corresponding command is Layer ➪ Add Layer Mask ➪ Reveal Selection.)

✦ **Hide the selection.** You can also choose to reverse the prospective mask, making the area inside the selection transparent and the area outside opaque. To do this, choose Layer ➪ Add Layer Mask ➪ Hide Selection. Or better yet, Alt-click (Win) or Option-click (Mac) the layer mask icon in the Layers palette.

✦ **Hide everything.** To begin with a black mask that hides everything, choose Layer ➪ Add Layer Mask ➪ Hide All. Or press Ctrl+D (⌘-D on the Mac) to deselect everything and then Alt-click (Win) or Option-click (Mac) the layer mask icon.

Box around the mask thumbnail tells you it's active

Link icon | Layer Mask thumbnail

Layer Mask icon

Figure 12-37: The layer mask thumbnail (white box to right of the layer thumbnail) indicates the presence of a mask.

✦ **View the mask.** Photoshop regards a layer mask as a layer-specific channel. You can actually see it listed in italics in the Channels palette. To view the mask on its own — as a black-and-white image — Alt-click (Win) or Option-click (Mac) the layer mask thumbnail in the Layers palette. Alt-click (Win) or Option-click (Mac) again to view the image instead.

✦ **Layer mask overlay.** To view the mask as a red overlay, Shift+Alt-click (Win) or Shift-Option-click (Mac) the layer mask icon. Or simply press backslash (\), which is above Enter (Return on the Mac).

Tip

After you have both the layer and mask visible at once, you can hide the mask by pressing \, or you can hide the layer and view only the mask by pressing the tilde key (~). So many alternatives!

✦ **Change the overlay color.** Double-click the layer mask thumbnail to access the Layer Mask Display Options dialog box, which enables you to change the color and opacity of the overlay color.

✦ **Turn off the mask.** You can temporarily disable the mask by Shift-clicking the mask thumbnail. A red *X* covers the thumbnail when it's disabled, and all masked pixels in the layer appear opaque. Click the thumbnail to put the mask back in working order.

✦ **Switch between the layer and mask.** As you become more familiar with layer masks, you'll switch back and forth between the layer and mask quite frequently, editing the layer one minute and editing the mask the next. You can switch between the layer and mask by clicking their respective thumbnails. As mentioned, look to the icon to the right of the eye icon to see whether the layer or the mask is active.

Tip

You can also switch between the layer and mask from the keyboard. Press Ctrl+tilde (Win) or ⌘-tilde (Mac) to make the layer active. Press Ctrl+\ (Win) or ⌘-\ (Mac) to switch to the mask.

✦ **Link the layer and mask.** A little link icon appears between the layer and mask thumbnails in the Layers palette. When the link icon is visible, you can move or transform the mask and layer as one. If you click the link icon to turn it off, the layer and mask move independently. (You can always move a selected region of the mask or layer independently of the other.)

✦ **Convert the mask to a selection.** As with all masks, you can convert a layer mask to a selection. To do so, Ctrl-click (Win) or ⌘-click (Mac) the layer mask icon. Throw in the Shift and Alt (Win) or Option (Mac) keys if you want to add or subtract the layer mask with an existing selection outline.

✦ **Apply the mask to a group.** You can also apply a mask to a group of layers. Just select the group and click the layer mask icon. The mask affects all layers in the group. If a layer in the group contains its own mask, no worries; Photoshop's smart enough to figure out how to mix them together. For another method of masking multiple layers, see the section "Masking groups of layers."

When and if you finish using the mask—you can leave it in force as long as you like— you can choose Layer ➪ Remove Layer Mask. Or just drag the layer mask thumbnail to the trash can icon. Either way, an alert box asks whether you want to discard the mask or permanently apply it to the layer. Click the button that corresponds to your innermost desires.

Pasting inside a selection outline

One command, Edit ⇨ Paste Into (Ctrl+Shift+V or ⌘-Shift-V), creates a layer mask automatically. Choose the Paste Into command to paste the contents of the Clipboard into the current selection, so that the selection acts as a mask. Because Photoshop pastes to a new layer, it converts the selection to a layer mask. But here's the interesting part: By default, Photoshop turns off the link between the layer and the mask. This way, you can Ctrl-drag (or ⌘-drag on the Mac) the layer inside a fixed mask to position the pasted image.

Tip

Once upon a time in Photoshop, there was a command that made it possible to paste a copied image in back of a selection. Although the command is gone, its spirit lives on in — you'll be shocked — a keyboard shortcut. Just press Alt (Win) or Option (Mac) when choosing Edit ⇨ Paste Into. Or just press Ctrl+Shift+Alt+V (⌘-Shift-Option-V on the Mac). Photoshop creates a new layer with an inverted layer mask, masking away the selected area.

Masking groups of layers

About now, you may be getting a little tired of the topic of layer masking. There's one more important facet of this very broad topic left to discuss, and then we'll move on. The facet? You can group multiple layers into something called a *clipping mask*, in which the lowest layer in the group masks the others. Where the lowest layer, or *base layer*, is transparent, the other layers are hidden; where the lowest layer is opaque, the contents of the other layers are visible.

Note

Despite the similarities in name, a clipping mask bears no relation to a clipping path. That is, a clipping mask doesn't allow you to prepare transparent areas for import into other applications. Nope, a clipping mask is used purely for controlling the editable parts of its layer pals, all of whom are sitting on top of him. Quite a sport, that clipping mask.

You can create a clipping mask in three ways:

✦ Alt-click (Win) or Option-click (Mac) the horizontal line between any two layers to group them into a single unit. Your cursor changes to the mask cursor, labeled in Figure 12-38, when you press Alt (Win) or Option (Mac); the horizontal line becomes broken after you click. To break the layers apart again, Alt-click (Win) or Option-click (Mac) the dotted line to make it solid.

✦ Select the higher of the two layers you want to combine into a clipping mask. Then choose Layer ⇨ Create Clipping Mask or press Ctrl+G (⌘-G on the Mac). To make the layers independent again, choose Layer ⇨ Release Clipping Mask or press Ctrl+Shift+G (⌘-Shift-G on the Mac). In Figure 12-39, you see the results of the clipping mask. The effects applied to the clipping mask — the type — are also applied to the layer above it.

✦ Select the layers you'd like to be part of the mask, and then choose Layers ➪ Create Clipping Mask. If you link your layers, the command will be dimmed. You can, however, click the line between selected layers to create a clipping mask, as described earlier.

✦ Next, choose Layer ➪ Create Clipping Mask From Linked. Keep in mind that this works only if all the linked layers are next to each other in the stacking order.

Note   If you're familiar with Illustrator, you may recognize Photoshop's clipping mask as a relative of Illustrator's clipping mask, in which one object in the illustration acts as a mask for a collection of additional objects. In Illustrator, however, the topmost object in the group is the mask, not the bottom one. So much for consistency.

Figure 12-38: Alt-click (Win) or Option-click (Mac) the horizontal line between two layers to group them into a clipping mask.

Figure 12-39: Use one layer as a mask for another. The Layers palette shows you the relationship between the clipping mask and the rest of the image.

Working with Layer Comps

Photoshop's Layer Comps palette (shown in Figure 12-40), is designed to track certain aspects of an image and save their status at any given time. Essentially, it records snapshots of the Layers palette as individual states, or *layer comps,* which are saved with the image file on disk.

Figure 12-40: Time travel is finally a reality with the Layer Comps palette.

The key to successfully working with layer comps is to be extremely conscious of what they are and aren't capable of tracking. A saved layer comp can store and recall information about the visibility, opacity, and blend modes of the layers in an image, as well as the position of each layer. Layer comps can also record whether or not styles are applied to each layer and the settings of those styles. What you need to keep in mind, however, is that layer comps don't even attempt to track any pixel changes to your images. This applies to painting, creating gradients, using the Patch tool; any operation that alters the pixels (as well as text contents) of an image is not recorded in the Layer Comps palette. The palette will turn the other way and pretend you've done nothing at all.

That said, layer comps can be a great and useful asset, especially when you're at the stage of assembling the final pieces into a composition. To save a layer comp, open the Layer Comps palette by choosing Window ⇨ Layer Comps or by clicking the Layer Comps tab in the Options bar's docking well (the palette is docked there by default). Next, click the new layer comp icon (labeled in Figure 12-40) to access the New Layer Comp dialog box, shown in Figure 12-41. Here, you set a name for your layer comp and any comments that might help you identify the state you're saving. This dialog box is also where you specify exactly what gets tracked by this layer comp. Three option are available to you:

✦ **Visibility.** Select this option to track the visibility of layers and layer masks.

Figure 12-41: The New Layer Comp dialog box lets you specify exactly what type of layer data you want to track.

✦ **Position.** This option tracks the position of each separate layer in relation to the others. Again, it's important to note that position changes within layers — say, if you marquee a section of a layer and drag it over to a corner — cannot be restored through layer comps.

✦ **Appearance (Layer Style).** This option saves all layer style attributes, including knockouts and effects, as well as the Opacity value and blend mode assigned to each layer.

Click OK to confirm your settings and, presto, you've created a new layer comp. You can tell that you're looking at a saved state of your image because the little icon in the left column of the Layer Comps palette sits alongside your new layer comp, as shown in Figure 12-42. As soon as you make any layer-comp-friendly changes to your image, such as moving a layer or adjusting its opacity, the icon will snap back to the topmost layer comp, known as the Last Document State. This means that trackable changes have been made to the image since your last saved layer comp. You can save this new state as another layer comp, if you want, and continue working. To return to a saved state, simply click in the space to the left of the layer comp.

Figure 12-42: Nearly all the functions available to you in the Layer Comps palette menu can be accessed from icons in the palette.

Working with the Layer Comps palette is pretty easy once you get used to it, but there are a few things you should know:

✦ Use the left- and right-pointing arrows at the bottom of the palette to cycle through your various layer comps. Click the right-pointing arrow to view the next saved layer comp down the list and click the left-pointing arrow to view the previous layer comp. To cycle through only specific comps, Ctrl-click (⌘-click on the Mac) or Shift-click to select them and then click the arrows.

✦ To the right of the arrow icons is the update layer comp icon (it's the one with two arrows that form a circle). Click this icon to assign changes to an existing selected layer comp. The icon in the left column of the palette leaps over to whatever layer comp you've selected and the current state of the Layers palette is applied to this layer comp.

✦ To delete a layer comp, simply select it and click the trash can icon, just as you would to delete a layer in the Layers palette. Here, you also have the added benefit of being able to select and drag multiple layer comps to the trash icon at once.

✦ You can always return the image to its most recent unsaved layer state by clicking in the space next to the Last Document State item in the palette.

All of these options can also be accessed from the Layer Comps palette menu, as shown in Figure 12-42. The palette menu also lets you duplicate any selected layer comp or access its options without having to double-click it.

Caution   Fragile creatures that they are, layer comps have a tendency to break down every once in a while. Luckily, though, they're pretty good at letting you know when they're unhappy. Whenever you make a change that will throw any of your layer comps out of whack—such as merging layers or converting a layer into a background—the affected comps will display a little triangle with an exclamation point. You can either undo the destructive move or click one of the triangle icons, in which case you'll be presented with a warning explaining exactly how you've betrayed the layer comp. From this warning, you have the option of "clearing" the layer comp, which is a way of updating the comp to account for the changes you've made. Right-click (Control-click on the Mac) any of the triangles and choose Clear Layer Comp Warning to clear that particular layer comp, or choose Clear All Layer Comp Warnings to clear all the layer comps without having to wrangle with the warnings for each.

Summary

In this chapter, you learned all about layers—from creating and cloning them to floating the background layer, to reordering layers, to merging layers and converting layers to selections. You also learned about combining layers using links, grouping layers, and moving, scaling, rotating, and aligning layers, too. The use of Smart Guides was also covered, making much of this a lot easier.

To make further use of layers, this chapter also showed you how to make drop shadows, halos, and spotlights, and to work with the new Smart Objects. You learned to use the Measure tool, to select the Lock Transparency option, and to work with layer masks and the Layer Comps palette.

✦   ✦   ✦

The Wonders of Blend Modes

✦ ✦ ✦ ✦

In This Chapter

Modifying the
Opacity and
Fill values

Using blend modes to
mix the active layer
with those behind it

Sandwiching a
heavily filtered
image between two
unfiltered originals

Employing the
Advanced Blending
options

Creating knockouts

Fading pixels
according to
brightness values
using the Blend If
sliders

Mixing same-sized
images with the Apply
Image command

Using the Add and
Subtract blend modes

Modifying selection
outlines and masks
using the Calculations
command

✦ ✦ ✦ ✦

Blend modes permit you to mix the color of a pixel with that of every pixel in a straight line beneath it. A single blend mode can pack as much power as a mask, a filter, and a retouching tool combined. And, unlike some of those combined options, blend modes don't physically alter an image's pixels — they're temporary. As long as one image remains layered in front of another, you can replace one calculation with another as easily as you change a letter of text in a word processor.

To appreciate the most rudimentary power of blend modes, consider Figure 13-1. Here you see several clones of our bony old pal. Each one has been mixed with the background using a random sampling of blend modes from Photoshop's Layers palette. The skeleton image itself never changes; each repeated layer contains the same collection of pixels. In all, there are six layers: five skeletons and the background, each skeleton layer subject to the blend mode labeled in the figure.

You delve into the specifics of every one of these blend modes later in this chapter — as well as the other 18 that didn't make it into the previous example. However, before you get ahead of yourself a few basics are in order.

In this chapter, you investigate three fundamental ways to mix pixels:

✦ **The Layers palette.** You can combine the active layer with underlying pixels using the Opacity and Fill values, along with the blend mode pop-up menu, all members of the Layers palette, as seen in Figure 13-2. Opacity and Fill options are examined in detail in the next section. Blend modes are covered in the section after that.

Normal   Hard Light   Linear Dodge   Linear Light   Difference

Figure 13-1: Six identical layers mixed in a variety of ways with the background image using a different blend mode option

Figure 13-2: The blend mode menu, and Opacity and Fill sliders located on Photoshop's Layers palette

✦ **Blending options.** Right-click a thumbnail in the Layers palette (Control-click on the Mac) and choose Blending Options to display the Blending Options panel of the extensive Layer Style dialog box. Along with the Blend Mode, Opacity, and Fill Opacity options, you get an assortment of advanced blending options, including the Knockout pop-up menu and Blend If sliders. The Knockout options let you use one layer to cut a floating hole into one or more layers below it. Using the Blend If sliders, you can drop colors out of the active layer and force colors to show through from layers below. For more information about these and other options, read the section "Advanced Blending Options."

✦ **Channel operations.** The so-called channel operations permit you to combine two open images of identical size, or one image with itself. Photoshop offers two commands for this purpose, Image ⇨ Apply Image and Image ⇨ Calculations. Largely archaic and completely lacking in sizing and placement functions, these commands are unique in that they provide access to two otherwise hidden blend modes, Add and Subtract. Simply put, unless a technique involves the Add or Subtract mode, or you want to clone two images into a third image window, you can mix images with greater ease, flexibility, and feedback using the Layers palette. For more on this lively topic, see the section "Whole Image Calculations."

Blend modes are not Photoshop's most straightforward feature. There may even come a time when you utter the words, "Blend modes are stupid." They demand a generous supply of experimentation, and even then they'll try to fool you. The key is to combine a basic understanding of how blend modes and other compositing features work with your natural willingness to experiment, grow, and bond with pixels. Sometime when you don't have a deadline looming, take a multilayered composition you have lying around and hit it with a few calculations. Even if the result is a disaster that you wouldn't share with your best friend, let alone a client, you can consider it time well spent.

Opacity and Fill

The Opacity value permits you to mix the active layer with the layers beneath it in prescribed portions. By way of example, consider Figure 13-3. The left side of the image shows a grouping of the skeletons at full opacity. In the example on the right, the Opacity setting was reduced, thereby transforming the group of skeletons into mere ghosts of their former selves.

The option directly below Opacity in the Layers palette is the field for controlling Fill opacity. Where Opacity controls the translucency of *everything* associated with a layer, Fill adjusts the opacity of the filled areas of a layer independently of any layer effects you add to it. Take a gander at Figure 13-4, where a drop shadow and outer bevel have been added to each of the skeleton layers. (You can add a layer effect to a layer by choosing an option from the cursive *f* icon at the bottom of the Layers palette, as discussed in Chapter 14.) Opacity affects pixels and layer effects alike; Fill affects pixels and leaves effects unchanged.

Figure 13-3: Skeletons at 100 percent Opacity (left) and faded by 50 percent (right) directly beneath the Opacity field.

Figure 13-4: By adding a layer effect or two, the difference between Opacity and Fill becomes obvious. Opacity makes layer and effects translucent (left); Fill alters the layer independently of its effects (right).

Fill is also more absolute than Opacity. You can lower the Opacity value to 1 percent, just shy of altogether transparent. But Photoshop lets you take Fill all the way down to 0 percent. Why? Because that allows you to reduce the fill of a layer to nothing while leaving the effects intact. Figure 13-5 shows the results of lowering the Fill value to first 20 and then 0 percent.

Figure 13-5: Using the Fill value, you can subordinate a layer to its effect (left) or fade the layer away entirely (right).

Tip   When a selection or navigation tool is active, you can change the Opacity setting for a layer from the keyboard. Press a single number key to change the Opacity in 10 percent increments. That's 1 for 10 percent, 2 for 20 percent, up to 0 for 100 percent, in order along the top of your keyboard. If you have the urge to be more precise, press two keys in a row quickly to specify an exact two-digit Opacity value.

Hankering to change the Fill just as easily? Then press Shift. Shift-1 changes the Fill value to 10 percent, Shift-0 makes it 100 percent. Shift plus two numbers enters a two-digit value.

You also can change the setting by clicking and dragging the Opacity or Fill slider in the Layers palette (labeled back in Figure 13-2). Click the arrowhead to the right of the option to display the slider and then drag the triangle to change the value. Or press the up and down arrows to nudge the triangle along; press Shift with the arrow key to nudge the value in 10 percent increments. Press Enter or Return to confirm the slider setting, or press Escape to restore the previous setting.

Note   Incidentally, both the Opacity and Fill options are dimmed when working on the background layer or in a single-layer image. There's nothing underneath, so there's nothing to mix. Naturally, this goes double when editing a black-and-white image, an indexed image, a single channel, or a mask, because none of these circumstances supports layers.

Blend Modes

Photoshop offers a total of 23 blend modes, starting with Normal and ending with Luminosity. If you've been reading the chapters sequentially, you'll notice this isn't the first time blend modes have been touched upon. In fact, given that the blend modes mimic the brush modes described in Chapter 5 both in name and in function, we're covering some familiar territory. But you'll soon find that there's a big difference between laying down a color or pattern with a brush and merging the myriad colors that inhabit a single layer. This difference is the stuff of the following pages.

To demonstrate the effects of Photoshop's blend modes, we'll be compositing the series of images shown in Figure 13-6, in more or less the order shown. The background layer (being a true background layer) can have no blend mode applied to it. Also note that the face includes a drop shadow layer effect, fading off to the left.

Tip   You can apply every one of the blend modes to a layer from the keyboard by pressing Shift+Alt (Shift-Option on the Mac) plus a letter, provided that the active tool doesn't offer its own brush mode options. (If the tool supports brush modes — as in the case of the Brush tool, Pencil, Clone Stamp, Healing Brush, and others — the shortcuts set the mode for the tool and not the layer.)

Photoshop's 23 blend modes, in order of appearance, are:

✦ **Normal (N).** In combination with Opacity and Fill settings of 100 percent, this option displays every pixel in the active layer normally, regardless of the colors in the underlying layers. When you use opacity values (whether Opacity or Fill) of less than 100 percent, the color of each pixel in the active layer is averaged with the composite pixel in the layers behind it. Figure 13-7 shows examples applied to the face layer on its own.

Composite pixel refers to the pixel color that results from all the mixing that's going on beneath the active layer. For example, your document may contain hordes of layers with all sorts of blend modes in effect, but as long as you're working on, say, Layer 23, Photoshop treats the image formed by Layers 1 through 22 as if it were one flattened image filled with a bunch of static composite pixels.

Figure 13-6: The default order of the images is the order pictured here — the face on top, followed by the Blistered Paint pattern (one of the predefined patterns included with Photoshop), then the gradient, and the tranquil background at the bottom. However, if it better suits the discussion, sometimes the pattern and gradient layers get pushed around.

Figure 13-7: The face layer subject to the Normal mode when combined with Opacity values of 100 percent (top) and 60 percent (bottom). The superimposed character indicates the keyboard shortcut Shift+Alt+N (Shift-Option-N on the Mac) and 6 for 60 percent opacity.

✦ **Dissolve (I).** This option affects feathered or softened edges. If the active layer is entirely opaque with hard edges, Dissolve has no effect. But when the edges of the layer fade into view, as seen in Figure 13-8, Dissolve randomizes, or *dithers*, the pixels. If you look closely, you'll see that Dissolve does not dither pixels in the drop shadow; as discussed in Chapter 14, layer effects are governed by their own, independent blend modes. Things change, however, when you drop the Opacity value below 100 percent, in which case Dissolve dithers all pixels, as demonstrated in the second example in the figure.

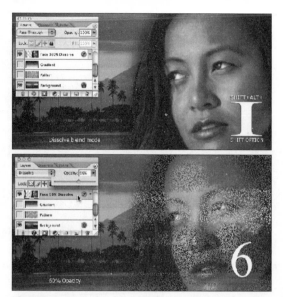

Figure 13-8: Here the Dissolve mode has been applied to a layer at an Opacity setting of 100 percent (top) and 60 percent (bottom). Instead of creating translucent pixels, Dissolve turns pixels on and off to simulate transparency.

✦ **Darken (K).** The first of the four darkening modes, Darken applies colors in the active layer only if they are darker than the corresponding pixels below. Keep in mind that Photoshop compares the brightness levels of pixels in a full-color image on a channel-by-channel basis. So although the blue component of a pixel in the active layer may be darker than the blue component of the underlying composite pixel, the red and green components may be lighter. In this case, Photoshop would assign the blue component but not the red or green, thereby subtracting blue and shifting the pixel toward yellow. Darken is most useful for covering up light portions of an image while letting dark areas show through.

To illustrate Darken and the other darkening modes, a light background was established by setting the pattern layer on top of the background and lowering its Opacity to 25 percent. Then the gradient layer was placed on top of that and set to the Screen mode, which left the white portion of the gradient visible and dropped out the black portion. The face layer was then added and set to the Darken mode, as shown at the bottom of the figure. The result (Figure 13-9) is a face that appears smooth in both the midtones and the shadows and patterned in the light areas, with relatively sharp transitions between the two.

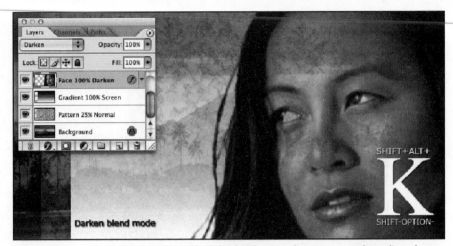

Figure 13-9: A backdrop composed of the background, pattern, and gradient layers followed by an application of the face in the Darken mode. Only those pixels in the face that are darker than the pixels in the patterned backdrop remain visible.

✦ **Multiply (M).** Multiply is one of the rare blend modes that emulates a real-world scenario. Imagine that the active layer and the underlying composite are both photos on transparent slides. The Multiply mode produces the same effect as holding these slides up to the light, one slide in front of the other. Because the light has to travel through two slides, the outcome invariably combines the darkest elements from both images. So unlike Darken, Multiply universally darkens, resulting in smooth transitions that are ideal for preserving contours and shadows, as shown in Figure 13-10.

Tip

If the Multiply mode produces too dark an effect, reduce the Opacity or Fill value. If it isn't dark enough, clone the layer by pressing Ctrl+J (⌘-J on the Mac). This technique holds true throughout Photoshop: Provided that two layers share a common blend mode, you can merge the layers and preserve the effect.

✦ **Color Burn (B) and Linear Burn (A).** Where the Multiply mode darkens your images, the two Burn modes can literally char them. They both use colors in the active layer to reduce brightness values, resulting in radical color transformations. As demonstrated in Figure 13-11, Color Burn results in crisp, often colorful, toasted edges; Linear Burn creates a smoother, less vibrant effect. Both modes have an uncanny ability to draw colors from background layers. For example, even though the background is lightened by applying Screen to the pattern layer in Figure 13-11, you see more contrast in this figure than in the Multiply example from Figure 13-10. So for high-contrast stamping effects, these are the blend modes to use.

Figure 13-10: The Multiply blend mode produces the same effect as holding two overlapping transparencies up to the light.

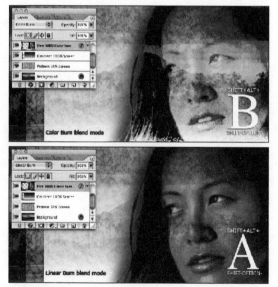

Figure 13-11: After applying Screen to the pattern layer, Color Burn (top) and Linear Burn (bottom) blend modes are applied to the face layer. Even though the background is lighter, many portions of the face appear darker than they did after a single application of Multiply.

✦ **Lighten (G).** The next four options use the active layer to lighten those below it. If you select Lighten, for example, Photoshop applies colors in the active layer only if they are lighter than the corresponding pixels in the underlying image. As with Darken, Photoshop compares the brightness levels of all channels in a full-color image.

To set the stage for the lightening figures, the background layers were modified, restoring the pattern layer to Normal and switching the gradient layer to Multiply. As a result, Photoshop dropped out the whites in the gradient and kept the blacks. The Lighten blend mode was then assigned to the face. The drop shadow was also modified — which would have otherwise remained black — by changing its color to white and its blend mode to Screen. The result (Figure 13-12) is a drop glow, which is described in Chapter 14.

Figure 13-12: Here a dark background was prepared by assigning Multiply to the gradient layer Then, Lighten was applied to the face layer and its drop shadow changed to white.

✦ **Screen (S).** From a creative standpoint, Screen is the opposite of Multiply. Rather than creating a darker image, as you do with Multiply, you create a lighter image, as demonstrated in Figure 13-13.

You can use the Screen blend mode to emulate film that has been exposed multiple times. However, you should only apply Screen when working with images that are sufficiently dark so that you avoid over lightening. Screen is equally useful for creating glows, retaining just the light colors in a gradient, and creating light noise effects such as snow and stars.

Figure 13-13: The Screen mode produces the same effect as shining two projectors at the same screen. In this case, one projector contains the background layers, and the other contains the face (top). Want a more pronounced ghosting effect? Just duplicate the Screen layer (bottom).

✦ **Color Dodge (D) and Linear Dodge (W).** When you apply one of the two Dodge modes, each color in the layer becomes a brightness-value multiplier. Light colors such as white produce the greatest effect, and black drops away. As a result, the Dodge modes are Photoshop's most dramatic whitening agents — imagine mounting your image on a gel and projecting it from a spotlight. Of the two, Color Dodge produces the sharper, rougher effect; Linear Dodge smoothes out the transitions (see Figure 13-14). Because they send so much of an image to white, the Dodge modes are most useful for simulating hot spots and other intensely bright effects.

✦ **Overlay (O), Soft Light (F), and Hard Light (H).** Photoshop's six Light modes darken the darkest colors and lighten the lightest colors, thereby allowing the midtones to intermix, so that foreground and background remain independently identifiable. Of the six, the first three — Overlay, Soft Light, and Hard Light — are the oldest and arguably the most useful, so the discussion begins with them.

Each of these three modes alternatively multiplies the blacks and screens the whites, but to different degrees. For example, where Overlay favors the background layers, Hard Light emphasizes the active layer. In fact, the two are direct opposites — Layer A set to Overlay in front of Layer B produces the same effect as Layer B set to Hard Light in front of Layer A. Meanwhile, Soft Light is a modified version of Hard Light that results in a more subtle effect than either Hard Light or Overlay.

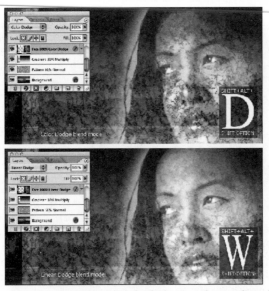

Figure 13-14: After slightly darkening the gradient layer
and fading the pattern layer, Color Dodge (top) and
Linear Dodge (bottom) were applied to the face.
Never subtle, both modes simultaneously bleach
the image and draw out some of the dark outlines
from the Blistered Paint pattern.

When experimenting with these modes, my advice is to always start with
Overlay. If Overlay produces too strong an effect, reduce the Opacity or Fill
value to favor the composite pixels. Figure 13-17 shows three compositions
created using the background, face, and pattern layers. Throughout, the face
is set to Normal, fully opaque. To add texture to the image, the blend mode for
the pattern layer was set to Overlay. But as you can see in the first example,
this overwhelms the image. By pressing 5 to reduce the Opacity to 50 percent,
the second image results.

Alternatively, you can switch from Overlay to Soft Light, as was done in the
final example of Figure 13-15. On first glance, the second and third examples
in the figure — one showing Overlay at 50 percent and the other Soft Light at
full opacity — look almost identical. But on closer inspection, you notice that
where the balance of lights and darks is roughly equivalent, their distribution
is quite different. The Overlay example favors the details in the face; the Soft
Light example favors the marbleized edges of the Blistered Paint pattern.

Figure 13-15: With the pattern layer in front, the Overlay mode (top) was applied, and its Opacity setting changed to 50 percent (middle). Last, the layer was set to Soft Light mode with an Opacity of 100 percent (bottom).

If the Overlay mode at 100 percent seems too subtle, consider switching to the Hard Light mode, shown in Figure 13-16, which provides the best marriage of emphasis on the face and balance with the background.

Figure 13-16: Here the face layer was set to Hard Light in front with the gradient set to Screen behind it.

✦ **Vivid Light (V) and Linear Light (J).** Where Overlay and family combine Multiply and Screen, the next two Light modes combine Dodge and Burn. Vivid Light combines Color Dodge and Color Burn, where Linear Light combines Linear Dodge and Linear Burn. Figure 13-17 shows examples.

This time, the Opacity setting was reduced for the gradient layer to 50 percent and brought back the pattern layer, also at 50 percent Opacity but set to Soft Light. Sandwiched in between is the face, set to Vivid Light at top and Linear Light at bottom.

Figure 13-17: The effect of setting the face to the Vivid Light (top) and Linear Light (bottom) modes. Because the effects are so hot, a Soft Light pattern layer and a Screen gradient layer were sandwiched between them, each with Opacity settings of 50 percent.

✦ **Pin Light (Z).** One of the simplest modes in all of Photoshop, Pin Light keeps the darkest blacks and the lightest whites, and then makes everything else invisible.

You'll find Pin Light particularly useful for modifying edge filters. In Figure 13-18, the gradient layer has been set to Pin Light to enhance its extremes. The face layer has been returned to Normal and then cloned to a new layer, with the Filter ➪ Sharpen ➪ Unsharp Mask applied. A mask with an Amount of 100 percent and a Radius of 20 pixels was applied, and by applying the Pin Light mode, the lightest and darkest edges of the sharpened layer were retained. The result is a more subtle effect that still manages to exhibit thick, high-contrast outlines.

Figure 13-18: After returning the face to the Normal mode, the gradient layer was set to Pin Light. Then the face was cloned and the edges sharpened using the Unsharp Mask filter. The Pin Light mode was applied to keep just the lightest and darkest pixels.

✦ **Hard Mix (L).** The Hard Mix blend mode combines the pixels in your layers using the Vivid Light blend mode and then performs a color threshold operation on them. The results that Hard Mix produces don't fit a standard definition of "pretty," as shown in Figure 13-19. Hard Mix mixes two layers and pushes the colors to their absolute extreme. All in all, Hard Mixed pixels come in only eight colors: black, white, red, green, blue, cyan, magenta, and yellow, the end result being quite similar to the Posterize command (Image ⇨ Adjustments ⇨ Posterize).

You may be wondering why you'd ever want to achieve this effect, and you may also be wondering what exactly you just did to your image. Essentially, Hard Mix pushes the colors in an image's blended pixels to their absolute extreme: A hint of auburn becomes a harsh, deafening red; a sprinkle of cool aquamarine is transformed into bright, brash blue; you get the picture. All in all, Hard Mix leaves you with only eight colors for your pixels: black, white, red, green, blue, cyan, magenta, and yellow. Consider the fact that you're probably downsizing from roughly 16 million colors, and you begin to understand why the effect looks less than appealing.

Believe it or not, a color threshold created with the Hard Mix blend mode has its uses, rare as they may be. For a closer look at some effects you might be able to pull from thresholds, check out Chapter 17.

Figure 13-19: Here only the face layer was set to Hard Mix. Although it is by no means smooth or anti-aliased, Hard Mix managed to isolate the eyes from the other details in the face (by completely obliterating those details).

✦ **Difference (E) and Exclusion (X).** Difference inverts lower layers according to the brightness values in the active layer. White inverts the composite pixels absolutely, black inverts them not at all, and the other brightness values invert them to some degree in between. In the first example of Figure 13-20, the Difference mode was applied to the face layer, which is set against the gradient layer set to Screen. The light colors from the background show through the black pixels around the eyebrows, nose, and mouth, while the light areas in the face invert the lake and mountains.

Exclusion works just like Difference except for one, er, difference. Illustrated in the second example in Figure 13-20, Exclusion sends midtones to gray — much as Pin Light sends midtones to transparent — creating a lower-contrast, often smoother effect.

✦ **Hue (U).** Hue and the remaining three blend modes make use of the HSL color model to mix colors between the active layer and the underlying composite. When you select Hue, Photoshop retains the hue values from the active layer and mixes them with the saturation and luminosity values from the underlying image.

Hue, Saturation, Color, and Luminosity blend modes affect only color images, so trying to demonstrate their effects here in grayscale would be a little pointless. In fact, if you tried to use any of these options in a grayscale document you'd find them dimmed.

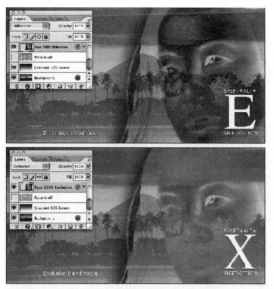

Figure 13-20: When you apply the Difference mode (top), white pixels invert the pixels beneath them; black pixels leave the background untouched. The Exclusion mode (bottom) performs a similar effect, but instead of inverting medium colors, it changes them to gray.

✦ **Saturation (T).** When you select this option, Photoshop retains the saturation values from the active layer and mixes them with the hue and luminosity values from the underlying image. Saturation produces such subtle effects that you'll typically want to apply it in combination with other blend modes. For example, after applying a random blend mode to a layer, you might duplicate the layer and then apply the Saturation mode to either boost or downplay the colors, much like printing a gloss or matte coating over an image.

✦ **Color (C).** This option combines hue and saturation. Photoshop retains both the hue and saturation values from the active layer and mixes them with the luminosity values from the underlying layers. Because the saturation ingredient of the Color mode produces such a slight effect, Color frequently produces a very similar effect to Hue.

✦ **Luminosity (Y).** The Luminosity blend mode retains the lightness values from the active layer and mixes them with the hue and saturation values from the composite pixels below. So just as the Color mode uses the layer to colorize its background, the Luminosity mode uses the background to colorize the layer.

Blend modes are amazing. They permit you to try out so many permutations that you can lose yourself for hours. Predicting the outcome of these permutations might require a brain on par with Einstein's, but let's leave prediction to Nostradamus. Experimenting with Photoshop's different blend mode settings requires no intelligence at all, just the willingness to begin the experimentation in the first place — and that's where this book comes in.

An excellent technique to incorporate into your scientific method is *sandwiching*. This refers to the process of placing a heavily filtered version of an image between two originals. This technique is based on the principal that more than half the blend modes — including Normal, Dissolve, Color Dodge and Burn, the seven Light modes, and the four HSL modes — change depending on which of two images is on top.

For example, Figure 13-21 shows two layers, A and B, and the result of blending them with the Overlay mode. When the moon is on top, as in the third example, the Overlay mode favors the man; but when the man is on top, Overlay favors the moon.

Layer A
(The face of the moon)

Layer B
(The face of the man)

Overlay: A over B
(Spotlight on the man)

Overlay: B over A
(The man in the moon)

Figure 13-21: After establishing two layers, moon and man, the moon was placed on top and Overlay applied to get the third image. Then the order of the layers was switched and Overlay applied to the man to get the last image.

Overlay just happens to be balanced by its opposite, the Hard Light blend mode, which favors the layer to which it's applied. So, you could have achieved the exact effect shown in the last example in Figure 13-21 by placing the man under the moon and setting the moon to Hard Light.

Therefore, you see that the order in which you stack your layers is as important as the blend mode you select. Even modes that have no stacking opposites — Color Dodge, Linear Light, and others — produce different effects depending on which layer is on top.

Note   Like Overlay, Color Dodge favors the composite pixels below the active layer. This holds true for Color Burn as well. Meanwhile, Linear Light, Pin Light, and all the other modes with Light in their name favor the active layer. Modes that do not change based on layering order — Multiply, Screen, Difference, and the like — favor neither front nor rear layer.

Sandwiching a filtered image

When you sandwich a filtered image between two originals you can lessen the effect of the filter and achieve different effects than those discussed in Chapter 11. Layers and blend modes give you the flexibility to experiment as much as you want and for as long as you please.

Returning to our bathing beauty again in Figure 13-22, her face was copied to a new layer and then Filter ➪ Sketch ➪ Charcoal was applied with the foreground and background colors set to their defaults, black and white. The right-hand image lists the specific settings.

Figure 13-22: The ingredients for our blend mode sandwich include the original image layer (left) and a cloned version on an independent layer subject to the Charcoal filter (right).

Like most filters under the Sketch submenu, Charcoal absolutely destroys the detail in the image, replacing all brightness values with the foreground and background colors, in this case, black and white. Fortunately, because Charcoal was applied to a clone of the image, a blend mode to restore some of the detail can be used. Figure 13-23 shows two of the many possibilities that exist — one using the Multiply mode, which kept the blacks in the Charcoal effect and threw away the whites, and the other using Pin Light, which allowed colors from the original image to show through the gray areas of the Charcoal rendering.

Figure 13-23: Each of two blend modes applied to the filtered layer in front of the original image

So far we've only really been working with an open-faced sandwich. By once again cloning the background layer and moving it above the Charcoal layer, so that the filtered image resides between two originals, you can increase your opportunity for blend mode variations. In this full sandwich, the original images serve as our bread while the Charcoal layer is the sandwich contents. Figure 13-24 provides a small menu of sandwich choices.

Creating a Difference sandwich

Check out the last example in Figure 13-24 and you'll see a purist's sandwich, Pin Light on the cheese and Pin Light on the bread. In Photoshop, that's one of the best, most reliable sandwich combinations you can create. If blend modes were condiments, Pin Light would be mustard — it works for everything.

Tip   When it comes to things that "work for everything," you just can't forget the Difference mode. By applying Difference to both the filtered layer and the cloned original on top, you do a double-invert, first inverting the filter into the original image and then reinverting the original into the composite. The result is a subtler and utterly unique combination.

Figure 13-24: When you're really hungry, only a full sandwich will do. Here you see there are layers, each with a different blend mode.

Advanced Blending Options

To display the Advanced Blending options, you have three options: First, you can double-click the layer thumbnail. Second, if you want to modify the Advanced Blending options for a specialty layer — such as type or an adjustment layer — right-click the layer name or thumbnail (Control-click on the Mac) and choose the Blending Options command. You can also right-click in the image window with one of the selection tools and access Blending Options that way. Third, you can press Alt (or Option) and double-click the layer name. So you decide.

In any case, you'll see the vast and stately Layer Style dialog box. This one multi-paneled window holds controls for adding layer effects, changing the opacity and blend mode of a layer, and achieving some special blending tricks, which will be discussed here. By default, you should see the Blending Options panel, pictured in Figure 13-25. If you're working in some other area of the dialog box, click the Blending Options item at the top of the list on the left side of the dialog box.

You already know how the two General Blending options, Blend Mode and Opacity, work. The same goes for the Fill Opacity slider (though as you'll see, it takes on broader meaning in this dialog box). These are the same options found in the Layers palette and discussed in the first half of this chapter. The next few sections explain the Advanced Blending options, spotlighted in Figure 13-25. Like so many aspects of blend modes, these options can be perplexing at first. But after you get the hang of them, they enable you to gain a degree of control over your layers unrivaled by any other image editor.

Many of the Advanced Blending options affect the performance of layer effects, such as drop shadows, glows, bevels, and so on. These effects fall into the broader category of layer styles, which is discussed at length in Chapter 14.

Figure 13-25: Using the Advanced Blending options, you can turn a layer into a floating hole, make specific color ranges invisible, and more.

Blending interior layer effects

It should be said at the outset that the Fill Opacity value behaves exactly like the Fill option in the Layers palette. Type a value in one option and it appears in the other as well. They are as one. The same goes for the Blend Mode setting in the dialog box and the selected mode in the Layers palette. However, you're about to discover a few ways to modify the performance of the Fill Opacity and Blend Mode options that are possible only from the Advanced Blending options.

As you may recall, the Opacity value controls the translucency of all aspects of a layer, including pixels and layer effects alike. This is a fact of life, regardless of any other settings that may be in place. Meanwhile, the Blend Mode and Fill Opacity settings modify the interaction of pixels independently of most or all layer effects. This caveat "most or all" is where things get interesting.

You see, Photoshop divides layer effects into two groups that you can control independently of each other. *Interior effects* fall inside the boundaries of the filled areas of a layer and consist of the Inner Shadow, Inner Glow, Satin, and three Overlay effects. *Exterior effects* fall either outside or both inside and outside the boundaries of a layer. These consist of the Drop Shadow, Outer Glow, Bevel and Emboss, and Stroke effects.

Using blend modes and Fill Opacity, Photoshop permits you the option of modifying interior effects independently from exterior effects. The catalyst at the heart of this behavior is the Blend Interior Effects as Group option. When deselected, as by default, blend modes and Fill Opacity affect the pixels on a layer only. But if you select this option, Photoshop applies the blend mode and Fill Opacity to the interior layer effects as well — only the exterior effects remain unchanged.

Figures 13-26 and 13-27 show examples. In Figure 13-26, you see a layer to which a red Inner Glow as been assigned as well as two exterior effects — Drop Shadow and Stroke. When the Fill Opacity is lowered to 60 percent, the pixels that make up the yacht within the circle drop away, but the layer effects remain unchanged. However, if you also select the Blend Interior Effects as Group option, Photoshop reduces the opacity of the Inner Glow effects as well.

Figure 13-26: The results of taking a layer subject (the yacht) to an interior effect and two exterior effects (top), reducing the Fill Opacity value to 60 percent (middle), and then selecting the Blend Interior Effects as Group option (bottom).

Figure 13-27: The default image (top), and the effect of the Difference blend mode when applied to the yacht layer with the Blend Interior Effects as Group option deselected (middle) and selected (bottom).

Note, however, that neither Fill Opacity nor blend mode affects the exterior layer effects — even when those exterior effects actually fall inside the boundaries of the layer. The Stroke effect, for example, is set to trace the inside of the layer. In fact, the only effect that truly exists outside the layer is the drop shadow. However, as far as Photoshop is concerned, an exterior effect is an exterior effect, regardless of where it happens to fall.

Tip

Found just beneath the Blend Interior Effects as Group option, the Blend Clipped Layers as Group option controls whether the upper layers in a clipping mask blend along with the base layer or remain unchanged. By default, this option is selected, blending all layers in a clipping mask as a single unit. To adjust the blending of the base layer in a clipping mask by itself, simply deselect the option. Then, only the Opacity slider will impact the other layers in the group.

Masking and unmasking effects

The Transparency Shapes Layers, Layer Mask Hides Effects, and Vector Mask Hides Effects options permit you to manage the boundaries of interior and exterior effects alike.

✦ **Transparency Shapes Layer.** Deselecting this option deactivates the transparency mask that is normally associated with a layer, permitting layer effects and clipped layers to spill outside the boundaries of a layer to fill the entire image window. If the layer includes a layer mask, effects and clipped layers fill the mask instead. So it serves two purposes: First, you can fill an image or clipping mask with a Color Overlay or other interior effect associated with a layer. And second, you can substitute a transparency mask with a layer or vector mask. You'll be seeing both of these in the following pages.

✦ **Layer Mask Hides Effects.** When selected, this option uses the layer mask to mask both the pixels in the layer and the layer effects. When deselected, as by default, the layer mask defines the boundary of the layer, and the effect traces around this boundary just as it traces around other transparent portions of the layer.

✦ **Vector Mask Hide Effects.** Photoshop's shape tools allow you to draw vector-based shapes that you can fill with flat colors, gradients, patterns, or even layered images. When working inside a layer inside a shape, you can use the Vector Mask Hides Effects option to specify whether the shape defines the outline of the layer (selected) or clips layer effects just as it clips pixels (deselected). For complete information on defining a layer mask, see Chapter 14.

Typically, you use these options to change Photoshop's default behaviors because something has gone wrong and you want to correct it. Don't like how your layer effects look? Select or deselect one of these options and see whether it makes a difference. Of course, it helps to have a little experience with these options before you start randomly hitting switches, so let's work through an example.

Take a look at Figure 13-28. Here, the basic elements of the previous two figures are taken and thrown in with a few items for a quaint little postcard effect. A head shot of a woman eating watermelon has been clipped to the circular layer of the yacht on the beach (which now becomes her backdrop), and a color Overlay layer effect included, set to a blending mode of Saturation and an Opacity of 60 percent to punch up the colors of the clipped layers. The circular layer's blending options have both the Blend Interior Effects as Group and Blend Clipped Layers as Group options deselected.

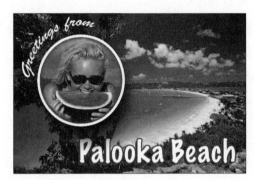

Figure 13-28: Beginning with the woman masked inside the circle (top), a layer mask was added to the circle layer using the Gradient tool (middle). But instead of fading the effects, the mask shoved the Inner Glow so far upward the effects began to obscure the face (bottom).

Now let's say you want to add a layer mask to the circular layer. Nothing fancy, just a gradient from black at the bottom of the image to white near the middle, as shown in the second example in Figure 13-28. Naturally, this makes the layer transparent at the bottom and opaque toward the middle, but it has an unexpected consequence. Rather than fading into view, that red Inner Glow effect begins meshing at the point where the layer becomes fully opaque. At first glance you might say, "Gee — guess I can't combine this type of layer mask here." Not at all — simply consult your Advanced Blending options and make some adjustments.

In the first image in Figure 13-29, the problem was fixed by simply selecting the Layer Mask Hides Effects option. This way, rather than constraining the effects, the layer mask fades them out just like a good gradient mask is supposed to do.

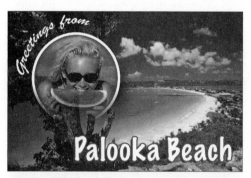

Figure 13-29: After fading out the Inner Glow and Stroke effects by selecting the Layer Mask Hides Effects option (top), the Transparency Shapes Layer option was deselected (middle). A vector mask was added and the Vector Mask Hides Effects option was deselected (bottom).

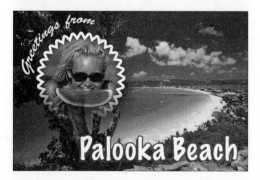

The second example of Figure 13-29 shows what happens when the Transparency Shapes Layer option is deselected (it's selected by default). Suddenly, the layer effects are no longer constrained by the boundaries of the circular layer and grow to fill the entire layer mask. Edge-dependent effects, such as Inner Glow, Drop Shadow, and Stroke disappear.

Next, a vector mask was added to the circular layer. To do this, the Ctrl key (⌘ on the Mac) was pressed and the layer mask icon at the bottom of the Layers palette was clicked. After selecting the Custom Shape tool and selecting a shape from the menu in the Options bar, the plus key (+) was pressed to make sure the Add to Path Area button was active and the shape was drawn. Photoshop automatically traced the Drop Shadow, Inner Glow, and Stroke effects around the shape. However, if for some reason this weren't to occur, you would only have to visit the Advanced Blending options and deselect the Vector Mask Hides Effects option.

Dumping whole color channels

That takes care of the most complex of the options. All that remain are the Channels options. Located directly below the Fill Opacity slider in the Layer Style dialog box, the Channels options let you hide the layer inside one or more color channels. For example, deselecting R makes the layer invisible in the Red channel, sending colors careening toward vivid red or turquoise (all red or no red, respectively), depending on the colors in the layers underneath.

Some opinion/advice here: You may find the Channels options useless. There are exceptions, of course — in a CMYK image it can prove helpful to drop a layer inside, say, the Black channel — but for general RGB image editing, they just don't offer much. This is a shame, because if slightly retooled, they could. For example, it might be nice to be able to control the translucency of a layer on a channel-by-channel basis, but instead you have only on or off controls. Maybe in a future version of Photoshop....

Making knockouts

Nestled in the middle of the Advanced Blending section of the Layer Style dialog box sits the Knockout pop-up menu (Figure 13-30). Knockouts turn the contents of the active layer into a floating hole that can bore through one or more layers behind it. It's like a layer mask, except that you can use it to mask multiple layers and any associated layer effects simultaneously. You can also apply layer effects to the knock-out, making them extremely flexible.

To create a knockout, you specify how deep the hole goes using the Knockout pop-up menu. Then use the Fill Opacity or Blend Mode option to define the translucency of the hole. The Knockout pop-up menu provides the following three options:

✦ **None.** This default setting turns the knockout function off. The layer is treated as a standard layer, not a hole.

Figure 13-30: Selecting Shallow or Deep from the Knockout pop-up menu determines how deep a hole you're going to punch through the layers of your image.

✦ **Shallow.** Choose this option to cut a hole through a group of layers in a set and expose the layer immediately below the set. In a clipping mask where the Blend Clipped Layers as Group option is deselected, Shallow burrows down to the layer directly below the base layer of the group. When the Blend Clipped Layers as Group option is selected, the knockout layer burrows down to the base layer in the group. If the layer resides inside neither a set nor a clipping mask, the Shallow option typically cuts a hole down to the background layer.

✦ **Deep.** The final setting bores as far down as the background layer, even if the knockout layer resides in a set. A notable exception occurs when working inside a clipping mask. If the Blend Clipped Layers as Group option is selected, Deep burrows down to the base of the clipping mask, just like Shallow.

Those are your Knockout options, but making one has less to do with what option you choose and more to do with your Fill Opacity settings, your layer order, and any groups you've got in place.

Figure 13-31 shows the basic ingredients used to create a knockout. In the example, there's a ratty scan of a crow from the local paper as the top — and eventual knock-out — layer (the crow is surrounded by transparency, represented by Photoshop's checkerboard pattern), followed by an Ode-to-Escher pattern beneath that. These two layers are placed in a group. Next down in the layer stack is a gradient that reflects the colors in the pattern. All these layers ride above a black background layer.

With the crow and pattern placed in a layer group, you can then use the two knock-out options to punch through to either the gradient layer (Knockout: Shallow) or through to the background layer (Knockout: Deep). Figure 13-32 shows the first option.

Figure 13-31: Using this collection of layers and layer groups, you can punch through to either the gradient layer or the black background layer — depending on the knockout option you use.

Figure 13-32: With the knockout option for the crow layer set to Shallow and its Fill Opacity set to 0 percent, the layer only punches through to the very next layer beneath the layer group — the gradient layer.

Not satisfied with the results, the crow's knockout option was pushed to Deep — knocking all the way through to the background layer — and included a gradient Stroke layer effect, reversing the colors used in the gradient layer. Last, the URL for the site for which this crow would serve as a logo was thrown in (Figure 13-33).

Figure 13-33: The final product has the crow layer's knockout option set to Deep, and a gradient Stroke layer effect.

Dropping Out and Forcing Through

Found at the bottom of the Blending Options panel of the Layer Style dialog box, the Blend If sliders are among Photoshop's oldest and most powerful compositing features. Pictured in Figure 13-34, these sliders permit you to drop out pixels in the active layer and force through pixels from lower layers according to their brightness values. You can even use them in combination with the Knockout option. For example, if you set the Knockout to Deep, you force through pixels from the background layer instead of from the layer immediately below the active layer.

Figure 13-34: Use the This Layer sliders to drop pixels out of the active layer, and the Underlying Layer sliders to force pixels through from lower layers.

Here's how the three Blend If options work:

✦ **Blend If.** Select a color channel from the Blend If pop-up menu to apply the effects of the sliders according to the contents of a single color channel. If you choose Gray, as by default, Photoshop bases the changes on the grayscale composite. Each time you select a different Blend If option, the slider triangles change to the positions at which you last set them for that color channel. Regardless of how you set the sliders, Photoshop applies your changes evenly to all channels in the image; the selected channel is merely used for the calculation.

✦ **This Layer.** This slider lets you exclude ranges of colors according to brightness values in the active layer. You exclude dark colors by clicking and dragging the black triangle to the right; you exclude light colors by clicking and dragging the white triangle to the left. In either case, the excluded colors disappear from view.

✦ **Underlying Layer.** The second slider forces colors from the underlying layers to poke through the active layer. Any colors outside the range set by the black and white triangles will not be covered and are therefore visible regardless of the colors in the active layer.

✦ **Preview.** Don't forget to select the Preview option on the right side of the Layer Style dialog box so you can see the effects of your modifications in the image window every time you adjust a setting.

These options are far too complicated to fully explain in a bulleted list. You'll probably want to read the following sections, if only to make the authors feel better for having taken the time to write them.

Color range sliders

The first Blend If slider, This Layer, hides pixels in the active layer according to their brightness values. You can abandon dark pixels by clicking and dragging the left slider triangle and abandon light pixels by clicking and dragging the right triangle. To demonstrate the Blend If options, look at the composite image first introduced in Figure 13-6. Figure 13-35 shows examples of each:

✦ To create the first example in Figure 13-35, the blend mode was first set to Screen. Then the black slider triangle was dragged until the value immediately to the right of the words This Layer read 130, thereby hiding all dark pixels whose brightness values were 130 or lower.

✦ To create the second example, the blend mode was changed to Multiply, the black slider triangle was reset to 0, and the white slider triangle dragged to 175, which hid those pixels with brightness values of 175 or higher.

✦ The final image in the figure shows the second face layered in front of the first. With the help of the This Layer slider, one can combine the Screen and Multiply blend modes to produce an image that is both lighter and darker than its background.

Click and drag the triangles along the Underlying Layer slider to force pixels in the underlying layers to show through, again according to their brightness values. To force dark pixels in the underlying image to show through, drag the black slider triangle; to force light pixels to show through, drag the white slider triangle. Figure 13-36 gives you an idea of what happens when you repeat the same values and procedure using this slider.

Bear in mind, like every other adjustment made in the Layer Style dialog box, changes made to the Blend If slider bars are temporary. These options hide pixels; they don't delete them. As long as the layer remains intact, you can revisit the Blend If sliders and restore hidden pixels or hide new ones.

Figure 13-35: Examples of modifying the blend mode and This Layer settings in the Layer Style dialog box. The final image shows the face that was set to Multiply, layered in front of the copy set to Screen, to get a high-contrast effect.

Figure 13-36: Here the Underlying Layer settings were changed to force through the darkest (top) and lightest (middle) pixels from the sculpted face and tranquil background layers. The third image shows the two effects combined.

Fuzziness

The problem with hiding and forcing colors with the sliders is that you achieve some pretty harsh color transitions. Although printed at high resolutions, both Figures 13-37 and 13-38 exhibit occasional jagged edges. Luckily, you can soften the color transitions by dropping and forcing pixels gradually over a fuzziness range, which works much like the Fuzziness value in the Color Range dialog box, leaving some pixels opaque and tapering others off into transparency.

To taper the opacity of pixels in either the active layer or the underlying image, press Alt (or Option on the Mac) and drag one of the triangles in the appropriate slider. The triangle splits in half, and the corresponding value above the slider bar splits into two values separated by a slash.

The left triangle half represents the beginning of the fuzziness range — that is, the brightness values at which the pixels begin to fade into or out of view. The right half represents the end of the range — that is, the point at which the pixels are fully visible or invisible. Figure 13-38 shows a bit of fuzziness applied to the This Layer slider. Here are the specifics:

✦ In the top example, the blend mode was set to Screen. After splitting the black slider triangle by Alt-dragging (Option-dragging on the Mac), one half of the triangle was set to 40 and the other to 220. Colors with a brightness value of 40 or darker turn transparent, fade into view from 41 to 219, and become opaque from 220 on up.

✦ In the second image, the Multiply blend mode was selected and both halves of the black triangle restored to 0. Then the white triangle was Alt-dragged (or Option-dragged) to split it. The left half of the triangle was moved to 20 and the right half to 190. The result is an extremely gradual drop-off. Those few pixels with brightness values from 0 to 20 are opaque, the pixels from 21 to 189 become gradually translucent, and pixels of 190 and brighter are transparent.

✦ Finally, both effects are combined on separate layers, with the Multiply effect on top. As shown in the bottom example in Figure 13-38, the result is a perfect blending of Multiply and Screen, with the background images showing through in the midtones.

The Underlying Layer slider works best when you're trying to force through very bright or dark details, like highlights or shadows. It also helps to work with a foreground layer that has lots of flat areas of color for the background to show through. Keeping these little factoids in mind, here's what was done to create Figure 13-38:

✦ In the top image, the Linear Dodge mode is applied to the face layer. First, most of the dark colors are dropped out by setting the halves of the black This Layer triangle to 80 and 230. Then the black triangle for the Underlying Layer slider is split, leaving the left half at 0 and moving the right half to 190. This forces through virtually all of the darkest pixels from the rear layers, fading them out as they get lighter.

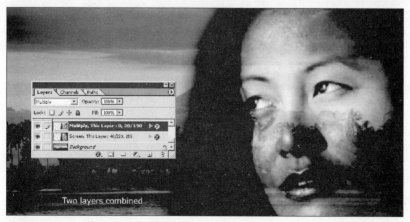

Figure 13-37: Alt-drag (or Option-drag on the Mac) a slider triangle to split it in half. You can then specify a range over which brightness values will fade into transparency.

Figure 13-38: Combining the Linear Dodge and Multiply blend modes, the This Layer and Underlying Layer sliders were both used to drop out foreground colors and force through background colors.

✦ In the second image, the face layer is duplicated and the Multiply mode applied. The black triangles of the This Layer sliders are set to 0, and the white triangle halves set to 110 and 180. Then, the Underlying Layer sliders are adjusted, setting the blacks to 0 also, and the white halves to 90 and 200.

✦ Finally, the two face layers are combined, with the Multiply effect on top. The result: A vibrant composition that contrasts elements of the palm-lined shore with the outline of the woman's face.

Whole Image Calculations

Image ⇨ Apply Image and Image ⇨ Calculations provide access to Photoshop's *channel operations*, which composite one or more channels with others according to predefined mathematical calculations. Once considered Photoshop's most powerful capabilities, channel operations have been eclipsed by the standard and more accessible functions available from the Layers and Channels palettes. Of course, there may come a day when Adobe decides to get rid of Apply Image and Calculations, but for now, they're part of the program, so you should at least read about them here.

Based on that encouraging and enthusiastic introduction to the Apply Image and Calculations commands, you'll no doubt be excited to learn what they do. The Apply Image and Calculations commands allow you to merge one or two identically sized images using 18 of the 23 blend modes discussed earlier plus two additional modes, Add and Subtract. In a nutshell, the commands duplicate the process of dragging and dropping one image onto another (or cloning an image onto a new layer) and then using the blend mode and the Opacity settings in the Layers palette to mix the two images together.

Although Apply Image and Calculations are more similar than different, each command fulfills a specific — if not entirely unique — function:

✦ **Apply Image.** This command takes an open image and merges it with the foreground image (or takes the foreground image and composites it onto itself). You can apply the command to either the full-color image or one or more of the individual channels.

✦ **Calculations.** The Calculations command works on individual channels only. It takes a channel from one image, mixes it with a channel from another (or the same) image, and puts the result inside an open image or in a new image window.

The primary advantage of these commands over other, more straightforward compositing methods is that they allow you to access and composite the contents of individual color channels without a lot of selecting, copying and pasting, cloning, floating, and layering. You also get two extra blend modes, Add and Subtract, which may prove useful.

The Apply Image and Calculations commands provide previewing options, so you can see how an effect will look in the image window. But thanks to the sheer quantity of unfriendly options offered by the two commands, it's probably a good idea to use them only occasionally, if at all. The Calculations command can be a useful way to combine masks and layer transparencies to create precise selection outlines. Apply Image offers the unique capability to composite images in different color models. For example, you could mix a layer or channel from an RGB image with another image in the CMYK mode.

However, if your time is limited and you want to concentrate your efforts on learning Photoshop's most essential features, feel free to skip Apply Image and Calculations. No one will know if you skip right on to the next chapter.

The Apply Image command

Channel operations work by taking one or more channels from an image, called the *source*, and duplicating them to another image, called the *target*. When you use the Apply Image command, the foreground image is always the target, and you can select only one source image. Photoshop then takes the source and target, mixes them together, and puts the result in the target image. Therefore, the target image is the only image that the command actually changes. The source image remains unaffected.

When you choose Image ⇨ Apply Image, Photoshop displays the dialog box shown in Figure 13-39. Notice that you can select from a pop-up menu of images to specify the Source, but the Target item — listed just above the Blending option — is fixed. This is the active layer in the foreground image.

If this sounds a little complicated, think of it this way: The source image is the floating selection and the target is the underlying original. Meanwhile, the Blending options are the blend modes pop-up menu and the Opacity value in the Layers palette.

Using the Apply Image command is a five-step process. You can always simply choose the command and hope for the best, but you'll get the most use out of it if you do the following:

STEPS: Applying the Apply Image Command

1. **Open the two images that you want to mix.** If you want to mix the image with itself to create some effect, just open the one image.

2. **Make sure that the two images are exactly the same size, down to the last pixel.** Use the Crop tool and Image Size command as necessary. (You don't have to worry about this step when mixing an image with itself.)

3. **Inside the target image, switch to the channel and layer that you want to edit.** If you want to edit all channels, press Ctrl+tilde (⌘-tilde on the Mac) to remain in the composite view.

Tip If you're thinking of editing a single channel, you should go ahead and display all channels on-screen. For example, after pressing Ctrl+1 (⌘-1) to switch to the Red channel, click in front of the RGB item in the Channels palette to display the eyeball icon and show all channels. Only one channel is active, but all are visible. This way, you can see how your edits inside the Apply Image dialog box affect the entire image, not just the one channel.

4. **Select the portion of the target image that you want to edit.** If you want to affect the entire image, don't select anything.

5. **Choose Image ➪ Apply Image.**

Obviously, that last step is a little more difficult than the concise instructions let on. In fact, it takes an entire section to explain all the details you'll need to know, and that section begins now.

Figure 13-39: The Apply Image dialog box lets you mix one source image with a target image and make the result the new target.

The Apply Image options

The following list explains how to use each and every option in the Apply Image dialog box:

✦ **Source.** The Source pop-up menu contains the name of the foreground image as well as any other images that are both open and exactly the same size as the foreground image. If the image you want to merge is not available, you must not have been paying much attention to Step 2. Press Esc to cancel, resize and crop as needed, choose Image ⇨ Apply Image, and try again.

✦ **Layer.** This pop-up menu lists all layers in the selected source image. If the image doesn't have any layers, Background is your only option. Otherwise, select the layer that contains the prospective source image. Select Merged to mix all visible layers in the source image with the target image.

✦ **Channel.** Select the channels that you want to mix from this pop-up menu. Both composite views and individual color and mask channels are included. Keep in mind that you'll be mixing these channels with the channels that you made available in the target image before choosing the command.

For example, if the target image is an RGB image shown in the full-color composite view, and you choose RGB from the Channel pop-up menu in the Apply Image dialog box, Photoshop mixes the Red, Green, and Blue channels in the source image with the corresponding Red, Green, and Blue channels in the target image. However, if you switched to the Red channel before choosing Apply Image and then selected the RGB option, the program mixes a composite grayscale version of the RGB source image with the Red channel in the target and leaves the other target channels unaffected.

✦ **Selection, Transparency, and Layer Mask.** If a portion of the source image is selected, the Channel pop-up menu offers a Selection option, which lets you apply the selection outline as if it were a grayscale image, just like a selection viewed in the Quick Mask mode. If you selected a specific layer from the Layer pop-up menu, you'll find a Transparency option that represents the transparency mask. If the layer includes its own layer mask, a Layer Mask option also appears.

None of the three options is particularly useful when you work in the composite view of the target image; you'll usually want to apply the Selection, Transparency, or Layer Mask option only to a single channel, as described in the section "The Calculations command."

✦ **Invert.** Select this option to invert the contents of the source image before compositing it with the target image.

✦ **Target.** You can't change this item. It merely shows which image, which channels, and which layers are being affected by the command.

✦ **Blending.** This pop-up menu offers access to 18 of the blend modes discussed in the section "Blend Modes" earlier in this chapter. The Dissolve, Hue, Saturation, Color, and Luminosity options are missing. Two additional options, Add and Subtract, are discussed in the section on the Add and Subtract options later in this chapter.

✦ **Opacity.** By now, you're well aware of how this one works. If you're not, stop now and go back and reread the book

✦ **Preserve Transparency.** When you're editing a layer in the target image — that is, you activated a specific layer before choosing Image ➪ Apply Image — the Preserve Transparency option becomes available. Select it to protect transparent portions of the layer from any compositing, much as if the transparent portions were not selected and are therefore masked.

✦ **Mask.** Select this option to mask off a portion of the source image. As stated previously, you can specify the exact portion of the target image you want to edit by selecting that portion before choosing the Apply Image command. You can also control which portion of the source image is composited on top of the target through the use of a mask. When you select the Mask option, three new pop-up menus and an Invert option appear at the bottom of the Apply Image dialog box. For complete information on these options, see the next section.

Compositing with a mask

The Mask option in the Apply Image dialog box provides a method for you to import only a selected portion of the source image into the target image. Select the Mask option and choose the image that contains the mask from the pop-up menu on the immediate right. As with the Source pop-up menu, the Mask menu lists only those images that are open and happen to be the exact size as the target image. If necessary, select the layer on which the mask appears from the Layer pop-up menu. Then select the specific mask channel from the final pop-up menu. This doesn't have to be a mask channel; you can use any color channel as a mask.

After you select all the necessary options, the mask works as follows:

✦ Where the mask is white, the source image shows through and mixes in with the target image, just as if it were a selected portion of the floating image.

✦ Where the mask is black, the source image is absent. Gray values in the mask mix the source and target with progressive emphasis on the target as the grays darken.

If you prefer to swap the masked and unmasked areas of the source image, select the Invert option at the bottom of the dialog box. Now, where the mask is black, you see the source image; where the mask is white, you don't.

Tip   You can even use a selection outline or layer as a mask. If you select some portion of the source image before switching to the target image and choosing Image ⇨ Apply Image, you can access the selection by choosing Selection from the Channel pop-up menu at the very bottom of the dialog box. Those pixels from the source image that fall inside the selection remain visible; those that do not are transparent. Use the Invert option to create an inverse of the selection. To use the boundaries of a layer selected from the Layer pop-up menu as a mask, choose the Transparency option from the Channel menu. Where the layer is opaque, the source image is opaque (assuming that the Opacity option is set to 100 percent, of course); where the layer is transparent, so too is the source image.

Add and Subtract

The Add and Subtract blend modes found in the Apply Image dialog box (and also in the Calculations dialog box) add and subtract the brightness values of pixels in different channels. The Add option adds the brightness value of each pixel in the source image to that of its corresponding pixel in the target image. The Subtract option takes the brightness value of each pixel in the target image and subtracts the brightness value of its corresponding pixel in the source image. When you select either Add or Subtract, the Apply Image dialog box offers two additional option boxes, Scale and Offset. Photoshop divides the sum or difference of the Add or Subtract mode, respectively, by the Scale value (from 1.000 to 2.000), and then adds the Offset value (from negative to positive 255).

Perhaps an equation will help. Here's the equation for the Add blend mode:

Resulting brightness value = (Target + Source) ÷ Scale + Offset

And here's the equation for the Subtract mode:

Resulting brightness value = (Target – Source) ÷ Scale + Offset

OK, so maybe that didn't help. Anyway, if equations only confuse you, just remember this: The Add option results in a destination image that is lighter than either source; the Subtract option results in a destination image that is darker than either source. If you want to darken the image further, raise the Scale value. To darken each pixel in the target image by a constant amount, which is useful when applying the Add option, type a negative Offset value. If you want to lighten each pixel, as when applying the Subtract option, type a positive Offset value.

Applying the Add command

The best way to demonstrate how the Add and Subtract commands work is to offer examples. To create the effects shown in Figures 13-40 and 13-41, use the woman's face and the background introduced way back in Figure 13-6. The difference is, for purposes of the Apply Image command, both photographs start out in separate image windows.

After switching to the Tranquil Background image and choosing Image ➪ Apply Image, the face image was selected from the Source pop-up menu. I selected the Add option from the Blending pop-up menu and accepted the default Scale and Offset values of 1 and 0, respectively, to achieve the first example in Figure 13-41. The face went blindingly white, much lighter than it would under any other blend mode, even the Dodge modes. To improve the quality and detail of the image, the Scale value was changed to 1.2 to slightly downplay the brightness values and an Offset value of –60 was used to darken the colors uniformly. The result of this operation is the more satisfactory image shown in the second example of the figure.

For the sake of comparison, the final example in Figure 13-41 shows what happens when introducing the background image into the face layer using the Add mode, with a Scale of 1.2 and an Offset of –60. Note that Add automatically respects the transparency mask of the face layer, regardless of whether or not you select the Preserve Transparency option.

Applying the Subtract command

To create the first example in Figure 13-41, the Subtract option was selected from the Blending pop-up menu, once again accepting the default Scale and Offset values of 1 and 0, respectively. This time, the face turns pitch black because the light values of the face are subtracted from the light values in the background image, leaving no brightness value at all. Meanwhile, shadow details such as facial features had little effect on the background because shadows range from very dark to black. Subtracting black from a color is like subtracting 0 from a number — it leaves the value unchanged.

The result seems too dark, so it was lightened by raising the Scale and Offset values. To create the second image in Figure 13-41, the Scale value was increased to 1.2, just as in the second Add example, which actually darkened the image slightly. Then the Offset value was raised to 180, thus adding 180 points of brightness value to each pixel. This second image is more likely to survive reproduction with all detail intact.

Subtracting the other direction — that is, applying the Subtract mode inside the face image — produces a radically different effect, as verified by the final example of Figure 13-41. Portions of the background are generally quite dark, so they have little effect when subtracted from the face. In fact, by Subtract standards, this is a remarkably successful blend.

Figure 13-40: Two applications of the Add blend mode from inside the flat Tranquil Background image (top and middle), each subject to different Scale and Offset values. When adding an image into an independent layer, Add always preserves transparency (bottom).

Figure 13-41: The Subtract command was used on the Tranquil Background image: the top image shows Scale and Offset values of 1 and 0 and the middle shows values of 1.2 and 180. When subtracting into the face, Subtract not only respects the transparency mask but also delivers a very different result (bottom).

The Calculations command

The Calculations command performs a different function than Apply Image, although its options are nearly identical. Rather than compositing a source image on top of the current target image, Image ➪ Calculations combines two source channels and puts the result in a target channel. You can use a single image for both sources, a source and the target, or all three (both sources and the target). Although Photoshop previews the effect in the foreground image window, the target doesn't have to be the foreground image. The target can even be a new image. But the biggest difference is that instead of affecting an entire full-color image, as is the case with Apply Image, the Calculations command affects individual color channels. Only one channel changes as a result of this command.

Choosing Image ➪ Calculations displays the dialog box shown in Figure 13-42. Rather than explaining this dialog box option by option which would take way too many pages and too much of your time the topic will be covered in a less structured but more expedient fashion.

When you open the dialog box, you select your source images from the Source 1 and Source 2 pop-up menus. As with Apply Image, the images have to be exactly the same size. You can composite individual layers using the Layer menus. Select the channels you want to mix together from the Channel options. In place of the full-color options — RGB, Lab, CMYK — each Channel menu offers a Gray option, which represents the grayscale composite of all channels in an image.

The Blending pop-up menu offers the same 20 blend modes — including Add and Subtract — found in the Apply Image dialog box. However, it's important to keep in mind how the Calculations dialog box organizes the source images when working with blend modes. The Source 1 image is equivalent to the source when using the Apply Image command (or the floating selection when compositing conventionally). The Source 2 image is equivalent to the target (or the underlying original). Therefore, choosing the Normal blend mode displays the Source 1 image. The Subtract command subtracts the Source 1 image from the Source 2 image.

Half of the blend modes perform identically regardless of which of the two images is Source 1 and which is Source 2. The other half — including Normal, Overlay, Soft Light, and Hard Light — produces different results based on the image you assign to each spot. Sound confusing? Don't worry. As long as you keep in mind that Source 1 is the floater, you'll be fine.

Tip   The only mode that can throw you off is Subtract, because you see Source 1 at the top of the dialog box and naturally assume that Photoshop subtracts Source 2, which is underneath it. Wouldn't you know it, though, this is exactly opposite to the way it really works? If you find yourself similarly confused and set up the equation backward, you can reverse it by selecting both Invert options. Source 2 minus Source 1 results in the same effect as an inverted Source 1 minus an inverted Source 2. After all, the equation (255 − Source 1) − (255 − Source 2), which represents an inverted Source 1 minus an inverted Source 2, simplifies down to Source 2 − Source 1. Are your eyes spinning like a cartoon character's yet?

As in the Apply Image dialog box, you can specify a mask using the Mask options in the Calculations dialog box. The difference here is that the mask applies to the first source image and protects the second one. So where the mask is white, the two sources mix together normally. Where the mask is black, you see only the second source image.

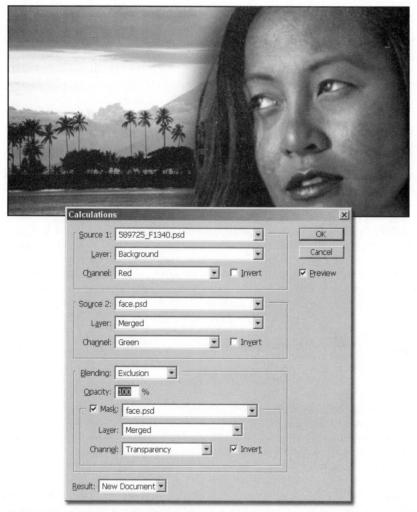

Figure 13-42: Use the Calculations command to mix two source channels and place them in a new or an existing target channel.

The Result option determines the target for the composited channels. If you select New Document from the Result pop-up menu, as in Figure 13-43, Photoshop creates a new single-channel image. Alternatively, you can stick the result of the composited channels in any channel inside any image that is the same size as the source images.

Combining masks

As described for the Apply Image command, the Channel pop-up menus may offer Selection, Transparency, and Layer Mask as options. Here, however, they serve a greater purpose. You can composite layer masks to form selection outlines, selection outlines to form masks, and make all sorts of other pragmatic combinations.

Figure 13-43 shows how the Calculations command sees selected areas. You see two selections, one for the penguin with his wings outstretched and one for penguins behind him that he directly overlaps. Whether you're working with masks, selection outlines, transparency masks, or layer masks, the Calculations command sees the area as a grayscale image. So in Figure 13-43, white represents selected or opaque areas, and black represents deselected or transparent areas.

Assuming that you've chosen Image ➪ Calculations and selected the images using the Source 1 and Source 2 options, the only remaining step is to select the proper blend mode from the Blending pop-up menu. Screen, Multiply, and Difference are the best solutions. Figure 13-44 shows the common methods for combining selection outlines. In the first example, the two have been added together using the Screen mode, just as in the preceding steps. In fact, screening masks and adding selection outlines are equivalent operations. To subtract the Source 1 selection from Source 2, the former was inverted (by selecting the Invert option in the Source 1 area) and the Multiply blend mode was applied. To find the intersection of the two masks, Multiply was applied without inverting.

The Calculations command doesn't stop at the standard three — add, subtract, and intersect. Figure 13-45 shows three methods of combining selection outlines that are not possible using single keystroke operations. For example, if you invert the Source 1 mask and combine it with the Screen mode, it's like inverting the first selection and adding it to the second. The Difference mode adds the selections but subtracts the area where they overlap, an operation known as exclusion. And inverting Source 1 and then applying Difference retains the intersection, subtracts the areas that do not intersect, and selects the area outside the penguin — which is equivalent to excluding two selections and then inverting the result. These may not be options you use every day, but they are extremely powerful if you can manage to wrap your brain around them.

Figure 13-43: The photo, followed by two selections expressed as grayscale images (also known as masks). The joyous, skyward-looking penguin will serve as the first source; the penguins behind him will be the second.

Screen
(same as add)

Invert + Multiple
(same as subtract)

Multiply
(same as intersect)

Figure 13-44: Here the penguin masks are combined using the Calculations command in concert with the Screen and Multiply modes, simulating the effects of adding, subtracting, and finding the intersection of two selection outlines.

Figure 13-45: Three nontraditional ways to combine selection outlines, all greatly facilitated by the Calculations command.

Summary

In this chapter, you learned to modify the Opacity and Fill values for image content, and discovered how these settings affect both layer content and the blend modes applied to your layers. You also learned more about blend modes, and how to use them to mix an active layer with those layers beneath it.

The use of filters and the sandwiching of heavily filtered images between unfiltered originals were also covered, along with the use of advanced blending options. You also discovered the need for and how to create knockouts, preserving transparency within an image. To further your ability to control visibility through your image layers, you learned to fade pixels according to brightness values using the Blend If sliders, and when and how to use the Add and Subtract blend modes.

In addition, you learned about mixing same-sized images with the Apply Image command, and how to modify selection outlines and masks using the Calculations command.

✦   ✦   ✦

Shapes and Styles

Adobe makes several products for creating art — going strictly by the products' intended or core strengths, you've got Photoshop for pixel-based images, Illustrator for vector images, and applications like After Effects for motion graphics and special video effects. Of course, in recent versions, Photoshop's capabilities have grown, and its core purpose has grown tentacles, reaching into areas previously considered the domain of other products. For example, Photoshop's shape tools make it possible to draw crisp, sharp shapes and lines, and they're the first topic in this chapter. The shape tools (there are six of them, for those of you who like to keep track of these things) create shape layers easily added to photos, scanned drawings or documents, or in your creation of totally original digital art.

Next up in this very stylish chapter are layer styles, which promise (among other things) quick and easy drop shadows and glows. This sort of "just add water" approach might sound like a cheap trick unworthy of inclusion in Photoshop's professional high-end tool set, but layer styles, whether used for quick effects such as shadows and glows or for loftier artistic goals, have proven to be an invaluable addition. Not only do layer styles give you painstaking control over drop shadows, glows, and bevels, but you can coat layers with gradients, patterns, and contoured wave patterns, as well as trace outlines around layers. When combined with the advanced blending options introduced in Chapter 13, layer styles blossom into a powerful special-effects laboratory, one of the most far-reaching and flexible Adobe has ever delivered. Furthermore, you can save the effects and reapply them to future layers.

✦ ✦ ✦ ✦

In This Chapter

Drawing object-oriented shapes

Setting polygon, line, and custom shape options

Combining shapes into compound paths

Defining custom shapes

Filling shapes with gradients, patterns, and imagery

Creating and modifying automatic layer effects

Working in the Layer Style dialog box

Duplicating effects

Saving effects and blending options as styles

✦ ✦ ✦ ✦

These features may not be the reason you set out to learn Photoshop in the first place, and there's no question that they'll take time and patience to fully understand. But you'll be rewarded with greater proficiency and versatility in the long run—and you'll be that much farther down the road to mastery when Adobe finally releases the application that does everything from brewing your coffee in the morning to putting soothing glows on even the most nightmarish image in your nightly dreams.

Drawing Shapes

Photoshop provides six *shape tools* that allow you to draw geometric and predefined shapes. By default, the shapes are separated into independent *shape layers*, which are a mix of objects and pixels. The vector-based outlines of the shapes print at the maximum resolution of your printer, while the interiors may consist of solid colors, gradients, or pixel-based patterns and images.

The pros and cons of shapes

Why should you love shapes? Let us count the ways:

✦ **Shapes are editable.** Unlike pixels, you can change a shape by moving points and control handles. Likewise, you can scale, rotate, skew, or distort shapes, or even transform specific points and segments inside shapes. Nothing is ever set in stone, and nothing weird happens when you resize or reshape.

✦ **Shapes help to disguise low-resolution images.** Sharply defined edges can add clarity to a printed image, and those sharply defined edges are achieved through the use of vector-based outlines.

✦ **You can color a shape with a layer style.** As shown later in this chapter, layer effects such as drop shadows and beveled edges, are equally applicable to shape layers as they are to standard image layers.

✦ **You can preview clipping paths directly in Photoshop.** Before object-oriented shapes, you were never quite sure if you traced an image properly with a clipping path until you imported it into InDesign, QuarkXPress, or some other application. Now you can preview exactly what your clipping path will look like directly in Photoshop.

✦ **Shapes expand with an image.** In Chapter 3, you were advised against using Image ➪ Image Size to resample an image upward on the grounds that it adds pixels without adding to the image quality. But you can enlarge shapes as much as you want. Because the shape is mathematically defined, it remains crystal clear no matter how big or small you make it. Layer styles likewise resize without a problem. Figure 14-1 shows a shape with a layer style applied (see exciting fill), resized (smaller original appears in upper left) with no loss of clarity or crispness to the edge.

Figure 14-1: Resizing doesn't require the addition of pixels to make up the difference, so making a shape layer's content larger doesn't result in a choppy edge or a muddied fill. Compare the shape on the upper left (the small original shape) with its resized copy in the lower right.

Now, of course this list of vector-based delights begs the question: If vectors are so great, why not forsake pixels and start drawing entirely with shape layers instead? Well, a shape can clip a continuous-tone photograph, but it can't replace one. Although there have been all kinds of experiments using objects and fractals, pixels are still the most viable medium for representing digital photographs. Because Photoshop's primary job is photo editing, pixels are (for the foreseeable future) the program's primary commodity.

Caution One downside to shape layers is compatibility. Photoshop has stretched TIFF and PDF files to accommodate any kind of layer—shape layers included—but that doesn't mean other programs have any idea what Photoshop is doing. Of all the formats, PDF is the most likely to work with other programs. Just be sure to proof the document on a laser printer before taking it to a commercial printer.

The shape tools

There's much to know and love about the shape tools. Now that you've read the list of Shape tool delights, get to know the tools so that your love can be real. To begin the getting-acquainted process, start by looking at the Shape tool and its flyout of alternate tools shown in Figure 14-2. You can click and hold the default Rectangle tool so that the flyout of six shape tools displays, or you can press U to select the Rectangle tool and then press U again (or Shift+U) to switch from one tool to the next. Each of the tools, no matter how you access it, works as follows:

✦ **Rectangle tool.** At one time, you had to draw a rectangular marquee and then fill it with color or a pattern in order to create a filled rectangle. This wasn't difficult, but it certainly wasn't very efficient or flexible. With the advent of the Shape tool, however, this antiquated method of shape creation is dead, and all you have to do to draw a rectangle is activate the Rectangle tool and then from one corner of the desired area (the area you'd like to see containing a shape) to the other, Shift-drag to draw a square, or Alt-drag (Win) or Option-drag (Mac) to draw the shape outward from the center. Oh, and if you want to set the fill color beforehand, set your foreground color to the color you want filling your shape. That's it.

Tip   While drawing a rectangle or any other shape, press the space bar to reposition the shape. Then release the space bar and continue dragging to resize the shape as you normally do.

Figure 14-2: There are six — count 'em — six shape tools. Click the Rectangle tool to display them en masse, or press U or Shift+U to switch between tools.

✦ **Rounded Rectangle tool.** When you select the Rounded Rectangle tool, a Radius value becomes available in the Options bar. If you think of each rounded corner as a quarter of a circle, the Radius value is the radius (half the diameter) of that circle. Bigger values result in more roundness.

✦ **Ellipse tool.** The Ellipse tool draws ovals. Shift-drag for circles; Alt-drag (Win) or Option-drag (Mac) to draw the oval outward from the center.

✦ **Polygon tool.** This tool draws regular polygons, which are straight-sided shapes with radial symmetry. Examples include equilateral triangles (3 sides), squares (4 sides), pentagons (5 sides), hexagons (6 sides), heptagons (7 sides), octagons (8 sides), decagons (10 sides), dodecagons (12 sides), and a bunch of other shapes with so many sides that they're virtually indistinguishable from circles. Type a Sides value in the Options bar to set the number of sides in the next polygon you draw. Or better yet, press the bracket keys, [and], to decrease or increase the Sides value from the keyboard. You can also draw stars and rounded shapes, as explained in the next section.

✦ **Line tool.** Wait a minute; how is a line a shape? Well, technically, the lines created with the Line tool *are* shapes — they're just very skinny rectangles, drawn at whatever angle you drag them. When you activate the Line tool, you get the chance to type a Weight value into the Options bar, which defines the thickness of the so-called "line." Next, just drag from point A to point B (assuming the line is intended to point to something or span a particular distance). The Options bar also allows you to apply arrowheads (true pointing jobs, or other shapes created by adjusting the width, length, and concavity of the heads) to one or both ends of your line. Snazzy.

✦ **Custom Shape tool.** The Custom Shape tool makes up for the fact that it's very hard (if not impossible) to do more than draw simple polygons with the other shape tools. If you opt to see all the available Custom Shape tool shapes, you're presented with more than 250 shapes — everything from stars to paw prints to flowers to things that look like the symbols in the Zapf Dingbats or Monotype Sorts font libraries.

Drawing the shape

The act of drawing a shape can be as simple as clicking and dragging with a tool. How that shape manifests itself, however, depends primarily on which of the first three Options bar buttons pictured in Figure 14-3 is clicked. The first option creates a new shape layer when you draw with the Shape tool. The second option creates a work path, available for inspection in the Paths palette. And the final option creates a pixel-based shape. In this latter scenario, Photoshop doesn't add a new layer; it merely recolors the pixels on the active layer. Although simple in theory, the program offers you a wealth of additional controls. Just to make sure you understand all the ins and outs, here's the long way to approach the process of drawing a shape layer.

STEPS: Creating a New Shape Layer

1. **Select the shape tool you want to use.** Remember, U is the keyboard shortcut for the shape tools.

2. **Specify the color.** Select a color for the shape from the Color palette (note the Color button on the Options bar, or use the Foreground Color button on the Toolbox). If you want to fill the shape with a gradient, a pattern, or an image, you can do that after you finish drawing the shape, as explained in the section "Editing the stuff inside the shape."

3. **Specify how you want to draw the shape.** Pictured in Figure 14-3, the first three buttons in the Options bar determine what the Shape tool draws. Because we're creating a shape layer, you'll want to make sure that the first button is selected.

Figure 14-3: Use the options in the Options bar to specify the appearance of a shape *before* you draw it.

4. **Modify the geometry options.** Click the down-pointing triangle to the right of the tool buttons in the Options bar (labeled in Figure 14-3) to see a pop-up palette of options geared to the selected shape tool. These permit you to constrain rectangles, ellipses, and custom shapes; indent the sides of a polygon to create a star; round off the corners of a polygon or star; and add arrowheads to a line.

The one unusual option is Snap to Pixels, which is associated with the two rectangle tools. Object-oriented shapes don't have any resolution, so their sides and corners can land in the middle of pixels. To prevent potential anti-aliasing in rectangles, select the Snap to Pixels option to precisely align them with the pixels in the image.

5. **Modify other tool-specific settings.** Depending on the tool, you may see options to the right of the Geometry Options triangle. The Polygon tool offers a Sides option; the Line tool offers a Weight option. When drawing a custom shape, click the Shape button to display a pop-up palette of presets, as shown in Figure 14-3. You can load more shapes by choosing the Load Shapes command or by choosing a predefined presets (.csh) file from the presets palette menu.

6. **Apply a layer style.** When drawing a shape layer, you can assign a layer style to your shape before drawing it. The Layer Style pop-up palette offers all presets available in the Styles palette, as discussed at the end of this chapter.

7. **Draw the shape.** Because you set the tool to draw a shape layer in Step 3, Photoshop automatically creates a new layer. As shown in Figure 14-4, the Layers palette shows a colored fill (labeled "Layer contents" in the figure) with a clipping path — or *vector mask* in Photoshop parlance — to the right of it, masking the fill. If you assigned a layer style, a list of one or more effects appears under the layer name.

8. **Switch tools and draw more shapes.** By default, Photoshop creates a new shape layer for each new shape that you draw. If you prefer to keep adding to the same shape layer so that all shapes will share the same fill, click the Add to Shape Area button in the Options bar (labeled in both Figures 14-3 and 14-5). Then draw a new shape.

Figure 14-4: A shape layer is actually a vector mask that masks a color or other contents directly in Photoshop. Here, you also see the polygon's options and the settings for drawing a star.

Have a (Masked) Ball

Still not dazzled by all these ways to perform near feats of magic with shape layers? Jeez — how jaded *are* you? Don't answer that. Instead, consider that you can also add a layer mask to a shape layer. Dazzled yet? That's right, Photoshop lets you combine pixel masking and vector masking on one layer, as shown in this figure.

Why would you do such a thing? The combination permits you to have soft and razor-sharp edges all in the same layer. For example, to achieve the results shown in the figure, you would Ctrl-click (⌘-click on the Mac) the vector mask and then load that as a layer mask by clicking the Add Layer Mask icon at the bottom of the Layers palette. In other words, the layer mask is identical to the vector mask. So what does that do for you? As shown in the next figure, you could then apply, say, the Gaussian Blur to the layer mask and then apply the Crystallize filter (or virtually any other filter that strikes your fancy). The result is soft filtered edges along the inside of the vector shape but then a hard edge after that. The layer mask masks the layer, and then the vector mask masks that. Cool, no?

Note   If you press Enter, Return, or Esc, the current shape layer is deactivated, signifying that you no longer want to add shapes to that layer. This change is visible in the Layers palette; notice that the vector mask thumbnail no longer has a selection border around it. To reactivate the layer, simply click the thumbnail.

You now have one or more shape layers that you can use as you please. From this point, it's a matter of editing the shape, as explained in the following sections.

Combining and editing shapes

So you've drawn your shape. Now what? Well, if you don't like a segment, you can change it. Don't like a point? Move it. Hate the entire shape? Delete it. Here's how:

✦ **Using compound path options.** As explained in Step 8 in the preceding section, you can draw multiple shapes on a single layer. Because they all share a single fill, Photoshop thinks of the shapes as being bits and pieces of a single, complex path. In drawing parlance, such a path is called a *compound path*. This presents Photoshop with a dilemma when the bits and pieces overlap. Because the pieces of the compound path share a fill, they could just merge together. Or perhaps you'd rather use one shape to cut a hole in the other. Or maybe you'd like the intersection to be transparent. You have to tell Photoshop which of these possible outcomes you prefer.

You specify your preference by selecting one of the last four compound path buttons, shown in Figure 14-5. (As mentioned previously, the first button, which is on by default, makes Photoshop create every shape on its own shape layer.) Click the second button or press the plus key (+) to add the new shape to the others, or press Shift as you draw shape after shape, adding each one to the active shape layer. Click the third button or press the minus key (–) to subtract the new shape from the others. The fourth button retains the intersection, while the fifth makes the intersection transparent.

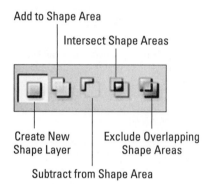

Add to Shape Area

Intersect Shape Areas

Create New
Shape Layer

Exclude Overlapping
Shape Areas

Subtract from Shape Area

Figure 14-5: The five compound path buttons; the last four are available when editing or adding to an existing shape layer.

✦ **Selecting shapes.** You have access to all but the first compound path button when selecting shapes with the arrow tool. Press A to get the black arrow tool — if you get the white arrow instead, press A again (or Shift+A if the Use Shift Key for Tool Switch option is selected) — and then click a shape to select it. Or Ctrl-click (⌘-click on the Mac) a shape when using a shape tool.

✦ **Moving and transforming.** Click and drag a selected shape to move it. Select the Show Bounding Box option in the Options bar to access the transformation controls. Or press Ctrl+T (⌘-T on the Mac) to enter the free transform mode. Then click and drag a handle to scale, drag outside the bounding box to rotate, and Ctrl-drag (Win) or ⌘-drag (Mac) a handle to skew or distort. If you need a transformation refresher, see Chapter 12.

✦ **Arranging and combining shapes.** After selecting a shape with the arrow tool, you can apply any of the four available compound path buttons. As you do, bear in mind that the topmost shape takes precedence, and the stacking order is entirely dependent on the order in which you draw the shapes – with more recent shapes in front. (The Layer ➪ Arrange commands affect whole layers; they can't be used to reorder shapes.) After you get the effect you're looking for, the relationship created by selecting two or more paths and clicking the Combine button in the Options bar causes Photoshop to fuse the selected paths into one.

Caution   Technically, you can combine multiple shapes that don't overlap, but it's not advisable. At first, the shapes behave as if they're grouped together. But try to combine other paths with them, and your results may not be what you expected.

✦ **Selecting points and segments.** Press A (or Shift+A) to get the white arrow tool, which selects individual points and segments. Move individually selected points by dragging them; transform such points by pressing Ctrl+T (Win) or ⌘-T (Mac). To select an entire shape, Alt-click (Win) or Option-click (Mac) it.

✦ **Adding and deleting points.** The best tool for reshaping a shape is the Pen tool. First select part of the shape with one of the arrow tools. Then click a segment to insert a point; drag on a segment to add a smooth point; click a point to remove it. You can also use the Convert Point tool, as well as any other technique that's applicable to paths.

✦ **Disabling a vector mask.** Shift-click the vector mask thumbnail in the Layers palette to turn it off and make visible the entire contents of the layer. Shift-click the thumbnail again to turn the vector mask on.

✦ **Duplicating a vector mask.** As far as Photoshop is concerned, shapes are just another kind of path. So it's not surprising that you can access the paths in an active shape layer from the Paths palette. Drag the *Vector Mask* item onto the tiny page icon at the bottom of the Paths palette to duplicate the shapes so you can use them elsewhere as standard paths (as discussed in Chapter 8).

✦ **Deleting a vector mask.** Click the vector mask thumbnail and then click the trash can icon at the bottom of the Layers palette to delete the shapes from the layer. You can also just drag the thumbnail to the trash can icon. To add a new shape to the layer, first choose Layer ➪ Add Vector Mask ➪ Hide All. Then draw shapes in the layer to expose portions of the layer's contents.

✦ **Defining your own custom shape.** If you create a shape that you think you might want to repeat in the future, select the shape with either arrow tool and choose Edit ➪ Define Custom Shape. Then name the shape and press Enter or Return. Photoshop adds the shape to the presets so you can draw it with the Custom Shape tool. If you want to keep it around, it's a good idea to save the shape with the Preset Manager, as discussed in Chapter 2.

The moral of the story is, shapes work a lot like paths, bearing many of the accuracy-maintaining and change-supporting attributes that you may have grown to love. If you're forgetting exactly what it is that you're supposed to love about paths, go back to Chapter 8 and rekindle your affection.

Editing for inner beauty

When it comes to shapes, all they have is their insides. Of course, you can apply a stroke to a shape, but that's discussed later, and it's only a veneer, anyway. So with the knowledge that a shape is only as good as what's inside it, here are a few ways to modify the color and general appearance of shape layers:

✦ **Change the color.** To change the color of a shape layer, double-click the layer contents thumbnail in the Layers palette. Then select a new color from the Color Picker dialog box. Or better yet, change the foreground color and then press Alt+Backspace (Option-Delete on the Mac).

✦ **Change the blending options.** You can change the blend mode and Opacity value for a shape layer using the standard controls in the Layers palette. Or double-click anywhere on the layer except the name or the layer contents thumbnail to display the Blending Options section of the Layer Style dialog box. As discussed in Chapter 13, these options work the same for shape layers as they do for normal layers. You can also apply or modify layer effects, as is explained later in this chapter.

✦ **Change the layer style.** Another way to apply or switch out layer effects is to apply a predefined style from the Styles palette. Just click a preset in the Styles palette and Photoshop automatically applies it to the active layer. After that, you can edit an effect by double-clicking its name in the Layers palette.

The Linked button labeled back in Figure 14-3 comes into play when you make a change to the layer style or color of a shape layer. If the button is selected, changes you make to the style or color are applied, or "linked," to the currently active shape layer. If the button isn't selected, the style or color change applies to the next shape layers you create.

✦ **Rename the shape layer.** Double-click the name of a shape layer to rename it. This works for renaming any kind of layer.

✦ **Fill with a gradient or repeating pattern.** Is a solid color fill too boring for you? Don't limit yourself. To fill the active shape layer with a gradient, choose Layer ➪ Change Layer Content ➪ Gradient. Or choose Layer ➪ Change Layer Content ➪ Pattern to apply a repeating pattern. Figure 14-6 shows the dialog box for each. Most of the options are familiar from the Gradient tool discussion in Chapter 6. The only new options are in the Pattern Fill dialog box. Scale lets you resize the pattern inside the shape; Link with Layer makes sure the shape and pattern move together; and Snap to Origin snaps the pattern into alignment with the origin.

After applying a gradient or pattern, you can edit it just by double-clicking the layer contents thumbnail in the Layers palette. Photoshop calls these kinds of editable contents *dynamic fills*.

Tip   You can reposition a gradient or pattern inside a shape just by dragging anywhere inside the image window while the dialog box is on-screen.

Figure 14-6: Gradients and patterns inside a shape layer are considered dynamic fills, which means you can edit them simply by double-clicking the layer contents thumbnail and editing the options shown here.

✦ **Make a color adjustment shape.** Where layer content is concerned, shape layers have unlimited potential. You can even fill a shape with a color adjustment. Just choose Levels ➪ Curves ➪ Hue/Saturation, or any of the other color-correction classics from the Layer ➪ Change Layer Content submenu. Read Chapter 17 for complete information.

✦ **Paint inside a shape layer.** Wish you could paint or edit the contents of a shape layer? Well, thanks to subtle genetic alterations to Photoshop's core subroutines, you can. Assuming the shape is filled with a solid color, gradient, or pattern (this technique is not applicable to adjustment layers), choose Layer ➪ Rasterize ➪ Fill Content. From this point on, the fill is no longer dynamic. This means you can't double-click its thumbnail to edit it. However, you can edit it like any other layer full of pixels, paint, clone with the Stamp tool, blur, sharpen, dodge, burn, whatever your heart desires.

✦ **Fill a vector mask with an image.** Applying a vector mask to an image is a more delicate operation. Fortunately, there are several ways to do it, so you can select your favorite. Method number one: Draw a shape not as a new shape layer but rather as a working path (see coverage of the shape drawing process earlier in this chapter). Then select the layer that you want to mask (it must be a floating layer, not the background) and choose Layer ⇨ Add Vector Mask ⇨ Current Path.

Tip

After establishing a work path, Ctrl-click (Win) or ⌘-click (Mac) the add layer mask icon at the bottom of the Layers palette to make the path clip the active image layer.

✦ **Go from clipping mask to vector mask.** What if you've already made a shape layer, and you want to fill that shape with an image? Again, there are a few approaches, but the easiest is to paste the image onto a layer in front of the shape layer. Then press Ctrl+G (Win) or ⌘-G (Mac) to group it with the shape layer.

✦ **Fuse image and shape layer.** That's enough to create the same visual effect as a shape masking an image, but it involves two layers instead of one. If you want for any reason to fuse the two layers together, you have to take a special approach. First, select the shape layer and choose Layer ⇨ Rasterize ⇨ Fill Content to convert the dynamic fill to pixels. Then select the image layer and press Ctrl+E (Win) or ⌘-E (Mac) to merge it with the shape layer below.

Skin-Deep Beauty: Layer Styles

With Photoshop 5, Adobe introduced a series of *layer effects* that automated the creation of shadows, glows, and beveled edges, applicable to individual layers in an image. Version 6 took those rudimentary tools several steps further, dramatically improving the quality of the existing effects and adding effects that overlay colors, stroke outlines, and create textures and contours. It also let you define exactly how effects are blended with background layers and permitted you to save them as preset *layer styles* for later use. Not much has changed since then, but why mess with a good thing, right? Photoshop's layer styles save you tons of time, make it easy to apply consistent effects throughout one or more images, and to also customize effects for a totally unique look.

To apply a layer effect, start with content on an independent layer, such as shown in the image in Figure 14-7. You can use any kind of layer, including a text layer (see Chapter 15) or a shape layer. After activating the layer in question, click the Add Layer Style icon at the bottom of the Layers palette — the one that looks like a florin (cursive *f*) — and choose any of the commands following Blending Options. Or double-click anywhere on the layer other than the layer name to display the Layer Style dialog box, and then select an effect from the left-hand list. Or, you can right-click (Ctrl + Click on the Mac) and choose Blending Options from the resulting pop-up menu. Once in the resulting dialog box, select or deselect the check box to turn the effect on and off; highlight the effect name to edit its settings. Figures 14-8 and 14-9 show inner shadows and inner and outer glows, and you can select from the following ten effects to apply similar effects to your images:

Figure 14-7: Select a layer (here a Shape layer, with the "Ornament 2" shape drawn), click the Add Layer Style icon at the bottom of the Layers palette and choose an effect from the menu shown at the top here. Then, as needed, adjust the settings in the very comprehensive Layer Style dialog box.

✦ **Drop Shadow.** The Drop Shadow command applies a common, everyday drop shadow, as seen in the first example of Figure 14-8. You can go with the default setting for the size, shape, and color of the shadow, or tweak it, specifying your own color, opacity, blend mode, position, size, and contour for the shadow. Photoshop makes it pretty — and pretty easy.

✦ **Inner Shadow.** This command applies a drop shadow inside the layer, as demonstrated in the second example in Figure 14-8. The command simulates the kind of shadow you'd get if you were looking through a piece of paper that was cut through — casting a shadow through the cutout onto the paper beneath it.

Figure 14-8: A 3-D look, with a shadow cast beneath the layer (left) or simulating a shadow seen through the layer (right) can be easily created with the Drop or Inner Shadow effects. Here, the same settings for both drop and inner shadow were used — Distance 10, Size 6.

✦ **Outer Glow.** The Outer Glow command creates a traditional halo, as seen in the first example in Figure 14-9. You can adjust the color, size, and other aspects of the glow, to meet your illumination needs.

✦ **Inner Glow.** This command creates a glow from within — applying the effect inside the layer rather than outside, as demonstrated in the second example in Figure 14-9.

Figure 14-9: Choose an Inner Glow or an Outer Glow, or both — effects can be applied in combination, too. Here, an Outer Glow emanates from the edges of the content (left) and an Inner Glow shows a fire within (right). Both glows are set to a Size of 10.

Tip

To create a neon strip around the perimeter of a layer, apply both the Outer Glow and Inner Glow commands. Figure 14-10 shows an example of a neon edge (top right), as well as other effects you can obtain by mixing and matching shadows and glows.

Figure 14-10: Combining two or more layer styles gives you virtually unlimited options — especially when you factor in all the options for each style. Clockwise from the upper left, these are: Drop Shadow and Inner Shadow, Outer Glow and Inner Glow, Inner Shadow and Outer Glow, and Drop Shadow and Inner Glow.

✦ **Bevel and Emboss.** The Bevel and Emboss option produces one of five distinct edge effects, as defined using the Style pop-up menu. The first four appear in Figure 14-11; the fifth one is exclusively applicable to stroked layers and requires the Stroke effect to be turned on. You can add a three-dimensional beveled edge around the outside of the layer, as in the first example in the figure. The Inner Bevel effect produces a beveled edge inside the layer. The Emboss effect combines inner and outer bevels. The Pillow Emboss effect reverses the inner bevel so the image appears to sink in and then rise back up along the edge of the layer. By tweaking the settings for a bevel, you can achieve a soft effect or a hard, chiseled look. The depth and intensity of the beveled effect is also adjustable.

Figure 14-11: Choose Layer ➪ Layer Style ➪ Bevel and Emboss to select one of several beveling options. Here, all four types of bevels are set to a Depth of 200 and a size of 10. Clockwise from the upper left, these are Outer Bevel, Inner Bevel, Pillow Emboss, and Emboss.

✦ **Contour and Texture.** The Contour and Texture options aren't actual effects unto themselves. Instead, you use them to modify the Bevel and Emboss effect. The Contour settings create waves in the surface of the layer that result in rippling lighting effects. Texture stamps a pattern into the surface of the layer, which creates a texture effect. Figure 14-12 illustrates these two options. On the left is an example of an Inner Bevel with the Contour set to Ring, and a Range of 30%. On the right is another example of Inner Bevel, this time with the Contour set to Ring, a Range of 30%, Texture set to Pattern (River Rocks Inverted).

Figure 14-12: Create even more interesting effects by adding Contour and/or Texture options to your beveled layer.

✦ **Satin.** This option creates waves of color, as in Figure 14-13. You define the appearance of the waves using the Contour options. One of the stranger effects, Satin can be difficult to predict. As long as you keep the Preview option selected, though, you can experiment and play with settings for all the styles you're applying until you see a desirable result.

Figure 14-13: Satin, all by itself, looks...satiny... but may not create a very distinct effect without a bevel to go with it. On the right, the satin effect is confined and its edges sharpened by adding a contoured Inner Bevel.

✦ **Color, Gradient, and Pattern Overlay.** These three options fill the layer with a coating of solid color, gradient, or repeating pattern, respectively. They work almost identically to the three dynamic fills available to shape layers, as discussed earlier in this chapter. All three can be quite useful when defining your own style presets. Figure 14-14 shows the Gradient and Pattern Overlay effects, applied with a drop shadow, too.

✦ **Stroke.** Use this option to trace a colored outline around a layer, as shown in Figure 14-15. The default stroke is rarely, if ever, useful — it's red and quite thick. You can change the color and thin it out as needed, and you can also choose to apply it to the inside or outside of the layer's edge. The Stroke effect is often preferable to Edit ➪ Stroke because you can edit it long after creating it. By comparison, Edit ➪ Stroke is a permanent effect.

Figure 14-14: On their own the Gradient (top left) and Pattern (top right) overlays are relatively interesting, but they really pop when combined with other styles, such as bevels, glows, and shadows. The bottom left and right images show a Gradient and Pattern Overlay, combined (opacity of gradient reduced to show pattern). The bottom right image also has an Inner Bevel applied.

Figure 14-15: On the left, a 3-pixel stroke (placed Outside) is added to the layer, on a shape to which the Satin effect was already applied. On the right, instead of Satin, a Bevel is applied with an Inside 5-pixel stroke.

To apply a blending option and see its options at the same time, click the name of the effect — for example, click the words "Drop Shadow" and you see the settings for the shadow in place. If you only wanted to see the options and not apply the style, this might seem like a problem, but it's no big deal to turn the style off (deselect the check box to the left of the style name) if you don't want it and just wanted to look at the settings.

If you prefer keyboard shortcuts, try some of these to help you navigate the Layer Style dialog box, which truly is a vast labyrinth of options: To switch between effects without turning them on or off, press Ctrl (or ⌘ on the Mac) plus a number key. Ctrl+1 (⌘-1 on the Mac) highlights Drop Shadow, Ctrl+2 (⌘-2) highlights Inner Shadow, Ctrl+3 (⌘-3) highlights Outer Glow, and so on, all the way to Ctrl+0 (⌘-0) for Stroke. You cannot get to Blending Options, Contour, or Texture from the keyboard.

The advantages of layer effects

The quick and automatic, almost "canned," nature of the layer styles may cause some more advanced designers and photographers to turn up their noses. It seems so amateur, after all, to just click a button and have a drop shadow appear, or to create a glow or beveled edge without having to go through countless steps and use several tools — expertly, craftily, with great skill and creativity. Of course, new Photoshop users and people who don't consider themselves expert designers will love layer styles, and we can all learn from those users and their very reasonable response.

Why sniff at something just because it's fast or easy? It would be harder and require more effort to push your car to the store than to drive it, but we all hop in and hit the gas rather than hoofing it to the mall. Why? Because the car was meant to make it fast and easy to get from place to place.

So hop in, hit the accelerator, and make use of layer styles with no guilt, no sense of taking the easy way out. Still feeling like a cheater? Consider these real benefits to using layer styles:

✦ They stick to the layer. Move or transform the layer and the effect tags along with it.

✦ The effect is temporary. As long as you save the image in one of the three layered formats — native Photoshop (PSD), TIFF, or PDF — you can edit the shadows, glows, bevels, overlays, and strokes long into the future.

✦ Layer effects are equally applicable to standard layers, shape layers, and editable text. This is unusual because both shape layers and editable text prohibit many kinds of changes.

✦ Thanks to the Contour presets, layer effects enable you to create effects that would prove otherwise exceedingly difficult or even impossible.

✦ You can combine multiple effects on a single layer.

✦ You can copy an effect from one layer and paste it onto another.

✦ You can save groups of effects for later use in the Styles palette.

✦ The effects show up as items in the Layers palette. You can expand and collapse a list of effects, as well as temporarily disable and enable effects by clicking the familiar eyeball icons.

✦ Layer effect strokes print as vector output, so they're guaranteed to be smooth.

That's it. How many good reasons do you need? Just accept that layer styles are great, use them, and just get over it.

Inside the Layer Style dialog box

The Layer Style dialog box offers 13 panels containing more than 100 options. The first panel, Blending Options, was discussed in Chapter 13. The remaining 12 panels are devoted to layer effects. Select the desired effect from the list on the left; use the check box to turn the effect on and off.

Although there are tons of options, most are self-explanatory. For example, you select a blend mode from the Blend Mode pop-up menu. (For explanations of these, see Chapter 13.) Next, you make the effect translucent by typing a value in the Opacity option box. Easy enough?

Other options appear multiple times throughout the dialog box. All the options that appear in the Inner Shadow panel appear also in the Drop Shadow panel; the options in the Outer Glow panel appear in the Inner Glow panel; and so on. Once you've played with the settings for an Outer Glow or a Drop Shadow, tweaking the settings for the Bevel or Stroke styles won't present any mystery. Figure 14-16 shows the Bevel and Emboss settings, which include most of the settings you'll encounter for any of the other effects — adjusting angles, contours, depth, size, spread, and opacity, as well as choosing where in the layer to place the effect in question.

Figure 14-16: The Bevel and Emboss settings are pretty representative of the other effects' settings — master these and you're ready to tackle anything the Layer Style dialog box throws at you.

The following items explain the options in the order in which they appear throughout the panels. Each option is explained only once, so if an option appears in multiple panels (or versions of the dialog box, for different styles, to put it another way), check this list for more information or clarification:

✦ **Blend Mode.** This pop-up menu controls the blend mode. So much for the obvious. But did you know that you can use the Blend Mode menu to turn an effect upside-down, select a light color and apply the Screen mode to change a drop shadow into a directional halo, or use a dark color with Multiply to change an outer glow into a shadow that evenly traces the edge of the layer? Don't be constrained by the traditional or allegedly intended uses of shadows and glows. Layer effects can be anything.

✦ **Color swatch.** To change the color of the shadow, glow, or beveled edge, click the color swatch. When the Color Picker is open, click with the eyedropper cursor in the image window to select a color from the layered composition. When editing a glow, you can apply a gradient in place of a solid color. Click the gradient preview to create a custom gradation or select a preset from the pop-up palette.

✦ **Opacity.** Use this option to make the effect translucent. Remember, a little bit of effect goes a long way. When in doubt, reduce the Opacity value for more subtle results.

✦ **Angle.** Associated with shadows, bevels, the Satin effect, and gradients, this value controls the direction of the effect. In the case of shadows and bevels, the option controls the angle of the perceived light source. With Satin, it controls the angle at which contour patterns overlap. And with a gradient, the Angle value represents the direction of the gradient.

Tip   You can avoid the numerical Angle option by either clicking and dragging inside the little compass or clock-looking device in the dialog box or simply dragging inside the image window. When the Drop Shadow or Inner Shadow panel is visible, click and drag inside the image window to move the shadow with respect to the layer. You can also drag the contour effect when working in the Satin panel. Other draggable effects include Gradient Overlay and Pattern Overlay, although dragging affects positioning, not angle.

✦ **Use Global Light.** In the real world, the sun casts all shadows in the same direction. By selecting the Use Global Light option, you tell Photoshop to cast *all* direction-dependent effects — drop shadows, inner shadows, and the five kinds of bevels — in the same direction. If you change the angle of a drop shadow applied to Layer 1, Photoshop rotates the sun in its digital heaven and so changes the angle of the pillow emboss applied to Layer 9, thus preventing you from applying conflicting shadows and other light-direction-dependent effects to different parts of the image.

Conversely, if you deselect the option, you tell Photoshop that physics and the laws of nature be damned, you're going to dictate where the sun is on each layer and there may be conflicts, but who cares. You can change an Angle value in any which way you like and none of the other layers will care — or at least they won't let on if they do.

Tip   If you have established a consistent universe, you can edit the angle of the sun by choosing Layer ⇨ Layer Style ⇨ Global Light. Change the Angle value and all shadows and bevels created with the Use Global Light turned option selection will move in unison. You can also set the Altitude for bevels.

✦ **Distance.** The Drop Shadow, Inner Shadow, and Satin panels feature a Distance value that determines the distance between the farthest edge of the effect and the corresponding edge of the layer. Like Angle, this value is affected when you click and drag in the image window.

✦ **Spread and Choke.** Associated with the Drop Shadow and Outer Glow panels, the Spread option expands the point at which the effect begins outward from the perimeter of the layer. If you were creating the effect manually (as discussed in Chapter 12), this would be similar to applying Select ➪ Modify ➪ Expand. Spread changes to Choke in the Inner Shadow and Inner Glow panels, in which case it contracts the point at which the effect begins. Note that both Spread and Choke are measured as percentages of the Size value, explained next.

✦ **Size.** One of the most ubiquitous settings, the Size value determines how far an effect expands or contracts from the perimeter of the layer. In the case of shadows and glows, the portion of the Size that is not devoted to Spread or Choke is given over to blurring. For example, if you set the Spread for Drop Shadow to 0 percent and the Size to 30 pixels, Photoshop blurs the shadow across 100 percent of the 30-pixel size. If you set the Spread to 100 percent, 0 percent is left for blurring. The shadow expands 30 pixels out from the perimeter of the layer and has a sharp edge. This makes the effect seem larger, but only the opaque portion of the effect has grown.

Size and Depth observe a similar relationship in the Bevel and Emboss panel, with Depth taking the place of Spread or Choke. When adjusting a Satin effect, Size affects the length of the contoured wave pattern. And in Stroke, Size controls the thickness of the outline.

✦ **Contour.** Photoshop creates most effects — namely shadows, glows, bevel, and the Satin effect — by fading a color from a specified Opacity value to transparent. The rate at which the fade occurs is determined by the Contour option. Click the down-pointing arrowhead to select from a palette of preset contours; click the contour preview to design your own. If you think of the Contour preview as a graph, the top of the graph represents opacity and the bottom represents transparency. So a straight line from top to bottom shows a consistent fade. A spike in the graph shows the color hitting opacity and then fading away again. Figure 14-17 shows a few examples applied to a new layer.

The most challenging contours are associated with Bevel and Emboss. The Gloss Contour option controls how colors fade in and out inside the beveled edge, as if the edge were reflecting other colors around it. The indented Contour effect — below Bevel and Emboss in the Layer Style list — wrinkles the edge of the layer so that it casts different highlights and shadows.

✦ **Anti-aliased.** If a Contour setting consists of sharp corners, you can soften them by selecting this option. Most presets have rounded corners, making anti-aliasing unnecessary.

✦ **Noise.** Associated strictly with shadows and glows, the Noise value randomizes the transparency of pixels. It's like using the Dissolve blend mode, except that you have control over how much randomization to apply. The Noise value does not change the color of pixels; that is the job of an option called Jitter.

Figure 14-17: Four different Contour presets, all set to a 60% Spread, with Noise set at 65%, 10 pixels in Size, and a 25% Range. Clockwise from upper left, the following Contours are in place: Linear, Cove-Deep, Ring, and Ring Double. The Contour setting controls how the halo drops from opacity to transparency, and sometimes back again.

✦ **Layer Knocks Out Drop Shadow.** In the real world, if an object was translucent, you could see through it to its own shadow. However, this turns out to be an unpopular law of nature with most image editors. So when creating a drop shadow, Photoshop gives us the Layer Knocks Out Drop Shadow option, which when selected makes the drop shadow invisible directly behind the layer. Deselect the option for a more natural effect.

✦ **Technique.** Moving out of the Shadow panels and into Outer Glow, the first unique option is the Technique pop-up menu. Also available when creating bevel effects, Technique controls how the contours of the effect are calculated. When a glow is set to Softer, Photoshop applies a modified Gaussian Blur to ensure optimal transitions between the glow and background elements. Your other option is Precise, which calculates the effect without the Gaussian adjustment. Of course, the effect may remain blurry, but strictly as a function of the Spread and Contour settings. Precise may work better in tight corners, common around type and shape layers. Otherwise, stick with Softer.

The Bevel and Emboss panel doesn't provide the same kind of blurring functions that you get with shadow and glow effects, so the Technique option works a bit differently. The default setting, Smooth, averages and blurs pixels to achieve soft, rounded edges. The two Chisel settings remove the averaging to create sawtooth abrasions into the sides of the layer. Chisel Hard results in thick cut marks; Chisel Soft averages the perimeter of the layer to create finer cuts. Increase the Soften value (described shortly) to blur the abrasions.

✦ **Source.** When working in the Inner Glow panel, Photoshop wants to know where the glow starts. It can glow inward from the perimeter of the layer (Edge, as seen in the left example in Figure 14-18) or outward from the middle (Center, as seen on the right in Figure 14-18).

Inner Glow set to Edge,
Size 25 pixels, Choke 7%, Contour
Ring, Range 50%, Jitter 20%

Inner Glow set to Center, Size 15 pixels, Choke 35%,
Contour Rolling, Slope Descending, Range 15%, Jitter 20%

Figure 14-18: The two options — Edge and Center — for the Source setting in the Inner Glow panel are applied to these two palm shapes. The Eraser was also applied (after the shapes were rasterized), set to Flowing Stars, affecting the Inner Glow's impact on the layer. After that, for more visual interest, a simple Inner Bevel was applied.

✦ **Range.** The two Glow panels and the Contour panel (subordinate to Bevel and Emboss) use Range values to modify the Contour settings. This value sets the midpoint of the contour with respect to the middle of the size. Figure 14-19 shows the two extremes — values less than 50 percent and greater than 50 percent — and their impact on the results.

Outer Glow Contour is Linear, Range 15%
Inner Glow has Ring Contour, Range 15%

Outer Glow Contour is Linear, Range 75%
Inner Glow has Ring Contour, Range 75%

Figure 14-19: Less is really more when it comes to Range settings. Here you see the same two hands shown in Figure 14-18, but now there's an Outer Glow, too.

✦ **Jitter.** Where the Noise value randomizes the transparency of pixels, Jitter randomizes the colors. This option is operable only when creating gradient glows in which the gradation contains two or more colors (not a color and transparency).

✦ **Depth.** The first unique Bevel and Emboss setting is Depth, which makes the sides of a bevel steeper or shallower. In most cases, this translates to increased contrast between highlights and shadows as you raise the Depth value.

The Texture panel includes its own Depth setting. Here, Photoshop renders the pattern as a texture map, lighting the white areas of the pattern as high and the black areas as low. The Depth value determines the depth of the texture. The difference is you can type a negative value, which inverts the texture. Meanwhile, you also have an additional Invert option, which, when selected, reverses the lights and darks in the pattern. So a positive Depth value with Invert selected produces the same effect as a negative Depth value with Invert deselected.

✦ **Direction.** When working in the Bevel and Emboss panel, you see two radio buttons: Up and Down. If the Angle value indicates the direction of the sun, Up, when selected, positions the highlight along the edge near the sun and the shadow along the opposite edge. Down, when selected, reverses things, so the shadow is near the light source. Presumably, this means the layer sinks into its background rather than protrudes from it. But, in practice, the layer usually appears merely as though it's lit differently.

✦ **Soften.** This value sets the amount of blur applied to the beveled highlights and shadows. Small changes make a big difference when Technique is set to one of the Chisel options.

✦ **Altitude.** The Bevel and Emboss panel includes two lighting controls, Angle and Altitude. The Angle value is just that: the angle of the sun with respect to the layer. Altitude, demonstrated in Figure 14-22, measures the height in the "sky" of the light source. A maximum value of 90 degrees puts the sun directly overhead (noon); 0 degrees puts it on the horizon (sunrise). Values in the medium range — 30 to 60 degrees — generally produce the best results. If you find the effect to be too sharp, you can temper it with the Soften setting, as also shown in Figure 14-20.

Figure 14-20: These two hands are each getting sun from different directions, using different Gloss Contour settings. On the left, the sun's Angle is 145 degrees, with an Altitude of 22 degrees with a Gloss Contour set to Cone Deep. The Size of the Bevel is 10, and a Depth of 200% is set. On the right, the Size and Depth of the Bevel are the same, but the sun is at a 45-degree angle, at an Altitude of 11 degrees. The Gloss Contour is Cone Inverted.

✦ **Scale.** The Texture and Pattern Overlay panels include Scale values, which scale the pattern tiles inside the layer. Values greater than 100 percent swell the pattern; values lower than 100 percent shrink it.

✦ **Link/Align with Layer.** When selected, this option centers a gradient inside a layer. If you want to draw a gradient across many layers, deselect the option to center the gradient inside the canvas. When editing a pattern, this option links the pattern to the layer so the two move together.

✦ **Position.** The final Layer Style option appears in the Stroke panel. The Position pop-up menu defines how the width of the stroke aligns with the perimeter of the layer. Photoshop can draw the stroke outside the edge of the layer, draw the stroke inside the edge, or center the stroke exactly on the edge.

Modifying and Saving Effects

After you apply a layer effect, Photoshop stamps the layer with a florin symbol (*f*), as shown in Figure 14-21. Clicking a triangular toggle switch lets you expand and collapse the displayed list of applied effects to permit more room for layers in the palette. If the triangle points up, it indicates the effects are displayed; if the triangle points down, the effects are hidden. From that point on, you can edit an effect by double-clicking its name in the Layers palette. Or double-click the florin symbol to display the Blending Options panel of the Layer Style dialog box.

Disabling effects

To temporarily disable all effects applied to a layer, choose Layer ➪ Layer Style ➪ Hide All Effects. Or, just click the eyeball in front of the word "Effects" in the Layers palette. Click the eyeball spot again to show the effects. You can likewise hide and show individual effects — without permanently disabling them — by clicking eyeballs. Photoshop even goes so far as to save hidden effects. This makes it easy to bring an effect back to life later without reentering settings.

 florin symbol

Figure 14-21: The florin symbol (*f*) indicates that one or more layer effects have been applied to the layer. Use the toggle to hide and show the list of effects.

To permanently delete an effect, click and drag it to the trash icon at the bottom of the Layers palette. To delete all effects, drag the word "Effects" to the trash.

Tip   Right click (or Ctrl + Click on the Mac) the florin symbol to display a pop-up menu from which you can choose Clear Layer Style. This deletes all effects on the layer in question.

Duplicating effects

After you apply an effect to a layer, the effect becomes an element that you can copy and apply to other layers. Select the layer with the effects you want to duplicate and choose Layer ⇨ Layer Style ⇨ Copy Layer Style. Or right-click (Control-click on the Mac) the layer name in the Layers palette and choose Copy Layer Style from the shortcut menu. Then select another layer, right-click (Win) or Control-click (Mac) it, and choose Paste Layer Style. To paste a copied effect onto multiple layers at a time, link them together (as explained in Chapter 12) and choose the Paste Layer Style to Linked command.

Note   The Copy and Paste Layer Style commands bypass the Clipboard. This means you can copy an image and then copy an effect without displacing the image.

Tip   Paste Layer Style duplicates all effects associated with one layer onto another. But what if you want to duplicate only a single effect? Just click and drag the effect name from one layer and drop it below another in the Layers palette. Be sure you see a bar below the layer name when dropping the effect — otherwise, it won't take.

Scattering effects to the four winds

When you apply an effect, Photoshop is actually doing all the manual layer work for you in the background. This means if Photoshop doesn't seem to be generating the precise effect you want, you can take over and edit the layers to your satisfaction. Choose Layer ⇨ Layer Style ⇨ Create Layers to resolve the automated effect into a series of layers and clipping masks. In some cases, a warning appears telling you that one or more attributes of an effect cannot be represented with layers. Go ahead and give it a try; you can always undo. If you like what you see, inspect it and edit at will.

Caution   After choosing Create Layers, you're on your own. From that point on, you lose the ability to edit the effects from the Layer Style dialog box (unless, of course, you decide to go back in time with the History palette).

Note   If you like layer effects (and you should, you really should), there's no doubt you'll eventually find yourself experiencing a curious phenomenon. After you've gone and applied a bunch of different effects, particularly Color, Gradient, and Pattern Overlays, your layer may no longer respond to blend modes.

Saving effects as styles

Photoshop lets you save layer effects and blending options for later use by creating layer styles, which appear as items in the Styles palette. There are three ways to create a style:

✦ **Click the New Style icon.** When working in the Layer Style dialog box, click the New Style icon to display the options shown at the bottom of Figure 14-22. Name your style and then select the check boxes to decide which settings in the Layer Style dialog box are preserved. The first check box saves the effects covered in this chapter; the second saves the blending options discussed in the previous chapter.

Create New
Style button

Figure 14-22: Click in the Styles palette (top) to display the New Style dialog box (bottom).

✦ **Click in the Styles palette.** Choose Window ➪ Styles to view the Styles palette. Then move your cursor inside the palette (shown in Figure 14-22) and click with the Paint Bucket. Photoshop responds by showing you the New Style dialog box (also shown in figure 14-22). Set the options as described previously.

✦ **Drag and drop a layer.** Start with both the Layers and Styles palettes open. Click and drag any layer, active or not, and drop it in the Styles palette. Again, Photoshop shows you the New Style dialog box.

After you press Enter or Return, Photoshop saves the style as a new preset. As with any preset, you can apply it to future images during future Photoshop sessions. Just click a style to apply it to the active layer, or drag the style and drop it on any layer name (active or not) in the Layers palette.

Don't forget that Photoshop ships with a big bunch of preset styles that you can explore at your leisure. Load a set of styles from the Styles palette menu, apply one to your favorite layer, and take a look at how it's put together in the Layer Style dialog box. This sort of play — testing, trying things on for size — is a really effective way to get a feel for the amazing variety of effects that are possible in Photoshop.

Tip A style may include blending options, layer effects, or both. Applying a new style to a layer replaces all blending options and effects associated with that style. If you would rather add the blending options and effects from a style to the existing blending options and effects associated with a layer, Shift-click an item in the Styles palette.

Note Sadly, there is no way to update a style — and even if you could, the style and layer are not linked, so updating the style would have no effect on the layer. Photoshop lets you create new styles, rename existing styles, and delete old ones — but that's about it.

Summary

In this chapter, you learned about object-oriented shapes and how to create them. Tricks for setting up your polygon, line, and custom shape options were covered, along with techniques for combining shapes into compound paths. You also learned about defining custom shapes and filling shapes with gradients, patterns, and images.

Because shapes reside on their own layers, you also learned about creating and modifying automatic layer effects, and how to apply layer-based styles through the Layer Style dialog box. This included must-have information on duplicating effects and saving effects and blending options as styles for future use.

✦   ✦   ✦

Fully Editable Text

In This Chapter

A brief history
of text in Photoshop

Creating vector type

Producing text-based
selection outlines

Rasterizing text

Adding type
directly to an image

Creating vertical
columns of type

Entering text
in a bounding box

Selecting and
editing existing text

Formatting text using
the Character and
Paragraph palettes

Using the Check
Spelling and Find
and Replace Text
commands

Creating text
on a path

Warping text layers

Converting
text to shapes

Photoshop's handling of type has come a long way. The journey has taken us from a Type tool that was about as forgiving and friendly as trying to write with an indelible-ink pen while riding in an old truck on a bumpy road to the very efficient, useful, and powerful tool we have today. If you weren't there for those bumpy rides, consider yourself lucky.

The lack of layers before version 3 was the biggest problem; once you typed the text, it was part of your image, take that, so there. There was also no spell-check, so if you weren't a spelling bee champion or the most accurate typist, it was very frustrating.

With the release of version 5 came something new and welcome — editable bitmapped type. Suddenly, you could type your text and then (gasp) go back and edit it. You could adjust the font, size, and color of the type, responding to the ubiquitous need for changes after first creating an image and adding type to it. You could adjust kerning and leading, giving you the ability to essentially typeset your images and not just rely on the defaults. Photoshop 5.5 expanded the type possibilities further, but with version 6, type finally evolved — into a graceful, intelligent part of the application. Some of the advances that users of Photoshop 5.5 and above can count on:

✦ Scale text as large as you want, without any repercussions, just as you could with any vector object — because the text is vector text.

✦ Create and edit text by typing directly on the image canvas — no more side trips to the Type tool dialog box required.

✦ Create text inside a frame and then apply paragraph formatting to control hyphenation, justification, indents, alignment, and paragraph spacing. You can even create lists that use hanging punctuation and control word and character spacing in justified text, as you can in Quark XPress, Adobe PageMaker, and InDesign.

✦ Make per-character adjustments to color, width, height, spacing, and baseline shift.

✦ Bend, twist, and otherwise distort text using a simple Warp Text dialog box instead of wrestling with the Wave filter or other distortion filters.

✦ Convert characters to shapes that you can then edit, fill, and stroke just as you do objects you create with the shape tools (which are explored in Chapter 14). Alternatively, you can convert text to a work path.

✦ Rasterize text so that you can apply any filters or tools applicable to ordinary image layers.

Photoshop 7 introduced a few useful type features, such as the type mask tools and the Check Spelling command, but you still couldn't put type on a drawn path, a feature by now standard to most illustration and layout programs. The closest Photoshop got was the Warp Text command, which is nice but fairly limited.

That limitation disappeared in Photoshop CS. Photoshop CS2, while not offering major changes in the Type tool, continues to offer great features with regard to creating and editing type. In addition to supporting text on a path, Photoshop can also create and modify text around and even inside shape layers and paths. Finally, Photoshop's text features are fully in line with those found in page-layout, illustration, and even advanced word-processing programs. You should be able to make them a regular part of your text routine in no time.

Note   This book doesn't cover the options for formatting Chinese, Korean, and Japanese text, which become available when you select the Show Asian Text Options check box on the General panel of the Preferences dialog box. Like the rest of Photoshop's type controls, these options should be familiar to you if you work regularly with type in these languages. But if you're not sure what each control does, check the Photoshop online help system for details.

The Five Flavors of Text

Photoshop's Type tool produces vector type. But that's not all. You can also create a text-based selection outline or work path, convert each character to a separate vector object, or create a bitmap version of your text. Here's a rundown of your type choices:

✦ To create regular text, select the Type tool (also known as the Horizontal Type tool), click in the image window, and begin typing. Or, to create paragraph text, click and drag with the Type tool to create a text frame and then type your text in the frame. You then can choose from a smorgasbord of type-formatting options, apply layer effects, and more. There are a few things you can't do, at least while the type is still considered type, such as apply the commands in the Filter menu or use the standard selection tools. You can apply these features if you rasterize the type, but that's covered later on. As for selecting text, the inability to use the selection tools on type is no big deal — you can just use the Type tool to drag through and select existing test, just like you use your mouse to select text in a word processor, or you can double-click the T icon on the Type layer, and all the text on that layer is selected.

✦ To produce a text-based selection outline, select the Horizontal or Vertical Type Mask tool from the Type tool flyout menu (see the upcoming Figure 15-5) and create your text. Photoshop covers your image with a translucent overlay, just like when you work in the Quick Mask mode, and your text appears transparent. You can apply all the same formatting options that are available when you work with ordinary text. When you commit the text (by clicking on another tool or clicking the green checkmark at the far right end of the Type tool's Options bar), the overlay disappears and your selection outline appears.

Tip

You can also create type masks using the regular Type tool. Simply type and format your text as usual. Then Ctrl-click (⌘-click on the Mac) on the type layer in the Layers palette to generate the selection outlines. What's the advantage of this approach? Simple — type on a layer is forever editable; a type mask is not. Therefore, it is hard to see any real advantage to using the Type Mask tools at all.

✦ After creating text, choose Layer ➪ Type ➪ Convert to Shape to turn each character into an individual vector shape that works just like those you create with the shape tools (covered in Chapter 14). You then can edit the shape of individual characters, an option explored in the section "Editing text as shapes" later in this chapter.

✦ Choose Layer ➪ Type ➪ Create Work Path to generate a work path from text. One reason to use this option is to create a clipping path based on your text.

✦ Finally, you can convert text to bitmapped type by choosing Layer ➪ Rasterize ➪ Type. After rasterizing the text, you can apply Photoshop's filters and other pixel-based features to it.

Caution

After you rasterize text or convert it to a shape or work path, you can't go back and run the spell-checker or change the text formatting as you can while working with vector text or type masks. So, be sure that you're happy with the spelling, capitalization, and font before you convert it. And here's a tip embedded right here in this caution: You can save a copy of the vector text in a new layer so that you can get it back if needed.

When you save images in the PSD, PDF, or TIFF format, you must select the Include Vector Data option to retain the vector properties of your text. If you deselect this option or save in a format that doesn't support vectors, Photoshop rasterizes your text. Saving a backup copy of the image in the native Photoshop format is a good idea.

Text as Art

Before diving into the nuts and bolts of creating text, it would probably be useful and inspiring for you to see some examples of out-of-the-ordinary ways to use type in your images. By combining the powers of the Type tool with the program's effects, filters, paint, and edit tools, and layering features, and you can create an almost unlimited array of text effects — you can even produce text that stands alone as a powerful image in its own right. Here goes:

✦ **Create translucent type.** Because Photoshop automatically creates type on a new layer, you can change the translucency of type simply by adjusting the Opacity value for the type layer in the Layers palette. Using this technique, you can merge type and images to create subtle overlay effects, as illustrated in Figure 15-1.

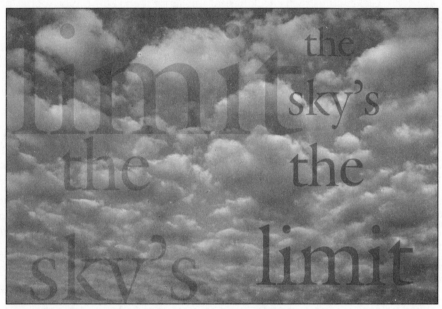

Figure 15-1: Not only is the type layer translucent due to reduced opacity (set to 30 percent on the smaller type object and 15 percent on the larger one), the type layer was easily duplicated and resized to create a graphic statement that enhances the meaning of the type itself.

✦ **Use type as a selection.** By creating a type mask, you can use type to select a portion of an image, and then move, copy, or transform it. To create Figure 15-2, for example, text from Figure 15-1 was used. The selection was copied (including the sky background, grabbed with the text selection) and pasted into a new image window. Further enhancements came through new type, a strip of sky on its own layer, and a text selection that was used to delete part of that sky.

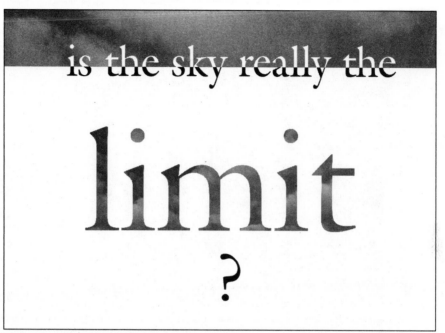

Figure 15-2: The word "limit" was turned into a selection in Figure 15-1 and then copied into this image, bringing the sky with it. A new type layer was also turned into a selection and cut away from the strip of sky at the top, creating the white top half of the text.

✦ **Apply layer effects.** Photoshop's layer effects are fully applicable to type. In Figure 15-3, the type object is again pasted into an image (the sky photo again), but a layer style was applied by right-clicking on the layer and choosing Blending Options from the pop-up menu. The Magic Wand tool was then used to select some of the clouds. That selection was copied and pasted it into a new layer, which was then subjected to the same pillow embossing applied to the type layer. A follow-up blurring with a Blur filter was the final touch.

✦ **Edit type as part of the image.** After rasterizing text (by choosing Layer ⇨ Rasterize ⇨ Type), you can paint type, erase it, smear it, apply a filter or two, or do anything else that you can do to pixels. In Figure 15-4, the Chrome filter was applied, and then the Edit, Transform, Distort command was used to make the type look like it's coming at the viewer. One little tip — the Image, Adjustments, Variations command was used to darken the sky layer a bit so that the type would stand out on top of it.

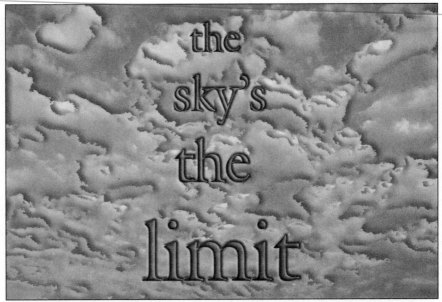

Figure 15-3: Text from Figure 15-1 is embossed with a deep and soft pillow effect. Portions of the clouds from the sky layer were duplicated and the same style applied — followed by a Gaussian Blur filter, for further cloud-like softness.

Figure 15-4: Here majestic-looking type, runs up into the sky, mirroring the statement both literally (thanks to the Chrome filter) and figuratively. Filters and Transform commands are no problem once you rasterize your type.

Using the Type Tool

In virtually any drawing or desktop publishing program, the Type tool enables you to create new and edit existing text. The following steps assume that you're creating text for the first time in your image — we'll talk about adding to existing text later.

STEPS: Creating Text in Photoshop

1. **Select the Type tool by clicking its icon in the toolbox or pressing T.** Photoshop activates the Type tool, displays the I-beam cursor in the image window, and displays type controls in the Options bar. You can access additional formatting options by displaying the Character and Paragraph palettes shown in Figure 15-5.

2. **Select the font, type size, and other formatting attributes from the Options bar and palettes.** The upcoming sections explain your options.

3. **Click or drag in the image window.** If you click, Photoshop places the first character you type at the location of the blinking insertion marker, just as a word-processing program works. You can press Enter or Return to insert a line break, or just keep typing and the text string will go on as long as you do. Of course, you're likely to run off the edge of the image window, but the type will be visible if you increase the Canvas size enough to accommodate it. Adobe calls this process of clicking on a single point and then typing, *point text*.

   Alternatively, you can create paragraph text by clicking and dragging rather than clicking with the Type tool to draw a frame — called a *bounding box* — to hold the text. Now your text flows within the frame, wrapping to the next line automatically when you reach the edge of the bounding box. If you create your text this way, you can apply standard paragraph-formatting attributes, such as justification, paragraph spacing, and so on. In other words, everything works pretty much like it does in every other program in which you create text in a frame. Pressing Enter or Return starts a new paragraph in the bounding box.

4. **Type your text.** If you make a mistake, press Backspace (Win) or Delete (Mac) to delete the character to the left of the insertion marker. On the PC, pressing Delete wipes out the character to the right of the insertion marker.

5. **Edit the text, if necessary.** To alter the character formatting, select the characters you want to change by clicking and dragging over them or using the selection shortcuts listed in Table 15-1. Then choose the new formatting attributes from the Options bar, Character palette, or Paragraph palette. If you don't select any text, paragraph formatting affects all text in the bounding box (the bounding box appearing only if you're working with paragraph text). If you're editing point text, any change you make to your formatting options while the cursor (insertion point) is still active within the text (but while no text is selected) will apply to new text that you type at the insertion point only. To make changes to existing text, the text must be selected. This enables you to change single characters or words to a new font, size, or color.

   You can also choose the Check Spelling command to spell-check your text, as well as use the Find and Replace Text feature to search for words in large chunks of text.

Figure 15-5: Choose Window ➪ Character or Window ➪ Paragraph to display the text palettes — the rest of the type tools and features appear automatically when you click to activate the Type tool.

6. **Click the OK (check mark) button on the right end of the Options bar to commit the text.** You can also simply click on another tool, such as the Move tool to let Photoshop know you've finished dealing with the Type layer for now. If you want to keep the Type tool active, use the OK button. Oh — and don't worry — "committing the text" simply takes you out of the text-editing mode. As long as you don't convert the text to a regular image layer, work path, or shape, you can edit it at any time.

Tip

If the Options bar is hidden or you just don't like reaching to click the button, you can commit text by selecting any other tool, clicking any palette but the Character or Paragraph palette, or pressing Ctrl+Enter (⌘-Return on the Mac).

Note

While you're in the text-editing mode, most menu commands are unavailable. You must commit the text or cancel the current type operation to regain access to them. To abandon your type operation, click the Cancel button — the "no" symbol at the right end of the Options bar — or press Esc.

When you create the first bit of type in an image, Photoshop creates a new layer to hold the text — you'll see the layer created as soon as you began typing changes from "Layer 1" (or whatever generic layer number you're up to in the image at hand) to a layer named using the first 30 characters of the text you've typed.

After you commit the type, clicking or dragging with the Type tool has one of two outcomes. If Photoshop finds any text near the spot where you click or drag, it assumes that you want to edit that text and, therefore, selects the text layer and puts the Type tool into Edit mode. For paragraph text, the paragraph is selected as well. If no text is in the vicinity of the spot you click, the program decides that you must want to create a brand-new text layer and responds accordingly. You can force Photoshop to take this second route by Shift-clicking or Shift-dragging with the Type tool, which comes in handy if you want to create one block of text on top of another.

Tip

If you don't like the type layer being named for the text you've typed, you can double-click the name in the Layers palette and type something new.

Creating Vertical Type

The Vertical Type tool is entirely dedicated to creating vertically oriented text. To get this tool, press T (or Shift+T) when the regular Type tool is active. In truth, the Vertical Type tool is nothing more than the standard Type tool lifted from the Japanese version of Photoshop. As shown in the first example of Figure 15-6, it creates vertical columns of type that read top to bottom, and right to left, as in Japan. If you want to make columns of type that read left to right, you have to create each column as an independent text block.

Tip

If you want to do what I do (and hey, who doesn't), type the text with the Horizontal Type tool, and then rotate it with the Edit ⇨ Transform ⇨ Rotate command, or press Ctrl + T (⌘ + T for Mac users) to enter Transform mode. In order to access these tools, however, you cannot be using the Type tool at the time — be sure to commit to your type and/or switch to the Move tool (which commits your type) before trying to do any kind of transformation. Then point to a corner handle, and when your mouse pointer turns to a curved arrow, click and drag to rotate the text. You can refer to the Options bar to see if you've achieved the desired angle of rotation.

After you click the image, you have access to the Standard Vertical Roman Alignment command in the Character palette menu. (If the palette isn't open, click the Display/Hide palettes button at the right end of the Options bar. It's labeled in Figure 15-5.) By default, the option is selected, which gives you upright characters such as those on the left side of Figure 15-6. Choose the command again to rotate the text 90 degrees clockwise and flip characters on their side, as shown in the right side of the figure. You can also deselect this feature before typing, which can be easier on the eyes if you're not from a country that typically reads right to left.

Figure 15-6: By default, vertical type reads right to left, as shown in the first example. If you deselect the Standard Vertical Roman Alignment option in the Character palette menu, your characters appear like those on the right.

You also can choose Layer ➪ Type ➪ Horizontal and Layer ➪ Type ➪ Vertical to change vertically oriented type to horizontally oriented type, and vice versa.

Creating and Manipulating Text in a Frame

If you click and drag the Type tool within your image window, Photoshop draws a bounding box to hold your text, as shown in Figure 15-7. If you want to create a bounding box that's a specific size, Alt-click (Win) or Option-click (Mac) with the Type tool instead of dragging. Photoshop displays the Paragraph Text Size dialog box, in which you can specify the width and height of the box. Press Enter or Return, and Photoshop creates the bounding box, placing the top-left corner of the box at the spot you clicked.

The bounding box looks just like the one that appears when you choose Edit ➪ Free Transform (and you can do this to point text as well), and some of its functions are the same with regard to paragraph text:

✦ Click and drag a corner handle to resize the box. Shift-drag to retain the original proportions of the box. The text reflows to fit the new dimensions of the box.

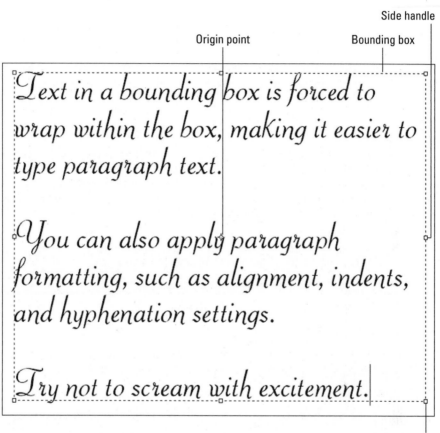

Figure 15-7: Click and drag the box handles to transform the frame alone or the frame and text together.

✦ Ctrl-drag (Win) or ⌘-drag (Mac) a corner handle to scale the text and box together. Ctrl+Shift-drag (⌘-Shift-drag on the Mac) to scale proportionally. To scale text alone, use the character formatting controls in the Options bar or in the Character palette. Either way, you can scale up or down as much as you want without degrading the text quality, thanks to the vector orientation of the Type tool.

✦ To rotate both box and text, move the cursor outside the box and drag, just as you do when transforming selections, crop boundaries, and layers. Shift-drag to rotate in 15-degree increments. The rotation occurs respective to the origin point, which you can relocate by dragging, as usual.

Using the bounding-box approach to type, however, has more benefits than simply being able to use the transformation techniques just described. You also can apply all sorts of paragraph-formatting options to control how the text flows within the bounding box, as described in the section "Applying paragraph formatting."

Note   Keep in mind that you also can scale, skew, rotate, and otherwise transform the text layer after you commit the text to the layer. In addition, you can size and rotate text using the options in the Character palette.

Tip   If you ever decide that you'd like to work with your text as regular text instead of paragraph text, cancel text-editing mode by clicking the OK or Cancel button in the Options bar. Then select the text layer and choose Layer ➪ Type ➪ Convert to Point Text. Photoshop splits the paragraph text into individual lines. To go back to paragraph text, select the text layer and choose Layer ➪ Type ➪ Convert to Paragraph Text.

Before you can modify any type, you have to select it. You can select all text on a text layer by simply double-clicking the layer thumbnail in the Layers palette. (This automatically switches you to the Type tool as well.) You can select individual characters by clicking and dragging over them with the type tool, as in any word-processing program. You also have access to a range of keyboard tricks listed in Table 15-1.

Table 15-1
Using the Keyboard to Select Text

Text Selection	Keystrokes
Select character to left or right	Shift+left or right arrow
Select entire word	Double-click the word
Select entire line	Triple-click the line
Move left or right one word	Ctrl+left or right arrow (⌘-left or right arrow)
Select word to left or right	Ctrl+Shift+left or right arrow (⌘-Shift-left or right arrow)
Select to end of line	Shift+End
Select to beginning of line	Shift+Home
Select one line up or down	Shift+up or down arrow
Select range of characters	Click at one point, Shift-click at another
Select all text	Ctrl+A (⌘-A)

After selecting type, you can replace it by typing new text — no need to delete and then type the replacement text. You can also cut, copy, or paste text (perhaps a paragraph you already have in a document) by pressing the standard keyboard shortcuts (Ctrl/⌘+X, C, or V) or by choosing commands from the Edit menu. You can undo a text modification by pressing Ctrl+Z (⌘-Z on the Mac) or choosing Edit ➪ Undo. However, if you type a few characters and then choose Undo, you wipe out all the new characters, not just the most recently typed one. If things go terribly wrong, press Esc or click the Cancel button in the Options bar to cancel the current type operation.

Tip

Selected text appears highlighted on-screen, as is the convention. If the highlight gets in your way, press Ctrl+H (Win) or ⌘-H (Mac) to hide it. This shortcut hides all on-screen helpers, including guides.

Applying Character Formatting

The Options bar gives you easy access to the collection of formatting controls shown in Figure 15-8. The Character palette and its palette menu, also shown in the figure, offer some of these same controls plus a few additional options. If you use Adobe InDesign, the palette should look familiar to you — with a few exceptions, it's a virtual twin of the InDesign Character palette.

To open the palette and its partner, the Paragraph palette, click the Display/Hide palettes button in the Options bar. Alternatively, you can choose Window ⇨ Character or press Ctrl+T (⌘-T on the Mac) when in the text-editing mode.

Figure 15-8: Photoshop provides many character-formatting controls in the Options bar and the Character palette, including increased support for OpenType features.

Note

You can apply formatting on a per-character basis. For example, you can type one letter, change the font color, and then type the next letter in the new color. You can even change fonts from letter to letter, either as you type or by selecting existing text character by character.

The next several sections explain the character-formatting options. All apply to both paragraph and regular text. You can specify formatting before you type or reformat existing type by selecting it first.

Tip   If you ever want to return the settings in the Character palette to the defaults, make sure that no type is selected. Then choose Reset Character from the bottom of the palette menu.

Font

Select the font (typeface) and type style you want to use from the Font and Style pop-up menus. Photoshop offers a full list of designer-style options. For example, whereas Times is limited to Bold and Italic, the Helvetica family may yield such stylistic variations as Oblique, Light, Black, Condensed, Insert, and Ultra Compressed. The fonts that are available through Photoshop are dependent on the fonts that are installed on your computer. In general, if you have access to a font in your word processor, you'll find it in the Font list in Photoshop, and vice versa.

Tip   If you're working with multiple linked text layers, you can quickly change the font or type style on all linked layers in one fell swoop by pressing Shift while choosing an option from the Font or Style pop-up menu.

The Character palette menu contains a whole lot of additional style options, which you can see in Figure 15-8. Click these options in the menu to toggle them on and off. A check mark next to the style name means that it's active; clicking it again will turn it off.

Many of the style options in the palette menu are also available in the row of buttons near the bottom of the palette. They include the following (in order from left to right on the palette itself and top to bottom in the palette menu):

✦ Faux Bold and Faux Italic enable you to apply bold and italic effects to the letters when the font designer doesn't include them as a type style. Use these options *only* if the Style pop-up menu doesn't offer bold and italic settings. You get better-looking type by applying the font designer's own bold and italic versions of the characters.

✦ Choose All Caps and Small Caps to convert the case of the type. Small Caps only works on text that was typed using the Shift key to capitalize the first letter in words — such As This Text Here. The Small Caps effect will make all the letters capital, but the ones typed with the Shift key will be taller.

Tip   Pressing Ctrl+Shift+K (Win) or ⌘-Shift-K (Mac) toggles selected text from uppercase to lowercase, as it does in InDesign and QuarkXPress. Remember that this shortcut works only when text is selected. If you're working with the Type tool and haven't selected text, the shortcut affects any new text you create after the insertion marker; with any other tool, it brings up the Color Settings dialog box.

✦ Superscript and Subscript shrink the selected characters and move them above or below the text baseline, respectively, as you might want to do when typing mathematical equations or chemical formulas. If Superscript and Subscript don't position characters as you want them, use the Baseline option to control them, as explained in the section "Baseline."

Tip

You can also "cheat" and type the tiny character in its own type layer and then use the Move tool to place it right where you need it — just above or just below the text (on another layer) to which it relates.

✦ Underline Left and Underline Right apply to vertical type only and enable you to add a line to the left or right of the selected characters, respectively. When you work with horizontal type, the option changes to Underline and does just what its name implies. Strikethrough draws a line that slices right through the middle of your letters.

Note

It's a bit confusing when working with vertical type to have two Underline options available in the menu — left and right — but only one Underline button on the palette itself. Activating the button turns on whichever type of underlining you used last; it's probably safer to ignore the Underline button when using vertical text and just use the palette menu.

Tip

Keep in mind that you can always produce these styles manually by using the Pencil or Brush tool — a choice that enables you to control the thickness, color, and opacity of the line and even play with blend modes. Just click to set a starting point, and then Shift-click to draw a straight line with these tools.

Although version 7 included support for a few OpenType font features, such as Old Style and Ligatures, Photoshop CS greatly expanded its OpenType support — and this support continues in CS2. Longtime favorites of designers and layout artists, OpenType fonts contain information for up to thousands of extra or alternate characters. The OpenType options are available only in the palette menu and appear dimmed unless an OpenType font is selected. Among the new options in Photoshop is Ordinals, which lets you automatically create those little letter combinations that are often coupled with ordered numbers, such as 1st, 2nd, 3rd, and so on. Swash gives you those pretty, swooping letters that often extend below the baseline and out under the other letters in the word.

One of the more useful OpenType options is Ligatures. A ligature is a special character that produces a stylized version of a pair of characters, such as *a* and *e*, tying the two characters together with no space between, like so: æ. The rest of the OpenType options are specialized, and you're more likely to use them in a layout program such as Adobe InDesign. As with the Asian fonts, if you're going to be working with them, you probably already know what they do. If you're still curious, check the manual for a description of each option. The expanded OpenType support is an improvement that most Photoshop users won't need, but it gives you some great new options nonetheless.

Size

You can measure type in Photoshop in points, pixels, or millimeters. To make your selection, press Ctrl+K and then Ctrl+5 (⌘-K and then ⌘-5 on the Mac) to open the Units and Rulers panel of the Preferences dialog box. (You must exit the Text mode to do so.) Select the unit you want to use from the Type pop-up menu. Of course, for the traditionalists among us, you can always choose Edit ➪ Preferences ➪ Units and Rulers if you're not good at remembering countless keyboard procedures.

Tip   You can type values in any of the acceptable units of measurement, and Photoshop automatically converts the value to the unit you select in the Preferences dialog box. For example, if you've set the units to pixels but want to type a point value when selecting a size, leave the units setting alone (don't reset the preference, in other words) and type the size, plus "pt," and Photoshop will change the size and display the pixel equivalent of the point size you typed in the Size field.

Cross-Reference   See Chapter 2 for more information about measurement units in Photoshop and how to choose the measurement units that are right for you and your individual projects.

If the resolution of your image is 72 ppi, points and pixels are equal. There are 72 points in an inch, so 72 ppi means only 1 pixel per point. If the resolution is higher, however, a single point may include many pixels. Therefore, you want to select the point option when you want to scale text according to image resolution and select pixels when you want to map text to an exact number of pixels in an image. (If you prefer, you can use millimeters instead of points; 1 millimeter equals 0.039 inch, which means 25.64 mm equals 72 points — not easy to remember, perhaps, but if you're working with other metric measurements in a project, it's good to know.)

Whatever unit of measure you choose, type is measured from the top of its *ascenders* — letters such as *b*, *d*, and *h* that rise above the level of most lowercase characters — to the bottom of its *descenders* — letters such as *g*, *p*, and *q* that dip below the baseline. That's the way it's supposed to work, anyway. But throughout history, designers have played pretty loose and free with type size. To illustrate, Figure 15-9 shows four fonts, including a display font (Tekton) and a script font (Brush Script). Each line is set to a type size of 180 pixels, and then placed between two solid lines exactly 180 pixels apart. The dotted horizontal lines indicate the baselines. As you can see, the only font that comes close to measuring the full 180 pixels is Tekton. The Brush Script sample is relatively minuscule, and neither Times New Roman or Arial comes close to spanning the entire 180-pixel height of the space between the two lines. So if you're looking to fill a specific space, be prepared to experiment — if you have your heart set on a particular font, you may end up applying a much larger font size than you expected in order for the type to take up the desired space in your design.

Tip   You can change the type size by selecting a size from the Size pop-up menu or double-clicking the Size value, typing a new size, and pressing Enter or Return. But the quickest option is to use the following keyboard shortcuts: To increase the type size in 2-point (or pixel) increments, press Ctrl+Shift+> (or ⌘-Shift-> on the Mac). To similarly decrease the size, press Ctrl+Shift+< (or ⌘-Shift-< on the Mac). Add Alt (or Option on the Mac) to raise or lower the type size in 10-point (or pixel) increments. If you select millimeters as your unit of measurement, Photoshop raises or lowers the type size by 0.71 mm, which is equivalent to 2 points.

Figure 15-9: Four samples of 180-pixel type set inside 180-pixel boxes. From top to bottom they are Tekton, Times New Roman, Brush Script, and Arial. As you can see, type size is an art, not a science.

Leading

Also called line spacing, *leading* is the vertical distance between the baseline of one line of type and the baseline of the next line of type, as illustrated in Figure 15-10. You set leading using the Leading pop-up menu in the Character palette, labeled in Figure 15-8. Again, either select one of the menu options or double-click the current value, type a new value, and press Enter or Return. Leading is measured in the unit you select from the Type pop-up menu in the Preferences dialog box.

If you choose the Auto setting, Photoshop automatically applies a leading equal to 120 percent of the type size. The 120 percent value isn't set in stone, however. To change the value, open the Paragraph palette menu and choose Justification to display the Justification dialog box. Type the value you want to use in the Auto Leading option box and press Enter or Return.

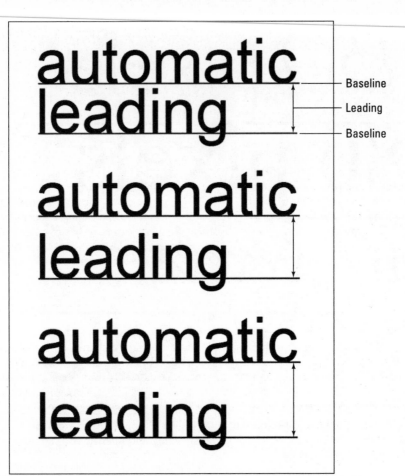

Figure 15-10: Leading is the distance between any two baselines in a single paragraph of text. Here, you can see three examples of 100-pixel type, each with a different leading. The top example is 80 pixel leading, the middle is 100 pixel leading, the bottom is 120 pixel leading.

Note   In most cases, you'll want to select Metrics or the Optical option (which was new in Photoshop CS), which relies on Photoshop's built-in artificial intelligence to examine the shapes of letters and determine the proper spacing. One advantage of Optical kerning is that it provides professional results with even the most nonprofessional custom fonts.

Leading Shortcuts

There are easier ways to adjust leading that allow you to tweak the settings in small increments and make your adjustments "by eye," tweaking until it looks the way you want it to. First, you can select the lines (or characters, in the case of kerning) that you want to adjust, and then click in the Leading field box in the Character palette. Now, use your up-arrow key to increase the leading or the down arrow to decrease it. Keep pressing the key/s until the desired spacing is achieved. Another technique: When adjusting the leading between a pair of lines, select the bottom of the two. Then press Alt+up arrow (Option-up arrow on the Mac) to decrease the leading in 2-point (pixel) increments and move the lines closer together. Press Alt+down arrow (Option-down arrow on the Mac) to increase the leading and spread the lines apart. To work in 10-point (pixel) increments, press Ctrl+Alt+up or down arrow (⌘-Option-up or down arrow on the Mac). Again, if you work in millimeters, the leading value changes by 0.71 mm and 3.53 mm — the equivalent of 2 points and 10 points, respectively. Obviously, the second method is going to be a thrill for those of you who love keyboard shortcuts, and the first one is more low-tech, but just as effective. Choose the one that's right for you.

Kerning

Technically, *kern* is the predetermined amount of space that surrounds each character of type and separates it from its immediate neighbors. (Some type-heads also call it *side bearing*.) Therefore, *kerning* became the verb based on that term — to adjust the kern around characters, thus changing the space between them. You establish kerning using the Kerning pop-up menu in the Character palette. Select 0 to use the amount of side bearing indicated by the specifications in the font file on your hard drive.

Some character combinations, however, don't look right when subjected to the default kern. The spacing that separates a *T* and an *h* doesn't look so good when you scrap the *h* and insert an *r*. Another pair that can look funky in certain fonts is an *r* and an *n*, which may look like an *m*. You may have your own pet pairs that look wrong to you in some or all fonts. You can select Metrics from the Kerning pop-up menu and ask Photoshop to look further into the font specifications and pull out a list of special-needs letter pairs. Once it has done that, it applies a prescribed amount of spacing compensation.

Figure 15-11 shows a few ways to fix the awkward spacing that default kerning can create. The first word pair shows the before and after uses the Optical kern to create enough spacing between the *r*'s. The second pair shows the before and after of using Metrics (auto kerning) on the *T* and the *r*. Finally, the third pair shows how to avoid having your *r* and *n* combination from looking like an *m* by using Manual kerning to create a slight separation.

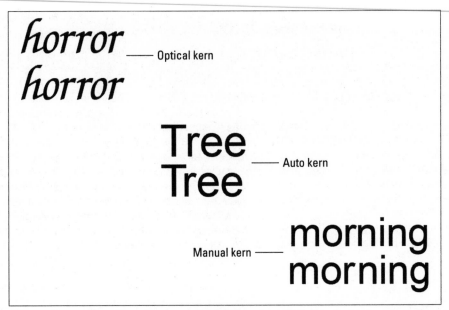

Figure 15-11: Examples of some problematic pairs and their adjusted versions.

Still, there may be times when the prescribed kerning isn't to your liking. To establish your own kerning, click between two badly spaced characters of type. Then select any value other than 0 from the Kerning pop-up menu. Or double-click the current kerning value, type a value (in whole numbers from –1000 to 1000), and press Enter or Return. Type a negative value to shift the letters closer together. Type a positive value to kern them farther apart. The last line in Figure 15-11 shows examples of tighter manual kerns.

Tip   To decrease the Kerning value (and thereby tighten the spacing) in increments of 20, press Alt+left arrow (Option-left arrow on the Mac). To increase the Kerning value by 20, press Alt+right arrow (Option-right arrow on the Mac). You can also modify the kerning in increments of 100 by pressing Ctrl+Alt+left or right arrow (⌘-Option-left or right arrow on the Mac). You can also just click in the Kerning field and use the up and down arrows on your keyboard to adjust the spacing until you like what you see. Of course, select the pair of improperly kerned characters first, so Photoshop knows which ones you want to adjust.

Incidentally, the Kerning and Tracking values (explained shortly) are measured in $\frac{1}{1000}$ em, where an *em* (or *em space*) is the width of the letter *m* in the current font at the current size. This may sound weird, but it's actually very helpful. Working in ems ensures that your character spacing automatically updates to accommodate changes in font and type size.

Fractional Widths and System Layout

If kerning is too annoying for you, try turning off Fractional Widths, found in the Character palette menu. (Click the option name to toggle the feature on and off.) When type gets very small, the spacing between letters may vary by fractions of a single pixel. Photoshop has to split the difference in favor of one pixel or the other, and 50 percent of the time the visual effect is wrong. It's better, in most cases, to turn the feature off and avoid the problem entirely.

However, turning off Fractional Widths isn't always a complete solution. A better choice when using small type for onscreen display — for example, in a graphic that will be used in a Web page — is to turn on the System Layout option in the Character palette menu. Doing so turns off anti-aliasing — in fact, choosing System Layout when you have an active text layer makes Photoshop automatically perform three tasks, the first of them setting anti-aliasing to None. This anti-aliasing method is the best option for small on-screen type and a particularly good choice when you need to match the type used in on-screen interface elements.

Tracking

The Tracking value, which you set using the pop-up menu to the right of the Kerning pop-up, is almost identical to Kerning. It affects character spacing, as measured in em spaces. The Tracking value even reacts to the same keyboard shortcuts. The only differences are that you can apply Tracking to multiple characters at a time, and Photoshop permits you to apply a Tracking value on top of either automatic (as in Metrics or Optical) or manual kerning. Tracking is usually applied to body text, such as paragraphs, whereas kerning is typically used in single lines of text, such as headlines or character pairs.

Horizontal and vertical scaling

The Size pop-up menu scales text proportionally. But using the two scaling options labeled, you can scale the width and height of letters individually. A value of 100 percent equals no change to the width and height. Type a value larger than 100 percent and you make the character/s larger. If you type a value lower than 100 percent, the character(s) shrink.

Photoshop applies horizontal and vertical scaling with respect to the baseline. If you're creating vertical type, the Vertical value affects the width of the column of letters and the Horizontal value changes the height of each character.

You also can distort text after you create it by applying the Edit ➪ Free Transform command to the text layer. If you want to keep the proportions of the letters — not stretching them in any one direction but simply enlarging or reducing them — press and hold Shift as you click and drag from a corner handle. You can also distort the text entirely by stretching it up, down, or totally out of whack with the Ctrl (or ⌘ on the Mac) key as you click and drag, making the text lean forward or backward. You can also distort the bounding box by skewing the sides, and the characters will reshape as a group to fit the new shape of the bounding box. This applies to both point and paragraph text, both of which are contained in a bounding box while you're in Free Transform mode. Now, if you apply the Free Transform approach to type resizing and then decide you want the letters back at their original proportions, just open the Character palette and type scaling values of 100 percent to reapply the size last set through the Character palette or Type Options bar.

Cross-Reference

See Chapter 12 for more information on the uses of Free Transform, most of which can be applied to type.

Tip

By converting text to shapes, you can reshape characters with even more flexibility, clicking and dragging points and line segments as you do when reshaping paths and objects created with the shape tools.

Baseline

The Baseline value, which you set using the bottom-left option box in the Character palette (see Figure 15-8), raises or lowers selected text with respect to the baseline. In the lingo of the typesetting world, this is called *baseline shift*. Raising type above the baseline results in a superscript. Lowering type results in a subscript.

Typically, when type is raised or lowered relative to the baseline, the shifted type is also shrunken — and both superscript and subscript formatting, when applied through any word processor, automatically includes a size reduction in the process. The baseline shift value in the Character palette doesn't shrink the type for you, though, so if you're trying to create the look of scientific notation, a chemical formula, or a footnote, you'll want to reduce the font size on your own. You can do that with the Size value, or by using the Superscript or Subscript style buttons at the foot of the Character palette instead of adjusting the baseline shift. By using these two buttons, you get both a shift and a size reduction — but no control over the amount of either. Examples of both superscript and subscript (with font size reductions also applied) appear in Figure 15-12.

The top example shows the 3 raised with the Superscript Style button on the Character palette. The asterisk was lowered with the Baseline Shift value, which is also in the Character palette. Its size was not changed. In the middle example, the 2s were reduced in size and then the baseline shift was adjusted to -30. Finally the bottom example creates a fraction by reducing the size of both numbers and adjusting their baseline shift. Then, the size of the slash was increased so its top lines up with the top of the first number and its bottom lines up with the bottom of the second number.

You can also raise type to create a built fraction, as shown in Figure 15-12. Select the number before the slash (the *numerator*) and type a positive value into the Baseline option box. Reduce the type size of the number (the *denominator*) after the slash but leave the Baseline value set to 0.

$$10^3=5(X*100)$$

Plants love CO_2
and H_2O.

$120/_{300}$

Figure 15-12: Here we've got scientific notation and a chemical formula. The last example is a fraction, and both numbers are reduced in size as well as shifted relative to the baseline.

Tip   Press Shift+Alt+up arrow (Shift-Option-up arrow on the Mac) to raise the Baseline value by 2 or Shift+Alt+down arrow (Shift-Option-down arrow on the Mac) to lower the value by 2. To change the value in increments of 10, add in the Ctrl key (or ⌘ key on the Mac).

Color

Click the Color swatch in the Options bar or in the Character palette to display the Color Picker dialog box. You can apply color on a per-character basis. The color you select affects the next character you type and any selected text. it is good to set the color first, and then start typing, at least in cases where all the type in the type layer will be the same color. By default, when you activate the Type tool, the current Foreground color is used and appears on the Options bar, which may or may not be convenient at the time. If it's not convenient, then use the Color swatch to open the Color Picker and choose another color.

Tip   When applying color to selected text, you can't preview the new color accurately because the selection highlight interferes with the display. Press Ctrl+H (⌘-H on the Mac) to toggle the selection highlight (as well as all other on-screen guides) on and off so that you can better judge your color choice.

Anti-aliasing

The Anti-alias pop-up menu, found both in the Character palette and in the Options bar, offers five choices — None, Sharp, Crisp, Strong, and Smooth. While it's nice to be all of those things (well, except "None"), type can only be one of them at a time, and whichever option you choose, the entire layer gets the effect. You can't apply anti-aliasing to individual characters on a layer, as you can other character formatting options.

In Figure 15-13, you can see several examples various anti-aliasing settings. Choose None from the pop-up menu, as in the first line, to turn off anti-aliasing (softening, for those of you who've forgotten what anti-aliasing does) and give characters hard, choppy edges, which is good for very small type. Sharp, in the second line, applies a slight amount of anti-aliasing, creating sharp contrast. Crisp is similar to Sharp but a little bit softer, as in the third line. If you notice jagged edges, try applying the Smooth setting as in the fourth line. Finally, if anti-aliasing seems to rob the text of its weight, you can thicken it up a bit with the Strong setting as in the bottom line. Sharp, Crisp, Strong, and Smooth produce more dramatic effects at small type sizes.

> # 30 pts. of choppy type, set to None.
>
> # Ouch! At 30 pts., set to Sharp.
>
> # Crisp at 30 big crackling points.
>
> # You big, Strong 30 pt. type, you.
>
> # Ah, 30 pts. and oh, so Smooth.

Figure 15-13: The differences can be subtle, and are most obvious on the smaller type. If you're not sure which one you need, try 'em all and see which one looks best on a case-by-case basis.

Applying Paragraph Formatting

Photoshop offers a comprehensive set of paragraph-formatting options, including ways to set your justification, alignment, hyphenation, line spacing, and indents. With the exception of the alignment, all these controls appear only in the Paragraph palette and affect text that you create inside a bounding box. (See the section "Creating and Manipulating Text in a Frame" for information about this method of adding text.) Point text, not typed into a bounding box, can be aligned, but the other paragraph formatting cannot be applied to it.

Figure 15-14 shows you the lay of the land in the Paragraph palette and also shows the palette menu, which offers additional paragraph formatting choices.

Figure 15-14: You can control the flow and position of text created in a bounding box by using the options in the Paragraph palette.

Note   If your bounding box contains more than one paragraph, you can apply formatting to individual paragraphs. Click with the Type tool inside a paragraph to alter the formatting of that paragraph only, or click and drag through the paragraph to select it, being careful not to select the blank lines above or below it. To format multiple paragraphs, you must click and drag over them. If you want to format all paragraphs in the bounding box, double-click the type layer thumbnail in the Layers palette, which selects every word, space, and blank line in the bounding box. You also can click the type and then press Ctrl+A (Win) or ⌘-A (Mac) to select everything in the box.

Tip   When no text is selected, you can restore the palette's default paragraph settings by choosing Reset Paragraph from the Paragraph palette menu.

Alignment

The alignment options, found both in the Paragraph palette and in the Type tool's Options bar, let you control how lines of type align with each other. This is close to what's occurring in a word processor when you use alignment tools there, but in the case of a word processor, you're also aligning relative to the page. As there is no page in Photoshop, the type is aligned to itself. If you're using the Horizontal Type tool, Photoshop lets you left-align, center, or right-align text. The lines on the alignment buttons indicate what each option does, and they change depending on whether you're formatting vertical or horizontal type — if you're using the Vertical Type tool, the lines run up and down, but align to the top (right alignment), bottom (left alignment), or vertical center (center alignment) of the button.

If you create bounding-box text, Photoshop aligns text with respect to the boundaries of the box. For example, if you draw a bounding box with the right alignment option selected, the text cursor appears at the right edge of the box and moves to the left as you type. For vertical type, the right-align and left-align options align text to the bottom and top of the bounding box, respectively. You must choose a different alignment option to relocate the cursor; you can't simply click at another spot in the bounding box.

When you create point text — that is, by simply clicking in the image window instead of drawing a bounding box — the alignment occurs with respect to the first spot you click and affects all lines on the current text layer.

Tip   You can change the alignment using standard keyboard tricks. Press Ctrl+Shift+L (⌘-Shift-L on the Mac) to align selected lines to the left. Ctrl+Shift+C (⌘-Shift-C on the Mac) centers text, and Ctrl+Shift+R (⌘-Shift-R on the Mac) aligns it to the right.

Roman Hanging Punctuation

One additional alignment option controls the alignment of punctuation marks. You can choose to have punctuation marks fall outside the bounding box so that the first and last characters in all lines of type are letters or numbers. This setup can create a cleaner looking block of text, and approximates the look of full justification in a word processor. Choose Roman Hanging Punctuation from the Paragraph palette menu to toggle the option on and off.

Justification

Speaking of justification, the justification options (second set of three buttons across the top of the Paragraph palette) adjust text so that it stretches from one edge of the bounding box to another. The different options, labeled in Figure 15-15, affect the way Photoshop deals with the last line in a paragraph.

Assuming that you're using the Horizontal Type tool, choose Justify left to align the line to the left edge of the box; Justify right to align to the right edge; and center to align the type exactly between the left and right edges. With Force justify, Photoshop adjusts the spacing of the last line of text so that it, too, fills the entire width of the bounding box. This option typically produces unsightly results, especially with very short lines, because you wind up with huge gaps between words. However, if you want to space a word evenly across an area of your image, you can use Force justify to your advantage. Click and drag the bounding box to match the size of the area you want to cover, type the word, and then choose the Force justify option. If you later change the size of the bounding box, the text shifts accordingly.

Photoshop lets you apply a couple of the justification options from the keyboard: Press Ctrl+Shift+J (⌘-Shift-J on the Mac) to left-align the last line; press Ctrl+Shift+F (⌘-Shift-F on the Mac) to Force justify the last line.

Figure 15-15: The justification options let you control how Photoshop adjusts your text when justifying it.

You can further control how Photoshop justifies text by using the spacing options in the Justification dialog box, also shown in Figure 15-15. To open the dialog box, choose Justification from the Paragraph palette menu. You can adjust the amount of space allowed between words and characters, and you can specify whether you want to alter the width (scaling) of *glyphs* — a fancy word meaning the individual characters in a font. Here's what you need to know:

✦ The values reflect a percentage of default spacing. The default word spacing is 100 percent, which gives you a normal space character between words. You can increase word spacing to 1000 percent of the norm or reduce it to 0 percent.

✦ The default letter spacing is 0 percent, which means no space between characters. The maximum letter spacing value is 500 percent; the minimum is –100 percent.

✦ For glyphs, the default value is 100 percent, which leaves the characters at their original width. You can stretch the characters to 200 percent of their original width or squeeze them to 50 percent.

To establish your ideal settings for these options, use the Desired column and type the values there. Whenever possible, Photoshop uses these values—when it can't accommodate you, it refers to the Minimum and Maximum options to tell it how much it can alter the spacing or character width when justifying text. If you wind up with text that looks like sardines jammed into the bounding box, increase the Minimum values. Similarly, if the text looks spacey and becomes hard to read, decrease the Maximum values. You can type negative values to set a value lower than 0 percent.

Note You can't type a Minimum value that's larger than the Desired value or a Maximum value that's smaller than the Desired value; nor can you type a Desired value that's larger than Maximum or smaller than Minimum.

Tip If you want a specific character width used consistently throughout your text, use the Horizontal scale option in the Character palette rather than the Glyph spacing option. You can apply Horizontal scaling to regular text as well as paragraph text.

As for the Auto Leading option at the bottom of the Justification dialog box, it determines the amount of leading used when you select Auto from the Leading pop-up menu in the Character palette. As luck would have it, if you're seeking information on additional paragraph spacing controls, the next sections pertain to just that.

Indents and paragraph spacing

The five option boxes in the Paragraph palette control the amount of space between individual paragraphs in the same bounding box (like the space before and space after settings control paragraph spacing in a word processor) and between the text and the edges of the bounding box (like adjusting margins, if you think of the bounding box as though it's a tiny page). Photoshop's indent options work the same as their counterparts in just about any word processing or graphics program that supports the use of type, so there shouldn't be any surprises there, either. Here are the details:

✦ Type values in the top two option boxes to indent the entire paragraph from the left edge or right edge of the box.

✦ To indent only the first line of the paragraph, type a value into the first-line indent option box, the second of three boxes on the right. Type a positive value to shove the first line to the right; Type a negative value to push it to the left, so that it extends beyond the left edge of the other lines in the paragraph, which creates a hanging indent.

✦ Use the bottom option boxes to increase the space before a paragraph (left box) and after a paragraph (right box).

Note In all cases, you must press Enter or Return to apply the change. To set the unit of measurement for these options, use the Type pop-up menu in the Units & Rulers panel of the Preferences dialog box; you can choose from pixels, points, and millimeters. As is the case with options in the Character palette, however, you can type the value using a unit of measurement other than that which is currently the preferred unit by typing the value followed by the desired unit's abbreviation ("in" for inches, for example, while pixels, points, or millimeters is the current unit). When you press Enter or Return, Photoshop converts the value to the unit you selected in the Preferences dialog box. (See Chapter 2 to find out more about setting preferences for units.)

Hyphenation

In most cases, you probably won't be typing text that requires hyphenation in an image. If you need to type that much text, you're better off doing it in your page-layout program (such as PageMaker, InDesign, or QuarkXpress), and then importing the image into that layout.

Even knowing that most images won't or shouldn't contain so much text that hyphenation is needed, Photoshop still offers the Hyphenate option in the Paragraph palette. When you select this option, the program automatically hyphenates your text using the limits set in the Hyphenation dialog box, shown in Figure 15-16. Choose Hyphenation from the Paragraph palette menu to display the dialog box and make any changes. If you move the dialog box so that you can see your text, the Preview option (on by default) can help you adjust the settings so that they meet the needs of your text and you won't have to close and reopen the dialog box in order to find the right settings.

Figure 15-16: If you want to hyphenate text in a bounding box, set the hyphenation controls here.

This dialog box, like several others related to text formatting, comes straight from Adobe InDesign and Illustrator. The controls work as follows:

✦ Type a value in the Words Longer Than option box to specify the number of characters required before Photoshop can hyphenate a word.

✦ Use the After First and Before Last options to control the minimum number of characters before a hyphen and after a hyphen, respectively.

✦ Type a number in the Hyphen Limit option box to tell Photoshop how many consecutive lines can contain hyphens.

✦ Finally, specify how far from the edge of the bounding box Photoshop can place a hyphen by typing a value in the Hyphenation Zone box.

✦ Deselect the Hyphenate Capitalized Words option if you want Photoshop to keep its mitts off words that start with an uppercase letter.

Line breaks and composition methods

When you create paragraph text that includes several lines, you may not like the way that Photoshop breaks text from line to line. Maybe you feel it's jumping the gun when it gets close to the right edge of the bounding box, or maybe you wish it were more conservative and didn't cram things so close to the sides of the box. Whatever your complaint is, you may be able to get some resolution by changing the equation that Photoshop uses to determine where lines break.

If you choose Adobe Every-line Composer from the Paragraph palette (available only if you have an active type layer with text in a bounding box), the program evaluates the lines of text in the active bounding box as a group and figures out the best place to break lines. In doing so, Photoshop takes into account the Hyphenation and Justification settings that are in place at the time. Typically, this option results in more evenly spaced text and fewer hyphens — and that's a good thing when most of the time, bounding boxes are small, and if you use a lot of long words, such as medical or legal terminology, your right edge (if your type is left-aligned) can end up with so many hyphens, it looks fringed.

Adobe Single-line Composer takes a line-by-line approach to your text, using a few basic rules to determine the best spot to break a line. The program first attempts to fit all words on the line by adjusting word spacing, opting for reduced spacing over expanded spacing where possible. If the spacing adjustments don't work for the given type, Photoshop hyphenates the last word on the line and breaks the line after the hyphen.

Remember, these options may not be an issue very often because most people don't create long blocks of text in Photoshop. If you want to control line breaks for a few lines of text, you can just create your text using the regular, point text method instead of putting the text in a bounding box. Then you can just press Enter or Return at the spot where you want the line to break, adding a hyphen to the end of the line if needed.

Checking your spelling

Found in the Edit menu, the Check Spelling command compares the words in your document with the words in Photoshop's built-in dictionary. If you've typed a word not found in the dictionary, Photoshop brings this to your attention by displaying the Check Spelling dialog box, shown in Figure 15-17.

The unrecognized word appears in the Not in Dictionary option box, and Photoshop offers you its favorite replacement word in the Change To option box. Other choices can be found in the Suggestions list. If you have made an error but none of Photoshop's suggested words is correct, you can type the correct word in the Change To option box.

After you have the appropriate replacement word in the Change To option box, click Change. If you've made the same mistake throughout the rest of the text, click Change All. If the highlighted word is correct but simply isn't in Photoshop's vocabulary, you can click Ignore to tell it to ignore the word, click Ignore All to tell it to ignore that and all other instances of the word. If you will be using the word a lot in the future, click Add to add the word to the dictionary — be sure it's spelled correctly, though, before doing so. After you finish making corrections, click Done to exit the dialog box.

Figure 15-17: The Check Spelling dialog box offers helpful suggestions for replacing words it doesn't recognize. Here, you can see that it doesn't recognize itself. Hmmmm...

If you're in the text-editing mode — defined as when there's an insertion marker blinking away in your text — Photoshop performs the spell-check on only the currently active layer, and on only the text that follows the placement of the insertion marker. In other words, if you want to check the entire text layer, make sure the insertion marker is at the beginning of the text block. Better yet, you can check spelling on all text layers at once. Just make sure that no active insertion marker appears in any text layer when you choose Edit ➪ Check Spelling, and make sure the Check All Layers option is selected in the Check Spelling dialog box.

Note   You can specify the dictionary used by the Check Spelling command by choosing Window ➪ Character and selecting a language from the pop-up menu in the bottom-left corner of the Character palette. The language you choose will also be used to determine proper hyphenation when words need to be broken over two lines.

Finding and Replacing Text

In the unlikely event that you find yourself entering tons and tons of text into an image in Photoshop, you can choose Edit ➪ Find and Replace Text to display the dialog box shown in Figure 15-18. As you may have guessed, this dialog box lets you search for specific words in your text and replace them with other text. In reality, you don't have to have a ton of text for this to be useful — even in an image with just a few type layers, it can be easy to miss something like a name, date, or even a symbol. Using Find and Replace can be a handy way to check for things you tend to do, such as pressing the percent (%) sign instead of the dollar sign ($) when typing, or forgetting to capitalize certain names or words. You can click Find Next to skip to the next instance of the content you are looking for.

Figure 15-18 Find one or all instances of a particular word, phrase, or single character and insert more desirable content.

If you've ever used a similar command in a word-processing program, there are no big surprises here. Type the word, phrase, or symbol you're looking for in the Find What option box. If you want to replace that word with another, type the new word in the Change To option box. Click Find Next to locate the next instance of your word relative to the placement of the insertion marker; click Change to replace the word; click Change All to replace all instances of the word; and click Change/Find to replace the current instance and highlight the next. The remaining options are common in Find/Replace commands found in word processors. The one quirky thing about

Photoshop's version of the command is that if you start your search in the middle of a text block, Photoshop doesn't wrap around when it reaches the end of the text and start looking at the beginning. That's the main use for the Forward option; leave it selected and Photoshop searches forward from the text insertion marker; deselect it and Photoshop looks backward.

Fitting Type on a Path

Photoshop CS introduced the ability to place text on a path, and this long-overdue feature remains in CS2. Even if you're not sure why this was considered long over-due or why tears would be shed if it was removed from Photoshop, this one little addition opens up a boatload of possibilities for the creation and placement of Photoshop text. Imagine not being able to draw text both around and inside paths you create with the shape tools. Imagine if all you had was the very limited Warp Text tool that gives you the ability to type text in an arc or along a wave. Yawn. In Photoshop CS2, not only can you place text along a path, you can even place two different pieces of text on the same side of the same path and keep them entirely independent of each other. Try *that* with the Warp Text option.

Perhaps the most impressive thing about Photoshop's new text-on-a-path capability is how easy it is to use. Instead of adding a new tool for creating path text or for cre-ating the text path itself, Photoshop lets you use the regular Type tool to create path text, and you can drop text of any font, size, or formatting onto any path in your image. The following steps show you how:

STEPS: Creating Text on a Path

1. **Draw a path in your image.** Press P to select the Pen tool and click to set a few points to form an open path in your image. If you create a path with a few smooth curves using the Bézier handles discussed in Chapter 8, you'll provide a better line for the type. You can add text to any path you draw, but hard edges (corners, spikes, very sharp curves) cause harsh character jumps, and they're usually quite undesirable.

2. **Add text to the path.** Press T to select the Type tool and position your cursor over the path you just drew. Your cursor changes from the normal I-beam to one with a little diagonal line crossing through the bottom of it. Click once to make the path active, and then type — it's that easy.

3. **Format your text to taste.** From here on, any formatting changes work just as they do when you're working with regular text, as shown in Figure 15-19. You can change the font, adjust the size of characters, increase the tracking to spread them out over the course of the path, and even alter the baseline for a specific character or word. Manual kerning comes in handy here, because Photoshop's Optical and Metrics options may not be able to accommodate the fine-tuning you require along certain paths and with certain words and fonts.

Note   When you create text on a path, the letters orient themselves according to the direction in which the path was originally drawn. For example, if you draw a path from left to right and then add text to it, the text appears as it normally does. But if you draw the path from right to left, no matter where on the path you click with the Type tool, the text appears upside-down and headed in the wrong direction.

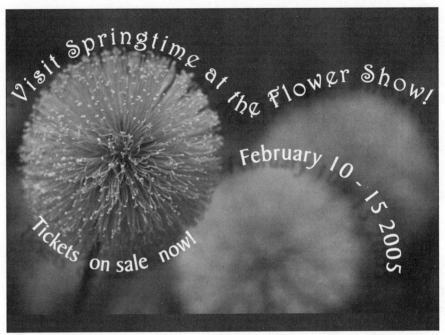

Figure 15-19: Just think how dull this same text might be if it just slogged along on a straight line.

4. **Press A to select the Arrow tool.** Position the cursor over a path with text on it until your pointer changes to an I-beam cursor with a black arrow protruding from one side. This protruding arrow tells you that you can now use the tool to slide the text along on the path. If you accidentally typed your text upside-down, drag the text all the way to the end of the path and continue dragging to pull the text back up to the correct side. You can also use the Arrow tool to move the path around your image. To do so, move the cursor away from the path until you once again see the standard Arrow tool cursor. Then click and drag to reposition the text and path in unison.

Tip   The point at which you originally click on a path with the Type tool is designated as the start point of your text. By default, an endpoint is also set at the far end of your line. You can click and drag this point with the Arrow tool back toward the start point to remove letters from the end of your text. Any letters that fall beyond your end point will get clipped and disappear.

By now, you're probably sitting on the edge of your chair, one hand clasped over your mouth, which fell open as you read about dragging your text along a path. Well, close your mouth and use that hand to keep turning pages — in the following steps, you learn to add text inside a closed path, and you wouldn't want to miss that, would you?

STEPS: Adding Text inside a Path

1. **With the Paths button selected in the Options bar, draw a shape.** Press U (or Shift+U) to select the desired shape tool and click the Paths button in the Options bar. Click and drag to draw a shape in the image. You can play it safe your first time out and draw a circle or a square, but you can also try something more interesting, such as the shape you see in Figure 15-20. When choosing a path, remember that sharp or tight corners can be difficult for the type to follow without losing legibility.

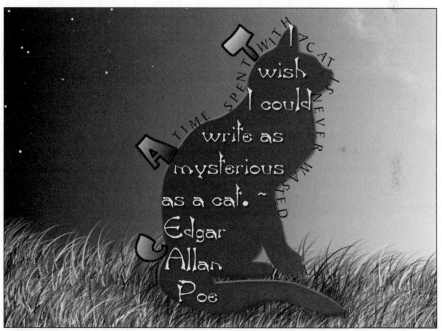

Figure 15-20: You can place text inside a shape and also around a shape. In fact, you can place more than one type layer along the same path — here indicated by the two strings of text in two different fonts.

2. **Select the Type tool and position your cursor at the center of the shape.** As you hover, the cursor should look like an I-beam with parentheses around it. Click once and begin to type your text. Notice that the text appears inside the shape, like the text inside the cat in Figure 15-20. The shape essentially functions as a bounding box for the text, thus molding the text to its shape. When you finish typing text, click the OK button in the Options bar.

3. **Choose Window ➪ Paths to bring up the Paths palette.** You should see the path you created with the shape tool, as well as an identical path that Photoshop created when you typed the text. This is just Photoshop's way of keeping track of how text has been typed on a path. Click the top Work Path item.

4. **Click somewhere else in the shape with the Type tool,** or Shift-click if necessary to force Photoshop to create a new text layer. Then type some new text. In Figure 15-20, note that there is text on the outer edge of the shape, too.

Note   Just because you've fit type to a path doesn't mean that the shape of the path is set in stone. On the contrary, you can reshape a path freely with the Convert Point tool — any text fitted to the path will bend and move according to your edits.

In addition to letting you place different layers of text at different areas of the same shape, Photoshop remarkably enables you to place different layers of text *on the same area* of one path or shape. Review Figure 15-20 and note that there are two strings of the same text on the perimeter of the shape — one of them is in Baker Signet, the other in Kruffy, an artistic font. Each string is on its own layer, yet they occupy the same space. How was this done? First, the original Work Path was reselected from the Paths palette, and then clicked around the same area in the path that was originally used. Then, two layers of text are placed on the same line. This was possible because every time you create a new set of path text, Photoshop actually duplicates the path you click — so presumably, you can have several type layers on what appears to be the same path. A word of caution, however — Photoshop can get bogged down very quickly while working with this new feature, and it might slow down or even seize up, depending on your hardware and memory. To eliminate the kind of delay that makes you want to scream and run around in circles (which can draw unwanted attention if you work in an office), you might want to do your basic formatting, such as setting the font and text size, on a regular text layer and then copy and paste it onto a path.

Warping Text

Prior to the addition of Photoshop's tools for fitting text to a path, the Warp Text feature was the only way to make editable text bend in a circle, an arc, or a wave. With the Warp Text tool, you can also control the nature of the warp, adjusting its horizontal and vertical distortion. You can choose from 15 different warp shapes and choose to curve type, distort it, or both.

Tip   You can warp paragraph text or regular text, but the warp affects all existing text on the layer, making it a little difficult to use on paragraph text and sometimes tricky to use on a long string of point text. If you want to reshape just a part of a line of text — for example, to make the last few letters in a word bend upward — put that bit of text on its own layer and position the two layers so that the text looks continuous.

Note   You can't warp type to which you've applied the faux bold style (applied through the Character palette), nor can you warp bitmap fonts or fonts for which the designer hasn't provided the paths, or outlines, that make up the font characters.

To warp text, select the text layer, click the text warp button in the Options bar, labeled in Figure 15-21, or choose Layer ➪ Type ➪ Warp Text. Photoshop displays the Warp Text dialog box, shown in the figure.

Figure 15-21: Use the controls in the Warp Text dialog box to bend, stretch, and curve type.

After choosing a warp style from the Style pop-up menu, set the orientation of the warp by selecting the Horizontal or Vertical radio button. Then adjust the Bend, Horizontal Distortion, and Vertical Distortion sliders until you get an effect that fits your needs. You can preview your changes in the image window.

Note You can warp text that you create on a path, but you basically lose all ability to perform any more path-related adjustments with the text.

Some tips for making effective use of the Warp tool:

✦ When you select the Horizontal radio button, the warp occurs as the shape in the Style pop-up menu suggests. If you choose Vertical, the warp is applied as if you turned the shape on its side.

✦ Use the Bend value to change the direction of the curve. A positive Bend value curves the text upward, and a negative value curves the text downward.

✦ You can use the Horizontal and Vertical Distortion options to create perspective effects. Horizontal Distortion puts the origin point of the perspective to the left if you type a positive value and to the right if you type a negative value.

✦ Vertical Distortion places the origin point above the text if you type a positive value and below the text if you type a negative value.

✦ If you edit warped text, Photoshop reapplies the warp to the layer after you finish editing the text.

Tip

The effects of a warp can be enhanced by tweaking the tracking, kerning, and other character-spacing and scaling formatting. If you have trouble achieving the distortion or perspective effect you're after, try choosing Edit ➪ Free Transform to manipulate the text layer. Remember that you must get out of the text-editing mode to access the Free Transform command.

Editing Text as Shapes

As stated earlier in this chapter, you can convert each letter in a text layer to individual shapes by choosing Layer ➪ Type ➪ Convert to Shape. The command converts all text on a layer, so if you want to turn only some of your text to shapes, put that text on its own layer and leave the text that must remain editable on its own layer, too. If the Convert to Shape command is dimmed, that means you're in the text-editing mode — to leave that mode and make the command accessible, click the OK (check mark) or Cancel ("no" symbol) button in the Options bar to exit the editing mode.

After you make the conversion to a shape, each character works just like a shape that you create with the shape tools. Photoshop creates points and line segments as it sees fit for each letter, as shown in Figure 15-22. This enables you to fool with the shape of each letter by clicking and dragging points and segments, as you can see in Figure 15-22. You can also apply all the same effects to your new text shapes as you can to any shape.

Cross-Reference

See Chapter 14 for a complete list of your options.

Caution

Before you convert text to shapes, make sure that you don't need to make further changes to character or paragraph formatting or do any editing. Photoshop sees your text purely as shapes after the conversion, so you can't edit the text using the Type tool anymore. For safety's sake, you should save the text to a new layer or image before choosing Convert to Shape — you can hide the backup layer and only use it if it turns out your converted text needs editing.

Figure 15-22: Sure, you can make editable text look cool, but can you reshape the individual letters? Not without converting them to shapes first. Here, text has been converted to shapes, the shapes have been pushed, pulled, and stretched like mad, and some interesting background elements have been added to pull the image together.

Tip   Like regular shapes, type shapes appear jagged around the edges because of the tiny outline that Photoshop displays around the shape. To hide the outline and smooth the on-screen appearance of the text, press Ctrl+H (⌘-H on the Mac). Of course, this command also hides the marching ants, guides, and other on-screen aids. The View ➪ Show ➪ Target Path command enables you to toggle just the shape outlines.

Summary

After a short retrospective on the use of text in Photoshop, this chapter showed you how to insert text, to edit existing text, and several ways to use text artistically — including the creation of vector type, text-based selection outlines, and rasterized text. You learned how to create paragraph text in a bounding box, and to build vertical text, as well as how to use the Character and Paragraph palettes to customize the appearance of your individual type characters and the flow of your text within its own layer.

To make sure text is not only beautiful, but also correct, you learned to use the Check Spelling, and Find and Replace commands, and finally, to take your type to a whole new level, you learned to fit your text to a path and to warp your text using a variety of preset shapes.

✦   ✦   ✦

Color and Output

✦   ✦   ✦   ✦

In This Part

Chapter 16
Essential Color
Management

Chapter 17
Mapping and
Adjusting Colors

Chapter 18
Printing and
Publishing with
Photoshop

Appendix A
The Keyboard,
Menus, and Making
Photoshop Your Own

✦   ✦   ✦   ✦

Essential Color Management

✦ ✦ ✦ ✦

In This Chapter

Setting up your monitor

Selecting an RGB working space

Embedding a color profile in a saved image

Converting colors from one working space to another

Using the Color Settings command

Assigning profiles to untagged images

Establishing color management policies

Reacting to and disabling alert messages

Changing the Intent setting

Setting up a custom CMYK space

Saving and loading CMYK settings

✦ ✦ ✦ ✦

Most artists react very warmly to the word "color" and a bit more coolly to the word "management." One's reaction is normally a matter of temperament, and you may be able to empathize. Put the two words together, though, and you can clear a room in seconds. The term *color management* has been known to simultaneously frighten and bore the most steadfast of graphic artists, photographers, and computer users.

It's no exaggeration to say that color management is the least understood topic in all of computer imaging. Most people, if they think about it at all, expect to calibrate their monitors and achieve reliable if not perfect color. But in point of fact, there's no such thing as perfect color. So-called *device-dependent color*—synthetic color produced by a piece of hardware—is a moving target. The best that Photoshop or any other piece of software can do is to convert from one target to the next.

For what it's worth, most consumer monitors (and video boards, for that matter) are beyond calibration, in the strict sense of the word. You can try using a hardware calibrator (one of those devices where you plop a little suction cup onto your screen), but calibrators often have less to do with changing screen colors than identifying them. Even if your monitor permits prepress-quality calibration—as in the case of $3,000-plus devices sold by different vendors over the years, including Radius, Mitsubishi, and LaCie—it's not enough to simply correct the colors on-screen; you also have to tell Photoshop what you've done.

Therefore, color management is first and foremost about identifying your monitor. You have to explain your screen's weaknesses to Photoshop so that it can make every attempt to accommodate them. In days gone by, Photoshop used the screen data to calculate CMYK conversions and that was it. These days, Photoshop embeds a *profile* that identifies the source of the image and uses this information to translate colors from one monitor to another. Photoshop also permits you to work in multiple profile-specific color spaces at the same time — great for artists who alternatively create images for print and for the Web. Photoshop also permits you to specify exactly what to do with images that lack profiles.

The Color Settings command is that interesting combination of wonderful and bewildering. It can just as easily mess up colors as fix them, but if you read this chapter, you and your colors should be able to ride the currents safely from one digital destination to the next. And best of all, color management in Photoshop is consistent with color management in recent versions of Illustrator and other Adobe applications, so you can learn one, and then the others will make a lot more sense.

A Typical Color-Matching Scenario

For Windows users, Photoshop CS2 devotes three features to color management; Mac users have only two. Formerly a standard component of Photoshop on both platforms (prior to version CS), the Adobe Gamma control panel, which characterizes your monitor, is now a Windows-only utility accessible in the Control Panel. Mac users can use the built-in Display Calibrator Assistant, available from the Color section of the Displays system preferences.

The second color management feature, common to both platforms, is the Color Settings command, found under the Edit menu for Windows users and under the Photoshop menu on the Mac. Choose the command or press Ctrl+Shift+K (⌘+Shift-K on the Mac) to display the Color Settings dialog box, which lets you edit device-dependent color spaces and decide what to do with profile mismatches. Finally, choose File ➪ Save As and use the resulting Save As dialog box to decide whether to embed a profile into a saved image or include no profile at all.

Now, we could just explain each of thee color-management features, each on its own, and hope you can put it all together, but that might prevent you from being able to see the bigger picture and understanding the concepts as a whole. Therefore, we begin our tour of color management by showing the various control panels, commands, and options in action. In this introductory scenario, an RGB image has been created on the Mac and opened on a Windows system. The Mac is equipped with a high-end monitor and the PC is hooked up to relatively low-end monitor, so we're covering two extremes and allowing for the many users whose monitors fall somewhere in between.

Despite the change of platforms and the even more dramatic change in monitors, Photoshop maintains a high degree of consistency, so the image looks the same at both ends of the spectrum. The specifics of setting up your system will obviously vary, but this tour should give you an idea of how color management in Photoshop works.

Setting up the source monitor

If you own a monitor with calibration capabilities, start by calibrating it. You can use OS X's built-in Display Calibrator Assistant. You can access this feature by clicking the Calibrate button in the Color panel of the Displays system preferences, as shown in Figure 16-1. The Display Calibrator Assistant utilizes ColorSync, which is Apple's system-wide color management system.

Figure 16-1: On the Mac, clicking the Calibrate button on the Color panel of the Displays system preferences launches the Display Calibrator Assistant.

The Macintosh Display Calibrator Assistant

If you feel particularly confident (and even if you don't), go ahead and select the Expert Mode option. That gives you access to a few more options, but you may also find that you can't access every option in the Display Calibrator Assistant (or for that matter of the Adobe Gamma control panel on the PC). Some monitors, particularly LCDs, don't allow for every adjustment — again, your situation may vary from the one depicted and described here, but the overall concept is the same.

The Adobe Gamma control panel

For the Windows/PC users, Photoshop ships with the Adobe Gamma control panel. Under Windows systems before XP (which includes Windows 2000, often considered a concurrent OS), choose Settings from the Start menu, and then choose Control Panel. After the Control Panel window appears, double-click the Adobe Gamma icon. (Make sure you're viewing all Control Panel options.) Under Windows XP, the Control Panel is available immediately under the Start menu. If you're using Windows 2000 or an earlier version of Windows, you can access the Control panel through the Start menu's Settings command. If you don't see the Adobe Gamma icon in the Control Panel window, select the Appearance and Themes option, and then double-click the Adobe Gamma icon. (If the Control Panel displays a warning that your video card doesn't support systemwide color management, don't lose any sleep over it — many video cards don't.) Select the Step By Step (Wizard) option and click Next to walk through the setup process one step at a time. If you see a control panel like the one on the right side of Figure 16-2, click the Wizard button to continue.

When using the Adobe Gamma Wizard, all you have to do is answer questions and click Next to advance from one screen to another. For example, after adjusting the contrast and brightness settings, Gamma asks you to specify the nature of your screen's red, green, and blue phosphors. If you own a Trinitron or Diamondtron monitor — which you'll know because you paid more for it — select the Trinitron settings. Or select Custom and type values according to your monitor's documentation. If the documentation does not suggest settings, ignore this screen and click Next to move on. This will not be a big problem, so don't worry if you don't know or can't find all of your monitor's specs and suggested settings.

As with the Native Gamma section of the Mac Display Calibrator Assistant, the next screen, pictured in Figure 16-3, is the most important. It asks you to balance the red, green, and blue display functions of your monitor. But to do so, you need to deselect the View Single Gamma Only option; this presents you with separate controls over each of the three monitor channels. Then use the sliders to make the inner squares match the outer borders. You are in essence calibrating the monitor according to your unique perceptions of it, making this particular brand of characterization a highly personal one.

The next screen asks you to set the white point, which defines the general colorcast of your screen from 5,000 degrees Kelvin for slightly red to 9,300 degrees for slightly blue. A medium value of 6,500 degrees is a happy "daylight" medium. To find the best setting for your monitor, click Measure. Then click the gray box that appears the most neutral — neither too warm nor too cool — until you get dumped back into the Gamma Wizard. Click Next.

Gimme Gamma

The term *gamma* refers to the amount of correction required to convert the color signal generated in the monitor (let's call it *x*) to the color display that you see on-screen (*y*). Imagine a simple graph with the input signal *x* along the bottom and the output *y* along the side. A gamma of 1.0 would result in a diagonal line from the lower-left to the upper-right corner. A higher gamma value tugs at the center of that line and curves it upward. As you tug, more and more of the curve is taken up by darker values, resulting in a darker display. So a typical Mac screen with a default gamma of 1.8 is lighter than a typical PC screen with a default gamma of 2.2. For a real-time display of gamma in action, see Chapter 17 for a discussion of the Curves dialog box.

Figure 16-2: Select the Step By Step option (upper-left dialog box) to advance one step at a time through the Adobe Gamma Wizard. Depending on your version of Windows (2000 is shown here), you can have up to eight steps, including selection of the Wizard, each with its own dialog box.

After you click Finish, the Gamma utility asks you to name your new monitor profile and save it to disk. Name it whatever you want, but don't change the location because the profile has to stay in the default location to be made available to Photoshop and other applications.

Figure 16-3: Deselect the View Single Gamma Only option to modify each of the three color channels independently.

Adobe Gamma generates a custom monitor profile and automatically alerts Photoshop to the change. Your screen may not look any different than it did before you opened Gamma, but you can rest assured that Photoshop is now officially aware of its capabilities and limitations.

Selecting the ideal working space

Now that you've identified your monitor, it's time to select an RGB *working environment*, which is a color space other than the one identified for the monitor. This is the strangest step, but it's one of the most important as well. Fortunately, all it requires is a bit of imagination to understand fully.

On the Mac, switch to Photoshop and choose Photoshop ⇨ Color Settings (Windows users choose Edit ⇨ Color Settings). Photoshop displays the dialog box shown in Figure 16-4. You're immediately faced with a dizzying array of options — think of it like being shoved off the diving board when being taught to swim — but Photoshop does make a small attempt to simplify the process. The program offers several collections of predefined settings under the Settings pop-up menu. Among the settings are Color Management Off, which deactivates Photoshop's color management entirely; ColorSync Workflow, which is useful in all-Macintosh environments; and Emulate Photoshop 4, which both turns color management off and mimics version 4's screen display. With the release of Photoshop CS (and maintained in CS2, there are a few new settings, but mostly, these let you assign a working space that's standard for Adobe products in either Europe, Japan, or North America.

Each of these options has its relative advantages in certain settings, but most people will gravitate toward two other options. If you create most of your images for the Web, select the Web Graphics Defaults option. This directs Photoshop's color functions so that they're most amenable to screen display. On the other hand, if most of your artwork finds its way into print, and if you live in the United States or a country that supports U.S. printing standards, select U.S. Prepress Defaults.

If you develop images for both print and Web use and aren't sure if you should commit to settings for one over the other, select U.S. Prepress Defaults, as shown in Figure 16-4. Why? Among its other attractions, the U.S. Prepress Defaults option sets the working RGB color space to Adobe RGB (1998), arguably the best environment for viewing 24-bit images on-screen.

Adobe RGB includes a wide range of theoretical RGB colors, whether they can truly be displayed on a monitor or not. You may see some *clipping*, which is when two or more color spaces appear as one, on-screen, but Photoshop has greater latitude when interpolating and calculating colors.

After selecting U.S. Prepress Defaults, click OK. The source environment is fully prepared, and you can now save an image and send it on its way.

Tip   If you're using Windows 2000, your Settings option for Web graphics may appear as "North America Web/Internet," and your other Settings choices may be worded differently than in XP as well.

Figure 16-4: Select the U.S. Prepress Defaults option to access the Adobe RGB (1998) color space, which affords a large theoretical RGB spectrum.

Embedding the profile

The final step on the Mac side in this scenario is to *embed* the Adobe RGB profile into a test image. (Embed simply means that Photoshop adds a little bit of code to the file stating where it was last edited.) For this, choose File ➪ Save As, which displays the dialog box in Figure 16-5. After naming the file and specifying a location on disk, select the Embed Color Profile option, which embeds the Adobe RGB color profile into the test image. Then click Save to save the file.

Caution   To save a profile with an image, you have to select a file format that supports profiles. This includes the native Photoshop (PSD) format, TIFF, JPEG, EPS, and PICT. The two DCS formats also save profiles, but because DCS supports only CMYK images, it converts the RGB image to CMYK and saves a CMYK profile. If you select another format — GIF, PNG, BMP, or the like — the Embed Color Profile option becomes dimmed.

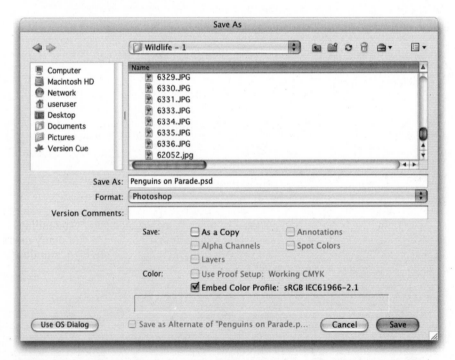

Figure 16-5: Select the Embed Color Profile option to append the Adobe RGB profile to the image saved on the Mac.

Note The Embed Color Profile option always embeds the device-independent profile defined in the Color Settings dialog box. This is very important — it does *not* embed the monitor profile. Photoshop handles the conversion from monitor space to RGB space internally without the help of either the Color Settings or Save As commands. This permits Photoshop to accommodate a world of different monitors from a single RGB working space.

Setting up the destination space

After saving the test image with the embedded Adobe RGB profile, you can transfer the file from your Mac to your PC. You can do this by e-mailing the file to yourself (if you have two computers, one Mac and one PC), or by sending it to a network folder that you can access from the PC (if you're on a network). With either transfer method — or if you want to bring the file over on a CD — no translation occurs; this is a simple file copy from one computer to another. Before you can open the image and display it properly on the PC, you have to set up the RGB colors. Start by characterizing the monitor, using the Adobe Gamma Wizard, as discussed previously in the section "The Adobe Gamma control panel."

After you finish with Adobe Gamma, go into Photoshop and choose Edit ⇨ Color Settings or press Ctrl+Shift+K. If you really want to the two systems to match, select U.S. Prepress Defaults from the Settings pop-up menu, just as you did (if you took my sage advice) on the Mac. For the purpose of educational experimentation, however, you can try forcing Photoshop to perform a conversion — so choose Web Graphics Defaults from the Settings option, as shown in Figure 16-6. This sets the RGB Working Spaces pop-up menu to the utterly indecipherable sRGB IEC61966-2.1.

The truncated name for this working space is *sRGB*, short for *standard RGB*, the ubiquitous monitor space touted by Hewlett-Packard, Microsoft, and a host of others. Although much smaller and drabber than Adobe RGB, the sRGB space is perfect for Web graphics because it represents the colors projected by a run-of-the-mill PC monitor. It also happens to be Photoshop's default setting. Given that many users will never visit this dialog box, sRGB is fast becoming a cross-platform standard.

Defining color management policies

The Color Settings command determines not only how Photoshop projects images on-screen but also how it reads embedded profiles. The three Color Management Policies pop-up menus control how Photoshop reacts when it tries to open an image whose embedded profiles don't match the active color settings. When Web Graphics Defaults is active, the RGB pop-up menu is set to Off, which tells Photoshop to resist managing colors when it opens an RGB image. Disabling color management entirely is probably not a good move, especially when it threatens to ruin your color-conversion scenario. Instead, set the option to Convert to Working RGB, as shown in Figure 16-7.

Figure 16-6: On the Windows side, select the Web Graphics Defaults (North America Web/Internet if you're using Windows 2000) to set the working environment to sRGB. This forces Photoshop to make a conversion.

Finally, Photoshop wants to know how it should behave when it encounters an image with a profile other than sRGB. Should it convert all colors in the image to the sRGB environment? Or should it ask permission before proceeding? If you want to be able to make this choice on a case-by-case basis, select the Ask When Opening option from the Profile Mismatches options, as shown in Figure 16-7.

Converting the color space

When you're ready to open the test image (assuming you're working along here— if not, you can refer back to these pages when you're doing this "for real") choose File ➪ Open. As Photoshop opens the test image, it detects the embedded Adobe RGB profile and determines that it does not match the active sRGB profile. Slightly flipped out by this development, Photoshop displays the alert box shown in Figure 16-8. You can select from three conversion options:

Figure 16-7: Set the first of the Color Management Policies to Convert to Working RGB to convert the image from the Adobe RGB working space to the sRGB space.

Figure 16-8: The alert box gives you the option of converting the colors from the foreign image or opening the image as is.

✦ **Use the embedded profile.** Photoshop is perfectly capable of displaying multiple images at a time, each in a different color space. Select this option to tell Photoshop to use the Adobe RGB space instead of sRGB to display the image it's about to open. No colors are converted in the process.

✦ **Convert document's colors to the working space.** This option converts the colors from the Adobe RGB space to sRGB. Because Convert to Working RGB was selected in the preceding section, this option is selected by default. Had the Ask When Opening option not been activated, Photoshop would have performed the conversion without asking you.

✦ **Discard the embedded profile.** Select this option to ignore the embedded profile and to display the image in the sRGB space without any color manipulations. Thanks to the low saturation inherent in sRGB, the result would be a significantly grayer, gloomier image.

Select the Convert Document's Colors to the Working Space option and click OK. Photoshop spends a few seconds converting all pixels in the image from Adobe RGB to the smaller sRGB and then displays the converted image on-screen. The result is an almost perfect match — much better than the sort of results you could achieve without profile-based color management.

Color Conversion Central

Color Settings is the command that puts Photoshop's color conversion functions in play. It defines the color space parameters and at the same time makes the color conversions happen. This section explains the specific options as they're grouped in the Color Settings dialog box. You'll also find some suggestions for using particular settings, in case you're interested in a little advice.

Description

This portion of the Color Settings dialog box comes last, but it's also the most important. It tells you what every one of the Color Settings options does. Just position the cursor over an option to see a detailed description. To see how an option in a pop-up menu works, select the option and then position your cursor over it. With help like this, what do you need us for?

No seriously, what *do* you need us for? Before we take the rest of the chapter off — there's laundry to do, after all — we will tell you that if you save your own color settings, you can type a description that shows up in the Description section when you load your settings.

Working spaces

Because every color model except Lab varies according to the hardware — the screen or the printer — Photoshop has to tweak the color space to meet your specific needs. There's no such thing as a single, true CMYK color model, for example. Instead, there are lots of printer-specific CMYK color models. These color models inside color models are called *working spaces*. You define the default working spaces that Photoshop uses when opening unprofiled images, creating new ones, or converting mismatched images using the four Working Spaces pop-up menus:

✦ **RGB.** The RGB environment defines what you see on-screen. Rather than limiting yourself to the circumscribed range of colors that your particular brand of monitor can display — known as the monitor's *gamut* — you can work in a larger, richer color environment, filled with theoretical color options that will serve your image well when projected on other monitors and output from commercial presses. Unless you work strictly on the Web and never create artwork for print, select the Adobe RGB (1998) option. If you're working with images destined for After Effects, Adobe recommends that you choose the Monitor RGB working space. Notice that your monitor space also appears in the pop-up menu — this shows that your monitor was correctly tagged with Adobe Gamma or the Display Calibrator Assistant.

Tip

If you're a Web artist and want to preview how an image will look on a different kind of monitor, choose View ⇨ Proof Setup menu after closing the Color Settings dialog box. For example, choose View ⇨ Proof Setup ⇨ Windows RGB to see how the image looks on a typical PC monitor. Choose Macintosh RGB for a typical Mac monitor or Monitor RGB to turn off the RGB working space and see the image as it appears without conversion. Then use Ctrl+Y (Win) or ⌘-Y (Mac) to turn the preview on and off.

✦ **CMYK.** Use this option to specify the kind of printer you intend to use to print your final CMYK document. This option defines how Photoshop converts an image to the CMYK color space when you choose Image ⇨ Mode ⇨ CMYK Color. It also governs the performance of the CMYK preview (View ⇨ Proof Setup ⇨ Working CMYK). Finally, it decides how the colors in a CMYK image are converted for display on your RGB monitor. So any time you open a CMYK image, the RGB working space becomes dormant and this option kicks into gear. For more information about characterizing a CMYK device, see the section "Custom CMYK Setup."

✦ **Grayscale.** This command defines how Photoshop displays a grayscale image (created using Image ⇨ Mode ⇨ Grayscale). You can adjust the gray values in the image to account for a typical Macintosh or PC display (Gray Gamma 1.8 or Gray Gamma 2.2, respectively). Or preview the image according to how it will print, complete with any of several Dot Gain values. (*Dot gain* is the factor by which halftone dots grow when absorbed into paper, as discussed in the section "Custom CMYK Setup.") My preferred setting is Gray Gamma 2.2. It's dark enough to account for dot gains of more than 25 percent, so it accurately reflects the printing conditions typical of grayscale work. Plus it predicts how grays display on a typical PC monitor. Everybody wins.

✦ **Spot.** From a printing perspective, a spot-color separation behaves like an extra grayscale print. Specify the dot gain value that correlates to your commercial printer. If you don't know that value, Dot Gain 20% is a safe bet.

Tip

To permit the image to change on the fly according to the active working space, choose Edit --> Assign Profile and select the Don't Color Manage This Document option. A pound, or number, symbol (#) appears in the title bar to show that the image is no longer tagged with a color profile. Now whenever you change the image's working space in the Color Settings dialog box, the image is updated in kind. Select the Preview option to view changes without exiting the dialog box.

If the Assign Profile command leaves pixels unchanged so that they appear to change on-screen, there must be a command that converts pixels so that they appear consistent on-screen. That command is Edit ⇨ Convert to Profile, which displays the dialog box pictured in Figure 16-9. The options in the lower half of the dialog box — Engine, Intent, and so on — also appear in the Color Settings dialog box when you enter the advanced mode, so you'll be hearing more about them later. For now, just select the color space that you want to convert the image to from the Destination Space pop-up menu and press Enter or Return.

Tip

At first glance, the Destination Space pop-up menu may seem complicated, offering RGB, CMYK, and grayscale working spaces, and even allowing you to create your own. Surprisingly, this vast array of options may result in less work for you. The Destination Space option permits you to switch color modes. For example, if you open an RGB image, choose the Convert to Profile command, and select a CMYK space such as U.S. Web Coated (SWOP). Photoshop not only remaps the colors, it converts the RGB channels to CMYK. Convert to Profile has an edge over Image ⇨ Mode ⇨ CMYK Color — you can switch color modes and nail a specific working space in one operation.

Assigning a Profile

An open profiled image remains in its working space regardless of how you change the settings in the Color Settings dialog box. Suppose that you open an image in sRGB, and then change the working space to Adobe RGB. The open image remains unchanged on-screen, safe in its sRGB space. If you prefer the image to change to the new space, choose Edit ⇨ Assign Profile. Then select the Working RGB option. The figure here shows the Assign Profile dialog box. Because Assign Profile leaves the color values of all pixels unchanged, Photoshop merely displays the old pixels in the new space, which permits the colors to shift on-screen. So perhaps perversely, not converting pixels results in a visible color shift, whereas converting pixels does not.

Figure 16-9: Convert to Profile is the complement to Assign Profile. Choose it to switch an open image to a different color space and convert the pixels. The result is an image that looks the same on-screen as it did before.

Color management policies

Highlighted in Figure 16-10, the next set of options controls how Photoshop reacts when opening an image that either lacks a profile or contains a profile that doesn't match the specified Working Spaces options previously listed. These are the options that are most likely to cause confusion because they're responsible for the error messages Photoshop delivers when opening images. The trick is to keep the error messages to a minimum while keeping control to a maximum. Here are some suggestions for each option accompanied by what is hopefully enough explanation for you to make your own educated decisions:

✦ **RGB.** The first three pop-up menus establish default policies that Photoshop suggests or implements according to the options that follow. For example, when opening an untagged RGB image, tag it with the working RGB profile, which in my case is Adobe RGB. Select Convert to Working RGB and deselect the Missing Profiles option. This way, when no profile is evident, Photoshop assigns the Adobe RGB profile without any further fanfare. However, if the image contains a profile, you could go either way. An image tagged with an sRGB profile is probably a Web image, so you could go ahead and open it in the sRGB space without conversion. However, if you have an image tagged with the Apple RGB profile—intended to match a typical Apple Macintosh screen—you might want to convert it to Adobe RGB. Therefore, set Profile Mismatches to Ask When Opening. This way, Photoshop will ask you what you want to do every time you open an image with a non-matching RGB profile. It will suggest that you convert the image to Adobe RGB, but permit you to override it if you prefer.

✦ **CMYK.** Whereas RGB color is a function of your monitor and the RGB working space, accurate CMYK is all about matching colors to a specific output device. Therefore, if you're accepting CMYK images from clients and colleagues, you probably want to be very careful about making arbitrary conversions. By setting CMYK to Preserve Embedded Profiles, you tell Photoshop to open a tagged CMYK image in its own color space and override the default CMYK space specified in the Working Spaces option mentioned previously. Again, setting Profile Mismatches to Ask When Opening gives you the option to change your mind and convert the image to your working CMYK space if it seems appropriate. If the image has no profile, Photoshop leaves it untagged, giving you the option of testing multiple CMYK working spaces and assigning the one that fits best. This is case-by-case decision making at its best.

✦ **Gray.** Making automatic color manipulations to color images is all very well and good, but clipping is bound to occur, and with millions of theoretical colors at your disposal, the clipping is unlikely to do any visible harm. Grayscale images are another story. Blessed with just 256 brightness values, they are significantly more fragile than color images, and few grayscale images are tagged properly, which makes Photoshop's automatic adjustments less than reliable. You, therefore, would be well served to correct grayscale images manually (as explained in Chapter 17) and keep Photoshop out of the process. Set the Gray option to Off.

Figure 16-10: Here are the settings recommended for the five Color Management Policies options. They tell Photoshop to ask you when opening images with mismatches, but otherwise proceed automatically.

✦ **Profile Mismatches.** These two options tell Photoshop how to behave when opening an image whose profile does not match the working color space. If you select Ask When Opening, Photoshop asks your permission to perform the conversion suggested in the previous pop-up menus. This prompt also gives you the option of opening the image in its native color space or leaving the image untagged. Back in the Color Settings dialog box, select the Ask When Pasting option to tell Photoshop to warn you when you copy an image from one working space and paste it into another. As for the Ask When Pasting option, deselect that, too, and let Photoshop do its work unhindered.

✦ **Missing Profiles.** When you open an image that lacks an embedded profile, Photoshop likes to ask you whether you want to manage the colors or not. I say deselect the Ask When Opening option — enough alert messages already! — and let Photoshop take its cues from the RGB, CMYK, and Gray pop-up menus. According to Figure 16-10, this means Photoshop will tag most unprofiled RGB images with an Adobe RGB profile and leave unprofiled CMYK and grayscale images alone. An exception occurs when opening newer unprofiled images. If you save an image without a profile using version 5 or later, Photoshop inserts a tag that explicitly states, "I have no profile." In this case, the file will open untagged and Photoshop resists color managing the image until you tell it to do otherwise.

The Color Management Policies options are particularly dense, so no one will blame you if you find yourself reading and rereading the text trying to make sense of it. If you can't for the life of you make heads or tails of it, try this instead: Set your options to match the ones suggested in Figure 16-10. Then work in Photoshop for a few days or weeks and see how it feels. The good news about suggestions is that they're just that, and the settings they affect can be reset as needed. In the suggested positions, they won't hurt your images, even if you don't know what you're doing. With a little time and practice, you'll get a feel for how the settings work. Then come back, read the text again, and see if it makes more sense.

More options

Up to this point, admiration for Photoshop's color management tools has out-weighed frustration with its complexity. But the moment More Options is clicked patience evaporates. Suddenly, this really is too much. The next portion of the Color Settings dialog box that is covered is the stuff that appears when you click More Options. This button brings with it many frustrations, and it's tempting to just skip it. But that's not something a bible can do — skip entire sections of pivotal dialog boxes — so here you go.

Think of More Options as the key to the color management underworld. When you click it, you unleash two categories of demonic preference settings: Conversion Options and Advanced Controls. Shown in Figure 16-11, each set of options possesses its own special brand of loathsome and horrible power. Save yourself now, dear reader — run while you still can.

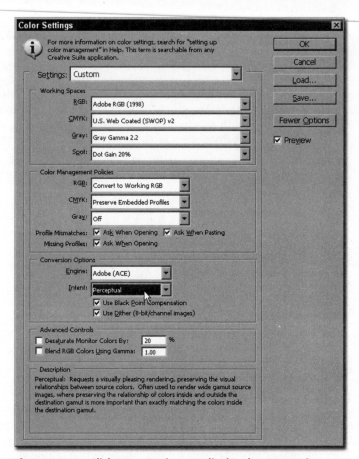

Figure 16-11: Click More Options to display the Conversion Options and Advanced Controls, as well as define your own CMYK working space. The button changes to Fewer Options, and that will seem like a good idea.

Wait — you're still here? Brave soul. Oh, well, as long as you're here you might as well go over it. Here goes:

✦ **Engine.** The first of the Advanced Mode options is Engine, and it does just what it sounds like it does. The force behind the color management process is the engine. If you don't like one engine, you can trade it for another. If you work in a Macintosh-centric environment, for example, you might want to select Apple ColorSync. You should probably stick with the Adobe Color Engine, or ACE. Not only is ACE a great engine, it ensures compatibility with Illustrator, InDesign, and other Adobe applications.3

✦ **Intent.** Whenever you remap colors, a little something gets lost in the translation. The trick is to lose as little as possible, and that's the point of Intent. In previous versions of Photoshop, the option was set by default to Relative Colorimetric, which converts every color in the source profile to its closest equivalent in the destination profile. Although such a direct transfer of colors may sound attractive, it can create rifts in the image. The closest equivalent for two similar colors in the source profile might be a single color in the destination, or they might be two very different colors. As a result, gradual transitions may become flat or choppy. Wisely, Adobe has now set Perceptual as the default, which sacrifices specific colors in favor of retaining the gradual transitions between colors, so important to the success of continuous-tone photographs.

Tip

Is Perceptual *really* better? Well, we think so, but don't take our word for it. Instead, position your cursor over the word Perceptual and read the Description text (shown in Figure 16-11), which tells you that Perceptual "requests a visually pleasing rendering, preserving the visual relationships between source colors." The truth is, most people at Adobe believe Perceptual to be the better choice. Who are we to disagree?

✦ **Use Black Point Compensation.** Like any other colors, Photoshop wants to convert black and white to new values. Whites are compensated naturally by the Intent setting, which may in many cases map white to a different color in the name of smoother transitions. But if you let black map to a lighter color, you can end up with wimpy gray shadows. To keep your blacks their blackest, select this option.

✦ **Use Dither (8-bit/channel images).** Just so we're all on the same page, a 24-bit image contains 8 bits per channel. So don't think we're talking about 8-bit GIF images here; this option uses *dithering* (random patterns of pixels) to smooth out what might otherwise be harsh color transitions. Ostensibly, it can result in higher file sizes when saving an image in the native PSD format or TIFF with LZW compression. But the effect is usually minimal. Leave this option selected.

✦ **Desaturate Monitor Colors By.** The Adobe RGB space in particular has a habit of rendering such vivid colors that the brightest areas in the image flatten out on screen. Because they may or may not have a direct outcome on the appearance of the final image, whether in print or on the Web, such flat areas can be a bit misleading. To better see details in bright areas of color, select the Desaturate Monitor Colors option. Note that this option affects only the screen view; the colors will continue to print as vividly as ever. Use this option only for running previews in the Color Settings dialog box. Leaving this option selected for extended periods of time can be more deceiving than deselecting it.

✦ **Blend RGB Colors Using Gamma.** When this option is deselected, as by default, Photoshop blends layers according to the gamma of the working color space. For example, the gamma of Adobe RGB is 2.2, the same as a typical PC screen and a few shades darker than a typical Macintosh screen. On occasion, however, this may result in incongruous highlights around the edges of layers. If you encounter this, try selecting this option. Photoshop recalculates all blends using a theoretically more desirable gamma value.

Custom CMYK Setup

To prepare an image for reproduction on a commercial offset or web press, you first need to specify how you want Photoshop to convert the image from the RGB to CMYK color space. This step also affects the conversion from CMYK to RGB, which in turn defines how CMYK images appear on-screen.

You specify the CMYK space by choosing Edit ➪ Color Settings. Then select the color profile you want to use from the CMYK pop-up menu in the Working Spaces section of the dialog box. You can select a predefined color profile, or you can define a custom CMYK conversion setup by choosing Custom CMYK from the CMYK pop-up menu. When you choose Custom, Photoshop displays the Custom CMYK dialog box shown in Figure 16-12.

Figure 16-12: Use the options in the Custom CMYK dialog box to prepare an image for printing on a commercial offset or web press.

The following list explains each and every option in the Custom CMYK dialog box. If you're not a print professional, some of these descriptions may seem a little abstruse. After reading this section, you may want to talk with your commercial printer and find out what options, if any, he or she recommends.

✦ **Name.** Okay, so this one's not so abstruse after all. Type a name for your custom CMYK settings here.

✦ **Ink Colors.** This pop-up menu offers access to a handful of common press inks and paper stocks. Select the option that most closely matches your printing environment. (Your commercial printer can easily help you with this one.)

The default setting, SWOP (Coated), represents the most common press type and paper stock used in the United States for magazine and high-end display work. Regardless of which setting you choose, Photoshop automatically changes the Dot Gain value to the most suitable setting.

✦ **Dot Gain.** Type a value from –10 to 40 percent to specify the amount by which you can expect halftone cells to shrink or expand during the printing process, a variable known as *dot gain*. When printing to uncoated stock, for example, you can expect halftone cells to bleed into the page and expand by about 25 to 30 percent. For newsprint, it varies from 30 to 40 percent. In any case, Photoshop automatically adjusts the brightness of CMYK colors to compensate, lightening the image for high values and darkening it for low values.

✦ **Separation Type.** When the densities of cyan, magenta, and yellow inks reach a certain level, they mix to form a muddy brown. The GCR (*gray component replacement*) option avoids this unpleasant effect by overprinting these colors with black to the extent specified with the Black Generation option. If you select the UCR (*under color removal*) option, Photoshop removes cyan, magenta, and yellow inks where they overlap black ink. GCR is almost always the setting of choice except when printing on newsprint.

Curve Control

For more control, select Curves from the Dot Gain pop-up menu. As shown in the figure, this brings up the Dot Gain Curves dialog box, which permits you to specify how much the halftone dots expand on a separation-by-separation basis. If the All Same option is selected, deselect it. Then use the Cyan, Magenta, Yellow, and Black radio buttons in the lower-right corner of the dialog box to switch among the four separations and modify their output independently. To do this, locate the lone point in the center of the curved line in the graph on the left side of the dialog box. Drag this point up to add dot gain, which in turn darkens the display of CMYK colors on-screen; drag the point down to lighten the display. If you need more control, you can add points to the graph by clicking on the curved line. Points added to the left side of the curve affect the display of light colors; points added to the right side of the curve affect dark colors.

✦ **Black Generation.** Available only when the GCR option is active, the Black Generation pop-up menu determines how dark the cyan, magenta, and yellow concentrations must be before Photoshop adds black ink. Select Light to use black ink sparingly; select Heavy to apply it liberally. The None option prints no black ink whatsoever, and the Maximum option prints black ink over everything. You may want to use the UCA Amount option to restore cyan, magenta, and yellow ink if you select the Heavy or Maximum option.

✦ **Black Ink Limit.** Type the maximum amount of black ink that can be applied to the page. By default, this value is 100 percent, which is solid ink coverage. If you raise the UCA Amount value, you'll probably want to lower this value by a similar percentage to prevent the image from over darkening.

✦ **Total Ink Limit.** This value represents the maximum amount of all four inks permitted on the page. For example, assuming you use the default Black Ink Limit and Total Ink Limit values of 100 and 300 percent, respectively, the darkest printable color contains 100 percent black ink. The sum total of cyan, magenta, and yellow inks, therefore, is the difference between these values: 200 percent. A typical *saturated black* — a mix of inks that results in an absolute pitch-black pigment — is 70 percent cyan, 63 percent magenta, 67 percent yellow, and 100 percent black. And 70 + 63 + 67 + 100 =, you guessed it, 300.

✦ **UCA Amount.** The opposite of UCR, UCA stands for *under color addition,* which enables you to add cyan, magenta, and yellow inks to areas where the concentration of black ink is highest. For example, a value of 20 percent raises the amount of cyan, magenta, and yellow inks applied with black concentrations between 80 and 100 percent. This option is dimmed when the UCR option is selected.

✦ **Gray Ramp.** The Gray Ramp graph on the right side of the Custom CMYK dialog box shows the effects of your changes. Four lines — one in each color — represent the four inks. Although you can't edit the colored lines in this graph by clicking and dragging them, you can observe the lines to gauge the results of your settings. If you have an urge to grab a curve and yank it, choose Custom from the Black Generation pop-up menu. The ensuing dialog box lets you edit the black curve directly while you preview its effect on the C, M, and Y curves in the background.

Tip   To see how your changes affect an open CMYK image in Photoshop, do this: Before choosing the Color Settings command, choose Edit ⇨ Assign Profile and select the Don't Color Manage This Document option. Then choose Edit ⇨ Color Settings and select the Preview option. From then on, the image is updated every time you press Enter or Return to accept changes from the Custom CMYK dialog box.

Saving and Loading Color Settings

As you've seen, it can be a painstaking process of trial and error to arrive at the perfect color settings. Furthermore, the perfect settings for one job might be highly imperfect for another. Clearly, there's a pressing need for a way to save and load color settings — and just as clearly, Photoshop is the sort of obliging application to provide a way to do it.

You might logically surmise that the Load and Save buttons on the right side of the Color Settings box will come into play here — and you'd be correct. After you have your settings just the way you want them, click Save. You'll be prompted to save your settings in a Settings folder located deep within the bowels of your hard drive. (Should you ever need to find it again, here's the path: Under Windows, it's Program Files\Common Files\Adobe\Color\Settings. On the Mac, it's located in your User folder at Library\Application Support\Adobe\Color\Settings.) Clicking Load takes you to the same folder, where you can choose the saved settings that you want to load.

And that's not all. Not only can you save and load individual CMYK Working Spaces settings, but with the dreaded Advanced Mode option activated, you can save Working Spaces files for RGB, Grayscale, and Spot color settings as well. You'll find the load and save commands under the individual pop-up menus for each space.

But what if you work with multiple commercial prepress houses? Wouldn't it be nice to be able to select different custom working spaces from the CMYK pop-up menu without having to constantly open setup files using the Load CMYK option? Yes, it would, and here's how you do it.

STEPS: Create a Profile that Appears in the CMYK Pop-up Menu

1. **In the Color Settings dialog box, choose Save CMYK from the CMYK pop-up menu, and give the file a name ending in the *.icm* extension to create an ICM file.** Other than the extension, the name you give it here isn't really that important; the original name you assigned when you first created the settings with the Custom CMYK command is the name you'll see when you actually load the settings.

2. **Save the ICM file to the Recommended folder.** For Photoshop to see the CMYK profile, you have to save it to a specific folder. On the PC, the path for that folder is C:\Program Files\Common Files\Adobe\Color\Profiles\ Recommended. On the Mac, start with the Library folder at the root level of your hard drive, and then go to Application Support\Adobe\Color\Profiles\ Recommended. When you finally arrive inside the Recommended folder, save the ICM file.

3. **Quit Photoshop.** Regardless of which version of Photoshop you're using, quit it by choosing File ➪ Exit (Photoshop ➪ Quit on the Mac).

4. **Launch Photoshop.** By starting (or restarting) Photoshop, you force the program to load the ICM profile.

5. **Confirm that the profile has loaded.** Press Ctrl+Shift+K (⌘-Shift-K on the Mac) to display the Color Settings dialog box, and then click the CMYK pop-up menu in the Working Spaces area. You should see the profile you saved in the menu.

Tip   Because the ICM file created in the preceding steps resides in the Recommended folder, it appears in the CMYK pop-up menu even when More Options has not been clicked. Any ICM files saved in the Profiles folder but outside the Recommended folder appear only when Advanced Mode is turned on.

Synchronizing Bridge Color Settings

As discussed in Chapters 3 and 18, Photoshop CS2's Bridge feature enables you to both organize your images and use them in creative ways that go beyond the Save for Web and Print commands in the main Photoshop workspace. You can use the Bridge to scan images or to capture images from a digital camera or video phone, as well as other sources.

So what's all this synchronizing business? It's simple, actually—unbelievably so, considering all the dialog boxes and steps and settings you have to deal with in Photoshop—choosing color settings, embedding them, dealing with those dreaded More Options. When you work with images in the Bridge, though, assuming you want to make sure you've got the same color settings in place as you do in the main Photoshop workspace, all you have to do is choose Edit ➪ Creative Suite Color Settings. The resulting dialog box appears in Figure 16-13. You can also open this dialog box by pressing Ctrl + Shift + K.

Figure 16-13: The Suite Color Settings dialog box offers 13 color management choices, including Color Management Off. Choose the one that matches your Photoshop settings so you're in synch with the Bridge.

So anyway, you want to synchronize your color settings. You may not have *known* that is what you want to do, but you do. Synchronization is something you want to maintain because, as the dialog box itself tells you, it provides "consistent color management." What's life without consistency? Interesting, you say? Well, yes. But in Photoshop, consistency is a good thing.

Once the Suite Color Settings dialog box is open, you can scroll through the 13 options, reading the short blurb about each one, and then you can make a selection by clicking on the setting you want to use, the one that matches your Photoshop color settings choice. If you click the Show Expanded List of Color Settings Files option, and then click Apply, the list expands (what a surprise) to show 18 additional settings, the last of which being Web Graphics Defaults, so if you're a Web artist and have your Photoshop color settings set for the Web, you may want to expand the list and choose this one. The expanded list, showing the tail end of the 18 additional settings, appears in Figure 16-14.

Figure 16-14: More, more, more. 18 more color settings to choose from, including U.S. Prepress Defaults, Web Graphics Defaults, and Photoshop 4 Emulation.

Tip   The Show Saved Color Settings Files takes you to Windows Explorer (it opens a new Windows Explorer window, even if you have such a window open already) and shows you the location of the settings files—a handy tool if you can't remember the exact path (C:\Documents and Settings\Default\Application Date\Adobe\Color\ Settings).

Once you click the setting you want to use, click Apply, and the dialog box closes. That's all there is to it. You can reset the selection as needed, matching your Photoshop settings for individual images or for groups of photos that need different handling—images bound for a Web Gallery rather than a printed Contact Sheet, for example. Luckily, all the hard work is done on the Photoshop side, and all you have to do in the Bridge is match the main color management method, and you're good to go.

Summary

In this chapter, you learned about controlling how Photoshop displays and uses color. This included everything from testing the way your image will appear on different monitors to embedding a color profile to making sure that your color settings in Photoshop follow your images to the Bridge and beyond.

✦   ✦   ✦

Mapping and Adjusting Colors

✦ ✦ ✦ ✦

In This Chapter

Mapping colors
with Invert, Equalize,
Threshold, and
Posterize

Tweaking colors with
Hue/Saturation

Raising and lowering
saturation levels

Colorizing grayscale
images

Correcting colors
with Replace Color,
Selective Color,
Variations, Photo
Filter, and Match
Color commands

Using the Histogram
palette

Boosting brightness
and contrast levels

Editing specific color
values with Curves

Using the Shadow/
Highlight command

Fixing exposure
problems

Correcting multiple
layers at once with
adjustment layers

Correcting Camera
Raw images

✦ ✦ ✦ ✦

Color mapping is one of those terms that doesn't really explain itself. Color converting might be a better term, or maybe color organization. Anyway, it's color mapping that we're stuck with, and the term simply refers to the process of shuffling colors around. For example, to map Color A to Color B simply means to take all the A-colored pixels and convert them to B-colored pixels. Photoshop provides several commands that enable you to map entire ranges of colors based on their hues, saturation levels, and most frequently, brightness values.

Color Effects and Adjustments

Why would you want to change colors around? Maybe to achieve some special effect or to improve the clarity of an image or to make some portion of the image stand out more so than it does under its current color scheme. In Figure 17-1, the image at the bottom is greatly improved by some color mapping that's been applied to the original version of the same image at the top—the colors stand out, edges are crisper and cleaner, and detail is much more evident. The image in the middle shows the sort of "special" effects you can also achieve when tinkering with color settings.

While some mapping is done to create special—sometimes psychedelic—effects, most of the time the sort of correction or improvement shown in the bottom image in Figure 17-1 is the goal. You're making straightforward repairs, alternatively known as color adjustments and corrections. The reasons to need or want to make such adjustments or corrections are plentiful. Scans are never perfect, no matter how much money you spend on a scanning device or a service bureau. They can always benefit from tweaking and subtle adjustments, if not outright overhauls, in the color department.

Figure 17-1: From bad to bizarre to better — color adjustments can serve
many different purposes. The top image (original) is faded and blurry, and
a gradient map makes it interesting — but not clearer or crisper, as it
appears in the bottom image after some corrections were made to light
and color levels.

Of course, Photoshop's color adjustment functions can't make something from nothing. In creating the illusion of more and better colors, most of the color adjustment operations that you perform actually take some small amount of color *away* from the image. Somewhere in your image, two pixels that were two different colors before you started the correction change to the same color. The image may look ten times better, but it will in fact be less colorful than when you started.

Remembering this principle is important because it demonstrates that color mapping is really a balancing act. The first several operations you perform may make an image look progressively better, but the tenth may send it into decline — the perfect example of less being more, or knowing when to quit. This knowledge, however, of when to quit or when correction has become corruption is hard-won. There's no magic formula; the amount of color mapping you need to apply varies from image to image. But if you follow basic principles — use the commands in moderation, know when to stop, and save your image to disk before doing anything drastic — you should be happy with your results the majority of the time.

Note   Many of the commands discussed in the following sections can also be applied as *adjustment layers*. Adjustment layers are an extremely flexible tool, giving you all the advantages of the color correction commands without the drawback of having your original image permanently altered. Adjustment layers are discussed in full at the end of this chapter, but it's a good idea to know they're "out there" from the beginning of any discussion of color mapping and image correction — it can help you put all the techniques covered between now and then in better perspective, evaluating the differences between techniques, weighing pros and cons, and so on. So now you know.

When Colors Need Therapy

Photoshop stores all of its color mapping commands under the Image ⇨ Adjustments submenu. (The one exception is Photoshop CS2's Camera Raw dialog box, which can be accessed only by opening a Camera Raw file, which will be looked at this later in the chapter.) Basically, these commands fall into three categories:

✦ **Color mapping.** Commands such as Invert and Threshold are quick-and-dirty color mappers, swapping, for example, the original colors for their color opposites (Invert). They don't correct images, but they can be useful for creating special effects and adjusting masks.

✦ **Easy color corrections.** Brightness/Contrast and Color Balance are true color-correction commands, but you may feel that they sacrifice functionality for ease of use.

✦ **Expert color corrections.** The third, more complicated variety of color-correction commands provides better control, but they take a fair amount of effort to learn. Levels, Curves, and Hue/Saturation are examples of color correcting at both its best and most complicated.

This chapter contains little information about the second category of commands for the simple reason that so little information is required. You issue a command from the Image ➪ Adjustments submenu, and either the automatic adjustment takes place with no interaction required from you, or a dialog box opens, you drag a slider, you see if you like the previewed change, and if so, you click OK. If not, you close the dialog box without making any changes, and that's it.

Now, it's important to state up front that some of the quick and automatic adjustment tools aren't going to wow you, even when you consider their incredible speed and ease of use. Some exceptions: Auto Color, which usually does a pretty good job of adjusting an image's midtones and removing color casts; Auto Levels and Auto Contrast, which are decent quick fixers; and Variations, which offers deceptively straightforward sophistication — but it's not really that automatic compared with the others, in that you have several choices of color and lighting adjustments you can make and you can confine the adjustments to specific ranges of color.

No matter how you end up feeling about the individual commands and the three types of adjustments that can be made, you're about to master them — so grab a really dysfunctional photo and let the color therapy begin.

Quick and Automatic Color Effects

The first category of commands, the color mapping tools, all occupy one of the lower sections in the Image ➪ Adjustments submenu. These commands — Invert, Equalize, Threshold, and Posterize — produce immediate effects that are difficult or require too much effort to duplicate with the more full-featured commands.

Invert

When you choose Image ➪ Adjustments ➪ Invert or press Ctrl+I (⌘-I on the Mac), Photoshop converts every color in your image to its exact opposite, as in a photographic negative. As shown in Figure 17-2, you can take some or all of a photo and swap every color — black becomes white, white becomes black, yellow becomes blue, red becomes green, and so on. The brightness value of every primary color component changes to 255 minus the original brightness value, if you want to get all technical about it.

Figure 17-2: You can take some or all of your image and turn it to its negative. Here, the left half of the image has been inverted, showing you the before and after in one image.

Note   Now you might have already thought, "Hey, this means I can scan a negative and convert it to a positive image with this command!" Well, not really, at least not that simply. By itself, the Invert command is not sufficient to convert a scanned color photographic negative to a positive. Negative film produces an orange cast that the Invert command does not address. After inverting, you can use the Variations command to remove the colorcast. Or avoid Invert altogether and use the Levels command to invert the image. Both Variations and Levels are explained later in this chapter.

One really good thing about the Invert command is that it's just about the only color-mapping command that retains the rich diversity of color in an image. (The Hue/Saturation command also retains color diversity under specific conditions.) For example, if you apply the Invert command twice in a row, you arrive at your original image without any loss in quality. Cool, no?

Of course, bear in mind that when you're working on a full-color image, the Invert command simply inverts the contents of each color channel. This means the command produces very different results when applied to RGB, Lab, and especially CMYK images. Typically, the Invert command changes most pixels in a CMYK image to black. Except in rare instances — such as in night scenes — the black channel contains lots of light shades and few dark shades. So when you invert the channel, it becomes extremely dark.

Note   Just so you know, when applying color corrections in the CMYK mode is discussed, it's assumed that you're applying them after choosing Image ⇨ Mode ⇨ CMYK Color. Applying corrections in the RGB mode when View ⇨ Proof Setup ⇨ Working CMYK is active produces the same effect as when Working CMYK is not selected. The only difference is that the on-screen colors are limited slightly to fit inside the CMYK color space. You're still editing inside the same old Red, Green, and Blue color channels, so the effects are the same.

Tip   As mentioned in Chapter 12, inverting the contents of the mask channel is the same as applying Select ⇨ Inverse to a selection outline in the marching ants mode. In fact, this is one of the most useful applications of the filter.

Equalize

When you invoke the Equalize command, Photoshop searches for the lightest and darkest color values in a selection and then it maps the lightest color in all the color channels to white, maps the darkest color in the channels to black, and distributes the remaining colors to other brightness levels in an effort to evenly distribute pixels over the entire brightness spectrum. This doesn't mean that any one pixel will actually appear white or black after you apply Equalize, however. Instead, one pixel in at least one channel will be white and another pixel in at least one channel will be black. In an RGB image, for example, the red, green, or blue component of one pixel would be white, but the other two components of that same pixel might be black. The result is a higher contrast image with white and black pixels scattered throughout the color channels.

If no portion of the image is selected when you choose Image ➪ Adjustments ➪ Equalize, Photoshop automatically maps the entire image across the brightness spectrum. If you select a portion of the image before choosing the Equalize command, Photoshop displays a dialog box containing the following two radio buttons:

✦ **Equalize Selected Area Only.** Select this option to apply the Equalize command strictly within the confines of the selection. The lightest pixel in the selection becomes white, the darkest pixel becomes black, and the others remap to shades in between. Figure 17-3, at the top, shows an image that's been Equalized in only one selected area.

✦ **Equalize Entire Image Based on Selected Area.** If you select the second radio button, which is the default setting, Photoshop applies the Equalize command to the entire image based on the lightest and darkest colors in the selection. All colors in the image that are lighter than the lightest color in the selection become white and all colors darker than the darkest color in the selection become black. Figure 17-3, at the bottom, shows the same image with the Equalize command applied to the entire image based on the same selection.

What you may find with the Equalize command is that it can rely too heavily on the automation of its procedure to be of much use as a color-correction tool. You simply don't have enough control over the equalization process, or the equation it's using to distribute colors over the entire spectrum of light to dark. You can create some interesting special effects, though, and sometimes it can be a helpful command, depending on the photo in question, its problems, and your goals for it.

Tip If you really want to automatically adjust the colors in an image from black to white regardless of the color mode and composition of the individual channels, choose Image ➪ Adjustments ➪ Auto Levels or press Ctrl+Shift+L (⌘-Shift-L on the Mac). If you want to adjust the tonal balance manually and therefore with a higher degree of accuracy, the Levels and Curves commands are really great. They're all explained at length later in this chapter.

Threshold

The Threshold command converts all colors to either black or white, based on their brightness values. When you choose Image ➪ Adjustments ➪ Threshold, Photoshop displays the Threshold dialog box shown in Figure 17-4. The dialog box offers a single Threshold Level option box and a slider bar, either of which you can use to specify the medium brightness value in the image. Photoshop changes any color lighter than the value in the Threshold option box to white and changes any color darker than the value to black.

Figure 17-4: The histogram in the Threshold dialog box shows the distribution of brightness values in the selection. The weird mountain-range silhouette thing is what's known as a *histogram*.

Tip   Generally speaking, you achieve the best effects if you change an equal number of pixels to black as you change to white (and vice versa). So rather than moving the slider bar to 128, which is the medium brightness value, move it to the point at which the area of the vertical lines to the left of the slider triangle looks roughly equivalent to the area of the vertical lines to the right of the slider triangle.

The example on the left in Figure 17-5 shows the result of applying the Threshold command with a Threshold Level value of 128 (right smack in the middle of the slider), while the image on the right shows a Threshold level of 50 — providing the equivalent areas of white and black as suggested in the previous paragraph.

The dialog box also includes a graph of all the colors in the image — even if only a portion of the image is selected. This graph is called a *histogram*. The width of the histogram represents all 256 possible brightness values, starting at black on the left and progressing through white on the right. The height of each vertical line in the graph demonstrates the number of pixels currently associated with that brightness value. Therefore, you can use the histogram to gauge the distribution of lights and darks in your image. You may have trouble imagining that looking at the histogram in a dialog box could ever translate to a useful tool for perceiving and adjusting color, but with enough experience, the histogram becomes an invaluable tool, permitting you to greatly improve the colors that you see on-screen. You may even get excited enough about histograms to spend some time using the Histogram palette, discussed later in this chapter.

To show how color adjustment tools can be used with various filters for a variety of interesting results, check out Figure 17-6. In each example of the same photo, you can see how four different filters, each followed by use of the Threshold command, can turn photos into something completely different.

Figure 17-5: Use the histogram and your own eyes — trained on the preview — to determine when the Threshold command is delivering interesting or simply destructive results.

Tip   If you want to achieve a colorful Threshold effect, try applying the Threshold command independently to each color channel. In an RGB image, for example, press Ctrl+1 (⌘-1 on the Mac) and then choose Image ⇨ Adjustments ⇨ Threshold. Then press Ctrl+2 (⌘-2 on the Mac) and repeat the command, and press Ctrl+3 (⌘-3 on the Mac) and do it again. Alternatively, you can make Photoshop perform this process for you by using the new Hard Mix blend mode, discussed in Chapter 13. Don't forget that you can also apply the same effect to two channels at once by selecting one channel and Shift-clicking the second.

Figure 17-6: Experiment with these (Ocean Ripple, Plaster, Stained Glass, and Crosshatch, working clockwise from upper left), and other filters preceded by the Threshold command (set to 50). You can also experiment with using more than one filter — and swapping the order of their application.

Posterize

Where Threshold boils down an image into only two colors, Posterize can retain as many colors as you like. Of course, you can't control how colors are mapped, as you can when you use Threshold — the Posterize dialog box provides neither a histogram nor a slider bar. Instead, Posterize automatically divides the full range of 256 brightness values into a specified number of equal increments.

To use this command, choose Image ➪ Adjustments ➪ Posterize and type a value in the Levels option box. The Levels value represents the number of brightness values that the Posterize command retains. Higher values result in subtle color adjustments; lower values produce more dramatic effects, as shown in Figure 17-7, where just two levels and then a near normal-looking 16 levels are applied.

Figure 17-7: On the left, Posterize was applied at two levels. On the right, 16 were applied, which makes the image look almost "normal," like the original photo with millions of colors.

Like Threshold, the Posterize command is also something you can play with in conjunction with filters to get some really interesting results. You can apply it before a filter or after it — or along with more than one filter. By reducing the number of levels and thus simplifying the color palette in the image, the Posterize command makes various filters perform differently than they would on a photo with millions of colors.

Quick and Automatic Corrections

Photoshop offers four quick, automatic correctors under the Image ⇨ Adjustments submenu. Introduced in Photoshop 7, the Auto Color command is the most useful of them. Desaturate removes all color from a selection, leaving it looking like a grayscale image, and the Auto Levels and Auto Contrast commands automatically adjust the contrast of an image according to what Photoshop deems to be ideal brightness values. Auto Levels examines each color channel independently; Auto Contrast examines the image as a whole. Note that Auto Color, which works only with RGB images, looks at the entire image as it attempts to automatically correct the image's midtones and remove colorcasts.

Gray areas

The Desaturate command is quite useful for removing color from selected areas or from independent layers. You can use it to reduce or remove color from an entire image, but for that you'd probably be better off using the Image ⇨ Mode ⇨ Grayscale command. Using the Mode command will also dispose of the extra channels that would otherwise consume room in memory and on disk. Now, there are reasons to circumvent this alleged benefit — you might want to use the Desaturate command to get rid of color in an entire photo for the following reasons:

✦ You want to retain the option of applying RGB-only filters, such as Lens Flare and Lighting Effects. You'd lose these options if you convert to Grayscale.

✦ You intend to downsize the colors using Image ⇨ Mode ⇨ Indexed Colors and save the final image as a GIF file for use on the Web.

Tip   You can use Edit ⇨ Fade (Ctrl+Shift+F or ⌘-Shift-F) to reduce the effects of Desaturate or any other command under the Image ⇨ Adjustments submenu. As always, the Fade command is available immediately after you apply the color correction; if you alter a selection outline, Fade becomes unavailable.

Note   Desaturate isn't the only way to remove colors from an image. You can also invert the colors and mix them with their original counterparts to achieve a slightly different effect. Just press Ctrl+I (⌘-I on the Mac) to invert the area you want to desaturate. Then press Ctrl+Shift+F (⌘-Shift-F on the Mac), change the Opacity setting to

50 percent, and—here's the important part—select Color from the Mode pop-up menu. You can get a close approximation of converting an image to the Grayscale mode simply by creating a new layer, filling it with black, and switching the blend mode to Color. You can also use the Channel Mixer, which gives you the most exacting control over converting to grayscale. For details, see Chapter 4.

The Auto Levels command

Image ➪ Adjustments ➪ Auto Levels (Ctrl+Shift+L or ⌘-Shift-L) goes through each color channel and changes the lightest pixel to white, changes the darkest pixel to black, and stretches all the shades of gray to fill out the spectrum. In Figure 17-8, you see a very dull gray image on the left, and a more dynamic version of the same image on the right. The right-hand image was improved through the Auto Levels command because Photoshop increased the lights and darks, which increased the contrast. You might get better results by applying Levels and dragging the sliders by hand, as you can see from this example; this very quick, automated tool is not too shabby.

Figure 17-8: After the use of the Auto Levels command, you see more contrast, more discernable detail, more interest.

You might be thinking that Auto Levels is a whole lot like Equalize, and you'd be right—except that unlike the Equalize command, which considers all color channels as a whole, Auto Levels looks at each channel independently. This results in more dynamic, profound results, based on the color Mode for the photo. Like

Invert, Equalize, and other automatic color mapping commands, Auto Levels is designed for use in the RGB mode. If you use it in CMYK, you may not like the results.

Note By default the Auto Levels command produces the same effect as the Auto button in the Levels dialog box, as discussed later in this chapter.

The Auto Contrast command

If you find that Image ➪ Adjustments ➪ Auto Levels (which modifies values on a channel-by-channel basis) results in an unpleasant skewing of the balance of colors in an image you can use Image ➪ Adjustments ➪ Auto Contrast (Ctrl+Shift+Alt+L or ⌘-Shift-Option-L). The Auto Contrast command adjusts the composite levels, which preserves the colors.

Not sure which one to use? If a low-contrast image suffers from a colorcast that you want to correct, try Auto Levels. If the image is washed out but the colors are okay, try Auto Contrast. If you're working on a grayscale image, the two commands work the same, so choose whichever is more convenient. Given that neither command is perfect, you may want to make additional Levels and Variations adjustments (see these commands covered in detail later in this chapter) — or try Auto Color, which is up next.

The Auto Color command

The Auto Color command is such a smart and useful tool that it serves as the exception to the rule that one must be somewhat reserved in praise for or use of any command that starts with the word "Auto." Auto Color is great at tweaking skin tones and making other subtle changes — something you'll notice right away, especially in photos where the Auto Levels and Auto Contrast commands don't seem to make much, if any, difference in the image.

To use it, choose Image ➪ Adjustments ➪ Auto Color or press Ctrl+Shift+B (⌘-Shift-B on the Mac) to apply the Auto Color command. To get a sense of how the command works, and how it compares with Auto Levels in particular, take a look at Figure 17-9, which shows how each command affects an image on a channel-by-channel basis. You'll want to remember that Auto Color works only when applied to images in the RGB mode.

Tip Auto Color is different from Auto Levels in that rather than setting the darks to black and the lights to white, Auto Color neutralizes an image's highlights, midtones, and shadows, thereby restoring balance to other colors in the image. That's the plan, anyway. If you don't see the results that this command promises, you can always customize it using the Levels and Curves commands — a process discussed later in this chapter.

Auto levels

red

green

blue

red

Auto colors   green

blue

Figure 17-9: The effects of Auto Levels (top row) and Auto Color (bottom row) on the individual channels of an RGB image show you how the two "Auto" commands do their respective jobs. Auto Color turned the red and green channels slightly darker than did Auto Levels, but the blue channel is slightly lighter. If you forget the "before" version of this image, check Figure 17-8 to see it in its pristine, un-Auto'd state.

Adjusting Hues and Colorizing Images

In this section, you'll be looking at the commands that change the distribution of colors in an image. You can move the hues across the color spectrum, change the saturation of colors, adjust highlights and shadows, and even tint an image. Four of these commands — Hue/Saturation, Selective Color, Photo Filter, and Match Color commands — are applicable only to color images. The other two — Replace Color and Variations — can be applied to grayscale images, too. You might find that they're better suited to color images, but it depends on the photo as to whether or not these commands are the most effective choice for a grayscale image. If you're more interested in editing grayscale photographs, you can check out the Levels, Curves, and new Shadow/Highlight commands, all of which are covered toward the end of the chapter. For those of you who want to correct colors, however, read on.

Tip

Remember how Ctrl+Alt+F (⌘-Option-F on the Mac) redisplays the last filter dialog box so that you can tweak the effect? Well, a similar shortcut is available when you apply color corrections. Press Alt (or Option on the Mac) when choosing any of the commands described throughout the rest of this chapter to display that command's dialog box with the settings last applied to the image. If the command has a keyboard equivalent, just add Alt (or Option on the Mac) to restore the last settings. Pressing Ctrl+Alt+U (or ⌘-Option-U on the Mac), for example, brings up the Hue/Saturation dialog box with the settings you last used.

Using the Hue/Saturation command

The Hue/Saturation command provides two functions. First, it enables you to adjust colors in an image according to their hues and saturation levels. You can apply the changes to specific ranges of colors or modify all colors equally across the spectrum. And second, the command lets you colorize images by applying new hue and saturation values while retaining the core brightness information from the original image.

This command is perfect for colorizing grayscale images. You can give your images the Ted Turner treatment with just a little effort. Just scan and change the Hue value to 140 degrees.

When you choose Image ➪ Adjustments ➪ Hue/Saturation or press Ctrl+U (⌘-U on the Mac), Photoshop displays the Hue/Saturation dialog box, shown in Figure 17-10. Before looking at how to use this dialog box to produce specific effects, it would be a good idea to introduce the options, starting with the three option boxes:

> ✦ **Hue.** The Hue slider bar measures colors on the 360-degree color circle, as explained back in the section of Chapter 4 that discussed the HSB model. You can adjust the Hue value from –180 to +180 degrees. As you do, Photoshop rotates the colors around the Hue wheel. Consider the example of flesh tones. A Hue value of +30 moves the flesh into the orange range; a value of +100 makes it green. Going in the other direction, a Hue of –30 makes the flesh red and –100 makes it purple.

Figure 17-10: The Hue/Saturation dialog box as it appears when editing all colors in a layer (top) or just a specific range of colors (bottom)

Note When the Colorize option is selected, Hue becomes an absolute value measured from 0 to 360 degrees. A Hue value of 0 is red, 30 is orange, and so on, as described in Chapter 4.

✦ **Saturation.** The Saturation value changes the intensity of the colors. Normally, the Saturation value varies from –100 for gray to +100 for incredibly vivid hues. The only exception occurs when the Colorize option is selected, in which case saturation becomes an absolute value, measured from 0 for gray to 100 for maximum saturation.

✦ **Lightness.** You can darken or lighten an image by varying the Lightness value from –100 to +100.

Caution

Because this value invariably changes *all* brightness levels in an image to an equal extent—whether or not Colorize is selected—it permanently dulls highlights and shadows. It's advisable that you avoid this option at virtually all costs and rely instead on the Levels or Curves command to edit brightness and contrast.

Tip

Like a lot of sliders and settings in the program, Photoshop now lets you "scrub" to adjust the values. Position your cursor over the name of one of the sliders (such as Hue) until you get a hand cursor with two arrows protruding from it. Drag left to decrease the value of the slider, drag right to increase it. Shift-drag to change the value in increments of 10.

✦ **Edit.** The Edit pop-up menu controls which colors in the active selection or layer are affected by the Hue/Saturation command. If you select the Master option, as by default, Hue/Saturation adjusts all colors equally. If you prefer to adjust some colors in the layer differently than others, choose one of the other Edit options or press the keyboard equivalent—Ctrl+1 (Win) or ⌘-1 (Mac) for Reds, Ctrl+2 (Win) or ⌘-2 (Mac) for Yellows, and so on.

Each Edit option isolates a predefined range of colors in the image. For example, the Reds option selects the range measured from 345 to 15 degrees on the Hue wheel. Naturally, if you were to modify just the red pixels and left all non-red pixels unchanged, you'd end up with some jagged transitions in your image. So Photoshop softens the edges with 30 degrees of fuzziness at either end of the red spectrum (the same kind of fuzziness described in Chapter 9).

Tip

You can apply different Hue, Saturation, and Lightness settings for every one of the color ranges. For example, to change all reds in an image to green and all cyans to gray, choose the Reds option and change the Hue value to +50 and then choose Cyans and change the Saturation value to –100.

✦ **Color ramps.** You can track changes made to colors in the Hue/Saturation dialog box in two ways. One way is to select the Preview option and keep an eye on the changes in the image window. The second way is to observe the color ramps at the bottom of the dialog box. The first ramp shows the 360-degree color spectrum; the second ramp shows what the color ramp looks like after your edits.

✦ **Color range controls.** You can use the color ramps also to broaden or narrow the range of colors affected by Hue/Saturation. When you choose any option other than Master from the Edit pop-up menu, a collection of color range controls appears between the color ramps. The range bar identifies the selected colors and also permits you to edit them.

Figure 17-11 shows the color range controls up close and personal. Here's how they work:

• Drag the central range bar to move the entire color range.

• Drag one of the two lighter-colored fuzziness bars to broaden or narrow the color range without affecting the fuzziness.

- Drag the range control (labeled in Figure 17-11) to change the range while leaving the fuzziness points fixed in place. The result is that you expand the range and condense the fuzziness, or vice versa.

- Drag the triangular fuzziness control to lengthen or contract the fuzziness independently of the color range.

Tip

By default, red is the central color in the color ramps, with blue at either side. This is great when the range is red or some other warm color. But if you're working with a blue range, the controls get split between the two ends. To move a different color to the central position, Ctrl-drag (Win) or ⌘-drag (Mac) in the color ramp. The spectrum revolves around the ramp as you drag.

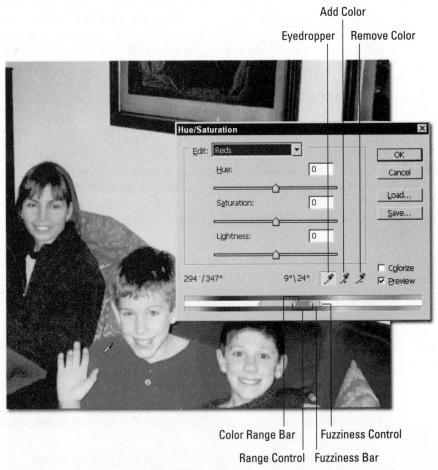

Figure 17-11: Choose which range you want to edit, and then use the color range controls — the eyedroppers and spectrum sliders — to modify the range or the fuzziness.

✦ **Eyedroppers.** To lift a color range from the image window, click inside the image window with the Eyedropper cursor. The cursor automatically changes to an eyedropper when you move it outside the Hue/Saturation dialog box, and then when you click on a color, Photoshop centers the range on the exact color you click.

To expand the range to include more colors, Shift-click or drag in the image window. To remove colors from the range, Alt-click (Option-click on the Mac) or drag in the image. You can also use the alternative plus and minus Eyedropper tools, but Shift and Alt (Shift and Option on the Mac) work well, too.

✦ **Load/Save.** You can load and save settings to disk in case you want to reapply the options to other images using the Load/Save options. These options are especially useful if you find a magic combination of color-correction settings that accounts for most of the color mistakes produced by your scanner.

✦ **Colorize.** Select this option to apply a single hue and a single saturation level to the entire selection or layer, regardless of how it was previously colored. All brightness levels remain intact, although you can adjust them incrementally using the Lightness slider bar (a practice that should be avoided, as mentioned earlier).

Color ranges are not permitted when colorizing. The moment you select the Colorize option, Photoshop dims the Edit pop-up menu and sets it to Master.

✦ **Restore.** Wait — there is no Restore button in this dialog box. Or is there? If you Alt + click (Windows) on the Cancel button (or Option-click if you're on a Mac), the Cancel button becomes a Restore button. While in Restore mode, you can restore the options in the Hue/Saturation, Levels, and Curves dialog boxes to their original settings by clicking Restore. You can also press Option-Escape on the Mac to achieve the same result.

To track the behavior of specific colors when using Hue/Saturation or any of Photoshop's other powerful color adjustment commands, display the Info palette (press F8) before choosing the Hue/Saturation command. Then move the cursor inside the image window. As shown in Figure 17-12, the Info palette tracks the individual RGB and CMYK values of the pixel beneath the cursor. The number before the slash is the value before the color adjustment; the number after the slash is the value after the adjustment. Note that the Info palette only shows these before and after numbers while the adjustment dialog box is open — if you're just sampling pixels with the Eyedropper, there is only one value shown in the palette — the color values for the pixel you're sampling at the time.

Photoshop's Histogram palette also updates continuously as you work in the Hue/Saturation dialog box or with any of the other color adjustment commands. The Histogram palette is discussed a little later in this chapter.

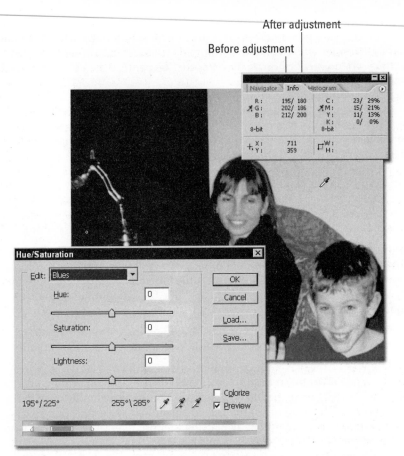

Figure 17-12: When you move the Eyedropper outside a color adjustment dialog box and into the image window, the Info palette lists the color values of the pixel beneath the cursor before and after the adjustment.

Remember, you don't have to settle for just one color readout. Shift-click in the image window to add up to four fixed color samples, just like those created with the color sampler tool, described in Chapter 4. To move a color sample after you've set it in place, Shift-drag it.

In the case of the Hue/Saturation dialog box, you can set color sample points only when the Edit pop-up menu is set to Master. After you set the samples, select some other options from the pop-up menu to modify a specific range. As long as you select only the Master option and edit only the Hue value, Photoshop retains all colors in an image. In other words, after shifting the hues in an image +60 degrees, you can later choose Hue/Saturation and shift the hues −60 degrees to restore the original colors.

Note Just as the Saturation option works like the Color control on a television, the Hue value serves the same purpose as the Tint control, and the Lightness value works like the Brightness control. Note that increasing the Saturation has the effect of heightening the contrast of the color channels — display the Channels palette before opening the Hue/Saturation dialog box and display just one channel. Watch as you drag the Saturation slider, and then switch channels to see the impact on each one individually. You will have to close the dialog box to switch channels, though.

Tip The Saturation option is especially useful for toning down images captured with low-end scanners and digital cameras, which have a tendency to exaggerate certain colors.

Correcting out-of-gamut colors

Another common use for the Saturation option is to prepare RGB images for process-color printing. As explained in Chapter 4, many colors in the RGB spectrum are considered out-of-gamut, meaning that they fall outside the smaller CMYK color space. Photoshop provides a means for recognizing such colors while remaining inside the RGB color space. Choose View ➪ Gamut Warning or press Ctrl+Shift+Y (⌘-Shift-Y on the Mac) to color all out-of-gamut colors with gray (or some other color that you specify using the Preferences command). The pixels don't actually change to gray; they just appear gray on-screen as long as the command is active. To toggle View ➪ Gamut Warning off, choose the command again.

How do you eliminate these out-of-gamut colors? Consider these options:

✦ Let Photoshop take care of the problem automatically when you convert the image by choosing Image ➪ Mode ➪ CMYK Color. This tactic can be a bit risky because Photoshop simply cuts off colors outside the gamut and converts them to their nearest CMYK equivalents, and this can result in flattened hues. Choosing View ➪ Proof Setup ➪ Working CMYK gives you an idea of how dramatic the flattening might be while permitting you to continue working in the RGB color space. Sometimes the effect is hardly noticeable, in which case no additional attention may be warranted.

✦ Another method is to scrub with the Sponge tool. Although it theoretically offers selective control — you just scrub at areas that need attention until the gray pixels created by the Gamut Warning command disappear — the process leaves too much to chance and can do more damage than simply choosing Image ➪ Mode ➪ CMYK Color. If you want to try this method, be ready to go back in History if you don't like the results.

✦ The third and best solution involves the Saturation option in the Hue/Saturation dialog box.

If you're surprised to read the last item (and wondering why it's listed last if it's the best bet), don't be — read on for a procedure you can try to bring your colors back into the CMYK color space.

STEPS: Eliminating Out-of-Gamut Colors

1. **Create a duplicate of your image to serve as a CMYK preview.** Choose Image ➪ Duplicate to create a copy of your image. Then choose View ➪ Proof Setup ➪ Working CMYK. Alternatively, you can press Ctrl+Y (or ⌘-Y on the Mac) to invoke color proofing. By default, Photoshop selects the working CMYK space. This image represents what Photoshop does with your image if you don't make any corrections. It's good to have around for comparison.

2. **Return to your original image and choose Select ➪ Color Range.** Then select the Out Of Gamut option from the Select pop-up menu and press Enter (Win) or Return (Mac). You have now selected all antigamut pixels throughout your image.

3. **To monitor your progress, choose View ➪ Gamut Warning to display the gray pixels.** Don't forget to press Ctrl+H (⌘-H on the Mac) to get rid of the marching ants.

4. **Press Ctrl+U (or ⌘-U on the Mac) to display the Hue/Saturation dialog box.**

5. **Lower the saturation of individual color ranges.** Don't change any settings while Master is selected; it's not exacting enough. Instead, experiment with specifying your own color ranges and lowering the Saturation value. Every time you see one of the pixels change from gray to color, it means that another pixel has now left the "out of gamut" ranks and is officially within the CMYK color space.

6. **When only a few hundred sporadic gray spots remain on-screen, click OK to return to the image window.** Choose Image ➪ Mode ➪ CMYK Color and watch as Photoshop forces them into the gamut.

Bear in mind that the differences between your duplicate image and the one you manually forced into gamut may be very subtle and you might not really notice any immediate improvement. When the image is printed, however, the difference will be more obvious and will produce a better-looking image with a more dynamic range of colors.

Avoiding gamut-correction edges

The one problem with the previous procedure is that the Color Range command selects only out-of-gamut pixels without even partially selecting their neighbors. As a result, you desaturate out-of-gamut colors while leaving similar colors fully saturated, an effect that may result in jagged and unnatural edges.

Tip

One solution is to insert a step between Steps 2 and 3 in which you do the following: Select the Magic Wand tool and change the Tolerance value in the Options bar to 12 (for example — feel free to tinker). Next, choose Select ➪ Similar, which expands the selected area to incorporate all pixels that fall within the Tolerance range. Finally, choose Select ➪ Feather and type a Feather Radius value that's about half the Tolerance — in this case, using the Tolerance setting of 12, 6 is half of that.

This solution isn't perfect—ideally, the Color Range option box wouldn't dim the Fuzziness slider when you choose Out Of Gamut—but it does succeed in partially selecting a few neighboring pixels without sacrificing too many of the out-of-gamut pixels, and makes for a smoother result.

Colorizing images

When you select the Colorize option in the Hue/Saturation dialog box, the options perform differently. Every pixel in the selection receives the same hue and the same level of saturation, and only the brightness values remain intact to ensure that the image remains recognizable. In most cases, you'll only want to colorize grayscale images or bad color scans. After all, colorizing ruins the original color composition of an image. For the best results, you'll want to set the Saturation values to somewhere in the neighborhood of 25 to 75.

Tip   To touch up the edges of a colorized selection, change the foreground color to match the Hue and Saturation values you used in the Hue/Saturation dialog box. You can do this by choosing the HSB Sliders command from the Color palette menu and typing the values in the H and S option boxes. Set the B (Brightness) value to 100 percent. Next, select the Brush tool and change the Brush mode to Color by pressing Shift+Alt+C (Shift-Option-C on the Mac).

Shifting selected hues

The Replace Color command allows you to select an area of related colors and adjust the hue and saturation of that area. When you select Image ⇨ Adjustments ⇨ Replace Color, you get the dialog box shown in Figure 17-13. The Replace Color dialog box bears a strong resemblance to the Color Range dialog box—in fact, it varies in only a few respects. It's missing the Select and Selection Preview pop-up menus, and it offers three slider bars, just like the ones in the Hue/Saturation dialog box.

For further comfort or confusion (however the similarities with other tools strike you), this dialog box works the same as selecting a portion of an image using Select ⇨ Color Range and editing it with the Hue/Saturation command, as done previously. You don't have as many options to work with, but the outcome is the same. The Replace Color and Color Range dialog boxes even share the same default settings. If you change the Fuzziness value in one, the default Fuzziness value of the other changes as well.

So given that the Replace Color command's dialog box looks and acts like two other tools, why does it even exist? Because it allows you to change the selection outline and apply different colors without affecting the image. Just select the Preview option to see the results of your changes on-screen, and you can play with the settings and only click OK when you like what you see.

Figure 17-13: The Replace Color dialog box works like the Color Range dialog box described in Chapter 9, with the Hue/Saturation sliders thrown in.

Cross-Reference

If you're not clear on how to use all the options in the Replace Color dialog box, read the section in Chapter 9 on using the Color Range command. The content there tells you all about the Eyedropper tools and the Fuzziness option so you'll have a better idea of how they work.

Shifting predefined colors

The Selective Color command permits you to adjust the colors in CMYK images. Although you can use Selective Color also when working on RGB or Lab images, it makes more sense in the CMYK color space because it permits you to adjust the levels of cyan, magenta, yellow, and black inks.

Note

You may find that the Variations command provides better control and more intuitive options than the Selective Color command. Adobe created the Selective Color command to accommodate traditional press managers who prefer to have direct control over ink levels rather than monkeying around with hue, saturation, and other observational color controls. If Selective Color works for you, great. But don't get hung up on it if it never quite gels. You can accomplish all that Selective Color provides and more with the Variations command, described in the next section.

Choosing Image ⇨ Adjustments ⇨ Selective Color brings up the dialog box shown in Figure 17-14. To use the dialog box, choose the predefined color that you want to edit from the Colors pop-up menu and then adjust the four process-color slider bars to change the predefined color. When you select the Relative option, you add or subtract color, much as if you were moving the color around the musical chairs using the Hue slider bar. When you select Absolute, you change the predefined color to the exact value entered in the Cyan, Magenta, Yellow, and Black option boxes. The Absolute option is therefore very much like the Colorize option in the Hue/Saturation dialog box.

Figure 17-14: Select a predefined color from the Colors pop-up menu and adjust the slider bars to change that color.

If you examine the Selective Color dialog box closely, you'll notice that it is very much like the Hue/Saturation dialog box. You have access to predefined colors in the form of a pop-up menu instead of radio buttons, and you can adjust slider bars to alter the color. The two key differences are that the pop-up menu lets you adjust whites, medium grays (Neutrals), and blacks — options missing from Hue/Saturation — and that the slider bars are always measured in the CMYK color space.

Tip
As mentioned at the outset, the Selective Color command produces the most predictable results when you're working on a CMYK image. When you drag the Cyan slider to the right, for example, you're actually transferring brightness values to the cyan channel. However, you have to keep an eye out for a few anomalies, particularly when editing Black. In the CMYK mode, areas of your image that appear black include not only black but also shades of cyan, magenta, and yellow, resulting in what printers call a *rich black* (or *saturated black*). Therefore, to change black to white, you have to set the Black slider to –100 percent and also set the Cyan, Magenta, and Yellow sliders to the same value.

Filtering colors

Since the dawn of color film, photographers have used different filters and balanced film stocks to correct the color balance in their photos. Different types of light sources produce a variety of *color temperatures*: Natural daylight generally takes on a bluish cast, or a higher color temperature, whereas artificial light often produces more shades of reds and yellows, or a lower color temperature. When not shooting on film that has been prebalanced to account for these casts, photographers will often place a color filter over the lens to compensate — adding blue to an indoor scene will counteract the yellows, for example. It's similar to how folks who work in video need to set the white balance on their cameras before they shoot.

Although it has long let you correct the colorcast of an image through Variations (which is discussed next), Photoshop also offers a handy tool through the Photo Filter command. Choose Image ⇨ Adjustments ⇨ Photo Filter to display the Photo Filter dialog box, as shown in Figure 17-15. You are presented with the following options:

   ✦ **Filter.** The Filter pop-up menu includes four specific filter options followed by a list of colors you can use to fix various colorcasts on your image. The first two options, Warming Filter (85) and Warming Filter (81), simulate filters that a photographer would use when the color temperature is too cool, or bluish. Warming Filter (85) produces an orange colorcast, and Warming Filter (81) adds more of a tan tint to your image. Conversely, Cooling Filter (80) and Cooling Filter (82) add to your image a dark and rich cast of blue or a light cast of blue, respectively, to account for the yellows of artificial light. The rest of the options in the pop-up menu are different color presets that let you achieve photographic effects similar to those provided by some real-life filters.

   ✦ **Color.** You can also specify any color and use it as though it were a filter. This is a great way to compensate for an unusual colorcast, such as a color light source in a scene that you'd like to neutralize. Click the color swatch to open the Color Picker and select a color. Alternatively, once the Color Picker is open, you can click anywhere in your image to choose a particular color.

   ✦ **Density.** The Density slider adjusts the amount of color correction that the Photo Filter command will apply. You can also manually type a value in the option box above the slider. Remember, you can always adjust the amount of correction after you click OK by choosing Edit ⇨ Fade Photo Filter and changing the Opacity value.

   ✦ **Preserve Luminosity.** Select this option to ensure that the brightness values will not be darkened by your color adjustments.

Tip   You can apply the Photo Filter command also as an adjustment layer, ensuring that none of the changes you make is permanent. You'll take a look at adjustment layers later in this chapter.

Figure 17-15 You can use Photoshop's Photo Filter dialog box to simulate various lens filters and correct the overall colorcasts of your images.

Using the Variations command

The Variations command is Photoshop's most essential color-correction function *and* its most un-Photoshop-ish in that it's amazingly simple and highly effective all at the same time. Typically, control comes with complexity, but not so here.

When it comes to control and effectiveness, you can adjust hues and luminosity levels based on the brightness values of the pixels, something Hue/Saturation cannot do. You can also see what you're doing by clicking little thumbnail previews (see Figure 17-16), which takes much of the guesswork out of the correction process. This is where the "alarmingly simple" description comes in.

On the other hand, the Variations dialog box takes over your screen and prevents you from previewing corrections in the image window — not a big deal, but if you're used to seeing a preview in the image window, this can be jarring. Another problem (equally slight, really) is that you can't see the area outside a selection, which can be disconcerting when making color adjustments to just part of your image. You won't know until you click OK if the adjustment you made to the selection works in context, but you can slide the dialog box aside to see the entire original image. Just click the title bar of the dialog box and drag it.

Figure 17-16: Click the "More" thumbnails to add more of one color or another to your image. Refer to the Current Pick to see your results before okaying them. Start over by clicking the Original thumbnail, and use the radio buttons to choose which aspect of the image to change. The slider adjusts sensitivity.

The Variations command is really great for correcting an image in its entirety, although it can be useful for adjusting selections (with the previously mentioned issues kept in mind). Whether you like it for the whole image or just part of it, here's how it works: To infuse color into the image, click one of the thumbnails in the central portion of the dialog box. The thumbnail labeled More Cyan, for example, shifts the colors toward cyan. The thumbnail even shows how the additional cyan will look when added to the image.

Notice that each thumbnail is positioned directly opposite its complementary color, with the Current Pick between them. More Cyan is across from More Red, More Blue is across from More Yellow, and so on. In fact, clicking a thumbnail shifts colors not only toward the named color but also away from the opposite color. For example, if you click More Cyan and then click its opposite, More Red, you arrive at the original image.

Note   Although this isn't exactly how the colors in the additive and subtractive worlds work — cyan is not the empirical opposite of red — the colors are theoretical opposites, and the Variations command makes the theory a practicality. After all, you haven't yet applied the color to the image, so the dialog box can calculate its adjustments in a pure and perfect world. Cyan and red ought to be opposites, so for the moment, they are.

To control the amount of color shifting that occurs when you click a thumbnail, move the slider in the upper-right corner of the dialog box. Fine produces minute changes; Coarse creates massive changes. Just to give you an idea of the difference between the two, you have to click a thumbnail about 40 times when the slider is set to Fine to equal one click when it's set to Coarse.

The radio buttons at the top control which colors in the image are affected. Select Shadows to change the darkest colors, Highlights to change the lightest colors, and Midtones to change everything in between.

Note

In fact, if you're familiar with the Levels dialog box, you might have noticed that the first three radio buttons have direct counterparts in the sliders in the Levels dialog box. For example, when you click the Lighter thumbnail while the Highlights option is selected in the Variations dialog box, you perform the same action as moving the white slider in the Levels dialog box to the left — that is, you make the lightest colors in the image even lighter.

Selecting the Saturation option lets you increase or decrease the saturation of colors in an image. Only one thumbnail appears on each side of the Current Pick image: one that decreases the saturation and another that increases it. The Variations command modifies saturation differently than Hue/Saturation. Hue/Saturation pushes the saturation of a color as far as it will go, but Variations attempts to modify the saturation without changing overall brightness values. As a result, an image saturated with Hue/Saturation looks lighter than one saturated with Variations.

As you click the options — particularly when modifying saturation — you may notice that unexpected colors spring up in the thumbnails. These brightly colored pixels are gamut warnings, highlighting colors that exceed the boundaries of the current color space. For example, if you're working in the RGB mode, these colors extend beyond the RGB gamut. Although the colors won't actually appear inverted as they do in the dialog box, it's not a good idea to exceed the color space because it results in areas of flat color, just as when you convert between the RGB and CMYK spaces. To view the thumbnails without the weirdly colored pixels, deselect the Show Clipping option.

Using the Match Color command

With Adobe's introduction of the Match Color command in Photoshop CS, the Photoshop user community wondered if Adobe had really added a true color-matching tool. Well, even with the release of Photoshop CS2, the answer is no, and the wait continues — the Match Color command has nothing to do with emulating the color of a match. It does, however, adjust the colorcast of one image to match that of another, which can still be pretty useful.

In case you were wondering how such a tool might be useful, imagine that you have a series of photos taken outdoors, on a day when the sun was coming in and out over the course of your shoot and the lighting was really different in several of the shots. Or you were taking photos of people indoors, and in the later afternoon, when the room got hotter, people started to look a bit flushed, or the sunlight coming into the room was starting to change and it no longer drowned out the fluorescent lighting from overhead in the room. Any of these scenarios would present you with the need to change a colorcast, making one photo's cast match another's. Brighten the cloudy photos, smooth out the ruddy cheeks, soften the pasty fluorescent glow.

You begin by opening both the image you want to adjust and the image whose color you want to match. If you want Match Color to base its analysis on a particular part of the image, such as skin tones, select the colors you want to isolate in both the source and destination images. Make sure the destination image is in the active image window and choose Image ⇨ Adjustments ⇨ Match Color to display the dialog box shown in Figure 17-17.

Figure 17-17: The Match Color command in Photoshop lets you adjust the colorcast of one image to match another.

The following list explains the options available to you in the Match Color dialog box:

✦ **Target.** The Target is automatically set as whatever image was active when you chose the command, and you can't change this. If your destination image contains a selection, the Ignore Selection when Applying Adjustment option is available. If you don't select this option, the effect will apply to only the selected area in your image, which may not be the desired result. If you've made a selection in your destination image and you don't want to confine the effect to that selection, select the option.

✦ **Image Options.** The Image Options let you make adjustments to the lightness, saturation, and strength of the Match Color command. The Luminance slider defaults to a value of 100 and lets you increase or decrease the brightness of your destination image. Color Intensity works much like the Saturation slider in the Hue/Saturation command. The Fade slider saves you the step of applying Match Color and then choosing Edit ⇨ Fade Match Color. Increase this value to gradually bring in color elements from your unaltered destination image. A value of 100 will exactly match your pre-Match Color image.

Select the Neutralize option to tell Photoshop to examine the destination image, without factoring in any values from the source image, and attempt to remove any colorcast that it finds. You may find that sometimes it works really well and sometimes it just dulls your image. If you don't get the results you want, try using the Photo Filter command, discussed earlier in this chapter, to manually target and correct a colorcast.

✦ **Image Statistics.** These options let you specify a source image and determine how it is interpreted. The source can be any other open image, or even a layer within the destination image itself. The latter is particularly useful if, for example, you're trying to composite a person from another photo on a separate layer into your destination image. If your source image contains a selection, select the Use Selection in Source to Calculate Colors option to only analyze the statistics, or characteristics, of the selected region. When this option is deselected, Match Color determines the statistics of the source by looking at all the pixels in the image. Similarly, selecting the Use Selection in Target to Calculate Adjustment option makes changes to the target image using colors found in only the selected area of that image. If you selected similarly colored areas in both your target and source images, it's a good idea to leave both of these options selected.

Use the Source pop-up menu to choose the source image from among all open images. If you select None, you still have access to the Neutralize option and other Image Options settings. If you select a source with more than one layer, you can specify the layer from which you're culling statistics in the Layer pop-up menu. You also have the option of choosing a merged composite of all the layers in the source image.

Finally, the Match Color dialog box offers you the option of both saving and then loading the statistics it has calculated from a source image. This can be useful in a couple of ways. First, it means you don't need to have a source image open when applying the Match Color command. It also means you can save the statistics of an image and use them to adjust an unlimited number of other images, on other machines, long after the original source image is out of the picture.

Note   The Match Color command only works with images in the RGB mode.

Enhancing colors in a compressed image

Now that you know several methods for adjusting hues and saturation levels with Photoshop, it's time to discuss some of the possible challenges you may face in using them. The danger of rotating colors or increasing the saturation of an image is that you can bring out some unstable colors. Adjusting the hues can switch ratty pixels from colors that your eyes aren't very sensitive to — particularly blue — into colors your eyes see very well, such as reds and greens. Drab color can also hide poor detail, which becomes painfully obvious when you make the colors bright and vivid — all the problems in the image will come screaming out at you once you've heightened the colors.

Unstable colors may be the result of JPEG compression, as in the case of the digital photo. Or you may be able to blame bad scanning or poor lighting — the potential causes are abundant, and we've all been victims. No matter what's caused your color problems, you can correct the problem using the Median and Gaussian Blur commands, explained in the following procedure. Grab a particularly color-challenged digital photo and play along.

STEPS: Boosting the Saturation of Digital Photos

1. **Select the entire image and copy it to a new layer.** You can speed this process along with the keyboard shortcuts Ctrl+A and Ctrl+J (⌘-A and ⌘-J on the Mac).

2. **Press Ctrl+U (or ⌘-U on the Mac) to display the Hue/Saturation dialog box.** Then raise the Saturation value to whatever setting you desire. Don't worry if your image starts to fall apart — that's the whole point of these steps. Pay attention to the color and don't worry about the rest.

3. **Choose Filter ➪ Noise ➪ Median.** Median is a great tool for fixing JPEG color problems, and a Radius value of 4 or 5 pixels works well for most images. You can take it even higher when working with resolutions of 200 ppi or more. This destroys the detail, but that's not important in this exercise, because you're only concerned with color right now.

4. **Choose Filter ⇨ Blur ⇨ Gaussian Blur.** As always, the Median filter introduces its own edges, and because you don't want strong edges here, you can be fairly aggressive with the Gaussian Blur settings.

5. **Select Color from the blend mode pop-up menu in the Layers palette.** Photoshop mixes the blurry color with the crisp detail underneath.

If your image is still a little soft, flatten the image and sharpen it until you like the results.

Making Custom Brightness Adjustments

You may find the Lighter and Darker options in the Variations dialog box to be more effective and controllable than the Lightness slider in the Hue/Saturation dialog box because you can specify whether to edit the darkest, lightest, or medium colors in an image. Focusing on these areas gives you the ability to target trouble spots, which is handy if not all of your pixels are in need of lighting adjustment. If your needs are even more specific, you may find that neither command is adequate for making very precise adjustments to the brightness and contrast of an image. If this is the case, Photoshop provides three expert-level commands for adjusting the brightness levels in both grayscale and color images:

✦ **Levels.** This command is great for most color corrections. It lets you adjust the darkest values, lightest values, and midrange colors with a minimum of complexity and a maximum amount of control.

✦ **Curves.** This command is great for creating special effects and correcting images beyond the help of the Levels command. Levels didn't really do it all? Using the Curves command, you can map every brightness value in every color channel to an entirely different brightness value. Hop from channel to channel, and let Curves work its magic until you're happy with the results.

✦ **Shadow/Highlight.** This command is great for altering the brightness levels of certain sections of an image without harming other sections. It provides for a different approach than the Levels command and is particularly good at fixing backlighting problems in images.

Note As with any application with a large number of fevered devotees, Photoshop's two brightness commands, Levels or Curves, have spurred some debates as to which is the more effective. Levels, it has been argued, provides a histogram, which is thought to be absolutely essential for gauging the proper setting for black and white points. Not to be outdone, Curves lets you map out a virtually infinite number of significant points on a graph. Of course, with Photoshop CS came the Histogram palette, and it remains a powerful weapon in Photoshop CS2. No longer confined to the Levels dialog box, the mighty histogram is right there under the Info and Navigator tabs in a shared palette. Every user and every user's photo will have special needs, and no one tool will serve or please them all — at least not all the time. Is there really a best here? Probably not.

The Histogram palette

As discussed earlier in the section on the Threshold command, a histogram is a graph depicting the intensity of different values in your image. While the histogram in the Threshold command displays only brightness values, the Histogram palette is capable of showing not only the brightness values but the combined color values and the individual color values in an image as well. Keep the palette on-screen and you're never more than a quick look away from knowing the distribution of levels in your image at any given time.

Choose Window ➪ Histogram to display the Histogram palette. While at first it may seem like there's not a whole lot to the palette, give it a chance. It saves you the trouble choosing the Levels command, but you don't have access to any other information or the ability to select different channels. Or do you? Click Expanded View in the palette menu, and you'll gain access to Channels. The basic, not terribly illuminating view as well as the Expanded View are shown in Figure 17-18.

Figure 17-18: The Histogram palette's Expanded View (on the right) gives you an impressive amount of information about the intensity levels of your pixels.

The expanded view is where you can explore the real power of the Histogram palette. It contains the following options:

✦ **Channel.** The Channel pop-up menu lets you determine the types of values displayed by the Histogram palette. By default it's set to the color mode in which you're working. If you're editing an image in either the Grayscale or Indexed Color modes, this menu is unavailable.

From the Channel menu, you can choose to display the default combined tonal levels or any of the color channels individually. Choose Show Channels in Color from the palette menu to display the individual channels in the colors they represent. Any additional channels you have created can also be selected from the Channel pop-up menu. Choose Luminosity to display a histogram of only the brightness levels in your image. Finally, you can call up an overlapping composite graph of all the color channels by choosing Colors.

✦ **Uncached Refresh.** Whenever you make an adjustment to an image that affects its brightness or color intensity levels, the histogram redraws itself to compensate. It saves time doing this by analyzing the already existing cache of the image and guessing how the change you've made will affect the graph. The Preferences setting that enables the Levels command to use the image cache is covered in Chapter 2.

Regardless of how you've set your preferences, the Histogram palette will automatically regenerate based on the image cache unless you click Uncached Refresh, labeled in Figure 17-19, which tells the palette to redraw the graph based on the current image. Photoshop provides a number of other ways to refresh the histogram. You can also click the cached data warning icon (labeled in Figure 17-19) that appears in the top-right corner of the histogram whenever you're viewing a graph created from the cache. Additionally, you can accomplish the same thing by doubling-clicking the histogram itself. Finally, you can choose the Uncached Refresh option from the palette menu.

✦ **Source.** In a multilayered image, you can tell the Histogram palette to display values for either the Entire Image or just the Selected Layer from the Source pop-up menu. If the image contains any adjustment layers, select one of them and choose Adjustment Composite from the Source pop-up menu to display a histogram of the adjustment layer and any visible layers below it.

Below the Source menu in the expanded view, you'll find statistical information about the image or layer, which you can toggle on or off by choosing Show Statistics from the palette menu. The statistics give you some useful information about the intensity values in your image, plus you can find out about the intensity Level at the spot under your cursor. You can also view the Count, which tells you the total number of pixels in the image that match a particular intensity.

One of the great strengths of the Histogram palette is the fact that it updates on the fly even while you're working in one of the color adjustments dialog boxes (but only if you have selected the Preview option). Even better, the palette doesn't simply replace the original histogram with the new one; it keeps the original histogram visible behind the adjusted histogram in a grayed-out version. Figure 17-19, along with a display of a separate histogram graph for each color channel in your image. To display these multiple-channel histograms, choose All Channels View from the palette menu.

Tip   When you select a portion of an image, the Histogram palette displays intensity levels and statistics for only the selected area.

Although many of the other palettes become frozen when you're working in a dialog box, you never lose access to the options in the Histogram palette — given its needing to be used in conjunction with so many of them. One exception? You can't access the Histogram palette options when the Filter Gallery window is open.

Oh, and don't panic if you go to the palette and see a circle with a line through it where the histogram should be — this is simply what's displayed when there is no image open in the Photoshop workspace.

Figure 17-19: While it's no shrinking violet, the Histogram palette's All Channels view can be really useful when you need a quick view of the color intensity distribution in your image. Coupled with the historical view provided by Expanded View, this palette tells quite a story.

The Levels command

When you choose Image ⇨ Adjustments ⇨ Levels or press Ctrl+L (⌘-L on the Mac), Photoshop displays the Levels dialog box shown in Figure 17-20. The dialog box offers a histogram, matching the combined tonal histogram found in the Histogram palette, as well as two sets of slider bars with corresponding option boxes and a three automated Eyedropper options in the lower-right corner. You can compress and expand the range of brightness values in an image by manipulating the Input Levels options (drag the sliders). Then you can map the original brightness values to new brightness values by adjusting the Output Levels options.

Figure 17-20: Use the Levels dialog box to map brightness values in the image (Input Levels) to new brightness values (Output Levels).

The options in the Levels dialog box work as follows:

✦ **Channel.** Select the color channel that you want to edit from this pop-up menu. You can apply different Input Levels and Output Levels values to each color channel. However, the options along the right side of the dialog box affect all colors in the selected portion of an image regardless of which Channel option is active.

✦ **Input Levels.** Use these options to modify the contrast of the image by darkening the darkest colors and lightening the lightest ones. The Input Levels option boxes correspond to the slider immediately below the histogram. You map pixels to black (or the darkest Output Levels value) by typing a number from 0 to 255 in the first option box or by dragging the black slider. For example, if you raise the value to 50, all colors with brightness values of 50 or less in the original image become black, darkening the image as shown in the first example of Figure 17-21.

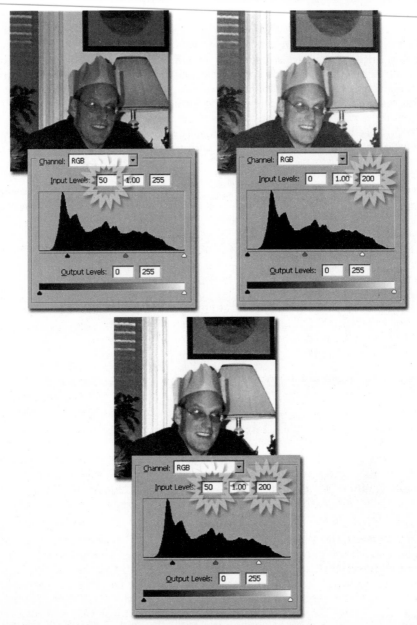

Figure 17-21: The results of raising the first Input Levels value to 50 (left), lowering the last value to 200 (right), and combining the two (bottom).

You can map pixels at the opposite end of the brightness scale to white (or the lightest Output Levels value) by typing a number from 0 to 255 in the last option box or by dragging the white slider. If you lower the value to 200, all colors with brightness values of 200 or greater become white, lightening the image, as shown in the second example of Figure 17-21. In the last example of the figure, the first value was raised and the last value lowered, thereby increasing the amount of contrast in the image.

Tip The Input Levels value is to select the numeric field and then press the up- or down-arrow key. Each press of an arrow key raises or lowers the value by 1. Press Shift with an arrow key to change the value in increments of 10.

Tip If you press and hold Alt (or Option on the Mac) while dragging the black and white Input Levels sliders, you can watch where the first shadows appear and where the first highlight detail begins in your RGB image.

✦ **Gamma.** The middle Input Levels option box and the corresponding gray tri-angle in the slider bar (shown in Figure 17-22) represent the midtone, or *gamma value*, which is the brightness level of the medium-gray value in the image. The gamma value can range from 0.10 to 9.99, with 1.00 being dead-on medium gray. Increase the gamma value or drag the gray slider to the left to lighten the medium grays (also called *midtones*). Lower the gamma value or drag the gray slider to the right to darken the medium grays.

Figure 17-22: The middle slider under the Histogram controls midtones. Drag it to adjust \\ middle box, or type a new number in the box and see the slider move to indicate the new midtone level.

Tip You can edit the gamma value also by pressing the up- and down-arrow keys. Pressing an arrow key changes the value by 0.01; pressing Shift+arrow changes the value by 0.10.

✦ **Output Levels.** Use these options to curtail the range of brightness levels in an image by lightening the darkest pixels and darkening the lightest pixels. You adjust the brightness of the darkest pixels—those that correspond to the black Input Levels slider—by typing a number from 0 to 255 in the first option box or by dragging the black slider. For example, if you raise the value to 100, no color can be darker than that brightness level (roughly 60 percent black), which lightens the image. You adjust the brightness of the lightest pixels—those that correspond to the white Input Levels slider—by typing a number from 0 to 255 in the second option box or by dragging the white slider. If you lower the value to 175, no color can be lighter than that brightness level (roughly 30 percent black), darkening the image. If you raise the first value and lower the second value, you dramatically decrease the amount of contrast in the image. Note that any change to the Output Levels values will decrease the contrast of the image. Figure 17-23 shows two halves of the same image—the left half has darks made lighter, and the right half has lights made darker.

Tip

You can fully or partially invert an image using the Output Levels slider triangles. Just drag the black slider to the right and drag the white slider to the left past the black slider. The colors flip, whites mapping to dark colors and blacks mapping to light colors.

✦ **Load and Save.** You can load settings to disk and save settings to disk using these buttons.

✦ **Auto.** You might assume that the Auto button in the Levels dialog box performs the same function as the Auto Levels command, discussed earlier in this chapter. And if you were working in a version of the program before Photoshop 7, you'd be right. Photoshop 7, however, added the Options button into the mix. Since then, the effect of clicking Auto in the Levels dialog box (as well as in the Curves dialog box) has depended on the settings in the Auto Color Correction Options dialog box, described next.

✦ **Options.** Clicking Options in the Levels (or Curves) dialog box brings up the Auto Color Correction Options dialog box, shown in Figure 17-24. The top section, Algorithms, determines the type of correction you want to apply. Instead of the long, somewhat confusing names, these three choices could be labeled Auto Contrast, Auto Levels, and Auto Color, because that's what the choices are equivalent to. In fact, you can rest your cursor over each name to see an informative tool tip telling you just this. Select the Snap Neutral Midtones option and you'll apply Auto Color's automatic gamma correction as well. If you select the Save as Defaults option, your settings will be remembered the next time you click Auto in the Levels and Curves dialog boxes.

The Target Colors & Clipping settings come into play not only when you click Auto in the Levels and Curves dialog boxes but also when you choose the Auto Levels and Auto Contrast commands in the Adjustments submenu. (This is assuming that Save as Defaults is selected.) Here you can choose colors to assign to the target values for the highlights, midtones, and shadows in your image. You also have access to the Clip values for the highlights and shadows. Type higher values to increase the number of pixels mapped to black and white; decrease the values to lessen the effect. Figure 17-25 compares the effect of the default 0.50 percent values to higher values of 5.00 and 9.99 percent (the highest setting the field accepts). As you can see, raising the Clip value produces higher contrast effects.

Figure 17-23: Lighten your darks and darken your lights. The result of raising the first Output Levels value to 100 (left), lowering the second value to 175.

Figure 17-24: Customizing the settings in the Auto Color Correction Options dialog box lets you take the "auto" out of Photoshop's auto correction commands.

Figure 17-25: The effect of the default Clip values in the Auto Color Correction Options dialog box (.50% on the left) and the effect after raising the values (5.00% in the middle and 9.99% on the right).

Note The Clip settings have an effect on only Auto Levels and Contrast, not Auto Color. The reason is that Auto Color seeks to neutralize shadows and highlights, as opposed to clipping away the darkest and lightest colors.

Tip You can combine the Auto Color Correction Options with the Auto Color command to create a truly useful tool. If you have a batch of photos you need to correct that share similar problems — maybe you've scanned an overexposed roll of film from a recent holiday — make adjustments to the first photo with the Target Colors & Clipping settings and make sure you select the Save as Defaults option. Now when you open subsequent photos, you can simply choose Image ⇨ Adjustments ⇨ Auto Color — or, press Ctrl+Shift+B (⌘-Shift-B on the Mac) — to instantly apply the same color correction.

✦ **Eyedroppers.** Select one of the Eyedropper tools in the Levels dialog box and click a pixel in the image window to automatically adjust the color of that pixel. If you click a pixel with the black Eyedropper tool (the first of the three), Photoshop maps the color of the pixel and all darker colors to black. If you click a pixel with the white Eyedropper tool (the last of the three), Photoshop maps it and all lighter colors to white. Use the gray Eyedropper tool (middle) to change the color you clicked to medium gray and adjust all other colors accordingly.

Tip

One way to use the Eyedropper tools is to color-correct scans without a lot of messing around. Include a neutral swatch of gray with the photograph you want to scan. (For those who own a Pantone swatch book, Cool Gray 5 or 6 is your best bet.) After opening the scan in Photoshop, choose the Levels command, select the gray Eyedropper tool, and click the neutral gray swatch in the image window. This technique won't perform miracles, but it will help you distribute lights and darks in the image more evenly. You then can fine-tune the image using the Input Levels and Output Levels options.

Tip

By default, the Eyedroppers map to white, gray, and black. But you can change that. Double-click any one of the three Eyedroppers to display the Color Picker dialog box. For example, suppose you double-click the white Eyedropper, set the color values to C:2, M:3, Y:5, K:0, and then click a pixel in the image window. Instead of making the pixel white, Photoshop changes the clicked color — and all colors lighter than it — to C:2, M:3, Y:5, K:0, which is great for avoiding hot highlights and ragged edges.

To give you a sense of how the Levels command works, the following steps describe how to improve the appearance of a low-contrast, shadow-heavy image:

STEPS: Correcting Brightness and Contrast with the Levels Command

1. **Press Ctrl+L (or ⌘-L on the Mac) to display the Levels dialog box.** Probably, most of the colors for this image are clustered on the left side of the histogram, showing that there are far more dark colors than light.

2. **Press Ctrl+1 (or ⌘-1 on the Mac) to examine the Red channel.** Assuming that you're editing an RGB image, Ctrl+1 (⌘-1 on the Mac) displays a histogram for the Red channel.

3. **Edit the black Input Levels value as needed.** Drag the black slider to below the point at which the histogram begins.

4. **Edit the white Input Levels value.** Drag the white slider to below the point at which the histogram ends.

5. **Edit the gamma value.** Drag the gray slider to the center of the histogram. Imagine that the histogram is a big mass, and you're trying to balance the mass evenly on top of the gray triangle.

6. **Repeat Steps 2 through 5 for the Green and Blue channels.** Ctrl+2 (or ⌘-2 on the Mac) takes you to the Green channel; Ctrl+3 (or ⌘-3 on the Mac) takes you to Blue. At this point, your image probably has a preponderance of Red about it. To correct this, you need to edit the Green and Blue channels in kind. Feel free to switch back and forth between channels as much as you like to get everything just right.

7. **Press Ctrl+~ (tilde) (or ⌘-~ on the Mac) to return to the composite RGB histogram.** After you get the color balance right, you can switch back to the composite mode and further edit the Input Levels. You may notice that your RGB histogram has changed. Although the histograms in the individual color channels remain fixed, the composite histogram updates to reflect the red, green, and blue modifications.

8. **Press Enter (or Return on the Mac) to apply your changes.**

The Curves command

If you want to be able to map any brightness value in an image to absolutely any other brightness value, the Curves command is what you need. When you choose Image ➪ Adjustments ➪ Curves or press Ctrl+M (⌘-M on the Mac), Photoshop displays the Curves dialog box, shown in Figure 17-26, which offers access to the most complex and powerful color-correction options on the planet.

Here's a quick sketch of how the Curves dialog box options work:

✦ **Channel.** The concept of channels isn't new, certainly — and the use of channels within an adjustment dialog box is nothing new in the case of Curves, either. You select the color channel that you want to edit from this pop-up menu, and then apply different mapping functions to different channels by drawing in the graph below the pop-up menu. Of course, as always, the options along the right side of the dialog box affect all colors in the selected portion of an image regardless of which Channel option is active.

✦ **Brightness graph.** The brightness graph is where you map brightness values in the original image to new brightness values. The horizontal axis of the graph represents input levels; the vertical axis represents output levels. The *brightness curve* charts the relationship between input and output levels. The lower-left corner is the origin of the graph (the point at which both input and output values are 0). Move right in the graph for higher input values and up for higher output values. The brightness graph is the core of this dialog box, so upcoming sections explain it in more detail.

Brightness curve

Brightness Graph

Brightness bars   Curve tools   Eyedroppers

Figure 17-26: Click on the curved line in the Curves dialog box and drag the line up or down, from one or more points on the line. The brightness in the active photo is thereby adjusted.

Tip

By default, a grid of horizontal and vertical dotted lines crisscrosses the brightness graph, subdividing it into quarters. For added precision, you can divide the graph into horizontal and vertical tenths by Alt-clicking (Win) or Option-clicking (Mac) in the graph to toggle between tenths and quarters.

✦ **Brightness bar.** The horizontal brightness bar shows the direction of light and dark values in the graph. When the dark end of the brightness bar appears on the left — as by default when editing an RGB image — colors are measured in terms of brightness values. The colors in the graph proceed from black on the left to white on the right, as demonstrated in the left example of Figure 17-27. Therefore, higher values produce lighter colors. This setting measures colors in the same direction as the Levels dialog box.

If you click the brightness bar, white and black switch places, as shown in the second example of the figure. The result is that Photoshop measures the colors in terms of ink coverage, from 0 to 100 percent of the primary color. Higher values now produce darker colors. This is the default setting for grayscale and CMYK images.

Figure 17-27: Click the brightness bar to change the way in which the graph measures color: by brightness values (left) or by ink coverage (right).

✦ **Curve tools.** Use the Curve tools to draw the curve in the brightness graph. The Point tool (labeled in Figure 17-28) is selected by default. Click in the graph with this tool to add a point to the curve. Drag a point to move it. To delete a point, Ctrl-click (Win) or ⌘-click (Mac) it.

The Pencil tool lets you draw free-form curves simply by dragging in the graph, as illustrated in Figure 17-28. This pencil works much like Photoshop's standard Pencil tool, in that you can draw straight lines by clicking one location in the graph and Shift-clicking a different point.

✦ **Input and Output values.** The Input and Output values monitor the location of your cursor in the graph according to brightness values or ink coverage, depending on the setting of the brightness bar. You can modify the Input and Output values when working with the point tool. Just click the point on the graph that you want to adjust and then type new values. The Input number represents the brightness or ink value of the point before you entered the Curves dialog box; the Output number represents the new brightness or ink value.

When editing multiple graph points from the keyboard, you may want to activate the points from the keyboard. To advance from one point to the next, press Ctrl+Tab (or Control-Tab on the Mac). To select the previous point, press Ctrl+Shift+Tab (or Control-Shift-Tab on the Mac). To deselect all points, press Ctrl+D (or ⌘-D on the Mac).

Pencil tool cursor

Figure 17-28: Use the Curves dialog box Pencil tool to draw free-form lines in the brightness graph. If the lines end up jagged or spiky, you can soften them by clicking Smooth.

Smooth tool

Pencil tool

Tip

You can change the Output value also by using the up- and down-arrow keys. Click the point you want to modify, and then press the up- or down-arrow key to raise or lower, respectively, the Output value in increments of 1. Press Shift+up or down arrow to change the Output value in increments of 10. Note that these techniques — and the ones that follow — work only when the Point tool is active because you can't change points with the Pencil tool.

✦ **Load and Save.** Use these buttons to load and save curve settings to disk, respectively.

✦ **Smooth.** Click Smooth to smooth out curves drawn with the Pencil tool. Doing so leads to smoother color transitions in the image window. This button is dimmed unless the Pencil tool is active.

✦ **Auto.** This button is identical to the Auto button available in the Levels dialog box — it allows you to apply, automatically, the settings you can establish in the Options dialog box (opened by clicking Options, discussed in the next paragraph) when Auto is clicked. For more details on this concept, see the section "The Levels command" earlier in this chapter — the Levels dialog box has an Auto button, too.

✦ **Options.** Identical to the Options button in the Levels dialog box, this opens the Auto Color Correction dialog box, wherein you can set the Target Colors and Clipping settings discussed in the Levels command coverage earlier in

this chapter. Whatever you set in this dialog box is applied by the aforementioned Auto button.

✦ **Eyedroppers.** If you move the cursor out of the dialog box and into the image
window, you get the standard eyedropper cursor. Click a pixel in the image to
locate the brightness value of that pixel in the graph. A circle appears in the
graph, and the Input and Output numbers list the value for as long as you
hold down the mouse button, as shown in the first example in Figure 17-29.

The other eyedroppers work as they do in the Levels dialog box, mapping pix-
els to black, medium gray, or white (or other colors if you double-click the
Eyedropper icons, which opens the Color Picker). For example, the White
Point Eyedropper tool changes whichever pixel you click on to white.

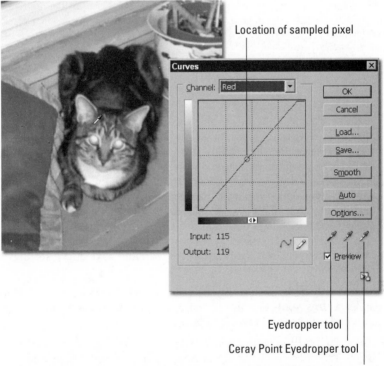

Location of sampled pixel

Eyedropper tool

Ceray Point Eyedropper tool

White Point Eyedropper tool

Figure 17-29: Use the standard eyedropper cursor (the first of the three
buttons) to locate a color in the brightness graph. Click with one of the
Eyedropper tools from the Curves dialog box to map the color of that pixel
in the graph. You then can edit the location of the point in the graph by
dragging it.

Tricks for Curves

The eyedropper tools aren't the only way to add points to a curve from the image window. Photoshop offers two more keyboard tricks that greatly simplify the process of pinpointing and adjusting colors in the Curves dialog box. Bear in mind, both techniques work only when the Point tool is active.

✦ To add a color as a point along the Curves graph, Ctrl-click (or ⌘-click on the Mac) a pixel in the image window. Photoshop adds the point to the channel displayed in the dialog box. For example, if the RGB composite channel is visible, the point is added to the RGB composite curve. If the Red channel is visible, Photoshop adds the point to the red graph and leaves the green and blue graphs unchanged.

✦ To add a color to all graphs, regardless of which channel is visible in the Curves dialog box, Ctrl+Shift-click (or ⌘-Shift-click on the Mac) a pixel in the image window. In the case of an RGB image, Photoshop maps the red, green, and blue brightness values for that pixel to each of the red, green, and blue graphs in the Curves dialog box. The RGB composite graph shows no change — switch to the individual channels to see the new point.

Note   Bear in mind that Photoshop maps the value to each color channel independently. So when editing a full-color image in the Curves dialog box, you need to switch channels to see the results of clicking with the eyedropper. You can further adjust the brightness value of that pixel by dragging the corresponding point in the graph, as demonstrated in the last example of the figure.

Tip   Remember, keep an eye on the Histogram palette to view dynamic, constantly updating results while working in the Curves dialog box.

Gradient maps

The Gradient Map command permits you to apply a gradation as a Curves map. In other words, you can use a gradient map to adjust the brightness values of an image so that they match the values in a custom gradient. Just choose Image ➪ Adjustments ➪ Gradient Map to display the dialog box pictured in Figure 17-30. Make sure the Preview option is selected. Then click the down-pointing arrowhead to the right of the gradient preview to display the familiar gradient drop-down palette, and select a gradient from the palette.

How does this work? Well, any gradient can be expressed as a Curves graph, progressing through a variety of brightness values in each of the three (RGB) or four (CMYK) color channels. When applied as a gradient map, the beginning of the gradient maps black; the end of the gradient maps white. If you apply the Violet, Orange preset, for example, the dark colors in the image map to violet and the light colors map to orange. Noise-type gradients (introduced in Chapter 6) produce especially interesting effects.

Figure 17-30: Choose the Gradient Map command to apply a preset gradient as a Curves map.

Practical applications: Continuous curves

Note   Due to the complex nature and general usefulness of the Curves dialog box, this and the following section explore practical applications of its many options, concentrating first on the Point tool and then on the Pencil tool. As the coverage progresses, it is assumed that the brightness bar is set to edit brightness values, so that the gradation in the bar lightens from left to right. If you set the bar to edit ink coverage — where the bar darkens from left to right — you can still achieve the effects described, but you must drag in the opposite direction. For example, if the discussion tells you to lighten colors by dragging upward, you would drag downward. To avoid any confusion, you might want to set your brightness bar to edit brightness (rather than ink) so that what you're looking at matches what's described here.

When you first open the Curves dialog box, the brightness curve appears as a straight line strung between two points, as shown in the first example of Figure 17-31, mapping every input level from black (the lower-left point) to white (the upper-right point) at an identical output level. If you want to perform seamless color corrections, the Point tool is your best bet because it enables you to edit the levels in the brightness graph while maintaining a continuous curve. If you were to try to do that with the Pencil tool, you may not be able to maintain the curve's integrity.

To lighten the colors, click near the middle of the curve with the Point tool to create a new point and then drag the point upward, as demonstrated in the second example of Figure 17-32. To darken the image, drag the point downward, as in the third example.

Figure 17-31: Click to create a single point in the curve with the Point tool (top) and then drag it upward (middle image) to lighten the image evenly or downward (bottom image) to or darken it evenly. Note that the Output value changes to reflect the conditions on the curve line.

Figure 17-32: Create two points in the curve to change the appearance of contrast in an image, whether by increasing it mildly (top image), decreasing it (middle image, where points are dragged in opposite directions), or boosting it dramatically (bottom image, where a steeper curve is created).

You can also create two points in the curve to boost or lessen the contrast between colors in the image. In the first example of Figure 17-32, there's one point very near the white point in the curve and another point very close to the black point. The curve was dragged down on the left point and up on the right point to make the dark pixels darker and the light pixels lighter, which translates to higher contrast.

In the second example of the figure, the opposite was done — the left point was dragged up to lighten the dark pixels and the right point was dragged down to darken the light pixels. As you can see in the second image, this lessens the contrast between colors, making the image more gray.

In the final example of Figure 17-32, the contrast was heightened considerably by dragging the right point down and to the left. This has the effect of pushing the right half of the curve farther upward, creating a steep curve and increasing the brightness of the light pixels in the image.

Practical applications: Arbitrary curves

You can create some bizarre color variations by adjusting the brightness curve arbitrarily, mapping light pixels to dark, dark pixels to light, and moving everything in between in all sorts of directions. Figure 17-33 is an example of the kind of curve you can create and the results you can achieve in your image — turning a simple tabby housecat into a psychedelic feral feline.

Tip

If you're interested in something a little more subtle, try applying an arbitrary curve to a single channel in a color image. You could, for example, apply relatively basic color manipulations in the Green and Blue channels, followed by an arbitrary adjustment to the Red channel.

When drawing arbitrary curves, you may find the Pencil tool to be more flexible than the Point tool — although you will probably want to follow the Pencil tool with a click of the Smooth button so that any unwanted zigs, zags, or jags in the line can be ironed out in favor of smooth waves.

The Shadow/Highlight command

Sometimes it seems that the camera, be it digital or film, sees more than we do with our eyes. This is normally an observation made when a photo exposes some detail that no one noticed had the scene in question not been captured in a still photo, where every little object could be studied. In truth, the lens on any camera, but especially a digital camera can't hold a candle to the human eye in terms of capturing light and color.

Figure 17-33: Click along the curve and add several points, and then drag them up and down. For darker results, keep the first point low, and add as many waves as you need for the results you want.

Modern cameras try their best to keep up with complicated and varied lighting situations, but unlike your eyes, which can probably adjust and absorb the next scene after just one blink, when it comes to a camera, you're often stuck having to choose between sacrificing the darker areas of an image or overexposing the lighter areas because the camera just can't keep up. For example, how many times have you photographed someone against the sky, only to find the sky perfectly exposed and your subject so dark you can barely make out his or her features?

Thanks to Photoshop's Shadow/Highlight command, the camera's limitations can be accommodated. It's a great tool for both the too-bright and the too-dark photo (or portions thereof), pulling detail out of the shadows and shielding your eyes from blinding highlights. You may find that that you're happier with its results on images with dark shadows, however, but you'll be glad to have it in your arsenal for a variety of lighting problems.

To use the command, choose Image ⇨ Adjustments ⇨ Shadow/Highlight and select the Show More Options check box to view the dialog box shown in Figure 17-34. As soon as you choose the command, you'll see a change take place in your image, as the command does a little bit of its job right away. You can further the effects by adjusting the three areas of the dialog box — Shadows, Highlights, and Adjustments — and the sliders within them.

The Shadow/Highlight command examines the image and, according to your settings, deems certain spots to be "shadows" and others "highlights." From there, you adjust the sliders to tell Photoshop just how much brightening or darkening it should perform on those areas. It's a smart feature that's deceptively easy to master. The first two sections of the dialog box, Shadows and Highlights, contain identically named sliders. Naturally, the Shadows section controls the lightening of shadows in an image, and the Highlights section controls the darkening of brighter areas. Here's a list of the options available in both sections:

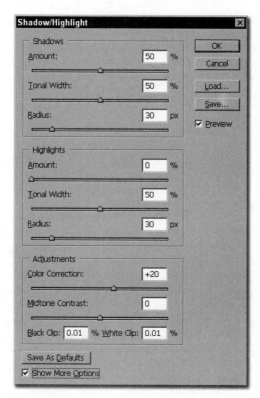

Figure 17-34: The Shadow/Highlight dialog box lets you correct exposure problems in specific areas of an image without harming other areas.

✦ **Amount.** In the Shadows section, the Amount slider lets you specify the degree to which the shadows in an image will be lightened. In the Highlights section, the slider controls how much the highlights will be darkened. A value of 0 percent yields no change in the image; a value of 100 percent results in maximum lightening of the shadows (in the Shadows section) or darkening of the highlights (in the Highlights section). The default Shadows Amount setting of 50 percent is a safe place to start when lightening shadows in an image.

✦ **Tonal Width.** This setting adjusts the range of the pixels that get modified by the command. In the Shadows section, higher values increase the range of shadow areas that gets lightened and lower values concentrate on only the darker regions of the image. In the Highlights section, higher values increase the range of light areas that gets darkened and lower values restrict the adjustment to only the lighter regions. The default Tonal Width value in both sections is 50 percent. If you find that the command is lightening too much of an image, lower the value in the Shadows section to correct it.

✦ **Radius.** The Shadow/Highlight command determines which areas are shadows and which are highlights by examining each pixel compared to the pixels that surround it. This prevents every stray dark pixel from being classified as a shadow and subsequently lightened, for example. Adjust the Radius sliders to determine the size of each pixel's neighborhood, or in other words, the number of surrounding pixels that are taken into account when each pixel is categorized as shadow or highlight.

Radius is the setting you'll most likely need to adjust on an image-by-image basis. The default setting of 30 pixels is a good place to start, but keep in mind that by increasing the Radius value you apply a less exacting change to the image, and by decreasing the value you lose some of the contrast.

Below the Shadows and Highlights sections is a third area labeled Adjustments. It contains the following options:

✦ **Color Correction.** Occasionally, the Shadow/Highlight command can make the colors in an image a little less vivid. The Color Correction slider lets you adjust the saturation of the color in the affected portion of the image. In grayscale images, this option is replaced with a general Brightness setting.

Tip   You can achieve an interesting effect by increasing the Amount value in the Shadows section and ramping down the Color Correction setting. The result is an image in which all pixels formerly in the shadowed areas become grayscale. In addition to producing an interesting effect, it also lets you glimpse exactly which pixels are being affected.

✦ **Midtone Contrast.** This setting is fairly self-explanatory. It increases or decreases the contrast of the midtone pixels in the image. Generally speaking, higher values mean a darker image and lower values produce a lighter, more even result.

✦ **Black Clip and White Clip.** These values let you adjust the maximum settings for how dark the adjusted shadow pixels will be and how light the adjusted highlight pixels will be. While the limit for both values is 50 percent, it is advisable to never even approach that high a value. On the contrary, keep these settings as low as you can to provide for smooth transitions and healthy contrast levels in your images.

The Shadow/Highlight dialog box lets you save your settings and then load them later using the Save and Load buttons on the right. If you want to designate your current settings as the default for the command, click Save As Defaults at the bottom of the dialog box. Finally, select the Show More Options check box to toggle between the default reduced view, which gives you access to only the two Amount sliders, and the expanded view, which presents you with all the options just discussed.

Tip   Okay, this has been mentioned before, but it's worth repeating: The Histogram palette is a great way to keep track of brightness and tonal changes to an image. It keeps up with you expertly while you're working in the Shadow/Highlight dialog box.

Figure 17-35 shows a photo of a bird's nest and birds in a tree, against a bright blue sky (yes, it's all gray in your view, I know). The details of the branches and nest are lost to the shadows, however, and need to be revealed so that the image looks like less of a silhouette. In the second image (accompanied by the Shadow/Highlight dialog box), you can see the settings that worked for this image — your results and settings will vary, depending on your image and its problems.

Correcting exposure

It might seem like the Shadow/Highlight command is all you'd need for a photo that's too dark or too light, with detail-smothering shadows and blinding, eye-piercing highlights. For some photos, that would be true — Shadow/Highlight and its extensive set of tools would be all you need. On the other hand, if all-over exposure is the problem and one shadowy or glaring area isn't what you're trying to fix, the Exposure command, new to Photoshop CS2, is your answer. As shown in Figure 17-36, the dialog box is very simple — three sliders and three eyedroppers for setting black, gray, and white points. There's also a Preview option, so you can see your adjustments take effect in the image window, as you make them.

Figure 17-35: The Shadow/Highlight command reveals details that would otherwise be lost to intense shadows, while leaving the correctly exposed portions of the image just as they were. The original photo is on the top.

Figure 17-36: Adjust your photo's overall Exposure with three simple sliders. Used alone or with the help of other Adjustment submenu commands, the Exposure tools can fix under- or overexposed photos quickly.

Some details about your Exposure options:

✦ **Exposure.** This slider does just what you'd expect — it increases or decreases exposure, depending on how far you drag it to the left or right. Drag to the right, and the image brightens, drag to the left and it darkens. Sometimes, this is the only slider you need to use, depending on the nature of the problems caused by the exposure of the original image. If the colors look fine after just a slight increase in the exposure (brightening an underexposed image, for example), you won't need to tinker with the other two sliders at all. On the other hand, if sliding the Exposure setting in either direction creates colorful havoc, the Offset and Gamma sliders (to be explained next) may need a tweak.

✦ **Offset.** Set to 0.00 by default, increasing it both decreases contrast and brings all the pixels closer to gray. Decreasing the Offset increases contrast and brings all pixels closer to black.

✦ **Gamma.** This setting adjusts the brightness of the midtone values. Set to a default of 1.00, an increase in Gamma brightens the colors, eventually shifting the entire image to white. Drag the other way, and the colors are darkened.

✦ **Eyedroppers.** Click the Set Black Point button (the first of three eyedropper buttons) and then click on the pixel in your image that's closest to black. The image exposure adjusts as soon as you click the pixel. The middle button, Set Gray Point, establishes a midpoint for your photo's pixel range, and the Set White Point button is used to establish the white or lightest pixel in the photo. In the photo in Figure 17-37, the black point could be any of the shadows on the birds or tree, a midpoint or gray pixel could be on the tree's bark where the sun has illuminated it slightly, and a white point would be where the bark is torn away exposing the bare, very light flesh of the tree branch. Figure 17-37 shows an original photo with exposure problems — the same one used to demonstrate Shadow/Highlight, to show that two different tools can be used to attack the same problem — and includes the "after" version and the Exposure dialog box so you can see the settings that fixed the photo.

Figure 17-37: Before (top) and after (bottom). The underexposure resulting in darks that hide details and a sky that's really too dark can be remedied by increasing the exposure and increasing Offset and Gamma just a tiny bit.

Adjustment Layers

Every one of the commands discussed in this chapter is applicable to a single layer at a time. If you want to correct the colors in multiple layers, you have to create a special kind of layer called an *adjustment layer*. Adjustment layers are layers that contain mathematical color correction information. The layer applies its corrections to all layers beneath it, without affecting any layers above.

You can create an adjustment layer in one of two ways:

✦ Choose Layer ➪ New Adjustment Layer. This displays a submenu of color adjustment commands, ranging from Levels and Curves to Invert, Threshold, and Posterize. The menu appears in Figure 17-38.

✦ Click the button that looks like a black and white cookie at the bottom of the Layers palette, also shown in Figure 17-38. The first three options — Solid Color, Gradient, and Pattern — are dynamic fill layers, as discussed in Chapter 14. Choose any one of the remaining 12 options to make a new adjustment layer.

Create New Fill or Adjustment Layer button

Figure 17-38: The Fill and Adjustment Layer menu offers four Fill options and 12 Adjustment Layer choices.

If you choose a command from the Layer ➪ New Adjustment Layer submenu, Photoshop displays the New Layer dialog box, which permits you to name the layer, assign a color, and set the blend mode, as shown in Figure 17-39. You can also group the adjustment layer with the currently selected layer, which means that the adjustment layer will affect only that layer. If you choose an option from the Create New Fill or Adjustment Layer button in the Layers palette (labeled in Figure 17-38), Photoshop bypasses the New Layer dialog box and targets the selected correction. Choosing Curves, for example, displays the Curves dialog box — Invert is the only option that produces no dialog box. Change the settings as desired and press Enter or Return as you normally would. If you press and hold Alt or Option while clicking the adjustment layer icon in the Layers palette, you'll get the New Layer dialog box just as if you'd chosen from the menu commands.

Figure 17-39: First, the New Layer dialog box, which appears if you start the Adjustment Layer process from the menu — name your layer and choose its Color and Mode. Second, the Layers palette after an Adjustment Layer has been added — the name of the layer is determined by the choice made from the submenu of adjustments that can be made.

Layer Mask thumbnail

Link icon

Adjustment Layer icon

Regardless of the color adjustment you select, it appears as a new layer in the Layers palette, as shown in Figure 17-39. Photoshop marks adjustment layers with special icons that look like miniature versions of their respective dialog boxes. This way, you can readily tell them apart from image layers. As you can also see in Figure 17-39, adjustment layers automatically come with accompanying layer masks. You can take advantage of this fact, ignore the mask, or delete the mask by dragging it to the trash can icon.

The advantages of layer-based corrections

The whole concept of using Adjustment Layers to apply corrections to multiple layers may not seem so revolutionary, given that there are other ways to make your adjustments affect multiple layers. Before you write off everything said so far about Adjustment Layers as some sort of hype, though, consider these points:

✦ **They're forever editable.** As long as the adjustment layer remains intact, stored in one of the three formats that support layers (native Photoshop PSD, TIFF, or PDF), you can edit the color correction over and over again without damaging the underlying pixels. Unlike standard color corrections that alter selected pixels directly, adjustment layers have no permanent effect on the pixels.

Caution   When editing the settings for an adjustment layer, be sure to double-click the first icon that precedes the layer name (labeled "Adjustment layer icon" in Figure 17-40). Double-clicking elsewhere displays the Layer Mask Display Options or the Layer Style dialog box, or it allows you to rename the layer.

✦ **They offer versatile layer masking.** You can also adjust the affected area to your heart's content. Unless it's grouped with another layer, an adjustment layer covers the entire image like a tight-fitting blanket. An adjustment layer doesn't contain pixels, so painting inside the layer changes its layer mask. Paint with black to remove the correction from an area; use white to paint the correction back in.

Tip   In fact, if a selection is active when you create a new adjustment layer, Photoshop automatically creates a layer mask according to the selection outline.

✦ **You can reorder your corrections.** As with any layers, you can shuffle adjustment layers up and down in the stacking order. For example, if you decide you don't want the correction to affect a specific layer, just drag the adjustment layer to a level in the Layers palette below the layer you want to exclude. If you're juggling multiple adjustment layers, you can shuffle the adjustment layers to change the order in which they're applied. This includes the standard reordering keyboard shortcuts, Ctrl+[and Ctrl+] (⌘-[and ⌘-] on the Mac).

Figure 17-40: The two adjustment layers applied in this image brightened the sky (Levels, applied to the sky layer) and the tree branches, nest, and birds (Curves). After applying both layers and choosing not to apply Levels to the top layer, the desired effect was achieved. You can revisit the original in Figure 17-36.

✦ **You can Fade corrections.** As you know, you can use the Edit ➪ Fade command on a standard color correction right after you apply the correction. With an adjustment layer, however, you can use the Fade command on a correction.

✦ **You can correct using blend modes without ballooning file sizes.** Some people prefer to correct overly light or dark images using blend modes. For example, such a person might take an image, copy it to a new layer, and apply the Multiply mode to darken the layer or Screen to lighten it. The problem with this approach is that it increases the size of the image in memory. Duplicating the image to a new layer requires Photoshop to double the size of the image in RAM. If you darken or lighten through an adjustment layer, no such size increase or memory hogging occurs.

Tip

Adjustment layers permit you to apply this same technique without adding pixels to RAM. Create a new adjustment layer with the Levels option selected, and after the Levels dialog box appears, press Enter or Return to ignore it. Next, select Multiply or Screen from the blend mode pop-up menu in the Layers palette. The adjustment layer serves as a surrogate duplicate of the layers below it, mimicking every merged pixel. It does all this without any file size increase.

✦ **You can change one adjustment to another.** After applying one kind of adjustment layer, you can convert it to another kind of adjustment layer. For example, you could swap an existing Levels adjustment for a Curves adjustment. To do so, choose the desired color adjustment from the Layer ➪ Change Layer Content submenu. Photoshop doesn't try to preserve the prior color adjustment when making the conversion — in other words, it can't convert the Levels information into Curves data — but it does preserve the layer mask, the blend mode, and other layer attributes.

Correcting a flat image using layers

Although many artists use adjustment layers to edit multilayer compositions, adjustment layers are equally applicable to flat photos. As you learned in the section "The Shadow/Highlight command" earlier in this chapter, an image that appears black may actually contain several thousand colors just itching to get out. Adjustment layers make it easier than ever to free these colors and make them fully visible to the world.

Because the image needed lightening and serious control over the amount of lightening applied, the Curves command was used first, and applied to the top-most layer (and therefore to the layers beneath it). To tweak the tree branches and birds some more, the Levels command was used next (selecting Levels from the submenu of Adjustment Layer options).

Dragging the center Input slider (the gray one, under the Histogram) created the brightness desired without increasing contrast too much.

Every image is different — and so will be your choice of adjustment techniques, the layers to which you apply them, and how you use the individual correction tools' dialog boxes. Expect to spend some time creating and throwing out adjustment layers until you find the perfect one or combination of two or more, and with time, you'll find that you can size up an image visually and know exactly which tools to use and how to apply them. The experimentation stage, which is really a lot of trial and error, is an essential step in getting from wherever you are now with Photoshop to the expertise you seek. Even then, you'll still do a lot of experimenting, and like the authors of this book, you'll always be learning something new.

Correcting Camera Raw Images

The images produced by modern digital cameras can be nothing short of breathtaking. Yet by the time a photo leaves a digital camera and enters an image-editing program like Photoshop, even a non-compressed TIFF can be many steps removed from what the CCD or CMOS (the camera's "eye") saw. That's because the camera itself takes that input from the sensor and performs a slew of processes meant to make the image more presentable. These can include white balance adjustments, color and brightness correction, and sharpening and compression passes over an image. It's almost as if there was a tiny little person inside your camera, using a tiny little computer running a tiny little version of Photoshop, and that little guy is trying to make your photos look better.

Although many people would welcome the help of the tiny guy — after all, the picture generally looks brighter, more balanced, and sharper by the time it's opened — the real digital photo pro knows that almost any improvement comes at a cost. In truth, a lot of the original information captured by the camera is lost with the corrections. And who is that suspicious little guy inside the camera, anyway? Why should we trust him to correct our images willy-nilly? He may know a few things about image editing, but there's certainly no way he could have a big helpful book like this one inside the camera for reference. For professional digital photographers and graphic designers, every last pixel counts, and there's no way those big-leaguers are going to trust the judgment of some little guy who lives in a camera over their own judgment. "Eliminate the little middle man!" is the professional's rallying cry.

Luckily, all hope is not lost. Some midrange and high-end digital cameras now offer the option of saving images as Camera Raw files, which skip all of that post-processing and save a perfect, pristine representation of the exact image as originally captured. It's very much akin to a digital negative. Between the releases of Photoshop 7 and Photoshop CS, Adobe quietly introduced a plug-in for the program that was capable of opening and making adjustments to certain RAW files. This phenomenally expanded version of the Camera Raw plug-in gives you access to better image detail and a wider range of colors than would be available otherwise. In many cases, raw format images offer more than 24 bits of information in a full-color file; some cameras provide up to 30 or 36 bits, meaning you have billions and billions of potential colors to work with. For professionals who need to get the absolute most out of their digital images, getting access to this raw data is nothing short of a godsend. Camera Raw lets you *be* the little guy in the camera, taking the pixels captured by the camera's sensor and manipulating them *yourself* before you open the image up in Photoshop proper.

It's important to know that RAW files are proprietary, meaning that each and every manufacturer adheres to a different and unique format. At this time, Photoshop supports RAW files created by several different cameras from Canon, Fujifilm, Leaf, Minolta, Nikon, and Olympus. Additionally, Adobe has pledged to continue expanding support to more manufacturers and models over the life of the product. Check `www.adobe.com/products/photoshop/cameraraw.html` to see if your camera has been added to the list.

Instead of the gigantic, unmanageable files you might expect them to be, RAW files are very efficiently compressed, and Adobe's Camera Raw dialog box can make adjustments at an impressive speed. The only way to access the Camera Raw features in Photoshop CS2 is to open a file saved in a RAW format. Instead of displaying the image, Photoshop first brings up the massive Camera Raw dialog box, as shown in Figure 17-41.

Tip

Before we delve into the labyrinth of Camera Raw settings, here's a little-known tip: Holding down the Shift key will bypass the Camera Raw dialog box altogether and immediately open the image inside Photoshop. If you've used Camera Raw on the image before, the last settings you used will be automatically applied as the image opens. If you've never opened the image before, Camera Raw's default settings for your camera will be used instead.

Figure 17-41: Think of the new Camera Raw dialog box as your first stop along the road to correcting RAW images with Photoshop.

Along the bottom of the Camera Raw dialog box are various settings you can adjust to determine how your image will take shape once you're through with the Camera Raw settings and you bring the image into Photoshop for regular editing. You can set the target color space of the image (probably the same as the color settings you're currently using), the number of bits per channel desired, even the size and printing resolution of the image. Camera Raw uses slightly different interpolation methods than Image Size, but the results are very good. And if you're going to downsample anyway, it will probably save you some Camera Raw processing time if you go ahead and downsample now. If your camera uses non-square pixels, the default Size amount is automatically set to try to maintain the same approximate number of pixels when the image is converted to square pixels in Photoshop. To achieve this, one dimension (width or height) will be upsampled, and the other downsampled. Setting Size to the next highest choice will cause the pixel count to be maintained along the high-resolution dimension of the image; the low-resolution dimension will be upsampled so as to achieve square pixels (almost certainly a better choice for non-square pixel images).

You can rotate the preview using the rotation buttons at the bottom right of the preview window, if you haven't already done so with the Bridge. The Camera Raw dialog box also sports a full-color histogram, mapping the red, green, and blue color channels in their respective colors. The other colored areas show where these channels overlap; white represents luminance. But the real power of the Camera Raw feature lies in the image adjustment options found in the panels on the right side of the dialog box.

Making color adjustments

As you can see in Figure 17-41, the Adjust panel in the Camera Raw dialog box is composed of two sections: settings for adjusting white balance, and settings for adjusting the tonal qualities of an image. *White balance* is a process where something white (such as a sheet of paper) is typically used to calibrate the camera; with many cameras, this information is recorded at the time an image is shot and saved as metadata in the RAW file. When available, the Camera Raw dialog box uses this white balance information as the default when it opens an image; hence the As Shot setting in the White Balance pop-up menu. If Camera Raw can't read white balance info from your camera, it makes a decent guess. In this case, As Shot is the equivalent of the Auto setting. The pop-up menu also contains several other options that reflect various lighting conditions that may have been present when the image was first shot. The options contain different presets for the Temperature and Tint sliders below. The White Balance pop-up menu is a good place to start when adjusting white balance. It's quite possible you'll be happy with one of the preset options. If not, you can tweak the two sliders below the pop-up menu by hand:

✦ **Temperature.** This setting lets you modify the color temperature of an image. Increase the Temperature value (which is measured in Kelvin) to bring out the more yellow colors in the image, as seen in the middle example in Figure 17-42. The right example shows a decrease in Temperature to cool the image into the realm of blue.

Temp. 5550 (as shot)   Temp. 6600

Temp. 4600

Figure 17-42: Camera Raw's Temperature slider takes an image (left) and lets you warm up (right) or cool down (bottom) the color temperature. Appearing in shades of gray here, you will be able to reproduce the effect with your own images and view them in color on your screen.

✦ **Tint.** The Tint slider adjusts and compensates for different color tints the image may contain. Drag the slider to the left to increase the amount of green in the image and drag it to the right to remove green and add in magenta values.

Tip

You can also set the white balance manually by selecting the white balance tool (it's the eyedropper located in the top-left corner of the dialog box) and clicking at a spot in the image that you'd like to assign as neutral, either white or gray. The White Balance settings in the Adjust panel snap into a position that adjusts the selected pixel to white and the other pixels in the image accordingly.

Below the White Balance settings are five sliders that let you make adjustments to the tonal qualities of an image. Generally, it's a good idea to adjust these controls in the order they're presented:

✦ **Exposure.** Quite simply, the Exposure setting adjusts the brightness of the image. But if you look a couple of sliders down, you'll see one labeled Brightness, so now you may quite rightly be wondering, "What gives?" The Exposure slider is based on the f/stop of a camera (a setting of +1.00 is the equivalent of opening the lens one stop wider), and adjusts in much larger increments than the Brightness setting. In fact, adjust this value more than a little and you're bound to encounter some *clipping*, which occurs when pixels are pushed to pure white or black and lose all detail. It's best to adjust this setting until it begins to clip, ramp it back a smidge, and then do your finer brightness adjustments with the Brightness slider.

✦ **Shadows.** Increase this value and watch as more and more pixels get sucked into darkness and, eventually, pure black. It might appear as though the Shadows slider is just upping the contrast in the image, but it's really performing a function that's more in line with the black point slider in the Input Levels section of the Levels command, discussed in Chapter 16.

Tip

Alt+drag (or Option-drag on the Mac) the Exposure or Shadows slider triangles to see a dynamic depiction of any and all clipping pixels in the image. Different colors mean there is clipping only in one or two color channels. For Exposure, black means no clipping; contrariwise, white means no clipping for Shadows. Figure 17-43 shows the clipping display for the Exposure slider.

Figure 17-43: Holding down Alt or Option while using the Exposure slider on the image seen at left brings up a graphic display of which pixels are being clipped to pure white as seen on the right). In this case, the brightest clouds are clipping.

✦ **Brightness.** As mentioned above, this setting makes gentle adjustments to the general brightness levels of the image.

✦ **Contrast.** This setting increases (higher values) or decreases (lower values) the contrast in the midtone colors of the image.

✦ **Saturation.** This is your basic saturation option that you've encountered a number of times before. Decrease the value to –100 to remove all colors from an image; increase the value to +100 to get colors so vibrant you may need to close your eyes.

Sharpening and smoothing

Click the Detail tab to access options you can use to adjust the sharpness and smoothness of a RAW image in Camera Raw. The Detail panel contains the following three settings:

✦ **Sharpness.** The Sharpness slider works in much the same way as the Unsharp Mask filter. The biggest difference lies in the fact that the Camera Raw dialog box does not give you controls for Radius or Threshold. This is because Camera Raw calculates these factors for you using information based on the camera model and the ISO (or light sensitivity) for the image. You'll probably want to wait to adjust sharpness as a final step with Unsharp Mask once you've opened the image inside Photoshop, but it's possible for Camera Raw to apply its Sharpness setting to only image *previews*, not the image itself. With the Camera Raw dialog box open, Macintosh users can choose Photoshop ➪ Camera Raw Preferences, and then choose Preview Images Only from the Apply Sharpening To pop-up menu (as shown in Figure 17-44). Windows (and Macintosh) users can access the Camera Raw Preferences by selecting the Advanced radio button in the Camera Raw dialog box, clicking the right-pointing arrowhead next to the Settings pop-up menu, and choosing Camera Raw Preferences.

Figure 17-44: In the Advanced mode, Camera Raw has its own preferences dialog box. Here Camera Raw is told to only sharpen the previews for raw images. After opening a Camera Raw image in Photoshop, use Unsharp Mask to sharpen it as a final step.

✦ **Luminance Smoothing.** This slider adjusts the amount of blurring that the Camera Raw dialog box applies in an attempt to reduce grayscale noise in an image. Depending on the ISO and general quality of the camera, a little bit of noise — those random speckles that lower the quality of an image — is a common occurrence. Increase this setting to smooth out some of the noise, but don't go overboard — too much smoothing and you'll lose valuable detail in the image.

Note The Camera Raw dialog box fully supports multiple undos through the usual keyboard shortcut, Ctrl+Alt+Z (or ⌘-Option-Z on the Mac), so don't be afraid to experiment.

✦ **Color Noise Reduction.** This slider performs the same function as Luminance Smoothing, except it works towards decreasing the amount of colored noise artifacts in the image.

Correcting for the camera lens

A camera lens is an imperfect thing. As a result of lens imperfections, which are generally more prevalent in less expensive lenses, many times an image will look terrific in the center, but subtle problems will start to creep in toward the edges and in the corners. Clicking the Advanced radio button in the Camera Raw dialog box gives you access to two additional panels full of settings. The first of these, Lens, is designed to compensate for the imperfections of a camera lens.

✦ **Chromatic Aberration R/C.** One of the problems that lenses can introduce into an image is *color fringing*, where sharp edges seem to have a fringe of pixels running along them. This happens when the color channels are slightly different sizes, creating a sort of *misregistration* like a bad printing job of the Sunday funnies. Commonly, this fringe runs red on the side of the edge toward the center of the image and cyan along the other side. The Chromatic Aberration R/C slider, shown in Figure 17-45, fixes this by slightly scaling the size of the red channel in relation to the green.

Figure 17-45: Adjusting the Chromatic Aberration R/C slider lets you better align the image's color channels.

✦ **Chromatic Aberration B/Y.** Similar to the Chromatic Aberration R/C slider, this control can eliminate a blue/yellow fringing problem on high-contrast edges found along the sides and in the corners of images by slightly scaling the blue channel in relation to the green.

Tip

If your image has both kinds of fringing, hold down the Alt (or Option) key as you adjust one slider to temporarily turn off the effects of the other slider. And remember that these sliders do nothing to the center of an image. This type of chromatic aberration only occurs along the sides and in the corners of images.

✦ **Vignetting Amount.** As shown in the top image in Figure 17-46 imperfections in lenses can also cause the edges and corners of an image to be darker than the center, creating a sort of vignette that frames the image. Drag the Vignetting Amount slider triangle to the right to lighten the edges of the image, which helps to eliminate the problem. And should you *want* this type of vignetting, drag the Vignetting Amount slider triangle to the left.

✦ **Vignetting Midpoint.** This controls the vignetting transition from dark to light. Drag to the left to increase the range of the vignetting compensation; drag to the right to decrease it.

Figure 17-46: The top image shows typical vignetting, where the edges of the image are darker than the center. Here, adjusting the Vignetting Amount to +52 and Vignetting Midpoint to 63 fixed the problem handily, as shown in the bottom image.

Tweaking the profile

If you're using Camera Raw, then it's safe to assume that Photoshop has a profile based on the model of your camera. But it's possible that your particular camera might not exactly match the one Adobe used when they created the profile for your model. If you find your camera has a repeatable, predictable problem you always need to compensate for, you might want to use the controls available in the Calibrate tab of the Advanced Camera Raw settings. The first option, Shadow Tint, lets you fix a color cast lurking in the dark areas of the image. As with the Exposure and Shadows sliders in the Adjust tab, holding down the Alt or Option key gives you a look at any clipping that might occur as a result of your adjustments.

The remaining six sliders exist so you can give your Camera Raw settings a little extra tweak. Each color channel has both a hue and a saturation slider, allowing you to account for slight differences between your actual camera and the model of your camera that Adobe used to build its Camera Raw profile. There's no right or wrong way to use these sliders. The whole idea is to adjust things until they look right to you. If, after all the controls in the Adjust, Detail, and Lens tabs, those skin tones still don't look quite right, this is your chance to fix them.

Opening and saving images with Camera Raw

If you feel you've thoroughly botched things with the Camera Raw dialog box, just hold down the Alt or Option key and, as with many Photoshop dialog boxes, the Cancel button changes to a Reset button. Click it, and the image will be restored to its state when you first began this session of Camera Raw adjustments. You may also notice that the OK button changes to an Update button; clicking this updates the associated Camera Raw settings to reflect your changes and closes the Camera Raw window, but it doesn't open the image in Photoshop. And holding down the Shift key makes the OK button turn into a Skip button, in case you want to open an image with its default settings (disregarding any changes you may have already made).

Once you are happy with your Camera Raw settings, click OK, and Photoshop will proceed to apply your adjustments and open the image. Note that you can't save the image back to the RAW format. Just to thoroughly confuse things, there *is* a Photoshop RAW format available when you choose Save As, but that's a different format useful at times for saving images you plan to transfer between different computer systems. Photoshop is incapable of writing the RAW format used by your digital camera. After you adjust the Camera Raw settings, Photoshop essentially opens a copy of your image, leaving the original file untouched.

Yet, here's an odd thing: The original file is untouched, but you will probably notice that the Bridge preview of your RAW image has changed to reflect the adjustments you made. How can this be? Well, the changes you make with Camera Raw get saved in one of two places. By default, the changes are stored in the Camera Raw database, located on the Mac in the Preferences folder of the user, and under Windows in the user's Application Data folder. When the Bridge displays a RAW format image, it draws the preview both from the image and from the settings for that image in the database. The problem with this is that your Camera Raw settings will fail to travel with your images to another computer. Adobe's solution can be found in the Camera Raw Preferences dialog box, which you can access by selecting the Advanced radio button, clicking the right-pointing arrowhead next to the Settings pop-up menu, and choosing Preferences. Choosing Sidecar ".xmp" Files from the Save Image Settings In pop-up menu instructs Photoshop to store the Camera Raw settings for an image not in the default database, but rather in a small file located in the same folder as the image. The data file shares the same base name as the image. For example, the image "watermelon.orf" would have its settings stored in a file called "watermelon.xmp." Keep these sidecar files along with the main image files when you move images or burn CDs, and your Camera Raw settings will travel with you.

Saving your Camera Raw settings

Whether you decide to have your image's Camera Raw settings saved in the main Camera Raw database or in an individual XMP file, it's a darned good thing you *can* save them, isn't it? It would be a drag to have to try to recreate those Camera Raw settings from scratch if you should decide to open the image from the original raw file. But when you think about it, a lot of the image problems you compensated for exist not just in that image, but in every image you take with that camera. Wouldn't it be great if you could save the settings from that image and apply them to other images? Apparently, Adobe figured you'd say "Yes!" because Camera Raw lets you do just that.

When you open an image in the Camera Raw dialog box, by default the Settings pop-up menu is set to Camera Default, meaning that the default Camera Raw settings for your camera are being applied. Choosing Selected Image means that if you've ever opened that image with Camera Raw before, your last settings will be automatically applied. Previous Conversion uses the settings from the last opened raw format image that came from the same camera. To save your current settings so that they can be used by other images, click the right-pointing arrowhead next to the Settings pop-up menu and choose Save Settings. You can name the settings anything you like, but make sure you save them inside the suggested Camera Raw folder (which is inside the Presets folder in the application folder on your hard drive, in case you're curious). From then on, the settings will be available in the Settings pop-up menu. If for some reason you ignore the advice and choose to save the settings somewhere else, you'll need to use the Load Settings command (available in the same pop-up menu as the Save Settings command) to access them in the future.

When the Advanced mode is activated, it's also possible to save just a subset of settings. Maybe your camera consistently introduces chromatic aberration and vignetting to images, so you always want to apply those settings to images from that camera, but you'd rather tweak the other settings on an image-by-image basis.

Click the right-pointing arrowhead next to the Settings pop-up menu and choose Save Settings Subset. You'll be presented with a column of check boxes, allowing you to specify which settings you want included in the subset. The Subset pop-up menu contains a few preset options, designed to save you from having to click a bunch of check boxes. From there, click the Save button, and save your subset in the Camera Raw folder. If you want to delete settings you previously saved, choose them from the Settings pop-up menu, click the ever-popular right-pointing arrowhead, and choose Delete Current Settings.

It's also possible to override Camera Raw's default settings for your camera model by choosing Set Camera Default from the pop-up menu that appears when you click the right-pointing arrowhead. Thereafter, the Camera Default option in the Settings pop-up menu will load your current settings. To restore Camera Raw's default settings for your camera, choose Reset Camera Default.

Applying your saved Camera Raw settings

Applying saved Camera Raw settings to a RAW image before opening it in Photoshop is pretty straightforward. Start by double-clicking the RAW image to open it in the Camera Raw dialog box. If you saved your settings in the Camera Raw folder as Photoshop suggested (see the preceding section), then the settings will appear at the bottom of the Settings pop-up menu. Just choose the settings, click OK, and go to work inside Photoshop.

But remember what happens to the OK button when you hold down the Alt or Option key inside the Camera Raw dialog box? It turns into an Update button, and clicking that button updates the Camera Raw settings for that image by changing the data saved in either the Camera Raw database or the image's XMP sidecar file. You then can see the change evident in the thumbnail and preview within the Bridge.

Note It's important to remember that Camera Raw never actually changes a single pixel of the RAW format file. It can only change the data applied to that file which is saved in the database or the XMP file, and then open a copy of the image in Photoshop with that data applied. But you can't save back to your camera's RAW format from Photoshop, so the original RAW file — reflecting exactly what your camera's sensors saw — is always there on your hard drive.

Because Photoshop is such a flexible tool, it should come as no surprise that you can actually update RAW images with new Camera Raw settings without even opening the images. With one or more RAW format images selected in the Bridge, either choose Edit ⇨ Apply Camera Raw Settings from the Bridge menu bar or just right-click (or Control-click on the Mac) one of the images and choose Apply Camera Raw Settings. You're presented with the small Apply Camera Raw Settings dialog box, where you can select an option from the Apply Settings From pop-up menu. (If you have more than one image selected in the Bridge, the standard Selected Image option will instead appear as First Selected Image.) Click Update, and the Camera Raw data for the selected raw file or files will be updated without opening the images.

And in case that seems all too simple for a complicated feature like Camera Raw, you're exactly right. Clicking the Advanced radio button opens what is basically the Camera Raw dialog box without the preview but with the Save Settings Subset dialog box, as shown in Figure 17-47. You can load saved settings, modify them, apply them, and save them as new settings or as just a subset of settings. Seriously, go nuts. Just click Update when you're done, and the data for the selected image or images will automatically update to show the fruits of your labor.

Figure 17-47: Right-clicking a RAW image in the Bridge and choosing Apply Camera Raw Settings lets you update Camera Raw data for images without actually opening them. Pictured here is the Advanced mode of the Apply Camera Raw Settings dialog box.

Summary

In this chapter, you learned about mapping colors with Invert, Equalize, Threshold, and Posterize, and tweaking colors with the Hue/Saturation dialog box. You learned how to raise and lower saturation levels, and to colorizing grayscale images.

You also learned about correcting colors with Replace Color, Selective Color, Variations, Photo Filter, and Match Color commands, and to use the Histogram palette. The process of boosting brightness and contrast levels, editing specific color values with Curves, and using the Shadow/Highlight command were also covered, along with techniques for fixing exposure problems and correcting multiple layers at once with adjustment layers. Finally, Photoshop's support for Camera RAW was covered, including techniques for correcting Camera Raw images.

✦   ✦   ✦

Printing and Publishing with Photoshop

✦ ✦ ✦ ✦

In This Chapter

Terms to help you communicate with your commercial printer

How to print grayscale and color composites

Setting up and previewing your print job in Photoshop

How to assign transfer functions to distribute brightness values

A discussion of the color-separation process

How to apply color trapping

How to convert a grayscale image into a duotone, tritone, or quadtone

Adding spot-color highlights to a CMYK image

Publishing to paper and the Web, with Photoshop and via the new Bridge

Creating Web graphics and animations

✦ ✦ ✦ ✦

Technically, printing is pretty straightforward. You choose the Print command, press Enter or Return, wait for something to come out of your printer, and then you admire yet another piece of forestry that you've destroyed. Of course, printing can also be a ridiculously complicated subject, involving dot-gain compensation, hardware calibration, undercolor removal, toxic processor chemicals, separation table generation, infinitesimal color parameters, and then the publishing requirements for graphics to be used on the Web, and you're liable to spend your otherwise valuable time trying to figure out what the heck's going on.

This chapter is intended to help make sense of it all, and to give you some guidance that you can use to figure out what the heck's going on in your printing and publishing projects. Although the chapter is *not* intended to cover every possible facet of printing and publishing digitized images, it does take you through the process of preparing and printing the four major categories of output: composites, color separations, duotones, and Web graphics. By the end of the chapter, you'll be familiar with all of Photoshop's printing and publishing options for both paper and Web production. You'll also be prepared to communicate with professionals at your service bureau or at a commercial printer, if need be, and to learn from their input and expertise.

Understanding Printing Terminology

While not a glossary in the traditional sense, the following is a general list of the printing and publishing terms you'll encounter as you work with commercial printers, your own printer, and Web hosts. Ready? Here you go:

✦ **Service bureau.** A *service bureau* is a shop often filled with young graphic artists, printer operators, and about a billion dollars' worth of hardware. A small service bureau is usually outfitted with a few laser printers, photocopiers, and self-service computers. Big service bureaus offer scanners, imagesetters, film recorders, and other varieties of professional-quality input and output equipment.

Service bureaus once relied exclusively on the Macintosh. This has changed, but a substantial number of Mac-based service bureaus remain. Most service bureaus are equally ready to help Photoshop users on both Windows and Mac platforms, but many will take your Windows Photoshop file and run it through a Mac. There's nothing wrong with this — Photoshop is nearly identical on the two platforms — but cross-platform problems may crop up. If you're a PC user, try to be sure your service bureau knows how to address cross-platform incompatibilities and has a general working knowledge of Windows. How can you be sure? Ask.

✦ **Commercial printer.** Generally speaking, a *commercial printer* takes up where the service bureau leaves off. Commercial printers reproduce black-and-white and color pages using offset presses, web presses, and a whole bunch of other age-old technology. The process is less expensive than photocopying when you're dealing with large quantities, say, more than 100 copies, and it delivers professional-quality reproductions.

✦ **Output device.** This is just another way to say *printer. Output devices* include printers, imagesetters, film recorders, and a whole bunch of other machines.

✦ **Laser printer.** A *laser printer* works much like a photocopier. First, it applies an electric charge to a cylinder, called a *drum*, inside the printer. The charged areas, which correspond to the black portions of the image being printed, attract fine, petroleum-based dust particles called *toner*. The drum transfers the toner to the page, and a heating mechanism fixes the toner in place. Most laser printers have resolutions of at least 300 dots (or *printer pixels*) per inch. The newer printers offer higher resolutions, such as 600 and 1200 dots per inch (*dpi*).

✦ **Color printers.** *Color printers* fall into three categories. Generally speaking, inkjet and thermal-wax printers are at the low end, and dye-sublimation printers occupy the high end. *Inkjet printers* deliver colored dots from disposable ink cartridges. *Thermal-wax* printers, which aren't much in vogue these days, apply wax-based pigments to a page in multiple passes. Both kinds of printers mix cyan, magenta, yellow, and, depending on the specific printer, black dots to produce full-color output. Inkjet output quality can be quite good, but if you want truly photographic quality prints, you must migrate up the price ladder to *dye-sublimation printers*. Dye-sub inks permeate the surface of the paper, literally dying it different colors. Furthermore, the cyan, magenta, yellow, and black pigments mix in varying opacities from one dot to the next, resulting in a continuous-tone image that appears nearly as smooth on the page as it does on-screen.

✦ **Imagesetter.** A typesetter equipped with a graphics page-description language (most often PostScript) is called an *imagesetter*. Unlike a laser printer, an imagesetter prints photosensitive paper or film by exposing the portions of the paper or film that correspond to the black areas of the image. The process is like exposing film with a camera, but an imagesetter knows only two colors: black and white. The exposed paper or film collects in a lightproof canister. In a separate step, the printer operator develops the film in a processor. Developed paper looks like a typical glossy black-and-white page. Developed film is black where the image is white and transparent where the image is black. Imagesetters typically offer resolutions between 1200 and 3600 dpi. But the real beauty of imageset pages is that blacks are absolutely black (or transparent), as opposed to the irregular gray you get with many laser-printed pages.

✦ **Film recorder.** A *film recorder* transfers images to full-color 35mm and 4-x-5-inch slides, perfect for professional presentations. Slides also can be useful to provide images to publications and commercial printers. Many publications can scan from slides, and commercial printers can use slides to create color separations. So, if you're nervous that a color separation printed from Photoshop won't turn out well, ask your service bureau to output the image to a 35mm slide. Then have your commercial printer reproduce the image from the slide.

✦ **PostScript.** The *PostScript* page-description language was the first product developed by Adobe — the same people who bring you Photoshop — and is now a staple of hundreds of brands of laser printers, imagesetters, and film recorders. A *page-description language* is a programming language for defining text and graphics on a page. PostScript specifies the locations of points, draws line segments between them, and fills in areas with solid blacks or *halftone cells* (dot patterns that simulate grays). Some newer printers instead use *stochastic screens* that simulate grays and colors using almost-random patterns.

✦ **Spooling.** Printer *spooling* allows you to work on an image while another image prints. Rather than communicating directly with the output device, Photoshop describes the image to the system software. Under Windows 2000, you set spooling options using the Printer control panel. Choose Settings ➪ Printers, right-click the icon for your specific printer, and choose Properties from the pop-up menu. In the printer's Properties dialog box, switch to the Details panel and click the Spool Settings button. Under Windows XP, the spooling settings are in the Advanced panel of the Properties dialog box. When Photoshop finishes describing the image — a relatively quick process — you are free to resume working while the system software prints the image in the background. This isn't an issue anymore under Mac OS X, which has spooling turned on at all times.

✦ **Calibration.** Traditionally, *calibrating* a system means synchronizing the machinery. In the context of Photoshop, however, calibrating means to adjust or compensate for the color displays of the scanner, monitor, and printer so what you scan is what you see on-screen, which in turn is what you get from the printer. Colors match from one device to the next. Technically, this is impossible; a yellow image in a photograph won't look exactly like the on-screen yellow or the yellow printed from a set of color separations. But calibrating is designed to make the images look as much alike as possible, taking into account the fundamental differences in hardware technology. Expensive hardware calibration solutions seek to change the configuration of scanners, monitors, and printers. Less expensive software solutions, including those provided by Photoshop, manipulate the image to account for the differences between devices.

✦ **Brightness values and shades.** As described in Chapter 4, there's a fundamental difference between the way your screen and printer create gray values and colors. Your monitor shows colors by lightening an otherwise black screen; the printed page shows colors by darkening an otherwise white piece of paper. On-screen colors, therefore, are measured in terms of *brightness values*. High values equate to light colors; low values equate to dark colors. On the printed page, colors are measured in percentage values called *shades* or, if you prefer, *tints*. High-percentage values result in dark colors, and low-percentage values result in light colors.

✦ **Composite.** A *composite* is a page that shows an image in its entirety. A black-and-white composite printed from a standard laser printer or imagesetter translates all colors in an image to gray values. A color composite printed from a color printer or film recorder shows the colors as they actually appear. Composites are useful any time you want to proof an image or print a final grayscale image from an imagesetter, an overhead projection from a color printer, or a full-color image from a film recorder.

✦ **Proofing.** To *proof* an image is to see how it looks on paper before the final printing. Consumer proofing devices include laser printers and color inkjet printers, which provide quality and resolution sufficient only to vaguely predict the appearance of your final output. Professional-level proofing devices include the Rainbow dye-sublimation printer and Matchprint laser proofer, both developed by Imation; DuPont's toner-based Cromalin; and Creo's Iris, the latter of which uses a special variety of inkjet technology.

✦ **Bleeds.** Simply put, a *bleed* is an area that can be printed outside the perimeter of a page. You use a bleed to reproduce an image all the way to the edge of a page, as in a slick magazine ad. For example, this book includes bleeds. Most of the pages — such as the page you're reading — are encircled by a uniform 2-pica margin of white space. This margin keeps the text and figures from spilling off into oblivion. A few pages, however — including the parts pages and the color plates — print all the way to the edges. In fact, the original artwork goes 2 picas beyond the edges of the paper. This ensures that if the paper shifts when printing — as it invariably does — you won't see any thin white edges around the artwork. This 2 picas of extra artwork is the bleed. In Photoshop, you create a bleed by clicking the Bleed button in the Print with Preview dialog box.

✦ **Color separations.** To output color reproductions, commercial printers require *color separations* (or slides, which they can convert to color separations for a fee). A color-separated image comprises four printouts, one each for the cyan, magenta, yellow, and black primary printing colors. The commercial printer transfers each printout to a *plate*, which is used in the actual reproduction process.

✦ **Duotone.** An 8-bit grayscale image in Photoshop can contain as many as 256 brightness values, from white on up to black. A 16-bit grayscale image can contain thousands of brightness levels. Most printers can convey significantly fewer shades. A laser printer, for example, provides anywhere from 26 to 65 shades. An imagesetter provides from 150 to 200 shades, depending on resolution and screen frequency. And this assumes perfect printing conditions. You can count on at least 30 percent of those shades to get lost in the reproduction process. A *duotone* helps to retain the depth and clarity of detail in a grayscale image by printing with two inks. The number of shades available to you suddenly jumps from 150 to a few thousand. Photoshop also lets you create *tritones* (three inks) and *quadtones* (four inks). Note that using more inks translates to higher printing costs.

✦ **Spot color.** Most color images are printed as a combination of four *process color* inks — cyan, magenta, yellow, and black. But Photoshop also lets you add premixed inks called *spot colors*. As mentioned in Chapter 4, the most popular purveyor of spot colors in the United States is Pantone, which provides a library with hundreds of mixings. But many large corporations use custom spot colors for logos and other proprietary emblems. Most spot colors fall outside the CMYK gamut and thus increase the number of colors available to you. In addition to using spot colors in duotones, Photoshop lets you add a spot color channel to any image.

But what about the Web? This chapter's title and introduction give the impression that Web publishing will be covered — and it will be. Look to the latter sections on the Save for Web dialog box (also covered in Chapter 3), and for tips on animating Web graphics and slicing images for use on the Web. Further, the Bridge, and its commands for creating Web-based output from one or more of your Photoshop creations, will be covered in nearly excruciating detail.

Printing Composites

Now that you're armed with a bit of printing jargon, you're ready to learn how to put it all together. This section explores the labyrinth of options available for printing composite images. Later in this chapter, you'll learn about color separations and duotones.

Like any Windows or Macintosh application, Photoshop can print composite images to nearly any output device you can hook up to your computer. Assuming that your printer is turned on, properly attached, and in working order, printing a composite image from Photoshop is a five-step process, as outlined next. The sections that follow describe each of these steps in detail.

STEPS: Printing a Composite Image

1. **Choose your printer.** Use the Printers control panel on your PC or the Print Center utility on the Mac to select the output device to which you want to print. If your computer is not part of a network, you probably rely on a single output device, in which case you can skip this step.

2. **Choose File ⇨ Print with Preview or press Ctrl+Alt+P (⌘-Option-P on the Mac).** This command displays the Print with Preview dialog box, where you can position the image on the page, scale the print size of the image, and select a few other options, as discussed later in this chapter.

   Before you select those settings, however, click Page Setup to specify the page size and orientation of the image on the page. Then return to the Print with Preview dialog box and select the Show More Options check box to display and select still more output options.

3. **Adjust the halftone screens, if needed.** Choose Output from the pop-up menu below the Show More Options check box. Then click Screen to change the size, angle, and shape of the halftone screen dots. This step is purely optional and useful mostly for creating special effects.

4. **Adjust the transfer function again, if needed.** Click Transfer to map brightness values in an image to different shades when printed. This step is also optional, though frequently useful.

5. **Click Print to open the Print dialog box.** Depending on your printer, you may also be able to access specialized output functions here. After you've tweaked all relevant print settings, click Print to send the image to the printer.

If you already have your printer set up to your satisfaction, you can simply choose the File ⇨ Print command or press Ctrl+P (⌘-P on the Mac) to skip Steps 2 through 4 and go directly to the Print dialog box. Or press Ctrl+Alt+Shift+P (⌘-Option-Shift-P on the Mac) to access the Print One Copy command located under the File menu.

Caution

At this point, you may be wondering about drag-and-drop printing, where you click and drag a file and drop it onto a printer icon at the desktop. Although this approach may seem more convenient, Photoshop still has to launch and access the same functions as when you use the manual process. And in the worst-case scenario, the operating system may print your image from the wrong application. Drag-and-drop printing is great for making quick copies of text files with your word processor, but when printing photographs and other artwork, don't look for shortcuts.

Choosing a printer through Windows

To select a printer in most Windows systems, choose Start ➪ Settings ➪ Printers. Right-click your printer of choice and select Set As Default Printer from the resulting pop-up menu. If you want to add a printer, double-click the Add Printer icon and be sure to have either your Windows CD-ROM or a drivers disk from your printer manufacturer.

Under Windows XP, choose Start ➪ Control Panel, select Printers and Other Hardware, and then select Printers and Faxes. Double-click the desired printer, and in the resulting window, choose Set As Default Printer from the Printer menu. To add a printer, choose the Add a Printer option from the Printer Tasks menu and follow the steps in the Add Printer Wizard.

Printer drivers help the PC hardware, Windows, and Photoshop translate the contents of an image to the printer hardware and the page-description language it uses. You generally want to select the driver for your specific model of printer. But you can, if necessary, prepare an image for output to a printer that isn't currently hooked up to your computer. For example, you can use this technique before submitting a document to be output on an imagesetter at a service bureau.

Most high-end graphics applications can take advantage of *PostScript printer description (PPD)* files. A single driver can't account for the myriad differences between different models of PostScript printers, so each PPD serves as a little guidance file, customizing the driver to accommodate a specific printer model. Windows lets you attach a PPD file globally to your PostScript printer, for which you need both the PPD file and the INF file to tell Windows what to install. (Adobe offers its own printer driver called AdobePS — available at www.adobe.com — which doesn't require INF files. The setup program works for only Adobe-licensed PostScript printers, however.)

Tip

Windows also lets you switch printers from inside an application. Just choose File ➪ Page Setup (Ctrl+Shift+P) in Photoshop and select the printer you want to use from the Name pop-up menu. Under Windows XP, click the Printer button in the Page Setup dialog box. In any version of Windows, the Print dialog box also has a drop-down list that allows you to choose from printers you're already set up to use — say a network printer you have network permission to use, and a local printer to which you're physically attached. Click the drop-down list and make a choice.

Choosing a printer on a Mac

If your printer is on a network, you may first need to ensure that you are properly connected to the network. After that, open the Printer Setup utility, located in the Utilities folder of the Applications folder, and select a printer from the Printer List.

Most of the time, you'll want to select the printer driver for your specific model of printer. But as mentioned previously, you can use this technique to prepare an image for output on an imagesetter or another device that isn't currently hooked up to your computer.

First, connect your printer and have it turned on. The Printer List window will open, and your printer should display the list of connected printers. If you haven't set up your printer previously, click Add. A new window will open, with a drop-down menu at the top of the window that allows you to choose the type of connection (such as USB, AppleTalk, or FireWire). Choose the method you will use for your new printer. All the printers that are connected and turned on will appear in a new menu. Click the new printer's name and click Add.

Setting up the page

The next step is to define the relationship between the current image and the page on which it prints. You handle most aspects of this part of the printing process in the Print with Preview dialog box, shown in Figure 18-1. To open the dialog box, choose File ➪ Print with Preview or press Ctrl+Alt+P (⌘-Option-P on the Mac). If the options shown at the bottom half of the figure aren't visible, click More Options to display them. If the bottom half of the dialog box is visible, More Options appears as Fewer Options.

The settings in the Print with Preview dialog box relate to the printer, paper size, and page orientation you select in the Page Setup dialog box. So unless you want to use Page Setup options that you already established, click Page Setup to transport to that dialog box. Alternatively, you can open the dialog box by choosing File ➪ Page Setup or by pressing Ctrl+Shift+P (⌘-Shift-P on the Mac) when the Print with Preview dialog box isn't open. The next section explains the important choices you need to make in the Page Setup dialog box; after that, you'll learn about several other print settings.

Note   Some of Photoshop's print options may appear in several different dialog boxes. For example, you may find image-scaling controls in the Page Setup dialog box, as well as in the Print with Preview dialog box. For most print attributes, Photoshop doesn't care where you specify your print options. But if you want to scale the image for output, use the Scaled Print Size controls in the Print with Preview dialog box. If you scale the image in the Page Setup dialog box, the Scale, Height, and Width values in the Print with Preview dialog box may not reflect accurate values. Or better yet, specify these settings using the Image Size command, as discussed in Chapter 3.

The Page Setup dialog box

The Page Setup dialog box varies depending on what kind of printer you use. Figure 18-2 shows the Mac OS X (bottom) and Windows 2000 (top) Page Setup dialog boxes.

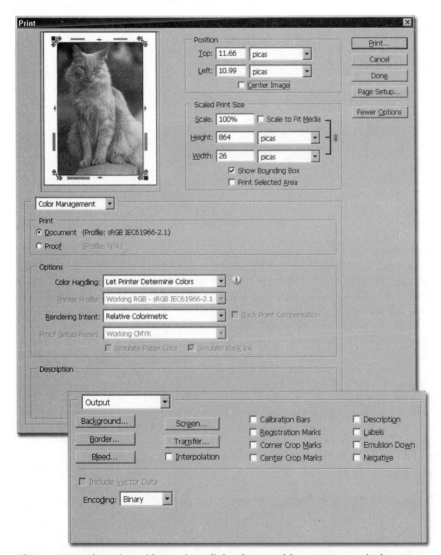

Figure 18-1: The Print with Preview dialog box enables you to precisely position and scale the image, and handle almost all other print setup chores. Here you see the Color Management version of the lower half of the dialog box, plus the Output version, too.

Even though the Page Setup dialog box offers different options for different printers, you should always have access to the following (or their equivalents):

Figure 18-2: Use the Page Setup dialog box to choose the page size and image orientation.

✦ **Paper size.** Select the size of the paper loaded into your printer's paper tray. The paper size you select determines the *imageable area* of a page — that is, the amount of the page that Photoshop can use to print the current image. For example, the Letter option calls for a page that measures 8.5 x 11 inches, but only about 7.5 x 10 inches is imageable.

✦ **Source (Windows only).** Virtually all printers include paper cartridges, but some permit you to manually feed pages or switch between cartridges. Use this option to decide where your paper is coming from.

✦ **Orientation.** You can specify whether an image prints upright on a page (Portrait) or on its side (Landscape) by selecting the corresponding Orientation option. Use the Landscape setting when an image is wider than it is tall.

Position and scaling options

All the options described so far are constant regardless of what application you're using. However, the settings in the Print with Preview dialog box (shown earlier in Figure 18-1) are unique to Photoshop. These settings enable you to position the image on the page and perform a few other handy printing adjustments:

✦ **Position.** If you want the image to print in the middle of the page, leave the Center Image option selected. Otherwise, deselect the Center Image option and type values in the Top and Left option boxes to position the image with respect to the top-left corner of the page. You can select from five different measurement units for these options. If you're not overly concerned about placing the image exactly at a certain spot, deselect the Center Image option and then just click and drag the image in the preview on the left side of the dialog box.

The preview updates to show you the current image position.

✦ **Scaled Print Size.** If you want to adjust the image size for only the current print job, use these controls. They have no effect on the actual image file — they merely scale the image for printing. You can type a scale percentage; values greater than 100 percent enlarge the image, and values less than 100 percent reduce the image. Or type a specific size in the Height and Width option boxes. If you want Photoshop to adjust the image automatically to fit the page size, select the Scale to Fit Media option.

The Show Bounding Box option, when selected, displays handles at the corners of the preview image. For faster scaling, you can drag the handles until the image is the approximate print size you want.

✦ **Print selection.** If you selected a rectangular area before opening the dialog box, you can print just the selection by clicking the Print Selected Area option. Any scaling and position settings still apply to the printed output.

Tip Photoshop prints only visible layers and channels, so you can print select layers or channels in an image by hiding all the other layers or channels. (To hide and display layers and channels, click the eyeball icon next to the layer or channel name in the Layers or Channels palette, respectively.) To print a single layer or channel, Alt-click (Win) or Option-click (Mac) the eyeball.

Output options

To display the special print options shown at the bottom of Figure 18-1 click More Options and then select Output from the pop-up menu immediately below. (If any options are dimmed, your printer doesn't support them.)

The five Output buttons work as follows:

✦ **Background.** To assign a color to the area around the printed image, click this button and select a color from the Color Picker dialog box, described in Chapter 4. This button and the one that follows (Border) are designed specifically to accommodate slides printed from a film recorder. If you select either of these options, Photoshop updates the preview to show them.

✦ **Border.** To print a border around the current image, click this button and type the thickness of the border in the Width option box. The border automatically appears in black.

✦ **Bleed.** This button lets you print outside the imageable area of the page when outputting to an imagesetter. (Imagesetters print to huge rolls of paper or film, so you can print far outside the confines of standard page sizes. Most other printers use regular old sheets of paper; any bleed — were the printer to acknowledge it — would print off the edge of the page.) Click Bleed and type the thickness of the bleed in the Width option box. Two picas (24 points) is generally a good bet. (Bleeds are defined in the section "Understanding Printing Terminology" at the beginning of this chapter.)

✦ **Screen.** Click this button to enter a dialog box that enables you to change the size, angle, and shape of the printed halftone cells, as described in the upcoming section "Changing the halftone screen."

✦ **Transfer.** The dialog box that appears when you click this button enables you to redistribute shades in the printed image, as explained in an upcoming section.

Most of the Output options — all except Negative, Emulsion Down, Interpolation, and Include Vector Data — append special labels and printer marks to the printed version of the image. Figure 18-3 illustrates how they look when printed. For all options except Interpolation and Include Vector Data, Photoshop shows the result of selecting the option in the image preview.

✦ **Interpolation.** If you own an output device equipped with PostScript Level 2 or later, you can instruct Photoshop to anti-alias the printed appearance of a low-resolution image by selecting this option. The output device resamples the image up to 200 percent and then reduces the image to its original size using bicubic interpolation (as described in Chapter 2), thereby creating a less-jagged image. This option has no effect on older-model PostScript devices.

✦ **Calibration Bars.** A *calibration bar* is a 10-step grayscale gradation beginning at 10 percent black and ending at 100 percent black. The function of the calibration bar is to ensure that all shades are distinct and on target. If not, the output device isn't properly calibrated, which just means that the printer's colors are out of whack and need realignment. When you print color separations, the Calibration Bars option instructs Photoshop to print a gradient tint bar and a progressive color bar, also useful to printing professionals.

✦ **Registration Marks.** Select this option to print eight cross hairs and two star targets near the four corners of the image. Registration marks are imperative when you print color separations; they provide the only reliable means to ensure exact registration of the cyan, magenta, yellow, and black printing plates. When printing a composite image, however, you can ignore this option.

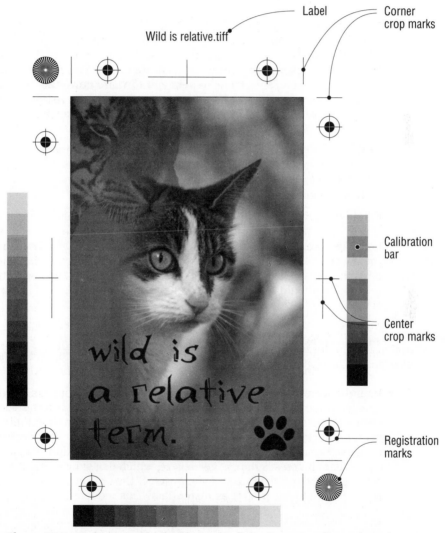

Figure 18-3: An image printed with nearly all the Output options selected.

✦ **Corner Crop Marks.** Select this option to print eight hairline crop marks — two in each of the image's four corners — which indicate how to trim the image in case you anticipate engaging in a little traditional paste-up work.

✦ **Center Crop Marks.** Select this option to print four pairs of hairlines that mark the center of the image. Each pair forms a cross. Two pairs are located on the sides of the image, the third pair is above it, and the fourth pair is below the image.

✦ **Description.** To print a description below the image, select this option. Then press Enter or Return to exit the dialog box, choose File ➪ File Info, and type a caption in the Description field of the Description section of the File Info dialog box. The description prints in 9-point Helvetica. This is strictly an image-annotation feature, something to help you 17 years down the road, when your brain starts to deteriorate and you can't remember why you printed the image in the first place. You might also use the description to keep images straight in a busy office where hundreds of people have access to the same images.

✦ **Labels.** When you select this option, Photoshop prints the name of the image and the name of the printed color channel in 9-point Helvetica. If you process many images, you'll find this option extremely useful for associating printouts with documents on disk.

✦ **Emulsion Down.** The emulsion is the side of a piece of film on which an image is printed. When the Emulsion Down option is deselected, film prints from an imagesetter emulsion side up. When the option is selected, Photoshop flips the image so the emulsion side is down. Like the Negative option, discussed next, this option is useful only when you print film from an imagesetter, and this option should be set in accordance with the preferences of your commercial printer.

✦ **Negative.** When you select this option, Photoshop prints all blacks as white and all whites as black. In-between colors switch accordingly. For example, 20 percent black becomes 80 percent black. Imagesetter operators use this option to print composites and color separations to film negatives.

✦ **Include Vector Data.** If your image contains any vector objects or type for which outline data is available (not outline or protected fonts), select this option to send the actual vector data to a PostScript printer. If there are no vector objects in your image, the option will be dimmed. Your vector objects then can be scaled to any size without degrading the quality. Including the vector data increases the image file size, which can slow printing and cause other printing problems. But if you deselect the option, everything in the image is sent to the printer as raster data. This reduces the file size, but you no longer can scale the vector objects or type with impunity. They're subject to the same quality loss that occurs when you enlarge any pixel-based image.

✦ **Encoding.** Select an option from this pop-up menu to control the encoding method used to send the image file to the printer. In normal printing situations, leave the option set to the default, Binary. If your network doesn't support binary encoding (highly unlikely) or your printer is attached through the local parallel printer port instead of the network, select the ASCII option to transfer PostScript data in the text-only format. The printing process takes much longer to complete, but at least it's possible. If your printer supports PostScript Level 2 or later, you can also choose to use JPEG compression to reduce the amount of data sent to the printer. (This option is applicable to only PostScript printers.)

Color management options

After you click More Options in the Print with Preview dialog box, you can display color management settings by selecting Color Management from the pop-up menu, as shown back in Figure 18-1. These settings enable you to convert the image color space for printing only. You may want to do this to print a proof of the image on a printer other than the printer you'll use for final output. To convert the color space of the actual image file, you need to use the techniques discussed in Chapter 16.

You can select from two Source Space options, Document and Proof. These options tell Photoshop whether you want to print the image according to the color profile officially assigned to the image file or according to the Proof Setup profile (the so-called "soft proofing" profile). Document uses the actual color profile; Proof uses the profile currently selected in the View ⇨ Proof Setup submenu.

The Profile options control whether Photoshop converts the image to a different profile during the printing process. If you select Same As Source from the Profile pop-up menu, no conversion occurs. To convert to a different profile, select the profile from the pop-up menu. You can then specify the rendering method by selecting it from the Intent pop-up menu.

You can convert to any color space offered by Photoshop, Kodak's ICC CMS (Win), or Apple's ColorSync (Mac). Ideally, you want to select the specific profile for your brand of printer. If you can't find such a profile, you'll probably want to stick with the RGB color space (specified in the Color Settings dialog box). Another option is to choose Working CMYK, which prints the image just as if you had converted it to the CMYK color space. Unfortunately, most consumer printers are designed to accommodate RGB images and fare pretty badly when printing artwork converted to CMYK.

Tip   If you own a color printer, it would be time well spent if you took an hour out of your day and conducted a few tests with the other Print Space options. For example, if you select Apple RGB, your printed image will darken several shades. This might throw you. Because the Apple RGB profile features the lightest of the monitor gammas — 1.8 — you might expect the image to print lighter. But what Photoshop is really doing is converting the colors as if the printer were as naturally light as an Apple RGB monitor. To maintain consistent color, the conversion therefore darkens the image to account for this unusually light device. Select the Wide Gamut setting and the colors appear lighter and washed out, again accounting for this hypersaturated Space setting. So think opposite.

Caution

Yet another alternative is to convert an RGB image to the grayscale color space during printing. But it's generally a bad alternative. Asking Photoshop to perform this conversion on the fly dramatically increases the output time, as well as the likelihood of printing errors. It's better and much faster to simply convert the image to the grayscale mode (Image ⇨ Mode ⇨ Grayscale) and then print it.

Cross-Reference

Again, if you're unfamiliar with any of these terms or just don't know which options are best for your printing situation, review Chapter 16, where color management is discussed in detail.

Changing the halftone screen

Before discussing the Screen option, available when you select Output from the pop-up menu in the Print with Preview dialog box, you should learn a bit more about how printing works. To keep costs down, commercial printers use as few inks as possible to create the appearance of a wide variety of colors. Suppose you want to print an image of a pink flamingo wearing a red bow tie. Your commercial printer could print the flamingo in one pass using pink ink, let that color dry, and then load the red ink and print the bow tie. But why go to all this trouble? After all, pink is only a lighter shade of red. Why not imitate the pink by lightening the red ink?

Unfortunately, with the exception of dye-sublimation printers, high-end inkjets, and film recorders, output devices can't print lighter shades of colors. They recognize only solid ink and the absence of ink. So how do you print the lighter shade of red necessary to represent pink?

The answer is *halftoning*. The output device organizes printer pixels into spots called *halftone cells*. Because the cells are so small, your eyes cannot quite focus on them. Instead, the cells appear to blend with the white background of the page to create a lighter shade of an ink.

The cells grow and shrink to emulate different shades of color. Large cells result in dark shades; small cells result in light shades. Cell size is measured in printer pixels. The maximum size of any cell is a function of the number of cells in an inch, called the *screen frequency*.

For example, suppose the default frequency of your printer is 60 halftone cells per linear inch and the resolution is 300 printer pixels per linear inch. Each halftone cell must, therefore, measure 5 pixels wide by 5 pixels tall ($300 \div 60 = 5$), for a total of 25 (5^2) pixels per cell. When all pixels in a cell are turned off, the cell appears white; when all pixels are turned on, you get solid ink. By turning on different numbers of pixels — from 0 to 25 — the printer can create a total of 26 shades.

Photoshop enables you to change the size, angle, and shape of the individual halftone cells used to represent an image on the printed page. To do so, click Screen in the

Print with Preview dialog box (after clicking More Options and choosing Output from the pop-up menu). The Halftone Screen dialog box shown in Figure 18-4 appears.

Figure 18-4: Use the Halftone Screen dialog box to edit the size, angle, and shape of the halftone cells for any one ink.

In the dialog box, you can manipulate the following options:

✦ **Use Printer's Default Screen.** Select this option to accept the default size, angle, and shape settings built into your printer's ROM. All other options in the Halftone Screen dialog box automatically become dimmed to show that they are no longer in force.

✦ **Ink.** If the current image is in color, you can select the specific ink you want to adjust from the Ink pop-up menu. When you work with a grayscale image, no pop-up menu is available.

✦ **Frequency.** Type a new value in this option box to change the number of halftone cells that print per linear inch. A higher value translates to a larger quantity of smaller cells; a smaller value creates fewer, larger cells. Frequency is traditionally measured in *lpi*, or *lines per inch* (as in lines of halftone cells), but you can change the measurement to lines per centimeter by selecting Lines/cm from the pop-up menu to the right of the option box.

Tip

Higher screen frequencies result in smoother looking printouts. Raising the Frequency value, however, also decreases the number of shades an output device can print because it decreases the size of each halftone cell and, likewise, decreases the number of printer pixels per cell. Fewer printer pixels mean fewer shades. You can calculate the precise number of printable shades using the following formula:

```
Number of shades = (printer resolution ≡ frequency)² + 1
```

✦ **Angle.** To change the orientation of the lines of halftone cells, type a new value in the Angle option box. In the name of accuracy, Photoshop accepts any value between negative and positive 180 degrees.

Caution

When printing color composites to inkjet and thermal-wax printers, and when printing color separations, Photoshop calculates the optimum Frequency and Angle values required to print seamless colors. In such a case, you should change these values only if you know exactly what you're doing. Otherwise, your printout may exhibit weird patterning effects. When printing grayscale images, though, you can edit these values to your heart's content.

✦ **Shape.** By default, most PostScript printers rely on roundish halftone cells. You can change the appearance of all cells for an ink by selecting one of six alternate shapes from the Shape pop-up menu. If you know how to write PostScript code, you can select the Custom option to display a text-entry dialog box and code away.

✦ **Use Accurate Screens.** If your output device is equipped with PostScript Level 2 or later, select this option to subscribe to the updated screen angles for full-color output. Otherwise, don't worry about this option.

✦ **Use Same Shape for All Inks.** Select this option if you want to apply a single set of size, angle, and shape options to the halftone cells for all inks used to represent the current image. Unless you want to create some sort of special effect, leave this option deselected. The option is unavailable when you are printing a grayscale image.

✦ **Auto.** Click this button to display the Auto Screens dialog box, which automates the halftone editing process. Type the resolution of your output device in the Printer option box. Then type the screen frequency you want to use in the Screen option box. After you press Enter or Return to confirm your change, Photoshop automatically calculates the optimum screen frequencies for all inks. This technique is most useful when you print full-color images — because Photoshop does the work for you, you can't make a mess of things.

✦ **Load and Save.** You can load and save settings to disk in case you want to reapply the options to other images. These buttons are useful if you find a magic combination of halftone settings that results in a really spectacular printout.

Tip

You can change the default size, angle, and shape settings that Photoshop applies to all future images by Alt-clicking (Win) or Option-clicking (Mac) Save. When you press Alt (Win) or Option (Mac), the Save button changes to read ->Default. To restore the default screen settings at any time, Alt-click (Win) or Option-click (Mac) Load (<-Default).

Cross-Reference

The Halftone Screens dialog box settings don't apply to printing images only directly from Photoshop. You can export these settings along with the image for placement in QuarkXPress or some other application by saving the image in the Photoshop EPS format. Make sure you select the Include Halftone Screen option in the EPS Format dialog box, as discussed in Chapter 3. This also applies to transfer function settings, explained in the following section.

Caution If you decide to include the halftone screen information with your EPS file, be sure the settings are compatible with your intended output device. You don't want to specify a low Frequency value such as 60 lpi when printing to a state-of-the-art 3600-dpi imagesetter, for example. If you have any questions, be sure to call your service bureau or commercial printer before saving the image.

Specifying a transfer function

A *transfer function* enables you to change the way on-screen brightness values translate — or *map* — to printed shades. By default, brightness values print to their nearest shade percentages. A 30 percent gray pixel on-screen (which equates to a brightness value of roughly 180) prints as a 30 percent gray value.

Problems arise, however, when your output device prints lighter or darker than it should. Depending on your printer, you might compensate for this overdarkening effect by clicking Transfer in the Print with Preview dialog box after clicking More Options and choosing Output from the pop-up menu. The resulting Transfer Functions dialog box, shown in Figure 18-5, can be a big help in fixing printer problems.

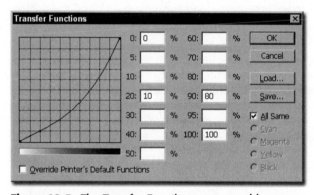

Figure 18-5: The Transfer Functions curve enables you to map on-screen brightness values to specific shades on paper.

The options in the Transfer Functions dialog box work as follows:

✦ **Transfer graph.** The *transfer graph* is where you map on-screen brightness values to their printed equivalents. The horizontal axis of the graph represents on-screen brightness values; the vertical axis represents printed shades. The *transfer curve* charts the relationship between on-screen and printed colors.

The lower-left corner is the origin of the graph—the point at which both the on-screen brightness value and the printed shade are white. Move to the right in the graph for darker on-screen values; move up for darker printed shades. Click in the graph to add points to the line. Click and drag up on a point to darken the output; drag down to lighten the output.

Cross-Reference

For a more comprehensive explanation of how to graph colors on a curve, read about the incredibly powerful Curves command in Chapter 17.

✦ **Percentage option boxes.** The option boxes are labeled according to the on-screen brightness values. To lighten or darken the printed brightness values, type higher or lower percentage values in the option boxes. There is a direct correlation between changes made to the transfer graph and the option boxes. For example, if you type a value in the 50 percent option box, a new point appears along the middle line of the graph.

✦ **Override Printer's Default Functions.** As an effect of printer calibration, some printers have custom transfer functions built into their read-only memory (ROM). If you have problems making your settings take effect, select this option to instruct Photoshop to apply the transfer function you specify, regardless of the output device's built-in transfer function.

✦ **Load and Save.** Use these buttons to load settings to disk and save settings to disk, respectively. Alt-click (Win) or Option-click (Mac) the buttons to retrieve and save default settings.

✦ **Ink controls.** When you print a full-color image, five options appear in the lower-right corner of the Transfer Functions dialog box. These options enable you to apply different transfer functions to different inks. Select the All Same option to apply a single transfer function to all inks. To apply a different function to each ink, deselect the option, and then select one of the radio buttons and edit the points in the transfer graph as desired.

Printing pages

When you finish slogging your way through the Page Setup and Print with Preview dialog boxes, you can initiate the printing process by clicking Print in the Print with Preview dialog box or by choosing File ➪ Print. The Print dialog box appears, shown in its Mac and Windows 2000 forms in Figure 18-6.

Several options in this dialog box also appear in the Print with Preview dialog box or the Page Setup dialog box, both discussed earlier in this chapter. The few remaining options you need to understand work as follows:

Figure 18-6: The Print dialog box as it appears on the Mac (bottom) and in Windows 2000 (top)

✦ **Copies.** Type the number of copies you want to print in this option box. You can print up to 999 copies of a single image if you want to. Will you want to? Probably not.

✦ **Print Range (Pages on the Mac).** No such thing as a multipage document exists in Photoshop, so you can ignore these options for the most part. If you selected an image area with the rectangular marquee tool, you can print just the selected area by choosing the Selection radio button (Win) or the Print Selected Area check box (Mac), if available. Alternatively, you can select the Print Selected Area option in the Print with Preview dialog box. You may want to use this option to divide an image into pieces when it's too large to fit on a single page.

✦ **Print to File (Destination on the Mac).** Exclusively applicable to PostScript printing, this option lets you save a PostScript-language version of the file on disk rather than printing it directly to your printer. Under Windows, deselect the Print to File option to print the image to an output device as usual. Select Print to File to write a PostScript-language version of the image to disk. To save a PostScript file to disk on the Mac, choose Output Options from the unnamed pop-up menu in the middle of the dialog box (it's the one displaying Copies & Pages in Figure 18-6), select the Save as File option, and choose PostScript from the Format menu.

Tip Because Photoshop offers its own EPS option in the Save dialog box, you'll probably want to ignore this option. In fact, the only reason to select Print to File is to capture printer's marks, as shown back in Figure 18-3. If you do, a second dialog box appears, asking where you want to save the PostScript file. You can navigate just as in the Open and Save dialog boxes. For the best results, select the Binary radio button.

Note Mac OS X offers a handy Preview button at the bottom of the Print dialog box; click it to generate a PDF file of the image and display it in Adobe Reader (if you have Reader installed). To save the image to Adobe PDF without opening it in Adobe Reader, click Save As PDF.

Press Enter or Return in the Print dialog box to start the printing process on its merry way. To cancel a print in progress, click Cancel. If you neglect to cancel before Photoshop spools the print job, don't worry because you can still cancel. On the PC, choose Settings ⇨ Printers from the Windows Start menu to display the Printers dialog box. Right-click the icon for the printer you're using and then select Open. Or you can double-click that tiny printer icon that appears on the far-right side of the taskbar. Either way, Windows shows you a window listing the current print jobs in progress. You can pause or cancel the selected print job by choosing a command from the Document menu. On the Mac, you can cancel the print job from the Printer Setup Utility, which appears in the Dock automatically when you start printing.

Printer-specific options

In addition to the options in the Page Setup and Print dialog boxes, you may be able to control certain print attributes specific to the selected printer. To explore these options in the Print dialog box, click Properties on the PC or choose the appropriate command from the middle pop-up menu on the Mac. Figure 18-7 shows the Windows version of the printer Properties dialog box for a Lexmark inkjet printer and the list of printer features available through the Mac Print dialog box.

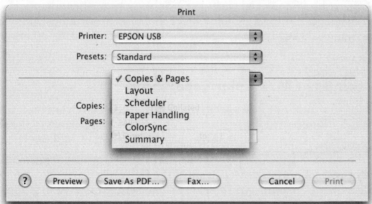

Figure 18-7: In the Print dialog box, click Properties button (Windows, top) or choose Printer Features from the pop-up menu (Mac, bottom) to access more settings that are specific to the type, manufacturer, and model printer you use.

Creating Color Separations

Unless you're a printing professional, you'll rarely have to print color separations directly from Photoshop. You'll more likely import the image to QuarkXPress, PageMaker, InDesign, or a similar application before printing separations. It's even more likely that you'll take the image or page-layout file to a commercial printer and have a qualified technician take care of it.

So why discuss this process? Two reasons. First, it's always a good idea to at least peripherally understand all phases of the computer imaging process, even if you have no intention of becoming directly involved. This way, if something goes wrong on the printer's end, you can decipher the crux of the problem and either propose a solution or strike a compromise that still works in your favor.

Second, before you import your image to another program or submit it to a commercial printer, you'll want to convert the RGB image to the CMYK color space. (You don't absolutely *have* to do this — with Photoshop's improved color-matching functions, you can exchange RGB images with greater confidence — but it's always a good idea to prepare your images down to the last detail, and CMYK is invariably the final destination for printed imagery.)

Outputting separations

Accurately converting to CMYK is the trickiest part of printing color separations; the other steps require barely any effort at all. So without further ado, here's how you convert an image to the CMYK color space and print separations. Many of the steps are the same as when printing a grayscale or color composite, others are new and different.

STEPS: Printing CMYK Color Separations

1. **Calibrate your monitor and specify the desired RGB environment.** Use the techniques discussed in the sections in Chapter 16 that pertain to the Gamma control panel, the Macintosh Display Calibrator Assistant, and selecting the ideal working space.

2. **Identify the final output device.** If you're lucky, your commercial printer may provide a CMYK table that you can load. Otherwise, you have to grapple with some weird settings. The good news is that you need to complete this step only once each time you switch hardware. If you always use the same commercial printer, you can set it up and forget about it.

3. **Convert the image to the CMYK color space.** Choose Image ➪ Mode ➪ CMYK Color to convert the image from its present color mode to CMYK.

4. **Adjust the individual color channels.** Switching color modes can dramatically affect the colors in an image. To compensate for color and focus loss, you can edit the individual color channels as described in the section on color channel effects in Chapter 4.

5. **Trap your image, if necessary.** If your image features many high-contrast elements and you're concerned that your printer might not do the best job of registering the cyan, magenta, yellow, and black color plates, you can apply

Image ➪ Trap to prevent your final printout from looking like the comics in the Sunday paper. When working with typical "continuous-tone" photographs, you can skip this step.

6. **Choose your printer.** Select the printer you want to use, as described earlier in this chapter.

7. **Turn on a few essential printer marks.** Choose File ➪ Page Setup or press Ctrl+Shift+P (⌘-Shift-P on the Mac) to specify the size of the pages and the size and orientation of the image on the pages, as described in the section on the Page Setup dialog box, earlier in this chapter. In the Print with Preview dialog box, also introduced earlier, be sure to select the Calibration Bars, Registration Marks, and Labels options at the very least. (You need to select the Show More Options check box and then select Output from the pop-up menu to display these options.)

8. **Adjust the halftone and transfer functions as needed.** Click Screen and Transfer in the Print with Preview dialog box to modify the halftone screen dots and map brightness values for each of the CMYK color channels, as described earlier in this chapter. This step is entirely optional.

9. **Send the job to the printer.** In the Print with Preview dialog box, make sure the Show More Options check box is selected and choose Color Management from the pop-up menu. Then choose Separations from the Profile pop-up menu in the Print Space section of the dialog box. This tells Photoshop to print each color channel to a separate piece of paper or film. Finally, click Print to open the Print dialog box and initiate the print job.

Note   You can create color separations also by importing an image to a page-layout or drawing program. Instead of choosing your printer in Step 6, save the image in the DCS format, as described in Chapter 3.

Steps 1 through 4 were covered at length in Chapters 4 and 16. Steps 6 through 9 are repeats of concepts explained in previous sections of this chapter. This leaves Step 5 — trapping — which is explained in the following section.

Color trapping

If color separations misalign slightly during the reproduction process (a problem called *misregistration*), the final image can exhibit slight gaps between colors. Suppose an image features a 100 percent cyan shape against a 100 percent magenta background. If the cyan and magenta plates don't line up exactly, you're left with a shape that has a white halo partially around it. Not good.

A *trap* is an extra bit of color that fills in the gap. For example, if you choose Image ➪ Trap and type 4 in the Width option box, Photoshop outlines the shape with an extra 4 pixels of cyan and the background with an extra 4 pixels of magenta. Now the registration can be off a full 8 pixels without any halo occurring.

Continuous-tone images, such as photographs and natural-media painting, don't need trapping because no harsh color transitions occur. In fact, trapping actually harms such images by thickening up the borders and edges, smudging detail, and generally dulling the focus.

One of the primary reasons to use the Trap command, therefore, is to trap rasterized drawings from Illustrator or FreeHand. Some state-of-the-art prepress systems trap documents by first rasterizing them to pixels and then modifying the pixels. Together, Photoshop and Illustrator (or FreeHand) constitute a more rudimentary but, nonetheless, functional trapping system. When you open an illustration in Photoshop, the program converts it into an image according to your size and resolution specifications, as described in Chapter 3. After the illustration is rasterized, you can apply Image ➪ Trap to the image as a whole. Despite the command's simplicity, it handles nearly all trapping scenarios, even going so far as to reduce the width of the trap incrementally as the colors of neighboring areas grow more similar.

Caution   If you plan on having a service bureau trap your files for you, do not apply Photoshop's Trap command. You don't want to see what happens when someone traps an image that's already been trapped. If you're paying the extra bucks for professional trapping, leave it to the pros.

Printing Duotones

It's been a few pages since the printing terminology section of this chapter, so here's a quick recap: A *duotone* is a grayscale image printed with two inks. This technique expands the depth of the image by allowing additional shades for highlights, shadows, and midtones. If you've seen a glossy magazine ad for perfume, designer clothing, a car, or just about any other overpriced commodity, you've seen a duotone. Words like *rich*, *luxurious*, and *palpable* come to mind. Photoshop also enables you to add a third ink to create a tritone and a fourth ink to create a quadtone.

Creating a duotone

To convert a grayscale image to a duotone, tritone, or quadtone, choose Image ➪ Mode ➪ Duotone. Photoshop displays the Duotone Options dialog box shown in Figure 18-8. By default, Monotone is the active Type option, and the Ink 2, Ink 3, and Ink 4 options are dimmed. To access the Ink 2, 3, or 4 options, select Duotone, Tritone, or Quadtone, respectively, from the Type pop-up menu.

Specify the color of each ink you want to use by clicking the color swatch associated with the desired ink option. You can define colors with the Color Picker or with the Custom Colors dialog box. It's easy to switch back and forth between the two by clicking the Custom or the Picker button, depending on which dialog box you currently are using.

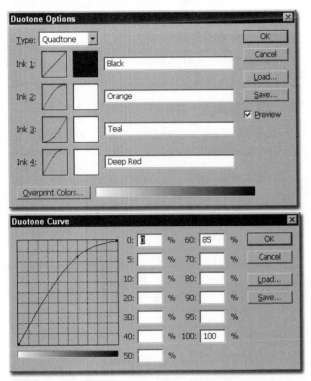

Figure 18-8: The Duotone Options dialog box enables you to apply multiple inks to a grayscale image. If you click the Ink 1, 2, 3, or 4 curve, the Duotone Curve dialog box opens (bottom image).

Photoshop takes the guesswork out of creating a duotone by previewing your settings in the image window when the Preview option is selected. Keep in mind that the preview may not exactly match your output when using certain Pantone inks. (This is a common problem when previewing Pantone inks in any program, but it's always a good idea to keep in mind, particularly because Photoshop mixes inks to create its duotone effects.) The next time you create a duotone, Photoshop displays the same colors you defined in your last visit to the Duotone Options dialog box.

When creating duotones, tritones, and quadtones, prioritize your inks in order — from darkest at the top to lightest at the bottom — when you specify them in the Duotone Options dialog box. Because Photoshop prints inks in the order in which they appear in the dialog box, the inks will print from darkest to lightest. This ensures rich highlights and shadows and a uniform color range.

After selecting a color, you can use either of two methods to specify how the differently colored inks blend. The first and more dependable way is to click the curve box associated with the desired ink option. Photoshop then displays the Duotone Curve dialog box (also shown in Figure 18-8), which works just like the Transfer Functions dialog box described in the section "Specifying a transfer function." This method permits you to emphasize specific inks in different portions of the image according to brightness values.

The second method for controlling the blending of colors is to click Overprint Colors. An Overprint Colors dialog box appears showing how each pair of colors will mix when printed. Other color swatches show how three and four colors mix, if applicable. To change the color swatch, click it to display the Color Picker dialog box.

The problem with this second method is that it complicates the editing process. Photoshop doesn't actually change the ink colors or curve settings in keeping with your new specifications; it just applies the new overprint colors without any logical basis. And you lose all changes made with the Overprint Colors dialog box when you adjust any of the ink colors or any of the curves.

To return and change the colors or curves, choose Image ➪ Mode ➪ Duotone again. Instead of reconverting the image, the command now lets you edit the existing duotone, tritone, or quadtone.

Reproducing a duotone

If you want a commercial printer to reproduce a duotone, tritone, or quadtone, you must print the image to color separations, just like a CMYK image. Because you already specified which inks to use and how much of each ink to apply, however, you needn't mess around with all those commands in the Color Settings dialog box. Just take the following familiar steps.

STEPS: Printing a Duotone, Tritone, or Quadtone

1. **Choose the printer you want to use.** Select a printer as described previously in this chapter.

2. **Set the page size, orientation, and printer marks options.** In the Page Setup dialog box (Ctrl+Shift+P or ⌘-Shift-P), specify the size of the pages and the size and orientation of the image on the pages, as described in the section "The Page Setup dialog box." Then select the Registration Marks option in the Print with Preview dialog box (Ctrl+Alt+P or ⌘-Option-P).

3. **Adjust the halftone screens, if desired.** If you're feeling inventive, click Screen to change the size, angle, and shape of the halftone screen dots for the individual color plates, as described in the section "Changing the halftone screen."

4. **Specify output to color separations.** Still in the Print with Preview dialog box, choose Color Management from the pop-up menu. Then choose the Separations option from the Profile pop-up menu in the Print Space section of the dialog box to print each ink to a separate sheet of paper or film.

To prepare a duotone to be imported to QuarkXPress, Illustrator, or some other application, save the image in the EPS format, as described in Chapter 3. As listed in Table 4-1 of Chapter 4, EPS is the only file format other than the native Photoshop format that supports duotones, tritones, and quadtones.

Editing individual duotone plates

If you'll be printing your duotone using CMYK colors and you can't quite get the effect you want in the Duotone Options dialog box, you can convert the duotone to the CMYK mode by choosing Image ➪ Mode ➪ CMYK Color. Not only will all the duotone shades remain intact, but you'll also have the added advantage of being able to tweak and add colors using Photoshop's standard color correction commands and editing tools. You can even edit individual color channels, as described in Chapter 4.

If your duotone includes Pantone or other spot colors, converting to CMYK is not an option. But you can still access and edit the individual color channels. To separate the duotone inks into channels, choose Image ➪ Mode ➪ Multichannel. Each ink appears as a separate spot color in the Channels palette, as shown in Figure 18-9. You can experiment with different color combinations by turning eyeball icons on and off. You can even switch out one spot color for another by double-clicking the channel name and then clicking the color swatch.

Figure 18-9: Image ➪ Mode ➪ Multichannel was chosen to separate a quadtone into four independent spot-color channels, and then the Deep Red channel was double-clicked to access the Spot Channel Options dialog box.

To save a duotone converted to the multichannel mode, you have just two options: native Photoshop (as always) and DCS 2.0. For complete information on the latter, see Chapter 3.

Spot-Color Separations

Photoshop permits you to add spot colors to your images. Although it's unlikely that you'll use spot colors to widen the gamut of your photographs — after all, scanners can't scan spot colors and Photoshop can't automatically lift them out of, say, the RGB color space — you may want to toss in a spot color to highlight a logo, a line of type, or some other special element.

For example, suppose you have a full-color image of a jet ski. The logo along the side of the boat is fully visible, just as the client wants it, but the color is off. Normally, the logo appears in Pantone 265 purple. But the CMYK equivalent for this color looks about three shades darker, four shades redder, and several times muddier. The only solution is to assign the proper spot color — Pantone 265 — to the logo. The following steps tell how.

STEPS: Adding a Spot Color to an Image

1. **Select the logo.** You can use the Magic Wand tool or a more exacting method, as described in Chapters 8 and 9.

2. **Fill the selection with white.** Press D to get the default foreground and background colors and then press Ctrl+Backspace (⌘-Delete on the Mac). It's important that you erase the old logo so that it appears in pure spot color without any mixing with the CMYK inks. But do *not* deselect your selection — it must remain active in order for Step 5 to work.

3. **Create a new spot channel.** As explained in Chapter 4, the easiest way to do this is to Ctrl-click (Win) or ⌘-click (Mac) the page icon at the bottom of the Channels palette. But you can also choose New Spot Channel from the Channels palette menu if you prefer.

4. **Set the color to Pantone 265.** Click the Color swatch in the New Spot Channel dialog box. Then select Pantone 265 from the Custom Colors dialog box. (If the Color Picker appears instead, click Custom.)

5. **Press Enter or Return, or click OK twice.** Photoshop adds the new spot color to the Channels palette and fills the selection. Your logo automatically appears in the spot color. (Cool, huh?)

6. **Choose Image ⇨ Trap.** It's a good idea to trap the spot color so that it covers up any gaps that may result from misregistration. Enter a value of 1 or 2 pixels and press Enter or Return. Photoshop spreads the logo but leaves the CMYK image alone. Very intelligent program, that Photoshop.

7. **Save the image.** You have two choices of formats, native Photoshop or DCS 2.0. If you want to import the image to a different program, use DCS.

Naturally, you don't want to trust Photoshop's on-screen representation of the spot color any more than you would in Illustrator, QuarkXPress, or any other program.

The screen version is an approximation, nothing more. Therefore, it's a good idea to have a Pantone swatch book on hand so that you know exactly what the color should look like when printed. (If the printed logo doesn't match the swatch book, it's the printer's fault, not Photoshop's.)

Optimizing Images for Web Publication

While audio and video content may be cooler, and text-based content, databases, and hyperlinks are the main stock and trade of the Internet, it's the bitmapped graphics that rule the Web. They make the Web intelligible and invite us to come back for more. From the moment Marc Andreessen introduced the <img> tag to embedded graphics into HTML documents, it's been those graphics that have brought the masses to the Web. Because Photoshop is the world's number one image editor, it's no surprise Photoshop has become as inextricably linked to the Web as Netscape, Internet Explorer, Macromedia Flash, Apple QuickTime, and a hundred other programs. It's just another happy accident in Photoshop's strange and alarming success.

Choosing the Right Web Graphic Format

The Web provides a highly satisfying outlet for creative expression. How else can you get your work in front of hundreds of thousands of viewers without breaking a sweat? But as is the case with just about everything in life, success on the Web depends not just upon your artistic prowess, but also upon your understanding of the right and wrong ways to prepare your images.

If you have any experience with the Web, you know that small images are speedy images. Physically small images are flexible, because they can coexist with text and other elements on a page displayed on a low-resolution screen. Meanwhile, disk size affects speed. A 20K image that fills your screen takes less time to download and display than a 50K file no larger than a sticky note. It's the act of getting the data through the network lines, routers, cables, and modems that takes the time.

So, in a nutshell: Optimizing an image for use on the Web is a process of reducing that image to its smallest possible file size (to facilitate quick downloading), while maintaining the highest level of clarity and fidelity.

At the time of this writing, three graphic file types are supported by Web browsers: These are the Graphics Interchange Format (GIF), the Joint Photographic Experts Group (JPEG) format, and the Portable Network Graphics format (PNG). The trick is to know which format to use for the type of image you've created. What follows is a rundown of the strengths and weaknesses of these three Web file formats.

Graphic Interchange Format

When talking about image formats, we have to talk about bits. Bits are the smallest unit of data computers work with, and the number of bits a format can devote to each pixel determines the maximum number of colors the format can display. Time for some new terms:

✦ **Bit depth.** This is the total number of bits a file format is capable of devoting to each pixel. This stat determines the total number of colors a format can display in a single image, which is our next term.

✦ **Color depth.** This is the total number of colors a format can display in a single image. For example, GIF files can display a total of 256 colors in a single image, therefore GIF files have a color depth of 256. Pretty simple so far, yes?

A format's color depth is calculated this way: we begin by taking the number of states a bit has — which is two (one state being on, the other being off) — and raise that number to the power indicated by the format's bit depth.

GIF is an 8-bit format, meaning it can devote 8 bits of data to each pixel. So, using our handy little equation, this makes its color depth 2^8 — or 2x2x2x2x2x2x2x2 — which totals 256. This is the first of GIF's strengths — a low color depth helps ensure a low file size.

GIF's next major strength is how it compresses file data. GIF uses a compression method called LZW, after its creators Lempel, Ziv, and Welch. If you've been creating TIFF files for ages, then you've already seen this option in the TIFF Options dialog box. When turning an image into a GIF file, this compression method exploits inefficiencies in the file's data structure, effectively removing unused space within the file. Consequently no additional information is removed from the image. In technobabble, LZW compression is called a "lossless" compression method because no image data is lost in the process.

If GIF only supports a maximum of 256 colors in an image, than it follows that you wouldn't try to optimize an image with thousands of colors into this format. GIF is best suited for images with a limited number of total colors, preferable with a high degree of contrast where the edges at which two colors meet are sharply defined. Figure 18-10 shows a prime candidate for GIF optimization.

Granted, Figure 18-10 is produced as a grayscale image here, but regardless, it only has a handful of colors in it. Furthermore, those colors aren't jumbled together along a continuous tone gradient. The image is divided into distinct regions of solid color. GIF loves these — unlike its cousin JPEG, which you'll examine in a just a second, who has a nasty habit of introducing pixilated noise (called artifacts) into regions of solid color.

Figure 18-10: LZW compression favors images with large zones of single colors.

Another of GIF's strengths is its support for transparency. Sadly, GIF doesn't support multiple levels of transparency. GIF supports binary transparency, meaning a pixel is either transparent or it's not, unlike the Portable Network Graphics format, discussed momentarily. GIF is also capable of animation (the bane of the early Web), and we'll grudgingly look at this feature later in the chapter.

GIF's major strengths — a limited number of total colors per image, a lossless compression method, and a liking for regions of solid color — when looked at from another perspective, are also the format's major weaknesses. After all, what do you do if your image has millions of colors that fade from one to the next all over the place? For example, how do you deal with the average color photograph? We thought you'd never ask.

JPEG File Interchange Format

Members of the Joint Photographic Experts Group represent a wide variety of companies and academic institutions throughout the world who meet to discuss and create the standards for still-image compression. The standards they developed for continuous-tone images — images with an unlimited range of color or shades of gray — were used by C-Cube Microsystems to create the JPEG File Interchange Format.

JPEG has a bit depth of 24, giving it a color depth of 2^{24} or 16,777,215 colors. Its method of compression reduces file size by removing "unessential" data from the image. What is this unessential data? The JPEG format takes advantage of certain limitations inherent in the human eye. You see (no pun intended), our eyes perceive minute changes in brightness better than they perceive equally minute changes in color. JPEG's compression method favors changes in brightness, discarding colors the eye won't necessarily miss, while still reproducing up to 16,777,215 million colors. When viewing the image on a 72 dpi monitor, we humans perceive an image we consider highly detailed.

Because JPEG compression removes data it is referred to as a "lossy" compression method. The degree of compression is adjustable, allowing you to choose how much data is lost. The higher you compress the file, the smaller its size. The less you compress it, the better the image quality.

The type of images best optimized in the JPEG format can be deduced from the name—photographs and photo-realistic images. In other words, images with millions of colors or shades of gray, heavy degrees of gradation, where large zones of single colors are few. Figure 18-11 shows a good candidate for the JPEG format (top), with the results of trying to optimize Figure 18-10 as a JPEG (bottom).

Portable Network Graphics Format

The PNG format has an interesting history. When Unisys, the owner of the patent on LZW compression, began demanding royalty payments eight years after the format's introduction, some confusion erupted and there were those who thought the royalties would be levied against anyone who so much as used a GIF image in a Web site. This confusion turned out to be a boon for graphics artists when the Internet Engineering Task Force produced its answer to GIF—PNG, a format that used a lossless compression method AND came in 8-bit and 24-bit flavors, effectively combining the best aspects of both GIF and JPEG.

Used in its 8-bit version, PNG and GIF are fairly even in their abilities to produce quality images with low file sizes. PNG tends to produce slightly large files, but only by a kilobyte or two, and is fine for optimizing the same sort of images GIF should be used for.

The 24-bit version of PNG does not, however, compare with JPEG. Because the compression method is lossless (removing no additional data from the image), files optimized in this format tend to be double in size than when optimized in the JPEG format.

As mentioned earlier, PNG supports transparency. It offers binary transparency equivalent to GIF's. It also has a more impressive version, called *alpha transparency*, which gives the format something Photoshop users can wrap their brains around—a *mask channel*. In total, PNG supports 256 levels of transparency from fully opaque to completely transparent, with 254 stops in between. Most modern browsers support PNG's variable transparency, including WebTV and Microsoft Internet Explorer for Macs. Unfortunately, the Windows version of Internet Explorer (the most widely used browser in the world) is still a hold-out.

The Save For Web Dialog Box

In the mid 1990s, Photoshop received a fair amount of flak for its relatively paltry collection of Web-savvy features. Adobe explained to Web designers they were missing the point—Photoshop was for print graphics and a separate program Adobe had acquired, ImageReady, was for the Web. But most Web designers ignored this advice and continued to grouse, so Adobe eventually caved, and started to do the right thing.

Figure 18-11: Avoid using JPEG to optimize images with large zones of a single color. JPEG compression introduces distortions (called *artifacts*) when attempting to render them (bottom).

Beginning in Photoshop 5.5, Adobe expropriated a bevy of features from ImageReady 1.0 and hot-wired them directly into Photoshop. Then midway into the process it said, "Oh to heck with it!" and tossed in ImageReady for good measure.

While most of ImageReady's commands work the same as those in Photoshop, ImageReady is built around a central optimization window that would change things fairly dramatically if it were integrated into Photoshop. Enter the Save For Web dialog box, shown in Figure 18-12, which is a condensed version of the ImageReady interface, containing all its key optimization features. Here you preview your optimized image, selecting the format, compression, and color options. To display the Save For Web dialog box, choose File > Save for Web, or click the Save for Web button in the shortcuts bar.

Figure 18-12: The Save For Web dialog box

Note   To be sure, ImageReady offers its share of unique capabilities. It might even deserve its own book, albeit one considerably smaller than this one. However, when you take into account that with each successive version Photoshop incorporates more of ImageReady's functionality, some argue it's only a matter of time before ImageReady goes the way of the dinosaur. But for the present, the section "Turning to ImageReady" at the end of this chapter outlines some of the interesting things ImageReady can do so that you can get started with the program.

In the Save For Web dialog box you compare your original image with the optimized results, deciding which optimization settings prove best for your image. The annotation area beneath the original image displays the file name and file size. Beneath the optimized image, the current optimization settings, file size, and estimated download time are shown.

The download time is based on the dialog box's currently selected Internet access speed. To change the selected Internet access speed, click the small arrow to the right of the optimized image to display the Preview pop-up menu, shown in Figure 18-13, and select the access speed of your choice.

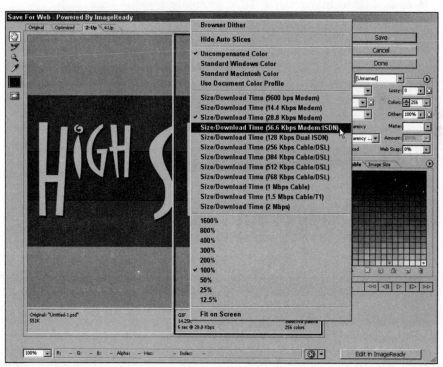

Figure 18-13: The Preview pop-up menu allows you to choose among multiple modem, ISDN, cable, or DSL speeds.

The Save For Web dialog box also allows you to view the differences in Gamma correction between platforms. Gamma measures the intensity to voltage response of a signal sent to a computer system's monitor. The Windows and Macintosh platforms, for example, use significantly different Gamma correction methods. Macintosh systems have partial gamma correction integrated into their hardware. Windows systems have no such gamma correction, though some graphics card manufacturers do provide this functionality. Because Macintosh has Gamma correction, images created on Windows PCs look washed out on Macintosh systems. Conversely, images created on Macintosh systems look darker to Windows users.

To preview differences in Gamma Correction, access the Preview pop-up menu by clicking the small arrow to the right of the optimized image, and choose one of the following display options:

✦ **Uncompensated Color.** This default option displays the image with no color adjustment.

✦ **Standard Windows Color.** This option displays the image with the color adjusted to simulate the Gamma of a standard Windows monitor.

✦ **Standard Macintosh Color.** This option displays the image with color adjusted to simulate the Gamma of a standard Macintosh monitor.

✦ **Document Color Profile.** This option displays the image with its current color profile if it has one.

These options only adjust the color display in the Save For Web dialog box alone. The original and optimized images are not physically modified in any way. Windows users should view their images in Standard Macintosh Color, and Mac users in Standard Windows color to see the differences. If the change is too great, the typical remedy is for Macintosh users to slightly lighten their images and Windows users to slightly darken their images.

Optimizing Images into GIF and PNG-8 Formats

GIF and PNG are both indexed color formats. When images are optimized into either format, Photoshop indexes the colors used, storing them in a *color lookup table* (CLUT). Limiting the color palette in this way helps to reduce file size while preserving image quality.

To reiterate, GIF and PNG-8 are best suited to images with a limited range of colors to begin with (under 256), where zones of color are crisply defined. Optimization settings are adjusted in the Settings area of the Save For Web dialog box, shown in detail in Figure 18-14.

Dithering Algorithm menu

Color Reduction Algorithm menu

File Format menu   Optimization preset menu

Colors menu

Dither percentage

Matte Color menu

Figure 18-14: The options in the Settings area change based on the file format you choose. GIF and PNG-8 have identical Settings options.

Optimization presets

The Optimization preset menu provides seven GIF and one PNG-8 preset. These are:

- ✦ GIF 128 Dithered
- ✦ GIF 128 No Dither
- ✦ GIF 32 Dithered
- ✦ GIF 32 No Dither
- ✦ GIF 64 Dithered
- ✦ GIF 64 No Dither
- ✦ GIF Web Palette
- ✦ PNG-8 128 Dithered

The numbers 128, 64, and 32 represent total number of colors Photoshop maintains in the image. The Web Palette preset pushes each color in the image to its closest corresponding value in the Web Safe color palette — the palette of 216 colors identical to all browsers, operating systems, and monitors when running in 8-bit, 256-color mode.

In the color indexing process common to GIF and PNG, choosing Dithered or No Dither indicates whether some colors lost by optimization are simulated by alternating pixels in a checkerboard-like pattern using colors left within the CLUT.

Custom GIF and PNG-8 optimization settings

Custom optimization settings are adjusted using the remaining menus, pop-ups, and sliders in the Settings area.

To specify your chosen file format, select GIF or PNG-8 from the File Format menu. Next, choose a method for establishing the CLUT of the image by making a selection from the Color Reduction Algorithm menu.

In Photoshop, CLUTs fall into three categories: Dynamic options, Fixed options, and Custom options.

Dynamic Color palette options

Using Photoshop's dynamic options, CLUTs are based on colors present in the image and the number of colors chosen from the Colors menu.

The Color Reduction Algorithm menu's dynamic options are:

✦ **Perceptual.** The perpetual palette creates a customized CLUT using colors in the image to which human eyes are more sensitive.

✦ **Selective.** The selective palette — similar to the perceptual palette in its inclination toward colors favored by human visual response — creates a table that is more sensitive to areas of single flat colors. This algorithm prevents such colors from being merged with other colors in the image, and preserves any existing Web-safe colors. This palette tends to be the best for Web graphics.

✦ **Adaptive.** The adaptive palette creates a CLUT by sampling the predominant colors within the image. For example, if the image you're optimizing has a preponderance of yellows and greens, choosing the adaptive palette creates a CLUT slanted to those two colors.

Fixed Color palette options

Instead of using colors present in the image as the basis from which the CLUT is derived, Photoshop's fixed options use predefined palettes from which to build the CLUT.

The fixed options include:

✦ **Web.** The Web palette consists of 216 colors common to Windows, Macintosh, Netscape Navigator, and Internet Explorer out of the 256 colors available in 8-bit mode. Choosing this option pushes the image's existing colors to their closest Web palette equivalent.

✦ **Mac OS.** Choosing this palette pushes existing colors to their closest equivalents in the default 256 system colors of the Macintosh operating system's 8-bit color mode.

✦ **Windows.** Choosing this palette pushes existing colors to their closest equivalents in the default 256 system colors of the Windows operating system's in 8-bit color mode.

Custom Color palette options

When you select Custom from the Color Reduction Algorithm menu, this maintains your current color table as a fixed palette that doesn't update with changes to the image.

Once the Color reduction algorithm is selected, choose the maximum number of colors you want the image to contain using the Colors pop-up menu. The maximum number of colors available is 256, because you're creating an indexed color file when optimizing as GIF or PNG-8. The fewest colors possible are two.

If you chose either Web or Custom for the color reduction algorithm, you can choose Auto in the Colors menu, which tells Photoshop to decide the optimal number of colors in the color table based on the frequency of colors in the image.

Applying dither settings

Dithering creates the illusion of different colors and shades by varying a pattern of pixels using colors within the image's existing palette. For example, Figure 18-15 shows how a simple checkerboard pattern of black and white pixels can appear gray.

Original   Zoomed in 1600%

Figure 18-15: The image appears gray, but on closer examination we see it is actually made up of alternating black and white pixels.

Dithering can happen in one of two ways — through Photoshop's optimization process (application dither), or through the Web browser if the user has their system set to 8-bit color mode (browser dither). The likelihood, however, that contemporary computer users have their system set to 8-bit color mode when the typical graphics card is capable of 24- or 32-bit color is slim. Application dither, then, is your primary concern.

The reason to apply dither is to prevent colors from *banding* — where the chosen color reduction method has eliminated any continuous tone, leaving nothing but solid bands of color, as shown in Figure 18-16.

To dither an image in the Save For Web dialog box, simply make a selection from the Dithering Algorithm menu. Your options are:

- ✦ **Diffusion.** The Diffusion algorithm, instead of using an obvious checkerboard-like pattern, diffuses the pattern of dithered pixels. This algorithm works in conjunction with the Dither percentage slider. The higher the dither percentage, the more latent colors you simulate, increasing the overall file size.

- ✦ **Pattern.** The Pattern algorithm dithers pixels in a clear, linear pattern.

- ✦ **Noise.** The Noise algorithm creates a randomized pattern of dithered pixels.

Figure 18-17 shows a close-up of the differences between Diffuse, Pattern, and Noise.

Figure 18-16: The original image on the left contains a gradient, that when optimized without dither creates the banded results on the right.

Figure 18-17: Where Diffuse creates a more random dither, Pattern creates a noticeable checkerboard-like effect. Noise generates a randomized pattern.

GIF and PNG-8 Transparency and Matte settings

Unlike native Photoshop files, whose layers can have varying degrees of opacity, in a GIF or PNG-8 file a pixel is either opaque or transparent. This presents a dilemma when Photoshop needs to optimize a drop-shadow or anti-aliased edge. Here, Photoshop translates any pixels of partial transparency into a fully opaque pixel, calculating the appropriate color based on that of the original semiopaque color and the color you choose for the matte.

To preserve transparent regions when optimizing images in GIF or PNG-8 formats, simply select the Transparency option. Any completely transparent pixels will remain so, while semitransparent pixels are blended with your chosen matte color (typically, the intended Web page's background color) to simulate a gradual transition.

The matte color is selected using the Matte Color menu. The Matte Color menu provides the following options:

✦ **None.** Disables matte color. Pixels of less than 50 percent transparency are made entirely opaque, while pixels of more than 50 percent transparency are made completely transparent.

✦ **Eyedropper Color.** Uses the color last selected with the Save For Web dialog box's eyedropper, shown beneath the Eyedropper tool on the left side of the dialog box. Clicking this color swatch also invokes the Photoshop Color Picker from which to make a selection.

✦ **Black.** Sets the matte color to black.

✦ **White.** Sets the matte color to white.

✦ **Other.** Invokes the Photoshop Color Picker from which to make a selection.

The Photoshop Color Picker can also be invoked by clicking the Matte Color menu's text field directly.

Interlacing graphics

To interlace an image, select the Interlace option in the Settings area. When an optimized image is interlaced, browsers start by displaying it at a lower resolution and bring it up to full resolution over seven progressive scans. The purpose of this is to get something to the site visitor's screen ASAP so there are no blank areas on the screen while the visitor waits for the entire page to download.

In the days of 14.4 and 28.8 Kbps modems, interlacing graphics was a common practice. While it resulted in insignificant increases in file size, at least the visitor wasn't staring at text with a bunch of square holes punched in it waiting for something to appear. With contemporary Internet connection speeds being light years faster than this, interlacing images isn't really necessary, and doing so can even hurt performance because imposing seven scans may take longer than simply allowing the image to download unencumbered.

Optimizing Images into JPEG and PNG-24 Formats

JPEG and PNG-24 are meant for optimizing continuous-tone images. This is facilitated by their 24-bit color depth, supporting 16,777,216 colors. The JPEG format uses a *lossy* compression method that removes color data, while PNG-24 (like PNG-8 and GIF) uses *lossless* compression that results in significantly larger file sizes than JPEG.

Figure 18-18 shows the Save For Web dialog box's Settings area options for JPEG and PNG.

Figure 18-18: JPEG settings are shown on the left and PNG-24 settings on the right.

Optimization presets

Photoshop offers three presets for JPEG, and one for PNG-24:

- ✦ JPEG Low
- ✦ JPEG Medium
- ✦ JPEG High
- ✦ PNG-24

In Photoshop, JPEG compression is represented by a scale of 0 to 100. The three presets of Low, Medium, and High represent compressions of 10, 30, and 60, respectively. The higher the number, the greater the degree of compression—which decreases the overall image quality. Your mission is to achieve a balance between image quality and file size.

Custom JPEG and PNG-24 optimization settings

The JPEG Quality Level menu offers one setting not provided by the presets—Maximum—which equals a compression value of 80. The Quality slider manually adjusts the compression value to any point on the 0-100 scale.

The Optimized option available for JPEG optimization should always be selected. It improves color optimization and produces smaller files.

JPEG and PNG-24 transparency and matte settings

Unlike GIF and PNG-8, JPEG lacks transparency support, so a matte color must be used to fill such zones created in the original image. The JPEG Matte menu is identical to those used by GIF and PNG-8, described earlier in the chapter.

PNG-24 supports up to 256 levels of transparency by selecting the Transparency option, and consequently doesn't need a Matte option. Unfortunately, while Netscape Navigator 7.x correctly renders PNG-24 transparency, Microsoft Internet Explorer never has.

Progressive JPEG and interlaced PNG-24

Like GIF and PNG-8, PNG-24 provides an interlacing option, and the same rules apply. JPEG provides similar functionality with a feature referred to as Progressive JPEG.

Where interlacing GIF and PNG files increases their overall file size, using the progressive option results in smaller JPEG files. But again, forcing the image into a series of progressive scans can actually make the download take longer.

Resizing Images

Beneath the Save For Web dialog box's Settings area sits the Image Size area (Figure 18-19), which allows you to adjust an image's dimensions without going back to the Photoshop workspace.

Figure 18-19: The Image Size area resembles the Pixel Dimensions area of the Image Size dialog box.

Tip

Don't use the resizing features of the Save For Web dialog box for radically altering an image's dimensions. Knocking an image 5 pixels one way or the other (provided such a number doesn't account for 50 percent of an image's initial width or height) is fine. But, if you're starting with a high-resolution image that's over 300 dpi, with dimension values in the thousands of pixels, do your reducing out in the main Photoshop interface where you have the rest of the program's tools at your disposal to maintain sharpness and clarity.

The image's original dimensions are shown in the Original Size area, with the New Size area beneath, where you can type new values. Adjust the image's dimensions proportionally by selecting the Constrain Proportions option, which also activates the Percentage field.

Creating Animated GIF Images

The only thing that the GIF format offers over PNG is support for animation. Although a primitive animation standard compared to Macromedia's vector-based Flash program, it can be very effective when used properly. "Properly used" is the operative phrase here. Anyone reading this who still remembers the Web of the early 1990s, when every home enthusiast was packing his or her pages with animated whirly-winks will appreciate the veracity of that statement. In fact, nearly all Web advertising relies on animated GIF files.

If you open an animated GIF file in Photoshop, it automatically separates each one to an independent layer. Figure 18-20 shows an animated GIF file opened in Photoshop. You can see the layers of frames in the Layers palette on the right and the Animation palette (Window ➪ Animation), with each layer assigned to a frame, along the bottom.

To make your own animation, add frames to the Animation palette, and then move and adjust the visibility of layers and effects.

STEPS: Creating an Animation

1. **Create an image in which each layer acts as an individual frame of the finished animation.**

2. **Access the Animation palette (Window ⇨ Animation).** The first frame is already waiting, displaying whatever layers you currently have active in the Layers palette.

3. **Click the New Frame button (labeled in Figure 18-20) to insert the next frame, and make any necessary changes to the visibility of your various layers to advance the action in your animation.**

4. **Increase or decrease the amount of time a frame stays on-screen using the pop-up menu located directly beneath the frame on the Animation palette.**

Figure 18-20: A simple animation, showing the Layers and Animation palettes

5. **If your animation simply requires moving an object from point A to point B, create only a single layer.** Place the object in its starting position in frame 1, click the New Frame button in the Animation palette, and go back to your layer and reposition the object in its final location. From here click the Animation palette's Tween button (meaning to create the frames "in between," shown in Figure 18-20) to have Photoshop create all the frames in between. The Tween dialog box (Figure 18-21) provides fields to specify how many frames Photoshop should place between your two starting frames, as well as which direction the tween should go (tweening between the selected frame and the frame before it or after it, depending upon which frame you have selected at the time).

Figure 18-21: The Tween dialog box allows you to specify how many frames Photoshop should place between your two starting frames, as well as which direction the "tween" should go.

Slicing and Dicing an Image

Some Web designers who come from a graphic arts background like to rough out their pages in Photoshop, which allows them to assemble all the buttons, special text, and other elements the way that they want them to appear on the final Web page. Then they can cut the elements apart and save them out to later assemble in HTML.

Consider the image in Figure 18-22. This simple image contains a text layer whose position in the finished Web page will actually be occupied by physical page text typed into the HTML code. The simplest way to combine text blocks and graphics on a Web page is to create an HTML table. And Photoshop's slicing feature can divvy up your image and generate the required HTML table code for you all in a one sitting.

Illustrated in Figure 18-23, *slices* are rectangular containers that permit you to add structure to a Web page design. The slices in the figure act like children's blocks, each of which contains just enough of the graphic to fit together into a seamless whole. The blocks marked in blue (appearing in dark gray here) are the *user slices*, the ones that the designer drew. They indicate the boundaries of the text. The remaining blocks are *auto slices*, which Photoshop creates automatically to fill in the gaps. In the figure, a total of six auto slices are needed to keep all slices exactly rectangular.

Figure 18-22: Here's a mock-up of an image destined for Web use.

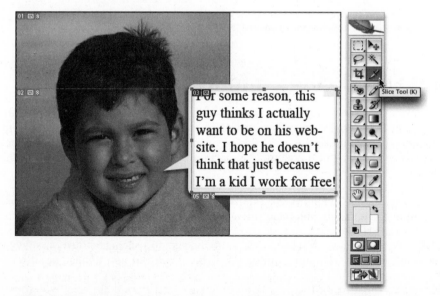

Figure 18-23: Use the Slice tool (right) to subdivide a Web page design into rectangular blocks. Photoshop later assembles the blocks into an HTML table, which adds structure to the otherwise free-flowing arrangement of elements on a Web page.

Creating slices

Photoshop provides two Slice tools, one for drawing slices and one for editing them. Press K to select the Slice tool (highlighted in Figure 18-23), which lets you draw slices. That tool shares a flyout with the Slice Select tool, which you use to move and scale slices.

Draw a rectangle around the portion of the image that you want to slice into an independent image; Shift-drag to constrain the shape of the slice to a square. For each slice that you create, a number appears in the upper-left corner of the slice, as shown in Figure 18-23. Here are a few other things you should know:

✦ As you draw your user slices, Photoshop automatically fills in the auto slices, which it differentiates using dotted outlines. The program also numbers the slices from left to right and then top to bottom. User slice numbers appear in blue; auto slice numbers appear in gray.

✦ Simple tables are reliable tables. This means you want to draw as few slices as absolutely possible. In Figure 18-23, just one slice has been drawn around the text block. Avoid overlapping slices and avoid having two slices that almost, but don't quite, touch, because both result in Photoshop having to draw extra auto slices.

If you need help aligning your slices, choose View ➪ Snap To ➪ Slices to snap one user slice into agreement with another. Although this option is deselected by default, there is no good reason not to always have it selected.

You can also align slices on the fly. While drawing a slice, press and hold the space bar to move the slice as you drag. Release the space bar to put the slice down and return to sizing it.

✦ To create a slice that surrounds everything on a particular layer, select the layer in the Layers palette and then choose Layer ➪ New Layer Based Slice. If you later change the layer's contents, Photoshop redraws the slice boundary as necessary to include the new pixels.

Use this technique when saving slices that contain layer effects, such as drop shadows. This way, you can edit the effect without having to worry about redrawing the slice manually if the new effect takes up more space.

✦ Photoshop can also make slices from guides. First drag one or more guidelines from the horizontal and vertical rulers (View ➪ Rulers) to establish divisions inside your image. Then select the slice tool and click the Slices From Guides button in the Options bar.

✦ To hide and show the slice boundaries, press Ctrl+H (⌘-H on the Mac). By default, this hides all on-screen aids, including selection outlines and guides.

(If it doesn't, choose View ➪ Show ➪ Show Extras Options and then select the Slices option and try again.) To toggle the slice boundaries on and off independently, choose View ➪ Show ➪ Slices.

✦ After you get your slices just so, choose View ➪ Lock Slices to fix them in place. That way, you won't accidentally alter a slice boundary. To delete all slices, choose View ➪ Clear Slices.

Editing slices

Need to change a slice boundary? Grab the Slice Select tool (Shift+K) and click a slice to select it. You can also Shift-click and drag in the image window to select multiple slices. Then edit the slice or slices as described in the following list.

Tip   To temporarily access the Slice Select tool while the Slice tool is active, press and hold Ctrl (⌘ on the Mac). This means you can Ctrl-click (⌘-click) on a slice with the Slice tool to select it. Conversely, if the Slice Select tool is active, holding Ctrl (⌘) gets you the slice tool.

✦ A selected user slice displays corner handles. Click and drag a handle to change the size and shape of the slice. You can also drag inside a selected slice to change its location. Press Backspace (or Delete) to delete it.

✦ To duplicate a slice, press Alt (or Option) and drag the slice.

✦ When the Slice Select tool is active, you can promote an auto slice to a user slice. Click the auto slice and then click the Promote to User Slice button in the Options bar. Then adjust the boundaries of the slice as desired. If the Slice tool is active, right-click on an auto slice (on the Mac, Control-click) and choose Promote to User Slice.

Tip   To change a user slice to an auto slice, simply select and delete the user slice. Photoshop has to fill the vacated space, and does so with an auto slice.

Setting slice options

Double-click a selected slice with the Slice Select tool to display the Slice Options dialog box (see Figure 18-24), which lets you assign a name to the slice image file, add a link, and set other slice attributes described in the following list. You can also access a version of this dialog box with slightly different options (as you'll see) by double-clicking a slice inside the Save For Web window.

✦ **Slice Type.** You can fill a slice with either an image or text. To keep the slice an image, leave this option unchanged. If you would prefer to fill the slice with text, select No Image.

Figure 18-24: Double-click a slice with the Slice tool to name the slice file that Photoshop eventually saves to disk, assign a hyperlink, and insert a status bar message.

For example, the third slice in Figure 18-23 features a placeholder for a text introduction to a Web site. To convey this text to the HTML document, select the text using the Type tool and copy it to the Clipboard by pressing Ctrl+C (⌘-C on the Mac). Then switch to the Slice tool, double-click the slice, and switch the Slice Type to No Image. Photoshop gives you a text-entry box into which you can place text. Simply click inside it and press Ctrl+V (⌘-V) to paste in the text, as shown in Figure 18-25. Although Photoshop cannot preview this text correctly inside the standard image window, it will save the text when you choose File ⇨ Save As. Then open the resulting HTML page in your favorite browser.

Tip

You can likewise insert HTML tags into the text-entry area, but if you do, things get a bit trickier. In Figure 18-25, an *<a href>* tag has been added (colorized for emphasis) around the word *money*. This should turn the word into a hyperlink, but instead, the Web page merely ends up displaying the tags as text. The solution is to visit the Save For Web dialog box, double-click the slice, and select an option not otherwise found in Photoshop — Text is HTML. Highlighted in Figure 18-26, this option correctly interprets HTML tags and once selected, remains selected as long as you work on the image.

✦ **Name.** Photoshop automatically names the slices after the saved image name followed by an underscore and number. If you want to override the automatic naming convention, type your preferred slice name here. (Note that this option and the four that follow apply only when you select Image as the Slice Type.)

Figure 18-25: Select the No Image option to fill a slice with text and HTML tags.

Figure 18-26: Available only inside the Save For Web dialog box (and ImageReady), select the Text is HTML option to properly interpret HTML tags in the text-entry area.

✦ **URL.** To turn the slice into a button, type the appropriate pathname to the page to which you want to link.

✦ **Target.** If you need to target your link, for example if your site is frames-based, type the appropriate frame name or reserved HTML target value (_blank, _parent, etc) in this option box.

✦ **Message Text.** Type a message to appear in the status bar at the bottom of the browser window when a visitor hovers the cursor over the slice. For those familiar with JavaScript, Photoshop handles this using an *onMouseOver= "window.status"* event handler.

✦ **Alt Tag.** To provide a text alternate for a button, type the text into this option box.

✦ **Dimensions.** To specify the exact placement and size of a slice boundary, type the pixel coordinates into the X and Y options and the dimensions into the W and H options. This can be useful when trying to delete auto slices by getting the user slices into exact alignment.

✦ **Slice Background Type.** If your image contains transparent areas, you can fill them with a color selected from this pop-up menu. The Matte option uses the matte color specified in the Save For Web optimization settings. Choose Other to select a color from the Color Picker. Note that you can't preview this background color in Photoshop; you must use a browser.

Saving slices

After you create and edit your slices to absolute perfection, you'll want to perform both of the following kinds of saves:

✦ **Save the image itself.** To save your original image with all slice information, layers, and other doodads intact, choose File ➪ Save As and select either the Photoshop (PSD) or TIFF format. (Depending on your platform, other formats may also store slices, but PSD and TIFF are the safest.) When you reopen the image, choose the slice tool to redisplay the slice boundaries and make any further changes.

✦ **Save the HTML table and slice files.** To output the image in Web-ready form, choose File ➪ Save For Web. This command enables you to save all the slices as individual image files and create the HTML page that will reassemble the slices in the Web browser.

Publishing from the Bridge

So far in this chapter, you've looked at the various printing options that Photoshop provides. Next, the many automated methods of publishing images for presentation in print or for use on the Web are up for discussion.

New Feature Through the new Bridge, Photoshop CS2 gives you expanded capabilities for organizing images that you will use in your printed contact sheets and picture packages, for posting images in galleries on the Web, designing automatic PDF presentations for your friends and family, and even merging multiple images into one large panorama. You can also use the Bridge to print and publish the resulting creations — in fact, you may prefer spawning these publication jobs from within the Bridge if you're there already, organizing your photos. You don't have to, though — if you're comfy in Photoshop, you can print anything from there.

If you're going to print and publish from within Photoshop, the commands reside in the File ➪ Automate submenu. If you're in the Bridge, you'll find the same commands there, in the Tools ➪ Photoshop submenu. Despite the virtually accurate statement that both environments offer the same commands in their respective menus, there are a few differences between these two submenus. They are:

✦ **The Bridge offers an Image Processor command.** This opens the dialog box shown in Figure 18-27. Through this dialog box, you can send images from the Bridge to Photoshop for "processing." This is meant to be used for images coming from your digital camera, primarily — "processing" means saving in a particular format (you pick this through the File Type section of the dialog box), and running actions and inserting copyright information. You can save the files in up to three formats — JPEG, PSD, and TIFF. If you're not sure of what other settings to use, select the Open first image to apply settings option, and the Camera Raw dialog box opens for the first image in the batch. You can use the dialog box to set things up for the first and all subsequent images in the batch.

✦ **Photoshop offers a Create Droplet command.** This opens a dialog box through which you can create an executable file (.exe extension, for Windows users, no extension appears for Mac droplets) for automating the use of Photoshop actions. You can create droplets, store them as icons — say on your Desktop — and then click and drag images (or folders thereof for batch processing) onto the icons and the specified actions are performed on the image(s). You can also swap droplets between Mac and Windows, if you so desire — a Windows droplet much be dropped onto the Photoshop icon on the Mac desktop, at which point Photoshop will accommodate the platform changes and automatically run it, stopping, as needed to prompt you for any required settings, commands, or file names.

✦ **Photoshop has a Conditional Mode Change command.** Choose File ➪ Automate ➪ submenu, and it produces the dialog box shown in Figure 18-28. This dialog box lets you take all the open images (open in image windows in Photoshop) and convert them to a particular mode, selected from the dialog box. Using the Source Mode section of the dialog box, select the check boxes next to the current modes represented by your open images, and then choose the Target Mode from the drop-down list. Click OK, and the images' modes are changed. If you're not sure which mode to choose, or wonder if your open images can even be changed to the mode you're about to select as the target, read Chapter 4.

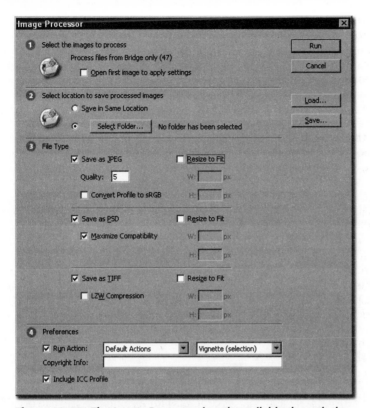

Figure 18-27: The Image Processor is only available through the Bridge, and for good reason — it sends images selected on the Bridge to Photoshop.

Figure 18-28: Need to change all your open images to a different mode in one fell swoop? Choose Conditional Mode Change from the File ⇨ Automate submenu.

✦ **Fit Image command.** This offers the dialog box shown in Figure 18-29. This can be a handy procedure to run an image through before printing, as it constrains the image to a particular width and height, measured in pixels. If your image is bound for the Web — and you haven't fired up the Save for Web dialog box yet — you can resize it with this dialog box first, and then go about the optimization process described earlier in this chapter and also in Chapter 3.

Figure 18-29: Need an image to be this wide by this tall? Choose Fit Image from the File ➪ Automate submenu and enter your desired dimensions there.

So, you can print and publish your images, singly or in groups, from either the Bridge or from right within Photoshop. For the next several sections of this chapter, you'll learn how to combine multiple images into printable and Web-displayable creations for business, personal, and artistic use.

Printing contact sheets

Choose File ➪ Automate ➪ Contact Sheet II to display the dialog box shown in Figure 18-30. The options here permit you to take a folder of images and arrange them as thumbnails on a page, greatly expediting the creation of image catalogs. You specify the location of the folder, the number of columns and rows in the grid, and the color mode, and Photoshop does the rest. You also have the ability to look into folders in the specified folder (very useful) and label image thumbnails according to their file names (even more useful). You can even select the typeface and type size for the labels from the Font and Font Size pop-up menus.

Figure 18-31 shows a contact sheet. You can add your own content later — additional captions, shapes, drawings, even layers from other images — and jazz the sheet up as desired. Right out of the box, however, it's a pretty cool way to print out a bunch of photos to be reviewed for use elsewhere, or just to share them all on one page.

New Feature

Photoshop CS2 introduces some useful improvements to the Contact Sheet II command. As with the other automated functions, the command is now fully accessible directly from the Bridge. Likewise, you can set Contact Sheet II to create a contact sheet from selected images in the Bridge, instead of from an entire folder. Photoshop CS2 also gives you the ability to deselect Auto-Spacing and manually enter Vertical and Horizontal spacing values instead. Finally, the Thumbnails section of the dialog box now includes a useful new Rotate For Best Fit option that, when selected, automatically rotates the images to make better use of the available space.

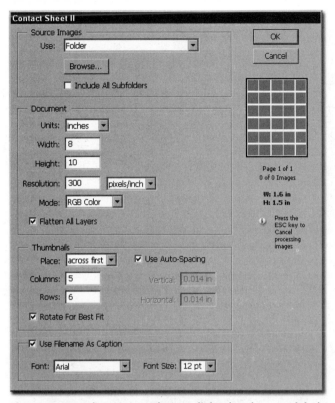

Figure 18-30: The Contact Sheet II dialog box lets you label thumbnails with their corresponding file names.

Creating a picture package

In addition to Contact Sheet II, Photoshop offers two other commands under the File ➪ Automate submenu that organize multiple images onto a single page. You can also access them both from the Bridge through the Tools ➪ Photoshop submenu. The first of these is called Picture Package. Originally designed for printing multiple copies of an image in different sizes on one page, the Picture Package command can now fill a page with multiple copies of multiple images scaled to common print sizes such as 5 x 7 inches, 4 x 5 inches, and wallet snapshots. If you're a photographer, or you simply want to print some pictures of the kids for Grandma, this command does it all. After choosing a layout from the Layout menu, you can replace any image in the layout with a different one by clicking the image thumbnail in the preview to bring up the Select an Image File dialog box. You can also replace any image by clicking and dragging it in from your desktop and dropping it on top of another image.

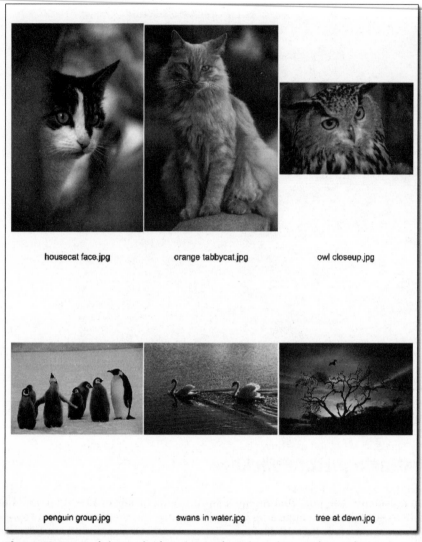

housecat face.jpg　　orange tabbycat.jpg　　owl closeup.jpg

penguin group.jpg　　swans in water.jpg　　tree at dawn.jpg

Figure 18-31: Each image in the contact sheet is on its own layer. The configuration of the images is dictated by your choices in the Contact Sheet II dialog box.

The Label section of the Picture Package dialog box, shown in Figure 18-32, lets you add text to your image. The options are pretty self-explanatory, but it's worth pointing out that the Custom Text option box keeps you from having to quit the Picture Package command to jump over to File ➪ File Info just so you can type a caption.

Figure 18-32: Save a tree — print a Picture Package. By tiling several images on a single sheet of paper — how about photo paper? — you can share one image in several sizes or multiple images in a variety of layouts.

You can create and edit custom layouts for the Picture Package command. Click Edit Layout (shown in Figure 18-32) to display the Picture Package Edit Layout dialog box, shown in Figure 18-33. From the Layout section of this dialog box, you can create a template that sets a custom Name, Page Size, Width, and Height for the picture package. But the real power of the Edit Layout command is the ability to completely rearrange or even create from scratch a template that sets the actual positions and sizes of the images in your picture package.

By default, the Picture Package Edit Layout dialog box opens with the most recently selected layout template displayed. The dialog box also displays just one of your images, even if you clicked the individual tiles in the main dialog box and selected alternate images. Pay this no mind and just arrange the images without respect to what's in them, and your package will in the end reflect the images you chose in the main Picture Package dialog box.

Figure 18-33: Photoshop gives you total control over the scale and position of the images in a picture package.

To alter the layout, just click one of the instances of the image, or "image zones" as Photoshop calls them, and drag it around the window. As soon as an image zone is selected, you gain access to handles that let you scale it. You can also manually type the Size and Position values for each individual zone in the Width, Height, X, and Y option boxes. The buttons in the Image Zone section of the dialog box let you add and remove zones at will. You can even place image zones on top of each other. Finally, the Grid section is where you specify whether or not the image zones snap to a grid and, if so, the size of the boxes within the grid. Click Save to save your new layout template as a text file or overwrite an existing template.

Creating a Web Photo Gallery

Again geared toward professional and aspiring photographers, the Web Photo Gallery command assembles a folder or selected group of images into a Web page, complete with HTML pages and JPEG images. In the Web Photo Gallery dialog box, shown in Figure 18-34, first select a page style from the Styles pop-up menu. The preview on the right side of the dialog box shows a sample page created using that style. You can also type an e-mail contact. You can make further design choices by selecting the various items in the Options pop-up menu. For each item, you get a different set of accompanying design options:

✦ **General.** Choose between *.htm* and *.html* extensions. Additionally, you can choose to preserve the images' metadata when they're converted to JPEG files. You can also elect to use UTF 8 encoding, which will enable older operating systems to view the generated Web pages.

✦ **Banner.** Name your page and add the photographer's name, contact info, and the date. You also can select the font and type size for these items.

✦ **Large Images.** Add a border around your images, resize images, add titles, and apply JPEG compression.

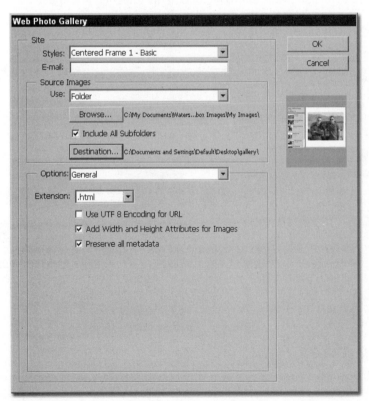

Figure 18-34: The Web Photo Gallery assembles your images for display on a Web page.

✦ **Thumbnails.** Specify the thumbnail size and the number of columns and rows of thumbnails. You can also add borders around the thumbnails, add captions based either on the image file name or the description info typed in the File Info dialog box, and specify a font and type size.

✦ **Custom Colors.** Set the colors for the page background, banner, text, and links.

✦ **Security.** Create a text message that will be embedded into each image, making people much less likely to steal the images from your Web site for their own nefarious purposes. You can type custom text, use the File Info description or the name of the file, choose the placement of the text, and choose whether you want the text to be rotated at an angle on the image.

The Source Images options let you choose either a folder of images or a group of selected images in the File Browser for use in your Web Photo Gallery, allow you to determine whether to include folders nestled in a specified folder, and also choose where the resulting files should finally end up. Figure 18-34 shows a Web page created with the settings from Figure 18-35.

Figure 18-35: The visitor can click the thumbnails on the left to change the displayed large image on the right. It's a very basic page (using the Centered Frame 1 Info Only style here), but it's a clean design, and it's simple to navigate.

Web pages created using the Web Photo Gallery command aren't going to win any design awards, but the command is easy to navigate and it gets the job done. And if you know a little HTML, you can use the pages as a jumping-off point for a more sophisticated site.

The Web Photo Gallery includes styles that let a visitor or client submit feedback about your images directly from the Web page. Choose one of the three Styles that contain the word Feedback and Photoshop will include a live tab in the finished Web Photo Gallery in which a visitor can type text or click a check box to mark the currently selected image as "approved." The Feedback styles can even program the generated Web page to e-mail visitor comments back to you by automatically opening the local mail program and generating a message instantly.

Tip
Photoshop also lets you define custom Web Photo Gallery page styles. Using an HTML editor, you can create a batch of HTML files that contain the instructions for formatting the various elements of the page. To get an idea of how to build a custom style, take a look at the HTML files provided for the Photoshop default styles, found in the Presets\Web Photo Gallery folder. After creating your custom pages, store them together in a new styles folder in the Web Photo Gallery folder.

Creating a PDF presentation

In addition to letting you create an HTML-based slide show using the Web Photo Gallery command, Photoshop lets you create PDF-based slide shows using the new PDF Presentation command. As you're probably aware by now, PDF is Adobe's increasingly widespread and immensely robust format for delivering digital information on-screen. While originally designed as a sleek, efficient format for text layout and vector-based shapes, recent PDF versions have added support for sound and even video clips embedded directly in PDF files. This means PDF is also a great way to transmit and distribute multipage files containing high-quality images, and the new PDF Presentation command lets you do this without leaving Photoshop.

New Feature
Choose File ➪ Automate ➪ PDF Presentation to bring up the PDF Presentation dialog box, shown in Figure 18-36 — again, you can also access it through the new Bridge and its Tools ➪ Photoshop menu. In the Source Files section, click Browse to display the Open dialog box and choose any images you'd like to include in the PDF file. If any images are currently open, you can select the Add Open Files option to add those to the list. Click and drag any of the listed files up or down the list to change the page order of the resulting PDF file. If you've opened this dialog box from the Tools ➪ Photoshop submenu in Photoshop CS2's new Bridge, any selected files will be included by default.

Below the Source Files section you'll find the Output Options. Here, you can select the View PDF after Saving option to automatically display the PDF file in Adobe Reader after the saving process is complete. More importantly, however, is the option that lets you choose whether the PDF file will be a static, multipage document or a slide show, which Photoshop refers to as a Presentation. Choose Presentation and the Presentation Options at the bottom of the dialog box become available (shown in Figure 18-36) to you. Here, you set the speed at which the slide show advances, whether or not it will loop continuously, and what type of transitions will take viewers from one image to another while they watch it. You can experiment to see which transition you like best. Figure 18-37 shows the PDF document window, and a panel of the images included, along with the main image that would appear in the individual slide during the show.

Figure 18-36: The PDF Presentation feature lets you create PDF slide shows and even set snazzy transitions between the images — here, "Box Out" is chosen.

When the show runs, the screen displays the images, full-screen, with a black background. Press Esc to end the show, and if you didn't set automatic timings (through the Presentation Options portion of the dialog box), you can press Enter to move from slide to slide.

There are a number of reasons to create a PDF slide show instead of a Web Photo Gallery for distributing your images. A PDF file is just that — one file — as opposed to the numerous files that make up a Web Photo Gallery. Thus, you can burn a PDF file onto a CD or e-mail it to friends, family members, or coworkers to view on-screen using Adobe Reader software, available for free from www.adobe.com.

Figure 18-37: Open the PDF file and watch the show — all you need is Adobe Reader.

Using Photomerge to create a panorama

Until the last release of Photoshop (version CS), the ability to create a panoramic composite from a group of images was something you could only do with Photoshop Elements. The Photomerge command in Photoshop is virtually identical to the Elements version — and that's not a drawback, despite Elements being a sort of "lite" version of Photoshop. There's nothing pared down about the Photomerge feature, and it's quite effective at taking a series of images and merging them into a single, wide, panoramic shot. Of course, the only catch is that the images you plan to merge need to have been shot under specific circumstances — the same setting, the same size film, the same orientation of the camera. If you painstakingly stood there at the Grand Canyon, however, and took a series of shots of a very wide view and now you have each section of the view represented by two or more images, you're good to go with Photomerge.

To get started, choose File ⇨ Automate ⇨ Photomerge or open the Bridge and choose Tools ⇨ Photoshop ⇨ Photomerge. If you don't access the command through the Bridge, choosing it will display the Photomerge dialog box, as shown in Figure 18-38. At first glance, you might think Photomerge is a simple command. All you need to do is choose which files you'd like to merge and whether or not Photoshop should "Attempt to Automatically Arrange Source Images" (as per the option at the bottom of the dialog box). Right? Alas, those sweet naïve dreams are soon shattered when you click OK and find yourself presented with the giant, imposing beast of a dialog box shown in Figure 18-39. This, as they say, is where the magic happens.

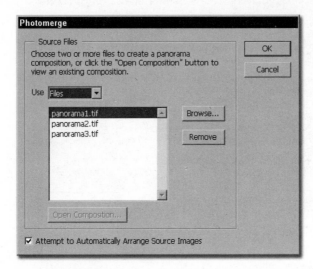

Figure 18-38: The Photomerge dialog box lets you choose the images that will make up your panorama.

By default, Photomerge tries its best to make sense of the pixels in your images and match certain areas of one photo with similar areas of another. But it's something of a gamble; most of the time you'll see at least a few portions of your image that could use some fixing. You adjust the individual placement and rotation of the images in a panorama using the Select Image and Rotate Image tools available in the upper-left corner of the dialog box. The bottom two tools — the Zoom and Hand tools — work the same as they do everywhere else in the program. Between these two sets of tools is the Set Vanishing Point tool, which is covered in a moment.

Tip

If you adjust the settings without getting the results you want, try removing one of the images if the area it covers is already captured by the other images on-screen. To remove an image, simply select the arrow tool, click the image, and drag it to the lightbox strip at the top of the screen, labeled in Figure 18-39. Giving the Photomerge command too much information about your scene can be a bad thing, and you may want to leave some of the images up in the Lightbox until you're ready to incorporate them. The Lightbox is also the all-purpose depository for any image that Photoshop cannot figure out how to fit within the panorama. If you'd like to reintroduce an image, simply click and drag it from the Lightbox and drop it back into the work area.

Select Image

Rotate Image

Set Vanishing Point   Lightbox

Red line indicates good alignment   Navigator slider

Figure 18-39: The very large Photomerge dialog box makes every attempt to create a panorama from a group of photographs, but you usually need to manually adjust the images to get the best results.

By default, Photomerge assembles the images into a flat, jagged puzzle that rotates the images to fit each other but does not distort them in any way. If you'd like Photomerge to try bending and distorting the photos in an attempt to make them fit better, select the Perspective option — shown selected in Figure 18-39. When the Perspective option is selected, the command contorts the images and presents a more accurate, nearly 3-D view of your scene. You can select the Set Vanishing Point tool and alter the perspective by clicking the different images in the composition.

The two options in the Composition Settings section of the Photomerge dialog box let you correct certain problems inherent in the Photomerge process. For example, the Perspective setting does a great job of distorting the images to ensure that they all fit together in the composition, but it also often results in a sort of "bowtie" shape for your final composition. The Cylindrical Mapping option, available only when the Perspective option is selected, corrects this by bending the more extreme corners of the composition back toward the center. Even more useful is the Advanced Blending option, which attempts to smooth over the common color and luminance shifts between images that can be dead giveaways of a computer-generated panorama. Both Composition Settings options make for pretty intense renders, so you might want to click the Preview button to see a lower-resolution preview while working in the dialog box.

Selecting the Keep as Layers option creates a new image consisting of a layer for each original image and a background layer. This new image maintains the positioning determined by the Photomerge command but loses all the blending.

Tip   Powerful as it may be, the Advanced Blending option can sometimes let you down when trying to stabilize the colors among the images in a panorama. A good trick for getting around this is to perform a color correction pass on your individual images before you merge them using the new Match Color command, as described in Chapter 17.

If you've carefully arranged the images in your panorama and would like to return sometime later and continue adjusting the settings, click Save Composition As to save a version of your Photomerge settings for these particular images that you can open and edit at any time. To do so, choose File ➪ Automate ➪ Photomerge and then click Open Composition in the first dialog box that appears.

As mentioned earlier, the way in which the original images were photographed is perhaps the most important factor in determining the results of a panorama created with Photomerge. The most crucial thing to keep in mind when shooting photos that you plan to merge is that the greater the consistency in focal length, camera angle, exposure, and position, the easier it will be for Photoshop to merge the resulting images. Adobe recommends an image-to-image overlap of 15 to 40 percent and that you avoid using any sort of lens that will distort your images (such as a "fisheye"). Finally, the use of a tripod or another stabilizing surface can mean the difference between an expert merge and an expressionist fiasco.

Summary

In this chapter, you discovered terms to help you communicate with your commercial printer and learned how to print grayscale and color composites. You also learned about setting up and previewing your print job in Photoshop and how to assign transfer functions to distribute brightness values. Through a discussion of the color-separation process, you should now understand how to apply color trapping, and know about adding spot-color highlights to a CMYK image. Finally, you learned about publishing to paper and the Web, with Photoshop and via the new Bridge, and how to create Web graphics and animations.

✦   ✦   ✦

The Keyboard, Menus, and Making Photoshop Your Own

When you imagine people making creative, artistic use of a computer, you probably don't think of them typing—instead, you probably think of them moving the mouse and drawing, or using a tablet and pen to paint on-screen. Well, Photoshop's significant and unique reliance on the keyboard to make many things happen flies in the face of that imaginary computer artist.

If you are using Photoshop, the keyboard, used to invoke the seemingly unlimited list of commands and features, is at least as important as the mouse or tablet to the creative process. In Photoshop CS2, that reliance is taken a step further—with enhanced capabilities for customizing keyboard shortcuts, any discomfort with using and remembering the shortcuts is eliminated. For the things you'd rather do from the menus, there are new ways to customize their functioning and appearance as well.

If you're new to Photoshop, you may not realize that Photoshop provides no menu command that lets you delete multiple layers at a time. There is no command that hides all palettes, nor is there an option that brings up the last-used color correction settings. Every one of these options is out of your reach if you don't know the right key. The keyboard may seem like an unlikely artistic tool, but it is a powerful and an essential ally in Photoshop.

Photoshop's keyboard artistry comes in two varieties:

+ **Shortcuts.** Some keystrokes (single keys) and keystroke combinations (two or more keys, pressed simultaneously) produce immediate effects. For example, pressing Ctrl + Backspace (⌘ + Delete on the Mac) fills a selection with the current background color, while pressing M all by itself activates the Marquee tools, which you might then use to make a selection, which you might then fill

+ **Modifiers.** Some keys change the behavior of a tool or command. Pressing Shift while dragging with the Lasso tool adds the lassoed area to the previous selection. Because they modify other keystrokes and combinations, the Shift, Alt, and Ctrl keys (Shift, Opt, and ⌘ on the Mac) are known collectively as *modifiers.*

The goal of this Appendix is to help you become familiar with all that you can do with the keyboard in Photoshop. You may think of the keyboard only as some dry tool for typing text and numbers, but as you read on, you'll see that it's much, much more — it's what helps unleash the power of Photoshop's tools so that you can truly unleash your own imagination.

Hidden Shortcuts and Modifiers

Shortcuts permit you to initiate various Photoshop commands and features without having to stop what you're doing and click a toolbox button or pull down a menu to make a selection. Some shortcuts are fairly obvious, and you'll find them easy to remember, either because the alpha characters used make sense or because the key combinations are ubiquitous.

For example, you can choose File ⇨ New by pressing Ctrl+N (⌘+N on the Mac), and that's memorable because N stands for "new." You can choose Edit ⇨ Undo by pressing Ctrl+Z (or ⌘-Z), choose Select ⇨ All by pressing Ctrl+A (⌘-A), and those same shortcuts do the same thing in just about any word processing program.

Many of Photoshop's keyboard shortcuts are displayed in the form of tool tips, which are pop-ups that appear when you hover over a tool with your mouse. Some are listed in menus to let you know the keyboard equivalent of a given command. But many of Photoshop's shortcuts are hidden, and it's only in a book like this, or by digging through Photoshop's Help files, that you'll find out about them. What's weird is, the hidden shortcuts turn out to be some of the most important ones in the bunch.

Windows Alt-key combos

Under Windows, you can perform many operations using *hot keys*, which are the underlined letters you see in menus and dialog boxes. To access one of these functions, press Alt + the underlined letter. This can be very useful when choosing commands that lack a Ctrl-key shortcut. For example, normally, you would choose Image ➪ Adjustments ➪ Channel Mixer to access the Channel Mixer, but with hot keys, you can press Alt+I, release the Alt key and press A, and then press X. After the Channel Mixer dialog box appears, you can press Alt+G to select the Green value, Alt+B for Blue, and so on.

You can even access commands that have no underlines. To access the Unsharp Mask, you normally choose Filter ➪ Sharpen ➪ Unsharp Mask, but with hot keys, you can press Alt+T to bring up the Filter menu, S to highlight Sharpen, Enter to display the Sharpen submenu, and U to choose Unsharp Mask. For Filter ➪ Stylize ➪ Extrude, press Alt+T, S, S, S, Enter, E, E, Enter. I know, even as I'm writing this, I'm thinking it sounds really cumbersome. But you may find you like it. For example, I had to rely on hot keys instead of the mouse when I had an accident involving tree roots, glass, and a dark night — I was bandaged like a boxer for weeks

For more mouseless excitement, you can also whip through the menus with the arrow keys. After you press Alt + the underlined letter to display a menu, use the up and down arrows to highlight commands in the menu. Use the left and right arrows to display neighboring menus. To choose a highlighted command, press Enter. To hide the menus and return focus to the image window, press Esc twice. Suddenly that keyboard is looking like someone you need to know, eh?

The shortcut menu

One of the best and least documented tricks in Photoshop is right-clicking (Control-clicking on a Mac). It's not really a hidden concept if you use a lot of other software, because right-clicking is fairly common in Windows and most Windows applications, and for Mac users, Control-clicking isn't exactly a foreign concept.

When you right-click or Control-click the mouse button in the image window, Photoshop displays a shortcut menu of commands tailored to your current activity and/or the item you right-clicked/Control-clicked. For example, if you right-click or Control-click a layer in the Layers menu, you get the pop-up menu shown in Figure A-1. There are other ways to get at some of these commands, but this way is very quick and easy, especially if you're already using your mouse to paint or draw in the image window. You're already in the neighborhood, so why not right-click while you're there?

Shortcut menus are considered *context sensitive*, because they're triggered in and their commands relate to where you literally are in the program. While some tools and on-screen elements have no shortcut menus associated with them, most do, and you'll find that simply seeing what the menu has to offer is educational unto itself.

Tip   As with the regular menus, you can press the up- and down-arrow keys to highlight commands in the context-sensitive pop-up menus. To choose a command, press Enter. To hide the menu, press Esc.

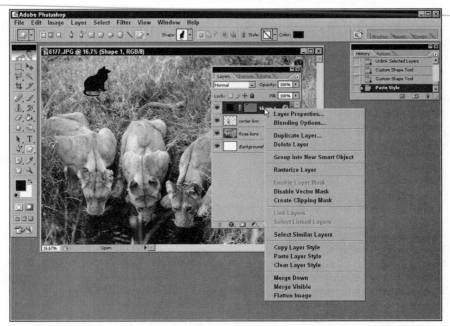

Figure A-1: You're never really alone in Photoshop. Just about anywhere you wander, a right-click (or a Control-click) will provide a handy and comforting list of commands that help you get your bearings and also let you get some work done while you're there.

Toolbox shortcuts

Usability has always been one of Photoshop's great strengths, and the ability to activate toolbox tools with a single keystroke is a perfect example of this. You can keep your dominant hand on the mouse and use the other hand to press the key (or use your mouse hand, if you prefer) — all without stopping to perform some digital gymnastics to reach two or three keys at the same time. Also the shortcuts work even when the Toolbox is hidden. Once you get used to the shortcuts, you may find that the only time you look at the Toolbox is to check which tool is selected.

Figure A-2 shows the Toolbox and all of the keys that give you quick access to the tools. The way it works is simple, press the appropriate key, as shown in the figure — no Ctrl key, Option key, or other modifier key required. Many of the shortcuts make sense. For example, M selects the Marquee tool, and L is for Lasso tool. Some only make sense in a strange way — I for Eyedropper. But then there are the ones you have to wonder about, such as O for DOdge or R for BluR. Well, they *sort of* make sense — at least those letters are in the tool names, but they're not entirely memorable.

Full Screen menu (Windows)

Figure A-2: Press these keys to select tools and activate controls. The bold letters indicate keys that toggle between alternate tools or settings.

Ctrl + Shift + M
(⌘ + Shift + M)

Letters shown in black boxes (white text) switch between one or more tools that share a common slot. For example, press G to access either the Gradient tool or the Fill Bucket. By default, you have to press Shift in combination with one of these letters to toggle to an alternative tool. However, you can eliminate the need for Shift by choosing Edit ⇨ Preferences ⇨ General (Ctrl+K) and deselecting the Use Shift Key for Tool Switch option, as explained in Chapter 2, and that may make using these toggle-able keys easier, given that they make up the majority of the shortcuts.

Tip   Notice that at the top of the Toolbox in Figure A-2 there is a small pop-up menu arrow. You may not see this on your Toolbox because it's usually hidden. Press F twice to view the image against a black backdrop—this places you in Full Screen mode. Assuming the menu bar is hidden, click the right-pointing arrow at the top of the Toolbox to open a top-secret stash that includes every single one of Photoshop's commands. This is because in Full Screen mode, the menus are hidden. Pretty neat, huh? Just press F again to return to a normal workspace and view.

Palette shortcuts

Photoshop also lets you access palette options from the keyboard, and a list of the palettes, their purpose, and shortcuts for access appears below. Note that each of the shortcuts works even when the palette is hidden:

✦ **Palette function keys.** Press F5 to show or hide the Brushes palette. Press F6, F7, F8, or Alt+F9 (Option+F9 on the Mac) to toggle the display of the Color, Layers, Info, or Actions palette, respectively. If for some weird reason the Options bar is hidden, press Enter or Return to bring it back.

✦ **Hide or show all palettes.** Press Tab to hide or show all palettes, including the Toolbox, Options bar, and the status bar on the PC. To hide or show the standard palettes only — that is, everything except the Toolbox, Options bar, and the status bar — press Shift+Tab.

✦ **Brush size.** Press left bracket ([) to decrease or right bracket (]) to increase the brush size when a paint or edit tool is active.

✦ **Brush hardness.** Press Shift with a bracket key to change the hardness of a brush. Shift+] gives the brush a sharper edge; Shift+[makes it softer. Again, a paint or edit tool must be active.

✦ **Brush preset.** Press comma (,) or period (.) to cycle between preset brushes. If this doesn't work for you, try pressing Shift+comma, which selects the first preset, the single-pixel brush. Then press period to move forward. Shift+ period jumps to the last preset brush.

✦ **Gradient style.** Select the Gradient tool and press a bracket key, [or], to switch among the five gradient styles.

✦ **Gradient preset.** Press comma or period to step backward or forward, respectively, through the predefined gradients. Press Shift+comma or Shift+period to switch to the first or last gradient in the list.

✦ **Shape layer styles.** Select any of the shape tools and press , (comma) or . (period) to step backward or forward through the predefined layer styles. Press Shift+comma or Shift+period to jump to the first or last style in the list.

✦ **Shape attribute.** With the Rounded Rectangle tool active, press a bracket key, [or], to decrease or increase, respectively, the corner radius. Select the Polygon tool and press a bracket key, [or], to decrease or increase the number of sides in the next polygon or star you draw. For the Line tool, press a bracket key, [or], to decrease or increase the line weight.

✦ **Custom shape preset.** Select the Custom Shape tool and press a bracket key, [or], to step backward or forward through the predefined shapes. Press Shift+[or Shift+] to switch to the first or last shape in the list.

✦ **Brush opacity.** When a paint or edit tool is active, press a number key to change the Opacity, Strength, or Exposure value in the Options bar. Press 1 to change the value to 10 percent, press 2 for 20 percent, and so on, up to 0 for 100 percent. Or use an exact value by typing two numbers in a row. For example, type 87 for 87 percent or 05 for 5 percent.

✦ **Airbrush.** If a tool offers an airbrush icon in the Options bar, press Shift+Alt+P (Shift-Option-P on the Mac) to toggle it on or off.

✦ **Airbrush flow.** If a tool offers the Airbrush, it includes both an Opacity value and a Flow value. When the Airbrush is turned off, press Shift with a number key to change the Flow value. When the Airbrush is on, press a number key to change the Flow value; press Shift with a number key to change the Opacity value.

✦ **Layer opacity.** When any tool other than a paint or edit tool is selected — that is, any tool in the first, third, or fourth group in the Toolbox — pressing a number key changes the Opacity value for the active layer. Again, press one number to modify the Opacity setting in 10 percent increments; press two numbers to specify an exact Opacity setting.

✦ **Fill opacity.** Press Shift with a number key to change the Fill value for the active layer, which modifies the opacity of the pixels in a layer without affecting the layer effects.

✦ **Brush mode.** When a paint or edit tool is active, you can cycle through brush modes by pressing Shift+plus (+) or Shift+minus (–). Shift+plus takes you down the brush mode pop-up menu and Shift+minus takes you back up.

✦ **Blend mode.** When some other tool is selected, Shift+plus and minus affect the blend mode applied to the active layer. You can also access a particular blend mode by pressing Shift and Alt (or Option) with a letter key. For example, Shift+Alt+M selects the Multiply mode; Shift+Alt+S selects Screen; Shift+Alt+N takes you back to Normal.

✦ **Lock setting.** Press the forward slash (/) to toggle on and off the lock icon that controls transparency in the Layers palette. If one or more of the lock icons is already active, press / to turn off all four. Press / again to return the options to their former configuration. Layer locking can be extremely useful for protecting the contents of layers, as explained in Chapter 12.

✦ **Switch layer.** Press Alt+] to ascend through the layers. Press Alt+[to descend. Press Shift+Alt+] to activate the top layer in the composition. Press Shift+Alt+[to go all the way down to the bottom of the stack, usually the Background layer.

✦ **Arrange layer.** Press Ctrl+] (or ⌘+] on the Mac) to move the active layer one level forward in the stack; press Ctrl+[to move it back. Press Ctrl+Shift+] to move the layer to the top of the stack. Press Ctrl+Shift+[to move it to the bottom, usually just in front of the Background layer.

Customizing Keyboard Shortcuts

Photoshop CS gave us what many Photoshop users have been requesting for a very long time — the ability to edit keyboard shortcuts. Being able to customize them is key to their being useful, because a keystroke or combination that's hard to remember or difficult to reach with one hand's fingers is one you won't use.

So now, you don't have to live with the totally illogical and hard to remember strokes, such as J to activate the Healing Brush (J? why J?) or the inscrutable Ctrl+Shift+E (⌘+Opt+E) to merge all visible layers. Photoshop CS gave us the ability to simply and easily edit existing keyboard shortcuts, as well as assign shortcuts to commands that formerly had none. CS2 continues to provide this level of customizability and has enhanced it to include the ability to customize menus as well. Choose Edit ⇨ Keyboard Shortcuts to bring up the Keyboard Shortcuts and Menus dialog box shown in Figure A-3. You can access this command also by pressing Ctrl+Shift+Alt+K (⌘+Shift+Option+K), which ironically is one of the most difficult and convoluted shortcuts in all of Photoshop, but at least you know how to change it now!

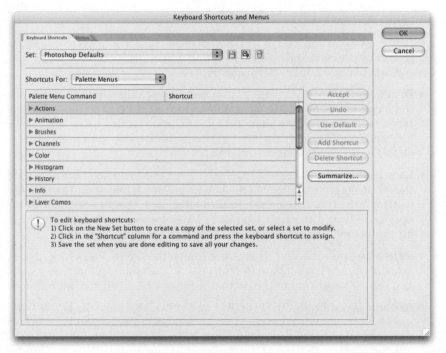

Figure A-3: The Keyboard Shortcuts and Menus dialog box lets you change your keyboard shortcuts and menus so that they look and work the way you need them to.

Despite its power to really change the way you interface with Photoshop, the Keyboard Shortcuts and Menus dialog box is quite easy to use. First, from the Set pop-up menu, select the collection of shortcuts to which you'd like to make edits. You can modify the default set or create new ones for different users or types of image-editing work. Use the three icons to the right of the Set pull-down menu to save the set, create a new set, or discard the entire set, respectively. From there, select a category from the Shortcuts For pop-up menu and then simply explore the various subsections in the list below. If you dig around enough, you can find almost every single command, function, and filter in the program — aside from this appendix and references to them throughout this book, this might be the best place to find all the shortcuts you never knew existed.

To assign a new shortcut to a command, simply click in the blank area labeled Shortcut to the right of the command name and press the desired shortcut key or combination of keys. As soon as you click the spot in the dialog box, the currently assigned key or combination highlights, so the next thing you type replaces it. If there is no key or combination currently assigned, just type whatever you want to be the shortcut. Then click Accept to make the change/addition permanent.

If you happen to type a keyboard shortcut that is already assigned to another function in the program, Photoshop displays a warning at the bottom of the dialog box, as shown in Figure A-3, and gives you the option to accept or undo your changes. You can also use the buttons along the right side of the dialog box to save and discard changes, as well as add and delete shortcuts. Lastly, you can click Summarize to generate and display an HTML Web page that lists the currently active keyboard shortcuts, which is a handy list to tack up close to your computer.

Customizing menus

Photoshop's menus can also be made friendlier, using the Menus tab in the Keyboard Shortcuts and Menus dialog box. You can turn on commands that currently have no menu representations so that they do appear in menus, and you can change the color of menu commands so that they stand out for you.

Tip   If you want to assign colors to menus and menu commands, be sure that Show Menu Colors is selected in the General Preferences dialog box (choose Edit ➪ Preferences ➪ General).

To change a menu command's visibility and/or color, choose the Set (Photoshop Defaults or a custom set you or another user who shares your computer may have created), and then choose either Application Menus or Palette Menus from the Menus For list. Application Menus refers to the main menus across the top of the workspace — File, Edit, Image, and so on. The Palette Menus are the menus that are available by clicking the tiny triangle button in the upper-right corner of various palettes.

Once you select a Set and a Menu group, choose a particular menu to change. In Figure A-4, the File menu (from the Applications Menus) is chosen, and its commands are displayed by clicking the triangle to the left of the word File. For each menu command, there's an entry in the Visibility and Color columns. Click to insert or remove the eye icon, displaying or hiding that particular command, respectively. If you click the Color option (None, by default), a list of colors appears, also shown in Figure A-4.

Figure A-4: Use the Menus tab in the Keyboard Shortcuts and Menus dialog box to change the visibility and color of any application or palette menu. Directions remind you how at the bottom of the dialog box.

Go through and change all the commands you want, hiding some and showing others, changing colors for those you want to have stand out, or grouping related commands by a common color. After you make all your changes, click OK and the changes will take effect.

Tip   When you hide commands, the Show All Menu Items command is added to that menu, If you ever want to see the hidden commands again, you can Ctrl+click on the menu in question, and all hidden commands will be visible. Or, just click the Show All Menu Items command to redisplay those commands you've hidden.

Creating a new menu set

If you want to keep the Photoshop Defaults set of menus just as they are "out of the box," you can create your own custom menu set and customize it instead. Just make your changes — hiding and coloring commands as desired — and then click the second of three buttons to the right of the Set list. This opens a Save dialog box. Name the new set and click Save to make it a reality. The file extension for menu set files is .MNU, and by default, they're stored in the Menu Customization folder, a subfolder of the Presets folder found in your Adobe folder. Don't monkey with the default location for your new .MNU file — if you do, it won't appear automatically in the Set list for future use or modification.

The Great-Grandmother of All Shortcut Tables

A shortcuts table has always been a part of the Photoshop Bible. What kind of Bible would it be if such a handy and powerful list weren't included? The table, however, has grown and improved over the years, and Deke did a great job of turning it into the fabulous table that it is today.

Any tool is more useful if you know how to use it properly. The table that follows these paragraphs doesn't really need much introduction, but there are a few things to keep in mind. If these reminders seem insulting to your intelligence, we apologize, but ask that you simply skip ahead to the table and don't mutter under your breath. We're just trying to help.

✦ First, don't press Shift just because a key combination involves a character that normally requires the Shift key. For example, the shortcut for the Zoom In command is Ctrl+plus (⌘+plus on the Mac). Technically, + is the Shifted version of =, so you might think you have to press Ctrl+Shift+= to get this shortcut combination to work. That would be wrong, of course, but we respect that sort of thorough, literal thinking. Remember that the plus sign is used because it implies zooming while the equal sign does not. So when you see Ctrl+plus, just press Ctrl+=.

✦ Second, if you're a Windows user, note that many of Photoshop's keyboard shortcuts involve both the Ctrl and Alt keys. Ctrl+Alt+O, for example, invokes the Open As command, and Ctrl+Alt+Z undoes an operation from the History palette. Unfortunately, Windows likes to reserve Ctrl+Alt combinations to launch applications, and if you, as a Windows user, set up a keyboard shortcut to invoke a particular application, Windows will commandeer that command and you won't be able to successfully use it within Photoshop. So be careful when creating Windows shortcuts and avoid the following when assigning file-launching shortcuts, which are very much used in Photoshop: B, D, E, F, J, K, L, M, N, O, P, S, T, U, W, X, Z, plus, minus, semicolon, and 0 through 9. This doesn't leave you too many other options, but which is more important, Photoshop or Windows? That's right.

Tip   Don't know how to create a Windows shortcut to start an application? Here you go: Create a shortcut icon for the application by dragging the Programs menu command and icon from the Programs menu (press and hold Ctrl while dragging so that you make a copy of the command) onto the Desktop. Then right-click the new shortcut icon, choose Properties, click the Shortcut tab, and type the character and modifier key/s of your choice into the Shortcut Key option box.

It's time to wade right into the table and immerse yourself in Photoshop's keyboard shortcuts. Some will be familiar and others won't be. Some will invoke a command or feature you have never used, and others may be the keyboard access to something you do 50 times a day, and now you can't believe how much time you've been wasting clicking buttons and menus. Throughout the table, operations are listed in the left column. Windows shortcuts in the center column, and Mac shortcuts are in the right column. There is no implied priority in this order — Windows first, or Mac in the "right" column — it's just how it all worked out.

Table A-1
Photoshop's Shortcuts and Modifiers

Operation	Windows Shortcut	Macintosh Shortcut
Menu Commands		
Actual Pixels	Ctrl+Alt+0 (zero)	⌘+Option+0 (zero)
Auto Color	Ctrl+Shift+B	⌘+Shift+B
Auto Contrast	Ctrl+Shift+Alt+L	⌘+Shift+Option+L
Auto Levels	Ctrl+Shift+L	⌘+Shift+L
Bring Layer Forward	Ctrl+right bracket (])	⌘+right bracket (])
Bring Layer to Front	Ctrl+Shift+right bracket (])	⌘+Shift+right bracket (])
Browse	Ctrl+Shift+O	⌘+Option+O
Canvas Size	right-click title bar	*None*
Clear	Backspace or Delete	Delete
Close	Ctrl+W or Ctrl+F4	⌘+W
Close All	Ctrl+Shift+W or Ctrl+Shift+F4	⌘+Option+W
Color Balance	Ctrl+B	⌘+B
Color Balance, with last settings	Ctrl+Alt+B	⌘+Option+B
Color Settings	Ctrl+Shift+K	⌘+Shift+K
Copy	Ctrl+C	⌘+C
Copy Merged	Ctrl+Shift+C	⌘+Shift+C
Curves	Ctrl+M	⌘+M
Curves, with last settings	Ctrl+Alt+M	⌘+Option+M
Cut	Ctrl+X	⌘+X

Operation	Windows Shortcut	Macintosh Shortcut
Desaturate	Ctrl+Shift+U	⌘+Shift+U
Deselect	Ctrl+D	⌘+D
Duplicate	click left icon at bottom of History palette or right-click title bar	click left icon at bottom of History palette
Exit/Quit	Ctrl+Q or Alt+F4	⌘+Q
Extract	Ctrl+Alt+X	⌘+Option+X
Fade last operation	Ctrl+Shift+F	⌘+Shift+F
Feather selection	Ctrl+Alt+D	⌘+Option+D
File Info	right-click title bar	*none*
Fill	Shift+Backspace	Shift+Delete
Fill from history	Ctrl+Alt+Backspace	⌘+Option+Delete
Filter, repeat last	Ctrl+F	⌘+F
Filter, repeat with new settings	Ctrl+Alt+F	⌘+Option+F
Fit on Screen	Ctrl+0 (zero)	⌘+0 (zero)
Free Transform	Ctrl+T	⌘+T
Free Transform, from clone	Ctrl+Alt+T	⌘+Option+T
Gamut Warning	Ctrl+Shift+Y	⌘+Shift+Y
Group with Previous layer	Ctrl+G	⌘+G
Help Contents	F1	⌘+Shift+?
Hue/Saturation	Ctrl+U	⌘+U
Hue/Saturation, with last settings	Ctrl+Alt+U	⌘+Option+U
Image Size	right-click title bar	*none*
Inverse Selection	Ctrl+Shift+I	⌘+Shift+I
Invert	Ctrl+I	⌘+I
Layer Via Copy	Ctrl+J	⌘+J
Layer Via Cut	Ctrl+Shift+J	⌘+Shift+J
Levels	Ctrl+L	⌘+L
Levels, with last settings	Ctrl+Alt+L	⌘+Option+L
Liquify	Ctrl+Shift+X	⌘+Shift+X
Lock Guides	Ctrl+Alt+semicolon (;)	⌘+Option+semicolon (;)

Continued

Table A-1 *(continued)*

Operation	Windows Shortcut	Macintosh Shortcut
Merge Down/Linked/Layer Set	Ctrl+E	⌘+E
Merge Visible	Ctrl+Shift+E	⌘+Shift+E
Merge Visible, into current layer	Ctrl+Shift+Alt+E	⌘+Shift+Option+E
New, document	Ctrl+N	⌘+N
New, with default settings	Ctrl+Alt+N	⌘+Option+N
New Layer	Ctrl+Shift+N	⌘+Shift+N
New Layer, skip options	Ctrl+Shift+Alt+N	⌘+Shift+Option+N
Open, existing document	Ctrl+O	⌘+O
Open As	Ctrl+Alt+O	⌘+O
Page Setup	Ctrl+Shift+P	⌘+Shift+P
Paste	Ctrl+V or F4	⌘+V or F4
Paste Into	Ctrl+Shift+V	⌘+Shift+V
Pattern Maker	Ctrl+Shift+Alt+X	⌘+Shift+Option+X
Preferences	Ctrl+K	⌘+K
Preferences, last panel	Ctrl+Alt+K	⌘+Option+K
Print	Ctrl+P	⌘+P
Print One Copy	Ctrl+Shift+Alt+P	⌘+Shift+Option+P
Print with Preview	Ctrl+Alt+P	⌘+Option+P
Proof Colors	Ctrl+Y	⌘+Y
Redo	Ctrl+Z	⌘+Z
Reselect	Ctrl+Shift+D	⌘+Shift+D
Revert	F12	F12
Rulers, show or hide	Ctrl+R	⌘+R
Save	Ctrl+S	⌘+S
Save As	Ctrl+Shift+S	⌘+Shift+S
Save as a copy	Ctrl+Alt+S	⌘+Option+S
Save For Web	Ctrl+Shift+Alt+S	⌘+Shift+Option+S
Select All	Ctrl+A	⌘+A
Send Layer Backward	Ctrl+left bracket ([)	⌘+left bracket ([)

Operation	*Windows Shortcut*	*Macintosh Shortcut*
Send Layer to Back	Ctrl+Shift+left bracket ([)	⌘+Shift+left bracket ([)
Show/Hide Extras (for example, selection edges, slices, annotation)	Ctrl+H	⌘+H
Show/Hide Grid	Ctrl+Alt+quote (")	⌘+quote (")
Show/Hide Guides	Ctrl+semicolon (;)	⌘+semicolon (;)
Show/Hide Selected Path	Ctrl+Shift+H	⌘+Shift+H
Snap (for example, guides, grid, document bounds)	Ctrl+Shift+semicolon (;)	⌘+Shift+semicolon (;)
Step Backward in History	Ctrl+Alt+Z	⌘+Option+Z
Step Forward in History	Ctrl+Shift+Z	⌘+Shift+Z
Transform Again	Ctrl+Shift+T	⌘+Shift+T
Transform Again, repeat and clone	Ctrl+Shift+Alt+T	⌘+Shift+Option+T
Undo	Ctrl+Z	⌘+Z
Ungroup Layers	Ctrl+Shift+G	⌘+Shift+G
Zoom In	Ctrl+plus (+)	⌘+plus (+)
Zoom Out	Ctrl+minus (−)	⌘+minus (−)

Navigation

Scroll image with Hand tool	spacebar+drag or drag in Navigator palette	spacebar+drag or drag in Navigator palette
Scroll up or down one screen	Page Up or Page Down	Page Up or Page Down
Scroll up or down slightly	Shift+Page Up or Shift+Page Down	Shift+Page Up or Shift+Page Down
Scroll left or right one screen	Ctrl+Page Up or Ctrl+Page Down	⌘+Page Up or ⌘+Page Down
Scroll left or right slightly	Ctrl+Shift+Page Up or Ctrl+Shift+Page Down	⌘+Shift+Page Up or ⌘+Shift+Page Down
Switch to upper-left corner	Home	Home
Switch to lower-right corner	End	End
Magnify to custom zoom ratio	Ctrl+spacebar+drag or Ctrl+drag in Navigator palette	⌘+spacebar+drag or ⌘+drag in Navigator palette
Zoom in and change window size to fit (assuming default settings)	Ctrl+Alt+plus (+)	⌘+plus (+)

Continued

Table A-1 *(continued)*

Operation	Windows Shortcut	Macintosh Shortcut
Zoom in without changing window size	Ctrl+spacebar+click or Ctrl+plus (+)	⌘+spacebar+click or ⌘+Option+plus (+)
Zoom out and change window size to fit (assuming default settings)	Ctrl+Alt+minus (–)	⌘+minus (–)
Zoom out without changing window size	Alt+spacebar+click or Ctrl+minus (–)	Option+spacebar+click or ⌘+Option+minus (–)
Zoom to 100%	Ctrl+Alt+0 (zero) or double+click zoom tool icon	⌘+Option+0 (zero) or double-click zoom tool icon
Fit image on screen	Ctrl+0 (zero) or double-click hand tool icon	⌘+0 (zero) or double-click hand tool icon
Apply zoom value but keep magnification box active	Shift+Enter	Shift+Return
Cycle through full screen and normal window modes	F	F
Change screen mode for all open windows	Shift+click screen icon in toolbox	Shift+click screen icon in toolbox
Toggle display of menu bar in full screen modes	Shift+F	Shift+F
Bring forward next open image window	Ctrl+Tab	Ctrl+Tab

Painting and Editing

Operation	Windows Shortcut	Macintosh Shortcut
Display crosshair cursor	Caps Lock	Caps Lock
Erase to History	Alt+drag with Eraser	Option+drag with Eraser
Select Brush tool or Pencil tool	B or Shift+B	B or Shift+B
Select Airbrush (while Brush tool is active)	Shift+Alt+P	Shift+Option+P
Cycle between Stamp tools	S or Shift+S	S or Shift+S
Select Healing Brush or Patch tool	J or Shift+J	J or Shift+J
Specify area to clone	Alt+click with Clone stamp or Bealing Brush	Option+click with Clone Stamp or Healing Brush

Operation	Windows Shortcut	Macintosh Shortcut
Cycle between Focus tools	R or Shift+R	R or Shift+R
Sharpen with Blur tool or blur with Sharpen tool	Alt+drag	Option+drag
Dip into foreground color when smearing	Alt+drag with Smudge tool	Option+drag with Smudge tool
Cycle between the Dodge, Burn, and Sponge tools	O or Shift+O	O or Shift+O
Darken with Dodge tool or lighten with Burn tool	Alt+drag	Option+drag
Paint or edit in a straight line	click, and then Shift+click	click, and then Shift+click
Change Opacity, Strength, or Exposure in 10% increments	number (1 through 0)	number (1 through 0)
Change Opacity, Strength, or Exposure in 1% increments	two numbers in a row	two numbers in a row
Change Flow in 10% increments	Shift+number (1 through 0)	Shift+number (1 through 0)
Change Flow in 1% increments	Shift+two numbers in a row	Shift+two numbers in a row
Select brush mode	Shift+right-click with paint or edit tool or Shift+Alt+ letter	Shift+Control-click with paint or edit tool or Shift+Option+letter
Cycle through brush modes	Shift+plus (+) or Shift+ minus (−)	Shift+plus (+) or Shift+minus (−)
Reset to Normal brush mode	Shift+Alt+N	Shift+Option+N
Change brush diameter in increments proportional to brush size	bracket key, [or]	bracket key, [or]
Change brush hardness in 25 percent increments	Shift+bracket, [or]	Shift+bracket, [or]
Cycle between brush presets	comma (,) or period (.)	comma (,) or period (.)
Select first or last brush preset	Shift+comma (,) or Shift+period (.)	Shift+comma (,) or Shift+period (.)
Display Brushes palette	F5 or right-click with paint or edit tool	F5 or Control-click with paint or edit tool
Delete preset brush from Brushes palette	Alt+click preset	Option+click preset

Continued

Table A-1 *(continued)*

Operation	*Windows Shortcut*	*Macintosh Shortcut*
Edit preset name in Brushes palette	double-click preset	double-click preset
Applying Colors and Styles		
Switch foreground and background colors	X	X
Reset foreground and background colors to black and white	D	D
Lift foreground color from image	Alt+click with Paint tool or click with Eyedropper	Option+click with Paint tool or click with Eyedropper
Lift background color from image	Alt+click with Eyedropper	Option+click with Eyedropper
Lift color from different application	click with Eyedropper in image window, and then drag outside window into other application	click with Eyedropper in image window, and then drag outside window into other application
Place fixed color sampler in image	click with Color Sampler tool or Shift+click with Eyedropper	click with Color Sampler tool or Shift+click with Eyedropper
Delete fixed color sampler	Alt+click with Color Sampler tool or Shift+Alt+click with Eyedropper	Option+click with Color Sampler tool or Shift+Option+click with Eyedropper
Display or hide Color palette	F6	F6
Lift foreground color from color bar at bottom of Color palette	click color bar	click color bar
Lift background color from color bar	Alt+click color bar	Option+click color bar
Cycle through color bars	Shift+click color bar	Shift+click color bar
Specify new color bar	Right-click color bar	Control-click color bar
Lift foreground color from Swatches palette	click swatch	click swatch
Lift background color from Swatches palette	Ctrl+click swatch	⌘+click swatch
Delete swatch or style from palette	Alt+click swatch or style	Option+click swatch or style

Operation	Windows Shortcut	Macintosh Shortcut
Add new swatch or style to palette	click in empty area of palette	click in empty area of palette
Add new swatch or style without naming	Alt+click in empty area of palette	Option+click in empty area of palette
Apply style to active layer	click icon in Styles palette	click icon in Styles palette
Add effects in style to those applied to active layer	Shift+click icon in Styles palette	Shift+click icon in Styles palette
Fill selection or layer with foreground color	Alt+Backspace	Option+Delete
Fill layer with foreground color, preserve transparency	Shift+Alt+Backspace	Shift+Option+Delete
Fill selection on background layer with background color	Backspace or Delete	Delete
Fill selection on any layer with background color	Ctrl+Backspace	⌘+Delete
Fill layer with background color, preserve transparency	Ctrl+Shift+Backspace	⌘+Shift+Delete
Fill selection with source state in History palette	Ctrl+Alt+Backspace	⌘+Option+Delete
Display Fill dialog box	Shift+Backspace	Shift+Delete
Select Gradient Tool or Paint Bucket	G or Shift+G	G or Shift+G
Change gradient style	bracket key, [or]	bracket key, [or]
Cycle between gradient presets	comma (,) or period (.)	comma (,) or period (.)
Select first or last gradient preset	Shift+comma (,) or Shift+period (.)	Shift+comma (,) or Shift+period (.)

Type

Select all text on text layer	double-click T in Layers palette	double-click T in Layers palette
Select all text when already working inside text layer	Ctrl+A	⌘+A
Select single word	double-click word with type tool	double-click word with Type tool

Continued

Table A-1 *(continued)*

Operation	Windows Shortcut	Macintosh Shortcut
Select word to left or right	Ctrl+Shift+left or right arrow	⌘+Shift+left or right arrow
Increase type size 2 pixels	Ctrl+Shift+greater than (>)	⌘+Shift+greater than (>) (or points)
Decrease type size 2 pixels	Ctrl+Shift+less than (<)	⌘+Shift+less than (<)
Increase type size 10 pixels	Ctrl+Shift+Alt+greater than (>)	⌘+Shift+Option+greater than (>)
Decrease type size 10 pixels	Ctrl+Shift+Alt+less than (<)	⌘+Shift+Option+less than (<)
Kern together 2/100 em	Alt+left arrow	Option+left arrow
Kern apart 2/100 em	Alt+right arrow	Option+right arrow
Kern together 1/10 em	Ctrl+Alt+left arrow	⌘+Option+left arrow
Kern apart 1/10 em	Ctrl+Alt+right arrow	⌘+Option+right arrow
Toggle underlining	Ctrl+Shift+U	⌘+Shift+U
Toggle strikethrough	Ctrl+Shift+slash (/)	⌘+Shift+slash (/)
Toggle all uppercase text	Ctrl+Shift+K	⌘+Shift+K
Toggle small caps text	Ctrl+Shift+H	⌘+Shift+H
Toggle superscript text	Ctrl+Shift+plus (+)	⌘+Shift+plus (+)
Toggle subscript text	Ctrl+Shift+Alt+plus (+)	⌘+Shift+Option+plus (+)
Restore 100% horizontal scale	Ctrl+Shift+X	⌘+Shift+X
Restore 100% vertical scale	Ctrl+Shift+Alt+X	⌘+Shift+Option+X
Tighten leading 2 pixels	Alt+up arrow	Option+up arrow
Expand leading 2 pixels	Alt+down arrow	Option+down arrow
Tighten leading 10 pixels	Ctrl+Alt+up arrow	⌘+Option+up arrow
Expand leading 10 pixels	Ctrl+Alt+down arrow	⌘+Option+down arrow
Switch to Auto leading	Ctrl+Shift+Alt+A	⌘+Shift+Option+A
Raise baseline shift 2 pixels	Shift+Alt+up arrow	Shift+Option+up arrow
Lower baseline shift 2 pixels	Shift+Alt+down arrow	Shift+Option+down arrow
Raise baseline shift 10 pixels	Ctrl+Shift+Alt+up arrow	⌘+Shift+Option+up arrow
Lower baseline shift 10 pixels	Ctrl+Shift+Alt+down arrow	⌘+Shift+Option+down arrow
Left-align text	Ctrl+Shift+L	⌘+Shift+L

Operation	Windows Shortcut	Macintosh Shortcut
Center-align text	Ctrl+Shift+C	⌘+Shift+C
Right-align text	Ctrl+Shift+R	⌘+Shift+R
Justify all text	Ctrl+Shift+F	⌘+Shift+F
Justify all text except last line	Ctrl+Shift+J	⌘+Shift+J
Insert nonbreaking hyphen	Ctrl+Alt+hyphen (-)	*none*
Insert nonbreaking space	Ctrl+Alt+X	Option+spacebar
Show or hide highlight while editing text	Ctrl+H	⌘+H
Move live text	Ctrl+drag	⌘+drag
Accept changes to text	Enter on keypad or Ctrl+Enter	Enter or ⌘+Return
Cancel changes to text (cannot undo)	Esc	Escape
Highlight font option when Type Tool active but no type highlighted	Enter	Return
Change formatting for multiple linked text layers	Shift+choose setting from Options bar or type value and press Shift+Enter	Shift+choose setting from Options bar or type value and press Shift+Return
Display Character palette	Ctrl+T when text highlighted	⌘+T when text highlighted
Display Paragraph palette	Ctrl+M when text highlighted	⌘+M when text highlighted
Selections		
Select everything	Ctrl+A	⌘+A
Deselect everything	Ctrl+D	⌘+D
Restore last selection outline	Ctrl+Shift+D	⌘+Shift+D
Hide or show marching ants	Ctrl+H	⌘+H
Feather selection	Ctrl+Alt+D	⌘+Option+D
Reverse selection	Ctrl+Shift+I	⌘+Shift+I
Toggle between Rectangular and Elliptical Marquee tools	M or Shift+M	M or Shift+M
Draw out from center with Marquee tool	Alt	Option
Constrain marquee to square or circle	Shift	Shift

Continued

Table A-1 *(continued)*

Operation	Windows Shortcut	Macintosh Shortcut
Move marquee as you draw it	space bar	space bar
Cycle between Lasso tools	L or Shift+L	L or Shift+L
Add corner to straight-sided selection outline	Alt+click with Lasso tool or click with Polygonal Lasso tool	Option+click with Lasso tool or click with Polygonal Lasso tool
Add point to magnetic selection	click with Magnetic Lasso tool	click with Magnetic Lasso tool
Delete last point added with Magnetic Lasso tool	Backspace	Delete
Increase or reduce magnetic lasso width	bracket, [or]	bracket, [or]
Close polygon or magnetic selection	double-click with respective Lasso tool or press Enter	double-click with respective Lasso tool or press Return
Close magnetic selection with straight segment	Alt+double-click or Alt+Enter	Option+double-click or Option+Return
Cancel polygon or magnetic selection	Esc	*None*
Add to selection	Shift+drag (marquee, lasso) or Shift+click (magic wand)	Shift+drag (marquee, lasso)or Shift+click (magic wand)
Subtract from selection	Alt+drag (Marquee, Lasso) or Alt+click (Magic Wand)	Option+drag (Marquee, Lasso)or Option+click (Magic Wand)
Retain intersected portion of selection	Shift+Alt+drag (Marquee, Lasso)or Shift+Alt+click (Magic Wand)	Shift+Option+drag (Marquee, Lasso) or Shift+Option+click (Magic Wand)
Select Move tool	V or press and hold Ctrl	V or press and hold ⌘
Move selection	drag with Move tool or Ctrl+drag with other tool	drag with Move tool or ⌘+drag with other tool
Constrain movement vertically or horizontally	press Shift while dragging selection	press Shift while dragging selection
Move selection in 1-pixel increments	Ctrl+arrow key	⌘+arrow key
Move selection in 10-pixel increments	Ctrl+Shift+arrow key	⌘+Shift+arrow key

Operation	Windows Shortcut	Macintosh Shortcut
Clone selection	Alt+drag selection with Move tool or Ctrl+Alt+drag with other tool	Option+drag selection with Move tool or ⌘+Option+drag with other tool
Clone selection in 1-pixel increments	Ctrl+Alt+arrow key	⌘+Option+arrow key
Clone selection and move the clone in 10-pixel increments	Ctrl+Shift+Alt+arrow key	⌘+Shift+Option+arrow key
Clone selection to different image	Ctrl+drag selection from one window and drop it into another	⌘+drag selection from one window and drop it into another
Move selection outline independently of its contents	drag with Selection tool	drag with Selection tool
Move selection outline in 1-pixel increments	arrow key when Selection tool is active	arrow key when Selection tool is active
Move selection outline in 10-pixel increments	Shift+arrow key when Selection tool is active	Shift+arrow key when Selection tool is active
Copy empty selection outline to different image	drag selection from one window into another with Selection tool	drag selection from one window into another with Selection tool
Change opacity or blend mode of floating selection, when used immediately after applying a filter	Ctrl+Shift+F	⌘+*Shift+F*
Paste image into selection	Ctrl+Shift+V	⌘+Shift+V
Paste image behind selection	Ctrl+Shift+Alt+V	⌘+Shift+Option+V
Layers		
Display or hide Layers palette	F7	F7
View single layer by itself	Alt+click eyeball icon in Layers palette	Option+click Eyeball icon in Layers palette
Create new layer above current layer	click Page icon at bottom of Layers palette or Ctrl+Shift+Alt+N	click Page icon at bottom of Layers palette or ⌘+Shift+Option+N
Create new layer below current layer	Ctrl+click Page icon at bottom of Layers palette	⌘+click Page icon at bottom of Layers palette

Continued

Table A-1 (continued)

Operation	Windows Shortcut	Macintosh Shortcut
Create new layer above current layer and assign name	Alt+click Page icon at bottom of Layers palette or Ctrl+Shift+N	Option+click Page icon at bottom of Layers palette or ⌘+Shift+N
Create new layer below current layer and assign name	Ctrl+Alt+click Page icon at bottom of Layers palette	⌘+Option+click Page icon at bottom of Layers palette
Clone selection or entire layer to new layer	Ctrl+J	⌘+J
Clone selection or entire layer to new layer and assign name	Ctrl+Alt+J	⌘+Option+J
Transfer selection to new layer	Ctrl+Shift+J	⌘+Shift+J
Transfer selection to new layer and assign name	Ctrl+Shift+Alt+J	⌘+Shift+Option+J
Convert floating selection to new layer	Ctrl+Shift+J	⌘+Shift+J
Create adjustment layer	choose from Dual-tone icon menu at bottom of Layers palette	choose from Dual-tone icon menu at bottom of Layers palette
Create and name adjustment layer	Alt+choose from Dual-tone icon menu at bottom of Layers palette	Option+choose from Dual-tone icon menu at bottom of Layers palette
Add layer set	click Folder icon in Layers palette	click Folder icon in Layers palette
Add and name layer set	Alt+click Folder icon in Layers palette	Option+click Folder icon in Layers palette
Ascend one layer	Alt+right bracket (])	Option+right bracket (])
Descend one layer	Alt+left bracket ([)	Option+left bracket ([)
Ascend to top layer	Shift+Alt+right bracket (])	Shift+Option+right bracket (])
Descend to background layer	Shift+Alt+left bracket ([)	Shift+Option+left bracket ([)
Go directly to layer containing specific image element when using Move tool	Ctrl+click or Alt+right+click layer in image window	⌘+click or Control+Option+click layer in image window
Go directly to layer containing specific image element when using any tool except Move tool	Ctrl+Alt+right-click layer in image window	⌘+Control+Option+click layer in image window

Operation	Windows Shortcut	Macintosh Shortcut
Select from layers that overlap when using Move tool	Right-click layer in image window	Control-click layer in image window
Select from layers that overlap when using any tool except Move tool	Ctrl+right-click layer in image window	⌘+Control-click layer in image window
Lock transparency of layer	slash (/)	slash (/)
Toggle between current lock configuration and no locks in Layers palette	slash (/)	slash (/)
Convert layer's transparency mask to selection outline	Ctrl+click layer name in Layers palette	⌘+click layer name in Layers palette
Add transparency mask to selection	Ctrl+Shift+click layer name	⌘+Shift+click layer name
Subtract transparency mask from selection	Ctrl+Alt+click layer name	⌘+Option+click layer name
Retain intersection of transparency mask and selection	Ctrl+Shift+Alt+click layer name	⌘+Shift+Option+click layer name
Move layer	drag with Move tool or Ctrl+drag with other tool	drag with Move tool or ⌘+drag with other tool
Move layer in 1-pixel increments	Ctrl+arrow key	⌘+arrow key
Move layer in 10-pixel increments	Ctrl+Shift+arrow key	⌘+Shift+arrow key
Clone and move layer	Alt+drag with Move tool or Ctrl+Alt+drag with other tool	Option+drag with Move tool or ⌘+Option+drag with other tool
Clone and move layer in 1-pixel increments	Ctrl+Alt+arrow key	⌘+Option+arrow key
Clone and move layer in 10-pixel increments	Ctrl+Shift+Alt+arrow key	⌘+Shift+Option+arrow key
Clone layer to another open image	Ctrl+drag layer from one window and drop it into another	⌘+drag layer from one window and drop it into another

Continued

Table A-1 *(continued)*

Operation	Windows Shortcut	Macintosh Shortcut
Clone layer to new image	Alt+drag layer onto page icon at bottom of Layers palette, choose New from Document menu	Option+drag layer onto page icon at bottom of Layers palette, choose New from Document menu
Bring layer forward one level	Ctrl+right bracket (])	⌘+right bracket (])
Bring layer to front of file	Ctrl+Shift+right bracket (])	⌘+Shift+right bracket (])
Send layer backward one level	Ctrl+left bracket ([)	⌘+left bracket ([)
Send layer to back, just above background layer	Ctrl+Shift+left bracket ([)	⌘+Shift+left bracket ([)
Link layer containing specific image element with active layer	Ctrl+Shift+Alt+right-click layer in image window	⌘+Control+Shift+Option+ click layer in image window
Unlink layer that contains specific image element from active layer	Ctrl+Shift+Alt+right-click layer in image window	⌘+Control+Shift+Option+ click layer in image window
Unlink all layers from active layer	Alt+click brush icon in front of layer name in Layers palette or Ctrl+Shift+Alt+ right-click active layer in image window	Option+click brush icon in front of layer name in Layers palette or ⌘+Control+Shift+Option+ click active layer in image window
Change opacity of active layer in 10% increments	number (1 through 0) when Selection tool is active	number (1 through 0) when Selection tool is active
Change opacity of active layer in 1% increments	two numbers in a row when Selection tool is active	two numbers in a row when Selection tool is active
Change opacity of pixels in active layer in 10% increments, independently of effects	Shift+number (1 through 0) when Selection tool is active	Shift+number (1 through 0) when Selection tool is active
Change opacity of pixels in active layer in 1% increments, independently of effects	Shift+two numbers in a row when Selection tool is active	Shift+two numbers in a row when Selection tool is active
Edit layer name	double-click layer name in Layers palette	double-click layer name in Layers palette

Operation	Windows Shortcut	Macintosh Shortcut
Edit blending options for layer	double-click thumbnail in Layers palette or Alt+double-click layer name	double-click thumbnail in Layers palette or Option+double-click layer name
Edit settings for fill or adjustment layer	double-click thumbnail in Layers palette	double-click thumbnail in Layers palette
Change blend mode when Selection tool is active	Shift+Alt+letter	Shift+Option+letter
Cycle between blend modes when Selection tool is active	Shift+plus (+) or Shift+minus (–)	Shift+plus (+) or Shift+minus (–)
Reset to Normal blend mode when Selection tool is active	Shift+Alt+N	Shift+Option+N
Adjust "fuzziness" in Layer Style dialog box	Alt+drag This Layer or Underlying Layer slider triangle	Option+drag This Layer or Underlying Layer slider triangle
Merge layer with next layer down	Ctrl+E	⌘+E
Merge linked layers	Ctrl+E	⌘+E
Merge grouped layers	Ctrl+E	⌘+E
Merge all layers in active set	Ctrl+E	⌘+E
Merge all visible layers	Ctrl+Shift+E	⌘+Shift+E
Copy merged version of selection to Clipboard	Ctrl+Shift+C	⌘+Shift+C
Clone contents of layer into next layer down	Ctrl+Alt+E	⌘+Option+E
Clone contents of linked layers to active layer	Ctrl+Alt+E	⌘+Option+E
Clone contents of all visible layers to active layer	Ctrl+Shift+Alt+E	⌘+Shift+Option+E
Delete active layer	click Trash icon in Layers palette	click Trash icon in Layers palette
Delete active layer without warning	Alt+click Trash icon in Layers palette	Option+click Trash icon in Layers palette
Delete multiple linked layers and sets	Ctrl+click Trash icon in Layers palette	⌘+click Trash icon in Layers palette
Delete multiple linked layers and sets without warning	Ctrl+Alt+click Trash icon in Layers palette	⌘+Option+click Trash icon in Layers palette

Continued

Table A-1 *(continued)*

Operation	Windows Shortcut	Macintosh Shortcut
Edit specific layer effect	double-click effect name in Layers palette	double-click effect name in Layers palette
Switch between effects in Layer Styles dialog box	Ctrl+1 through Ctrl+0	⌘+1 through ⌘+0
Save flattened copy of layered image	Ctrl+Alt+S	⌘+Option+S
Brush and Blend Modes		
Normal	Shift+Alt+N or Shift+Alt+L	Shift+Option+N
Dissolve	Shift+Alt+I	Shift+Option+I
Behind	Shift+Alt+Q	Shift+Option+Q
Clear	Shift+Alt+R	Shift+Option+R
Darken	Shift+Alt+K	Shift+Option+K
Multiply	Shift+Alt+M	Shift+Option+M
Color Burn	Shift+Alt+B	Shift+Option+B
Linear Burn	Shift+Alt+A	Shift+Option+A
Lighten	Shift+Alt+G	Shift+Option+G
Screen	Shift+Alt+S	Shift+Option+S
Color Dodge	Shift+Alt+D	Shift+Option+D
Linear Dodge	Shift+Alt+W	Shift+Option+W
Overlay	Shift+Alt+O	Shift+Option+O
Soft Light	Shift+Alt+F	Shift+Option+F
Hard Light	Shift+Alt+H	Shift+Option+H
Vivid Light	Shift+Alt+V	Shift+Option+V
Linear Light	Shift+Alt+J	Shift+Option+J
Pin Light	Shift+Alt+Z	Shift+Option+Z
Hard Mix	Shift+Alt+L	Shift+Option+L
Difference	Shift+Alt+E	Shift+Option+E
Exclusion	Shift+Alt+X	Shift+Option+X
Hue	Shift+Alt+U	Shift+Option+U
Saturation	Shift+Alt+T	Shift+Option+T
Color	Shift+Alt+C	Shift+Option+C
Luminosity	Shift+Alt+Y	Shift+Option+Y

Operation	Windows Shortcut	Macintosh Shortcut
Saturate (Sponge tool)	Shift+Alt+S	Shift+Option+S
Desaturate (Sponge tool)	Shift+Alt+D	Shift+Option+D
Shadows (Dodge and Burn tools)	Shift+Alt+S	Shift+Option+S
Midtones (Dodge and Burn tools)	Shift+Alt+M	Shift+Option+M
Highlights (Dodge and Burn tools)	Shift+Alt+H	Shift+Option+H
Replace (Healing Brush)	Shift+Alt+Z	Shift+Option+Z
Pass Through (layer set)	Shift+Alt+P	Shift+Option+P
Cycle to next mode	Shift+plus (+)	Shift+plus (+)
Cycle to previous mode	Shift+minus (−)	Shift+minus (−)
Channels and Masks		
Switch between independent color and mask channels	Ctrl+1 through Ctrl+9	⌘+1 through ⌘+9
View composite RGB, Lab, or CMYK image	Ctrl+tilde (~)	⌘+tilde (~)
Activate or deactivate color channel	Shift+click channel name in Channels palette	Shift+click channel name in Channels palette
Create channel mask filled with black	click Page icon at bottom of Channels palette	click Page icon at bottom of Channels palette
Create and name channel mask filled with black	Alt+click Page icon at bottom of Channels palette	Option+click Page icon at bottom of Channels palette
Create channel mask from selection outline	click Mask icon at bottom of Channels palette	click Mask icon at bottom of Channels palette
Create and name channel mask from selection outline	Alt+click Mask icon at bottom of Channels palette	Option+click Mask icon at bottom of Channels palette
View active channel mask as rubylith overlay	tilde (~)	tilde (~)
Convert channel mask to selection outline	Ctrl+click channel name in Channels palette or Ctrl+Alt+number (1 through 0)	⌘+click channel name in Channels palette or ⌘+Option+number (1 through 0)

Continued

Table A-1 *(continued)*

Operation	Windows Shortcut	Macintosh Shortcut
Add channel mask to selection	Ctrl+Shift+click channel name	⌘+Shift+click channel name
Subtract channel mask from selection	Ctrl+Alt+click channel name	⌘+Option+click channel name
Retain intersection of channel mask and selection	Ctrl+Shift+Alt+click channel name	⌘+Shift+Option+click channel name
Enter or exit quick mask mode	Q	Q
Toggle quick mask color over masked or selected area	Alt+click Quick Mask icon in Toolbox	Option+click Quick Mask icon in Toolbox
Change quick mask color overlay	double-click Quick Mask icon	double-click Quick Mask icon
View quick mask independently of image	tilde (~)	tilde (~)
Add spot color channel	Ctrl+click Page icon at bottom of Channels palette	⌘+click Page icon at bottom of Channels palette
Create layer mask filled with white when nothing selected	click Mask icon at bottom of Layers palette	click Mask icon at bottom of Layers palette
Create layer mask filled with black when nothing selected	Alt+click Mask icon	Option+click Mask icon
Create layer mask from selection outline	click Mask icon	click Mask icon
Create layer mask that hides selection	Alt+click Mask icon	Option+click Mask icon
Switch focus from layer mask to image	Ctrl+tilde (~)	⌘+tilde (~)
Switch focus from image to layer mask	Ctrl+backslash (\)	⌘+backslash (\)
View layer mask as rubylith overlay	backslash (\) or Shift+Alt+click layer mask thumbnail in Layers palette	backslash (\) or Shift+Option+click layer mask thumbnail in Layers palette
View layer mask independently of image	backslash (\), and then tilde (~) or Alt+click layer mask thumbnail in Layers palette	backslash (\), and then tilde (~)or Option+click layer mask thumbnail in Layers palette
Add vector mask to layer	Ctrl+click Mask icon in Layers palette	⌘+click mask icon in Layers palette

Operation	Windows Shortcut	Macintosh Shortcut
Convert current path to vector mask	Ctrl+click Mask icon in Layers palette with path active	⌘+click Mask icon in Layers palette with path active
Toggle display of vector mask	click vector mask thumbnail or press Enter when shape or arrow tool is active	click vector mask thumbnail or press Return when shape or arrow tool is active
Disable layer mask or vector mask	Shift+click mask thumbnail in Layers palette	Shift+click mask thumbnail in Layers palette
Toggle link between layer and mask	click between layer and mask thumbnails in Layers palette	click between layer and mask thumbnails in Layers palette
Copy layer mask or vector mask from one layer to active layer	drag mask thumbnail onto Mask icon at bottom of Layers palette	drag mask thumbnail onto Mask icon at bottom of Layers palette
Convert layer mask to selection outline	Ctrl+click layer mask thumbnail or Ctrl+Alt+ backslash (\)	⌘+click layer mask thumbnail or ⌘+Option+ backslash (\)
Convert vector mask to selection outline	Ctrl+click vector mask thumbnail	⌘+click vector mask thumbnail
Add layer mask or vector mask to selection	Ctrl+Shift+click mask thumbnail	⌘+Shift+click mask thumbnail
Subtract layer mask or vector mask from selection	Ctrl+Alt+click mask thumbnail	⌘+Option+click mask thumbnail
Retain intersection of layer mask or vector mask and selection	Ctrl+Shift+Alt+click mask thumbnail	⌘+Shift+Option+click mask thumbnail

Paths and Shapes

Operation	Windows Shortcut	Macintosh Shortcut
Cycle between standard, Free-form, and Magnetic Pen tools	P or Shift+P	P or Shift+P
Add corner to end of active path	click with Pen tool or Alt+click with Freeform Pen tool	click with pen tool or Option+click with Freeform Pen tool
Add smooth arc to end of active path	drag with Pen tool	drag with Pen tool
Add cusp to end of active path	Alt+click, and then drag with Pen tool	Option+click, and then drag with Pen tool
Add point to end of active magnetic selection	click with Magnetic Pen tool	click with Magnetic Pen tool

Continued

Table A-1 *(continued)*

Operation	*Windows Shortcut*	*Macintosh Shortcut*
Delete last point added with standard or Magnetic Pen tool	Backspace	Delete
Draw freehand path segment	drag with Freeform Pen tool or Alt+drag with Magnetic Pen tool	drag with Freeform Pen tool or Option+drag with Magnetic Pen tool
Increase or reduce Magnetic Pen tool path width	bracket, [or]	bracket, [or]
Close magnetic selection	double-click with Magnetic Pen tool or click first point in path	double-click with Magnetic Pen tool or click first point in path
Close magnetic selection with straight segment	Alt+double-click or Alt+Enter	Option+double-click or Option+Return
Cancel magnetic or freeform selection	Esc	Escape
Select Arrow tool	A or press Ctrl when Pen tool is active	A or press ⌘ when Pen tool is active
Move selected points	drag point with Arrow tool or Ctrl+drag with Pen tool	drag point with Arrow tool or ⌘+drag with Pen tool
Select multiple points in path	Shift+click with Arrow or Ctrl+Shift+click with Pen tool	Shift+click with Arrow or ⌘+Shift+click with Pen tool
Select entire path	Alt+click path with white arrowor Alt+click path in Paths palette	Option+click path with arrow or Option+click path in Paths palette
Clone path	Alt+drag path with Arrow or Ctrl+Alt+drag with Pen tools	Option+drag path with Arrow tool or ⌘+Option+drag with Pen tool
Access Convert direction tool when Pen tool is active	Alt while hovering cursor over anchor point	Option while hovering cursor over anchor point
Access Convert Direction tool when Arrow tool is active	Ctrl+Alt while hovering cursor over anchor point	⌘+Option while hovering cursor over anchor point
Convert corner or cusp to smooth arc	Alt+drag point with Pen tool	Option+drag point with Pen tool
Convert arc to corner	Alt+click point with Pen tool	Option+click point with Pen tool

Operation	Windows Shortcut	Macintosh Shortcut
Convert arc to cusp	Alt+drag handle with Pen tool	Option+drag handle with Pen tool
Insert point in selected path	click segment with Pen tool	click segment with Pen tool
Remove point from path	click point with Pen tool	click point with Pen tool
Convert path to selection outline	Ctrl+click path name in Paths palette or Ctrl+Enter when Pen or Arrow tool is active	⌘+click path name in Paths palette or ⌘+Return when Pen or Arrow tool is active
Add path to selection	Ctrl+Shift+click path name in Paths palette	⌘+Shift+click path name in Paths palette
Subtract path from selection	Ctrl+Alt+click path name in Paths palette	⌘+Option+click path name in Paths palette
Retain intersection of path and selection	Ctrl+Shift+Alt+click path name in Paths palette	⌘+Shift+Option+click path name in Paths palette
Apply brushstroke around perimeter of path	Enter on keypad when Paint or edit tool is active	Enter when Paint or Edit tool is active
Revert around perimeter of path	Enter on keypad when History Brush is active	Enter when History Brush is active
Save and name path for future use	double-click Work Path item in Paths palette	double-click Work Path item in Paths palette
Hide path (it remains active)	Ctrl+Shift+H	⌘+Shift+H
Deactivate path	click in empty portion of Paths palette or Enter when Pen or Arrow tool is active	click in empty portion of Paths palette or Return when Pen or Arrow tool is active
Cycle between shape tools	U or Shift+U	U or Shift+U
Move shape as you draw it	space bar	space bar
Add next shape you draw to active shape layer	plus (+)	plus (+)
Subtract next shape you draw from active shape layer	minus (−)	minus (−)
Adjust roundness of next rounded rectangle you draw	bracket key, [or]	bracket key, [or]
Change number of sides on next regular polygon or star you draw	bracket key, [or]	bracket key, [or]

Continued

Table A-1 *(continued)*

Operation	Windows Shortcut	Macintosh Shortcut
Change weight of next straight	bracket key, [or]	bracket key, [or]line you draw
Cycle between custom shapes	bracket key, [or]	bracket key, [or]
Cycle between layer styles	comma (,) or period (.)	comma (,) or period (.)
Change color of active shape layer to foreground or background color	Alt+Backspace or Ctrl+Backspace	Option+Delete or ⌘+Delete
Hide shape outlines (shape layer remains active)	Ctrl+Shift+H	⌘+Shift+H
Deactivate shape outlines	Enter when Pen or Arrow tool is active	Return when Pen or Arrow tool is active
Delete shape layer when shape outlines are active	Backspace or Delete	Delete
Crops and Transformations		
Select Crop tool	C	C
Move crop boundary as you draw it	space bar	space bar
Move crop boundary	drag inside boundary	drag inside boundary
Scale crop boundary	drag boundary handle	drag boundary handle
Scale crop boundary proportionally	Shift+drag corner handle	Shift+drag corner handle
Scale crop boundary with respect to origin	Alt+drag boundary handle	Option+drag boundary handle
Scale crop boundary proportionally with respect to origin point	Shift+Alt+drag corner	Shift+Option+drag corner
Rotate crop boundary (always with respect to origin)	drag outside boundary	drag outside boundary
Rotate crop boundary in 15° increments	Shift+drag outside boundary	Shift+drag outside boundary
Distort crop boundary	draw crop boundary, select Perspective check box in Options bar, drag boundary handle	draw crop boundary, select Perspective check box in Options bar, drag boundary handle
Constrain distortion effect in Perspective mode	Shift+drag corner handle	Shift+drag corner handle

Operation	Windows Shortcut	Macintosh Shortcut
Scale crop boundary in Perspective mode	Alt+drag handle	Option+drag handle
Accept crop	Enter	Return
Cancel crop	Esc	Escape
Freely transform selection, layer, or path	Ctrl+T	⌘+T
Duplicate selection, layer, or path and freely transform	Ctrl+Alt+T	⌘+Option+T
Move image in Free Transform mode	drag inside boundary	drag inside boundary
Move transformation origin	drag cross-hair target	drag cross-hair target
Scale image	drag boundary handle	drag boundary handle
Scale image proportionally	Shift+drag corner handle	Shift+drag corner handle
Scale image with respect to origin	Alt+drag boundary handle	Option+drag boundary handle
Rotate image (always with respect to origin)	drag outside boundary	drag outside boundary
Rotate image in 15° increments	Shift+drag outside boundary	Shift+drag outside boundary
Skew image	Ctrl+drag side handle	⌘+drag side handle
Skew image along constrained axis	Ctrl+Shift+drag side handle	⌘+Shift+drag side handle
Skew image with respect to origin	Ctrl+Alt+drag side handle	⌘+Option+drag side handle
Skew image along constrained axis with respect to origin	Ctrl+Shift+Alt+drag side handle	⌘+Shift+Option+drag side handle
Distort image	Ctrl+drag corner handle	⌘+drag corner handle
Symmetrically distort opposite corners	Ctrl+Alt+drag corner handle	⌘+Option+drag corner handle
Constrain distortion to achieve perspective effect	Ctrl+Shift+drag corner handle	⌘+Shift+drag corner handle
Constrain distortion to achieve symmetrical perspective effect	Ctrl+Shift+Alt+drag corner handle	⌘+Shift+Option+drag corner handle
Apply specific transformation in Free Transform mode	right+click in image window	Control+click in image window

Continued

Table A-1 *(continued)*

Operation	Windows Shortcut	Macintosh Shortcut
Apply numerical transformation in Free Transform mode	enter values in Options bar	enter values in Options bar
Accept transformation	Enter	Return
Cancel transformation	Esc	Escape
Replay last transformation	Ctrl+Shift+T	⌘+Shift+T
Duplicate selection, layer, or path and replay last transformation	Ctrl+Shift+Alt+T	⌘+Shift+Option+T
Rulers, Measurements, and Guides		
Display or hide rulers	Ctrl+R	⌘+R
Display or hide Info palette	F8	F8
Change unit of measure	right-click ruler or drag from X,Y pop-up in Info palette	Control-click ruler or drag from X,Y pop-up in Info palette
Reset ruler origin	double-click ruler origin box	double-click ruler origin box
Select Measure tool	I, I, I (or I, Shift+I, Shift+I)	I, I, I (or I, Shift+I, Shift+I)
Measure distance and angle	drag with Measure tool	drag with Measure tool
Move measure line	drag measure line	drag measure line
Change length and angle of measure line	drag endpoint of measure line	drag endpoint of measure line
Measure angle between two lines (protractor option)	Alt+drag endpoint	Option+drag endpoint
Match rotation of entire image to measure line	Choose Image ⇨ Rotate ⇨ Arbitrary	choose Image ⇨ Rotate ⇨ Arbitrary
Match rotation of single layer to measure line	Choose Edit ⇨ Transform ⇨ Rotate	choose Edit ⇨ Transform ⇨ Rotate
Create guide	drag from ruler	drag from ruler
Move guide	drag guide with Move tool or Ctrl+drag with other tool	drag guide with Move tool or ⌘+drag with other tool
Change horizontal guide to vertical or vice versa	press Alt while dragging guide	press Option while dragging guide
Snap guide to ruler tick marks	press Shift while dragging guide	press Shift while dragging guide

Operation	Windows Shortcut	Macintosh Shortcut
Display or hide guides	Ctrl+semicolon (;)	⌘+semicolon (;)
Lock or unlock guides	Ctrl+Alt+semicolon (;)	⌘+Option+semicolon (;)
Display or hide grid	Ctrl+quote (")	⌘+quote (")
Toggle guide and grid snapping	Ctrl+Shift+semicolon (;)	⌘+Shift+semicolon (;)
Edit guide color and grid increments	Ctrl+double+click guide	⌘+double-click guide
Filters and Automation		
Repeat filter with last-used settings	Ctrl+F	⌘+F
Repeat filter with different settings	Ctrl+Alt+F	⌘+Option+F
Fade effect of last filter	Ctrl+Shift+F	⌘+Shift+F
Scroll preview box in corrective filter dialog boxes	drag in preview box or click in image window	drag in preview box or click in image window
Zoom preview box in corrective filter dialog boxes	Ctrl+click and Alt+click	⌘+click and Option+click
Zoom full image preview	Ctrl+plus (+) and Ctrl+minus (−)	⌘+plus (+) and ⌘+minus (−)
Increase selected option box value by 1 (or 0.1)	up arrow	up arrow
Decrease value by 1 (or 0.1)	down arrow	down arrow
Increase value by 10 (or 1)	Shift+up arrow	Shift+up arrow
Decrease value by 10 (or 1)	Shift+down arrow	Shift+down arrow
Adjust Angle value (where offered) in 15° increments	Shift+drag in Angle wheel	Shift+drag in Angle wheel
Reset options in corrective filter dialog boxes	Alt+click Cancel button	Option+click Cancel buttonor Option+Escape
Create high-contrast clouds effect	Alt+choose Filter ⇨ Render ⇨ Clouds	Option+choose Filter ⇨ Render ⇨ Clouds
Specify numerical center in Lens Flare dialog box	Alt+click in preview	Option+click in preview
Clone light in Lighting Effects dialog box	Alt+drag light	Option+drag light
Delete Lighting Effects light	press Delete	press Delete

Continued

Table A-1 *(continued)*

Operation	Windows Shortcut	Macintosh Shortcut
Adjust size of footprint without affecting angle of light	Shift+drag handle	Shift+drag handle
Adjust angle of light without affecting size of footprint	Ctrl+drag handle	⌘+drag handle
Select Forward Warp or Push Left tool in Liquify dialog box	W or O	W or O
Select Twirl Clockwise or Turbulence tool	C or T	C or T
Select Pucker or Bloat tool	S or B	S or B
Select Reconstruct or Mirror tool	R or M	R or M
Select Freeze Mask or Thaw Mask tool	F or D	F or D
Change Liquify brush diameter in 1-pixel increments	Bracket key, [or]	bracket key, [or]
Change Liquify brush diameter in 10-pixel increments	Shift+bracket, [or]	Shift+bracket, [or]
Undo last brushstroke in Liquify dialog box	Ctrl+Z	⌘+Z
Undo brushstroke prior to last one	Ctrl+Alt+Z	⌘+Option+Z
Redo undone brushstroke	Ctrl+Shift+Z	⌘+Shift+Z
Select the select image, rotate image, or set vanishing point tool in Photomerge dialog box	A, R, or V	A, R, or V
Select Zoom or Hand tool	Z or H	Z or H
Temporarily access Hand tool	Spacebar	Spacebar
Step backward	Ctrl+Z	⌘+Z
Step forward	Ctrl+Shift+Z	⌘+Shift+Z
Show individual image border	Alt+move pointer over image	Option+move pointer over image

Color Adjustments

Choose Levels command	Ctrl+L	⌘+L

Operation	Windows Shortcut	Macintosh Shortcut
Switch between channels in Levels or Curves dialog box	Ctrl+1 through Ctrl+3, or Ctrl+tilde (~) for composite	⌘+1 through ⌘+3, or ⌘+tilde (~) for composite
Preview black and white points in Levels dialog box	Alt+drag black or white Input Levels triangle	Option+drag black or white Input Levels triangle
Specify alternate colors for black point, white point, and midtone	double-click black, white, or gray Eyedropper tool	double-click black, white, or gray Eyedropper tool
Invert image in Levels dialog box	swap black and white Output Levels triangles	swap black and white Output Levels triangles
Repeat last Levels correction	Ctrl+Alt+L	⌘+Option+L
Choose Curves command	Ctrl+M	⌘+M
Add point in Curves dialog box	click graph line	click graph line
Add specific color as new point on composite curve in point mode	Ctrl+click in image window	⌘+click in image window
Add color as new point on independent channel curves	Ctrl+Shift+click in image window	⌘+Shift+click in image window
Nudge Input value for selected point	left or right arrow key	left or right arrow key
Nudge Output value for selected point	up- or down-arrow key	up- or down-arrow key
Select next curve point	Ctrl+Tab	Control+Tab
Select previous curve point	Ctrl+Shift+Tab	Control+Shift+Tab
Delete curve point	Ctrl+click point	⌘+click point
Select multiple curve points	Shift+click point	Shift+click point
Deselect all points	Ctrl+D	⌘+D
Repeat last Curves correction	Ctrl+Alt+M	⌘+Option+M
Choose Hue/Saturation command	Ctrl+U	⌘+U
Add colors to Hue/Saturation range when Edit set to anything but Master	Shift+click or drag in image window	Shift+click or drag in image window
Subtract colors from Hue/Saturation range when Edit set to anything but Master	Alt+click or drag in image window	Option+click or drag in image window

Continued

Table A-1 *(continued)*

Operation	Windows Shortcut	Macintosh Shortcut
Edit all colors in Hue/Saturation dialog box	Ctrl+tilde (~)	⌘+tilde (~)
Edit predefined color range	Ctrl+1 through Ctrl+6	⌘+1 through ⌘+6
Repeat last Hue/Saturation correction	Ctrl+Alt+U	⌘+Option+U
Desaturation colors	Ctrl+Shift+U	⌘+Shift+U
Undoing Operations		
Undo or redo last operation	Ctrl+Z	⌘+Z
Undo operation prior to last one	Ctrl+Alt+Z	⌘+Option+Z
Redo undone operation	Ctrl+Shift+Z	⌘+Shift+Z
Undo to specific point	click item in History palette	click item in History palette
Duplicate previously performed operation	Alt+click item in History palette	Option+click item in History palette
Select state to revert to with History Brush	click in front of item in History palette	click in front of item in History palette
Create snapshot from active state	click camera icon at bottom of History palette	click camera icon at bottom of History palette
Create duplicate image from active state	click leftmost icon at bottom of History palette	click leftmost icon at bottom of History palette
Revert selection to active History state	Ctrl+Alt+Backspace	⌘+Option+Delete
Revert entire image to saved state	F12	F12
Miscellaneous		
Display or hide all palettes, Toolbox, and status bar	Tab	Tab
Display or hide palettes except Toolbox, Options bar, and status bar	Shift+Tab	Shift+Tab
Hide Toolbox, Options bar, and status bar	Tab, and then Shift+Tab	Tab, and then Shift+Tab

Operation	Windows Shortcut	Macintosh Shortcut
Display Options bar	Enter	Return
Move panel out of palette	drag panel tab	drag panel tab
Dock palette	drag panel tab into docking well	drag panel tab into docking well
Snap palette to edge of screen	Shift+click palette title bar	Shift+click palette title bar
Fully collapse palette	Alt+click collapse box or double-click panel tab	Option+click collapse box or double-click panel tab
Delete item without warning from any palette that includes trash can	Alt+click Trash icon	Option+click Trash icon
Preview how image sits on printed page	click Doc box in status bar	click Doc box at bottom of image window
View size and resolution of image	Alt+click Doc box in status bar	Option+click Doc box at bottom of image window
View image tile information	Ctrl+click Doc box in status bar	⌘+click Doc box at bottom of image window
Change preference settings	Ctrl+K	⌘+K
Display last-used Preferences dialog box panel	Ctrl+Alt+K	⌘+Option+K
Bring up dialog box with last-used settings	Alt+choose command from Image ⇨ Adjustments submenu	Option+choose command from Image ⇨ Adjustments submenu
Duplicate image and bypass dialog box	Alt+choose Image ⇨ Duplicate	Option+choose Image ⇨ Duplicate
Cancel operation	Esc	⌘+period or Escape
Activate No or Don't Save button when closing image	N	D
Activate Don't Flatten button when changing color modes	D	D
Activate Flatten button when changing color modes	F	F

✦   ✦   ✦

Index

8-bit channel, 179

f (florin symbol) layer effect indicator, 764, 765

(number symbol) color profile indicator, 824

16-bit channel, 182

32-bit channel, 81, 182

3D Transform filter, 550

A

.abr files, 238

ACE (Adobe Color Engine), 828

ADCT (Adaptive Discrete Cosine Transform), 140

Add Anchor Point tool, 26, 395

Add Blend mode, 724–725

Add Color tool, 453

Add Noise filter
  Amount option, 437, 439, 526, 528
  banding, removing using, 436–437
  Edit menu Fade option, using with, 528
  Gaussian option, 526, 528
  mask pixels, jumbling using, 439
  Monochromatic option, 526–527
  Pointillize filter, using with, 528–529
  Uniform option, 526

Add Point tool, 403–404

adjustment layer introduced, 613

Adobe Color Engine (ACE), 828

Adobe software
  After Effects, 823
  Illustrator
    clipping mask, 673
    color compatibility, 828
    compression, 142
    exporting to, 131, 134, 415–416, 419, 945
    Pen tool, 393
    rasterizing Illustrator file, 131–133
    trapping rasterized drawing from, 942
  InDesign, 134, 781, 828
  PageMaker, 134
  Reader, 126

Adobe Web site, 12, 905, 923

AdobePS printer driver, 923

After Effects software, 823

.ai files, 132

alpha transparency introduced, 950

Alt-key menu shortcut, 988–989

ambient light introduced, 607

American Standard Code for Information Interchange
  (ASCII) EPS document, 135

Animation palette, 963–965

ANPA (American Newspaper Publishers Association)
  color, 189

Anti-alias menu, 792

anti-aliasing introduced, 132

Apply Camera Raw Settings dialog box, 914–915

Apply Image dialog box, 720–724

Apply Settings From menu, 914

Apply Sharpening To menu, 909

Art History Brush tool
  Area option, 350
  Cancel cursor, 351–352
  History palette, using with, 341, 347–350
  introduced, 24
  source state, 309, 341, 351–352
  Style menu, 348
  Tolerance option, 350

ascender introduced, 784

ASCII (American Standard Code for Information
  Interchange) EPS document, 135

Assign Profile dialog box, 824–825, 832

Audio Annotation tool, 27, 149–150

Auto Color Correction Options dialog box, 878, 880

Auto Screens dialog box, 934

auto slice introduced, 966

Average filter, 537–538

.axt files, 455

B

Background Contents menu, 82

Background Eraser tool, 24, 308, 444–447, 452

background layer introduced, 625

Backspace key, applying color fill using,
  266, 274–275, 299

banding introduced, 277

Bas Relief filter, 477, 547, 549

base layer introduced, 673

Behind mode, 254

Bézier control handle, 396–397, 399, 400, 403

Bézier curve, 396–397, 399

Bezier tool, 393

bit depth introduced, 17

Bitmap dialog box, 184–188

bitmap introduced, 4

black arrow (Path Selection) tool, 25, 359, 396, 402, 407

Black Generation menu, 832

Blast filter, 502

bleed introduced, 920–921

Blend menu, 633, 728
blend mode
    Add, 724–725
    CMYK, behavior in, 635
    Color, 696, 697
    Color Burn, 688–689
    Color Dodge, 691, 692, 699
    Darken, 687–688
    Difference, 696, 697, 700, 704, 730
    Dissolve, 686–687
    Exclusion, 696, 697
    Hard Light, 691–693, 699
    Hard Mix, 695–696
    hierarchy, 698–701
    Hue, 696
    keyboard shortcut list, 1014–1015
    Layers palette, adjusting using, 679–681
    Lighten, 690
    Linear Burn, 688–689
    Linear Dodge, 691, 692
    Linear Light, 694
    Luminosity, 696, 697
    menu, 757
    Multiply, 688, 689, 716, 718, 730–732
    Normal, 684–686
    Overlay, 691–693, 698
    Pin Light, 694–695
    RGB, behavior in, 635
    Saturation, 696, 697
    Screen, 687, 689, 690–691, 730, 732
    Soft Light, 691–692
    Subtract, 724, 725–727, 728
    Vivid Light, 694
Blistered Paint pattern, 685, 692–693
Bloat tool, 590
Blur
    filter, 219, 470, 471, 773
    tool, 24, 218, 219, 220, 334
BMP files, 123–124, 173
Book menu, 188
bounding box introduced, 133
Box Blur filter, 512–514
Bridge
    accessing, 54, 77, 85, 89–90
    Apply Camera Raw Settings dialog box, 914–915
    cache, managing using, 110–111
    Camera Raw Preferences dialog box, 108–109, 839, 912–913
    contact sheet, publishing, 974–975
    Creative Suite panel, 107–108
    Details view, 92, 96–97
    droplet, publishing, 972

Duplicate Image dialog box, 115
Edit Layout option, 977
Edit menu
    Apply Camera Raw Settings option, 914
    Creative Suite Color Settings option, 107, 834
    Preferences submenu, 100
    Replace Metadata option, 115
    selection options, 93, 98, 99, 111
Favorites panel, 100–102
File Info dialog box, 112–115
File menu, 97, 101, 112, 116, 120
file type, specifying when publishing image, 972
Filmstrip view, 96, 109
Find dialog box, 103–104
Folders panel, 91
Image menu, 115
Image Processor option, 972
Keywords panel, 104–107
Label menu, 102
Metadata panel, 92, 96, 102–104
mode change, conditional, 972
opening image, 93
panorama, publishing, 983–986
PDF presentation, publishing, 981–983
picture package, publishing, 975–978
Preferences dialog box, 104, 105
Print with Preview dialog box, 112
rating image, 102
rotating image, 99–100
Save As dialog box, 116, 117–120
Save dialog box, 116, 117
Save for Web dialog box, 120–122, 125
Select an Image File dialog box, 975
sizing image when publishing, 974
slide show, 94
Thumbnails view, 95–96
Tools menu, 110, 111–112, 972, 975, 981
Versions and Alternates view, 97–98
View menu, 91, 92, 94, 96, 97
Web photo gallery, publishing, 978–981
Window menu, 109
workspace, 90, 91–92, 109
brush mode
    Color, 261
    Color Burn, 256
    Color Dodge, 256
    Darken, 254, 496, 528
    Difference, 259–260, 442
    Dissolve, 254
    Exclusion, 260, 442
    Hard Light, 257
    Hard Mix, 259

Healing Brush tool, 317, 318
Hue, 260–261
keyboard shortcut list, 1014–1015
Lighten, 256
Linear Burn, 256
Linear Dodge, 256, 258, 496, 531
Linear Light, 258, 259
Luminosity, 261
Multiply, 254–255, 317, 523, 633
Overlay, 257, 259
Pin Light, 258, 260
Saturation, 261
Screen, 256, 317
Soft Light, 257, 259
Vivid Light, 258
Brush tool
    Airbrush option, 217
    indexing color, considerations when, 179
    introduced, 23
    line, drawing using, 217, 221, 222, 224
    Options bar, 217
    path, stroking using, 409
    selection perimeter, applying to, 426, 465–466, 467
    underlining text using, 783
Brushes palette
    Airbrush option, 248
    Brush Presets option, 231, 238
    Brush Tip Shape option, 233–234, 238, 410
    Color Dynamics option, 217, 247
    Delete Brush option, 240
    Dual Brush option, 246
    Expanded View option, 231
    Load Brushes option, 240
    lock icon, 247
    Master Diameter option, 232
    Noise option, 248
    page icon, 241
    Protect Texture option, 249
    Replace Brushes option, 240
    Save Brushes option, 239
    Scattering option, 246
    Shape Dynamics option, 241–246
    Smoothing option, 249
    Texture option, 246
    Wet Edges option, 248
Burn tool
    darkroom equivalent, 219
    drop shadow, darkening using, 640
    Exposure option, 251
    Highlights mode, 261–262
    introduced, 25
    Midtones mode, 261–262

Options bar, 261
Range option, 253
red eye, removing, 323
Shadows mode, 261–262

C

Calculations dialog box, 728–730
Calibrator Assistant software, 813
Camera Raw dialog box
    accessing, 839, 905
    Adjust panel, 906
    Advanced option, 909, 910, 913
    Apply Sharpening To menu, 909
    Brightness option, 908
    bypassing when opening RAW file, 905
    Calibrate panel, 912
    Chromatic Aberration options, 910
    Color Noise Reduction option, 909
    Contrast option, 908
    Detail panel, 908–909
    Exposure option, 907–908
    Eyedropper tool, 907
    Lens panel, 910
    Luminance Smoothing option, 909
    preview area, 906, 909
    Reset option, 912
    Saturation option, 908
    Settings menu, 913, 914
    Shadow Tint option, 912
    Shadows option, 908
    Sharpness option, 909
    Skip option, 912
    Subset menu, 914
    Temperature option, 906–907
    Tint option, 907
    undo support, 909
    Update option, 914
    Vignetting options, 910–911
    White Balance menu, 906
Camera Raw Preferences dialog box, 108–109, 839, 912–913
Cancel cursor, 351–352
Canvas Extension Color menu, 300
Canvas Size dialog box, 155–156, 160, 299–300
Chalk & Charcoal filter, 547, 549, 699–700
channel introduced, 198
Channel menu
    Apply Image dialog box, 722, 724
    Extract dialog box, 452
    Histogram palette, 873
    Layer Mask option, 722

(continued)

Channel menu *(continued)*
 Save Selection dialog box, 457
 Transparency option, 636, 722, 724
Channels palette
 accessing, 199
 active channel, 200
 channel icon, 458
 composite view, 201
 Delete Channel option, 208
 displaying channel, 200–201, 210
 Duplicate Channel option, 207, 488
 mask, displaying in, 459
 Merge Channels option, 209
 Merge Spot Channel option, 208
 New Channel option, 207
 New Spot Channel option, 208, 946
 Palette options, 207
 Quick Mask option, 435, 437, 459
 Split Channels option, 209
 visibility icon, 200, 210
Character palette
 accessing, 34, 781
 Alignment option, 777–778
 All Caps option, 782
 Anti-alias menu, 792
 Baseline option, 790–791
 Color swatch, 791
 Faux Bold option, 782
 Faux Italic option, 782
 Fractional Widths option, 789
 InDesign, 781
 Kerning menu, 787–788
 Leading menu, 785–787
 OpenType options, 783
 Reset Character option, 782
 rotating text using, 780
 scaling text using, 779, 796
 Size option, 790
 Small Caps option, 782
 Strikethrough option, 783
 Subscript option, 783, 790
 Superscript option, 783, 790
 System Layout option, 789
 Tracking option, 788, 789
 Underline options, 783
Check Spelling dialog box, 775, 798–799
checkerboard layer, 61, 82, 442–443, 623–624
choking introduced, 521
chroma keying introduced, 62
Chrome filter, 560, 561–562, 773–774
CIE (Commission Internationale d'Eclairage), 177
Cineon image format, 125

Clear mode, 254
Clipboard
 exporting path to Illustrator using, 415–416
 layer effect, bypassing when copying, 765
Clone Stamp tool
 accessing, 307
 airbrush icon, 312
 Aligned option, 312–314, 329, 334
 background element, eliminating using, 331–335
 blending mode, 313
 Blur tool, smoothing cloned area edge using, 334
 Brush option, 312
 Dust & Scratches filter compared, 325
 Flow option, 312
 Healing Brush tool compared, 315, 316, 318
 History Brush tool, using with, 329
 image, copying area from another, 311, 312
 introduced, 23
 layer, copying area from another, 311, 312
 Layers palette Lock transparency option, using
  with, 668, 669
 Mode option, 312
 Move tool versus, 384
 Opacity option, 312, 329
 Options bar, 312
 source point, 309, 310
 transparency, cloning using, 624
 Vanishing Point filter, using with, 597
closed path introduced, 397
Clouds filter, 601–603
CLUT (color lookup table), 954, 956, 957
CMYK (cyan-magenta-yellow-black) color
 blend mode, behavior in, 635
 channel, 198–199, 201, 204, 212, 708
 Color Halftone filter, applying to, 555
 DCS file support, 173, 818
 described, 174–175
 editing, 175–176
 EPS file support, 173
 gamut, 170, 177, 455, 859–860, 921
 GIF file support, 173
 Image menu Auto Levels option, using with, 851
 information about CMYK value, displaying, 171, 857
 JPEG file support, 173
 Lab color, converting to/from, 179
 management policy, 825–826, 827
 Mezzotint filter, applying to, 557
 number of colors, 146, 172
 PCX file support, 173
 PDF file support, 173
 PICT file support, 173
 PNG file support, 173

previewing, 176–177
printing, 213, 830–832, 931, 940–941, 945
profile
    creating, 833
    missing, 827
    SWOP, 824, 831
proofing, 176–177, 842
RGB, converting to/from, 174, 176, 212, 213, 940
Scitex CT file support, 130, 173
Selective Color dialog box, adjusting CMYK color
        using, 862–863
separation, 940–941
spectrum, displaying, 192
subtractive color model, 174–175
TIFF file support, 173
working space, 822, 823, 825, 828, 830
CMYK menu, 825–826, 830, 833–834
color adjustment introduced, 837
Color Burn mode
    blend, 688–689
    brush, 256
color correction introduced, 837
Color Dodge mode
    blend, 691, 692, 699
    brush, 256
color fringing introduced, 910
Color Halftone filter, 472, 476, 555
Color Libraries dialog box, 188, 189, 208
color lookup table (CLUT), 954, 956, 957
color management introduced, 811
color mapping introduced, 837
Color menu, 287
Color mode
    blend, 696, 697
    brush, 261
color model introduced, 172
Color palette
    accessing, 190
    alert icons, 191
    background color icon, 191, 196
    color bar, 192
    Color Picker dialog box versus, 28
    Copy Color as HTML option, 192, 196
    defining color using, 168
    Eyedropper tool versus, 218
    foreground color icon, 191, 195–196
    hexadecimal color number, retrieving using,
            192, 196
    Load Swatches option, 194
    Make Ramp Web Safe option, 191
    Options bar, 740
    Replace Swatches option, 194

selecting color from, 168, 191, 740
    Web Color Sliders option, 191
Color Picker dialog box
    accessing, 28
    alert triangle, 170
    Color field, 169
    Color Libraries option, 188, 208
    Color palette versus, 28
    color slider control, 169
    current color area, 170
    Duotone Options dialog box, using with, 942
    Eyedropper tool, accessing temporarily from, 298
    hexadecimal value entry, 171
    Only Web Colors option, 170
    Photo Filter dialog box, using with, 864
    previous color area, 170
    Print with Preview dialog box, using with, 928
    Quick Mask mode, using with, 435
    text, applying color to using, 791
    Web-safe alert cube, 170
Color Picker plug-in, 51
color printer introduced, 918
Color Range dialog box
    accessing, 453
    Add Color tool, 453
    Eyedropper tool, 453–454
    Fuzziness option, 453, 454, 488, 714–718
    Linear Dodge blend mode, using with, 716, 718
    Magic Wand tool compared, 453, 454, 456
    Matte options, 455
    Multiply blend mode, using with, 716
    preview area, 453, 455
    Remove Color tool, 453
    Select menu, 455, 457, 860, 861
    This Layer option, 712, 716
    Underlying Layer option, 712, 713, 715, 716
Color Reduction Algorithm menu, 956–957
Color Replacement tool, 23, 219, 228–230
Color Sampler tool, 27, 196–198, 657, 658
color separation introduced, 921
Color Settings dialog box
    accessing, 812
    Advanced Controls options, 828
    Blend RGB Colors Using Gamma option, 829
    CMYK menu, 825–826, 830, 833–834
    Color Management Off option, 816
    Color Management Policies options, 821–822,
            825–827
    Conversion options, 828
    Convert to Working RGB option, 821–822
    Desaturate Monitor Colors By option, 829

                                        (continued)

Color Settings dialog box *(continued)*
    Description area, 822
    Emulate Photoshop 4 option, 816
    Engine option, 828
    Gray menu, 826
    Intent option, 829
    Load option, 833
    Missing Profiles option, 827
    More Options option, 827–828
    Preview option, 824, 832
    Profile Mismatches options, 820, 825–826, 827
    RGB menus, 825
    Save option, 833
    Source Space options, 931
    U.S. Prepress Defaults option, 817
    Use Black Point Compensation option, 829
    Use Dither option, 829
    Web Graphics Defaults option, 817, 819, 820
    Working Spaces options, 822–823, 833
color temperature introduced, 864
Colored Pencil filter, 545, 548
Colors menu, 863, 956, 957
ColorSync software, 813, 828
commercial printer introduced, 918
Commission Internationale d'Eclairage (CIE), 177
composite page introduced, 920
composite pixel introduced, 684
compound path introduced, 742
Contact Sheet II dialog box, 974–975, 976
Conté Crayon filter, 547
Contiguous tool, 22
Continuous Tone (CT) image format, 130, 173
Convert Point tool, 26, 398, 404, 804
convolution kernel introduced, 545
Cooling filter, 864
corrective filter, 470–471
Craquelure filter, 550
Crop tool, 22, 157–160, 161
Crosshatch filter, 473, 847
Crystallize filter, 550, 555
CS (Creative Suite), 107–108
CT (Continuous Tone) image format, 130, 173
Curves dialog box
    accessing, 882
    Auto option, 885
    brightness options, 882–884, 888–889
    Channel option, 882
    contrast options, 890–891
    Curve tools option, 884
    Eyedropper tool, 886–887
    Histogram palette, using with, 887
    Input option, 884

    Load option, 885
    Output option, 884
    Pencil tool, 884, 885, 891
    Save option, 885
cusp point introduced, 399
Custom CMYK dialog box, 830–831, 832
Custom Colors dialog box, 942, 946
Custom Pattern palette, 186–187
Custom Shape tool, 26, 708, 739
cyan-magenta-yellow-black color. *See* CMYK color

D
Darken mode
    blend, 687–688
    brush, 254, 496, 528
DCS (Desktop Color Separation) image format, 136–137, 173, 818
DeBabelizer software, 148
De-Interlace filter, 476
Delete Anchor Point tool, 26, 395
Delete key, applying color fill using, 266, 274–275, 299
Delete Point tool, 404
Depth Map, 509–510, 511
descender introduced, 784
Desktop Color Separation (DCS) image format, 136–137, 173, 818
Despeckle filter, 530
Destination Space menu, 824
destructive filter, 471–472
device-dependent color introduced, 811
DIC (Dianippon Ink and Chemical) color, 189
Difference Clouds filter, 439, 601–603
Difference mode
    blend, 696, 697, 700, 704, 730
    brush, 259–260, 442
Diffuse filter, 544
Diffuse Glow filter, 545
Digimarc software, 114
dipping effect introduced, 225
Direct Selection (white arrow) tool, 25, 396, 402, 404, 744
directional blurring filter, 498–499
DiskTop software, 88
dismissing path introduced, 398
Displace filter, 476, 545
displacement map (dmap), 545
Display Calibrator Assistant (Mac OS X), 813, 823, 940
Display Properties dialog box, 124
Dissolve mode
    blend, 686–687
    brush, 254
Dithering Algorithm menu, 958

dithering introduced, 686

dmap (displacement map), 545

docking well, 16, 31, 36–37

Dodge tool

    darkroom equivalent, 218

    Exposure option, 251

    Highlights mode, 261–262

    introduced, 25

    Midtones mode, 261–262

    Options bar, 261

    Range option, 253

    Shadows mode, 261–262

Dot Gain menu, 831

dpi (dots per inch), 918

Dry Brush tool, 246

Duotone Curve dialog box, 943, 944

Duotone Options dialog box, 942–943

Duplicate Image dialog box, 115

Dust & Scratches filter

    Clone Stamp tool compared, 325

    detail loss caused by, 325–326

    Gaussian Blur filter, using with, 536

    halftone from scanner, cleaning up using, 535–537

    Healing Brush tool compared, 325

    introduced, 325

    Median filter, using with, 536

    moiré pattern, removing using, 536

    Radius option, 535, 536

    Threshold option, 535, 536

    Unsharp Mask filter, using with, 536

dye-sublimation printer introduced, 919

dynamic fill introduced, 746

E

Easter egg, displaying, 207

Edge Highlighter tool, 447, 449, 451

Edge Touchup tool, 451

Edit Log Items menu, 55

Edit menu

    Assign Profile option, 824–825, 832

    Bridge

        Apply Camera Raw Settings option, 914

        Creative Suite Color Settings option, 107, 834

        Preferences submenu, 100

        Replace Metadata option, 115

        selection options, 93, 98, 99, 111

    Check Spelling option, 798–799

    Clear option, 404

    Color Settings option, 812, 816

    Convert to Profile option, 824

    Copy Merged option, 634

    Define Brush option, 237–238

    Define Custom Shape option, 744

Define Pattern option, 23, 186, 307

Fade option

    adjustment layer, applying to, 903

    Chrome filter, using with, 562

    filter intensity, reducing using, 476–477, 483, 528

    Healing Brush tool, using with, 330

    Image menu Adjustments effect, reducing using, 849

    Median filter, using with, 530–531

    Opacity value, 230, 250, 330

Fill option, 168, 266, 272–274, 626

Find and Replace Text option, 799–801

Free Transform option, 639–640, 661, 666, 789–790

History palette, 339, 342

Hue/Saturation dialog box, 855, 858

Keyboard Shortcuts option, 994

Match Color dialog box, 869

Paste Into option, 672–673

Paste option, 78

Photo Filter dialog box, 864

Preferences submenu

    File Handling option, 100–101

    Files & Clipboards option, 415

    General option, 48, 991, 995

    Units & Rulers option, 27, 784

Preset Manager option, 33

Purge option, 342

Stroke option, 298, 303, 408, 754

Transform submenu

    Again option, 663

    Distort option, 391, 406, 579

    Flip options, 391, 406, 569, 661

    Path option, 405

    Perspective option, 406, 595

    Points option, 405

    Rotate option, 391, 406, 569, 777

    Scale option, 390, 406

    Skew option, 391, 406

    Warp option, 391–392, 406, 661, 664–665

    Undo option, 160, 230, 336, 337

    Undo State Change option, 339

effects filter, 472–473

8-bit channel, 179

Ellipse tool, 26, 739

Elliptical Marquee tool

    adding to/subtracting from selected area, 373–374, 375–377, 389–392

    aspect ratio, 360

    circle, constraining selection outline to, 83, 294, 360, 375

    dragging selected area, 389

(continued)

Elliptical Marquee tool *(continued)*
  gradient, applying to selection outline, 281
  introduced, 21
  layer, dragging using, 616
  Options bar, 295
  Pinch filter, using with, 565
  Spherize filter, using with, 565
Embedded Profile Mismatch dialog box, 821
Emboss
  filter, 474, 557–559
  Layer Style dialog box Emboss options, 751–752
EPS (Encapsulated PostScript) image format
  anti-aliasing, 132
  ASCII EPS document, 135
  clipping path, 418–419
  color, 173, 818
  compression, 134–135
  exporting, 133–136, 416–418, 934–935, 938
  file size, 419
  halftone screen information, 135–136, 934–935
  metadata, 114
  parsing, 133
  placing EPS file, 133
  printing, 133, 134, 135–136
  rasterizing image for, 131–133
  translation engine, 132
  transparency, 416
Equilibrium DeBabelizer software, 148
Eraser tool
  background color, applying using, 168, 308, 343
  Erase to History option, 344
  History Brush tool versus, 344
  introduced, 24
  layer
    applying erase operation to, 295, 303, 308, 343
    mask, Eraser tool versus, 343
  mask boundary, editing using, 451
  Opacity option, 343
  Options bar, 342, 343
  undoing change using, 338, 341, 342–344
Exclusion mode
  blend, 696, 697
  brush, 260, 442
EXIF (Exchangeable Image File), 57, 93, 114
eXtensible Metadata Platform (XMP), 108, 114
exterior effect introduced, 702
Extract dialog box, 447–452
Extrude filter, 476, 544, 546
Eyedropper tool
  accessing temporarily from another tool, 196, 198,
    298, 453
  Camera Raw dialog box, 907
  Color palette versus, 218

Color Range dialog box, 453–454
Curves dialog box, 886–887
Hue/Saturation dialog box, 856–858
Image menu Shadow/Highlight option, 897
introduced, 27
Levels dialog box, 875, 881
Measure tool, using with, 657, 658
Sample Size option, 369
selecting color, 168, 195–196, 288

F

Facet filter, 506, 555
Fade dialog box
  Emboss filter, using with, 558
  Gaussian Blur filter, using with, 496
  Luminosity option, 550, 558
  Median filter, using with, 530–531
  Opacity option, 250, 477, 496, 531
  Overlay option, 550
Favorites feature, 100–101, 102
feathering introduced, 381
Fibers filter, 603–604
File Buddy software, 88
File Info dialog box
  Bridge, 112–115
  Description area, 930
  History panel, 54–55
File menu
  accessing, 73
  Add to Favorites option, 101
  Automate submenu
    Conditional Mode Change option, 972, 973
    Contact Sheet II option, 974–975
    Create Droplet option, 972
    Crop and Straighten Photos option, 162
    Fit Image option, 974
    Multi-Page PDF to PSD option, 126
    PDF Presentation option, 981
    Photomerge option, 983
  Bridge, 97, 101, 112, 116, 120
  Browse option, 77, 90
  Close and Go to Bridge option, 90
  Exit option, 833
  Export option, 416, 418
  Import option, 78, 126, 151
  New option, 63, 76–77
  Open As option, 88, 146
  Open option, 77, 84, 126
  Open Recent option, 78, 100–101
  Page Setup option, 923
  Place option, 133
  Preview option, 17
  Print dialog box, 922

Print with Preview option, 73, 922, 924
Revert option, 337
Save As option, 116, 120, 635, 812
Save for Web option, 952
Save option, 83, 125, 126
Show Info option, 49
Fill and Adjustment Layer menu, 899
Fill dialog box, 273, 408
Fill tool. *See* Paint Bucket tool
film recorder introduced, 919
Filmstrip view, 96, 109
Filter Gallery feature, 472, 553–555
Filter menu
   Add noise option, 330, 439
   Average option, 537
   Brush Strokes submenu, 472–473, 547
   Chrome option, 561
   Clouds option, 602
   Color Halftone option, 555
   Colored Pencil option, 545
   Cooling Filter option, 864
   Craquelure option, 550
   Crystallize option, 555
   Custom option, 545
   Despeckle option, 530
   Difference Clouds option, 439, 602
   Diffuse Glow option, 545
   Diffuse option, 544
   Displace option, 545
   Dust & Scratches option, 535
   Emboss option, 557
   Extract option, 447
   Facet option, 506, 555
   Fibers option, 603
   Filter Gallery option, 553
   Find Edges option, 488, 560
   Fragment option, 542, 555
   Fresco option, 545
   Gaussian Blur option, 489
   Glowing Edges option, 472, 477, 560
   Grain option, 529
   Halftone Pattern option, 529
   High Pass option, 461, 463–464, 492
   Lens Blur option, 508
   Lens Flare filter, 542
   Lighting Effects option, 604
   Liquify option, 585
   Maximum option, 488, 521
   Median option, 489, 530, 532
   Mezzotint option, 555–556
   Minimum option, 521
   Mosaic option, 556
   Mosaic Tiles option, 550

   Motion Blur option, 499
   Ocean Ripple option, 427
   Offset option, 552
   Palette Knife option, 545
   Patchwork option, 550
   Pattern Maker option, 307
   Photocopy option, 494
   Pointillize option, 427
   Polar Coordinates option, 580
   Radial Blur option, 503
   Ripple option, 571
   Rough Pastels option, 545
   Shape Blur option, 515
   Sharpen Edges option, 480
   Sharpen More option, 480
   Sharpen option, 480
   Shear option, 579
   Smart Blur option, 506
   Smudge Stick option, 545
   Stained Glass option, 550
   Texturizer option, 550, 551
   Trace Contour option, 560
   Twirl option, 566
   Unsharp Mask option, 489
   Video submenu, 552
   Warming Filter option, 864
   Watercolor option, 545
   Wave option, 576
   Wind option, 500, 552
   ZigZag option, 569
Find and Replace Text feature, 775, 799–801
Find dialog box, 103–104
Find Edges filter, 488, 560–561
florin symbol (*f*), layer effect indicator, 764, 765
Focoltone color, 189
focus point introduced, 606
Font menu, 782, 974
Font Size menu, 974
footprint introduced, 606
Format menu, 125, 134, 136
Forward warp tool, 588, 589
Fragment filter, 542, 555
Free Transform mode, 639–640, 661, 666, 789–790
Freeform Pen tool, 25, 358, 395, 400–401, 403
FreeHand software, 131–133, 414, 415, 942
Freeze Mask tool, 593
Fresco filter, 545, 548
fringe pixel introduced, 630

G

Gallery Effects filters, 529
Gamma control panel utility, 813–816, 819, 823, 940
gamma value introduced, 877

Gaussian Blur filter
  Amount option, 491
  anti-aliasing compared, 497–498
  Average filter, using with, 538
  bell curve, 382
  Box Blur filter compared, 516–518
  color in compressed image, enhancing using, 870–871
  Darken mode, using with, 496
  Dust & Scratches filter, using with, 536
  Fade dialog box, using with, 496
  Find Edges filter, using with, 560–561
  layer mask, applying to, 742
  low-contrast area, blurring using, 507
  Median filter
    compared, 530, 531
    using with, 532
  Minimum filter, using with, 521–523
  pixel value, 292
  preset blurring filter compared, 496–497
  Radius option, 489, 491, 495–496, 522
  Remove option, 491, 493
  Select menu Feather option compared, 520–521
  shadow effect, creating using, 521–525
  Smart Blur filter, using with, 507
  softening selection outline using, 381–382
  text, applying to, 774
  Threshold option, 494
  Unsharp Mask filter, using with, 532
GCR (gray component replacement), 831
GIF (Graphics Interchange Format)
  animation, 121, 125, 949, 963–965
  bit depth, 948
  color, 121, 125, 173, 948, 954
  compression, 125, 948–949
  exporting, 120
  JPEG compared, 948
  optimizing, 954–960
  PNG compared, 950
  transparency, 125, 949, 960
  Web image, using for, 948–949, 954–955
Glass filter, 574, 576
Glowing Edges filter, 472, 477, 560, 561
glyph introduced, 795
Gradient Editor dialog box
  accessing, 279
  Color menu, 287
  color stop control, 286, 287–288
  Dither option, 280
  fade bar, 286, 289
  Gradient Type menu, 285, 290–291
  loading preset gradient, 279–280
  midpoint marker control, 286–287, 288, 289–290

  Mode option, 280
  Name text box, 285
  opacity options, 280, 286, 289
  Reverse option, 280
  Save option, 292
  Transparency option, 280–281
Gradient palette, 279, 284, 285, 292–293, 438
Gradient tool
  default gradient, 278
  foreground color, changing using, 167–168
  indexing color, considerations when, 179
  introduced, 24
  Lab mode color, 178
  layer mask, adding using, 706
  Options bar, 178, 266, 279, 282–283, 438
  Quick Mask mode, using with, 435–442
  style options, 282–283, 294, 295
Grain filter, 529
Graphic Pen filter, 549
Graphics Interchange Format. *See* GIF
gray component replacement (GCR), 831
Gray menu, 826
.grd files, 292
grid, 65, 656, 657
guide
  action/title-safe zone, 79
  adding, 652–653, 967
  color, 64
  displaying/hiding, 654
  keyboard shortcut list, 1022–1023
  line style, 64
  positioning, 654
  snapping to, 654

H

Halftone Pattern filter, 529
Halftone Screen dialog box, 933–934
Hand tool, 27, 46, 584, 587
Hard Light mode
  blend, 691–693, 699
  brush, 257
Hard Mix mode
  blend, 695–696
  brush, 259
HDR (High Dynamic Range) image, 183
Healing Brush tool
  accessing, 308
  Aligned option, 318, 329
  background element, eliminating using, 331
  brush mode, 317, 318
  Clone Stamp tool compared, 315, 316, 318
  Dust & Scratches filter compared, 325
  Edit menu Fade option, using with, 330

Flow option, 251
Hardness option, 316
History Brush tool, using with, 329
introduced, 23, 24
Multiply mode, 317
Opacity option, 330
Options bar, 317, 319
Pattern option, 318
Replace mode, 318
Sampled option, 318
Screen mode, 317
source
    point, 310, 318
    state, 309
texture, replacing using, 316
Use All Layers option, 319
Help menu, 12, 154
High Dynamic Range (HDR) image, 183
High Pass filter, 461, 463–464, 471, 492–493
HiJaak TransverterPro software, 148
Histogram palette
accessing, 872
All Channels View option, 874
Channel menu, 873
Curves dialog box, using with, 887
Expanded View option, 872
Hue/Saturation dialog box, using with, 857
Image menu Shadow/Highlight option, using
    with, 895
Source menu, 873
Uncached Refresh option, 873
History Brush tool
Cancel cursor, 351–352
Clone Stamp tool, using with, 329
correcting multiple mistakes using, 330
Eraser tool versus, 344
Flow option, 251
Healing Brush, using with, 329
History palette, using with, 24, 309, 330, 341, 346
introduced, 24
Opacity option, 344
Options bar, 344
source state, 309, 347
History Eraser tool, 344
History Log feature, 54–55
History palette
accessing, 338
Allow Non-Linear History option, 339, 340,
    341, 342, 344
animation, 336
Art History Brush tool, using with, 341
brushstroke, undoing using, 230
Clear History option, 342

closing image, history loss when, 337
Edit menu, 339, 342
Eraser tool Erase to History option, 344
File menu Revert operation, undoing using, 337
filter operation, undoing using, 471
History Brush, using with, 24, 309, 330, 341, 346
History Options dialog box, 340, 341
logging, 55
memory considerations, 52, 339, 341
Move tool, using with, 385
number of undo operations possible, changing, 339
Smart Object operation, undoing using, 650
Stamp Layers option, 634
state
    deleting, 342
    displaying, 336, 338–339, 341
    returning to previous, 339–341
    saving, 336, 337, 341, 452
    source state, 341
stepping, undo-independent, 336
HKS color introduced, 189
Horizontal Type Mask tool, 25, 359, 771
Horizontal Type tool. *See* Type tool
hot key introduced, 988
hot spot introduced, 606
Hue mode
blend, 696
brush, 260–261
Hue/Saturation dialog box
accessing, 853
color ramp area, 855
color range controls, 855–856
Colorize option, 854–855, 857, 861, 863
Edit menu, 855, 858
Eyedropper tool, 856–858
Histogram palette, using with, 857
Hue slider, 853
Lightness option, 854
Load option, 857
Preview option, 855
Restore option, 857
Saturation option, 854, 859, 860, 861
Save option, 857
Huffman encoding, 134–135, 140, 142
Hyphenation dialog box, 797–798

I

I-beam cursor, 775–776, 801
ICM files, 833–834
Illustrator software
clipping mask, 673
color compatibility, 828

(continued)

Illustrator software *(continued)*
    compression, 142
    exporting to, 131, 134, 415–416, 419, 945
    Pen tool, 393
    rasterizing Illustrator file, 131–133
    trapping rasterized drawing from, 942
Image Interpolation menu, 663
Image menu
    Adjustments submenu
        Auto Color option, 840, 849, 851–852, 880–881
        Auto Contrast option, 840, 851, 878
        Auto Levels option, 213, 840, 843, 850–851, 878
        Channel Mixer option, 211
        Curves option, 461, 871, 882–887
        Desaturate option, 849–850
        Edit menu Fade option, reducing adjustment effect using, 849
        Equalize option, 842–843, 850–851
        Gradient Map option, 887–888
        Hue/Saturation option, 853–861
        Invert option, 212, 464, 488, 840–842
        Levels option, 197, 463–464, 561, 871, 875–882
        Match Color option, 867–870
        Photo Filter option, 864
        Posterize option, 695, 848–849
        Replace Color option, 861
        Selective Color option, 862–863
        Shadow/Highlight option, 891–898
        Threshold option, 184, 493, 494, 843–847
        Variations option, 773, 842, 862, 865–867
    Apply Image option, 681, 719, 720–724
    Bridge, 115
    Calculations option, 681, 719, 728–730, 732–733
    Canvas Size option, 155–156, 160, 299
    Crop option, 161
    Image Size option, 41, 52, 72, 152, 497
    Mode submenu
        Bitmap and Image option, 254
        Bitmap option, 183–184, 188
        CMYK Color option, 136, 147, 176, 212, 213
        Duotone option, 172, 942, 944
        8 Bits/Channel option, 179
        Grayscale option, 182, 202, 204, 823, 849
        Indexed Color option, 124, 179, 849
        Multichannel option, 147, 172, 212, 945
        RGB option, 179, 213
        16 Bits/Channel option, 182
        32 Bits/Channel option, 81, 182
    Pixel Aspect Ratio option, 83
    Resample Image option, 73
    Reveal All option, 158
    Rotate Canvas submenu
        Arbitrary option, 160, 658, 660
        degree of rotation, specifying, 660
        Flip Horizontal option, 660
        Flip Vertical option, 660
        introduced, 99
    Trap option, 941, 942, 946
    Trim option, 157
Image Processor dialog box, 972, 973
Image Size dialog box
    Resample Image option, 153–154, 497–498
    Resolution option, 73, 74, 362
ImageReady CS2 software
    file format, 122
    integration into Photoshop functionality, 951–952, 953
    introduced, 9
    PSD native format, 122
    Toolbox, accessing from, 30
imagesetter introduced, 919
InDesign software, 134, 781, 828
Indexed Color dialog box, 179–181
Info palette
    CMYK value, tracking using, 857
    Color Sampler tool, 198
    coordinate display, 386
    Current Tool option, 20
    Document Dimensions option, 18
    Document Profile option, 18
    document size display, 17
    Edit menu Free Transform option, 666
    Efficiency option, 19
    image position display, 17–18
    introduced, 14
    Options dialog box, 16
    RGB value, tracking using, 857
    Scratch Sizes option, 18–19
    Timing option, 20
inkjet printer introduced, 918
interior effect introduced, 702–703
interior point introduced, 403
interpolation introduced, 52

J
Jasc Paint Shop Pro software, 215
JPEG File Interchange Format, 949–950
JPEG (Joint Photographic Experts Group) format
    ADCT calculation, 140
    bit depth, 949
    color, 125, 141, 173, 949–950, 951

compression
  artifact produced by, 951
  cumulative, 141
  Huffman encoding, use of, 140, 143
  lossy, 124, 139, 950
  PICT compared, 128–129
  printing file having JPEG encoding, 128, 135
  quality, 125, 140, 141, 962
exporting JPEG file, 120, 121, 127, 140–141
GIF compared, 948
implementation, proprietary, 148
line drawing, using for, 141
mask channel support, 459
metadata, 114
optimizing, 961–962
photograph, using for, 950
Picture CD use of, 145
PNG compared, 950
quantization matrix, 140
screen shot, using for, 141
Web image, using for, 141, 947, 949–950
JPEG Options dialog box, 140–141
Justification dialog box, 785, 795–796

K

Kerning menu, 787–788
keyboard shortcut
  automation-related, 1023–1024
  blend mode-related, 1014–1015
  brush mode-related, 1014–1015
  channel-related, 1015–1017
  color-related, 1004–1005, 1024–1026
  context sensitive, 989
  cropping-related, 1020–1022
  customizing, 991, 993–997
  described, 988
  Edit menu Keyboard Shortcuts option, 994
  editing-related, 1002–1004
  filter-related, 1023–1024
  guide-related, 1022–1023
  layer-related, 1009–1014
  mask-related, 1015–1017
  measurement-related, 1022–1023
  menu-related, 998–1001
  modifier key, 988, 997
  navigation-related, 1001–1002
  painting-related, 1002–1004
  palette-related, 991–993, 1026–1027
  path-related, 1017–1020
  Ruler-related, 1022–1023
  selection-related, 1007–1009
  shape-related, 1017–1020
  style-related, 1004–1005

  Toolbox-related, 990–991
  transformation-related, 1020–1022
  type-related, 1005–1007
  undo operation-related, 1026
  Windows environment, 988–989, 997–998
Keyboard Shortcuts and Menus dialog box,
    994, 995, 996
Knockout menu, 681, 708–711

L

Lab color
  channel, 178, 206
  device independence, 179
  gradient, 178
  haloing, removing using, 483
  light independence, 177
  luminosity, 178
  pigment independence, 177
Large Document Format image, 57, 130, 649–650
laser printer introduced, 918
Lasso tool
  adding to/subtracting from selected area, 373–374,
    375–377, 389–392
  dragging selected area, 389
  edge detection, 358
  feathering selection, 363, 381–382
  introduced, 22
  layer, dragging using, 616
  Opacity option, 303
  Options bar, 374
Layer Comps palette, 675–678
Layer Mask Display Options dialog box, 672, 901
Layer menu
  Add Layer Mask submenu, 670
  Add Vector Mask submenu, 744, 747
  Apply Image dialog box, 722
  Arrange submenu, 627, 743
  Background From Layer option, 626
  Change Layer Content submenu, 745
  Convert to Layer option, 650
  Convert to Paragraph Text option, 780
  Convert to Point Text option, 780
  Convert to Shape option, 771, 806
  Create Clipping Mask options, 673
  Create Work Path option, 771
  Current Path option, 747
  Defringe option, 631
  Duplicate Layer option, 619
  Edit Contents option, 649
  Export Contents option, 651
  Fill Content option, 746, 747
  Flatten Image option, 133, 634–635

(continued)

Layer menu *(continued)*
   Free Transform option, 52
   Gradient option, 745
   Group Into New Smart Object option, 648
   Group Layers option, 646–647
   Hide All option, 670, 744
   Hide Selection option, 670
   Horizontal option, 778
   Layer option, 617
   Layer Style submenu
      Bevel and Emboss option, 752
      Copy Layer Style option, 765
      Create Layers option, 765
      Drop Shadow option, 626, 636
      Global Light option, 758
      Hide All Effects option, 764
      Paste Layer Style option, 765
      Stroke option, 299
   Layer Via Copy option, 617
   Layer Via Cut option, 617
   Layers palette, relation to, 618
   Match Color dialog box, 869
   Matting submenu, 631, 632
   Merge Layers option, 634
   Merge Visible option, 634
   New Adjustment Layer submenu, 899–900
   New Layer Based Slice option, 967
   New submenu, 617, 626
   Pattern option, 745
   Rasterize submenu, 746, 747, 771, 773
   Release Clipping Mask option, 673
   Remove Black Matte option, 632
   Remove Layer Mask option, 672
   Remove White Matte option, 632
   Replace Contents option, 651
   Reveal All option, 670
   Reveal Selection option, 670
   Smart Objects submenu, 348, 649, 650, 651
   Transform option, 52
   Type option, 771, 773
   Type submenu, 771, 778, 780, 805, 806
   Vertical option, 778
   Warp Text option, 805
Layer Style dialog box
   accessing, 299
   Altitude option, 763
   Anti-aliased option, 759
   Bevel and Emboss option, 751–752,
      757, 759, 762–763
   Blend Clipped Layers as Group option,
      705, 706, 709
   Blend If options, 712–713

Blend Interior Effects as Group option,
   703–705, 706
Blend Mode option, 702, 757
Blending options, 633, 681, 712, 745, 764
Channel options, 708
Chisel options, 761, 763
Choke option, 759
color options, 713–718, 754, 758
Contour options
   Angle, 758
   bevel effect, using with, 759
   color, fading using, 759
   Cove-Deep, 760
   emboss effect, using with, 759
   Gloss, 759, 763
   Linear, 760
   Noise, 760
   Range, 752, 761–762
   Ring, 752, 760
   Ring Double, 760
   Rolling, 761
   satin effect, using with, 753, 758
   Slope Descending, 761
   Spread, 760
   Technique, 760–761
   Texture, 752
Depth option, 759, 762
Direction option, 762
Distance option, 758
Drop Shadow options, 749, 751, 757, 758–759, 760
General Blending area, 633, 701
Gradient option, 754
Inner Glow options, 703, 706–707, 749–750, 751,
   761–762
Inner Shadow options, 749, 751, 757, 758
Jitter option, 762
Knockout menu, 681, 708–711
Layer Mask Hides Effects option, 705, 707
Layers palette, saving effect for use in, 756
Link/Align with Layer option, 763
new style icon, 766
Noise option, 759, 760, 762
Opacity options, 681, 702, 703, 758
Outer Glow options, 749–751, 757, 759, 761–762
Pattern Overlay options, 754, 763
Position option, 763
Satin option, 753, 755, 758
Scale option, 763
Size option, 759
Soften option, 763
Spread option, 759, 760
Stroke options, 299, 300, 754, 763

Styles palette, saving effect for use in, 756
Technique option, 760–761, 763
Texture option, 752–753, 763
Transparency Shapes Layer option, 705, 707–708
Use Global Light option, 758
Vector Mask Hides Effects option, 705
Layer Style palette, 741
Layers palette
    accessing, 303
    add layer mask icon, 747
    add layer style icon, 748
    Background option, 625, 626
    Blend menu, 633
    blend mode, adjusting using, 679–681
    Create New Fill or Adjustment Layer option,
        899–900
    Create New Layer option, 619
    eyeball icon, 620, 623, 764
    Fill option, 632–633, 679–680, 681–684
    Group options, 620, 622, 644–647
    Layer menu, relation to, 618
    Layer Style dialog box effect, saving for use in, 756
    link icon, 672
    Link Layers option, 643
    Lock all option, 651–652
    Lock pixels option, 343, 651–652
    Lock position option, 651–652
    Lock transparency option, 274, 275, 343, 651–652,
        667–669
    Mode options, 252, 645
    Opacity option, 620, 632, 679–680, 681–684, 772
    Options bar, sending Layers palette tab to, 617
    selecting layer in, 620–621, 622–623
    Smart Objects menu, 648
    thumbnail display, 617, 620, 671, 744, 780
    transparency mask, converting to selection outline
        using, 521
    trash icon, 635, 765
    visibility icon, 200
Leading menu, 785–787
Lempel-Ziv-Welch compression. See LZW compression
Lens Blur filter, 508–512
Lens Correction filter, 582–584
Lens Flare filter, 542–543, 849
Levels dialog box, 867, 875–882
Levels menu, 746
Lightbox feature, 984–985
Lighten mode
    blend, 690
    brush, 256
Lighting Effects filter, 604–608, 849
limitcheck error introduced, 133
Limits menu, 445

Line tool
    Arrowhead options, 301–302, 739
    introduced, 26
    Options bar, 301, 302, 303, 739, 741
    shape tool, as, 739
    stroke, applying using, 298, 300–301
    Weight option, 739, 741
Linear Burn mode
    blend, 688–689
    brush, 256
Linear Dodge mode
    blend, 691, 692, 716, 718
    brush, 256, 258, 496, 531
Linear Light mode
    blend, 694
    brush, 258, 259
lines per inch (lpi), 933
Liquify filter
    accessing, 585
    Bloat tool, 590
    Brush Density option, 586
    Brush Pressure option, 586, 590
    Brush Rate option, 587
    Brush Size option, 586
    drop shadow, retouching using, 640
    Forward warp tool, 588, 589
    freezing/thawing technique, 587, 593–594
    Hand tool, 587
    Mesh options, 587–588
    Mirror tool, 590–591
    Pucker tool, 589
    Push Left tool, 590
    Reconstruct options, 594–595
    Reset option, 594
    Restore All option, 594
    Show Backdrop option, 587
    Show Mesh option, 587
    Turbulence tool, 591–593
    Twirl tools, 588–589
    Undo option, 594
    zooming, 587
lpi (lines per inch), 933
luminosity introduced, 178
Luminosity mode
    blend, 696, 697
    brush, 261
LUT (look-up table), 179
LZW (Lempel-Ziv-Welch) compression
    color, 949
    GIF, 125, 948–949
    Huffman encoding compared, 142
    lossless, 142

(continued)

LZW (Lempel-Ziv-Welch) compression *(continued)*
    recompressing file compressed by, 143
    TIFF, 122, 124, 459
    ZIP compression versus, 142

M

Mac OS palette, 957
Magic Eraser tool
    Anti-aliased option, 444
    Contiguous option, 444
    History Eraser tool, relation to, 344
    introduced, 24
    layer, action limited to, 308
    Magic Wand tool compared, 442, 444
    Opacity option, 444
    Options bar, 443–444
    saving image state before using, 452
    Tolerance option, 443–444
    transparency, 442
    Use All Layers option, 444
Magic Wand tool
    adding to/subtracting from selected area, 373–374,
        389–392
    Anti-aliased option, 368
    Average filter, using with, 537
    Color Range dialog box compared, 453, 454, 456
    color, using to eliminate out-of-gamut, 860
    Contiguous option, 368
    introduced, 22
    layer, dragging using, 616
    Magic Eraser tool compared, 442, 444
    Options bar, 368, 373
    predictability, 358
    Quick Mask selection outline, cloning using, 433
    smoothing selection outline, 376
    spot color, selecting using, 946
    Tolerance option, 368–371, 377, 378, 454, 860
    Use All Layers option, 368, 371–372
Magnetic Lasso tool
    anchor point, 365, 367
    backtracking along selection line, 365, 366
    edge detection, 365, 367
    feathering selection, 333, 381–382
    Frequency option, 367
    introduced, 22
    Options bar, 358, 366–367, 373
    straight segment, selecting, 365
    Width option, 366–367
Magnetic Pen tool, 358–359, 395, 401, 403
Make Work Path dialog box, 413–414
marching ants selection feature, 28, 356–357, 424
mask introduced, 424
Match Color dialog box, 867–870

Matte Color menu, 960
Maximum filter, 488
Measure tool, 27, 160, 657–659, 660
Median filter
    color in compressed image, using to enhance,
        870–871
    Despeckle filter compared, 530
    Dust & Scratches filter, using with, 536
    Fade dialog box, using with, 530–531
    Gaussian Blur filter
        compared, 530, 531
        using with, 532
    introduced, 471
    pixel averaging, 530–531
    Radius option, 489, 530, 531
    Unsharp Mask filter, using with, 532
menu system, customizing, 995–997
Merge Channels dialog box, 209
Mezzotint filter, 555–557
midtone value introduced, 877
Minimum filter, 521–523
Miramar Systems PC MACLAN software, 83
Mirror tool, 590–591
misregistration introduced, 910
MNU files, 997
modifier keystroke introduced, 988
Mosaic filter, 474, 556
Mosaic Tiles filter, 550
Motion Blur filter, 478, 499–500, 501, 502
Move Grid tool, 584
Move tool
    accessing, 385, 616, 642
    Auto Select Layer option, 642
    cloning selection using, 384, 386–387
    constraining movement to specific direction, 385
    guide, positioning using, 654
    History palette, using with, 385
    introduced, 22
    layer, moving using, 616, 620–621, 642
    nudging, 385
    selection, moving using, 383, 384, 385–388, 616
    Smart Guide, using with, 652
    tracking movement, 386
.msh files, 587
Multichannel mode, 147, 172, 212, 945
Multiply mode
    blend, 688, 689, 716, 718, 730–732
    brush, 254–255, 317, 523, 633

N

NAA (Newspaper Association of America) color, 189
Name dialog box, 193
Navigator palette, 47–48, 196–197

nesting layer group introduced, 645
New dialog box, 76, 78–79, 82, 83, 115
New Document Preset dialog box, 80
New Layer Comp dialog box, 676–677
New Layer dialog box, 619, 900
New Spot Channel dialog box, 208
New Style dialog box, 766
Newspaper Association of America (NAA) color, 189
noise introduced, 526
Normal Blend mode, 684–686
Note Paper filter, 547
Notes tool, 26–27, 149
NTSC Colors filter, 552
number symbol (#) color profile indicator, 824
NuVista video board, 131

O

Ocean Ripple filter, 427, 574–576, 847
Open dialog box, 77, 84–86, 87
OpenType font support, 781, 783
Optimization Preset menu, 956
Options bar
    Actual Pixels option, 40
    airbrush icon, 217, 227, 248, 251
    Anti-alias menu, 792
    Author text box, 149
    Auto Add/Delete option, 404
    Auto Erase check box, 218
    Brush tool, 217
    Burn tool, 261
    check mark icon, 407
    Clear All option, 151
    Clear option, 161
    Clone Stamp tool, 312
    Color palette, 740
    Color Replacement tool, 229
    Combine option, 407, 743
    Delete option, 158
    Display/Hide palettes option, 777, 781
    displaying/hiding, 30, 31
    docking floating palette to, 36–37
    Dodge tool, 261
    Edit menu Free Transform option, 666
    Elliptical Marquee tool, 295
    Eraser tool, 342, 343
    Exposure option, 250, 251
    Feather option, 362, 381
    Finger Painting option, 224, 225
    Fit on Screen option, 40
    Flow option, 250, 251
    Font option, 151

    Front Image option, 161
    Gradient tool, 178, 266, 279, 282–283, 438
    Guides option, 967
    Healing Brush tool, 317, 319
    Hide option, 158
    History Brush tool, 344
    Ignore Palettes check box, 42
    Lasso tool, 374
    Layers palette tab, sending to, 617
    Line tool, 301, 302, 303, 739, 741
    Magic Eraser tool, 443–444
    Magic Wand tool, 368, 373
    Magnetic Lasso tool, 358, 366–367, 373
    Magnetic option, 359, 401
    Mode options, 252–261, 442
    moving, 31
    navigating using Tab key, 39
    Opacity option, 250–252
    Paint Bucket tool, 267–270
    Patch tool, 320, 322
    Path Selection (black arrow) tool, 407
    Path tool, 373
    Paths option, 394, 395, 803
    Pen tool, 373, 398
    Pencil tool, 218
    Perspective option, 158
    Polygon tool, 739, 741
    Print Size option, 41
    Promote to User Slice option, 968
    Range menu, 261
    Rectangular Marquee tool, 374–375
    Resize Windows to Fit check box, 42, 43, 44
    Rounded Rectangle tool, 739
    Sample Size menu, 196
    Scroll All Windows option, 46
    Shape Area option, 741
    Shape tool, 373
    Shield option, 158
    Show Bounding Box option, 405, 661, 743
    Size option, 151
    sizing, 31
    Smudge tool, 224–226
    Snap to Pixels option, 740
    Sponge tool, 226–227
    Strength option, 224, 250
    Style menu, 360–361, 362, 375
    transformation boundary icon, 391
    Type tool, 775, 776, 791, 793
    Warp option, 406
    Zoom All Windows option, 42
Options dialog box, 16
output device introduced, 918

Overlay mode
blend, 691–693, 698
brush, 257, 259
Overprint Colors dialog box, 944

P

Page Setup dialog box
Mac environment, 924–925
Orientation option, 926
Paper Size option, 926
Printer option, 923
Source option, 926
Windows environment, 924–925
PageMaker software, 134
Paint Bucket tool
foreground color, changing using, 167–168, 266, 267
introduced, 24
Options bar, 267–270
Pattern palette, 267
selection area fill, applying using, 275–277
Paint Shop Pro software, 215
Painter software, 215
Palette Knife filter, 545
Palette Options dialog box, 207
Pantone color, 190, 194
Paragraph palette
accessing, 34, 775, 781
Adobe Every-line Composer option, 798
Alignment options, 794
Hyphenate option, 797–798
Indent options, 796
Justification options, 785, 794–796, 798
Reset Paragraph option, 793–794
Roman Hanging Punctuation option, 794
Patch tool, 23, 308, 320–322, 325
Patchwork filter, 550
Path Selection (black arrow) tool, 25, 359, 396, 402, 407
Path tool, 373
Path-Drawing mode, 395
Paths palette
accessing, 393
Clipping Path option, 418, 419
Fill Path option, 408
Make Selection option, 394, 398, 412–413
Make Work Path option, 412, 413–414
Operation options, 412
Save Path option, 397, 414
Stroke Path options, 397, 408, 409, 410
Stroke Subpath option, 409
Vector Mask item, 744
Work Path option, 394, 410, 418, 804
Pattern palette, 267, 274

Pattern Stamp tool, 23, 307
PC MACLAN software, 83
PC Paintbrush software, 125–126
PCX files, 125–126, 173
PDF (Portable Document Format)
channel support, 459
color, 173
compression, 127
exporting, 126, 127–128, 938
layer support, 737, 756
mask channel support, 459
metadata, 114
opening PDF file, 126
presentation, publishing using Bridge, 981–983
printing PDF having JPEG encoding, 128
PSD converting to, 126
text vector property, preserving in, 771
vector data, saving to, 771
Pen tool
Bézier control handle, 396–397, 399, 400, 403
cusp point, 399
dragging straight segment drawn by, 403
Illustrator, 393
introduced, 25
Options bar, 373, 398
path, drawing using, 358, 394–395, 396–401
point manipulation, 395, 744
Pencil tool
Auto Erase option, 218, 343
Curves dialog box, 884, 885, 891
introduced, 23
line, drawing using, 217–218, 221
Options bar, 218
underlining text using, 783
Photo CD image format, 144–145, 179
Photo Filter dialog box, 864–865
Photocopy filter, 494, 547, 549
Photomerge dialog box, 983–986
Photo-Paint software, 123
Photoshop menu, 812, 816, 833, 972
Photoshop Raw image format, 130, 146–148
PICT image format, 128–129, 173, 459
Picture CD image, 145
Picture Package dialog box, 976–977
Picture Package Edit Layout dialog box, 977–978
Pin Light mode
blend, 694–695
brush, 258, 260
Pinch filter, 564, 565–566
Pixar image format, 129, 459
pixel introduced, 4
Plastic Wrap filter, 473

PNG (Portable Network Graphics) image format
    color, 130, 173, 818, 960
    compression, 130, 950, 962
    exporting, 120
    GIF compared, 950
    interlaced PNG-24, 130, 950, 962
    JPEG compared, 950
    mask channel support, 950
    optimizing, 954–962
    transparency, 949, 950–951, 960
    Web image, using for, 120, 130, 954–955
point text introduced, 775
Pointillize filter, 427, 528–529, 556, 607
Polar Coordinates filter, 580–582
Polygon tool, 26, 739, 741
Polygonal Lasso tool, 22, 358, 363–364, 376
Portable Document Format. See PDF
Portable Network Graphics image format. See PNG
        image format
Posterize dialog box, 848–849
PostScript page-description language, 919
PPD (PostScript printer description) file, 923
Prairie Group DiskTop software, 88
Preferences dialog box
    accessing, 49–50
    Bridge, 104, 105
    Display & Cursors panel, 59–60, 177, 199, 642
    File Handling panel, 55–59, 86, 117, 130
    General panel, 51–55, 339, 770
    Guides, Grid & Slices panel, 64–66, 656–657
    Image Interpolation menu, 663
    Memory & Image Cache panel, 68–69
    navigating, 50
    Plug-Ins & Scratch Disks panel, 66–67
    Tool Switch option, 357
    Transparency & Gamut panel, 60–62
    Type panel, 69–70
    Units & Rulers panel, 18, 27, 62–64, 784, 796
Prefs file, 48–49, 236
Premiere Pro software, 138–139
Preset Manager dialog box
    accessing, 33
    Brushes panel, 239
    Delete option, 24, 240, 293
    Done option, 34
    Gradients panel, 293
    introduced, 33
    Load option, 34, 240, 280
    Preset Type menu, 33, 293
    Rename option, 34, 240
    Save Set option, 34, 239
    Swatches panel, 194–195

Presets palette, 231, 232
Preview application (Apple), 87
Preview menu, 953, 954
Print Center utility (Mac), 922
Print dialog box
    accessing, 922
    Cancel option, 938
    Copies option, 937
    Destination option, 938
    File menu, 922
    Mac environment, 936
    Pages option, 937
    Preview option, 938
    Print One Copy option, 922
    Print Range option, 937
    Print to File option, 938
    Printer Features option, 938–939
    Properties option, 938–939
    specifying printer using, 923
    Windows environment, 936
Print with Preview dialog box
    Background option, 928
    Bleed option, 928
    Border option, 928
    Calibration Bars option, 928, 941
    Color Picker dialog box, using with, 928
    Crop Marks option, 930
    Description option, 930
    Emulsion Down option, 930
    Encoding option, 930–931
    Include Vector Data option, 930
    Interpolation option, 928
    Labels option, 930, 941
    More Options option, 931
    Negative option, 930
    Position option, 927
    Print option, 936
    Print Selected Area option, 927, 937
    Print Space options, 931
    Profile menu, 931, 941, 944
    Registration Marks option, 929, 941, 944
    Scale option, 74
    Scaled Print Size option, 927
    Screen option, 928, 932–933, 941, 944
    Show Bounding Box option, 927
    Transfer option, 928, 935
    Wide Gamut option, 931
printer driver introduced, 923
Printer Setup utility (Mac), 923–924
Printers control panel (Windows), 922, 923
Profile menu, 931, 941, 944
proofing image introduced, 920

protractor feature, 658
PSB files, 57, 130, 649–650
PSD files
    Apple Preview application, opening in, 87
    backward compatibility, 122
    compatibility, maximizing, 58
    compression, 122
    ImageReady native format, 122
    layer support, 634
    metadata, 114
    PDF, converting to, 126
    slice support, 971
    support by third party software, 123
    thumbnail display, 85
    transparency, 416
    vector data, saving to, 771
Pucker tool, 589
Push Left tool, 590

Q

QuarkXPress software
    compression, 142
    DCS image format, 136–137, 173
    exporting to, 123, 134, 414, 625, 945
    transparency, 416, 625
Quick Mask mode
    accessing, 430
    adding to/subtracting from selected area, 430
    channel
        displaying image simultaneously with, 460–461
        Quick Mask mode as temporary channel, 437
    cloning selection outline, 433, 434
    color display of protected area, changing, 434–435
    displaying mask independently of image, 424–425
    feathering selection outline, 433
    filtering selection outline, 521–525
    Gradient tool, using with, 435–442
    introduced, 28
    inverting image using, 439
    Minimum filter, using with, 521
    movie frame, selecting in, 138–139
    outline of selection, displaying, 430
    Patch tool, 322
    Select menu Feather option versus, 433
    transforming selection outline, 433

R

Radial Blur filter, 295, 476, 503–505
Range menu, 261
raster line introduced, 298
Rasterize Generic EPS Format dialog box, 132
RAW files, 904

Reader software, 126
Rectangle tool, 26, 738
Rectangular Marquee tool
    adding to/subtracting from selected area, 373–374,
        375–377, 389–392
    Anti-aliased option, 362
    aspect ratio, 360
    dragging selected area, 389, 616
    introduced, 21
    Options bar, 374–375
    Quick Mask selection outline, cloning using, 433
    square, constraining selection outline to, 360,
        374–375
    Twirl filter, using with, 568, 569
Red Eye Removal tool, 24, 309, 322–323
red-green-blue color. See RGB color
registering selection introduced, 388
Remove Color tool, 453
Remove Distortion tool, 584
Replace Color dialog box, 861–862
Resample Image menu, 153
ResEdit software, 88
Resize Image Wizard, 154
Reticulation filter, 473
RGB menus, 825
RGB (red-green-blue) color
    additive primary model, 172
    blend mode, behavior in, 635
    brightness value, displaying, 883
    channel, 176, 182–183, 198–199, 201–204, 722
    CMYK, converting to/from, 174, 176, 212, 213, 940
    Color Halftone filter, applying to, 555
    composite curve, 887
    DCS file support, 173, 818
    described, 172–173
    EPS file support, 173
    gamut, 859
    GIF file support, 173
    grayscale image, converting to/from, 261, 932
    histogram, displaying, 881–882
    Image menu Auto Levels option, using with, 851, 852
    JPEG file support, 173
    Lighting Effects filter, applying to, 604
    management policy, 825, 827
    monitor color, desaturating, 829
    number of colors, 146, 171, 172
    PCX file support, 173
    PDF file support, 173
    PICT file support, 173
    Pixar file support, 129
    PNG file support, 173
    printing, 174, 179, 931

profile
    assigning, 824–825
    embedding, 818–819
    missing, 827
    proofing, 176, 842
    Scitex CT file support, 130, 173
    shifting predefined RGB color, 862–863
    sRGB, 819, 820, 822, 825
    TIFF file support, 173
    tolerance, 368
    Web image, using for, 172
    working space, 145, 816, 817, 819, 823
RGB Working Spaces menu, 819
Ripple filter, 292, 472, 571–573
RLE (Run-Length Encoding) compression, 123
Rotate Image tool, 984
Rough Pastels filter, 545, 548
Rounded Rectangle tool, 26, 739
Ruler feature
    displaying/hiding, 62, 652
    guide
        action/title-safe zone, 79
        adding, 652–653, 967
        color, 64
        displaying/hiding, 654
        keyboard shortcut list, 1022–1023
        line style, 64
        positioning, 654
        snapping to, 654
    keyboard shortcut list, 1022–1023
    unit of measurement, specifying, 18, 27, 63, 784
Run-Length Encoding (RLE) compression, 123

S

Sample Size menu, 196
Sampling menu, 447
sandwiching introduced, 698
saturation introduced, 174
Saturation mode
    blend, 696, 697
    brush, 261
Save As dialog box
    accessing, 83
    Bridge application, 116, 117–120
    Embed Color Profile option, 818–819
    location text box, 83
    name text box, 83
Save dialog box
    Alpha option, 142
    Annotations option, 149
    As a Copy option, 133
    Bridge, 116, 117

    Format menu, 125, 134, 136
    Layers option, 123, 142
    Use Adobe Dialog option, 118
Save for Web dialog box
    Bridge, 120–122, 125
    Color Reduction Algorithm menu, 956–957
    Colors menu, 956, 957
    Diffusion option, 958–959
    Dithering Algorithm menu, 958
    Document Color Profile option, 954
    Gamma Correction options, 954
    Image Size area, 962–963
    ImageReady, based on, 951–952
    Mac OS palette, 957
    Matte Color menu, 960
    Noise option, 958–959
    Optimization Preset menu, 956
    Pattern option, 958–959
    Preview menu, 953, 954
    Standard Macintosh Color option, 954
    Standard Windows Color option, 954
    Text is HTML option, 969, 970
    Uncompensated Color option, 954
    Web palette, 957
    Windows palette, 957
Save Selection dialog box, 457–458
Save Settings Subset dialog box, 915
Scattered Leaves brush tool, 246–247
Scitex printer, 130
scratch disk, 67
scratch file, 18, 66, 67
screen frequency introduced, 932
Screen mode
    blend, 687, 689, 690–691, 730, 732
    brush, 256, 317
scrubbing introduced, 666
Select an Image File dialog box, 975
Select Image tool, 984
Select menu
    Color Range dialog box, 455, 457, 860, 861
    Deselect option, 372, 408
    Feather option
        Gaussian Blur filter compared, 520–521
        layer edge, feathering using, 632
        Patch tool, using with, 322
        Quick Mask feathering versus, 433
        Radius value, 275, 381, 382, 383
    Grow option, 376, 377
    Hide Extras option, 383
    Inverse option, 275, 373, 426, 460
    Load Selection option, 459–460, 636

(continued)

Select menu (continued)
    Modify submenu
        Border option, 299, 376
        Contract option, 376, 524, 632
        Expand option, 376, 488, 759
        Smooth option, 376
    Out of Gamut option, 455
    Reselect option, 372–373
    Save Selection option, 457
    Similar option, 377
    Transform Selection option, 389–390
selection masking introduced, 425
Selection Preview menu, 455
Selective Color dialog box, 862–863
service bureau introduced, 918
Set menu, 994
Settings menu, 913, 914
Shape Blur filter, 515–518
shape layer introduced, 736
Sharpen
    filter, 219, 470, 471, 487
    tool, 24, 218, 220
Sharpen Edges filter, 487
Sharpen More filter, 487
Shear filter, 579–580
Shift key, navigating Toolbox using, 54
Shortcuts For menu, 995
Show menu, 452
Single-Column Marquee tool, 22, 358, 360
Single-Row Marquee tool, 22, 358, 360
16-bit channel, 182
Size menu, 571, 784, 789
SkyTag File Buddy software, 88
Slice Options dialog box, 968–971
Slice Select tool, 23, 968
Slice tool, 22, 966–967, 969
Smart Blur filter, 506–508
Smart Guides feature, 65, 652, 656
Smart Object feature, 647–651
Smart Sharpen filter, 326, 489–492
SMPTE (Society of Motion Picture and Television
        Engineers), 138
Smudge Stick filter, 545
Smudge tool
    effect created by, 218, 220
    Finger Painting option, 225–226
    introduced, 24
    Options bar, 224–226
    selection perimeter, applying to, 426–427, 428
    Strength option, 224–225
    Use All Layers option, 226, 227
Society of Motion Picture and Television Engineers
        (SMPTE), 138

Soft Light mode
    blend, 691–692
    brush, 257, 259
Solarize filter, 544
Source menu
    Apply Image dialog box, 722
    Histogram palette, 873
    Lens Blur filter, 509
    Match Color dialog box, 869
Specifications for Web Offset Publications (SWOP)
        color, 824, 831
spell-checker feature, 775, 798–799
Spherize filter, 564, 565
splash screen, 12
Sponge tool, 25, 219, 226–228, 859
spooling introduced, 919
Spot Channel Options dialog box, 945
spot color introduced, 921
Spot Healing Brush tool, 23, 319–320, 325
spreading introduced, 521
sRGB (standard RGB) color, 819, 820, 822, 825
Stagger filter, 502
Stained Glass filter, 473, 550, 847
Stamp filter, 547
status bar, 15
Straighten tool, 584
Stroke dialog box, 298–299
stroke introduced, 265
Stroke Path dialog box, 408–409
Style menu
    Art History Brush tool, 348
    Lighting Effects filter, 606–607
    Options bar, 360–361, 362, 375
    text options, 782
    Warp Text dialog box, 805
Styles menu, 978
Styles palette, 745, 756, 766–767
subpath introduced, 394
Subset menu, 914
Subtract Blend mode, 724, 725–727, 728
Suite Color Settings dialog box, 834–836
Surface Blur filter, 518–520
Swatches palette, 168, 192–194
SWOP (Specifications for Web Offset Publications)
        color, 824, 831

T

Tagged Image File Format. See TIFF
Technique menu, 760–761
Texture Fill filter, 550
texture map introduced, 607
Texturizer filter, 550, 551
TGA (Targa) image format, 131, 459

Thaw Mask tool, 593
thermal-wax printer introduced, 918
32-bit channel, 81, 182
3D Transform filter, 550
Threshold dialog box, 843–846
TIFF Options dialog box, 142–144
TIFF (Tagged Image File Format)
    channel support, 142, 459
    clipping path, saving as, 418
    color, 173, 818
    compression, 57, 122, 124, 142–143, 459
    EPS export, relation to, 134
    exporting, 142–144, 418, 466
    file size, 419
    grayscale image, using for, 466
    layer support, 57, 737, 756
    mask channel support, 459
    metadata, 114
    slice support, 971
    text vector property, preserving in, 771
    tiling, 144
    vector data, saving to, 771
Tiles filter, 476, 544, 546
Tool Presets palette, 31–32, 241
tool tip feature, 20, 53
Toolbox feature
    accessing tool from, 15, 20–21
    background color icon, 28
    displaying/hiding, 30
    editing tool icons, 216
    foreground color icon, 28
    full screen icons, 29–30
    image ready icon, 30
    keyboard shortcut list, 990–991
    marching ants icon, 28
    moving, 38
    navigating using Shift key, 54
    painting tool icons, 216
    Quick Mask mode icon, 430
    standard window icon, 29
    switch colors icon, 28
Tools menu
    Bridge application, 110, 111–112, 972, 975, 981
    Folder Option option, 49
    Photoshop submenu, 972
TouchUp Image format, 131
Toyo color, 189
Trace Contour filter, 560
Transfer Functions dialog box, 935–936
transfer graph introduced, 935
transformation introduced, 660
transparency mask introduced, 289

TransverterPro software, 148
trap introduced, 941
TrueVision video board, 131
Trumatch color, 190, 194
Turbulence tool, 591–593
Tween dialog box, 965
Twirl
    filter, 292, 566–569
    Liquify filter Twirl tools, 588–589
Type menu, 785, 942
Type tool
    accessing, 770, 775, 780
    Alignment options, 793–794
    Check Spelling option, 775
    creating text frame using, 770, 778–779
    creating type mask using, 771
    cursor, 775, 801
    editing text using, 775, 777
    entering text using, 775–776, 801–802
    Find and Replace Text option, 775
    formatting paragraph using, 793
    introduced, 25
    Options bar, 775, 776, 791, 793

U

UCA (under color addition), 832
UCR (under color removal), 831
Unsharp Mask filter
    Amount option, 481, 482–483, 485, 489
    applying repeatedly, 482–483
    channel, applying to, 483
    channel, focusing using, 210
    Dust & Scratches filter, using with, 536
    edge detection, 463, 480–481, 483–484, 486
    Gaussian Blur filter, using with, 532
    Median filter, using with, 532
    Pin Light Blend mode, using with, 694
    previewing effect, 482
    Radius option, 481, 482, 483–485, 489
    resolution considerations, 484
    sharpening filter compared, 487
    Smart Blur filter, using with, 507
    Threshold option, 481, 482, 484, 486, 487
U.S. Web Coated color profile, 824, 831
Use menu, 274
user slice introduced, 965

V

Vanishing Point filter, 595–601
Variations dialog box, 871
vector mask introduced, 741
vector object introduced, 4

Vertical Type Mask tool, 25, 359, 771
Vertical Type tool, 25, 777, 794
View menu
    Actual Pixels option, 40, 76
    Bridge application, 91, 92, 94, 96, 97
    Extras option, 357, 426
    Fit on Screen option, 40
    Gamut Warning option, 62, 177, 859, 860
    Grid option, 656
    New Guide option, 654
    Pixel Aspect Ratio Correction option, 82
    Print Size option, 41
    Proof Setup submenu
        Windows RGB option, 823
        Working CMYK option, 823, 842, 859, 860
    Rulers option, 652
    Show submenu
        All option, 151
        Annotations option, 151
        Clear Slices option, 968
        Grid option, 656
        Guides option, 654
        Layer Edges option, 629
        Lock Slices option, 968
        None option, 151
        Selection Edges option, 357
        Show Extras option, 357, 399, 654, 968
        Slices option, 968
        Smart Guides option, 65
        Target Path option, 399, 807
    Slide Show option, 94
    Snap To submenu, 654, 656, 967
    Thumbnails option, 86
    Zoom options, 42
view size introduced, 40
virtual memory introduced, 19
Vivid Light mode
    blend, 694
    brush, 258

W
Wacom drawing tablet, 240
Warming filter, 864
Warp mode, 391–392
Warp Text dialog box, 804–806
Watercolor filter, 346, 545, 548
Wave filter, 576–579

WBMP (Wireless Bitmap) image format, 131
Web palette, 957
Web Photo Gallery dialog box, 978–981
Welcome Screen, 12–13
white arrow (Direct Selection) tool, 25, 396,
        402, 404, 744
White Balance menu, 906
Wind filter, 500–503, 552
Window menu
    Animation option, 963
    Arrange submenu, 39, 45, 210
    Bridge application, 109
    Brushes option, 231
    Channels option, 200
    Character option, 776
    Color option, 190
    Histogram option, 872
    History option, 338
    Info option, 666
    Layer Comps option, 676
    Navigator option, 47
    New Window option, 45, 210
    Paragraph option, 776
    Paths option, 393
    Status Bar option, 15
    Styles option, 766
    Swatches option, 192
    Tile Horizontally option, 39
    Tile Vertically option, 39
    Tool Presets option, 31–32, 241
    Workspace option, 38, 109
Windows palette, 957
Wireless Bitmap (WBMP) image format, 131
Working Spaces menus, 822–823

X
xerography introduced, 139
XMP (eXtensible Metadata Platform), 108, 114

Y
YCC image format, 144–145

Z
ZigZag filter, 569–570
Zip compression, 127, 142
zoom ratio introduced, 40
Zoom tool, 27, 41–42, 474–475, 584